MW01623327

EXODUS

EXODUS

AN EXEGETICAL COMMENTARY

VICTOR P. HAMILTON

BakerAcademic
a division of Baker Publishing Group
Grand Rapids, Michigan

Published by Baker Academic
a division of Baker Publishing Group
P.O. Box 6287, Grand Rapids, MI 49516-6287
www.bakeracademic.com

Printed in the United States of America

Library of Congress Cataloging-in-Publication Data

Hamilton, Victor P.
Exodus : an exegetical commentary / Victor P. Hamilton.
p. cm.
Includes bibliographical references and index.
ISBN 978-0-8010-3183-0 (cloth)
1. Bible. O.T. Exodus—Commentaries. I. Title.
BS1245.53.H36 2011
222′.1207—dc23 2011017701

Dedicated to

Nathan
Benjamin
Madeline
Bethany
Abigail
Holly
Lindy
Natalie
Rachel
Samuel
Evelyn
Zechariah
Lillian

Our thirteen grandchildren, who provide us with hours of delight, but whose interests probably run more toward playing Wii than reading this commentary on Exodus.

Contents

Part 2: Liberation from Egypt (6:2–15:21) *95*

Part 3: Testing Time in the Wilderness (15:22–18:27) *237*

Part 4: Covenant and Law at Sinai (19:1–24:18) *291*

Preface

It has been my privilege since retiring from teaching Old Testament at Asbury College to devote full time to research and writing. This commentary is the first product of that time. I wish to express my appreciation to the administration of Asbury College for appointing me as "Scholar-in-Residence," and for allowing me to keep my office on campus. That has provided me a quiet place for much of my reflection and writing. Thanks also to the staff of the B. L. Fisher Library/Information Commons at Asbury Theological Seminary for their assistance. I have spent many an hour in that building, with full access to their invaluable resources, both books and periodicals.

Needless to say, without the encouragement and guidance of many individuals at Baker Academic, among them Jim Kinney, Brian Bolger, and a host of others, this book would never have seen the light of day. A big thank-you to all of them for their professional gifts in moving my manuscript to publication. A special thanks to Wells Turner, who has superbly supervised this project from start to finish in his capacity as a senior editor at Baker and has passed on to me a number of very helpful suggestions. This is the third book of mine that Baker has published, and it has been an honor to work with their staff. I wrote the book. They helped me write a better book.

I wish to reserve the highest accolade for my wife, Shirley, who has typed the entire manuscript for me. She has invested almost as much time in this project as I have. Additionally, she frequently interacted with me on the text, made many invaluable suggestions, and asked a lot of penetrating and helpful questions. For those kinds of contributions I am forever grateful to her.

Last of all, I thank our Lord for his sustaining grace and guidance. To him and him alone be all the glory. My prayer is that this commentary will not only find a place in the conversation within the biblical academy but will also be a reference book that a pastor can consult with profit when preparing to share this portion of God's Word with parishioners.

Abbreviations

Bibliographic and General

[ ]	encloses versification of the MT or the LXX when this differs from the English, as with Ps. 46:10 [11]
ABD	*Anchor Bible Dictionary*, ed. D. N. Freedman, 6 vols. (New York: Doubleday, 1992)
ANEP	*The Ancient Near East in Pictures Relating to the Old Testament*, ed. J. B. Pritchard, 2nd ed. (Princeton: Princeton University Press, 1969)
ANET	*Ancient Near Eastern Texts Relating to the Old Testament*, ed. J. B. Pritchard, trans. and annotated by W. F. Albright et al., 3rd ed. (Princeton: Princeton University Press, 1969)
AT	author's translation
BDB	F. Brown, S. R. Driver, and C. A. Briggs, *A Hebrew and English Lexicon of the Old Testament* (Oxford: Clarendon, 1907)
CAD	*The Assyrian Dictionary of the Oriental Institute of the University of Chicago*, ed. I. J. Gelb et al. (Chicago: University of Chicago Press, 1956–)
cf.	*confer*, compare
chap(s).	chapter(s)
COS	*The Context of Scripture*, ed. W. W. Hallo et al., 3 vols. (Leiden: Brill, 1997–2002)
CTA	*Corpus des tablettes en cunéiformes alphabétiques découvertes à Ras Shamra-Ugarit de 1929 à 1939*, ed. A. Herdner, Mission de Ras Shamra 10 (Paris: Imprimerie nationale, 1963)
EA	El-Amarna tablets: ed. J. A. Knudtzon, *Die el-Amarna-Tafeln* (1908–15; reprinted, Aalen: O. Zeller, 1964); continued in A. F. Rainey, *El-Amarna Tablets, 359–370*, 2nd rev. ed. (Kevelaer: Butzon & Bercker, 1978)
EncJud	*Encyclopaedia Judaica*, 16 vols. (Jerusalem: Encyclopaedia Judaica, 1971–72)
esp.	especially
et al.	and others

fem.	feminine
GKC	*Gesenius' Hebrew Grammar*, ed. E. Kautzsch, trans. A. E. Cowley (Oxford: Clarendon, 1910)
GNB	Good News Bible
IDB	*Interpreter's Dictionary of the Bible*, ed. G. A. Buttrick, 4 vols. (Nashville: Abingdon, 1962)
IDBSup	*Interpreter's Dictionary of the Bible: Supplementary Volume*, ed. K. Crim (Nashville: Abingdon, 1976)
ISBE	*International Standard Bible Encyclopedia*, ed. G. W. Bromiley, rev. ed., 4 vols. (Grand Rapids: Eerdmans, 1979–88)
JB	Jerusalem Bible
KJV	King James Version
KTU	*Die keilalphabetischen Texte aus Ugarit*, ed. M. Dietrich et al., 2nd ed., Alter Orient und Altes Testament 24/1 (Neukirchen-Vluyn, Germany: Neukirchener Verlag, 1976)
lit.	literally
loc. cit.	*loco citato*, in the place cited
LXX	Septuagint, ancient Greek version of the Old Testament
masc.	masculine
Message	*The Message*, Eugene H. Peterson
MT	Masoretic Text of the Hebrew Scriptures
NAB	New American Bible
NASB	New American Standard Bible
NEB	New English Bible
NIV	New International Version
NJPS	*Tanakh: The Holy Scriptures; The New Jewish Publication Society Translation according to the Traditional Hebrew Text* (1999)
NKJV	New King James Version
NLT	New Living Translation
NRSV	New Revised Standard Version
NT	New Testament
OT	Old Testament
pl.	plural
PRU	*Le palais royal d'Ugarit*, ed. C. F. A. Schaeffer et al. (Paris: Imprimerie nationale, 1955–)
REB	Revised English Bible
RSV	Revised Standard Version
sg.	singular
SP	Samaritan Pentateuch
TEV	Today's English Version
TNIV	Today's New International Version
trans.	translator, translated by
UT	*Ugaritic Textbook*, by C. H. Gordon. Analecta orientalia 38 (Rome: Pontifical Biblical Institute, 1965)
v(v.)	verse(s)
Vulg.	(Latin) Vulgate
x	times a term/idea occurs, such as *nāṣal* in Exod. 18:10 [2x]

Old Testament

Gen.	Genesis	Song	Song of Songs
Exod.	Exodus	Isa.	Isaiah
Lev.	Leviticus	Jer.	Jeremiah
Num.	Numbers	Lam.	Lamentations
Deut.	Deuteronomy	Ezek.	Ezekiel
Josh.	Joshua	Dan.	Daniel
Judg.	Judges	Hosea	Hosea
Ruth	Ruth	Joel	Joel
1–2 Sam.	1–2 Samuel	Amos	Amos
1–2 Kings	1–2 Kings	Obad.	Obadiah
1–2 Chron.	1–2 Chronicles	Jon.	Jonah
Ezra	Ezra	Mic.	Micah
Neh.	Nehemiah	Nah.	Nahum
Esther	Esther	Hab.	Habakkuk
Job	Job	Zeph.	Zephaniah
Ps(s).	Psalms	Hag.	Haggai
Prov.	Proverbs	Zech.	Zechariah
Eccles.	Ecclesiastes	Mal.	Malachi

Old Testament Apocrypha

Jdt.	Judith	Sir.	Sirach
1–4 Macc.	1–4 Maccabees	Tob.	Tobit

New Testament

Matt.	Matthew	1–2 Thess.	1–2 Thessalonians
Mark	Mark	1–2 Tim.	1–2 Timothy
Luke	Luke	Titus	Titus
John	John	Philem.	Philemon
Acts	Acts	Heb.	Hebrews
Rom.	Romans	James	James
1–2 Cor.	1–2 Corinthians	1–2 Pet.	1–2 Peter
Gal.	Galatians	1–3 John	1–3 John
Eph.	Ephesians	Jude	Jude
Phil.	Philippians	Rev.	Revelation
Col.	Colossians		

Other Ancient Sources

Alleg. Interp.	Philo, *Allegorical Interpretation*
Ant.	Josephus, *Antiquities of the Jews*

Bib. Ant.	Pseudo-Philo, *Biblical Antiquities*
Drunk.	Philo, *On Drunkenness*
Jub.	*Jubilees*
Names	Philo, *On the Change of Names*
Spec. Laws	Philo, *On the Special Laws*
Virt.	Philo, *On the Virtues*

Transliteration Patterns

Greek

α	*a*	ξ	*x*
β	*b*	ο	*o*
γ	*g/n*	π	*p*
δ	*d*	ρ	*r*
ε	*e*	σ/ς	*s*
ζ	*z*	τ	*t*
η	*ē*	υ	*y/u*
θ	*th*	φ	*ph*
ι	*i*	χ	*ch*
κ	*k*	ψ	*ps*
λ	*l*	ω	*ō*
μ	*m*	῾	*h*
ν	*n*		

Notes on the Transliteration of Greek

1. Accents, lenis (smooth breathing), and *iota* subscript are not shown in transliteration.
2. The transliteration of asper (rough breathing) precedes a vowel or diphthong (e.g., ἁ = *ha*; αἱ = *hai*) and follows ρ (i.e., ῥ = *rh*).
3. *Gamma* is transliterated *n* only when it precedes γ, κ, ξ, or χ.
4. *Upsilon* is transliterated *u* only when it is part of a diphthong (i.e., αυ, ευ, ου, υι).

Hebrew

א	ʾ	בָ	*ā*	*qāmeṣ*
ב	*b*	בַ	*a*	*pataḥ*
ג	*g*	הַ	*a*	furtive *pataḥ*
ד	*d*	בֶ	*e*	*sĕgôl*
ה	*h*	בֵ	*ē*	*ṣērê*
ו	*w*	בִ	*i*	short *ḥîreq*
ז	*z*	בִ	*ī*	long *ḥîreq* written defectively
ח	*ḥ*	בָ	*o*	*qāmeṣ ḥāṭûp*
ט	*ṭ*	בוֹ	*ô*	*ḥôlem* written fully
י	*y*	בֹ	*ō*	*ḥôlem* written defectively
ך/כ	*k*	בוּ	*û*	*šûreq*
ל	*l*	בֻ	*u*	short *qibbûṣ*
ם/מ	*m*	בֻ	*ū*	long *qibbûṣ* written defectively
ן/נ	*n*	בָה	*â*	final *qāmeṣ hēʾ* (בָה = *āh*)
ס	*s*	בֶי	*ê*	*sĕgôl yôd* (בֶי = *êy*)
ע	ʿ	בֵי	*ê*	*ṣērê yôd* (בֵי = *êy*)
ף/פ	*p*	בִי	*î*	*ḥîreq yôd* (בִי = *îy*)
ץ/צ	*ṣ*	בֲ	*ă*	*ḥāṭēp pataḥ*
ק	*q*	בֱ	*ĕ*	*ḥāṭēp sĕgôl*
ר	*r*	בֳ	*ŏ*	*ḥāṭēp qāmeṣ*
שׂ	*ś*	בְ	*ĕ*	vocal *šĕwāʾ*
שׁ	*š*			
ת	*t*			

Notes on the Transliteration of Hebrew

1. Accents are not shown in transliteration.
2. Silent *šĕwāʾ* is not indicated in transliteration.
3. The spirant forms ב ג ד כ פ ת are usually not specially indicated in transliteration.
4. *Dāgēš forte* is indicated by doubling the consonant. Euphonic *dāgēš* and *dāgēš lene* are not indicated in transliteration.
5. *Maqqēp* is represented by a hyphen.

Commentaries on Exodus

The entries below represent a sampling of some of the more important commentaries, and therefore the listing is not exhaustive.

Alter, R. 2004. "Exodus." In *The Five Books of Moses: A Translation with Commentary*, 297–535. New York and London: Norton.

Brenner, A., ed. 1993. *A Feminist Companion to Exodus to Deuteronomy*. Feminist Companion to the Bible 6. Sheffield: Sheffield Academic Press.

Bruckner, J. K. 2008. *Exodus*. New International Biblical Commentary on the Old Testament. Peabody, MA: Hendrickson. Reprinted, Grand Rapids: Baker Academic.

Brueggemann, W. 1994. "Exodus." In *The New Interpreter's Bible*, edited by L. E. Keck et al., 1:675–981. Nashville: Abingdon.

Cassuto, U. 1967. *A Commentary on the Book of Exodus*. Jerusalem: Magnes.

Childs, B. S. 1974. *The Book of Exodus: A Critical, Theological Commentary*. Old Testament Library. Philadelphia: Westminster.

Clements, R. E. 1972. *Exodus*. Cambridge Bible Commentary. Cambridge: Cambridge University Press.

Coats, G. W. 1998. *Exodus 1–18*. Forms of the Old Testament Literature 2A. Grand Rapids: Eerdmans.

Dozeman, T. B. 2009. *Exodus*. Eerdmans Critical Commentary. Grand Rapids: Eerdmans.

Driver, S. R. 1911. *The Book of Exodus*. Cambridge Bible for Schools and Colleges. Cambridge: Cambridge University Press.

Durham, J. I. 1987. *Exodus*. Word Biblical Commentary 3. Waco: Word.

Enns, P. 2000. *Exodus*. NIV Application Commentary. Grand Rapids: Zondervan.

Fokkelman, J. P. 1987. "Exodus." In *The Literary Guide to the Bible*, edited by R. Alter and F. Kermode, 56–65. Cambridge, MA: Belknap.

Fretheim, T. E. 1991. *Exodus*. Interpretation: A Bible Commentary for Preaching and Teaching. Louisville: John Knox.

Goldingay, J. 2010. *Exodus and Leviticus for Everyone*. Old Testament for Everyone. Louisville: Westminster John Knox.

Gowan, D. E. 1994. *Theology in Exodus: Biblical Theology in the Form of a Commentary*. Louisville: Westminster John Knox.

Greenberg, M. 1969. *Understanding Exodus*. New York: Behrman.

Houtman, C. 1993–2000. *Exodus*. 4 vols. Historical Commentary on the Old Testament. Kampen: Kok; Leuven: Peeters.

Hyatt, J. P. 1971. *Commentary on Exodus*. New Century Bible. London: Oliphants.

Jacob, B. 1992. *Exodus*. Translated by Y. Elman. Hoboken, NJ: Ktav.

Janzen, J. 1997. *Exodus*. Westminster Bible Companion. Louisville: Westminster John Knox.

Kaiser, W. C., Jr. 1990. "Exodus." In *The Expositor's Bible Commentary*, edited by Frank E. Gaebelein, 2:287–437. Grand Rapids: Zondervan.

Longman, T., III. 2009. *How to Read Exodus*. Downers Grove, IL: InterVarsity.

Meyers, C. 2005. *Exodus*. New Cambridge Bible Commentary. Cambridge: Cambridge University Press.

Motyer, J. A. 2005. *The Message of Exodus: The Days of Our Pilgrimage*. The Bible Speaks Today. Downers Grove, IL: InterVarsity.

Noth, M. 1962. *Exodus: A Commentary*. Old Testament Library. Philadelphia: Westminster.

Oswalt, J. 2008a. "Exodus." In *Cornerstone Biblical Commentary*, edited by Philip W. Comfort, 1:259–560. Carol Stream, IL: Tyndale.

———. 2008b. "Exodus." In *NLT Study Bible*, 122–91. Carol Stream, IL: Tyndale.

Pixley, G. V. 1987. *On Exodus: A Liberation Perspective*. Translated by R. R. Barr. Maryknoll, NY: Orbis Books.

Propp, W. H. C. 1999. *Exodus 1–18: A New Translation with Introduction and Commentary*. Anchor Bible. New York: Doubleday.

———. 2006. *Exodus 19–40: A New Translation with Introduction and Commentary*. Anchor Bible. New York: Doubleday.

Sailhamer, J. H. 1992. *The Pentateuch as Narrative: A Biblical-Theological Commentary*, 241–322. Grand Rapids: Zondervan.

Sarna, N. 1986. *Exploring Exodus: The Heritage of Biblical Israel*. New York: Schocken.

———. 1991. *Exodus*. JPS Torah Commentary. Philadelphia: Jewish Publication Society.

Smith, M. S. 2010. *Exodus*. The New Collegeville Bible Commentary Series: Old Testament 3. Collegeville, MN: Liturgical Press.

Stuart, D. K. 2006. *Exodus*. New American Commentary. Nashville: Broadman & Holman.

Tigay, J. H. 2004a. "Exodus." In *The Jewish Study Bible*, edited by A. Berlin and M. Z. Brettler, 102–202. Oxford: Oxford University Press.

Waltke, B. 2007. *An Old Testament Theology: An Exegetical, Canonical and Thematic Approach*, 346–478. Grand Rapids: Zondervan.

Introduction

The Narrative and Theology of Exodus

Before the book of Exodus begins to narrate an *exodus* ("a way out") of Hebrews from Egypt, it first describes an *eisodus* ("a way into") of a Hebrew family into Egypt. There cannot be, and need not be, an exodus unless there has been an eisodus. One need not ever have to get "out" of debt unless first of all one has gotten "into" debt. In a nutshell, the book of Exodus is about how the Lord God turns an *eisodus* into an *exodus* and why he does so, about how the Lord God changes a "going down" into a "coming up."

Why the Lord brings his people out of Egypt is as important, if not more important, than *how* he delivers Israel from Egypt. If the book of Exodus is about the exodus event, then the book should be concluded by the end of chap. 14, or by 15:21 if one wants to include Miriam's and Moses's lyrical response. But what is one to do with 15:22–40:38, all of which are postexodus events in the Exodus book?

The first answer, but not the most important answer, to *why* God delivers his people from Egypt is to rescue them from the excruciating oppression to which Pharaoh and Egypt are subjecting them. Why would the first two chapters of Exodus address this potential holocaust on foreign soil if it is only of minimal interest to the author (and to God)? Accordingly, I believe that liberation theology is correct in looking to this book of Scripture, at least to its first part, to fuel the passion of its message of "setting the captive free," especially when the captors are desensitized, megalomaniacal, bureaucratic governments that rule with an iron fist and keep the masses in line and impoverished.

I cannot imagine that the Lord of Scripture is moved to action when he hears Israel's moaning under its bondage at Egyptian hands but looks the other direction or plugs his ears lest he hear Philistines moaning under bondage at Assyrian hands or Canaanites moaning under bondage at Hittite hands. Gratuitous suffering, whoever the perpetrator and victim are, is something to which the Lord is never indifferent. He feels about Philistine and Canaanite boy babies as he does about Hebrew boy babies.

There is, however, a second answer to why God delivers Israel from Egypt that, in my judgment, surpasses the above first answer. I argue that even if the Hebrews have been enjoying a blissful life in Egypt, that if Egypt for them has turned out to be a paradise, a French Riviera or a Hawaii, the Lord would still take them out of that land.

The reason for that is that Israel's misery is not the Lord's primary motivating factor. Rather, it is to fulfill the covenant he has made with Abraham, Isaac, and Jacob, of which Genesis speaks. That covenant includes Israel's settlement in the land of Canaan. See the emphasis on the "land" that God promises repeatedly throughout Genesis to the patriarchs (Gen. 12:1–2; 13:14–17; 15:7, 18; 17:8; 22:17b; 24:7; 26:3–4; 28:13b; 35:12; 48:4; 50:24). The suffering Israelites never ask God to act on it, as later Moses does. Before Moses asks God to "remember" his pact with Abraham, Isaac, and Jacob (Exod. 32:13), God already "remembered" his promise to those three (2:24). So Moses is a little late in asking God to do something God has already done. Hence, we can say that the most crucial reason for the exodus is to fulfill a covenantal promise.

Having said that, it is unlikely that the Hebrews were interpreting their exodus that way. For them what is happening is not a salvation "to" but a salvation "from." It is a deliverance from tyranny, a moment when light beats back the darkness, as it did at creation, a time when hope is birthed.

Many Christian writers have observed the "salvation" theme, at least through the first fifteen chapters of Exodus. After pointing that out, they then proceed to make the parallels between old-covenant salvation and new-covenant salvation. Some of these parallels are quite legitimate: (1) a tyrant rules the nest, be he Pharaoh or Satan; (2) Israel/the individual are in bondage to a power greater than themselves; (3) Israel/the individual are totally incapable of liberating themselves; (4) salvation is a deliverance, a liberation from bondage; (5) only God (in Christ) can provide such an exodus.

However, there are at least two major differences between "salvation" in Exod. 1–15 and "salvation" in the Second Testament. For one thing, as I understand it, salvation in the Second Testament is, for the most part, salvation from sins I/we have committed. By contrast, salvation in Exod. 1–15 is salvation from sins others have committed against me/us (Egypt against Israel).

The second difference is related to the first difference. In Second-Testament salvation, the experience alters the relationship between the individual/group saved and one's/its Savior. The alien becomes a citizen. An enemy becomes a friend. Those who are far away are now brought near. Reconciliation has taken place. See, for example, the radical way Paul speaks in Eph. 2:1–22 of conversion and the major changes it introduces into the divine-human relationship.

Salvation in Exod. 1–15 does not change the relationship between Yahweh and Israel; rather, it confirms and reestablishes a relationship that already exists. The Lord saves Israel not so that Israel may *become* God's people but because Israel already *is* God's people, and such a deliverance is essential for the realization of the plan and purpose that God has for his people down the road. As early as the burning-bush incident, with the moment of liberation yet a good way off, Moses hears his God already referring to Israel as "my people" (Exod. 3:7, 10).

This understanding of salvation may help explain why Exodus prefers to use much more extensively the verbs *ʿālâ* ("bring up") and *yāṣāʾ* ("bring out") for the exodus, what one might call "locomotive verbs," rather than the more-explicit "salvation-family verbs" (*yāšaʿ*, *pādâ*, *gāʾal*, *mālaṭ*, *ʿāzar*, *nāṣal*). These are present in Exodus, or in parallel portions of the Torah, but only sparingly. For example, the verb *yāšaʿ* ("save," and the verb from which the proper names "Joshua" and "Jesus" are formed) appears only once in Exodus (14:30) with God as the subject, and the noun *yĕšûʿâ* ("salvation") also only once (15:2). (Jethro's daughters use this verb in 2:17 to tell their father what Moses has done for them at the well.) Contrast that with the Hiphil of *yāṣāʾ* ("bring out"), of which there are well over twenty instances in Exodus. Vocabulary-wise, lots of *yāṣāʾ*, little of *yāšaʿ*. See further the perceptive insights of Barr (1973) on this topic.

Following the exodus and the first taste of freedom, Israel finds itself in a wilderness (much like Hagar does in Gen. 16 and 21) that is threatening enough to make life back in Egypt desirable, at least to some, as impossible as that sounds. God does not lead his people from carnage directly to Canaan. After the exit from suffocating land, the way to promised land is through unpromising land. As Birch et al. (2005: 123) says, "God's salvation does not guarantee life without hardships. The world outside of bondage is also a world with dangers and struggles. . . . In the context of such struggle, even bondage can begin to look attractive."

The God of chaps. 1–14 who "sees, hears, remembers, is concerned about, and comes down" is now in chaps. 15–18 (and beyond) the God who "tests." Wilderness time is testing time. The Israel who has "cried" in chaps. 1 and 2 is now the Israel who "complains." The God of chaps. 1–14 who graciously provides for Israel's liberation now graciously provides for Israel's hydration, their obstinacy notwithstanding. If God can prevent death brought on by cruelty and barbarism, can he also prevent death brought on by hunger and thirst? There is no indication that God ever entertains any second thoughts about leading recalcitrant Israel out of Egypt ("Maybe I should have left the ingrates there"). He did think of "destroying" them (32:10) but never of "leaving them in the lurch," although annihilation might be considered as bad as abandonment, maybe even worse. But as in Gen. 1:1–2:4a, anything God starts, he finishes. No Pharaoh, no anybody, will derail a plan that is in God's heart.

Israel, according to the structure of Exodus and Numbers, spends a good bit of time in the wilderness (Smith 1999):

Exodus	Numbers
1:1–15:21 in Egypt	1:1–10:10 at Sinai
15:22–18:26 in the wilderness	10:11–21:35 in the wilderness
19–40 at Sinai	22–36 in Transjordan

(Actually there is more wilderness time in Exodus and Numbers than the chart suggests, for Sinai too is part of the wilderness. Perhaps, then, a better way to outline Exodus would be: (1) in Egypt [1:1–12:30]; (2) beyond Egypt [12:31–18:27]; (3) at Sinai [19–40].)

Far and away the most critical revelations that appear in the wilderness era are those that take place at Mount Sinai. Far and away the most critical aberration that appears in the wilderness era is what takes place at Mount Sinai. Hence, this mountain is a place of great sanctity and gross sacrilege.

Under the category of "critical revelations," one includes these: (1) the Lord's offering of a covenant to his people (chap. 19); (2) the revelation of the Lord's law that articulates the guidelines by which his covenant people are to order their lives (chaps. 20–23); (3) the sealing of that covenant in a most moving ceremony (chap. 24); (4) the building of a place of worship where God will meet with his people (chaps. 25–31, 35–40). It is of no little interest that the disclosure of these monumental matters takes place in the wilderness. God speaks to his people about these most holy matters in a decidedly unholy place before they enter the holy land.

Furthermore, God's two most important revelations to his people take place when Israel is *not* on the move: Exod. 19:1–Num. 10:10 while camped at Sinai; and the legislation in Deuteronomy (12–29) while camped in the Plains of Moab, in the Transjordan.

Seven or eight times the text of Exodus cites Israel on the move from place X to place Y: 12:37a; 13:20; 14:1–2; 15:22a; 15:27; 16:1; 17:1; 19:1–2. Little significant revelation takes place during these journeys until the last one. God chooses to speak most clearly to his people when (a) they are camped rather than on the move, and (b) when they are alone in a wilderness, rather than in a land filled with all sorts of "people-ites." Most often, as far as I can determine, God speaks to Moses when they are alone. The posture of stillness and solitude creates an atmosphere that allows God to speak and his people to hear (see Ps. 46:10 [11]). That we are yet uncertain about Mount Sinai's location indicates that the reader should focus more on *what* God says than on *where* he says what he says, beyond recognizing the general "wilderness" area.

The Lord does not offer a covenant to his people until after (a) he has delivered Israel from Egypt and from Pharaoh, and (b) he has led and provided for them in the wilderness. A God who is a saving God and a sustaining God now desires to become the covenant God of those he has saved and sustained. Clearly this covenant does not initiate a relationship between God and Israel, for we just observed that as early as Exod. 3 God labels Israel as his people. Thus the covenant raises an existing relationship between two parties (Yahweh and Israel) to a higher and more intimate level. It is the difference, to use a human analogy, between fiancé/fiancée and spouse/spouse.

The covenant at Sinai is not distinct from the covenant God has made with Abraham. Rather, it fulfills that covenant. There is not one covenant with the patriarchs and another covenant with their offspring some four centuries later. What God has started in Gen. 12 he is bringing to completion in Exod. 19–24. Abraham, the "friend" of God (Isa. 41:8; 2 Chron. 20:7; James 2:23), anticipates Israel as the Lord's "treasured possession." God's word to Abram, "Walk before me, and be blameless" (Gen. 17:1b), anticipates his word to Israel about being "a holy nation" (Exod. 19:6). God's promise to Abram that all nations "will be blessed through you" (Gen. 12:3; 18:18) anticipates God's word to Israel to be "a kingdom of priests," for as Moses has heard his "call to ministry" in Exod. 3–4, Israel now hears its "call to ministry" in Exod. 19. The emphasis on God's honoring Abraham's obedience (Gen. 22:15–18) echoes the call to faithful obedience on Israel's part throughout Exod. 20–24. God not only blesses; he also uses, beyond calculation, those who lovingly obey him.

Part of the covenant that God makes with his people at Sinai includes the commandments of the Decalogue (20:1–17) and the more detailed laws of the Book of the Covenant (20:22–23:19). Law never comes before covenant in the Bible, so it is inconceivable, for example, that chap. 20 could precede chap. 19. But covenant never exists apart from law, anymore than a marriage ceremony can delete the exchange of vows. If the purpose of covenant is to elevate (or initiate) a relationship between two parties, then the purpose of law is to help protect and nourish that relationship by providing guidelines or boundaries that, if faithfully honored, will go a long way in preserving and extending that relationship. And because this covenant relationship is one between nonequals, Yahweh the master and Israel the servant, it is Yahweh who determines the guidelines and sets the boundaries.

There is no clear-cut prioritizing or scaling of these *miṣbōt* (commandments) that permits the contemporary reader of Scripture, Jewish or Christian, to focus in on 20:1–17, but to brush aside as irrelevant 20:22–23:19. (For a thoughtful treatment of the "relevance" of all this Sinai legislation for modern believers, see Sprinkle 2006.) I find, on the one hand, no evidence that the Book of the Covenant stands in the shadow of the Decalogue, as if the latter is on the front burner and the former is on the back burner. The God who says, "You shall have no other gods before me" (Exod. 20:3), also says (through Moses), "Do not cook a young goat in its mother's milk" (23:19b). The Lord is sovereign enough to be able to tell his people not only how to worship him, but also how to prepare the meals one eats in the privacy of one's home. On the other hand, other passages in Scripture graphically spell out the consequence for worshiping other gods. I am not aware of any passage that tells what happens to the individual who, behind the closed doors of the home, boils a kid in its mother's milk. Plus, the significance of the Decalogue over the Covenant Code shows forth in that the Lord speaks the former directly to his people, and the only time he does so in Exodus, while he delivers the contents of the Covenant Code to Israel through Moses. (In my commentary section to follow, especially the last verse of chap. 19, I shall present the argument of some that the Lord also delivers the Decalogue through Moses.)

Any covenant-making moment calls for a ceremony, be it a bar/bat mitzvah, a christening, a baptism, or a wedding to solemnize the moment. Exodus 24 records the moment of covenant ratification in which, with a blood covenant, Yahweh bonds with Israel, and Israel bonds with Yahweh. In chaps. 19–23 Israel has heard. Now in chap. 24 Israel must respond to what it has heard. Its response is clear: "We will do everything the Lord has said; we will obey." Who would not want to obey a God who has both saved and sustained one in perilous places and times? The more one trusts him, the easier it is to obey him.

Earlier I said that if Exodus were primarily about the exodus, then the book could have concluded by the end of chap. 14. If the primary purpose of God's delivering his people is that he might engage them in a covenant and solicit their obedience, then Exodus could conclude with chapter 24.

The last portion of Exodus, chaps. 25–31, 35–40, demonstrates that God's concern is to move his people beyond obedience, as crucial as that is, to worship, to having a place where God can dwell among them (*miškān*) and meet with them (*ʾōhel môʿēd*). Divine, legal pronouncements give way to divine presence. Exodus begins by briefly referring to Jacob's "going down" to Egypt (Gen. 46:3 uses *yārad*) and ends by referring to the Lord's "coming down" from the mountaintop to dwell among his people (although chap. 40 does not use *yārad* language). The God who has "come down" in Exod. 3:8 to rescue his people is the God who in Exod. 40 comes down to remain with his people. It is a "coming down" that shifts in emphasis from deliverance to dwelling, from saving to staying. Alter (2004) has picturesquely described the change from the pulsating narrative of Exodus up to this point to the ordered liturgy in chap. 25 and following. He says that chaps. 25–31, 35–40 provide a "beautiful ordering of sacred space, a zone of choreographed repetition set off against the unsettled peregrinations of the Wilderness generation. The satisfaction this material gives its audience is not story but pageantry" (2004: 305).

As early as 3:12 ("When you have brought the people out of Egypt, you will *worship* God on this mountain") the worship theme surfaces. Pharaoh's refusal is a refusal to release Israel so that the people might worship Yahweh ("Let us take a three-day journey into the desert to offer sacrifices to the Lord our God" [3:18b]). In chap. 19 Moses instructs the people how best to prepare for a worshipful encounter with God, an experience akin to his own at the burning bush. Surely it is no accident that the Book of the Covenant begins (20:24–26) and ends (23:14–19) with worship-related emphases. And in 24:1 Moses and others are to come up and worship, albeit at a distance, Moses excepted. But in chap. 40, nobody needs to "go up" to worship, for the divine glory came down and "settled upon" the shrine. G. I. Davies (1999: 149) has appropriately called Exodus "a theology of liberation for worship."

Exodus concludes with two powerful contrasts. In the penultimate chapter, one reads that the Israelites do "just as the LORD had commanded" (39:43). That positive comment contrasts with chap. 32, in which Israel does everything the Lord has forbidden. Similarly chap. 40 in several places says that "Moses did . . . just as the LORD commanded him." The actions of Moses in chap. 40 contrast vividly with his actions earlier in chaps. 3 and 4, where Moses is unwilling to do what the Lord is commanding him to do.

In the opening chapters of Exodus, it is Pharaoh who determines Israel's movements. In the last chapter of Exodus (vv. 36–38) and onward, it is the cloud and glory of God that determine Israel's movements. In the process Israel has shifted masters. Pharaoh controls their lives in the early chapters of Exodus. Yahweh controls their travels in chap. 40. Israel moves on only when the cloud lifts. Otherwise, they stay put. As Isbell (1982: 45) correctly observes, "The real issue throughout the narrative [of Exodus] is not slavery vs. freedom, but merely the identity and character of the master whom Israel must serve."

There are any number of ways to outline the contents of the book of Exodus. I cite a few that I find creative and compelling.

1. Westermann 1967: 55–56:

I. God's Saving Act: Deliverance out of Distress (chaps. 1–14)
  A. The Distress (chaps. 1–11)
  B. The Deliverance (chaps. 12–14)
II. Man's Response in Praise (15:1–21)
III. God's Action: Preservation (15:22–18:27)
  A. From Thirst (15:22–27; 17:1–7)
  B. From Hunger (chap. 16)
IV. [Israel's] Response in Obedience (chaps. 19–31)
V. Transgression and Renewal (chaps. 32–40)

2. Smith 1997: 190:

I. Egypt
  A. Chapters 1–2: Moses's movement from Egypt to Midian
  B. Two calls and two confrontations
    i. 3:1–6:1: Moses's first call and confrontation with Pharaoh

i′. 6:2–14:31: Moses's second call and Yahweh's confrontation with Moses
The conflict between the powers of Egypt and Sinai
15:1–21: Victory at the sea

II. Sinai
A′. 15:22–18:27: Israel's movement from Egypt to Midian
B′. Two covenants and two sets of tablets
i. Chaps. 19–31: Israel's first covenant with Yahweh; the first tablets
i′. Chaps. 32–40: Israel's second covenant with Yahweh; the second tablets

3. Janzen (1997: 9–11), who sees Exodus as "a Story in two acts":

A. Oppression, Redemption, Covenant (1–24)
B. Planning a Place for Presence (25–31)
A′. Sin, Redemption, Covenant (32–34)
B′. Preparing a Place for Presence (35–40)

Among other connections between the "two acts," Janzen notes that in *A* Israel comes under dire threat from Egypt because of a "change" in Egypt's leadership, while in *A′* Israel comes under dire threat from Yahweh because of a "change" for the worse in Israel's behavior. In *A* the Lord intercedes with Moses to go to Egypt to bring Israel out, while in *A′* Moses intercedes with the Lord not to wipe out Israel. In *A* the Lord's saving his people from Egypt and Pharaoh is followed by the Lord's entering into a covenant with his people, while in *A′* the Lord's saving his people from his own wrath is followed by a renewal of the covenant.

4. Longman (2009: 34) offers the following concise outline, stating that it captures the book's three major themes of deliverance, law, and presence:

I. God saves Israel from Egyptian bondage (1–18)
II. God gives Israel his law (19–24)
III. God commands Israel to build the tabernacle (25–40)

5. At the risk of overusing rhyming words, I offer my own outline:

1. Oppression (1:1–2:25)
2. Trepidation (3:1–4:31)
3. Rejection (5:1–23)
4. Reaffirmation (6:1–30)
5. Confrontation (7:1–12:30)
6. Liberation (12:31–14:31)

7. Celebration (15:1–21)
8. Itineration (15:22–17:15)
9. Administration (18:1–27)
10. Legislation (19:1–24:18)
11. Specifications (25:1–31:18)
12. Deviation (32:1–33:23)
13. Reconciliation (34:1–35)
14. Construction (35:1–40:33)
15. Glorification (40:34–38)

PART 1

Oppression in Egypt

(1:1–6:1)

Little does Jacob realize when God speaks to him nocturnally, instructing him to go down to Egypt (Gen. 46:3–4), that the sojourn will last well beyond his lifetime, 430 years in fact (Exod. 12:40). While on that occasion he hears God's promises to "make you into a great nation," and "I will surely bring you back again," more than likely he is uninformed of what God has earlier said to his grandfather. That is, for 400 of those 430 years Jacob's descendants will be "enslaved and mistreated" (Gen. 15:13). For one reason or another, God does not bring that grim prospect up to Jacob. God's emphasis is on the termination of the servitude rather than on the duration of the servitude.

Hence, there is a considerable chronological gap between the end of Genesis, concluding with the death of 147-year-old Jacob, the last 17 years of which he lives in Egypt (Gen. 47:28), and the death of 110-year-old Joseph (Gen. 50:26).

For the first portion of those 400 years, any mistreatment and oppression of the Hebrews in Egypt must be mild and sporadic. Presumably Exodus begins toward the end, or least the second half, of those four centuries. As far as biblical record goes, they are years that the text passes over in virtual silence. There is no record of God's speaking even once during that interlude. The last time the text has recorded God as speaking to anybody is Gen. 46:2–4, and that is briefly in a nocturnal vision to Jacob. Before that, one has to go back to Gen. 35:1, 10. Fast-forwarding the tape, one finds that God is not heard from again until Exod. 3:4.

The Hebrews' fortunes go downhill rapidly when an anonymous Pharaoh "who did not know about Joseph" comes to the Egyptian throne (Exod. 1:8). One suspects that if he knew about Joseph and his salvific leadership that also spared Egypt through difficult times, such knowledge would override and cancel out any suspicions he entertains about these "foreigners" who live on his turf and who, in his imagination, pose a colossal threat to the well-being of his empire.

The first two chapters of Exodus provide a summarization of these brutal times for the Hebrews. The Lord's word to Abram in Gen. 15:13 is now coming to pass graphically and ominously. Still, no word from God, no word that would rend the heavens and stop this ruthless oppressor dead in his tracks. Thankfully the actions of some God-fearing women limit the death toll, but the torment continues.

That is, until God encounters a shepherd by a bush and calls him to be the instrument whom God will use to liberate his people from Egypt and lead them to a promised land. That shepherd is Moses. Chapters 3 and 4 of Exodus record his "call." It is a "call account" that has more than its share of bumps and sharp curves. But God sticks with a trying-to-get-out-of-it Moses as much as he sticks with a trying-to-get-out-of-it Jonah. In neither case does the Almighty adopt a take-it-or-leave-it disposition.

Chapter 5 records Moses's first attempt to persuade Pharaoh to release the Hebrews. Judged by the yardstick of "success in ministry," Moses's efforts are an unmitigated disaster. Both Pharaoh and his own flock of sheep reject Moses and his message. No wonder, then, that if in chap. 2 it is the Hebrews who are "crying out" (either just crying out, or crying out to God), at the end of chap. 5 it is Moses who is crying out to God. The one commissioned and sent by God to deliver the Hebrews from their lamenting can only articulate his own angry (and honest) lament.

Multiplying in Egypt

(1:1–7)

Translation

[1]And these [are] the names of the sons of a man named Israel who came to Egypt, each with his own househeld: [2]Reuben, Simeon, Levi, Judah, [3]Issachar, Zebulun and Benjamin, [4]Dan and Naphtali, Gad and Asher. [5]Those souls issuing from Jacob's thigh numbered seventy. Joseph was already in Egypt. [6]Joseph, along with all his brothers and that entire generation, died. [7]Still, the Israelites were fertile and prolific; they multiplied and became extremely mighty, so that the land was filled with them.

Grammatical and Lexical Notes

1:1. The first word in Exodus is "and" (*wĕʾēlleh*, "*And these* [are] the names of . . ."), indicating that Exodus, rather than being a distinct book, is simply the continuation of the narrative that Genesis has begun. However, the LXX does not start with "and" and has its own name: "Exodus." These facts indicate that for the Greek translator(s) Exodus was considered a distinct book that could stand by itself (Wevers 2004: 21).

1:6. Although the subject of the verb "died" is plural ("Joseph, his brothers, that entire generation"), the verb is singular. There are several examples in Exodus of a compound subject with a singular verb, the reason for which is to highlight the principal person in the narrative (Exod. 4:29; 7:6, 10; 12:30; 15:1; 16:6; 29:21b).

1:7. "Was filled with them" illustrates an accusative of relation after a verb in the Niphal (cf. 1 Kings 7:14, "Huram was full of wisdom"; 2 Kings 3:20, "and the land was full of water"; Ezek. 10:4, "and the court was full of the radiance of the LORD's glory.").

1:7. One way Hebrew expresses the superlative (here indicated by "extremely") is by doubling the word: *mĕʾōd mĕʾōd*. Genesis examples include 7:19 ("rose greatly"); 17:2, 20 ("greatly increase"); 17:6 ("very fruitful"); 30:43 ("grew exceedingly prosperous").

Commentary

Exodus (in the Hebrew at least; see above note on 1:1) begins with the word **1:1**
"and" ("and these [are]"). This conjunction links the story of Exodus with Genesis, one taking up where the other leaves off. Leviticus ("and-called to Moses") and Numbers ("and-spoke the Lord") begin similarly. Genesis through Numbers is one story, a Tetrateuch.

Actually Exodus does not pick up exactly where Genesis leaves off. Exodus 1 goes back to the genealogy of Jacob's family in Gen. 46:8–27 rather than the end of Genesis. The repetition of the introductory "these are the names of . . ." from Gen. 46:8 indicates the writer's intention to link Gen. 46:8–27 with Exod. 1:1–5. In the latter passage he does so by resuming the subject of the former, thus arching over the intervening account, 46:28–50:26 (Talmon 1978: 14–15).

For a similar introductory phrase to name lists see Exod. 6:16 ("These are the names of the sons of Levi"); 2 Sam. 23:8 ("These are the names of David's mighty men"); 1 Kings 4:7–8 ("Solomon also had twelve district governors. . . . These are their names"). An Aramaic text from the fifth century BC begins as follows: "Now these are the names of the women who were found at the gates in Thebes and were taken prisoners" (Cowley 1923: 127, text #34).

1:2–4 Although these opening verses are taken from Gen. 46:8–27, the order in which the names are listed is different. Actually the best parallel to Exod. 1:2–4 is Gen. 35:23–26 (which also includes Joseph). Genesis 46:8–27 lists first the sons by Leah (vv. 8–15), then those by her maidservant, Zilpah (vv. 16–18), then the sons by Rachel (vv. 19–22), and finally the sons by Rachel's maidservant, Bilhah (vv. 23–25).

Exodus 1:2–4, however, arranges the sons chiasmically according to matriarchal origin:

A the sons of Leah (Reuben, Simeon, Levi, Judah, Issachar, and Zebulun)
  B Rachel's second son (Benjamin)
  B′ the sons of Rachel's maidservant, Bilhah (Dan, Naphtali)
A′ the sons of Leah's maidservant, Zilpah (Gad, Asher).

1:5 The Hebrew word for "thigh" (*yerek*) may sometimes refer to the genitalia, male or female. For example, what part of the anatomy is involved in those passages in Genesis (24:2, 9; 47:29) in which somebody puts his hand under the "thigh" of another as he makes a promise to that person? Literally, the thigh, or possibly the genitals? Similarly, the reference to the "thigh" of the suspected adulteress wasting away or sagging (Num. 5:21, 22, 27) is probably a euphemism for her procreative organs.

Verse 5 and Deut. 10:22 tell us that Jacob has seventy descendants. "Seventy" is a frequent number in Scripture and elsewhere (Burrows 1936). There are seventy nations (Gen. 10); seventy elders of Israel (Exod. 24:1; Ezek. 8:11); seventy other elders (Num. 11:16); seventy submissive kings (Judg. 1:7); seventy struck by the Lord (1 Sam. 6:19); Gideon's seventy sons (Judg. 8:30); seventy offspring riding seventy donkeys (Judg. 12:14); Ahab's seventy sons (2 Kings 10:1). Luke 10:1 says that Jesus sent out seventy or seventy-two of his disciples (there is good ancient manuscript evidence for both numbers).

In some instances it seems to be a precise number, and in others it symbolizes a large group of people.

In a Canaanite text from Ugarit that describes Baal as preparing a divine banquet (*KTU* 1.4 vi:46), this line appears: "Baal/Hadad invites the seventy sons of Athirat / he supplies the gods with rams (and) with wine." Parker (1997: 134, 171n135) adds this observation, "The number of gods perhaps survive in the later Jewish notion of the seventy angels, one for each of the seventy nations ([Babylonian Talmud,] *Shabbat* 88b; *Sukkah* 55b)."

The LXX, along with a Dead Sea Scroll text of Exodus (4QEx[a]), reads "seventy-five" instead of "seventy." Stephen too uses this number (Acts 7:14), as do Josephus (*Ant.* 2.7.4 §176) and the book of *Jubilees* (44.33). The difference is because Gen. 46:20 LXX adds five names to the families of Manasseh and Ephraim (details in R. Klein 1974: 14–15).

Unlike in Numbers, there is no indication that this first generation's death is **1:6**
in any way linked to a judgment from God. The first generation of Israel in Egypt fares much better than the first generation of Israel who flees Egypt.

In Genesis the problem is too much infertility. Here so much fertility will **1:7**
arouse the paranoid fears of Pharaoh. Apparently there are few, if any, Sarahs or Rebekahs or Rachels in Goshen.

There are numerous places, especially in Genesis, where the words "be fruitful/fertile" (*pārâ*) and "multiply" (*rābâ*) occur together. The two are used with animals (Gen. 1:22; 8:17), Adam (1:28), Noah (9:1, 7), Abraham (17:2, 6), Ishmael (17:20), Isaac (26:4, 24), and Jacob (28:3; 35:11; 48:4). Of these many parallels, the closest to Exod. 1:7 is Gen. 1:28, for they are the only two verses among the lot with a sequence of five nonidentical verbs ("be fruitful/increase/fill/subdue/rule" and "were fertile/prolific/multiplied/became mighty/filled with them"). "The climax of Genesis 1 is Exodus 1: the divine power to proliferate found its highest expression in the emergence of Israel" (Porten and Ruppaport 1971: 368).

The word I have rendered "prolific" is the verb *šāraṣ*, "to swarm, teem" (Gen. 1:20–21). The related noun, *šereṣ*, refers to the "swarming things" of Gen. 1:20 (aquatic creatures) and 7:21; 8:17 (land creatures). Leviticus 11:20 ("all winged swarming creatures") forbids their consumption. The use of this verb to describe Israel's phenomenal growth in Egypt, and its connections elsewhere with lower forms of life, suggests that their growth was "insect-like" (Gruber 1992: 101). More than normal conceived. Fewer than normal miscarried. More than normal survived to adulthood.

The parallel pair *pārâ*/*šāraṣ*, here side by side, occur again in distant parallelism in Ps. 105, parts of which (vv. 23–36) reflect on this section of Exodus: Ps. 105:24a and 30, "The Lord made his people very fruitful [*pārâ*]. . . . The land teemed [*šāraṣ*] with frogs." So the story goes from teeming Israelites in Egypt in Exod. 1 to teeming frogs in Egypt in Exod. 8.

An Anxious Pharaoh

(1:8–14)

Translation

[8]A new king who did not know Joseph came to power in Egypt. [9]He said to his advisers, "Indeed the people of the sons of Israel outnumber us and are more powerful. [10]Come now, let us deal wisely with him lest he multiply. Should war break out, he might join our enemies, fight against us, and go up from the land." [11]Then they put over him taskmasters to crush him with forced labor. He built store cities (Pithom and Rameses) for Pharaoh. [12]But the more they sought to crush him, the more he multiplied and became even more prolific, with the result that the Egyptians dreaded the sons of Israel. [13]The Egyptians imposed backbreaking labor on the sons of Israel. [14]They embittered their lives with excruciatingly hard work involving mortar and bricks and other kinds of demanding labor out in the field, all sorts of backbreaking labors that they imposed on them.

Grammatical and Lexical Notes

1:8. For two other places where *wayyāqom* ("arose, came to power") stands at the head of a sentence and follows the notice of someone's death, see Gen. 23:3 and Ruth 1:6.

1:9. "Advisers" (*ʿam*) hides the fact that the Hebrew word occurs twice in this verse: "Look," he said to his *people*; and "the *people* of the sons of Israel." For the first "people" the LXX uses *ethnei* ("people"), but for the Israelite people it uses *genos* ("race"). The latter term is used for Israel, "to indicate a foreign people, since the Israelites were foreigners in the land of Egypt" (Wevers 2004: 24).

1:9. Here Pharaoh introduces his words of concern with *hinnēh* ("indeed"). In 5:5 he introduces similar words of concern with *hēn*. Although at times interchangeable, *hinnēh* introduces something new in the discourse, while *hēn* reestablishes and reasserts previous knowledge (Garr 2004b: 342–44).

1:9. *rab . . . mimmennû* ("outnumber us") may be rendered either "too numerous for us" or "more numerous than we." See commentary below.

1:10. *hābâ* ("Come now"), an exclamation, is from the verb *yāhab*, "give." This word before a cohortative ("Come now, let us deal wisely") recalls the similar construction in Gen. 11:3, 4, 7 ("Come, let us make bricks"; "Come, let us build ourselves a city"; "Come, let us go down").

1:10. I retain the masculine singular (him/he) throughout vv. 10–12 until the plural surfaces in v. 14, rather than replace the Hebrew masculine pronouns and verbs with "it" or "she" or "they."

1:10. "break out" is from *qārāʾ* II, "befall, happen," and not from *qārāʾ* I, "call." The subject ("war") is a feminine singular noun, but the verb ("break out") is feminine plural. GKC §145e cites instances of feminine collective nouns with plural verbs. Dahood (1971: 348–49) upholds the Hebrew consonantal text by parsing the verb as a Qal passive of the energetic mood ("when war is declared").

1:10. Ironically, Pharaoh speaks of the possibility of Israel "going up" (*ʿālâ*) from Egypt long before the Lord does (Exum 1994: 43–44).

1:11. The Hebrew for "forced labor" is *siblâ* (also in 2:11; 5:5, where NIV renders it "working"; and 6:6–7, where NIV renders it "yoke"). The Hebrew root *sbl* is the same as the Akkadian *zabalu*, which Held (1968: 92) notes was commonly used with transporting clay, bricks, and straw.

1:11. Although the correct translation for *miskĕnôt* is "store cities," the LXX translates with *ochyras* ("strong/fortified cities"). To the Greek translator, these Hebrew-built places were "cities built up for strong defence against possible attack rather than places for storing commodities" (Wevers 2004: 24–25).

1:12. "The more . . . the more" is *kaʾăšer . . . kēn*, on which see R. Williams 1976: §264; Waltke and O'Connor 1990: 641.

1:12. "Dreaded" is the meaning of the verb *qûṣ* when it is followed by the expression *mippĕnê* ("from the face of"), as here and in Num. 22:3 (Moab of Israel) and Isa. 7:16 (Ahaz of neighboring kings). However, followed instead by the preposition *bĕ*, *qûṣ* means "to loathe, be disgusted with" (Gen. 27:46: "I am disgusted with living because of these Hittite women," Rebekah says to Isaac).

1:13. "Imposed backbreaking labor" is literally "compelled them to labor [Hiphil] in harshness." The last word is *bĕpārek*. The expression resurfaces three times in Lev. 25 (vv. 43, 46, 53) telling how Israel is not to treat her slaves. The root is related to Aramaic *pĕrak* ("rub, pulverize") and Akkadian *paraku* ("hinder, oppose"). Hebrew *bĕpārek* has the same force as Akkadian *ina parikti*.

1:14. The Hebrew behind "embittered" is *mārar*, which some have rendered as "toughened." See commentary below.

1:14. *ʿābĕdû bāhem* near the end of the sentence shows that the (intransitive) Qal of *ʿābad* requires the *bêt* of means. If the (transitive) Hiphil is used, as in v. 13, the *bêt* is unnecessary. The use of *ʾēt* before a nominal expression (*ʾēt kol-ʿăbōdātām*) is perhaps surprising after a string of nouns with the prefixed preposition *bĕ*. The latter expression demonstrates the use of *ʾēt* before a noun in apposition to a noun with preposition, and introducing an explicative clause.

Commentary

The Bible could easily have identified who this "new king" was. It identifies the 1:8
midwives by name (v. 15), but not this regal figure who more than likely was the most powerful person on the planet at that time. For all the pharaohs identified as such throughout Genesis and Exodus, one has to wait until Solomon's time until one is named—Shishak (1 Kings 11:40; 14:25–26; 2 Chron. 12:1–11).

When the verse says that this Pharaoh does not "know" Joseph, "know" could mean "has never heard of." Or it could mean "once knew, but has forgotten him" (as with Joseph and the cupbearer, who "did not remember Joseph; he forgot him" [Gen. 40:23]). More than likely "know" has a stronger, more belligerent thrust. The new Pharaoh refuses to acknowledge the worth of Joseph's contribution to Egypt's well-being. He repudiates the legitimacy of Joseph's time in office, refuses to acknowledge him and to extend any further courtesy to Joseph and his kin. A change of ruler may be a turning point in the career of one who is powerfully positioned in the royal court. For a parallel, think of Daniel's predicament after the death of Nebuchadnezzar.

One cannot miss the parallels between the times of transition in leadership noted in Exod. 1:6, 8 and Judg. 2:8, 10: (1) Exod. 1:6: "Joseph, along with all his brothers died," and Judg. 2:8, "Joshua, the son of Nun . . . died"; (2) Exod. 1:6, "and that entire generation," and Judg. 2:10, "After that whole generation had been gathered to their fathers"; (3) Exod. 1:8, "a new king arose over Egypt who did not know Joseph," and Judg. 2:10, "another generation arose [NIV, "grew up"] who did not know the Lord." Which ignorance imperils God's people more, a new Pharaoh who does not know Joseph, or a new generation of Israelites who do not really know their covenant Lord?

1:9 The Hebrew word for "advisers" is "people" (*ʿam*), but surely Pharaoh is not making a broad, nationwide announcement; rather, he is speaking to the advisers in his administration, those who counsel him and help expedite his decisions. Still, notice the almost back-to-back use of *ʿam*: "He said to his people, 'Indeed the people of . . .'" One people mushrooming, and another people alarmed.

Pharaoh is concerned either that these immigrant Israelites are increasing too rapidly (becoming "too numerous") or that they actually outnumber his own people. Elsewhere the expression carries comparative force ("far more numerous than" [Num. 14:12; Deut. 9:14]; "much larger than" [Deut. 7:1]; "greater and more populous than" [Deut. 4:38; 9:1]; "stronger than we" [1 Kings 20:23]; "stronger than I" [2 Sam. 22:18]). Pharaoh is speaking either truthfully or hyperbolically as part of his fearmongering tactics.

If this new king is Rameses II (1279–1213 BC), and that is not at all certain, then his fears seem even stranger. One historian reports that "he had an enormous harem, and as the years passed his children multiplied rapidly. He left over a hundred sons and at least half as many daughters, several of whom he himself married. He thus left a family so numerous that they became a Ramessid class of nobles" (Breasted 1967: 388). To this, Sternberg (1998: 123–24) adds, "Were all the Egyptian menfolk breeders of anything like their sovereign's caliber, the predicament of hosting a race 'too numerous and mighty' for us would hardly loom so large, not even to the xenophobes of antiquity."

1:10 The "Come now, let us . . ." recalls that phrase throughout the City/Tower of Babel story in Gen. 11. The further reference to "mortar and bricks" (Exod. 1:14) repeats some of the materials mentioned in Gen. 11:3. The builders do what they do "lest" they be scattered (Gen. 11:4), and Pharaoh is fearful "lest" Israel multiply. In both cases somebody comes up with a plan to do something that is not God's will, and so on both occasions God frustrates the plan. No city with a tower, and no genocide.

Pharaoh refers to "our enemies," indicating that Egypt has other nations who do not like Egypt and are prepared to go to war against that nation.

Israel might become a large fifth column, aiding the international bloc of such enemies.

The verb "crush," here and in v. 12 (*ʿānâ* II in the Piel), carries the idea of forc- 1:11
ing someone into submission. That explains why in some passages it takes on the meaning of "rape," something a man does to a woman (Gen. 34:2; Deut. 22:24; Judg. 20:5; 2 Sam. 13:12, 14, 22, 32). The verb also describes what a woman might do with a man, Delilah binding Samson and "subduing" him (Judg. 16:5–6, 19). It is also used to describe what one woman may do to another woman (Gen. 16:6; NIV's "Sarai 'mistreated' Hagar" seems a bit weak in light of other uses of the verb). What Sarah, an (early) Israelite, did to an Egyptian, an Egyptian Pharaoh will do to Sarah's descendants. To that degree, Sarah foreshadows Pharaoh's role, just as Hagar's story prefigures Israel's story (Trible 1984: 69).

The Hebrew for "store cities" is *ʿārê miskĕnôt*. It is difficult to miss the similarity in sound between *miskĕnôt* ("storage") and the word *miškān* ("tabernacle") throughout Exod. 25–40. Exodus begins with God's people building cities of *miskĕnôt* for Pharaoh; it concludes with God's people building a *miškān* for their God. The first building project is imposed and harsh. The second one is God-revealed and an honor with which to be involved.

Wherever the Bible mentions such cities, it is always in connection with royal activity: Gen. 41:35, 48 (in Egypt); Exod. 1:11 (in Egypt); 1 Kings 9:19; 2 Chron. 8:4, 6 (Solomonic); 2 Chron. 16:4 (in Naphtali, associated with Baasha, king of Israel); 2 Chron. 17:12 (Judean, built by Jehoshaphat); 2 Chron. 32:28 (associated with Hezekiah). Frick (1977: 136) suggests that "store city" "refers to the building of royal granaries or warehouses in already existing cities rather than to the building of an entire city. Such structures were used to store the taxes of grain, wine and oil collected by the government."

Of all these references to "store cities" in the OT, those belonging to Pharaoh in Exod. 1 and those belonging to Solomon invite comparison. What Pharaoh does with the aliens living in his backyard, David (1 Chron. 22:2) and Solomon (2 Chron. 2:17–18) do with the aliens living in their backyard. If Sarah's oppressing Hagar anticipates Pharaoh's oppressing the Israelites, David and Solomon's use of outsiders to do the hard and dirty work of construction recalls Pharaoh's decree.

The identities of Pithom and Rameses remain a mystery. Egyptologists usually connect Rameses with Pi(r)-Rameses ("House/Domain of Rameses"), a northeast delta metropolis built up and expanded by Rameses II (1279–1213 BC). His predecessor, Seti I (1294–1279 BC), had built a summer palace there. Pithom is thought to represent Egyptian Pi(r)-Atum, "House of (the god) Atum." It is either Tel er-Retabeh or Tel el-Maskhutah, both of which are south and west of Pi(r)-Rameses. (On these two sites, see especially the studies of Redford 1963; Uphill 1968; 1969; Hoffmeier 1997: 116–21; Kitchen 2003:

254–59; and A. Collins 2008, who regrettably dismisses the reference to these two cities as anachronistic additions.)

For some who have addressed the date of the exodus, the reference to "the city of Rameses" in Exod. 1:11 seems to seal the case for a date in the thirteenth century BC. Others who argue for an earlier date for the exodus (the mid-fifteenth century BC) suggest that Rameses in Exod. 1:11 is an editorial updating of an earlier name that has gone out of use. See the debate among Wood (2005; 2007) and Hoffmeier (2007).

1:12 Pharaoh's harsh measures directed at the Israelites have the opposite effect from what he was hoping. They continue to thrive and multiply, their severe conditions notwithstanding. Acts provides examples from the NT era where the believers, although harassed and persecuted, continue to multiply. Illustrations of this phenomenon can be found in almost any century.

1:13 The verse seems to repeat v. 11, with "backbreaking labor" (*bĕpārek*) replacing "forced labor" (*siblâ*). The former Hebrew expression occurs in Lev. 25:43, 46, and 53, all of which forbid the ruthless treatment of a fellow Israelite. What the Egyptians do to the Israelites (Exod. 1), Israelites ought not to do to one another (Lev. 25). Apparently they sometimes crossed that line. Ezekiel (34:4), addressing the shepherds/kings of Israel, charges them with this indictment, "You have not strengthened the weak. . . . You have ruled them harshly and brutally [*bĕpārek*]."

1:14 The attempt to exploit and degrade the Israelites has either "embittered" their lives, or only "toughened" their lives. How does one translate the verb *mārar*? The root is reflected in Naomi's words in Ruth 1:20, "'Don't call me Naomi,' she told them. 'Call me *mārāʾ*, for the Lord has *mārar*-ed me.'" Does Eccles. 7:26 say, "I found more *bitter* than death the woman who is a snare," or does it say, "I found *stronger* than death"?

One reason for going with "be/make strong" is that the root *mrr* carries that meaning in Ugaritic, Arabic, and Aramaic (Gordon 1965: 438; Dahood 1958: 308–9), and so, maybe also in some OT passages. It is unlikely, however, that the writer of Exodus intended to suggest that the Egyptians were strengthening/toughening the Israelites, any more than Naomi was saying that the Lord had strengthened her (Pardee 1978: 258). Kutler (1984: 114) tries to retain "strong" over "bitter" but with a negative connotation: "And they 'exacerbated' their lives with hard work."

Two God-Fearing Midwives

(1:15–22)

Translation

[15]The king of Egypt said to the Hebrewess-born midwives, one of whom was named Shifrah and the second named Puah; [16]he said, "When you midwife the Hebrewesses, look upon the birthstool. If it is a son, you shall kill him; but if it is a girl, she shall live." [17]The midwives feared God and did not do as the king of Egypt had instructed them, but let the male children live. [18]Then the king of Egypt called the midwives and said to them, "Why have you done this thing and let the children live?" [19]The midwives answered Pharaoh, "Because not like the Egyptian women are the Hebrewesses, because they are lively. Before the midwife comes to them, they have given birth." [20]God dealt well with the midwives. The people multiplied and became very strong. [21]Because the midwives feared God, he established households for them. [22]Pharaoh commanded all his advisers, "All the born sons you shall throw Nileward, but all the daughters you shall let live."

Grammatical and Lexical Notes

1:15. "To the Hebrewess-born midwives" renders the Hebrew literally: preposition (*la*), plus nominal participle in the construct (*mĕyallĕdōt*), plus the plural feminine adjective (*hāʿibrîyōt*). This makes it clear that the midwives are Hebrewesses. If we repoint the preposition *la* to *li*, then we have preposition (*li*), plus verbal participle (*mĕyallĕdōt*), plus plural noun (*hāʿibrîyōt*)—"to those who midwife the Hebrewesses." This is the reading in the LXX and Vulgate, and it suggests that the midwives were Egyptians.

1:16. "Birthstool" (*haʾobnāyim*) is literally "two stones" (the dual). Its only other occurrence is in Jer. 18:3, "I went down to the potter's house, and I saw him working at the 'wheel.'" Did the midwives' stool look like the potter's wheel? Or does *ʾobnāyim* refer to something else? See commentary below.

1:17. The Piel of *ḥāyâ* (here and in vv. 18 and 22) does not carry the normal factitive use of the Piel ("make live") but means "let live."

1:18. For other "Why?" (*maddûaʿ*) questions in Exodus that spring from anger or reproach, see 5:14 ("Why didn't you meet your quota of bricks?") and 18:14 (Jethro to Moses, "Why do you alone sit as a judge?").

1:19. The midwives use no verbs until the end of the sentence. (I have supplied "are" for sense.) For other instances of clauses introduced by *kî* in which the predicate appears before the subject in a nominal clause, compare verses like "because detestable to the Egyptians [are] all shepherds" (Gen. 46:34), or "because fools [are] my people" (Jer. 4:22).

1:19. How best to render *ḥāyôt* ("lively, vigorous, instinct with life") remains unclear. A doubling of the middle consonant (*ḥayyôt*) gives the meaning, "They are like (wild) animals." Compare the phrase "multiplying like rabbits."

1:21. God either establishes "households" (*bāttîm* [or *bottîm*]) for these midwives or makes "houses" for them.

1:22. "All the sons . . . daughters" demonstrates the use of *kol* before a singular noun that is a noun of category or species, and hence the equivalent of the plural.

1:22. BDB 409b suggests that the Hebrew word for "born" in "all the born sons" (*yillôd*) is an adjective, and is an irregular punctuation for the Qal passive participle *yālûd*. Possibly the Pual of *yālad* uses two forms of the passive participle, *yullad* and *yillôd*, the latter to be explained through dissimilation. See Hendel 2000: 44n28, 45.

Commentary

1:15 As I indicated in my grammatical note on this verse, the Hebrew text clearly presents the midwives as Hebrew. Other ancient translations of Scripture (the Septuagint and Vulgate) and Josephus (*Ant.* 2.9.2 §§206–7) think of them as Egyptians. The difference between the two comes down to one vowel change in the opening preposition, *la* versus *li*. One might argue for their Hebrew origin because their names, Shifrah and Puah, are Semitic rather than Egyptian names. The latter name, Puah, is the same as Ugaritic *pgt*, "young woman," and the sister of Aqhat in the famous Canaanite story. Shifrah seems to be related to the verb *šāpar*, "be beautiful, fair." The same name appears in an Egyptian text that lists ninety-five household workers, forty-five of whom are Asiatics with Semitic names. One of these forty-five is identified simply as "the female Asiatic Shifrah" (*COS* 3:35). That v. 17 says they "feared God" might also tip the scales in favor of their being Hebrew, and if the text said, "They feared the Lord," it would have removed all doubt.

However, there are arguments to support their Egyptian origin. First, Hagar of Gen. 16 and 21 has a Semitic rather than Egyptian-sounding name although she is Egyptian. And might "they feared God" of v. 17 be rendered "they feared the gods [*hāʾĕlōhîm*]"? (Note that v. 21 uses a masculine, singular verb ["established"] with the subject *hāʾĕlōhîm*, suggesting "God" and not "gods" in v. 17 too.) Last of all, which group of women, Egyptian or Hebrew, would be more likely to implement Pharaoh's order about massive male infanticide?

Interestingly, the LXX transliterates "Shifrah" as *Sepphōra*, which is the same rendering it uses for "Zipporah," Moses's Midianite wife in the next chapter. Could it be that a non-Hebrew woman who rescues the newborn Moses from death at Pharaoh's hands later marries him and saves him from death at God's hands in 4:24–26?

Commentators continue to be vexed over how just two women could handle the obstetric needs of a people who earlier in the chapter are said to be multiplying and becoming very numerous. Are they actually two supervisors, midwives-in-chief, over a much larger group of underlings? Does the low number reinforce the imaginative, folktale character of the whole narrative? Do these two restrict their work to a very small region of Goshen alongside their unnamed counterparts who preside at births elsewhere in Goshen? Or, and this is the position I would advance, does the implicit emphasis on these two overworked midwives parallel the emphasis elsewhere in the chapter on the overworked Hebrews in Egypt? For both groups it is unrelieved, around-the-clock labor. See Sternberg 1998: 235–37.

There continues to be a difference of opinion on how to reproduce in English 1:16
"look upon *hā'obnāyim*": "look upon the birthstool," or "look upon the two stones [i.e., testicles]." The former is the much more common, but the latter is not without its advocates (e.g., Meek 1963: 270; Fewell and Gunn 1993: 91; and Blenkinsopp 2003: 271). If we go with "birthstool," then the reference is likely to some object on which the parturient mother sat, with an opening to allow the newborn to pass from the mother and into the hands of the midwife.

Pharaoh's instructions about killing the boy babies (Hiphil of *mût*) with the midwives as the subject, and the girl babies living (Qal of *ḥāyâ*) with the girl baby as subject, recalls Gen. 12:12. Abraham says to Sarah in Egypt, "Then they [the Egyptians] will kill me [Qal of *hārag*], but let you live [Piel of *ḥāyâ*]." Female lives are safe; male lives are on the chopping block. Both pharaohs will keep the ladies and eliminate the men.

Commentators have long puzzled over the logic of Pharaoh's decree. For example, Greenberg (1969: 29) remarks, "The condemnation of male infants seems either self-defeating or inadequate. If Pharaoh wanted to exploit Israel's manpower, the decree was self-defeating; if he wanted simply to reduce the Israelite population, he should have condemned the females, or at least included the females." Maybe, however, Pharaoh's intention is to get rid of the boys so that eventually he can have all the girls for himself and his people. Do with the boys what David does with Uriah so that he can have all these Hebrew Bathshebas for himself and his cronies. The attractiveness of that possibility is surely heightened by the witness of the midwives in v. 19 that the Hebrew women reproduce rapidly. In bluffing Pharaoh, they may be confirming him, albeit unintentionally, in his diabolical scheme.

The midwives have "feared" God more than Pharaoh. Sometimes people act 1:17
the way they act and do what they do because God has appeared to them (as with Moses in chap. 3). Out of that divine encounter, a pattern for living and ministry is shaped. Not so here. God, as far as we know, has never appeared or spoken to these midwives. Their response is instinctive and immediate. They will not render unto Pharaoh what belongs to God.

The phrase "fear/revere God" has already appeared a number of times in Genesis: (1) Abraham rationalizes and justifies his lying about Sarah to Abimelech by saying, "There is no fear of God in this place" (Gen. 20:11);

(2) Abraham's willingness to offer Isaac proves beyond a shadow of doubt to the angel of the Lord that Abraham fears God (Gen. 22:12); (3) an incognito Joseph tests his brothers' sincerity by keeping Simeon as hostage until they bring Benjamin to Egypt. He says to them, "Do this and you will live, for I fear God" (Gen. 42:18). The phrase appears again in Exod. 18:21, part of Jethro's advice to Moses, "Select capable men from all the people—men who fear God, trustworthy men," and in Exod. 20:20, Moses's words to his people right after the revelation of the Decalogue, "Do not be afraid. God has come to test you, so that the fear of God will be with you to keep you from sinning."

M. Fox (2000: 70) notes that the "fear of God is valued because it motivates right behavior even when socially enforced sanctions do not exist, and therefore cannot be effective." For example, no legal authority would punish Abimelech and the Philistines if they kill the alien Abraham. Only the fear of God, which Abraham believes does not exist there, would restrain them. Abraham has no legal obligation to kill his son. Only his fear of God motivates him. But when Pharaoh speaks to two Hebrew midwives and orders them "to jump," their logical response should be, "How high?" Instead, they ignore the ultimatum. For them, "to fear God" means making a decision, when presented with alternatives, that will be most pleasing to God, come what may.

In v. 16 the text has Pharaoh using "live" in the Qal of the verb ("she shall live"). In v. 17 the narrator uses the Piel of that verb ("they let the male children live"). In v. 16 Pharaoh speaks (via the Qal stem) of natural survival, based on gender. Verse 17 speaks of a brave choice (via the Piel stem) by these midwives to save lives. In the following verse, v. 18, the narrator has Pharaoh use the Piel stem ("let live") when interrogating the midwives.

1:18 Pharaoh's question, "Why have you done this thing?" turns the midwives' behavior into a sin of commission, whereas v. 17 has described it as a sin of omission: "They did not do as the king of Egypt had instructed them." For another king who questions an underling as to why he has violated directions that the king has placed on him, see Solomon's words to Shimei in 1 Kings 2:42–45.

1:19 The midwives reject Pharaoh's accusation of a sin of commission on the grounds that they have played no role whatsoever in the birth of these babies. They have neither abetted nor aborted one single birth. The reason? The Hebrewesses are able to give birth even before the midwife arrives! True? Fabricated? Hyperbole? Are these captive women "lively/vigorous" (*ḥāyôt*), or do they reproduce like "(wild) animals" (*ḥayyôt*)? The consonantal text permits either reading. On the one hand, the Masoretic Text vocalizes it as *ḥāyôt*, a word that appears only here in the Bible. On the other hand, *ḥayyôt* is more common, as is its singular form *ḥayyâ*. The singular in Gen. 1 is both a generic term for animals (1:28, 30) and for wild beasts (1:24–25). If the word the midwives use is *ḥāyôt*, then they are complimenting Hebrew women over

Egyptian women. If the word they are using is *ḥayyôt*, then they are denigrating the Hebrew women as part of their ruse, using what today we would call an ethnic slur, a tactic comparable to the insult strategy used by Abigail to David about her husband, Nabal, in 1 Sam. 25:24–25 (Frymer-Kensky 2002: 319).

Their strategy of deception is comparable to what Rachel employs with her father, Laban, when he is searching for his gods: "I cannot stand up in your presence; I am having my period" (Gen. 31:35). A woman (or women) deceives a man by appealing to something unique to the experience of a woman. It is likely that Pharaoh knows as little about labor pains and delivery of a child as Laban does about menstruation (Fewell and Gunn 1993: 92).

Throughout Scripture, God honors faithfulness and right behavior. The mid- **1:20–21**
wives do not act the way they do, however, in hopes that God will "bless" them for their salvific act. They do not say, "God, we spared the little Hebrew tykes; now you owe us one." Their response is spontaneous and not self-motivated, not doing something for God in anticipation that he will do something for them. For all they know, the midwives might be executed on the spot. And in the next chapter, Moses's mother receives nothing from the Lord for her brave act of defiance (except the survival of her baby boy).

Nevertheless, God "established households" for them. As Brichto (1973: 43) asks, "What reward could be more fitting than posterity for the women who preserved the posterity of Israel?" The same Hebrew expression, *ʿāśâ bayit*/*bāttîm*, occurs in 2 Sam. 7:11 in the covenantal promise God makes to David, "He will establish a house for you," and in Solomon's repetition of that promise (1 Kings 2:24). David wants to "build" (*bānâ*) a house for God (2 Sam. 7:5), but God will "establish" (*ʿāśâ*) a household for David. That is, David seems to be interested in projects, while God is interested in people. Paul (1992) has observed that Hebrew *ʿāśâ bayit* is the etymological equivalent of the Akkadian idiom *bitam epeshu*, "to found a family."

There is surely some irony in the fact that because the midwives befuddle this pharaoh, God gives each a house(hold). Most Egyptologists (Gardiner 1961: 52; Lambdin 1953: 153) believe that "Pharaoh" in Egyptian means something like "Great House." Those who pull the wool over the eyes of King Great House end up with their own houses.

I take "people" as "advisers" (here, and back in v. 9), rather than seeing this as **1:22**
a nationwide pronouncement. Pharaoh's command to this group to "throw" (*šālak*) male babies into the Nile may conceal a Hebrew term for exposure and abandonment rather than literal throwing (Cogan 1968). Does Hagar throw (*šālak*) or "leave" Ishmael under a bush (Gen. 21:15)? In the allegory of unfaithful Jerusalem (Ezek. 16), is newly born Jerusalem "thrown" out into the open field, or "left, abandoned" in the open field (Ezek. 16:5)? In many cases, as White (1975: 287, 302) has observed, *šālak* may refer to the placing

of a dead body into a grave, or the placing of a living person into what surely will be his grave (Gen. 37:20, 22, 24; 2 Sam. 18:17; 2 Kings 13:21; Jer. 38:6).

When speaking to the midwives about newborn Hebrew girls, Pharaoh uses the verb "live" (*ḥāyâ*) in the Qal (v. 16). When speaking to his advisers about them, he shifts to the Piel of this verb (*tĕḥayyûn*), "you shall let live." To a female audience: "The little girls will live." To a male audience: "Let the little girls live." Possibly, as I indicated earlier (see my comments at v. 16), this may be his way of suggesting to his male senior staff that with the young males killed off, the young females will be all theirs when they are older. Recall that when Abram speaks about males letting Sarah live (the Piel of *ḥāyâ* in Gen. 12:12), he is suggesting that the males will let her live only for the purpose of later "taking" her. One wonders if Pharaoh's directive to Moses to depart Egypt with only the men, but leave the women (and children) behind, runs along the same lines (Exod. 10:10–11).

The Birth and Naming of Moses

(2:1–10)

Translation

1 Now a man from the tribe/house of Levi went and married the daughter of Levi. 2 The woman conceived and birthed a son. Seeing how beautiful he was, she hid him three months. 3 When she was no longer able to hide him, she got for him a papyrus basket, and caulked it with tar and pitch. She lowered the child into it and placed it in the marsh at the riverbank. 4 His sister positioned herself at a distance to know what might be done to him.

5 Pharaoh's daughter went down to bathe by the river, her maidens walking on the bank of the river. She saw the basket in the middle of the marsh and sent her maid, and she took it. 6 She opened and saw him—the child—and the infant was crying. She had compassion on him and said, "From the children of the Hebrews is this." 7 Then his sister said to Pharaoh's daughter, "Shall I go and call for you a wet nurse from among the Hebrewesses, that she might nurse for you the child?" 8 Pharaoh's daughter answered, "Yes." The girl went and called the mother of the child. 9 And Pharaoh's daughter said to her, "Take this child and nurse him for me, and I will pay your wages." The woman took the child and nursed him. 10 The child reached boyhood, and she brought him to Pharaoh's daughter, and he became a son to her; she called his name Moses and said, "Because out of the water I drew him."

Grammatical and Lexical Notes

2:1. "House" (*bayit*) may sometimes mean "tribe," as in Num. 17:8 (v. 23 MT), "Aaron's staff, which represented the 'house/tribe' of Levi, had not only sprouted . . ."

2:2. "Conceived" (*hārâ*) and "birthed" (*yālad*) occur frequently together in birth scenes, e.g., Gen. 21:2 (Sarah); 30:5, 7 (Bilhah); 1 Sam. 1:20 (Hannah).

2:2. The basic difference between *kî-ṭôb* ("how beautiful") here and the frequent use of *kî-ṭôb* ("that it [was] good") throughout Gen. 1 (vv. 10, 12, 18, 21, 25, 31 [*hinnēh-ṭôb*]) is that this Exodus passage includes the pronominal predicate: *kî-ṭôb hûʾ*. To that degree, Gen. 6:2 is a closer parallel to Exod. 2:2 than any of the Gen. 1 passages: "The sons of God saw that they were beautiful" (*kî ṭōbōt hēnnâ*).

2:3. The shift from the Piel of *ṣāpan* ("hide") in v. 2 to the Hiphil of that verb in v. 3 indicates simply variation as opposed to verbatim repetition as a part of Hebrew rhetoric. See Ratner 1992: 145–46.

2:3. The etymology of *tēbâ* ("basket, ark") is not evident. Cohen (1972) rejects the usual connection with Egyptian *ḏb3t*, which is never used for any kind of sailing vessel or floatable receptacle.

2:3. Literally, "with 'the' tar and 'the' pitch," in which the article is the generic article rather than the definite article.

2:3. "In the marsh" seems a preferable reading of *bassûp* than "among the reeds." See Ward 1974.

2:4. *wattētaṣṣab* (Hitpael, 3rd fem. sg. of *yāṣab*) should read *wattityaṣṣēb*, for it appears that a *y* (*yôd*) has fallen out of the verbal form (BDB 426).

2:4. Only here is the Qal infinitive construct of *yādaʿ* written as *lĕdēʿâ*. The usual form is *lādaʿat*.

2:5. For *yad* ("hand") with the meaning "border, bank," see Num. 13:29 ("along the 'hand' of the Jordan") and Deut. 2:37 ("neither the land along the 'hand' of the Jabbok").

2:5. The Hebrew word for "maid(ens)" in the first part of the verse is the feminine form (*naʿărâ*) of the masculine word for "infant" in v. 6 (*naʿar*). However, the Hebrew word for "maid" in the second half of the verse is *ʾāmâ*. *Naʿărâ* seems to connote a higher status, female attendants who accompany their supervisor. *ʾĀmâ* may refer to women who do more servile work for their superior. See Macdonald 1976.

2:5. The subject of "and she took it" at the end of the verse could be either "her maid" ("sent her maid to get it") or Pharaoh's daughter. If it is the latter, then it is an instance of taking by means of sending someone else, as in Gen. 20:2, "Then Abimelech . . . sent for Sarah and took her."

2:6. The *ʾet* before "the child" follows an already determined object ("saw him") in order to introduce an expression defining that object more precisely. Hence my use of dashes. See Elwode 1994: 173.

2:6. Of the *hinnēh* before "the infant was crying," BDB 244a (sub c) says that *hinnēh* is frequent "in historical style, esp. . . . after verbs of seeing or discovering, making the narrative graphic and vivid, and enabling the reader to enter into the surprise or satisfaction of the speaker or actor concerned."

2:7. For the phrase *ʾiššâ mêneqet* ("wet nurse"), see Yee (2009), who places the incident under the category of "resistance literature."

2:7–8. "Shall I go? . . . Yes," is "Shall I go? . . . Go." There is no word in Biblical Hebrew for "yes" as an affirmative reply to a yes-or-no question. The way it says "yes" is by repeating the verb in the answer without the interrogative particle ("Shall I go? Go"), in which "go" equals "yes." Compare David's words in 1 Sam. 23:2 and God's answer, "Shall I go and attack these Philistines?" The Lord answers him, "Go." Or David's question to the Lord, "Will Saul come down?" to which the Lord responds, "He will come down" (1 Sam. 23:11). Or his question, "Will the citizens of Keilah surrender me and my men to Saul?" to which the Lord responds, "They will surrender" (1 Sam. 23:12). See Greenstein 1989: 54–55.

2:8. The Hebrew for "girl" is *ʿalmâ*. Its normal rendering in the Septuagint is *neanis* (here; Ps. 68:25 [67:26]; Prov. 30:19; Song 1:3; 6:8). Of course, the most debated use of *ʿalmâ* is in the celebrated prophecy of Isa. 7:14, which the LXX renders with *parthenos* rather than *neanis*.

2:9. "I will pay your wages" is, literally, "I will give your wage." This is an illustration of how a pronominal suffix on a noun ("your wages") often indicates a dative idea ("I will give to you the wages"). Thus Lev. 26:4, "I will give your rains," means, "I will give you rains."

2:10. I shall comment below on the relationship between "Moses" (*mōšeh*) and "I drew him out" (*mĕšîtihû*).

Commentary

2:1 The verse does not name the parents of the child whose birth is mentioned in the following verse. They are identified only by tribal origin (tribe of Levi) and by function. Once married, they procreate. The baby too is unnamed (until the last verse of the unit), as are the baby's older sister and the Egyptian princess. Reinhartz (1998: 106) suggests that the "anonymity of the women draws attention to their typified roles." One woman is a creative and nurturing mother; the second woman is a quick-thinking young girl and a protector of her baby brother; the third woman defies her father's ultimatum and demonstrates compassionate maternity as more than merely a biological process.

There may be some connection between the fact that Levi, the ancestor of the tribe of this baby's parents, is the third-born child in his family (Gen. 29:34), and this baby, as we will shortly discover, is the third-born child in his family.

The baby's parents are subsequently named, in Exod. 6:20, and later in Num. 26:59, as (father) Amram and (mother) Jochebed. In Exod. 2:2–3 Jochebed is the subject of no less than nine verbs (eleven verbs if we include v. 9), yet is unnamed. In 6:20 she is the subject of only one verb, yet is named. Furthermore, the chap. 6 reference informs us that Amram marries his aunt on his father's side. This is a marital relationship that Moses, speaking for God, later outlaws, either with a consanguineal aunt (Lev. 18:12–13) or with an affinal aunt (18:14).

That Amram marries his aunt raises the possibility that Moses's mother is a good bit older than his father. How much older, or how old? Taking the expression "daughter of Levi" in Exod. 2:1 and Num. 26:59 literally, rather than reading it as a metonym for a distant relative, Brichto (1998: 335–36) computes that Jochebed is forty years older than her husband and that she is 176 in the year she gives birth to Moses! To which Brichto adds: "And Sarah thought it past belief to bear a child at ninety by a husband aged one hundred!" So then, there are two miracles in this story: the miraculous preservation of the baby from the king's edict, and a mother who, pushing the second-century mark, conceives and gives birth.

Jochebed has the distinction of being the first person in Scripture with a name part of which includes a portion of one of God's names. For other *Jo-* names, think of Jo-el, Jo-nathan, Jo-ab and the like. *Jo* is an abbreviated form of "Yahweh." Her name means "Yo/Yah/Yahweh is glorious." By contrast, all theophoric names in Genesis are *-el* names (*el* an abbreviation for *ʾĕlōhîm*), such as Isra-el or Ishma-el. Exodus begins by telling us about Moses, whose mother is *yôkebed*, and it ends by telling us that *yôkebed*'s son cannot enter the tent because it is filled with the Lord's *kābôd*.

If we had no other data, then we might assume that this baby is the mother's 2:2
firstborn. However, the mention of an older sister (whose birth goes unnoticed), and later the mention of an older brother, Aaron (whose birth also goes unnoticed), shows that this is not the case. For a parallel, 2 Sam. 12:24–25 seems to suggest that Bathsheba births Solomon shortly after the death of their first newborn son. Yet 1 Chron. 3:5 tells us that Bathsheba has had three sons, Shammua, Shobab, and Nathan, before Solomon. Moses is the special child of Jochebed, and hence the siblings are ignored or briefly cited, just as Solomon

is the special child of Bathsheba. Miriam and Aaron will be to Moses what Andrew is to Peter, "Simon Peter's brother," as the NT frequently identifies him. As we all know, it can be difficult to be a minor prophet when God calls one of your siblings to be a major prophet.

There are other women in Scripture who are willing to put their own life at risk to save the life of a male who is at risk. One thinks of Michal, who saves David from her father (1 Sam. 19:11–17). A closer parallel is Rahab, who hides the two Hebrew spies from the local authorities (Josh. 2:4). These are the only two places in the Bible where a woman "hides" (*ṣāpan*) a man from another man or men.

2:3 The Hebrew word for "basket" is *tēbâ*. The only other place in the Bible where it appears is in Gen. 6–9 (about twenty-six times) to refer to the "ark" that Noah builds. For that reason, the KJV has Moses's mother building an "ark of bulrushes" for her baby. Obviously the two are quite different in size! Jochebed does not make a three-story floating zoo for her baby's bassinet. The appearance of this word in these two places, and only in these two places, ties together the lives of Noah and Moses. Two individuals, both major role players in God's plan of redemption, are saved from certain death by drowning by finding salvation inside a *tēbâ*.

"By faith Moses's *parents* hid him for three months after he was born" (Heb. 11:23). Yet the Hebrew of Exod. 2:3 suggests that Amram is possibly away from home at the time, drafted into the labor workforce of Pharaoh.

Jochebed's actions are an ironic reversal of Abraham's in Gen. 22. Abraham obeys God's order to kill Isaac, yet Isaac is spared. Jochebed disobeys Pharaoh's order to kill Moses, yet Moses is spared. In one incident, God honors obedience. In the other, he honors defiance.

2:4 This first encounter between Moses and his older sister is positive. Unfortunately their last recorded encounter is not (Num. 12). Exodus 2:4 is the only time the Hitpael of *yāṣab* ("positioned herself") appears with a feminine subject in Exodus, or in the entire Bible, for that matter. For masculine subjects with this verb in Exodus (with NIV renderings), see 8:20 [v. 16 MT]; 9:13 ("confront"); 14:13 ("stand firm"); 19:17 ("stood"); 34:5 ("the Lord stood with Moses there").

One wonders if the mother places the basket in the river at just any point, a river by the way that is infested with crocodiles, or whether she places the receptacle near the point in the river where she has frequently seen the princess come to bathe. With crocodiles, Moses has no chance. With a princess, there is at least a slight opening. Trust in Pharaoh's daughter and trust in God are not mutually exclusive. Thus Fewell and Gunn (1993: 93) are correct when they say, "Jochebed places the fate of their baby at the feet of Pharaoh's daughter, somehow trusting that this young woman could never carry through the brutal policy of her father." But so is Janzen (1997: 21) correct: "This is a desperate commitment of the child into God's hands when all her resources are at an end."

The bathing may be either for hygienic purposes or a part of some religious **2:5**
ritual. She is at the river either to clean her body or clean her soul, or maybe both. Because the princess is in the water and not her maidens, she is the one to see the basket. Would the maidens perhaps have handled things differently if they had spotted the basket first? Would they have dared to flout the king's decree as his own daughter does? Surely their lives are not as significant to His Royal Highness as is that of this daughter.

In some ways, as Fretheim (1991: 38–39) has pointed out, the princess's move- **2:6**
ments in chap. 2 parallel God's in chap. 3. In 2:5 she "came down" to the Nile; in 3:8 God says, "I have come down." In 2:5 she "saw" a basket; in 3:7 God says, "I have seen the misery of my people." Twice, the text says, she "saw" something (2:5, 6). Twice, says the text, God "saw" something (3:7, 9). In 2:6 she hears a baby crying; in 3:7 God says of his people, "I have heard them crying."

The verb "took compassion on [*ḥāmal*]" appears only here in Exodus, but elsewhere is used of divine compassion (Mal. 3:17, "I will *spare* them, just as in compassion a man *spares* his son who serves him"). Numerous times in the prophets, God threatens not to *ḥāmal*, not to show compassion/pity (e.g., Ezek. 5:11; 7:4, 9; 8:18; 9:10).

One could translate "she took pity on him," but I prefer "had compassion." One difference between "pity" and "compassion" is that pity means "to feel for," while compassion means "to feel with." In the parable of the Good Samaritan (Luke 10:25–37), the priest and the Levite have pity, but no compassion. They feel sorry for the victim, but it stops there. Not so with the Samaritan. And not so with this princess. She does not simply feel a brief tinge of sorrow, and then get on with her bathing. Not without reason could (at least parts of) Exod. 2:1–10 be called "the parable of the Good Egyptian(ess)."

We cannot know for sure whether Miriam speaks as a Hebrewess about a He- **2:7–9**
brew to an Egyptian lady, or whether she pretends herself to be an Egyptian. For sure, Miriam never identifies herself as the baby's sister.

Numerous commentators have suggested that the story is told in such a way as to make the princess look stupid and naive. She is conned into surrendering the child, and ends up paying his biological mother to nurse him. However, she is not so foolish after all. Gunn and Fewell (1993: 93) properly ask, "Is she so simple to think that this young Hebrew girl's appearance is coincidental? Is she so slow to be unable to connect the woman who instantly materializes, her breasts filled with milk, with the child's mother?"

That she is willing to surrender the child, at least until weaning, says something profound about her respect for the honesty and integrity of these "Hebrews." After all, Jochebed can go "underground" with her baby, and the princess may never see him or her again. If David can hide from Saul, why cannot Jochebed hide from the princess? There are plenty of places to conceal mother and child's whereabouts in Goshen. Maybe the princess insists that Jochebed and son stay near her house, where she can keep an eye on them, just as David brings Mephibosheth into his house, where he can keep an eye on this Saulide (2 Sam. 9).

2:10 Imagine the emotional trauma Jochebed must experience in handing her two- or three-year-old child, at the completion of the lad's weaning, over to the Egyptian princess, more than likely never to see him again. But there might be a better future, or even the possibility of a future, for her baby in the palace rather than in the brickyards, if he even lives that long. For other mothers who, for one reason or another, are willing to give up their young child to another, recall Hannah and Samuel (1 Sam. 1:28; 2:11, 19), and the prostitute who is willing to give her son to the other prostitute rather than have him killed (1 Kings 3:16–27, esp. v. 26). Mary, within eyesight of her Son on the cross, is another such mother.

For the first time the name "Moses" appears. His name is used 767 times in the OT, 647 of which are in the Torah (290x in Exodus, 86x in Leviticus, 233x in Numbers, and 38x in Deuteronomy), 80x in the Prophets, and 40x in the Writings (statistics from Nigosian 1993: 345–46).

A father often names the child (Gen. 4:26; 5:3, 29; 16:15; 35:18b; 41:50–51; Exod. 2:22), sometimes in response to God (Gen. 17:19; Isa. 8:3; Hosea 1:4, 6, 9). A child could also receive a name from the mother, either biological (Gen. 4:1, 25; 16:11 [in response to God]; 19:37–38; 29:31–30:24; 35:18a; 38:3–5; Judg. 13:24; 1 Sam. 1:20; 4:21; 2 Sam. 12:24; 1 Chron. 7:16; Isa. 7:14), or adoptive (Exod. 2:10), and from female neighbors (Ruth 4:17).

Esther 2:7 ("Mordecai had taken her [Esther] as his own daughter when her father and mother died") and Exod. 2:10 provide the only two instances of adoption in the OT. At least the Latin Vulgate reads it as such, translating the Hebrew as *adoptavit* in both verses, although the possibility of fosterage rather than adoption cannot be ruled out (Paul 1980: 182n28). Interestingly, though there is a legion of family laws in the legal sections of the Torah, there is not one anywhere about adoption.

The Hebrew "he became to" (*hāyâ lĕ*) appears elsewhere in Scripture. For starters, *hāyâ lĕ* means to gain a special status in relation to somebody. Thus when Deut. 7:6 says, "The Lord your God has chosen you . . . to be to him [*hāyâ lĕ*] his treasured people," the verse speaks of that unique relationship. The first commandment in the Decalogue (Exod. 20:3 = Deut. 5:7) says, "There shall not be to you [*hāyâ lĕ*; i.e., 'not have'] any other gods." "Have" here means "to be in relationship with."

This idiom is the idiom used for establishing family relationships (Exod. 2:10; Deut. 24:2; Judg. 14:20; 15:2; 2 Sam. 7:14; Esther 2:7, 15). Also, *hāyâ lĕ* is the phrase for establishing a covenant relationship between God and Israel (Exod. 6:7; Lev. 26:12). Thus, when Moses becomes a son to the princess, he assumes a relationship to her that is unique, familial, and covenantal.

There continues to be much debate about the meaning of the name "Moses." Most scholars believe that she gives the weaned child an Egyptian name. The foundational study in support of that reading is Griffiths (1953). Numerous names of the pharaohs end with *-mose* (Ah-*mose*, Thut-*mose*, Ra*meses*), in which the first part of the name is the name of an Egyptian god, and the "mose" part reflects either the verb *msy*, "to be born," or the noun *ms*, "child, son." Thus, Thutmose means either "(the god) Thut is born" or "son of (the god) Thut." Here, it is suggested, we have the retention of the second part of the baby's Egyptian name with the deletion of the deity's name.

Kitchen (2003: 296–97) disagrees with this explanation. For one thing, many Egyptians (not pharaohs) were simply called "Mose" without any name of a deity. Second, one would expect Egyptian *s* to appear as *s* (*sāmek*) in Hebrew, not as *sh* (*šîn*) as with *Mōšeh* here. Kitchen himself suggests that the adopting daughter probably names him *Māšû*, "one drawn out," which somebody later changes to *Mōšeh*.

Many interpreters have observed that her name and her explanation for that name do not fit. If she calls him this "because I drew him out of the water," should she not call him *Māšûy*, passive participle, "One-who-was-drawn-out," rather than *Mōšeh*, active participle, "one-who-draws-out"? One writer, J. Ackerman (1974: 94–95), suggests that by mixing up her participles, the princess blunders into this name as an incompetent Hebraist!

It is not unheard of in the Bible for a non-Hebrew to give a Hebrew name to a Hebrew person. Pharaoh Neco renames Eliakim "Jehoiakim" (2 Kings 23:34), and Nebuchadnezzar changes Mattaniah to "Zedekiah" (2 Kings 24:17). This is not an exact parallel, however. It is one thing for a foreigner to change the Hebrew name of a king to another Hebrew name. It is another thing for a foreigner to give a Hebrew name to somebody who is nameless.

Possibly, as Marks (1995: 29–32) points out, the name "Moses" contains a double etymology, one public, one disguised, just as Moses at the beginning has a double identification. He is Egyptian and Hebrew. He is Hebrew in 2:11–15a but Egyptian in 2:15b–22. Thus, maybe it is the words of the narrator "he became a son to her" that provide the background for the name. Son/*ben* = *mōšeh*/*mš*/son, for the Egyptian word for "son" is *mesu*, a name similar in sound to *Mōšeh*. As Sternberg (1998: 335) says, "His very name testifies to his sonship. He became to her what she called him."

To be sure, the verb *māšâ* never appears in Exodus as one of the "exodus" verbs such as "brought up, brought out, delivered," even though the name the princess gives to him seems to be given almost prophetically. Moses will "draw" his people "out of" Egypt. The verb appears in the Song of David when David speaks of his Lord: "he reached down from on high and took hold of me, he 'drew me out' of deep waters" (2 Sam. 22:17 = Ps. 18:16 [17]). The closest use is Isa. 63:11, whose translation is far from certain: "He remembered the days of old, Moses and his people," or "He remembered the days of old, (the days) of him who drew his people out [*mōšeh ʿammô*]."

Many writers have noticed the parallel between the events surrounding the births of Moses and King Sargon the Great of Akkad (ca. 2350–2294 BC). The latter's birth account reads as follows (translation of Beyerlin 1978: 98–99):

> I am Sargon, the mighty king, the king of Akkad.
> My mother was an *enitum* [a priestess?]; I do not know my father.
> The brother of my father loved the hills.
> My city is Azupiranu, which lies on the banks of the Euphrates.
> The *enitum*, my mother, conceived me and bore me in secret.
> She laid me in a basket of rushes, sealed my cover with asphalt,
> And cast me on the river, which did not rise over me.
> The river bore me to Akki, the drawer of water.
> Akki, the drawer of water, lifted me out as he dipped his ewer.
> Akki, the drawer of water, (took me) as son and reared me.
> Akki, the drawer of water, made me his gardener.
> When I was a gardener, Ishtar gave me her love,
> And for [fifty-]four years I exercised the kingship.

On the one hand, it would be difficult to see any parallels between Moses and Sargon beyond the child set adrift by his mother in some kind of infant receptacle, and his subsequent discovery and rescue by another individual. On the other hand, there are numerous parallels within Scripture between Moses and other characters. For example, think of similar motifs with Joseph and Moses (see Carmichael 1996: 16–17):

1. Joseph is taken from a pit and escapes murder; Moses is taken from the water and escapes drowning.
2. A close relative plays a role in the deliverance of each: Joseph's brother Reuben, Moses's sister Miriam.
3. Non-Israelites play a role in the deliverance of each: the Midianites with Joseph, Pharaoh's daughter with Moses.
4. Joseph's brothers misunderstand Joseph (Gen. 37), and Moses's brothers misunderstand Moses (Exod. 2:11–15).
5. Both end up in a foreign, but neighboring, country—Joseph in Egypt, Moses in Midian—and live there for a good while.
6. Each marries a daughter of a priest in that foreign country, and fathers two sons: Joseph—Ephraim and Manasseh; Moses—Gershom and Eliezer.
7. Joseph outperforms Egypt's wise men (Gen. 41), and Moses outperforms Egypt's wise men (Exod. 7:8–12).

An even closer parallel to Moses than Joseph, and one that is seldom connected with Moses, is Hagar in Gen. 16 and 21 (see Dozeman 1996: 28–33):

1. Both assume two roles that blatantly contrast with each other. Hagar is household slave and surrogate wife. Moses is Hebrew slave and Egyptian prince.
2. Hagar's shift from household slave to surrogate wife arouses Sarah's hostility. Moses's shift from Egyptian prince to Hebrew liberator arouses Pharaoh's hostility.
3. To escape Sarah's hostility, Hagar flees (*bāraḥ*) into the wilderness (Gen. 16:6). To escape Pharaoh's hostility, Moses flees (*bāraḥ*) into the wilderness (Exod. 2:15).
4. While in the wilderness, Hagar encounters "the angel of the Lord" (Gen. 16:7), as does Moses (Exod. 3:2).
5. Hagar is instructed to return to her mistress, from whom she has fled (Gen. 16:9). Moses is instructed to return to Pharaoh, from whom he has fled (Exod. 3:10).
6. While in the wilderness, Hagar receives a gracious promise from the angel (Gen. 16:11–12), as does Moses (Exod. 3:12).
7. Hagar gives God a new name ("You-are-the-God-who-sees-me" [Gen. 16:13]). To Moses, God reveals God's new name ("Yahweh/Lord" [Exod. 3:13–15]).
8. Hagar's second encounter with God is near a bush (Gen. 21:15); Moses's first encounter with God is near a bush (Exod. 3:2).
9. Hagar goes to the wilderness a second time when Sarah demands her expulsion (Gen. 21:10, *gāraš*). Moses (for the second time) and his people will find themselves in the wilderness, driven there by Pharaoh and *his* people (Exod. 10:11; 12:39, *gāraš*).
10. Both times, God either sanctions (Gen. 21:12–13) or orchestrates (Exod. 11:1) the expulsion, in effect transforming expulsion into liberation.
11. Food and beverage for the expelled are limited to what one can carry on one's shoulders (*šĕkem*, Gen. 21:14 and Exod. 12:34).
12. The absence of (drinkable) water threatens the life of Hagar's child (Gen. 21:15–16), as it does for Moses's people (Exod. 15:22–26).
13. Thirst produces a desperate cry (Gen. 21:16–17 [Hagar's? Ishmael's?]) that leads to a divine response of provision of water (21:19). Moses's cry to the Lord (Exod. 15:25a) leads to a divine response of provision of water (Exod. 15:25b).

All these parallels, hardly incidental, suggest that Hagar is the prototype for Moses, just as her son, Ishmael, provides the paradigm for Israel with their mutual wilderness experiences (Dozeman 1996: 33). In light of the ongoing Israeli-Arab conflict in the Middle East, it would be interesting to reflect on the implications of the biblical writers' using Hagar as a paradigm of Moses, and Ishmael as a paradigm of Israel.

Of course, the most transparent parallel just to Exod. 2:1–10 is Matthew's account of Jesus's birth (Matt. 1–2). What Pharaoh is to infant Moses, Herod is to infant Jesus. What Jochebed and Miriam are to Moses, Mary and Joseph are to Jesus. What Pharaoh's daughter is to Moses, the magi are to Jesus. In both birth instances, God sovereignly watches over and preserves the life of a little one who in adult years will emerge as the one chosen by God to save his people from their sins, either from the sins others have committed against them (Moses), or from the sins they themselves have committed (Jesus).

Hebrews 11:24 says, "By faith Moses, when he had grown up, refused to be known as the son of Pharaoh's daughter" (just as Joseph [Gen. 39:8, 10] and Vashti [Esther 1:12] similarly "refused" an invitation or opportunity). That must not have been an easy refusal. It is one thing to say "no" to the "treasures of Egypt." It is another thing to say "no" to somebody who has risked her life to save your life, who has invested years of her own life to nurture you, who takes you under her wing. Faith may involve saying "no" to good things as well as to things patently evil.

Moses's First Attempt at Mediation

(2:11–15)

Translation

[11]In those days, after Moses had reached manhood, he went out to his brothers and witnessed their hard labors. He witnessed an Egyptian assaulting a Hebrew, one of his brothers. [12]Looking this way and that, he witnessed nobody around. He fatally assaulted the Egyptian, and buried him in the sand. [13]The next day he went out, and behold, two Hebrew men were brawling. He said to the instigator, "Why are you assaulting your fellow?" [14]And he retorted, "Who appointed you prince and judge over us? Do you intend to kill me just as you killed the Egyptian?" Moses panicked and thought, "Surely the deed is known." [15]When Pharaoh learned of the deed, he sought to kill Moses. Moses fled from Pharaoh and settled in the land of Midian, where he sat down by a well.

Grammatical and Lexical Notes

2:11. "In those days" (*bayyāmîm hāhēm*) can refer to either past time (cf. Gen. 6:4) or to future time (Deut. 17:9; 19:17; 26:3).

2:12. The Hebrew for "hid/buried" is *ṭāman*. It occurs thirty-one times in the OT. Thirteen of those times it is followed by the preposition *bĕ* ("bury in") as here. Jacob buries pagan memorabilia under an oak tree (Gen. 35:4). Achan buries the items he has stolen in the ground (Josh. 7:21). Jeremiah buries his belt in the crevice in the rocks (Jer. 13:4–7). See Balentine 1980: 142.

2:13. *bayyôm haššēnî*, "on the second day," should here be rendered "on the next day." See Josh. 10:32; Judg. 20:24–25; Neh. 8:13; Ezek. 43:22 (all of which the NIV translates—erroneously, I believe—as "the second day").

2:13. Many translations omit *wĕhinnēh* in their rendering. Its omission subtracts from Moses's shock at seeing what he saw. Andersen (1974: 95) says, "A *wĕhinnēh* clause is used to report a surprise development after verbs of motion." See, for example, Exod. 4:6, 7 and 16:10 for the same phenomenon.

2:13. "Instigator" is "the wicked one" (*lārāšā ʿ*). Fontaine (1982: 114–15) suggests that a "wicked one" is "someone who is judged to be guilty of violence or illegal activities against the right civil authority." She cites the following passages where the word carries this nuance, as in Exod. 2:13: Deut. 25:2; Prov. 17:23; 18:5; 19:28; 20:26; 29:12.

2:13. On the use of the imperfect *takkeh* ("Why are you 'assaulting' your fellow?"), S. Driver (1998: 44–45) remarks that in why questions "instead of the outspoken, categorical perfect, the imperfect as more courteous, more adapted to a tone of entreaty or deprecation is often preferred."

2:14. There is some problem with how to render *lĕʾîš*, which admittedly disappears from my translation and also from the NIV. There are at least three possibilities: (1) the preposition *lĕ* prefixed to the noun is a vocative *lamedh*: "Who appointed you, O mortal, prince and judge over us?" (Dahood 1981: 413–14); (2) *ʾîš*, based on parallels from Tell el-Amarna, where "man of X" = "prince of X," may here mean "ruler": "Who appointed you a ruler, a prince and judge over us?" (Crown 1974: 111); (3) most simply, as Hess (1990: 5) has observed, when *ʾîš* is in construct to a following noun, it can be used to designate offices, professions, and nationalities. Thus in v. 11 *ʾîš miṣrî* and *ʾîš ʿibrî* mean, respectively, "an Egyptian" and "a Hebrew." In Lev. 21:9 *ʾîš kōhēn* designates a "priest," and in Joel 2:7 *ʾîš milḥāmâ* designates a "fighter."

2:14. Melamed (1961: 131) was the first to suggest that "prince and judge" may be a hendiadys: a figure of speech in which one idea is expressed by two nouns connected by "and." For the same two nouns together (*śar, šōpēṭ*) elsewhere, see 2 Chron. 1:2; Prov. 8:16; Amos 2:3; Mic. 7:3; Zeph. 3:3.

2:14. The Hebrew verb *ʾāmar* ("to say"), when linked syntactically to infinitives, may express intent. So *halĕhorgēnî ʾattâ ʾōmēr*, "Do you intend to kill me?" Compare 1 Kings 5:5 [19]; 8:12; 2 Chron. 13:8; 28:10; Ezek. 20:8.

2:14. *ʾākēn* (surely) is an interjection, perhaps with the force in English "O, my!" Goldbaum (1964: 135) calls the word a "quasi-adverb," while Andersen (1974: 185) calls it "an utterance-initial asseverative." Compare Jacob's "Surely the Lord is in this place, and I am not aware of it" (Gen. 28:16), and Agag's words to Samuel, "Surely the bitterness of death is past" (1 Sam. 15:32).

2:15. "Settled" and "sat down" are exactly the same word in the Hebrew (*wayyēšeb*).

2:15. "By a well" is, literally, "by the well" (*habbĕʾēr*). The noun is definite either because a well-known well is meant, or else a well is always found near where people live. In 3:2 the Lord's angel appears to Moses from within "*the* bush, and *the* bush, although on fire, did not burn up." See Ehrensvärd 2001: 305.

Commentary

2:11 For "reached manhood," the Hebrew reads "became great" (*wayyigdal*, literally rendered in the LXX as *megas*). Fleishman (1992: 43–44) says that the root *g-d-l*, when used of a child's growing up, refers to "the stage of babyhood, when one is no longer a suckling, as well as the passage from childhood to the stage of early manhood." When a child has reached such a stage, he is able to choose his way of life and interests (Gen. 21:20; 25:27), take part in his father's business (2 Kings 4:18), marry (Gen. 38:11; Ruth 1:13), deprive other heirs from receiving a share of the father's estate (Judg. 11:2), and theoretically, give sound advice to others based on mature understanding and reason, but will not necessarily always do so (1 Kings 12:8, 10).

All this is to say that when God calls Moses into spiritual leadership (chaps. 3 and 4), Moses is not a child. Unlike Jeremiah, who tries to disqualify himself from ministry by protesting, "I cannot speak, for I am a youth" (Jer. 1:6), no octogenarian can get off saying, "I am only a *naʿar*." In the fourth and fifth centuries, the church father Jerome (*In Hieremiam* 6.5) suggests that Moses's resistance is met with severe rebuke by God because he is a grown man. By contrast, God treats Jeremiah's resistance more leniently because he is just a lad at the time.

Like Jacob's daughter, Dinah, who "went out to see the daughters of the land" (Gen. 34:1), Moses "went out to see" the toils of his people. The Hebrew for "and witnessed" is *rāʾâ bĕ*. The verb followed by this preposition is used frequently for looking at some kind of trouble or disaster. See Gen. 21:16; 29:32; 44:34; 2 Sam. 16:12.

The verb *nākâ*, "assault, strike, batter," occurs either in finite or participial form three times here—vv. 11, 12, 13—and balances the three uses of *hārag* ("kill") in vv. 14–15. We are not told if the Egyptian in v. 11 or Moses in v. 12 uses any weapon in the physical attack. Normally the verb does occur with a listed weapon. Thus David strikes Goliath with a stone (1 Sam. 17:49–50), Abishai wants to strike Saul with a spear (1 Sam. 26:8), and Abner strikes Asahel with a spear (2 Sam. 2:23). David uses this verb when he speaks of having "struck" a lion and a bear, and hence Goliath would be no big deal (1 Sam. 17:36). He does not mention whether on those occasions he uses any weapon, or just his bare hands, as Samson, who tears asunder (*šāsaʿ*) the lion with his bare hands (Judg. 14:6).

In several instances *nākâ* means "to kill." That is its meaning in passages like Lev. 24:21 ("whoever 'kills' an animal must make restitution, but whoever *kills* a man must be put to death") or Lev. 24:17–18 ("If anyone 'kills' a human being . . . Anyone who 'kills' an animal . . ."). In 1 Sam. 17:9 Goliath challenges Saul to choose a man to fight him with these words: "If he is able to fight and 'kill' me, . . . but if I overcome him and 'kill' him. . . ." Clearly in Exod. 2:12 *nākâ* carries the meaning "kill" (hence my translation "fatally assaulted") for what Moses does to the Egyptian. The verb in v. 11 need not necessarily carry that nuance.

The verb *nākâ* occurs later in Exodus to describe what God will do, or has done, to Egypt and the Egyptians (3:20; 7:17, 25; 9:15; 12:12, 13, 29). Moses and Aaron also do their share of "striking" either water (7:20) or land (8:16, 17 [13, 14]). The hail God sends "struck" the land (9:25), and the flax and barley (9:31; NIV "destroyed"). Could it be that Moses's striking anticipates God's striking?

"Looking this way and that" does not necessarily mean that Moses wants to **2:12**
avoid detection, to make sure nobody is looking. Maybe he is looking to see if anybody else will come along to avenge the beating, and when there is no one, he takes care of the matter himself. The language is close to Isa. 59:16 ("He [the Lord] saw that there was no one, he was appalled that there was no one to intervene"), and 63:5 ("I looked, but there was no one to help. I was appalled that no one gave support").

Whether it is Moses's intention to kill the Egyptian, or simply give him a good beating in return (which tragically gets out of hand and goes too far) remains a moot point. In one sense, Moses's actions in v. 12 are more violent than those of the Egyptian in v. 11. The Egyptian wounds and bruises; Moses kills. In so acting, Moses is repeating his ancestral heritage. Exodus 2:1 and 6:16–20 inform us that Moses's great-grandfather is Levi (Levi-Kohath-Amram-Moses). Levi, we recall, has a capacity for violence that astounds even his father, Jacob. Levi is one of two of Jacob's sons who avenge their sister's humiliation by wreaking violence on the perpetrators (Gen. 34:25–29). Both Levi and Moses come to the aid of a sister and a brother, respectively. Father Jacob rebukes Levi (Gen. 34:30), and a sibling Hebrew taunts Moses (Exod. 2:14).

2:13 "Brawling" (*nāṣâ*) connotes physical fighting rather than verbal sparring. See Exod. 21:22: "If men who are *fighting* hit a pregnant woman . . ."; Lev. 24:10: "And a *fight broke out* in the camp between him and an Israelite"; Deut. 25:11: "If two men are fighting . . ."; 2 Sam. 14:6: "I your servant had two sons. They *got into a fight* with each other"; Ps. 60, the superscription [v. 2 MT]: "A *Miktam* of David. For Teaching. When he *fought* Aram Naharaim."

The Bible abounds with strife scenes involving family or community members. It is as ancient as the Cain-Abel debacle (Gen. 4) and continues with the quarreling between Abram's and Lot's herdsmen (Gen. 13) and quarrels among neighbors over access to wells (Gen. 21:25–32; 26:18–21). A father-in-law is at the throat of his son-in-law over alleged thievery (Gen. 31:25–55), Israelite brothers on the west side of the Jordan are suspicious of and belligerent toward Israelite brothers on the east side of the Jordan (Josh. 22:10–34), and tribal groups (Ephraim) bellyache against their political/military leader (Judg. 8:1–13; 12:1–6).

2:14 Moses has been physically involved in stopping the Egyptian (v. 12). Here he is only verbally involved (v. 13). He takes no overt action other than to express his amazement and disappointment that two tired, overworked Hebrew brothers would fight with each other rather than join their resources to fight a common enemy. And yet he finds himself the target of insult from his own people.

In the previous chapter (1:11) the Egyptians "put [taskmasters] over" (*śîm ʿal*) the Hebrews. Now one Hebrew asks Moses derogatorily, "Who appointed/put you [*śîm ʿal*] over us?" The rebuke is not all that different from what the Sodomites direct at Lot when he seeks to protect his two male visitors: "'Get out of our way,' they replied. And they said, 'This fellow came here as an alien, and now he wants to play the judge!'" (Gen. 19:9). That Genesis incident is about somebody "knowing" something ("Bring them out to us, so that we may *know* them" [Gen. 19:5]). This Exodus incident is about somebody "knowing" something: "Surely the deed is 'known.'"

In Luke 12:13–15 a man approaches Jesus and asks him to tell his brother to divide the family inheritance with him. In words recalling Exod. 2:14 Jesus responds with, "Man, who appointed me a judge or an arbiter between you?" This must be Jesus's way of defining his mission, and it does not include being a local magistrate in a family dispute over property. There are individuals charged with that responsibility, but it is outside the orbit of Jesus's calling and ministry. Similarly, there are those individuals charged with waiting on the tables of the elderly, but it is outside the orbit of the apostles' calling and ministry (Acts 6:1–4).

There is only one possible way Pharaoh could have found out about the killing. **2:15**
The only other person around in v. 12, apart from himself and the deceased Egyptian, is the Hebrew to whose rescue Moses has come. It is this fellow Hebrew who must have tattled on Moses, for whatever reason, to the local authorities.

Pharaoh's wrath is first of all unleashed at all boy babies (Exod. 1:22), and then it is directed at one special baby (2:15). Herod's wrath is the reverse of this. First it is directed at one special baby (Matt. 2:3–8), and then at all Bethlehem boy babies when his plan fails (2:16). The Greek of parts of Exod. 2:15 LXX and Matt. 2:13 are strikingly similar: *kai ezētei anelein Mōysēn* and *gar Herōdēs zētein to paidion tou apolesai auto*.

To flee to a remote, wilderness region (for such is Midian) when one's life is in homicidal danger is not a bad idea. Elijah does it after he has killed several hundred preachers, all of whom he feels were deluded (1 Kings 19:3–4). Like Moses, in this remote area Elijah encounters God by a bush/tree, then eventually makes his way back to Israel, as Moses does to Egypt. Jesus does so too, not because he has killed anybody, but because his miracles so confound the religious authorities that "from that day on they plotted to take his life" (John 11:53). What does Jesus then do? Verse 54 says, "Therefore Jesus no longer moved about publicly among the Jews. Instead he withdrew to a region near the desert." But in chap. 12 of John, Jesus returns to the place from which he has fled, just as Moses and Elijah eventually do.

Barclay (1992: 31) notes that the Septuagint translates the Hebrew *bāraḥ* ("fled") by *anechōrēsen*, which it uses only two more times for the fifty-three occurrences of *bāraḥ*. The Septuagint uses the verbs *pheugō* (27x) and *apodidraskō* (23x) for the other fifty. Barclay asks, "Is this an attempt to remove the ignominy of a flight (*pheugein* would be the more obvious translation) by describing it in more polite terms as 'withdrawal'?" This reading seems to be in sync with Heb. 11:27, which says that Moses, "by faith . . . left Egypt, not fearing the king's anger," although, to be sure, Moses leaves Egypt twice, just as Hagar leaves Abraham's home twice (Gen. 16 and 21). Also, *pheugō* is the term that Stephen uses in Acts 7:29 when he is retelling this incident.

In Acts 7:23–29, Stephen has a unique take on Exod. 2:11–15. First, he omits some data from Exod. 2, such as any reference to Moses's "looking this way and that," any reference to Moses's burying the Egyptian in the sand, and any reference to Moses's fleeing Egypt to avoid Pharaoh's death threat. He adds some new data, such as the notice that Moses is forty years old at the time. Stephen seems to suggest (v. 26 at least, but see v. 27) that both Hebrews are entangled with each other, while Exod. 2 suggests one is the attacker and the other is the victim. Most crucial is Stephen's addition of two phrases not found in the Exodus text. The first is Acts 7:25, "Moses thought that his own people would realize that God was using him to rescue them, but they did not." The second is Acts 7:27, "But the man who was mistreating the other *pushed Moses aside.*" First, Moses's own people misunderstand him. Then his own people mistreat him. Can we see here a subtle attempt by Stephen to compare what Moses's kin have done to him with what Jesus's kin have done to him? Both have been misunderstood. Both have been abused, especially when they assume the role of mediator. Furthermore, Stephen's reference to Moses's assuming that his people will know that God has sent him as the Hebrews' rescuer is very interesting. It suggests that already, before the burning bush and God's first self-disclosure to Moses in Exodus, a divine dream has been taking shape in Moses's soul. Here is God's shaping the direction of a human life long before God even shows up!

Moses Flees to Midian

(2:16–22)

Translation

[16]The priest of Midian had seven daughters. They came and drew water, and filled the troughs to water their father's flock. [17]Shepherds, however, came and drove them away. Moses got up and rescued them. Then he watered their flock. [18]They returned to Reuel their father, and he said to them, "Why have you now come so quickly?" [19]They replied, "An Egyptian man delivered us from the shepherds. What's more, he even drew water for us and watered the flocks." [20]"Where is he, then?" he said to his daughters. "Why did you abandon the man? Invite him to break bread." [21]Moses agreed to stay with the man. He gave Zipporah, his daughter, to Moses (as wife). [22]She birthed a son, and he called his name Gershom, for he said, "A sojourner I have been in a foreign land."

Grammatical and Lexical Notes

2:18. "Why have you now come so quickly?" is literally, "Why did you run/hasten (with respect to) coming today?" The infinitive construct (*bōʾ*, "coming") follows a finite verb ("run/hasten"). In such a case, Waltke and O'Connor (1990: 602) suggest that one "render the infinitive as a finite verb ['come'] and the finite verb by an adverb ['quickly']." The adverbial use of *hayyōm* (lit., "the day") to mean "now," on this occasion, as opposed to other days, is frequent in the OT. See De Vries 1975c: 160.

2:19. For the translation of *gam* as "What's more" before an infinitive absolute and a finite verb form, see Van der Merwe 2009: 326.

2:19. The translation "he even drew" reflects the infinitive absolute of "drew out" (*dālōh*) followed by the finite form of that same verb (*dālâ*), i.e., "drawing out, he drew out." In addition to its three occurrences here (vv. 16, 19 [2x]), the verb *dālâ* appears only twice more in the OT. One is Prov. 20:5, "The purposes of a man's heart are deep waters, but a man of understanding draws them out." The other is Ps. 30:3 [4] AT, "O Lord, you drew me up from the grave." When this verb has a human subject (Exod. 2; Prov. 20), the Qal stem is used. When the verb has a divine subject (Ps. 30), the Piel stem is used, perhaps to underscore the intensity and grandeur of a divine drawing up or out. Moses's "drawing out" water in chap. 2 may anticipate his "drawing out," that is, freeing Israel from Egypt in chap. 3 (v. 10, Hiphil of *yāṣāʾ*, and the first use of this important verb in Exodus in conjunction with Israel's departure from Egypt).

2:20. "Where is he, then?" (*wĕʾayyô*) seems to be a better representation of the *wāw* than simply "And where is he?" The Lord uses the same interrogative particle (*ʾay*), also with pronominal suffix, when he asks the hiding Adam, "Where are you [*ʾayyekkâ*]?" in Gen. 3:9.

2:20. "Why?" at the head of the father's question in v. 18 is *maddûaʿ*. "Why?" at the head of the question in v. 20 is *lāmmâ*. I agree with Barr (1985: 28) when he says, "The Hebrews mixed up the two very thoroughly, and it is doubtful whether anyone in biblical times was conscious of the difference between them." Compare the two same interrogatives in 2 Sam. 11:20 ("Why [*maddûaʿ*] did you get so close to the city to fight?") and 2 Sam. 11:21 ("Why [*lāmmâ*] did you get so close to the wall?"). Also Job asks in Job 3:11, "Why [*lāmmâ*] did I not perish at birth?" and in 3:12 asks, "Why [*maddûaʿ*] were there knees to receive me?"

2:20. "Break bread" is "eat bread." Since the next verse says that the priest gives his daughter to Moses as wife, some have suggested that "eat," *ʾākal*, is a euphemism for sexual intercourse. Passages where it is claimed that "eat" means "have sex with" are Gen. 39:6; Exod. 32:6; Prov. 30:20; Dan. 10:3; Hosea 4:10. I see this as a possibility only in the Proverbs and Hosea references.

2:22. The verb *hāyîtî* can be rendered "I have been" (expressing a continuing state), what one would call in English grammar a present perfect, and compare NEB's "I have become." Or it may be rendered "I was" (expressing a previous state that no longer exists). The former nuance seems to be the one Moses is using.

Commentary

2:16 It is not clear whether Midian is the place Moses intentionally chooses for refuge or whether he stumbles into Midian by accident. Midian is consistently associated with peoples to the southeast of Israel, such as Ishmaelites (Judg. 8:24–28), Medanites (Gen. 37:28, 36, for which most versions read "Midianites"), and Moabites (Num. 22–25). At times, their relationship with Israel is warm and friendly (Exod. 2:15–22; 3:1; 4:18–19; Num. 10:28–32). At other times, it is hostile (Num. 31:1–54; Josh. 13:21; Judg. 6–8; 9:17).

The priest's seven daughters (the opposite of Job's seven sons; Job 1:2) may have chores restricted to watering their father's flocks, but their responsibility may extend to shepherding too. Genesis 29:9 ("Rachel came with her father's sheep, for she was a shepherdess") shows that it is not unheard of for women to tend flocks. Carrying water from wells was both a woman's work (Gen. 24:11–21; 1 Sam. 9:11) and a man's work (Deut. 29:10–11; Josh. 9:27; Mark 14:13).

2:17 The verb used for what the male shepherds do to the daughters ("drove away") is *gāraš*. It will reappear later in the story to refer to what Pharaoh will do to Israel, or to Moses and Aaron. He will "drive them out" (Exod. 6:1; 10:11; 11:1; 12:39). This is the first of several verbs appearing in this paragraph that will resurface at later points in the narrative.

The second part of this verse describes what Moses does for the daughters. He "rescued them," the Hiphil of *yāšaʿ*. The verb reappears in 14:30 ("That day the LORD saved/rescued Israel"). The related noun *yĕšûʿâ*, "rescue, salvation," appears in 14:13 AT ("Stand firm and you will see the rescue/salvation the LORD will bring you today") and in 15:2 ("The LORD . . . has become my salvation").

One might expect such a "salvation" verb or noun to be all over the place in Exodus–Deuteronomy, given that much in these books focuses one way or another on God's "saving/delivering" his people out of incarceration in Egypt to the freedom he has for them. Such is not the case, however. The Hiphil of *yāšaʿ* occurs three times (Exod. 2:17; 14:30; Deut. 20:4 [NIV, "to give you victory"]). The Niphal of *yāšaʿ* occurs but twice (Num. 10:9; Deut. 33:29). The noun *yĕšûʿâ* ("salvation") appears only four times (Gen. 49:18; Exod. 14:13; 15:2; Deut. 32:15). Thus vocabulary-wise, God is presented as a "saving" God in only eight passages in this first part of the OT. (Here I exclude Exod. 2:17, with Moses as the actor.) By contrast, over fifty times this root is used in the Psalms to describe God's saving activities. This first part of the Bible seems to prefer locomotive verbs ("brought out") to salvation verbs, unlike the Psalter (see Barr 1973).

The first, but certainly not the last, name we find in Scripture for this priest of **2:18**
Midian is Reuel (*rĕʿûʾēl*). This name is like a number of others in Scripture that are composed of X + nominative case vowel *û* + *ʾēl*. Parallel structured names include the likes of Penuel (Gen. 32:31 [32]; 1 Chron. 4:4; 8:25); Kemuel (Gen. 22:21; Num. 34:24; 1 Chron 27:17); Samuel (1 Sam. 1:20); Pethuel (Joel 1:1). "Reuel" could mean "friend of God/El," or more likely "God/El is a friend." See Dahood 1987: 94; Layton 1990: 91–94.

This priest has a number of other names. The very next chapter (Exod. 3:1) calls him "Jethro" (also see 18:2, 5, 9, 12, 27). Exodus 4:18 identifies him as "Jether" (an alternate writing of Jethro, *yeter* versus *yitrô*). Numbers 10:29 and Judg. 4:11 call him Hobab, with Num. 10:29 adding he is the son of Reuel. Additionally Judg. 1:16 and 4:11 call him a "Kenite" rather than a Midianite. The closest of these additional names to Reuel is Hobab. That name is a passive, shortened form meaning "loved one, friend [of God?]." Moses uses this root *ḥ-b-b* when in Deut. 33:3 he says of the Lord, "Surely it is you who love/befriend the peoples" (*ḥōbēb ʿammîm*).

I am not sure if all these differences can be worked out and resolved smoothly. One possibility is that Hobab and Jethro are the same person, and Reuel is their father (Num. 10:29). If that is so, "daughters" in v. 16 would have to be read as "granddaughters," and "father" in v. 18 would have to be read as "grandfather." Parallels to that possibility are the use of "son" for "grandson" in Gen. 29:5 and the use of "father" for "grandfather" in Gen. 32:9 [10]. Possibly, Reuel is a clan name rather than a personal name, and the Hebrew *ḥōtēn* (father-in-law) in Num. 10:29 should be read as *ḥătan*, "son-in-law." Hobab is then Moses's son-in-law (Albright 1963). This explanation would have to assume that Moses has a daughter. Second, Exod. 2:18 would have to be read as "They returned to their father [Jethro son of] Reuel." Both are unproved assumptions.

There is an easier explanation for how Reuel/Jethro/Hobab can be called in one place a "Midianite" and in another a "Kenite." Midian is not so much the name of one people but of a confederation of peoples, one of which is the Kenites (Dumbrell 1975). "Kenites" means "smiths," metalworkers at the mines in the mountain regions of Sinai/Midian. They may also be a clan of priests, of which Reuel is one (Mazar 1965; Milgrom 1990: 78).

The daughters quickly return to their father to share this stranger's benevolent act on their behalf. The verb behind "quickly" is *māhar*. It occurs forty-one times in Genesis–2 Kings, eleven of which have a woman or women as the subject. Rachel does something quickly three times (Gen. 24:18, 20, 46). Abigail does something quickly four times (1 Sam. 25:18, 23, 34, 42). See also Sarah (Gen. 18:6), Samson's mother (Judg. 13:10), the witch/medium of Endor (1 Sam. 28:24), and here Reuel's daughters.

2:19 The daughters must have thought of Moses as "an Egyptian man" because of his appearance or language. They never stop to ask his name, nor does he volunteer it. Their words to their father sound much like the Samaritan woman's message to the men of her village, "Come, see *a man* who told me everything I ever did" (John 4:29). Their (mis)taking of Moses as an Egyptian man recalls Joseph's brothers (mis)taking their younger sibling as an Egyptian man (Gen. 42:8).

The occasion on which Moses draws (*dālâ*) water for the daughters, who himself was drawn (*māšâ*) from the water, foreshadows later events in which God will use Moses to provide water for those who need it (Exod. 15:22–26; 17:1–7; Num. 20:1–3).

2:20 Such an act of kindness and bravado, Reuel thinks, ought not to go unrewarded, even if the individual is non-Midianite. Presumably between v. 20 and v. 21 the daughters return to the well, where Moses has lingered, offer expressions of gratitude, and then invite him to meet their father and be a guest at the family meal.

Fretheim (1991: 44) has nicely caught the difference in tone between 2:11–15 and 2:16–22: "Moses is not welcome in the Israelite community, but here is shown considerable hospitality by *strangers*. . . . Israel does not appreciate his acts of justice on its behalf; the Midianites welcome it. Israelites engage in accusations of Moses; the daughters of Reuel publicly sing his praises. Those who stand within the community of faith are abusive; those without faith in Israel's god exemplify genuine relationships."

2:21 Three times in Scripture a prospective wife and husband (or the husband's proxy) first meet at a well. The bride-to-be draws, or offers to draw, water from the well, then runs quickly to tell her family about the stranger. The woman's family invites the man to her home for a meal. Then there is the betrothal. See Gen. 24:1–67; 29:1–24; Exod. 2:16–21. Of the three, this one is clearly the shortest. On the significance of the repeating of similar scenes or events in Scripture, see Culley (1976: 41–43) and Alter (1981: 47–62, esp. 56–58).

Of the three scenes, Exod. 2 gives less attention to Zipporah than Gen. 24 does to Rebekah or Gen. 29 to Rachel. All that we have here is, "He gave Zipporah, his daughter, to Moses (as wife)." The phrase "X gave his daughter [her name supplied] to Y (as wife)" appears in passages like Gen. 41:45 ("Pharaoh . . . gave him Asenath . . . to be his wife"); Josh. 15:17 ("Caleb gave his daughter Acsah to him in marriage"); Judg. 1:13 ("So Caleb gave his daughter Acsah to him in marriage"); 1 Chron 2:35 ("Sheshan gave his daughter [no name supplied] in marriage to his servant Jarha"). This idiom is the background for a question still used in some weddings: "Who gives this woman to this man?"

Connected with the first two of these at-the-well scenes, Isaac "loved" Rebekah (Gen. 24:67, note the well in v. 11), and Jacob "kissed" Rachel (29:11, and, by the way, the only instance in the Old Testament of a man kissing a woman, the desire of the beloved in Song 1:2 notwithstanding) and was willing to wait a long time for her because "of his love for her" (29:20). None of those terms appear in Exod. 2. Rebekah was "very beautiful" (Gen. 29:17 AT). No adjectives like that appear in Exod. 2. As Fuch (2000: 103) says, "Zipporah's feelings and thoughts, even her appearance or the feelings she might have evoked in Moses, are unknown. The scene does not distinguish her from her other sisters, . . . neither does it explain why Reuel chose her rather than any of her other sisters."

Moses's marriage to a Midianite is an illustration of an exogamous marriage. (Marriage within one's group, be it social, ethnic, or religious, is by contrast an endogamous marriage.) Some exogamous marriages in the Bible (and some endogamous ones too!) lead to disastrous results. One thinks of Samson's marriage to a Philistine (Judg. 14), or Solomon's multiple exogamous marriages (1 Kings 11:1–13), or Ahab's marriage to the Phoenician Jezebel (1 Kings 16:31), or Esau's marriage to Hittites (Gen. 26:34–35). This is an argument that Rebekah uses (Gen. 27:46) to persuade Isaac to let Jacob go back home (to Paddan Aram) to find a bride, as if to say, "Do you really want another exogamous marriage on our hands? Do you want Jacob acting like Esau?" This is part of her strategy or ruse to get her beloved Jacob safely away from Esau.

However, some marriages to "outsiders" seem to work out quite well in spite of the "unequal yoking." Joseph marries an Egyptian (Gen. 41:45). Moses marries a Midianite. Naomi's sons marry Moabites (Ruth 1:4). Bathsheba marries Uriah the Hittite. David marries the "daughter of Talmai king of Geshur" (2 Sam. 3:3). And Deut. 21:10–14 allows Israelite troops to marry women captured in war. What Deuteronomy seems to offer is not a flat-out veto on all mixed marriages, but only on such marriages with peoples who live in the land that God is giving Israel (Deut. 7:3). One wonders how, much later, Ezra reconciles his obvious enthusiasm for Moses and the Mosaic law with Moses's marriage and his own stringent views on and suggestions about aborting such marriages (Ezra 9; see also Neh. 13:23–27; Mal. 2:10–12).

Both ancient Jewish writers (e.g., Josephus, *Ant.* 1.15 §§240–41) and early Christian writers (e.g., Eusebius, *Praeparatio evangelica* 9.291) were able to justify Moses's marriage into a Midianite family by recalling that Genesis traced the ancestry of Jethro back to Abraham through the latter's marriage to Keturah (Gen. 25:2, 4). Hence, both Zipporah and Moses are directly descended from Abraham. It would appear that a child born to an Israelite father and non-Israelite mother has an Israelite heritage. Ephraim and Manasseh are the ancestors of two major tribes in Israel. Although sons of an Egyptian mother, they are Joseph's heirs and through them his lineage is traced. Gershom has an Israelite father and a Midianite mother, yet Moses's priestly line is traced through Gershom (Judg. 18:30). Absalom has an Israelite father and a non-Israelite mother (2 Sam. 3:3), and would have been heir to the throne as David's eldest living child if he had not been killed. Even the son of a foreign concubine is the heir of an Israelite father. First Chronicles 7:14 states that Manasseh's Aramean concubine bore him Asriel and Machir. Machir becomes the father of Gilead, the ancestor of a Tranjordanian Israelite group. Yet when the parental identities are reversed, and the son has an Israelite mother and a non-Israelite father, it is debatable whether he has an Israelite heritage. See Lev. 24:10–16, 23.

2:22 In one breath Zipporah marries (v. 21). In the next breath (v. 22) she reproduces, but her husband names the child. As Whedbee (1998: 143) says, "In naming his son, he in fact names himself." The child's name is Gershom for, Moses says, "I have been a sojourner [*gēr*] in a foreign land." The pattern is close to that of the process back in v. 10: "She called his name [*wattiqrāʾ šĕmô*] X, and she said [*wattōʾmer*] because [*kî*] . . ." Here we have "And he called his name [*wayyiqrāʾ šĕmô*] X because [*kî*] he said [*ʾāmar*] . . ."

Moses refers to himself as a "sojourner in a foreign land [*bĕʾereṣ nokrîyâ*]." Compare the similar expression in Ps. 137:4 AT, "How can we sing the Lord's song in a foreign land [*ʾadmat nēkār*]?" In Exod. 2:22, what is the foreign land? Egypt? Midian? I am inclined to think it is Midian. Ask an older Moses many years later what his "foreign land" was, and he would probably say Egypt. But at this stage of his life, Egypt is his home, the only home he has known except for the first couple years of his life while in the care of his mother.

A sojourner/*gēr* is an outsider, an alien, a stranger. Abraham identifies himself as such to the Hittites when looking for a family burial plot (Gen. 23:4). The Lord reveals to Abram that his descendants will be "sojourners/strangers" in a country not their own for a good long while (Gen. 15:13). One reason God's people are admonished to love the *gērîm* is because they themselves have been *gērîm* in Egypt (Exod. 22:21 [20]; 23:9; Lev. 19:34; Deut. 10:19). Even when Israel has settled in Canaan, its status in it is theologically and logically that of a *gēr* (Lev. 25:23), since the land belongs to the Lord. Thus, not only is the *gēr* an alien; he is also a protected alien, often lumped together with the poor (Lev. 23:22) and with orphans and widows (this triad orphan-widow-*gēr* occurs eleven times in Deuteronomy: 10:18; 14:29; 16:11, 14; 24:17, 19, 20, 21; 26:12, 13; 27:19). (See the good studies on *gēr* in the monograph of Kidd and Ramirez 1999; Milgrom 2000a: 1416–20, 1493–1501.)

Surely at this stage Moses attaches no theological content to this word as Mosaic law later would. He uses it simply to describe his circumstance of the moment. He is away from home, forced to flee that setting, and now is living in a foreign land as what today we might call an "immigrant." (I believe the first person to suggest that *gēr* be translated "immigrant" in some passages, as in Exod. 2:22, was Meek 1930: 172.)

Some commentators dismiss the explanation of Gershom as popular etymology and instead suggest that Gershom be derived from the verb *gāraš*, "drive away/out, expel." That was the verb v. 17 used to describe what the shepherds do to Reuel's daughters: "they drove them away." The Hebrew for "they drove them away" rhymes with Gershom, *wayĕgāršûm* and *gēršōm*. Furthermore, later *gāraš* appears in the Exodus narrative to describe Pharaoh's driving Israel out of Egypt (6:1; 11:1; 12:39), or Pharaoh's driving Moses and Aaron out of his presence (10:11). If, perchance, Gershom is a variant of Gershon (both are sons of Levi, one immediate, one eventual), the connection with *gāraš* could be better sustained, for "Gershon" seems to incorporate this verb. With the affix *-ōn*, the name would mean "expeller, conqueror." But surely this is to assign to Moses prophetic knowledge that is premature. Verse 22 focuses on the circumstances of Moses's present, not his future.

A God Who Hears and Remembers

(2:23–25)

Translation

[23]After a good long while the king of Egypt died. Israel's sons were groaning because of the hard labor. They cried out, and their cry for help because of the hard labor reached God. [24]God heard their moaning, and God remembered his covenant with Abraham, with Isaac and with Jacob. [25]God saw Israel's sons and God knew. . . .

Grammatical and Lexical Notes

2:23. The verb for "groan" is *ʾānaḥ* and occurs only in the Niphal (cf. Prov. 29:2; Isa. 24:7; Lam. 1:8; Joel 1:18). When it is followed by a preposition, the preposition may be "over" (*ʿal*; Ezek. 9:4, "put a mark on the foreheads of those who groan [*ʾānaḥ*] and lament *over* all the detestable things") or "with" (*bĕ*; Ezek. 21:6 [11], "Groan . . . groan before them *with* broken heart and bitter grief"). Here the following preposition is *min* ("because of, from"). Dahood (1975: 94–95) claims to uncover *ʾānaḥ min* elsewhere by revocalizing the last two words of Isa. 51:19 from *mî ʾănaḥămēk* ("Who can comfort you?" [NRSV]) to *mî ʾānaḥ mēk*, "Who will groan over you?"

2:23. For other places where *zāʿaq* ("cry out") and the noun *šawʿâ* ("cry for help") or the verb *šāwaʿ* ("cry for help") occur together, see Job 19:7 ("though I cry [for help], . . . though I call for help" [using *ṣāʿaq* instead of *zāʿaq*]); Job 35:9 ("Men cry out; . . . they plead for relief"); Lam. 3:8 ("Even when I call out or cry for help"); Hab. 1:2 ("How long, O Lord, must I call for help . . . or cry out to you?").

2:24. For "moaning" (*nĕʾāqâ*), see 6:5; Judg. 2:18. In Ezek. 30:24 the king of Egypt "moans/cries out" because of Babylonian domination.

2:25. Most versions feel constrained to add an object to "knew" (i.e., NIV, "was concerned about them"). It is peculiar to find "know" (*yādaʿ*) used absolutely, without object, as here. The Greek LXX apparently felt so, read the verb as a passive, and also supplied an object: "and he made himself known to them" (*kai egnōsthē autois*). Such a shift or addition is not necessary. Lundbom (1999: 602) argues that this is an illustration of a terse ending, a thought intentionally left unfinished. He compares it to his translation of Jer. 10:18, "For thus said Yahweh: 'Look, I am slinging out the dwellers of the land at this time, and I will afflict them so that they may find out . . . !'" Or second, possibly *yādaʿ* means not primarily "know" but "care for, be concerned about," on the basis of Arabic *wadiʿa* (see D. Thomas 1934; 1948; Barr 1968: 22). That use of *yādaʿ* is reflected in NIV's translation of Job 9:21, "Although I am blameless, I have no concern for [lit., "I do not know"] . . . my life."

Commentary

What a contrast between v. 22 and v. 23! Verse 22, birth; v. 23, death. Verse 2:23
22, a baby; v. 23, an old king. Verse 22, newborn baby identified; v. 23, dead Pharaoh anonymous.

Alive or dead be the Pharaoh, his captive Israelites still, because of the surmounting pressure in which they find themselves, have "moaned" and cried out (or "screamed"). The verse does not explicitly say they cry out to God. They just cry out. Two later verses in the Pentateuch (Num. 20:16; Deut. 26:7) do refer to this cry as a cry to the Lord. Occasionally in the Bible one may cry (*zāʿaq* or *ṣāʿaq*) out of anger, but most often one cries out (to an authority), particularly when one is under duress: Gen. 41:55, the Egyptians crying to Pharaoh for food; 1 Sam. 28:12, the witch of Endor crying out to Saul; 2 Sam. 19:4 [5], David crying out to his murdered son Absalom; 2 Kings 4:40, the famine-driven men crying out to Elisha; 2 Kings 6:5, the prophet, whose axe head flew off, crying out to his master.

For specific instances of crying out to the Lord, see passages like Exod. 14:10; 15:25; 17:4; Num. 11:2; Josh. 24:7; and so forth. Even when crying out to God is noted, such crying does not necessarily carry any spiritual or theological component (like crying out to God over one's sin). The crying is simply the loud and agonized crying of someone in acute distress and calling for help. God's being moved to action by *zāʿaq* that is not necessarily directed at him has a good parallel in Gen. 18:20. God heard "the cry" against Sodom and Gomorrah and moved into action.

The God of v. 24 is a God who hears and remembers. How could anybody 2:24
cry out from pain (to whomever), and God not hear? How could God be God and be oblivious to such wailing? Does recalling that Hebrew *šāmaʿ* means not only "hear" but also "obey" suggest that for God not to hear is for God not to obey, as strange as that might sound? Thankfully, he is neither deaf nor indifferent. If Exod. 2:23–25 is about a community that "*has a bold voice for hurt*," it is also about a God who "*has an attentive ear for hurt*" (Brueggemann 1997: 47, italics original).

The verb "remember" (*zākar*) in the basic Qal stem appears 169 times in the OT. Of these 169 times, God is the subject 73 times. He is a God who remembers. He remembers the recipient of the covenant (Noah, Gen. 8:1; Abraham, 19:29). Fourteen times God remembers the covenant he has made with somebody, as here: Gen. 9:15, 16; Exod. 2:24; 6:5; Lev. 26:42 [3x], 45; Pss. 105:8; 106:45; 111:5; Jer. 14:21; Ezek. 16:60. John the Baptist's father, Zechariah, picks up on this when he speaks of the Lord as one who has come "to show mercy to our fathers and to remember his holy covenant" (Luke 1:72). "Remember" sounds like such a human-related verb that using it of God may seem strange. If by "remember" v. 24 is stating that the crying of the people jogs God's memory about a covenant he has made earlier, then it is indeed strange! That is hardly what it means, however. For God to remember is not to recollect accidentally, but to take action deliberately on what is recalled. Or as Childs (1962: 34) has put it, "God's remembering always implies his movement toward the object of his memory. . . . The essence of God's remembering lies in his acting toward someone because of a previous commitment." This truth suggests that God saves his people not because he dislikes slavery, but because of his prior covenant with this people. Even if they had not cried out, even if life in Goshen had been serene and idyllic, God still would have delivered them. He cannot be faithful to his covenant and do otherwise. Hence, I find myself unable to agree with Knierim (1995b: 131) when he says, in conjunction with Exod. 3:7–8, that "without their [Israel's] current oppression there would be no cause for him [God] to lead them out of Egypt. They may have stayed in Egypt forever."

Alongside this emphasis on God's remembering is the biblical emphasis elsewhere on God's not remembering. What he remembers is his covenant with us. What he does not remember is our sins (Jer. 31:34; Heb. 8:12).

2:25 There are four uses of *ʾĕlōhîm*, "God," in these three verses (NIV deletes one of them). There are also four verbs of which *ʾĕlōhîm* is the subject: "heard . . . remembered . . . saw . . . knew." Propp (1996: 471) observes that "in the MT, the four *ʾĕlōhîm*s fall like hammer blows, accompanied by alternating verbs of perception and cognition: 'heard . . . remembered . . . saw . . . knew.'"

God Encounters Moses for the First Time

(3:1–6)

Translation

[1]Moses was shepherding the flocks of Jethro, his father-in-law, priest of Midian. He drove the flocks deep into the steppe and reached God's mountain, Horeb. [2]The Lord's angel showed himself to him in [as?] a fiery flame from within a certain bush. He caught sight, yes, the bush there ablaze with fire, yet the bush intact, unconsumed. [3]Thought Moses, "I must turn aside and inspect this mysterious phenomenon! How is it the bush is not burned away?" [4]When the Lord observed that he was turning aside for a closer look, God called out to him from within the bush: "Moses! Moses!" "Yes-s-s sir," said he. [5]"Approach no closer," he said. "Remove your shoes from your feet, for the spot upon which you are standing is holy ground." [6]Further he said, "I am the God of your father, yes, the God of Abraham, the God of Isaac, and the God of Jacob." Whereupon Moses cloaked his face, fearful of gazing upon Divinity.

Grammatical and Lexical Notes

3:1. "Was shepherding" is composed of the finite form *hāyâ* plus the participle *rōʿeh*. Such a construction suggests continuous action in the past (GKC §116r).

3:1. The verb *nāhag* is used for herding/driving animals in Gen. 31:18; 1 Sam. 23:5; 30:20; Job 24:3. It is used for herding/driving people in Gen. 31:26; Deut. 4:27; 28:37; 1 Sam. 30:2, 22; and so forth.

3:1. "Deep into" is, literally, "behind, after" (*ʾaḥar*), hence KJV's unique "backside of the desert." Some Hebrew grammarians argue for the translation "west" ("he drove the flock to the west side of the steppe"). See Waltke and O'Connor 1990: 193; R. Williams 1976: §359.

3:2. The phrase *wayyērāʾ malʾak YHWH ʾēl* ("The Lord's angel showed himself to . . .") occurs in the OT only here and in Judg. 6:12; 13:3.

3:2. The preposition *bĕ* can be rendered either "in" ("in a fiery flame") or "as" ("as a fiery flame"). If it is the latter, then the preposition is the so-called *bêt essentiae* (GKC §119i).

3:2. The verb *rāʾâ* ("see") appears first in the Niphal ("showed himself," *wayyērāʾ*) with "Lord" as its subject, and then in the Qal ("He caught sight," *wayyarʾ*) with Moses as its subject, followed by *wĕhinnēh* ("and yes . . ."). The only other time we have this in the Pentateuch is Gen. 18:1–2 AT, "The Lord *appeared* to Abraham. . . . Abraham looked up *and saw and behold,* three men." For Magonet (1975: 305) such a variation on the verb "see" within the same verse in Exod. 3:2 allows the reader to hear this incident through the objective eyes of the narrator, who knows all along who is in this bush, and through the subjective eyes of the participant, Moses, who knows nothing of the Divinity that is in the bush.

3:2. Fire's attributes or properties include light and heat. Fire itself, however, is a metaphor for love. The Hebrew word for "passionate ardor" in Ezek. 16:30 ("How hot your passionate ardor [*libbâ*] is" versus NIV's "how weak-willed you are") may show that *libbâ* seems to be a fusion of the word *labbah* ("flame"), used here in Exod. 3:2, and *lēb* ("heart").

3:2. "He caught sight, yes . . ." is the verb *rā'â* followed by *wĕhinnēh* ("he looked and behold . . ."). For other *rā'â hinnēh* passages, see Gen. 1:31; 41:22; Josh. 5:13; Ezek. 2:9; Zech. 1:8. Compare 1 Kings 19:6: "he [Elijah] *looked around* and *there* by his head was a cake of bread . . . ," except *nābaṭ* is used for "look" instead of *rā'â*. This formula enables the narrator to look through the eyes of the character and present to him what he sees. Just as *lē'mōr* introduces direct speech, so *hinnēh* introduces direct sight (on which see Sadka 2001: 485).

3:2. For other instances where *bā'ar* ("ablaze") and *'ākal* ("consumed") are used together, compare Num. 11:1 AT ("Fire from the LORD burned [*bā'ar*] and consumed [*'ākal*] some of . . ."). See also Job 1:16; Isa. 9:18 [17]; 10:17; Lam. 2:3c.

3:2. "(Un)consumed" illustrates one form of the Qal passive participle, a *qattul* form (*'ukkāl*). We have already seen the other form it may take, a *qittôl* form, in *yillôd* in 1:22.

3:3. "I must turn aside" is my attempt to capture the *-na'* after the verb (*'āsurâ-nnā'*). Waltke and O'Connor (1990: 579) call this a "cohortative of resolve" and compare God's words about the clamor coming from Sodom and Gomorrah: "I will go down [*'ērădâ-nnā'*] and see" (Gen. 18:21). Christiansen (2009: 385) takes another approach. He notes passages where *-nā'* occurs in speech that is a soliloquy, and so cannot have its usual meaning of "please, I beg you." He references Gen. 18:21; Exod. 3:3; 2 Sam. 14:15; Ps. 122:8 and suggests that in such instances the particle "functions to signal that the speaker is proposing a course of action with which the addressee may or may not agree or choose to accommodate."

3:3. Freedman (1969) reads the *lō'* before *yib'ar* ("is not burned away") as an emphatic rather than a negative: "Why 'indeed' the bush continues to burn." G. Driver (1973: 110) also reads the *lō'* as an affirmation by exclamatory negation: "Why, is it not burning?" = "What can I imagine? Of course, it's burning."

3:4. For other uses of *sûr lĕ* ("turn aside to/for"), see Judg. 14:8 ("Some time later . . . he [Samson] turned aside to look at the lion's carcass"). *Sûr 'el* occurs with the same nuance in Gen. 19:2, 3 ("My lords, . . . please turn aside to your servant's house").

3:4. Emphatic vocatives like "Moses! Moses!" occur in Gen. 22:11 ("Abraham! Abraham!"); 1 Sam. 3:10 ("Samuel! Samuel!"); 2 Sam. 18:33 ("O my son Absalom! My son, my son Absalom!"); 2 Kings 2:12 ("My father! My father!"); Ps. 22:1 [2] ("My God! My God!"). Although not vocatives, similar repetition appears in phrases like "Amen, Amen" (Pss. 72:19; 89:52 [53]); "has fallen, has fallen" (Isa. 21:9); "Comfort, comfort" (Isa. 40:1); "Peace, peace" (Jer. 8:11). See Muilenburg 1953: 102.

3:4. For the rendering of *hinnēnî* as "Yes-s-s sir," see Brichto 1991. For other instances of "here I am; yes" see Gen. 22:1 (Abraham to God); 22:11 (Abraham to the angel); 27:1 (Esau to Isaac); 31:11 (Jacob to the angel); 37:13 (Joseph to Jacob; NIV "Very well"); 46:2 (Jacob to God); 1 Sam. 3:4, 5, 6, 8, 16 (Samuel to the Lord or Eli); Isa. 6:8 (Isaiah to God). The normal spelling is *hinnēnî*, but in two instances the Masoretic editors have *hinnennî*, that is, with two doubled n's. Interestingly, they are both occasions on which a father is addressing a younger but favored son (Gen. 22:7 [Abraham to Isaac] and 27:18 [Isaac to Jacob disguised as Esau]).

3:5. The last part of this verse includes a *casus pendens* ("the spot upon which you are standing") followed by a nominal clause in which the predicate precedes the resumptive subject pronoun ("holy ground it [is]"). The purpose of such a construction is to lend emphasis to the predicate. See Gen. 40:12, "the three branches—three days [are] they"; Exod. 32:16, "The tablets—the work of God [were] they"; Ezek. 37:11, "These bones—the whole house of Israel [are] they." See T. Zewi (2000: 54), who calls such sentences "Tripartite Nominal Sentences."

3:6. "Divinity" is an attempt to capture the thrust of the definite article "the" on "God" (*hā'ĕlōhîm*).

Commentary

Shepherding is what Moses has been doing for a good long while. If one thinks about it, it is a good preparation for another kind of shepherding to which God will call Moses. If Jesus can transform those he has called from one kind of fisherman into another kind of fisherman, why cannot the Lord God transform one kind of shepherd into another kind of shepherd? That may explain why there are several "ex-shepherds" in the Bible when God calls them to forsake shepherding. God takes both David (2 Sam. 7:8) and Amos (Amos 7:14–15) from tending the flock and redirects their lives. So we say to all shepherds, "Watch your back!" 3:1

God does not reveal himself to Moses so spectacularly when Moses is praying, or fasting, or meditating, or engaging in some profound metaphysical thought. It happens while he is alone, working, and probably unexciting menial work at that.

On this particular day Moses leads his flock far beyond the usual grazing grounds, "deep into the steppe." "Steppe" is often translated "wilderness" or "desert," which suggests an arid wasteland. Here, however, *midbār* suggests uncultivated, more remote pasturelands. That this territory can hardly be "desert" is proved by Exod. 34:3, which in speaking of this same area has God say to Moses, "Not even the flocks and herds may graze in front of the mountain." So Moses is, geographically, out of his comfort zone, perhaps driving his sheep "to the highlands after the lowland grass had dried up or had been consumed" (Greenberg 1969: 68).

The narrator tells us that this place is "Horeb," which is another name for Sinai, maybe in the sense that "The Big Apple" is another name for New York City, or "The Windy City" is another name for Chicago. To call it "God's mountain" is proleptic, for that is what it will become when Moses comes a second time, with his people, to this place (Exod. 19). But for now it is just another hill. *A* mountain will become *the* mountain, just as here *a* place will become *the* place.

God sometimes, or maybe many times, shows up unexpected, unannounced, 3:2
and unbidden. He does so to Jacob by the river Jabbok in Transjordan while Jacob is expecting to run into Esau, not into God (Gen. 32:22–32). He does so to Ezekiel by the Kebar River or Canal in Babylon (Ezek. 1:1). He does so to Saul of Tarsus on the road to Damascus (Acts 9). Moses could surely say, "Even if I make my bed in Midian, thou art there." God's appearing as an angel to a shepherd on just another day of shepherding, and the fear that appearance engenders in the shepherd(s), recalls the scene in Luke 2:8–20. One assumes that both revelations are nocturnal, Luke 2:8–20 for sure, and Exod. 3:2 probably so because of the revelation by fire. Two differences separate the two incidents. First, to the best of our knowledge, Moses never shares the particulars of this bush revelation with anybody. The shepherds do share their

experience (Luke 2:15–17). Second, Luke's shepherds return to shepherding after the encounter (2:20). After his encounter with God, Moses's return to shepherding will be either short-lived or nonexistent.

"The angel of the Lord" can be rendered "the messenger of the Lord." ("Malachi," for example, means "my angel," or "my messenger.") It is unlikely to be a supernatural being distinct from God. Rather, we should understand the phrase to refer to a manifestation of God that is visible to the human eye, either in anthropomorphic form or in fiery form. This "angel/messenger" appears to men (Abraham: Gen. 22:11, 15; Jacob: Gen. 31:11; 48:16; Moses: Exod. 3:2; Gideon: Judg. 6:11; Samson's father, Manoah: Judg. 13:13, 15, 16 [2x]) and to women (Hagar: Gen. 16:7, 9, 11; 21:17; the mother of Samson: Judg. 13:3, 6, 9). Hagar, by the way, is the first person in Scripture to whom this angel/messenger appears and is the only one to whom the angel/messenger comes on two separate occasions separated by many years (Gen. 16 and 21).

Several of these references speak of angel/God/Lord as if interchangeable and undistinguishable, reinforcing the idea that the Lord himself is the angel, and the angel is the Lord himself. Compare, for example, Hagar's words about the angel in Gen. 16:13, or the angel's own words to Abraham in 22:12, or the angel's words of self-identification to Jacob in 31:13, or the narrator's words about the angel in the bush (Exod. 3:2) and God in the bush (3:4b). Manoah calls the angel "God" (Judg. 13:22).

Fire is a frequent medium by which God reveals himself. God's fire always does one of two things in Scripture. Either it destroys (think of Sodom and Gomorrah's fire), or it purifies (think of Isa. 6). When John the Baptist speaks of Jesus "baptizing with the Holy Spirit *and fire*" (Matt. 3:11; Luke 3:16; Mark 1:8 omits "with fire"), one wonders whether he is speaking of fire as something destructive or something purifying or both. God is never interested merely in amplifying himself or in impressing us with some pyrotechnic display. The reading in Codex Vaticanus renders "in/as a fiery flame" as *en pyri phlogos*. That exact phrase appears in 2 Thess. 1:7, "This will happen when the Lord Jesus is revealed from heaven in blazing fire [*en pyri phlogos*] with his powerful angels." Close to this Greek phrase is *en phlogi pyros*, used in Isa. 66:15 to refer to the Lord's "flames of fire" (also the in-text reading of Exod. 3:2 LXX). At least the blazing fire in Exod. 3 purifies the bush. Pity any bug or larva that is nesting in it! There is not a single thing left there except bush and fire.

Like Hagar, Moses encounters God by a bush. There are two Hebrew words for "bush." Hagar's bush is a *śîḥ* (Gen. 21:15); Moses's bush is a *sĕneh*. Outside of Exod. 3:2–4, the second word occurs only one more time in the OT, in one line of Moses's blessing on the Joseph tribe (Deut. 33:13–17). In the second line of Deut. 33:16 Moses prays that the Josephites might be blessed with "the favor of him who dwelt in the burning bush" (*šokĕnî sĕneh*). On this his final speech in his life, Moses recalls the centerpiece of his first encounter with God. It is hard to miss the similarity in sound between *sĕneh*/bush and *sînāy*/Sinai.

Sinai is a subsequent encounter with God enveloped in fire. To that degree, the blazing bush (Exod. 3) anticipates the blazing mountain (Exod. 19).

There seem to be some resonances of Exod. 3:2b in Jer. 20:9. Exodus 3 speaks of a bush "ablaze with fire" (*bōʿēr bāʾēš*) that nevertheless is "not consumed" (*ʾênennû ʾukkāl*). In Jer. 20:9 the prophet laments that God's word is "in my heart like a [burning] fire (*kĕʾēš bōʿeret*). . . . I am weary of holding it in; indeed, I cannot (*wĕlōʾ ʾûkāl*)," with Moses's *ʾukkāl* matching Jeremiah's *ʾûkāl*. The fire that keeps the bush aflame, which Moses is powerless to put out, is inexhaustible. The fire that burns in Jeremiah's heart, which Jeremiah is powerless to put out, is nonstop.

It is the bush, not the angel/messenger, that catches Moses's attention. Often, **3:3**
before God is able to say something to somebody, he must arrest that individual's attention in one way or another. Moses calls the incinerating bush "this mysterious phenomenon," literally, "this great sight" (*hammarʾeh haggādōl hazzeh*). When Num. 8:4 refers to the lampstand, another source of light, it uses the word *marʾeh*: "The lampstand was made exactly like the 'pattern/depiction/view' the Lord had shown Moses" (B. Robinson 1997: 118). (Exodus 25:40 uses the synonym *tabnît* for "pattern/replica" in conjunction with the making of the lampstand, with *marʾeh* suggesting a picture while *tabnît* suggests a model.) Like the bush, the lampstand is arboreal in form. Like the bush, the lampstand is to burn continually (Exod. 27:20–21). The fire that pushes back the darkness of the Midianite sky anticipates the fire that pushes back the darkness in the holy place in the sanctuary. And possibly those who have been baptized with the Holy Spirit's fire (Matt. 3:11) will be those whom God most uses to push back the darkness of the day.

If we include v. 7 in our discussion, then seven times some form of the root **3:4**
r-ʾ-h, either in verbal ("see") or nominal form ("sight"), occurs. In v. 2 God lets himself be seen. Also in v. 2 Moses "caught sight" of this flaming bush. In v. 3 Moses wants to move closer to "see" this "sight." Now in v. 4 it is the Lord who sees something. And in v. 7 the Lord says to Moses, "Seeing, I have seen." A few verses later, when God begins to speak to Moses about mission, the emphasis will be on "he that has ears to hear, let him hear." But here the emphasis is on "he who has eyes to see, let him see."

It may appear puzzling that in the middle of v. 4 God switches names, or the narrator switches God's name. It is the Lord (*YHWH*) who has seen Moses moving closer, but it is God (*ʾĕlōhîm*) who addresses Moses from the bush. The Greek of the LXX smooths out the differences by simply reading "Lord/*kyrios*" both times. Commentators who subscribe to the Documentary Hypothesis—sometimes known as the JEDP theory, which argues for the composite formation of the Pentateuch—offer another solution. Whoever wrote v. 4a could not be the same person who wrote v. 4b, for the same author would not have changed God's name in midstream. It is the source J that gave us v. 4a, and E gave us v. 4b. The source critics divide 3:1–6 into the following literary units: E (vv. 1, 4b, 6) and J (vv. 2–3, 4a, 5).

Maybe there is another possibility. Because *ʾĕlōhîm* is a kind of catchall designation for all heavenly beings (God/god/gods/angels), might not *ʾĕlōhîm* be a reference to "the Lord's angel," who, according to v. 2, is in the fiery bush, and here addresses Moses from within the fiery bush? Elsewhere when this divine messenger appears, he not only shows up, but he also converses and commands, either on earth (Gen. 16) or from heaven (Gen. 22). The narrator knows that the voice from the bush is the Lord's (v. 4a), but for Moses it is simply the voice of some (unknown) *ʾĕlōhîm* (v. 4b).

In a grammatical note, I have already commented on the use of double vocatives here: "Moses! Moses!" To the OT examples I listed there, we could add Jesus's "Martha, Martha" (Luke 10:41), "Simon, Simon" (Luke 22:31), "Saul, Saul" (Acts 9:4). The bottom line is that, whether we are in the First or Second Testament, when God calls your name twice, you'd better listen up.

Of all the times God calls somebody by name twice, the closest parallel to Exod. 3:4 is God's call to Jacob in Gen. 46: (1) "And God said to Israel, 'Jacob! Jacob!'" (Gen. 46:2a); "And he said, 'Moses! Moses!'" (Exod. 3:4a); (2) "and he said, 'Here am I'" (Gen. 46:2b); "And he said, 'Here am I'" (Exod. 3:4b); (3) "I am God, the God of your father" (Gen. 46:3a); "I am the God of your father" (Exod. 3:6a). Unlike Moses, however, Jacob does not hide his face, nor is he fearful. Maybe the reason is because Gen. 46 describes Jacob's last encounter with God, while Exod. 3 describes Moses's first encounter with God.

3:5 God's/the angel's words to Moses, "Approach no closer," are close to Moses's final encounter with an awesome, glorious God after the completion of the tabernacle. Exodus 40:35 says, "Moses could not enter the Tent of Meeting because . . . the glory of the Lord filled the tabernacle." In between the first "Approach no closer" and the final "could not enter" is the emphasis in chaps. 19 and 24 that Moses alone *can* enter into the direct presence of God, into the dense cloud atop Sinai, a holy of holies on the mountain's peak. Prohibited in chaps. 3 and 40, but permitted in chaps. 19 and 24. Locked out in chaps. 3 and 40; invited in, say chaps. 19 and 24. No beaming face in chaps. 3 and 40; a beaming, luminous face for Moses in 34:29–35.

Holiness language is remarkably absent in Genesis. It appears only in God's sanctification of the Sabbath (Gen. 2:3), and in Judah's thinking that his daughter-in-law, Tamar, is a "shrine prostitute" (NIV; lit., "a holy one" [*qĕdēšâ*, Gen. 38:21]). Nobody in Genesis is called holy or even challenged to be holy. Noah is "righteous" (*ṣaddîq*) and "blameless" (*tāmîm*, Gen. 6:9), but not "holy" (*qādōš*). The Lord calls Abraham to be blameless (*tāmîm*, Gen. 17:1), but he never calls him to be holy. Holy places and holy people appear in the Bible only in conjunction with the covenant and covenantal law that God gives to his chosen people, Israel.

Here somewhere on the Sinai steppe, God identifies the place of his presence as "holy ground." More literally the Hebrew phrase *ʾadmat-qōdeš* should be translated "land of holiness." *Qōdeš* is not an adjective modifying the feminine noun *ʾădāmâ*. Rather, *qōdeš* is a noun in the absolute state; the preceding noun (*ʾădāmâ*) is in construct form and goes with *qōdeš*. "Holy ground" would be *ʾădāmâ qĕdōšâ*. I am not aware of any feminine noun in the Hebrew Bible that is followed by the adjective *qĕdōšâ* used attributively. For example, the only way Biblical Hebrew can refer to Jerusalem as "the holy city," and "city" is a feminine noun, is to write "(the) city of holiness" (*ʿîr haqqōdeš*, Isa. 52:1; Neh. 11:1, 18). It is not unusual in the Bible for the promised land to be called "holy." See, for example, Exod. 15:13 ("your holy dwelling") or Isa. 11:9 ("my holy mountain"). It is also not unusual for the Bible to refer to all land outside the promised land as "defiled" (Josh. 22:19), "pagan" (Amos 7:17), and the like. Normally, then, the wilderness is the antithesis of holiness. They go together like oil and water. The one thing that can transform common, unholy ground into extraordinary, holy ground is a theophany, a (spectacular) divine manifestation. And if God can transform unholy ground into holy ground by the glow of his presence, might he not also be able to transform an unholy life? What God can do with the *ʾădāmâ*, might he not also do with the *ʾādām*? One does not have to restrict the significance of this story to the exiles who are pining away in their own unholy surroundings, yet the exiles would derive much hope from it (as does Wyatt 1979; 1986). It shows what God can do when he shows up anytime, anywhere, to anybody.

A shod Moses, standing on such holy ground, can only remove his shoes. There are several possibilities to explain why. First, because people make shoes from the carcass of an animal, the shoes are inherently unclean or impure, and nothing unclean or impure is to enter God's presence. Second, shoes protect one's feet from injury or dirt. One need not fear either of these in God's presence, and so the need for shoes to cover one's feet becomes superfluous. Third, upon entering a sacred precinct, one removes the shoes as a sign of respect for the deity. This is practiced when Muslims enter a mosque, and in some places throughout Christendom. (I think of a Christian from India whom I have often heard preach. Before he approaches the pulpit, he always removes his shoes.) A fourth possibility is that this story reflects the idea of a host (in this case, God) inviting his guest (in this case, Moses) to remove his shoes before entering the host's home as an act of gracious hospitality (see Janzen 1997: 28–29). In such an understanding, Moses, who at the end of chap. 2 describes himself as an "alien," is now a "guest" of God.

Many commentators have noticed that in the portions of Exodus dealing with priestly vestments (28; 39), mention is made of a covering for every part of the body except the feet. This suggests that when the clerics enter into the holy place for ministry, they do so barefoot.

The closest parallel to Exod. 3:5 is Josh. 5:13–15. At the threshold of the ministry to which God has (or will shortly) call them, God appears in fiery form and soldier form, telling both to remove their shoes, for each is on holy ground. Moses will not face Egypt alone, and Joshua will not face Jericho alone.

There are a few differences between the two scenes. "Ground" is absent in Josh. 5 ("is holy" versus "is holy ground"), and in Josh. 5 "shoe" and "foot" are morphologically singular (versus "shoes" and "feet" in Exod. 3). More important, there is some difference in the sequence of events. In Joshua, first comes the emphasis on circumcision (Josh. 5:1–9), then the appearance of a sword-wielding divine figure (Josh. 5:13), then the divine theophany/epiphany, then the start of Joshua's ministry. With Moses the sequence is first the encounter with God at the bush, a subsequent encounter with God on his way back to Egypt (4:24), then the appearance of a knife-wielding Zipporah and circumcision (4:25–26), and finally the start of his ministry. The similarity, even if in somewhat of a reverse order, between these portions of the lives of Moses and Joshua reinforces the common divine calling on these two lives. What Moses starts, Joshua will complete. God's grace is exhibited through two barefoot generals (also see Alter 1992: 119).

3:6 In v. 3 Moses is curious. In v. 6 he is "fearful"—although his persistent verbal jousts with God throughout chaps. 3 and 4, and again in chap. 5, show that his fear of God does not make him tight-lipped before God. Fearful, but argumentative! Scared, but brash!

It is not unusual for Scripture to tell us of God's hiding (or not hiding) his face (*sātar pānîm*). There are twenty-three references to this: Deut. 31:17; 32:20; Job 13:24; 34:29; Pss. 10:11; 13:1 [2]; 22:24 [25]; 27:9; 30:7 [8]; 44:24 [25]; 51:9 [11]; 88:14 [15]; 102:2 [3]; 143:7; Isa. 8:17; 54:8; 59:2; 64:7 [6]; Jer. 33:5; Ezek. 39:23, 24, 29; Mic. 3:4. The phrase is most common in the Psalter and the Prophets. What is unusual is for Scripture to say that a person "hid his face/*sātar pānîm*." Apart from Isaiah's prophetic mention of the suffering servant who "did not hide my face" (Isa. 50:6), but from whom all the rest of us hid our faces (53:3), Exod. 3:6 is the only reference to a person hiding (with the verb *sātar*) his face from God. (The Hebrew Bible may occasionally use other verbs for "hiding," as in the seraphs covering/hiding [*kāsâ* and not *sātar*] their faces; Isa. 6:2.)

A phrase related to "covering the face" is "covering the eyes." Its verb of choice for "cover, hide" is *ʿālam*, whether the subject is human (Lev. 20:4; 1 Sam. 12:3; Prov. 28:27; Ezek. 22:26) or divine (Isa. 1:15).

The phrase that God uses to identify himself to Moses ("I am the God of your father, yes, the God of Abraham, the God of Isaac, and the God of Jacob") appears twice in the NT. Stephen briefly mentions this Exodus incident in Acts 7:30–33, with the quote of Exod. 3:6 appearing in Acts 7:32. There are some slight differences between the two, and for a person about to be stoned to death, the minimal departures are understandable. In Exod. 3:6 God begins by saying, "I am the God of your father" (sg.). In Acts 7:32 Stephen has God saying, "I am the God of your fathers" (pl.). Also, Stephen omits "God of" before Isaac and Jacob, whereas Exod. 3:6 had "God of" three times, once before each name of the patriarchs. Third, Exod. 3:5–6 has God first tell Moses to remove his shoes (v. 5), and then God identifies himself as the father of the ancestors (v. 6). Stephen reverses these two so that Acts 7:32 = Exod. 3:6, and Acts 7:33 = Exod. 3:5.

The other reference in the NT to Exod. 3:6 is in Matt. 22:32 (= Mark 12:26; Luke 20:37). On this occasion some Sadducees approach Jesus and raise the question about the woman who has serially married seven brothers, but has had children by none. At the time of resurrection, to which one of the seven will she be spouse? they ask. Jesus's answer (and we will take Mark's account for our discussion) is in Mark 12:24–27. The climax of Jesus's response is in Mark 12:26, when he quotes Exod. 3:6 as a proof text for the resurrection, and then adds in v. 27a, "He is not the God of the dead, but of the living."

How can Jesus cite Exod. 3:6 as pointing to resurrection? We can agree that, without a knowledge of Jesus's citing this passage in the context he does, it is unlikely that anybody would read into the Exodus verse a resurrection emphasis in its original context. In Exod. 3:6 God is simply introducing himself to Moses by way of his connection with the patriarchs; he is not talking about postmortem existence. Furthermore, we can agree with Meier (2000: 11), who observes that there is no Jewish exegetical tradition, before or after Jesus in ancient times, that uses Exod. 3:6 to argue for resurrection, and to that degree Meier describes Jesus's take on Exod. 3:6 as "idiosyncratic."

The standard way of making this all fit is to focus on Jesus's use of the verb "am" in the present tense. "I 'am' [*eimi*] the God of . . . ," not "I 'was' the God of . . . ," although there is no verb "am" in either in Mark 12:26 or Luke 20:37, but only in Matt. 22:32. The former two are nominal sentences. So understood, Jesus implies that the patriarchs are still alive, for he is a God of the living, not of the dead. N. Wright (2003: 424) points out that a Pharisaic and rabbinic view of the resurrection involves two stages: (1) an intermediate stage in which the dead are in some way or another still alive; (2) a final stage in which the dead will be eternally reembodied. In Mark 12:26 Jesus is saying that the patriarchs are in stage 1, waiting for stage 2.

Perhaps there is more to it than this, however (see Janzen's illuminating study [1985: 43–58]). The Sadducees' question arises over the hypothetical question of seven sibling brothers, all of whom fail to impregnate the same woman. Seven successive episodes and experiences of sterility. Now for Jesus to refer to God as "the God of Abraham, Isaac, and Jacob" should ring a bell at this point. All three have great difficulty in impregnating their wives. It does not appear that Sarah, or Rebekah, or Rachel can conceive. Sarah's womb is "dead" (Rom. 4:19; Gen. 18:11). Genesis 30:1 has childless Rachel saying to Jacob, "Give me children, or I'll *die*" (which could be read, "Give me children, or else I'm *dead*").

But is not God a God who can give life to the dead? If he can resurrect a womb from the dead, and form offspring in that womb, can he not also resurrect a body from the dead? Can God do with the whole body what he can do with one part of the body? One must allow one of the following two realities to guide how one approaches these possibilities: either resignation to the realities of the moment, or total trust in God's promises. Abraham, Paul says, recognized reality: (1) "he faced the fact that his body was as good as *dead*" (Rom. 4:19), but (2) he did not permit that reality to control him. And the reason he did not is because he allowed "the promise of God" (4:20) to anchor him.

If Abraham knew that his body was "as good as dead," so also the Israelites in Egypt know they are "as good as dead with no possibility of a future generation," given the pogroms Pharaoh has launched: death through removal of males and death through oppression. But the God who "remembered" Rachel (Gen. 30:22) is the God who, upon hearing the groans of his own in Egypt, "remembered" his covenant with the ancestors (Exod. 2:24). That seems to be the point that Jesus is making in the Synoptics, even if he moves the issue to postmortem existence. That is to say, God has an excellent track record when it comes to sabotaging death, any kind of a death. Why should he quit now?

God's "Go" and Moses's "No"

(3:7–12)

Translation

7The LORD then said, "Long have I seen the degradation of my people who are in Egypt, and their cry because of his taskmasters I have heard. I know his pain. 8And I have come down to deliver him from Egypt's hand, and to bring him up from that land to a land fertile and spacious, to a land oozing milk and sap, to the place of the Canaanite, and the Hittite, and the Amorite, and Perizzite, and the Hivvite, and the Jebusite. 9So now, the cry of Israel's sons has reached me; also, I have certainly seen the oppression that Egyptians are imposing on them. 10So now go, and I will send you to Pharaoh, and free my people, Israel's sons, from Egypt." 11Moses then replied to the Divinity, "Who am I that I should go to Pharaoh, and that I should free Israel's sons from Egypt?" 12He said, "I AM [am] with you. And here is the sign for you that it is I who have sent you: When you have freed the people from Egypt, (all of) you will worship the Godhead at this very mountain."

Grammatical and Lexical Notes

3:7. The root *n-g-ś* ("treat harshly") appears in the Hebrew Bible thirteen times in participial form, as here, and in the majority of these instances the reference is to "taskmaster" or "slave driver." For other uses of this participle in Exodus see 5:6, 10, 13, 14. A celebrated use of this root in the Niphal is the prophet's words about the one he labels "the (suffering) servant of the Lord": "He was oppressed [*niggaś*] and afflicted [*naʿăneh*]" (Isa. 53:7a). There may be a connection between Isa. 53:7 and Exod. 3:7. In the latter the Lord speaks of Israel's "taskmasters," and Isa. 53:7 speaks of the servant being "oppressed," with both the participle and the verb coming from the same root, *nāgaś*. In Exod. 3:7 the Lord has observed the "degradation" of his people, and in Isa. 53:7a the servant is "afflicted," with both the noun and the verb being from the root *ʿ-n-h*.

3:7. I tend to go with the textual evidence that reads "pain" at the end with a singular suffix (*makʾōbô*) rather than MT's plural suffix (*makʾōbāyw*). It brings the noun into conformity with the singulars elsewhere in the context.

3:8. The basic meaning of *nāṣal* ("deliver') is "remove, rescue, get something out of the way," like sheep (David says in 1 Sam. 17:35 that he "rescued" his father's sheep from the mouths of predators), or riches (Rachel and Leah say to Jacob in Gen. 31:16 that God has "taken away" from their father Laban all the wealth that properly belongs to them). In only a few instances (maybe seven or eight) is the verb used of God's delivering/saving people. Five of these are in Exod. 18 (4, 8, 9, 10 [2x]). It is the verb that Jethro's daughters use in 2:19 (also Hiphil) to explain to their father how "an Egyptian man" rescued them from the shepherds.

3:9. Both v. 9 and v. 10 begin with *wĕʿattâ*, "and now." Sheppard (1985: 208) remarks that "the use of such an introduction within speeches, prayers or oracles denotes a turning point in the discussion. Two such openings in close proximity in the same discourse commonly occur, and often lend to the force of the second a sense of 'therefore' with a climactic conclusion." He cites as parallels to Exod. 3:9 in 1 Sam. 25:26–27; 26:19–20; 2 Sam. 2:6–7; 7:28–29. Add to those verses Gen. 44:30, 33: "So now [*wĕʿattâ*], if the boy is not with us when I go back to . . . my father . . . Now then [*wĕʿattâ*], please let your servant remain here"; 1 Sam. 24:20–21 [21–22]: "And now [*wĕʿattâ*] I [Saul] know that you will surely be king. . . . Now [*wĕʿattâ*] swear to me. . . ."

3:9. *wĕgam-rāʾîtî*, "I have certainly seen," carries the same force as *rāʾōh rāʾîtî* ("Long have I seen") in v. 7, for both are analogous grammatical constructions.

3:9. *laḥaṣ* ("oppression") appears sometimes in the Bible, as does *ʿōnî* ("degradation," 3:7), with food or water words. Examples are Deut. 16:3, *leḥem ʿōnî*, "the bread of affliction"; 1 Kings 22:27 (= 2 Chron. 18:26), "Put this fellow in prison and feed him with the bread of affliction (*leḥem laḥaṣ*) and water of affliction (*ûmayim laḥaṣ*)." Such "food" God will replace with "milk and sap/honey."

3:11. My rendering "the Divinity" is an attempt to capture the definite article *hā-* on *hāʾĕlōhîm*, as is my translation "the Godhead" for *hāʾĕlōhîm* in v. 12.

3:11. I am not aware of all the differences between the two forms of the first-person pronoun "I," *ʾănî* and *ʾānōkî* (used here). Unlike *ʾănî*, however, *ʾānōkî* is used elsewhere in expressions of self-abasement (see David's two "Who am I?" questions, using *ʾānōkî*, in 1 Sam. 18:18 and 2 Sam. 7:18).

3:11. For other instances of a "who"/*mî* question followed by a clause introduced with "that"/*kî*, see Judg. 9:28 ("*Who* is Abimelech, and *who* is Shechem, *that* we should be subject to him?"); 1 Sam. 17:26 ("*Who* is this uncircumcised Philistine *that* he should defy the armies of the living God?"); 2 Sam. 7:18 ("*Who* am I . . . *that* you have brought me this far?"); 2 Kings 18:35 NRSV ("*Who* among all the gods of the lands have delivered their countries from my hands, *that* the Lord should deliver Israel from my hand?"); Isa. 36:5 AT ("*Whom* do you depend on *that* you rebel against me?"); Isa. 57:11 ("*Whom* have you so dreaded and feared *that* you have been false to me?"). Close to Exod. 3:11, *mî ʾānōkî kî*, is Exod. 16:7 AT, *wĕnaḥnû mâ kî* ("*What* are we *that* you should grumble against us?").

3:12. The *kî* after the opening "he said" introduces a direct quotation, and therefore need not be translated. For other uses in the Hebrew Bible of *kî* functioning as quotation marks, see Gen. 21:30; 22:16–17; 26:22; 29:32–33; 37:35; and others. For instances of a sentence headed by *kî* that is an explicit reply to a question, see Gen. 20:10–11; 31:30–31; Judg. 6:15–16; 1 Kings 21:5–6.

3:12. The first part of God's response in v. 12 can be rendered simply "I will be with you," but since the verb for "I will be" (*ʾehyeh*) appears a few verses later in the celebrated v. 14, *ʾehyeh ʾăšer ʾehyeh*, normally rendered "I am who I am" (NRSV), I choose to raise the possibility of translating *ʾehyeh* the same in v. 12 as in v. 14.

3:12. Weinfeld (1977: 179–80) cites a line from one of the early second-millennium BC prophecies at Mari, *lu ittum*, "Let it be a sign," and basically the cuneiform equivalent of *wĕzeh* (*lĕkā*) *hāʾôt* in v. 12, as proof that signs played an important role in the Mari prophecies as well as in biblical prophecies.

3:12. I insert "(all of)" before "you will worship" to show that the "you" in "worship" is a plural "you" (*taʿabdûn*).

Commentary

3:7–9 The misery/hardship/degradation (*ʿŏnî*) that the Lord sees (*rāʾâ*) in Israel, brought on by Egypt, invites comparison with the misery/hardship (*ʿonyî*) God saw (*rāʾâ*) in Jacob, brought on by Laban (Gen. 31:42). Pharaoh is told that Israel has fled (Exod. 14:5); Laban is told that Jacob has fled (Gen. 31:22). The Egyptians pursued (*rādap*) Israel and overtook them (*nāśag*, Exod. 14:9); Laban pursued (*rādap*) Jacob (Gen. 31:23) and overtook him (*nāśag*, Gen. 31:25). See Geohegan 2004: 48–49. Laban is not only a *nābāl* ("fool," and *Laban* spelled backward), but he is also a pharaoh.

What the narrator has previously said about God's concern for his oppressed people in Egypt (2:24–25), God now says about himself to Moses. He is a God who "sees, hears, and knows" (v. 7), who "comes down" and "brings up" (v. 8). The cries of his people "reach" him, and he "sees" their horrific circumstances. But the time of his decision to go beyond hearing and seeing to liberating is his alone to make. God has not recently learned of the pain of his people in Goshen, nor does he stumble upon their plight accidentally. Like many of God's people, incarcerated Israel will have to learn, maybe with some bewilderment and anger, that God's delays are not necessarily God's denials. "In His time, in His time, / He makes all things beautiful in His time," say the lyrics of the song (Diane Ball, © Maranatha Music 1986; cf. Eccles. 3:11).

The Scripture references several instances of God's "coming down" (Gen. 11:5, 7; 18:21; Exod. 3:8; 19:20; Num. 11:25; 2 Sam. 22:10 = Ps. 18:9 [10]), and the prayers of his people that he "come down" (Ps. 144:5; Isa. 64:1–2). In this instance we know that the Lord has already come down, for he has spoken to Moses from within the bush. In Gen. 3 this phrase is not used, but surely the story assumes that God has come down, for Adam and Eve hear the sound under God's feet as he walks in the garden (3:8). Nowhere does the Scripture say that God comes down to talk to, say, Abraham or Noah, but surely he does not (always) speak from above. The language presupposes that God's dwelling is in the heavens, but when the situation calls for it, "God can leave the office" (Goldingay 2003: 306). Interestingly, God comes down to bring Israel up!

Sometimes the purpose of God toward Israel is to bring Israel out of Egypt (*yāṣāʾ*, Hiphil), but as in v. 8, sometimes his purpose is to bring Israel up to a new land (*ʿālâ*, Hiphil). The basic meaning of *yāṣāʾ*, in the context of slaves or prisoners, is "go free, be released." Note the slave law in Exod. 21:2–11, where *yāṣāʾ*, "go out," means "release." For the Hiphil of *yāṣāʾ* in Exodus to refer to the release from Egypt, see 6:6 and 20:2.

By contrast the Hiphil of *ʿālâ*, "bring up," focuses not on liberation, but on settlement in the new land (Gen. 50:24; Exod. 3:8, 17; 32:1; 33:1). According to Wijngaards (1965: 91, 98), the Hiphil of *yāṣāʾ* is used more for the exodus event (83x) than is the Hiphil of *ʿālâ* (41x). Taking both verbs together, one sees that God's saving/delivering work is both a saving "from" and a saving "to," a deliverance from bondage and an old way of life, and an entry into freedom and a revolutionary new way of life.

The land to which God will bring his people is one that is "fertile and spacious, oozing with milk and sap/honey." This description of Canaan appears about twenty times in the Bible. Antedating any of these twenty references to

Canaan's fertility is an Egyptian story, the story of Sinuhe, which dates to the early second millennium BC. After his flight from Libya and Egypt, Sinuhe arrives in Palestine. His description of this land is as follows: "It was a good land, named Yaa (= Canaan). Figs were in it, and grapes. It had more wine than water. Plentiful was its honey, abundant its olives. Every (kind of) fruit on its trees." Stern (1992: 554) cites two lines from a Canaanite/Ugaritic text (fourteenth to twelfth centuries BC) that is the story of Baal's death and resurrection, he who is the god of fertility (*KTU* 1.6 [*CTA* 6], III): "The heavens rain fat/oil (*šmn*), the wadis flow with honey (*nbtm*)."

It is odd to think of a land flowing/oozing with milk. Although milk is a symbol of purity (Gen. 49:12; Song 5:12) or wealth (Isa. 60:15–16), to the best of my knowledge the only time it is a symbol of fertility is in Joel 3:18 [4:18], "the mountains will drip new wine, and the hills will flow with milk." For that reason some have suggested a slight vowel variation in the word, changing *ḥālāb* ("milk") to *ḥēleb* ("fat"). The two words occur in subsequent verses in Exod. 23:18b, 19b: "The fat [*ḥēleb*] of my festival offerings must not be kept until morning. . . . Do not cook a young goat in its mother's milk [*ḥālāb*]." Some scholars have suggested that 23:19b should be read as the "mother's fat" rather than the "mother's milk." Additionally, "fat," but never "milk," combines in construct relationship with various nouns to form idioms of superlativity ("best oil" [Num. 18:12]; "best wine" [18:12]; "best wheat" [Deut. 32:14]; "the best land" [Gen. 45:18]). See Margalit 1987: 403–4. One argument against changing "milk" to "fat" is that "fat" is normally used to denote animal fat rather than liquid fat. If we retain "milk," then it is goat's milk, not cow's milk, that is one feature of Canaan's fertility.

I have chosen to render *dĕbāš* as "sap" rather than "honey" because the reference is to fruit rather than to bees' honey, meaning the nectar of dates and possibly other fruits. See, however, Forti (2006), who argues not only for "honey" but for "bees' honey." The only place I am aware of where *dĕbāš* refers to bees' honey is in the Samson story, Judg. 14:6–9. The Bible uses the word *yaʿar* for bees' honey (1 Sam. 14:26; Song 5:1) or *nōpet* (Ps. 19:10 [11]; Prov. 5:3; 24:13; 27:7; Song 4:11). Although the Bible refers to Canaan as a land full of *ḥālāb* and *dĕbāš*, however one translates the words, Lev. 2:11 prohibits the use of *dĕbāš*/honey in any offering made to the Lord by fire. You can eat it, put it on your toast, add it to other dishes as a sweetener, but do not offer it to God. We cannot be sure why Levitical law prohibits honey and yeast in offerings whose fragrance God will inhale. It is unlikely that the traditional explanation is correct: because of honey's widespread use in pagan cults. If that were so, the law would prohibit other items that Israelite sacrifice shares with heathen sacrifice (flour, incense, salt, blood, etc.). I suggest another reason why Sinaitic law forbids leaven and honey: because God desires no artificial inflation (yeast) or artificial flavoring (honey) in our offerings. Our offering is to be what it is without any attempt at artificial enhancement.

Canaan is not only a land flowing with milk/fat and honey/sap; it also is a land flowing with people, lots of them, six different groups to be exact. According to Ishida (1979: 461), there are twenty-seven passages in the OT that enumerate the indigenous peoples of Canaan. The longest lists mention twelve groups (Gen. 10:15–18; 1 Chron. 1:13–16). The shortest lists mention only two groups (Gen. 13:7; 34:30; Josh. 5:1; Judg. 1:4–5). The most common number is six (eleven times: Exod. 3:8, 17; 23:23; 33:2; 34:11; Deut. 20:17; Josh. 9:1; 11:3; 12:8; Judg. 3:5; Neh. 9:8, but the sequences of peoples enumerated may vary). Perhaps the reason for difference in the numbers is due to how finely one distinguishes one group from another, a different branch or subbranch. I suspect that if one checks out all the references to how many Native American groups resided in pre-Pilgrim America in many different sources, there would be a considerable variation in the total numbers.

There is an absolutely stunning passage in Isa. 19:19–25 about the noble future God has planned for Egypt, just as in Exod. 3 there is an equally stunning passage about the future God has planned for Israel. There are many shared key words in Isa. 19:19–25 and chaps. 3–11 of Exodus, suggesting that some dimension of inner-biblical exegesis is at work here (see table).

Exodus 3 and Isaiah 19:19–25 Compared

	Exodus 3	Isaiah 19:19–25
1.	God calls Israel "my people" (Exod. 3:7).	God calls Egypt "my people" (Isa. 19:25).
2.	God has heard his people crying out (Exod. 3:7).	God will hear Egypt when Egypt cries out to him (Isa. 19:20).
3.	The people are crying out because of the oppression (*laḥaṣ*) the Egyptians are imposing on them (*lōḥăṣîm*; Exod. 3:9).	Egypt will cry out to the Lord because of their oppressors (*lōḥăṣîm*; Isa. 19:20).
4.	God will send (*šālaḥ*) Moses to Pharaoh (Exod. 3:10).	God will send (*šālaḥ*) a savior and defender to Egypt (Isa. 19:20b).
5.	God gives Moses a sign (*ʾôt*) that he is the one to go to Egypt and that God's presence will go with him (Exod. 3:12).	Egypt's building an altar to the Lord in Egypt will be a sign (*ʾôt*) of the Lord's presence in Egypt with the Egyptians (Isa. 19:19–21).
6.	God plans to deliver (Hiphil of *nāṣal*) Israel (Exod. 3:8).	God plans to deliver (Hiphil of *nāṣal*) Egypt (Isa. 19:20).
7.	Key words found throughout Exod. 7–11 are highlighted in Isa. 19:21–22.	God promises that Egypt will "know" the Lord, and although he will strike Egypt with a plague (*nāgap*), he will also "respond to their pleas" (*ʿātar*; Isa. 19:21–22).
8.	The Lord is Israel's healer (*rāpāʾ*, Exod. 15:26).	The Lord is also Egypt's healer (*rāpāʾ*, Isa. 19:22 [2x]).

What is one to make of all these parallels? What God has in store for Israel, he has in store for Egypt. As Fishbane (1980: 354) says, "Through a manifest and deliberate reworking, Israel's paramount memory of salvation has been extended to its most ancient enemy." Such is the God of Israel, a God of the nations, who weeps over their sins, who longs for their liberation from oppression, who makes his divine resources available to all.

3:10 In light of how in vv. 7–9 God has so consistently talked to Moses about himself and what he intends to do, Moses may think that he is to be a spectator to this dynamic work of God. But no! God is going to send Moses to be the agent through whom God will do his work. Presumably the Lord has the resources and ability to act independently, to deliver Israel by himself, without Moses's assistance. Seldom in Scripture, however, does God act so unilaterally. The scriptural pattern seems to be God's using people to reach people. Four times God will say to Moses "Go!": 3:10 (*lĕkâ*); 4:12 (*lēk*); 4:19 (*lēk*); 6:11 (*bôʾ*).

3:11 Moses's self-belittling response to God's "go" in v. 11 is the first of five excuses or dodges he will make to God (3:13; 4:1; 4:10; 4:13). Many commentators have noticed a common pattern or structure in various call narratives scattered throughout Scripture, for which they often use the German word *Berufungsschema* (see Habel 1965): a commission (v. 10); an objection (v. 11); a reassuring word from God or a rejoinder (v. 12a); a sign of some sort (v. 12b). The best parallels to Moses's call in Exod. 3:9–12 are Gideon's (Judg. 6:14–17), Saul's (1 Sam. 9–10), and Jeremiah's (Jer. 1:4–10). Perhaps the closest parallel to Moses's objection in v. 11, although not part of a call narrative, is what Samuel says to the Lord when the Lord instructs Samuel to go to Bethlehem and anoint David: "How can I go? Saul will hear about it and kill me" (1 Sam. 16:2).

Quite possibly what fuels Moses's self-doubts on this occasion are very vivid and painful memories of failed efforts many years earlier to come to the rescue of one of his people (Exod. 2:11–15a). Past defeats and humiliations tend to dog us more than past victories. Time does not always heal all wounds. On occasions the passing of time exacerbates them. The failure to deliver the wounded Hebrew is much more in his memory bank than is the successful deliverance of the priest's seven daughters at the well.

There seems to be a world of difference between David's two "Who am I?" questions, the first asked of Saul (1 Sam. 18:18), the second asked of God (2 Sam. 7:18b), and Moses's "Who am I?" David's are genuine expressions of humility and modesty. Why should he be the king's son-in-law? Why should God build of and for David a house that will last forever? In neither case, then, does Saul or God need to offer David a reassuring word as God does with Moses in 3:12. If David's "Who am I?" points to genuine humility, Moses's "Who am I?" is a cop-out, an attempt to disqualify himself, an attempt not to say with Isaiah, "Here am I. Send me!" (Isa. 6:8), but rather to say, "Here am I. Send him!"

There is a profoundly more important statement in Scripture than "Who am I?" It is found in Paul's statement while caught in the storm aboard a ship on the Mediterranean. To his frightened fellow passengers, he says, "Last night an angel of the God *whose I am* and whom I serve stood beside me" (Acts 27:23). Moses is focused on "Who am I?" In v. 12 God will attempt to shift the focus of Moses to "whose I am."

God does not rebuke Moses, at least not yet. He does not say, "Don't talk like that." He simply makes the promise "I am with you." This is the only time in Exodus where God makes this promise to Moses. Pharaoh uses the phrase somewhat sarcastically in 10:10, and Moses's father-in-law, Jethro, repeats this promise to Moses (18:19). **3:12**

Although appearing only once in Exodus in God's mouth, this exact promise appears over a hundred times in the OT. In most of these occasions the promise is made to a leader of some sort (patriarchs, kings, military leaders/judges, priests and prophets, or by a leader to a people). (Jeremiah is the only prophetic book of fifteen or sixteen to contain this same promise: Jer. 1:8, 19; 15:20; 20:11.) To be sure, similar promises appear elsewhere in the Moses story with a slight variation in language: "will meet with you" (Exod. 25:22; 30:6, 36); "not go with you" (33:3, 5); "my presence/face will go with you" (33:14). Gowan (1994: 57) remarks that such phrases as "I am with you," "God/the Lord is with you," or "May the Lord be with you" belong "to a clearly defined set of circumstances; that is, when the addressee faces danger or a task where the risk of failure is very great." Moses is surely facing a daunting task. He more than likely will not find out "who he is," but what he will discover is the dynamic power of presence, God's presence.

God's response to fear(fulness) is not to explain it away as illusory, but to replace it with another, more powerful belief: trust in his presence. DeNeff (2002: 27–28) uses the story of his young daughter who feared the bogeyman in her bedroom. Trying to tell her there is no bogeyman was to no avail. The father's only recourse was to sit at the foot of his daughter's bed and stand guard while she slept. "If the bogeyman comes out," he said, "he'll have to get through me, and I'm tougher than the bogeyman." Says DeNeff, "There was no sense in denying fear; it had to be replaced with trust in her father." Rather than explain away his apprehensions, God said to Moses, "For Pharaoh to get to you, he'll have to go through me."

The sign that God gives Moses to confirm this promise is in some ways rather strange: "When you have freed the people from Egypt, you will worship the Godhead at this very mountain." That is to say, the sign will appear only after Moses has stepped out in obedience. The sign is promised in Exod. 3. The sign is manifested in Exod. 19. Between chaps. 3 and 19 there must be considerable time—time for Moses to gather his family and make the trip back to Egypt, time for Moses to make his first appearances before Pharaoh, time for the ten plagues to run their course, maybe about a year, time for the first several months to pass between leaving Egypt and arriving at Sinai (Exod. 19:1). Furthermore, Moses is the only one to know about this sign, at least this early. For his people, Sinai is a resting place. For Moses, Sinai is a fulfillment of God's promise of presence. Can we imagine Moses, upon reaching Sinai, looking heavenward and raising two thumbs to the sky, as if to say "Yes!"?

Such signs are not common in the OT, but 1 Kings 13:3 ("this is the sign the LORD has declared: The altar will be split apart and the ashes on it will be poured out") and 2 Kings 19:29 ("This will be the sign for you, O Hezekiah . . .") provide two examples. In the first of these (1 Kings 13), a sign is first promised (13:3), then fulfilled (13:5), in order to authenticate the accuracy of the prediction in 13:2 that three centuries later God will raise up a godly king by the name of Josiah, to rid the land of idolatry. In the second of these (2 Kings 19), the Lord gives to Hezekiah, king of Judah, a sign that spells out what he and his people will eat for the next three years, for the invading Assyrians have either decimated or confiscated the available food from the recent harvest throughout Judah. Isaiah 44:28–45:1, although not called a "sign," is another illustration—if these words about Cyrus are the words of the eighth-century-BC prophet Isaiah and not some later "Second Isaiah." Yet one surely has the sign that Isaiah gives to Ahaz about a virgin/young girl being with child and birthing a son (7:14).

For others who receive "signs" from the Lord, compare Gideon (Judg. 6:17), Eli (1 Sam. 2:34), Saul (10:7), Jonathan (14:10), Hezekiah (2 Kings 19:29 = Isa. 37:30; 2 Kings 20:9–11 = Isa. 38:7–8), and the shepherds near Bethlehem (Luke 2:12).

If God Knows Your Name, Do You Need to Know His?

(3:13–22)

Translation

[13]Moses said to the Godhead: "If I were to come to Israel's sons and say to them, 'The God of your fathers has sent me to you,' and they then say to me, 'What is his name?'—what do I say to them?" [14]God said to Moses, "I-WILL-BE-WHO-I-WILL-BE." He said, "Say to Israel's sons, 'I-WILL-BE has sent me to you.'" [15]God also said to Moses, "So say to Israel's sons, 'The LORD, the God of your fathers, the God of Abraham, the God of Isaac, and the God of Jacob, has sent me to you.' This is my Name for all time, my Title throughout all generations. [16]Go, gather Israel's elders and say to them, 'The LORD, the God of your fathers, appeared to me—the God of Abraham, Isaac, and Jacob—saying, I have indeed marked you and what was done to you in Egypt, [17]and I have said, I will bring you up from the degradation of Egypt to the land of the Canaanite, and the Hittite, and the Amorite, and the Perizzite, and the Hivite, and the Jebusite into a land oozing milk and sap.' [18]And they will listen to your voice, and you shall come, you and Israel's elders to Egypt's king, and (all of) you will say to him, 'The LORD, the God of the Hebrews chanced upon us, and so, let us go, please, a journey of three days into the steppe, that we may sacrifice to the LORD our God.' [19]I, I know that Egypt's king will not let you go, not even with a strong hand. [20]I will stretch forth my hand and strike Egypt with all my marvelous deeds that I will do in his midst, and after this he will send you on your way. [21]And I will grant this people favor in Egypt's eyes so that when (all of) you go, you will not go empty-handed. [22]Rather, a woman will ask a gift of her neighbor and of the sojourner in her house ornaments of silver and ornaments of gold, and robes, and you shall dress your sons and daughters with them. Thus shall you despoil the Egyptians."

Grammatical and Lexical Notes

3:13. When *hinnēh* before a participle or finite verb is followed by an interrogative clause in the apodosis, it carries the meaning "if." Compare 2 Kings 4:13 AT, Elisha said to him, "Tell her, 'If [*hinnēh*] you have gone to all this trouble for us, what can be done for you?'"

3:15. The last line of the verse may be read as a line of poetry: "This has been my name from eternity, and this will be my title throughout all generations." This is Dahood's (1977: 107) rendering. It necessitates, however, reading the preposition *lĕ* before "eternity" as "from," and the same preposition before "all generations" as "to/throughout."

3:15. For *šēm* ("name") and *zeker* ("title") in parallelism elsewhere, see Ps. 135:13 (almost the same as the last part of Exod. 3:15) and Prov. 10:7, "The memory [*zeker*] of the righteous will be a blessing, but the name [*šēm*] of the wicked will rot." Avishur (1975: 38–39) provides instances of these two words together in Aramaic, Phoenician, and Akkadian.

3:15. "Throughout all generations" in Ps. 135:13 (see the previous note on this verse in the Psalter) is *lĕdōr-wādōr*, with an intervening *wā-* ("and") between the double use of *dōr*. "Throughout all generations" in Exod. 3:15 is *lĕdōr dōr*, without an intervening *wā-*. The former is known as a syndetic construction (with the "and"), and the Exodus one as an asyndetic one (without the "and"). The syndetic construction is more common in later books of the Bible: Esther 1:8, "each man" is *ʾîš wā ʾîš*; 3:4, "day after day" is *yôm wāyôm*; Ezra 10:14, "each town" is *ʿîr wā ʿîr*. The asyndetic construction is found in passages like Num. 4:19, where "each man" is *ʾîš ʾîš*; or Deut. 14:22, where "each year" is *šānâ šānâ*; or Gen. 39:10, where "day after day" is *yôm yôm*. Gevirtz (1963: 26; 1986: 26–27) opines that there is no essential difference between X w-X and XX.

3:16. The verb *pāqad* ("marked") means "visit." When God visits, he visits for weal or woe. There are two divine visitations in Exodus, both remarkably different from each other. In Exod. 3:16 God visits to show his interest in and concern for his people (NIV, "watched over"). (In Exod. 4:31 NIV translates the same verb as "was concerned about.") However, when God comes for another visit in 32:34, it is not a friendly, caring visit. On that occasion he comes to pronounce judgment, or as the NIV has it, "punish." How interesting that the same verb in one place means "watch over, be concerned about" and in another place means "punish"! The Greek verb in the Septuagint is *episkeptomai*. As this verb is used in the Greek OT to describe a great, divine act of deliverance, it (or its related noun) is so used in NT Greek (Luke 1:68, 78; 7:16; 19:44; 1 Pet. 2:12). When James (1:27) says that pure religion is manifested in "visiting" orphans and widows, meaning people who cannot care for themselves, he is saying that in the same way that God visits to help those in their distress, we are to visit those who are in their own distress.

3:18. "Come" in "you shall come" is singular (*ûbāʾtā*), even though the subject of the verb is plural ("you and Israel's elders"). Naude (1977: 77) points out that where an independent pronoun forms the first conjunct of a coordinate subject, the person, gender, and number of the verb follows the independent pronoun. Compare Gen. 34:30: "I will be destroyed [*nišmadtî*], I and my household."

3:18. The Niphal of *qārâ* ("happened") sometimes refers to establishing contact, often by chance, hence my rendering "happened." See Num. 23:3–4; 2 Sam. 1:6; 18:9. Rabin (1961: 399) suggests that *qārâ* may be related to Arabic *qara*, "invite to a feast," and so translates v. 18 as "God has asked us to hold a banquet for him." Barr (1968: 102–3) seems to agree with Rabin.

3:19. The last three words of this Hebrew verse, *wĕlōʾ bĕyād ḥăzāqâ* ("and not by/in a strong hand"), are notoriously difficult. Early versions of the Bible read *wĕlōʾ* ("and not") as "except, unless." Witness the Septuagint's *ean mē meta cheiros krataias* and Vulgate's *nisi per manum validam* (both of which change *wĕlōʾ* into *kî ʾim*). A copy of Exodus from the Qumran scrolls (4QExod[b]) does read *kî ʾim* in line with the Septuagint and Vulgate. Elwode (1990) reads the *wa-* in *wĕlôʾ* as a rare use of *wa-* as an adversative or exceptive particle. Addinall (1999: 298) leaves the passage as it appears in the MT: "It is a phrase of general meaning including every power on earth or in heaven which could enter the mind of Pharaoh."

3:20. For the Egyptian background to God's "stretching out his hand" and the significance of God's "hand" in Exodus, see Hoffmeier (1986) and Seely (2004).

3:21. "To find favor" (*māṣāʾ ḥēn*) is a very common phrase in Scripture (in Exodus: 33:12, 13; 34:9). "To grant favor" (*nātan ḥēn*) occurs only about seven times (Gen. 39:21; Exod. 3:21; 11:3; 12:36; Ps. 84:11 [12]; Prov. 3:34; 13:15).

3:22. For the verb *šāʾal* meaning not "borrow," or not even just "ask," but rather "ask as a gift," see Daube (1947: 49–50).

3:22. For the word "neighbor" (*šākēn*) and "sojourner" (*gēr*) together in parallelism, or related words from the same root in parallelism, see the references in Avishur 1984: 647. For example, in Gen. 26:2

the Lord tells Isaac, "Do not go down to Egypt; live [*š-k-n*] in the land where I tell you to live." Then he says to Isaac in the very next verse (v. 3), "Stay [*g-w-r*] in this land for a while."

3:22. *nāṣal* appears frequently in Exodus in the Hiphil with the meaning "rescue, deliver" (e.g., 2:19; 5:23; 6:6). In the Piel, however, as here, it means "strip off, (de)spoil, plunder," and for the so-called plundering of the Egyptians, see the seminal studies of Morgenstern 1949 and Coats 1968.

Commentary

God's promise to Moses in v. 12 of both divine presence and eventual delivery **3:13–15**
from Egypt and safe arrival at Sinai is good, but not good enough. Alongside such promises, Moses wants information. Maybe Moses does not really hear those promises of v. 12, and now he is ready with a second question he directs at God. He moves from "Who am I?" in v. 11 to "Who are you?" in v. 13. I like the way NIV begins v. 13 with "Suppose I go," as if Moses has said to God, "I'm not saying I'm going; I'm speaking only hypothetically, for argument's sake."

Moses wants to know God's name primarily for his own benefit, in case his fellow Hebrews in Egypt ask him to identify by name the God he claims has sent him to them. God gives him three answers. Note the three uses of "God said" (vv. 14a, 14b, 15 [NIV eliminates the one at the start of 14b]) in the introduction to the divine response. Before I explore some of the technicalities of this passage, let me fast-forward the tape and point out that there is no later passage in Exodus, once Moses has arrived in Egypt, that has the Goshen Hebrews approaching Moses and saying, "Before we will even listen to you and trust you, identify by name the God you claim sent you to us." Nobody asks Moses for such information. Maybe, like some of us, Moses excels at raising problems and issues that never emerge as problems and issues.

The amount of secondary literature on Exod. 3:13–15, especially v. 14, is staggering. A revision of Eccles. 12:12 might read, "Of the writing of articles, monographs, essays, and dissertations on Exod. 3:14, there is no end." For example, Sæbø's essay (1981; ET 1998) on the verse begins with an almost two-page bibliographic note (1998: 78–79) of previous studies on Exod. 3:14. It is certainly not an exhaustive compilation either, for I notice a number of omissions of studies published before 1980. Also, if the bibliography were extended to include studies published since 1980, one would produce a bibliographic footnote of at least comparable length.

There are at least three main issues here. The first is, Who does not know God's name? Does Moses not know it? Do the Hebrews in Egypt not know it? Do perhaps neither Moses nor this people know it? Or may it be that Moses does not know whether his fellow Hebrews know it?

A case for the Hebrews in Egypt being the ones who are ignorant can be made. After all, they have been in Egypt for a good long while. I doubt that God is ever more than a generation away from being forgotten (Judg. 2:10).

How many generations would the name "Jesus" last on the lips of displaced Christians who are shorn of sacred book, sacred song, sacred celebrations, opportunities for sacred worship?

The majority of biblical commentators think that what the writer of Exodus implies is that Moses himself does not know the name. The Hebrews, thinks Moses, will inquire about God's name not because they are ignorant of it. Rather, they will ask about the name because they know it and will not listen to somebody who cannot name the name of the God they know (e.g., Seitz 1999: 152). In effect, this makes God's name a password, a badge of acceptance among his peers. It surely is possible that Moses might not know God's special name, given that he has spent all of his postweaning years in Egypt or in Midian.

The second issue revolves about how to render *ʾehyeh ʾăšer ʾehyeh*. The traditional way (cf. NIV and NRSV) is "I AM WHO I AM." But that is just one of several literal translations of the Hebrew. The term *ʾehyeh* is a first-person imperfect of the verb *hāyâ* ("be") and equals the English "I was," "I am," and "I will be." Plus, "WHO" in "I AM WHO I AM" may also mean "WHAT, THAT," thus adding to the possibilities. Let us go with "WHO" and suggest some legitimate translations, and here I will use lowercase letters: (1) "I am who I am"; (2) "I am who I was"; (3) "I am who I shall be"; (4) "I was who I am"; (5) "I was who I was"; (6) "I was who I shall be"; (7) "I shall be who I am"; (8) "I shall be who I was"; (9) "I shall be who I shall be." For that matter, how should we translate *ʾehyeh* back in v. 12, "I 'will' be with you," or "I 'am' with you"? Promise or present reality? To the best of my knowledge, there are few places, if any, in the Hebrew Bible where *ʾehyeh* is a name for God ("I AM") outside of Exod. 3:14. Greenberg (1969: 82) cites Hosea 1:9b as one possibility (NIV, "For you are not my people, and I am not your God"; Greenberg: "For you are not my people, nor [am] I Ehyeh to you") and suggests another: Ps. 50:21b (NIV, "You thought I was altogether like you"; Greenberg: "You imagined Ehyeh to be like you").

It is still debated to what degree Jesus's "I am" statements (*egō eimi*) throughout the Gospel of John are inspired by God's *ʾehyeh* in Exod. 3:14. It is unlikely, however, that the pathological anger that Jesus's "Before Abraham was [born], I am!" (John 8:58) produces in his hearers is generated by their fuming over his grammatical gaffe. "He does not know even how to parse the verb 'be'! Let's kill him." To the high priest's question "Are you the Christ, the Son of God?" Matthew (26:64) has Jesus reply "Yes, it is as you say." In Mark 14:62 Jesus's response is simply "I am." But in Luke 22:70 Jesus's response is "You are right in saying I am." One cannot miss the irony in Luke of the chief priest inadvertently terming Jesus as *egō eimi*.

In Exod. 3:15 God shifts, when giving his name, from first person to the much more familiar third person, which would be *yihyeh* ("He-was/is/will be"), but that is not the form used here. Rather, it is *y-h-w-h* ("Jehovah/

Yahweh/Lord"). Scholars refer to this name for God as the tetragram, or the tetragrammaton, because of its four consonants. What vowels should go with it and how it was pronounced or should be pronounced seem to be anybody's guess, if there ever was a known, accepted pronunciation. A number of names in the OT are simply third-person masculine singular imperfect verbs, such as Isaac (*yiṣḥāq*, "he laughs"), Jacob (*yaʿăqōb*, "he protects"), and Jephthah (*yiptāḥ*, "he opens"). Unlike *ʾehyeh*, which occurs as a name for God once in the OT (or maybe three times), *y-h-w-h* appears 6,823 times.

Modern biblical scholarship encourages the pronunciation of *y-h-w-h* as "Yahweh" rather than the traditional "Jehovah." One reason for this, at least for the proper name's first part, is the number of names that end in *-iah* (= Y/*yah*). So understood, the name "Yahweh" is a third-person masculine singular verb (like the verbal names above), and in the Hiphil stem. Hence, its meaning is "He-causes-to-be-what-is."

There are a few problems with this reading, however. First, we have no instance of the use of the Hiphil stem of *hāyâ* anywhere in the Hebrew Bible. Again, if this is the correct reading of the tetragrammaton, should not v. 14 have been *ʾāyeh ʾăšer ʾāyeh* ("I will cause to be what I cause to be") rather than *ʾehyeh ʾăšer ʾehyeh*? Finally, such a reading completely ignores the context in which God speaks to Moses of his name. Moses is to go back to Egypt and tell his people, who are being brutally abused by the Egyptians, and for whom there is no apparent end in sight to the nightmare, that the God who has dispatched him to them is the God "who causes to be what is"!

The third issue emanating from these verses is whether God's reply to Moses is a response or a rebuff, sense or nonsense, answer or evasion, sharing or withholding vital information, a revealing or a hiding of his name. For those interpreters who take the second of these options, the thrust of v. 14 is "I will be whoever I want to be, and who/what that is is none of your business." So Sandmel (1961: 113) can say, "'I am' . . . is simply a good-natured pun, the humor of which has long escaped the long-faced grammarians." Carroll's (1994: 47) comment is more acerbic: "I read the simple punning tautology of 3:14 as a dismissive rejection of Moses's kvetching questions. . . . It says nothing and then twits Moses by inviting him to speak nonsense to the people of Israel. It is playful rather than serious linguistics." The best response I have seen to that approach is Fretheim's statement: "It is difficult to believe that the thousands of uses of Yahweh in the OT are only a testimony to God's holding back his name" (1991: 64).

There are, to be sure, two other occasions when somebody asks God for his name but is denied an answer. To Jacob's "Please tell me your name" (Gen. 32:29a [30a]), God replies, "Why do you ask my name?" (32:29b [30b]). When Samson's father, Manoah, asks, "What is your name?" (Judg. 13:17), the answer he receives is much like the one Jacob receives: "Why do you ask my name?" (13:18). But there are two important differences between those two passages and the Exodus passage. First, Jacob and Manoah ask for their own benefit. Moses asks out of his concern for others ("if they ask me . . ."). Second, Moses is the first person in Scripture that God "sends" on a prophetic mission. God is not "sending" Jacob or Manoah anywhere. How possibly can a God-sent Moses establish credibility with his people if he dances around the name of the God who has dispatched him to Egypt?

Let us go, then, with the idea that God's answer is a real answer. It seems that the name implies more than merely God's existence (as the Septuagint has it, "I am the one who is" or "I am the Existing One," in which it replaces the Hebrew finite form of the verb "to be" with a participle of "to be"). More than ontology is at stake.

I suggest that the dominant idea is presence (see, e.g., Isbell 1978). Goldingay (2003: 333) makes a very apropos statement: "Moses asks after God's name. . . . Yhwh responds by providing not a label but a theology." That is to say, God will always be there for his people, in a distant Egypt too, even if that divine presence is questioned and imperceptible. He will always be whatever his people need him to be in any given moment, in any given place. If they need a deliverer, that's YHWH. If they need grace and mercy and forgiveness, that's YHWH. If they need purifying and empowerment, that's YHWH. If they need rebuke and chastisement, that's YHWH. If they need guidance, that's YHWH. For God is a "I-will-be-what-I-will-be" God and a "I-will-be-what-I-need-to-be-for-you" God.

3:16–20 That there are "elders" in the community, even when Israel is ghettoed in Goshen, suggests some form or degree of organized, centralized government for these Hebrews. They appear throughout Exodus (4:29; 12:21; 17:5–6; 18:12; 19:7–8; 24:1, 9–11, 13–14). On their place and significance throughout the OT, see the fine study of Reviv 1989. As Dozeman (2006: 117) has pointed out, beginning with v. 16 the emphasis in Moses's call shifts from the identity of the Lord to the authority of Moses: "Say to Israel's elders, 'The LORD . . . appeared to me.'"

Not only is Moses told what to say to the elders about God (vv. 16b–17), but he is also told that the elders will listen to him (*šāmaʿ lĕ*, v. 18). That promise makes Moses's word in 4:1 all the more interesting: "What if they do not listen [*šāmaʿ bĕ*] to me?" Even God, who on this occasion says they will listen to Moses, says later to Moses in 4:8, "If they do not listen to the voice [*šāmaʿ lĕ*; NIV, "pay attention to"] of the first sign," and in 4:9, "and if they do not listen to [*šāmaʿ lĕ*] your voice." So God spells out for Moses the possibility of both accomplishment and setback, fruitfulness and frustration, reception and rejection. Anybody in ministry can identify with Moses here.

Verse 18 has given some readers pause. God seems to resort to deceptive measures when he instructs Moses and the elders to ask Pharaoh to allow them to go on a three-day journey into the open places to sacrifice to God, a kind of a three-day miniretreat. Is Moses to talk in such a way to lead Pharaoh to believe that they will return to Egypt after a long weekend away? Is Greenberg (1969: 85) on target here? "Where wicked, superior force must be overcome for a just cause, an effective deception is as much a part of God's arsenal as miracle." Maybe twentieth-century Christians like Corrie Ten Boom and Brother Andrew would agree. There is an interesting phrase at the end of Ps. 18:25–26 [26–27] (= 2 Sam. 22:26–27), part of David's thoughts about God: "To the faithful you show yourself faithful, to the blameless you show yourself blameless, to the pure you show yourself pure, but to the crooked [*ʿiqqēš*] you show yourself shrewd [*titpattāl*]."

Numbers 33 is a lengthy, some would say tedious, chapter that outlines geographically the stages Israel takes in her journey out of Egypt: "They left X and camped at Y. They left Y and camped at Z," and so forth. The only verse in the chapter that tells the time it took to cover one of these stages is v. 8, "They left Pi Hahiroth, . . . and when they had traveled for *three days* . . ." (also see Exod. 15:22, "For 'three days' they traveled in the wilderness"). Both verses imply that God's people keep their word.

God does not want his people to leave Egypt "empty-handed" (*rêqām*). That **3:21–22**
same concern is reflected in Deuteronomy's "servant/slave" law (Deut. 15:12–18). Verse 13 states, "When you release him [the servant/slave], do not send him away empty-handed [*rêqām*]." Jacob does not want Laban to send him away empty-handed (*rêqām*, Gen. 31:42). Boaz will not send Ruth back to Naomi empty-handed (*rêqām*, Ruth 3:17). It is clear that most often *rêqām* is found with verbs of motion (e.g., "send").

To that end, Israelite women are to ask their Egyptian counterparts for silver, gold, and clothing. This comes to fruition in 11:2–3 and 12:35–36, the only places in Exodus (along with 3:21) where God "granted favor" to his people before the Egyptians or before anybody (*nātan ḥēn*, 3:21; 11:3; 12:36). The differences in the three passages are that in 3:22 the Hebrew women are to do this, in 11:2 the Hebrew men and women are to do this, while in 12:35 the "Israelites" (men only?) do this.

It is an odd combination. In v. 20 God promises to pummel the Egyptians. At the end of v. 22 he instructs his people to "plunder" [NIV] the Egyptians. Are the Egyptians gullible or generous? What people who just have had the daylights smacked out of them are going to be so philanthropic to those who have caused so much agony and turmoil? Might we see vestiges of Prov. 16:7 here, "When a man's ways are pleasing to the LORD, he makes even his enemies live at peace with him"? It certainly is a fulfillment of God's promise to Abram in Gen. 15:14, "But I will punish the nation they serve as slaves, and afterward they will come out with great possessions."

Perhaps we can compare Jacob's "stealing" from Laban (Gen. 30) as a just compensation for withheld wages. Think of all those free man-hours Pharaoh has obtained from the Hebrews. Surely they are entitled to some financial/material compensation. On this matter of taking something valuable from one's nemesis, one possible parallel is the story in 1 Sam. 6, in which the Philistines return the ark to Israel along with other valuable items. The Israelites take golden jewelry from the Egyptians, and the Philistines return the ark along with gold objects. Both Exod. 3:22 and 1 Sam. 6:8 use the phrase *kĕlê zāhāb*, "vessels of gold," to refer to valuable commodities given to Israel by a foreign nation that has humiliated Israel (Damrosch 1987: 191). The best parallel to these three passages in Exodus is King Cyrus's instructions to a group of people to provide silver and gold, goods and livestock, and freewill offerings to those returning from captivity in Babylon to Jerusalem (Ezra 1:4, 6). However, as Knowles (2004: 57–58) has observed, correctly I believe, it is likely that the donors are not Persians, but Judean exiles who have chosen to stay in Babylon.

In a touching note, v. 22b instructs the Hebrew women to clothe their own children with some of these donated fabrics. In reflecting on why this is added, Greenberg (1969: 87) says tellingly: "The recovery of dignity by the liberated slaves would be signalized by their being able to provide good things for their children. Of even greater moment than their own enrichment was their capacity to assert parental solicitude toward their children." This notation also explains why, when Pharaoh later suggests that only the Hebrew males leave to worship, and that they leave their children (and women) behind (10:10–11), Moses in effect replies, "Over my dead body!" Satan still says to us, "Go and worship your God, but leave your children behind." Leaving children behind or keeping them out of "adult" worship time, or barring them from sacrament observance, may be a contemporary parallel. After all, did not Jesus die for children as well as for adults?

Divine Reassurance through Authenticating Signs

(4:1–9)

Translation

[1]Moses replied and said, "But, truth be told, they will not believe me nor heed my voice for they will say, 'The LORD never revealed himself to you.'" [2]Then the LORD said to him, "What is that in your hand?" And he said, "A staff." [3]And he said, "Throw it to the ground." Moses threw it to the ground, and it became a snake. Moses fled from it. [4]And the LORD said to Moses, "Reach out your hand and grasp its tail." He reached out his hand and held it tightly, and it became a staff in his palm. [5]"So that they may believe that the LORD God of their fathers, the God of Abraham, the God of Isaac, and the God of Jacob has revealed himself to you," [6]the LORD again said to him, "Bring, pray, your hand into your bosom." And he brought his hand into his bosom, and then brought it out. Amazingly, his hand was leprous, blanched like the snow. [7]And he said, "Put back your hand into your bosom." And he put back his hand into his bosom. Then he brought it out from his bosom. Amazingly, it came back like his own skin. [8]"If they do not believe you nor heed the voice of the first sign, they will believe the voice of the following sign. [9]If they do not believe either of these signs, nor heed your voice, you shall take some of the Nile's water which you are to pour on the dry ground, and the water which you take from the Nile will become blood on the dry ground."

Grammatical and Lexical Notes

4:1. "But, truth be told" is a translation for *wĕhēn*, which I owe to Garr (2004b: 336). Often *hēn* is an interjective particle ("*Behold*, they will not believe me"). On occasion *hēn* may carry the meaning "if" ("*if* they will not believe me") and corresponds to Ugaritic *hm*. See GKC §159w; Stec 1987.

4:1. "Believe (in)" is the Hiphil of *ʾāman* and occurs five times in this section (vv. 1, 5, 8 [2x], 9). When the Hiphil of this verb is followed by a direct object that is a person, a preposition is added to the person's name. It may be *lĕ* or *bĕ*. Where the individual that is believed in is God, the preferred preposition is *bĕ* (Gen. 15:6; Exod. 14:31a; Num. 14:11; 20:12; Deut. 1:32; 2 Kings 17:14; Pss. 78:22, 32; 106:12; Jon. 3:5). Sometimes the preposition with "God/Lord/his promises" is *lĕ* (Deut. 9:23; Ps. 106:24). Where the individual believes in a human being, the preferred preposition is *lĕ* (Gen. 45:26 [Jacob's sons]; Exod. 4:1, 5, 8, 9 [Moses]; 1 Sam. 27:12 [David]; 2 Chron. 32:15 [Hezekiah]). A few times the preposition is *bĕ* (Exod. 14:31b; 19:9 [Moses]).

Novick (2009: 579–82) takes the distinction between *ʾāman* (Hiphil) plus preposition *bĕ* versus *lĕ* further. He argues that *hʾmyn bĕ* generally attaches to persons (God and human) and refers to trustworthiness (e.g., "Though the speech [of a malicious person] is charming, do not *believe* him" [Prov. 26:25]). On the other hand, *hʾmyn lĕ* attaches more to belief in a person's speech than to the person himself (e.g., "A simple man *believes* anything" [Prov. 14:15]). Hence, the issue in Exod. 4 is not faith in Moses per se but whether they will believe his verbal claim to be God's messenger. Tellingly, *h'myn bĕ* occurs in parallelism with *bāṭaḥ bĕ*, but *h'myn lĕ* never does: "Will you rely on him [*bāṭaḥ bĕ*] for his great strength . . . ? Can you trust him [*h'myn bĕ*] to bring in your grain . . . ?" (Job 39:11–12); "For they did not believe in [*h'myn bĕ*] God or trust in [*bāṭaḥ bĕ*] his deliverance" (Ps. 78:22).

4:2. The subject of the second "said" in this verse is clearly Moses, but he is not explicitly identified. In narrative scenes such a shift in speaker from one "and he said" to another "he said" without the explicit identification of the subject of the second "he said" is common. For examples of this, see Judg. 3:19; 1 Sam. 12:5; 16:11.

4:4. The verb in the first clause that God uses for what Moses is to do with the snake is "grasp" (*'āḥaz*). The verb the narrator uses in the second clause for what Moses actually does with the snake is "hold tightly" (*ḥāzaq*). Avishur (1984: 635–58) cites numerous examples where the verbs in command/performance statements differ. Two examples from Exodus will suffice: (1) Exod. 7:18 (command), "And the Egyptians will not be able [*lā'â*] to drink the water," and Exod. 7:21 (performance), "And the Egyptians were not able [*yākōl*] to drink the water"; (2) Exod. 10:12 (command), "so that the locust may consume all the grass of the land left behind [*šā'ar*]," and Exod. 10:15 (performance), "And the locusts consumed all the grass of the land . . . that the hail had left behind [*yātar*]."

4:6. "Again" goes with "said" rather than with "Bring," so it is "Said again," and not "Again, bring." When *'ōd* means "again," it invariably follows its verb. Compare Hosea 3:1, "The Lord said to me again, 'Go, love your wife' . . . ," and not as NIV has it, "The Lord said to me, 'Go, show your love to your wife again.'" See Gordis 1971: 241.

4:6. The LXX avoids the word "leprous" and reads "became as snow" (*hōsei chiōn*), possibly to sidestep the idea that Moses, if only momentarily, becomes unclean through leprosy or some kind of skin disease like psoriasis. Josephus (*Ant.* 2.12.3 §273) also avoids any word for leprosy by simply saying that Moses's hand became "white of color resembling chalk." See Houtman 1985.

4:7. For "came back," the LXX uses the verb *apekatestē* to speak of the restoration of a previous condition of health. See also Lev. 13:16 (raw flesh turning white) and Mark 8:25 (sight restored).

4:8. Referring to "signs" having voices is strange, yet it is used, metaphorically and by association, with the emphasis elsewhere in these verses on the people heeding Moses's voice (vv. 1, 9).

4:9. Tov (2001: 90) gives numerous examples where the Samaritan Pentateuch (SP) replaces unusual verb forms with more regular ones, here *yišmĕ'û* for MT's *yišmĕ'ûn*.

Commentary

4:1 The Lord's guaranteed promise in 3:18 that the Hebrews in Egypt will listen to Moses does not cut it with Moses. He does not share or embrace God's optimism. Later in the narrative, 4:29–31 and 14:31 support the Lord's optimism, but 6:9, 12 support Moses's "realism." Moses, apparently, is bold or brazen enough to call God's bluff, to get in God's face, to correct the Almighty. Getting through to Pharaoh, thinks Moses, will not be nearly as difficult as getting through to his own people.

4:2–9 One might think that the Lord may severely rebuke Moses at this point for doubting God's promise. But there is no "Oh ye of little faith." Instead, the Lord gives three signs to Moses, things he is to do, that might remove any doubt among his audience. In the first, something supportive (a staff) becomes something serpentine (a snake, the same Hebrew word for "snake" in Gen. 3 [*nāḥāš*]), and then the transformation reverses itself. God's use of the word "throw" recalls Pharaoh's haunting use of that same verb back in 1:22 about "throwing" Hebrew babies into the water.

Second, something healthy (an unblemished hand) becomes something harmful (a diseased hand), and then the transformation reverses itself. "Bosom" refers to the "fold in a robe above the midsection where the hands are placed" (Lundbom 2004a: 512). On one's bosom or lap, one may carry objects or money (Prov. 21:14), infants (Num. 11:12), and small animals (Isa. 40:11).

Third, something pure (the waters of the Nile) is to become something putrid (blood). There is no reversal with this third sign. Unlike the first two signs, which Moses then does before the people in chap. 4, the third sign remains on hold until a later time (chap. 7).

This will not be the last time Moses is involved with the phenomena of these signs. He will encounter them again. Number 1, staff and snake, will resurface in 7:8–13; number 3, water and blood, will resurface in 7:14–24; number 2, leprous hand, will resurface in Num. 12. Turning a staff into a snake and vice versa is a "sign" to persuade belief in God's people in 4:8. But turning a staff into a snake to persuade belief in/from Pharaoh is a "miracle/portent" (7:9). Maybe this is one distinction between "signs" and "wonders" (although elsewhere the two nouns may be synonyms). "Signs" are for believers, while "wonders" are for nonbelievers. Signs bring courage and encouragement. Wonders frighten the tar out of people or bring them to their knees (cf. 1 Cor. 14:22–25).

In giving these signs to/through Moses, God does not guarantee that their observance will erase all skepticism. He simply says in vv. 8–9, "Should they not believe you, . . . should they not believe either of these signs." God does not let Moses know ahead of time about the eventual response of the people. He keeps the results to himself, and leaves Moses hanging in faith.

The NT takes a good and not-so-good view of the relationship between signs and belief. On the one hand, Jesus says, "Unless you people see miraculous *signs* and wonders you will never *believe*" (John 4:48). He says that because of people's making statements like, "What miraculous *sign* then will you do that we may . . . *believe* in you?" (John 6:30). On the other hand, in summing up Jesus's ministry, John says, "Jesus did many other miraculous *signs*. . . . But these are written that you may *believe* . . ." (John 20:30–31). The difference between the two is the difference between signs demanded and expected, and signs lovingly given to nudge the sincere seeker to faith.

Mouthing Off to God about Your Mouth

(4:10–12)

Translation

[10]And Moses said to the LORD, "Please, my Lord, not a man of words [am] I, either before or since your speaking to your servant, for heavy-mouthed and heavy-tongued [am] I." [11]And the LORD said to him, "Who gave a mouth to man, or who makes one dumb or deaf, clear-sighted or blind? Is it not I, the LORD? [12]So now, go. I, I will be with your mouth, and teach you what to say."

Grammatical and Lexical Notes

4:10. "Please, my Lord" (*bî ʾădōnāy*) is an expression that "denotes submission, request, supplication, a formula by which a person of lower status addresses a ruler" (Garsiel 2002: 236). See Gen. 44:18; Exod. 4:13; Num. 12:11; Judg. 6:13, 15; 1 Sam. 1:26.

4:10. Moses ends both of his statements with the longer form of the independent pronoun "I" (*ʾānōkî*); see my comments on Moses's *mî ʾānōkî* back in 3:11. Revell (1995: 204–5) says, "Where the clause ascribes to the speaker some characteristic or quality that is distasteful or shameful, or is a disqualification for some position, *ʾānōkî* [versus *ʾănî*] is used."

4:10. "Heavy-tongued" (*kĕbad lāšôn*) is present in God's word to Ezekiel at the time of his calling: "You are not being sent to a people of obscure speech and *difficult language* [*kibdê lāšôn*]," in Ezek. 3:5–6.

4:10. "Your servant" appears in the prayers of Moses (Num. 11:11; Deut. 3:24), of David (1 Sam. 23:10, 11a, 11b), of Solomon (1 Kings 8:28, 29, 30, 52), and fifty-seven times in the Psalms.

4:11. The Hebrew for "clear-sightedness" is *piqqēaḥ*, with the doubling of the middle consonant *q*. In Exod. 23:8 the word appears in the plural without the doubling of the middle consonant: "Do not accept a bribe, for a bribe blinds those who see [*piqḥîm*]." Gevirtz (1984b: 515) provides a few other illustrations of this phenomenon, for example, *pissēaḥ* ("lame") in Isa. 35:6 and *pisḥîm* ("[the] lame") in 2 Sam. 5:6, or the word for "blind" (*ʿiwwēr*) in Exod. 4:11 and *ʿiwrôt* in Isa. 42:7.

4:11. The verb behind *piqqēaḥ* (*pāqaḥ*) is the one used in Gen. 3:5, 7 (in the Niphal) for the serpent's claim that sin would open one's eyes. It is also the verb used in Gen. 21:19 when God opens Hagar's eyes to see the nearby well of water.

4:11. There are three negative terms here ("dumb, deaf, blind") and one positive ("clear-sighted"). The order of words, then, is AABA (negative/negative/positive/negative). In other series of words, note the pattern AAAB (negative/negative/negative/positive): "The LORD Almighty has a day in store for all the proud and lofty, for all that is exalted (and they will be humbled)" (Isa. 2:12); the pattern ABAA (individuals/groups/individuals/individuals) occurs in Ps. 148:11, "kings of the earth and all nations, you princes and all rulers of the earth."

Commentary

Moses's fourth statement of protest to God (after those in 3:11, 13; 4:1) is **4:10**
that he does not believe he has the necessary speech gifts to be persuasive enough as an intermediary. There are four possible explanations for his comment: (1) it is simply another excuse, another attempt to evade God's will for his life; (2) he suffers from some kind of speech defect, either congenital or through injury; (3) it is difficult for Moses to express himself in Hebrew, given his lengthy residence in Egypt and Midian; (4) his apprehension will surely manifest itself when he has to speak in front of people with an embarrassingly quivering voice. Or maybe it is some combination of the four.

Many Jewish traditions suggest that it is a speech defect. For example, a midrash (*Exodus Rabbah* 1.26) says that as a child Moses accidentally burned his mouth with a live coal. Ibn Ezra, the medieval Jewish exegete, says of Moses, "He was born that way, with a heavy mouth. He could pronounce the sounds of the language only partly and with difficulty."

While a few commentators argue for the view that Moses is simply saying that he is not eloquent, not a charismatic speaker (Weinberg 1980: 191–93), most tend to veer toward the view that Moses indeed does have some sort of speech impediment (e.g., Tigay 1978; and Greenberg [1983: 68–69], who renders the last part of v. 10 as "for I am clumsy-mouthed and clumsy-tongued").

Three reasons seem to support this reading. First, it is likely that the second line ("Heavy-mouthed and heavy-tongued [am] I") supplies a reason why Moses has said in the first line, "Not a man of words [am] I," rather than simply rephrasing the first line. Second, the Greek Septuagint's *ischnophōnos* ("weak-voiced") suggests a speech impediment. Third, the closest parallel to *kĕbad lāšôn* ("heavy-tongued") is Ezek. 3:5 (*kibdê lāšôn*, with *kābôd* in the plural construct), and clearly the reference there is to speech which is unintelligible because it is a foreign speech. In effect, God says to Ezekiel, "I am not sending you to a people whose tongue you cannot understand. I am sending you to your fellow exiles." Here is a case where a term for a physical affliction that causes halting or unintelligible speech (Exod. 4) has been extended to function as a metaphor for speech that is unintelligible because it is unknown (Ezek. 3).

The parallels between Moses's call to prophetic ministry and Jeremiah's are at this point very transparent (see Holladay 1964: 155):

1. Both begin with a precative interjection:
    "Please [*bî*], my Lord" (Exod. 4:10).
    "Ah [*ʾăhāh*], my Lord" (Jer. 1:6).
2. Both end their sentence with the longer form of the independent personal pronoun *I*:
    "Not a man of words am I [*ʾānōkî*] . . . and heavy-tongued am I [*ʾānōkî*]" (Exod. 4:10).
    "For only a child am I [*ʾānōkî*]" (Jer. 1:6).

3. Both use a form of the root *d-b-r* ("speak") preceded by the negative particle *lôʾ*:
   "Not [*lôʾ*] a man of words [*dĕbārîm*] am I" (Exod. 4:10).
   "I do not [*lôʾ*] know how to speak [*dabbēr*]" (Jer. 1:6).

These similar apprehensions of Moses and Jeremiah parallel Jesus's words of reassurance to his apprehensive disciples: "Do not worry about what to say or how to say it. . . . You will be given what to say, for it will be . . . the Spirit of your Father speaking through you" (Matt. 10:19–20 = Mark 13:11; Luke 12:11–12). Despite all the parallels between the calls of Moses and Jeremiah, there is one clear way in which they are different. Jeremiah is the only prophet I am aware of who is told not only that there will be an unfavorable response to his message (many prophets are so informed ahead of time) but also that there will be real threats against his life. It is one thing to know that your people will not believe in you (Exod. 4:1). It is another thing to know that they will fight against you aggressively (Jer. 1:8, 19).

For all his denial of being a good speaker, Moses seems to be doing quite well in his verbal combat with God! Stephen will later refer to Moses as "*powerful in speech* and action" (Acts 7:22), a statement remarkably similar to what somebody earlier said about Prophet Jesus: "He was a prophet, *powerful in* deed and *word*" (Luke 24:19). The Greek brings out the similarity of the two even better:

dynatos en logois kai ergois autou (Acts 7:22)
prophētēs dynatos en ergō kai logō (Luke 24:19)

4:11–12 If Moses is a poor communicator because of defective speech, then it is because God has made him that way. Nobody needs to come along and say, "Who sinned, Moses or his parents, that he should stammer?" God never healed Moses of his speech impediment, but what God did do was display his glory through a physically flawed instrument. Moses's imperfections become the means through which God's way and purpose will advance and come to completion.

Here Am I, Send Him

(4:13–17)

Translation

[13]And Moses said, "Please, my Lord, send, I beg, [your message] in the hand of [him whom] you will send." [14]The LORD's anger burned against Moses, and he said, "Surely Aaron your brother, the Levite—I know he really speaks well. At this very moment he is coming out to meet you. And when he sees you, he will rejoice heartily. [15]You shall speak to him and place the words in his mouth. I, I will be with your mouth and with his mouth. I will instruct [both of] you about what you are to do. [16]He will speak for you to the people. He will be to you as a mouth, and you will be to him as God. [17]This staff take in your hand so that you may do with it wonders."

Grammatical and Lexical Notes

4:13. The words in square brackets are added for sense. Normally after a noun in construct (*bĕyad*, "in the hand of") one expects another noun, but here a verb follows (*tišlāḥ*, "you will send"). What we have here is a relatively rare instance of a construct form before an asyndetic relative, verbal clause. See GKC §155.2; Waltke and O'Connor 1990: 156.

4:14. "Surely" is Hebrew *hălōʾ*, the interrogative particle *ha-* and the negative particle *lôʾ*. When these two words are conjoined, as here and in v. 11b, the combined word may acquire a strongly affirmative sense. See G. Driver 1973: 107–8. In rhetorical questions especially, not all clauses that have an interrogative morpheme are functionally interrogative.

4:15. For "to place [words] in one's mouth," see Num. 22:38; 23:5, 12, 16; Deut. 31:19 (omitted in NIV's translation); 2 Sam. 14:3, 19; Isa. 51:16. A *śîm bĕpeh* related phrase is *nātan bĕpeh* (Deut. 18:18; Jer. 1:9; 5:14).

4:15. The familiar word "torah" comes from the verb *yārâ*, "cast, shoot [e.g., an arrow]." The Hiphil of this verb, as here, means "aim, direct toward," and hence, "show the way, instruct."

4:17. *ʾăšer* ("so that") is here a conjunction of purpose.

4:17. When *ʾôt* ("wonder, sign, miracle") follows *ʿāśâ* ("do, make"), *ʾôt* is usually in the plural, *ʾōtōt*, as here. See Num. 14:11, 22; Deut. 11:3; 34:11; Josh. 24:17. Twice the singular *ʾôt* follows *ʿāśâ*, Judg. 6:17 and Ps. 86:17, both of which begin with "Give me a sign" or "Work a sign/miracle for me."

Commentary

4:13 This is the last of Moses's five statements of objection to God's call on his life: "Send somebody else!" His "Send whom you will send" sounds like God's earlier "I WILL BE WHO I WILL BE" (v. 14). Does he really believe there is somebody more qualified than he? Is he convinced that out there somewhere somebody has better credentials, a more impressive résumé, than he?

4:14–17 This is the first time in Scripture where God is said to get angry at anybody. The book of Genesis never says that God's anger flares up at Adam, or Abraham, or Jacob because of something they have done. Even the flood of Noah's day comes from God's grieving heart, and not from an angry heart (Gen. 6:6).

There are numerous times when Scripture records God's anger being directed at his people, yet only a few times when God's anger is directed at individuals. A good parallel to Exod. 4:14 is 2 Sam. 6:7 (= 1 Chron. 13:10): "The LORD's anger burned against Uzzah." The difference between the two is that God does not then terminate Moses's life as he did Uzzah's. That the Lord's anger does not flare up until after Moses's fifth provocative statement reinforces the claim that he is a God who is "slow to anger" (Exod. 34:6; Num. 14:18; Pss. 86:15; 103:8; 145:8; Joel 2:13; Jon. 4:2).

To a certain degree God makes a concession (Childs 1974: 79) to Moses. What Moses lacks (oratorical gifts), Aaron has in abundance. But here's the catch. Aaron can indeed speak so compellingly, so persuasively, that later he will successfully engineer the golden-calf debacle (chap. 32)! Moses's questioning of God and his attempt at evasive actions paves the way for an eloquent Aaron to emerge, but at what a cost! Better for Moses to have said, "I know there are individuals more credentialed than I, but if I am the person you want, and if you will go with me and with my mouth, then I am available. Give me your marching orders!"

Moses and Aaron become a tag team, but they are not equal. What Elohim is to Moses, Moses is to Aaron ("You will be to him as God"). The cleric is under the layman. The priest is under the prophet. But that is still a good twosome. On only two other occasions does Israel operate under two such leaders: (1) the settlement in Canaan (Joshua the layman and Eleazar the priest; see Josh. 14:1; 17:4; 19:51; 21:1; 24:29, 33); (2) the postexilic period (Nehemiah the layman and Ezra the priest). See Japhet 2006: 503.

Egypt Beckons

(4:18–23)

Translation

[18]Moses went and returned to Jether, his father-in-law, and said to him, "May I go, please, and return to my brothers who are in Egypt, and see whether or not they are alive?" Jethro said to Moses, "Go in peace." [19]The LORD (had) said to Moses in Midian, "Go, return to Egypt. Dead are all the men seeking your soul." [20]And Moses took his wife and sons, mounted them on his donkey, and returned to the land of Egypt. And he took the staff of the Divinity in his hand.

[21]The LORD said to Moses, "As you go to return to Egypt, see all the portents that I have placed in your hand. Do them before Pharaoh's face. However, I, I will make very tough his heart, and he will not send forth the people. [22]And you shall say to Pharaoh, 'Thus is what the LORD said: My son, my firstborn, is Israel. [23]And I said to you, "Send forth my son that he may worship me." You refused to send him forth. So, I, I will slay your son, your firstborn.'"

Grammatical and Lexical Notes

4:18. Jether (*yeter*) is an alternate form of Jethro (*yitrô*).

4:19. Translating *wayyōʾmer* as a pluperfect ("had said") is possible but not necessary. The command in v. 19 need not have been given before Moses's words to Jethro in v. 18. Clearly Jethro does not (over)hear these words, which depart significantly from the words he heard from his son-in-law.

4:20. "Sons" at this point of the story is a bit of a problem since Moses, as far as we know, now has only one son, Gershom (2:21–22). The second son, Eliezer, does not appear until 18:4. Presumably Moses fathers both sons before he leaves Midian.

4:20. "His donkey" (lit., "the donkey") is likely an instance of the definite article functioning as a possessive pronoun. See Barr (1989: 313, 316) and Ehrensvärd (2000: 308).

4:22. "Thus said/says the LORD" occurs only in Exodus among the five books of the Pentateuch (here and 5:1; 7:17; 8:1 [7:26]; 8:20 [16]; 9:1; 10:3; 11:4; 32:27). The plagues section of Exodus accounts for most of these.

4:23. "Slay" is *hārag*. It appears first in the Bible to refer to Cain's killing Abel (Gen. 4:8, 25), to what Cain thinks may happen to him (Gen. 4:14), something God prevents by placing a protective mark on Cain (Gen. 4:15). It is the verb used in Exod. 2:14 for Moses's killing the Egyptian, and in 2:15 for what Pharaoh seeks to do to Moses. It first appears in the Bible with God as subject in Gen. 20:4 in the mouth of Abimelech (NIV, "Lord, will you *destroy* an innocent nation?").

Commentary

4:18–20 Moses's explanation to Jethro for his reason for leaving Midian and going to Egypt is correct, but not totally truthful. We simply do not know whether Moses ever shares with his Midianite father-in-law his encounter with God at the bush and the details of that encounter. Impressive here is Jethro's response: "Go in peace." Contrast Jacob's wanting to leave the house of Laban, his non-Israelite father-in-law, with Laban's daughters, who are Jacob's wives (Gen. 31), and Moses's wanting to leave the house of Jethro, his non-Israelite father-in-law, with Jethro's daughter who is Moses's wife (Janzen 1997: 42). Think of what loss there would be to Jethro when the only other male in the household is gone. Does Jethro think that Moses's absence will be only temporary, and so is this the reason for his not acting Labanesque?

Verses 19 and 20 anticipate some dynamics in Matthew's account of Jesus's birth. First is the phrase used to refer to Herod's death in Matt. 2:14–15 ("and left for Egypt, where he stayed until the death [*teleutē*] of Herod"). *Teleutē* ("death") is a hapax legomenon in NT Greek, and is more than likely modeled on the reference to the death of the king of Egypt in Exod. 4:19 LXX, "For the king of Egypt has died" (*eteleutēsen ho basileus Aigyptou*; the same Greek is in 2:23). The death of Pharaoh opens the door for Moses to leave Midian and return to Egypt, just as the death of Herod opens the door for Jesus to leave Egypt and return to Palestine. Second, "Dead are all the men seeking your soul" anticipates Matt. 2:20, "For those who were trying to take the child's life are dead":

> *tethnēkasin gar pantes hoi zētountes sou tēn psychēn* (Exod. 4:19)
> *tethnēkasin gar hoi zētountes tēn psychēn tou paidiou* (Matt. 2:20)

Most interesting here is the preservation of the plural participle *hoi zētountes* in the Matthew reference even though Herod is the only one trying to kill the infant Christ. The retention helps to maintain the parallel with Exod. 4:19. Third, in Exod. 4:20 Moses takes his wife and child(ren) and returns to Egypt. In Matt. 2:21 Joseph takes his wife and child and leaves Egypt.

4:21–23 For the first time, even before leaving Midian, Moses finds out that the Lord intends to toughen/make strong/harden/make obstinate the heart of Pharaoh. The fulfillment of that promise will be found in the plagues section of Exodus (9:12; 10:20, 27; 11:10; 14:4, 8, all of which use the Piel of *ḥāzaq*, as does 4:21). I will comment at length on this later in the commentary. Suffice it to say here that Moses does not object upon hearing this revelation. He certainly does object, repeatedly, when God calls him to go to Egypt. He does not say anything like, "Well, why then should I go?" or "Why are you going to do something like that?" Perhaps at this point God is testing Moses with something like,

"Will you trust me even if immediate success on your mission is unlikely? Will you focus more on obedience than on results?"

God's declaration that he will slay Egypt's firstborn as a just response to Pharaoh's refusal to release his stranglehold on Israel, God's firstborn, may be an illustration of the talionic principle throughout Scripture. There is often a correspondence between the nature of the punishment and the nature of the trespass that generates the punishment. Take an eye, you lose an eye. Take a tooth, you lose a tooth. Persuade Adam and Eve to eat something they should not eat, and you eat dust for the rest of your existence (Gen. 3). Suck the life out of my firstborn, and you lose your firstborn.

The Bloody Bridegroom

(4:24–26)

Translation

[24]It happened on the way at the inn that the LORD encountered him and sought to put him to death. [25]And Zipporah took a flint and cut away the foreskin of her son and made it touch his feet. She said, "A bridegroom of blood(s) are you to me." [26]And he backed away from him. Then she said, "A bridegroom of blood(s) by the circumcision(s)."

Grammatical and Lexical Notes

4:24. *mālôn* ("inn") is presumably a place one would stop for a night's rest while on a journey (Gen. 42:27), but not necessarily so. In hotter climates one might stop at such a place to escape the blistering, hot sun in the daylight hours.

4:24. The Septuagint softens the first part of the verse by saying, "An angel of the Lord met him." It does the same with two later passages in Exodus: 19:3, "Moses went up to God" (MT); "Moses went up into the mountain of God" (LXX); 24:10, "And they saw the God of Israel" (MT); "And they saw the place where the God of Israel stood" (LXX).

4:24. Biddle (2002: 632) says that *pāgaš* ("encounter") appears fourteen times in the Hebrew Bible, and in most of these the reference is to a dangerous, disastrous encounter (Exod. 4:24, 27; 2 Sam. 2:13; Job 5:14; Prov. 17:12; Isa. 34:14; Jer. 41:6; Hosea 13:8), or to a meeting where one of the two parties expects the worst (Gen. 32:17 [18]; 33:8; 1 Sam. 25:20). For these passages he suggests the translation "to (be) ambush(ed), fall upon, fall prey to." I am not sure if Exod. 4:27 fits into this (Aaron meeting Moses). Both 4:24 and 4:27 use exactly the same verbal form, *wayyipgĕšēhû*.

4:24. When *bāqqēš* ("sought, tried") appeared earlier in Exodus with Moses as the object of the verb and Pharaoh as subject of the verb, NIV rendered "tried to kill Moses" (2:15) and "wanted to kill you" (4:19), but here with God as the subject of the verb instead of Pharaoh, NIV shifts to "was about to kill him."

4:24. Exodus 4:23 uses the Qal participial form of *hārag* for God's intention to kill Egypt's firstborn, but 4:24 uses the Hiphil infinitive construct of *mût* for God's seeking to kill Moses. Another place where *wayĕbaqqēš hămîtô* ("and he sought to put him to death") occurs is Jer. 26:21, "And he [Jehoiakim] sought to put him [Uriah the prophet] to death." Also, 1 Sam. 19:2 ("My father Saul is looking for a chance to kill you") and 1 Kings 11:40 ("Solomon tried to kill Jeroboam") are similar, except that they have the preposition *lĕ* before the infinitive construct "kill."

4:25. Biblical information about instruments used in circumcision is scant. Here it is a "flint" (*ṣōr*), and in Josh. 5:2 it was "flint knives" (*ḥarbôt ṣurîm*).

4:25. For other references to the Hiphil of *nāgaʿ* used with a following preposition to refer to the touching of some part of the body, see Isa. 6:7 ("with it [the hot coal] he touched my mouth. . . . This has touched your lips": both Hiphil of *nāgaʿ* followed by *ʿal*), and Jer. 1:9 ("Then the Lord reached out his hand and touched my mouth": also the Hiphil of *nāgaʿ* followed by *ʿal*). In Exod. 4:25 it is the Hiphil of *nāgaʿ* followed by *lĕ*.

4:25. It is a matter of some dispute whether in the Bible "feet" is sometimes a euphemism for the genitalia, male or female. Passages that have been cited to support this reading include: Gen. 49:10; Exod. 4:25; Deut. 28:57 NRSV; Judg. 3:24 KJV; 1 Sam. 24:3 KJV; 2 Sam. 11:8; 2 Kings 18:27 (= Isa. 36:12); Isa. 6:2; 7:20; Ezek. 16:25 KJV. It is claimed that other parts of the body are referred to euphemistically: "hand" (Song 5:4; Isa. 57:8); "knee" (Ezek. 7:17; 21:12); "thigh" (Gen. 24:2, 9; 46:26 KJV; 47:29; Exod. 1:5 KJV; Judg. 8:30 KJV). Some of these passages clearly point to "feet" or to some other part of the anatomy as a euphemism, but for others it seems quite a stretch. See Pope 1994a: 281; 1992.

Some have argued that "foot" (*pous*) in Mark 9:45 ("And if your foot causes you to sin . . .") is also a euphemism for penis, but this is unlikely since the verse goes on to say, "It is better for you to enter life crippled than to have two feet and be thrown into hell." Mark's linking of sins involving the foot (9:45) and sins involving the eye (9:47) recalls Job 31:1, 5: "I made a covenant with my *eyes*. . . . If my *foot* has hurried after deceit. . . ."

4:25. Clearly the Septuagint is not any more sure than modern writers are what "bridegroom of blood(s)" (*ḥătan-dāmîm*) means. In both vv. 25 and 26 LXX reads, "I have stopped the blood of the circumcision of my child" (*estē to haima tēs peritomēs tou paidiou mou*).

4:25. The Hebrew word for "blood" is written in the plural, *dāmîm*, hence my rendering "bridegroom of blood(s)." Whether it is a normal plural or some other kind of a plural is debatable. Frolov (1996: 520) observes that elsewhere in the Hebrew Bible the plural of "bloods," with a noun standing in construct with it and denoting a person or a group of people, always suggests something negative, something evil: "man of bloods" (2 Sam. 16:7–8, the language Shimei used of King David; Ps. 5:6 [7], "bloodthirsty and deceitful men the Lord abhors"); "men of bloods" (Pss. 26:9; 55:23 [24]; 59:2 [3]; 139:19; Prov. 29:10, all of which NIV translates as "bloodthirsty men"); "house of bloods" (2 Sam. 21:1, [NIV, "Saul and his blood-stained house"]); "city of bloods" (Ezek. 22:2; Nah. 3:1).

4:25. Adding to the confusion of the meaning of *dāmîm* is that the word in construct before it (*ḥātān*) can mean "bridegroom" and also "son-in-law" (Gen. 19:12, 14; Judg. 19:5; 1 Sam. 18:18; 22:14; Neh. 6:18; 13:28). Should we then translate "bridegroom of blood(s)" or "son-in-law of blood(s)"? Moses is hardly a bridegroom, and Gershom is a son, not a son-in-law.

4:26. "Circumcision(s)" (another plural, *mullâ*/*mûlōt*) appears only here in the Hebrew Bible.

Commentary

David Penchansky (1999: 67) begins his study of this incident with these words: **4:25–26**
"Biblical scholars love this passage *because* it is totally incomprehensible." And if it is incomprehensible to the scholar, what about the other 98 percent of Bible students and readers? Similarly, part of the title of Walters's 2002 study of this passage is "The Devil Is in the Ambiguities."

Here are some of the "incomprehensibles": First, whom does God seek to put to death, Moses, or one of his sons, and if one of his sons, which one, Gershom or Eliezer? Second, if Moses is the target, why would God want to end the life of his servant whom God has just recruited and finally persuaded to go to Egypt on a divine mission? Third, what has Moses done that has so angered Divinity, or has he done nothing amiss? Is it a sin of omission or a sin of commission? Fourth, why does v. 25 say the Lord "sought" or "tried" to kill Moses? Cannot God, being God, do what he desires to do? Can God be stopped in his tracks? Fifth, how does Zipporah, a Midianite, immediately size up the situation and do what is necessary to avert divine wrath against her husband or one of her sons? And since the Midianites are itinerant metalworkers, does that explain how Zipporah has the skills to wield a cutting instrument to perform surgery on the delicate anatomy of another (Wyatt 2009: 414n29)? Sixth, whose feet does Zipporah touch (Moses's? a son's? the Lord's?), and why, or is "feet" actually a reference to the membrum of Moses or one of her sons? Seventh, what does the phrase "bridegroom of blood," peculiar to vv. 25 and 26, mean? Eighth, who is the "you" in Zipporah's "A bridegroom of blood are you to me"? Whom is she addressing: Moses? Her son? The Lord? Ninth, why does the Lord stop his assault only after Zipporah says what she says at the end of v. 25?

I cannot claim to answer all (or any?) of these questions with certainty. In a nutshell, I interpret the story as follows. The object of divine attack is Moses (but see Howell [2010: 68–69], who argues that it was Gershom the Lord sought to kill). One would think that if it was the son whose life was in danger, Moses would have been the one to leap into action instead of being passive. The reason for the attack? Moses's failure, for whatever reason, to minister paternally to his son by circumcising him. In the words of the woman of Song 1:6, Moses has been taking care of everybody else's vineyard but in the process has neglected his own vineyard. The shedding of blood via an act of circumcision averts divine wrath, as does the "touching" of the blood to the Hebrews' houses in Egypt during the night of that first Passover (Exod. 12). I am aware that a major objection to this time-honored explanation circles around several questions: "Why would God wait so long to hold Moses accountable for his sin of omission? Does God not know of this oversight when he first appears to Moses at the bush, but never once raises it during the call narrative?" All true, but is not Scripture replete with instances of an enormous chasm that often exists between sinful acts and their day of reckoning? Does not the God of Scripture repeatedly say, "Yet forty days . . ."?

If there is an incident in Scripture parallel to this one, it involves Balaam in Num. 22 (see Embry 2010). In Exodus, Moses is journeying to Egypt; in Numbers, Balaam is journeying to Moab. The Lord is upset over something Moses has or has not done and meets him on the way; God is angry that Balaam went to Moab (Num. 22:11) and meets him on the way. The only two places where the Lord is said to be angry with somebody (*wayyiḥar-ʾap*) but the reader is not sure why are Exod. 4:14 and Num. 22:22. Zipporah was the means of Moses's deliverance; the donkey (*ʾātôn*, a female animal, "she-ass") was the means of Balaam's deliverance. One cannot miss the connection between

Zipporah and "Balak, the son of Zippor." Finally, although the Hebrew word for the "staff" with which Moses struck the water is *maṭṭeh*, and the Hebrew word for the "staff" with which Balaam struck the donkey is *maqqēl* (Num. 22:27), the LXX translates both *maṭṭeh* and *maqqēl* with *rhabdos*. "Staff" does not appear in Exod. 4:24–26, but it is present elsewhere in the chapter (vv. 2, 4, 17, 20).

In addition to the Exodus commentaries (esp. those of Cassuto 1967; Childs 1974; Greenberg 1969; and Propp 1999), I have been much stimulated by the studies of Lindstrom (1983: 41–55); B. Robinson (1986); Frolov (1996); and Kirsch (1997).

I would like, however, to highlight two brilliant observations by Fretheim. First, Fretheim (1991: 79) teases in-depth meaning out of the text by saying "the Lord 'tried' to kill." Says Fretheim, "This softens the divine action. . . . God only seeks and does not make a 'direct hit.' . . . God leaves room for mediation, allows time for Zipporah to act, even implicitly invites it. . . . Zipporah moves into the temporal spaces allowed by God's seeking. The divine move is thus a threat, not an attempt to kill that God fails to pull off."

Again, Fretheim (1991: 80) notes that unlike the women in chaps. 1–2, who save Moses, or his kin, from the wrath of Pharaoh, Zipporah saves Moses from the wrath of the Lord. To that degree her interceding, mediating ministry that spares her husband from divine wrath anticipates Moses's own later intercessory ministry of prayer that will spare (most of) his golden-calf-building people from divine wrath (chap. 32).

This is a cogent and healthy observation, one that honors the role of Zipporah. One wonders if in the following paragraph (vv. 27–31) Moses shares any of this incident with Aaron. One wonders if he thanks Zipporah. Does he say anything like, "Man, just think, I came within spitting distance of Sheol, but thanks to you, I am alive to tell about it"?

I have noticed a trend among some conservative commentators who, by contrast with Fretheim, tend to paint Zipporah as the villain! For example, among older conservative writers, Keil and Delitzsch (1865: 459) put the onus on Moses for not circumcising Gershom, but suggest that he has omitted circumcising him "from regard to his Midianitish wife, who . . . disliked this operation." In other words, if only she had gotten on board, this would never have happened.

Among more-modern conservatives, Kaiser (1990: 332–33) takes a similar view. He speaks of "her revulsion and disgust with this rite of circumcision" and of Moses's neglect to circumcise their son "out of deference for his wife's wishes." Her "You are a bridegroom of blood to me" is Zipporah's way of unleashing a verbal vendetta at Moses. Allen (1996: 268) also speaks of Zipporah's distaste for circumcising children or youth, but interprets her "You are a bridegroom of blood to me" as directed at God, a way of cussing out God (maybe in Midianitese) for sanctifying such a grotesque operation.

Moses and Aaron Reunite

(4:27–31)

Translation

[27]And the LORD said to Aaron, "Go to meet Moses on the steppe." And he went and encountered him at the mountain of God, and he kissed him. [28]And Moses informed Aaron about all the words of the LORD with which he sent him, and all the signs with which he charged him. [29]And Moses went, along with Aaron, and they assembled all the elders of Israel's sons. [30]And Aaron spoke all the words that the LORD had spoken to Moses, and he did the signs before the people. [31]The people believed when they heard that the LORD had visited Israel's sons and had seen their abuse. They bowed down and they worshiped.

Grammatical and Lexical Notes

4:31. The first part of the verse reads, literally, "And the people believed, and they heard that the LORD visited Israel's sons." Clearly, the second half of this precedes in sense the first part. It was what they heard that led to their belief. One way in which Hebrew permits a pluperfect reading of a verb ("had visited/seen") is by presenting the events or phrases out of order, that is B before A, or effect before cause. See Zevit (1998: 69).

4:31. The Septuagint renders "and they heard" (*wayyišmĕʿû*) by the Greek verb *chairō*, "and they rejoiced" (= *wayyiśmĕḥû*). While I cannot explain this grammatically, it is an understandable change. *Chairō* occurs about eighty times in the Greek OT, and in over a quarter of these the reference is to a joy that greets a divine saving act, or announcement, or promise.

4:31. The expression *pāqad ʾet* (and in 3:16) is quite different from *pāqad ʿal* in 32:34b. The NIV renders the verb in 3:16 as "watched over," in 4:31 as "was concerned about," and in 32:34b as "punish." In 3:16 and 4:31 God "visits" his people to deliver them. In 32:34b God "visits" his people to punish them. God "turns his attention to" (= the basic meaning of *pāqad*) Israel for two radically different purposes. The Septuagint's verb here for a divine "visit," *episkeptomai*, resurfaces in Luke's frequent use of this verb in reference to moments of God's historical intervention (Luke 1:68, 78; 7:16; 19:44; Acts 7:23 [the only one that NIV translates as "visit"]; 15:14). In his comments on Luke 1:68, Fitzmyer (1981: 383) observes that the religious sense of "visit" is unattested in extrabiblical Greek.

Commentary

4:27–31 It has been years, possibly decades, since Moses and Aaron have seen each other. The reuniting of the two brothers after such a long separation parallels to a degree Jacob's reunion with Esau after a long separation from him. God encounters Jacob dramatically in a nocturnal wrestling match, and "touched" a part of his body (Gen. 32:25 [26]). God encounters Moses dramatically, possibly during the night hours, and Zipporah "touched" a part of his body or their son's body. It is Esau who goes to meet Jacob, just as here Aaron goes to meet Moses. Upon glimpsing Jacob, Esau runs toward Jacob, embraces him and kisses him (Gen. 33:4). Upon meeting Moses, Aaron kisses him. There are two differences between the two scenes. First, Moses is not fearful of his reunion with Aaron, for he has no reason to think that Aaron is out for revenge, as Jacob does while he faces that inevitable reconnect with Esau. Second, Jacob and Esau's reunion is short-lived. Shortly thereafter, they separate and go their individual ways. By contrast, Moses and Aaron are together until Aaron's death. That the meeting between Moses and Aaron takes place at "the mountain of God," the same venue where the Lord has appeared to Moses in the fiery bush (3:1), indicates that Moses has not traveled very far yet on his way back to Egypt.

Verse 28b speaks of the signs with which the Lord has "charged" or "commanded" Moses (*ṣāwâ*). This verb appears in Exodus with the Lord as the subject (in the Piel stem) in 4:28; 6:13; 7:2, 6, 10, 20; 12:28. It is also the verb that Exod. 1:22 and 5:6 use (in the Qal stem) for Pharaoh's commands to oppress and destroy God's people. In these opening chapters of Exodus, contrast what Pharaoh commands with what God commands. It is as if "Yhwh's commands are thus a means of rescuing Israel from Pharaoh's commands" (Goldingay 2003: 379).

Here it is Aaron, not Moses, who performs the signs about which God has spoken to Moses back in 4:2–7. This, as Janzen (1997: 46) has observed, accomplishes two things, First, it helps Moses set aside some of his earlier statements he has made to God about his perceived lack of gifts. Second, Aaron is a recognized figure among the Israelites in Egypt. Moses is not. It can be easier to believe in a friend and an acquaintance than in a stranger.

Moses and Aaron's First Meeting with Pharaoh

(5:1–9)

Translation

[1]Afterward Moses and Aaron came to Pharaoh and said, "Thus said the LORD, God of Israel, 'Send away my people that they may keep a pilgrim-feast for me on the steppe.'" [2]And Pharaoh said, "Who is the LORD that I should heed his voice to send away Israel? I do not know the LORD, and furthermore, Israel I will not send away." [3]And they said, "The God of the Hebrews chanced upon us. Let us go, please, a journey of three days into the steppe that we may sacrifice to the LORD our God, lest he fall upon us with pestilence or sword." [4]And the king of Egypt said to them, "Why, Moses and Aaron, do you cause the people to refrain from its tasks? Go back to your burdensome labor." [5]And Pharaoh said, "Look, numerous now are the people of the land, and you want to keep them away from their burdensome labor!" [6]On that day Pharaoh commanded the taskmasters over the people and its foremen, saying, [7]"No longer shall you give straw to the people for brickmaking as in time past. They themselves will go and gather their own straw. [8]And the amount of bricks they were making previously you shall continue to demand of them. Do not reduce it, for they are idlers. Therefore they cry out, saying, 'Let us go and let us sacrifice to our God.' [9]Let the labor be heavy on the men, and let them do it and do not heed deceptive words."

Grammatical and Lexical Notes

5:1. The Qal of *šālaḥ* ("send away") has appeared frequently so far in Exodus (2:5; 3:12, 13, 14, 15; 3:20a; 4:4 [2x], 13 [2x], 28). Here (and in 3:20b; 4:21, 23 [2x]) the Piel is used, and all refer to Pharaoh sending (or not sending) Israel away. The Piel of *šālaḥ* may mean to "send away, release, let loose" without the possibility of return (e.g., Hagar [Gen. 21:14]; Tamar [2 Sam. 13:17]; a wife, where the verb means "to divorce" [Deut. 22:19, 29]). This is not always the case with the Piel of *šālaḥ*, however. Noah "sent out" a dove (Gen. 8:8), but it returns to the ark (Gen. 8:9).

There is a very interesting use of the Piel of *šālaḥ* in Ps. 81:11–12 [12–13] to refer back to exodus events: "But my people would not listen to me. . . . So I *sent them off* [NIV, 'I gave them over'] in the stubbornness of their hearts to follow their own devices." Here is a rare use of the Piel of *šālaḥ* to refer to a God-inflicted punishment. For Pharaoh to *šālaḥ* Israel is to release Israel from captivity. For Yahweh to *šālaḥ* Israel is to give Israel over to her own ways and devices, a captivity that in the long run may prove more destructive than that in Goshen.

5:3. This verse repeats much of 3:18, yet 5:3 (and 7:16; 9:1, 13; 10:3) uses the shorter plural form of "the Hebrews" (*hā ʿibrîm*), while 3:18 uses the longer plural form (*hā ʿibrîyîm*).

5:3. In 3:18 the verb for "chanced upon" is *niqrâ* (ending with a *hê*). In 5:3 the verb for "chanced upon" is *niqrāʾ* (ending with an *ʾālep*).

5:3. Moses's and Aaron's use of "lest" (*pen*) recalls Pharaoh's earlier use of "lest"/*pen* in 1:10, "lest they multiply."

5:3. Like other verbs of contact (e.g., *nāgaʿ*, "touch"), *pāgaʿ bĕ* can also mean "fall upon, strike." When the verb signifies simply meeting somebody, with no hostile intent, it may take an ordinary accusative, as in 5:20.

5:4. The verb for "cause to refrain" (here the Hiphil of *pāraʿ*) looks a lot like the name "Pharaoh" (*parʿōh*), on which see Garsiel (1991: 58–59). A similar pun may be found in Jer. 46:2, which tells how Nebuchadnezzar "slew" (*nākâ*) Pharaoh Neco (*nĕkô, nĕkōh*). The LXX renders *pāraʿ* with *diastrephō*, "make crooked," and in a figurative sense, "pervert." It is the verb in Luke 23:2, a charge brought against Jesus, "We have found this man *subverting* our nation."

5:5. The phrase "the people of the land" (*ʿam hāʾāreṣ*) appears sixty to seventy times in the OT and has engendered much study. I am inclined to agree with Nicholson (1965: 59–66) that the expression is not necessarily a technical term, as many have suggested, but is a fluid phrase, one whose meaning varies from context to context. The SP applies the expression in 5:5 to the Egyptians, and not to the Hebrews, as in MT ("numerous now are the people of the land [the Hebrews]"). It does so by reading MT's *ʿam hāʾāreṣ* as *mēʿam hāʾāreṣ* ("they [the Hebrews] are more numerous than the people of the land"). For other clear uses of "people of the land" referring to non-Israelites, see Gen. 23:7; 42:6 (NIV's "to all its people" is "to all the people of the land").

5:6. The Septuagint renders "taskmasters" (*nōgĕśîm*), here and in vv. 10, 13, as *ergodiōktai*, which actually means "overseers, foremen." Würthwein (1979: 67) suggests that "the efforts of translators to make the OT intelligible to their compatriots in Egypt led them to use terms native to their Egyptian and Alexandrian environment which were not the exact equivalents of the Hebrew expressions."

5:6. The Hebrew word for "foreman" is *šōṭēr*. Behind the noun is a putative verb, *šāṭar*, which means "to write," as can be seen in Akkadian *šaṭaru* ("write") and Aramaic *šĕṭaraʾ* ("document, writ"). The LXX translates the word here as *grammateusin* ("scribes"). However, in the Bible there are no references to the *šōṭĕrîm* writing. In Deut. 1:15 they are simply civilian "officials," and in Deut. 16:18 they appear alongside judges. Possibly one function of the *šōṭĕrîm* was to assist judges in secretarial work (see *ANEP*, no. 231 for an illustration from Egypt of scribes recording judicial information). In Deut. 20:5, 8, 9 and Josh. 1:10; 3:2 they help maintain military discipline. It is clear that the *nōgĕśîm*/"taskmasters" are Egyptians, while the *šōṭĕrîm*/"foremen" are Hebrews.

5:7. Although the verb in "you *shall no longer* give" (*lōʾ tōʾsipûn lātēt*) is *ʾāsap*, LXX reads the verb as if it is *sûp*: "You shall stop giving any longer" (*ouketi prostethēsetai didonai*). See Tov 2008: 390.

5:7. Hebrew *lāban lĕbēnâ* ("make brick")—and compare the two cognate (related) words together in Gen. 11:3—appears in a Ugaritic text: "Seeing Athirat is a slave-girl to mould the bricks (*hm.ʾmt.atrt. tlbn.lbnt*), let a house be built for Baal" (Gibson 1978: 60). One may also compare Akkadian *libatta labanu* (Held 1965: 277n5).

5:7 The use of the independent pronoun before the verb in *hēm yēlĕkû* ("they themselves will go") draws attention to the subject: "they, not you, will gather the straw." For a parallel, note David's word to the Lord after his sin of taking a census (2 Sam. 24:17). He uses the pronoun *ʾānōkî* before "I have sinned" and again before "I have done wrong," as if to say, "It is I who have sinned, not the people."

5:7. *Qāšaš* ("gather") is a denominative verb formed from *qaš*, "stubble, straw, chaff," and means "to assemble, gather (into a bunch or bale)." First Kings 17:10 uses the verb for gathering sticks to make a fire, and Zeph. 2:1 uses it for assembling people.

5:8. The Hebrew for "reduce, diminish" is *gāraʿ*. It is a mathematical term meaning "subtract." In addition to v. 8, see also vv. 11, 19; Lev. 27:18; Num. 27:4; 36:3–4.

5:8. "Idlers" is in Hebrew *nirpîm*, a Niphal plural participle of *rāpâ*, "sink, relax." This verb occurs in 4:26, when the Lord "backed away from, withdrew from" Moses after Zipporah has circumcised their son.

5:9. With "*No* longer shall you give straw" in v. 7, and with "Do *not* reduce it" in v. 8, Pharaoh uses the negative particle *lōʾ* for "not." Here with "do *not* heed deceptive words" he uses the negative particle *ʾal* for "not." Bright (1973: 188) notes that in the Pentateuch *lōʾ*, the stronger of the two particles, is always in the mouth of God or Moses, except for four times in Pharaoh's mouth (Exod. 5:7, 8, 19; 8:28 [24]), and twice when Isaac spoke to Jacob (Gen. 28:1, 6).

Commentary

5:1 How well does Moses follow divine directives? For that matter, how well do we? In Exod. 3:18 God tells Moses how to approach Pharaoh and what to say; 5:1 is about Moses carrying through on that. However, if one compares the two passages, they are quite different. I list the following. First, in 3:18 it is Moses and the elders who are to go; here, it is Moses and Aaron who go. Second, Moses changes the Lord's "The Lord, the God of the Hebrews" into "The Lord, the God of Israel." Third, in 3:18 the Lord speaks of taking only a three-day journey away. Moses omits that here. Fourth, God instructs Moses to use the cohortative ("Let us go"). Instead, Moses uses the Piel of *šālaḥ* and the imperative mood at that ("Send away!"). Fifth, the Lord has Moses using the particle *nāʾ*, "please, pray" ("Let us go, please"). Here there is no "please, pray." The difference between the two is obvious. God's language is courteous and diplomatic. Moses's language is abrasive, in-your-face confrontation. As Sternberg (1998: 271) says, Moses "would rather hammer than talk the rock of Egypt into disgorging its prey." He then goes on to describe Moses's tactics as "curt, peremptory, uncompromisingly Israelite, . . . certain to offend." In a similar fashion Goldingay (2003: 340, italics original) remarks that Moses and Aaron "speak *to* the king like messengers announcing a message *from* a king."

5:2 There are two ways to interpret Pharaoh's response. One way is to read it as a statement of arrogance and defiance, even insult. "Nobody is Lord here except myself. In my backyard I'm Lord. So who is this Lord of whom you speak?" Similar derogatory, insulting "who . . . ?" questions appear in passages like Judg. 9:28 ("Who is Abimelech, and who is Shechem, that we should be subject to him?"); 1 Sam. 17:26 ("Who is this uncircumcised Philistine that he should defy the armies of the living God?"); 1 Sam. 25:10 ("Who is this David? Who is this son of Jesse?"). On the phenomenon of "insult formulas" in Scripture, see Coats 1970.

Alternatively, Pharaoh's "Who is the Lord that I should heed his voice?" may be read as an expression of understandable ignorance. Again to quote Sternberg (1998: 272), "After all, if an earlier Pharaoh 'did not know Joseph' (1:8), a recent Egyptian celebrity, this one may genuinely 'not know the Lord' associated with an outlandish slave-class theology." I might add that an earlier passage in Exodus indicates that Moses himself does not know the Lord as LORD (3:13–15). Even the Lord makes it clear that he "did not make himself known" as LORD/YHWH to any of the patriarchs (6:3). The bottom line is that up until this point nobody in Scripture is said to know/not know the Lord (Eslinger 1996: 194). If Abraham did not really and fully know YHWH as YHWH, should we expect this pharaoh to know? But if 5:2 highlights a pharaoh who does not know (*yādaʿ*) the Lord, let us not forget that Exodus earlier highlights a God, a God of the Hebrews, who does know (*yādaʿ*) in 2:25. A God who knows and a pharaoh who does not know; that contrast will erupt powerfully in the forthcoming chapters in Exodus.

Moses's second attempt to persuade Pharaoh is much less confrontational than **5:3**
v. 1, and is much more like 3:18. For example, he introduces "LORD" only later in the verse, rather than beginning with "LORD" as he did in v. 1. He drops the imperative ("send away") for the cohortative ("let us go"), and he repeats God's earlier "God of the Hebrews," "please," and "a journey of three days." Uniquely, Moses adds, "lest he fall upon us with pestilence or sword." "Of what use would a dead workforce be to you?" Moses suggests. Then again, of what use would a disappeared workforce be to Pharaoh? If the Hebrews are dead or if they have vanished, either way Pharaoh is left holding the bag.

Moses's use of more diplomatic language is no more successful than his bel- **5:4–9**
ligerent tone in v. 1. Maybe his original brusqueness in v. 1 has negated any chance of success in v. 3, regardless of how many modifications he makes in his strategy. Sometimes you get only one real chance up to bat. Blow it here, and the game is over.

What do Moses's people reap from Moses's obedience to God? Not what one would call blessings. Instead, an overworked, exhausted people have even higher demands and expectations placed on them. No time for worship will be allotted. No cutting back on production rates will be tolerated. The Egyptians will provide no straw. Some of their own people will keep a watchful, supervising eye ("the foremen") on them, a classical example of the old divide-and-conquer strategy as a means of "keeping people/underlings in their place." These programs Pharaoh justifies, but surely not seriously, because he dubs the Hebrews as "idlers" (v. 8). This is what Meyers (2005: 67) calls "a classic case of 'blame the victim' as a justification for tyranny."

All of this picturing of enslaved, brickmaking Hebrews is very realistic, based on what we have found in ancient Egypt. Various sources, especially from the New Kingdom Period in Egyptian history (i.e., ca. 1570–mid 1100s BC), provide evidence of large groups of slaves toiling in the delta region. In particular the tombs of Rekhmire at Thebes (fifteenth century BC) give ample illustrations of slaves of Semitic stock working as brickmakers and bricklayers. An inscription over one scene of bricklayers reads, "The taskmaster says to the builders: 'The rod is in my hand; be not idle'" (N. Davies 1943: 123).

Pharaoh's last word, "Do not heed/listen to deceptive words" (v. 9b), is amazingly similar to a warning Jeremiah gives to a group of people who, he believes, are about to be duped. His "Do not listen to your prophets. . . . They prophesy lies" (Jer. 27:9–10, 14, 16) shares with Exod. 5:9 both the verb "listen" and the noun "lies/deceptive words" (*šeqer*). In Jeremiah's mouth that phrase is a God word. In Pharaoh's mouth that phrase is a concocted farce.

No Straw, but a Lot of Stench

(5:10–21)

Translation

[10]And the people's taskmasters and foremen went out and said to the people, "Thus said Pharaoh: 'I am not giving straw. [11]As for you, get straw for yourselves wherever you may find it because your heavy labor will not be reduced one iota.'" [12]And the people spread out all over the land of Egypt to gather stubble for straw. [13]The taskmasters kept urging them, saying, "Complete your tasks every single day as when the straw was available." [14]And the foremen of Israel's sons, whom Pharaoh's taskmasters had appointed over them, were scolded, saying, "Why did you not complete your prescribed allotment of bricks as before, not yesterday nor today?"

[15]And the foremen of Israel's sons came and cried out to Pharaoh, saying, "Why do you do this to your servants? [16]Straw is not given to your servants, and 'bricks,' they keep on saying to us, 'make.' Look how your servants are being harassed, and the fault lies with your people." [17]And Pharaoh said, "Idlers, you are idlers! That is why you keep on saying, 'Let us go and sacrifice to the LORD.' [18]And now, go, serve. Straw will not be given to you, but the quota of bricks you must produce." [19]And the foremen of Israel's sons saw themselves in harm's way, hearing it said, "You shall not reduce for a single day your brick output." [20]They came across Moses and Aaron, standing there to meet them as they exited from Pharaoh. [21]They said to them, "Let the LORD look upon you and judge, for you have made us a stench in Pharaoh's eyes and in his servants' eyes by putting a sword in their hand to kill us."

Grammatical and Lexical Notes

5:10. One "thus said Pharaoh" is overwhelmed and consumed by multiple "thus said the LORD" (4:22; 7:17; 8:1 [7:26]; 8:20 [16]; 9:1, 13; 10:3; 11:4) throughout these opening chapters of Exodus.

5:13. "Every single day" or "every day" (and "a single day" in v. 19) is *dĕbar-yôm bĕyômô*, literally, "the thing/word of a day in its day." For this idiom elsewhere see 16:4; Lev. 23:37; 1 Kings 8:59; 2 Kings 25:30 (= Jer. 52:34), and so forth. It is like the expression "every Sabbath" in Num. 28:10 (*šabbat bĕšabbattô*, lit., "Sabbath in its Sabbath").

5:14. It is common, and quite possible, to translate *wayyukkû* (from *nākâ*) as "were beaten." I choose to give the verb here (and in v. 16, "harassed") its nonphysical sense: "scold, berate." Note that NIV adds words not found in the Hebrew when it retains "beaten": "were beaten and *were asked*, 'Why . . . ?'"

5:14. The Hebrew for "prescribed allotment" is *ḥōq*, elsewhere in the Bible often translated "law, decree." The noun is built off the verb *ḥāqaq*, "dig, engrave in stone," and perhaps reflects the idea of engraving laws on stone. Extended meanings of *ḥōq* beyond "law, decree" are "assignment, prescribed allotment."

5:15. For other instances of a cry (*ṣāʿaq*) to a king, see 1 Kings 20:39; 2 Kings 6:26; 8:3, 5.

5:16. The end of the verse looks strange, for a verbless phrase dangles by itself. It reads, literally, "Look how your servants are being harassed/beaten, and the sin of your people [*wĕḥāṭāʾt ʿammekā*]." The Septuagint reads the last two words as a full, independent clause ("And look, your servants are beaten. Therefore, you are being unjust to your people").

5:19. The word "themselves" (*ʾōtām*) in "saw themselves" illustrates the reflexive use of the object pronoun.

5:21. "You have made us a stench" reads, literally, "You have made foul our odor" (*hibaʾštem ʾet-rêḥēnû*). An abbreviated form of this phrase appears in Gen. 34:30, Jacob's words to Simeon and Levi: "You have brought trouble on me by making me a stench" (*ʿăkartem ʾōtî lĕhabʾîšēnî*), with the word *rēyaḥ* ("odor, scent") understood (B. Levine 1974: 60n18). Caird (1980: 146) cites this as an instance of synesthesia: using a term to express an idea that connects with one of our senses (smell, touch, etc.). Compare the reference in 10:21 to darkness that can be "felt." The Septuagint's verb, *bdelyssomai*, simply means "to make repulsive." That the text speaks about making the Israelites a stench "in the eyes" of Pharaoh, and not "in the nose" of Pharaoh, shows that "the writer is not much thinking of its olfactory force" (Alter 2004: 337).

Commentary

5:10–21 Unlike Jesus's yoke and burden, which are "easy" and "light" (Matt. 11:29–30), the Pharaoh's yoke is life-sapping and exasperating. Unlike Jesus, who promises to "give" rest to those who are weary, Pharaoh will "give" no straw to his weary, exhausted, brickmaking subjects. Unlike Jesus, whose expectations are realistic, Pharaoh's are unrealistic. Jesus offers to share the yoke (any load, any burden you have to pull, he helps you pull it; anywhere you go, he goes with you if the two of you are yoked). Pharaoh imposes his yoke. For Pharaoh the key word is work quotas and production schedules. For Jesus the key word is rest.

Understandably, the Israelite foremen can take their wrath out only on Moses and Aaron. They surely have gotten nowhere with Pharaoh (vv. 5–18). It is as if Moses's own people turn to him and say, "It's because of your big mouth that we're in such trouble now. Nobody invited you. Why don't you go back to where you came from?" This will not be the last time the congregants will quarrel vigorously and condemningly with their pastor.

Asking God the Hard Questions

(5:22–6:1)

Translation

[22]Moses returned to the LORD and said, "My Lord, why have you harmed this people? Why have you sent me? [23]Since I came to Pharaoh to speak in your name, he has harmed this people, and you have done nothing at all to rescue your people." [6:1]And the LORD said to Moses, "Now you will see what I am about to do to Pharaoh, for by means of a strong hand he will send them away, and by means of a strong hand he will drive them away from his turf."

Grammatical and Lexical Notes

5:22. "Sent" in v. 22, with God as the subject, is the Qal of *šālaḥ*, while in 6:1 "send away," with Pharaoh as subject, is the stronger Piel of that verb.

5:22. Another way to translate "Why have you harmed this people?" (*hărēʿōtâ*, the Hiphil of *rāʿaʿ*) is "Why have you done evil to this people?" The same goes for "harmed" with Pharaoh as subject in v. 23 (*hēraʿ*). God/LORD is the subject of *rāʿaʿ* (Hiphil) twelve times in the Hebrew Bible, although NIV never renders any of these twelve as "do evil." Instead, it uses the following expressions: (1) "brought trouble" (Exod. 5:22; Num. 11:11); (2) "bring disaster" (Josh. 24:20; Jer. 25:29; 31:28; Zech. 8:14); (3) "brought tragedy" (1 Kings 17:20); (4) "harm" (Jer. 25:6); (5) "brought to grief" (Mic. 4:6); (6) "do bad" (Zeph. 1:12); (7) "crushed" (Ps. 44:2 [3]); (8) "brought misfortune" (Ruth 1:21). Three of these twelve use the verb in a question directly addressed to God (Exod. 5:22; Num. 11:11; 1 Kings 17:20).

Commentary

Two or more why questions, asked in rapid succession, appear throughout **5:22–23**
Scripture in the same verse. Think of the Lord's "*Why* are you angry? *Why* is your face downcast?" to Cain (Gen. 4:6); or Laban's questions to Jacob, "*Why* did you run off secretly and deceive me? *Why* didn't you tell me?" (31:27); or the words of Sisera's mother about her son in the Song of Deborah, "*Why* is his chariot so long in coming? *Why* is the clatter of his chariots delayed?" (Judg. 5:28).

Then there are instances of back-to-back why questions in adjacent verses. For example, Pharaoh asks Abraham, "*Why* didn't you tell me she was your wife? *Why* did you say, 'She is my sister'?" (Gen. 12:18b, 19a). Other examples include the two why questions the Egyptians address to Joseph (Gen. 47:15, 19), and the two why questions the Israelites put to Moses (Num. 20:4–5; see Barr 1985: 29).

In narrative literature it is rare for anybody to ask God two why questions. In Judg. 21:3 the Israelites ask God, "*Why* has this happened to Israel? *Why* should one tribe be missing from Israel today?" Nobody does this more often than Moses: here in 5:22; 32:11–12 ("*Why* should your anger burn against your people . . . ? *Why* should the Egyptians say . . . ?"); Num. 11:11–12 ("*Why* have you brought this trouble on your servant? . . . *Why* do you tell me to carry them in my arms?").

Moses begins a long tradition of truth-telling and truth-talking in biblical prayer. He employs no nice clichés or shibboleths. He has failed and is discouraged, rejected, confused, and bewildered by God's apparent withdrawal to the sidelines, by his unwillingness to become involved with his people's desperate needs. As audacious as it sounds, Moses believes that God's not doing anything brings as much evil to Israel as Pharaoh's doing horrific things brings evil to Israel. God's omission is as crushing to Israel as Pharaoh's commission.

6:1 So how does God respond to that charge? He ignores it! God does not appear shocked in the least by Moses's insolent speech. He does not reprimand Moses for making irresponsible and blasphemous accusations against God. Instead, he says to Moses, "Just wait until you see what I do with Pharaoh." The future lies in God's "mighty hand," not in Moses's mighty (big) mouth. There are numerous places in the Torah where Moses unloads before God. A classic case is Num. 11. The people complain and get burned (Num. 11:1–9); Moses complains and gets blessed (Num. 11:10–17). What is the difference? How do you complain about the toast without becoming toast? Perhaps it is because whenever the people complain, they complain *about* God, whereas when Moses complains, he complains *to* God. Moses never talks about God negatively "behind God's back." And God can take such frontal language, such searching questions, if for no other reason than that he has amazingly strong self-esteem. Critique never gets him down.

PART 2

Liberation from Egypt

(6:2–15:21)

By the end of Exod. 5, it seems that God's intention to deliver Israel from Egypt via Moses has come to a grinding and embarrassing halt. Pharaoh appears to have won. God and Moses appear to have lost. Before Pharaoh, Moses is bruised. As a result, before God he is brazen (5:22–23). Maybe Moses is correct. God needs to commission someone more qualified and persuasive (4:13) if Pharaoh is ever to cry "uncle."

But no! God will stick with Moses while he sticks it to Pharaoh and Egypt. As Paul states it in Rom. 11:29, "for God's gifts and his call are irrevocable." To that end, this section commences with God's reaffirming his call upon a discouraged, angry Moses, who still feels bedeviled by his lack of necessary speech skills (6:12, 30). Silver-tongued orator or inarticulate bungler, Moses is Yahweh's chosen.

Earlier, in 3:20 ("I will strike Egypt with all my marvelous deeds that I will do") and in 4:21 ("all the portents"), the Lord has revealed to Moses his intentions on how he plans to deal with a recalcitrant Pharaoh and Egypt. Chapters 7–14 will spell out the nature of those "portents."

The "marvelous deeds" will consist of ten plagues, beginning with the waters of Egypt becoming bloodied (7:14–24) and climaxing with the death of all of Egypt's firstborn (11:1–9 and 12:29–30). The purpose of these plagues is never to make Pharaoh and Egypt pay for their "sins." Rather, it is so that Pharaoh and Egypt may "know" that Yahweh alone is Yahweh even in Egypt, or anywhere else, for that matter (7:5, 17; 8:10, 22 [6, 18]; 9:14, 29; 11:7; 14:4, 18). In the process, Israel too will come to "know" her Lord in a deeper way (6:7; 10:2).

What is meant by Pharaoh and Egypt coming to "know" that Yahweh is Lord more than likely does not refer to what we would call "conversion." Conversion is the dramatic change that God works in the life of somebody who happily and completely surrenders one's life to God for such a transformation. If that is the purpose of the plagues, then God fails to see that purpose realized. At the end of Exod. 15:21 Pharaoh is not "saved." He is dead! Not delivered, but drowned.

I suggest that the language of "knowing" the Lord in Exod. 6–15 is akin to that which Paul uses in Phil. 2:10–11 when he speaks of every knee bowing at the name of Jesus and every tongue confessing that Christ is Lord. It is unlikely that Paul is advocating a kind of universalism, a massive explosion of entries into the kingdom that leaves nobody on the outside. Rather, he is suggesting that even those who refuse to bow their hearts will, one day, still be compelled to bow their knees before this Christ.

To that end, all this emphasis in part 2 throughout Exod. 6–14 on Pharaoh's "knowing" the Lord springs from something Pharaoh has boasted of in part 1—"I do not know the LORD" (5:2). Now he will have a chance to find out.

The amount of material in Exodus devoted to the exodus itself is slim (12:31–42; 13:17–14:31). The emphasis is, instead, on what has led up to it and prepared for it (1:1–12:30) and what follows it (15:1–40:38).

What immediately follows the account of the exodus is Moses's/Miriam's/the peoples' poems of celebration of this event (15:1–21). The movement is from story to song, from a crossing to a celebration, from a drowning to a deliverance. Sobbing Israel who has "cried" throughout the early chapters of Exodus now becomes singing Israel. And why not?

God, Not Moses, Is Lord

(6:2–9)

Translation

[2]And God spoke to Moses, and he said to him, "I [am] LORD. [3]I showed myself to Abraham, to Isaac, and to Jacob as El Shadday. But I (my name LORD, that is) did not make myself known to them. [4]And also I have confirmed my covenant with them by giving to them the land of Canaan, the land of their sojourning in which they have sojourned. [5]And also I have heeded the cry of Israel's sons whom Egyptians continue to enslave, and I have remembered my covenant. [6]Upon my word, say to Israel's sons, 'I [am] LORD, and I will bring you out from underneath the burden of Egypt. I will deliver you from your slavery, and I will redeem you by means of an outstretched arm and mighty chastisements. [7]And I will take you to myself as a people, and I will be for you as God. And you will know that I [am] the LORD your God who is bringing you out from underneath the burden of Egypt. [8]And I will bring you to the land about which I swore with my hand, to give it to Abraham, to Isaac, and to Jacob. I will give it to you as a possession. I [am] LORD.'" [9]So Moses spoke thusly to Israel's sons, but they did not heed Moses because of demoralization brought on by exhaustion and their crushing labor.

Grammatical and Lexical Notes

6:2. "Spoke . . . said" is a verbal hendiadys introducing direct speech: both verbs refer to the same discourse.

6:3. Both "I showed myself" (*wāʾērāʾ*) and "did not make myself known" (*nôdaʿtî*) are Niphals, but what kind of Niphals: (1) direct passives ("I was seen" and "I was not known"); or (2) what grammarians call a *Niphal tolerativum* ("I let myself be seen" and "I did not let myself be known"); or (3) reflexives, as I have it ("I showed myself" and "I did not make myself known")?

6:3. Some grammarians would understand the preposition *bĕ* on *bĕʾēl šaddāy* to be a double-duty preposition: it must be supplied before *šĕmî* in the second clause even though it occurs only once in the text: "I showed myself to Abraham . . . *as* [*bĕ*] El Shadday, but [*by, bĕ*] my name LORD I did not make myself known to them." See, for example, Dahood 1974a: 393; Sarna 1991: 242; Milgrom 1990: 96. Others (e.g., Garr 1992: 386, 395) argue that a second *bĕ* should not be supplied in the second clause for it is a different type of clause: "But I, my name LORD, was not known to them." Although that sounds awkward in English, Hebrew grammar permits a double-subject construction, here, "my name" and "LORD," which is in apposition to "my name." In such a case the verb agrees with the possessive suffix on the noun, here "my" (for examples from elsewhere in the Hebrew Bible, see Garr 1992: 389).

6:3. The Septuagint renders the Hebrew Niphal *nôdaʿtî* ("I was not known/did not make myself known") as a Hiphil, *hôdaʿtî* with its *edelōsa* ("I did not make known to them"). I shall argue in the commentary below why I believe this is wrong.

6:4. "Make a covenant" (*kārat bĕrît*) occurs about eighty times in the OT. The expression used here, *hēqîm bĕrît* ("establish/confirm a covenant") is much less frequent. The former most often refers to making a new covenant, while the latter (with the Hiphil of *qûm*) usually refers to maintaining a covenant already concluded. However, in a few places (e.g., Gen. 6:18 and maybe here in Exod. 6:4) *hēqîm bĕrît* also carries the sense of establishing a new covenant.

6:4. The phrase "the land of their sojourning" is plural (*ʾereṣ mĕgurêhem*): "the land of their sojournings" (and the same goes for the phrase in Gen. 28:4, *ʾereṣ mĕgurêkā*). More than likely this is a qualitative plural that focuses on the event of sojourning. A parallel use of the plural is in Num. 15:2, "When you come into the 'land of your settlement(s)' [NIV, "home"] [*ʾereṣ môšĕbōtêkem*] . . ."

6:6. For the translation of *lākēn* as "upon my word," see Goldbaum 1964: 134.

6:6. The OT speaks of the exodus as God's bringing Israel "out" of Egypt (the Hiphil of *yāṣāʾ*) and as God's bringing Israel "up" from Egypt (the Hiphil of *ʿālâ*). See my comments on these two verbs back at 3:7–9. The first of these is more frequent when God speaks in the first person (Exod. 6:6, 7; 7:4, 5; 12:17; 16:32; 20:2; 29:46).

6:6. A common rendering of *šĕpāṭîm* ("chastisements") is something like "acts of judgment" (NIV). The word occurs but four times in the Torah. Twice it is something God has done to Egypt on behalf of Israel (Exod. 6:6; 7:4), and twice it is a divine act directed at Egypt's gods (Exod. 12:12; Num. 33:4).

6:7. Ehrlich (1985: 15–16) notes that there are forty-four uses of *hāyâ lĕ* ("be to/for") in the Hebrew Bible. In twenty-eight of these the order is verb>object>predicate noun with prefixed preposition *lĕ* (here, "I-will-be">"for/to you">"as/*lĕ*-God"). He remarks that the phrase does not "imply human or divine possession in its narrow sense. Rather, . . . it circumscribes the parameters of the relationship."

6:9. "Demoralization brought on by exhaustion" is my attempt to translate the Hebrew phrase (*miq*) *qōṣer rûaḥ*, literally, "[because of] the shortness of wind/spirit." On the one hand, some would suggest that the meaning of the phrase in Exod. 6:9 is determined by the opposite phrase in Eccles. 7:8b, "and 'patience' [*ʾerek-rûaḥ*, lit., "long of wind/spirit"] is better than pride." Thus Exod. 6:9, according to this interpretation, suggests that the people did not listen to Moses because they were impatient. See, for example, Gordis (1955: 110; 1976b: 287, 297) and B. Levine (2000: 86). I suggest that the related phrase *qĕṣar-rûaḥ* in Prov. 14:29b does mean "impatient, quick-tempered": "but a 'quick-tempered' man displays folly" (NIV). In Exod. 6:9 the proximity of the phrase to "and because of . . . their crushing labor" seems to rule out "impatience." The only other two passages where the phrase appears are Mic. 2:7b, ("Is the Spirit of the Lord shortened/angry/impatient/impotent?") and Job 21:4b, ("Why should I not be impatient?" [NIV]). See the study of Haak (1982), and note the Septuagint's *oligopsychias*, "discouragement, faint-heartedness."

Commentary

6:2 Both in 6:1 and 6:2 God seems to brush aside or ignore Moses's blunt words directed at, and critical of, God in 5:22–23. He does not upbraid Moses for so impugning God and his character, as he does, say, with Jeremiah's outbursts and diatribe against God (compare Jeremiah's word to/about God in Jer. 15:18b with God's response in 15:19–21).

Instead, all that God does is to reaffirm in Moses's hearing Yahweh's lordship. God both begins and ends his statement with "I am Lord" (vv. 3, 8). He also punctuates his words with the same phrase (v. 6). For the Lord to both commence and conclude with this assertion has a parallel in Lev. 18, a chapter devoted to family law, especially forbidden sexual unions in the family. It begins, "I am the LORD your God" (v. 2b). Then come the laws (vv. 3–30a). It concludes, "I am the LORD your God" (v. 30b). The phrase "I am LORD," or its variant "I am the LORD your God," "constitutes a self-presentation formula that adds authority to the proclamation that follows" (Weinfeld 1991: 284). Although it is common for the Lord to begin his words with such a formula, I am unaware of any place where Moses introduces his words with "I am Moses." *ʾĂnî YHWH* is appropriate. *ʾĂnî mōšeh* is not quite as appropriate.

There remains some doubt about how to translate El Shadday/Shaddai **6:3**
(*Šadday*). Thanks to the Vulgate's use of *omnipotens* for this term and the Septuagint's use of *pantokratōr* in the almost twenty instances of *Šadday* in Job, the popular rendering is "God Almighty." It is unlikely that there is any connection between the noun "Shadday" and the verb *šādad*, "destroy, devastate, lay waste." Some have connected "Shadday" with Akkadian *shadu*, "mountain" (i.e., "[God of] the Mountain"). Also, Akkadian *shadu rabbu* ("great mountain") was a way of referring to kings and gods. As such, "Shadday," ending with the diphthong *-ay*, would carry the adjectival force of a gentilic, giving the meaning "One of the mountain" or "the One residing on the mountain." That would be a great name for God, given the frequent references elsewhere to him as "Rock" (Deut. 32:18, 31, 37; 2 Sam. 22:47 = Pss. 18:46 [47]; 31:3; Isa. 51:1). One may compare "Shadday" with the postexilic prophet "Haggay" (English versions read "Haggai"). Both names double the middle consonant and end with the diphthong *-ay*. If "Shadday" means "One of the mountain," then "Haggay" would mean "One of the pilgrimage," that is, a participant, a celebrant, in a pilgrimage.

Only twice does the identification "I am El Shadday" appear in Genesis, once to Abraham (17:1) and once to Jacob (35:11). These two instances supply the background for the opening claim of Exod. 6:3, "I showed myself to Abraham, to Isaac and to Jacob as El Shadday." There is no instance of El Shadday appearing to Isaac anywhere in Genesis, and only Isaac (Gen. 28:3) and Jacob (43:14; 48:3) use the name El Shadday in dialogue.

So here is the problem. What might God mean in v. 3b when he says to Moses that he did not make himself known, meaning his name "LORD/YHWH," to the patriarchs? What is one to do with the frequent references to and uses of "LORD/YHWH" throughout the patriarchal narratives by the patriarchs themselves, and even before Gen. 12? For instance, Eve says, "With the help of the LORD/YHWH I have brought forth a man" (Gen. 4:1). In Gen. 5:29 Lamech says of his son Noah, "He will comfort us in the labor and painful toil . . . caused by the ground the LORD/YHWH has cursed." In Gen. 9:26 Noah says, "Blessed be the LORD/YHWH, the God of Shem!" Thus, as far back as antediluvian times, Eve, Lamech, and Noah know, speak, and use the name LORD/YHWH.

What about the patriarchal period? Focusing on only the Abraham narrative, I note that Abraham uses it (Gen. 14:22 is the first: "I have raised my hand to the LORD/YHWH, God Most High"; see also 15:2, 8; 22:14; 24:3, 7, 12, 42 [some of these in chap. 24 are by the servant of Abraham]). Sarah uses it (16:2, 5). The Lord himself uses it in dialogue with Abraham (18:14), and in an internal conversation with himself about Abraham (18:19). Finally, the "angel/messenger" of the LORD/YHWH uses it (to Hagar, in 16:11; to Abraham, in 22:16). And we could add to that the numerous uses of LORD/YHWH by the narrator as in the phrase "And the LORD said." The name "YHWH" occurs in Genesis 148 times, 96 of which are by the narrator. See, for example, Gen. 13:4: "Abram called on the name of the LORD."

Eve, Lamech, Noah, Abraham, Abraham's servant, Sarah, God himself, and God's angel—all use "LORD/YHWH" conversationally before Exod. 6:3. How does one then make the two pieces of data fit? Which is correct: God was known as LORD before the time of Moses (Genesis), or he was not known as LORD before the time of Moses (Exod. 6:3)?

Higher criticism has handled this conundrum quite conveniently. It suggests that in biblical Israel there were two literary/theological traditions that clashed with each other over when God first made himself known as LORD/YHWH. The older of the two is the "J" (for "J/Yahwist") tradition, which asserted that knowledge of God as LORD/YHWH goes back almost to creation and the beginning of humanity. The younger of the two, by centuries, is the "P" (for "Priestly") tradition, which affirmed, in opposition to "J," that knowledge of God as LORD/YHWH emerged only in the Mosaic era. One's immediate response to this is that it would be unexpected and strange, maybe even inexplicable, that different "camps" in ancient Israel would have disagreed with each other over such an important, fundamental issue as the revelation of God's (proper) name: YHWH.

What, then, are the alternatives to the explanation offered by the documentary hypothesis? One possibility is that put forward by G. Driver (1973: 109), one of the most learned Hebraists of the twentieth century. For Driver, the problem is that we have misunderstood the grammar of Exod. 6:3. He believes that the last part of v. 3 is an illustration of "affirmation by exclamatory negation": "Did I not (of course I did) let myself be known to them as to my name Yahweh!" To the best of my knowledge, no Exodus commentator has picked up and endorsed this suggestion.

Brichto (1998: 24–34), ever an astute maverick in biblical studies, reflects on the idea that Israelite monotheism had no need for a proper noun as the name of deity (if that is what YHWH is supposed to be) because proper names are labels by which one individual is differentiated from other members of the same group. And since deity is a class with but one member, it/he need not be differentiated from other members of that class or group by means of a distinguishing, proper name.

Brichto further suggests that when Genesis states that one of the patriarchs called on the name of the LORD/YHWH, such a phrase does not necessarily involve knowledge of that name by the suppliant, but rather may simply mean, "called on the name [of God/god whom we know as] YHWH." Furthermore, the statement in Exod. 6:3b not only applies to those who came before Moses, but also to those who come after Moses, including ourselves. "For in the sense of a name as a phenomenon of speech, an oral or auditory phenomenon, the name reflected in the written characters YHWH was never made known to anyone" (Brichto 1998: 34).

All true, but one suspects that more is at issue here than multigenerational ignorance about the pronunciation of the enigmatic tetragrammaton.

A recent suggestion is that of Moberly (1992: 36–79), who agrees with one of Brichto's observations: use of the name "LORD/YHWH" in Genesis, either by the narrator or by one of the characters, does not necessarily mean that the name "LORD/YHWH" was known before the time of Moses. To that degree, Moberly agrees with the higher critical interpretation of Exod. 6:3. Rather, he contends that what we have in Genesis is a retelling and a reshaping by later writers (who know the name YHWH) of earlier stories in which they put in the mouths of earlier characters the name of God that these earlier characters would have used, if they had lived in the time of the later storytellers.

That means that for Moberly we do not have in Genesis the actual words of these patriarchal figures, because every use of "LORD/YHWH" in Genesis is anachronistic. What we do have, according to Moberly, is characters' words when talking to/about God that are appropriate to the worldview of the narrator but inappropriate to the worldview of the characters, and this gives me some problems. If this is true, why not extend the observation to a lot of other matters in Genesis and label much of the phenomena of the narrator's or characters' speeches as anachronistic? To be fair to Moberly, however, it is only this one item (knowledge of God qua YHWH) that Exodus mentions.

I believe a more helpful direction to go is to connect what God says in v. 3 with what he says in the following verses (vv. 4–8), where the subject matter is what God is about to do for his people in Egypt, and something he has never done for anybody before this. That involves covenant (vv. 4–5), deliverance and redemption (vv. 6–7), settlement in Canaan (v. 8). A knowledge of God as LORD/YHWH will emerge from the experience of these events that would be impossible without the experience of these events, even if one were cognizant of the vocable Y-H-W-H.

Accordingly, Eslinger (1996: 196) states that to "know Yahweh" "describes a unique cognitive state borne of a particular experience derived from special intervention by Yahweh in human affairs." Seitz (1999: 157, 158) puts it this way: "The issue is not knowledge of the name per se, but how God most fully makes himself known as Yahweh. . . . This knowledge turns on the events of the exodus. . . . Abraham did not know him as he would be known in the exodus." After his detailed and complex study of the grammar of Exod. 6:3, Garr (1992: 408) renders the verse interpretively as follows: "I appeared to Abraham, Isaac, and Jacob (in limited form) as El Shaddai (who makes covenantal promises). But I was not the object of (full) covenantal knowledge to them as conveyed by my name Yahweh (who keeps covenantal promises)."

Regardless of how one tries to make the claim of Exod. 6:3 "fit" with the presence of YHWH in Genesis, all will agree that Exod. 6:3 is not pointing to some minor, relatively insignificant change of how God is known or reveals himself. For Janzen (2009: 24), Exod. 6:3 "marks an epoch-making shift from one paradigm of divine-human relations to another." He suggests that the older paradigm, the patriarchal model, evidenced here by the name El Shadday, is the "original default position." The newer paradigm, the Mosaic model, evidenced here by the introduction of Y-H-W-H, is the "customized default position." How Moses and his fellow Israelites related to and understood God is both similar to and different from how the patriarchal and matriarchal individuals related to and understood God. The apostle Paul seems to agree with this distinction when he repeatedly, especially in Romans and Galatians, summons followers of Jesus to take Abraham as their model of "how it is done" (see, e.g., Rom. 4; Gal. 3:6–29).

6:4–5 These two verses continue God's private revelation to Moses. What information Moses is to transmit to his people will be found in vv. 6–8. In these two verses God speaks of the past (v. 4), his promised covenant with the patriarchs (to be actualized in the era of Moses), and the present (v. 5), the groans of his people in Egypt. There are two mentions of covenant here, one in v. 4 and one in v. 5, but only one about groanings, as if to say, God has made this covenant with his people, groanings or no groanings. The idea of covenant flows from the sovereign, graceful mind and heart of God. It is not an idea he has hatched in order to fix and reverse the turmoil of those in Goshen, but that he will do too.

6:6–8 The message that Moses is to deliver to his people involves three emphases, really four: (1) Yahweh's lordship (vv. 6a, 8b); (2) redemption (the three divine "I wills" of v. 6); (3) adoption (the two divine "I wills" of v. 7); (4) settlement in a new home (the two divine "I wills" of v. 8).

Particularly interesting in the second emphasis is God's use of the verb "redeem" (*gā'al*) in the latter part of v. 6. For other uses of this root to refer to the divine action at the exodus, see Exod. 15:13; Pss. 74:2; 77:15 [16]; 78:35; 106:10. With God as subject, the verb also refers to the later restoration from Babylon of those in exile (Isa. 43:1; 44:23; 48:20; 52:9). The verb also is used for occasions on which God changes death to life, and hopelessness to hope (Ps. 103:4; Lam. 3:58; Hosea 13:14). The basic idea in "redeem, redemption," then, is to restore something to its original condition. In the case of oppressed Israel, he will restore the people to their earlier condition of liberty.

There is another term in Biblical Hebrew for "redeem" and it is *pādah*, but it is restricted in Exodus to persons "redeeming" persons, such as parents and adults "redeeming" their firstborn, both sons and animals (Exod. 13:13 [3x]). The basic difference between the two is that *pādah* means "to buy what was originally not one's own" (the firstborn belongs to God, and hence the parent/adult must "buy" him from God), while *gāʾal* means "to buy back what was originally one's own." Thus, in redeeming Israel the Lord is restoring the family relationship and bringing Israel back into the family fold.

The participial form of *gāʾal* (*gōʾēl*) is used for the individual called *gōʾēl haddām* ("the blood-avenger," or better, "the blood-redeemer"), a near kinsman of the murdered person who avenges the death of his relative by taking the blood of the slayer (e.g., Num. 35:9–15, 19, 21, 25, 27). Second Samuel 13 records the incident of Absalom avenging his sister's abuse and violation at the hands of their half brother Amnon. Chapter 13 nowhere calls Absalom "a blood-redeemer," but the wise woman of Tekoa, in the very next chapter, does use this term in a veiled reference to the sordid events in chap. 13 (see 2 Sam. 14:11). This reference shows that a blood-redeemer avenged not only murder, but also horrific abuse and humiliation inflicted on a relative. Could this idea provide the background for what God is doing when he, as Redeemer, redeems Israel from its oppression (see Unterman 1995)? In redeeming Israel from its oppression, he punishes those who are the perpetrators of that oppression.

Many translations gloss over an important point in their rendering of v. 7a by reading it something like "I will take you as my own people" (NIV), but the Hebrew reads, literally, "I will take you to me/myself [*lî*] as a people." The wording is similar to the ending of 19:4, "and (how) I brought you *to myself*." Before God desires to bring Israel to Canaan, he desires to bring Israel to himself. As Janzen (1997: 54–55) correctly says, "God's aim and desire are not simply to bring us into the land but to bring us into intimate relation with God." Fellowship and intimacy trump relocation.

The phrase "I will take you to myself as a people, and I will be for you as God" and the more common phrase "I will be for you as God, and you will be for me as a people" (reversing the order of the two halves of the verse) are widely recognized as covenant formulas. The language appears to derive from marriage and adoption formulas found in the Israelite and ancient Near Eastern world (see Sohn 1999). So, after v. 6 draws attention to God's "family" relationship with his people by using the verb *gāʾal*, v. 7 does so by using phraseology akin to that used in marriage and adoption contexts.

According to v. 8 the Lord has solemnized this covenant by swearing with uplifted hand. For this concept, see Abram's words in Gen. 14:22–23, "I have raised my hand to the Lord, God Most High, . . . that I will accept nothing belonging to you." Closest to Exod. 6:8 is Ezek. 20:5, "On the day I chose

Israel, I swore with uplifted hand." There is an ironic reference to Exod. 6:8 in Num. 14:30, "Not one of you will enter the land I swore with uplifted hand to make your home." In Exod. 6:8 God swears that he will bring the generation of the exodus into the land, but in Num. 14:30 he swears that he will not bring that generation into the land but only their children. One subsequent divine swearing with an uplifted hand cancels out an earlier divine swearing with an uplifted hand.

6:9 This exciting, good news about what God is about to do falls on deaf ears, not because of unbelief or sin, but because of severe, oppression-induced exhaustion. There is such a thing as a good "broken heart" (Ps. 51:17 [19]) and a numbing "broken heart." Brueggemann's (1994: 735) comment is apropos: "The text accepts the fact that the depth of despair can (at least in the short term) defeat the hope of God. In this utterance, despair prevails."

Levites and Lips

(6:10–30)

Translation

[10]And the LORD spoke to Moses, saying, [11]"Go, speak to Pharaoh, king of Egypt, that he send away Israel's sons from his turf." [12]Moses spoke directly in the presence of the LORD, "If Israel's sons did not heed me, how then will Pharaoh heed me, and I [am] uncircumcised of lips?" [13]And the LORD spoke to Moses and to Aaron, and he gave them commands regarding Israel's sons and regarding Pharaoh, king of Egypt, to bring out Israel's sons from the land of Egypt.

[14]These [are] the heads of their patriarchal houses: The sons of Reuben, Israel's firstborn—Enoch and Pallu, Hezron and Karmi. These are the clans of Reuben. [15]And the sons of Simeon—Jemuel and Jamin and Ohad, and Jachin and Zohar and Saul, son of the Canaanitess. These are the clans of Simeon. [16]And these [are] the names of the sons of Levi according to their lineage—Gershon and Qohath and Merari. And the years of the life of Levi were a hundred and thirty-seven years. [17]The sons of Gershom—Libni and Shimei according to their clans. [18]And the sons of Qohath—Amram and Izhar and Hebron and Uzziel. And the years of the life of Qohath were one hundred and thirty-three years. [19]And the sons of Merari—Mahli and Mushi. These are the clans of the Levites according to their lineage. [20]And Amram took as wife Jochebed, his aunt, and she bore him Aaron and Moses. And the years of the life of Amram were a hundred and thirty-seven years. [21]And the sons of Izhar—Qorah and Nepheg and Zichri. [22]And the sons of Uzziel—Mishael and Elzaphan and Sithri. [23]And Aaron took Elisheba, daughter of Amminadab, sister of Nahshon, to himself as wife, and she bore him Nadab and Abihu, Eleazar and Ithamar. [24]And the sons of Qorah—Assir and Elqanah and Abiasaph. These are the clans of the Qorahite. [25]And Eleazar, son of Aaron, had taken for himself from the daughters of Putiel a wife for himself, and she bore him Phinehas. These [are] the heads of the patriarchal houses of the Levites according to their clans.

[26]It was the very same Aaron and Moses to whom the LORD said, "Bring out Israel's sons from the land of Egypt with their battalions." [27]They were the ones speaking to Pharaoh, king of Egypt, to bring out Israel's sons from Egypt, the same Moses and Aaron.

[28]And it happened on the day of the LORD's speaking to Moses in the land of Egypt, [29]that the LORD spoke to Moses, saying, "I [am] the LORD. Speak to Pharaoh, king of Egypt, everything that I am speaking to you." [30]And Moses said in the presence of the LORD, "If I [am] uncircumcised of lips, how will Pharaoh heed me?"

Grammatical and Lexical Notes

6:12. "In the presence of the LORD" is *lipnê YHWH*, an expression that appears 236x in the Hebrew Bible. In many of these, but not in all, the emphasis is on direct, personal communication between man and God, speaking face to face. See Fowler's (1987) study of this phrase.

6:12. "If . . . how then . . . ?" is *hēn . . . wĕʾêk . . .* ? (also in v. 30). There are seven or eight instances in the Hebrew Bible where *hēn* (or *hinnēh*) introduces the protasis of a sentence, while *wĕʾêk* introduces an interrogative apodosis. For *hēn . . . wĕʾêk*, see Gen. 39:8–9, "Since/If [*hēn*] my master trusts me with everything . . . how then [*wĕʾêk*] could I do such a wicked thing?" Also 26:9, "Since/If [*hēn*] she is your wife, why [*wĕʾêk*] did you say, 'She is my sister'?" And 44:8, "Since/If [*hēn*] we brought back to you the silver . . . inside . . . our sacks, why then [*wĕʾêk*] would we steal silver or gold from your master's house?" For *hinnēh . . . wĕʾêk*, see 2 Kings 10:4, "If [*hinnēh*] two kings could not resist him, how [*wĕʾêk*] can we?" Also Isa. 20:6, "Since/If [*hinnēh*] this is what happened to those we relied on, . . . the king of Assyria, how then [*wĕʾêk*] can we escape?" See Labuschagne 1973: 12; Zewi 1998: 80.

6:12. The Septuagint renders "uncircumcised" in "uncircumcised [NIV, "faltering"] of lips" as *alogos*, literally, "wordless" or "without word." Tov (2001: 126) translates *alogos* freely as "lacking verbal fluency," and then remarks, "The overall meaning of the context is more influential for determining equivalents." In 6:30 the Septuagint renders "uncircumcised" (*ʿăral*) with *ischnophōnos* ("weak-voiced"), the same word it employs back in 4:20 for Moses's first mention of his lack of speaking skills.

6:14. "Their patriarchal houses" (*bêt-ʾăbōtām*) is, literally, "the houses of their fathers." Within such patriarchal houses there are "clans" (*mišpĕḥōt*; vv. 14b, 15b, 17b, 25b). The same terms appear in the census list of Num. 1. In Num. 1:4 the "head of each patriarchal house" (*rōʾš lĕbêt-ʾăbōtāyw*) is to assist Moses in the census taking, with many "clans" (*mišpĕḥōt*) constituting one patriarchal house (Num. 1:20, 22, etc.).

6:15. "Ohad" is present among the descendants of Simeon in Gen. 46:10 too, but not in Num. 26:12–14 or in 1 Chron. 4:24, suggesting that this particular clan of Simeonites later disappeared.

6:15. "Saul, son of the Canaanitess," or "Saul, son of a Canaanite woman," is translated in the Septuagint as "Saul, the one who came from the Phoenician woman" (*ho ek tēs Phoinissēs*), although Gen. 46:10 refers to him as "the son of the Canaanite woman" (*huios tēs Chananitidos*). The reading of the LXX in Gen. 46:10 is more understandable, for the Simeonites were located in the southern part of Palestine and had no contact with the northern Phoenicians. Could then "the one who came from the Phoenician woman" be an attempt by a later translator, when maybe distinctions between "Canaanite" and "Phoenician" have blurred, "who, to demonstrate his learning, has here decided to 'modernize' the text" (Lemche 1991: 59)?

6:20. "Moses and Aaron" are mentioned together, in that order, 78x in the OT. The reverse, "Aaron and Moses," in that order, appears only five times, and all are in genealogical texts (Exod. 6:20; Num. 3:1; 26:59; 1 Chron. 6:3 [5:29]; 23:13). See Milgrom 1990: 15.

6:20. For Amram's 137 years, LXX has 132 years. As Larsson (1983: 406) suggests, such an alteration allows for a descending series of ages (Isaac at 180>Jacob at 147>Levi at 137>Qohath at 133>Amram at 132>Aaron at 123>Moses at 120).

6:20. For the MT's "and she bore him Aaron and Moses," both LXX and SP have "and she bore him Aaron and Moses *and Miriam*."

6:23. The name *ʾĕlîšebaʿ* (Elisheba) is the Hebrew form of "Elizabeth." What "Elizabeth" means is debatable, but two possibilities are "My God is the One by whom to swear" or "My God is Seven."

6:25. "Phinehas" is an Egyptian name (as "Putiel" may be, even though it ends with the theophoric element *-ēl*). Phinehas means "The Dark One/The Nubian." The following line appears in an Egyptian inscription about Amenhotep II (1427–1400 BC): "His mace struck Naharin, while his bow trampled Nubia [*tʾ nhsy*]" (*COS* 2:20). The name "Phinehas" (*pînĕḥās*) shares the *n-ḥ-s* consonants with the Egyptian word for "Nubia" (*nhsy*).

6:26. Although the pronoun *hûʾ* is singular (reflected in my translation "very same") it refers to a plural predicate, "Moses and Aaron." Rendsburg (1989: 500) points out, referencing Gardiner 1952: 103, that the Egyptian third-person masculine singular pronoun *pw* is used for masculine/feminine and singular/plural.

6:26. "Battalions" is the Hebrew word *ṣābāʾ/ṣĕbāʾôt*, sometimes translated elsewhere as "host/hosts" or as "army/armies." It is the same word that often appears (in the plural form) with YHWH, "Lord of hosts/armies," a name for God made famous in Martin Luther's "A Mighty Fortress Is Our God": "Were not the right Man on our side, / The Man of God's own choosing: / Dost ask who that may be? / Christ Jesus it is He; / 'Lord Sabaoth' his name."

Commentary

I have decided to take 6:10–30 together as one unit, for it presents a beautifully constructed chiasm on the pattern ABCB′A′ (Walsh 2001: 71–73).

A Dialogue of YHWH with Moses (6:10–12)
  B Narrator's report: YHWH speaks to Moses and Aaron (6:13)
    C Genealogies related to Moses and Aaron (6:14–25)
  B′ Narrator's report: YHWH speaks to Moses and Aaron (6:26–27)
A′ Dialogue of YHWH with Moses (6:28–30)

If in 6:1 the Lord seems to ignore Moses's brash words in 5:22–23, here he **6:10–13**
seems again to ignore his people's refusal to listen, or inability to listen in 6:9, by again instructing Moses to go to Pharaoh.

Moses's response is predictable. Greenberg (1969: 136) nicely captures the thrust of Moses's response in v. 12: "If Israel, who had only to gain from my messages, and who had once believed me will not listen, how much less will Pharaoh, who has only to lose and who never believed me!" This type of talk is an illustration of an argument in the language of the discipline of logic known as *a minore ad maius* (from lesser/minor to greater/major), or in Jewish rabbinical tradition as *qal wahomer* (Jacobs 1972). Such an argument goes like this: if situation A is true, how much more is situation B true. For some other examples besides Exod. 6:12, see Deut. 31:27 ("If you have been rebellious against the Lord while I am still alive and with you, how much more will you rebel after I die!"); 2 Kings 5:13 ("If the prophet had told you to do some great thing, would you not have done it? How much more, then, when he tells you, 'Wash and be cleansed'!"); Jer. 3:1 ("'If a man divorces his wife, . . . should he return to her again? [implied answer: 'No'] . . . Would you now return to me?' declares the Lord"); Jer. 12:5 ("If you have raced with men on foot and they have worn you out, how can you compete with horses?"); Jer. 49:12 ("If those who do not deserve to drink the cup must drink it, why should you go unpunished?").

Instead of a "how much more" statement, we may occasionally find a "how much less" statement: 1 Kings 8:27 ("The heavens, even the highest heaven, cannot contain you. How much less this temple I have built!"); Job 15:15–16

("If God places no trust in his holy ones, if even the heavens are not pure in his eyes, how much less man, who is vile and corrupt!").

6:14–25 Suddenly Exod. 6 shifts from the dialogue between God and Moses, and the latter's protest about his uncircumcised lips, to a genealogy, most of which focuses on Levi and his Levitical descendants. The first thing to notice about this genealogy is that it lists only the first two children of Jacob (Reuben [v. 14], Simeon [v. 15]), and the second generation of those two families. From there on (that is, ten out of twelve verses) it is all about the third son, Levi, and his descendants through five succeeding generations. None of Jacob's other sons or their progeny appear. Who's who in vv. 16–25 looks like this (with the number representing the number of the generation):

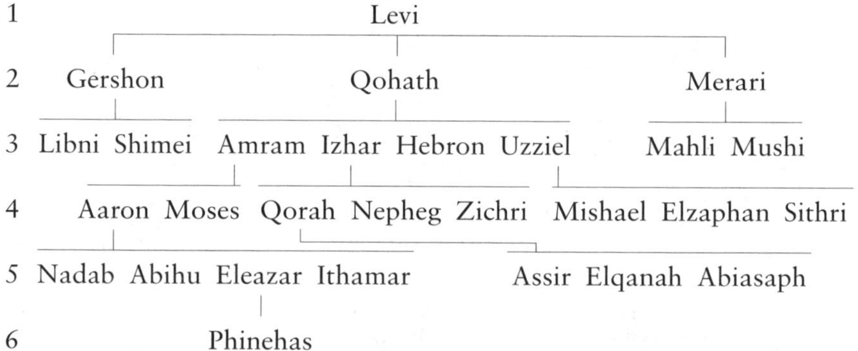

Let us begin by making some general observations about this genealogy. First, it is a six-generation Levitical genealogy, stretching from Levi to Phinehas. Both individuals are capable of violent action when they feel some wrong has to be dramatically righted. Recall what Levi, along with his brother Simeon (and they are next to each other in Exod. 6), does to the fellow who has violated their sister and the rapist's townsmen (Gen. 34:25–29), and what Phinehas does to the couple who are having sex within the sacred precincts (Num. 25:7–8, an act that gains Phinehas immortality in later Jewish literature; see Sir. 45:23; 1 Macc. 2:26; 4 Macc. 18:12).

Second, unlike most genealogies in Scripture or elsewhere, it includes the names of women (Matt. 1:1–17 is another exception to the rule): Jochebed, Elisheba, an anonymous daughter of Putiel (wife of Eleazar, Aaron's daughter-in-law, Phinehas's mother), and Miriam in v. 20 if we follow the reading of the LXX and the SP. What makes the presence of these women so unique here is that this genealogy is about who has the proper bloodlines to serve as high priest or just as priests, an office restricted by sex to males. There are no "priestesses" in the OT.

Third, it is a genealogy that places (for once) Moses in the shadow of Aaron. It does so on the one hand by the omission of any of Moses's descendants, and on the other hand by the inclusion of Aaron's wife, her pedigree, all his sons, his anonymous daughter-in-law and her pedigree, and finally his grandson Phinehas. The situation is analogous to Num. 3:1, which begins by saying, "This is the account of the family of Aaron and Moses," but the rest of the chapter lists only the descendants of Aaron. All this is understandable. For priests like Aaron, bloodlines are critical. It is a position into which one is born, as with monarchy. Nobody in the Bible is ever "called" to be a priest. With the charismatically chosen prophets, it is different, however. There is no "father-son" prophetic team in Scripture. Both Shear-Jashub (Isa. 7:3) and Maher-Shalal-Hash-Baz (Isa. 8:3) are sons of Isaiah, but neither of them is the "next Isaiah." A double portion of Hosea's spirit never falls on his sons, Jezreel (Hosea 1:4) and Lo-Ammi (Hosea 1:8), or on his daughter, Lo-Ruhamah (Hosea 1:6–7).

Fourth, this genealogy dares to point out that both Israel's supreme prophet (Moses) and high priest (Aaron) are the offspring of a marriage between Amram and his paternal aunt, Jochebed. In later biblical law, Amram's marriage to Jochebed is both forbidden (Lev. 18:12) and punishable (20:19). If Moses and Aaron were birthed after the promulgation of such laws, they both would be identified as children who used to be known as "bastards." Apparently Sinaitic law does not apply ex post facto. This marriage is in line with other "irregularities" in Genesis that are outlawed in Leviticus: (1) Abraham's marriage to his sister on his father's side (Gen. 20:2, 12 and Lev. 18:9; 20:17); (2) Jacob's simultaneous marriage to two sisters while both sisters are alive (Gen. 29:23, 28 and Lev. 18:18); (3) Judah's incestuous sex with his daughter-in-law (Gen. 38:18 and Lev. 18:15; 20:12); (4) Reuben's adultery with his father's wife/concubine while the father is still living (Gen. 35:22 and Lev. 20:10–11).

Furthermore, Exod. 6:23 tells us that Aaron does not marry a fellow Levite(ss), but instead marries Elisheba/Elizabeth. Her father is Amminadab, and her brother is Nahshon (a name meaning "snakelike" [the Hebrew word *nāḥāš*, "serpent/snake," as in Gen. 3, and *-ôn*, a characterizing affix]). Both her father and her brother are links in the line from Judah to David and to Jesus (Ruth 4:20; 1 Chron. 2:10–11; Matt. 1:4; Luke 3:32–33). Her brother, Nahshon, is the individual from the tribe of Judah who assists Moses in taking the census (Num. 1:7). That means that the Levitical priest Aaron is married to a Judahite, and that the second generation of high priests comes from mixed tribal groups, Levitical and Judahite. Thus, in the ancestry of Jesus Christ, our High Priest and King of kings, there is an interesting mixture of Levi and Judah.

Fifth, the various bits of information given about Aaron distinguish him sharply from another priest in the OT, Melchizedek (Gen. 14:18–20; Ps. 110:4). Aaron has parents, offspring, and pedigree. So at several points he is unlike Melchizedek: (1) he is not *apatōr* ("without father"); (2) he is not *amētōr* ("without mother"); and (3) he is not *agenealogētos* ("without genealogy/pedigree"). See Heb. 7:3.

Sixth, although most of this genealogy is devoted to the "sons" of Levi, most of them never appear again in Scripture. Of those who do reappear, a few are disasters and very "un-Levitical." Moses's first cousin, Qorah (or Korah), ends up being swallowed by the ground for orchestrating a revolt against Moses (Num. 16). Two of Aaron's own sons, Nadab and Abihu, die for offering "unauthorized fire" before the Lord, and their corpses are disposed of by their Levitical cousins Mishael and Elzaphan (Lev. 10:1–7). (The deceaseds' two brothers, Eleazar and Ithamar, have been recently consecrated as priests and dare not become impure from contact with a corpse.) The one shining light seems to be Phinehas. And yet, in spite of all these Levites who fail to honor their position, the work of God and the plan of God move inexorably forward.

Finally, this genealogy provides generational information that demonstrates the fulfillment of God's promise to Abram in Gen. 15:16: "In the *fourth generation* your descendants will come back here." The first generation of Israelites subject to enslavement in Egypt is represented by Levi's children (Gershon, Qohath, and Merari). Moses's father, Amram, and others represent the second generation. The third generation is that of Moses, Aaron, and their cousins who do not enter Canaan. Aaron's son, Eleazar, who does enter Canaan and serves alongside Joshua, represents the fourth generation.

At least once "the fourth generation" designates the length of time God's punishment of sin and the consequences for sin persevere ("punishing the children for the sin of the fathers to the third and fourth generation of those who hate me," Exod. 20:5b = Deut. 5:9b). But at least twice in Scripture "the fourth generation" carries redemptive significance, once in the return to Canaan from Egypt (Gen. 15:16), and once in the return to Canaan from Babylon ("All nations will serve him [Nebuchadnezzar] [= generation 1] and his son [= generation 2] and his grandson [= generation 3] until the time for his land comes; then many nations and great kings will subjugate him [= generation 4]," Jer. 27:7).

6:26–30 These last five verses repeat much of 6:10–13. There are two changes, however. First, in v. 12 Moses speaks of the difficulty of his mission because of Pharaoh's obstinacy, then shifts to his own lack of eloquence. In v. 30 he reverses those two, speaking first of his own lack of oratorical skills, then moving to Pharaoh's refusal to listen. That is to say, in v. 12 he tries to convince God that Moses himself is the real problem, but in v. 30 he tries to convince God that Pharaoh is the real problem.

The other difference is that after the genealogy, but not before it, God speaks in v. 26 of Moses's bringing the Israelites out of Egypt "with their battalions." What does that phrase add? Tigay (2004a: 116) has nicely caught the thrust of the additional phrase: "The Israelites would not leave Egypt as fleeing slaves but as an army marching to the promised land in military formation."

An Octogenarian God Who Is Not God

(7:1–7)

Translation

[1]And the LORD said to Moses, "See, I have made you god to Pharaoh, and Aaron your brother will be your prophet. [2]You (it is who) will speak everything with which I have charged you, and Aaron your brother will speak to Pharaoh, and he will send away Israel's sons from his turf. [3]I, I shall toughen the heart of Pharaoh, that I may multiply my signs and my portents in the land of Egypt. [4]But Pharaoh will not heed (either of) you. I shall set my hand against Egypt, and I shall bring out my battalions, my people, Israel's sons, from the land of Egypt with mighty acts of authority, [5]that the Egyptians might know that I [am] LORD when I stretch out my hand over Egypt and bring out Israel's sons from their midst." [6]And Moses did, and Aaron, just as the LORD had charged them. They did it. [7]Moses was eighty years old and Aaron eighty-three years old when they spoke to Pharaoh.

Grammatical and Lexical Notes

7:1. "See" (*rĕʾēh*) may be used before appointments, as here (Gen. 41:41, "*See*, I put you in charge of the whole land of Egypt"; Exod. 31:2, "*See*, I have chosen Bezalel son of Uri"; Jer. 1:10, "*See*, today I appoint you over nations and kingdoms"). It may also appear before the announcement of a gift (Deut. 1:8, "*See*, I have given you this land"; Deut. 1:21, "*See*, the LORD your God has given you the land"; Josh. 6:2, "*See*, I have delivered Jericho into your hands").

7:1. There is no need to add "like" before "God" as does the NIV ("I have made you *like* God to Pharaoh"). There is no preposition attached to "god," such as one finds in Gen. 3:5, "You shall be like God [*kēʾlōhîm*]." It is just *ʾĕlōhîm*.

7:1. The Septuagint's and Vulgate's rendering of "I have made you god to Pharaoh" is almost the same as the Hebrew. We have seen other places where especially the Septuagint "softens" the Hebrew (see my grammatical comment at 4:24). Not so here. *Targum Onqelos*, however, renders the verse, "Behold, I set you as Rab [Teacher] to Pharaoh, and Aaron your brother shall be your Meturgeman [Interpreter]." Similarly, *Targum Neofiti* has, "Behold, I have set you as lord and prince for Pharaoh, and Aaron your brother shall be your Meturgeman." Josephus (*Ant.* 3.7.7 §180) refers to Moses as a "divine man" (*theios anēr*).

7:1. There continues some debate about the meaning of the word *nābîʾ* ("prophet"). Albright (1957: 303) has led the way in reading the word as a passive ("one who is called") by appealing to Akkadian *nabu* ("to call") and *nabitu* ("one who is called"). Fleming (1993) has more recently argued for an active meaning ("one who invokes God") by observing the active, as well as passive, uses of Akkadian *nabu* and *nabitu* ("one who invokes the gods").

7:2. The parenthetical addition in "you (it is who) will speak" is to bring out the presence of the independent pronoun "you" before the verb, otherwise unnecessary because the subject is already contained in the verb *tĕdabbēr*. The same goes for v. 3, *waʾănî ʾaqšeh* ("I, I shall toughen"). In 4:16, a verse very similar to 7:2 and one that also puts Moses and Aaron side by side, we find the same use of the independent pronoun: *hûʾ yihyeh-lĕkā lĕpeh wĕʾattâ tihyeh-lô lēʾlōhîm* ("he, he will be to you as a mouth, but you, you will be to him as God").

7:3. The verb used here for "toughening" Pharaoh's heart is *qāšâ* (Hiphil). (The verb for heart-toughening back in 4:21 was *ḥāzaq* [Hiphil].) Outside of Exodus, *q-š-h* is used with "heart" in Ezek. 3:7 AT, "For the whole house of Israel is hardened and *obstinate* [*qĕšê-lēb*]." The root is used with "face(s)" in Ezek. 2:4a, "The people to whom I am sending you are *obstinate* [*qĕšê pānîm*] and stubborn." The root is also used with "neck" (*qĕšēh-ʿōrep*) in the familiar "stiff-necked" (Exod. 32:9; 33:3, 5; 34:9; Deut. 9:6, 13; 31:27). A stiff heart! A stiff face! A stiff neck!

7:4. The "you" is a plural "you" (*ʾălēkem*), hence my "(either of) you."

7:4. A variant of *nātan yād bĕ* ("set my hand against") is *šālaḥ yād bĕ* (Exod. 22:8 [7]; 1 Sam. 24:10 [11]; 26:11; Ps. 55:20 [21], all with a human subject).

7:5. Exodus refers to God's "stretch out (my) hand" both by *nāṭâ yād* (here in 7:5) and *šālaḥ yād* (3:20; 9:15; 24:11). The two phrases occur frequently throughout the Bible. Regardless of whether it is *nāṭâ yād* or *šālaḥ yād*, one does not want to be on the receiving end whenever God stretches out his hand, especially when the phrase is followed by a preposition like *ʿal* or *ʾel* ("against, to[ward])"!

7:6. Note the repetition of "did" in "And Moses *did* [*wayyaʿaś*] . . . they *did it* [*kēn ʿāśû*]." A similar repetition occurs in the last verse of Num. 1 (v. 54 AT): "The Israelites *did* [*wayyaʿăśû*] everything just as the Lord commanded Moses. They *did it* [*kēn ʿāśû*]." The repetition of the beginning of the sentence at the end of the sentence indicates the conclusion of the account. For the same reiteration in an Exodus verse elsewhere, see 12:28; 39:32, 43.

Commentary

7:1 It is unusual for any mortal in the Bible to be called an *ʾĕlōhîm*, especially if we translate the word as "G/god." Earlier (4:16) God has spoken of Moses as being an *ʾĕlōhîm* to his brother Aaron. In the earlier reference there is no indication that Moses ever says to Aaron, "Big brother, don't forget who I am. I am an Elohim to you." The (parenthetical) verse in Num. 12:3 suggests, to the contrary, that Moses "was a very humble man, more humble than anyone else on the face of the earth." Designated twice by God as an *ʾĕlōhîm*, and yet the quintessential model of humility and modesty! What a combination! Recall God's later word to Moses about wiping out Israel because of their idolatry and apostasy, starting over from scratch, climaxed by, "Then I will make you into a great nation" (Exod. 32:10b). What an offer! Moses has the opportunity of being not only an *ʾĕlōhîm* but also an *abrāhām*. That is authority and privilege at two levels, divinity and patriarchy. But Moses rejects the offer and instead goes with the ministry of intercession for the idolaters. In Exod. 34:29 Moses is completely unaware of the brilliant glow on his face. He never fancies himself to be "Mr. Incandescent."

In the account that follows 7:1, there is no indication that being an *ʾĕlōhîm* will give Moses a "leg up" on Pharaoh, that Pharaoh, upon seeing such a supernal, charismatic figure, will genuflect before him and forthrightly submit to any of his directives. If Moses is an *ʾĕlōhîm*, nobody has told Pharaoh.

John 10:22–39 records an instance in which much tension flows between Jesus and his opponents over Jesus's calling himself God. To buttress his case, Jesus quotes Ps. 82:6, "Is it not written in your Law, 'I have said you are gods'?" Then he goes on to ask his detractors rhetorically, "If he called them 'gods,' . . . what about the one whom the Father set apart as his very own and sent into the world?" (John 10:35–36). "God" to designate Moses is the closest parallel in that First Testament for "God" applied to Jesus in the NT (Exod. 4:16; 7:1). Elsewhere in John, Jesus is emphatically linked with Moses (as in John 1:17), thus making the Moses/god and Jesus/God connection even more suggestive.

In this verse, two individuals are given expanded roles. Moses, an *ʾādām*, becomes an *ʾĕlōhîm*. Aaron, an eventual *kōhēn* ("priest"), becomes a *nābîʾ* ("prophet"), which is the same as "he [Aaron] will be to you [Moses] as a mouth" in 4:16. So a prophet is somebody who is a mouth for somebody else. Never again after 7:1 will either of these gentlemen be so styled. Subsequent chapters in Exodus will reveal which of the two does a better job with their new titles: Moses as an *ʾĕlōhîm*, or Aaron as a *nābîʾ*? Throughout the plagues, Aaron is speechless. He goes in tandem with Moses to Pharaoh (as in 7:10), but all the recorded speech is Moses's. The emphasis is on things Aaron does (stretching out his hand, as in 8:6 [2]), not on any words he speaks.

The emphasis on Moses's "saying [*d-b-r*] everything I command [*ṣāwâ*] you" **7:2**
highlights two verbs ("say/speak, command") that occur together elsewhere only in Deut. 18:18 ("I will raise up for them a prophet. . . . I will put my words in his mouth, and he will *tell* them everything I *command* him") and in Jer. 1:7 ("Do not say, 'I am only a child.' You must go to everyone I send you to and *say* whatever I *command* you"). The parallels in vocabulary suggest that, to a certain degree at least, Jeremiah is a second Moses. As a mediator of the "old" covenant, the first prophet anticipates another prophet who, alone among OT prophets, will articulate a "new" covenant.

After I have discussed all the plagues, I will have a separate treatment of Pha- **7:3**
raoh's hardened heart and all the theological issues that raises. Suffice it to say here, there may be a connection between the references to Pharaoh's hardened heart and the one use of "hardness of heart" language in Mark. After a Sabbath healing, Jesus is quite aware that he is in trouble with the Pharisees for violating such a taboo. As to those who are more concerned with traditions than with meeting human need, Jesus "looked around at them in anger and, deeply distressed at their *stubborn/hardened* hearts, said . . ." (Mark 3:5). Now we want to notice that the Greek words for "Pharaoh" and "Pharisees" are close to each other (*Pharao*, *Pharisaios*). Pharaoh was the prototypical enemy

and nemesis of God's people and the incarnation of ungodliness, while the Markan Pharisees thought of themselves as the spiritual guardians, the sanctified ones, of the nation. Yet, as Marcus (2000: 253) has observed, Pharaoh and Pharisees played a similar role in the respective testaments: Pharaoh's hardness of heart ultimately leads to the revelation of God's glory. The Pharisees' hardness of heart has a similar salvific effect, for their plotting Jesus's death leads to Jesus's death, an occasion on which God's glory bursts forth and his redemptive program kicks into high gear.

7:4 Even though the Lord has made Moses "god" to Pharaoh (v. 1), Pharaoh will not listen to him. If Moses cannot understand why Pharaoh will not listen to an *'ĕlōhîm*, let him ask Elohim, who has had, and will have, copious experiences of his people's not listening to him.

What the angel tells Abraham not to do to Isaac (Gen. 22:12, "Do not lay a hand on the boy"), and what the man refuses to do to David's son Absalom (2 Sam. 18:12, "I would not lift my hand against the king's son"), the Lord will do to Egypt: "I shall set my hand against/lay my hand on Egypt." This is the exact phrase the NT uses about Jesus: "And the chief priests . . . sought to lay hands on him" (Luke 20:19 KJV) or "they laid hands on him" (NIV, "seized him"; Mark 14:46); "Every day I was with you in the temple courts, and you did not lay a hand on me" (Luke 22:53). Of and to his own followers, Jesus says, "They will lay hands on you and persecute you" (Luke 21:12). There are numerous scenes in Scripture about somebody laying hands on another, but not all have the same meaning. The OT phrase "to lay hand(s) on" may denote hostile action, often ending in death (1 Kings 20:6; Acts 4:3). It also carries the nuance of judgment (Isa. 5:25; 11:14–15; 25:11). (My late father justified an occasional spanking of his sons by claiming that the laying on of hands was scriptural!) Pity the poor person or nation on whom God lays his hand. It will not be a pretty picture.

7:5 In chap. 6 the Lord uses the phrase "I am LORD" to the Israelites five times (6:2, 6, 7, 8, 29). Beginning with chap. 7, the Lord uses the same phrase to the Egyptians also five times (7:5, 17; 8:22 [18]; 14:4, 18). It is as if "God wished to be known [as Lord] as much by Egypt as by Israel" (Fokkelman 1987: 64).

For references elsewhere to God's "mighty hand and outstretched arm" as a symbol of deliverance, see Deut. 4:34; 5:15; 7:19; 11:2; 26:8. It is not unheard of in Egyptian literature to find references to the "arm" of the Pharaoh. Rameses II is called "The Strong-Armed." Pharaoh Apries (Hophra) took on the titulary name "Possessed of a Muscular Arm." And his father, Psammeticus II, gave himself the epithet "Mighty-Armed" (references in Lundbom 2004a: 102).

7:6–7 For other places where information is supplied about someone's age at the time of the event(s) by means of a circumstantial clause, see Gen. 16:16 ("Abram [was] eighty-six years old when Hagar bore him Ishmael"); Gen. 17:24–25

("Abraham [was] ninety-nine years old when he was circumcised, and his son Ishmael was thirteen"); Gen. 25:26b ("Isaac [was] sixty years old when Rebekah gave birth to them").

There is a bit of a puzzle with the chronology here. In 7:7 Moses is eighty and Aaron is eighty-three. Aaron dies forty years later at the age of 123 (Num. 33:39), meaning that Moses is 120 at his older brother's death. Yet at his own death Moses is still 120 (Deut. 34:7). That must mean that everything from Num. 33 onward in the Torah (through the end of Deuteronomy) took place during that last year of his life.

Taming and Transforming the Tannin

(7:8–13)

Translation

[8]And the Lord spoke to Moses and to Aaron, [9]"Should Pharaoh say to (both of) you, 'Provide a portent for yourselves,' you shall say to Aaron, 'Take your staff and hurl it before Pharaoh.' It will become a serpent." [10]So Moses came, and Aaron, to Pharaoh, and then they did just as the Lord had charged. Aaron hurled his staff before Pharaoh, and his servants, and it became a serpent. [11]And Pharaoh in turn summoned the sages and sorcerers, and the Egyptian magicians too did the same by their magical arts. [12]Each one hurled his staff, and they became serpents. But Aaron's staff swallowed their staffs. [13]Still Pharaoh's heart remained tough, and he did not heed them, just as the Lord had said.

Grammatical and Lexical Notes

7:9. The Hebrew word for "serpent" (and in vv. 10, 12 [plural]) is not *nāḥāš* as in 4:3–4 (Moses throws his staff on the ground and it becomes a *nāḥāš*), but *tannîn*. I shall have more to say about this word in the commentary section. Suffice it to say now, *tannîn*, in singular or plural form, appears fourteen or fifteen times in the Hebrew Bible. In all but one of these the Septuagint translates *drakōn* (compare our English word "dragon"). The one exception is Gen. 1:21, "God created the great sea creatures (*hattannînim haggĕdōlîm*)." There LXX uses *kētos* ("whale"). Similarly, the Vulgate translates with the Latin *draco* in most of these passages. The Vulgate follows LXX in Gen. 1:21, however, by using *cetus* ("whale"). Interestingly, the Vulgate uses *coluber* ("snake") for Aaron's rod that becomes a serpent in vv. 9 and 10, but uses *draco* in v. 12 for the Egyptian staffs that become serpents. The Vulgate also uses *draco* for the Lord's later reference to this incident in 7:15, and the Hebrew word there is *nāḥāš*. The two Hebrew words for "serpent/snake" occur side by side in Isa. 27:1: "In that day, the Lord will punish with his sword . . . Leviathan the gliding 'serpent' [*nāḥāš*], Leviathan the coiling 'serpent' [*nāḥāš*]; he will slay the 'monster' [*tannîn*] of the sea." Thus we have seen that NIV translates *tannîn* three ways: (1) "creatures of the sea" (Gen. 1:21); (2) "snake" (Exod. 7:9, 10, 12); (3) "monster" (Isa. 27:1). The word *tnn* has appeared in a Ugaritic text (*ʿnt* III: 34f.), part of which lists the enemies of Baal: "How many foes rise up against Baal, enemies / against the rider on the clouds? Verily I have smitten / Yam beloved of El, made an end of the mighty god Nahar. / Verily I have muzzled the *tannin*, muzzled him" (trans. H. L Ginsberg, *ANET* 137).

7:10. "And then they did" (*wayyaʿăśû*) obviously follows "So Moses came" (*wayyābōʾ*). Moses and Aaron first had to come before Pharaoh, and then do what the Lord told them to do. Compare Gen. 4:1, "And she [Eve] conceived [*wattahar*], and then gave birth to [*wattēled*] Cain." On the use of the imperfect plus *wāw* consecutive in a sequence to describe a situation subsequent to a previous action, see Arnold and Choi 2003: 84–85.

7:11. I owe the rendering of *gam* (often translated "also") as "in turn" to Labuschagne 1966: 197.

7:11. More than likely *ḥarṭōm* ("magician") is of Egyptian origin and can be connected with the Egyptian title *hry-hb* or *hry-tp*, a magician-priest or priest-magician (see Redford 1970: 49, 203–4). In an earlier study, Lambdin (1953: 150–51) expresses his misgivings about this on two linguistic levels: (1) an Egyptian *t* (the *t* in *hry-tp*) should appear in Hebrew as a *tāw* (*t*) and not as a *ṭêt* (*ṭ*), which is what we have in *ḥarṭōm*; (2) it is strange that Egyptian *p* (in *hry-tp*) should appear in Hebrew as "m"/*mêm* (*hry-tp* = *ḥarṭōm*). The Hebrew word appears in only two books of the Bible, and always in the plural (Gen. 41:8, 24; Exod. 7:11, 22; 8:7, 18, 19 [3, 14, 15]; 9:11). In the Aramaic portion of Daniel the word appears in the singular in Dan. 2:10, 27, and in the plural in 4:7 [4] and 5:11.

7:11. The phrase *hēm ḥarṭummê miṣrayim* ("the Egyptian magicians *too*") illustrates a pronoun followed by a noun in apposition ("they, the magicians of Egypt") as a way of drawing emphasis to the subject of the verb (see Waltke and O'Connor 1990: 232–33).

7:12. The verb for "remained tough" is the same as the one the Lord uses of Pharaoh's heart back in 4:21 (*ḥāzaq*). The difference is that 4:21 uses the Hiphil causative ("I will toughen"), while here the form is that of a Qal stative verb ("remained [in a state of] tough[ness]"), without designating either the Lord or Pharaoh as the source or cause of the toughness.

Commentary

7:8 Some commentators believe that Exod. 7:8–13 is actually the first of the plagues rather than simply a prelude or introduction to the plagues. The unit certainly shares some features with (some of) the plagues: God tells Moses to do something with a staff through his "second," Aaron, and Aaron does it. Egyptian magicians are involved, replicate the act, leaving Pharaoh unimpressed and unmoved.

One key ingredient is missing, however. Unlike in the plagues, beginning with 7:14, there is no damage or injury to any person or any animal, or to anybody's crops or fields or drinking water. Nobody's life is threatened. It is more of a contest than a plague.

The unit surely shares parallels/contrasts with the scene back in 4:1–5. (1) In each, Moses or Aaron throws a staff to the ground, and the staff becomes a snake (*nāḥāš*/*tannîn*). (2) Moses's turning a staff into a snake is called a "sign" (*ʾōt*, 4:8); Aaron's turning a staff into a snake is called a "portent, wonder, marvel, miracle" (*môpēt*, 7:9). (3) The sign of transformation in 4:1–5 is to persuade the Israelite people to believe (4:5); the miracle of transformation in 7:8–13 is to be performed before Pharaoh, should Pharaoh request it, but without any specifically stated purpose or desired result ever stated.

7:9–10 It continues to remain a mystery how a staff could suddenly become a snake/serpent. Kitchen (2003: 249) speaks for many when he says, "If charmed and deftly pressured at its neck muscles, the Egyptian cobra can be rendered immobile (cataleptic), becoming a 'rod'—and, of course, released." If that explanation is correct, then it qualifies Aaron as an excellent snake handler, and so to his résumé of priest and prophet is now added "snake handler." It would also make it easy to explain how in v. 11 Egyptian artisans can do the same, given the specialization of some of them in "serpentineology."

Aaron's staff becomes a *tannîn*. As we saw in my grammatical note at 7:9, the NIV renders this word "snake" in Exod. 7, but as "sea creature" in Gen. 1 and "monster" in Isa. 27:1. One point of interpretation is whether *tannîn* in Exod. 7 is a synonym for *nāḥāš*, or whether we need to use a stronger word in English like "reptilian monster, crocodile." In favor of the synonym reading is the word of the Lord to Moses during the blood plague in 7:15, "And take in your hand the staff that was changed into a snake" (*nāḥāš*, not *tannîn*). Also, in two passages it is used in parallel with a Hebrew word meaning "cobra": (1) Deut. 32:33, "Their wine is the venom of serpents [*tannîn*]; the deadly poison of cobras [*peten*]"; (2) Ps. 91:13, "You will tread upon the lion and the cobra [*peten*]; you will trample the great lion and the serpent [*tannîn*]."

In other passages, however, it assumes a more monster-like meaning. Thus, in Ezek. 29:3 the Lord speaks against the pharaoh of Egypt with these words, "I am against you, Pharaoh king of Egypt, you great monster [*tannîn*] lying among your streams [a crocodile?]." Again to Pharaoh in Ezek. 32:2 the Lord says, "You are like a lion among the nations; you are like a monster [*tannîn*] in the seas." Similarly Jer. 51:34 has the exiles in Babylon say, "Nebuchadnezzar king of Babylon has devoured us; . . . like a serpent/monster [*tannîn*] he has swallowed us," with both Jer. 51:34 and Exod. 7:12 using the same verb for the "swallowing" (*bālaʿ*) actions of a *tannîn*. Finally, in three other passages (Ps. 74:13; Isa. 27:1; 51:9) the *tannîn* is an enemy of God, one doomed to destruction at the hands of the Almighty, and for these three NIV appropriately uses "monster." So, is Exod. 7:8–13 about snakes or crocodiles, mundane reptiles or reptilian monsters? It is safe to say that a meaning a word carries in one context is not necessarily the meaning it must have every other time it occurs. Hence, I see no problem with rendering "serpent" in Exod. 7 and "monster" most times elsewhere. For additional studies on this word, see Kiessling 1970; Wakeman 1973: 68–79; Oswalt 1977; P. Guillaume 2004.

7:11–12 On this occasion part of Pharaoh's retinue includes his sages, or wise men (*ḥăkāmîm*), a term familiar to us from Gen. 41:8: "In the morning his [Pharaoh's] mind was troubled, so he sent for all the magicians and *wise men* of Egypt." B. Levine (1981: 199; 2000: 252) suggests rendering the Hebrew word something like "skilled diviner(s)." He does so by appealing to the ninth- or eighth-century-BC Aramaic inscription involving the Balaam of the book of Numbers, from Deir ʿAlla on the east side of the Jordan River. In lines 29–31 of that inscription, Balaam addresses the enemies of Shagar-and-Ishtar with these words: "(29) Heed the admonition, adversaries of Sha[gar-and-Ishtar], (30) [*ḥ*]*km*/skilled diviner, (31) To skilled diviners [*lḥkmn*] one shall take you." V. Sasson (1986: 302), however, objects to reading the term as "ones skilled in divination." He suggests that "Pharaoh, in his panic, . . . assembled all persons whom he thought could help counter the machinations of the Israelites. Among these were the *ḥkmym* who may well have been learned scribes who had nothing to do with magic or its practice. As in Gen. 41:8, *ḥkmym* seems to be a blanket term for professional men of learning, to be distinguished from magicians (*ḥrṭmym*)."

The Bible never speaks approvingly of all wisdom and wise men in whatever shape or form. Even Proverbs suggests that without the fear of the Lord, there is no real wisdom. The fear of the Lord is inherently and self-evidently a religious virtue. That is not the case with wisdom. In the Bible, wisdom often is the precursor to much damage and destruction. Think of the "wise" counsel Jonadab gives to Amnon about how to bed Tamar (2 Sam. 13:3–5), or Hushai's deceitful (but looking oh so wise) counsel to Absalom (2 Sam. 17:5–13), or David's "wise" counsel to Solomon from his deathbed (1 Kings 2:5–9), to say nothing of the "clever" serpent of Gen. 3. If there is a wisdom from above that is delightful (James 3:17), there is a wisdom from below that may be demonic. If the wise men of Matt. 2 illustrate the first, then maybe the wise men of Exod. 7 illustrate the second.

The other part of his retinue are individuals called "sorcerers" (*mĕkaššĕpîm*). The root *k-š-p* appears in the Bible in three forms; (1) the noun *kešep*, "sorcery," only in the plural, *kĕšāpîm* (2 Kings 9:22; Isa. 47:9, 12; Mic. 5:12; Nah. 3:4); (2) the verb *kiššēp*, "practice sorcery" (2 Chron. 33:6), and in participial form in Exod. 7:11; 22:18 [17]; Dan. 2:2; Mal. 3:5; (3) the noun *kaššāp*, "sorcerer" (Jer. 27:9).

Magic in the Bible takes two forms: divination and sorcery. The difference between the two, as Milgrom (1990: 471) has argued, is that divination is the attempt, through the observation of omens, to predict the future. Sorcery, by contrast, is the attempt to alter the future, usually by recourse to some form of black magic, and hence is the more unacceptable and demonic of the two forms of magic. The Akkadian cognates of the Hebrew root, *kashapu*, "bewitch, cast an evil spell," and *kashshapu*, "sorcerer," reinforce this dark side of magic in the name of religion. Although the OT bans the practice of sorcery (Deut. 18:10) and threatens its practitioners with death (Exod. 22:18 [17]), Queen Jezebel still introduces it in Israel (2 Kings 9:22), and King Manasseh sanctions its practice in Judah (2 Chron. 33:6).

We are not told how the magicians are able to do the same with their staffs. It is like asking, "How could those whom Jesus said he never knew drive out demons and perform many miracles?" (Matt. 7:22). How, in the end times, can "false Christs and false prophets . . . perform great signs and miracles" (Matt. 24:24)? From where does Simon the sorcerer get his ability to do what provokes awe and amazement (Acts 8)? We do know that these Egyptian magicians use their "magical arts/spells." By contrast, Aaron says nothing, does nothing except throw his staff on the ground.

Although the text speaks of Aaron's staff swallowing the other staffs, I assume that this means staff(s) changed into snake(s). Staffs/rods do not swallow staffs/rods. There are a number of other "swallowing" (*bālaʿ*) scenes in the Bible, none of them pretty. Think of the sea's *swallowing* the Egyptians (Exod. 15:12), or the ground's *swallowing* Korah and the other malcontents (Num. 16:30, 32), or the fish's *swallowing* Jonah (Jon. 1:17). The apostle Paul promises us a day when victory will *swallow* up death (1 Cor. 15:54).

7:13 None of this impresses Pharaoh. Why should it? If a work of God can be imitated and reproduced by others (minus the loss of a few rods), then why should one come to faith? It is unlikely that anybody whose mind-set is "Anything you can do, I can do better" is on the verge of submission and capitulation.

Plague 1: Water into Blood

(7:14–25)

Translation

14 And the LORD said to Moses, "Pharaoh's heart is heavy. He refuses to send the people away. 15 Go to Pharaoh in the morning as he is going out toward the water. Position yourself to meet him by the bank of the Nile, and the staff, which was changed into a snake, you shall take in your hand. 16 And say to him, 'The LORD, the God of the Hebrews, has sent me to you to say, "Send away my people that they serve me out in the steppe," but up to now you have not heeded. 17 Thus says the LORD, "This is how you will know that I [am] the LORD." See, I am about to strike with the staff which is my hand the waters in the Nile, and they will be changed into blood. 18 And the fish in the Nile shall die, and the river will stink, and the Egyptians will find it impossible to drink the water from the Nile.'" 19 And the LORD said to Moses, "Speak to Aaron, 'Take your staff and stretch out your hand over the waters of Egypt, over their rivers, over their Nile-branches, over their marsh ponds, indeed over their every last body of water, that they may become blood.' There will be blood throughout the entire land of Egypt, even among the timber and the stones."

20 Moses and Aaron did so just as the LORD had charged. He raised his staff and struck the water in the Nile right before Pharaoh, and right before his courtiers, and all the water in the Nile was changed into blood. 21 The fish in the Nile died. The river stank. And the Egyptians could not drink water from the Nile. There was blood throughout all the land of Egypt. 22 The magicians of Egypt did the same with their magical arts. So Pharaoh's heart remained tough, and he did not heed them as the LORD had said. 23 Pharaoh turned and went into his palace-house, and he did not take even this to heart. 24 All the Egyptians had to dig around the Nile for water to drink because they could not drink the waters of the Nile.

25 Seven days passed after the Lord's striking the Nile.

Grammatical and Lexical Notes

7:15. "As he is going out to . . ." (*hinnēh yōṣēʾ*) shows the use of the participle to refer to a circumstance accompanying a future event (Waltke and O'Connor 1990: 627).

7:15. "*Position yourself* to meet him *by*" is *nāṣab . . . ʿal*. This phrase may mean "stand beside" or "stand over," with the latter of these suggesting a position of authority. For example, the reference in 1 Sam. 19:20 to Samuel "standing over the prophets" (NIV, "Samuel standing there as their leader") suggests such a nuance. Again, the phrase "foreman of his harvesters" (NIV) in Ruth 2:5–6 is, "he who is standing over the harvesters." In Jacob's famous dream at Bethel, is the Lord "standing over" the stairway, or is he "standing beside" Jacob (Gen. 28:13)? In Exod. 17:9 Moses "stood on top of" (*niṣṣāb ʿal*) the hill while Joshua and his troops engaged the Amalekites in battle.

7:15. The most frequent meaning of *hāppak lĕ* (especially in the Niphal) is "be changed." Something is transformed into something else: a staff into a snake (Exod. 7:15), water into blood (7:17, 20), raw flesh into white skin (Lev. 13:16), sorrow into joy (Esther 9:22), sling stones into chaff (Job 41:28 [20]), a rock into a pool and a hard rock into springs of water (Ps. 114:8), streams into pitch and dust into sulfur (Isa. 34:9), a choice vine into a wild vine (Jer. 2:21), dancing into mourning (Lam. 5:15), sun into darkness (Joel 2:31 [3:4]).

7:16. "Up to now" (*ʿad-kōh*) at the end of the Hebrew sentence is present again with this nuance at the start of 1 Kings 18:45, *wayĕhi ʿad-kōh wĕʿad-kōh*, "*Meanwhile*, the sky grew black with clouds, the wind rose." In the 1 Kings verse the phrase refers to the passage of time during which Elijah's order to his servant for Ahab is being fulfilled.

7:17. For *bĕzōʾt* meaning "This is how" or "by this," see Gen. 34:15 and 22, "*This is how* [NIV, "on one condition only"] we will give our consent to you"; Gen. 42:15, Joseph to his brothers, "And *this is how* you will be tested"; Lev. 16:3, "*This is how* Aaron is to enter the sanctuary area." The closest parallel to Exod. 7:17 ("*This is how you will know* I am the Lord") is Num. 16:28 ("*This is how you will know* that the Lord has sent me to do all these things, and that it was not my idea").

7:18. The verb *lāʾâ* ("find it impossible, not be able") is a rare word in Biblical Hebrew. See Gen. 19:11, "Then they struck the men . . . with blindness so that they *could not* find the door." It may be cognate with Akkadian *laʾu*, "be weak." Dahood (1979) has argued for the presence of this verb in Judg. 1:19, "Judah took possession of the hill country, but was 'not able' to drive the people from the place because they had iron chariots." The Hebrew for "was not able to drive out" (*lōʾ lĕhōrîš*) looks strange. Both LXX and Vulgate add a verb after *lōʾ* and before *lĕhōrîš* that would be the equivalent of Hebrew *y-k-l*, "be able," which is what one finds in the parallel verse, Josh. 15:63. Dahood has suggested that *lʾ* is a defective spelling for *lāʾâ*, and hence the insertion of another verb for sense is unnecessary.

7:19. "Nile-branches" reflects the use of the plural of the Hebrew word for "Nile" used here (*yĕʾōrêhem*). For other uses of "Nile" (*yĕʾōr*, the Hebrew form of Egyptian *ʾrw*, "great river") in the plural, see Ps. 78:44 [NIV, "rivers"]; Isa. 7:18 [NIV, "streams"]; Ezek. 29:3 [NIV, "streams"]. The Egyptians called every branch or tributary of the Nile in the delta region a "Nile."

7:19. "Their marsh ponds" is *ʾagmêhem*. The Akkadian cognate of the Hebrew word *ʾăgam*/*ʾăgammîm* is *agammu*, "swamp, marsh," and might be an Akkadian loanword in Hebrew (Mankowski 2000: 25–26).

7:19. My rendering of *kol-miqwēh mêmêhem* is "their every last body of water," for which NIV has "all the reservoirs." The key word here is *miqwēh*. There is no doubt that it means "pool, reservoir" when it is associated with "water(s)" (*mayîm*) as in Gen. 1:10 (NIV, "the gathered waters") and in Lev. 11:36, "A spring, however, or a cistern for *collecting* water remains clean." Sometimes *miqwēh* seems to mean "hope" as well as "pool." For example, which is the better way to translate the reference to God in Jer. 14:8 and 17:13 (also see Ezra 10:2) as *miqwēh yiśrāʾēl*: "Hope of Israel" or "Pool of Israel"? The same goes for Jer. 50:7b, "For they sinned against . . . the *miqwēh ʾăbôtêhem*" ("the Hope of their fathers" or "the Pool of their fathers"?). How could the same word mean both "hope" and "pool"? To those living through drought or in very arid conditions, a reservoir may be their only hope of survival. In Jer. 17:13 that double meaning seems especially present: "O Lord, the Hope/Pool of Israel, all who forsake you will be put to shame . . . because they have forsaken the Lord, *the spring of living water*."

7:19. "Among the timber/trees and the stones" is my fairly literal rendering of the notoriously difficult *ûbāʿēṣîm ûbāʾăbānîm*. Almost all modern translations of the Bible supply a word like NIV's "even in the wooden *buckets* and stone *jars*." But there is no "buckets" or "jars" in the Hebrew. The LXX translates literally: *en te tois chylois kai en tois lithois* ("in the trees and in the stones"). The Vulgate is the first to employ a word for the receptacles/vessels made from these materials with its *tam in ligneis vasis quam in saxeis* ("even in vessels of wood and stone"). Some recent studies have tried to make sense of the text as it is without adding words for clarification. Pope (1994b) appeals to a Ugaritic text, sometimes known as "The Poem of the Beautiful and Gracious Gods," in which the expression *labnm wl'ṣm* ("mid stones and shrubs") refers to an arid and barren desert area. So understood, Exod. 7:19 is stating that not one square inch of Egypt is spared. Water becomes blood even in the most remote areas. Houtman (1986) observes that elsewhere in the Bible "wood" and "stone" are sometimes used together for building materials (e.g., 1 Kings 5:18 [32], "The craftsmen of Solomon and Hiram . . . cut and prepared the *timber* and the *stone* for the building of the temple"). Hence, the reference is not, as Pope maintains, to blood out in the "sticks," but to the fact that even inside and throughout buildings in Egypt made of wood and stone, blood has penetrated and is pervasive. Lemmelijn (1999) pushes the conversation further with his note that "stone and wood" or "wood and stone" (in the singular, unlike the plurals of Exod. 7:19, but probably a collective singular) is the phrase the Bible often uses to refer to the materials from which people build their gods. See Deut. 28:36, 64; 29:17; 2 Kings 19:18; Isa. 37:19; Ezek. 20:32. Thus the phrase in Exod. 7:19 states, "even on their (idols of) stone and wood." I cannot choose between these three suggestions, but all, and especially the first two, are sufficient to show that the Hebrew of the phrase does not need additions for clarification.

7:20. The preposition *bĕ* attached to "his staff" (*bammaṭeh*) after the transitive verb "he raised" gives to the preposition the force of the accusative *'et*. Compare Job 16:10, "Men open their mouths [*bĕpîhem*] to jeer at me."

7:22. The Hebrew for "remained tough" is exactly the same as that in 7:13.

7:23. For other references to *šît lēb* ("take to heart"), see 1 Sam. 4:20 ("[not] pay any attention"); 2 Sam. 13:20 ("Don't take this thing to heart"); Ps. 48:13 [14] ("consider well"); Prov. 22:17 ("apply your heart"); 24:32 ("I applied my heart"); 27:23 ("give careful attention to").

7:23. In negative clauses *gam*-X (here *gam-lāzō't*) can mean "either" ("he paid no thought to this one *either*" [Andersen 1974: 163]) or "even" ("and he did not take *even* this to heart"), where an added event or statement is unexpected (Arnold and Choi 2003: 132).

Commentary

Previous references to Pharaoh's heart used the verbs *ḥāzaq* (4:21, "make **7:14**
tough"; 7:13, "remained tough") and *qāšâ* (7:3, "toughen"). Here the verb is *kābēd*, and it is a stative verb: Pharaoh's heart is "heavy, weighted down," again without implying who is the cause of the heaviness. The verb *kābad/kābēd* will appear again, both as a transitive and intransitive verb, in the second plague (8:15 [11]), in the fourth plague (8:32 [28]), in the fifth plague (9:7), in the seventh plague (9:34), in the eighth plague (10:1). In chaps. 7–14, it appears seven times in the sense of "harden/is heavy." It is the verb that the Philistine priests and diviners use with their own people after they have stolen the ark (1 Sam. 6:6): "Why do you *harden* your hearts as the Egyptians, and Pharaoh did?" In addition to "heart," the verb is used with the "ears," as in Isa. 6:10, "*Make* their ears *dull*"; Isa. 59:1, "nor his ear [God's] too *dull* to hear"; Zech. 7:11, "stubbornly . . . they *stopped up* their ears."

There could be many reasons why Pharaoh would go out in the morning to **7:15**
the river: (1) bathing, (2) checking the level of the Nile, (3) engaging in some ritual act of worship, or (4) simply taking a morning walk. The scene recalls

Pharaoh's daughter, who came down to the same river to bathe (2:5). The best parallel to Exod. 7:15 is the Lord's directives in Isa. 7:3, "Then the Lord said to Isaiah, 'Go out, you and your son Shear-jashub, to meet Ahaz at the end of the aqueduct of the Upper Pool, on the road to the Washerman's Field.'" Two later plagues begin with a similar early morning meeting with Pharaoh either by the river, the fourth plague (8:20 [16]), or without a specifically designated place, the seventh plague (9:13).

Pharaoh, like Abraham, is a morning person. Frequently Genesis tells us that Abraham gets up early in the morning to do something or go somewhere (Gen. 19:27; 21:14; 22:3). Things terrible and things tremendous happen early in the morning. For Pharaoh, early in the morning turns out to be a mess. For the women at the empty tomb (Mark 16:2; Luke 24:1; John 20:1), early in the morning turns out to be a miracle.

7:16–18 First there is a message from God that Moses is to deliver to Pharaoh (vv. 16–18), and then a message from God that Moses is to deliver to Aaron (v. 19). In the first message the recipient of that message discovers that he is the object of God's wrath. In the second message the recipient discovers that he is the mediator of that wrath.

In announcing that the Nile waters will turn into blood, God is aiming his first blow at the very life-support system of Egypt. He could not commence at a more critical point. Take away the Nile and its benefits, and Egypt, regardless of what military behemoth it is, dissolves. To cite something of a parallel about the cruciality of access to fresh water, think of what the modern state of Israel might be forced to do if a neighboring Arab country were to try to divert the waters of the Jordan so that Israel would be cut off from its supply. If an attacking nation is moving against a walled city whose people must venture outside those walls to fetch water, the best way to guarantee confining the target "like a bird in a cage" (as Sennacherib described it) is to cut off their water supply. Furthermore, if the Nile has a divine patron, if there is a Nile god who is one of Egypt's supreme benefactors, then he is about to be declawed, defanged, decimated, and defeated.

The purpose of all this is so that Pharaoh might "know" that the God of Israel is "Lord" in Egypt too, as well as anywhere and everywhere else. Later verses in Exodus will also refer to the purpose of the plagues, that Pharaoh may "know," and then expressly add something like "in all the earth." Exodus 8:22 [18] says that the purpose of the plague of flies is "so that you will know that I am Lord in the *land/earth*." The plague of hail comes on "so you may know there is none like me in all the *earth*" (9:14), and "so you may know the *earth* is the Lord's" (9:29). (NIV translates the Hebrew word *ʾereṣ* "land" in 8:22 [18], but "earth" in 9:14 and 29.) One wonders if some of this language from Exodus about God being Lord in every part of the earth resurfaces in a NT passage. After Jesus has forgiven a paralytic, his critics are aghast and begin to expostulate to themselves. Jesus says to them, "But that you may *know* that the Son of Man has authority *on earth* to forgive sins . . ." (Mark 2:10). Marcus (2000: 218) remarks, "If Mark is aware of these echoes of Exodus, it is significant that he has transformed a divine oracle against the ancient, archetypal Gentile enemy of Israel into a prophetic judgment against Israel's own religious leaders."

Three times there is a reference to "striking" (*nākâ*) the Nile, vv. 17, 20, 25. **7:19–21**
In the first and the last, the Lord is the subject ("I am about to strike"; "after the LORD's striking the Nile"). In the middle one, v. 20, the subject of "he raised his staff and struck the water in the Nile" could be either Moses or Aaron, but presumably it is Aaron, as v. 19 suggests. So, who does the striking? God or Aaron? Maybe both? When God does something, he may do it independently, but most often when God does something, he does it by using available human instruments. For Aaron to do faithfully what he is told to do is for God to do something.

This first plague both recalls and anticipates other events in Exodus. The reference to Aaron's "striking" the water recalls Moses's earlier "striking" the Egyptian (2:12), and his later "striking" the rock from which drinkable water flows (17:6), plus God's "striking" Egypt's firstborn (12:12, 13, 29). The reference to the foul odor from dead fish (7:18, 21) recalls the complaint of Moses's fellow Hebrews that he is responsible for making them a stench to Pharaoh (5:21b). The phrase "they could not drink the water" (7:21) because it was bloodied is the same as that used later, in 15:23, "When they came to Marah, *they could not drink its water* because it was bitter." Bloodied waters and bitter waters! Finally, the use of "every"/*kol* throughout this unit is prominent: 7:19, "over their *every* last body of water"; v. 19, "the *entire* land of Egypt"; v. 20, "*All* the water in the Nile was changed into blood"; v. 21, "*all* the land of Egypt." Pharaoh's own "all"/*kol* appears back in 1:22, "*Every* boy that is born you must throw into the Nile." The Lord's "every" suggests a measure-for-measure response to Pharaoh's "every."

Some of the plagues are unheard of in Egypt, for example, deep darkness in the land of everlasting sun. Other plagues may represent phenomena with which Egyptians are familiar, such as a Nile that looks like blood.

An Aramaic text from Upper Egypt, dating to the third century BC and sometimes called A Prayer for the Rising of the Nile, has these lines: "The river is poor in flood water / The river will die and it will be bitter" (*COS* 1:316). A much earlier Egyptian text, The Admonitions of Ipuwer, first delivered around 2000 BC but probably inscribed much later, has this line: "Indeed, the river is blood, yet one drinks from it" (*COS* 1:94).

Hort (1957: 87–95) has argued that what transpires here is an unusually high and threatening rise of the Nile brought on by an excess in the flow of water from the White Nile (especially) and the Blue Nile, the confluence of which produces the Nile. The larger the flow of water, the more red earth each river sweeps along in its channel. Add to this movement of red earth the mass appearance of flagellates in the water. At night they consume huge amounts of oxygen, thus producing a large fish kill. Unlike in some later plagues, Goshen, the area in which the Hebrews live in the delta region, is not exempted. For Hort, this plague would start in July–August and gradually (not quickly like some of the other plagues) run its course by October–November.

7:22 There is a problem here. If all the water in Egypt has turned into blood (vv. 20–21), how can the magicians do the same (v. 22)? Should there be no water left in Egypt for the magicians to use? The same issue is present in the fifth plague, where we read in 9:6, "*All* the livestock of the Egyptians died." Later, however, in the seventh plague the Lord instructs the Egyptians to bring their livestock indoors to avoid the plague of hail (9:19)! If all the livestock of the Egyptians have died, from where do the Egyptian "firstborn of the cattle" come that God intends to kill (11:5; 12:29)?

Maybe "all" here does not have its literal meaning, that is, 100 percent, but "most of" (although I admit that this is a strange rendering of *kol*). Could it be that the plague touches only surface water and not subterranean water that is found through digging (v. 19)? Could it be that the changing of water to blood is only temporary, and that shortly the blood reverts to water, at which time the magicians convert (some of) it back to blood?

7:22 The magicians' ability to imitate the work of the Lord and the Lord's servant a second time only ensconces Pharaoh further in his heart's obstinacy. There is nothing here to startle him, persuade him, convict him, terrorize him, or soften him.

7:23 Reflecting on the dismissive attitude of Pharaoh, Brueggemann (1994: 743) muses, "One wonders whether the smell could penetrate even the sealed-off apartments of their up-to-date ventilation systems."

7:24 Apart from the reference in the plague of darkness (10:23, "No one could see anyone else or leave his place for three days"), "seven days" is the only other time notation in the plagues pericope. According to Klingbeil (1997: 509), the phrase "seven days," or one very much like it, occurs eighty-five times in the OT. Genesis references to "seven days" include Gen. 7:10; 8:10–12; 31:23; 50:10. References to "seven days" in Exodus after 7:24 include 12:15–19; 13:6–7; 22:30 [29]; 23:15; 29:30, 35–37; 34:18.

The book of Jonah shows that the Lord may send a great wind that can whip up a fierce storm on the high seas. But the great wind that he would rather send is the Pentecostal wind of his Spirit. God can change water into blood. But he would rather, I think, turn water into wine.

Plague 2: A Frog Infestation

(8:1–15 [7:26–8:11])

Translation

8:1 [7:26]The LORD said to Moses, "Go to Pharaoh and say to him, 'Thus said the LORD: Send away my people that they may worship me. 8:2 [7:27]If you yet refuse to send away, I am about to strike at your territory with frogs. 8:3 [7:28]The Nile will teem [with] frogs. They will come up and enter into your house, and into your bedchamber, and onto your couch, and into your servants' houses, and upon your people, and into your ovens, and into your household vessels. 8:4 [7:29]And upon you, and on your people, and upon all your servants the frogs will come up.'" 8:5 [8:1]The LORD said to Moses, "Say to Aaron: 'Extend your hand with your staff over the rivers, over the Nile channels and over the ponds, and bring up the frogs upon the land of Egypt.'" 6 [2]And Aaron extended his hand over the waters of Egypt, and the frog(s) came up and covered the land of Egypt. 7 [3]But the magicians did the same with their magical charms, and brought up frogs over the land of Egypt.

8 [4]Pharaoh summoned Moses and Aaron, and said, "Entreat the LORD that he remove the frogs from me and from my people, and I will send away the people that they may sacrifice to the LORD." 9 [5] Moses said to Pharaoh, "Assume the honor over me (to decide) as to when I should entreat for you, and for your servants and for your people, to cut off the frogs from you and your houses. They will remain only in the Nile." 10 [6]"By tomorrow," he said. And he [Moses] said, "As you ordered, so that you may know there is none like the LORD our God. 11 [7]And the frogs will vanish from you, and from your house, and from your servants, and from your people. They will remain only in the Nile." 12 [8]And Moses, along with Aaron, went out from Pharaoh, and Moses cried to the LORD regarding the frogs he had placed on Pharaoh. 13 [9]The LORD did in accord with Moses's word. The frogs died out in the houses, out in the courtyards, and out in the fields. 14 [10] And they piled them up in great heaps, but the land stank. 15 [11]When Pharaoh saw that there was respite, he stiffened his heart and would not heed them, just as the LORD had said.

Grammatical and Lexical Notes

8:2 [7:27]. What part of speech is *mā᾿ēn* ("refuse")? It surely is not the third-person Piel perfect *mē᾿ēn* one finds in 7:14. BDB 549a calls it an "adj. verb" and translates "refusing." Since the verb occurs only in the Piel, *mā᾿ēn* may be the Piel participle. If so, consonantal *m-᾿-n* represents *m-m-᾿-n*. This would be an illustration of what is known as haplography, the excision, either accidental or intentional, of one of two identical and successive consonants (see Reider 1952: 78; Watson 1971: 48–50).

8:2 [7:27]. The Hebrew word for "frog" (*ṣĕpardēʿa*) occurs in the Hebrew Bible only in this one paragraph and in two Psalm references to this particular plague (Pss. 78:45b; 105:30).

8:3 [7:28]. I place "with" in brackets to show that I have added it for sense. Literally, the phrase says, "And the Nile will teem/swarm frogs," suggesting a transitive verb.

8:3 [7:28]. "Your bedchamber" is *ḥădar miškābĕkā*. The expression appears four more times in the Hebrew Bible: 2 Sam. 4:7, 11; 2 Kings 6:12; Eccles. 10:20. I will comment further on this phrase in the following section. The LXX uses the word *tameion* ("innermost/hidden/secret room"), the same word Jesus uses in Matt. 24:26 ("the inner rooms") and in Luke 12:3 ("what you have whispered in the ear in the inner rooms").

8:5 [8:1]. The prefixed preposition in "with your staff" is *bĕ* (*bĕmaṭṭekā*), showing that *bĕ* carries not only the usual meaning of "in," but is also used to indicate accompaniment (Arnold and Choi 2003: 105).

8:6 [8:2]. In "the frog(s) came up and covered the land of Egypt," "frog" is singular (hence my brackets around the final *s*), as are the verbs (*watta ʿal, wattĕkas*). This is a case of the singular used as a collective. Compare Num. 21:7, "Pray that the Lord will take the snake(s) [lit., "the snake," *ʾet-hannāḥāš*] away from us." When God speaks to Moses in 8:3–4 [7:28–29], he uses both the plural of "frogs" and the plural form of "come up." There is another difference between God's word about this in 8:4 [7:29] and the narrator's word about this in 8:6 [2]. When God refers to "frogs" in 8:4 [7:29], the form of the Hebrew word is *haṣĕpardĕʿîm* (without the *dagesh* in the *ṣādê* in spite of the added definite article). When the narrator uses the word "frog" in 8:6 [2] in the singular, the form of the Hebrew word is *haṣṣpardîʿa* (with the *dagesh* in the *ṣadê* because of the added definite article). On such morphological variations as part of Biblical Hebrew rhetoric, see Ratner 1992: 149.

8:9 [8:5]. There is much debate about how best to render *hitpāʾēr ʿālay lĕmātay* . . . ("Assume the honor over me [to decide] as to when . . ."). The Septuagint has *taxai pros me*, "Appoint for me." *Targum Onqelos* renders, "Glorify yourself on account of me." There are considerable variations in English translations: "Glory over me: when shall I entreat for thee?" (KJV); "You may have this triumph over me: for what time shall I plead on behalf of you?" (NJPS); "Kindly tell me when I am to pray for you" (NRSV); "I leave to you the honor of setting the time for me to pray for you" (NIV); "You may vaunt over me as to when I shall entreat for you" (Alter 2004: 353). Rabin (1961: 397) connects Hebrew *pāʾar* with a similar-sounding verb in Arabic that means "choose the (exact) time," and with Akkadian *paru* ("seek") and *iptaru* ("choose") to come up with, "Choose the exact time when I should pray for you." The verb *pāʾar* occurs most often in the later chapters of Isaiah (Piel, "make glorious, adorn, enhance" [55:5; 60:7, 9, 13]; Hitpael, "display glory/splendor, bring glory to oneself" [44:23; 49:3; 60:21; 61:3]). There are two passages quite close to Exod. 8:9 [5], for in both of them, as here, the verb *pāʾar* (in the Hitpael) is followed by the preposition *ʿal*: (1) Judg. 7:2 AT, "The Lord said to Gideon, 'You have too many men. . . . In order that Israel may not boast against me/may not vaunt itself against me [*pen yitpāʾēr ʿālay*] . . .'"; (2) Isa. 10:15a, "Does the ax raise itself above him [*hăyitpāʾēr haggarzen ʿal*] who swings it?"

8:10 [8:6]. What is the best way to render the preposition *lĕ* prefixed to "tomorrow," literally, "for tomorrow" (*lĕmāḥār*)? The expression occurs four more times in the Hebrew Bible (Exod. 8:23 [19]; Num. 11:18; Josh. 7:13; Esther 5:12). In three of these (Exod. 8:10, 23 [6, 19]; Esther 5:12) the NIV ignores the preposition and simply translates "tomorrow." In the other two (Num. 11:18; Josh. 7:13) NIV uses the phrase "in preparation for tomorrow." However, the reading "*by* morning" is suggested by the related phrase *labbōqer* (Exod. 34:2, "Be ready by morning" [not "in the morning"]; and Ps. 30:5 [6], "Weeping may remain for a night, but rejoicing comes by the morning" [not "in the morning"]). On the temporal use of the preposition *lĕ*, see Meek 1948: 238.

8:13 [8:9]. The parallel pair "houses/courtyards" (*bayit/ḥāṣēr*) is present in 1 Chron. 28:6 ("Solomon your son is the one who will build my *house* and my *courts*") and in Zech. 3:7 ("If you will walk in my ways, . . . then you will govern my *house* and have charge of my *courts*"). Compare also the lines in the Phoenician incantation text from Arslan Tash: "in the house [*bt*] which I enter you shall not enter, and in the courtyard [*wḥṣr*] which I tread you shall not tread." Also a Ugaritic text contains these lines: "Baal has no house [*bt*] like the gods, and a court [*wḥzr*] like the sons of Asherah." See Avishur 1975: 24; 1984: 221, 540.

8:14 [8:10]. "In great heaps" is *ḥŏmārim ḥŏmārim*. The doubling of the word in the plural, for emphasis, appears again in 2 Kings 3:16b, "Make this valley full of ditches [*gēbîm gēbîm*]," and in Joel 3:14 [4:14], "Multitudes, multitudes [*hămônîm hămônîm*] in the valley of decision." See Waltke and O'Connor 1990: 119.

8:15 [8:11]. *Wĕhakbēd* ("[Pharaoh] stiffened") is the Hiphil infinitive absolute of *kābēd*, "be heavy." Rubinstein (1952: 363) suggests that there are forty-five instances in the Hebrew Bible where one or more verbs are connected with a preceding finite verb by the conjunctive *wāw*, and are subordinated to such a verb by their infinitive absolute form, as here, instead of using the consecutive *wayyiqṭōl* form. See Waltke and O'Connor 1990: 594–97.

Commentary

Unlike in the preceding plague of blood, the Lord this time instructs Moses **8:1 [7:26]**
simply to "go to Pharaoh." There is no "go to Pharaoh in the morning as he goes out to the water" as in 7:15. The phrase "go to Pharaoh" must refer to the king's home/palace. The same phrase also introduces the fifth plague (the plague on livestock, 9:1), and the eighth plague (the plague of locusts, 10:1). Presumably this meeting could take place anytime during the day, since no time marker like "in the morning" is added.

The words "if you yet refuse to send away," which the Lord addresses to **8:2 [7:27]**
Pharaoh via Moses and again to Pharaoh in 9:2 and 10:4, seem to suggest that in behaving so stubbornly and resistingly, Pharaoh is acting out his own independent, freewill decision. Accordingly, he will be held accountable for his foolish display of autonomy.

I suggest that the phrase "if you yet refuse to send away, I am about to . . ." is functionally equivalent to the phrase "if he/you will not . . . (then) . . . ," common in both biblical law and in nonlegal material. Thus the phrase functions as a warning of forthcoming sanction, which the speaker holds out before the one who violates the stipulation, either by an act of omission or commission. Examples from legal texts are legion. Here are a few from nonlegal texts: (1) Gen. 24:8, Abraham says to his servant, "If the woman is unwilling to come back with you, then you will be released from this oath of mine"; Gen. 34:15–17, Jacob's sons say to the Shechemites about their sister, "We will give our consent to you on one condition only. . . . But if you will not agree to be circumcised, we'll take our sister and go"; 1 Sam. 12:15, Samuel says to his people, "But if you do not obey the Lord, and if you rebel against his commands, [then] his hand will be against you." See the perceptive study by Brin 1995 (esp. 360).

Additionally, Moses's "if you refuse" sounds a lot like "if you do not" in the preaching of the prophets, especially Jeremiah. Examples from Jeremiah include 13:17, "But if you do not listen . . ."; 17:27, "But if you do not obey me . . ."; 22:5, "But if you do not obey these commands . . ."; 38:21, "But if you refuse to surrender . . ." The latter is especially close to Exod. 8:2 [7:27]. Both begin with "And/but if you refuse [*wĕʾim-māʾēn ʾattâ*]" followed by the preposition *lĕ* prefixed to the infinitive construct of a verb (*lĕšallēaḥ*, *lāṣēʾt*). Two other emphases are common to Moses and Pharaoh and the prophets. The frequently expressed desire of God that Pharaoh and Egypt "know that I am LORD" is one that appears numerous times in Ezekiel (5:13; 6:10, 14; 7:27; 12:15, 16; etc.). Second, the emphasis on heart hardening and obduracy throughout this section of Exodus parallels God's call to Isaiah to "make the heart of this people calloused, make their ears dull, and close their eyes" (Isa. 6:10). The Hebrew verb in "make dull their ears" is *kābēd*, one of the three verbs this plague section of Exodus uses for heart hardening. See Van Seters 1986: 34.

Throughout Scripture are refusal scenes that turn out to be calamitous for the one doing the refusing—Pharaoh for one, and see my reference to Jer. 38:21 in the preceding paragraph. Hence Heb. 12:25 rightly cautions, "See to it that you do not *refuse* him who speaks. If they did not escape when they *refused* him who warned them on earth, how much less will we?" But there are also refusal scenes in Scripture that are wholesome and appropriate: "But he [Joseph] *refused*. . . . And although she spoke to Joseph day after day, he *refused* to lie beside her" (Gen. 39:8, 10 AT); "But . . . Queen Vashti *refused* to come" at the king's command (Esther 1:12); "By faith Moses, when he had grown up, *refused* to be called a son of Pharaoh's daughter" (Heb. 11:24).

God's threat to "strike" (*nāgap*) Egypt with frogs is interesting. Strike with frogs! This is the verb that the later Passover chapter (Exod. 12) uses for God's striking the Egyptians: "When the LORD goes through the land to *strike down* the Egyptians, . . . he will not permit the destroyer to enter your houses and *strike* you *down*" (12:23); "It is the Passover sacrifice to the LORD, . . . when he *struck down* the Egyptians" (12:27). The same verb appears in Exod. 32:35, but this time Israel is the object of a divine striking: "And the LORD *struck* the people with a plague because of what they did with the calf Aaron had made." Maybe its use in 8:2 [7:27] (with frogs!) is an anticipatory use of a later, and much more devastating, striking.

8:3–4 [7:28–29] The use of the verb "teem, swarm" (*šāraṣ*) recalls its use in the earlier chapters of Genesis (Gen. 1:20; 7:21; 8:17 [NIV, "move along"]; 9:7 [NIV, "multiply"]; and see Ezek. 47:9). Those references are to a God-blessed, God-ordained swarming. This reference is to a swarming because of a God-mandated judgment. Closer to the verb's use in 8:3 [7:28] is its use in Exod. 1:7 to refer to the proliferation of Israel in Egypt (NIV has collapsed this verb with another, *wayyirbû*, to produce "multiplied greatly"). So we have chap. 1: swarming Israel; chap. 8: swarming frogs.

The Hebrew for "bedchamber," as I indicated above in my grammatical notes, occurs only here and in 2 Sam. 4:7, 11; 2 Kings 6:12; Eccles. 10:20.

As Lasine (2001: 77–78) has observed, these references have some things in common. In three of the four the bedchamber draws attention to the king's vulnerability. Pharaoh cannot prevent the invasion of frogs. Ishbosheth cannot prevent an assassination plot (2 Sam. 4:7, 11). The king of Aram/Syria cannot prevent the enemy acquiring secret information (2 Kings 6:12). By contrast, the fourth reference, Eccles. 10:20, talks of a king who is invulnerable because even the birds inform him and bring him private knowledge about his people.

As in the first plague (7:19–20), Aaron plays a significant role. It is he who **8:5–6**
again extends his hand and staff, but this time there is no striking the river as **[8:1–2]**
he does in 7:20. (The verb for the Lord/Aaron "striking" the Nile in 7:17, 20, 25, and in 8:16–17 [8:12–13], is *nākâ*, while the verb for God's "striking" with frogs in 8:2 [7:27] is *nāgap*.) The inundation of the frogs, even into homes and kitchen ovens in Egyptian houses, is similar to the description that the wailing women of Jeremiah's day give about Jerusalem: "Death has climbed in through our windows and has entered our fortresses" (Jer. 9:21a). Brueggemann (1994: 745) calls this episode "saturation bombing with frogs."

The mention of the frogs "covering" the land points forward to two later coverings. The returning waters of the sea "covered" the Egyptian chariots and horsemen (Exod. 14:28; 15:5). Second, for hungry Israel, God sends abundant quail, which "came and *covered* the camp" (16:13). A covering that brings death. A covering that "came and covered the camp." A covering that brings death, or at least great annoyance and discomfort (frogs and seawater). A covering that brings life (quail).

Once again Pharaoh's magicians can do what Aaron and Moses can do (7:22), **8:7 [3]**
but at what a cost. Multiplying the amount of bloodied waters, or adding to the proliferation of frogs—either hardly seems to be something for which they would want to congratulate themselves. They can bring on bloodied waters; they cannot remove them. They can multiply the number of frogs; they cannot eliminate them. Pagan magic can introduce evil, but once having introduced it, cannot get rid of it. As the following verses will indicate, God's work can be imitated but never equaled.

In asking Moses to pray for him (his magicians apparently are not "prayer **8:8 [4]**
warriors"), Pharaoh uses the verb *ʿātar*. It appears about twenty times in the Hebrew Bible, most often in the plagues account (8:8 [4]; 8:9 [5]; 8:28 [24]; 8:29 [25]; 8:30 [26]; 9:28; 10:17, 18). The only other intercessor in the OT with whom this verb is linked is Isaac (Gen. 25:21, "Isaac prayed [*ʿātar*] to the Lord on behalf of his wife"). By contrast, the Hebrew verb *pālal* appears frequently to refer to the ministry of intercession by those so gifted: Abraham (Gen. 20:7); Moses (Num. 21:7; Deut. 9:20); Samuel (1 Sam. 7:5; 12:19, 23); an unidentified "man of God" (1 Kings 13:6); Hezekiah (2 Chron. 30:18);

Nehemiah (Neh. 1:6); Job (Job 42:8, 10); Jeremiah (Jer. 7:16; 11:14; 14:11; 37:3; 42:4); the people of God (Ps. 72:15; Jer. 29:7). See Balentine 1984: 163.

Pharaoh will ask Moses to pray for him four times: 8:8 [4]; 8:28 [24]; 9:28; 10:17. These are the only instances in the Bible of someone asking somebody else to pray for him/them that use the imperative mood of the verb *ʿātar* (Hiphil). Other kings who request prayer from a prophet include Jeroboam from a "man of God" (1 Kings 13:6) and Zedekiah from Jeremiah (Jer. 37:3). Both of these use the imperative form of *pālal* (Hitpael). The later verb form is the one that appears in Num. 21:7 when the Israelites say to Moses, "We sinned. . . . Pray that the Lord will take the snakes away from us." This Numbers reference is particularly close to Exod. 10:17, for they are the two that conjoin a confession of sin with a request for intercessory prayer for a removal of sin/snakes.

8:9 [5] Moses does not hurry off to his prayer room. He does not fall to his knees on the spot. Rather, he throws the ball back into Pharaoh's court by insisting that the king set the time for Moses's intercession that would terminate the frog plague. Moses has no sweaty palms. He can involve even Pharaoh in his prayer time, so convinced is Moses that there is one who reigns over Pharaoh. Childs (1974: 56) calls this a "classic example of 'one-upsmanship.'"

8:10–11 [6–7] If we translate *lĕmāḥār* as simply "tomorrow" (see my grammatical note), then Pharaoh, for some reason, is willing to tolerate twenty-four more hours of frogs. His magicians cannot get rid of them, and he will not be rid of them for at least another day by his own choosing. If, however, we translate "by morning," then Pharaoh's word to Moses is "Get rid of them as quickly as possible."

Moses's reference to God's incomparability ("there is no one like the Lord our God") is a biblical topos (see Deut. 4:35, 39; 32:39; 2 Sam. 7:22; Isa. 44:6; 45:5–6, 21–22; 46:9; Joel 2:27). One is reminded of what a teacher of the law said when Jesus answered his question perceptively: "Well said, teacher. You are right in saying that God is one and that there is no other but/besides him" (Mark 12:32). Mark's language (*kai ouk estin allos plēn autou*) is closest to Isa. 45:21–22 (*kai ouk estin allos plēn emou*, "and there is no other but/besides me").

8:12 [8] On the four occasions on which Moses is said to pray for Pharaoh, all four state that before Moses prays for Pharaoh, Moses "went out from/left Pharaoh" (8:12 [8]; 8:30 [26]; 9:33; 10:18). Why leave Pharaoh before praying? Why pray privately? Would not Pharaoh be duly impressed by hearing this giant man of prayer on his knees or face before his very eyes? By contrast, when Moses intercedes for his own people, he seems to do it on the spot. He does not withdraw. See, for example, references to his praying for his beleaguered people in Num. 11:2, or for his leprous sister in Num. 12:13. (Passages like Exod. 5:22 or 32:11–13, 30–31, with language like "Moses returned to the

Lord" or "I will go up to the Lord," suggest that even for Israel, at least on some occasions, Moses prays in private.) Unlike the intercessory prayers of Moses for Israel or a sibling (as mentioned above), the content of Moses's intercessory prayers for Pharaoh is not recorded. Perhaps, as Milgrom (1991: 588, 660) has noted, Moses's leaving Pharaoh's presence and praying in private to God would help remove any thinking from Pharaoh's mind that Moses is some kind of pagan magician who, with the right words and actions, can even command and manipulate the deity to perform his bidding.

Moses's prayer, though unrecorded, moves the Lord to respond. All the frogs **8:13–14**
die. But they leave a calling card: their stench. What Moses has been earlier **[9–10]**
to his own people (5:21), these dead amphibians now are to Pharaoh and the Egyptians. A stinking river in 7:21 and stinking dead frogs in 8:14 [10]!

Twice again after this episode, Pharaoh asks Moses to pray to Moses's god to **8:15 [11]**
remove the plague; for such a prayer, Pharaoh promises to release the Israelites. Moses prays. The Lord removes the plague. Pharaoh reneges on his promise when the plague disappears and hardens his heart. With 8:15 [11] compare 8:30–32 [26–28] and 9:33–35. It may be surprising that this scene plays out three times. Might not Moses, or God, see through Pharaoh's duplicity and say something like "Oh no, you are not going to sucker me again with that ruse"? Does God answer prayer even when he knows the asking person has ulterior motives? Does he answer "foxhole religion" prayers even if he knows that the pray-er will, if delivered, forget any promise made to God? Apparently yes. At least sometimes.

Plague 3: Learning a Lesson from Lice

(8:16–19 [8:12–15])

Translation

16 [12]And the LORD said to Moses, "Say to Aaron: 'Extend your staff and strike the dust of the land, and there will be lice in all the land of Egypt.'" 17 [13]And they did so, and Aaron extended his hand with his staff, and struck the dust of the land, and there were lice in man and in animal. All the dust of the land became lice in all the land of Egypt. 18 [14]And the magicians (tried) to do so with their magical charms, to bring out the lice, but they were unable, and there were lice in man and in animal. 19 [15]The magicians said to Pharaoh, "The finger of God/a divine being it is!" And Pharaoh's heart was stiff, and he did not heed them, just as the Lord had spoken.

Grammatical and Lexical Notes

8:16–18 [12–14]. In these three verses the Hebrew word for "lice" (or "gnats" or "mosquitoes") occurs five times. But it appears in two different forms, *kinnim/kinnîm* (vv. 16 [12], 17b [13b], 18a [14a]) and *kinnām* (vv. 17 [13a], 18b [14b]). Thus the sequence is *kinnim>kinnām>kinnîm>kinnîm>kinnām*. The difference between the two is that *kinnim/kinnîm* is the regular masculine-plural form. Since *kinnām* is a collective noun, it is used with a third-person feminine singular verb (*wattĕhî*) in vv. 17 [13] and 18b [14b]: "there were lice." We saw this same phenomenon in the preceding unit. There "frogs" (*ṣĕpardĕʿîm*) is the regular masculine plural noun, and it appears with a masculine plural verb. But when "frog" appears in the singular as a collective (*haṣpardēʿa*), the verbs used to refer to their "coming up and covering" the land are both feminine singular verbs (*wattaʿal, wattĕkas*, 8:6 [2]).

8:19 [15]. The phrase "hand of the LORD" is common in Scripture, twenty-seven times in Exodus alone, if one includes related words such as "right hand" or "finger." See, for example, 9:3 AT, "The hand of the LORD is about to be against your livestock" (full references in Seely 2004: 39n7). The equivalent phrase occurs in both Ugaritic (*yd ilm*) and in Akkadian (*qat ilī*). To the best of my knowledge, the expression "the finger(s) of God" is unique to the Bible, except for a few Egyptian texts, mostly magical in nature, that refer to the "finger of ——" (the name of some Egyptian deity).

Commentary

8:16–17 [12–13] At the beginning of the plague of blood, the Lord tells Moses to "go out to Pharaoh in the morning, as he is going out to the water" (7:15). At the beginning of the plague of frogs, the Lord simply tells Moses to "go to Pharaoh" (8:1 [7:26]). Here, at the start of the third plague, nobody goes to Pharaoh and gives him an ultimatum. The plague just commences after Aaron holds out his staff.

In the morning at the river		Go to Pharaoh		No warning/announcement	
Plague	Reference	Plague	Reference	Plague	Reference
1	7:15	2	8:1 [7:26]	3	8:16 [12]
4	8:20 [16]	5	9:1	6	9:8
7	9:13	8	10:1	9	10:21

I have chosen to translate the Hebrew word *k-n-m* as "lice," primarily because in Postbiblical Hebrew the word *k-n-h* means "maggot." Apart from this paragraph, the word appears in the Hebrew Bible again only in a Psalm reference to this plague (Ps. 105:31), and in Isa. 51:6, "The heavens will vanish like smoke . . . and its inhabitants die like flies [NIV]/gnats [NRSV]."

As in the two previous plagues, the Israelites also experience the devastating effects of this third plague. They do not escape the bloodied waters, the inundation of frogs, and the pervasive lice. It is not until the fourth plague (8:22 [18]), and consistently thereafter, that God does not permit the plague's destruction to touch his people.

The phrase "bring out the lice" could mean either "produce" them (NIV, NRSV) **8:18 [14]**
or "get rid of/take out" the pests (Alter 2004: 354). For these magicians, this is either imitation act 3, or expulsion act 1. Either way, they fail. Either they cannot make them appear, or else they cannot make them disappear.

So, if they cannot do anything, either way, what or who is responsible for the **8:19 [15]**
lice? Their answer? "God's finger." This phrase appears only twice more in the OT (Exod. 31:18b; Deut. 9:10), both of which credit the finger of God with writing the law on the two tablets of (lime)stone (see Klingbeil 2000). Weinfeld (1991: 408) suggests that in contrast to "the hand of God," the expression "the finger of God" "indicates some extraordinary performance." Note that in Ps. 8:3 [4] creation is the work of God's "fingers" rather than of his "hands."

The one NT use of this phrase is in Luke 11:20, "But if I drive out demons *by the finger of God*, then the kingdom of God has come to you." In the Matthew parallel (12:28) Jesus uses "the Spirit of God" instead of "the finger of God." I cannot sufficiently explain the reason for this change, but I offer one suggestion. The shift in Luke allows for an even sharper contrast between Luke 11:1–13 (Jesus's teaching on prayer) and Luke 11:14–20 (Jesus and demonic exorcism), and adds to the Moses-like dimension of Jesus's prophetic ministry. First, in Luke 11:13 Jesus refers to "your Father in heaven," while in Luke 11:16 some test Jesus by asking for a sign "from heaven." Second, in Luke 11:4b Jesus teaches us to pray, "And lead us not into testing/temptation," while in Luke 11:16 Jesus's critics "test" him. Third, Jesus teaches us to forgive the sins perpetrated against us (Luke 11:4a), while Jesus's critics accuse him of sin by being in collusion with Beelzebub (Luke 11:15), an accusation that Jesus readily rejects with his "finger of God" reference in Luke 11:20. God has sent Moses, who sends Aaron to Pharaoh. God has sent Jesus, who sends the seventy (Luke 10) into a world where hostile criticism and rejection are sure to raise their ugly head.

Plague 4: Inundated with Insects

(8:20–32 [8:16–28])

Translation

20 [16]And the LORD said to Moses, "Rise
early in the morning and position your-
self before Pharaoh. As he comes to the
water, say to him, 'Thus said the LORD: send
away my people that they may worship me.
21 [17]If you are not about to send away my
people, I am about to send against you, and
against your servants, and against your
people, and against your houses the insect
swarm. And the houses of Egypt will be full
of the insect swarm, and the ground too, on
which they stand. 22 [18]But I shall separate
on that day the land of Goshen on which
my people are standing so that there will
be no insect swarm there, in order that
you may know that I am LORD in the midst
of the land. 23 [19]I will make a distinction
between my people and between your
people. By tomorrow this sign shall come
to pass.'" 24 [20]And the LORD did thus. The
heavy insect swarm came into the house
of Pharaoh, and into the house of his ser-
vants, and in all the land of Egypt. The land
was ravaged because of the insect swarm.
25 [21]Pharaoh summoned Moses and
Aaron and said, "Go, sacrifice to your
god in the land." 26 [22]And Moses said, "It
would not be proper to do thus, for then
the abomination of Egypt we would sacri-
fice to the LORD our God. Since we would
sacrifice the abomination of Egypt before
their very eyes, would they not stone us?
27 [23]A journey of three days will we make
into the steppe, and sacrifice to the LORD
our God as he said to us." 28 [24]Pharaoh
said, "I myself will send you away that you
may sacrifice to the LORD your God on the
steppe. Only you must not go any farther
than necessary. Entreat for me." 29 [25]And
Moses said, "When I leave your presence,
I shall entreat the LORD that the insect
swarm turn away from Pharaoh, from his
servants, and from his people tomorrow.
Only let not Pharaoh continue to be du-
plicitous by reneging on sending off the
people to sacrifice to the LORD."
30 [26]Then Moses left Pharaoh and
prayed to the LORD. 31 [27]And the LORD
did as Moses commanded, and the insect
swarm turned away from Pharaoh, from
his servants, and from his people. Not
one remained. 32 [28]And Pharaoh made his
heart heavy also on this occasion, and he
did not send the people away.

Grammatical and Lexical Notes

8:20 [16]. The construction *hinnēh* plus participle [*yôṣēʾ*] ("as he comes to") to refer to a circumstance accompanying a future event is the same as in 7:15.

8:21 [17]. "About to send away" and "I am about to send" are both participles of *šālaḥ*, the first a Piel participle, and the second a Hiphil participle. The first is a participle in a prefuture time, while the second is a participle in future time (Watts 1964: 135). God's future sending is a possible divine response to Pharaoh's possible nonsending.

8:21 [17]. The preposition "against" is *bĕ*, what I would call "the *bêt* of hostility." "To send against" (*šālaḥ* [Hiphil] plus preposition *bĕ*) always refers to divine punishments: Lev. 26:22 (with wild beasts); 2 Kings 15:37 (with other kings); Ezek. 14:13 and Amos 8:11 (through famine).

8:21 [17]. The use of the stative verb "will be full of" (*ûmālĕʾû*) following the participle "I am about to send" is used to express a state of being that is to come to pass in the future. See Rainey 2003: 25.

8:21 [17]. The Hebrew word for "insect swarm" (*ʿārōb*) occurs only in this paragraph and in two psalm references to this plague (Pss. 78:45; 105:31). Is there any possible connection between *ʿārōb* and *ʿēreb*, the "mixed" multitude that leaves Egypt with Israel (Exod. 12:38)? This insect swarm is so massive, so dense, so concentrated that each insect seems to mix with and be indistinguishable from another.

8:23 [19]. I will discuss below the word *pĕdut*, which I have rendered "distinction." That translation owes as much to Vulgate's *divisio* and Septuagint's *diastolē* as anything, for the meaning of the Hebrew word is far from obvious. In the NT the Greek word *diastolē* appears three times in Paul's writings—in Rom. 3:22, "This righteousness from God comes through faith in Jesus Christ to all who believe. There is no *difference/distinction* [between Jew and Gentile]"; Rom. 10:12: "For there is no *difference* between Jew and Gentile"; 1 Cor. 14:7, "How will anyone know what tune is being played unless there is a *distinction* in the notes?"

8:23 [19]. The formula *bên . . . ûbên* ("between . . . and between") in "*between* my people *and between* your people" has already appeared in Gen. 1:7 ("So God made the firmament, and separated *between* the waters beneath the firmament *and between* the waters above it"), and in Gen. 13:3 ("He [Abram] went from place to place until he came to Bethel, to the place *between* Bethel *and between* Ai"). See the astute study of Barr 1978.

8:24 [20]. The verb "ravage, spoil, go to ruin" (*šāḥat*) appears again in the Niphal to describe the "corrupt" earth of Noah's day (Gen. 6:11, 12), Jeremiah's "ruined" linen belt that he hides in the crevice in the rocks (Jer. 13:7), and the "marred" pot the prophet sees at the potter's house (Jer. 18:4).

8:26 [22]. "Proper" is *nākôn* (the Niphal participle of *kûn*). It appears in David's great confession of sin prayer, Ps. 51:10b [12b], "And renew a *steadfast/right* spirit within me."

8:26 [22]. "Since" in "since we would sacrifice" is *hēn*. It might also be rendered "If." For "since," see Garr 2004b: 335–36. For "if," see Long 1976: 388–89. For parallels to an opening *hēn* clause followed by a question, as here, see Jer. 3:1, "If [*hēn*] a man divorces his wife, . . . should he return to her again?"; Hag. 2:12, "If [*hēn*] a person carries consecrated meat in the fold of his garment, and that fold touches some bread, . . . does it become consecrated?"

8:26 [22]. As Sivan and Schniedewind (1993: 212) have argued, *wĕlōʾ yisqĕlunû* is an unmarked rhetorical question ("Would they not stone us?") rather than an asseveration ("Surely they will stone us"). A parallel to a *hēn . . . wĕlōʾ* sentence is present in Isa. 32:1, 3, "When [*hēn*] a king reigns in righteousness, . . . will not [*wĕlōʾ*] the eyes of the seeing see and the ears of the hearing hear?" (AT, which varies from NIV's "See, a king will reign in righteousness. . . . Then the eyes of those who see will no longer be closed, and the ears of those who hear will listen").

8:28 [24]. "I myself will send you away" brings out the force of the independent pronoun in *ʾānōkî ʾăšallaḥ ʾetkem*.

8:28 [24]. "You must not go any farther than necessary" combines the Hiphil infinitive absolute of *rāḥaq* followed by the Hiphil imperfect of the same verb: "going far, you shall not go far."

8:28 [24]. On the restrictive force of *raq* ("only") to indicate clarification, see Arnold and Choi 2003: 141. For parallels, compare Abraham's word to his servant about Isaac: "Only [*raq*] do not take my son back there" (Gen. 24:8); and the Lord's word to the Satan about Job: "Everything he has is in your hand. Only [*raq*] do not send forth your hand against him [NIV, "but on the man himself do not lay a finger"]" (Job 1:12).

8:28 [24]. The imperative "entreat for me" is a masculine plural imperative (as it was in 8:8 [4]), just as the "you" in "you must not go any farther" is a masculine, plural "you." Maybe Pharaoh wants as many people as possible to be praying for him.

8:29 [25]. The word *hinnēh* followed by an independent pronoun and participle (*hinnēh ʾānōkî yôṣēʾ*) could be "Behold/Look, I am leaving your presence," or more likely, "*When* I leave your presence . . ." Similarly, dying Jacob's words to Joseph in Gen. 48:21 (*hinnēh ʾānōkî mēt*) could be translated "Behold/Look, I am about to die," or "When I die. . . ." See Zewi 1998: 77.

8:29 [25]. I have rendered *hātēl* as "to be duplicitous." BDB 1068b links it with *tālal* II, "mock, deceive, trifle with," here in Hiphil infinitive construct form. This verb appears twice in Job. 13:9, first as Hiphil infinitive construct with attached preposition followed by the Hiphil imperfect: "Could you *deceive* him [God] as you might *deceive* men?" (NIV); "Will you *fool* Him as one *fools* men?" (NJPS). The verb is also used for "cheating" Jacob in Gen. 31:7, and with Samson who "made a fool of" Delilah (Judg. 16:10, 13, 15). Or might the form in question be from the verb *hātal*, "mock, deceive" (1 Kings 18:27, "Elijah began to *taunt* [NIV]/*mock* [NRSV] them")?

8:30 [26]. The Septuagint's verb for "entreat, pray for" (*euchomai*), also in v. 28, appears a number of times in NT passages that focus on prayer, but a classic one is James 5:16 ("Confess your sins to each other, and *pray for* each other").

Commentary

In many ways this fourth plague is similar to the three that have preceded it, **8:20–32 [16–28]** especially the first two (bloodied waters and frogs). A few items, however, separate this plague from the ones before. For one thing, the magicians, present in the first three plagues (7:22; 8:7 [3]; 8:19 [15]), are conspicuously absent this time. Their absence matches Aaron's (relative) absence from this fourth plague. (Pharaoh makes a cursory reference to Aaron in v. 25 [21].) In the first three plagues, God has said to Moses, "Tell Aaron . . ." (7:19; 8:5 [1]; 8:16 [12]). This time there is no "Tell Aaron. . . ." Aaron has extended his staff or hand over the land before (7:20; 8:6 [2]; 8:17 [13]), but not this time. It is as if the confrontation now advances from one between Aaron and the magicians to one between Moses and Pharaoh, from one between lieutenants to one between captains.

A second major innovation is that for the first time the Lord protects his people from the plague's impact (v. 22 [18]). It is as if the truth of Ps. 91:7 is literally fulfilled: "A thousand may fall at your side, ten thousand at your right hand, but it will not come near you." (This is a verse the famous missionary to India, Amy Carmichael, took from Scripture when a devastating, sweeping disease of some type threatened the lives of the young girls in her orphanages.) This God-ordained sparing of Israel shows that Israel's survival in Egypt is no serendipity, no fluke, no luck of the draw. Rather, as Magonet (1997: 61) has so trenchantly put it, "This degree of discrimination moves the events beyond a natural cataclysm into a precise divine intervention."

As I indicated above in my first grammatical note on 8:23 [19], determining the meaning of the Hebrew word *pĕdut* ("distinction"?) is a bit of a puzzle. As we shall see, the Hebrew uses a different word for the "distinction" that God makes between Egypt's livestock and Israel's livestock (Exod. 9:4) in the next plague. All agree that *pĕdut* comes from the verb *pādâ*, "to redeem," and that in the three other places where the noun *pĕdut* occurs, it means "redemption" or "ransom": Pss. 111:9, "He provided *redemption* for his people"; 130:7, "O Israel, put your hope in the LORD, for . . . with him is full *redemption*"; Isa. 50:2, "Was my arm too short to *ransom* you?" In these three later references the Hebrew uses a long *u* vowel in *pĕdût*, while the spelling of the word in Exod. 8:23 [19] is with a short *u* vowel: *pĕdut*.

It perhaps seems strange for God to say, "I will put a redemption/ransom between my people and between your people." One does not redeem between X and Y; rather, one redeems X from Y. Perhaps G. I. Davies (1974: 491) is on the right track when he suggests an emendation of *p-d-t* to *p-(r)-d-t* (from the verb *pārad*, "separate"), in which the *r* was omitted through haplography and the confusion caused by the similarity of the *r* and *d* in the early Hebrew script. At least twice *pārad* is followed by the preposition "between," as in 2 Kings 2:11 AT, "Suddenly a chariot of fire appeared and *separated between* the two of them [Elijah, Elisha]"; Ruth 1:17 AT, Ruth to Naomi, "If anything but death *separates between* you and me." The prepositional phrase with "between" precedes *pārad* in Prov. 18:18 AT, "Casting the lot settles disputes and keeps apart ["separates between"] strong opponents."

Seldom in Scripture or in life does God erect an invisible shield that protects his followers from the devastation that crushes others. Sometimes, to be sure, "it will not come near you" happens. More times than not, it does come near. Here it is not the case that God is granting his people a serene immunity because they are, after all, his people. Rather, this shield of protection is to be another means by which God will make it possible and inviting for Pharaoh to know him as Yahweh (v. 22b [18b]).

A third innovation in this plague is Pharaoh's moving beyond asking for prayer to making a partial concession to Moses for an exodus. The Israelites may leave, but they must not go too far (v. 28b [24b]). This partial concession is like two later partial concessions: (1) You may go, but leave your children (and women) behind (10:10). (2) You may go but leave your flocks/possessions behind (10:24). The Lord's followers might still hear the same lure to compromise from the predatory one who seeks to devour those followers of the Lord: (1) Worship God, but don't take it too far. Confine it to one hour on Sunday morning. (2) Worship God, but let me have your children. (3) Worship God, but leave your possessions out of it.

Finally, the Lord tells Moses to tell Pharaoh to release the Israelites so that they can "worship" their God (v. 20 [16]). In his response, Pharaoh uses the word "sacrifice" (v. 25 [21]) rather than "worship." The same change has happened in the frog plague ("worship" in 8:1 [7:26], but "sacrifice" in 8:8 [4]). This time, however, Moses raises the point that the Egyptians would find the

Israelites' manner of worship so offensive that they would kill them if the sacrifices were offered on Egyptian soil. But what is it about Hebrew worship that the Egyptians would find so obnoxious if done in their backyard? Would it be analogous to Muslims in a country like Saudi Arabia and their hostility to the open expression of the practice of Jewish or Christian faith? Would it be analogous to the response of conservative Protestants if they were to observe devoted Roman Catholics offering up prayers to the Blessed Virgin in the sanctuary of a fundamentalist Baptist church? Or is Moses making this all up? Maybe in urging Pharaoh to desist from duplicity, he is using a bit of duplicity himself.

The data in Gen. 46:31–34 may provide another clue. Joseph instructs his family members to identify themselves to Pharaoh as shepherds. Joseph assumes that Pharaoh will assign them the area of Goshen, thus isolating Joseph's family from the Egyptians, "for all shepherds are detestable to the Egyptians." Nomadic (and maybe smelly) shepherds at worship are worse than nomadic (and maybe smelly) shepherds at shepherding, especially if one considers oneself a sophisticated urbanite. Of course, Joseph's statement about shepherds being on the typical Egyptian's dislike list is strange in light of what Pharaoh says about his own livestock: "And if you know of any among them with special ability, put them in charge of *my own livestock*" (Gen. 47:6, italics added).

Plague 5: Heavy Pestilence, Heavy Heart

(9:1–7)

Translation

[1]And the LORD said to Moses, "Go to Pharaoh, and you shall speak to him, 'Thus said the LORD, the God of the Hebrews: Send away my people that they may worship me. [2]But if you continually refuse to send away and instead continue to maintain your hold on them, [3]then indeed the hand of the LORD is about to be against your livestock that are out in the field, against the horses, against the donkeys, against the camels, against the cattle, and against the sheep—a pestilence very severe. [4]But the LORD will differentiate between the livestock of Israel and between the livestock of Egypt, and not a thing of Israel's sons will perish.'" [5]And the LORD established a fixed time, saying, "Tomorrow the LORD will do this thing in the land." [6]And the LORD did this thing the next day. All the livestock of Egypt perished, but of the livestock of Israel's sons, not a single one perished. [7]When Pharaoh sent, indeed not even a single livestock had perished. Pharaoh's heart remained heavy, however, and he did not send away the people.

Grammatical and Lexical Notes

9:2. The Hiphil of *ḥāzaq*, if followed by a direct object that is a person, means "seize, take control of, maintain one's hold over/on": "Lift the boy up and *seize/take* him by the hand" (Gen. 21:18); "If out in the country a man happens to meet a girl pledged to be married and *seizes/rapes* her" (Deut. 22:25; the meaning "seize/rape" is present also in Judg. 19:25, and as a prelude to rape in 2 Sam. 13:11 ["grabbed her"]); "The people of Israel are oppressed. . . . All their captors *hold them fast*, refusing to let them go" (Jer. 50:33, which is particularly close to Exod. 9:2).

9:2. Andersen (1974: 117) calls "if you continually refuse to send away and instead continue to maintain your hold on them" an instance of "coordination instead of apposition," in which the second sentence essentially repeats the first sentence.

9:3. "About to be" (*hôyâ*) provides the only illustration of the participle of *hāyâ* ("be") in the Hebrew Bible. Ogden (1967: 484) suggests that the reason for it here may be to bring this passage into line grammatically with surrounding passages that spell out the consequences for Pharaoh's stubbornness, all of which use the participle: "with the staff that is in my hand I am about to strike [*makkeh*] the waters of the Nile" (7:17); "If you refuse to let them go, I will plague [*nōgēp*] your whole country with frogs" (8:2 [7:27]); "or this time I will send [*šōlēaḥ*] the full force of my plagues against you" (9:14); "I will bring [*mēbîʾ*] locusts into your country tomorrow" (10:4).

9:4. The verb for "differentiate" is *pālâ* (Hiphil). It is the verb used in 8:22 [18], and will appear again in 11:7. All these times it refers to God's saving his people in Goshen from the plague that is devastating the other parts of Egypt. For other Hiphil uses of *pālâ*, see Pss. 4:3a [4a], "Know that the Lord *has set apart* the godly for himself"; and 17:7a, "*Make distinct* your acts of kindness" (NIV, "Show the great wonder of your love"). There is another Hebrew verb, *pālāʾ*, ending in an *ʾālep* rather than in a *hê*, which also means "separate, set apart." Perhaps *pālāʾ* is a phonetic variant of *pālâ*. Compare

Num. 6:2, "When anyone, a man or woman, *sets himself apart* [*pālā'*] . . . [NIV, "If a man or woman wants to make a special vow . . ."]." In speaking of God's acts of kindness, Ps. 17:7 uses the form *pālâ*, while Ps. 31:22 uses the form *pālā'* to speak of God's acts of kindness—suggesting that the two verbal forms are variants of each other.

9:7. "Remained heavy" (*wayyikbad*) is a stative verb. The verb does not indicate who has caused Pharaoh's heart to be heavy. It simply says that at that moment it is in a state/condition of heaviness. On the translation of such Hebrew verbs, Waltke and O'Connor (1990: 364) say, "English accurately renders the Hebrew by inserting a form of the 'dummy verb' *to be* ["was, remained" heavy], marking the situation represented by the utterance with respect to those meanings carried by the macrofunctional verb [here, *k-b-d*]."

9:7. This verse contains two different stems for "send," *šālaḥ*. Pharaoh "sent" some of his men to investigate (*šālaḥ*, Qal), but still he refused to "send away" the Israelites (*šālaḥ*, Piel).

9:7. The "severe" pestilence (v. 3) and Pharaoh's "heavy" heart both use some form of *k-b-d* (the pestilence is *kābēd*, but his heart is still *yikbad*). See the title I have given above for 9:1–7.

Commentary

The "hand of the LORD" (v. 3) is a hand that Pharaoh would prefer not to see. **9:1–7**
While there are copious references to "the hand of Yahweh" throughout Exodus and the rest of Scripture, I am particularly interested in those that connect the Lord's hand with death by pestilence (Exod. 9:3, 15; 1 Sam. 5:6, 7, 9, 11; 6:3, 5, 9; 2 Sam. 24:16–17 [= 1 Chron. 21:15, 17]). In a few Psalm passages (32:4; 38:2 [3]; 39:10 [11]) the "hand of the LORD" is a term associated with sickness.

Apparently not only does God visit the sins of the fathers on their children. He also visits the sins of the fathers on their livestock. All of God's creation, human and nonhuman, are liable to be caught up in the disastrous consequences of one malevolent human being. The ripple effect of one's stubbornness and stupidity can be massive.

Given that "animals" appear in the next plague of boils (9:9, 10), and in the following plague of hail (9:19, 22, 25), the "all" in "All the livestock of Egypt perished" (v. 6) must mean "most of." Perhaps the same goes for the "all" in "*all* the dust throughout the land of Egypt became gnats" (8:17 [13]). We must assume something along these lines, if the events subsequent to the statements in 7:20 and 8:17 [13] are to make sense. And surely the "all" that grew in the fields that were stripped by the hail (9:25) excluded the wheat and spelt (9:32).

Four times in these plagues (8:23 [19]; 9:5, 18; 10:4), in the announcement part of the plague, God tells Pharaoh what he is going to do "tomorrow." Twice "tomorrow" appears after the plague has already come on (8:10 [6]; 8:29 [25]). Unlike what Jesus says in Matt 6:34, "Do not worry about tomorrow," maybe Pharaoh had better start worrying a bit about tomorrow. Maybe he needs to start singing, "Don't stop thinking about tomorrow," especially if such meditation and reflection will move him toward a change of heart, an about-face. But don't hold your breath.

Plague 6: Pharaoh Not Bothered by Boils

(9:8–12)

Translation

8And the LORD said to Moses and to Aaron, "Take for yourselves a handful of furnace-ash, and let Moses scatter it heavenward right before Pharaoh's eyes. 9And it shall become dust over the entire land of Egypt, and it shall become on man and on animal a rash, quickly erupting into blisters in the entire land of Egypt." 10And they took the furnace-ash and stood before Pharaoh. Moses scattered it heavenward, and it became a rash quickly erupting into blisters on both man and on animal. 11The magicians were not able to stand before Moses because of the rash, for the rash was on the magicians and the entire land of Egypt. 12The LORD toughened Pharaoh's heart, and he did not listen to them, just as the LORD had said to Moses.

Grammatical and Lexical Notes

9:8. The Hebrew word for "ash, soot" (*pîaḥ*) occurs only in Exod. 9:8, 10.

9:8. The Hebrew word for "furnace" (*kibšān*) appears again only in v. 10 and in Gen. 19:28 and Exod. 19:18. For reasons I cannot fully explain, it is formed from the verb *kābaš*, "subdue, bring into bondage." Does a fiery furnace somehow "subdue" what is placed inside of it by reducing it to ashes? A similar-sounding verb, *kābas*, with a final *sāmek* rather than a final *šîn*, means "to wash, launder" and appears to be cognate with Akkadian *kabasu*, "to tread down, subjugate, trample," suggesting laundering by pounding or beating the clothes.

9:8. Most often "scatter" (*zāraq*) is used in a sacramental context (e.g., Lev. 1:5, 11; 3:2, 8, 13; 7:14; 8:19, 24) for "dashing" the blood against the sides of the altar. Parallel nonsacramental uses of *zāraq* to Exod. 9:8, 10 are Job 2:12 (Job's friends "sprinkled" dust on their heads upon seeing an almost unrecognizable Job), and Ezek. 10:2 (in which the Lord instructs the man clothed in linen to "scatter" burning coals over the city).

9:9. "Rash" or "boil" is *šĕḥîn*. I shall have more to say about this word in the commentary section. It is cognate with Ugaritic *shhn*, "burn," and Akkadian *shahanu*, "grow hot" (see Elman 1976). The Aramaic word *shhn* is present in a prayer of Nabonidus, the last king of Babylon, from Cave 4 at Qumran: "(Concerning) the words of the prayer of Nabonidus, [the Great] king, [when he was stricken] with a pernicious *inflammation* (*shhn᾽ b᾽ysht᾽*) by the decree of God" (trans. B. Levine, in *COS* 1:286).

9:9. *Pāraḥ* ("quickly erupting into, breaking out as") appears in Lev. 13:12 for some kind of skin-disease eruption. The basic meaning of the verb is "blossom."

9:9. The Hebrew *᾽ăbaʿbuʿōt* ("blisters, boils, pustules") appears only in Exod. 9:9, 10.

Commentary

9:8–11 This sixth plague begins like the third plague of gnats (8:16 [12])—no meeting with Pharaoh early in the morning by the river; no going to confront Pharaoh in his palace. The plague simply begins without any advance warning, although Moses and Aaron do what they do "right before Pharaoh's eyes."

On this occasion Moses takes a handful of furnace-ash and throws it above his head. The ash returns earthward, covering man and beast with a fine dust that in turn leads to the sudden outbreak of some sort of skin inflammation. Not only can the Egyptian magicians not cure the blisters on themselves and their people; they also cannot even "stand before" Moses, so incapacitated are they by their blister-covered skin.

The word for these "boils" is *šĕḥîn*. It appears in Lev. 13:18, "When someone has a *boil* on his skin . . ." How best to translate it is up for grabs. Tigay (1996: 263) suggests "skin anthrax," while B. Levine (1989: 79) suggests "dermatitis" for Lev. 13:18 and "dermatitis infection" for its uses in Exod. 9. It is a visible and very uncomfortable disease. Sometimes its flare-up is connected with a judgment sent by God (Exod. 9:9–10; Deut. 28:27, 35), yet perfectly innocent and good people may experience this pain too (the one with a skin disease in Lev. 13:18; Hezekiah, 2 Kings 20:7 [= Isa. 38:21]). Satan too has these in his arsenal, and he afflicts Job with them (Job 2:7).

9:12 Surely it is significant that the very first reference to the Lord's actually toughening/hardening Pharaoh's heart comes not until the end of the sixth plague's narration. When it comes to a real divine touch on Pharaoh's heart that confirms the king in his recalcitrance, we have now moved from promise (4:21; 7:3) to performance, and in between the two there has been a lengthy interlude. It is not that the Lord has a difficult time in implementing his promise. Hardly! It is, rather, the case that God will put his promise on hold, keeping the door of opportunity open, if only a bit, thus extending Pharaoh's chance to act responsibly. At some point, however, the Lord will implement his word. God, who heretofore has attempted to soften Pharaoh's heart (by giving him six opportunities—by the testimony of his own magicians in 8:19 [15]; by the prayers of Moses in 8:8 [4]; 8:28 [24]; and later, in 9:28; 10:17; by moving Pharaoh to making a partial concession in 8:8 [4]; 8:25–28 [21–24])—now hardens Pharaoh's heart.

Plague 7: God's Hail, Moses's Hands

(9:13–35)

Translation

[13]And the LORD said to Moses, "Get up early in the morning and position yourself right before Pharaoh, and you shall say to him, 'Thus said the LORD, the God of the Hebrews: Send away my people that they may worship me. [14]For at this time I am about to send all my plagues to/upon your heart and against your servants, and against your people, so that you may know that there is none like me in all the earth. [15]Because by now I should/could have put forth my hand and struck you and your people with pestilence, and you would have been erased from the earth. [16]And yet for this very thing I have let you stand firm—in order to show you my power, and that my name be proclaimed in all the earth. [17]Yet you still barricade my people rather than sending them away. [18]For sure I am on the verge of raining down at this very time tomorrow very heavy hail, the likes of which has never been in Egypt from the day of its founding until now. [19]So now, send, gather in your livestock and everything that is yours outside in the field. Every last man and animal that is found outside in the field and not brought inside, the hail shall come down upon them and they will perish.'" [20]As for the one who feared the LORD's word among Pharaoh's servants, he brought his slaves and his livestock inside, [21]but whoever instead ignored the LORD's word left his slaves and his livestock behind, in the field outside.

[22]The LORD said to Moses, "Extend your hand over the heavens, that there be hail in all the land of Egypt, upon man and upon animal, and upon all the vegetation outside in the field in the land of Egypt." [23]Just as Moses extended his staff over the heavens, the LORD uncorked thunder and hail, and fire came earthward, and the LORD rained hail over the land of Egypt. [24]And there was hail and fire burning by itself in the midst of the hail, very heavy. There was none like it in all the land of Egypt since it had become a nation. [25]The hail struck throughout all the land of Egypt. Everything that was in the field outside, from man to beast, and all the vegetation of the field, the hail struck. Even every tree in the field outside it decimated. [26]Only in the territory of Goshen, where Israel's sons were, was there no hail.

[27]Pharaoh sent for and summoned Moses and Aaron, and said to them, "I have sinned this time. The LORD [is] the righteous one, and I and my people [are] the wicked ones. [28]Entreat the LORD; enough of God's thunder and hail! I shall send you away, and you will not have to stay put." [29]And Moses said to him, "As I leave the city I will spread my palms to the LORD. The thunder(s) will cease, and the hail will be no more, so that you may know that the earth belongs to the LORD. [30]As for you and your servants, I have known that you do not fear the LORD God." [31]The flax and the barley were decimated because the barley was with soft-seeded ears, and the flax was in stalks; [32]but the wheat and the emmer were not decimated because they were (still) dark/unripened. [33]Moses went out from being with Pharaoh, out of the city, and spread his palms to the LORD. The thunders and the hail ceased, and rain did not fall earthward. [34]When Pharaoh saw that the rain had ceased, along with the hail and thunders, he sinned again. He made his heart heavy, he and his servants. [35]Pharaoh's heart was tough. He did not send away Israel's sons, just as the LORD had said by the hand of Moses.

Grammatical and Lexical Notes

9:14. The word for "plague(s)" is *maggēpâ* and comes from the verb *nāgap* ("strike, smite"), which appears at the start of the second plague (8:2 [7:27]), and will appear in conjunction with the initial observance of Passover (Exod. 12:23, 27). The Lord will use this noun to describe the demise of Ezekiel's wife: "With one *blow/stroke* I am about to take away from you the delight of your eyes" (Ezek. 24:16).

9:14. There is no need to emend "send *to your heart*" (*ʾel-libbĕkā*) to "send *these upon you*" (*ʾelleh bĕkā*), as some have suggested. That the Lord intends to send these plagues to/upon Pharaoh's heart is the text's way of saying, "The Lord will strike Pharaoh precisely in the organ that perpetuates his transgression—his heart" (Shemesh 2005: 346).

9:14. The phrase "none like me" is *ʾên kāmōnî*. In 2 Chron. 14:11 [10] Asa, godly king of Judah, says similarly of the Lord, "There is none like you" (*ʾên-ʿimĕkā*), showing that a rare but attested meaning of *ʿim* is "like."

9:15. Muilenburg (1961: 138) has observed that the expression *kî ʿattâ* ("Because by now") introduces a climactic affirmation or gives force to a predication. Examples from Genesis include the following: 22:12, "*Because now* I know that you fear God"; 26:22, "*Because now* the Lord has given us room"; 31:42, "You would *surely* have sent me away empty-handed"; 43:10, "*because [by] now* we could have gone and returned twice."

9:15. The sequence *kāḥad* [Niphal] *min* more often means "be hidden from" (2 Sam. 18:13; Pss. 69:5 [6]; 139:15; Hosea 5:3) than "be destroyed/erased from."

9:16. "And yet for this very thing" renders just one word in Hebrew (*wĕʾûlām*). BDB 19a calls it an "adverb, but indeed, a strong adversative." Compare its use in Jacob's words to Joseph about Joseph's two sons: "*Nevertheless*, his younger brother [Ephraim] will be greater than he [Manasseh]" (Gen. 48:19).

9:16. The Hiphil of *ʿāmad* ("I have let you stand firm") has a parallel use in 1 Kings 15:4: "For David's sake the Lord his God gave him [Abijah, king of Judah] a lamp in Jerusalem by raising up a son to succeed him, and by *making strong/maintaining* Jerusalem." See also Prov. 29:4, where the Hiphil of *ʿāmad* is used to describe the king whose faithful practice of justice *gives stability* to his country.

9:17. "Barricade my people" may also be translated "You exalt yourself against my people." The verb *sālal* ("lift up, cast up") is related to the noun *sōlĕlâ*, a mound or siege ramp cast up against a city.

9:18. *Kāʿēt māḥār* ("at this very time") indicates not approximation, but temporal precision. See Goldingay 1993.

9:18. The *mappîq* (a dot in the center of a final consonantal *hê*) in *hiwwāsĕdâ* (should be *hiwwāsĕdah*, "her founding") is absent. A similar absence of the *mappîq* is in Lev. 6:2, "The burnt offering is to be on its fireplace [*môqĕdâ* without the *mappîq*; should be *môqĕdah*] on top of the altar."

9:18. "Never been" is simply "has not been" (*lōʾ hāyâ*). It illustrates the intensive meaning of *hāyâ*. Mark 13:19 ("because those will be days of distress unequaled from the beginning, when God created the world, until now—and never to be equaled again") may be echoing several passages in Exodus that describe the unprecedented severity of the plagues on Egypt, such as this one in Exod. 9:18: "I am on the verge of raining down . . . very heavy hail, the likes of which has never been in Egypt from the day of its founding until now." See also Exod. 10:14 and 11:6 for similar "nothing like it ever again" language.

9:19. For two other uses of the Hiphil imperative of the uncommon verb *ʿûz* ("gather in"), see Jer. 4:6 and 6:1 ("flee for safety").

9:20. The phrase "the word of the Lord" occurs in the Pentateuch only here and in v. 21, as well as in Gen. 15:1, 4; Num. 15:31; Deut. 5:5. By contrast, it appears in 1 and 2 Kings fifty times, in Jeremiah fifty-two times, in Ezekiel sixty times.

9:20–21. On the use of explicit preverbal noun subjects used in coordination to bring out a contrast (the heedful and the unheedful), see Andersen 1974: 151–52. On the use of the *qāṭal* verb form in the apodosis of v. 20 (*hēnîs*, "brought") versus the use of the *wayyiqṭōl* verb form in the apodosis of v. 21 (*wayyaʿăzōb*, "left"), see Niccacci 1996. According to Steiner (2000: 265–66), the *wāw* prefixed to "he left" in v. 21 functions like the comma in English ("As for him who paid no regard to the word of the Lord, he left . . . in the open").

9:21. "Ignore" is *lōʾ-śām libbô ʾel* (lit., "did not set/direct his heart to"). Often, when the word *lēb*/"heart" follows the verb *śîm*, it is preceded by a preposition, for example, Deut. 11:18, "Fix (*śîm*) these words of mine in/on (*ʿal*) your hearts." But *lēb* may also be the direct object of *śîm* (here and Deut. 32:46; 1 Sam. 9:20; 25:25; Job 1:8; 2:3; Hag. 1:5, 7; 2:15, 18 [2x]). Note the variety of ways the NIV renders *śîm lēb*: "ignored" (Exod. 9:21); "Take to heart" (Deut. 32:46); "Do not worry about them" (1 Sam. 9:20); "Pay no attention to" (1 Sam. 25:25); "Have you considered . . . ?" (the two Job passages, 1:8 and 2:3); "give careful thought to" (the four Haggai passages, 1:5, 7; 2:15, 18).

9:23. There is a different order of subject/verb in the first two clauses of the verse: "and-stretched Moses" (verb:subject); "the Lord uncorked" (subject:verb). Although there is a cause-to-effect relationship between clause 1 and 2, Moses's actions and the Lord's are to be understood as almost simultaneous.

9:23. The verb "came" in "and fire came earthward" has the unusual and more archaic form *wattihălak*, where the expected third-person feminine singular imperfect would be *tēlēk* or *wattēlek* (if the *wa-* is added).

9:24. The expression "and fire burning by itself" (*wĕʾēš mitlaqqaḥat* [a Hitpael feminine singular participle of *lāqaḥ*, "taking hold of itself"]) appears again only in Ezek. 1:4, "I saw a windstorm, . . . an immense cloud with *flashing lightning*." Greenberg (1983: 43) suggests "a fire caught onto itself," and then adds, "i.e., not having an object onto which it has caught but merely burning there 'in the air' as a fiery mass."

9:25. More than likely the phrase *mēʾādām wĕʿad-bĕhēmâ* ("from man[kind] and-to beast/animal") is a merism: a literary device that expresses totality by using two words that are opposite and are joined by the conjunction "and." For example, "I have looked up and down for my car keys" (see Honeyman 1952: 12; Avishur 1984: 92, 94). Note also the chiasmus in the first clause (verb>subject>object: "struck">"the hail">"every man and beast in the field") and the second clause (object>verb>subject: "and all the vegetation of the field">"smote">"the hail").

9:27. "This time" (*happāʿam*) is, literally, "the time." Here the definite article has what Hebrew grammarians call "deictic" force: it points to a particular occasion in the present time. Compare Jeremiah's word to the pseudoprophet Hananiah: "This very year [*haššānâ*, lit., "the year"] you are going to die" (Jer. 28:16). See Arnold and Choi 2003: 32.

9:27. The verbs "is" and "are" in the second half of the verse are added for sense. There are no verbs in the Hebrew of v. 27b. On conjoined verbless clauses, see Andersen 1974: 128.

9:28. *Qōlōt ʾĕlōhîm* is like the expression *rûaḥ ʾĕlōhîm* in Gen. 1:2. Should we translate the latter as "the S/spirit of God" or as "a very mighty wind"? Should we translate the former as "the thunder of God" or as "a very loud thunder"? Is *ʾĕlōhîm*, usually understood as "God," ever used to express the superlative? The NIV ignores *ʾĕlōhîm* altogether in 9:28 ("We have had enough thunder and hail").

9:29. "As I leave the city" (*kĕṣēʾtî ʾet-hāʿîr*) provides an uncommon instance of the use of *ʾet* after an intransitive verb of motion; also see v. 33. For other instances of *yāṣāʾ ʾet*, see Gen. 44:4; Num. 35:26; Eccles. 7:18. For *ʾet* after other verbs of motion, compare Ezek. 21:20 [25] (*bôʾ ʾet*, "come against"); Judg. 19:18 (*hālak ʾet*, "go to"); 1 Sam. 30:21 (*nāgaš ʾet*, "approach, come up to").

9:29. The meaning "cease" for *ḥādal* is rare. A much more common meaning is "hold oneself back, refrain from" (see D. Thomas 1956).

9:30. As several writers have observed (e.g., P. Thompson 1971: 200n2; Humphreys 2001: 260n34), this is the only place in the Pentateuch where the name "Lord God" (*YHWH ʾĕlōhîm*) appears outside of Gen. 2:4–3:23.

9:31–32. I shall have more to say on these two verses in the commentary section. For now, note the ABBA sequence of nouns in v. 31. Ceresko (1975) claims to have uncovered 119 examples of this sequence in the Hebrew Bible.

A flax (*pištâ*)
B barley (*śĕʿōrâ*)
B′ barley (*śĕʿōrâ*)
A′ flax (*pištâ*)

In vv. 33–34 is another illustration of this sequence, which Ceresko did not note ("thunders and the hail"/"the hail and the thunders").

9:33. In the Qal, *nātak* refers to the pouring out of water (Job 3:24). In the Niphal it refers to the falling of rain (here and 2 Sam. 21:10) or of divine wrath (Jer. 42:18; Nah. 1:6). In the Hiphil it refers to the melting down of silver (2 Kings 22:9 [NIV, "paid out"]; Ezek. 22:20).

9:35. Rainey (1996: 3.55) connects the phrase "said by the hand of Moses" with Amarna *u qa-bi-ti i-na qa-tí Pa-wu-ra a-wa-ta$_5$ an-ni-ta$_5$*, literally, "I spoke this word by the hand of Pawura." For "speaking by the hand" of somebody, see 1 Kings 15:29; 16:12, 34; etc.

Commentary

The word "all/every(thing)" (*kol*) appears twelve times in the narration of this **9:13–19** plague: "*all* my plagues" (v. 14); "none like me in *all* the earth" (v. 14); "be proclaimed in *all* the earth" (v. 16); "*everything* that is yours" (v. 19); "*every* last man" (v. 19); "*all* the land of Egypt" (v. 22); "upon *all* the vegetation" (v. 22); "in *all* the land of Egypt" (v. 24); "throughout *all* the land of Egypt" (v. 25); "*everything* that was in the field" (v. 25); "and *all* the vegetation" (v. 25); "even *every* tree in the field" (v. 25).

This may explain why the Lord uses the word "plague" in v. 14 in the plural. There is an intensity, a pervasiveness, about this plague that separates it from its predecessors. With the exception of the Hebrews in Goshen (v. 26), no animal is safe, no person is safe, no vegetation is safe. Another reason why the Lord uses the plural "plagues" may be that the reference in v. 14 is not only to this seventh plague, but also to any and all that may follow this one. God's arsenal is not down to its last shot.

Pharaoh thinks that there is none like him in all the earth. Wrong! What he desperately needs to discover is that there is none like Yahweh in all the earth (and that includes Pharaoh's backyard and his deities). Texts like v. 14a are not so much evidence for the monotheistic nature of Israel's God, that he and he alone exists as God (although such are present elsewhere, as in Isa. 45:6, 14, 21); rather, they point to his incomparability. Moses will sing rhetorically,

"Who among the gods is like you, O Lord?" (Exod. 15:11). Moses's concern is not to underscore the exclusiveness and uniqueness of Yahweh's divinity but to suggest that Yahweh has both a character and wonder-working power that separate him from other beings who aspire to and claim the title "deity." "Who is like you?" or "There is none like you" is a testimony about God found in Israel's historical narrative (1 Sam. 2:2; 2 Sam. 7:22; 1 Kings 8:23), in its prophetic corpus (Jer. 10:6; Mic. 7:18), and in its liturgical literature (Pss. 35:10; 71:19; 86:8; 89:8 [9]). That other peoples may also claim such exclusiveness for their deities demonstrates that the issue here is "not the uniqueness of a theology but the uniqueness of a reality" (Goldingay 2006: 38).

In my translation of v. 15 I have allowed for the renderings "I *could have* . . . struck you," or "I *should have* . . . struck you." The first suggests possibility, the second suggests intention. I am inclined to think that "should have" is preferable. God is not talking about options that were previously at his disposal. Rather, he is talking about what his normal procedure would be, given Pharaoh's intransigence. However, God decides to put "normal procedures" on hold because he has a plan for Pharaoh that goes far beyond simply annihilating him and will be more far-reaching than that.

This is what v. 16 is about. Most of us would probably slide by this text, if it were not for the fact that Paul quotes a Septuagint version of Exod. 9:16 in Rom. 9:17. The larger context of Rom. 9 is Paul's magisterial (and difficult-to-understand?) discussion of divine sovereignty and divine mercy, and how Jews and gentiles are on the receiving end of both.

There are a few differences between the Hebrew and Greek text of Exod. 9:16, as there are in Paul's quote of it in Rom. 9:17 (see Cranfield 1979: 2.485–88). For example, the Hebrew "I have made you stand" comes out in the LXX as "You have been preserved" (*dietērēthēs*). Paul, who is quoting the Septuagint, changes "You have been preserved" into "I have brought into existence" or "I have raised you up." He uses the verb *exegeirō*, a verb that elsewhere in the NT refers to raising the dead (1 Cor. 6:14) and recovering from sickness (James 5:15, *egeirō*, without the prefix *ex-*). The differences of the three versions of Exod. 9:17 aside, they all agree on one very important point: Pharaoh, like any of us, owes every breath he breathes to a gracious and merciful God, and in spite of his habitual arrogance, God has a plan to use the life of Pharaoh that will have worldwide implications and impact. The Lord might well have said to Pharaoh, "I have plans for you" (cf. Jer. 29:11).

One would think that a hailstorm over all Egypt would be about as common as a blizzard in San Diego from a nor'easter. It would be as unheard of as 24-7 darkness (the ninth plague) in the land of eternal sunshine. One can imagine the Egyptians saying the same thing that the Israelites say when God sends the manna to them: "What is it?" (Exod. 16:15). Recall that on those two occasions God "rained down" (*māṭar*) something: hail and manna (Exod. 9:18, 23; 16:4). Some have argued, to the contrary, that thunderstorms and hailstorms are regularly a seasonal phenomena in at least some parts of Egypt (e.g., Hort 1958: 48–49). But this storm is massive. No inlet or hamlet is spared.

Loss of property and limb is not inevitable, however menacing the hailstorm may be. In v. 19 the Lord gives advanced warning to the Egyptians to seek shelter for themselves and for their livestock, inside the safety of their homes and barns. This is like the tornado siren that warns those in its path to get inside their homes, head to the basement if they have one, and if not, seek shelter under a heavy table or in an inside room, and stay away from windows. God wants survivors rather than victims.

9:20–21 In 9:19, God's command to Pharaoh, relayed through Moses, is for the Egyptians to leave the outside and get into houses before the hail falls; this word is somehow circulated throughout Pharaoh's domain. It produces two opposite reactions: those who listen to, embrace, and respond to the warning with due haste, and those who scoff at it. Those are always the two options when a word from God goes forth to any people: obey/disobey, listen/do not listen, respond/ignore, fall at his feet and worship him/unless I see I will not believe, soften your heart/harden your heart.

9:22–26 Sometimes God is the God of the "gentle whisper," as he is for Elijah in 1 Kings 19:12, but at other times he is the God of violent storms that wipe out just about everything in their path. Jonah can identify with these storm-ravaged Egyptians. He experiences God's storm because he is running from God, and some Egyptians experience God's storm because they ignore God.

There are two different points in this plague where something without equal is present. There is no god like God (*kāmōnî*, "none like me," in v. 14b). And Egypt has never experienced a storm like this one (*kāmōhû*, "none like it," in v. 24b). Once again parts of God's beautiful and innocent creation (animals, vegetation) experience the disastrous effects of the sins of humans. That grim reality is as old, unfortunately, as the flood of Noah. Seldom are the consequences and fallout of sinful behavior restricted to the perpetrator(s).

It is understandable how the hailstorm misses Goshen (v. 26). We have all seen it rain heavily on one side of the street while the other side remains dry, but how do you keep swarms of flies from making it to Goshen (8:22 [18]), or prevent disease on livestock from spreading to farms in Goshen (9:4)?

9:27–30 In confessing "I have sinned" (v. 27), Pharaoh joins others who offer to God the same contrition: Achan (Josh. 7:20), Saul (1 Sam. 15:24; 26:21), David (2 Sam. 12:13; 24:10), Israel (Num. 14:40; Deut. 1:41; Judg. 10:15), Daniel (Dan. 9:5), Judas Iscariot (Matt. 27:4). But given another opportunity to return to his old ways, Pharaoh jumps at it, eventually leading him to a second penitential confession (10:16–17). As Greenberg (1969: 161) says, "He acknowledged guilt but went right on being guilty." But surely repentance is more than serial apologies. We are not to continue in sin so that grace may abound (Rom.

6:1). DeNeff (2002: 11) has written incisively, "Any repentance that does not lessen our impulse to commit the same sin again is not genuine repentance."

If Pharaoh shares "I have sinned" with others, he also shares his acknowledgment of Israel's God with other kings and dignitaries: "The LORD [is] the righteous one" (v. 27b). Moses's Midianite father-in-law does (Exod. 18:10–11). Balaam the Mesopotamian diviner does (Num. 22–24). Naaman the Aramean does (2 Kings 5:15). Nebuchadnezzar does (Dan. 4:34–35). Darius does (Dan. 6:26). And according to an addition to the book of Esther not found in Protestant Bibles (Add. Esth. 16:15–16), Artaxerxes does: "The Jews, who were consigned to annihilation by this thrice-accursed man [Haman], are not evildoers, but are governed by most righteous laws and are children of the living God, most high, most mighty, who has directed the kingdom both for us and for our ancestors in the most excellent order" (NRSV).

9:31–32 These two verses are an intriguing agricultural aside. Because of the hailstorm, the flax and barley (which could not be brought inside) are ruined, while the wheat and emmer are not because they are yet in an earlier stage of growth.

Flax growing in Egypt is abundantly attested in both texts and pictures. By contrast, the only references to the flax plant and the actual processing of flax in the OT are here in Exod. 9:31 and in Isa. 19:9, and interestingly, both texts have an Egyptian setting. All the other biblical references to *pištâ*/*pištîm* deal with the already-processed weaving material (e.g., Lev 13:48, 52). The one biblical reference to the flax plant growing in Canaan is the flax stalks on the roof of Rahab's house (Josh. 2:6). Again, only two texts in the OT list barley, wheat, and emmer, along with other grain varieties (Isa. 28:25; Ezek. 4:9), as part of the Palestinian crops, but "flax" is conspicuously absent. All of this suggests that flax, which is used to make linen, was imported to Canaan from Egypt.

Yet we have a Hebrew inscription discovered at Gezer in 1908, known appropriately as the Gezer Calendar, and written in the last half of the tenth century BC. The calendar lists eight agricultural periods. Four of the eight have a two-month span, and the other four have a one-month duration (trans. *ANET* 320; *COS* 2:222).

Three lines are of special interest:

yrḥ ʾṣd psht—"the month of hoeing (cutting up?) flax"
yrḥ qstr śʿrm—"the month of reaping barley"
yrḥ qstr wkl—"the month of reaping [wheat] and measuring"

If we calculate from the beginning of the year, "the month of hoeing flax" would be April. "The month of reaping barley" would be May. "The month of reaping wheat" would be June. These are, of course, approximations on the calendar, with a degree of harvest overlap, to be sure. In any case, the crops parallel the people and animals. What takes refuge inside survives. What remains outside perishes. What grows in the fields early is ripped to shreds. What has not yet popped up through the soil is not damaged by the storm. Inside/late means deliverance. Outside/early means destruction. (I have been much helped here by the discussions of Talmon 1963: 179–80; B. Levine 2000: 412.)

Two items are of interest in the final three verses of this plague's narrative. **9:33–35**
First, for the third time Pharaoh asks Moses to pray for him and promises to then release the people (8:8 [4]; 8:28 [24]). Moses prays. God answers the prayer by removing the plague (8:13 [9]; 8:31 [27]). Once the plague is removed, Pharaoh reneges on his promise (8:15 [11]; 8:32 [28]) and hardens his heart. Are we about to repeat that scenario again? Should not somebody (God? Moses?) be catching on to something here? Is Pharaoh the perfect con artist? What about the proverb, "Fool me once, shame on you. Fool me twice, shame on me"? What about fooling me three times? Surely Moses agrees on this occasion to pray once more for the ending of the plague, not because he believes in Pharaoh's sincerity, but because of what he believes about God and God's sovereign purpose in all of this. If Jesus prays three times that some painful reality might pass (Matt. 26:36–46), why can Moses not pray three times (or four times; see 10:18) that some other painful reality might pass? The frogs pass. The flies/gnats pass. The hailstorm passes. The cup does not pass.

The second item of interest here is that even after the narrative of the previous plague ends by saying, for the first time, that the Lord has toughened Pharaoh's heart (9:12), Pharaoh is still able to make his own heart heavy (9:34b). Divine hardening does not preclude the possibility of a self-hardening, down the road, or making one's own heart "heavy."

Plague 8: Lots and Lots of Locusts

(10:1–20)

Translation

[1]The LORD said to Moses, "Go to Pharaoh, for I, I have made heavy his heart and the heart of his servants, so that I may place these signs of mine right where he is, [2]and that you may tell in your son's ears and in your grandson's how I toyed with Egypt, and my signs that I placed on them in order that (all of) you may know that I am the LORD."

[3]Moses, along with Aaron, came to Pharaoh, and they said to him, "Thus said the LORD, the God of the Hebrews, 'How long will you refuse to humble yourself before me? Send off my people that they may worship me. [4]For if you continue to refuse to send off my people, for sure I am about to bring on, tomorrow, locust(s) in all of your territory. [5]It will cover over the eye of the land so that one will not be able to see the land. And it will consume the rest of the remaining remnant left you from the hail, and it will consume every tree growing for you in the field. [6]They will fill your houses and the houses of all your servants and the houses of all of Egypt such as your fathers and grandfathers have not seen from the day of their being on the ground until this day.'" Moses turned on his heels and left Pharaoh's presence.

[7]Pharaoh's servants said to him, "How long will this one be a snare to us? Send away the men that they may worship the LORD their god. Do you not yet know that Egypt is starving?" [8]Moses, and Aaron too, was brought back to Pharaoh, and he said to them, "Go, worship the LORD your god. Who, by the way, will be going?" [9]Moses said, "With our lads and elders we will go. With our sons and daughters, with our sheep and cattle we will go, for it is a festival of the LORD for us." [10]He said to them, "The LORD better be with you as I send you off along with your little ones! See that evil is in front of your faces. [11]Not so! Have the adult men go, and let them worship the LORD, for that is what you really want to do." And he drove them from Pharaoh's presence.

[12]The LORD said to Moses, "Extend your hand over the land of Egypt for the locust, that it come up over the land of Egypt, and consume all the herbage, everything that the hail left untouched." [13]Moses extended his staff over the land of Egypt, and the LORD drove an east wind into the land that entire day and entire night. Come morning, and the east wind had brought the locust. [14]The locust came up over all the land of Egypt, and came to rest in every territory of Egypt. Very dense! There was never a locust like it before, and after it there would never be the like. [15]It covered the eye of the entire land so that the land turned dark. It consumed all the herbage and every fruit of the tree the hail had left behind. Nothing green in tree and the grass in the field was left behind in all the land of Egypt. [16]Pharaoh quickly summoned Moses and Aaron, and said, "I have sinned against the LORD your god and against you. [17]So now, forgive, please, my sin just this once, and entreat the LORD your god that he remove from me this one death." [18]Moses left Pharaoh's presence and entreated the LORD. [19]The LORD turned around a sea wind, very strong. It carried the locust away and drove it into the Re(e)d Sea. Not one locust remained in all the territory of Egypt. [20]The LORD toughened Pharaoh's heart, and he did not send Israel's sons away.

Grammatical and Lexical Notes

10:1. "Right where he is" renders Hebrew *bĕqirbô* (lit., "in his midst"). This *šît bĕqirbô* ("place in his midst") is the same in 10:1, functionally, as *šālaḥ ʾel-libbĕkā* ("send to your heart") in 9:14.

10:2. There are two possibilities for *hitʿallaltî* (Hitpael from *ʿālal*): "dealt harshly with" (NIV) and "made fools of" (NRSV). The former meaning, physical abuse, is present in passages like Judg. 19:25 ("abused" in rape); 1 Sam. 6:6 ("treat harshly"); 1 Sam. 31:4 ("abuse"); Jer. 38:19 ("mistreat"). The latter meaning is present in Num. 22:29 ("make a fool of"). The LXX uses the verb *empaizō*, which means "insult" in Gen. 39:14, but "make sport of" in Exod. 10:2; Num. 22:29; Judg. 16:25, 27; 1 Sam. 6:6; 31:4; Ezek. 22:5. It is the verb (or related noun) that the NT uses for the mockings heaped on Jesus (Matt. 27:29, 31, 34; Luke 23:11), the jeering directed at persecuted believers (Heb. 11:36), and end-time "scoffers" (2 Pet. 3:3; Jude 18).

10:2. The phrase "signs and wonders/portents" (*ʾōtōt ûmōpĕtîm*) occurs as a pair often in Deuteronomy (4:34; 6:22; 7:19; 26:8; 29:3 [2]; 34:11). In Exodus the pair appears only in 7:3. "Signs" appears by itself in Exod. 4:9, 17, 28, 30; 10:1–2, and "wonders/portents" by itself in 4:21; 11:9–10.

10:3. "How long will you refuse?" uses the *qāṭal* form of the verb (*mēʾantā*), while "How long will this one be a snare to us?" in v. 7 uses the (more-expected) *yiqṭōl* form of the verb (*yihyeh*). I see no difference in meaning between the perfect form of the verb in v. 3 and the imperfect form of the verb in v. 7 (see Hughes 1970: 22–23). We can call *mēʾantā* a perfective future or a future perfective.

10:3. For "How long [*ʿad-mātay*]?" as an interrogative implying judgment, see 1 Sam. 1:14; 2 Sam. 2:26; Prov. 1:22; Jer. 4:14, 21; 12:4; 31:22; 47:5.

10:3. The verb "humble" (*ʿānâ*) occurs seventy-six times in the Hebrew Bible. Most often it means "afflict(ed), defeat(ed)," but about twenty times it means "to submit to one in authority." Usually that authority is God, but twice the verb is used of submitting to other people (Gen. 16:9, Hagar to Sarah; and Isa. 60:14, oppressor to the oppressed). See Dickson and Rosner 2004: 473. The meaning "afflict, defeat" is more common in the Piel and Pual stems, while "humble oneself" is more common in the Niphal stem. This difference is clear in the presence of *ʿānâ* in Isa. 53:4, which speaks of the Suffering Servant as "smitten by God and *afflicted* [Pual of *ʿānâ*]," while Isa. 53:7 says that the Servant "was oppressed, yet he was *submissive* [Niphal of *ʿānâ*]" (rather than NIV's "He was oppressed and 'afflicted'"). See Barré 2000: 16.

10:4. Throughout this plague, "locust" (*ʾarbeh*) appears in singular form as a collective noun. All the verbs with which the noun is used are singular except for the "they will fill" of v. 6.

10:5. Most translations render the phrase "the eye of the land" as "the surface of the land." I choose to stay with a literal translation. It occurs again in Num. 22:5, 11 when Balak, king of Moab, says to Balaam that the approaching Hebrews are so numerous that they cover the "eye of the land." It may also appear in Zech. 9:1 if Dahood's (1963) reading of *ʿên ʾādām* as "the eye of the earth" instead of "the eyes of men" (NIV) is on target. In English one finds parts of the body used with impersonal nouns: the eye of the storm, the eye of a needle, the mouth of a river, the neck of a bottle, the shoulder of a road, the foot of the mountain.

10:5. In the announcement part of this plague, the targeted area is "the eye of the land" (v. 5). But in the fulfillment part of this plague, the targeted area is "the eye of the 'entire' land," which adds the word "entire/*kol*" (v. 15).

10:5. The clause *wĕlōʾ yûkal lirʾōt* ("so that one will not be able to see") illustrates the use of a third-person masculine-singular passive verb (*yûkal*) to express an indefinite subject. See Arnold and Choi 2003: 168.

10:5. The phrase *yeter happĕlēṭâ hannišʾeret* ("the rest of the remaining remnant left you") provides a rare instance of three words in succession that are essentially synonyms. See Avishur 1984: 181, 249.

10:6. In a perceptive study of the phrase "until this day," Childs (1963) observes that it occurs seventy-six times in the Hebrew Bible. It is used in one of two ways. Either it has an etiological function (e.g., "Therefore that place has been called the Valley of Achor until this day" [Josh. 7:26]), or it is a nonetiological idiom. When it is used in the latter sense, it always occurs in the context of somebody's speech, as here in Moses's disputation with Pharaoh.

10:7. G. Driver (1954b: 131–36) suggests reading *môqēš* not as "snare/trap" but as "striker," the movable part of a trap that, when released, falls down on the back or neck, thus trapping the victim.

10:7. "Do you not yet know?" (*hăṭerem tēdaʿ*) illustrates a standard form of appeal to recall tradition (Isa. 40:21–24, "Do you not know? Have you not heard?"). The phrase is also used to call for recognition of what is self-evident or common knowledge (e.g., here and in Gen. 44:15, "Joseph said to them, 'What is this you have done? *Don't you know* that a man like me can find things out by divination?'"; Judg. 15:11 NRSV, "*Do you not know* that the Philistines are rulers over us?"; 2 Sam. 2:26 AT, "*Do you not know* that this will end in bitterness?"; 2 Sam. 3:38 NRSV, "*Do you not know* that a prince and a great man has fallen in Israel today?"; 2 Sam. 11:20, "*Didn't you know* they would shoot arrows from the wall?"). See Habel 1976: 263.

10:7. *ʾĀbĕdâ* is often translated "ruined," but the basic meaning of the verb *ʾābad* is "perish." And here the idea is perishing through starvation, since all harvestable crops have been decimated. Janzen (1994: 362) has suggested reading not "my father was a 'wandering' Aramean [*ʾărammî ʾōbēd*]" in Deut. 26:5, but "my father was a 'starving' Aramean."

10:8. For other instances of *ʾet* before the subject of a passive verb (*wayyûšab ʾet-mōšeh*), see Gen. 4:18, "Irad [*ʾet-ʿîrad*] was born to Enoch"; Gen. 27:42, "When the words [*ʾet-dibrê*] of Esau were told to Rebekah"; Gen. 29:27, "Finish this week, and this one [*ʾet-zôʾt*] will be given to you"; Exod. 21:28, "and its flesh [*ʾet-bĕśārō*] must not be eaten"; Num. 14:21, "as surely as all the earth [*ʾet-kol-hāʾāreṣ*] will be filled with the glory of the Lord." In such cases the *ʾet* is more an indicator of the subject of the verb rather than the object of the verb. Hoftijzer (1965: 14) remarks that in such instances "*ʾet* is used as a determinative to the subject enclosed in the verb." See also Elwode (1994: 179), who adds to the above passages Gen. 17:5; 21:5, 8; 40:20; Exod. 27:7; and others.

10:8. "Who, by the way, will be going?" is *mî wāmî hahōlĕkîm*, "Who and who are the ones going?" Probably the pronoun "who/*mî*" is repeated for emphasis.

10:10. Rendsburg (1988: 355) has suggested that *kî rāʿâ neged pĕnêkem* is an instance of bilingual wordplay—"that evil [*rāʿâ*] is in front of your faces," and "that Ra [*rāʿâ*] is in front of your faces." In his commentary on Exodus, Cassuto (1967: 126) seems to have anticipated Rendsburg when he rendered this last phrase as "know that the power of my god will oppose you."

10:11. The word for "men" in v. 7 that Pharaoh's servants encourage Pharaoh to dispatch as quickly as possible is *ʾănāšîm*. The word Pharaoh uses for these "men" in v. 11 is *gĕbārîm*, which I have translated as "adult men."

10:11. For *ʾet* to introduce a neuter pronoun ("for 'that' [*ʾōtāh*] is what you really want to do"), see Elwode 1994: 173. There is no need to see an abbreviation here (*ʾōtāh* = *ʾet hāʾĕlōhîm*, "for G/god is what you desire"), as argued by R. Weiss (1964). Rather, the feminine suffix in *ʾōtāh* refers to the feminine *ʿăbōdat YHWH*, "the service/worship of the Lord," implied by Pharaoh's "and serve [*wĕʿibdû*] the Lord." See G. Driver 1966: 1.

10:14. For the verb "came to rest in" (*nûaḥ bĕ*), used elsewhere with birds or insects coming down and settling on something, see Isa. 7:19, "(flies and bees) will all come and *settle in* the steep ravines and in the crevices in the rocks." Its most famous use is in Gen. 8:4, where Noah's ark, after floating on the water, "came to rest on" the mountains of Ararat. The idea behind the verb is not so much on "rest" as it is on motion that moves to settlement. See G. Robinson (1980: 33–37).

10:14. For *lĕpānāyw* ("before it") and *wĕʾaḥărāyw* ("and after it") as a merism, see Krašovec 1983: 236.

10:15. On the color word "green"/*yereq*, see A. Brenner (1982: 100–101).

10:16. *Wayĕmahēr . . . liqrōʾ*, "and he [Pharaoh] quickly summoned," is a variant form of *wayyiqrāʾ mĕhērâ*, "Quickly he called to . . ." (Judg. 9:54).

10:19. "A sea wind" (*rûʾaḥ-yām*) is a west wind, and is the opposite of the "east wind" (*rûʾaḥ qādîm*) of v. 13. As Alter (2004: 368, 369) has pointed out, "east wind" and "west wind" presuppose the geography of Canaan rather than that of Egypt. Locusts would swarm into Egypt from the south. And any wind blowing off the Mediterranean would blow into Egypt from the north.

10:19. The verb for "turned around" is *hāpak*, the one used in Gen. 19:21, 25, 29 (and in Deut. 29:23 [22]; Jer. 20:16; Lam. 4:6) for the overthrow/annihilation of Sodom and Gomorrah. In Genesis, God's "turning" brings on destruction. In Exodus, God's "turning" brings on the removal of destruction.

Commentary

Unlike any previous plague account, this is the only one to begin with a ref- **10:1**
erence to the Lord having hardened/made heavy Pharaoh's heart. The verb form is the Hiphil first-person perfect of *kābēd*. Elsewhere in this section of Exodus, this stem of *kābēd* occurs with Pharaoh as the subject (8:15 [11], 32 [28]). The point of beginning with such a thought is to show that for Pharaoh the window of opportunity has closed.

Most often the plagues are said to be for the benefit of Pharaoh and/or his **10:2**
people, that he/they may "know" who Israel's Yahweh is (5:2; 7:5, 17; 8:10 [6], 22 [18]; 9:14, 29; 14:4, 18). Once earlier (6:7) it is Israel's knowledge of God that is encouraged (also see 11:7). What sets aside 10:2 from all these other references is that the Israelite participants, in times to come, are to share this story with the second and third generations. The first generation of delivered Hebrews are to narrate this incredible event to their children and grandchildren and hence "induct them into the world of wonder, . . . to recruit the next generation of Israelites into this daring scenario of courage and confidence, passion and faith" (Brueggemann 1994: 762–63). If for no other reason, this is reason enough why Moses cannot agree to Pharaoh's later ploy that the Israelites leave their children behind (vv. 10–11). How does one tell "the old, old story" to the next generation if there is no next generation to whom it can be told?

Yet another difference between the eighth plague and the previous seven sur- **10:3–6**
faces in these four verses. In all of the earlier plagues (except for those that give no warning), the narrative begins by reporting the message that God gives to Moses to deliver to Pharaoh (7:14–18; 8:1–4 [7:26–29]; 8:20–23 [16–19]; 9:1–4, 13–18), but Moses's actual delivery of that message to Pharaoh goes unrecorded, or is lumped into some cursory phrase like "and Moses did so." Here that pattern is reversed. God's actual message to Moses is absent. What we have is the delivery of a message of God that the text has not previously mentioned. In the earlier plagues the emphasis is on how Moses receives the

message, but here the emphasis is on how Moses delivers the message. Such variation at this point in the pericope of the plagues "lends vividness to the confrontation of prophet and audience suitable to the climax of a series" (Greenberg 1997: 513–14).

Very few kings, to say nothing of the rest of us, have a good track record at humbling themselves (v. 3). It is difficult for the high and mighty to become the low and the least. But thank God for those Judean kings who follow the word that the Lord gives to Solomon: "If my people, who are called by my name, will humble themselves" (2 Chron. 7:14). Rehoboam does (2 Chron. 12:6–7, 12). Manasseh does (2 Chron. 33:12). Josiah does (2 Chron. 34:27). (All these references in Chronicles use the verb *kāna'* for "humble oneself" rather than *'ānāh*, as in Exod. 10:3.)

Locusts, as a manifestation of divine judgment, appear elsewhere in Scripture. One thinks immediately of the book of Joel. Another reference, and perhaps one closer to Exodus than Joel is, is Amos 4:4–13. The Lord has sent a number of plagues among his people, one of which was locusts (Amos 4:9b). These plagues are not primarily to punish Israel, or from God's seeking vengeance. Rather, as with the plagues on Pharaoh and Egypt, they are intended to move Israel to repentance ("Yet you have not returned to me" [Amos 4:11c]). In an attempt to open his people to an about-face, God engages in selective raining: "I sent rain on one town, but withheld it from another. One field had rain; another had none and dried up" (Amos 4:7b). Does that not sound like, "But in the land of Goshen there was no ——"? But all to no avail! As in Exodus, so in Amos 4, divine patience has worn thin, and the final hour of reckoning is imminent.

10:7 Pharaoh's servants' "How long?" addressed to their king matches Moses's "How long?" addressed to Pharaoh back in v. 3. Both are critical of Pharaoh. For Moses, it is Pharaoh's arrogance. For the servants, it is Pharaoh's blindness and indifference. Moses's critique is more direct and blunt ("How long will *you* . . . ?"). The servants' critique is more indirect ("How long will *this one* . . . ?").

Nevertheless, the servants' exasperation is but another in a string of Egyptian testimonies screaming out to Pharaoh that he is fighting a losing battle and that his sand castle is crumbling (see 8:18–19 [14–15]; 9:11, 20–21; 11:3, 8; 12:33). As Sternberg (1998: 151) has said, "As the plagues multiply, so do the fissures in the Egyptian camp."

10:8–11 Pharaoh asks, either sincerely or cynically, maybe facetiously, about who will be included in the departing party. After all, in v. 7 the servants have strongly recommended that Pharaoh send away "the men." This is Pharaoh's second attempt at compromise. His first was "Go, but do not go very far" (8:28 [24] paraphrased). Here is his second: "Go, but leave your children, your wives, and your possessions behind." After all, you don't include women and children in worship, do you? If it were already written and Pharaoh had known it, could he not say, "Your own law says that three times a year *all the men* are to appear before your God for worship" (Exod. 23:17; 34:23; Deut. 16:16)? And when Joseph and his household leave Egypt to go to Canaan to bury his father, Jacob, do they not leave their children, and flocks and herds, behind in Goshen (Gen. 50:8)? Of course, Joseph's full intention is to return to Egypt. Moses's intention is not to return.

Pharaoh's ploy may have several motivations. Leaving such individuals behind would almost guarantee the return of Moses and the other adult males. Or if they do not return, the Hebrew children could be soon and easily Egyptianized, and Pharaoh's supply of available Hebrewess women greatly increased. Possibly Pharaoh's suggestion shows that worship in his own Egyptian religion is oriented around males. As Gruber (1992: 52) has said, "The cultic dispensability of women is a characteristic Gentile attitude."

In essence, Moses responds to Pharaoh: "Either everybody leaves or nobody leaves!" One has to appreciate this in-your-face, no-holds-barred dogmatism. Will Moses's refusal to blink provoke Pharaoh into even greater hostility? There are some places and times where compromise works and is valid. There are other places and times where compromise does not work. In fact, it may be disastrous. If Moses goes in the direction of compromise, this would be one of those times.

The negotiations do not end with a gentlemen's agreement. Nothing approaching a consensus evolves. On the contrary, Pharaoh "drove/*gāraš*" Moses and Aaron from his presence. That is the verb Exod. 2:17 used for the Midianite shepherds who drive away Reuel's daughters as they try to draw water for their father's flocks. The Lord uses the verb prophetically in Exod. 6:1 to describe to Moses what Pharaoh will do to the Hebrews: "He will drive them out of his country." Later, Exod. 12:31 will speak of Israel being driven out of Egypt before they have time to prepare food.

The invasion of locusts is massive, destroying and consuming everything edible **10:12–15**
in its path. The end of v. 14 indicates that there has never been a locust plague like it, nor will there ever be one after it to equal it in damage and intensity. The phrase recalls other references that set one episode or person apart from all others: Josh. 10:14, "There has never been a day like it before or since [the day the sun stood still]"; 2 Kings 18:5, "There was no one like him [Hezekiah] among all the kings of Judah, either before him or after him"; 2 Kings 23:25, "Neither before nor after Josiah was there a king like him"; Matt. 24:21, "For there will be great distress, unequaled from the beginning of the world until now—and never to be equaled again"; Rev. 16:18, "No earthquake like it has ever occurred since man has been on earth." See Brin 2001: 110.

The widespread phenomenon of locust invasion throughout the Middle East shows up in three Aramaic inscriptions from Sefire (southeast of Aleppo) that were written in the mid-eighth century BC. In one of these texts we have these lines: "(And) [may Ha]dad pour (over it) every sort of evil (which exists) on earth and in heaven and every sort of trouble; and may he shower on Arpad [ha]il-[stones]! For seven years may the locust devour (Arpad)" (trans. Fitzmyer, in *COS* 2:214).

10:16–20 One more time Pharaoh says, "I have sinned." But this confession of sin does go a bit further than his earlier one (9:27). This time, instead of simply saying, "I have sinned," he adds two objects to the verb: "I have sinned against the Lord . . . and against you." The order of the objects of Pharaoh's sinning is much like that in the confession of the prodigal son: "I have sinned against heaven and against you" (Luke 15:18, 21). First, it is a sin committed against God and then a sin committed against another human, in that order. All sin, regardless of the perpetrator and the victim, is first sin against God. Hence Joseph can say to Potiphar's wife, "How then could I do such a wicked thing and sin against God?" (Gen. 39:9). David, after destroying the lives of two humans, says, "Against you [God], you only, have I sinned" (Ps. 51:4 [6]). This posture is what makes the difference between guilt for sin and sorrow for sin. Guilt says, "I am sorry I did it." Sorrow says, "I am sorry I did it to him." Guilt is feeling sorry for one's sins because they are destroying one's own life. Sorrow is feeling sorry for one's sins because they grieve and break God's heart.

I am not suggesting, however, that by the use of such language Pharaoh is nicely making such a theological distinction. While not totally identical, there are some interesting parallels between Pharaoh's behavior in Exod. 10 and King Saul's behavior in 1 Sam. 15 (Frisch 1996: 102–3). Both confess, "I have sinned" (*ḥāṭāʾtî*), Pharaoh in Exod. 10:16 and Saul in 1 Sam. 15:24. Both supply a divine and human object of their sinning in that sequence: Pharaoh ("against the Lord your god and against you"); Saul ("against the Lord's command and your instructions"). Both use the expression "So now, forgive, please, my sin" (Pharaoh in Exod. 10:17, *wĕʿattâ śāʾ nāʾ ḥaṭṭāʾtî*; Saul in 1 Sam. 15:25, *wĕʿattâ śāʾ nāʾ ʾet-ḥaṭṭāʾtî*). Moses is not moved by Pharaoh's confession: "Moses left Pharaoh's presence" (Exod. 10:18). Samuel is not moved by Saul's confession: "As Samuel turned to leave . . ." (1 Sam. 15:27). Both incidents focus on worship: "Have the adult men go, and let them worship the Lord" (Exod. 10:11); "Come back with me, so that I may worship the Lord" (1 Sam. 15:25). The analogy between the two biblical scenes suggests the self-motivation and flimsiness of the confession and repentance of both Pharaoh and Saul.

Plague 9: A Darkness That One Can Feel

(10:21–29)

Translation

[21]And the LORD said to Moses, "Extend
your hand over the heavens, and there
will be darkness over the land of Egypt,
a darkness that one can feel." [22]So Moses
extended his hand over the heavens, and
there was pitch-black darkness in all the
land of Egypt three days. [23]Not a man could
see his brother, and not a man rose from
his place three days. But for all of Israel's
sons, there was light in their dwellings.
[24]Pharaoh summoned Moses and said, "Go,
worship the LORD. Only your sheep and
cattle will be left here. Your little ones may
also go with you." [25]And Moses said, "You,
you shall give into our hands sacrifices
and burnt offerings that we may sacrifice
them to the LORD our God. [26]Also our live-
stock will go with us. Not a hoof shall be
left behind. For from it we shall take to
serve the LORD our God, and we, we cannot
possibly know with what we are to serve
the LORD until our coming there." [27]The
LORD toughened Pharaoh's heart, and he
was not willing to send them away. [28]And
Pharaoh said to him, "Leave me. Beware.
Do not again see my face, for when you see
my face, you shall die." [29]And Moses said,
"You have spoken in truth. I will not again
see your face."

Grammatical and Lexical Notes

10:22. The words *ḥōšek-ʾăpēlâ* ("pitch-black darkness") used together in this grammatical construction are unique to this passage. However, words similar to *ʾăpēlâ* occur with *ḥōšek* in Isa. 29:18, "And out of gloom [*ʾōpel*] and darkness [*ḥōšek*] the eyes of the blind will see"; Amos 5:20, "Will not the day of the LORD be darkness [*ḥōšek*], not light—pitch-dark [*ʾāpēl*], without a ray of brightness?" Close to Exod. 10:22 is the description in Joel 2:2 and Zeph. 1:15 of the day of the Lord as a "day of darkness and gloom" (*ḥōšek wāʾăpēlâ*).

10:23. The two words *ʾîš* ("man") and *ʾāḥ* ("brother/fellow") occur here in the form *ʾîš ʾet-ʾāḥîw* (and also in 32:27). The two words occur together elsewhere as *ʾîš ʾāḥîw* (Gen. 9:5), *ʾîš mēʿal ʾāḥîw* (Gen. 13:11), *ʾîš ʾel-ʾāḥîw* (Gen. 42:21, 28; Exod. 16:15; 25:20; 37:9). The feminine counterpart is *ʾiššâ ʾel-ʾăḥōtāh* ("A woman with her sister you shall not take" [Lev. 18:18 AT]).

10:25. For *nātan bĕyād* ("*give* into one's *hand*"), see Gen. 35:4, "So they *gave* Jacob all the foreign gods that were in their *hands* [NIV, "the gods they had"]"; 1 Sam. 9:8 AT, "Look, I have found in my *hand* a quarter of a shekel of silver, and I will 'give' it to the man of God." In all three texts, party A turns over something to party B, and it becomes the permanent possession of party B to do whatever they wish with it.

10:25. "That we may *sacrifice* them to the LORD our God" is, literally, "that we may *do* [*wĕʿāśînû*] them to the LORD our God." The verb *ʿāśâ* with the meaning "sacrifice" is common in priestly texts (Lev. 4:20; 5:10; 6:22 [15]; 14:19, 30; 15:15, 30; 16:24; 17:9).

10:28. The Niphal imperative of *šāmar* (*hiššāmer*, "beware") is often used in texts for warning someone to be careful: Gen. 24:6, "*Make sure* you do not take my son back there"; Gen. 31:24, 29, "*Be careful* not to say anything to Jacob, either good or bad"; Exod. 19:12, "*Be careful* that you do not go up the mountain" (but see my note on this verse); Judg. 13:4, "Now *see to it* that you drink no wine"; 1 Sam. 19:2, "*Be on your guard* tomorrow morning"; Job 36:21, "*Beware* of turning to evil"; Isa. 7:4, "*Be careful*, keep calm and don't be afraid." Often the Greek OT uses the verb *prosechō* for the Niphal of *šāmar*. Luke is especially fond of employing this Septuagintism (Luke 12:1, "Be on your guard against the yeast of the Pharisees"; Luke 17:3, "Watch yourselves"; Luke 20:46, "Beware of the teachers of the law"; Luke 21:34, "Be careful"; Acts 5:35, "Consider carefully"; Acts 20:28, "Keep watch over yourselves").

10:28. The word "day" in *bĕyôm rĕʾōtĕkā pānay* (lit., "in the day of your seeing my face") is best rendered "*when* you see my face." Hebrew *bĕyôm* is the same as Akkadian *um sha* ("on the day that" = "when"). For other instances where *bĕyôm* means "when," see Gen. 2:4, 17; 3:5; Exod. 32:34; Num. 7:1, 10, 84; Deut. 16:3 (*ʾet-yôm*).

10:29. "You have spoken in truth" is *kēn dibbartā*. The phrase occurs again only in Num. 27:7 ("What Zelophehad's daughters are saying is right" [*kēn . . . dōbĕrōt*]), and in Num. 36:5 ("What the tribe of the descendants of Joseph is saying is right" [*kēn . . . dōbĕrîm*]). For the opposite phrase *loʾ ken*/"not right," see 2 Kings 7:9; 17:9; Jer. 23:10; 48:30. *Kēn* is an adjective from the root *k-w-n*.

10:29. The expression "see the face (of another)" is sometimes used in the context of coming from afar to see someone: Jacob to Esau (Gen. 32:20 [21]; 33:10); Joseph's brothers to Joseph (Gen. 43:3, 5; 44:23, 26); Jacob to Joseph (Gen. 46:30; 48:11); Moses to Pharaoh (Exod. 10:28–29); Abner to David (2 Sam. 3:13); Absalom to David (2 Sam. 14:24, 28, 32). Porten and Greenfield (1968: 226–27) quote an Aramaic text from Hermopolis with these lines: "Greetings to the Temple of Nabu. To my sister Reia from your brother Makkibanit. I bless you by Ptah that he may show me your face in peace [*brktky lpth zy yḥzny ʾpyk bšlm*]." "To see the face of" also appears as an idiom for the personal attendants of a king. Thus 2 Kings 25:19 tells us that those whom the Babylonians remove from Jerusalem at its capture include "five men who see the face of the king" (*rōʾê pĕnê-hammelek* [NIV, "five royal advisers"]). Compare also in Esther 1:14 the names of the seven dignitaries of Persia and Media who "see the face of the king" (*rōʾê pĕnê hammelek* [NIV, "had special access to"]). Possibly this Hebrew phrase is a calque formation of Akkadian *dagil pani*, "servant, subject," but literally, "one who beholds the face of." See *CAD* D:23.

Commentary

10:21–23 As in the third plague (8:16 [12]) and in the sixth plague (9:8), this ninth plague, the plague of darkness, erupts without any warning to Pharaoh. Think of what might be going through the minds of Egyptians: 8:00 a.m.—still dark; 9:00 a.m.—still dark; 10:00 a.m.—still dark; 11:00 a.m.—still dark; noon—still pitch dark, and all this in the land of Re/Ra the sun-god! Solar eclipse? A black sirocco? Something else? God's promise to Moses that there will be "darkness over the land of Egypt" (*wîhî ḥōšek ʿal-ʾereṣ miṣrāyîm*) is quite close to the condition of the earth, while God was still silent, and before he spoke his first creative word: "and darkness was over the face of the deep [*wĕḥōšek ʿal-pĕnê tĕhôm*]" (Gen. 1:2).

This is no ordinary darkness. It is a "darkness that one can feel," what Alter (2004: 370) picturesquely describes as "the claustrophobic palpability of absolute darkness." "Felt darkness" is an intriguing metaphor in relation to sense experience. A parallel would be Elijah's encounter with the Lord at Horeb, while he is hiding in a cave. The NIV renders 1 Kings 19:12 as "After the earthquake came a fire, but the LORD was not in the fire. And after the fire came a gentle whisper." A literal translation of the last part of this verse is, "And after the fire the voice/sound of thinnest silence." Darkness one can feel, and silence one can hear.

This has to be more than a natural phenomenon (solar eclipse, sandstorm). For not only is there no sunlight, but also nobody lights candles, nobody starts a bonfire. That's a real blackout!

But in the homes of the Hebrews in Goshen, there is light (v. 23b). That is the way it should always be. Light should always stream out into the darkness from the homes of the Lord's people. Let the houses of God's people be lighthouses for all the houses plunged into darkness. Let the family of God be a light to all the darkened Egypts as the light is to the darkness in Gen. 1:3–4 and John 1:5.

It is tempting to see some connection between these three days of darkness and the three hours of darkness at Jesus's crucifixion (Matt. 27:45; Mark 15:33; Luke 23:44–45a). Could not darkness over all the land of Egypt that is associated with Israel's exodus be an appropriate parallel to the darkness over all the land associated with Jesus's "exodus"? Some writers have suggested that. See, for example, the comment of Albright and Mann (1971: 353) in their Matthew commentary in the Anchor Bible series. More than likely, the darkness at the time of Jesus's demise is to be connected with the darkness that will appear at the coming "day of the LORD": Isa. 5:30; 8:22; 13:10; 50:3; 60:2; Jer. 13:16; 15:9; Joel 2:2, 10, 31; Amos 5:18. Particularly apposite to the Gospel references is Amos 8:9, a reference to the day of the Lord on which the Lord will "make the sun go down at noon." Furthermore, one verse later, v. 10, the Lord says it will be a "time like mourning for an only son." That kind of language points to the scene at Calvary. See Moo 1983: 342–44.

Here is Pharaoh's third attempt at negotiating a compromise: "Go, but do not **10:24–26**
go very far"; "Go, but leave your children behind"; and now, "Go, and take your children, but leave your sheep/cattle behind." Worship God, but keep a lid on it. Worship God, but leave your children out of it. Worship God, but keep your possessions out of it.

Moses is insistent. "The sheep and cattle go too, and guess what? You are the one who will give them to us" (v. 25–26 paraphrased). Egyptian sheep and Egyptian cattle make a perfectly good and acceptable offering to Yahweh. They are not tainted because they are not Hebrew animals, anymore than the Solomnic temple is tainted because of the workmanship on it by Hiram/Huram and his trained crew of professionals from neighboring but "pagan" Tyre (1 Kings 7).

Pharaoh would understand what Moses means by "sacrifices," but would he understand what Moses means by "burnt offerings" (*ʿōlôt*)? Even before the Mosaic period, Noah presents to God such an offering (Gen. 8:20). Isaac is to be a burnt offering (Gen. 22:2, 7, 8, 13). There are three references to "burnt offering" (in the singular or plural) that use it to refer to Canaanite or Moabite sacrifices. See Num. 23:15; 2 Kings 3:27; 10:24. So yes, the word may be comprehensible to Pharaoh.

One wonders why, if the Hebrews leave Egypt with sheep and cattle, they will later say, "If only we had meat to eat!" (Num. 11:4)? Is this an instance of imaginary, invented, and palpably false fault finding? Is this a case of gratuitous complaining? The next verse (Num. 11:5) answers those questions: "We remember *the fish* we ate in Egypt." That's what they miss. Not the lamb, not the beef, but the fish, of which there was much in Egypt, thanks to the Nile River.

10:27–29 The emphasis on seeing/not seeing Pharaoh's face ever again is particularly ironic in a plague of such darkness that "not a man could *see* his brother/fellow" (v. 23a). Presumably at this point Pharaoh and Moses are conversing in total darkness, unless the three days have passed and the darkness has retreated. Moses will not say to Pharaoh as Jacob said to Esau, "To see your face is like seeing the face of God" (Gen. 33:10).

The Final Plague: The Firstborns' Death

(11:1–10)

Translation

[1]And the LORD said to Moses, "One additional plague I will bring on Pharaoh and on Egypt. After that he will send (all of) you away from this place. When he sends you away, he will completely and surely drive (all of) you from this place. [2]Speak, pray, in the hearing of the people that they ask/borrow, a man from his neighbor and a woman from her neighbor, objects of silver and gold." [3]And the LORD made the people favorable in the eyes of the Egyptians, while the man Moses (was) very important in the land of Egypt in the eyes of Pharaoh's servants and the people.

[4]And Moses said, "Thus said the LORD: Near midnight I will go forth among the Egyptians. [5]Every firstborn in the land of Egypt shall die, from the firstborn of Pharaoh who occupies his throne to the firstborn of the slave girl who is at the millstones, and all the firstborn of the animals. [6]There shall be an enormous outcry throughout all the land of Egypt of which the like has never been, and the like will never be again. [7]But at every one of Israel's sons no dog will snarl, at man or at animal, so that (all of) you may know that the LORD differentiates between Egypt and Israel. [8]All of your servants will come down to me and bow before me, saying, 'Leave, you and all the people who are at your heels.' After that I will go out." And he went out from Pharaoh, burning with anger.

[9]And the LORD said to Moses, "Pharaoh will not listen to (all of) you for the multiplying of my portents in the land of Egypt." [10]Moses and Aaron had done all these portents before Pharaoh, but the LORD had toughened Pharaoh's heart, and he did not send away Israel's sons from his turf.

Grammatical and Lexical Notes

11:1. How does one translate *wayyōʾmer*—"said" (the perfect as in NRSV) or "had said" (the pluperfect as in NIV)? I shall have more to say about this in the commentary section below. It is very rare, if ever, that the imperfect with *wa-* can introduce the pluperfect. For sure the imperfect with *wa-* can *continue* a pluperfect (e.g., Gen. 31:34, "Rachel had taken the household gods and had put them [*wattĕśimēm*] inside her camel's saddle"), but can it *introduce* it? The usual way Biblical Hebrew expresses a pluperfect is to place the subject of the sentence between the conjunction *wa-* and the verb in the *qāṭal* form, not in the *yiqṭōl* form: for example, Gen. 24:62, "Now Isaac had come [*wĕyiṣḥāq bāʾ*] from Beer Lahai Roi," or Gen. 31:19, "When Laban had gone [*wĕlābān hālak*] to shear his sheep. . . ." Unless Exod. 11:1 is an exception, "had said" seems preferable to "said."

11:1. The Hebrew word for "plague" is *negaʿ* (only here in Exodus) and is a generic term for plagues, diseases, and injuries. The noun comes from the verb *nāgaʿ*, "touch." Thus when God "touched" Jacob's thigh, the result was that he limped (Gen. 32:25, 32 [26, 33]). There is a parallel with the Akkadian verb *lapatu* ("touch") and the noun related to it, *liptu* ("touch, plague, disease"). God is almost always the author of *negaʿ* as a divine punishment (Gen. 12:17; Exod. 11:1; 2 Sam. 7:14;

1 Kings 8:37, 38; etc.). A husband may inflict *negaʿ* on the adulterer who has had sex with the man's wife (Prov. 6:33). In Lev. 13 and 14 the term appears sixty-one times (NIV, mostly "infectious") either as an absolute or in construct with *ṣāraʿat* ("skin disease") or *neteq* ("scab").

11:1. The word I have translated "completely" is *kālâ*. BDB 478b identifies it as a feminine noun, used here and in Gen. 18:21 as an adverb. Morgenstern (1949: 1–3) connects *kālâ* with *kallâ*, "bride, daughter-in-law," and reads, "After that he will send you away from this place *as one lets go a bride*" (italics added). For a more recent adherent, see Sternberg 1998: 645n18, 671n42. Only the NEB and its replacement, the REB, have followed this rereading with their "When he finally lets you go, he will drive you out forcibly as a man might dismiss *a rejected bride*." See also Daube (1963: 58), who reads *kallâ* too, but with even stronger meaning: "as you would let go [divorce] *a slave-wife*." It would seem odd to use the verb *gāraš* ("drive off/away") for what a father does with his bridal daughter.

11:2. "Pray" is the particle *-nāʾ*, and in addition to "pray," it may be translated "please" or "I beg you." It appears more than sixty times in the Bible, but only in five of those does God use it (Gen. 13:14; 15:5; 22:2; Exod. 11:2; Isa. 7:3). Does God ever say "please" or "I beg you"? In each of these five instances (and especially in the Genesis/Exodus ones) God is asking some person (Abraham, Moses, Isaiah) to do something that defies rational explanation or understanding (Hamilton 1995: 101).

11:3. For other instances of *nātan . . . ʾet-ḥēn . . . bĕʿênê* ("make X favorable in the eyes of Y"), see Gen. 39:21; Exod. 3:21; 12:36.

11:3. For the use of *gam* as introducing a circumstantial clause and carrying the meaning "while," see Andersen 1974: 164.

11:3. "Very important" is the word *gādôl*, usually translated "great." It may carry other meanings such as "rich" in Lev. 19:15, "Do not show partiality to the poor (*dāl*) or favoritism to the rich/great (*gādôl*)."

11:4. The preposition *kĕ* prefixed to *kaḥăṣōt hallayĕlâ* ("about midnight") shows that *kĕ*, when prefaced to time or numerical expressions, means "about, the like of." See BDB 453a–b.

11:5. The expression "from [*min*; prefixed *mi-*] the firstborn of Pharaoh . . . to [*ʿad*] the firstborn of the slave girl" is a merism. Honeyman (1952: 12–13) gives many illustrations of *min . . . ʿad* or *min . . . wĕʿad* in the Hebrew Bible.

11:5. For the meaning of the preposition *ʾaḥar* as "at" in *ʾaḥar harēḥāyîm* ("at the millstones"), see Scott 1949: 178. See Matt. 24:41, "Two women will be grinding with/at (*en*) a hand mill." Given the circular shape of a millstone, how does one know whether the one turning the millstone is behind it or in front of it? *Rēḥāyîm* is a dual formation since it consisted of an upper and lower stone.

11:5. Several passages in Scripture seem to indicate that grinding grain with the hand mill was a woman's job. The reference in Num. 11:8 is vague, but Exod. 11:5; Isa. 47:2 (part of a poem about "Queen Babylon" being dethroned); and Matt. 24:41 connect this task with women. Blenkinsopp (2000: 280) refers to the grinding with which Samson is charged (Judg. 16:21) as "an example of the practice of humiliating and feminizing male prisoners-of-war."

11:6. There is gender disaccord between the antecedent "outcry" (*ṣĕʿāqâ*, feminine) and "(none) like it" (*kāmōhû*, masculine). Wherever *kamōhû* is used in the Bible, it has that form, whether the antecedent is masculine or feminine. See Exod. 9:18, 24; 2 Kings 18:5; 23:25; Joel 2:2. Hence, this is not a case of bad incongruence as much as it is a case of the writer citing idiomatic usage.

11:7. "Snarl" in "no dog will snarl" is *ḥāraṣ . . . lĕšōnô*, literally, "put out, sharpen its tongue." The same phrase occurs in Josh. 10:21b, "And no one uttered a word against the Israelites" (*lōʾ-ḥāraṣ libnê yiśrāʾēl lĕʾîš ʾet-lĕšōnô*). The verb appears in 2 Sam. 5:24, in which the Lord gives David counsel on when to move from hiding to attacking the Philistines. There the verb is translated in the NIV as "[you shall] move quickly" (*teḥĕrāṣ*). In the parallel to this verse in 1 Chron. 14:15 the verb *yāṣāʾ* is used instead of *ḥāraṣ* (*tēṣēʾ*, "you shall move out"). So *ḥāraṣ* = *yāṣāʾ*, at least this one time.

Accordingly, the use of *ḥāraṣ* with a dog's tongue may reflect a dog's habit of letting its tongue loll out.

11:8. De Moor (1993: 492) argues for the translation of *bĕraglêkā* (NIV, "who follow you") or *bĕraglāyw* as "at your/his heels" here, and in Judg. 4:10; 5:15; 8:5; 1 Sam. 25:27; 2 Sam. 15:18; 1 Kings 20:10.

11:10. Here is a good instance where the pluperfect is called for: "Moses and Aaron *had* done all these portents" (*ûmōšeh wĕʾahărōn ʿāśû*). See the first grammatical note above. Strangely, the NIV renders it as a perfect ("Moses and Aaron *performed* all these wonders"). Hence, in my judgment, NIV uses the pluperfect in v. 1 where it should not, and does not use the pluperfect in v. 10 where it should.

Commentary

Unlike the previous nine plagues, on this occasion the Lord simply announces **11:1–3**
a forthcoming and final plague, but it does not become a reality until 12:29–36, and that is after the Lord has addressed his people through Moses about Passover and their observance of it. The separation between announcement and implementation indicates that this final plague is a bridge, climaxing what has gone before and introducing what is to follow. The tenth plague advances the narrative from plague to Passover.

The novel note sounded here is the reference in v. 3 to the high esteem in which the Egyptians hold both the Hebrews and Moses. And this after all the heartaches brought on Egypt in the earlier plagues! Will that sense of favor continue after the death of the firstborn? Moses's stature in the Egyptian community is comparable to that of Mordecai in the Persian community: "Mordecai was prominent in the palace; his reputation spread throughout the provinces, and he became more and more powerful" (Esther 9:4). The words "prominent" and "powerful" are both *gādôl*, the same word used of Moses in Exod. 11:3 ("great, important").

One thing this God-given affection of the Egyptians for the Hebrews and Moses accomplishes is it contrasts their feelings for Moses and his people with Pharaoh's feelings, or lack thereof, for Moses and his people. The Lord may have given Moses favor in the eyes of the Egyptians, but he did not give Moses favor in the eyes of Pharaoh. Their respect contrasts with his hostility.

This contrast, vivid in the Hebrew and English text, loses a bit of its punch in the translation of the LXX (N. Collins 1994). Here is the Septuagint's rendering of Exod. 11:2–3 (I put in italics the changes/additions in the Greek): "Speak therefore *secretly* (*kryphē*) into the ears of the people, and let each man ask from his man-neighbor and each woman from her woman-neighbor vessels of gold and silver *and clothing* (*kai himatismon*). And the Lord gave grace to his people before the Egyptians, *and they lent to them* (*kai exrēsan autois*). And the man Moses became very great before the Egyptians, *and before Pharaoh* (*kai enantion Pharaō*), and before all his servants." The two most striking additions in the Greek are that (1) the Hebrews are to ask "secretly" for the items, and (2) Moses becomes great "before Pharaoh" too.

11:4–8 We do not know to whom Moses speaks in these verses until we come to the end of v. 8, "And he went out from Pharaoh, burning with anger." But has not the previous plague ended by Pharaoh's ordering Moses never to appear before him again on penalty of death, an ultimatum to which Moses consents (10:28–29)? So what are the two doing together at the same time at the same place subsequent to the slammed-shut door of 10:28–29?

Numerous attempts have been made to suggest that 11:4–8 has been displaced from its original setting, supposedly somewhere near the end of chap. 10. I am not so sure. I think that years ago S. Driver, in his discourse on Hebrew tenses, made the most commonsense suggestion: "It would be quite in keeping with Pharaoh's character, when his passion cooled, to relent from the threat which is there expressed by him, and which is at any rate broken, subsequently (12:31), on both sides" (1998: 85). We all have had the experience, when angered, of spouting off and mouthing something that we later, when in a calmer frame of mind, recant.

Dozeman (1996: 19) has nicely pointed out the specificity of Moses's speech. It includes (1) the time—midnight; (2) the content—the death of the firstborn; (3) the scope—from Pharaoh's firstborn to the firstborn of animals, Israelite firstborn excepted; (4) the outcome—a great cry, and a plea from Pharaoh's servants that Moses and his people leave. The midnight hour presents two dramatically different possibilities. It can be a time to worship, to give thanks, to sing the praises of God (Ps. 119:62; Acts 16:25); or it can be, as here, a time of incalculable danger and vulnerability. I would take Paul and Silas's prison cell at midnight over Pharaoh's palace at midnight.

Pharaoh is angry at Moses at the end of chap. 10; Moses is angry at Pharaoh near the end of chap. 11. Moses, who is the first explicit object of divine anger in the Bible (Exod. 4:14), is now the one who vents his own wrath. But he does not cuss out Pharaoh as he leaves, nor does he hurl any invectives at him. Baloian (1992: 25, 53nn19–20, 54n23) observes that Moses becomes angry on five occasions (Exod. 11:8; 16:20; Lev. 10:16; Num. 16:15; 31:14) "but maintains a clear head." In Num. 20:10–12, however, Moses acts angrily with a "hot" head instead of a "cool" head.

What God intends to do in his tenth plague—the death of all the firstborn of Egyptian families and Egyptian animals—suggests massive carnage, thousands dying because of the sins of their king and their fathers. Is this a payback for what Pharaoh has done to God's son ("'Let my son go so he may worship me.' But you refused to let him go; so I will kill your firstborn son" [Exod. 4:23])? Or even retributive justice for what Pharaoh has done to Hebrew boy babies in 1:15–22? Brueggemann (1994: 771) suggests that God's actions here are "like the passion of a mother bear in defense of a cub. The mother is ferocious and unreasoned in its attack on anything or anyone that threatens the cub."

This explanation, while possible and at least partially accurate, leaves unanswered why the firstborn Egyptian animals are to perish too. Can there be any possible connection between the tenth plague (if we read the text forward and not just backward to chap. 4) and the law about the consecration of the firstborn in Exod. 13? On that occasion the firstborn among the Israelites ("whether man or animal," phrases reminiscent of the language of 11:4–8) are to be consecrated to the Lord. All the firstborn belong to God and thus are given to him. To be sure, biblical law allows for the "redemption" of all firstborn unfit for an offering to the Lord (13:13), but Egypt and its livestock cannot claim that offer of redemption. Adding Exod. 13, as well as Exod. 4, to the mix suggests that the motivation for the tenth plague is not only retributive, but also cultic (see Greenstein 1995: 555–58).

Nothing changes. The die has been cast. Pharaoh's response is irreversible and **11:9–10**
nontransformational. He can no longer act autonomously, if he ever could. For the fourth time the text informs us that the Lord has hardened Pharaoh's heart (plagues 6, 8, and 9 [9:12; 10:1, 20; 10:27]).

An Excursus on Heart Hardening

Biblical scholars and lay readers of Exodus have long pondered over how best to understand the hardening of Pharaoh's heart and the theological issues it inevitably raises. Must one choose between the exercise of divine sovereignty and the exercise of human free will, or is there some valid room for the exercise of both? Or are they mutually exclusive, thus mandating that one take an "either . . . or" path? More than likely a close study of the Exodus passages will not resolve that issue transparently. "Electionists" would like to make a watertight case for that position from their reading of these Scriptures, and "voluntarists" would like to make an equally watertight case for that position from their reading of these Scriptures. In my judgment, neither goal is possible. What I shall do is simply list some observations to be taken into the mix when reflecting on this issue.

1. When God for the first time reveals to Moses that he "will harden his [Pharaoh's] heart so that he will not let the people go" (4:21), Moses does not blink. He does not say, "You will do what?" He does not protest with "Well, if that's what you're intending to do, why should I go, if I know beforehand that I will get nowhere with Pharaoh?" I point this out for two reasons. First, this particular revelation to Moses does not baffle him, bother him, unsettle him, or throw him off track. Second, this acceptance of a divine message and intention is in bold contrast to Moses's response to God's first commission in chap. 3 that he go to Egypt and tell Pharaoh to let the Hebrews go. Moses can protest and argue and try to evade obedience, but he does not resist on this occasion.

2. The reader is struck by the frequency of hardness language in this section of Exodus and the infrequency of such language elsewhere in the OT. Some form of hardness-of-heart language appears twenty times between Exod. 4 and 14. Three different verbs are used (*ḥāzaq*, *kābēd*, *qāšâ*). Furthermore, the verbs appear in three different ways: in the Piel stem (8x), in the Hiphil stem (6x), and in what is known as a stative verb in the Qal stem (6x): a verbal form that simply states the condition or state of something without designating who or what caused that state. In the case of the Piel and Hiphil verbs, the form may be a perfect ("hardened") or an imperfect ("will harden"). In the case of the stative verbs, the best and most literal translation is "was hard." The subject of the verb may be the Lord, Pharaoh, or Pharaoh's heart. Here is the breakdown:

The Lord as Subject (10 references)

kābēd	*ḥāzaq*	*qāšâ*
10:1 Hiphil perfect	4:21 Piel imperfect	7:3 Hiphil imperfect
	9:12 Piel perfect	
	10:20 Piel perfect	
	10:27 Piel perfect	
	11:10 Piel perfect	
	14:4 Piel imperfect	
	14:8 Piel perfect	
	14:17 Piel participle	

Pharaoh as Subject (4 references)

kābēd	*ḥāzaq*	*qāšâ*
8:15 [11] Hiphil perfect		13:15 Hiphil perfect
8:32 [28] Hiphil perfect		
9:34 Hiphil perfect		

Pharaoh's Heart as Subject (6 references)

kābēd	*ḥāzaq*	*qāšâ*
7:14 stative (in adjectival form)	7:13 Qal stative	
	7:22 Qal stative	
9:7 Qal stative	8:19 [15] Qal stative	
	9:35 Qal stative	

This proliferation of hardness vocabulary (twenty times in eight chapters of Exodus) contrasts with the occasional use of hardness vocabulary elsewhere in the OT. For example, in Deut. 2:30 Moses says of Sihon, king of Heshbon, through whose territory Israel will pass on their way to Canaan: "For the Lord your God has made his spirit stubborn [*qāšâ*, Hiphil perfect] and his heart obstinate [*ʾāmaṣ*, Piel perfect—not used in Exodus]." Joshua 11:20 informs us that the Lord has hardened the hearts (Piel infinitive construct of *ḥāzaq*) of the Canaanites so that they will not surrender to Israel but instead will engage them in battle and be wiped out in the process. Again, the Lord, in his calling of Isaiah into ministry, tells the prophet in Isa. 6:10 to "make the heart of this people calloused [*šāman*, Hiphil imperative]; make their ears dull [*kābēd*, Hiphil imperative]." Ps. 95:8 urges the people of God, "Do not harden your hearts [*qāšâ*, Hiphil imperfect with *ʾal*]." See also Prov. 28:14b, "He who hardens his heart [Hiphil participle of *qāšâ*] falls into trouble." This selection of non-Exodus "hardening" texts illustrates both a divine hardening and a self-induced hardening.

3. The opposite of God's hardening a heart (with the result that the individual's behavior threatens God's people) is God's moving/stirring the spirit of somebody (with the result that that individual's behavior blesses God's people). See 2 Chron. 36:22 (= Ezra 1:1), "The Lord moved/stirred [Hiphil perfect of *'ûr*] the heart/spirit of Cyrus king of Persia." Apparently when God works on somebody's heart, he is particularly attracted to the hearts of non-Israelite kings (Pharaoh, Sihon, Cyrus) or non-Israelite peoples (Egyptians, Canaanites).

4. There is an exact fifty-fifty breakdown in the twenty uses of these verbs in Exod. 4–14 with regard to the subject of the verb. Ten times the subject is Yahweh, and ten times the subject of the verb is Pharaoh or Pharaoh's heart. Of the few instances in which Yahweh is the subject, perfect-tense forms of the verb outnumber imperfect-tense forms six to four. Execution outnumbers announcement. When Pharaoh himself is the subject, all the verbs are, as one would expect, perfect-tense verb forms.

5. I think it is significant that God's first statements of intention to harden Pharaoh's heart (4:21; 7:3) both occur before the beginning of the first plague. However, the first-person imperfect "I will harden" does not become a third-person perfect ("The Lord hardened") until near the end of the sixth plague (9:12). Between what God says he intends to do and his actually carrying out that intention, at least for the first time, Pharaoh hardens his own heart (plagues 2 and 4, in 8:15 [11]; 8:32 [28]), or the text simply says that Pharaoh's heart is hard (plagues 1, 3, and 5, in 7:22; 8:19 [15]; 9:7), a heart condition of his even before the first plague (7:13 [*ḥāzaq*], 14 [*kābēd*]).

6. Even after the Lord has hardened Pharaoh's heart for the first time (plague 6, in 9:12), Pharaoh is able to harden his own heart at the end of the very next plague (plague 7, in 9:34). This shows that the Lord's initial hardening of Pharaoh's heart does not once and for all terminate Pharaoh's ability to act of his own accord. After the seventh plague, however, the door on further autonomous behavior is slammed shut. The Lord does the hardening in plagues 8 (10:1, 20), 9 (10:27), and 10 (11:10).

7. Some of these texts that highlight the Lord's hardening emphasize that God does so in order that by hardening the king's heart, thus surely guaranteeing Pharaoh's refusal to capitulate, he might have the opportunity to multiply his signs and wonders in Egypt, rather than stopping after round one (see 7:3; 10:1; 11:9–10). If Pharaoh had been able to cooperate fully and agreeably from the start, the plagues would have been reduced by nine, for which most Egyptians would have been grateful!

8. Some of the texts that highlight Pharaoh's own hardening state that Pharaoh does so only after he asks for Moses to pray to Moses's God to take the plague away. Moses prays. God says yes. The plague vanishes. Then

Pharaoh hardens his heart (plagues 2, 4, and 7, in 8:15 [11]; 8:32 [28]; 9:34) and withdraws his promise to release the people. It is not a case that Pharaoh is able to hoodwink both Moses and God three times. That is, Pharaoh gets, but he never has to give. God (or Moses) never protests, as Esau does about Jacob, that he has been deceived by Pharaoh. Rather, it is an instance in which an ever-gracious God, who is well aware of Pharaoh's subterfuge, both honors the intercessions of his servant Moses and allows himself "to be made a fool of," all for the sake of a divine outreach to a lost Pharaoh.

9. We must not downplay the importance of divine sovereignty at work in this unit of Scripture. Pharaoh's role must not overshadow Yahweh's role. We can so emphasize Pharaoh's autonomy that God becomes essentially nothing more than a passive, hand-wringing, but hopeful bystander. As Goldingay (2003: 352) has said, "To say only that Yhwh knows what will happen puts Yhwh in a purely reactive position, whereas the First Testament reckons that a God worth calling 'God' is more intentional about world history than this implies. . . . From time to time events happen because God specifically wants them to. The Egyptian king's resistance is an example of something that comes about by God's personal action rather than merely by God's permission."

This is surely how Paul in Rom. 9–11 reads this incident: "God has mercy on whom he wants to have mercy, and he hardens whom he wants to harden" (9:18). Cannot the potter do with the clay as he wishes and chooses (9:20–21)? As a hardening has come upon Pharaoh and the Egyptians (for the sake of the Hebrews' deliverance), there has come a hardening on Israel (11:25), for the sake of the gentiles' deliverance. In both instances hardening is used redemptively.

10. It would be incorrect to think that because Pharaoh's refusal to listen is due to his God-hardened heart, then anybody's and everybody's refusal to listen to God's voice is God-ordained and God-purposed. Again I quote Goldingay (2003: 351): "But the specialness of the situation in this story means that what Yhwh does here is not necessarily a guide to what God regularly does—only to what he *can* do" (italics original).

11. If there is strong support in these plague episodes for determinism/predestination, then there is equally strong support for at least some measure of free will. I have already mentioned above (see point 5) that the Lord does not harden Pharaoh's heart until after the sixth plague, despite his intention to do so as early as 4:21. Second, in Exod. 6:10, 29 the Lord sends Moses back to Pharaoh to speak again with the king. Not once, but twice (6:12, 30), Moses argues that Pharaoh will not listen to him because he is such an unpersuasive communicator. The implication is that if only Moses were a silver-tongued orator, or if only God would send some oratorical Cicero, then Pharaoh would listen and respond appropriately. Note that Moses never suggests to God that Pharaoh will not listen to Moses because God has hardened his heart, thus cutting off the possibility of his listening properly. Moses is the "problem," not God, so thinks Moses. Third, the verb "refuse" is frequently used with

Pharaoh as subject (4:23; 7:14; 8:2 [7:27]; 9:2; 10:3, 4) in a speech that God gives Moses to transmit to Pharaoh. In three of these six, Moses is to begin by saying to Pharaoh, "If you refuse to let them go . . ." (8:2 [7:27]; 9:2; 10:4; also see 8:21, "If you do not let my people go . . ."). Fretheim (1991: 99) rightly argues, "This 'if' language is problematic if only a negative decision of Pharaoh is possible. That is, if God says 'if,' such language conveys to Pharaoh (and to Moses) that his 'refusal' is only a future possibility, not a certainty. . . . But if, in fact, Pharaoh's refusal is a certainty, then to hold it out as a possibility is deceitful." Finally, what about the phrase "He [Pharaoh] did not heed/listen to them [Moses and Aaron], just as the LORD had said" (7:13; plagues 1, 2, 3, 6, and 7, in 7:22; 8:15 [11]; 8:19 [15]; 9:12; 9:35)? The phrase is missing in plagues 4, 5, 8, and 9, and a variant is present in plague 10 (11:9a). Does "just as the LORD had said" refer to a divine decree, or is this the narrator's comment that what God has said (prophetically) of Pharaoh's behavior is indeed coming to pass. Pharaoh is responding just as God has said he would respond.

McAffee (2010: 350) helpfully observes that the phrase never directly modifies any sentence describing Pharaoh's heart. Rather, the phrase in every instance appears on the heels of two previous clauses; for example, 7:13: "(1) Yet Pharaoh's heart became hard, (2) and he would not listen to them, (3) just as the LORD had said." The most likely antecedent for these "he would not listen" in five out of six of the notations, argues McAffee, is 7:3–4: "and though I multiply my miraculous signs and wonders in Egypt, he will not listen to you."

I see something of a parallel between the phrase "Pharaoh did just as the LORD had said," and "Moses did (just) as the LORD commanded him" near the end of Exodus (ten times in Exod. 39: vv. 1, 5, 7, 21, 26, 29, 31, 32, 42, 43; eight times in Exod. 40: vv. 16, 19, 21, 23, 25, 27, 29, 32). I think the emphasis in both sections is not so much on divine decrees that Pharaoh (unwittingly) and Moses (wittingly) carry out. Rather, both passages emphasize the conformity in behavior of both Pharaoh and Moses to a divine word that God has spoken earlier about Pharaoh and to Moses.

12. Last of all, for all the emphasis on God's hardening Pharaoh's heart, there are several ways in which God seeks to soften Pharaoh's heart:

a. by the prayers of Moses (8:8 [4], 28 [24]; 9:28; 10:17)
b. by his magicians' testimony (8:19 [15])
c. by moving him to partial obedience (8:8 [4]; 8:25–28 [21–24]; 10:24)
d. by moving him to partial penitence (9:27; 10:16)
e. by continually giving Pharaoh another opportunity
f. by the witness and urging of his own courtiers (10:7)
g. by miraculously sparing the Hebrews from some of the plagues

Celebration of Passover

(12:1–28)

Translation

[1]And the LORD said to Moses and to Aaron in the land of Egypt, [2]"This month shall be for (all of) you the head [first] of months. It is the head [first] for (all of) you of the year's months. [3]Speak to the entire congregation of Israel. 'On the tenth of this month let each take for themselves a lamb for the fathers' house, a lamb for a house(hold). [4]If a house(hold) is too small to have a lamb, it shall take along with its neighbor who is near his house, in proportion to the number of persons; each according to his eating you shall compute for the lamb. [5]An unblemished lamb, a yearling male, you shall have. From the sheep or from the goats you may take (it). [6]It shall be for (all of) you something to be preserved until the fourteenth day of this month. The entire congregation of Israel shall slaughter it at twilight. [7]And they shall take from the blood, and put it on the two doorposts and on the lintel, on the houses in which they will eat it. [8]And they shall eat the meat on this night fire-roasted; along with flatbread [unleavened bread] together with bitter herbs they shall eat it. [9]Do not eat any part of it raw or boiled in water, but fire-roasted—its head together with its legs and entrails. [10]You shall not leave any of it until morning. What remains from it until morning you shall burn it in fire. [11]And this is how you shall eat it: your loins girded, sandals on your feet, your staff in your hand. You shall eat it as quickly as possible. It is a Passover to the LORD. [12]And I will pass through the land of Egypt on this night, and I will strike down every firstborn in the land of Egypt, from man to animal, and on all of Egypt's gods I will hand down punishments. I am the LORD. [13]And the blood will be a sign for (all of) you on the houses in which you are, and when I see the blood, I will stand watch over you. No plague shall become a Destroyer among you when I strike throughout the land of Egypt.

[14]"'And this day shall be for (all of) you a remembrance day, and you shall celebrate it as a festival to the LORD throughout your generations. As a perpetual statute you shall celebrate it. [15]Seven days you shall eat flatbread [unleavened bread]. Therefore on the first day you shall remove leaven from your houses. As for anyone who eats leavened bread, that person shall be cut off from Israel, from the first day until the seventh. [16]And on the first day a sacred convocation and on the seventh day a sacred convocation you shall have. No assigned activity should be carried out on them. Only what every person is to eat, that alone may be prepared for you. [17]You shall observe (the Feast of) Flatbread [Unleavened Bread], for on this very day I brought out your battalions from the land of Egypt. And you shall observe this day throughout your generations (as) a perpetual statute. [18]In the first month, on the fourteenth day of the month in the evening, you shall eat flatbread [unleavened bread] until the twenty-first day of the month in the evening. [19]Seven days no leaven shall be found in your houses, for whoever eats what has been leavened, that person shall be cut off from the congregation of Israel, whether an alien or native-born of the land. [20]Anything leavened you must not eat. Wherever you live, you must eat flatbread [unleavened bread].'"

[21]Moses summoned all the elders of Israel and said to them, "Go, pick out for yourselves sheep for your families, and

slaughter the Passover offering. [22]And you shall take a bundle of hyssop, and dip it in the blood, which is in the basin, and you shall touch some of the blood to the lintel and to the two doorposts from the blood that is in the basin. As for yourselves, none of you shall go out from the door of his house until morning. [23]And the LORD will pass through to plague the Egyptians and will see the blood on the lintel and on the two doorposts, and the Lord will stand watch over the door and not permit the Destroyer to come into your houses to plague you. [24]And you shall observe this matter as a statute for you and for your sons forever. [25]And when you come into the land that the LORD will give (all of) you as he has said, you shall observe this service. [26]And when your sons say to you, 'What does this service mean to you?' [27]you shall say, 'It is a Passover sacrifice to the LORD, who stood watch over the houses of Israel's sons in Egypt when he plagued Egypt, and our houses he rescued.'" The people bowed and worshiped.

[28]Israel's sons went and did just as the LORD had commanded Moses and Aaron. They did it.

Grammatical and Lexical Notes

12:2. The verse illustrates two clauses in apposition that are identical in meaning with the parallel items arranged in chiasmus ("month>head of months: head>months"). See Andersen 1974: 38.

12:3. To express the distributive "each," Hebrew employs the word *ʾîš* ("man"). Compare Gen. 40:5 AT, "The two of them [the cupbearer and the baker] had a dream, each his own dream [*ʾîš ḥălōmô*]."

12:3. S. Driver (1998: 154 §125) notes how infrequently *wĕ* is joined to the imperfect (*wĕyiqḥû*, "let each take" or "each shall take").

12:4. *Miksâ*, "cut, portion" (here and in Lev. 27:23) in the expression *bĕmiksat nĕpāšōt* ("in proportion to the number of persons") is the feminine counterpart of masculine *mekes* (Num. 31:28–29). The latter is a tax raised from the fighting men of Israel's military in the form of tribute. Both words are cognate with Akkadian *miksu*, a term connoting a tax consisting of a share of the yield, or simply meaning "dues, customs." See *CAD* M/II:63–65.

12:5. The Hebrew for "yearling" is *ben-šānâ*. In Lev. 12:6 the new mother is to bring to the priest a year-old lamb (*kebeś ben-šĕnātô*), with the pronominal suffix on "yearling." Perhaps this less-common suffixed form refers to an animal that is younger than one year old.

12:5. Note the meaning "or" for the *wāw* in "from the sheep *or* from the goats." See also v. 9, "raw *or* boiled in water."

12:6. *Mišmeret* ("something to be preserved") is a noun derived from the verb *šāmar*, "keep, observe, guard, protect" (in vv. 17 [2x], 24, 25).

12:6. *Šāḥaṭ* ("slaughter," here and in v. 21) is used again with the Passover sacrifice in Exod. 34:25. It is a favorite verb in the priestly literature of the OT (some forty of seventy-nine instances) where sacrifices are under discussion. It is the verb Gen. 22:10 uses to describe what Abraham intends to do to Isaac. For other instances of *šāḥaṭ* with human sacrifices, see Isa. 57:5, "You sacrifice your children"; Ezek. 16:21, "You slaughtered my children"; Ezek. 23:39, "They sacrificed their children to their idols." The verb also is used in describing mass slaughterings (Num. 14:16; Judg. 12:6; 1 Kings 18:40; 2 Kings 10:7, 14). Milgrom (1976c: 13–14) argues that the basic meaning of the verb is "slit the throat."

12:6. "At twilight" (*bên hāʿarbāyim*) is, literally, "between the two evenings," or "between the two settings." It occurs again in Exod. 16:12; Lev. 23:5; Num. 9:3. The expression refers to a period of time between sunset and nightfall. The dual form of "evenings" points to the time of sunset and the time of nightfall, which would normally be one and a half to two hours in duration.

12:7. One may "put the blood" (*nātan dām*) on objects such as doorposts (Exod. 12:7; Ezek. 45:19), or on persons (Exod. 29:20; Lev. 14:14, 25), or on the altar (Lev. 4:7, 25; Ezek. 43:20). However, when God is the subject of *nātan dām*, the meaning of the verb is "give, bestow, assign," as in Lev. 17:11.

12:8. The LXX rendering of "on this night" (*tautē tē nukti*), apart from Ruth 3:2, appears in the OT only in Exod. 12:8, 12. It appears in Jesus's parable about the coming of the kingdom of God (Luke 17:20–37): "I tell you, *on that night* two people will be in one bed; one will be taken and the other left" (17:34). Do both the exodus and the inauguration of God's kingdom commence at night? See Derrett 1996: 38.

12:8–9. For the very few other instances of *ṣālâ* (verb, "roast") and *ṣālî* (adjective, "roasted"), see 1 Sam. 2:15 and Isa. 44:16, 19.

12:8. I shall save my remarks on *maṣṣôt* ("flatbread, unleavened bread") for the commentary section.

12:8. The preposition *ʿal* here carries the meaning "together with" or "as well as," and also in Lev. 2:2. In the parallel verse in Numbers (Num. 9:11), there is a bit of a change. Exodus 12:8 prefixes the *wāw* to "flatbread," and uses the preposition *ʿal* before "bitter herbs." Numbers 9:11, conversely, uses the preposition *ʿal* before "flatbread," and prefixes the *wāw* to "bitter herbs." In Exod. 12:9 the preposition *ʿal* also carries the meaning "together with"—"*together with* its legs and *together with* its entrails."

12:9. The LXX renders the *ʾal* prohibitive ("You shall not eat") as *ou* with the future instead of its more normal rendering of the *ʾal* prohibitive as *mē* with imperative or aorist. Bright (1973: 196) notes that there are nine *lōʾ* prohibitives in Exod. 12, while v. 9 provides the lone instance of an *ʾal* prohibitive, which surely carries the same force as the other nine.

12:9. The word for "raw" (*nāʾ*) occurs only here in the Hebrew Bible.

12:9. "Boiled in water" is composed of an adjective (*ûbāšēl*) and a cognate Pual participle (*mĕbuššāl*), literally, "or boiled [meat] boiled in water."

12:9. The term *qereb* ("entrails") is synonymous with *mēʿeh* ("intestines") in Isa. 16:11, "My heart [*mēʿeh*] laments for Moab, . . . my inmost being [*qereb*] for Kir Hareseth." The Akkadian cognates are *qerbu(m)* II and *qerbitu*.

12:10. On verbal and nominal forms of the root *yātar* in passages not generally considered parallelistic (*tôtîrû*, "you shall (not) leave"; *wĕhannōtār*, "what remains/is left"), see Berlin 2008: 55. The verb form is a Hiphil imperfect, and the noun is a Niphal participle of the verb *yātar*.

12:11. "As quickly as possible" (*bĕḥippāzôn*) occurs only here, in Deut. 16:3, and in Isa. 52:12. The Isaiah verse is an interesting twist on Exod. 12:11. Exodus 12 speaks of the Hebrews leaving Egypt "in haste." However, Isa. 52:12 says that the descendants of the deportees to Babylon "will *not* leave in haste." The Septuagint's rendering, *meta spoudēs*, appears in Luke 1:39, "At that time Mary got ready and *hurried to* a town in the hill country of Judea." Although Exod. 12:11 calls for the Passover meal to be eaten "in haste," Matt. 26:20 (= Mark 14:18; Luke 22:14) has Jesus and his disciples "reclining" at the table during the meal. More than likely, the use of this verb (*anakeimai*) indicates that by NT times the Passover meal had become a banquet at which the participants ate leisurely and more slowly.

12:12. For previous (and frequent) uses of the root *nākâ* in Exodus ("strike down"), see Exod. 9:31, 32 (both Pual); Exod 2:11, 13; 3:20; 7:17, 20, 25; 8:16, 17 [12, 13]; 9:15, 25 (2x; all these are Hiphil); 5:14, 16 (both Hophal). When used in the context of death, *nākâ* means "to strike a fatal blow."

12:12. The objects of the verbs are arranged chiastically: verb ("I will strike down")>direct object ("every firstborn"): direct object ("all of Egypt's gods")>verb ("I will hand down punishments").

12:13. The verb for "pass through" in the preceding verse is *ʿābar*. The verb here for "stand watch over" (traditionally, "pass over") is *pāsaḥ*, on which I shall have more to say below. Similarly, I shall discuss at length *mašḥît* ("a Destroyer").

12:14. The way Biblical Hebrew says "celebrate a (pilgrimage) festival" is *ḥāgag ḥag*. The geminate verb *ḥāgag*, which occurs twice in this verse, is a denominative verb from the noun *ḥag* ("[pilgrimage] festival"), and its basic meaning is "turn, twist, dance out of happiness." The NIV translates the verb as "reveling" in 1 Sam. 30:16 and as "festive" in Ps. 42:4 [5]. We are familiar with the related Arabic noun *ḥagg*/*ḥajj*, "pilgrimage, procession."

12:15. The Hiphil of *šābat* followed by the preposition *min* ("remove from") appears again in Lev. 2:13, "Do not *leave* the salt of the covenant of your God *out of* your grain offerings"; Lev. 26:6 and Ezek. 34:25, "I will *remove* savage beasts *from* the land"; Deut. 32:26, "I said I would scatter them and *blot out* their memory *from* mankind."

12:16. The antecedent of *bāhem* could be either the first and seventh day ("on them"), or the celebrants ("among them").

12:16. *Yēʾākēl lĕkol-nepeš* ("what every person is to eat") illustrates the use of the preposition *lĕ* as an agent with a passive verb ("what may be eaten *by* every person"), on which usage of the preposition see R. Williams 1976: 50 §280; Waltke and O'Connor 1990: 385.

12:17. *Bĕʿeṣem hayyôm* ("on this very day") is a phrase first appearing in the Bible in connection with Noah (Gen. 7:13, "*On that very day* Noah . . . entered the ark"), and with Abraham (17:23, 26, "*On that very day* Abraham took his son Ishmael . . . and circumcised them. . . . Abraham and his son Ishmael were circumcised *on that same day*").

12:19. R. Williams (1976: 45 §250) identifies the preposition *bĕ* attached to "alien" (*baggēr*) and "native-born" (*ûbʾezraḥ*) as the *bĕ* of specification, indicating the parts of which the whole consists. He cites as a parallel Gen. 7:21, "Every living thing that moved on the earth perished—birds [*bāʿôp*], livestock [*ûbabbĕhēmâ*], wild animals [*ḥûbaḥayyâ*], and all [*ûbĕkol*] the creatures that swarm over the earth."

12:21. Hebrew *pesaḥ* appears in the LXX as *to pascha*. This is a transliteration of the Aramaic term for "Passover," *pisḥāʾ* or *pasḥāʾ*. It became a technical term in early Christianity and is not glossed in its Matthean usages (Matt. 26:2, 17, 18, 19) or in other NT passages (Acts 12:14; 1 Cor. 5:7; Heb. 11:28), although note the added comments in Luke 22:1 and John 6:4. The word has a range of meanings: (1) the Passover celebration on the night of the fifteenth of Nisan; (2) the Passover lamb itself (Exod. 12:21, LXX; Mark 14:12; 1 Cor. 5:7); (3) the seven-day holiday that began on the night of the feast (the usual NT meaning); (4) Easter (in Christian circles), aided by the closeness of *pascha* to the verb *paschein*, "to suffer." See Marcus 2009: 931–32.

12:22. The Septuagint renders the Hebrew "in the basin" (*bassap*) as "on the threshold" (*para tēn thyran*, and compare Vulgate's *in limine*). The LXX translators' thinking was that the blood was first poured on the threshold, thus preventing crossing, and then smeared on the lintel and two side posts as an added precaution. See G. Driver 1968: 181.

12:23, 25. Note the phrase used in v. 23 with the Lord as subject, *lōʾ yittēn* ("will not permit"), and here again with the Lord as subject, *yittēn* ("will give"). Something the Lord will *lōʾ yittēn*, and then something he will *yittēn*.

12:27. As in v. 12, there is a nice chiasmus here: "when he plagued Egypt [infinitive followed by direct object], and our houses he rescued [direct object followed by a perfect verb form]."

Commentary

For the first time in Exodus, God speaks to his people about the importance of **12:1–2**
certain days and certain months. More than likely the Hebrews, while working as slaves, are not addicted to, or even aware of, calendar watching. As Janzen (1997: 81) says, "When Pharaoh is in charge of time, one's days become an endless repetition of wearisome toil that in time may seem to go on forever. Past and future are just limitless extensions of an intolerable present." But my, what a monumental change happens in a person's life when God is in charge of one's time instead of Pharaoh! Expectation replaces resignation. Hope replaces numbness. Rhapsody replaces routine. Celebration replaces drudgery.

It is surely not a coincidence that the time of the exodus and the much later return from exile under Ezra both happen in "the first month of the year." Compare Exod. 12:2 with Ezra 7:9, "He [Ezra] had begun his journey from Babylon on the first day of the first month." At both chronological ends of the story of the Hebrew Bible, confinement of God's people in Egypt and Babylon ends during the first month.

The fundamental unit of time in Israelite society was the lunar month. In fact, sometimes the Hebrew word for "month" (*ḥōdeš*) is to be translated "new moon." The months of the year were designated by ordinal numbers: first month, second month, and so forth. This counting began in the spring of the year. Hence the "first month" of the year is the equivalent of our March–April, elsewhere called "Abib," and later around exilic times "Nisan." There is a good possibility that biblical Israel over its long history operated on more than one calendar, one that had a vernal inception, and one that had an autumnal inception.

The word "congregation/community" (*ʿēdâ*) occurs over a hundred times in **12:3**
Exodus–Joshua. Far and away its most frequent reference is to the entire nation, including women and children. Or the term may be used for all adult males (e.g., Num. 14:1–4), especially those bearing arms (Judg. 20:1). Lastly, *ʿēdâ* may be limited to tribal leaders meeting as an executive body (e.g., Josh. 22:16; Judg. 21:10). Thus *ʿēdâ* designates (a) all Israelites; (b) adult males; (c) national representatives. So which of the three is it here? I am inclined to think it is *c*, selected leaders who represent their "constituencies" back home. It is unlikely that Moses is able to address every single individual, as a national leader might do today on television or radio.

Two additional observations about *ʿēdâ*. First, although it appears over a hundred times in Exodus–Joshua, this is the first of those one hundred-plus times. God's people, heretofore called "Hebrews" or "sons of Israel," are now for the first time identified as a "community," a "congregation." The constituents of this assembly bond with one another, both in shared ancestry and in corporate worship of the one and same God.

Second, whenever the text explicitly states that Moses addresses "the entire congregation of Israel," one can be sure that what will follow is of extreme importance. Thus in Exod. 35:1 Moses's address to "the entire congregation of Israel" will be about matters relating to worship and the tabernacle. Similarly, the Lord instructs Moses to take a census of all able-bodied men in "the entire congregation of Israel" (Num. 1:2, 18; 26:2). Most telling, the only time in Leviticus when God instructs Moses to speak to "the entire congregation of Israel" is in Lev. 19:2 AT, and what follows is the topic of holiness—"Speak to the entire congregation of Israel, and say to them, 'Be holy, because I, the Lord your God, am holy.'"

12:4 If there are two chapters in the Bible that are heavily about eating, then it is Gen. 3 and Exod. 12. Genesis 3 uses some form of "eat" sixteen times. In Exod. 12:1–20 the Lord, beginning with v. 4, uses "eat" thirteen times, and five more times in the additional Passover instructions in vv. 43–49. What to eat? When to select the animal that is to be eaten? When to prepare it for eating? How to prepare it for eating? What to do with leftovers you cannot eat? With whom to eat it? At what speed to eat it, slowly or quickly? What side dishes come with the entrée? What to wear when you eat it? The OT seldom dissociates worship from eating. Dinner is not something that follows worship. Dinner is an integral part of worship.

There is no problem in rendering *śeh* as "lamb" (as also in v. 3), but the fact that the next verse allows for an animal "from the sheep or . . . goats" permits either "lamb" or "kid." This animal first shows up in Scripture in Isaac's question to his father, "Where is the *śeh* for the burnt offering?" (Gen. 22:7) and in Abraham's answer, "God himself will provide the *śeh* for a burnt offering, my son" (22:8). These two references to the *śeh* (plus Jacob's two references in Gen. 30:32 to Laban's spotted "sheep" and dark-colored "lamb(s)") are the only occurrences of the word before Exod. 12:3. Admittedly, "lamb" has caught on in Christian circles more than "kid." "Behold the kid of God" does not have the same ring to it as "Behold the lamb of God."

12:5 As I indicated in the previous paragraph, the animal may be taken from either the sheep or goats. Deuteronomy 16:2 expands the possibilities to include bovines: "Sacrifice as the Passover . . . an animal from your flock *or herd*." Tigay (1996: 153–54) correctly explains the addition: "The difference between Exodus and Deuteronomy may be due to the fact that the original *pesaḥ*, in Exodus, was offered by individual households, for which even a single head of small cattle might have been too much to consume (Exod. 12:4), whereas Deuteronomy deals with a time when the sacrifice would be made at the central sanctuary and many households could share a larger animal." He also suggests the possibility that Deuteronomy may evidence later farming realities in Israel, when cattle had become a significant part of the economy.

The phrase "unblemished lamb/kid" (*śeh tāmîm*; LXX, *probaton teleion*) anticipates the description of Jesus in 1 Pet. 1:18–19: "You were redeemed . . . with the precious blood of Christ, a lamb without blemish and defect [*amnou amōmou kai aspilou*]," which thus ties together Passover and Calvary.

Back in v. 3 God offers no explanation why he chooses the "tenth" day of the 12:6
month for the selection of the animal, and neither here in v. 6 does he clarify why he selects the "fourteenth" day of the month for its slaughtering. The liturgical calendar in Lev. 23:5–8 mentions the fourteenth day and ignores the tenth day. Why the gap is anybody's guess.

The lamb can be selected at any time on the tenth day but must be slaughtered on the fourteenth day "between the two evenings/settings." That is the reason it says in Luke 22:7, "Then came the day of Unleavened Bread on which the Passover lamb *had to be sacrificed*" or "*it was necessary for* the Passover lamb to be sacrificed." Such necessity is prompted by the chronological specificity of Exod. 12:6. Deuteronomy's equivalent phrase for "between the two evenings" is "in the evening, when the sun goes down [*bāʿāreb kĕbôʾ haššemeš*]" (Deut. 16:6).

The latter expression seems a bit more extended and open-ended. I suggest that the first Passover in Egypt, since individual families are celebrating it in homes, could be observed fairly simultaneously throughout all of Goshen. By contrast, Deut. 16 legislates that Passover be observed at "the place the LORD will choose as a dwelling for his Name" (Deut. 16:2, 6), meaning a central sanctuary. Certainly more time is needed for all the congregation of Israel to assemble at a central sanctuary and for each to sacrifice his sheep, goat, or bovine. Understandably, later sources extend "between the two evenings" earlier into the day: *Jub.* 49.10, 19, the last third of the day; Philo, *Spec. Laws* 2.145, after high noon. The LXX renders "between the two evenings" as *pros hesperan*, "toward evening," a phrase that appears in Luke 24:29, "But they urged him strongly, 'Stay with us, for it is *nearly evening* [*pros hesperan*].'"

Most often in Scripture when sacrificial blood is placed on an object or on a 12:7
person, it is placed on the outside or the extremities. Here the blood is put on the lintel and the doorposts. In the consecratory rite for new priests, blood is placed on the lobe of the right ear, the thumb of the right hand, and the big toe of the right foot (Exod. 29:20; Lev. 8:23–24). The same procedure is followed in the case of one cleansed of a serious skin infection (Lev. 14:14–17, 25–28). And recall how often the blood is smeared on the "horns" of the altar (Lev. 4:7, 18, 25, 30; etc.). Milgrom (1991: 249, 279) suggests that "the common denominator of all these rites is that the things that receive blood are extremities, the particular points of the object that a hostile force would strike first."

Meat is normally cooked in pans or ovens, but not this time. Bread is normally 12:8–9
prepared with leaven to help it rise, but not this time. No cooking utensils

equals no leaven. Fire will not make the meat inedible, but leaven will make the bread inedible on this occasion. Part of the sanctity of Passover is conveyed by the fact that one does things differently on this day, avoiding things that are quite permissible and ordinary on other days.

Hebraists have not yet agreed on the etymology of *maṣṣôt*. The BDB *Lexicon* connects *maṣṣôt* with the verb *māṣaṣ*, "to suck," or to *māṣâ*, "sip out, press out," but this sounds more appropriate with a liquid than with a solid. Others have suggested a connection with the Greek word *maza*, "barley bread." More recently, Goldstein and Cooper (1990: 20–21; Cooper and Goldstein 1992: 27–28) connect *maṣṣôt* with the verb *nāṣâ* I ("fight") and render *maṣṣôt* as "strife." They appeal to the following pairing in the expression in the parallel verse of Deut. 16:3: "But for seven days eat unleavened bread, the bread of affliction [*maṣṣôt leḥem ʿōnî*]." I take the translation "flatbread" from Alter (2004: 377), who remarks that the "conventional translation of 'unleavened bread' is less than felicitous not only because of its excess of syllables but [also] because it explicitly defines the bread by negation, the lack of leavening, whereas the Hebrew is a positive term."

The OT speaks of two other offerings that involve eating bread. One is the fellowship/thanksgiving offering (Lev. 7:12–13), and the other is the offering of the Nazirite who is terminating one's term in office (Num. 6:19–20). All three are offered and consumed by the laity, and all three share the same motive of thanksgiving. The fellowship offering is even closer to Exod. 12 with its additional instruction that "it must be eaten on the day it is offered; he must leave none of it till morning" (Lev. 7:16).

The text does not supply a reason for the inclusion of "bitter herbs." Later traditions (Mishnah *Pesaḥim* 10.5) historicize the addition by linking the herbs with the "bitter" experiences of the Hebrews in Egypt and even add a fourth item to the meal, the drinking of wine (*Pesaḥim* 10; *Jub.* 49.6). Other passages of Scripture speak of bitter water (Exod. 15:23; Num. 5:23–24) and bitter grapes (Deut. 32:32). One wonders if eating the bitter herbs in Exod. 12 is anything like drinking the bitter water in Num. 5, meaning water that is not only bitter in taste but also bitter in its effects.

Commentators have often pointed out, and have been much exercised by, an alleged blatant discrepancy between Exod. 12:9, which says the meat must "not be boiled" (*bāšal*) in water, and Deut. 16:7, which says that the meat is to be "boiled" (*bāšal*). So, no *bāšal*, or *bāšal* indeed? The NIV translates the Hebrew word "cooked" in Exod. 12:9 and "roast" in Deut. 16:7. To make matters more complicated, so it is maintained, the writer of 2 Chron. 35:13 badly and nonsensically fused the two traditions when he has Josiah "boil in fire" the Passover sacrifice. To quote Levinson (2000: 271n7), "In attempting to honor both requirements, the resulting harmonization conforms to neither. In his bid for harmonization, the Chronicler created a text that, quite literally, cannot be read; it can only be interpreted." I am not so sure Exodus and Deuteronomy contradict each other. In Akkadian the verb *bashalu* has multiple meanings. Thus *CAD* B:135 lists the following, "Boil, roast, become roasted, burn to ashes, fire (used with clay), fuse, melt, ripen, bake, cook." If cuneiform *b-sh-l* can refer to several kinds of cooking and food preparation in Akkadian, why cannot Hebrew *b-š-l* do the same?

The instruction to leave nothing until the next day and to incinerate anything **12:10**
that is left over is repeated in other Scripture passages on Passover (Num. 9:12; Deut. 16:4b). The same guidelines accompany the thank offering (Lev. 7:15; 22:29–30), the freewill offering (Lev. 7:16–17; 19:6), and the offerings of the priestly ordinands (Exod. 29:34; Lev. 8:32).

In the OT burning is a method of disposal for (1) impure objects such as fabrics infected with mildew (Lev. 13:52, 55, 57), (2) idolatrous impurities (Exod. 32:20; Deut. 7:5, 25; 9:21; 12:3; 1 Kings 13:2; 15:13; 2 Kings 10:26), (3) a Nazirite's hair (Num. 6:18), (4) persons executed (Gen. 38:24; Lev. 20:14; 21:9; Josh. 7:25), and (5) leftover portions of edible sacrifices (as here, Exod. 12:10; 29:34; Lev. 7:17; 8:32; 10:16–20; 19:6). For passages that say only "Do not leave anything till morning" and lack an explicit reference to burning, see Exod. 23:18b; 34:25b; Lev. 7:15; 22:30; Num. 9:12; Deut. 16:4b. See D. Wright 1987: 399.

"Your loins girded" is almost the same as the Lord's words to Jeremiah in Jer. **12:11**
1:17, "Gird up your loins" (NIV, "Get yourself ready!"), except that Exod. 12:11 uses *ḥāgar* for "gird," while Jer. 1:17 uses *ʾāzar* for "gird." The reference here is to a long, ankle-length tunic or robe, which needs to be tied at the waist with a girdle or belt when one is (a) setting out on a journey (Exod. 12:11; 2 Kings 4:29; 9:1), (b) beginning to run (1 Kings 18:46), or (c) engaging in war and spiritual warfare (Jer. 1:17; Ezek. 23:15). The common denominator is that the phrase underscores preparation for anything strenuous or difficult (see the Lord's use of this phrase to Job in KJV of Job 38:3 and 40:7 [NIV, "Brace yourself like a man"]).

Jesus uses the phrase with his disciples in Luke 12:35 (KJV), as does Paul with the Ephesians (6:14 KJV) and Peter in his First Epistle (1:13 KJV). The phrase means to "get ready for service," "get ready for confrontation." There may be a subtle connection between Exod. 12:11 (and other Torah passages) and Mark's account of Jesus's sending out the Twelve (Mark 6:8–11). Note these parallels: (1) take a staff; (2) no bread (bread will be provided: cf. Exod. 16); (3) no money in your belts; (4) wear sandals; (5) a single tunic (each Israelites' one set of clothing lasted through the wilderness wanderings: Deut. 8:4; 29:5). According to Marcus (2000: 389), these parallels suggest that the disciples' missionary journey on which Jesus is dispatching them is their participation in the new exodus that Jesus is launching.

One final NT connection here. Luke's comment in Luke 22:14 that Jesus and his disciples eat the Passover as "they reclined at the table" indicates that the practice of standing and quickly eating the Passover meal, ready for a hasty departure, has long been given up. (See the latter portion of my grammatical and lexical note on 12:11 above.)

12:12 Sternberg (1998: 278) notes that the word "Hebrew" (*ʿibrî*) comes from the verb "pass through" (*ʿābar*); here and in v. 23, he suggests an ironic translation of the opening of the verse as "and I will 'Hebrew' the land of Egypt." Pharaoh has killed God's firstborn, the *ʿibrîm*. Now God is about to *ʿābar* Egypt, to slay their firstborn.

There are different ways to translate *ʿāśâ šĕpāṭîm*: "bring judgment" (NIV); "execute judgments" (NRSV; Childs 1974: 179); "mete out punishments" (NJPS); "exact retributions" (Alter 2004: 378). The basic meaning of the phrase is "do justice." See Deut. 10:18; Ps. 146:7; Mic. 6:8, all of which use the phrase for acting justly for the poor and oppressed. When God is the subject of the phrase, the results, as far as the recipients go, may be negative (Exod. 12:12; 2 Chron. 24:24; Ps. 9:16 [17]; Ezek. 5:8) or positive (Pss. 9:4, 16 [5, 17]; 140:12 [13]). Ezekiel uses the phrase often with the meaning "inflict punishment." These objects of divine punishment are not only Sidon (28:22), Egypt (30:14, 19), and Moab (25:11), but God's own Israel as well (5:10, 15; 11:9; 16:41).

12:13 "Signs" appear in earlier biblical narratives: the rainbow of Noah's time (Gen. 9:12, 13, 17), Abraham's circumcision (17:11). This is the first "sign" in Exodus, which later identifies the Sabbath as a sign (31:13). In Numbers the altar plating made of the fire pans is a "sign," a warning (16:38 [17:3]), as is Aaron's staff (17:10 [25]).

Three of these passages use both the word "sign," *ʾôt*, and either the verb *zākar* ("remember") or the noun *zikkārôn* ("reminder, remembrance"): (1) Gen. 9:12, 13, 15; (2) Exod. 12:13, 14; (3) Num. 16:38 [17:3] and 16:40 [17:5]. In the first two the sign points to God's favorable intervention, whereas in the Numbers passage the sign is a warning to other would-be "Korahites."

For whose benefit is the sign? Can it be for God's assistance, to help him know the identity of the occupants of the houses, Egyptian or Hebrew? But are not the Hebrews already ghettoed in Goshen? Or is the sign for the benefit of the Hebrews? Only those who indicate that they are placing themselves under the divine mercy and protection offered by the blood will be spared. "Hebrewness" will not save them. Only the blood will. After all, v. 13 begins by saying, "The blood will be a sign for *you*," not, "the blood will be a sign for *me*."

The word "stand watch over" (traditionally, "pass over"), here and in vv. 23 and 27 is *pāsaḥ*. The three consonants of the verb, *p-s-ḥ*, are the same three consonants of the name of the sacrifice, *pesaḥ*. In 1 Kings 18:21 Elijah on Mount Carmel asks the prophets of Baal, "How long will you *waver* [Qal, *pāsaḥ*] between two opinions?" Later, in that same story, 1 Kings 18:26 says that these prophets "*danced* [Piel, *pāsaḥ*] around the altar they had made."

Second Samuel 4:4 speaks of Mephibosheth who "fell and *became crippled* [Niphal, *pāsaḥ*]." In conjunction with the translation "became crippled," I also mention the adjective *pissēaḥ*, "crippled," as in Lev. 21:18, which says of the priests, "No man who has any defect may come near; no man who is blind or lame [*pissēaḥ*]." Hence, following the NIV, we have three translations for the verb, depending on the stem in which it appears: "waver"; "danced"; "became crippled." And for good measure, Isa. 31:5 speaks of God's shielding, delivering, protecting (Qal, *pāsaḥ*), and rescuing Jerusalem. So, is it "waver," "danced," "became crippled," or "protected" in Exod. 12:13? Are we dealing here with two homonymic verbs, one of which means "limp, be lame" and the other "protect, stand watch over"?

It is the LXX that first introduces the translation of *pāsaḥ* as "skip/pass over" with its use of *paraeleusetai* ("he will pass by/over") in v. 23. Yet in both v. 13 and in v. 27 it employs a Greek verb (*skepazō*) meaning "protect": v. 13, "I will protect you" (*kai skepasō hymas*); v. 27, "protected" (*eskepasen*).

Perhaps we might bring all these meanings together, as Brichto (1992: 234) has suggested. The basic meaning of the verb points to one who is so seriously crippled that he is at a "standstill." Thus Elijah asks the prophets in 1 Kings 18:21 AT, "How long will you *stand* on both sides of the fence" (they are immobilized by their indecision). And in 1 Kings 18:26 the Baal prophets do not "dance around" the altar, but rather "stood still" (Brichto: "remained fixed in place") by the altar. In Exod. 12, then, one can appropriately render all three occurrences of *pāsaḥ* as "stand/stood watch over." The God of Exod. 12 is a protecting God for those inside, behind the blood.

Because, and only because, the Lord will stand watch over his people, a "Destroyer" (*mašḥît*) will not be able to enter their houses. (The term is anarthrous in v. 13, "a Destroyer," but articular in v. 23, "the Destroyer," *hammašḥît*.) In the earlier plagues the Hebrews need no blood on their doorposts to protect them from flies or locusts or darkness, but here, when the issue is survival and life or death, they need both the blood and the Lord's protecting presence over their houses.

Mašḥît is a Hiphil participle of the verb *šāḥat*, "destroy." As such, there are almost twenty instances of *mašḥît* as a verbal form. Here are three from Genesis: (1) Gen. 6:13, "I am surely going to destroy them and the earth" (*mašḥîtam*, participle plus pronominal suffix); (2) Gen. 19:13, "Because we are going to destroy this place" (*mašḥitîm*, plural participle, plus independent pronoun); (3) Gen. 19:14, "For the Lord is about to destroy the city!" (*mašḥît*).

In another almost twenty instances, *mašḥît* is a noun, meaning either "destroyer" or "destruction." In some of these the reference is clearly to somebody who performs a destructive act, such as a destroyer, and sometimes this is a military unit or commandos (1 Sam. 13:17 and 14:15 [NIV, "raiding parties"]; Jer. 4:7 [NIV, "a destroyer of nations has set out"], meaning the Babylonian lion; Jer. 22:7 [NIV, "destroyers"]). With the exception of Exod.

12, the "destroyer" is always a human agent. One of the few places where the Hebrew word should be translated more abstractly as "destruction" is Ezek. 21:31 [36], "men skilled in destruction."

So who is this nonhuman "Destroyer" in Exod. 12, and from where does he/it come? Contrary to much that has been suggested by some writers, I think we can eliminate the idea that this Destroyer is some desert demon or plague demon (Lindstrom 1983: 59–65). Note Kaufmann's (1972: 105) helpful remark: "But mark who the destroyer is: not a band of demons or satyrs, but YHWH himself or his death-dealing angel. From the realm of YHWH comes all activity—even destruction; no satyrs and no impurity are involved."

One suspects that the definite article on "Destroyer" in Exod. 12:23 is parallel to the definite article appended to the name of other divine agents—for example, "the satan" who is with the other "sons of God" (Job 2:1, and thirteen more times in Job 1–2) or "the Messenger" who speaks to Zechariah (Zech. 4:1). Verse 23a states that the Lord will "pass through to plague" (*lingōp*) Egypt, while v. 23b indicates that that is the mission of the Destroyer too (*lingōp* again). Such parallelism of activity recalls instances where the text oscillates between "Lord" and "angel" (e.g., Exod. 3:1–7). There is at work here both a process of hypostatization (at one point the work of God and of the Destroyer are the same), and differentiation (the Lord's presence at the threshold prohibits the Destroyer from entering).

12:14 To what does "this day" refer? To what has preceded or to what follows? Does v. 14a conclude Passover or introduce the festival of Unleavened Bread? Or both? I agree with Childs (1974: 197) when he states, "'This day' of v. 14 is 15 Nisan, the day of exodus, but it includes the night of Passover. The reference in v. 14 is to 'that night' (v. 12), but includes the entire day of the 15th."

"(A day of) remembrance [*zikkārôn*]" can, as here and in Lev. 23:24, simply refer to a special occasion as an act of commemoration. More often, a *zikkārôn* involves the display of some object as a visual reminder: Exod. 13:9, 16, a headband or *tēpîllîn* ("tefillin") on the forehead; Exod. 28:29, the names of Israel's tribes on the high priest's breastpiece; Zech. 6:14, the crown of the high priest Joshua to be placed in the temple. Isaiah (Isa. 57:8) chides those who "behind the door and doorpost place your memorial" (NIV, "you have put your pagan symbols").

12:15–20 As in Lev. 23:5–8 and Deut. 16:1–8, mention of the Festival of Unleavened Bread follows immediately after the mention of Passover. The two, while a pair, are distinct. Passover observance recalls what happened the night before the Hebrews left Egypt, while the Festival of Unleavened Bread recalls the baking of such bread in their haste to leave Egypt. Since the two spring festivals occurred back-to-back, and since unleavened bread was a part of Passover observance too (Exod. 12:8), later religious calendars in the Bible (e.g., Deut. 16) can speak of Passover as part of the Festival of Unleavened Bread.

The absence of leaven (yeast) for these seven days suggests nothing negative about leaven. Rather, its nonuse for these seven days in the bread one eats simply reminds the consumer that when God says "Go," he means, "Go now. Drop everything you're doing." When a smoke detector goes off in one's house, through its sharp beeps it is saying, "Evacuate immediately." Before leaving, the occupant may scoop up a few family photos, but one will not vacuum the carpets first! On all the other days of the year, eating leavened bread is normal and acceptable. But on a few days at least, in one's worship of God, one is prepared to set aside normal customs and habits and foods.

The closest the OT comes to picturing leaven as something not desirable is Lev. 2:11, which bans the use of yeast (no added/artificial inflation) and honey (no added/artificial sweetener) in the preparation of a grain/cereal offering.

The Synoptic Gospels record Jesus as saying, "Be on your guard against the yeast of the Pharisees and Sadducees" (Matt. 16:6), or "Watch out for the yeast of the Pharisees and that of Herod" (Mark 8:15), or "Be on your guard against the yeast of the Pharisees, which is hypocrisy" (Luke 12:1). Possibly Jesus is using "yeast" here as a symbol for what gives the above-named groups or individuals an exaggerated and falsely inflated sense of their own uniqueness and piety.

It is Paul in 1 Cor. 5:6–8 who most patently speaks of yeast in a negative way. He urges the Corinthian Christians to "get rid of the *old yeast* that you may be a new batch without yeast—as you really are. For Christ, our Passover Lamb, has been sacrificed. Therefore let us keep the Festival, not with the *old yeast*, . . . but with bread without yeast." I suggest that the apostle is using "yeast" as a symbol of a carnal, unsurrendered believer who continues to harbor within him elements of behavior that have "risen" and are operative in his being, elements that ought to have been "put to death." Paul names some of these traits: boasting, malice, wickedness, insincerity, untruthfulness. The apostle's counsel? "Get rid of it." Janzen (1997: 84) remarks, "When we have lived for some time in our own version of 'Egypt,' . . . the danger is that in leaving Egypt we will take with us the old yeast that will simply give rise to the same old habits and patterns."

It is not necessary to remove leaven from one's house during Passover even though the eating of some form of unleavened bread is banned on that occasion. It is only on the first day of Unleavened Bread that such removal is mandatory (Exod. 12:15b). Removing leaven probably does not mean destroying it, but rather removing it from one's pantry and sealing and storing it elsewhere.

The penalty for noncompliance is severe: "That person shall be cut off from . . . Israel." The penalty "cut off from" (*kārat min*) occurs frequently in the OT, especially in the priestly literature (see the studies of Milgrom 1991: 457–60; B. Levine 1989: 241–42). Milgrom suggests that there are nineteen cases of *kāret min* in the Pentateuch, which he subsumes under five categories: (1) sacred time; (2) sacred substance; (3) purification rituals; (4) illicit worship; (5) illicit sex. Levine labels the categories as (1) violation of the Sabbath and improper observance of festivals and holy days; (2) violation of certain laws of purity; (3) certain prohibited sexual unions regarded as a form of impurity; (4) cultic offenses, such as eating blood and fat and mishandling sacrificial substances; (5) failure to circumcise one's male children at the age of eight days.

Exodus 12:15 is an illustration of Milgrom's number one ("sacred time") and Levine's number one ("improper observance of festivals and holy days"). Most, but not all, of these cases involve private, secretive sins. (Working on the Sabbath [Exod. 31:14] is obviously public in nature.) Who polices your dinner menu? Who knows what kind of bread you eat in the privacy of your home, leavened or unleavened? Well, God knows, so he must be the one who does the cutting off. What then might "be cut off from" mean? The most common answer is ostracism or banishment. However, the one place in Leviticus–Numbers where the meaning "be excommunicated from" is most likely uses *kārat lĕ* instead of *kārat min* (Lev. 20:17): "They shall be excommunicated in the sight of their kinsfolk" (NJPS; NIV, "They must be cut off before the eyes of their people"). I suggest a range of meanings: (1) an earlier-than-expected death; (2) childlessness; (3) the elimination of the sinner's family and descendants; (4) failure to join and enjoy the hereafter with one's family already in the land of eternal bliss.

The one thing a celebrant is not to do, apart from the bread preparation, is work on the first and last days of the festival (Exod. 12:16). The NIV's "do not work at all" has rightly caught the meaning of *kol-mĕlā'kâ*. Both this Hebrew word for "work" (*mĕlā'kâ*) and the word for "angel/messenger" (*mal'āk*) come from the verb *lā'ak*, "to send, assign," and hence my translation "no assigned activity." Just as *šabbat šabbātôn* (Exod. 31:15; 35:2) means "absolute rest," so *kol-mĕlā'kâ* means "total desistance from any kind of work," or as Milgrom (2000b: 1977) has said, the phrase connotes that "every conceivable kind of exertion, skilled or unskilled, heavy or light, is proscribed."

12:21–27a These verses contain Moses's relaying to his people the data that God told him about Passover/Unleavened Bread in vv. 1–20. This establishes a pattern in Exodus. First, God speaks privately to Moses about some matter, and then Moses transmits that to his people. Compare, for example, what Moses is to do with what the Lord will tell him at Sinai ("This is what you are to say to the house of Jacob and what you are to tell the people of Israel," 19:3b), or what the Lord will tell him as the tabernacle project looms on the horizon ("Tell the Israelites . . . ," 25:2). An exception to this pattern may be the revelation of the Decalogue ("And God spoke all these words," 20:1), but see the grammatical and lexical note on 19:25 below.

Two things stand out in Moses's speech. First, it is amazingly much shorter than the Lord's. The Lord's speech takes twenty verses. Moses's transmission of that revelation takes six and half verses. Most of what the Lord has earlier said to Moses nowhere appears in Moses's speech. The Lord uses the verb "eat" thirteen times in vv. 1–20. It does not appear even once in Moses's speech. And where does he mention the tenth and fourteenth day, the girding of the loins, wearing sandals, the bitter herbs, and eating hastily?

These "omissions" do not suggest either that Moses has a short memory, or that he feels compelled to edit God's lengthy speech and give the people a digest. Neither God nor Moses is into synopses and summaries. Rather, I believe that Moses passes on God's instructions verbatim, but what we have preserved in the biblical text is a condensed account of his talk. The one highlighted item in Moses's speech is the proper use of the blood. What this accomplishes is that it underlines the importance of the blood on this occasion. Forgetting the bitter herbs, or eating leisurely and barefoot, while important, do not vitiate Passover. But the blood, that's something else! If there is no blood, there is no deliverance.

The second item here is that Moses anticipates the day when, once settled in Canaan, the children will ask their parents the meaning of this ceremony ("What does this service mean to you?" v. 26). We find this pattern of question (from the children) and answer (from the parents) again in Exod. 13:14–16; Deut. 6:20–25; Josh. 4:6–7, 21–22. More distant parallels are in Deut. 4:9b ("Teach them to your children and to their children after them"); Deut. 6:7 ("Impress them on your children. Talk about them when you sit at home"); Deut. 11:19 ("Teach them to your children"). In such cases, especially Exod. 12–13; Deut. 6; Josh. 4, as Long (1968: 78–84; 1997: 138–39) has observed, the purpose of such parental answers is not to explain the origin or cause(s) of something, but to explain its significance—why it is important for us, and why it is important for you.

The above catechistic passages highlight the God-given, educative ministry of parents to offspring. That is a strong theme in the Wisdom literature of the OT, especially Prov. 1–9 and 31, "Listen my son/child to your father's/mother's instruction." (On "Fathers as Teachers" in Proverbs, see M. Fox 2000: 80–82.) Weinfeld (1991: 357) remarks: "The education of children by telling them the history of their ancestors who were freed from oppression is something peculiar to the Israelite nation. . . . Pagan nations, who marked their gods by their mythological features, educated their children through mythology." He then quotes a line from the *Enuma Elish*, the Babylonian creation epic: "Let the father recite [the names of the God Marduk] and impart them to his son" (from the "Epilogue").

One final point I shall make about Moses's speech to his people: he seems to stress more strongly in v. 23 than the Lord does in v. 13 the importance of God's protecting presence. The blood itself, while critical, will not keep the Destroyer at bay. This immediately eliminates any idea that the blood of the *śeh* has intrinsic powers to stop destruction in its path, or that the blood is for the purpose of warding off malefic forces. At the same time, Moses's words to the Israelites make it clear that the Destroyer, if left unchallenged, will destroy everybody indiscriminately, Egyptian and Hebrew firstborn, blood or no blood, unless God is there to stop him/it. It is a biblical principle that when God punishes a community by a group of natural disasters, the righteous suffer along with the wicked. Recall Abraham discussing this with Yahweh in Gen. 18. For the righteous to survive, they must depart from the area. Thus Noah must build and go aboard his ark if he is not to drown along with everybody else. Lot and his family must flee from Sodom if they are not to be incinerated along with all the other Sodomites. Moses and Aaron must get away from the people to escape the death coming to Korah and to others (Num. 16:45 [17:10]). And here, if the Israelites are to escape the judgment coming on others, they need blood on their doorposts, and more important, the Lord's protecting presence.

12:27b–28 The Israelites do what the Lord has commanded, not what Moses and Aaron command. Passover is God's idea, not Moses's. Such an "execution formula" (Blenkinsopp 1976: 275–77) is common in Genesis–Numbers. It occurs in one of three ways: (1) "Moses [or somebody else] did what/just as the LORD commanded"; (2) "The people of Israel did what/just as the LORD commanded Moses"; (3) "The people of Israel did what/just as the LORD commanded Moses. Thus they did it."

The Tenth Plague and the Start of the Exodus

(12:29–42)

Translation

[29]It happened. At midnight the LORD struck down every firstborn in the land of Egypt, from the firstborn of Pharaoh who is sitting on his throne to the firstborn of the prisoner in the pit-house, and all the firstborn of animal. [30]Pharaoh got up at night, he and all his servants and all Egypt, and there was an enormous cry in Egypt, for there was no house(hold) in which there was no dead. [31]And he summoned Moses and Aaron at night, and he said, "Up, leave my people, (both of) you and Israel's sons. Go, worship the LORD as you spoke. [32]Also your sheep and cattle take, just as you said, and go, and bless also me."

[33]Egypt strongly urged the people to hurry to send them away, for they said, "All of us are dead." [34]The people carried off their dough before it leavened, their kneading pans wrapped in their garments on their shoulders. [35]And Israel's sons had done as Moses spoke. They asked from the Egyptians vessels of silver and vessels of gold and garments. [36]And the LORD had granted the people favor in the eyes of Egypt(ians), who lent to them, and they plundered Egypt(ians).

[37]And Israel's sons journeyed from Rameses to Sukkot, about six hundred thousand footmen, plus dependents. [38]Also a motley crew went up with them, along with sheep, cattle, and an awful lot of livestock. [39]They baked the dough that they brought out of Egypt (into) flatbread cakes, for it had not leavened. Because they had been driven out of Egypt, they were not able to dally around. Also (other) provisions they did not prepare for themselves.

[40]The stay/residence of Israel's sons that they stayed/resided in Egypt was four hundred and thirty years. [41]At the end of four hundred and thirty years, yes, to the exact day, all the LORD's battalions went out from the land of Egypt. [42]A night of watchkeeping [was] that for the LORD, to bring them out from the land of Egypt. That [day]—this night—belongs to the LORD, a watchkeeping for all Israel's sons for all their generations.

Grammatical and Lexical Notes

12:29. For other incidents that begin with a time reference in a prepositional phrase ("at midnight"), see Gen. 22:1 ("After these things" [NIV, "Some time later"]) and Gen. 41:1 ("When two full years had passed").

12:31. Coordinate commands in apposition in which *qûm* ("Up/Arise") is the first imperative are common in Genesis (Gen. 19:14; 21:18; 27:19, 43; 28:2; 31:13; 35:1; 44:4). See also Exod. 32:1. In Gen. 43:13 *qûm* is the middle of three imperatives.

12:31. The Hebrew imperative "leave" (*ṣĕʾû*) has a *dagesh forte* in the first consonant (indicating the doubling of the consonant, *ṣṣ*). We find the same two verbs in the imperative in Gen. 19:14, again with the *dagesh* in the initial letter: *ṣṣĕʾû*. In Deut. 2:24 AT ("Rise, journey, and cross the Arnon Gorge"), the second imperative ("journey") places a daghesh in the initial *sāmek*: *ssĕʿû*.

12:33. The verb I have translated "strongly urged" is *ḥāzaq* in the Qal stem. That is the verb that the plagues section of Exodus uses (in the Piel stem, transitive) for the Lord's "toughening/ strengthening" Pharaoh's heart (Exod. 4:21; 9:12; 10:20, 27; 11:10; 14:4, 8, 17 [Piel participle]). In all those references it is *ḥāzaq*, Piel, followed by the accusative indicator *ʾet*. Here it is *ḥāzaq*, Qal, followed by the preposition *ʿal*.

12:37. The last phrase ("plus dependents/little children [*miṭṭāp*]") makes no mention of any women. The Septuagint renders *ṭap* with *aposkeuē*. The primary meaning of the noun is "moveable property, baggage" (from the verb *aposkeuazomai*, "pack up and carry off"). In Gen. 15:14 it translates the Hebrew *rĕkuš*, Abram's descendants' possessions with which they will leave Egypt. Used in a military context, *aposkeuē* came to mean "baggage-train," meaning the soldier's baggage, wife, and children that accompany him. Thus in Exod. 12:37 *aposkeuē* includes both children and women. See Lee 1972: 432.

12:38. I shall have more to say on *ʿēreb rab* ("motley crew") below. For an excellent study of this expression, see Bar (2008), who argues that the phrase refers to mercenaries who have intermarried with the Israelites in Egypt.

12:38. The Hebrew word *kābēd* is behind my translation "lot" ("and an awful *lot* of livestock"). Like *ḥāzaq* in v. 33 (see note above on 12:33), *k-b-d* also figures prominently in the plagues with Pharaoh and/or his heart (7:14; 8:15, 32 [11, 28]; 9:7, 34). For *kābēd* meaning "numerous," see 1 Kings 3:9 (NIV, "great"); 2 Kings 6:14 (NIV, "strong"); 2 Kings 18:17 (NIV, "large").

12:39. The Hebrew for "flatbread cakes" (*ʿugōt maṣṣôt*) recalls the use of both of these words in Genesis: Abraham instructed Sarah to make some "bread" (*ʿugôt*, Gen. 18:6) for his visitors, and Lot made "flatbread" (*maṣṣôt*, Gen. 19:3) for his visitors. There are several other connections between the Passover and the Sodom/Gomorrah incident (see Geoghegan 2004: 50–59). (1) There is hurried activity in Gen. 18:6–7 (*māhar*) and hurried activity in Exod. 12:11 (*bĕḥippāzôn*) and 12:33 (*māhar*). (2) The verb "pass [by]," *ʿābar*, which is present in Gen. 18:3 ("do not pass your servant by") and 18:5 ("and then go on your way"), although appearing many times in the remainder of Genesis, does not resurface in the Hebrew Bible to refer to the Lord's movements (his passing by or over) until Exod. 12:12, 23. (3) Both incidents use some form of the verb *šāḥat* for "destroying" human life (Gen. 18:28, 31, 32; 19:13, 14, 29; Exod. 12:13, 23). (4) The Lord's promise to return to Abraham "at the appointed time" (*lammôʿēd*) next year in conjunction with Sarah's pregnancy (Gen. 18:14) points to Exod. 13:10, a reminder to keep the Festival of Flatbread on the heels of Passover "at the appointed time" (*lammôʿēd*). (5) The phrase "rise [and] go from" (*qûmû ṣĕʾû min*) occurs in only two places in the Hebrew Bible: Gen. 19:14 (Lot to his sons-in-law) and Exod. 12:31 (Pharaoh to Moses and Aaron).

12:39. I follow the ancient versions (LXX, SP, Vulgate) in reading *gērĕšûm* ("has been driven") for MT's *gōrĕšû*.

12:41. My use of "yes" in "yes, to the exact day" is an attempt to capture the force of the second *wayĕhi* in this sentence, a word that is ignored in most, if not all, translations I have consulted.

Commentary

12:29–32 These few verses record, albeit briefly, the implementation of the tenth plague, which the Lord first reveals to Moses in 11:1–3. Nobody in Egypt escapes the wrath of Yahweh. It cuts a swath of destruction from Egypt's palace to Egypt's pits (dungeons).

Earlier Pharaoh asks Moses to pray for him (8:8 [4], 28 [24]; 9:28; 10:17). On this occasion he asks Moses to bless him (v. 32), thus providing the first instance of the verb *bārak* in Exodus. In the earlier references, when Pharaoh has asked Moses to pray for him, the next verse or so records that Moses does indeed honor that request, regardless of Pharaoh's motivation in asking for prayer. However, on this occasion there is no record of Moses's blessing Pharaoh. Indeed, instances of people's blessing a king are rare in Scripture (Gen. 47:7, 10, Joseph and the Pharaoh; 1 Kings 8:66, Solomon's people; Ps. 72:15, part of a psalm that is a prayer for the king's success).

Maybe what Pharaoh wants from Moses's blessing is a cessation of this plague, but vv. 29–30 suggest the plague has already done its work and run its course. Does he, in making such a request, hope for some "payback," some sort of quid pro quo, for releasing the Hebrew people? Is this the prayer of a man at his wit's end? Can we hear Pharaoh say something like Jacob says to the "man": "I will not let you go unless you bless me" (Gen. 32:26b [27b])? Predictably, Pharaoh desires a blessing, but repenting for his disgraceful, arrogant behavior never crosses his mind.

This paragraph fulfills the earlier instructions that God has given his people **12:33–36**
about "borrowing/taking/asking a gift" from the Egyptians: silver, gold, and clothing. See my earlier comments at 3:21–22 and 11:2–3. Exodus 12 uses the verb *nāṣal* in two dramatically different ways. When written in the Hiphil stem, it means "spare, rescue" (v. 27; see earlier uses, 2:19; 3:22; 5:23; 6:6). But when written in the Piel stem, as here (v. 36 and in 3:22), it means "plunder, strip off, (de)spoil." When God "rescues" his people, he will "snatch away/take away" Egypt's slave workforce. When the Hebrews exit Egypt, they will "snatch/take away" some of its valuables.

Later in Exodus, the Israelites will do one of two things with these gifts of precious metals and fabrics. Either they will give gold, silver, and fabrics as an offering to help build the tabernacle (Exod. 25:1–7), or else they will give some of that gold jewelry to Aaron to help build the golden calf (32:2–3)! Janzen (1997: 95) states: "These gifts, then, are ambiguous, depending on how they are used: When used in obedience to God they serve the new beginning. . . . When used in disregard of God they serve to perpetuate the old past with its idolatry and oppression." Is that not true, I might add, of all of God's gifts that come to us from whatever source? The possibility for proper use is there, but so is the possibility for abuse.

The exodus from Egypt now starts. After leaving Rameses, their first stop is **12:37–42**
at Sukkot (NIV, Succoth). The latter city is in the eastern delta of the Nile, south and a bit east of Rameses. About a day's journey from Rameses, it was somewhere between Lake Timsah and the Bitter Lakes. The Hebrew word

sukkâ (pl., *sukkôt*) designates a "booth." Animals took shelter in these (Gen. 33:17 [NIV, "shelters"]), as did soldiers (1 Kings 20:16 [NIV, "tents"]), and even disgruntled prophets (Jon. 4:5). The word may be used as a double entendre in two later references referring back to Exod. 12:37. Leviticus 23:43 and Num. 33:5 speak of God's bringing Israel to Sukkot and/or having them dwell in *sukkôt*. In any case, Israel's first stop on the way to Canaan is at "Shelterville."

If 600,000 adult men leave Rameses (v. 37b), how many of those 600,000 make it to Sukkot with their families on the same day? After all, Sukkot is not a metropolitan area. This stratospherically high number reappears consistently in the biblical record: Exod. 38:26; Num. 1:46; 2:32 (603,550); 11:21 (600,000); 26:51, the second generation of Israelites (601,730).

There have been several attempts to read the word "thousand" (*ʾelep*) in "600,000" (*šēš-mēʾôt ʾelep*) as 600 "[something else]" beside "thousand." The candidates include some kind of a military unit like a "brigade" (Mendenhall 1958: 52–66), or rendering *ʾelep* as "families" or "clans." One support for seeing *ʾelep* as a military unit is the reference elsewhere to the Danites' "600" warriors (Judg. 18:11, 16, 17), Saul's "600" warriors (1 Sam. 13:15; 14:2), and David's "600" warriors (1 Sam. 27:2; 30:9; 2 Sam. 15:18), although none of these persons are said to have 600 *ʾelep*. Support for the meaning "family/clan" is found in that *ʾelep* elsewhere may mean that: (1) Gideon says in Judg. 6:15, "My clan [*ʾalpî*] is the weakest in Manasseh"; (2) in 1 Sam. 10:19 Samuel says to the people, "So now present yourselves before the LORD by your tribes and clans [*ʾalpêkem*]." For additional passages where *ʾelep* means "clan," see Num. 1:16; Josh. 22:14, 21, 30; 1 Sam. 23:23 (for all of which NIV uses "clan/s"), and maybe Isa. 60:22 (NIV, "a thousand"), in which I believe "1,000" is a typological number for a vast host, as in Deut. 1:11, "May the LORD . . . increase you a thousand times [*ʾelep pĕʿāmîm*]."

Having said all that, I am unaware of any Bible version that translates Exod. 12:37 something like "about 600 fighting units" or "600 families."

A round number like "600,000" lends itself to a more nonliteral interpretation, but specific numbers like "603,550" do not. I am left to conclude that whatever size the departing body of Israelites is, it is large enough for Pharaoh to say, "The Israelites have become much more numerous for us/than we" (Exod. 1:9 AT). Would 600 families lead him to that conclusion? In a chapter that forbids the use of yeast in baking bread on special occasions, must we assume that a good bit of "yeast" has been added to the number of Hebrews leaving Egypt?

The KJV's famous "mixed multitude" (12:38) is an attempt to capture the Hebrew *ʿēreb rab*. The first word appears in Ezek. 30:5, "Cush and Put, Lydia and all the *ʿēreb* [*kol-hāʿereb*; NKJV, "all the mingled people"; NIV, "all Arabia"] . . . will fall by the sword along with Egypt." See also Neh. 13:3, "When the people heard this law, they excluded from Israel all who were of foreign descent [*kol-ʿēreb*]." The word *ʿēreb*, however one translates it, contains two consonants, *r-b*, that are the opposite sequence of the *b-r* consonants in "Hebrew(s)," leading Sternberg (1998: 21) to say that *ʿēreb rab* is a "double near-anagram of *eber* or *ibri*."

In Numbers, the word for this group is *ʾăsapsup* (Num. 11:4). It is a noun formed from the verb *ʾāsap* ("to gather") and is likely a reference to foreigners "gathered around" Israel's boundaries. The LXX renders both expressions with *epimiktos* ("mixed crowd," and see this Greek word in Jdt. 2:20; Neh. 13:3 [= 2 Esdras 23:3 LXX]; Ezek. 30:5). The TNIV's "rabble" is okay in Num. 11:4, but an excellent English equivalent would be "riffraff," with the similarity of the two syllables in the English word matching the similarity of the two syllables in the Hebrew word (*ʾspsp*). Indeed, Cassuto (1967: 147–48) was the first to suggest that the second word in *ʿēreb rab* is not a separate word but a repetition of the second syllable of the first word. Thus Exod. 12:38's *r-b-r-b* = Num. 11:4's *s-a-p-s-u-p* = English's "riffraff."

Hagar, along with other menservants and maidservants, would be among the first "mixed multitude" to accompany a Hebrew (or proto-Hebrew) out of Egypt to Canaan (Gen. 12:16). Joshua 9 contains the story of how some Canaanites, albeit duplicitously, attached themselves to Israel after the conquest. Isaiah 56:3, 6 speak of God's mercy to those "foreigners [*ben* or *bĕnê hannēkār*] who bind themselves to the Lord." Lack of proper bloodlines and heritage does not bar one from God's kingdom.

There might be any number of reasons why such a group would join the Israelite exodus: (1) to escape their own oppression and poverty; (2) wanderlust; (3) they sense that these Hebrews serve a God completely different from the gods they serve, and they want to be a part of that, as if to say, "Where you go, I will go, and your God shall be my God" (see Ruth 1:16).

The note in vv. 40–41 about the stay in Egypt concluding after 430 years seems to clash with Gen. 15:13, which says this period of time will last 400 years. Even the LXX is sensitive to this, and so renders Exod. 12:40 as "Now the length of time the Israelite people lived in Egypt *and in the land of Canaan* was 430 years."

It is common to say that "430" is the exact number and "400" is a rounding-off number. I am not so sure. Indeed, part of the problem here is determining when this 430/400-year period begins. Hence, *Jub.* 14.13 tabulates the 430 years to be from the time of Isaac's birth to the exodus. I think the best explanation is that offered by Brichto (1998: 330–31), who has read both the Genesis and Exodus texts literally and carefully. The longer era, 430 years, refers to the number of years of the Hebrews' sojourn in Egypt. The smaller number, 400 years, refers to the period of servitude that began some thirty years after Jacob and his sons came to Egypt, and just after Joseph died.

The section ends (v. 42) by noting that this departure night is not a night on which the Hebrews exercise great bravado. Rather, it ends by focusing on the Lord of the Hebrews. Here is Heaven's Shepherd "keeping watch o'er his flock by night."

Further Instructions about Passover

(12:43–51)

Translation

[43]And the LORD said to Moses and Aaron, "This is the statute of the Passover offering: No foreigner shall eat of it. [44]Every man's slave, bought with silver, you shall circumcise him, then he shall eat of it. [45]No resident hireling shall eat of it. [46]In one house it shall be eaten. Do not take outside of the house any meat, nor break a bone of it. [47]The entire congregation of Israel shall observe it. [48]And if a sojourner sojourns with you, and observes the Passover offering to the LORD, let every male of his be circumcised. Then he is eligible to observe it. He shall be like a native-born of the land. But anyone uncircumcised shall not eat of it. [49]One law shall there be for the native-born and for the sojourner who sojourns in your midst."

[50]All of Israel's sons did/observed just as the Lord had commanded Moses and Aaron. They did it so. [51]And so it was on that very day the LORD brought out Israel's sons from the land of Egypt by their battalions.

Grammatical and Lexical Notes

12:45. That the verb "eat" is in the singular (*yōʾkal*) after the double subject *tôšāb wĕśākîr* may contribute somewhat to our understanding of this compound phrase.

12:47. In vv. 47, 48 (and maybe v. 50), "observe" is the verb *ʿāśâ*, "do, make." The most famous use of this sense of *ʿāśâ* is in the law about the Sabbath day in Deut. 5:15b, "Therefore the LORD your God has commanded you to observe [lit., "do, make"] the Sabbath day."

12:48. *Himmôl* illustrates the use of the infinitive absolute either as an imperfect, "he shall circumcise" (R. Williams 1976: 38–39 §209), or as a command, "let him circumcise" (Waltke and O'Connor 1990: 593–94).

12:48. It is possible that the preposition in *lô* ("every male *of his*") is a *lamedh* of agency ("Let every male be circumcised *by* him"). See Althann 1981: 239.

12:48. The verb for "eligible, qualified to" is *qārab*, whose more common meaning is "approach, come near."

12:48. There remains uncertainty about the etymology of *ʾezraḥ*, "native-born." Most likely it is a botanical term for a tree or plant that is rooted deeply in the soil. Compare Ps. 37:35, "I have seen a wicked and ruthless man flourishing like a green tree in its native soil," or, "flourishing like a robust native tree" (*kĕʾezrāḥ raʿănān*). Hence, an *ʾezraḥ* is one whose lineage has deep roots in his land.

Commentary

I noted above that the Lord uses the verb "eat" thirteen times in vv. 1–20, while **12:43–49**
Moses never uses it so much as once in vv. 21–27b. Now the Lord speaks again to Moses with additional instructions about Passover observance and will again use "eat" five times in these seven verses. The emphasis here is not on where to eat, or what to eat, or how to eat, or when to eat, but on who may eat. Who can participate and who cannot? The reason why these supplementary directives come after the start of the exodus is because a group of non-Hebrews have hopped onto the wagon and joined the march out of Egypt (v. 38).

Most translations identify four non-Hebrew and discrete socioeconomic entities in these verses: (1) the foreigner who may not participate under any circumstances (v. 43); (2) and (3) a temporary resident and/or hired worker who also may not celebrate the Passover under any circumstances (v. 45); (4) the alien, the *gēr*, who may participate, provided he and all the other males in his family have been circumcised (v. 48).

There is some debate about whether "temporary resident" (*tôšāb*) and "hired worker" (*śākîr*) represent two distinct groups, and if so, what the difference between them is. I noted above the use of a singular verb in v. 45 after these two subject nouns, thus raising the possibility that *tôšāb wĕśākîr* is a hendiadys. Hence my translation "resident hireling." Analogously, I suggest for *gērîm wĕtôšābîm* in Lev. 25:23 not NIV's "aliens and tenants" but "resident aliens," and for *gēr wĕtôšāb* in Lev. 25:35 not NIV's "alien or a temporary resident," but again, "resident alien." To go outside of Exodus and Leviticus, when Abraham introduces himself to the Hittites as *gēr-wĕtôšāb* (Gen. 23:4), is he describing himself as "an alien and a stranger" (NIV) or as a "resident alien"?

I note that *tôšāb*, unlike *śākîr*, can never stand by itself. It is always used in conjunction with another noun. So what is a *śākîr*? I suggest that he is a day laborer, either Israelite or non-Israelite (see Deut. 24:14, "Do not take advantage of a *śākîr*, . . . whether he is a brother Israelite or an alien"), probably quite poor, who returns to his home and family each evening after completing his work. I suspect that it is the *śākîr* whom Jesus has in mind in the parable of the vineyard workers: "The owner of the vineyard said to his foreman, 'Call the workers and pay them their wages'" (Matt. 20:8). By contrast, *tôšāb wĕśākîr* ("resident hireling") is a long-term employee who lives with his family on the owner's land, much like a migrant farm-working family would do today.

What then about the prohibition placed on the resident hireling at Passover? As I said above, such a person may be Israelite or non-Israelite. If the latter, he is in the category of the "foreigner" of v. 43, and so v. 45 may be directed at this outsider. If the former, he joins his own family for the celebration, even if he and his family live on the owner's property.

I find it interesting that in Num. 9:14, also about who may eat the Passover sacrifice, there is limited mention of the sojourner (no mention of his circumcision for example), and nothing at all about the foreigner or the slave or the *tôšāb wĕśākîr* of Exod. 12. Of course, this could be a case of intentional abbreviation in the repetition of previously formulated legislation.

When speaking of the *gēr*/the sojourner at Passover, Exod. 12 says that "one law shall there be for the native-born and for the sojourner" (v. 49; for this expression elsewhere, see Lev. 24:22; Num. 9:14; 15:29–30). In civil law, this means the *gēr* is not a second-class citizen to be deprived of rights granted to the native-born. But religious law, unlike civil law, does make some distinctions. The *gēr* is bound by the prohibitive commandments (= sins of commission), but not by the performative ones (= sins of omission). That is clear in Exod. 12. Verse 19 clearly says that whoever eats yeast or has it available in the house when they are not supposed to do so, sojourner or native-born, will be "cut off." However, the sojourners' choice to participate in Passover is theirs to make. There is no penalty for abstinence. Yet any male who chooses to participate must be circumcised.

Perhaps all this concern about eating/not eating is reflected in the words heard at Communion observances, and taken from 1 Cor. 11:27: "Whoever eats the bread or drinks the cup of the Lord in an unworthy manner will be guilty of sinning against the body and blood of the Lord."

There is one additional bit of new information found in these verses. That is the note at the end of v. 46 that not a bone of the animal is to be broken. It must be this detail to which John refers when he says of the crucified Christ, "These things happened so that the scripture would be fulfilled: 'Not one of his bones will be broken'" (John 19:36). It is possible that Ps. 34:20 [21] ("He protects all his bones, not one of them will be broken") has also influenced John, given the use of the passive voice in Ps. 34:20b and John 19:36. However, Ps. 34 is about the power of God to save and deliver his followers from trauma and pain. So why would John take a text from a psalm celebrating the escape of the righteous from tribulation, and apply it to a Jesus who has just breathed his last? (On this text from John 19, see Moo 1983: 314–16.) This exalted One, who has just expired without a broken bone in his body, has in his death broken and shattered all the hellish powers of evil.

12:50–51 See comments above at 12:27b–28.

Firstborn and Flatbread

(13:1–16)

Translation

1And the LORD spoke to Moses, saying,
2"Sanctify to me every firstborn, the breach
of every womb among Israel's sons, from
man to animal. It is mine."
3And Moses said to the people, "Re-
member this day on which you came out
of Egypt, from the slaves' house, for by
strength of hand the Lord brought (all of)
you out from this. Anything leavened shall
not be eaten. 4Today you are coming out, in
the month of Abib. 5Thus, when the LORD
brings you to the land of the Canaanite and
the Hittite and the Emorite and the Hivite
and the Jebusite which he swore/promised
to your fathers to give you, a land oozing
with milk and sap, you shall take part in
this service in this month. 6Seven days you
shall eat flatbread, and on the seventh day
a pilgrimage festival to the LORD. 7Flat-
bread shall be eaten for seven days. There
shall not be seen among you unleavened
stuff nor any yeast be seen among you in
all your territory. 8And you shall tell your
son on that day, 'Because this [is what] the
LORD did for me in my coming out of Egypt.'
9And it shall be for you a sign on your hand
and a mark/remembrance between your
eyes, so that the LORD's torah will be in
your mouth, for with a strong hand the
LORD brought you out of Egypt. 10And you
shall observe this statute at its fixed time
once every year.
11"Thus, when the LORD brings you
into Canaan land as he swore/promised
to you and to your fathers and gives it to
you, 12you shall transfer over every breach
of the womb to the LORD and every breach
of animal that is yours—the males to the
LORD. 13And every breach of a donkey you
shall redeem with a lamb, and if you do
not redeem (it), you shall break its neck,
but every firstborn human of your sons
you shall redeem. 14And should your son
ask you tomorrow, 'What is this?' you shall
say to him, 'By strength of hand the LORD
brought us out of Egypt, from the slaves'
house. 15And because Pharaoh was stub-
born about sending us away, the LORD
killed every firstborn in the land of Egypt,
from the firstborn of man to the firstborn
of animal. Therefore I am sacrificing to
the LORD every breach of the womb, the
males, but every firstborn of my sons I
redeem.' 16And it shall be a sign on your
hand and a symbol between your eyes, for
with strength of hand the LORD brought us
out of Egypt."

Grammatical and Lexical Notes

13:2. "Sanctify" (*qaddeš*, Piel) could be rendered "consecrate," or "set apart," but I prefer to retain the holiness overtones of the root *q-d-š*.

13:4. The LXX translates "coming out" here and in v. 8 with *ekporeuomai*, the verb that Mark 1:5 uses of John the Baptist: "All the people from the region of Judea . . . were *traveling out* to meet him" (AT). This could be another indication that Mark is invoking the exodus/Moses typology in the opening part of his Gospel.

13:5. Often the verb "swear" (*šāba'*, Niphal) means "promise." See Gen. 22:16–17; 26:3; 50:24; Exod. 33:1; Num. 11:12; 32:11; Deut. 1:8; 6:10, 18; etc.

13:5. The "you" in "*you* came out of Egypt" and "the LORD brought *you* out" in v. 3 is a plural "you." The same goes for the "you" in v. 4 ("*you* are coming out"). But starting with v. 5 and thereafter, the "you" is a singular "you" ("brings *you*"; "to give *you*"; "*you* shall take part in").

13:7. Before "seven days" one finds the particle *'ēt*. For other instances where duration of time is marked by *'et*, see Lev. 25:22, "While you plant [*'ēt*] the eighth year"; and Deut. 9:25, "I lay prostrate before the LORD [*'ēt*] those forty days and forty nights."

13:8. The relative particle *'ăšer* does not always appear, but is to be understood (hence, my square brackets). This can be seen by comparing Exod. 13:8 (*zeh 'āśâ*) with the similar wording in Gen. 6:15 (AT), *wĕzeh 'ăšer ta'ăśeh* ("This is how you are to make [the ark]").

13:9. Admittedly, "remembrance" is the more standard rendering of *zikkārôn*, but I think here that "mark [for remembrance?] between your eyes" provides a better parallel with "a sign on your hand," than does "remembrance between your eyes."

13:9. The phrase "between your eyes" in vv. 9 and 16 occurs also in a Ugaritic text describing the conflict between the gods Baal and Yam: "Strike the crown [*qdq*] of prince Yam / between the eyes [*bn. 'nm*] of judge Nahar" (cited in Gibson 1978: 44). Held (1968: 91n36) renders the phrase, "It (the club) strikes the head of Prince Yamm / on the forehead (it strikes) Ruler Nahar." Avishur (1980) notes that there are eight expressions of the type "between paired limbs" in the Bible (e.g., "between the knees," "between the arms"). He concludes that "between the eyes" designates the (fore)head or pate of a person.

13:10. The word *mô'ēd* ("fixed time") comes from the verb *yā'ad*, meaning "encounter, fix, designate a time/place/meeting."

13:10. "Once every year" is, literally, "from days to day." It is an expression used to refer to an event that occurs only one time a year. Thus, when 1 Sam. 1:3 tells us that Elkanah went up *miyyāmîm yamîmâ* to worship at Shiloh, it means not so much "year after year" but "once every year." Similarly this idiom appears in 1 Sam. 2:19, telling us that Samuel's mother, Hannah, makes him a new robe once a year.

13:12. "Transfer over" is the Hiphil of *'ābar*. The Qal of this verb appeared in the previous chapter (12:12, 23) for God "passing through" the land of Egypt Passover night.

13:13. The verb *'ārap* means "to break the neck (by striking the nape)." Besides donkeys (here and in 34:20), the verb is used for ending the lives of calves (Deut. 21:4, 6) and dogs (Isa. 66:3). The donkey/ass is a solid-hoofed, nonruminating animal and hence is inedible.

13:13. The pronominal suffix on *'ārap* (*ô*) more than likely does double duty and is to be understood as an object suffix on the immediately preceding word/verb: "if you do not redeem (it)" as well.

13:15. "I am sacrificing" (*'ănî zōbēaḥ*) illustrates the use of a participle in a durative circumstance involving repeated actions. See Waltke and O'Connor 1990: 626.

13:16. The etymology of *ṭôṭāpṭōt* ("symbols, circlets, frontlets") is far from certain. The word appears only three times in the Hebrew Bible (here, Deut. 6:8; 11:18), always as a feminine plural noun. The Septuagint's words (*asaleuton* [sg.]; *asaleuta* [pl.], "immovable") give a metaphorical meaning; that is, the ritual of Exod. 13 and the "words" of Deut. 6 and 11 are not to be "moved" from one's mind. Several explanations for the origin of the Hebrew word are possible but not conclusive: (1) a connection with an Arabic word (*ṭaftaf*) meaning "extremely" and "seam of a garment"; (2) a connection with another Arabic word (*ṭafa*) meaning "walking around, make a circuit"; (3) a possible comparison with the Postbiblical Hebrew verb *ṭpṭp* ("to drip") and the related noun *ṭippâ* ("drop"), suggesting that *ṭôṭāpṭōt* were pendants, which hang or drop down. See the study of this word by Tigay (1982), who settles on the meaning "headband," and Weinfeld (1991: 333–35).

Commentary

13:1–16 One of the first items that catches the eye of the reader of these sixteen verses is that it begins by talking about the setting apart of the firstborn (1–2), then moves to a discussion of the feast of Unleavened Bread/Flatbread (vv. 3–10), and finally returns to the matter of the firstborn (vv. 11–16)—thus forming an ABA′ structure. At this point chap. 13 shares three parallels with chap. 12. First, just as the presentation of the feast of Unleavened Bread/Flatbread in chap. 13 (vv. 3–10) is framed by a discussion of the firstborn (vv. 1–2, 11–16), so also in chap. 12 the feast of Unleavened Bread/Flatbread (12:15–20) is framed by a discussion of Passover (12:1–14, 21–27a). Second, chap. 12 begins with a speech of God to Moses (12:1–20), then moves to a speech of Moses to the people (12:21–27a). Similarly, chap. 13 begins with a speech of God to Moses (13:1–2), then moves to a speech of Moses to the people (13:3–16). The difference in the two is that in chap. 12 the Lord's speech is lengthy and detailed, while Moses's is brief. In chap. 13 the Lord's speech is brief, and Moses's is lengthy and detailed. Also, the Lord's speech to Moses in chap. 13 lacks the explicit instruction of 12:3 to communicate this information to the people, but Moses does it anyway. The third parallel is that both chapters conclude by moving to reporting the exodus itinerary (12:31–50; 13:17–22).

Within chap. 13 the data involving eating unleavened bread (vv. 3–10) and the offering of the firstborn (vv. 11–16) is presented in a parallel fashion. These parallels are (1) the phrase "When the Lord brings you to Canaan land" is repeated (vv. 5, 11); (2) the new land is a land that God "swore/promised" to give his people (vv. 5, 11); (3) a cultic observance follows upon reaching the land (vv. 6–7, flatbread; vv. 12–13, firstborn); (4) the son asks his father a question about the meaning of this rite (vv. 8a, 14a), and the father answers by mentioning the exodus from Egypt (vv. 8b, 14b–15); (5) both the dedication of the firstborn and the eating of unleavened bread have external reminders of their significance: "on your hand" and "between your eyes" (vv. 9, 16).

Perhaps the closest parallel to the structure of Exod. 13:3–16 is Deut. 6:4–25, a section following the second revelation of the Decalogue. It too has the phrase of Exod. 13:5, 11 in Deut. 6:10, "When the Lord your God brings you into the land he swore to give to your fathers." Just as Exod. 13 contains two catechistic passages (13:8, 14–15), so does Deut. 6 contain two catechistic passages (6:7, 20–25). Finally, Deut. 6 continues the emphasis on external reminders (6:8), urging the people both to carry these words on hands and foreheads and to write them on the doors and gates of one's house.

Since I have already discussed the Feast of Unleavened Bread/Flatbread in my commentary on chap. 12, I need not tarry with it here. Let me make two brief points. First, in chap. 12 the information on this festival is designed to be implemented immediately, while they are still in Egypt but preparing to leave, and on the heels of the first Passover observance. In chap. 13 the information about this festival is put on hold and is to be implemented only after successfully reaching Canaan. Thus chap. 12 is about "how you are to do it now" (although 12:17 envisions future observances), and chap. 13 is about "how you are to do it then." Given that distinction, it is likely that the "then" festival might differ a tad from the "now" festival. And this brings me to my second point. Chapter 12 designates both the first and seventh days as special occasions (12:16). Exodus 13 highlights the importance of only the seventh day (13:6b, "on the seventh day [observe] a pilgrimage festival to the LORD"). Maybe the change has something to do with the Israelites' first observing the festival as they prepare to exit Egypt, and doing subsequent observances once they are settled in the land and trying to balance the requirements of worship and work.

For the first (but not the last) time, the Lord and Moses bring up the subject of legislation vis-à-vis an Israelite family's firstborn (13:1–2, 11–16). Five subsequent references in the Torah will also address this topic: (1) Exod. 22:29–30 [28–29]; (2) Exod. 34:19–20; (3) Lev. 27:26–27; (4) Num. 18:14–18, (5) Deut. 15:19–23. And one of the most interesting things is that no two of these five passages, although the firstborn is the issue at hand in all of them, are identical. Each gives the dedication of the firstborn to God its own "twist." First, four different verbs are used for what the parent of the child or owner of the animal is to do with the firstborn. He may "sanctify/consecrate/set apart" (*qādaš*) the firstborn to the Lord (Exod. 13:2; Lev. 27:26; Deut. 15:19; see Num. 3:13, "I *set apart* for myself every firstborn in Israel"; and Num. 18:17, "You must not redeem the firstborn of an ox, a sheep, or a goat; they are *holy*"). Or second, he may "give" (*nātan*) the firstborn to the Lord (Exod. 22:29 [28]). Recall Hannah's words about her firstborn, Samuel, "I will *give* him to the LORD for all the days of his life" (1 Sam. 1:11), and Eli's words to Elkanah and Hannah, "May the LORD give you children by this woman to take the place of the one she prayed for and *gave* to the LORD" (1 Sam. 2:20). Third, one may "transfer over" (*ʿābar*) the firstborn to the Lord (Exod. 13:12a). While not dealing with firstborn, two other references show that this verb in the Hiphil stem means to shift somebody or something from one domain to another: Num. 27:7, 8 (AT), "And *turn over* their father's inheritance to them. . . . *Turn over* his inheritance to his daughters"; Esther 8:2, "The king took off his signet ring, which he had *reclaimed from* [had passed over from] Haman, and presented it to Mordecai." Finally, and fourth, one may "offer" (*qārab*) the firstborn to the Lord (Num. 18:15).

Here is another difference. Exodus 13:12b; 34:19–20; and Num. 18:15–18 speak of the firstborn of humans, pure animals, and impure animals. Exodus 22:29–30 [28–29] speaks only of the firstlings of humans and pure animals. Leviticus 27:26–27 and Deut. 15:19–23 speak only of the firstlings of clean and unclean animals. So there is no consistency in the laws about who/what is included in the firstling laws and who/what is not. Note also what is done with the meat of pure animals. Exodus 13:12–13 simply says it is transferred to the Lord, whatever that might mean (possibly incinerated). Numbers 18:18, however, says that the meat of the sacrificed animal goes to the priests ("Their meat is to be yours"), while Deut. 15:20 gives the meat back to the owner ("Each year you and your family are to eat them"). And what are we to do with Lev. 27:26, "No one, however, may dedicate/consecrate [*qādaš*] the firstborn of an animal"? That seems to disagree with Deut. 15:19, "Set apart/consecrate [*qādaš*] for the Lord your God every firstborn male of your herds and flocks." Is it to be *qādaš* or no *qādaš*?

I do not profess to be able to work out all these differences. Early rabbinical authorities and contemporary conservative scholars have tried to harmonize all of the above. However, I am not so sure one can end up with a nice and neatly tied package. More than likely some of these modifications can best be explained as due to changes and developments in biblical laws over an extended period of time.

One important subject calls for reflection. Whether a firstling who is a pure animal is given, or transferred to, or consecrated to the Lord, it is clear what happens to that animal. It is sacrificed. It dies. If an impure animal, it may be redeemed/ransomed (a donkey in Exod. 13:13 and 34:20; all unclean animals in Lev. 27:27 and Num. 18:15).

Being "redeemable" is a feature commonly connected with the firstlings of impure animals (Exod. 13:13; 34:20; Lev. 27:27; Num. 18:15). Firstlings of pure animals cannot be redeemed (Num. 18:17). The verb covers also the firstborn of humans. Firstlings of clean animals are sacrificed, but firstlings of humans are redeemed (Exod. 13:15; see also Exod. 34:20c; Num. 18:15b–16). In all these instances, the verb for "redeem/ransom" is *pādâ*, except for Lev. 27:27b, which uses *gā'al* (Lev. 27:27a uses *pādâ*). The bottom line is that for redemption to take place, something must give up its life, or somebody must pay a price to redeem the firstling.

So here is the issue. Is there any possibility that some of these "firstling" texts may support the idea that originally Israelites literally sacrificed their firstborn to the Lord, and did so because the Lord both commanded it and approved of it? Some interpreters have maintained they do (Fishbane 1985: 181–87; S. Ackerman 1992: 161; Levenson 1993: 3–31). A key text for such a position is Exod. 22:29b–30a [28b–29a], "You must give me the firstborn of your sons. Do the same with your cattle and your sheep." And does not God ask Abraham to slay his firstborn son (actually his second-born son, Sarah's firstborn son) in Gen. 22? Does not God say in Ezek. 20:25–26, in one of the most enigmatic pairs of verses in the Bible, "I also gave them over to statutes that were not good and laws they could not live by; I let them become defiled through their gifts—*the sacrifice of the firstborn*"? And Micah asks (rhetorically?), "Shall I offer my firstborn for my transgression?" (6:7). It seems to me quite a stretch to use such verses to argue that in its hoary past Israel practiced religious infanticide at the behest of its deity. I do not see either Ezek. 20 or Mic.

6 raising that possibility, although there may have been some eccentric group of believers here and there in biblical Israel who so read between the lines of their religious texts. If there ever was such a "cult," they never consulted, or else conveniently stepped around, Jer. 7:31, "They have built the high places of Topheth in the Valley of Ben Hinnom to burn their sons and daughters in the fire—something I did not command, nor did it enter my mind." (I have been much enlightened on these laws of the firstborn by these studies: Brin 1994: 165–284; Milgrom 1990: 431–32; 2000a: 1586–91; 2000b: 2415–17, 2388–91.)

Turning to the NT, one sees the frequent references there to Jesus as "the firstborn." Mary brings forth Jesus, her firstborn (Matt. 1:25; Luke 2:7). Twice Jesus is identified as "the firstborn from (among) the dead" (Col. 1:18; Rev. 1:5). Paul in Rom. 8:29 calls Jesus "the firstborn among many brethren," and in Col. 1:15 labels Jesus "the firstborn over all creation." The latter two seem to be using "firstborn" in the way we use "First Lady" to refer to a president's or governor's spouse (assuming that the one in office is a man). "First(born)" is a way to emphasize the person's uniqueness and magisterial standing. The Greek word is *prōtotokos*.

To say that Jesus is Mary's *prōtotokos* is simply to say that Mary had no child before she gave birth to Jesus, without suggesting one way or another whether she had any additional children. Luke 2:22–24 gives us the account of Mary and Joseph presenting her firstborn in the temple in accord with Exod. 13:2, quoted as "Every firstborn male is to be consecrated to the Lord" (Luke 2:23b NIV), or "Every male that opens the womb is to be considered sacred to the Lord" (AT). This is closer to the Hebrew of Exod. 13:2 than it is to the Septuagint's rendering of Exod. 13:2, *pan prōtotoken, prōtogenes dianoigon pasan mētran* ("every firstborn, the first-being opening every womb").

Luke makes it clear that it is the firstborn son/male (*arsēn*) that is to be consecrated to the Lord. We can also deduce that the son is the firstborn of its mother (and most likely of its father too, but not necessarily so). If passages like Exod. 13:12, 15; 34:19; and Deut. 15:19 speak of the "male" firstlings of cattle, then one can safely conclude that male children are the ones to be dedicated.

This opens up some ideas about how Christians "give" their children to God. Those who oppose the baptism of infants use as one of their arguments that there is no explicitly clear instance of an infant being baptized in the NT. That may or may not be true. In any case, the believing parents most often will "consecrate" or "dedicate" their children to the Lord, using the Hannah/Samuel story as a model or the Mary/Jesus story. But if infant baptism is "unscriptural," is not infant dedication just as unscriptural? To be sure, the OT affirms the practice of dedicating the firstborn son (of the mother), but says nothing about dedicating the second-born or third-born son, and so forth, and never anything about dedicating daughters. Hence, the believer who wishes to be scrupulously "scriptural" would have to limit infant dedication to the firstborn son.

From Egypt to Etham

(13:17–22)

Translation

[17]And it happened when Pharaoh sent away the people that God did not lead them by the way of Philistia land, even though it was near, for God said (to himself), "Lest the people change its mind when they experience battle and return to Egypt." [18]So God turned around the people by way of the wilderness road ending at the Re(e)d Sea. And Israel's sons went up girded for battle from the land of Egypt. [19]Moses took the bones of Joseph with him for he had made Israel's sons strongly swear, saying, "God will surely take care of you, and you shall take up my bones from this (place) with you." [20]And they journeyed from Sukkoth and camped at Etham, located at the edge of the wilderness. [21]And the LORD would go in front of them by day in a pillar of cloud to lead them on the way, and by night in a pillar of fire to give them light to go by day and night. [22]The pillar of cloud would not move an inch by day, nor the pillar of fire by night from before the people.

Grammatical and Lexical Notes

13:17. The Hebrew consonants behind "(not) lead them" are *n-ḥ-m*, and the same consonants (*n-ḥ-m*) are present in "change its mind" in the latter half of the verse. These are not, of course, the same verb. The first ("lead them") is the verb *nāḥâ* with pronominal suffix, while the second is the verb *nāḥam* in the Niphal stem.

13:17. "By way of Philistia land" (and "by way of the wilderness road ending at the Re[e]d Sea" in v. 18) shows that often in the OT routes are given their names by describing their terminal point. So the angel finds Hagar near a spring by "Shur Road," meaning the road leading to Shur. Compare also the reference to "the Desert of Edom Road" (2 Kings 3:8) and "the Arabah Road" (2 Kings 25:4).

13:17. One can translate *kî* with either concessive force, "even though it was near" (Arnold and Choi 2003: 184), or with causal force, "because it was near" (Aejmelaeus 1986: 206–7), or as the equivalent of *ʾăšer* used to introduce a relative sentence, "which was near" (Hoftijzer 1970: 438n4).

13:17. The adjective *qārôb* ("near") appears seventy-five times in the Hebrew Bible with literal and with metaphorical senses. When the adjective is used literally, it refers either to spatial (as in 13:17) or to temporal proximity (as in "the day of the LORD is near"). The adjective comes to take on nominal force ("neighbor, next of kin") as in Exod. 32:27, "Go back and forth through the camp . . . each killing his brother and friend and neighbor [*qārôb*]." See Lemke 1981.

13:18. I shall have more to say on *yam-sûp* ("Re[e]d Sea") below.

13:18. The Hebrew word for "girded for battle" is *ḥămušîm*, which appears again in Josh. 1:14; 4:12; Judg. 7:11. It is related to the word *ḥōmeš* ("five" or "fifth") and hence literally means "those girded around the fifth rib." This is the most likely place for one to be stabbed, in his *ḥōmeš* (2 Sam. 2:23;

3:27; 4:6; 20:10; NIV uses "stomach" for the first three of these and "belly" for the last one). Possibly *ḥămušîm* is analogous to another word for "girded warriors," *ḥălûṣîm*. Behind this latter word is the verb *ḥālaṣ* II, "to gird, arm," which is a denominative verb from *ḥălāṣāyîm*, "loins, midsection." See B. Levine 2000: 450.

13:19. "Bones" (*ʿaṣĕmôt*) may be a case of a *pars pro toto* reference to a corpse (and in Gen. 50:25 and Ezek. 6:5). In Akkadian *eṣemtu* ("bones") may also refer to the remains of the deceased. See *CAD* E:342 §1b.

13:19. Note the double use of the infinitive absolute before the finite verb for emphasis ("strongly swear"; "surely take care of").

13:21. "Would go (in front of)" is my attempt to bring out the force of continuous action on God's part in the participle *hōlēk*. Similarly in v. 22 *lōʾ-yāmîš* ("would not move an inch") has iterative force.

13:22. Sometimes when "day" and "night" appear together, "day" appears first, and then "night" (Gen. 1:14; here; 1 Kings 8:59; Pss. 42:8 [9]; 74:16). Sometimes the pair is reversed and "night" precedes "day" (Deut. 28:66; 1 Kings 8:29; Isa. 27:3 [although NIV curiously reads "day and night"]). In Exod. 13:21–22 *yômām* is the adverbial form of *yôm* ("day"), meaning "by day, in the daytime," while *lāyĕlâ* ("night") has no distinct adverbial form.

Commentary

13:17 God does not lead his people to Canaan via a route with the greatest threat or most intimidating obstacles. Sometimes he does do that. The Lord's concern is not with his own lack of power, but with his people's potential inclination to quail before opponents they consider more powerful than themselves. A return to Egypt would be preferable to a showdown with the Philistines. God's suspicions about his people's wanting to return to Egypt when the going gets rough are not ill founded. Numbers 14:3–4 has a group of malcontents say to Moses and Aaron, "Wouldn't it be better for us to go back to Egypt? . . . We should choose a leader and go back to Egypt."

Accordingly, to prevent Israel from changing its mind, God leads his people to Canaan by a route other than the Via Maris, the Way of the Sea. The Hebrew verb for "change one's mind" is *nāḥam*, an interesting verb with multiple English equivalents (e.g., "comfort, change one's mind, grieve, repent," etc.). Its first occurrence is in Gen. 5:29, with the meaning "comfort," words Lamech speaks about his son Noah. Its second occurrence is in Gen. 6:6–7, where the NIV says that God was "grieved" over the sorry state of humanity in Noah's time, a creation project he himself had launched. Parunak (1975: 519) suggests that the meaning of *nāḥam* in Gen. 6 and Exod. 13, and in several other passages, is "suffer emotional pain" because of a grief-stimulating situation. Morrow (1986: 216n17) refines that observation somewhat by observing that all the Scripture passages Parunak cites are associated with feelings of remorse or regret, which can accompany or cause a change of mind. In addition to Gen. 6:6–7 and Exod. 13:17, see Judg. 21:6, 15; 1 Sam. 15:11, 35; Job 42:6; Jer. 31:19. In the only other chapter in Exodus where this verb occurs (chap.

32), God is the subject of the verb. In 13:17 God does not want his people to *nāḥam*, but in 32:12 Moses wants God to *nāḥam*, and in 32:14 God does *nāḥam*! Fretheim (1991: 150) has accurately captured the dynamics here: "One might expect that God, with all the power at the divine disposal, would not back off from leading the people into any situation. God would just mow the enemies down. No, *the human situation makes a difference regarding God's possibilities* and hence affects the divine decisions" (italics original).

No need, however, for Israel to fear the Philistines as some sort of a Goliath-like colossus. Shortly, in Exod. 15:14, Moses will sing of the anguish gripping the Philistines as Israel approaches their borders. The feared will become the fearful. The taunter will become the tamed.

The Hebrew for "Red" or "Reed" Sea is *yam-sûp*. One wonders which of the **13:18**
two passages for Israel is more daunting, the Via Maris or the *yam-sûp*? That depends, in part, on how best to render *yam-sûp*: Red Sea or Reed Sea? It is an expression that occurs five times in Exodus (10:19; 13:18; 15:4, 22; 23:31), four times in Numbers (14:25; 21:4; 33:10–11), three times in Deuteronomy (1:40; 2:1; 11:4), and another twelve times or so in the rest of the Hebrew Bible.

The arguments for the translation "Reed Sea" are fourfold. First, Hebrew *sûp* is a loanword from Egyptian *ṯwf(y)*, "papyrus (reeds)." Second, when used by itself, *sûp* means "reed(s)," as in Exod. 2:3, where Moses's mother places the basket for her baby "among the reeds" (*bassûp*) by the bank of the Nile, and in 2:5, where Pharaoh's daughter spots the basket "among the reeds" (*bĕtôk hassûp*) of the river. Third, reeds grow only in marshy, freshwater bodies, so clearly the Red Sea cannot be intended. Fourth, *sûp* does not mean "Red," and that mistranslation comes to us erroneously from the LXX with its *Erythra Thalassa*, blindly repeated in Vulgate's *Mare Rubrum*.

I fully agree that by itself *sûp* means "reeds," but must it mean that in the combined expression *yam-sûp*? Is there any body of water in the delta region of Egypt that was ever known or identified as *yam-sûp*? If that can be answered positively, then that would certainly tilt the translation toward "Reed Sea." To the best of my knowledge, however, the answer is a resounding no. On this issue I am inclined to agree with Batto (1983: 35): "At no period in Israelite history is there any evidence that *yam sûp* ever referred to a body of water other than the Red Sea. . . . There is no reason whatever to posit the existence of a second *yam sûp*. In short, the hypothesis that the Israelites experienced deliverance . . . at some historical body of water . . . accurately preserved as the 'Reed Sea,' should be laid to rest forever. *Requiescat in pace!*"

Joseph's bones, perhaps preserved in some ossuary, are to be part of this **13:19**
Israelite procession. Joseph himself has requested that (Gen. 50:25). Canaan represents one's future, where one is headed. Joseph's bones represent one's past, where one has come from. Here the future and past are wedded, without either consuming the other. That is healthy. The two are nicely united in Jer.

6:16 (KJV): through the prophet the Lord encourages his people to "ask for the *old* paths," but in Jer. 31:31 he promises to make a "*new* covenant" with Israel. Brueggemann (1994: 790) remarks: "There is the danger the 'now generation' in the church . . . may scuttle all the old ancestors (their names and their bones) and seek to live in a vacuum, excessively focused on the present. Second, there is the danger that a preoccupation with ancestors may treat the past like a relic. . . . Against both temptations, the bones of Joseph are understood as an urgent, fervent bet on Israel's future with God."

13:20 We are not sure where Etham (*'ētām*) is. It is a stopping place, but an inconsequential place, a dot somewhere on a map. It could be an abbreviated form of Pithom (*pitōm*), mentioned in Exod. 1:11 (= *pr Itm*, "house of Atum"). Redford (1987: 142) points to an Egyptian site, *Hwt-Itm* in Lower Egypt, near Wadi Tumilat and between Lake Timsah and the Bitter Lakes. Ask the Hebrews decades later what they remember about Etham, and you will probably get a blank stare. Life is filled with places and moments like this, but they are part of the mix too.

13:20–21 These two verses seem not to refer to two distinct divine manifestations, a cloudy one for daytime, and a fiery one for nighttime. Rather, fire burns inside the cloud continuously. During the day it is not visible, whereas at night it can easily be seen in contrast to the surrounding darkness. Israel need not stumble through the foreboding wilderness by itself, trusting in its own wits or sense of direction. Rather, the Israelites need simply to keep their eyes on the cloud and the fire, and they will get to where God wishes to take them. The Israelites' equivalent of "Let us fix our eyes on Jesus" (Heb. 12:2) is "Let us fix our eyes on the cloud and on the fire."

Safe Passage through the Sea

(14:1–31)

Translation

[1]And the LORD spoke to Moses, saying, [2]"Speak to Israel's sons that they turn back/halt and encamp before Pi-Hahiroth, between Migdol and the sea, before Baal-zephon. Across from it you shall camp by the sea. [3]For Pharaoh has said of Israel's sons:

'Trapped [are] they in the land
Barred them in [has] the desert.'

[4]And I shall toughen Pharaoh's heart, and he will chase after them, but I shall be glorified through Pharaoh and through all his armed forces, and the Egyptians will know that I [am] the LORD." And they did so.

[5]It was told Egypt's king that the people had fled, and Pharaoh's heart, along with his servants', was changed regarding the people. And they said, "What is this we have done, that we have sent away Israel from our service?" [6]So he hitched his chariot, and his troops he took with him. [7]He took six hundred of the best chariots, indeed all of Egypt's chariots, and those trained in horsemanship over all of it. [8]The LORD toughened the heart of Pharaoh, king of Egypt, and he chased after Israel's sons, while the Israelites were coming out with a raised/high hand. [9]The Egyptians chased after them and caught up with them encamped by the sea—all the horses of Pharaoh's chariots, and his horsemen, and his armed forces—by Pi-Hahiroth before Baal-zephon.

[10]Pharaoh came closer, and Israel's sons looked up and behold, Egypt was closing in on them, and they were greatly afraid. Israel's sons cried out to the LORD, [11]and they said to Moses, "Was it because there were no graves in Egypt that you took us to die in the desert? What is this you have done to us in bringing us out of Egypt? [12]Is not this the very thing we spoke to you about in Egypt, saying, 'Leave us be that we serve Egypt, for it is better for us to serve Egypt than dying in the desert'?" [13]And Moses said to the people, "Do not be afraid. Take your position and see the LORD's salvation that he will do for you today, for just as you see the Egyptians today, you shall not again see them, not ever. [14]The LORD shall fight for you, and you, you will simply observe."

[15]And the LORD said to Moses, "What are you crying out about to me? Speak to Israel's sons that they continue the journey. [16]As for you, raise your staff and extend your hand toward the sea, and split it in twain that Israel's sons may come into the midst of the sea on dry land. [17]As for myself, I am about to toughen the Egyptians' heart so that they will come after them. I shall gain glory by means of Pharaoh and all his armed forces, his chariots, and his horsemen. [18]The Egyptians shall know that I am the LORD when I gain glory by means of Pharaoh, his chariots, and his horsemen."

[19]And the messenger of God who was going before Israel's camp journeyed on and went behind them. And the pillar of cloud journeyed from before them and stood behind them. [20]It came between Egypt's camp and Israel's camp, and there was the cloud and the darkness, and it illuminated [cast a spell upon?] the night, so that this [side] could not make contact with this [side] all through the night.

[21]Moses extended his hand toward the sea, and the LORD separated the sea by a powerful east wind all through the night. And he made the sea dry ground, and the waters were split in twain. [22]Israel's sons

came into the midst of the sea on dry land, the waters to them a wall on their right and on their left. 23 The Egyptians chased and went after them—all Pharaoh's horses, his chariots, and his horsemen into the midst of the sea. 24 And it happened in the morning watch that in a pillar of fire the LORD looked down on Egypt's camp, and he wiped out Egypt's camp. 25 He encumbered the wheels of its chariots and drove them heavily so that Egypt said, "Let me flee from before Israel, for the LORD is fighting for them against Egypt."

26 And the LORD said to Moses, "Extend your hand toward the sea that the waters come back over the Egyptians, over its chariots and over its horsemen." 27 So Moses extended his hand toward the sea, and the sea came back, as morning broke, to its normal state, with the Egyptians fleeing to get near it, and the LORD shook out the Egyptians in the midst of the sea. 28 The waters came back and covered the chariots and the horsemen belonging to all of Pharaoh's armed forces who were coming after them into the sea. Not a single one of them remained. 29 And Israel's sons went into the dry land in the midst of the sea, the waters (being) to them a wall on their right and on their left.

30 The LORD on that day saved Israel from Egypt's hand. Israel saw Egypt dead on the seashore. 31 And Israel saw the great hand with which the LORD had performed against Egypt, and the people feared the LORD and placed their trust in the LORD and in Moses his servant.

Grammatical and Lexical Notes

14:2. The more usual meaning of *šûb* is "turn, turn back, return to." Gordis (1976b: 220, 222) argues for the meaning "stop, halt" on the basis of "go forward" (which is the opposite of "come back"), whose negative is "not go forward," that is, "halt, stop."

14:2. In vv. 2 and 9 the LXX reads "before Pi-Hahiroth" as "before Pi-hahatserot," that is, "before the encampments" (*apenanti tēs epauleōs*), taking the *î/y* in "Hahiroth" as a *ṣ*. On the confusion of the letters *yôd* and *ṣadê*, see Talmon 1985: 396; Tov 2001: 245.

14:3. As several have noted (Albright 1968: 33; Kselman 1978: 162, 169), Pharaoh's words are a bicolon of poetry with a 6:8 syllable count, and hence I have reproduced them as verse. Reasons to see this as poetry include (1) the use of the formulaic pair "land/desert" (*ʾereṣ/midbār*); (2) assonance achieved by the repetition of the syllable *hēm* ("they, them") in both cola; (3) almost-rhyming words that end the cola (*bāʾāreṣ*/"in the land" and *hammidbār*/"the desert") with the *b-r* sequence in both nouns.

14:3. *Nĕbukîm* ("trapped") appears again in Esther 3:15 ("The king and Haman sat down to drink, but the city of Susu was *bewildered* [*nābôkâ*]," NIV) and in Joel 1:18 ("How the cattle moan! The herds *mill about* [*nābōkû*]," NIV). The verb means something like "squeeze, be in distress." Rabin (1961: 388) and Barr (1968: 323) connect the Hebrew verb with an Arabic one, *baka*, meaning "press, squeeze," used of rolling and squeezing a fruit between the palms.

14:4. "I will be glorified through" is the Niphal of *kābad* followed by the preposition *bĕ*. One finds a near parallel construction in Lev. 10:3, where *kābad* occurs with *qādaš*: "Among [*bĕ*] those who approach me I will show myself holy [Niphal of *qādaš*]; in the sight of [*wĕʿal-pĕnê*] of all the people I will be honored [Niphal of *kābad*]." For another instance of *kābad* (Niphal) plus *bĕ*, see Ezek. 28:22, part of a prophecy against Sidon: "I am against you, O Sidon, and I will gain glory within you [*wĕnikbadtî bĕtôkēk*]." What these three passages (Exod. 14:4; Lev. 10:3; Ezek. 28:22) have in common, apart from their use of *kābad* (Niphal), is they all speak about divine retribution against somebody whose behavior is out of line. See P. Segal 1989: 92.

14:4. "Armed forces" is the Hebrew word *ḥayil* (as in Deut. 11:4, "what he did to the Egyptian army [*lĕḥêl miṣrayim*]"). Individuals or groups serving as soldiers may be identified as *gibbôrê haḥayil* ("fighting men") in Josh. 1:14; Judg. 6:12; and others, or as *ʾanšê-ḥayil* ("valiant fighters") in Judg.

20:44, 46; and others. The word is overwhelmingly used of males, but occurs three times with women (Ruth 3:11; Prov. 12:4; 31:10).

14:5. Exodus 13:17 uses the verb *nāḥam* for Israel's changing its mind. This verse uses *hāpak* (Niphal) for Pharaoh's and the Egyptians' change of heart about releasing the captive Hebrews. It is the one that Gen. 19:25 (and others) use (in the Qal stem) for the "overthrow" of Sodom, and the one that Jonah uses for Nineveh's "overthrow" (Jon. 3:4, Niphal). In a few places *hāpak* may refer to a good change of heart as in 1 Sam. 10:6 ("and you [Saul] will be *changed* into a different person") and 1 Sam. 10:9 ("God *changed* Saul's heart"). The verb can even refer to a change in God's own heart for the better, as in Hosea 11:8 ("My heart *is changed* within me"). So when Jonah (3:4) proclaims, "Forty more days and Nineveh will be *hāpak-ed*," does that mean "overthrown" or "changed"? Could it be, as Halpern and Friedman (1980: 87) put it, that "Nineveh's transformation fulfills profoundly Jonah's prophecy"?

14:5. "Service," which here refers to demeaning service to Pharaoh, has appeared back in 13:5 to refer to the delightful service to Yahweh in the Passover ritual.

14:6. One would normally translate *ʿammô* as "his people," but the militaristic context of the passage calls for the translation "his troop(s)."

14:7. "Best chariots" is *rekeb bāḥûr*. There is some question about how to render *bāḥûr*. For example, when Num. 11:28 speaks of Joshua as Moses's *mĕšārēt mibbĕḥurāyw*, is Joshua Moses's "aide *since youth*," or Moses's "aide *from among his close associates*"? As a noun, *bāḥûr* has many meanings. The NIV uses "bridegroom" (= "young man"; Judg. 14:10); "young man" (1 Sam. 9:2); "chosen men" (2 Sam. 6:1); "best troops" (2 Sam. 10:9); "fighting men" (1 Kings 12:21); and so forth. As an adjective, it carries a military connotation in Exod. 14:7, and in Judg. 20:15, 16, 34; 1 Sam. 24:2; 26:2 ("chosen/finest men," all references to warriors). See Shafer 1977: 31, 31n10.

14:7. There has been much discussion of the word *šālišîm*, here rendered "those trained in horsemanship." What is its connection, if any, with the Hebrew word *šālōš*, "three"? Studies of this word include Mastin (1979); Vervenne (1987); Na'aman (1988); Schley (1990); Margalit (1992: 266); Särkiö (1993). The possibilities include (1) "soldiers wearing bronze, metal armor" on the basis of the Ugaritic cognate *ṯlṯ*, "bronze, copper" (Margalit); (2) a three-man squad or striking force of some type (Schley); (3) "the third man in the chariot," on the basis of the Akkadian cognate *shalashu* and Ugaritic *shlsh*, an officer of the third rank (Mastin; Na'aman); (4) a specially trained, professional soldier who does not belong to the standard war crew of a chariot, but who could temporarily be placed in a chariot in order to raise its effectiveness (Särkiö); (5) a special, military functionary, a knight, one with thorough military training in the use of arms and horsemanship (Vervenne). The NIV translates its five occurrences (in the singular) in 2 Kings in three ways: "officer" (7:2, 17, 19); "chariot officer" (9:25); "chief officer" (15:25).

14:8. The expression "with a raised/high hand" (*bĕyād rāmâ*) appears again in the parallel verse, Num. 33:3 ("The Israelites . . . marched out *boldly*"). The only other time is in Num. 15:30, where the NIV translates the phrase "sin *defiantly*," that is, the most egregious sins possible that God's people can commit. Israel can march out of Egypt *bĕyād rāmâ*, but the people had better not try sinning against Yahweh *bĕyād rāmâ*! For other places where *yād* ("hand") appears with *rûm* ("raise"), see Exod. 17:11, "As long as Moses held up his hands"; Deut. 32:27, Israel's enemies say, "It was our hand that was high [NIV, "has triumphed"]"; 1 Kings 11:26, "he [Jeroboam] lifted up his hand against [NIV, "rebelled against"] the king [Solomon]"; Mic. 5:9 [8], "Your hand will be lifted in triumph over your enemies." According to Labuschagne (1982a: 143–48), the phrase connotes a military or semimilitary expression, signifying readiness to fight and prevail, and could be translated in Exod. 14 and Num. 33 as "triumphantly."

14:9. The verbal pair "pursue" (*rādap*, Qal) and "catch up with" (*nāśag*, Hiphil) appears in Gen. 44:4 (Joseph's deputies and his brothers); Deut. 19:6 (the avenger of blood and a murderer); Deut. 28:45 (God's covenantal curses and the disobedient); Josh. 2:5 (Jericho's leaders and the two Hebrew scouts); 1 Sam. 30:8 (David's men and the Amalekites); 2 Kings 25:5 (= Jer. 39:5; 52:8; the Babylonian army and fleeing Zedekiah). See also Pss. 7:5 [6]; 18:37 [38]. Genesis 31:23, Laban's chasing after Jacob and his two daughters, uses the Piel of *dābaq* for "caught up with, overtook" rather than the Hiphil of *nāśag*, but 31:25 has the Piel of *nāśag*.

14:9. The Hebrew word for "horsemen" is *pārāšîm*. Since the singular is *pārāš*, one expects the plural form to be *pĕrāšîm*. The Masoretic vocalization suggests *parrāš* instead of *pārāš* for the singular form. The word occurs in conjunction with *rekeb*, "chariot(s)," seven times (out of fourteen in narrative portions of Scripture) in Exod. 14–15 (14:9, 17, 18, 23, 26, 28; 15:19). In the first (14:9), middle (14:23), and last (15:19) of these seven, *sûs*, "horse(s)," also appears, "forming a triplet that affirms the affinity of chap. 15 to the story in chap. 14" (Avishur 1984: 275–76). See also the study of Mowinckel (1962), who suggests that sometimes *pārāšîm* refers not to the chariot rider, the horseman, but to the "horse span" belonging to the chariot, a pair of horses or other animals harnessed and driven together.

14:10. "Come closer" is *hiqrîb*. The Hiphil, here lacking a direct object, has stative force, but of an intensive or elative character.

14:10. The phrase "look up/lift up one's eyes" appears fifty times in the Hebrew Bible, nineteen of which are in the Pentateuch. This is the only instance of it in Exodus, but it is frequent in Genesis (13:10, 14; 18:2; 22:4, 13; 24:63, 64; 31:10, 12; 33:1, 5; 37:25; 39:7 [a woman's eyes this time]; 43:29). See Reif's study of this phrase (1983).

14:10. Note that the verbs used in v. 9 with "Egyptians" are plural (*yirdĕpû*, "chased after" and *yaśśîgû*, "caught up with"), but here with "Egyptians" as subject (I used "Egypt") the verb is singular (*nōsēaʿ*, "was closing in on"). Some ancient versions, as in the SP, predictably change the singular participle into a plural participle. Why the shift from plural to singular when in both verses the subject is *miṣrayim*? Sternberg (1987: 256) asks, "Is it because the Israelites have eyes for nobody except Pharaoh 'drawing near' at the head of his army and personifying the might of Egypt? Or because they suddenly feel their military inferiority to the compact formation heading for them as one man?"

14:11. The double negative (*[ha]mibbĕlî ʾên*) in the rhetorical question "Was it because there were no . . ." is for the sake of emphasis. Compare Num. 12:2, "Has the Lord spoken only through Moses [*hăraq ʾak-bĕmōšeh*]?" See R. Williams 1976: 66 §394.

14:12. Israel's "leave us be" or "leave us alone" is the verb *ḥādal min*, a different verb than that of the Lord's later "leave me alone" to Moses in 32:10 (*nûaḥ lĕ*).

14:13. The Hitpael of *yāṣab* ("take your position") is a few times a technical term for the readiness required before a spectacular theophany (Exod. 19:17; Num. 11:16; Deut. 31:14). Sometimes it is Yahweh who does the standing (Exod. 34:5; 1 Sam. 3:10).

14:13. On the significance of "today" and "day" at this point in the narrative, and later in v. 30, see De Vries (1975a: 88; 1975c: 161), who says that the first "today" characterizes the godward side of the event, while the second "today" characterizes the event's manward side. Twice Moses uses *hayyôm* in v. 13 to characterize what Israel sees and will see, and then in v. 30 the narrator uses *bayyôm hahûʾ* to interpret the events as the Lord's decisive act of salvation "on that day."

14:14. Of the verb *ḥāraš* ("simply observe, be still/silent"), Margalit (1992: 474) says, "It is not merely the absence of speech, but inactivity, passivity." The verb *ḥāraš* here has the same nuance as the verb *dāmam* for the sun/moon "standing still" in Josh. 10:12–13.

14:16. I shall have more to say in the commentary section on the important verb *bāqaʿ*, "split in twain," here and in v. 21. For the moment, let me suggest that NIV's "divide" is a bit anemic. The verb suggests a much more powerful, violent act than that.

14:20. The Hebrew *wayyāʾer ʾet-hallāyĕlâ* is very difficult to render. The LXX is obviously confused as it guesses at "and the night passed" (*kai diēlthen hē nyx*), reading *wayyāʾer* as *wayyaʿăbōr*. The phrase is comprehensible enough ("it illuminated the night"), but the problem comes when one observes that the antecedent of "it" in v. 20 is the "cloud" of v. 19. How does a cloud light up anything? Speiser (1960) rejects the view that the verb in question is the causative form of *ʾôr*, "make bright as day, light up." Rather, the verb is *ʾārar*, "curse," either in the Qal or Hiphil stem; hence his translation, "Thus there was the cloud with the darkness, and *it cast a spell* (*wyʾr*) upon the night" (1960: 200, italics added; a rendering followed in the NJPS). This is unnecessary, I believe, once it is recalled, as I mentioned earlier (see my comment on 13:21–22), that there is one pillar, appearing as a cloud in the daytime but whose inner fire becomes visible at nighttime. M. Segal (2008: 256n12) also correctly rejects Speiser's reading and suggests instead that the verb *ʾôr*, when associated with clouds (Job 37:11, 15), indicates lightning. Thus, the verse would read "And there was cloud and darkness, and it [the cloud] illuminated the night" (i.e., lightning emerged from the cloud[s] and lit up the night sky).

14:21. The Hebrew word for "dry ground" in v. 21 is *ḥārābâ*, but the word for "dry ground" in v. 22 (and in 14:16, 29; 15:19) is *yabbāšâ*. The latter is the one used in the creation story in Gen. 1:9–10. The flood story oscillates between the two, using *ḥārābâ* in Gen. 7:22 and the verb *ḥārab* in Gen. 8:13 [2x], but the verb *yābaš* in Gen. 8:7, 14 for the drying up of the earth.

14:24. *ʾAšmōret habbōker* ("the very early morning watch") refers to the night watch just before dawn. Mark 13:35 speaks of four night watch periods: (1) "in the evening"; (2) "at midnight"; (3) "when the rooster crows"; (4) "at dawn."

14:24. The verb *hāmam* ("wiped out") frequently refers to God's actions in Israel's battles: Exod. 23:27 (NIV, "throw into confusion"); Deut. 7:23 (NIV, "throwing them into great confusion"); Josh. 10:10 (NIV, "throw into confusion"); Judg. 4:15 (NIV, "routed"); 1 Sam. 7:10 (NIV, "threw into panic"); 2 Sam. 22:15 (= Ps. 18:14 [15], NIV, "routed"); Ps. 144:6 (NIV, "rout"). In Deut. 2:15 disobedient Israel is the object of *hāmam* (NIV, "completely eliminated"). For the noun *mĕhûmâ*, "confusion/panic," see Deut. 7:23; 28:20; 1 Sam. 5:9, 11; 14:20; Isa. 22:5; Zech. 14:13.

14:25. The verb *sûr* ("encumbered") normally means "take off, remove." Perhaps the idea is that in the thick mud the wheels of the chariots soon "broke off" from the axle. LXX has "he 'bound' the wheels," reading *ʾāsar* rather than *sûr*.

14:27. On the temporal use of the preposition *lĕ* in *lipnôt bōker* ("as morning broke"), see Meek 1948: 237.

14:27. The Hebrew word for "normal state" is *ʾêtān*. Four times it is used with water (here; Deut. 21:4; Ps. 74:15; Amos 5:24), thus meaning a constant, ever-flowing, never-failing body of water. The word is also used for a firm, taut bow (Gen. 49:24); places that are enduring and permanent (Num. 24:21); constant agony (Job 33:19); the perpetual, unchanging way of traitors (Prov. 13:15). See D. Wright 1987: 396–97.

14:27. The part of the verse that reads "with the Egyptians fleeing to get near it [the sea]" sounds strange, for are they not already in the sea (vv. 23–26)? The Hebrew supports the "strange" reading, *nāsîm liqrāʾtô*. One would think that possibly the antecedent of "it" is the shoreline. Alter (2004: 395) provides the following explanation: "They [the Egyptians] flee, presumably in the direction from which they had come, but the flood of water comes down on them from that very direction."

14:27. "Shook out" is the verb *nāʿar*. The Lord "routed" the Egyptians as one would grab a garment by its corners and shake the dust from it, or as a tree would shake off its leaves in the fall.

14:28. Sarna (1959: 312) has shown that the verb *šāʾar* ("remain, be left over") can be followed either by the preposition *bĕ* (as here) or by *min* (1 Sam. 25:22; 2 Kings 10:14).

14:28. *Lōʾ . . . ʿad-ʾeḥād* ("not . . . a one," or lit., "not . . . until one") is like *kĕʾîš ʾeḥād* in Num. 14:15 ("to the last person," or lit., "as one man").

14:31. Verbs of mental acts are often followed by the preposition *bĕ*: (1) *ʾāman bĕ*, "believe in" (Gen. 15:6; Exod. 14:31; 1 Sam. 27:12; Mic. 7:5); (2) *bāṭaḥ bĕ*, "trust in" (Deut. 28:52; Judg. 9:26; the famous Prov. 3:5 uses the following: "Trust [*bāṭaḥ]* in [*ʾel*] the LORD with [*bĕ*] all your heart"); (3) *zākar bĕ*, "remember" (Jer. 3:16); (4) *šāmaʿ bĕ*, "listen to" (Gen. 22:18; 27:5).

14:31. "In the Lord and in Moses his servant" shows a phrase containing a name followed by the name of someone connected with the first person named, and then a noun denoting the relationship of the second person named to the first person named, and to which a pronominal suffix is attached. For other examples, see Gen. 25:10 ("Abraham and Sarah his wife"); 1 Sam. 13:16 ("Saul and Jonathan his son"); 2 Sam. 3:30 ("Joab and Abishai his brother").

Commentary

14:1–2 The exact location of Pi-Hahiroth, Migdol, and Baal-zephon are unknown. The last two are clearly Semitic names, while the first looks Egyptian with the prefix "Pi-." Yet, Pi-Hahiroth could be a Hebraized rendering of an original Akkadian phrase, *pi ḫiritu*, "the mouth of the canal" (*CAD* H:198).

Migdol is related to the Hebrew word *migdāl*, "fortress, (watch)tower." The latter appears as part of other place names in "Migdal-El" (Josh. 19:38); "Migdal-Peniel" (Judg. 8:9, 17); "Migdal-Gad" (Josh. 15:37); "Migdal-Eder" (Gen. 35:21; Mic. 4:8 [NIV, "watchtower of the flock"]). In Ezek. 29:10 and 30:6 Migdal is the northernmost town in Egypt in contrast to Aswan, the southernmost city. The Tell el Amarna cuneiform tablets from Egypt mention (EA 234:29) a site ^{URU}Ma-ag-da-li^{KI}. According to Jer. 46:14, Migdol is a border town in the eastern delta where news of an enemy approaching from the northeast would first be sounded. Some years ago the eminent Egyptologist Alan Gardiner (1920: 99–116 plus plates) published an article in which he claimed that there were actually four Migdols in the delta, three being forts, and the fourth a town of some size.

Baal-zephon means "Baal of the North" (although the *šĕwăʾ* [*ĕ*] under *ṣ* in "zephon" [*ṣĕpōn*] is strange [Aramaic influence?] instead of the expected *ā* vowel). It is odd to think of a place called "Baal of the North" yet actually in the south, in the Egyptian delta. In the Ugaritic texts, by contrast, Baal's abode is a mountain about twenty-five miles north of Ugarit, and about two and a half miles inland from the northern Mediterranean coast. In those texts the mountain is called either *spn* ("Sapan") or *ʾil spn* ("divine Sapan"). In modern Arabic it is Jebel ʾel-Aqraʿ ("Mount Baldy"). The name of such a city in the Egyptian delta must mean that the cult of Baal had been evangelistically imported into that area, and having moved out of "Jerusalem and Judea," was reaching "the uttermost ends of the earth." See also Isa. 14:13 and Ps. 48:1–2 for interesting takes on the north as the abode of Yahweh (Ps. 48:1–2) and "would-be Yahwehs" (Isa. 14:13).

14:3 Again, the Lord does not simply exhibit his power. He also uses a military tactic, making it appear through the fleeing Israel's "disoriented" wandering that they are hopelessly lost, and now are caught as sitting ducks, hemmed in on one side by the sea, and on the other by the Egyptians. Pharaoh may think that he can grab the cheese, but soon the snap bar will come down on his neck. Pharaoh gets to use a bit of poetry as he gloats in chap. 14, but Moses and Israel will get to use a lot of poetry in chap. 15 as they celebrate.

It is difficult to know how "the Egyptians will know I am Lord" if they are **14:4**
all dead! Will those drowning come to this knowledge before they expire? Or is the reference to possibly some survivors or the folks back home? The same conundrum surfaces in a number of verses in Ezekiel, such as 25:7, "I will destroy you, and you will know that I am the Lord"; or 26:6, "Her settlements on the mainland will be ravaged by the sword. Then they will know that I am the Lord."

As in the previous plague section, Pharaoh both acts on his own accord (vv. **14:5–9**
5–7) and at the Lord's behest (v. 8). Pharaoh harnesses and God hardens. Pharaoh has a change of heart, and God hardens his heart. Pharaoh believes the wilderness has closed in on the Israelites (end of v. 3), but little does he know that soon the waters will close in on him. Pharaoh is deft, and the Israelites are defiant (end of v. 8). Pharaoh misjudges Israel's movements, just as Israel misjudges God and Moses (vv. 11–12).

What Israel sees (v. 10) leads to its response in the form of an angry and sar- **14:10–13**
castic question addressed to Moses (v. 11), and a quote of their earlier words to Moses (v. 12). Israel, unfortunately, has a track record of acting at the first sign of trouble as if the situation is hopeless. In addition to Exod. 14:10–12, see 16:3; 17:3, 7; and Deut. 1:32 ("In spite of this, you did not trust in the Lord your God"). Living in Egypt during a crisis elsewhere is an attractive option for Abraham (Gen. 12:10–20), and now his posterity emulate his example. Josephus, in his account of this incident (*Ant.* 2.15.4 §327), mentions that the Israelites not only rebuke Moses on this occasion but also want to stone him. See Luke 13:34, "O Jerusalem, Jerusalem, you who kill the prophets and stone those sent to you." There is a refreshing world of difference in Israel's disposition between what Israel "sees" in v. 10, and what Israel "sees" in vv. 30–31. That latter seeing transforms Israel's "fear" from one kind of a fear (v. 10) to another kind of fear (v. 31). God delivers his people from drowning and from paralyzing fear.

Their statement to Moses in v. 12, "Is not this the very thing we spoke to you about in Egypt?" is remarkably like that of Jonah to God in Jon. 4:2, "Is this not what I said when I was still at home?" Both Israel and Jonah are away from their comfort zone. Jonah in a storm at sea and Israel in the desert may possibly perish. Both comment on a previous speech they have made to the addressee, and neither speech is quoted earlier in the text. Jonah is angry, and Israel is afraid. Jonah is pouting, and Israel is panicking. Jonah says it is better for him to live than die. The Israelites say it is better to serve the Egyptians than to die in the wilderness. Moses tries to calm the people (Exod. 14:13–14), while the Lord counterquestions Jonah (Jon. 4:4).

As I suggested at one point in the above paragraph, Israel's "Is not this the very thing we spoke to you about in Egypt?" is a claim not found earlier in the text. The SP, however, inserts it as an addition to Exod. 6:9. The SP does this elsewhere. For example, in Gen. 31:10–13 Jacob tells his wives of a dream he had, the details of which SP adds after Gen. 30:36. Tov (2001: 88–89) provides other illustrations.

Moses's reassuring words in v. 13 are quoted almost exactly in 2 Chron. 20:17, and there they are the words of encouragement of Jahaziel to King Jehoshaphat. For other instances of postexilic writers' quoting Pentateuchal Scripture verbatim, compare Ezra 9:12 with Deut. 7:2–3; 23:7; Neh. 1:5 with Deut. 7:9, 12; and Neh. 9:7 with Gen. 15:7. Weinfeld (1980: 425) suggests that these quotations in later OT books show that the Pentateuch had taken canonical form by the postexilic period.

Goldingay (2003: 478) points out that in the Pentateuch the Amalekites are the only people with whom Israel is instructed to "fight" (Exod. 17:9–10), but even here it is the Lord who will fight/war with the Amalekites (17:16b). Israel's fighting in Deut. 1:41–42 is self-directed and ends disastrously. Even in the first few chapters of Joshua, Israel is never said to "fight" the Canaanites. Goldingay says, "'Fighting' is something Israel's enemies do (e.g., Num. 21:21–26) and Yhwh does (e.g., Ex. 14:14; Deut. 1:30; 3:22 [and I would add Josh. 10:14b]." Who would want to fight the enemy when God volunteers to do the fighting?

Maybe, however, there are at least a few who try to fight. After all, if David can take on Goliath, why cannot Israel take on this Egyptian, military juggernaut? Rofé (1997a: 240–42; 1997b: 267) quotes postbiblical Jewish sources, especially the Tannaitic Midrash *Mekilta de Rabbi Ishmael*. The latter divides the Israelites at the sea into four groups: (1) one group said, "Let us throw ourselves into the sea"; (2) one group said, "Let us return to Egypt"; (3) one group said, "Let us fight them"; (4) one group said, "Let us cry out against them."

Moses's comforting words to the people, "Do not be afraid" (v. 13), are the same words even Israel's great ancestors have needed to hear when they have their backs against a wall: Abram (Gen. 15:1), Isaac (26:24), Jacob (46:3), and Hagar too (21:17). All these fears that God addresses are normal and real. They are not illusory. God does not lie to us about danger; nor does he plant in us the idea that they are figments of our imagination. What he reminds us is that in order for these frightening situations to get to us, they will first have to get past him. We can rest, not because of the absence of danger, but because of a God in whom we can trust.

One would expect v. 15 "What are *you* crying out about?" or "Why do *you* cry to me?" to be "What are *they* crying out about?" or "Why do *they* cry to me?" After all, it is the Israelites, not Moses, who cry out to the Lord (end of v. 10). Moses does cry out to the Lord in chap. 15 (v. 25), but no such cry is mentioned in chap. 14. God is moved to action when he hears his people crying out in 3:7. Here he is moved to ask a penetrating question. **14:15–18**

Earlier it is Moses who asks God a why question (Exod. 5:22; 6:12, 30). Now it is God's turn to ask Moses a why question. Maybe there is some unrecorded prayer that Moses has lifted heavenward on behalf of his beleaguered people, and God is telling Moses to stop praying. Or as leader of the people and as their spokesman, he is guilty by association. The shepherd is indicted along with the sheep.

The Israelites need not fear, for they have a lot of special company. They have God's angel/messenger (Exod. 14:19a; 23:20–23; 33:2; Num. 20:16). They have a cloud-encased fire (Exod. 14:19b–20; 13:21–22; Num. 9:15–23; 14:14; Deut. 1:33). Later, they will have the ark of the covenant (Num. 10:33; Josh. 3:3, 6, 11). Best of all, they have Yahweh's own presence, of which the first three are observable representatives of the Divine One in their midst, at both the front and rear of the camp. **14:19–21**

Childs (1974: 228) rightly rejects the idea, common in some circles, that the original event of the passage through the sea has a very "natural" explanation (and the better one at that), and that it was later writers, lamentably, who rewrote the story, giving it a "supernatural" narration. Childs writes, "The biblical writer is aware . . . of the two levels of divine activity which combined ordinary and wonderful elements." The strong east wind blowing all night—that is an ordinary element. God does not just snap his finger, and in an instant the waters part. The waters forming a wall on both sides of the Israelites without levees to hold back the water—that is a wonderful element. We have become, at least in the United States, very aware of the importance of strong levees to hold back rising floodwaters when a hurricane plows into a low-lying, vulnerable city.

There are several obvious connections between this incident and the creation story of Gen. 1 and the flood story of Gen. 6–8. In all three a *rûaḥ* (wind/spirit/Spirit) is connected with water (Gen. 1:2; 8:1; Exod. 14:21). In all three "dry ground" appears out of a watery mass (Gen. 1:9, 10; 7:22; 8:7, 13–14; Exod. 14:21–22). In the place where "dry ground" appears in back-to-back verses (Exod. 14:21–22), or the verb "dry up" appears in back-to-back verses (Gen. 8:13–14), the first noun is *ḥārābâ* (Exod. 14:21) and the second is *yabbāšâ* (14:22), while the first verb for "dry up" in Gen. 8:13 is *ḥārab* and the verb for "dry up" in 8:14 is *yābaš*. The first of these two verbs (and the related noun) means "to be free of moisture," while the second verb (and the related noun) designates the complete absence of waters. It is only logical that *ḥārābâ* precede *yabbāšâ*, and that *ḥārab* precede *yābaš*. To reverse them would be odd.

There is another feature shared by the flood story and the through-the-sea story: the use of the verb *bāqa'*, "cleave, divide, split (in twain)" with water (Gen. 7:11; Exod. 14:16, 21). Nehemiah 9:11; Ps. 78:13; and Isa. 63:12 also use *bāqa'* in referring back to Exod. 14. The verb appears in conjunction with water in Job 26:8, "He wraps up the water in his clouds, yet the clouds do not *burst* under their weight." The violent sense of the verb is conveyed by passages like 2 Kings 8:12; 15:16; Hosea 13:16 [14:1]; Amos 1:13, which use it for "ripping open" the womb of pregnant women; or Ezek. 29:7, which uses it to refer to "tearing open" one's shoulder; or Eccles. 10:9 (cleaving/splitting wood); or Judg. 15:19 (splitting open a rock so that water gushes forth).

The verb also appears in mythological texts from Ugarit. In a battle between Anat (Baal's wife/consort) and the god Mot ("Death") we find these words:

tiḫd.bn.ilm.mt	She seized Divine Mot.
bḥrb.tbq'nn	With a sword she split him.
bḫbr.tdrynn	With a pitchfork she winnowed him.
bisht.ṣhrpnn	With fire she burned him.
brḥm.tthnn	With millstones she ground him.

One observes the root *b-q-'* in the second line. It also occurs in the Ugaritic Legend of Aqhat when Baal "rips open" the eagles' livers (*ybq' kbdthm*) to see if vanished Aqhat's remains were inside them. The presence of *b-q-'* in Ugaritic mythological texts has led at least one scholar (Wakeman 1969; 1973: 123–27) to the conclusion that *bāqa'* must have similar mythological nuances in Exod. 14. That is, God triumphs over the (evil) sea by splitting it open, just as Anat triumphs over Mot by splitting open his body.

I fail to see the mythic roots of *bāqa'* in Genesis or Exodus. For one thing, both passages in Genesis and Exodus appear to have nothing to do with an underworld force against whom Yahweh fights and over whom he prevails. Exodus 14 is not about God's victory *over* the sea, but it is about God's victory *at* the sea. One really needs to read with unbridled imagination to see a "heaven versus hell" theomachy in either Gen. 7 or Exod. 14.

Of the fifty-one times where *bāqa'* occurs in the Hebrew Bible, I can find very few that use *bāqa'* of God's engaging in battle with some demonic monster. See Ps. 74:15, "It was you who *opened* up [*bāqa'*] springs and streams," after the immediately preceding verses have talked about God's splitting open (*pārar*, not *bāqa'*) the sea, crushing the heads of Leviathan, and breaking the heads of the monsters. In none of these passages like Isa. 51:9–10 or Ps. 74:12–17 is there any mention of the sea (or god of the sea, Yamm) being cleft (*bāqa'*). This is indeed where we would expect this verb. To be sure, such passages in the Bible, as Oswalt (1977) has demonstrated, show Israel's historicizing of pagan myth and appropriation of literary, mythical figures not native to her. But the OT's celebration of Yahweh's victory over Rahab, Leviathan, the Tannin, and the like does not suggest that Israel affirmed the actual existence of such chaotic monsters, anymore than Christians' use of "Sunday" or "Monday" shows that they believe in the sun god or the moon god.

This paragraph continues the series of contrasts present elsewhere in the chap- **14:22–28**
ter. Not one Israelite is lost. Not one Egyptian is spared. Each group is either all delivered or all drowned. There is a contrast between what Israel has seen that produces frantic fear, bordering on panic (v. 10), and what Israel sees that produces healthy fear (vv. 30–31). There is a contrast between what happens at night (v. 21) and what happens in the morning (v. 24). There is a contrast between Israel's fleeing from Pharaoh (v. 5), and Egypt's trying to flee from Israel (v. 27). If we go outside of the chapter, earlier uses of "not one of them remained" mean the complete removal of a plague from Egypt in 8:31 [27] (flies) and 10:19 (locusts). "Not a single one of them remained" here (v. 28) means a complete/total loss of life.

Pope (1977: 339) cites a number of postbiblical Jewish writings, among them a midrash (or commentary) on Exodus known as *Midrash Rabbah*, which gives a reason why the (male) horses pulling the chariots of Pharaoh pursued the Israelites into the sea (v. 23): God made the Israelites appear as mares to the Egyptian stallions, driving the latter wild with excitement at the presence or scent of an estrual mare. Pope produces evidence from Egyptian texts especially that such a strategy of using a female horse was an actual *ruse de guerre*. Maybe that concept explains what the lover says to his beloved in Song 1:9 NLT: "You are as exciting, my darling, as a mare among Pharaoh's stallions."

There are many parallels between the life and ministry of Moses and Elijah (Gnuse [2000: 216] cites ten). But here is one of them. The Lord enables Moses to part the water by using a rod and his hand. God enables Elijah to part the water by using a mantle (2 Kings 2:7–8). Both times the favored parties pass through "on dry ground." Moses, however, goes one step further. He not only parts the water, but with another wave of his hand he also brings the water back to its normal course. Perhaps in this second action of Moses we might discern an anticipation of how walls of Jericho fall inward on the residents of Jericho: here the walls of water fall inward on the Egyptians.

There is a seeing that leads to fear (v. 10), and there is a seeing that leads to **14:30–31**
faith (vv. 30–31). It is better to go from the seeing of v. 10 to the seeing of vv. 30–31 rather than vice versa. Sliding forward is always preferable to backsliding. Abram's faith is in the Lord (Gen. 15:6). Israel's faith is in the Lord, and in his servant Moses (in that order). Both God and servants of God become individuals upon whom one pins their hopes. For an excellent parallel to Exod.

14:31, one that uses the Hiphil of *ʾāman bĕ* with both divine and human object in that order, see 2 Chron. 20:20, the words of King Jehoshaphat to his people: "Listen to me Judah and people of Jerusalem! *Have faith in* the LORD your God; . . . *have faith in* his prophets."

Regrettably, Israel's faith in the Lord and in Moses is short-lived. Numbers 21:5 is the polar opposite of Exod. 14:31—"They spoke against God and against Moses." Israel, alas, has gone from *ʾāman bĕ* ("believe in") to *dābar bĕ* ("speak against").

Passages in the NT like Matt. 2:15 (quoting Hosea 11:1); Luke 1:68; Acts 13:17; 1 Cor. 10:1–2; Heb. 11:29; and Rev. 15:2–3 make reference to the sea event of Exod. 14 to illustrate a number of different things, such as the presence of God's power, the exercise of faith on that occasion, the limitations of that first exodus that point to a greater exodus and different kind of liberation.

There is one event in the Gospels whose connection with Exod. 14 may not be as obvious, and that is the story in Mark 5:1–20 (= Matt. 8:28–34 = Luke 8:26–39). It is the story of Jesus's transferring demons from a possessed man into two thousand pigs, who promptly rush down a steep bank into a lake and drown, and restoring the maniac to sanity. Might the swine's going headlong into the lake (Luke 8:31) and drowning recall the Egyptians' streaming headlong into the sea and drowning? Cave (1964: 97) says, "It was not unknown for Jews to apostrophize their enemies as swine." Derrett (1979: 5) notes that when the unclean spirits enter the pigs, they act very unpiglike. Instead of panicking and scattering as pigs would, they stampede herdlike as horses would. They march down the steep road to their death, à la Egyptians in Exod. 14.

There are a few vocabulary entries that also connect the two. Marcus (2000: 349) has a helpful chart that links some of the Greek phrases of Mark 5:1–20 with Exod. 14 and 15 LXX. For example, the Egyptians "ran" (*ephygon*) as the sea engulfed them (Exod. 14:27), and those tending the pigs "ran" off (*ephygon*) in Mark 5:14. In Exod. 15:2d, "And I will exalt him," *hypōsō*, is very similar to Mark 5:7, "What do you want with me, Jesus, Son of the Most High God [*tou theou tou hypistou*]?" Exodus 14:31 ends by saying, "When Israel saw . . . what the LORD *had done*," which matches Mark 5:19, "Go home to your family and tell them how much the Lord *has done* for you." In the OT story the Israelites live and the Egyptians die. In the Gospel story the demented man "lives" but the pigs die. There is one major difference between the two. The swine are guilty of no sin against God's people. They pay the ultimate price so that another may be freed and restored.

The Song at the Sea by Moses and the Men

(15:1–18)

Translation

[1]Then Moses and Israel's sons sang this song to the LORD, and they said, saying:

"Let me sing unto the LORD for he has surely risen on high,
horse and rider he shot into the sea.
[2]My strength and protection is Yah,
and he has become my salvation.
This one is my God, and I will glorify him,
My father's God, and I will exalt him.
[3]The LORD is a fighting man,
the LORD is his name.
[4]Pharaoh's chariots and armed forces he has shot into the sea,
all of Pharaoh's officers—even the best of them—drowned in the Red Sea.
[5](The) deeps were covering them,
they went down into the depths like a stone.
[6](With) your right hand, O LORD, dreaded for power,
(with) your right hand, O LORD, you shatter (your) foe.
[7]In the greatness of your exaltation you fell your assailants,
You send off your fury; it consumes them like straw.
[8]And with the breath of your nostrils cold waters piled up,
(the) streams swelled like a mound,
(the) deeps rose from the heart of the sea.
[9](The) enemy said, 'I'll pursue, catch up with, divide up (the) spoil,
my appetite will be sated, I'll draw my sword, my hand bring them to ruin.'
[10]You blew with your breath, (the) sea covered them,
they sank like lead in the majestic waters.
[11]Who is like you among the gods, O LORD,
who is like you, glorious in holiness, awe-inspiring in praise, a wonder-worker?
[12]You stretched out your right hand,
(the) earth swallowed them.
[13]You led forth in your kindness this people you redeemed,
you guided (them) in your strength to your holy abode.
[14]Peoples listened, they trembled,
anguish gripped Philistia's rulers.
[15]Then Edom's bulls were dismayed; as for Moab's rams, trembling seized them.
All of Canaan's rulers dissolved.
[16]Fell upon them terror and fear, by means of the greatness of your arm they became silent like stone,
until your people crossed over, O LORD, until this people you purchased/created crossed over.
[17]You bring them and plant them on your own mountain, the fixed place of your residence (that) you made, O LORD,
(the) sanctuary, O Lord, your hands firmly founded.
[18]The LORD is king for ever and ever."

Grammatical and Lexical Notes

15:1. *Yāšîr* would normally be translated "will sing," rather than "sang," but the *ʾāz* ("then") before it is a time indicator, showing *yāšîr* should be translated as a preterite rather than as an imperfect. See Greenstein 1988: esp. 8.

15:1. Although the verb "sang" is singular (*yāšîr*), the subject of the verb is plural or compound ("Moses and Israel's sons"). The rule seems to be that the predicate of a compound subject may agree with the first element of the compound subject if the predicate precedes the subject (here, and Gen. 21:32, "rose up [*wayyāqom*, sg.] Abimelech and Phicol . . . and returned to the land of the Philistines"). If the predicate follows the subject, it must be plural (e.g., Gen. 8:22, "Seedtime and harvest, cold and heat, summer and winter, day and night will never cease [*lōʾ yišbōtû*]"; see Kroeze 2001: 38).

15:1. *Rāmâ bĕ* often is translated as "thrown into," whereas I have rendered it "shot into." Except for its use in the Piel stem, when it means "deceive," the only other occurrences are participial forms ("shooters, bowmen") as in Ps. 78:9 ("the men of Ephraim, though armed with bows [*rômê-qāšet*]") and in Jer. 4:29 ("At the sound of horsemen and archers [wĕrōmēh qešet]").

15:2. Should the second word of line 1 (*wĕzimrāt*) be translated "song" or "protection" or something else? Loewenstamm (1969b) observes that "strength" and "song" are not synonymous, and so he offers the alternative "my strength and my glory." Shortly after this study, both E. Good (1970) and Parker (1971) rejected Loewenstamm's reading and suggested "protection, defense" instead, with Parker noting that whatever *zimrāt* means, it must go not only with "strength" before it, but also with "salvation" in the next line. Actually Gaster (1936–37) had offered this reading much earlier, as did Cross and Freedman (1955: 243). The ancient versions are divided. With its *boēthos kai skepastēs* ("a helper and a shelterer"), the LXX supports "strength"; the Vulgate's *fortitudo mea et laus mea Dominus* supports "song." Appeal for "protection, defense" is made to Ugaritic *dmr*, meaning both "song/sing" and "be strong, protect." In text RS 24:252 (= *KTU* 1.108) we have a sentence that begins with a long list of synonyms for "strength": *ʿzk. dmrk. lank. htkk. nrmtk. btk. ugrt. lymt. shpsh.wyrḥ.* "May your vigor, your *might*, your powers, your potency (and) your splendor be in the midst of Ugarit for (as long as) the days of sun and moon." Having said all this, I admit that the evidence for *z-m-r* with the meaning "protection, strength" in Biblical Hebrew is slim. Richardson (1971: 261) and Barré (1992: 628–29), for instance, read 2 Sam. 23:1's words about David, *nĕʾîm zimirôt yiśrāʾēl*, not as "Israel's beloved singer" (NIV footnote), but as "the beloved 'guardian' of Israel," or "the Favorite of the 'Strong One' of Israel." Barré also notes that in Jacob's words to his sons, "Put some of the *best products* [*zimrat*] of the land in your bags" (Gen. 43:11), *zimrat* obviously has nothing to do with "singing." Rather, the phrase should be compared with Gen. 4:12, where God says to Cain, "When you work the ground, it will no longer yield *its crops* [*kōḥāh*, lit., "its strength"] for you."

15:2. The form of "protection/song" is *zimrāt* and not the usual *zimrâ*. The expression *ʿozzî wĕzimrāt* occurs again in Isa. 12:2; Ps. 118:14. In form *zimrāt* is like *ben pōrāt* in Gen. 49:22 ("she-ass"? "fruitful vine"?). The suffix *-at* represents the feminine singular ending in an early poem before the shift of *-at* to *-â* (and so in Isa. 12:2 and Ps. 118:14 the identical couplet is a fossilized form). See Rendsburg 1992: 168.

15:2. As Zevit (2007: 158) has shown, in most Masoretic texts the *hê* grapheme is usually dotted with a *mappîq* when *YH* (*Yah*) is written as a free-standing word, as here, or when joined to a preceding word by a *maqqēp*. This shows that the final grapheme was taken as a consonantal *h*. When *YH* (*-iah*) is a part of a suffix, as in personal names (e.g., Jerem*iah*), the Masoretes did not mark the *h* with a *mappîq*.

15:2. "And has become . . ." (*wayĕhî*) is the only clear *wāw*-consecutive form in the hymn. Maybe in early Biblical Hebrew such a construction was used sparingly, especially in a poetic text. See V. Sasson 1997: 119–20.

15:2. The suffix "him" on "I will glorify him" is *-ēhû*, while the suffix "him" on "I will exalt him" is *-enhû* (with a *nûn*). Rainey (1988: 36) says the first verb and suffix is a jussive from the injunctive *yaqṭula*. But there is no difference in meaning between the two.

15:2. Dahood (1978; also see BDB 627a) argues that the root of *ʾanwēhû* (Hiphil) is *nāʾâ/nāwâ*, "be comely, beautiful." *Targum Onqelos* renders freely with "I will build for him a temple," a translation reflected in NJPS's "I will enshrine him." In such a rendering there is probably a desire to connect the first part of this poem with the second part of the poem and its mention of a sanctuary (v. 17).

15:3. The expression "fighting man, warrior" (*ʾîš milḥāmâ*) for Yahweh is a natural one here, coming on the heels of Moses telling his people back in 14:14 that their God will "fight" (*lāḥam*) for them, something even the Egyptians concede (14:25). Curiously, the LXX renders the first part of the verse as "The Lord will shatter/crush/stamp out war [*kyrios syntribōn polemous*]," doing what Talmon (1961: 371) describes as inserting "a pacifist note entirely absent from the Hebrew original."

15:4. *Yārâ* ("shot"), like *rāmâ* ("shot") in v. 1, is frequently used with shooting arrows (for a nearby Exodus reference, see 19:13, a warning to those who come too close to Sinai: "He shall surely be stoned or shot with *arrows*"). See also 1 Sam. 20:36–37; 2 Sam. 11:20; 2 Kings 13:17; 2 Kings 19:32 (= Isa. 37:33); Prov. 26:18.

15:4. *Ûmibḥar šālišāyw* ("and the best/select/chosen of his officers") is a partitive genitive, as GKC §128r recognizes. It is like *ḥakmôt śārôtêâ* ("the wisest of her ladies [answer her]") in Judg. 5:29. The line does not suggest that only the pick of Pharaoh's officers drowned, but it does suggest that not even the best of his troops escaped. As Noble (1997: 335–36) says, such a genitive "picks out as particularly worthy of comment the participation by a sub-group in something that is common to the group as a whole."

15:5. *Tĕhōmōt* ("deeps"), with a short "o" vowel at the end, appears as a masculine plural only in Exod. 15:5, 8 (and maybe Deut. 8:7). With a long "o" vowel at the end, *tĕhōmôt* in Ps. 78:15 is a feminine singular (*tĕhōmôt rabbâ*), but in Prov. 3:20 is a masculine plural (*tĕhômôt nibqāʿû*). Similarly, the singular form, *tĕhôm*, may be masculine (Job 28:14; Ps. 42:7 [8]; Jon. 2:6; Hab. 3:10), or feminine (nine times in all, e.g., Gen. 7:11). We cannot determine the gender or number of *tĕhôm/tĕhômôt* unless there is an accompanying adjective or verbal form, and there are sixteen of these uncertain cases. Feminine cases of *t-h-m* outnumber masculine ones by a ratio of about two to one.

15:5. Muraoka and Ragland (1998: 100) want to read *yĕkasyumû* as a "punctiliar-preterital *yiqṭōl*" ("covered" rather than "were covering"). What they ignore is the repeat of this verb in its *qāṭal* form in v. 10 ("the sea covered them [*kissāmô*]"). So why do we have the same verb in two different grammatical forms and with two different functions in the same poem? I argue that the *yiqṭōl* form in v. 5 is durative ("wave after wave overwhelmed them"), while the *qāṭal* form in v. 10 refers to a completed, irreversible, final action ("they were completely covered and sank to rise no more"). See V. Sasson 2001: 608–10.

15:6. The enigmatic form here is *neʾdārî*, usually translated something like "glorious/majestic [in power]." As the MT points it, it is a Niphal participle used in the construct, from the verb *ʾādar* (see BDB 12a). Cross and Freedman (1955: 245) and Freedman (1960: 105), following their mentor William F. Albright, repoint it to *neʾdōrî*, that is, an older form of the infinitive absolute, one that ends with an *-î*. The infinitive absolute is then used as a substitute for a finite verb. The main reason for not reading it as a participle is that the subject of line 1 (and 2), "your right hand," is feminine, while *neʾdārî*, the predicate in the sentence, is masculine. If we stay with the MT pointing, then *neʾdārî* modifies "Lord" rather than "right hand" ("Your right hand, O Lord, [who is] majestic in power"). The more "normal" form of the Niphal participle (*neʾdār*) appears in v. 11 ("majestic in holiness"), which SP emends to make it consistent with the form in v. 5. In v. 11 the participle modifies "Lord," and not anything like "right hand." D. Robertson (1969: 212–13n2) notes that the overwhelming majority of words ending in *-î* (excluding, of course, the pronominal suffix) occur on participles used as adjectives in appositional position.

15:6. I arrive at the translation "dreaded" by emending *neʾdārî* to *neʾdārê* along with Dahood (1972: 394–95). If that emendation is on target, then the discussion in the previous footnote becomes irrelevant. Butts (2010: 167–71) reads the *-î* on the end of *nĕʾdārî* ("dreaded") as a relic of the feminine morpheme *i* common in Semitic morphology, which obviates the need to emend *nĕʾdārî* to *nĕʾdārâ* to make it agree with feminine "your right hand" or to read the word as a masculine.

15:6. Depending on the context, *tirʿaṣ* is either a third-person feminine singular verb, whose subject has to be "your right hand," or a second-person masculine singular verb, whose subject here can only be the Lord. If it is the latter, "(With) your right hand" is an accusative of means preceding the verb.

15:6. Loewenstamm (1969a) calls a verse like 15:6 an "expanded colon." The first line is incomplete without the second line, which repeats and completes the thought of the first line. For an example of this elsewhere, look at Ps. 92:9 [10], "For surely your enemies, O Lord / surely your enemies will perish"; or 94:3, "How long will the wicked, O Lord / how long will the wicked be jubilant?"

15:7. "Exaltation" (*gāʾôn*) is from the verb that appears in v. 1 (and 21), *gāʾōh, gāʾâ* ("he has surely risen on high"). It is an appropriate word choice in the Song at "the Sea," since the verb *gāʾâ* is used with the surging of water (Ezek. 47:5), as is the noun *gāʾôn*, especially in the phrase "the swelling of the Jordan" (Jer. 12:5; 49:19; 50:44; Zech. 11:3, all of which NIV renders as "the thicket[s] of the Jordan").

15:7. A parallel to the simile at the end of the verse is present in Nah. 1:10 ("They will be consumed like dry stubble").

15:7. Seven verbs—one in v. 7 (*yōʾkĕlēmô*, "it consumes"), two in v. 9 (*timlāʾēmô*, "will be sated"; *tôrîšēmô*, "bring them to ruin"), one in v. 12 (*tiblāʿēmô*, "swallowed"), one in v. 15 (*yōʾḥăzēmô*, "seized"), two in v. 17 (*tĕbiʾēmô*, "bring," and *tiṭṭāʿēmô*, "plant")—all end in *-ēmô*, a rather strange ending for a verbal form. Hummel (1957: 92) reads *-ēmô* as an enclitic *mêm* rather than as a third-person masculine plural pronominal suffix (that is, the attachment of an "*m*" to a verb, the significance of which escapes us), but for a reason unclear to me mentions only v. 9. Emerton (1996) disagrees and believes there is no enclitic *mêm* in Biblical Hebrew, for if so, one would have to delete arbitrarily the final *wāw* from the end of these verbs, for example, *yōʾkĕlem* rather than *yōʾkĕlēmô*.

15:8. There is an interesting use or nonuse of the definite article in this poem. It seems not to be used with a noun that is the subject of a sentence, and hence my use of "(the)" in vv. 5, 8, 9, 10, 12. However, when the noun is collocated with the prepositions *bĕ, kĕ, lĕ*, the definite article is present: *kaqqaš*, v. 7 ("like straw"); *kaʿôperet*, v. 10 ("like lead"); *bāʾēlim*, v. 11 ("among the gods"); *baqqōdeš*, v. 11 ("in holiness" or "among the holy ones"); *kāʾāben*, v. 16 ("like a stone"). But this use is not consistent. Consider in v. 5 *bimṣôlōt* ("into the depths") without the article. See Barr 1989: 325–26.

15:8. The exact couplet *kĕmô-nēd* ("like a heap/a wall/a mound") reappears in Ps. 78:13b in the recalling of this incident: "he made the waters stand firm *like a wall*." The word for "heap, wall" is *nēd*, which occurs but a few times in the Hebrew Bible (these two, plus Josh. 3:13, 16; possibly in Ps. 33:7 and Isa. 17:11). By contrast, the word for the "wall" of water in 14:22, 29 is *ḥōmâ*, which occurs more than 130 times. Leonard (2008: 251) argues that shared language that is rare or distinctive (i.e., *nēd*) suggests a stronger connection between passages of Scripture than does more widely used vocabulary (i.e., *ḥōmâ*).

15:8. Wolters (1990), whom I partially follow, reads v. 8 not as reference to the first miracle of chap. 14, the piling up of the waters so that the Hebrews can pass through on dry ground, but as a reference to the second miracle of chap. 14, the walls of water collapsing and covering the Egyptians. He does so (1) by translating *neʿermû* as "swelled" rather than "piled up"; (2) by reading *niṣṣĕbû* as *niṣbû* ("swelled up," and a synonym for *neʿermû*); (3) by reading *nēd* ("mound/hill/stack") as "swelling up like a wineskin"; (4) by translating *qāpĕʾû* ("congealed/solidified") as "rose"; and (5) by translating the preposition *bĕ* in *bĕleb-yām* not as "*in* the heart of the sea," but "*from* the heart of the sea." Grabbe

(1993: 263–69), however, contends for the consensus reading and does not reference Wolters at all, even though his article was published three years later. My problem with Wolters's reading is that, if correct, v. 8 would have to follow v. 9, and be a duplicate of v. 10.

15:9. I have rendered *nepeš* ("soul") as "appetite," a meaning extracted from *nepeš* with the nuance of "throat." Compare Isa. 5:14, "Therefore the grave enlarges its appetite [*nepeš*], and opens its mouth [*peh*] without limit."

15:10. "Majestic waters" is *mayim ʾaddîrîm*. The standard phrase is *mayim rabbîm* (2 Sam. 22:17 = Ps. 18:16 [17] NIV, "deep waters"; Ps. 32:6 NIV, "the mighty waters"; Song 8:7 NIV, "many waters"; Jer. 41:12 NIV, "the great pool"; Ezek. 1:24 NIV, "rushing waters"; Hab. 3:15 NIV, "the great waters," etc.). Isaiah 17:12 offers *mayim kabbîrîm* ("great/mighty waters"). Psalm 93:4 combines two of the above with *mayim rabbîm ʾaddîrîm* (NIV, "the great waters").

15:11. M. Klein (1976: 534–35) notes that *Targum Onqelos* changes the two rhetorical questions of v. 11 into negative statements by the addition of the particle *lyt*: "There is *none* besides you, you are the Lord, O God. There is *none* but you majestic in holiness." Is the change due to a theological desire to eliminate the idea of the existence of other gods, or is this simply a stylistic way in which *Onqelos* renders rhetorical questions?

15:11. *Baqqōdeš* ("[glorious] in holiness") could also be translated "[glorious] among *the holy ones*," in which case *qōdeš* is a collective noun corresponding to *ʾēlîm* ("gods") in the line before it. That reading seems to be the one reflected in the LXX (*dedoxasmenos en hagiois*). The word surely carries that meaning in Deut. 33:2, "He came with myriads of holy ones [*mēribbōt qōdeš*]."

15:11. "Awe-inspiring" is the Niphal participle (*nôrāʾ*) of *yārēʾ*, "fear," a form that appears thirty-four times in the Hebrew Bible (BDB 431b). On using the Niphal participle for an attribute of God, see Strawn 2002: 790n31.

15:11. Watson (1989: 45) regards the line "awe-inspiring in praise, a wonder-worker" as an instance of internal parallelism or half-line parallelism.

15:12. "Earth" (*ʾereṣ*) seems here to be a reference to the underworld, a nether city, and is like the use of Akkadian *erṣitu/irṣitu*, which may also mean "underworld." This reading of *ʾereṣ* has been suggested for a number of passages. I cite three of them. What does "earth" mean in Isa. 14:12, when it says of some Luciferean figure that he has been "cast down to *the earth*"? And to what earth does a sinking Jonah refer when he says (Jon. 2:6), "*The earth* beneath barred me in forever"? A third passage, Jer. 17:13, says, "Those who turn away from you will be written in the dust [*ʾereṣ*]," whatever that means, but Dahood (1959b: 164–65) arrestingly translates it, "Those who turn from you shall be enrolled *in hell*."

15:13. This passage is one of the few places where the LXX translates *ḥesed* ("kindness") with *dikaiosynē* ("justice"). See Gen. 24:27; 32:10 [11]; Exod. 34:6–7.

15:13. The paralleling of *ḥesed* ("kindness") and *ʿōz* ("strength) is rare. See Ps. 59:16 [17]: "But I will sing of your strength [*ʿōz*], in the morning I will sing of your love [*ḥesed*]"; and Ps. 62:11–12a [12–13a]: "One thing God has spoken, two things have I learned: that you, O God, are strong [*ʿōz*] and that you, O Lord, are loving [*ḥesed*]" (references in Sakenfeld 1978: 221). The Lord's loving nature does not eliminate his capacity for power, and his capacity for power does not override his loving nature.

15:13. *Zû* may be either a demonstrative (Hab. 1:11, "this his strength," *zû kōḥô*), or a relative (Isa. 42:24, "against whom we sinned," *zû ḥāṭāʾnû lô*). Which is it here, a demonstrative ("*this* people you redeemed"), or a relative (the people *that* you have redeemed [BDB 262a])? See the study of Allegro 1955.

15:13. Hebrew *nāʾwâ* ("abode"), thanks to the study of Malamat (1962), is now linked with the word *nawum* from the early cuneiform tablets found at Mari. In standard Akkadian the word means "desert, uncultivated field." In Mari Akkadian it refers to the encampment of nomadic tribes.

Primarily *nāʾwâ* appears in the Hebrew Bible in a pastoral context, for example, the pasture of land of the shepherd (Jer. 23:10 and the famous Ps. 23:2). From this there developed a use of the word to designate a more fixed dwelling, either that of a person or of the Lord. See Frick 1977: 60, 74n221.

15:15. *ʾAllûpê* ("bulls") should be derived not from *ʾelep* II ("thousand"), but from the *ʾelep* that means "a head of large cattle, a bull" (compare Akkadian *alpu*). "Ram(s)" (*ʾêlê*), designating "rulers," is present in 2 Kings 24:15 (NIV, "leading men"). For human figures referred to by animals see Ezek. 17:3 ("eagle") and Ezek. 39:18 (rams/lambs/goats/bulls). See Miller (1970) for this phenomenon. If we have "bulls" and "rams" in v. 15 as designations for "rulers," then we can assume that *yōšĕbê* in vv. 14 and 15 should not be translated as "inhabitants," but as "rulers, chieftains." See Gottwald 1979: 511–34.

15:15. "Dissolved" is the verb *mûg* (Niphal) and may be rendered here "melted away." Israel's enemies dissolve until they disappear. An approaching army can do this to you (Exod. 15:15; Josh. 2:9; 1 Sam. 14:16; Isa. 14:31; Jer. 49:23 [NIV, "disheartened"]; Ezek. 21:15 [20]; Nah. 2:6 [7] [NIV, "collapses"]) but so too can the coming of God's glorious presence (Pss. 46:6 [7]; 75:3 [4] [NIV, "quake"]; Amos 9:5).

15:16. *Nāpal ʿal* ("fell upon") carries the sense of the sudden onset of overpowering forces, often bad for the individual(s) concerned (Ps. 105:38; Isa. 47:11; Dan. 10:7), but sometimes neutral or supernatural (Gen. 15:12; 1 Sam. 11:7).

15:16. The SP "corrects" *ʾêmātâ* ("terror") to more regular *ʾêmâ*. Hurvitz (1985: 119) refers to this form as "the poetic termination *-tā*, common without the definite article." He compares *yĕšûʿātâ* ("deliverance") in Ps. 3:2 [3]; *ʿezrātâ* ("help") in 94:17; and *ʿêpātâ* ("deepest night") in Job 10:22. I add *ʿawlātâ* ("wickedness") in Ezek. 28:15.

15:16. "Fell [upon them] terror and fear" is composed of a feminine singular verb and feminine noun ("terror") and masculine noun ("fear"). Normally when the subject of the verb is a masculine and feminine noun, the verb is masculine. Ratner (1990) has found thirty-eight examples in the Hebrew Bible where the feminine member of the nominal subject governs the gender of the verb (or adjective/pronoun/pronominal suffix), of which Exod. 15:16 is one. Sometimes the verb may be feminine because the feminine noun in the subject precedes the masculine noun.

15:16. The LXX translates "terror and fear" with *phobos kai tromos*. These two nouns often appear together (Gen. 9:2; Deut. 2:25; 11:25; Ps. 2:11; Isa. 19:16; 1 Cor. 2:3; 2 Cor. 7:15; Eph. 6:5; Phil. 2:12).

15:16. In the phrase *bigdōl zĕrôʿăkā* ("by means of the greatness of your arm"), it appears that the adjective *gādôl* ("great") is functioning as a substantive (see BDB 153b), unless one emends adjectival *gādôl* to a nominal *gōdel* ("greatness"). The noun does appear with "arm" in Ps. 79:11, "By the strength of your arm [*kĕgōdel zĕrôʿăkā*] preserve those condemned to die," and in parallel with "hand" in Deut. 3:24, "You have begun to show to your servant your greatness [*godlĕkā*] and your strong hand [*wĕʾet-yādĕkā haḥăzāqâ*]."

15:16. *Yiddĕmû* looks like a perfectly good Qal imperfect of *dāmam*. Cross and Freedman (1955: 249) read it as a Niphal, "They are struck down like a stone" (*yiddĕmû*>*yiddammû*). Dahood (1962) goes another direction and reads it as a Qal passive, or Hophal, of *nādâ*, "hurl" (*yiddĕmû*>*yuddum*, with enclitic *mêm*). If Dahood's interpretation is correct (and I think it is something of a stretch), then we have three verbs for "shoot/cast/throw": *rāmâ* in v. 1, *yārâ* in v. 4, and now *nādâ* in v. 16.

15:16. I have rendered *qānîtā* either "[this people] you purchased" or "[this people] you created." There is an ongoing debate about *qānâ* as to whether it indicates acquisition or creation, possession or production. The verb occurs eighty-three times, and I fully grant that in the vast majority of these the meaning is "acquire, possess." But I cannot go along with Irwin (1961) and Vawter (1986), who suggest that it never means "create." Thus, when in Gen. 4:1 Eve speaks of birthing Cain by using the verb *qānâ* (NIV, "I have brought forth"), surely a parent "acquires" a child by giving birth to/procreating him or her. Deuteronomy 32:6b asks rhetorically, "Is he not your Father, your Creator [*qānekā*, alongside of which NIV suggests in a footnote "who bought you"], who made you and formed you?" When Lady Wisdom says in the famous Prov. 8:22, "The Lord *qānâ*-ed me [NIV, "brought me forth"] as the first of his works," is she saying that Yahweh has created her or has acquired her? If it is the latter, then does that not suggest wisdom was preexistent and coeval with God? I think the strongest case for translating *qānâ* as "purchased" in Exod. 15:16 is found in the parallel phrases of "this people you redeemed [*gāʾal*]" in v. 13, and here in v. 16 "this people you purchased [*qānâ*]." It is surely a message of the Christian Bible that at the heart of redemption is the stark reality that somebody pays a (big) price. See D. McCarthy's remark (1967: 92, 398): "It is well to retain here the double meaning in the rather old-fashioned use of 'get,' for, though the root seems to mean 'form' in a general sense, 'acquire,' . . . it has the sense of 'produce' and 'procreate.'"

15:17. "On your own mountain" is, literally, "On the mount[ain] of your heritage (*bĕhar naḥălātĕkā*)." The Hebrew word *naḥălâ* ("possession, property, inheritance, heritage") can refer to both God's land (1 Sam. 26:19; 2 Sam. 14:16; Ps. 79:1; Jer. 2:7; 50:11) and to God's people (Deut. 4:20; 9:26; 1 Kings 8:51; Pss. 78:62, 71; 106:40; Jer. 10:16; Joel 3:2 [4:2]). It is the only expression in the OT that applies both to land and people. By contrast, the word *sĕgullâ* ("treasured possession") applies only to God's people (Exod. 19:5; Deut. 7:6; 14:2; 26:18) and is never used for Canaan. In the texts from Ugarit, Baal calls his residence on Mount Zaphon in the north *bqdsh.bgr.nḥlty* ("in the sacred mount[ain] of my heritage"), almost the exact same phrase we have in Exod. 15:17 (*KTU* 1.3 III:29–30; IV:19–20). The seminal study of this expression is that by Loewenstamm 1992: 322–60.

15:18. Hebrew *lĕʿōlām wāʿed* ("forever and ever") appears fifteen times in the Hebrew Bible, always in poetry (Exod. 15:18; Pss. 9:7 [6]; 10:16; 21:4 [5]; 45:6 [7], 17 [18]; 48:14 [15]; 52:9 [10]; 104:5; 119:44; 145:1, 2, 21; Dan. 12:3; Mic. 4:5). References in the Psalter count for twelve of these fifteen.

Commentary

Fancy listening to an all-male choir having more than half a million voices in **15:1–18**
it! Beside it even the famed Mormon Tabernacle Choir pales by comparison. This scene, with an enormous choir singing God's praises, anticipates the "thousands upon thousands, and ten thousand times ten thousand," who encircle the heavenly throne in the new Jerusalem (Rev. 5:11–12) to sing, "Worthy is the Lamb, who was slain." Or even better, if we are looking for a parallel in the Apocalypse, is the scene in Rev. 15 of a throng of the victorious redeemed standing beside "a sea of glass" and singing, to the accompaniment of musical instruments, the praises of their God, who has delivered them from their pharaoh, "the beast." It is not without significance that one song this seaside choir sings is "the song of Moses the servant of God" (Rev. 15:3).

To be sure, v. 1 seems to suggest that this is the song of an individual ("Let me sing"). There is no "we" or "us" or "our" in this song. It is characteristic of Songs of Victory, if that is what Exod. 15 may be called, for one to compose them in the first-person singular. See Deut. 31:30–32:1 ("And Moses recited the words of this song. . . . 'Listen, O heavens, and I will speak'"); Judg. 5:1, 3 ("On that day Deborah and Barak . . . sang this song: . . . 'I will sing to the Lord, I will sing; I will make music'"); 1 Sam. 2:1 ("Then Hannah prayed and said: 'My heart rejoices'"); 2 Sam. 22:1 ("David sang to the Lord the words of this song. . . . 'The Lord is my rock'").

What we actually have in Exod. 14–15 are back-to-back accounts of the exodus from Egypt. The one in Exod. 14 appears as prose; the one in Exod. 15 appears as poetry. The only parallel to this in the OT is in Judges, the account of Deborah's victory over the Canaanites: Judg. 4 tells it in prose; Judg. 5 tells it in poetry.

The purpose of the prose account is narration. The purpose of the poetic account is celebration. Exodus 14 tells the old, old story, while Exod. 15 sings the old, old story. You walk or march in chap. 14. You dance in chap. 15. Chapter 14 focuses on what God has done, and chap. 15 focuses on our appropriate response to what God has done. There is a holy hush in chap. 14. You sing fortissimo in chap. 15. And why not? God wipes away all fears after he has wiped out all Egyptians. In chap. 14 you are on the move. In chap. 15 you are standing on the seashore. You are holding your breath in chap. 14. Chapter 15 is the calm after the storm. Chapter 14 highlights dry ground. In chap. 15 there is not a dry eye. In chap. 14 (and 13) a cloud goes ahead of Israel. In chap. 15 (vv. 14–16) Israel's reputation goes ahead of the people. In chap. 14 Moses says nothing, but God asks him, "What are you crying out about to me?" (v. 15). In chap. 15 Moses is quite verbal, but God does *not* say, "What are you singing out about to me!" Chapter 14 is about "warship"; chap. 15 is about worship.

There has been extensive and intensive study of every facet of this poem, and of 15:19–21, which we will consider next. The scholarly literature that Exod. 15 has stimulated is massive. Suffice it to say, there are very few (there are some, to be sure) in the biblical academy who take the hymn's claims about its origins to be historically accurate: that Moses and his fellow male leaders spontaneously compose this song after exiting the sea on dry ground. That same position is taken on just about all hymns/prayers that appear in biblical narrative. For example, Moses did not actually compose the Song of Moses in Deut. 32:1–43 just before he gave up the ghost, nor did Hannah pray the prayer ascribed to her in 1 Sam. 2:1–10. Solomon did not offer up the prayer in 1 Kings 8:14–61 that 1 Kings 8:15–16 says he did. Jonah never prayed the prayer from the fish's innards that Jon. 2:2–9 ascribes to him there, nor did Ezra literally offer up the prayer connected to him in Ezra 9:6–15. For the NT, the same position is assumed for Mary's song (Luke 1:46–55) and Zechariah's song (1:67–79). In all the above instances, it is argued, the poetic compositions are so literally and rhetorically complex that the individual(s) named could not possibly have produced them "on the spot." See, for example, the study by S. Russell (2009: 127–76), who concludes that the language of 15:1–18 is metaphorical and not historical in any discernable sense. He makes much of the fact that the verb *ʿābar* ("pass by") in v. 16 lacks a direct or indirect object; accordingly, he gives the verb the meaning "tour, roam around, travel" (2009: 156) and opines that 15:1–18 "refers to the tour of the people of Yahweh as they journey to Yahweh's sanctuary" (2009: 176).

In the case of Exod. 15, the options for dating it run the gamut from very early to very late. The proponents for a late date for composition are clearly in the minority (e.g., M. Brenner [1991], who argues for a date in the mid-400s BC, and Noth [1962] in his Exodus commentary). The majority position is that if Exod. 15 is not the oldest poem in the Hebrew Bible, it is one of the oldest poems in that corpus. Its composition took place in the twelfth or early eleventh century BC (e.g., D. Robertson 1972; B. Russell 2007: 59–148). In between these two extremes for dating the poem is a middle ground that places its composition sometime around the time of David/Solomon (tenth century BC). My purpose is not to lay out and then evaluate all the arguments pro and con for an early/late date. Briefly, however, on the basis of what I have read and consulted, the arguments for an earlier composition seem to be more persuasive than do those for a postexilic dating.

Still, I am not totally convinced that attribution of any part of the poem to Moses and his contemporaries amounts to coloring Exod. 15 as a blatant pseudepigraph. Anybody familiar with Christian hymnody is well aware that some of these grand hymns have been so changed over the years that the original composer might have difficulty identifying it. Imagine, for example, John Newton, author of "Amazing Grace," asking about the last stanza ("When we've been there ten thousand years . . ."), "Where did that come from?" The author of the phrase "Here I raise mine Ebenezer" in the hymn "Come, Thou Fount of Every Blessing" thought the expression to be self-explanatory, but later hymnists have scrambled to replace it. And it is hardly likely that when Protestant parishioners sing "Faith of Our Fathers" on the third Sunday of June, they are reflecting on the martyrdom of faithful, Catholic clergy, as was Frederick Faber when he penned this song.

So my own position is that the basic themes and emphases and expressed sentiments throughout the song come from Moses and his fellow choir members. Subsequently, some individual(s), gifted in the creation of poetic verse and knowledgeable of Canaanite poetry, crafted these lyrics into the form of exquisite poetry. And who is not to say that even after that the poem underwent even further emendation? It must be remembered that alongside the many "archaic" forms of words throughout the poem, there are several "standard" forms (e.g., in v. 16 "upon them" is *ʿălêhem* rather than the archaic *ʿalēmô*, and "they became silent" is *yiddĕmû* rather than the older *yiddĕmûn*). For an analogy, think of a line, or lines, in a poem that contains language like "thou saidest," "methinks," "I wouldest," and "thereto I plight thee my troth," and language like "you said," "I think," "I would," and "so I promise to be faithful to you."

There are several ways in which one may divide up these eighteen verses. For starters, I observe that the song begins as a song *about* God (vv. 1–5, God is "he"), then shifts to a song *to* God (vv. 6–17, God is "you"), and concludes as a song *about* God (v. 18). We see verses addressing God as "you" outnumbering those that speak of God as "he" by a two-to-one ratio (twelve verses to six verses). In the doxological literature of the OT, I am not aware of how common this pattern is, but Ps. 23 is one good example of it. In vv. 1–3 the psalmist talks *about* the Shepherd, in vv. 4–5 he talks *to* the Shepherd, and in v. 6 he concludes with an affirmation *about* dwelling with God "forever." Conversation about God lacks the intimacy of conversation with God.

In terms of the poetic form of the song, the clearest expression of the semblance of unity is found in three "staircase parallelisms," which enter at strategic points in the song (for which see, among others, Perles 1926–27; Muilenburg 1966; Cohen 1975; Fokkelman 1998: 24–53):

v. 6	"Your right hand, O LORD, . . .
	your right hand"
v. 11	"Who is like you, . . .
	who is like you?"
v. 16b	"until your people crossed over, O LORD,
	until this people . . . crossed over"

In terms of strophic structure, I am inclined, along with many others, to divide the song into two parts, vv. 1–12 and vv. 13–18. In such a case, vv. 12 and 18 function as refrains or conclusions to both sections. It just happens that these two are the shortest of the eighteen verses, and each contains (in the Hebrew) only four words: v. 12, "you-stretched-out your-right-hand and-the-earth swallowed-them"; v. 18, "The-LORD is-king forever and-ever."

The basic reason for so dividing the song is as follows. Section A, vv. 1–12, focuses on and celebrates what the Lord has recently done for his people. He has given them safe and dry passage through the sea, while he has drowned their pursuers, Pharaoh and the Egyptians. Section B, vv. 13–18 (or 17), focuses on something that has yet to happen, but will happen, either in the near future or in the distant future. Thus in Exod. 15 Moses sings not only poetically, powerfully, and passionately but also prophetically.

The NIV translates most of the verbs in this section as future, and the NRSV takes most of them as past:

15:13a	NIV: "You *will lead* the people you have redeemed."
	NRSV: "You *led* the people whom you have redeemed."
15:13b	NIV: "You *will guide* them to your holy dwelling."
	NRSV: "You *guided* them . . . to your holy abode."
15:14a	NIV: "Nations *will hear and tremble*."
	NRSV: "The peoples *heard*, they *trembled*."
15:14b	NIV: "Anguish *will grip* the people of Philistia."

	NRSV: "Pangs *seized* the inhabitants of Philistia."
15:15a	NIV: "The chiefs of Edom *will be terrified*."
	NRSV: "The chiefs of Edom *were dismayed*."
15:15b	NIV: "The leaders of Moab *will be seized* with trembling."
	NRSV: "Trembling *seized* the leaders of Moab."
15:15c	NIV: "The people of Canaan *will melt* away."
	NRSV: "All the inhabitants of Canaan *melted* away."
15:16a	NIV: "Terror and dread *will fall* upon them."
	NRSV: "Terror and dread *fell* upon them."
15:16b	NIV: "They *will be* still as stone."
	NRSV: "They *became* still as stone."
15:16c	NIV: "until your people *pass by*."
	NRSV: "until your people . . . *passed by*."
15:17a	NIV: "You *will bring* them in and *plant* them."
	NRSV: "You *brought* them in and *planted* them."

Now, in one sense, both translations are correct. The NIV uses future-tense translations because the events of which Moses sings in those five verses have yet to happen. They are off in the future, either the immediate future or the distant future. A senior college student in the fall semester of the last year of school does not say, "This coming spring I graduated," but rather, "This coming spring I will graduate."

The NRSV, however, translates the verbs as if they refer to events that have already taken place. It does so because the verbs are all *qāṭal* verb forms: a verb form that refers to completed action, something like the aorist in Greek. Older grammarians called this "the prophetic perfect." Actions or events, yet to happen, could be described as having already taken place. Nowadays, Hebrew scholars explain the *qāṭal* forms as nonperfective preterites on the basis of parallel usages in related Semitic languages.

We see that vv. 5–7 in section A use *yiqṭōl* verb forms (the prefix conjugation) for past events, while vv. 13–17 in section B use *qāṭal* verb forms (the affixed conjugation) for events off in the future. This is just the opposite of what is expected by someone who knows the rules of "standard" Biblical Hebrew grammar. For another illustration of this phenomenon, consider what the Lord says to Joshua in Josh. 1:3: "Every place where you set your foot, to you *nĕtattîw*, as I promised Moses." How shall we render the verb (a *qāṭal* verb form) in italics: "I will give" (NIV), or "I have given" (NRSV)?

There is one other issue about the interpretation of vv. 13–17. And that is, to what time and place do phrases like "your holy abode" (v. 13), "crossed over" (v. 16), "your own mountain" (v. 17), and "(the) sanctuary" (v. 17) refer? If they refer to the immediate future, then the reference is to Israel's passing over/through the wilderness and arriving at Mount Sinai. If they refer to a more distant future, then the reference is to Israel's crossing over the Jordan River, entering into and conquering "the holy land," erecting a worship center at Shiloh, with David and Solomon's involvement in building a sanctuary/temple in Jerusalem as the climax. I believe there is intentional ambiguity here that allows successive generations to appropriate at least this part of the hymn to their own circumstances.

I am inclined to think, however, that the primary thrust of these final verses focuses on what is shortly coming down the pike rather than what is centuries away. As Halpern (1983: 39) has said, "It is more than possible that vv. 13–17 were seen not as an account of the conquest, but as a sixth recital [in this chapter] of the victory at sea, and as one culminating in the arrival of Israel at Sinai." Similarly, Smith (2001: 34) believes this poem stands at the fulcrum point of the book of Exodus: "The two halves of the poem in Exodus 15 recapitulate the events of the book in the priestly redaction: vv. 1–12 refer generally to events leading up to and including the victory at the sea rendered in the first half of the book, while vv. 13–18 anticipate the events following the victory at the sea, as described in the second half of the book."

Although chap. 14 ends by mentioning the people's placing their trust in the Lord *and in Moses*, in chap. 15 Moses does not share the dais with the Lord. This is a song of/by Moses, not a song to/about Moses. The song may ask rhetorically, "Who is like you among the gods, O Lord?" (v. 11), but it does not ask, "Who is like you among Yahweh's servants, O *Mōsheh*?" The only identifiable human to enter this poem is a certain pharaoh, much like Pontius Pilate, who made it into Christendom's Apostles' Creed. In both affirmations of faith, the "bad guy," a powerful titan in his day, appears, but only to disappear.

The last verse of the song, v. 18, speaks of God's eternal rule and is the first occurrence of this phrase in Scripture, using language that appears in a number of psalms that speak of God as king and of his reign (Pss. 29:10b; 47:6–7 [7–8]; 93:1; 95:3; 96:10; 97:1; 98:6; 99:1). To conclude, this sea song of Moses accomplishes two things. First, it demonstrates that Yahweh's victory over Pharaoh and his troops is not a fluke, an upset. There is no incredulous sportscaster like Al Michaels by the seashore, shouting out, "Do you believe in miracles?" at this David-over-Goliath victory. Second, the concluding and climactic emphasis about God's ruling, not just on this occasion but forever, allows later readers to appropriate for themselves the godly sentiments of this song whenever they face their own predatory pharaoh.

Sailhamer (2009: 36–37, 333, 572–73) has drawn attention to the presence of four major poems in the Pentateuch that follow on the heels of a block of narrative material: Jacob's (Gen. 49:1–27), Moses's (Exod. 15:1–18), Balaam's (Num. 22–24), and another of Moses's (Deut. 32–33). In three of these four poems, the phrase "in days to come" (*bĕʾaḥărît hayyāmîm*) occurs at a crucial point in the poem: Gen. 49:1 (at the start of Jacob's poem); Num. 24:14 (at the start of Balaam's important fourth oracle); Deut. 31:29 (just before the start of Moses's second poem). The only other instance of the phrase in the Pentateuch is Deut. 4:30. (For its use in prophetic literature, see Isa. 2:2; Jer. 23:20; 30:24; 48:47; 49:39; Ezek. 38:8 [with "years" instead of "days"], 16; Hosea 3:5; Mic. 4:1; Dan. 2:28; 10:14.)

The majority of commentators take the phrase, especially in the Pentateuch but even in the prophetic texts cited here, as not referring to the culminating period of history. Only in Dan. 2:28 and 10:14, it is claimed, is the phrase a reference to the messianic age. Instead, the phrase refers to the near future from the perspective of the speaker.

Sailhamer argues contrariwise that the phase in these pentateuchal poems is eschatological, and he provides references from the poems in support (e.g., Gen. 49:10–12). That being the case, why then is Exod. 15:1–18 the only major poem in the Pentateuch to lack the phrase, and why is it the only major poem in the Pentateuch to have the phrase "Yahweh reigns"? Sailhamer (2009: 572) contends that the other three poems point to a future kingdom that will be inaugurated in "the last days," while the focus of Exod. 15:18 is on the Lord's eternal reign and kingdom. He has always reigned. He reigns now. He will reign forever. This is not welcome news for any would-be pharaoh.

The Song at the Sea by Miriam and the Women

(15:19–21)

Translation

[19]When Pharaoh's horses along with his chariots and horsemen had gone into the sea, and the LORD turned back on them the seas' waters, while Israel's sons went on dry land in the midst of the sea, [20]Miriam, the prophetess, sister of Aaron, took the timbrel in her hand, and all the women went out after her with timbrels and dances. [21]And Miriam sang out to them:

"Sing to the LORD for he has surely
risen on high,
horse and rider he shot into the
sea."

Grammatical and Lexical Notes

15:20. The Hebrew word *tōp* ("timbrel"; LXX, *tympanon*; Vulg., *tympanum*) refers to some kind of handheld drum made from animal skin stretched over a circular frame of metal or wood. Normally it would be held in the left hand and struck with the palm or fingers of the right hand. It was used at victory celebrations (Exod. 15:20; Judg. 11:34; 1 Sam. 18:6; Ps. 68:25 [26]); as a part of prophetic ecstatic worship (1 Sam. 10:5); at yearly festivals (Ps. 81:2–3 [3–4]; Isa. 30:29–32); at moments of thanksgiving to God for his benefits (Jer. 31:4); and even at parties that can last late into the night (Job 21:12; Isa. 5:12; 24:8). They were also used in exuberant worship (2 Sam. 6:5; 1 Chron. 13:8; Pss. 149:3; 150:4).

15:20. Timbrels are mentioned along with dancing in Exod. 15:20; Judg. 11:34; 1 Sam. 18:6; Pss. 149:3; 150:4 (using either the verb *ḥûl*, the noun "dance" [*māḥôl*] or the noun "dancing" [*mĕḥôlâ*]); in 2 Sam. 6:5, 14, 16 (with the verb *kārar*); in Job 21:11–12 (with the verb *rāqad*). See the lengthy footnote in Bird 1997: 96.

15:21. The Hebrew for "to them" (*lāhem*) is the preposition with third-person masculine plural pronominal suffix, showing that Miriam is singing to Moses and the male Israelites, and not to the other women with her. Similarly, "sing" (*šîrû*) is a masculine plural imperative. She summons the men, rather than the women, to sing.

15:21. Whenever *ʿānâ* is followed by the preposition *lĕ*, as here, it means "to sing, recite (to the accompaniment of musical instruments)." See also Num. 21:17b; 1 Sam. 18:7; 21:11; 29:5; Ezra 3:11; Ps. 147:7; Song 2:10 (NIV, "spoke"); Isa. 27:2. However, when *ʿānâ* is followed by the accusative indicator *ʾet*, it means "answer." The connection between "sing" and "answer" may have derived from the antiphonal character of choral music. One sings and the other responds.

Commentary

Several questions surround the Song of Miriam. First, why are there seventeen 15:19–21
and half verses for Moses's song, but only one verse for Miriam's? Second, do we have the full version of her song, or an amazingly abbreviated form of it? Third, is this Miriam's own song or simply an antiphonal echo of Moses's? Fourth, which of the two songs is older? Many biblical scholars believe that Miriam's is older. If that is the case, why is her song reduced to one verse and placed after the song of her younger brother?

In addressing these questions, some feminist biblical scholars do not like what they see here. It is another instance of letting a less talented man up-stage a more talented woman. So for them, Miriam's song is the earlier one, maybe the only one. It is a case of male editors taking "the song out of her mouth and giving it to Moses," or creating a situation in which Miriam and the other women "are shouted down" by the voices of Moses and his male peers, or establishing one in which male voices almost "mute" female voices. See, as examples, the studies of A. Brenner 1985; Trible 1989; A. Brenner and Dijk-Hemmes 1993.

In response, I have no problem at all in agreeing that more than likely the Song of Miriam makes more sense if it precedes this Song of Moses. Her command "sing" in the imperative of v. 21 surely comes before his "let me sing" in the jussive of v. 1. See the remarks of Janzen (1992; 1997: 108–9). Furthermore, I am in agreement with those who suggest that placing her song after her brother's song creates an inclusio for the first fifteen chapters of Exodus. Thus Exod. 1–15 begins and ends by highlighting the significant role of women. They are both saviors and singers, midwives and minstrels. After chap. 15 women almost completely disappear from the book of Exodus.

I am inclined to think, however, that chap. 15, far from demoting Miriam, instead puts her on a pedestal. If male chauvinistic editors wanted to downplay her significance, then why not just eliminate her contributions altogether? We see a significant parallel between the two poems. There are, for both, narrative verses that set the stage for the poem to follow. What 14:26–31 is to 15:1–18 (the narrative background before the poem and necessary for the poem), 15:19 is to 15:20–21 (the narrative background before the poem and necessary for the poem). I suggest that what we have is not a voice and an echo, but a duet, with each contributing their part to the whole. As Kim (2000: 274–76) says, "There is a concept of unity and mutuality between Moses and Miriam. . . . These songs depict the affairs of the community in that both women and men take essential parts. When the community joins together for the common songs and celebration, there is a strong sense of solidarity. . . . Moses leads the brothers and Miriam leads the sisters. In the leadership of these two, . . . mutual complementarity functions as a key model for the unity and efficiency of the entire community."

It is common in the Bible for women to sing victory songs as they welcomed their victorious male warriors back from the battlefield. See Judg. 11:34 ("When Jephthah returned to his home in Mizpah, who should come out to meet him but his daughter, dancing to the sound of the tambourines!") and 1 Sam. 18:6–7 ("When the men were returning home after David had killed the Philistine, the women came out from all the towns of Israel to meet King Saul with singing and dancing. . . . As they danced, they sang"). In Exod. 15, who will sing the praises of the Victorious One of Exod. 14? We expect Miriam and the women to sing, as in Judg. 11:34 and 1 Sam. 18:6–7, and sing they will, but Moses and the men will sing too. That is the unexpected part. As Weitzman (1997: 29) has remarked, "Normally assigned the role of returning warriors, the males of Israel must in this case play the role usually imposed only upon females in the androcentric culture of ancient Israel, the role of cheerleader."

Miriam is the first woman in the Bible to be called a "prophetess" (v. 20a). Not even Moses has been called a prophet yet! Other members of her guild include Deborah (Judg. 4:4), Huldah (2 Kings 22:14), Isaiah's wife (Isa. 8:3), and Noadiah (Neh. 6:14). In the NT only Anna is called prophetess (Luke 2:36), apart from Jezebel's calling herself "a prophetess" in Rev. 2:20. Additionally, there are several verses referring to women as prophesying (Acts 2:17; 21:9; 1 Cor. 11:5). Of all these women, Miriam is most like Deborah. Both are called "prophetess," both have a reputation for writing poetry and singing, and both are involved in life-and-death situations from which they and their people are delivered by God's grace. We might call Miriam "the Torah's Fanny Crosby."

Miriam is also identified as "the sister of Aaron" (like other women in Scripture who are called the sister of an older brother, such as Dinah and Simeon and Levi [Gen. 34], or Tamar and Absalom [2 Sam. 13]). If "prophetess" emphasizes her prophetic role, then "brother of Aaron" hints at her priestly role, something unusual when one recalls that in the OT "women" and "priesthood" are mutually exclusive.

I can think of one more reason why Miriam's song comes where it is. There is no agreement on what her name means, although it is the same as "Mary" in the NT. Her name in Hebrew is *miryām*. Is it not interesting that the second part of her name, *-yām*, might recall the deliverance at the *yām-sûp*? And the first part of her name, *mir-*, has a sonant parallelism with the incident immediately following (vv. 25–26), which takes place at Marah. Both "*Miryām*" and "*Mārâ*" are feminine. Note 15:23, "He called *her* name Marah." Hebrew proper nouns ending in *-â* are feminine, such as Rebek*ah*, Le*ah*, Zippor*ah*. (Jon*ah* means "dove," but in the Bible the dove is a female bird. Noah sends "her" out from the ark and "she" returns. That raises the question of why any parents would name their son after a female bird! No*ah* is not an illustration since the *h* at the end of his name is the hard/fricative, *ḥ* [*ḥêt*], not the soft/aspirated *h* [*hê*]). So we move in Exod. 15 from Miryam's praise to Marah's petulance.

PART 3

Testing Time in the Wilderness

(15:22–18:27)

Part 2 of Exodus ends with Israel's singing about the Lord's victory over Pharaoh and his chariots at the sea (15:1–21). It may not be terribly challenging to express oneself tunefully when one observes such powerful acts of God, especially when the choristers are the beneficiaries of those mighty acts. In showing judgment on Egypt, the Lord shows mercy on Israel.

But here is the question as we move into part 3 of Exodus (15:22–18:27): will or can that song continue when the God who triumphs over others becomes the God who tests his people? For the first time in Exodus, and only the second time since Gen. 22:1, does God "test" anybody (Exod. 15:25b; 16:4b; see also 20:20; Deut. 8:2, 16; 13:3). Can the God who has prevented the Egyptians from living by drowning them prevent the Israelites from dying by providing sufficient beverage and food for their survival in an otherwise barren, forbidding wilderness?

To complain about the lack of drinkable water or a morsel of bread or meat in such unforgiving and inhospitable surroundings is not to quibble about nonnecessities or luxuries. Israel finds itself in another life-and-death situation. This time the threat is not from the Egyptian behemoth, but from potential life-sapping thirst and starvation, to say nothing of roving bands of desert robbers who would find vulnerable Israelites and anything they had with them an easy "take" (18:8–16).

In such circumstances, can the God who has pulverized the Egyptians be trusted to be a God capable of providing for the basic survival needs of the Hebrews and protecting them from assault? In some ways following where God wants to take his people can be more challenging and fraught with danger and risk than staying in Egypt. The Hebrews say so themselves to Moses as early as 14:11–12 and again in this part in 16:3.

Thrice in these wilderness chapters Israel is said to have "grumbled" (NIV) against Moses (and Aaron): 15:24; 16:2; 17:3. Yet the text never reports that they grumble directly against the Lord.

God answers prayers. Does he answer grumblings too? Is there such a thing as an (acceptable) grumbling prayer? The Hebrews grumble. Moses cries out to God. The Lord sends drinkable water (15:22–26; 15:27; 17:1–7) and food (16:1–36). Does he send these necessities because of the grumbling, or in spite of the grumbling, or because Moses cries out to him? Or because he is the kind of God who never half redeems anybody, releasing them from one kind of bondage only to allow them to wallow in another kind of bondage? He is the kind of God who, once having started a good work in people, will bring it to completion by whatever means necessary.

Friends may come from unexpected places. For every hostile Amalekite that comes across one's path (17:8–16), God will send a discerning and helpful Midianite into one's life (18:1–27). After all the trials that beleaguered Moses has experienced in 15:22–17:16, what more refreshing and pastoral thing could happen to him than a visit from his wise father-in-law, Jethro, a priest of Midian? No grumbling here. Aaron and Hur help a weary Moses by holding up his hands (17:11–12). Jethro helps a weary Moses by offering him counsel on how best to function as judge and bring qualified others into the judicial process, rather than Moses trying to be a lone ranger. Thankfully, Moses is not only a great speaker, his own reservations notwithstanding, but also a great listener. Sometimes two ears are better than one tongue.

Brackish Water, Sweet Water, Much Water

(15:22–27)

Translation

[22]Moses had Israel journey from the Red Sea, and they went out to the wilderness of Shur. They went three days in the wilderness and did not find water. [23]And they came to Marah, but were not able to drink water from Marah because they were bitter. Therefore, he called her name Marah. [24]The people protested against Moses, saying, "What shall we drink?" [25]He cried out to the LORD, and the LORD pointed out to him a stick, and he flung it into the water, and the water turned sweet.

There he set for him a statute and an ordinance, and there he tested him. [26]And he said, "If you indeed hear the LORD your God's voice, and what is right in his eyes do, and give ear to his commands, and keep all his statutes, all the sicknesses that I set upon Egypt I will not set upon you, for I am the LORD your healer."

[27]And they came to Elim, and there, twelve springs of water and seventy date palms, and they encamped there by the water.

Grammatical and Lexical Notes

15:22. The verb *nāsaʿ*, "journey," is common in the sections of Exodus and Numbers that detail Israel's wilderness wanderings, but this is the only one that uses the Hiphil ("had [Israel] journey") of that verb.

15:24. The verb *lûn* II ("protest, rail against, murmur") occurs both in the Niphal and Hiphil stems. For many of these references we have the Qere reading *yālinû* (Hiphil), "cause [the community] to mutter against," and the Ketib spelling *yillōnû* (Niphal), "muttered against." The difference between *lûn* II in the Niphal and Hiphil is that the Niphal is used to connote the actual grievance, while the Hiphil is used to describe the instigation of opposition on the part of others (e.g., Num. 14:36). Note that the verb here is plural (*wayyillōnû*) while the subject is singular (or collective? "the people," *hāʿām*). Most ancient versions (LXX, Vulg., SP) change the verb to a singular (as for *wayyālen*).

15:24. For *mah* ("*What* shall we drink?") with a negative meaning, in addition to this verse see 1 Kings 12:16 ("*What* share do we have in David, *what* part in Jesse's son?").

15:25. "Cried out" (*yiṣʿaq*) is a term used for Moses's intercessions in crisis situations (Exod. 17:4; Num. 12:13).

15:25. The MT reads "pointed out to him" (*wayyôrēhû*) as the Hiphil of *yārâ*, but LXX (*deichnymi*) and SP read *wayyarʾēhû*, the Hiphil of *rāʾâ*. The use of *yārâ* accomplishes two things. First, its use here in the Hiphil recalls its use in the Qal in 15:4 (God's shooting/throwing Pharaoh and his retinue into the sea). Second, if there is any possible connection between the sweetness of the water and the sweetness of God's ordinances (Ps. 19:10)—see the study of B. Robinson (1987)—then using the verb *yārâ*, from which one derives the noun *tôrâ*, is part and parcel of the writer's literary and theological artistry.

15:25. *ʿĒṣ* normally means "tree," but "stick, twig" is the meaning in some passages (Ezek. 37:16, 19).

15:25. For another reference where "sweet[ness]" (*m-t-q*) and "water" are connected, see Prov. 9:17a ("Stolen water is sweet"). The opposite of "sweet water" is "bitter water" in Num. 5:18, 24 (*mê hammārîm*).

15:25. English "There he set [for him]" misses the similarity in sound of the first two Hebrew words, *šām śām*. We can add to the use of *š/ś-m* words in this section. To "there" (*šām*) and "he set" (*śîm/śûm*), add "he called her *name*" (*šēm*) in v. 23, and "hear" (*šāmôaʿ a šāmaʿ*) in v. 26, and "keep" (*šāmar*) in v. 26. And *š/ś-m* is reversed into *m-š* in "Moses" (*Mōše[h]*) and "ordinance" (*mišpāṭ*) in v. 25.

15:25. In two verses (25–26) the verb *śîm/śûm* ("set, put, place") occurs three times, and each time it is followed by a different preposition: (1) v. 25, "he set for him" (*śîm lĕ*); (2) v. 26, "which I set upon Egypt" (*śîm bĕ*); (3) v. 26, "I will not set upon you" (*śîm ʿal*). I fail to see any significance in the choice of preposition.

15:26. The parallel pair "hear = give ear" (*šmʿ = ʾzn*) appears over twenty times in Hebrew poetry, but only twice in prose (here, and Deut. 1:45). See references in Globe 1974: 506–7n30.

15:26. In the long protasis of this verse are first of all two imperfects (*tišmaʿ* ["hear"] and *taʿăśeh* ["do"]), followed by two *wĕqāṭal* forms: *wĕhaʾăzantā* ("give ear to") and *wĕšāmartā* ("and keep"). On this shift, see Rainey 2003: 27–28.

15:27. Note the large empty space in the MT between the last word of v. 26 and the first word of v. 27. This indicates that the Masoretes believed that v. 27 goes with the start of the incident in chap. 16 rather than with the incident in 15:22–26.

15:27. The spelling of "Elim" (*ʾêlim*) is almost the same as "gods" in the phrase in 15:11, "Who among the gods [*baʾēlim*] is like you?" For another similarity in sound illustration, compare the word for "sickness" in 15:26 (*maḥălâ*) with the word for "dances" (*mĕḥōlōt*) in 15:20.

Commentary

15:22–26 Sometimes a person happily finds what one is not looking for, and we call that a serendipity. Sometimes a person unfortunately finds what one is not looking for, and we call that trouble and angst (Exod. 17:8–16). And sometimes, as in Exod. 15:22, a person does not find what one is looking for, and we call that disappointment bordering on hopelessness.

A three-day trek through an arid wilderness has turned up no water (also see Num. 33:8). As Talmon (1992: 188) has shown, "three days" or "the third day" is a common literary convention in the OT. As here, it suggests a survivable period of deprivation (1 Sam. 30:12; Jon. 1:17 [2:1]; 3:3; Acts 9:9). A journey of three days is common (Gen. 22:4; 30:36; 31:22; Exod. 3:18; 5:3; 8:27 [23]; Num. 10:33; 33:8). Three days, or the third day, may represent a period of purification (Exod. 19:10–11, 15–16), or the time of preparation for some important event (Josh. 1:11; Judg. 20:30; Esther 5:1; Ezra 8:15, 32). It also designates the time for recuperation after illness (Gen. 34:25; 1 Kings 3:18; 2 Kings 20:5, 8; Hosea 6:2), or the time to abandon a fruitless search (Josh. 2:16; 1 Sam. 9:20; 2 Kings 2:17).

Of all these references "to three days" or "the third day," the one closest to Exod. 15:22 is Num. 10:33. These two verses show that Israel's initial stage of journey *to* Sinai and *from* Sinai began with a three-day march. On both occasions that three-day march ends in a period of Israel's "muttering" (*lûn*) about something (Exod. 15:24; Num. 11:1). But here is the big difference. In Exod. 15 Israel's muttering is not punished, nor are they even reprimanded for their attitude. In Num. 11, by contrast, the people are reprimanded and punished (Num. 11:1, 10).

Why the difference? Is not muttering still muttering wherever it surfaces? Are not attitude sins still sins wherever they are expressed? Why does God ignore the ingrates in Exod. 15 but make them accountable in Num. 11? There are two possible answers, and perhaps both are on target. First, one might suggest that the people's complaint in Exod. 15 is legitimate. After all, having no water to drink anywhere, but especially in a wilderness, is a life-and-death crisis. One does not last long without water. A person can survive without oxygen for only a few moments, without water for only a few days, without food for only a few weeks. By contrast, the complaining in Num. 11 is about an imaginary need, not a real need. Numbers 11:1 says the people "complained about their hardships," but never states the basis for the complaining. What hardships? If it is a lack of water again (and it could be), Num. 11 does not specify that.

There is another possible answer for no divine response versus divine response. Exodus 15 is a precovenant sin (the people have yet to reach Sinai and enter into Yahweh's covenant with them). Numbers 11 is a postcovenant sin (Sinai is behind them). One could argue that precovenant sins carry less consequence than postcovenant sins. For example, fornication (i.e., sex *before* a marriage covenant is formed) is handled either by a marriage or a fine paid to the girl's father. Adultery (i.e., sex *after* a marriage covenant is formed) leads to stoning. This difference might explain why the "sins of the saints" are graver than the "sins of the sinners."

This is the first of several stops in Israel's wilderness wanderings where a place is named for certain extenuating circumstances. There are basically two different formulas that report and describe the conferment of a name and a rationale for it. One form is "And X called the name of Y so-and-so, for X said," and then follows the explanation for the name. An illustration of this pattern in Exodus is at 2:22, "And Moses named him Gershom, saying 'I have been an alien in a foreign land.'" The second formula, by contrast, is one that is introduced by "Therefore/that is why" (*ʿal-kēn*) he called its name/the name of that place so-and-so.

Long (1968: 6, 12) cites the etymology in Exod. 15:23 as the simplest form of the second pattern. He adds to Exod. 15:23: (1) Gen. 33:17 ("Jacob, however, went to Succoth, where he built a place for himself and made shelter for his livestock. *That is why* the place is called Succoth"), and (2) 2 Chron 20:26 ("On the fourth day they assembled in the Valley of Beracah, where they praised the Lord. *This is why* it is called the Valley of Beracah to this day"). In all three references (1) the locale is mentioned; (2) there is the report of a situation or event at this locale; (3) a name reflecting that situation or event is given to that place, which is introduced by *ʿal-kēn qārāʾ* ("Therefore/this is why he called . . .").

There are several miracle stories in the OT that involve someone's throwing something into something (see Culley 1976: 72–96). Second Kings 2:19–22 records the story of Elisha throwing salt (2:21) into the bad water, which then becomes good to drink. Second, 2 Kings 4:38–41 records Elisha making the poison stew edible by throwing (NIV has "put" in 4:41) meal/flour into the pot. Third, 2 Kings 6:1–7 is the famous story about the floating axhead, which happened after Elisha threw a stick (6:6) into the Jordan. This last story seems to be the closest to Exod. 15. In both incidents Moses/Elisha throws a stick (with *ʿēṣ* meaning "stick/branch/twig" in Exod. 15:24 and 2 Kings 6:6 rather than "tree") into a body of water. The one difference between the two stories, perhaps significant or insignificant, is that the Lord first points out the stick to Moses. Not so with Elisha. He just scoops up the nearest suitable branch lying on the ground and tosses it. Moses's throwing (*šālak*) something into a body of water comes on the heels of the Lord's throwing (*rāmâ*) something into a body of water (15:1). One throwing means survival. The other throwing means death.

Verse 25b calls this episode a time of testing for the Israelites ("And there he tested him"). The Hebrew verb is *nissâ*, one of three verbs for "testing." The other two are *bāḥan* and *ṣārap*. All three occur in Ps. 26:2, "Test me [*bāḥan*], O Lord, and try me [*nissâ*], examine [*ṣārap*] my heart and my mind," with the parallelism suggesting that there is probably not a significant difference between the three. The term *nissâ* is the one most commonly used. The object of divine testing (with *nissâ*) may be people (Exod. 15:25; 16:4; 20:20; Deut. 8:2, 16; 13:3 [4]; Judg. 2:22; 3:1, 4) or individuals (Gen. 22:1, Abraham; Ps. 26:2, David; 2 Chron. 32:31, Hezekiah). And sometimes it is Israel who tests the Lord (Exod. 17:2, 7; Num. 14:22; Deut. 6:16; Ps. 95:9). For all the OT references to God's testing somebody, there is only one place (maybe) in the NT where God appears as one who tests. This is in the (puzzling?) line of the Lord's Prayer in Matt. 6:13 (= Luke 11:4): "Lead us not into temptation," which may be rendered, "Do not put us to the test." Otherwise, it is the devil who tests/tempts.

On this particular occasion God's testing of his people has to do with a "statute and an ordinance" he set for them. Normally, especially in Deuteronomy, this phrase is in the plural ("statutes and ordinances"). The singular form, with the verb *śîm*, as here, appears in Josh. 24:25 (although curiously NIV renders with plurals, "decrees and laws"), and in 1 Sam. 30:25 with David. One might suggest that since Israel has not yet reached Sinai where the people will receive "the statutes and ordinances" that go with the covenant, the singular expression is used here to make that distinction. For now, it is about *ḥōq ûmišpāṭ*. Later it will be about *ḥuqqîm ûmišpāṭim*. To be sure, no specific "statute" or "ordinance" is spelled out. But the mention of such realities at this stage in Israel's march indicates that for Israel obedience does not begin as an expectation at Sinai. God's people are not free to live their lives any way they want before Sinai, and then justify it by claiming that God has not yet laid out any guidelines for their behavior. It could well be that what the "statute and ordinance" of v. 25a refers to is found in the language of v. 26: "Hear. . . . Do what is right. . . . Give ear. . . . Keep." The shift to the plurals in v. 26 ("commands, statutes") clearly has a proleptic, anticipatory look toward Sinai, and sounds very Deuteronomy-like. Verse 26 may be spoken by Moses ("And he said . . ."), for the references to the Lord are in the third person (e.g., "do what is right in *his* eyes," rather than "do what is right in *my* eyes"), but by the end of the verse, with the change to the first person, it is clear that the Lord is the speaker. Perhaps it is intentional that the identity of the speaker is blurred, with the Lord's voice intermingling with that of Moses.

Here God makes the unique promise that the people's obedience will save and spare them from "all the sicknesses that I set upon Egypt." The promise is somewhat like what God makes in Exod. 23:25: "Worship the LORD your God, and his blessing will be on your food and water. I will take away *sickness* from among you." The same promise appears again in Deut. 7:12–15: "If you pay attention to these laws, . . . the LORD will keep you free from every *disease*. He will not inflict on you the horrible *diseases* you knew in Egypt." The polar opposite of this promise is the one in Deut. 28:21, and this for disobedience: "The LORD will plague you with *diseases*"; and in Deut. 28:60–61: "He will bring upon you all the *diseases* of Egypt. . . . The LORD will also bring upon you every kind of *sickness*."

To what might "the sicknesses that I set upon Egypt" refer? Possibly characteristic Egyptian sicknesses like dysentery or elephantiasis. More likely the reference is to the plagues of chaps. 7–12, although the word "sickness" is never used to describe any of them. If this is correct, the plagues in Egypt begin with nobody being "able to drink the water" (Exod. 7:18, 21, 24). Similarly, Israel's journey Canaan-ward begins with nobody "able to drink the water." Egypt's water got a staff (Exod. 7:17). Israel's water got a stick.

The promise of v. 26 concludes with "For I am the LORD your healer." It is fair to say that secular medicine was virtually nonexistent in the biblical era, probably because healing was considered to be an act of God. For that reason the verb *rāpā'* ("heal") mostly has God as its subject, or the healing act is explicitly ascribed to him (Deut. 32:39; 2 Kings 20:8; Isa. 19:22; 57:18; Jer. 30:17; 33:6; etc.). God's agent in healing can be the priest (Lev. 13), or the prophet (1 Kings 17:17–24; 2 Kings 5:13–14). Prayer by a prophet may assist in the healing (Gen. 20:7, 17; Num. 12:10–13; 1 Kings 13:4–6), as may the sick person's own prayer (2 Kings 20:2–5; Ps. 6:2 [3]; Jer. 17:14). When the Hebrew

Bible uses the participial form *rōpēʾ*, as here, either in the singular or plural form for human healers/physicians, the reference is to foreigners (Gen. 50:2; 2 Chron. 16:12; Job 13:4; Jer. 8:22), and except for Gen. 50:2 such physicians are spoken of negatively. See especially what is said in 2 Chron. 16:12 about Asa turning to (non-Israelite?) physicians rather than to God.

This is not to say that the Yahweh of the OT is some kind of Israelite Asclepius, a professional healing god (most of whom would be second- or third-tier deities in pagan pantheons). Nor, at least in Exod. 15:26, is the Lord portrayed as the healer of individual persons. Rather, he is the physician of Israel (see Lohfink 1994: 71). It is healing to the nation that "Doctor Yahweh" desires to bring. It is the prevention of sickness that he wills for his people in 15:26. Thus the famous 2 Chron. 7:14 ends climactically by promising God's healing the land. And the sound medical advice that heaven's Physician is giving his people/patients in Exod. 15 is how to avoid behavior that will inevitably result in multiple forms of sickness.

15:27 There is no mention of the Israelites leaving Marah, such as we find many other times. Marah is the kind of place you get into and out of as quickly as possible. Also v. 27 indicates that Elim is the first place at which the Israelites camp after crossing the sea. Numbers 33, which lists all the stages of Israel's journey, mentions, by contrast, Israel camping at Marah (v. 8), and then leaving Marah for Elim (v. 9). But "left" and "camped in/by/at" in Num. 33 may be formulaic since every verse or two reads, "They left place A and camped at place B. They left place B and camped at place C."

Elim is as different from Marah as day is from night. Talk about going from the bitter to the better! No need for God to test his people at Elim. Bitter waters are no more, for now there are twelve springs of fresh water at this oasis, to say nothing of the seventy date palms. *Targum Pseudo-Jonathan* expands v. 27 by reading, "In Elim there were twelve fountains of water for the twelve tribes, and seventy palm trees corresponding to the seventy sages." The exact location of Elim is uncertain, but one proposal is the modern Uyun-Musa ("Springs of Moses"), a large oasis just south of Suez.

Often, after the trials and test of a Marah, God has an Elim prepared for his people. However, neither all Marahs nor all Elims are helpful to God's people. Dealing with nothing but Marah day after day would suck the life out of us. Dealing with nothing but Elim day after day would soften us and never stretch us. A healthy combination is, on the one hand, having our backs against the wall and learning to trust God, and on the other hand, those days when we feel we are "living on the mountain, underneath a cloudless sky," to quote an old Gospel song ("Dwelling in Beulah Land," by C. Austin Miles).

Manna from Heaven

(16:1–36)

Translation

[1]And they journeyed from Elim, and the entire congregation of Israel's sons came to the wilderness of Sin that is between Elim and Sinai on the fifteenth day of the second month of their going out from the land of Egypt. [2]The entire congregation of Israel's sons murmured against Moses and against Aaron in the wilderness. [3]Israel's sons said to them, "Would that we had died by the LORD's hand in the land of Egypt, when we sat by fleshpots, when we ate our fill of bread, for you have brought us to this wilderness to put to death this entire assembly by famine."

[4]And the LORD said to Moses, "I am about to rain upon (all of) you bread from heaven, and the people will go out and gather a day's supply on each day, so that I may test them whether they will walk in my teaching or not. [5]And it shall happen on Friday, when they shall consider what they are to bring in, it shall be the identical amount additional to what they gather each day." [6]And Moses, along with Aaron, said to all Israel's sons, "At evening time you shall know that the LORD brought you from the land of Egypt. [7]And at morning time you shall see the LORD's glory as he hears your murmurings against the LORD. As for us, what (are we) that you murmur against us?" [8]And Moses said, "When the LORD gives you in the evening meat to eat and your fill of bread in the morning, when the LORD hears your murmurings that you are murmuring against him—and what are we?—not against us (are) your murmurings; rather, (they are) against the LORD."

[9]And Moses said to Aaron, "Say to all the congregation of Israel's sons, 'Draw near to the LORD's presence, for he has heard your murmuring.'" [10]And it happened as Aaron was speaking to the entire congregation of Israel's sons, that they turned to the wilderness, and what but the LORD's glory appeared in a cloud. [11]And the LORD said to Moses, saying, [12]"I have heard the murmurings of Israel's sons. Speak to them, saying, 'At twilight you shall eat meat, and in the morning you shall have your fill of bread, and you shall know that I (am) the LORD your God.'"

[13]And it happened in the evening that the quail came up and covered the camp, and in the morning there was a falling of dew around the camp. [14]And the falling of dew disappeared, and there, on the face of the wilderness—small thin stuff, flaky, thin as frost on the ground. [15]And Israel's sons saw, and they said, each to his brother, "*Man huʾ?* What [is] it?" For they did not know what it was. And Moses said to them, "It is the bread that the LORD has given you as food. [16]This is the matter about which the LORD has commanded: 'Gather from it each person according to what he can eat, an omer to the head, the number of persons among you, each man for those in his tent you shall take.'" [17]And Israel's sons did so, and they gathered, more or less. [18]They measured by the omer. The one with more had no surplus, and the one with less did not lack. Each according to what he can eat they gathered. [19]And Moses said to them, "Let nobody leave any of it over until morning." [20]But they did not listen to Moses, and some men left over part of it until morning, and it bred worms and stank. And Moses was angry with them. [21]And they gathered it every morning, each man according to what he can eat. And when the sun blazed, it melted.

[22]And it happened on Friday they gath-

ered bread, the equivalent of two omers apiece, and all the spokesmen for the congregation came and told Moses. [23]And he said to them, "This [is] what the LORD has spoken: a complete rest, a holy Sabbath to the Lord [is] tomorrow. What you bake, bake, and what you cook, cook, and any surplus leave for yourselves for safekeeping until the morning." [24]And they left it until the morning, as Moses had commanded. It did not stink, and not a worm was in it. [25]And Moses said, "Eat it today, because a Sabbath (is) today to the LORD. Today you will not find it in the field. [26]Six days you shall gather it, but on the seventh day, a Sabbath, there will be none then."

[27]And it happened on the seventh day [that] some of the people went out to gather, but they came up empty. [28]And the LORD said to Moses, "How long are you refusing to keep my commandments and my teachings? [29]See, for the LORD has given you the Sabbath. Therefore he is giving you on Friday bread for two days. Sit each in his place, let no one go out from his home on the seventh day." [30]And the people rested on the seventh day.

[31]The house of Israel called its name Man(na). It was like coriander seed, white, and its taste like a wafer in honey. [32]And Moses said, "This is the matter about which the LORD commanded. A full omer of it is for safekeeping for your generations, so that they can see the bread with which I fed you in the wilderness when I brought you out of the land of Egypt." [33]And Moses said to Aaron, "Take a jar, and place in it a full omer of man(na), and set it before the LORD for safekeeping for your generations." [34]Just as the LORD commanded Moses, Aaron placed it before the Covenant for safekeeping. [35]And Israel's sons ate the man(na) forty years until they came to populated land. The man(na) they ate until they came to the edge of Canaan land. [36]As for an omer, one-tenth of an ephah it [is].

Grammatical and Lexical Notes

16:1. The Israelites may indeed have sinned in the wilderness of Sin, but that is not the reason for the name "Sin." Rather, the wilderness of *Sin* is a part of the *Sinai* area.

16:3. The Hebrew "Would that . . ." is *mî-yittēn*. It is often used in the Hebrew Bible (some twenty-five times) to express a wish contrary to fact. Some examples are Num. 11:29, "I wish that all the LORD's people were prophets [but they are not]"; Ps. 14:7, "Oh, that salvation for Israel would come out of Zion!"; Jer. 9:1 [8:23], "Oh, that my head were a spring of water and my eyes a fountain of tears!" The expression is common in Job: 13:5, "If only you would be altogether silent!"; 14:4, "Who can bring what is pure from the impure?"; 14:13, "If only you would hide me in the grave"; 19:23, "Oh, that my words were recorded, that they were written on a scroll"; 23:3, "If only I knew where to find him." In all the above verses, the Hebrew uses *mî-yittēn* to express "would that" or "I wish that" or "Oh, that" or "If only." R. Williams (1976: 91–92 §547) calls these "desiderative clauses."

16:3. If "died" were a noun, it would be written *môtēnū*. Hence, *mûtēnû* must be infinitive construct with pronominal suffix. See Orlinsky 1947: 123.

16:3. For *ʾākal lāśōbaʿ* ("eat one's fill"), see Lev. 25:19 ("You will eat your fill"); Lev. 26:5 ("Eat all the food you want"); Lev. 26:26 ("You will eat, but you will not be satisfied"); Prov. 13:25 ("The righteous eat to their heart's content"). The cognate word occurs in royal inscriptions that speak of the generosity of kings who provide for the needs of their citizens. See Ginsberg 1973: 138.

16:3. The Hiphil plural of *yāṣāʾ* ("you have brought us"), addressed to Moses and Aaron in an accusatory way by the people, has a parallel with the Hiphil plural of *ʿālâ* ("made us leave"), addressed to Moses and Aaron, also in an accusatory way, in Num. 20:5.

16:3. Verse 2 spoke of the "entire congregation (*ʿēdâ*) of Israel," while this verse speaks of the "entire assembly [*qāhāl*] of Israel." The two sometimes occur together, as in Lev. 4:13 ("congregation . . . assembly," although NIV uses "community" for both words). Or again, Num. 16:3, where this time NIV uses "community" for *ʿēdâ* and "assembly" for *qāhāl*. I discern no important difference between the two nouns.

16:4. Note that the first verb used with the (singular) subject "the people" (*hāʿām*) is the singular *wĕyāṣāʾ* ("go out"), while the second verb with this subject is plural, *wĕlāqĕṭû* ("and gather").

16:4. "A day's supply on each day" is my rendering of *dĕbar-yôm bĕyômô* ("the word/thing/matter of a day in its day"). The phrase has already appeared in Exod. 5:13 and 19. See also 1 Kings 8:59, "according to each day's need"; 2 Kings 25:30 (= Jer. 52:34), "Day by day the king gave"; Neh. 11:23, "in their daily activity." The phrase seems to be an administrative formula that was originally used in delineating the disbursement of food and other materials.

16:5. "Friday" is, literally, "the sixth day," *bayyôm haššiššî.*

16:5. I have translated the Hiphil of *kûn* (*wĕhēkînû*) as "consider" rather than as "prepare" (with which meaning the preposition *lĕ* often follows the verb), for the basic nuance of this verb in the Hiphil stem is "arrange/provide for a future state or event physically or *mentally*."

16:5. My translation of *mišneh* as "identical amount" departs from the more standard "twice as much." Rendering *mišneh ʿal* as "the identical amount additional to" at least includes the preposition *ʿal*, whereas translations like "twice as much (as)" ignore the preposition. See Tsevat 1994: 590–91.

16:6. Both "you shall know" in v. 6 and "you shall see" in v. 7 start with a *wāw* ("and"): *wiydaʿtem* and *ûrĕʾîtem*. Both illustrate the *wāw* consecutive with plural verb after an indication of time. See Waltke and O'Connor (1990: 538), who speak of such a construction as "the dependent notion of (con) sequence subordinated to adverbial expressions of time." Gordis (1976a: 54n51; see also BDB 254b) cites this as the use of the *wāw* to introduce the conclusion after a preliminary phrase. Another example of the same is Gen. 3:5, "For God knows that when you eat of it your eyes will be opened [*wĕnipqĕḥû ʿênêkem*]."

16:7. *Bōker* at the beginning of the verse (*ûbōker*), "at morning time," represents the adverbial use of *bōker* and is indistinguishable in use from *babbōker* ("in the morning") in v. 8.

16:7. *Naḥnû* ("as for *us*"), here and in v. 8, is the rarer form of the first-person common plural pronoun. It appears three more times in the Hebrew Bible in direct discourse (Gen. 42:11; Num. 32:32; 2 Sam. 17:12), and once in poetry (Lam. 3:42, probably to keep three *n-* words at the start of vv. 40, 41, 42 in the acrostic poem).

16:8. The Lord brings bread to his people in the morning and meat in the evening (the traditional time of the heavier meal). By contrast, the Lord brings Elijah meat and bread both in the morning and the evening (1 Kings 17:6). The LXX, perhaps influenced by Exod. 16:8, has the Lord bringing Elijah only bread in the morning and only meat in the evening.

16:8. "Not against us [*lōʾ-ʿālênû*], . . . rather [*kî*], they are against the Lord" shows that only after a negative may *kî* mean "rather." Compare Gen. 17:15 AT, "As for Sarai your wife, you shall not call her name Sarai; rather [*kî*], her name shall be Sarah"; 1 Sam. 6:3, "If you return the ark of the god of Israel, do not send it away empty; rather [*kî*; NIV, "but by all means"] send a guilt offering to him." See Gordis 1949: 191n6.

16:8. For other expressions of dialectic negation that use the pattern "Not A, but B," see Gen. 45:8, "It was not you who sent me here, but God"; and 1 Sam. 8:7, "it is not you they have rejected, but they have rejected me as their king."

16:9. The verb "draw near to" (*qārab*, as here, or *nāgaš*) often appears in a context of litigation in which the plaintiff approaches the judge, or both approach each other (Abraham to the Lord, Gen. 18:23; Judah to Joseph, Gen. 44:18; the Israelites before the Lord, here in Exod. 16:9; the disputants to Aaron and Hur, Exod. 24:14c; Zelophehad's daughters to Moses, Num. 27:1; the heads of the clans of Gilead to Moses, Num. 36:1; men in a dispute take their case to a judge, Deut. 25:1; the nations to the place of judgment, Isa. 41:1, 21). See Falk 1960: 353. "To draw near to the LORD's presence" mostly likely means to head in the direction of the cloud.

16:9. When one approaches another person, *qārab* is usually followed by the preposition *ʾel*. But when one approaches the Lord, the following preposition is normally *lipnê* as in Exod. 16:9. That is to say, there is not direct contact with divinity, but only proximity, an entering into his presence. Thus Leviticus and Numbers repeatedly say that one is to present (Hiphil of *qārab*) his offering "before" (*lipnê*) the LORD (e.g., Lev. 3:1, 7; 6:14 [7]; 10:1; Num. 3:4; 6:16). The distinction is not always maintained. See 1 Sam. 14:36d, "Let us inquire of God here [*qārab* + *ʾel*]"; and Ezek. 44:15, in which the Lord speaks of the Levitical priests who are to "come near [*qārab* + *ʾel*] to minister before me." See Milgrom 1991: 1012.

16:13. "Quail" (*śĕlāw*) never appears in the Hebrew Bible in a singular form (although the verbs used with the noun here, "came up" [*wattaʿal*] and "covered" [*wattĕkas*], are singular). Numbers 11:32 and Ps. 105:40 use the same form as Exod. 16:13, but Num. 11:31 treats it as a masculine plural with the form *śalwîm*. Rendsburg (1999: 30–31) believes the word, as we have it in Exod. 16:13, to be the plural of a segholate noun of the *mĕlak* type, a plural that could be either internal or external. Quail are pure birds and therefore edible.

16:13. One might translate *šikbat haṭṭal* "a layer of dew" (Barr 1968: 137n2), but I prefer to go with "a falling of dew" because of its similarity to the phrase *šikbat-zeraʿ* (lit., "a falling/outpouring of seed"). The latter is the biblical term for "semen" (Lev. 15:16, 17, 18, 32). The word *šĕkābâ* means "discharge, ejaculation, fall."

16:14. For *ʿālâ* meaning not only "ascend, lift up," but also "disappear," see Gen. 17:22 ("went up from him" = "disappeared from his sight"), and the same expression in Gen. 35:13. The Aramaic verb *sĕlēq* also means both "ascend" and "disappear."

16:14. The Hebrew word for "thin," appearing here twice, is *daq*. It is generally used in Scripture to refer to something thin (lit., "crushed") that can be felt or touched or seen, like Pharaoh's "thin/gaunt" cows (Gen. 41:3–4). The Akkadian cognate is *daqqu*, "small" (*CAD* D:107). In light of its references elsewhere, the use of *daq* (in feminine form) in *qôl dĕmāmâ daqqâ*, the "gentle whisper" or "still small voice" that Elijah hears in the cave, is most interesting (1 Kings 19:12). How does the prophet hear a "thin voice"? Could the use of the adjective for the "thin" voice in the Kings passage be explained as an allusion to the "thin" manna of Exod. 16? After all, the Elijah stories in Kings talk of God's nurturing Elijah and providing him with food in the morning and in the evening, as he does here with the manna for his people.

16:15. This is the only place *mān* (in *mān hûʾ*) occurs in the Hebrew Bible for "What?" The usual word for "what?" is *mah*, as later in the verse we have, "They did not know what it was [*mah-hûʾ*]." The form of the word is archaic and may have a Ugaritic cognate. See *UT* §19:1504. The term *mān-hûʾ* is a folk or popular etymology for "manna." Ron (2010) documents how many Jewish exegetes from the Middle Ages explain *mān* by connecting it with some root that has to do with food or provisions and thus turn the people's question into a statement: 1 Sam.1:5, "But to Hannah he [Elkanah] gave a double portion [*mānâ*]"; Dan. 1:10, the words of the Babylonian official to Daniel, "I am afraid of my lord the king, who has assigned [*minnâ*] your food and drink"; Jon. 1:17 [2:1], "But the LORD provided [*wayĕman*] a great fish to swallow Jonah."

16:16. According to Labuschagne (1982b: 270–71), "This is the matter about which the LORD has commanded" occurs seven times in Exodus–Numbers and thus is one of several series of sevens in this corpus (Exod. 16:16, 32; Lev. 8:5; 9:6; 17:2; Num. 30:1 [2]; 36:6).

16:20. On the verb *bāʾaš* ("stink"), see the study of Ackroyd (1951) who distinguishes between *bāʾaš* I ("stink") and *bāʾaš* II ("be ashamed"). It occurs here in v. 20 in the Qal, and in the Hiphil in v. 24. It has already appeared in Exod. 7:18, 21 and 8:14 [10] for the stench brought by the bloodied waters and fish kill, and the dead frogs, and earlier in Exod. 5:21, the stench that the Israelites are to Pharaoh, thanks to Moses, so his people think.

16:20. *Qāṣap ʿal* ("angry at") refers to human anger at other persons in Gen. 40:2 (Pharaoh at his two officials); Gen. 41:10 (Pharaoh at his servants); Lev. 10:16 (Moses at Eleazar and Ithamar); Num. 31:14 (Moses at the officers of the army); 1 Sam. 29:4 (the Philistine commanders at Achish); 2 Kings 13:19 (Elisha at the king); Jer. 37:15 (the people at Jeremiah).

16:21. "Every morning" is, literally, "in the morning, in the morning [*babbōker babbōker*]." On such repetition, see GKC §123c–d. Other examples are Gen. 39:10, "And although she spoke to Joseph day after day" (lit., "day day," *yôm yôm*); Exod. 36:4, "All the skilled craftsmen who were doing all the work on the sanctuary [everyone of them, *ʾîš-ʾîš*] left their work"; Deut. 14:22, "Be sure to set aside a tenth of all your fields produce each year [*šānâ šānâ*]."

16:22. The Hebrew word for "spokesman" is *nāśîʾ*, a word for which many translations, at least in some passages, use the word "prince." Compare, for example, the Hittites' words to Abraham, "You are a mighty *prince* among us" (Gen. 23:6; and for *nāśîʾ* here LXX uses *basileus*, "king"). The Hebrew word is a *qaṭil*-type noun. Other nouns similarly formed include *śākîr* ("hireling"), *ʾāsîr* ("prisoner"), *māšîaḥ* ("anointed one"), all with passive meaning, and *qāṣîr* ("harvester") with active meaning. The passive or active nuance of some *qaṭil* nouns is uncertain, especially *nābîʾ* ("prophet, a caller/one who is called"). Speiser's (1963a) study of this word remains the foundational examination of it, and he opts for "chieftain" when the text is talking about clans and tribes, and for "leader" when the focus is on larger units and states.

16:23. *Šabbātôn* ("a complete rest") often occurs in the expression "a Sabbath of Sabbaths," or "a Sabbath of complete rest" (*šabbat šabbātôn*). See Exod. 35:2; Lev. 16:31; 23:3; 25:4. It appears by itself here and in Lev. 23:24. The Hebrew word may be like other Hebrew words that end in *-ôn*, like *zikkārôn* ("memorial, remembrance") or *hērāyôn* ("pregnancy"), that is, words that carry an abstract sense, suggesting for *šabbātôn* something like "restfulness." See B. Levine 1989: 110.

16:23. *Šabbat-qōdeš* ("a holy Sabbath") is like *ʾadmat-qōdeš* ("holy ground") in Exod. 3:5. Both "ground" and "Sabbath" are feminine words, and since the adjective "holy" is never used attributively in the Hebrew Bible with any feminine noun, the Hebrew says "ground of holiness," or "Sabbath of holiness."

16:23. For "tomorrow" (*māḥār*) used as a substantive, rather than adverbially, where a solemn announcement is made of an imminent cultic observance, see Exod. 32:5 ("Tomorrow there will be a festival to the Lord"); 1 Sam. 20:5, 18 ("Look, tomorrow is the New Moon festival"). See De Vries 1975c: 5.

16:27. "Some of the people" is *min-hāʿām*, showing the partitive meaning of the preposition *min* (R. Williams 1976: 56 §324; Arnold and Choi 2003: 118).

16:29. "In his place" is *taḥtāyw*, referring to a static position. It appeared earlier, in 10:23, there with a prefixed *mem-*. See Arnold and Choi 2003: 126.

16:29. Dahood (1967: 431) provides references where *māqôm* ("place") means "home," such as Gen. 18:33; Amos 4:6; Mic. 1:3.

16:32. In "a full omer of it," the word "omer" has the article attached to it (*hāʿōmer*). Ehrensvärd (2000: 312) cites passages where the article is used with measurements. Examples are Exod. 26:2, "twenty-eight cubits [*bāʾammâ*] long and four cubits [*bāʾammâ*] wide," and Judg. 6:38, "a bowlful of water [*hassēpel māyim*]."

16:33. "Take a jar" is, in the Hebrew, "Take one pot." There are places where a noun is made expressly indeterminate by the addition of "one," as in "a (certain) man" (*ʾîš ʾeḥād*) of Judg. 13:2 and 1 Sam. 1:1; or "a (certain) woman" (*ʾiššâ ʾaḥat*) of Judg. 9:53.

16:35. Lemche (1991: 59–60) points out that Exod. 16:35 is one of two places (the other is Josh. 5:12) where the LXX translates "land of Canaan" as "land of the Phoenicians." Possibly this rendering reflects what the translators of the LXX conceptualized as "Canaan" in the third century BC.

16:36. Verse 36 is a nominal sentence, lacking a verb. Hoftijzer (1973: 490) suggests that "one-tenth" is placed before the pronoun *hu'*, rather than after the pronoun, to show that this is exactly the relation of the *omer* to the *ephah*. No more, no less.

Commentary

16:1 It is exactly one month since Israel has left Egypt (Num. 33:3, "The Israelites set out from Rameses on the fifteenth day of the first month"). The date now is the fifteenth day of the second month. A short while later (in about two weeks) the people will reach Mount Sinai (Exod. 19:1, "in the third month" or "on the third new moon," meaning the first of the month).

The Israelites spend the third week of this month gathering the manna. That leaves only one week of the second month left over, the fourth week, for all that happens in chaps. 17–18. That must be a hectic week! They have to travel to Rephidim (17:2); experience the miraculous supply of water from the rock (17:5–7); engage the Amalekites in successful battle (17:8–16); have enough time for Moses's father-in-law, Jethro, to travel from Midian to Rephidim and counsel his overworked son-in-law (18:1–27); and continue their wilderness journey from Rephidim to Mount Sinai.

16:2–3 The murmuring against Moses and Aaron is not isolated but massive. We have moved from "the people" murmuring (15:24) to the "entire congregation" murmuring. That is one of the unfortunate downsides of this kind of malaise. Once unleashed from isolated pockets, it spreads like wildfire, engulfing, consuming, and catching up everybody in its path. Nobody seems immune from it; no one challenges it or rises above it.

This is but one of three relapses into slave mentality on the part of recently freed Israel, a deep desire to be back in Egypt again (see 14:10–12 for the first instance, and 17:3 for the third instance). As Goldingay (2003: 455) remarks, "Only a few weeks' distance has given a rosy hue to their experience in the slave house." God wants to use this experience to orient his people to the future (v. 33 NIV, "generations to come"), but they are locked into their past. God wants his people to remember what can be. They only remember what it was like. The idea of security, but outside of the will of God, seems preferable to insecurity and uncertainty, but inside the will of God.

The Israelites' mind-set is not unlike that of criminals released from incarceration. Imprisonment, but with three meals a day and a place to lay one's head at night, seems more inviting than struggling with the challenges of liberty. Being told what to do and when to do it and how to do it may be easier than having to make one's own (responsible) decisions. In a strange way Egypt can become Eden. A ghetto can become a garden, or so it seems. Pharaoh can become a "nice guy," a life-giver, while Moses can become a villain, a life-taker.

The word "rain" has appeared frequently in the plagues unit as a noun (Exod. **16:4–5**
9:33, 34) and as a verb (9:18, 23). But there is a radical difference between the two rains in Exod. 9 and 16. The divine rain God sends in the seventh plague is a destructive rain, a rain of hail on the land of Egypt. However, the divine rain that God promises in chap. 16 (see Ps. 78:24, 27) to send is a beneficial, life-giving rain ("I am about to rain upon you bread from heaven"). If the exiles from Babylon can sing "Our God reigns" (Isa. 52:7), the escapees from Egypt can sing, "Our God rains."

God is no Ebenezer Scrooge when it comes to meeting the needs of his people. He is not miserly. He does not hoard. He does not dole out his blessings reluctantly in parsimonious pinches. The God who here says he will rain bread from heaven is the God who elsewhere promises to "pour out" his Holy Spirit (Acts 2:33; 10:45).

But what one does with those heavenly gifts is another matter. Like the warning on a label of a container with a prescribed medicine inside it, "To be used only according to directions," so God's blessings come with a similar qualification. Here the people are to gather only a day's supply of the bread (Exod. 16:4b), and even on Friday/the sixth day they are to gather the same amount as on the previous six days (v. 5), even though they cannot gather any on the seventh day. It is in observing these restrictions that the divine "test" ("so that I may test them") is found. Although the command is stated positively ("Go out and gather a day's supply"), one cannot miss the implied negative: "Do not gather two-day supply; especially do not double the amount on the sixth day." With few exceptions, God's word of permission is seldom separated from God's word of prohibition. Recall the "you may" and the "you must not" of Gen. 2–3.

Sometimes when God is said to test somebody, it is so that he may "know" (*yāda*ʿ) or "discover" something about the person he is testing (Gen. 22:1, 12; Deut. 8:2; 13:3 [4]; Judg. 3:4). Exodus 16:4 and Judg. 2:22 ("I will use them to test Israel and see whether they will keep the way of the Lord") do not use "know"/*yāda*ʿ, but the same nuance is accomplished by adding the interrogative particle *ha-* to a verb (*hăyēlēk*, "whether they will walk," in Exod. 16:4), or to a participle (*hăšōmĕrîm*, "and see whether they will keep," in Judg. 2:22).

Such texts as these have engendered much debate between open theists and classical theists on the matter of divine omniscience and foreknowledge. Does God know or not know whether his people will walk in his teaching? Is he in the dark about the people trying to gather manna on the seventh day, or does he already see that trespass on the radar? Does God both know that people will, in direct violation of Moses's specific command, leave some gathered manna over for the next day (vv. 19–20), but also know that they do not have to ignore that counsel?

I do not claim to be able to sort out all the theological issues here, and I see elements of great insight in both positions. There is, however, another dimension to these "testing in order to know/see" passages that I highlight. The clear purpose of all these "testing" passages is to underscore the importance to humanity of choices. There is no such thing as choices without consequences. But not only are humanity's choices important to humanity; they also are important to God. What one chooses to do when presented with alternatives matters to God. God is not a cold, passive, neutral experimenter. Such times of testing reveal God "as one who elects and enters into a covenant, in which the relationship thereby constituted is a real relationship which engages God as genuinely as it does Israel. The logic of God's 'need to know' is that of relationship and response" (Moberly 2000: 105).

16:6–8 Previously (v. 4), God has only promised that he will rain bread from heaven on the Israelites. He does not specify how or when, and he says nothing about meat. Without a further revelation from God, Moses now informs the people that the Lord will give his people meat in the evening and bread in the morning (v. 8). As a result, they will "know" in the evening something in a more profound way than ever before (v. 6), and they will "see" something in the morning more dazzling than ever before (v. 7). Recall all the references to Israel's "seeing" the display of divine power in chap. 14: vv. 13 [3x], 30, 31. The meat will point to a delivering Lord, while the bread will point to a glorious Lord.

What makes this specific speech of Moses so interesting is that it perfectly anticipates the information about meat in the evening and bread in the morning that the Lord makes to Moses later, in v. 12! Before God reveals it, Moses tells it, making then God's word to Moses in v. 12 not revelatory or informational, but confirmatory. Hence twice, in back-to-back chapters, Moses speaks prophetically about events yet to happen (15:13–17; 16:6–8), and both times he is right on, as subsequent events bear out.

According to v. 7 the Lord's glory (*kābôd*) is something one can "see." The Lord cannot be seen, but his glory can. The thought of the Lord's glory as a breathtaking and glorious visible manifestation of the divine is present elsewhere. In Numbers, the glory of the Lord "appears," usually in moments of crisis (Num. 14:10; 16:19; 16:42 [17:7]; 20:6). In these instances, the divine *kābôd* is represented by the cloud-encased fire that will later rest over the tabernacle.

In Exod. 24:17 the glory of the Lord "looked like a consuming fire." In Exod. 33:18 Moses asks God to "show" him his glory. In Ps. 19:1 David affirms that the heavens "declare" the glory of God. The prophet speaks of a day when "the glory of the LORD will be revealed, and all mankind together will *see* it" (Isa. 40:5). Ezekiel too speaks of seeing the Lord's glory (Ezek. 1:28).

And of the incarnate Word, John says, "We have *seen* his glory, the glory of the One and Only" (John 1:14). Paul in Rom. 8:18 speaks of a future glory that will be "revealed" in us. That glory is everywhere, for the whole earth is full of it (Isa. 6:3).

I suggest that the relationship of the Lord's glory to the Lord is like that of the reflection of the sun in a pool of water. The reflection is not the sun, but it is an accurate representation and likeness of the sun and may be looked at without damage to the eyes. When Paul indicts all of humanity for having sinned and fallen short of the glory of God (Rom. 3:23), the second half of this famous and oft-quoted Pauline verse suggests that God's salvation has a double edge to it. It includes not only the cancellation of one's sins, but also the restoration of the divine likeness, the divine glory in one's life, a likeness either lost or damaged in the fall, and from which we have fallen short.

There is one more thing to say about the glory of the Lord, and especially when it shows up suddenly and unbidden. The OT speaks both of God's regular presence and God's occasional and extraordinary presence. Goldingay (2003: 401) suggests that the difference between the two is the difference "between the fact of God's presence and the experience or sense of God's presence." Many Christians would call such breathtaking manifestations of the Spirit "revival," times when "the glory came." In the Christian college at which I was privileged to teach for thirty-six years, Asbury College, I witnessed several occasions on which that glory descended on our community spectacularly, stayed for a good while, and radically altered the trajectory of many lives. Whatever else the sudden manifestation of God's glory may accomplish on the occasions we are about to examine in our comments on vv. 9–12, we will see that one thing the coming of God's glory does is to shut up a lot of babbling mouths, and fairly quickly at that.

Childs (1974: 278) has noted that this narrative in Exod. 16 follows a simi- **16:9–12**
lar pattern of four episodes in Numbers: Num. 14:1–11; 16:3–21; 16:41–45 [17:6–10]; 20:2–8. Here are the parallels: (1) The Israelites murmur about something (Exod. 16:2–3; Num. 14:1–4; 16:13; 16:41 [17:6]; 20:2–5); (2) Moses (and Aaron, or Joshua) makes an initial response to the people (Exod. 16:6–8; Num. 14:6–9; 16:4–14; not in 16:41–45 [17:6–10] or in 20:2–8); (3) the glory of the Lord appears (Exod. 16:10; Num. 14:10; 16:19; 16:42 [17:7]; 20:6); (4) the Lord says something to Moses (and Aaron) right after the appearing of the glory (Exod. 16:11–12; Num. 14:11–12; 16:20–21; 16:43–45 [17:8–10]; 20:7–8). In the first and last of these five divine messages (Exod. 16:11–12 and Num. 20:7–8), the news is good news if one is an Israelite. In the middle three of these divine messages (Num. 14:11–12; 16:20–21; 16:43–45 [17:8–10]), the news is bad news if one is an Israelite.

One might expect to see this pattern also in Num. 11:4–35, another grumbling scene in which the people recall the manna God gave them, but now they crave meat as well. We have two murmuring scenes in which the lament is over food and its absence (Exod. 16; Num. 11). Unlike in Exod. 16; Num. 14; 16; and 20, in Num. 11 there is no explicit record of the glory of the Lord appearing, although God's "burning fire" (Num. 11:1) and his "burning anger" (Num. 11:33) must have been "glorious."

There are other differences as well. Exodus 16 records a pre-Sinai murmuring over food with God's provision of manna, but no word of judgment. Numbers 11 records a post-Sinai murmuring over food, with God's provision of quail, but the people pay a heavy price (11:33–34). Perhaps another major difference between the two incidents, as Balentine (1985: 64–65) has observed, is that in Num. 11 Moses twice engages the Lord in conversational prayer (11:11–14, 21–22), and twice the Lord answers (11:16–20, 23). By contrast, in Exod. 16 the Lord speaks to Moses (16:4–5, 11–12, 28–29), the Israelites speak to Moses (and Aaron; 16:3), Moses and Aaron speak to the people (16:6–8), Moses speaks to Aaron (16:9), Moses speaks to the people (16:15b–16, 19, 23, 25–26). But in Exod. 16, Moses never directly addresses God. He does so in 15:25 and 17:4 ("Then Moses cried out to the Lord"), but nowhere in chap. 16. For the record, note that in two of the parallel murmuring scenes in Numbers we have been discussing, there is mention of Moses's addressing God directly (Num. 14:13–19; 16:15, 22), but in the other two (16:41–50 [17:6–15]; 20:2–13) it is absent, as in Exod. 16. What is absent in Exod. 16 but present in all four Numbers narratives is the note that Moses (and Aaron) fall "facedown," either right after the people complain bitterly (Num. 14:5; 16:4, 22; 20:6) or after the divine glory has appeared and the Lord has addressed them (16:45 [17:10]). If "fell facedown" means "in prayer," then its absence from Exod. 16 is understandable. Then again, "fell facedown" in some of these Numbers passages might mean "fell down in fear, or grief, or despair, before the people," especially since even petitionary/intercessory prayer allows prostration, but does not require it.

16:13–18 Again there is the use of a phrase that appeared earlier in the plagues section (see my comments on "rain" bread from heaven in v. 4). In the second plague Aaron stretches out his arm over Egypt's waters, and frogs come up (*watta'al*) and cover (*wattěkas*) the land (8:6 [2]). Here it is quail that come up (*watta'al*) and cover (*wattěkas*) the land. As the first "rain" is in judgment but the second "rain" in blessing, so the earlier "coming up and covering" is in judgment, but the second "coming up and covering" is in blessing.

These quail, which are not mentioned again in this chapter after v. 8, represent a large number of birds migrating from Africa to Europe. On that long trek in the spring and fall, many would become exhausted and drop from the sky over areas of the Sinai peninsula, making them readily available to consumers.

Most of this section focuses on the supply of manna. The manna is described in vv. 14 and 31 as: (1) a small, thin seed like a coriander seed (a plant whose seeds are used in flavoring), and hence easy to pick; (2) white, hence easy to spot (on these color terms, see A. Brenner 1982: 88); (3) clean, since it falls on the dew, and hence safe to eat; (4) sweet in taste to the palate, and hence inviting to eat (Exod. 16:31, "like a wafer in honey"; Num. 11:8, "like something made with olive oil" [cf. NIV], but NJPS "like rich cream"); (5) something that could be eaten raw or cooked (Num. 11:8), hence adding some variety to one's daily consumption of food.

Modern naturalists, working in the Sinai region, have come across insect secretions in this area that are amazingly similar to the description of manna in Exod. 16 and Num. 11. Their explanation for this substance is as follows. Scale insects and plant lice (e.g., *Trabutina mannipara Ehrenberg* and *Naiacoccus serpentina Green*) live in some kinds of small tamarisk trees or shrubs. They ingest the sap from flower clusters on these trees and excrete it onto the branches, where it crystallizes and glistens like dew. It then falls to the ground as a sticky solid, but it must be harvested by morning or else creeping insects like ants will wipe out the edible food. The local Bedouin use it as a sweetener. It is available for harvesting only in late May, June, and July.

If this is the same as the biblical manna, then each gathers per person an "omer" a day, which is about 2.3 liters or 2.1 quarts (dry measure). As I said earlier, the people's "What is it?" is probably folk etymology for "man(na)." There is no other place in the Hebrew Bible where *man* occurs with the meaning "What?" apart from Exod. 16:15. In late Aramaic and Syriac, one does find *man* meaning "What?" but its more normal meaning in other Semitic languages like Arabic is "Who?" Perhaps the best way we can capture the Israelites' ignorance about this unknown substance is to render v. 15 something like "And they said to each other, looking puzzled, 'Whatchamacallit?'" It is something never experienced before. Israel wants something they have experienced before, Egypt's cuisine. The Lord is now giving them something they have never experienced before.

On this occasion one of the many miracles is that those who gather as much as they can end up with the same amount as those who are not as greedy (vv. 17–18). For one group, God downsizes their portion. For another group, God upsizes their portion. The situation is not unlike that in the early church (Acts 2:45; 4:32), where a spirit of generosity radically reduces the divide between the haves and have-nots in the apostolic, Christian community.

One wonders if this emphasis on the same amount of manna for all families may have provided some of the inspiration for later Deuteronomic law (Deut. 25:13–16) about honest weights and measures, a subject on which Wisdom literature weighs in heavily (Prov. 11:1; 16:11; 20:23). The law legislates against two differing weights in business transactions, one heavy, one light, one larger, one smaller, in order to increase the amount one receives and decrease the amount one must dispense. Not two different amounts of manna, and not two different weights, with the former serving as a God-given example in the use of just and faulty weights. On this possible connection, see Carmichael 1967: 200–204.

In one sense the supply of quail and manna is a natural event and a natural gift. We are not to believe that before the Israelites reach the Sinai area and after they leave it no quail or manna are ever found there. These things were present here long before the Israelites came and will be around long after the Israelites have moved on. It is not that God brings these gifts on ex nihilo for just this short time and only for his people. More than likely other desert groups like the Amalekites (Exod. 17:8–16) have survived by feeding on migratory birds and manna.

In another sense, the supply of quail and manna is a supernatural event and a supernatural gift. Elements in the story that point to this truth include the following: (1) everybody ends up with the same amount, regardless of how much they gather; (2) the double amount that God provides on Friday, and the fact that the portion left over for the Sabbath does not spoil; (3) the miraculous absence of edible granules every seventh day. Do even scale insects and plant lice observe the Sabbath?

In sum, we can see that God's provisions for his people are both natural and supernatural, as they are to us. Fretheim (1991: 181–82) writes,

> God's gifts to Israel are to be found not only in the unusual but also in the everyday. If the provisions of God in the wilderness are all subsumed under the extraordinary or miraculous, then the people of God will tend to look for God's providential care only in that which falls outside the ordinary. The all too common effect of this is to absent God from the ordinary and everyday and to go searching for God only in the deep sea and mountain top experiences. Consequently, the people of God will not be able to see in the very ordinariness of things that God is the one who bestows blessings again and again. The result will often be that, when the miraculous can no longer be discerned in one's life, there will be a profound experience of the absence of God altogether.

16:19–20 Moses's admonition to "leave none of it over until morning" parallels a similar command in conjunction with the consumption of the Passover lamb (Exod. 12:10; 34:25; Deut. 16:4), the disposing of the ram of ordination at the consecration or investiture of the priests (Exod. 29:34), the eating of the thanksgiving sacrifice (*tôdâ*), a subcategory of the fellowship/well-being offering [*šĕlāmîm*] (Lev. 7:15; 22:30). Note that the consumption of the votive offering (*nēder*) and freewill offering (*nĕdābâ*), also both subcategories of the fellowship/well-being offering, allow a second day by contrast: "but anything left over may be eaten on the next day" (Lev. 7:16). A similar injunction covers not keeping the fat of any festival offerings, but especially the Passover, until morning (Exod. 23:18b). On how the above verses fit together, see Haran (1978: 329–32), although he does not include Exod. 16:19 in his discussion of these "leave none until morning" verses.

The idea, at least behind Exod. 16:19, is twofold. First, either use it or lose it. Second, "So do not worry [about tomorrow], saying, 'What shall we eat?'" (Matt. 6:31). There are several things that may tempt one to try to save some for tomorrow. One might be anxiety, another might be greed, and another might be thinking one is a good steward. A penny saved may be a penny earned, but manna saved is manna forfeited.

Once more the Israelites demonstrate that they are not good listeners (v. 20a). Again, Moses seems more annoyed by this than is God (v. 20b). The Lord ignores their grumbling that is recorded in vv. 2–3, and here he ignores their refusal to listen. But not Moses, either time!

Earlier Moses has expressed concern that his people may not listen to him (Exod. 4:1). Unfortunately, in this case he turns out to be a prophet (6:12; 16:20b). It is not unexpected that Pharaoh would not listen to him (e.g., 7:13, 22; 8:15, 19 [11, 15]; 9:12), but one's own people, and comrades and parishioners? A hardened heart is behind Pharaoh's not listening, but no mention of that is present in Exod. 16.

Six days are for gathering. On the seventh day one is to forgo gathering and **16:21–30**
rest instead. This is the first of six Sabbath commands in Exodus (16:21–30; 20:8–11; 23:12; 31:12–17; 34:21; 35:2–3). There are six more in Leviticus and Deuteronomy (Lev. 19:3b, 30a; 23:3; 25:1–7; 26:2a; Deut. 5:12–15). To those twelve we may add aspects of Sabbath observance (Gen. 2:1–4; Num. 15:32–36; 28:9–10). None of these twelve (or fifteen) references call the seventh day a day of worship. There is no verse in the OT that says, "You shall go to 'church' on Saturday." Rather, the seventh day is a day for rest and abstention from all kinds of work. Here, even before the Sabbath is formally institutionalized in the Decalogue, the Lord already impresses on his followers the exceptional nature of the seventh day.

To that end, without their foreknowledge of it, God doubles the portion that the people gather on the sixth day. They gather the same as on other days, but lo! they have twice as much! To quote Childs (1974: 290), "God gives Israel, as it were, a surprise party." No wonder they are shocked and amazed and seek out Moses for explanation and clarification (v. 22b). And to add one more entry to the surprise party, the portion of manna left for eating on the seventh day does not rot (v. 24).

The idea of God's giving his people a surplus in order to carry them over a lean period when harvesting is outlawed occurs elsewhere in Scripture. When laying out the guidelines vis-à-vis the Sabbatical Year and the year of Jubilee (Lev. 25:1–23), God stipulates that in the seventh year the land may not be worked. One may eat only what grows naturally (25:4–6). Predictably, the people ask, "What will we eat in the seventh year?" (25:20). In Lev. 25:21 the anxious Israelites are assured that the crop of the sixth year will be so abundant that it will last beyond the end of the seventh year: "I will send you such a blessing in the sixth year that the land will yield enough for three years." One cannot miss the parallels: a double-sized portion of manna on the sixth day to cover the needs of people on the seventh day, and a double-sized harvest in the sixth year to cover the needs of people in the seventh year. How can one fret about the next day or the next year when one knows a God who makes those kinds of promises, who is always twenty-four hours or twelve months ahead of us? In return, he asks only that we honor his "sevenths."

Some elements about the Sabbath present in Exod. 16 explain how some Jewish believers observe the Sabbath today. For example, the custom of placing two loaves of bread (*leḥem mišneh*) on the dinner table at the Sabbath meal is rooted in Exod. 16:5, 22, where the word *mišneh* (v. 5, "identical amount"; v. 22, "the equivalent of") may well be translated "*double* [what they gather each day]" and "[they gathered] a *double portion* [of bread]." Also, the command in v. 29 that "no one go out from his home on the seventh day" has given rise to disputes about whether one may travel on the Sabbath, and if so, how and how far?

16:31–34 Not only will the manna provided on Friday last for twenty-four more hours, but some of it (an omer, that is, one day's supply) will last for generations to come (v. 32). Moses's instructions to Aaron are to place the omer of manna in a jar "before the LORD" (v. 33). Aaron instinctively knows what "before the LORD" means, for v. 34 informs the reader that he places the jarred manna "in front of / before the Covenant/Pact" (*lipnê hāʿēdut*).

So, what is an *ʿēdut*? It is a shortened form of *ʾărōn hāʿēdut*, "the ark of the covenant/testimony" (see Exod. 25:22; 26:33–34; 30:6, 26; 39:35; 40:3, 5, 21; Num. 4:5; 7:89). The longer phrase exists alongside another, *ʾărōn bĕrît* (e.g., Num. 10:33), and both designate the same object. But there is a problem here. In Exod. 16 the ark of the covenant does not yet exist! It first appears after Israel has reached Mount Sinai, when God speaks about its construction to Moses (Exod. 25:10–22), and Bezalel, the foreman who oversees the tabernacle's construction, builds it (37:1–9). Since 16:35 (the manna ends after forty years of wandering) was clearly written much later than the rest of the chapter (maybe by Joshua?), one might argue the same for vv. 32–34. The Lord must have spoken these words to Moses, and then Moses to Aaron, after the *ʿēdut* existed. But why, then, are they placed anachronistically in Exod. 16? For one thing, as in v. 35, the topic of both is something about manna, so why not include them both in the manna chapter? For another thing, we know that other biblical texts say the ark is to be the receptacle for the two tablets of the law (Exod. 25:16; Deut. 10:2, 5). But before the ark receives the tablets, it receives the jar. That is, in terms of the ark's contents, Scripture first tells us about a God of manna before it tells us about a God of mandates, a God who graciously provides before a God who lays down the law, or to put it in the most familiar terms, a God of grace, then a God of law, when it comes to what is inside this most holy box.

God, some would say, has an odd sense of humor. The second-generation **16:35**
Israelite vagabonds are preparing to engage the mighty Canaanites in battle in hopes of taking the land they believe God has promised to them. So, what does God do on the eve of the battle with a titan? First, he instructs all the males to be circumcised (Josh. 5:1–9). In such a postoperational physical state of recovering from the pain of adult circumcision, they are hardly ready for war. Second, as Exod. 16:35 says, God cuts off the food supply. The manna ceases. Lots of discomfort, no food, and now God says, "Go get them."

For the child who is learning how to ride a bicycle to which training wheels have been attached, there is a time when the training wheels must come off if the child is ever to gain confidence in riding a two-wheeler. To the inexperienced novice pilot, if he is ever to gain the confidence he needs to fly solo, he must one day hear his flight instructor say to him, "Now take it up and land it yourself." God does not cease to be a provider, any more than does a parent who turns the responsibility for providing for the child over to that child. That is part of the growing-up and maturing process as one takes responsibility for one's own needs and daily decisions. Jehovah-jireh is still Jehovah-jireh, even if you from now on have to get your own food.

Possibly, as Enns (2000: 328) has observed, this note (the NIV places the verse **16:36**
in parentheses) was added because when v. 36 was written (by whomever), the omer was no longer a commonly used measurement. The omer appears in the Bible only in Exod. 16. By contrast, the "ephah" is mentioned in eight different books, ranging from Torah books like Leviticus and Numbers, to historical books like Judges and 1 Samuel, to prophetic books like Ezekiel and Micah, and to short stories like Ruth. If one-tenth of an ephah equals one day's supply of food for one person, then Ruth's gleaning a full ephah of barley (2:17) is indeed magnanimous. No wonder Ruth 2:18 says, "Her mother-in-law saw how much she had gathered."

The Hebrew word "ephah" appears to be the same as the Egyptian measure *ipt*. Yet *ipt* is, according to Gardiner (1957: 198), about eighteen to twenty liters, while the Hebrew "ephah," being ten times an *ʿiśśārôn* [ten tenths], equals ten to twelve liters. Perhaps the difference is because the Egyptian *ipt* is based on the royal cubit, while the biblical ephah is based on the ordinary cubit.

One cannot read this incident without reflecting on how it provides the background for the phrase "Give us today/each day our daily bread" (Matt. 6:11; Luke 11:3) in the prayer Jesus teaches his followers to pray. There are some differences in how Matt. 6:11 and Luke 11:3 phrase this petition. For example, in Matt. 6:11 "give us" is an aorist imperative (*dos*), while in Luke 11:3 "give us" is a present imperative (*didou*). The difference may be because Matthew uses "today," while Luke uses "each day." But both employ *ton arton hēmon ton epiousion* for "our daily bread." Greek scholars have yet to find the adjective *epiousion* ("daily") outside of its occurrences in the Gospels. Hence, it has engendered much discussion about its meaning. Does it mean (1) "bread necessary for subsistence"; (2) "bread for the current day, today"; or (3) "bread for the coming day, the future"? I am inclined to agree with those who think that it most likely means option 3 above, "bread for the coming day," but the "coming day" not in the sense of "tomorrow" but in the sense of "today." In the so-called Lord's Prayer, Jesus may be teaching us not only *how* to pray but also *when* to pray, to start one's day with prayer. One does not pray ten minutes before going to bed, "Give us today our daily bread," nor does one pray just before falling asleep for the night, "and lead us not into temptation." The Lord's Prayer is a morning prayer, and like the manna, which was provided every morning, this petition is for God to provide bread for the day to come, meaning today, this unfolding day.

Paul in 2 Cor. 8:15, by quoting Exod. 16:18, in essence expands the Lord's Prayer petition "Give us our daily bread" to mean "give not only me, but give everybody their daily bread, and help me to share my God-given daily bread with others." That is managing one's manna in a God-glorifying way. It is to move beyond the prodigal son's self-centered "give me" (Luke 15:12) to Jesus's other-centered "give us."

The third appearance of the manna narrative in the NT is in conjunction with John's account of the feeding of the five thousand (John 6:1–15, 25–59). In vv. 30–31 the crowd quotes Scripture to Jesus in a disparaging way (like the devil and his "it is written" with Jesus in the wilderness?): "What miraculous sign then will you give? . . . Our forefathers ate the manna in the desert; as it is written: 'He [Moses] gave them bread from heaven to eat.'" Jesus's response in v. 32 is classic. First, he says, the "he" who provided the heavenly bread was not Moses, but Jesus's own heavenly Father. Second, Jesus changes the tense from the people's "he gave" to "he gives," thus claiming that the real manna is Jesus himself, the one who has come down from heaven, and his teachings. Eating the exodus manna did not grant immunity from (physical) death (v. 49). Neither will "eating" the real bread that came down from heaven save one from physical death, but it will save those who eat it from spiritual death (vv. 50–51). That is exactly what, in another context, Jesus says to Martha as she grieves over her brother's physical death (John 11:25–26).

Water from the Rock

(17:1–7)

Translation

[1]The entire community of Israel's sons journeyed from the wilderness of Sin by stages by order of the LORD, and they encamped at Rephidim, but there (was) no water for the people to drink. [2]The people complained against Moses and said, "Give us water that we may drink." And Moses said to them, "Why do you complain against me? Why are you testing the LORD?" [3]And the people thirsted for water there, and the people murmured against Moses and said, "Why this? You have brought us up from Egypt to kill me and my sons and my livestock by thirst." [4]And Moses cried out to the LORD, saying, "What shall I do with this people? Shortly they will stone me." [5]And the LORD said to Moses, "Pass before the people and take with you some of Israel's elders, and the staff with which you struck the Nile take in your hand, and go. [6]Watch! I will be standing in front of you there on the rock in Horeb, and you shall strike the rock, and water will issue from it, and the people will drink." And Moses did so before the eyes of Israel's elders. [7]He called the name of the place Massah and Meribah because of Israel's sons complaining and because of their testing the LORD, saying, "Is the LORD among us or not?"

Grammatical and Lexical Notes

17:1. "By stages" (*lĕmasʿêhem*) alludes to intermediate stations at which Israel stops on its wilderness journey, most of which remain unidentifiable, like Num. 33:13, "They left Dophkah [?] and camped at Alush [?]."

17:1. "By order of the LORD" is, literally, "by the mouth of the LORD (*ʿal-pî YHWH*)." This is its only occurrence in Exodus, but it is frequent in Numbers (Num. 3:16, 39, 51; 4:37, 41, 45, 49; 9:18, 20, 23 [3x]; 10:13; 13:3; 33:2, 38; 36:5). At least in Numbers the phrase "reinforces that all the particulars of priestly practice were directly ordained by God and were not merely matters of custom and convention" (B. Levine 1993: 158).

17:2. For *mah* (normally "What?") with the meaning "Why?" see BDB 553b. The particle appears with this nuance in 14:15, "What are you crying out about to me?" which could also be rendered "Why [*mah*] are you crying to me?"

17:2. The verb "contend" (*rîb*) may be followed by different prepositions: (1) *rib ʾet* (Judg. 8:1; Neh. 5:7; 13:11, 17); (2) *rîb bĕ* (Gen. 31:36; Judg. 6:32; Hosea 2:2 [4]); (3) *rîb ʿim* (Gen. 26:20; Exod. 17:2 [2x]; Num. 20:3; Judg. 11:25; Job 13:19; 23:6; 31:13; 40:2). All have the same semantic value, regardless of the following preposition, which is "make an accusation or complaint." In most of these references "the subject of the verb is the aggrieved party making an accusation against an aggrieving party" (Limburg 1969: 296).

17:3. There is an interesting shift from first-person plural to first-person singular ("You have brought *us* up from Egypt to kill *me* and *my* livestock"). Both LXX and Vulgate sidestep the change in number by reading "you have brought us up from Egypt to kill *us* and *our* sons and *our* livestock." In favor of the change to plural is a parallel verse in Num. 16:13, "You have brought us up . . . to kill us" (*heʿĕlîtānû . . . lahămîtēnû*). The Hebrew text can remain as it is, however. Alter (2004: 412), after noting that such a shift is good idiomatic usage in Biblical Hebrew, remarks, "The switch allows the sharpness of the complaint to become more vivid as the protological individual speaker representing the people laments his own imminent death and that of his children."

17:4. *ʿÔd mĕʿaṭ* means something like "(in) just a little while." See Ps. 37:10, "*A little while*, and the wicked will be no more"; Isa. 10:25, "*Very soon* my anger against you will end"; Jer. 51:33, "The time to harvest her [Babylon] will *soon* come"; Hosea 1:4, "Call him Jezreel, because I will *soon* punish the house of Jehu."

17:4. Few Hebrew verbs illustrate the Piel *privative* as clearly as does *sāqal*. In the Qal the verb means "to stone," as in Exod. 17:4, but in the Piel it means "remove/clear away stones" (Isa. 5:2; 62:10). Exodus 17:4 and Num. 14:10 are the only two references in the OT that speak of the people's desire to stone Moses. In the postbiblical *Exodus Rabbah* 7.3, God warns Moses and Aaron: "My children are obstinate, bad-tempered and troublesome. In assuming leadership over them you must expect that they will curse you and even stone you" (quoted by Donaldson [1981: 42] in conjunction with the account of Stephen's stoning in Acts 7).

17:5. "Pass before" (*ʿābar lipnê*) is not a common phrase in the Hebrew Bible. It appears four times as Jacob is getting ready to meet Esau after an extended stay in Mesopotamia: Gen. 32:16 [17]; 21 [22]; 33:3, 14.

17:5. The *min* attached to "elders" (*mizziqnê*) is a partitive *min* ("*some of* Israel's elders").

17:5. For "elders" in Exodus outside of 17:5, see 3:16; 4:29; 12:21; 18:12; 24:1, 9.

17:6. For "rock" Exod. 17:6 uses *ṣûr*. For "rock" in the parallel water story in Num. 20, the word is *selaʿ* (Num. 20:8, 10 [2x]). Deut 32:13b uses both in parallelism: "He nourished him with honey from the rock [*selaʿ*] and with oil from the flinty crag [*ṣûr*]." Deuteronomy 32:13b adds the word "flinty" (*ḥalmîš*) to show that the "crag" from which the water flows is a very hard rock rather than soft, porous limestone. Here honey and oil are poetic metaphors for fresh, sweet water that is good for drinking. For another reference to "honey" from the rock, see Ps. 81:16 [17]: "with honey from the rock I would satisfy you."

17:6. For the use of *yāṣāʾ* ("issue") with the flow of water, see Gen. 2:10; Num. 20:11; Judg. 15:19; Ezek. 47:1; Joel 3:18 [4:18]; Zech. 14:8.

17:7. For *ʿal* with the meaning "because of" ("*because of* Israel's sons complaining and *because of* their testing"), see R. Williams 1976: §291; Arnold and Choi 2003: 122.

17:7. "Or not?" stands for "Or is he not?" On the use of ellipsis or omissions with negatives, see Williams 1976: §§409, 563; Arnold and Choi 2003: 192.

Commentary

17:1–7 Israel's next encampment, after the initial supply of manna and quail, is at Rephidim, a place that cannot be situated too far from Mount Sinai/Horeb. The uncertainty on this occasion is over a lack of water. This time the Israelites not only murmur against Moses (v. 3), as they have done in 15:24 and 16:2, but they also complain (v. 2). The Hebrew word for "complain/make a complaint against" is *rîb*, and it is a (potentially) more threatening one than *lun* ("murmur"). Sometimes in the Bible *rîb* connotes violent conflict. For example, in Gen. 26:20–21, another story involving water and using the verb *rîb*, the herdsmen of Gerar quarrel (*rîb*) with Isaac's herdsmen over access to wells of water. Is it just a shouting match, or do they strike blows? That Gen. 26:20–21 reference is not unlike the one in Gen. 13:7, "And quarreling [*rîb*] arose between Abram's herdsmen and the herdsmen of Lot." Also, in Ps. 35:1 *rîb* is used in parallelism with *lāḥam*, "fight, do battle": "Contend [*rîb*], O Lord, with those who contend [*rîb*] with me; fight [*lāḥam*] against those who fight [*lāḥam*] against me."

Their ultimatum "Give us water to drink" implies that Moses and Aaron "have supplies of water but are withholding them mercilessly" (Pardes 2000: 46). Is Moses the arbiter over arid Sinai's waterworks? Can he simply snap his fingers and, presto, there is the water?

As Moses sees it, the peoples' complaining is really a test of the Lord: "Why are you testing the Lord?" (v. 2, 7). For God to test humans is acceptable (Gen. 22:1; Exod. 15:25; 16:4; 20:20; Deut. 8:2, 16; 13:3; Judg. 2:22; 3:1; 1 Chron. 29:17; 2 Chron. 32:31; Pss. 26:2; 81:7 [8]; 139:23; Isa. 48:10; Heb. 11:17; James 1:12). But when the shoe is on the other foot, and it is a person or persons testing God, that is another matter (Exod. 17:2, 7; Num. 14:22; Deut. 6:16; Pss. 78:18; 106:14; Luke 4:12; 1 Cor. 10:9). One of the few places where God invites testing from humans is in Mal. 3:10, "Bring the whole tithe into the storehouse. . . . Test [*baḥan*, one of three Hebrew verbs for "test"] me in this, . . . and see if I will not throw open the floodgates of heaven and pour out so much blessing." (In this verse from Malachi, note again the connection between "testing" and God pouring out a liquid-like blessing.)

So what is the problem with testing God? Janzen (1997: 118–19) says it well: "To test God is to pose an ultimatum in which we decide what shall count as evidence of God's presence, and then decide on God's presence or absence on the basis of whether God has met the test we have posed." Fretheim (1991: 189) similarly remarks that testing God is "seeking a way God can be coerced to act or show himself. It is to set God up, to try to force God's hand in order thereby to determine concretely whether God is really present or not." In essence, testing God is demanding that he jump through our hoops and make himself answerable and accountable to us. Sovereignty passes to us.

Although Exod. 17:2, 7 describe this incident as one in which the Israelites test the Lord, Ps. 81:7c [8c] refers to it as one in which he tests them: "I tested you at the waters of Meribah." Commenting on Deut. 6:16, Weinfeld (1991: 346) says, "The same event of distress may serve as a test by God as well as a test by man. God tests the man to see whether he remains faithful in spite of suffering, while man tests God in order to see whether he will prove himself as God and release him from suffering."

Once again the Lord ignores Israel's murmuring and complaining, and instead proposes a solution to Moses. While the Lord is standing before Moses on a rock (the Rock on a rock) at Horeb, Moses is to strike the rock with his rod, and water will gush from the rock.

It is common for a mortal to stand before God in worship (Jer. 7:10), in entering his presence (Deut. 19:17; 29:14–15), in service (KJV: 1 Kings 17:1; 18:15; 2 Kings 3:14; 5:16), in intercessory prayer (Jer. 15:1, 19 NRSV). But it is almost unheard of for the Lord to stand before anybody. In fact, some scholars believe that Gen. 18:22b ("but Abraham remained standing before the LORD") originally read, "but the LORD remained standing before Abraham." The Masoretes, it is argued, deliberately changed the text to remove the possibility that Yahweh would ever stand before any mere mortal. If the Lord is standing on the rock, and Moses is to bang the rock with his rod, what are the chances that his rod might hit or come down on the Lord? Talk about the hammer missing the nail! And might we see any connection between this incident in which the Almighty puts himself in a situation of great jeopardy for the purposes of providing water—and the incident in the passion narrative in which "one of the soldiers pierced Jesus' side with a spear, bringing a sudden flow of blood *and water*" (John 19:34)?

Are the people thankful for the water gift? To be sure, there is no report of the people's drinking the water from the rock. The provision comes near Sinai, and only Moses and the elders are there, while the rest of the people are back in Rephidim. Is there any doxology, even in advance of drinking this gracious gift from God? If so, none is reported. Instead, Moses gives a double name to Rephidim. Rephidim is now "Massah" ("Testingville") and "Meribah" ("Complainingburg"); Long (1968: 29–30) inexplicably sees no connection between the naming tradition in v. 7 and the preceding narrative material. In common with the account in Exod. 15:23, the etymology shares the giving of a name that is feminine in form (Marah, Massah, Meribah). In this case the new names, or the additional names, stand alongside the original name, Rephidim, which is masculine plural in formation.

According to Num. 33, Israel passes through forty-two stations between the starting point, Rameses, and the final encampment near the Jordan. Other names like Rephidim in the itinerary are Elim (33:9), Abarim (33:47), Iyim (33:45), and Abel Shittim (33:49). Names that are feminine plurals are more common: Pi Hahiroth (33:7), Hazeroth (33:17), Makheloth (33:26), Moseroth (33:30), and Oboth (33:43).

The etymology shares in common the explanation of Gideon's other name, Jerub-Baal, in Judg. 6:32 in that both etymologies employ the verb *rîb*: "He called the name of the place . . . Me*rib*ah [from *rîb*] because of Israel's complaining" (Exod. 17:7); and "So that day they called Gideon '*Jerub*-Baal,' saying, 'Let Baal contend [*yāreb*] with him, because he broke down Baal's altar'" (Judg. 6:32).

In Exod. 17 a double sin (testing God and murmuring) gives Rephidim two new names. In Deut. 33:8, part of Moses's blessing on the tribe of Levi, he says, "You tested him at Massah; you contended with him at the waters of Meribah." Since a poetic line consists of parallel clauses, Massah and Meribah must refer to the same incident.

There is one interesting and possibly puzzling reference to Exod. 17:1–7 in the NT. Referring to this episode, Paul says in 1 Cor. 10:3–4, "They all ate the same spiritual food and drank the same spiritual drink; for they drank from the spiritual rock that accompanied them, and that rock was Christ [the Messiah]."

The intriguing phrase of Paul's here is "for they drank from the rock *that accompanied them*." From where did Paul get that? Certainly not from Exod. 17.

For well over a century now (see the study of S. Driver 1889), biblical scholars have observed that postbiblical Jewish literature, both contemporary with Paul and later than Paul, speaks of a well or rock that journeys with the Israelites through the desert. For example, Philo, a Hellenistic Jewish contemporary of Paul, personifies the rock as the wisdom of God and suggests it accompanies the Israelites through their wilderness journey (*Alleg. Interp.* 2.86; Pseudo-Philo, *Bib. Ant.* 10.7). Thus Philo says (in *Bib. Ant.* 10.7), "Now he [Moses] led his people out into the wilderness; for forty years he rained down for them bread from heaven and brought quail to them from the sea and brought forth a well of water to follow them."

A post-Pauline reference is found in one of the sections of the Tosefta. (The Tosefta are rabbinical compilations of writings either omitted from the Mishnah, or else containing material supplementary to the Mishnah and, like the Mishnah, arranged according to six orders. They date from about the fourth century AD.) In Tosefta *Sukkah* 3.11 we encounter these words:

> And so the well which was with the Israelites in the wilderness was a rock, the size of a large round vessel, surging and gurgling upward, as from the mouth of this little flask, rising with them up onto the mountains, and going down with them into the valleys. Wherever the Israelites would encamp, it made camp with them, on a high place, opposite the tent of meeting. The princes of Israel come and surround it with their staffs, and they sing a song concerning it: *Spring up, O Well!* Sing to it (Num. 21:17–18). (quoted in Fee 1987: 448; see Neusner 1977–86: 2.220)

It seems fairly certain, then, that Paul is drawing on a postbiblical tradition about the continual supply of water for the Israelites while in the wilderness rather than from any explicit data in the OT. According to the esteemed NT scholar N. Wright (2004: 125), Paul, in order to make his point that Christians are those who share in the food and drink that is Messiah's gift of his own self, "goes along with this fanciful reading of the text."

Enns (1996; 2005: 149–51) goes further than Wright. For Enns, Paul's Hebrew Bible has already produced a rich history of interpretation, of which Paul is quite cognizant; from this "hermeneutical well" he does not hesitate to draw. "It is not just the words on the page but the interpretive tradition as well that made up Paul's Old Testament" (2005: 151).

It is not hard to see why Paul would speak of the rock that supplies water accompanying the Israelites, even if he is unaware of this reading. After all, the wilderness is not a rain forest! Here and there, to be sure, are some Elims, but they are not all over the place. Rivers, streams, and creeks hardly exist. Surely the absence of water is a compelling concern at more than just two locations, Rephidim in Exod. 17 and Kadesh in Num. 20. What about any of the other forty stations?

The Amalekite Ambush and Attack

(17:8–16)

Translation

[8]And Amalek came and fought with Israel at Rephidim. [9]And Moses said to Joshua, "Choose for us men, and go out, fight against Amalek. Tomorrow I shall station myself on the peak of the hill, with God's rod in my hand." [10]And Joshua did just as Moses had said to him in order to fight against Amalek, and Moses, Aaron, and Hur had gone up to the peak of the hill. [11]And so it was that whenever Moses would raise his hand, Israel was victor; but whenever he would lower his hand, Amalek was victor. [12]Whenever Moses's hands were heavy, they took a stone and placed it under him and he sat on it. And Aaron and Hur would support his hands, one on either side. So his hands remained firm until the setting of the sun. [13]Joshua disabled Amalek and his people with the edge of the sword. [14]And the LORD said to Moses, "Inscribe this as a reminder in a document, and read it aloud to Joshua: 'I will utterly blot out the memory of Amalek from under the heavens.'" [15]And Moses built an altar, and he called its name *YHWH Nissi* (The LORD [Is] My Banner). [16]And he said, "A hand on top of Yah's throne, a war for the LORD against Amalek from past to future."

Grammatical and Lexical Notes

17:8. For Amalek "fought with" Israel, the Hebrew is *lāḥam ʿim*. For Israel's "fighting against" Amalek (vv. 9–10), or God's "fighting against" Amalek (v. 16), the Hebrew is *lāḥam bĕ*.

17:9. For *bāḥar* in reference to "choosing" soldiers, see Josh. 8:3; 1 Sam. 13:2; 2 Sam. 10:9; 17:1; 1 Chron. 19:10. The related noun, *bāḥûr* ("chosen man"), designates soldiers or fighters in passages like 2 Sam. 6:1; 10:9; 1 Kings 12:21; and others.

17:9. Does "tomorrow" go with what precedes it ("and fight against Amalek *tomorrow*")? Or does it introduce what follows ("*Tomorrow* I shall station myself")? The LXX reads it the first way ("do battle with Amalek tomorrow"), but the Hebrew text places an *ʾatnāḥ* under "against Amalek," suggesting a major division of the verse, splitting the verse into two; hence, "Tomorrow I shall station myself." See Tov 2001: 68.

17:9. The Hebrew has Moses use the longer form of the first-person independent pronoun when he speaks to Joshua ("I [*ʾānōkî*] shall station myself"). Revell (1995: 209–10) notes that this longer form of the pronoun is sometimes used by a status-marked speaker in order to establish some kind of a bond or sense of solidarity with a nonstatus addressee (2 Sam. 2:6; 13:28).

17:9. For *niṣṣāb ʿal* meaning "to stand on top of something," see Exod. 33:21; 34:2. When Jacob in his dream at Bethel sees God *niṣṣāb ʿal* the ramp/ladder on which angels are traipsing (Gen. 28:13), is God standing "on top of" the ramp/ladder, or "beside" it?

17:11. The imperfect verb forms "raise, lower" are frequentative. Especially in conditional clauses, the verb is made frequentative by the addition of introductory *wĕhāyâ* (*wĕhāyâ kaʾăšer* . . .). The same goes for *wĕhāyâ* when it precedes a preposition joined to an infinitive construct, as in Exod. 33:8 ("And whenever Moses went out to the tent [*wĕhāyâ kĕṣēʾt*] . . ."). See Ogden 1971: 461.

17:11. "Hand" in "whenever Moses would raise/lower his hand" most likely means "arm." The Hebrew word for this, *yād*, occurs seven times in this unit (vv. 9, 11 [2x], 12 [3x], 16).

17:12. "One on either side" is *mizzeh ʾeḥād ûmizzeh ʾeḥād*. Without the numeral *ʾeḥād*, the phrase occurs back in 11:1, "Afterward he [Pharaoh] will send you off *from here* [*mizzeh*]; when he sends you off, he will surely drive you *from here* [*mizzeh*]." See also Exod. 25:19 and 37:8, "Make one cherub *on one end* [*miqqāṣâ mizzeh*] and the second cherub *on the other* [*miqqāṣâ mizzeh*]"; Exod. 26:13, "And the cubit *on one side* [*mizzeh*] and the cubit *on the other* [*mizzeh*]"; Exod. 32:15, "Moses . . . went down the mountain with the two tablets . . . inscribed *on both sides* [*mizzeh ûmizzeh*]"; Exod. 38:15, "And curtains . . . were *on the other side* [*mizzeh ûmizzeh*] of the entrance to the courtyard." The expression occurs where a pair of something is involved (Aaron and Hur, two ends, two tablets inscribed front and back, two sides).

17:12. This verse uses the adjectival form of *k-b-d* (*kĕbēdîm*) to refer to Moses's hands growing tired, but Gen. 48:10 uses the verbal form (*kābĕdû*) to refer to Jacob's failing eyesight. The difference is that the adjectival form describes the present state of Moses's hands, while the verbal form is used to report a process that has already transpired.

17:12. In "his hands remained firm," "firm" (*ʾĕmûnâ*) is a noun that is the predicate of a nominal sentence and functions as a qualifier. Compare Ezek. 16:22, "In all your detestable practices . . . you did not remember . . . when you were naked and bare [lit., "when you were nakedness (*ʿērōm*) and nudity (*wĕʿeryâ*)"]."

17:13. The Hebrew verb behind "disabled" is *ḥālaš*. It occurs only two more times in the Hebrew Bible: Job 14:10 ("But man dies *and is laid low*; he breathes his last and is no more") and Isa. 14:12 ("How you have fallen from heaven, O morning star, son of the dawn! You have been cast down to the earth, you who once *laid low* the nations!"). Also the cognate noun *ḥălûšâ* appears in Exod. 32:18 ("Moses replied, 'It is not the sound of victory, it is not the sound of *defeat*'"), and the noun *ḥallaš* in Joel 3:10 [4:10] ("Beat your plowshares into swords and your pruning hooks into spears. Let *the weakling* say, 'I am strong!'"). The question is whether the verb means "to inflict a crushing defeat," or whether Joshua and his people only weaken Amalek in a far-from-decisive victory. In a study of this verse, A. Guillaume (1963: 91) argues for the first of these possibilities with his rendering "Joshua seized the opportunity to smite Amalek without mercy." Support for this reading comes from parallel phrases to *ḥālaš* . . . *lĕpî-ḥāreb* ("by the edge of the sword"), such as "Hamor and his son Shechem they killed by the edge of the sword [*hārag lĕpî-ḥāreb*]" in Gen. 34:26 AT, and "All his [Agag's] people he [Saul] totally destroyed with the edge of the sword [*ḥāram lĕpî-ḥāreb*]" in 1 Sam. 15:8 AT. For proponents of those who argue for "disabled" because they believe the basic idea behind the verb is "weak" or "weakened," see McKay 1970: 453–54n4; Childs 1974: 311; Van Leeuwen 1980: 175–76. McKay, for example, renders the Luciferean passage in Isa. 14:12 not as "you who once laid low the nations!" (NIV), but as "you weakling above the nations."

17:13. "By the edge of the sword" (*lĕpî-ḥāreb*) occurs thirty-three times in the Hebrew Bible. Five of these are in the Pentateuch (Gen. 34:26; Exod. 17:13; Num. 21:24; Deut. 13:15 [16]; 20:13). Twenty-one are in Joshua–Judges. The remaining seven are 1 Sam. 15:8; 22:19; 2 Sam. 15:14; 2 Kings 10:25; Job 1:15, 17; Jer. 21:7.

17:14. *Zikkārôn* ("a reminder") shares one feature with most other *qiṭṭālôn* nouns like *higgāyôn* ("meditation") in Ps. 19:14 [15], *ḥizzāyôn* ("revelation") in 2 Sam. 7:17, *killāyôn* ("destruction") in Isa. 10:22, *niqqāyôn* ("innocence") in Ps. 26:6, *šibbārôn* ("destruction") in Jer. 17:18, and *timmāhôn* ("madness") in Zech. 12:4. In the construct state of each of these nouns, the doubled consonant reduces to a single consonant. Thus the construct case of the absolute *zikkārôn* is *zikrôn* (Lev.

23:24, "You are to have a day of rest, a sacred assembly, *commemorated with trumpet blasts* [*zikrôn tĕrû ʿâh*]"). See Gevirtz 1984b: 515n4.

17:14. "In a document" is, literally, "in *the* document/book [*bassēper*]," but this is not a case of real determination any more than is a phrase like "he spoke to me on the telephone." See Barr 1989: 313–14.

17:14. When the Hebrew Bible expresses the act of erasing written words from a document, it uses the verb *māḥâ* ("blot out"). See Exod. 32:32–33; Num. 5:23; Ps. 69:28 [29]; Isa. 44:22. For this verb referring to what God does to humanity in the days of Noah, see Gen. 6:7; 7:4, 23 ("wiped from/out"). Even when there is no reference to a book or scroll, the scribal image of erasing something from a book still persists in the phrase "his name [may not be] blotted/washed out" (Deut. 9:14; 25:6, 19; 29:20 [19]; Judg. 21:17; 2 Kings 14:27; Pss. 9:5 [6]; 69:28 [29]; 109:13). While *māḥâ* in such passages may include death, it refers to an even more terrible fate—to lose not only one's life but one's name and memory among one's descendants. For the use of *māḥâ* for the blotting/washing out of sins and shame, see Ps. 51:1, 9 [3, 11]; Prov. 6:33; Isa. 43:25; 44:22. See the remarks of Haran 1982: 169, 169n19.

17:15. Dahood (1982: 15) has found a parallel to *YHWH nissî* ("The Lord is my banner") in the Eblaite personal name *ni-si-mal-il/nissi-ma-ʾil*, "My banner is Il."

17:16. The textual and interpretive comments connected with v. 16 are legion, and I shall save any comment until the following section.

Commentary

Out of the blue, Israel finds itself under attack from the desert Amalekites. **17:8–13**
The reasons for this ambush are unclear. Possibly this is typical behavior for the Amalekites, who survive by preying pirate-like on innocent parties that pass through this region. Or maybe this is a case of turf war, and the Amalekites believe this approaching group is intent on taking over their area. If the Amalekites have heard about Israel's access to water from the rock at nearby Horeb (17:1–7), maybe they want access to that life-giving water too.

According to Gen. 14:7, the Amalekites have been around the Negev and Sinai peninsula area since the time of Abraham. Genesis 36:12, however, identifies Amalek as the grandson of Esau (Esau>Eliphaz>Amalek), or the great-great-grandson of Abraham (Abraham>Isaac>Esau>Eliphaz>Amalek). That means that Amalekites and Israelites are family, even if only distant relatives. So Amalekites fighting Israelites is not unlike Protestants and Catholics warring against each other, or Sunni and Shiite Muslims against each other.

Verses 9–10 provide the first reference to Joshua in the Bible. That he is introduced without any reference to family suggests he is a well-known person for whom no biographical data is necessary. One would think that Joshua's military activities on this occasion serve him well to be Israel's leader in the conquest of Canaan later on. Exodus 24:13 identifies Joshua as Moses's *mĕšerēt* ("aide, attendant"), but Exod. 33:11 calls him both Moses's *mĕšerēt* and *naʿar* (which NIV couples together as "young aide"). Numbers 11:28 labels Joshua Moses's "aide since youth" (*mĕšārēt . . . mibbĕḥurāyw*). These latter two references may be simply a reference to Joshua's young age. On the other hand, given that *bāḥûr* may designate a soldier/fighter (see my grammatical note at 17:9), *na'ar* at times might refer to one who served his lord in war (MacDonald 1976: 153–54).

The Amalekites are the only people in the Pentateuch against whom the Israelites fight successfully. The one and only other occasion the Israelites fight, thinking victory will be easy but in direct disobedience to God, is in Deut. 1:41–46, on which occasion the Amorites inflict total defeat on them.

The fight in which Israel engages in Exod. 17 is like most of those recorded in Josh. 6–12. With the exception of the battle against Jericho (Josh. 6) and Ai (Josh. 8), every other battle Israel fights is a defensive war. Israel fights (back) only when attacked (Josh. 9:1–2; 10:1–5; 11:1–5). Turning the other cheek might be good counsel for dealing with hostility in one-on-one relationships, but whether it should guide national policy may be another question.

Although there is not one mention of God/Lord in these six verses, Moses's name appears five times (vv. 9, 10 [2x], 11, 12). Furthermore, there is no indication that Moses seeks a revelation from God about how best to handle the situation. Earlier he does ask the Lord about his grumbling Israelites, "What am I to do with these people?" (17:4), but here he does not ask, "What am I to do with these Amalekites?" Rather, he sizes up the situation and acts independently or intuitively. That suggests to Coats (1975: 37) that Moses acts more as a hero than as a man of God in this particular episode.

I am not so sure. As Goldingay (2003: 344–45) has said, "Perhaps there are times for consulting God and times for taking action with the power God has given you." After all, God has already told Moses how to handle a crisis in 17:5–6. Why not build on that divine directive?

Aaron and Hur join Moses in an ascent to the top of a hill, surely something of an anticipation of Moses's solitary multiple ascents to the top of Mount Sinai, in chap. 19, joined by Aaron and Hur and others (at least partway) in chap. 24. Aaron and Hur appear together again in 24:14; in the prolonged absence of Moses at Sinai's summit, they are available to address any legal matters that might arise among the people at Sinai's base. Hur's grandson, Bezalel, is the foreman overseeing the tabernacle's construction (Exod. 31:2; 1 Chron. 2:19–20). Postbiblical Jewish literature sometimes "found" a husband for female figures in Scripture to whose husbands Scripture never refers (e.g., Dinah marries Job, and Rahab marries Joshua). Josephus (*Ant.* 3.2.4 §54) says that Miriam married Hur. This creates marital ties between the tribe of Levi (Miriam) and the tribe of Judah (Hur), as does the marriage of Levite Aaron to Judahite Elizabeth (Exod. 6:23). See Bauckham 2002: 36.

There continues to be much debate over what Moses is doing at the peak of a hill, rod in hand, with hands/arms raised skyward (vv. 9, 11). Many a sermon on intercessory prayer has plugged into Exod. 17:11. To cite but one instance, in a chapter on intercessory prayer, Foster (1992: 192) says, "While

Joshua engaged in physical combat, Moses engages in spiritual combat by raising hands of prayer over the conflict." Because the text makes no reference to Moses's praying, many commentators are hesitant to interpret it as a prayer scene. Elsewhere the Bible speaks of unspoken prayer, such as Hannah (1 Sam. 1:12–13), but there the text makes it quite explicit that Hannah is praying.

We can be certain of two things. First, this is the only time in the Moses narrative where a rod is employed (v. 9c) where smiting or striking something is not either specifically mentioned or implied (cf. Exod. 7:17, 20; 8:16–17 [12–13]; 17:5–6; Num. 20:9–11). The second is the significance of Moses's raising his hand(s)/arms(s). Occasionally this is something that God does: Isa. 5:25; 9:12, 17, 21; 10:4—all of which say, "Yet for all this, his anger is not turned away, his hand is still upraised"; Isa. 26:11, "O Lord, your hand is lifted high"; Ps. 89:13 [14], "Your hand is strong, your right hand exalted/ lifted up." See also Exod. 6:8; Num. 14:30; Deut. 32:40; Neh. 9:15; Ezek. 20:5; Dan. 12:7 for God's uplifted hand in oath taking. When a human raises his hand, it may be in conjunction with an oath (Gen. 14:22), used idiomatically (Pharaoh to Joseph in Gen. 41:44, "Without your word no one will lift hand or foot in all of Egypt"), and literally to raise one's hands above one's head (Num. 20:11). Raising the hand(s) is particularly a part of (semi-)military activity (Exod. 17:11; Deut. 32:27 ["Lest the adversary say, 'Our hand has triumphed,'" or "'Our hand was high'"]; 1 Kings 11:26, 27, "Jeroboam rebelled against Solomon," says, lit., "raised his hand against Solomon" [see KJV]). Most likely Mic. 5:9 [8], "Your hand will be lifted up in triumph over your enemies," refers to Israel's hand rather than to Yahweh's hand.

So if Moses is not praying, what is he doing? Symbolically and silently declaring their victory over the Amalekites? Directing the forces above against the Amalekites, as Joshua is directing the forces below? Providing inspiration and stimulation to his fighting troops? Plugging into heaven's power and resources (which is what one does when praying)? Indicating his total dependence on God by "looking above"? Skehan (1963: 109) quotes a passage from the Mishnah *Roš Haššanah* 3.8: "Every time that Israel[ites] were directing their thoughts upward, and keeping their heart subject to their Father, who is in heaven, they were prevailing, but if they did not, they were falling." The comment then goes on to make a parallel with the story of the bronze snake in Num. 21. Help comes only for those who look up at the serpent on the pole.

Not surprisingly, some have seen a parallel between Moses in the middle of Aaron and Hur, and Jesus on the cross between two criminals. The language of the LXX of Exod. 17:12 ("one on either side"), *enteuthen heis kai enteuthen heis*, is close to that of John 19:18 ("one on each side"), *enteuthen kai enteuthen*, but Moo (1983: 154) and I believe the similarity of language is accidental and without significance. Aaron and Hur are not shady characters. The thieves are criminals. Aaron and Hur are comrades.

There may be, however, another (indirect) NT connection. The Septuagint's translation of "support" in "Aaron and Hur *would support* his hands" uses *stērizō*. This verb occurs in the NT for somebody "strengthening" somebody else: Luke 22:32b, "And when you [Peter] have turned back, *strengthen* your brothers"; Acts 18:23, "Paul set out from there and traveled from place to place, . . . *strengthening* all the disciples"; Rom. 1:11, "I long to see you so that I may impart some spiritual gift *to make you strong*"; 1 Thess. 3:2, "We sent Timothy . . . to *strengthen* and encourage you in your faith"; 2 Thess. 2:16–17, "May our Lord Jesus Christ . . . encourage your hearts and *strengthen* you in every good deed and word"; 2 Thess. 3:3, "But the Lord is faithful, and he will *strengthen* and protect you from the evil one."

What Aaron and Hur do for Moses is the ministry of believer to believer. Aaron and Hur certainly need Moses, but even Moses needs an Aaron and a Hur. The battle with the Amalekites is not easy or over in the twinkling of an eye. It is protracted, sometimes two steps forward, sometimes two steps backward, a victory here, a setback there. In such a crisis, not even the gifted, charismatic, anointed Moses can afford to be a lone ranger. What Aaron and Hur are to an exhausted Moses in Exod. 17, his father-in-law, Jethro, will be to an exhausted Moses in Exod. 18.

17:14–16 For the first time in this episode, the Lord speaks, but only after Joshua has put the brakes on this attacking horde of Amalekites (v. 13). He tells Moses both to write something ("Inscribe this . . . in a document") and say something ("and read it aloud to Joshua"). The first of these directives is for subsequent generations who will read it, while the second of these directives is for the current generation who will hear it. Hurowitz (1998) has analyzed the relationship between written and oral transmission of some Mesopotamian texts; he observes that both forms of transmission exist side by side as supplementary (and not sequential, as is often suggested). He even cites the procedure in Exod. 17:14 as an illustration of this.

This is the first reference in the Bible to anybody writing something. No figure in Genesis is ever said to write something. Later references to Moses's scribal abilities are Exod. 24:4 ("Moses then wrote down everything the Lord had said"); Exod. 34:27 ("Then the Lord said to Moses, 'Write down these words'"); Num. 33:2 ("At the Lord's command Moses recorded the stages in their journey"); Deut. 31:9 ("So Moses wrote down this law and gave it to the priests"). In Exodus, God also is a writer (Exod. 34:1, "Chisel out two stone tablets, . . . and I will write on them"), as are Bezalel and Oholiab (Exod. 39:30, "They made the plate . . . and engraved on it, like an inscription on a seal: HOLY TO THE LORD"). For a survey of the degree of literacy in ancient Israel, see Young (1998).

Building an altar (v. 15) is something Noah starts (Gen. 8:20) and Abraham continues (12:7–8; 13:4, 18; 22:9), as does Isaac (26:25) and Jacob (35:7).

Moses will build another altar in Exod. 29:4, as does Aaron in 32:5 (cf. an Israelite's building an altar of which God does not approve, such as that of King Ahab, in 1 Kings 16:32). Joshua learns about altar building from his mentor, Moses (Josh. 8:30), but the altar the Transjordian tribes build (Josh. 22:10, 11, 16, 19, 23, 26, 29) almost leads to a bloody civil war between the "west" and the "east." Of all the altar-building scenes in the Bible, and there are many, the closest to Exod. 17:15 ("And Moses built an altar, and he called its name 'The LORD [Is] My Banner'"), even closer than Abraham's altar in Gen. 22, is Judg. 6:24. It says, "So Gideon built an altar to the LORD there and called it 'The LORD Is Peace.'" Building an altar is one way of memorializing for oneself, and for others who care to observe, a moment when God has dramatically intervened in one's life.

Verse 16 continues to puzzle commentators, myself included. Here are some of the issues. First, who is the "he" in "and he said," God or Moses? Second, what is the function of the *kî* after "and he said"? Does it have its normal causal sense ("because"), or does it introduce a quotation, or does it serve as some kind of interjection like "Yes!"? Third, does *yād* have its normal meaning of "hand," or the rarer meaning of "memorial," as in 1 Sam. 15:12; 2 Sam. 18:18; Isa. 56:5? Fourth, if *kēs* equals "throne," then why is it written differently from the way "throne" would normally be written: *kissēʾ*? Should *kēs* be emended to *nēs* ("A hand on the *banner* of the Lord") to bring v. 16 more in line with the name that Moses has given to the altar in v. 15? Fifth, why is there so much departure among the ancient versions in the translation of this verse from the Hebrew, and is this an indication those translators were as in doubt about the meaning of this verse as we are? For example, the LXX reads the name of the altar in v. 15 not as "The LORD is my banner," but as "The LORD is my refuge" (*Kyrios mou kataphygē*), apparently deriving *nissî* from *nûs*, "to flee." Again, instead of reading in v. 16a "a hand on top of Yah(weh)'s throne," the LXX reads, "for with a secret hand" (*hoti en cheiri kryphaia*). The LXX has arrived at that reading by (1) ignoring the introductory "and he said" and (2) by reading *kēs yâ* ("Yah's throne") as one word, *ksyh*, from the verb *kāsâ*, "to cover, conceal," hence, "with a secret hand." A look at the Vulgate and the various Targums shows the same degree of significant variation.

Moses does not build this altar in anticipation of what God might do, but in response to what God has done (which is usual). Since Moses is the subject of the two verbs in v. 15, it is most likely that Moses is the "he" in "and he said" at the beginning of v. 16. So what follows in the rest of v. 16 is something that Moses says. From there on, absolute certainty in interpretation of v. 16 halts.

First, because of the use of (uplifted) "hand" elsewhere in oaths, both in human oaths (Gen. 14:22) and in divine oaths (Exod. 6:8; Num. 14:30; Deut. 32:40), then possibly "A hand on top of/over/against Yah's throne" is some kind of an oath formula. To be sure, there is no use here of "swearing" or the uplifting of the hand, as in the other references; if such an expression appeared here too, it would make the meaning of v. 16 crystal clear. Among the ancient versions, *Targum Onqelos* best shows this interpretation. By means of a haggadic paraphrase, it renders, "A hand on top of Yah's throne" as "It is decreed by oath by the Fearful One, whose Shekinah is upon the Throne of Glory" (Vermès 1963: 163; 1975: 131).

For Houtman (1989: 116–18), "on top of the throne of Yah(weh)" in v. 16 is the same as "on top of the hill" in v. 9 (*'al-kēs yāh* in v. 16; *'al-rō'š haggib'â* in v. 9). On the peak of the hill, Moses is privy to God's immediate presence, as he will be when he ascends to the peak of a much higher place in chap. 19. In this hallowed place he builds an altar (possibly from the very stone on which he has been sitting, in v. 12?). For those who may be able to see it, that altar functions as a memorial (*yād*) to what the Lord has done on this occasion to the Amalekite perpetrators of this vile deed and to what he will continue to do to the distant Amalekite offspring.

In Deut. 12–25 the last of many laws, Deut. 25:17–19, comes out of the events of Exod. 17:8–16 (see Carmichael 1967: 205). It bids later Israelites not to forget what Amalek did to their ancestors. The law begins by stating, "Remember" (Deut. 25:17). It ends by stating "Do not forget!" (25:19). In what Brueggemann (1994: 822) calls "the institutionalization of hostility," the Lord commands his people to "blot out the memory of Amalek from under heaven." One reason this anti-Amalek commandment may come at the end of Deut. 25 is that a few verses earlier, when the code is discussing levirate marriage [vv. 5–10], the purpose of such a marriage is that the name of the deceased "not be blotted out from Israel." Deuteronomy 25:6, one law of "don't blot out," leads to a later law in Deut. 25:19 of "blot out."

Deuteronomy 25 does not say "Blot out Amalek"; rather, it says, "Blot out the memory of Amalek," as in Exod. 17:14. To be sure, this may mean, "Savage them; wipe them out; eradicate them." The Amalekites are a no-show in Judges (except where they partner with Moabites [Judg. 3:13] or with Midianites [Judg. 6:3, 33]), so no judge has to try to wipe out the memory of Amalek. Saul, at best, is mildly successful against them (1 Sam. 14:48; 15), but David is far more effective (1 Sam. 30), as is Hezekiah (1 Chron. 4:41–43). However, because there is still "Haman the Agagite" (Esther 3:1, 10; 8:3, 5; 9:24; referring to Agag, king of Amalek, in 1 Sam. 15:20?) in the Persian period, and a real nemesis to Israel, maybe Israel needs a better blotter. Possibly Israel needs not only to blot out the memory of Amalek from the history books, but also needs to blot out Amalek from its own memory log. Israel needs hallowed memories and not hateful memories. Anybody who has counseled an individual still struggling with a past of abuse, hurt, and grief knows of few things that heal as slowly as emotions that are raw and damaged due to trauma much earlier in life. The counselor also knows that few things are so exhilarating as seeing the counselee gradually experience the healing of those memories and be able "to blot out those memories."

Jethro, a Midianite Priest, Joins Moses in Worship of God

(18:1–12)

Translation

[1]And Jethro, priest of Midian, father-in-law of Moses, heard about everything that God had done for Moses and for Israel his people, that the LORD had brought out Israel from Egypt. [2]And Jethro, Moses's father-in-law, took Zipporah, wife of Moses, along with her dowry, [3]and her two sons, one of whose name was Gershom, for he said, "A sojourner I have been in a foreign land," [4]and the name of the other one, Eliezer, because (he said), "The God of my father (was) my help, and rescued me from Pharaoh's sword." [5]And Jethro, Moses's father-in-law, and his sons and his wife came to Moses, to the wilderness in which he was camping, the mountain of God. [6]And he had sent word to Moses, "I, your father-in-law, Jethro, am coming to you, along with your wife and her two sons with her." [7]So Moses went out to meet his father-in-law, and bowed down and kissed him, and each inquired about the other's well-being; then they went into the tent. [8]And Moses rehearsed for his father-in-law everything that the LORD had done to Pharaoh and to Egypt for Israel's sake, all the distress that overtook them on the way, and how the LORD had rescued them. [9]Jethro rejoiced over all the good that the LORD had done for Israel, how he rescued him from Egypt's hand.

[10]And Jethro said, "Blessed is the LORD, who rescued (all of) you from Egypt's hand and from Pharaoh's hand, who rescued the people from under Pharaoh's hand. [11]Now I know that greater (is) the LORD than all the gods, because of this thing they arrogantly did against them." [12]And Jethro, Moses's father-in-law, took a burnt offering and sacrifices to God, and Aaron came, and all Israel's elders, to eat food with Moses's father-in-law before God.

Grammatical and Lexical Notes

18:2. "Along with" is the preposition *ʾaḥar*, which normally means "after." For *ʾaḥar* meaning "with" (as in Ugaritic *aḥr*), see Dahood 1974b: 79.

18:2. *Šillûḥêhā* ("her dowry") occurs only two more times in the Hebrew Bible. It means "dowry" in 1 Kings 9:16 ("Pharaoh . . . captured Gezer . . . and then gave it as a *wedding gift* to his daughter, Solomon's wife"). The other reference is Mic. 1:14a, "Therefore you [Jerusalem/Judah] will give *parting gifts* to Moresheth Gath." According to Andersen and Freedman (2000: 232–33), what Mic. 1:14a is saying is that Jerusalem has given away her endowment by ceding territory to the northern nation, Israel.

18:4. Gordis (1971: 122; 1981: 412) and M. Fox (1980: 425) have both drawn attention to a category of quotation that sometimes omits the *verbum dicendi* in the naming formula, hence here ("and he said") is supplied.

18:4. The preposition *bě* prefixed to "my help" (*bě ʿezrî*) is the *bêt essentiae*, here rendered as a copula in a nominal sentence. Compare Ps. 146:5, "Blessed is he whose help [*bě ʿezrô*] is the God of Jacob."

18:5. Since Israel and Moses have not yet reached "the mountain of God," Sinai, perhaps we need to supply something like "(near) the mountain of God." Or since Moses has just been standing on top of a hill (17:10), maybe that too is God's mountain. Or since Rephidim is near Sinai, "God's mountain" designates a larger plot of ground than just the mountain itself.

18:6. Because Moses and Jethro do not meet each other until v. 7, *wayyôʾmer* in v. 6 must be rendered "And he had sent word to" rather than "And he said."

18:7. For *šāʾal lěšālôm* ("inquire about one's well-being, welfare"), see Gen. 43:27; Judg. 18:15; 1 Sam. 10:4; 17:22; 25:5; 30:21; 2 Sam. 8:10; 11:7; 1 Chron. 18:10. The NIV translates all the Samuel/Chronicles references as "greet" except for 2 Sam. 11:7 ("David asked him [Uriah] how Joab was, how the soldiers were and how the war was going"). The use of *šāʾal lěšālôm* on this occasion of Jethro and Moses's reuniting complements Jethro's final word to Moses earlier, when Moses asks Jethro's permission to return to Egypt: "Go in peace" (*lēk lěšālôm*) in Exod. 4:18. We have the same in Judg. 18. The priest tells the Danite spies heading to Laish, "Go in peace [*lēk lěšālôm*]" (18:6), and when they return to his house, they "greeted him [*šāʾal lěšālôm*]" (18:15). On the formula itself, see Wiseman 1982: 317–22; Talmon 1997: 84–86.

18:8. The Hebrew word for "distress" is *tělāʾâ*. Moses will later use it in correspondence with the king of Edom in Num. 20:14, "You know about all the *hardships* that have come down upon us." God's presence is surely with the Israelites as they make their way through the wilderness, but that does not lessen or remove the toil and pain and heartache that are a part of that migration.

18:9. The Hebrew form of "and he rejoiced" (*wayyiḥadě*) is unusual. Similar verb forms include *wayyišbě* ("and *captured* some of them") in Num. 21:1; *wayyiptě* ("so that my heart was secretly *enticed*") in Job 31:27; *yaptě* ("may God *extend* the territory of Japheth") in Gen. 9:27; *wayyēběkě* ("then Esau *wept* aloud") in Gen. 27:38; *wěyērdě* ("A ruler *will come out of* Jacob") in Num. 24:19. The exact same verbal form in Exod. 18:9 occurs in Job 3:6, "That night—may thick darkness seize it; may it not be *included* [*yiḥadě*] among the days of the year" (NIV; cf. NKJV's "As for that night, may darkness seize it; May it not *rejoice* among the days of the year"). The NIV translation of Job 3:6 ("included") actually reads the verb as a Niphal of *yāḥad* (*yēḥad*), "be one," rather than as the verb *ḥādâ*, "rejoice," as in Exod 18:9. Japhet (2003: 250–51) cites the approach of the medieval Jewish exegete from France, Rashbam, to both the Exod. 18 and Job 3 text, but especially to the latter. Rashbam notes that *ḥādâ* has a cluster of three unique consonants. First, the verb is a third *hê* verb: its final consonant is an *h*. Second, the middle consonant is *d* (*dālet*) one of the special *b-g-d-k-p-t* letters. Third, the first consonant is *ḥ* (*ḥêt*), one of the Hebrew gutturals. When such a verb appears in the jussive (as in Job 3:6), the *b-g-d-k-p-t* letter at the end of the verb form receives a *daghesh lene* and is vocalized with a *šěwāʾ*. See also GKC §§26r, 28d, 75r, which speaks of a *šěwāʾ mobile* at the end of such verb forms.

18:11. The phrase "Now I know that . . ." occurs several times in Scripture: Gen. 22:12; Judg. 17:13; 1 Kings 17:24; Ps. 20:6 [7]. Only in the first of these (Gen. 22:12) is the phrase used by the Lord or by one of his messengers.

18:11. The end of this verse (in the Hebrew) looks strange: *kî baddābār ʾăšer zadû ʿălêhem*, "because in the matter that they dealt arrogantly against them." My translation tries to make sense of what grammarians call an anacoluthon. Anacoluthon is a grammatical construction involving a break in sequence or coherence, such as "It makes me so—I just get angry."

18:12. One does not eat "with" (*ʿim*) God, but "before" (*lipnê*) God. See Deut. 27:7 ("Sacrifice fellowship offerings there, eating them and rejoicing in the presence of/before [*lipnê*] the Lord your God").

Commentary

So far Scripture has told us about three priests, all of them foreign. There is **18:1**
Melchizedek, the (Canaanite?) priest who blesses Abram (Gen. 14:18–20). Second, Joseph marries the daughter of the Egyptian Potiphera, priest of On/Heliopolis (Gen. 41:45, 50). And here we have Jethro, priest of Midian, father-in-law of Moses, and one whom the reader has first met back in chap. 2. Non-Israelite priests are identified by city ("Potiphera, priest of On" in Gen. 41:45) or by country ("Jethro, priest of Midian" in Exod. 3:1 and 18:1), or by god ("the priests of Dagon" in 1 Sam. 5:5 and "the priest of Baal" in 2 Kings 11:18 = 2 Chron. 23:17).

More important than Jethro's connection with Midian is his connection with Moses. Chapter 18 identifies Jethro as Moses's father-in-law twelve times (vv. 1, 2, 5, 6, 7, 8, 12 [2x], 14, 17, 24, 27). All twelve are the narrator's except for the one in v. 6, where Jethro identifies himself as Moses's father-in-law. The closest parallel to such repetition of relationship is in the story of David's bringing the ark to Jerusalem (2 Sam. 6): "Michal *daughter of Saul* watched from a window" (v. 16); "Michal *daughter of Saul* came out to meet him" (v. 20); "and Michal *daughter of Saul* had no children to the day of her death" (v. 23). One thing this repeated emphasis on Jethro's relationship to Moses accomplishes is that it makes even more bold the contrast between how one member of the "family" (Amalek in chap. 17) interacts with Moses and the Israelites, and how another member of the "family" (Jethro of Midian in chap. 18) interacts with Moses and the Israelites.

What the nations "heard" in the Song of Moses produces terror and trembling (Exod. 15:14). What God "heard" moves him to provide bread for his people (Exod. 16:7–8). Here, what Jethro has "heard" from afar moves him to come and see for himself if it is all true. Rahab too has "heard" from afar about Israel and Israel's God, but she does not need to do any traveling to confirm with her eyes what she has heard with her ears (Josh. 2:10). Closer to Jethro's example is the Queen of Sheba, who "heard" about Solomon's glory and had to come to see it for herself (1 Kings 10:1–13 = 2 Chron. 9:1–12). All three could say what Job says, "My ears had heard of you but now my eyes have seen you" (Job 42:5).

We are not sure at what point Moses has sent Zipporah and their two sons **18:2–4**
back to her father and to Grandpa Jethro. According to Exod. 4:20, Moses sets off for Egypt with Zipporah and their sons. It is understandable that Moses would not want his wife and children put in harm's way, and so at some point on the journey to Egypt, he has word sent to Jethro to come and take them back to Midian. A soldier's having to leave his family behind, not sure if he will see them again, is one of the most heart-wrenching moments whenever the soldier is summoned to war. Yet recall that Zipporah has handled herself quite adroitly when the one who threatens Moses's life is not the Egyptians

but God (4:24–26)! Zipporah seems to be an individual who is quite capable of taking the necessary steps to save not only her own life but also the life of her family.

To be sure, Exod. 4:20 refers to Moses's "sons," although Gershom is the only son mentioned before that. Now the reader is introduced to a second son, Eliezer. His name means "My God [Is] a Help(er)." The word for "help(er)" [*'ēzer*] is almost the same as that in Gen. 2:18, where the Lord God, upon affirming that it is not good for the male human to be alone, moves ahead and makes a "helper" (*'ēzer*) for him (Gen. 2:18). It is also the word in Samuel's famous stone that he sets up, Ebenezer (*'eben hā'āzer*) in 1 Sam. 7:12.

The name is exactly the same as that of Eliezer, the household servant that (childless) Abram comes within a whisker of adopting as his legal heir (Gen. 15:2), and almost the same as Eleazar, one of Aaron's surviving sons, and one who brings down Uncle Moses's wrath on himself (Lev. 10:12–20). It is a truth about God that Moses will mention later in his blessing of the tribes: "Be his *help* [Judah's] against his foes!" (Deut. 33:7); "There is no one like the God of Jeshurun, who rides on the heavens to *help* you" (Deut. 33:26); "He is your shield and *helper*" (Deut. 33:29).

Moses joins a host of other fathers who have two sons: Eber's sons Peleg and Joktan (Gen. 10:25); Joseph's sons Manasseh and Ephraim (Gen. 41:50–52); Elimelech's sons Mahlon and Kilion (Ruth 1:2); Eli's sons Hophni and Pinehas (1 Sam. 1:3; 2:34); Saul's two sons by Rizpah (2 Sam. 21:8); Simon and his brother Andrew (Matt. 4:18); Zebedee's sons James and John (Matt. 4:21). The mention of two daughters is less common, but we do have Laban's two daughters (Gen. 29:16) and Saul's two daughters (1 Sam. 14:49). The longest list of named sons that one father produces, exceeding even that of Jacob's twelve named sons, is Heman's (David's seer) fourteen sons (1 Chron. 25:4–5). We can be glad Scripture does not take the space to name all the seventy-some children that Gideon fathers (Judg. 8:30–31)!

It is difficult to pin down to what moment Moses is referring when at the end of v. 4 he says, "and rescued me from Pharaoh's sword." There have been many such moments, one after the other. Hence, it is likely that Moses is not thinking of one particular episode, but rather this is his testimony to God's saving power manifested again and again over at least a year's time. Eliezer is Moses's living Ebenezer.

18:5–6 Moses does not ask Jethro to visit him and, while he is at it, to bring Zipporah, Gershom, and Eliezer along. If Moses is just counting the days until he sees his wife and boys again, the text is silent about that. And yet there must have been some kind of ongoing communication. Otherwise, how would Jethro know where to find his son-in-law? Even for a Midianite, Rephidim is not the easiest place to find somewhere in a spacious wilderness.

Upon seeing the arrival of the family party, Moses is most respectful and affectionate toward Jethro ("went out to meet him . . . kissed him . . . they went into the tent"). But what about seeing Zipporah and the boys? I am sure that if I have seen neither my father-in-law nor my wife for a long time, I know which one I am going to kiss first! But that is a Westerner speaking. Middle Eastern cultures, both past and present, operate differently. **18:7–11**

The scene is reminiscent of that in Gen. 18:1–15, when three "men" appear to Abraham. He too goes out from his tent to meet them and bows low to the ground. Presumably Abraham invites the men into his tent, where they share a meal, as Jethro, Moses, and others do in Exod. 18:12. Sarah is not spoken to, neither does she speak (like Zipporah in Exod. 18). She cooks and listens and is rebuked by one of the visitors for her unspoken thoughts about her possibly becoming pregnant.

In v. 8 Moses is careful not to talk to Jethro about himself and his accomplishments or charismatic leadership. Rather, he puts the spotlight on his Lord: "everything that the Lord had done to Pharaoh and to Egypt" and "how the Lord rescued them." Yes, Moses does mention the "distress" along the journey, but in a way that does not elicit Jethro's pity, but rather in a way that exalts and magnifies the Lord. Since when is following the Lord's guidance a guaranteed distress-free experience? As the old gospel song has it, "Some through the waters, some through the flood, some through the fire, but all through the blood" ("God Leads Us Along," by George A. Young).

Jethro is one of several foreigners/outsiders in Scripture who pronounces a blessing in the presence of an Israelite or Israelite patriarch. One thinks of (1) Melchizedek's words of blessing before Abraham (Gen. 14:19–20); (2) Balaam's blessing on Israel throughout Num. 23–24, but especially Num. 24:5–9; (3) the Queen of Sheba's words of blessing in 1 Kings 10:9 before Solomon; (4) Hiram, king of Tyre, and his blessing for Solomon in 2 Chron. 2:11–12. On the blessing of foreigners in Ruth, see Moore 1998: 203–17.

As Towner (1968: 388–89) has noted, the phrase "Blessed is the Lord, who . . ." is often (but not always) comprised of four elements: (1) the Qal passive participle of *bārak* (*bārûk*) that is (2) connected with Yahweh; (3) an ascription clause that is in apposition to "Yahweh"; and (4) a predicative clause. We have these four elements here: (1) "Blessed [*bārûk*] is (2) Yahweh/the Lord, (3) who rescued you from . . . (4) Now I know . . ." Another good example of this pattern is Gen. 24:27, the words of Abraham's servant to Rebekah: (1) "Blessed [*bārûk*] is (2) Yahweh/the Lord, . . . (3) who has not abandoned his kindness and faithfulness to my master. (4) As for me, the Lord has led me on the journey." See also Ruth 4:14 (the women of Bethlehem to Naomi); 1 Sam. 25:32–33 (David to Abigail); 1 Sam. 25:39 (David to his own men?); 2 Sam. 18:28 (Ahimaaz, the priest's son, to David); 1 Kings 1:48 (the royal officials to Solomon); 1 Kings 10:9 = 2 Chron. 9:8 (the Queen of Sheba to Solomon); 2 Chron. 2:12 [11] (Hiram to Solomon); Ezra 7:27–28 (Ezra, about

Artaxerxes, king of Persia). Towner observes that these "Blessed is the LORD, who . . ." passages (1) are all noncultic; (2) frequently occur in conversation between two parties; (3) are not actually prayers but are rather kerygmatic utterances; and (4) all offer testimony to the goodness of God.

Jethro's "Now I know" is close to Rahab's "I know that the LORD has given this land to you" in Josh. 2:9, and is exactly the same as the Aramean Naaman's "*Now I know* that there is no God in all the world except in Israel" (2 Kings 5:15). The one difference between what Jethro says and what Naaman says is that Naaman's confession is a testimony to the unquestioned and exclusive monotheistic nature of Israel's God.

So when any "outsider" makes such an acknowledgment of Israel's God, does that mean, to use a word more at home in NT language, they have experienced conversion? Do, say, Jethro the Midianite and Naaman the Aramean become Yahwists? There is surely a difference between Jethro and Naaman. Jethro, on the one hand, is moved to say what he says because of what he has heard. He himself has experienced no deliverance. Naaman, on the other hand, is moved to say what he says because of the healing he has experienced. Perhaps, then, a better parallel to Jethro is King Nebuchadnezzar, who offers praise to the God who has delivered Shadrach, Meshach, and Abednego (Dan. 3:28). Each of the above takes a different path to their acknowledgment of Yahweh: Jethro because of what he has heard, Naaman because of what he has experienced, Nebuchadnezzar because of what he has seen.

Milgrom (1982) believes that the conversion of individuals is not attested in the OT until the postexilic period, and mass conversions do not appear until the period of the Hasmoneans (second and first centuries BC) and the advent of Christianity. For him, assimilation into the Israelite/Jewish faith is by intermarriage (e.g., the proposal made by Hamor the Hivite, speaking for his clan, that Jacob's family "intermarry with us, . . . [and then] you can settle among us" [Gen. 34:9–10]; or Ruth, who marries the Israelite Boaz) rather than by conversion.

Milgrom, however, does not discuss the likes of Jethro or Naaman or Nebuchadnezzar. If Jethro does not experience conversion, then what is he saying? He says what he says because of what he has heard Moses share, and does not Rom. 10:17 say that "faith comes from hearing the message"? It is possible that Jethro has simply come to the realization that this Yahweh of Israel is greater, more powerful, more involved with people's lives than any of his own Midianite gods, without rejecting the existence of the latter? The technical name for this kind of belief in which one acknowledges belief in one specific god, while at the same time affirming the true existence of other gods, is "henotheism." Conversion, if it is real, has a lasting impact on the one converted. Unfortunately, we do not know how Jethro's confession impacts and changes his life a week later, a month later, a year later. Does he return to his own people, as the Samaritan woman of John 4 does, and become an evangelist?

Mitchell (1987: 156–57) points out that "blessed is the LORD" in somebody's mouth is not necessarily a statement of faith. It may be simply an expression of admiration or a meaningful, appreciative, and ecumenical praise that transcends a one-way-to-God ideology. The *bārûk* formula does become a statement of faith, however, when the speaker declares his faith in God's deliverance, or when the confession is associated with acts of worship, as is the case with Jethro in v. 12.

Jethro seems to be the officiating priest. Moses is named twice but only as **18:12**
the son-in-law of Jethro. Aaron is named and is present, but he appears to do nothing priestly.

It is Jethro who takes a burnt offering (*ʿōlâ*) and sacrifices (*zĕbāḥîm*) and brings them to God. The latter term is not a catchall term for a whole bunch of other sacrifices in addition to the *ʿōlâ*. Rather, it is a reference to the *zebaḥ šĕlāmîm* (peace offering/fellowship offering) of Lev. 3. We know this is so because v. 12 tells us the party "eat" (part of) the sacrifices, and the *zebaḥ šĕlāmîm* (or just *šĕlāmîm*) is the only offering whose meat is consumed by the worshiper/donor.

The two sacrifices appear together in a number of passages. Besides Exod. 18:12 we have Exod. 10:25; Lev. 17:8; 22:18, 21; Num. 15:3, 8; Deut. 12:6, 11; Josh. 22:26, 28; 1 Sam. 15:22; 2 Kings 5:17; 10:24; Isa. 56:7; Jer. 7:21–22; Hosea 6:6. This is not to suggest that these two sacrifices are identical or interchangeable, although in some ways they are very similar. The different verbs used with each in the following four verses suggest some difference: (1) Exod. 32:6, one "sacrifices" (*ʿālâ*) burnt offerings, but "presents" (*nāgaš*) fellowship offerings; (2) Deut. 27:6–7, one "offers" (*ʿālâ*) burnt offerings, but "sacrifices" (*zābaḥ*) fellowship offerings; (3) Josh. 8:31, one "offers" (*ʿālâ*) burnt offerings, but "sacrifices" (*zābaḥ*) fellowship offerings; (4) 1 Kings 3:15, Solomon "sacrificed" (*ʿālâ*) burnt offerings, but "made" (*ʿāśâ*; ignored by NIV) fellowship offerings. What all these above references have in common is that they refer to two voluntary, spontaneous offerings (the *ʿōlâ* and the *šĕlāmîm*) of the individual(s) rather than to mandatory offerings required of everyone in the covenant community.

It is particularly striking to see a new convert, if that is what Jethro is, leading the likes of Moses, Aaron, and the elders in worship. A "babe in faith" leads those who hopefully are more mature in their faith.

Some early Jewish writers were not sure how to read Jethro. Philo (*Drunk.* 11.41–45) condemns Jethro as a blasphemer because Jethro dares to compare Yahweh to other gods (Exod. 18:11). Even Josephus, who is normally positive about Jethro, has Moses offer the sacrifice in v. 12 rather than Jethro (*Ant.* 3.3.1 §63), and has Aaron leading the rest of the worship in praise to God (*Ant.* 3.3.1 §64). See Feldman 1997: 591–94.

Jethro's Counsel to Moses

(18:13–27)

Translation

[13]And it happened on the morrow that Moses sat down to judge the people, while the people stood about Moses all day long. [14]Moses's father-in-law observed everything he was doing for the people, and he said, "What is this thing that you are doing for the people? Why are you sitting down alone while all the people take their place about you all day long?" [15]And Moses said to his father-in-law, "Because the people come to me to inquire of God. [16]For whenever one of them has a concern, he comes to me, and I judge between a man and his fellow, and I make known God's statutes and his teachings." [17]Moses's father-in-law said to him, "Not good is the thing you are doing. [18]For sure you will wear yourself out, yourself and also this people with you, for the thing is too heavy for you. You are not able to do it alone. [19]Now listen to me. I will advise you, and may God be with you. You be to the people in front of God, and it is you who shall bring concerns to God. [20]You shall enjoin upon them the statutes and teachings, and you shall make known to them the way in which they should go and the practices that they are to do. [21]As for you, seek out from all the people competent men, God-fearers, truthful men, haters of ill-gotten gain, and place them as chiefs of thousands, chiefs of hundreds, chiefs of fifties, and chiefs of tens. [22]They shall judge the people continually. Every major concern they will bring to you, but every minor concern they themselves shall judge. Ease up on yourself, and they will carry the burden with you. [23]If you do this thing, and God so commands you, you will be able to stand, and also each one of these people will go to his place in peace."

[24]Moses heeded his father-in-law's voice and implemented all he had said. [25]Moses chose competent men from all Israel, and appointed them heads over the people, officers of thousands, officers of hundreds, officers of fifties, officers of tens. [26]They judged the people continually. The more challenging matters they would bring to Moses, and every minor concern they themselves would judge. [27]And Moses sent off his father-in-law, and he went back to his own land.

Grammatical and Lexical Notes

18:13. *ʿĀmad ʿal* occurs earlier in Exodus with the meaning "stand on" (3:5, "the ground on which you are standing is holy"), but its meaning "stand by/about" is well attested (e.g., Gen. 18:8, "While they ate, he *stood near* them under a tree").

18:13. The expression *min-habbōqer ʿad-hāʿāreb* in vv. 13 and 14 ("from morning until evening") is a merism: hence my "all day long." See Honeyman 1952: 12; Avishur 1984: 92.

18:14. The Hebrew word for "thing" is *dābār*. It occurs ten times in this paragraph, nine times in the singular (vv. 14, 16, 17, 18, 22 [2x], 23, 26 [2x]), and one time in the plural (v. 19). Cassuto (1967: 222) suggests that the ten uses of *dābār* in this unit may anticipate two chapters later the "Ten Words," or

Ten Commandments. For the Sinai commandments referred to as Ten Words (the literal meaning of "Decalogue"), see passages like Exod. 34:28; Deut. 4:13; 10:4. The question here is how to translate *dābār* throughout Exod. 18:13–27: thing? matter? concern? dispute? case?

18:15. *Dāraš* (*ʾĕlōhîm*) may mean either "seek [God]" or "inquire [of God]." These two meanings account for about 100 of the 165 occurrences of *dāraš*. An illustration of the first meaning is in the famous Isa. 55:6, "Seek the Lord [*diršû YHWH*] while he may be found." In about twenty passages it is a prophet who is approached with a request to "inquire of God": the people of Moses (Exod. 18:15); young Saul and his companion of a seer (1 Sam. 9:9); Jeroboam's wife of Ahijah (1 Kings 14:5); Ahaz of his prophets and of Micaiah (1 Kings 22:7, 8 = 2 Chron. 18:4–7); Jehoram and Jehoshaphat of Elisha (2 Kings 3:11); Hazael of Elisha (2 Kings 8:8); Josiah of Huldah (2 Kings 22:13, 18 = 2 Chron. 34:21, 26); Zedekiah via representatives of Jeremiah (Jer. 21:2; 37:7); an idolater of a prophet (Ezek. 14:7); the exiles of Ezekiel (Ezek. 20:1, 3).

18:18. The word *nābēl* ("wear oneself out") means to "sink, drop down, wither." One can sink or drop down from exhaustion, as in Exod. 18:18, or one can sink or drop down from fear, as David says of his enemies, using this verb, "they all lose heart/courage" (2 Sam 22:46 = Ps. 18:45 [46]).

18:18. The word Jethro uses for Moses's task being too "heavy" is *kābēd*. It is the same word used back in 17:12 for Moses's "heavy/tired [*kĕbēdîm*]" arms. Moses himself has used it back in 4:10, when he informs the Lord that he is a man who is "heavy-mouthed and heavy-tongued" (*kĕbad-peh ûkĕbad lāšôn*).

18:19. The verb *yāʿaṣ* ("advise") is common enough in the Hebrew Bible, but it occurs only twice in the Pentateuch, and both times in exactly the same form (first-person imperfect with second-person masculine singular pronominal suffix). In addition to Exod. 18:19, in Num. 24:14 Balaam says to Balak, "I will *warn/inform* you of what this people [Israel] will do to your people in days to come."

18:19. Jethro's words to Moses, *hĕyēh ʾattâ lāʿām mûl hāʾĕlōhîm*, raise a translation issue. I have rendered it fairly literally with "You be to the people in front of God." Most translations paraphrase with something like "You must be the people's representative before God" (NIV), or "You represent the people before God" (NJPS). This is a quite acceptable rendering, for the preposition *mûl* ("in front of") is used here figuratively for the one and only time in the Hebrew Bible. For Moses to "be in front of God" means that he represents God to them. Back in 17:6 it is the Lord who stands in front of (*ʿāmad lipnê*) Moses.

18:20. While "enjoin upon, teach, instruct" is an appropriate rendering of *zāhar* (Hiphil) here, elsewhere it may take on the stronger meaning of "warn" (2 Kings 6:10, but especially in the account of Ezekiel's call to be a prophet—Ezek. 3:17, 18, 19, 20, 21). The connection between *teaching* (*ḥôq* and *tôrâ*, "statute" and "teaching/instruction") and *warning* is obvious, for one purpose of a law is to warn against the transgression of that law. There is another Hebrew verb, *ʿûd* (Hiphil), that means "warn," especially when followed by the preposition *bĕ* (e.g., Exod. 19:23, "about which you warned us") but sometimes may mean "instruct" (e.g., Neh. 9:34 and Ps. 50:7, although NIV usually translates these latter references with "warn" or "testify against").

18:20. The Septuagint's choice of *poreuesthai* for Hebrew *hālak/yālak* with metaphorical meaning ("the way in which they should *go*") reminds one of the frequent use of *peripatein* in the NT to refer to the "walk" of the believer in a path of virtue and holiness (Eph. 4:1; Col. 1:10; 1 Thess. 2:12; 1 John 2:6; etc.). *Poreuesthai* is also used in the NT with metaphorical meaning but normally in a negative way (1 Pet. 4:3; 2 Pet. 3:3; Jude 16, 18).

18:21. "Seek" is the verb *ḥāzâ*, one of the Hebrew verbs for "see." BDB 302b lists this reference as the one and only time where *ḥāzâ* means "provide." When Moses recalls this incident, he uses the verb "choose, pick" (*yāhab*; Deut. 1:13), which more often means "give" than "choose, pick" (Gen. 30:1, "*Give* me [Rachel] children or else I'll die"). *Ḥāzâ* can mean not only "see," but also "choose," just as another verb for "see" (*rāʾâ*) can also mean "choose" (e.g., 1 Sam. 16:1, "I am sending you [Samuel] to Jesse of Bethlehem. I have *chosen/seen* one of his sons to be king"). The root *ḥzh* is common enough in the Hebrew Bible, but in that part often called the "Primary History" (Genesis–Kings) the verb *ḥāzâ* appears only three other times (Exod. 24:11; Num. 24:4, 16), the participle *ḥōzēh* two times (2 Sam. 24:11; 2 Kings 17:13), and the noun *ḥāzôn* once (1 Sam. 3:1). The LXX's verb of choice for *ḥāzâ* is *kathistēmi*, used elsewhere for the description of leaders (Num. 3:10; 31:48; Deut. 1:13; 2 Sam. 3:39; 15:4; Ps. 2:6). For similar uses in the NT of this verb, see Luke 12:42; Titus 1:5; Heb. 5:1; 7:28.

18:21. *ʾAnšê-ḥayil* is the Hebrew for "competent/capable men." This is the Hebrew term for men who are respected for their abilities: Pharaoh to Joseph about Joseph's family in Gen. 47:6 ("If you know of any among them *with special ability*, put them in charge of my own livestock"); 1 Kings 1:42 ("a worthy man"); 1 Chron. 26:8 ("capable men"); Isa. 5:22 ("champions"). The phrase is used also for men known for their bravery: Judg. 3:29 ("strong"); 1 Sam. 14:52 ("a brave man"); 1 Sam. 31:12 ("valiant man"); Ps. 76:5 [6] ("warriors"); Eccles. 12:3 ("strong men"). Since the phrase connotes those who are brave, it stands to reason why it is also a term for "soldiers": Judg. 20:44, 46 ("valiant fighters"); 2 Sam. 11:16 ("strongest defenders"); 2 Sam. 23:20 ("a valiant fighter"); 2 Sam. 24:9 ("able-bodied men"); Nah. 2:3 [4] ("warriors"). How challenging it is to render *ʾanšê-ḥayil* into one English equivalent is illustrated by the fact that for the dozen or so Scripture passages I have just cited, NIV uses almost that many different wordings.

18:21. I have translated *bāṣaʿ* as "[haters of] ill-gotten gain." The verb *bāṣaʿ* ("cut off, break off, gain by violence") occurs sixteen times, and the noun *beṣāʿ* ("profit, unjust gain") twenty-three times. The noun is the word that Judah uses with his brothers when discussing how to get rid of Joseph: "What *gain* is there if we kill our brother and cover up his blood?" (Gen. 37:26 AT). In three verses, Proverbs addresses the negative fallout of going after *beṣāʿ* (Prov. 1:19; 15:27; 28:16). The noun is always used in a negative way, but not necessarily always in a violent context. Unlike *šāḥād*, which means only "bribe," *beṣaʿ* refers to any wrongful profit gained from the likes of bribe or extortion. See Harland (2000: esp. 318), who argues for "extortion" in Exod. 18:21.

18:21. Jethro suggests groups using numbers in descending order: 1000>100>50>10. By contrast, in the Gospels the tendency is to use numbers in ascending order: thus in the parable of the seeds, the seed that falls on good ground produces a crop 30>60>100 times (Mark 4:9, 20). An exception to this ascending order of numerals is Mark's account of the feeding of the five thousand, in which the throng sits down "in groups of hundreds and fifties" (Mark 6:40). Perhaps this order is another indication of the way in which Mark has presented the Gospel narrative as an Exodus story (Marcus 2000: 408).

18:22. The verb *qālal* in the Qal means "be swift, be lightly esteemed," but in the Hiphil (as here) it means, among other things, "make light, lighten." Compare what the Philistine priests say to their distraught people who are trying to dispose of the ark they have stolen: "Pay honor to Israel's god. Perhaps he will *lift* his hand [i.e., lighten the pressure] from you and your gods and your land" (1 Sam. 6:5).

18:22. In some places the verb *nāśāʾ* means "to bear a burden," and together with the cognate noun *maśśāʾ* ("burden") shows how demanding and overwhelming leadership can be (see Num. 11).

18:23. In v. 13 Moses "sat down" to judge, but here Jethro tells him that he "will be able to stand." Jethro wants his son-in-law to be strong enough to stand (i.e., endure) while he is sitting (as judge).

18:23. The NIV's rendering of *bĕšālôm* ("in peace") as "satisfied" is right on target. The phrase is much like what the still-incognito Joseph uses with his brothers when he tells them to go back home but leave Benjamin with him: "The rest of you, go back to your father *in peace*" (Gen. 44:17), as if that is possible! Wiseman (1982: 325) suggests that the phrase "in peace" "marks a successful conclusion of negotiation or assurance that the request for a desired state of relationship has been granted."

18:26. The adjective "major" in "major concern" in v. 22 is *gādôl*. Here it is the synonym *qāšeh* ("challenging"), from *qāšâ*. In both verses (22, 26), *qāṭōn* is used for "minor [concern]." Words related to *qāšâ* have a range of meanings in the Hebrew Bible. It is used for the taxing, difficult labor to which Pharaoh subjects the Hebrews (Exod. 1:14; 6:9; Deut. 26:6), and to which Solomon subjects his own people (1 Kings 12:4 = 2 Chron. 10:4). It is the word used for Joseph's speaking "harshly" to his brothers (Gen. 42:7, 30) and for the "surly" Nabal, husband of Abigail (1 Sam. 25:3). See further the discussion of *qāšâ* in A. Weiss 2006: 76–84.

18:27. What is one to do with the *lô* in *wayyēlek lô ʾel-ʾarṣô* ("and he went back to his own land")? Is it like the *lĕka* in the Lord's words to Abram in Gen. 12:1, *lek-lĕkā mēʾarṣĕkā* ("Leave your country")? Or does it indicate simply that Jethro returned "by himself" to Midian? Both BDB 515b (§§i.a and b) and Muraoka (1978: 495–98) cite the reflexive use of the preposition *lĕ* after (a) the imperative and (b) with verbs of motion, but neither mention Exod. 18:27.

Commentary

The reason Moses is sitting and the people are standing is that during legal **18:13–14**
proceedings the judge sits while the litigants stand. Kings, when they are judging, sit (Saul in 1 Sam. 22:6; Solomon in 1 Kings 3:16). See also Prov. 20:8, "When a king sits on his throne to judge. . . ." Psalm 122:5 speaks of "the thrones for judgment stand, the thrones of the house of David." A manslayer may flee to a city of refuge and "stand in the entrance of the city gate and state his case before the elders of that city" (Josh. 20:4; see also Num. 35:12; Deut. 21:18–19; Ruth 4:1–11). What is Mordecai doing "sitting at the king's gate" (Esther 2:19) after Esther has become the queen? I suspect that after she becomes queen, she has Mordecai appointed as a magistrate or judge as a reward for what he has done for her and to give him easier access to the royal quarters; see Gordis (1976a: 47–48). The only place I am aware of where a judge stands rather than sits is Ezek. 44:24: "In any dispute, the priests are to serve [lit., "stand," as in NKJV] as judges." G. Driver (1954a: 310) points out that Ezekiel's having judges stand while they expedite their legal responsibilities reflects Babylonian practices, where it was more common for judges to stand (*nazazu*) rather than sit (*ashabu*). And Ezekiel spends most of his life with the exiles in Babylon.

Judging is not an intermittent ministry of Moses. It has become an all-consuming ministry, one that goes on "all day long." Even if that is a bit of a hyperbole, it points to judging disputes as something that Moses does not do spasmodically. Apparently the people are not only grumbling against and testing God and Moses; they are also not getting along with one another. What kinds of disputes would Moses need to address? "You ate some of my family's manna." "You stole one of my cows." "You put too heavy a load on my wagon and made the wheels collapse." "Your son got too fresh with my daughter." "You took more water from the rock than you were supposed to, so I had less."

Jethro is the exact opposite of two other famous fathers-in-law, Laban and Saul. If you could get Moses, Jacob, and David together in a room and ask them to share memories of their fathers-in-law, can you imagine the radically different paths the conversation would take? Maybe Jacob and David would like to do to Laban and Saul what God says he will do to the Amalekites: blot out their memory. In relating to their respective sons-in-law, Laban is a shyster, Saul a savage, but Jethro a savior, for he was so solicitous about Moses's health. One kind of fatigue overtakes Moses in 17:12, where Aaron and Hur immediately give support. Another kind of fatigue overtakes Moses in chap. 18, where Jethro immediately gives counsel.

If Laban is the character in Genesis with whom Jethro contrasts, then Melchizedek is the character in Genesis with whom Jethro compares (Gen. 14:18–24). Both are foreign priests whose theology and God-statements are as orthodox as just about anything one will find in Scripture (Gen. 14:19–20; Exod. 18:10–11). Melchizedek's meeting up with Abram follows a war account (Abraham's successful recovery of Lot); Jethro's meeting up with Moses follows a war account (Exod. 17:8–16). Sailhamer (2009: 370–71) provides a helpful chart that picks up on some of these connections. The most salient one is his observation that the account of Melchizedek's encounter with Abram comes just before the account of the Lord's covenant with Abram (Gen. 14:18–24 and 15:1–19). Similarly, the account of Jethro's (second) encounter with Moses comes just before the account of the Lord's covenant with Moses and the Israelites at Sinai (Exod. 18:1–27 and chaps. 19–24). One difference between the two priests is that Melchizedek disappears from the Abraham narrative after chap. 14, while Jethro may reappear one more time, in Num. 10:29–32, when Moses asks "Hobab" (either yet another name for Jethro or Jethro's son and so Moses's brother-in-law) to go with the Israelites as a local guide through the wilderness.

18:15–16 The people repeatedly come to Moses for two diametrically opposite reasons. Sometimes they come to grumble and complain to him, but at other times, as he says in 18:15, they seek him out "to inquire of God." Imagine that one day somebody confronts you and says, "I do not like you. You are not a good person. You are just trying to kill me." And then the next day they approach you and request that you inquire of God about some issue on their behalf. Why would you speak so negatively of another person out of one corner of your mouth, and then out of the other corner of your mouth ask him to be an intermediary between you and God? Such is the fickleness of human nature.

The OT reveals that there are two divinely sanctioned ways one can "inquire of God" (see Long 1973). One is through a prophet, as in Exod. 18:15 and in all those passages I cited in my grammatical/lexical note on *dāraš* in v. 15. The other is through a priest. But there are some significant differences between the two. For example, when somebody asks a prophet to inquire of God, the verb for "inquire" is always *dāraš*. But when somebody seeks out a priest to inquire of God, the verb for "inquire" is *šāʾal* (Num. 27:21; Judg. 18:5; 20:18, 23; 1 Sam. 14:37; 23:2; 2 Sam. 2:1; 5:19, 23).

Here is a second difference. When a priest inquires of God, he does so by using the Urim and the Thummim, sacred lots used to determine God's will. So the Lord instructs Moses about Joshua with these words: "He is to stand before Eleazar the priest, who will obtain decisions for him by inquiring [*šāʾal*] of the Urim before the LORD" (Num. 27:21). How does the prophet inquire of God? Certainly not by using the Urim, a priestly prerogative. The most likely anwer is through intercession, but I do not believe that any of these prophetic inquiries records that when somebody seeks out a prophet for such an inquiry, the prophet then "prays." As Balentine (1984: 168) says, "To deliver a word from God does not necessarily imply that intercession has occurred."

There is a third difference. Most of the examples of priestly inquiry have to do with going/not going to war (e.g., 2 Sam. 5:19, "David inquired of the Lord [through the priest Abiathar], 'Shall I go up and attack the Philistines?'"). By contrast, prophetic inquiries are much broader: a lost animal (1 Sam. 9:1–9); sickness (Abijah, the son of Jeroboam in 1 Kings 14:1–5; Ben-Hadad, king of Aram, in 2 Kings 8:7–8); an interpretation of Scripture (2 Kings 22:13, 18); a military situation (1 Kings 22:7–8); under siege from the Babylonian behemoth (Jer. 21:2, which is an interesting scene of a priest [Pashhur] going to a prophet [Jeremiah] to "inquire of the LORD").

There is one difference between people going to Moses in Exod. 18 to inquire of the Lord and all the later prophetic inquiry passages. Even when such inquiries are at their height, such as during the ministry of northern Israelite prophets in the tenth and ninth centuries BC, like Micaiah and Elisha, such inquiries are not frequently reported. During the period of classical prophecy (eighth to fifth centuries BC), the biblical examples are even more isolated. For instance, there is not one reference anywhere in any one of the sixty-six chapters of Isaiah of anybody coming to Isaiah and asking the prophet to inquire of God. Moses, however, is peppered with such requests, leaving him little time for anything else. This all suggests that "inquiring of God" on behalf of another is not a common ministry of the prophets, Moses excepted.

In Exod. 18:16 Moses answers such requests by "mak[ing] known God's statutes and his teachings." We are not yet at Sinai, where God will reveal his *ḥôq* and his *tôrâ* to his people. Have there been revelations of such matters that are pre-Sinai and anticipatory of Sinai? Apparently so; see Exod. 15:25b. People know right from wrong long before Sinai. Cain knows that murder is wrong long before the revelation of the sixth commandment. Even Pharaoh knows it is not right to sleep with another man's wife (Gen. 12:17–20), and he has never heard of the seventh commandment (see also Gen. 20). Novak (1998: 55–58) argues for the existence in Israel and elsewhere of a "natural law," a law by which human reason tells the Israelites (and others) what is God's basic rule for humans in community.

18:17–26 Jethro not only discerns the problem (many of us are good at that), but he also proposes a solution that would eliminate the problem. His suggestion is that Moses select competent, virtuous people and appoint them as legal officers over groups of thousands, hundreds, fifties, and tens, to handle the more minor cases. Moses will be involved only in the more difficult ones. Later illustrations of Moses's alone tending to such severe issues include Lev. 24:10–16 (what to do with a blasphemer); Num. 9:6–13 (what if they cannot observe Passover at the regular time?); Num. 15:32–36 (what to do with the individual who is gathering sticks on the Sabbath). Joshua also, as Moses's successor, addresses the adjudication of such weighty matters as inheritance (Josh. 17:3–4).

There is possibly some connection between Moses's judicial reorganization and that launched by Jehoshaphat (2 Chron. 19:4–11). As in Exod. 18, the king devises a two-tiered system of justice in which the appointed leaders must be God-fearers and not tempted by partiality or bribes. Both Exod. 18:20 and 2 Chron. 19:10 use the verb *zāhar* (Hiphil) for the judges' teaching/warning the people about statutes and instructions. There are differences between the two reforms as well. For example, Jehoshaphat, unlike Moses, assumes no judicial role. And there is no mention of Jehoshaphat wearing himself out. Rather, his motivation is to get the nation back on track and be the kind of people that God has called them to be; an essential ingredient for that reform to take place is an overhaul of the judiciary. (See the helpful study by Knoppers 1994: 71–80.)

We may have something of a parallel to this division of labor (major/minor issues) in the book of Acts. The twelve apostles will have more than enough to do as they give themselves to "prayer and the ministry of the word" (Acts 6:4). The seven "male" deacons are "chosen" (6:3) to take care of the daily needs of certain widows who might otherwise be neglected (6:1). But not just any men will do. They too must demonstrate certain assets: "full of the Spirit and wisdom" (6:3a).

Moses follows and implements Jethro's counsel. In so doing, he demonstrates one of the characteristics of what Proverbs calls a wise man: 9:9a, "Instruct a wise man, and he will be wiser still" (AT); 12:15b, "A wise man listens to advice"; 19:20, "Listen to advice and accept instruction, and in the end you will be wise"; 20:18a, "Make plans by seeking advice."

But this is not just anybody's listening to advice. This is the one-and-only Moses, the deliverer of Israel, called, gifted, and anointed by God, the mediator between God and Israel, the one whom God will later have to inter in an unmarked spot (Deut. 34:5–6) lest the people worship him in death or try to consult his departed spirit. And this is a unique advice-giver: Jethro, a foreign priest. And what issues are more crucial than how a nation administers justice?

Can God use a "nonbeliever" to correct a blind spot in the life of a "believer"? Should not the people of God be open to much-needed truth, even when it comes from unexpected sources? Does not Jesus say that on some occasions the people of the world are wiser than the people of the light (Luke 16:8b)? If God can ordain praise from the lips of children and infants (Matt. 21:16), why can he not ordain counsel from the lips of a Midianite priest? Childs (1974: 332) nicely remarks, "Because the world of experience was no less an avenue through which God worked, the narrative can attribute the organization of a fundamental institution of Israel's law to practical wisdom without any indication that this might later be thought to denigrate its importance in the divine economy."

Some early Jewish authorities are not very positive about Jethro. Philo (*Names* 17.105; *Drunk.* 10.37) describes Jethro as only "seemingly wise" (*dokēsisophos*), as one who is concerned to talk to Moses only about human matters and not divine, eternal matters. Josephus's comments on Jethro are the direct opposite of those by Philo. For example, when Jethro first observes Moses's trying to do everything by himself, he says nothing, but holds his peace rather than embarrass his son-in-law. It is only after the surge of supplicants diminishes and disperses that Jethro takes Moses aside and speaks to him privately about his concern and suggestion (*Ant.* 3.3.1 §65). Actually, Josephus's Jethro starts by giving legal advice to Moses and then ends up giving him military advice: he tells Moses how to draw up his army and divide it into different-sized groups, from a thousand down to ten (*Ant.* 3.4.1 §70). Such teaching would "add greater appeal to Josephus' military-minded Roman readers" (Feldman 1997: 589, and from whom I have drawn the data in this paragraph).

We do not know the names of any of these leaders. If I were privileged to select them, among others I would chose the midwives of chap. 1, if Jethro had not limited his suggestion to *ʾanšê-ḥayil* ("competent *men*," although a few passages like Prov. 31:10 speak of an *ʾēšet-ḥayil*). No one can question their competence. They fear God (Exod. 1:21) and are "truthful" in a roundabout sort of way. They know how to act in a crisis and do what is most salutary. What we do know is that these officers are not to come from one small group of individuals like the elders. Rather, they are to be chosen "from all the people"—so maybe an elder here and a person who loads the stuff from Egypt onto wagons there.

Moses retells this event in Deut. 1:9–18, but there he makes it sound as if he appoints these leaders/officers while they are camped at Sinai, and not before they reach Sinai (as in Exod. 18): Deut. 1:6, "You have stayed long enough at this mountain. Break camp," then the recapitulation in Deut. 1:9–18 of Exod. 18:13–27, introduced with "At that time"; then Deut. 1:19, "Then, as the LORD our God commanded, we set out from Horeb [Sinai]." There are other differences as well (see Weinfeld 1991: 139–40). For instance, Moses never mentions

Jethro in Deut. 1 and that the appointment of this judiciary is Jethro's idea. Rather, it is done at Moses's initiative. Second, in Exodus, Moses selects the candidates, while in Deut. 1:13 the people choose the candidates. Third, the qualifications differ some with "competent, God-fearers, truthful" being replaced by "wise, understanding and respected." Fourth, in Deut. 1:16–17 Moses gives these minor judges instructions on impartial judging. The account in Exodus is silent about that.

The SP is aware of this "dischronologization" and tries to harmonize and dovetail the accounts into one smooth narrative. For helpful charts showing SP's redactional work and the differences between MT and SP, see Tigay 1975: 333–36.

Some of these differences are easily explainable. First, Moses in Deuteronomy is recalling a moment, an event, that has taken place almost forty years earlier. Some changes, deletions, and additions are to be expected. Second, it is most likely that when Moses selects these leaders, he takes suggestions from the people rather than acting totally autonomously. Since he listens to Jethro's counsel, why not to the counsel of his own people? How many leaders for groups of thousands down to tens would he need for a community of several million people? Tigay (1996: 11, 345n50) cites rabbinic sources (Babylonian Talmud, *Sanhedrin* 18a; *Sipre Deuteronomy* 13) that say Moses appoints 78,600 individuals. Third, the differences in qualifications are not significant (even without mentioning "God-fearers" in Deut. 1) and amount to what today one would call a reasonable paraphrase.

18:27 There are a lot of "sendings" in Exodus, beginning with God saying that he is "sending" Moses to Pharaoh (3:10). The verb "send" appears often in regard to whether or not Pharaoh will send Israel away and in conjunction with the plagues that God will send on Pharaoh and Egypt to convince Pharaoh to be a sender. An occurrence of "send" nearest to the one in 18:27 is the possible use of the same verb in 18:2. I have translated the Hebrew word in question "along with *her dowry*" (see the second grammatical and lexical note on 18:2 above). Both "dowry" and "send" share the same three consonants, *š-l-ḥ*. Alter (2004: 416) chooses to read *š-l-ḥ* as "send" in 18:2: "And Jethro . . . took Zipporah, *after her being sent away*." This translation creates a nice balance to the chapter, making it begin and end with a sending.

Presumably, Zipporah and her two sons remain with Moses from this point on, but none of them are mentioned again in the biblical narrative. There is a brief account of the death of Moses's sister, Miriam (Num. 20:1c), but no account of the death of his wife, Zipporah. There is an account of the death of Abraham's Sarah (Gen. 23) and an account of the death of Jacob's Rachel (Gen. 35:16–20) but not of Leah! Interestingly, there is a notice of the death of Rebekah's nurse (Gen. 35:8) but not of Rebekah herself! See too the note about the passing of Ezekiel's wife (Ezek. 24:15–18).

PART 4

Covenant and Law at Sinai

(19:1–24:18)

The recording of Moses's first dramatic encounter with God (3:2–4:17) immediately follows a passage of Scripture that focuses on Moses and Jethro, his Midianite father-in-law (2:15–3:1). The recording of Moses's (and Israel's) second dramatic encounter with God (19:1–25) immediately follows a passage of Scripture that also focuses on Moses and Jethro (18:1–27). In 4:21 it is Moses who returns to Egypt and says good-bye to Jethro. In 18:27 it is Jethro who says good-bye to Moses and returns to Midian.

With the departure of Jethro (chap. 18), Israel's journey through the wilderness resumes until it comes to a stop at one of the most crucial places in Scripture for biblical revelation. That is a mountain located somewhere in the desert of Sinai, in the southeast region of the Sinai peninsula. I say "somewhere" because the exact location of Mount Sinai remains a mystery. What Deut. 34:6b says of Moses's entombment ("But to this day no one knows where his grave is") one could say about Mount Sinai.

The importance of Sinai can be observed by noticing how long they stay there. Israel arrives at Sinai in the third month after they leave Egypt (19:1). They will not leave Sinai until "the twentieth day of the second month of the second year" (Num. 10:11). That indicates that Israel's encampment at Mount Sinai lasts for the better part of a year. Everything that God says or Moses passes on and everything that happens in Exod. 19:1–40:38 + Lev. 1:1–27:34 + Num. 1:1–10:10 transpires while God's people are resting at this holy site.

So what happens at Sinai, at least in this part 4 of Exodus? Well, for one thing, God shows up in a way that is more overwhelming and cataclysmic than any time previous in Exodus, with the possible exception of the burning-bush incident in chap. 3. The technical term for such a powerful, awesome divine appearance is "theophany." The unit both begins (19:9–25) and concludes (24:9–18) with such a stormy, pyrotechnic, overpowering revelation of the Holy One of Israel.

But the God of Israel is not interested in simply generating a breathless "Wow!" among his devotees. His purpose is not to present himself as heaven's superstar or megastar.

Two key items are on the divine agenda. The first is the Lord and Israel's entering into a covenant with each other. In chap. 19 God invites Israel into a covenant relationship with himself, and in 24:1–8 that covenant is formally confirmed. The covenant does not make Israel into God's people. They are already his people (e.g., 3:7, 10; 5:1). What the covenant does is to bring the Lord and Israel into a more binding, intimate relationship with each other "until death do us part."

For God's covenant people, that new relationship involves privilege ("my treasured possession," 19:5), a calling ("a kingdom of priests," 19:6a), and a certain kind of character ("a holy nation," 19:6a). One may note a parallel, as suggested in an earlier paragraph, between chaps. 2–4 and 18–19: (1) Moses and Jethro together + a divine theophany for Moses + God's call on Moses to go down to Egypt; and (2) Moses and Jethro together + a divine theophany for Moses + God's call on Israel to be a "kingdom of priests," to God himself and to other nations and peoples.

It is the third component in this description of the Lord's covenant people ("a holy nation") that points to the second item on the divine agenda. And that is the laws that must surely accompany the covenant, both the Ten Commandments (20:1–17) and the varied laws of the so-called Covenant Code (20:22–23:19). The laws are not about legalism; they are about holiness and holy living. Both as command and guidance, they provide guidelines and boundaries on how any community that labels itself holy is to behave. Israel observes these laws faithfully, not to achieve holiness or to become holy, but because Israel is holy, thanks to God's good grace.

God's Spectacular Self-Revelation at Sinai

(19:1–25)

Translation

[1]On the third new moon of the going out of Israel's sons from the land of Egypt, on this day they entered the Wilderness of Sinai. [2]They journeyed from Rephidim and entered the wilderness of Sinai, and they camped in the wilderness. Israel camped in front of the mountain. [3]Moses had gone up to God, and the LORD called to him from the mountain, saying, "Thus you shall say to the house of Jacob, and announce to Israel's sons: [4]'You yourselves have seen what I did to Egypt, and I carried (all of) you on eagles' wings, and I brought you to me. [5]And now, if you for sure will heed my voice and keep my covenant, you will become to me a unique treasure among all peoples, for the entire earth belongs to me. [6]As for you, you will become to me a royalty of priests and a holy nation.' These are the words that you shall speak to Israel's sons."

[7]And Moses went and summoned the elders of the people, and he set before them all these words that the LORD had commanded him. [8]All the people answered together and said, "Everything that the LORD has said we will do." And Moses brought back the peoples' words to the LORD. [9]And the LORD said to Moses, "Look, I am about to come to you in a dense cloud in order that the people may overhear as I speak with you, and also may put their trust in you forever." And Moses announced the people's words to the LORD.

[10]And the LORD said to Moses, "Go to the people and purify them today and tomorrow, and have them launder their cloaks. [11]They shall be prepared by the third day, for on the third day the LORD will come down in the sight of all the people on Mount Sinai. [12]You must establish boundaries for the people all around, saying, 'Take heed not to go up onto the mountain or even touch its edge. Anyone who touches the mountain shall be put to death. [13]No hand shall touch him, but he shall surely be stoned or shot (with an arrow); whether animal or man, he shall not live. When the horn blasts, they themselves shall go up the mountain.'" [14]And Moses came down from off the mountain to the people, and he purified the people, and they laundered their cloaks. [15]And he said to the people, "Be prepared by three days. Do not go near a woman."

[16]And it happened on the third day as the morning was coming, that there were thunderclaps and lightning flashes and a heavy cloud on top of the mountain and the sound of a ram's horn, very powerful, and all the people in the camp trembled. [17]And Moses brought out the people from the camp to meet God, and they positioned themselves at the mountain's base. [18]Mount Sinai was completely shrouded with smoke because the LORD had come down on top of it in fire. Its smoke was billowing like a kiln's smoke, and the whole mountain shook mightily. [19]And the sound of the ram's horn was growing progressively louder. Moses would speak, and God would answer him in a voice. [20]And the LORD came down on top of Mount Sinai, to the mountain's peak. The LORD summoned Moses to the mountain's peak, and Moses went up. [21]The LORD said to Moses, "Go down, warn the people lest they break through to the LORD to see, and many of them will perish. [22]Also the priests who come near to the LORD shall purify themselves lest the LORD burst forth against them." [23]But Moses said to the LORD, "The people are not able to come up to Mount

Sinai for you warned us, saying, 'Establish boundaries on the mountain and purify it.'" [24]And the LORD said to him, "Go down and come back up, you and Aaron with you, but the priests and the people shall not break through to go up to the LORD, lest he burst forth against them." [25]And Moses went down to the people, and he told them.

Grammatical and Lexical Notes

19:2. Is there any difference between "camping in front of the mountain" (*ḥānâ neged hāhār*) in Exod. 19:2 and "camping near the tent of meeting" in Num. 2:2 (*ḥānâ minneged sābîb lĕʾōhel-môʿēd*)? May the first be closer, but the second more removed (see NIV's "to camp around the tent of meeting some distance from it" for Num. 2:2)?

19:3. Rather than the Hebrew "Moses had gone up to God," LXX reads, "Moses went up to *the mountain of* God." On at least two other occasions, the LXX tries to soften the "bluntness" of the Hebrew. In 4:24 instead of "the LORD encountered Moses and sought to kill him," LXX has, "the *angel of* the Lord met Moses and sought to kill him." In 24:10 instead of "They saw the God of Israel," LXX has "They saw *the place* where the God of Israel stood." The Greek phrase *anabainō eis to oros* ("go up [to] the mountain") occurs twenty-four times in the Greek OT, eighteen of which are in the Pentateuch. The reference in Mark 3:13 to Jesus going up the mountain (same phrase in the Greek), and calling up those he wishes to be with him before giving them their marching orders, may point back to references about Yahweh's calling Moses up the mountain.

19:5. *Wĕʿattâ* ("And now") is both a conjunction and an interjection. It is often, but not always, followed by an imperative, and it marks the shift from the speaker's first statement to the speaker's expectation of some result that should follow from the addressee. Its Greek equivalent, *kai nyn*, is a Semitism and is prominent in the NT, ten times in Acts and nine times in the writings of John, according to Brown (1966–70: 2.742). An example is John 17:4–5, "I have brought you glory, . . . *and now* . . . glorify me."

19:5. "And keep my covenant" (*ûšĕmartem ʾet-bĕrîtî*) is not necessarily a sequel to "heed my voice," but a clarification and expansion of "heed my voice." On such a use of the *wāw*-consecutive perfect, see Arnold and Choi 2003: 90.

19:5. I shall have more to say about the Hebrew word *sĕgullâ* ("unique treasure") in the commentary section. For now, I note that the noun is formed like the following nouns: *gĕʾullâ* ("redemption"); *ʾăḥuzzâ* ("possession"); *kĕtûbâ* ("marriage document," without the doubling of the *b* [*bêt*]); *ḥănukkâ* ("dedication"). All these nouns are abstracts in the passive sense (e.g., "that which is redeemed," or "that which is possessed"). Presumably then, however we render *sĕgullâ* in English, it should be with an implied passive meaning. LXX translates with *periousios* ("superior"), the Aramaic Targums with *hbyb* ("beloved"), and the Vulgate with *peculium* (and the origin of KJV's famous "peculiar people"). The Latin word refers to that which is set aside because it is of special value.

19:6. For other places where "royalty/kingdom" (*mamlākâ*) and "nation" (*gôy*) occur together, see Ps. 46:6 [7], "Nations [*gôyim*] are in an uproar, kingdoms [*mamlākôt*] fall"; Jer. 1:10, "See, today I appoint you over nations [*haggôyim*] and kingdoms [*hammamlākôt*]"; Jer. 18:7, 9, "At any time I announce that a nation [*gôy*] or kingdom [*mamlākâ*] is to be uprooted . . . [or] be built up."

19:6. Whenever "holy" is used as an attribute adjective to describe the Lord's people, whether it is *gôy qādôš* or *ʿam qādôš*, the word "holy" is written with a long *ô*, what Hebrew grammarians call a *ḥōlem wāw*. But Deut. 26:19 ("You will be a people *holy* [*ʿām-qādōš*] to the LORD your God") is an exception. However, where the Lord says to Israel, "You shall be *holy*, because I am *holy*" (Lev. 11:44, 45; 19:2; 20:26), the adjective "holy" used with the Lord is written with the long vowel *ô*, while the adjective "holy" used with Israel is written with a short vowel *ō*, what Hebrew grammarians call a *ḥōlem* to distinguish it from a *ḥōlem wāw*. The difference in these latter references is surely due to the Masoretes wanting to distinguish between divine holiness and human holiness.

19:8. Note the plural verb "answered" (*wayya ʿănû*) with the singular noun "people" (*ʿām*) as subject of the verb, although the addition of "all" to "people" makes the noun virtually plural. Observe too that in v. 10, where "people" (without *kol* this time) occurs again in the singular, the pronominal suffixes that follow are plural ("purify *them*" and "have *them* launder *their* cloaks"). For another illustration of singular *ʿām* with plural verb, see Amos 3:6, "When a trumpet sounds in a city, do not the people tremble [*wĕʿām lōʾ yeḥĕrādû*]?"

19:9. "In a dense cloud" is not, in the Hebrew, composed of a noun and adjective, as with "heavy cloud" in v. 16 (*wĕʿānān kābēd*). Rather, the phrase has two nouns (*bĕʿab heʿānān*). For these two nouns together elsewhere, see Job 26:8, "He wraps up the waters in his clouds [*ʿāb*], yet the clouds [*ʿānān*] do not burst under their weight"; Job 37:11, "Also with moisture He saturates the clouds [*ʿāb*]; He scatters His bright clouds [*ʿānān*]" (NKJV); Isa. 44:22, "I have swept away your offenses like a cloud [*ʿāb*], your sins like the morning mist [*ʿānān*]."

19:10. The more usual word for "clothes/clothing" is *bĕgādîm*. The use here of *śĕmālōt* recalls the use of this word back in 3:22 and 12:35 to refer to the clothing the Egyptians gave the departing Hebrews. It is Egyptian clothing rather than Hebrew clothing that they are to launder.

19:11. For the perfect of *hāyâ* followed by a participle, see GKC §116 rem. 2, who believes such a construction emphasizes action continuing into the future, but Ogden (1971: 469) is not so sure. *Nākôn* after some form of the verb *hāyâ* has different meanings: Exod. 19:11, "They shall be prepared [*wĕhāyû nĕkōnîm*]"; Exod. 19:15, "Be prepared [*hĕyû nĕkōnîm*]"; Exod. 34:2, "Be ready [*hĕyēh nākôn*] in/by the morning"; Josh. 8:4, "All of you be on the alert [*wihĕyîtem kullĕkem nĕkōnîm*]"; 2 Sam. 7:16 = 1 Chron. 17:14, "Your throne [David's] will be established forever [*yihyeh nākôn ʿad-ʿôlam*]"; Mic. 4:1, "In the last days the mountain of the Lord's temple shall be established [*yihyeh har bêt-YHWH nākôn*]." In these references that use a form of *hāyâ* as an auxiliary verb with *nākôn*, we have the use of periphrasis: the use of two words instead of a single inflected word to express the same grammatical function (e.g., "more friendly" rather than "friendlier").

19:11. The phrases "They shall be prepared *layyôm haššĕlîšî*" in this verse and "Be prepared *lišlōšet yāmîm*" in v. 15 look as though they should read, "They should be prepared *for* the third day" and "Be prepared *for* three days." However, the meaning "by" for the preposition *lĕ* is present elsewhere, e.g., Gen. 17:21, "Isaac, whom Sarah will bear to you *by* this time [*lammôʿēd*] next year." See R. Williams 1976: §268. I argue for the same meaning for this preposition in Exod. 34:2, "Be ready *by* [NIV 'in'] the morning [*labbōker*]."

19:11. The reference here and in v. 16 to something starting on the third day, lasting for three days, and coming to fruition in three days may help resolve a conundrum in the Gospels. Matthew 16:21 and Luke 9:22 (and Paul in 1 Cor. 15:4) have Jesus rising *on* the third day, but the parallel passage (Mark 8:31) has Jesus saying that he will rise *after* three days. Exodus 19 describes an event that lasts for three days and ends on the third day. We have the same phenomenon in Gen. 42:17–18, "And he [Joseph] put them all in custody for three days. On the third day he said to them. . . ." Compare also Esther 4:16–5:1, "Do not eat or drink for three days. . . . On the third day Esther put on her royal robes." Most likely, then, "*on* the third day" and "*after* the third day" are interchangeable phrases. See Marcus 2009: 606.

19:12. The admonition "not to go up the mountain" is addressed to Israel (the "you" is plural, *lākem*) or, conceivably, to Moses and Aaron. Sailhamer (2009: 383, 385n54) has correctly pointed out that there is no expressed "no" or "not" in *hiššāmĕrû lākem ʿălôt bāhār*. The closest parallel I can find to Exod. 19:12 (Niphal imperative of *šāmar* followed by the infinitive) is what Laban, quoting God, says to Jacob in Gen. 31:29, "Be careful not to say [*hiššāmer lĕkā middabbēr*] anything to Jacob, either good or bad." What Exod. 19:12 lacks is the preposition *min* attached to the infinitive. If the Niphal imperative of *šāmar* is followed by an imperfect rather than by an infinitive, then to express a total prohibition the Hebrew inserts the word *pen*. See, for example, Deut. 4:23, "Be careful not to forget the covenant" (*hiššāmĕrû lākem pen-tiškĕḥû ʾet-bĕrît*), or Deut. 11:16, "Be careful, or you will be enticed" (*hiššāmĕrû lākem pen yipteh lĕbabkem*). Maybe, then, what Exod. 19:12 is prohibiting is an ascent of the mountain *now* by anybody—either by Moses or Aaron or by any of the Israelites. And when the time for ascent comes, they are to proceed with extreme caution.

19:12. In the clause "Anyone who touches the mountain shall be put to death," "shall be put to death" is *môt yûmāt*. The latter word is the Hophal of *mût* ("die"). Milgrom (1970: 5–7) has shown convincingly that there is a significant difference between "He/you shall die" (Qal) and "He/you shall be put to death" (Hophal), whether or not the infinitive absolute *môt* is present. In the former, God is the executioner, as in his word to Adam, "For when you eat of it, you will die [*môt tāmût*]" (Gen. 2:17). But when the Hophal is used, as here (*môt yûmāt*), the executioners are humans. This distinction is not always present outside of the Pentateuch.

19:13. The suffix on *bô* in *lōʾ-tiggaʿ bô yād* refers to the person guilty of contact with the mountain ("No hand shall touch *him*") rather than to the mountain itself ("No hand shall touch *it*"). Hebrew has no neuter, no "it." It has only masculine and feminine genders. So how is one to render the familiar Ps. 118:24, "This is the day the Lord has made; let us rejoice and be glad *bô*": "in *it*" or "in *him*"? Is the verse a call to celebrate the day the Lord has made, or is it a call to rejoice in the Lord, who has given us this day?

19:13. For the adversative *kî* ("but"), see Arnold and Choi 2003: 152.

19:13. There is a considerable difference in the Septuagint's rendering of "When the horn blasts." It instead reads, "when the voices and trumpets and cloud depart from the mountain" (*hotan hai phōnai kai hai salpinges kai hē nephelē apelthē apo tou orous*).

19:13. *ʾIm-bĕhēmâ ʾim-ʾîš* ("whether animal or man") recalls the nearly identical expression *lĕmē ʾîš wĕʿad-bĕhēmâ*, which occurs as a merism in 11:7.

19:13. "He shall not live" is another way of saying, through a negated antonym, "He shall be put to death," as in the preceding verse. On the use of negated antonyms, see Yaron 1993: esp. 146–47.

19:13. Commentators understandably have been baffled by *hēmmâ yaʿălû bāhār* ("They themselves shall/may go up the mountain"). Did not earlier verses prohibit the people from even touching the mountain, never mind ascending it? Althann (1976) believes he has solved the conundrum by making two slight alterations to the MT to come up with the reading "Whether man or beast, he shall not live if, when the ram's horn sounds, he goes up the mountain." A simpler suggestion is to take the pronoun *hēmmâ* as a reference just to Moses and to Aaron rather than to the entire community.

19:15. The Hebrew Bible has several synonyms for sex (licit and illicit): *nāgaš* ("go near") in Exod. 19:15; *yādaʿ* ("knew") in Gen. 4:1; *bôʾ ʾel* ("go into") in Gen. 16:4; *qārab ʾel* ("go near") in Gen. 20:4; *šākab* ("lay, violate") in Gen. 34:2; *šākab ʿim* ("lie with") in Gen. 39:8 and 2 Sam. 11:4; *ḥāzaq* ("overpower, rape") in Judg. 19:25.

19:16. In my translation I reproduce the first *wayĕhî* as "And it happened," and the second *wayĕhî* as "that there were." The *wayĕhî . . . wayĕhî* construction is like that in Ezek. 3:16 (and elsewhere): "And it was [*wayĕhî*] after seven days and was [*wayĕhî*] the word of the Lord to me" (AT).

19:16. The word for "thunderclaps" is *qōlōt*, the plural of *qôl*, which is the word for the *sound* of the ram's horn in v. 19, and for the *voice* with which the Lord answers Moses, also in v. 19. *Qôl* is one of a number of Hebrew words that is masculine in the singular, but feminine in the plural. For other examples, compare: *ʾōraḥ* ("way, path") and *ʾărāḥôt*; *dôr* ("generation") and *dōrôt*; *ḥalôm* ("dream") and *ḥălōmôt*; *lāšôn* ("tongue") and *lĕšōnôt*; *māqôm* ("place") and *mĕqômôt*; *nēr* ("lamp") and *nērōt*; *ʿôr* ("skin") and *ʿōrôt*; *šēm* ("name") and *šēmôt*. With some of these nouns, the plural form has a meaning different from the singular. "Voice/sound" (*qôl*) becomes "thunder [claps]" (*qōlōt*), and "tongue" (*lāšôn*) becomes "languages" (*lĕšōnôt*).

19:17. "At the mountain's base" is *bĕtaḥtît hāhār*. The word for "base" recalls the place name Tahath, at which the Israelites have camped briefly in their wilderness journey: "and camped at Tahath/'Foot [-of-the-Mountain].' They left Tahath/'Foot[-of-the-Mountain]'" (Num. 33:26–27).

19:18. For *mippĕnê ʾăser* with the meaning "because," see Jer. 44:23, "Because [*mippĕnê ʾăser*] you have burned incense and because [*waʾăšer*] you have sinned against the Lord" (AT); 1 Kings 3:19, "During the night this woman's son died because [*ʾăšer*] she lay on him"; 2 Sam. 12:6, "He must pay for that lamb four times over because [*ʾăšer*] he did such a thing and because [*wĕʿal ʾăšer*] he had no pity" (AT).

19:18. If many commentators take the preposition *bĕ* in Exod. 3:2 as a *bêt essentiae* in the expression *bĕlabbat-ʾēš* ("The Lord appeared to him *as* a flame of fire"), how then shall we render *bāʾēš* in this verse: "The Lord had come down on top of it *in* fire," or "*as* fire"?

19:18. The Hebrew word for "kiln/furnace" (*kibšān*) derives from the verb *kābaš* ("conquer"). The word for "launder, wash" (*kābas*, Piel in vv. 10, 14) is almost the same, with only the final sibilant different, a *sāmek* instead of a *šîn*. Hebrew *kābas* ("wash") seems to be cognate with Akkadian *kabasu*, "trample, crush," suggesting that one washes one's clothes by repeatedly hitting them.

19:19. For reasons I gave when explaining the plural *qōlōt* in v. 16 as "thunderclaps," *qôl* in the singular can only be translated "voice": "And God would answer him in a *voice*." Exodus 20:18 says that "when the people saw the thunder claps [*qôlōt*, pl.]. . . ." But the LXX reads a singular *qôl*: "When the people saw the voice [*tēn phōnēn*]." See also Deut. 4:11–12, "You came near and stood at the foot of the mountain. . . . You heard the sound of words but saw no form *except a voice* [*zûlātî qôl*]" (AT). To speak of a visible voice sounds strange until we understand that here the text is using *qôl* as a hypostasis (cf. Yadin 2003: 617–23). It is important that God's appearance has both visual and audible features. For God to appear but to say nothing would short-circuit the desired revelation. In the long run, it is not the sound effects that are most crucial, but the word that God speaks. When God speaks, he does so with a voice, not with a yell or a scream. And when God speaks, he utters "words" (*dĕbārîm*, as in 19:6–7; 20:1), not commands or orders, even if God's words have a commanding, warning tone to them.

19:20. *Rōʾš* to refer to the "top" or "summit" or "peak" of a mountain first appears in Gen. 8:5, "The tops of the mountains [*roʾšê hehārîm*] became visible."

19:21. The verb *ʿûd* (Hiphil), "warn," may be a denominative verb from *ʿēd*, "witness," call on someone to be a witness who will repeat certain significant information to a given audience. See J. Thompson 1965: esp. 225–26.

19:21. The verb for "break through to" is *hāras ʾel*. It occurs in Exod. 15:7 (without the preposition *ʾel*): "In the greatness of your exaltation you *fell/wreck/break* your assailants." The LXX renders both "break through to [the Lord]" (*hāras ʾel*) in v. 21 and "the priests who come near to [the Lord]" (*nāgaš ʾel*) in v. 22 with *engizō* ("approach, come near"). The NT uses *engizō* for approaching God only twice: Heb. 7:19, "A better hope is introduced, by which we *draw near to* God," and James 4:8, "*Come near to* God and he *will come near to* you."

19:22. On the verb *pāraṣ* (here and the end of v. 24) and the cognate noun *pōrîṣ*, see the study of Harland 1996. The basic meaning of the verb is "break down/through," as in 2 Kings 14:13, "Then Jehoash went to Jerusalem and *broke down* the wall of Jerusalem." The related noun *pereṣ* appears in the famous passage from Ezekiel: "I looked for a man among them who would build up the wall and stand before me in the *gap*" (22:30). A good parallel to the use of *pāraṣ* in Exod. 19:22 is 2 Sam. 6:8, for both deal with God's anger breaking out because of some infraction, either real or potential—"Then David was angry because the Lord's wrath *had broken out* against Uzzah, and to this day that place is called *Perez* Uzzah."

19:25. How does one render the last two words of the verse, *wayyōʾmer ʾălēhem*? One would normally use "and he said to them," but no recorded speech follows. Furthermore, the next verse in the

Bible (20:1) says, "And God spoke all these words, saying . . ." Possibly, as Sailhamer (1992: 55n89; 2009: 386–87, 396) has suggested, "and he said to them" in 19:25 indicates that Moses is the one who mediates the Decalogue to the Israelites. Thus at the end of v. 25 one would punctuate with a colon, and at the start of 20:1 place quotation marks. Another solution is to render *wayyōʾmer* not as introducing the contents of a speech ("he said"), but as a reference to the act of speaking ("And Moses went down to the people *and he told them*"). See Chavel 2003: 26–27n11; Watts 1995: 553n35.

Commentary

There are two extended encampments for Israel between leaving Egypt and arriving in Canaan. There are also two stages in its wilderness journeys, a pre-Sinai one and a post-Sinai one. We can structure these movements as follows: (1) Israel leaves Egypt and heads for Canaan, but stops at Sinai (Exod. 12:31–18:27); (2) Israel camps at Sinai for the better part of a year (Exod. 19:1–Num. 10:10); (3) Israel leaves Sinai and continues the journey to Canaan (Num. 10:11–36:13); (4) Israel camps in the Plains of Moab, east of the Jordan (Deut. 1–34). Such is the Israel of the Torah: traveling>camping>traveling> camping. Of these four segments, it is of interest that the great moments of God's revelation happen when Israel is encamped either at Sinai or on the Plains of Moab. To be sure, God can and does speak and communicate when Israel is traveling as quickly as possible from site to site, gathering up a day's supply of manna here, trying to fill up a pail with water from the rock there, and fighting off the Amalekites along the way. But it is difficult in such frenzied times to "be still, and know that I am God" (Ps. 46:10 [11]). It is when Israel halts the travels and puts down stakes into the ground, at least for a while, that the Lord's word to Israel becomes most extensive and most compelling.

Chapter 19 is one part, and the first part, of a unit that includes chaps. 19–24. Some writers have tied these six chapters together by suggesting that they are presented in a form of a chiasm. Sprinkle (2004: 242) suggests this pattern:

A Narrative: The covenant offered (19:3–25)
  B Laws (general): The Decalogue (20:1–17)
    C Narrative: The people fear (20:18–21)
  B′ Laws (specific): Book of the Covenant (20:32–23:33)
A′ Narrative: The covenant accepted (24:1–11)

Brettler (2005: 62) has a similar idea although his terminology and text divisions differ. He sees here what he calls "a double-decker sandwich":

A Revelation (19:1–25)
  B Decalogue (20:1–14) [20:1–17 MT]
A′ Revelation (20:15–18) [20:18–21 MT]

B′ Laws (20:19–23:33) [20:22–23:33 MT]
A″ Revelation (24:1–18)

As I have already indicated, Israel's stay at Mount Sinai is not only crucial 19:1–2
but also lengthy, almost a year. They arrive there in the third month of the first year of the exodus (Exod. 19:1) and depart on the twentieth day of the second month of the second year (Num. 10:11–12). They experience, or observe, about a year of plagues while in Egypt, and now they will experience, or observe, about a year of Yahweh's power on display.

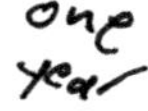

One would think, then, that such a pivotal place would be easily identifiable by modern geographers. The usual identification of Sinai is with *Jebel Musa* ("The Mountain of Moses"), deep in the southern Sinai. But "honest" maps, if they place Sinai there, will either put a question mark beside it, or else put something beside it in parentheses like "(traditional location)." There are several objections to the traditional identification (see Milgrom 1990: 280). First, fishing is good in the southern Sinai area, yet in Num. 11:5 the people are drooling over memories of the fish they ate while in Egypt. Second, at this time, with Egyptian-owned and -operated mines all over the southern Sinai, and sentries guarding those mines, would this group of Israelites that has recently escaped from Egypt be able to settle down in that area for the better part of a year?

Another possibility for Sinai is Jebel Sin Bisher, which is approximately 30 miles southwest of Sinai, and is 1,900 feet high. There were fewer Egyptians and no fishing. And it fits better with the eleven-day journey from Sinai to Kadesh-barnea (about 210 miles) that Deut. 1:2 mentions.

The bottom line is that we are not sure where Mount Sinai was. I suggest a parallel with the two encampments at this point. Our ignorance about Sinai's location matches our ignorance about where God buried Moses in Moab (Deut. 34:5–6). The human tendency is to make shrines of holy places and surreal beatific figures of holy people. We worship sites or saints. If there is such a thing as necrolatry (worshiping the dead), is there also such a thing as "mountainolatry"? For this reason, or for some other reason, the identification of these two "holy places" has slipped beyond our ken.

There is also a bit of a problem with the first phrase of Exod. 19:1, *baḥōdeš haššělîšî*. Since the noun *ḥōdeš* has two meanings, should we translate this phrase "On/in the third *month*" (NIV), or "On/in the third *new moon*" (NRSV)? Since v. 1 later says "on this day," many versions opt for "new moon" over "month." The phrase is comparable to that in Num. 20:1, "The Israelite community arrived at the Desert of Zin *baḥōdeš hāri'šôn*": "on/in the first month" (again without a day mentioned)? Or "on/in the first new moon"? An exact parallel to Exod. 19:1 is 2 Chron. 15:10. It says that godly Asa, king of Judah, launched his reforms by assembling everybody in Jerusalem *baḥōdeš haššělîšî* ("in the third month/new moon"). Not only is the Hebrew phrase exactly the same in both, and not only is no day specified in both, but in Exod. 19 and 2 Chron. 15 the emphasis is on a covenant and a covenant-making ceremony.

Regardless of which way we go, "month" or "full moon," no numbered day is mentioned. The TNIV (an NIV successor) reads "On [the first day of] the third month." Alexander (1999: 14) safely reads, "On [the day of] the third new moon." Oswalt (2008b: 156) reads, "On the fifteenth day of the month." So now we have two mysteries: where is Sinai, and on what day of the month do they arrive at Sinai, or what day is the third full moon? Geography and chronology have taken a backseat to other more critical matters.

19:3–8 Moses now makes his first of several ascents (v. 3) and descents (v. 7) of Mount Sinai (on the number of his ups and downs, see Arichea 1989). Right off the bat we have a "God" to "Lord" shift within the same verse (v. 3). Moses goes up to God, and the Lord calls out to him. We find that same phenomenon in Gen. 7:16, "The animals going in were male and female, . . . as *God* had commanded Noah. Then the Lord shut him in." Source critics will use such shifts in the divine name as an evidence of originally distinct accounts that have now been edited and combined into a single narrative. I note, however, that in the previous chapter, involving Moses and his non-Israelite father-in-law, "God"/*'ĕlōhîm* occurs eleven times while "Lord"/*YHWH* appears only four times. In this chapter, involving only Israelites, that ratio is reversed, "Lord"/*YHWH* sixteen times, and "God"/*'ĕlōhîm* only three times.

There are several different patterns employed in the OT that involve the narrative of commissioned communication (Vater 1980: esp. 373–74). In one pattern, A commissions B to transmit A's message to C, and then follows a brief notice of B's faithfully carrying out his commission. Exodus 19:3–7 is an excellent illustration of that. In vv. 3b–6 the Lord (A) instructs Moses (B) what to say to the people (C) at the base of Mount Sinai, and v. 7 tells us that Moses (B) obediently carries through on that commission. In another pattern, A commissions B to transmit A's message to C, but there is no record of B doing that. We have an illustration of that in Exod. 8:1–4 [7:26–29]. The Lord tells Moses what to say to Pharaoh, but there is no mention of Moses's relaying that message. Vater points out that the overwhelming number of these Pattern I and II narratives in the OT involve Moses, twenty-eight of thirty-six examples, or about 75 percent. Their pervasiveness emphasizes two things. First, they focus on the initiative and importance of the sender, who in most cases is the Lord. Second, they focus on the strategic role of the "sendee," who in most cases is Moses. More often than not, the Lord chooses to address his people intermediately rather than mediately.

What is to follow in vv. 3–8 is God's first offer of a covenant to his people while they are in Egypt or since they have left Egypt ("Now if you . . . keep my covenant . . . ," v. 5). Sklba (1972: 4) suggests that 19:4–8 is a complete covenant formula in abbreviated but essential terms: (1) the historical prologue, v. 4; (2) general stipulations, v. 5a; (3) blessing for obedience, vv. 5b–6; (4) acceptance by the people, v. 8.

Undeniably, covenant is a key (some would say *the* key) theological truth at the heart of the OT. In the early twentieth century, the famous German scholar Walther Eichrodt (1961; 1967) wrote his widely read and influential *Theology of the Old Testament* around the concept of covenant. Of interest here is that the Lord does not speak to his people anytime before chap. 19 about a covenant. So why wait until now? Why wait until after the exodus, until the sea has been crossed, until they are well into the journey to Canaan?

Greenberg (1969: 14) quotes a halakic midrash on the book of Exodus (*Mekhilta de Rabbi Ishmael*) from the very early Christian centuries that beautifully answers these kinds of questions:

> Why didn't the Torah begin with the Decalogue? A parable will explain it: A man entered a country and said, "Make me your king." The people replied, "What have you ever done for us that we should make you our king?" So, he built them walls, made them water-works, fought wars on their behalf. Then he said to them, "Make me your king," and they said, "Yes indeed!" Thus God liberated Israel from Egypt, divided the sea for them, gave them manna from heaven, provided them with a water supply, provisioned them with quail, fought Amalek on their behalf, then said to them, "Make me your king," whereupon they replied, "Yes indeed!"

The purpose of the Lord's offering Israel a covenant is not to "make" Israel God's people. They already are God's people. Earlier in Exodus the Lord has already called Israel "my people" (e.g., 3:7, "I have seen the misery of *my people* in Egypt"; 3:10, "I am sending you to Pharaoh to bring *my people* out of Egypt"), "my firstborn son" (4:22), "my son" (4:23). Also, Moses in conversation with the Lord has called Israel "your people" (5:23).

So what is happening at Sinai? A covenant is a means by which two parties enter into a new relationship with each other, or more often, a covenant elevates to a more intimate, dynamic level an already-existing relationship between two parties. One thinks of the covenant of marriage as an example. Two individuals, already committed to each other and in some serious sort of relationship, now take that relationship to the next level and, before God and others, covenant with each other.

The Lord begins in v. 4 by having Moses remind the people of what he has done to Egypt, and how he has carried Israel as a mother eagle carries her young on her wings (note the gynomorphic language for God [a mother eagle] instead of the more common andromorphic language). For other references to God's "wings," see Pss. 17:8; 36:7 [8]; 57:1 [2]; 61:4 [5]; 63:7 [8]; 91:4; and especially Deut. 32:11, "like an eagle that stirs up its nest and hovers over its young, that spreads its wings to catch them" (see Peels [1994], who argues that

Deut. 32:11 is about the eagle's protection of her young rather than about the eagle's teaching her young how to fly). The "bald" eagle (see Mic. 1:16) is one of God's most majestic creatures, as Agur, the sage, says in Prov. 30:18–19. The only thing they are not good for is eating, for Lev. 11:13 and Deut. 14:12 classify the eagle as one of the unclean birds, probably because it feeds on carrion (Job 39:27–30; Prov. 30:17).

In the previous chapter, Jethro has spoken to Moses about the need for Moses to appoint others to help him "carry" (*nāśā'*) the burden of so much litigation (Exod. 18:22). In 19:4 it is the Lord who has carried (*nāśā'*) his people. Scripture presents a picture of a God who is always carrying his people. Either God/god(s) carry the people, or else the people have to carry their god(s). For the latter, see Isa. 46:1, "The images [of the Babylonian gods] that are carried about [*nāśā'*] are burdensome, a burden [*massā'*] to the weary." In contrast to gods who must be carried, especially when they are in great danger because of the invading Persians [Isa. 46], Yahweh is the one who has carried (*nāśā'*) Israel (46:3) and will carry (*nāśā'*) Israel (46:4).

The last phrase "I brought you to me/myself" of v. 4 may be simply a way of expressing covenant terminology. But it may be more than covenantal vocabulary. The phrase suggests that God's primary purpose of bonding with Israel is for that rapturous enjoyment of each other's presence. Before Israel is chosen for service, Israel is chosen for fellowship. I suggest a parallel with Mark 3:14, "Jesus appointed twelve . . . that they might be with him and that he might send them out to preach." First fellowship, then service.

The key word used to describe Israel, God's covenant people, in v. 5 is "unique treasure" (*sĕgullâ*). It is used twice in the Hebrew Bible in a secular way to refer to royal treasure (Eccles. 2:8, "I amassed silver and gold for myself and the *treasure* of the kings and provinces"; 1 Chron. 29:3, "Besides, in my devotion to the temple of my God I [David] now give my personal *treasures* of gold and silver for the temple of my God"). In Mal. 3:17 the Lord uses it for the faithful postexilic community ("'They will be mine' says the Lord Almighty, 'in the day when I make up *my treasured possession*'"). Elsewhere, as in Exod. 19:5, the word refers to the chosen and special status of the people of Israel (Deut. 7:6; 14:2; 26:18; Ps. 135:4). In the Exodus passage and the three passages from Deuteronomy, the invitation to be God's *sĕgullâ* is coupled with the call to holiness. First in Exodus is the invitation to be Yahweh's *sĕgullâ* (19:5), then the call to holiness (19:6). That is the sequence too in Deut. 26, shown in 26:18 and then 26:19. But in Deut. 7:6 and 14:2 the sequence is reversed, with the emphasis on holiness preceding the invitation to be Yahweh's *sĕgullâ* (Deut. 7:6a, then 7:6b; 14:2a, then 14:2b). Regardless of the sequence, the coupling of these two phrases is a deterrent against emphasizing "unique treasure" to the exclusion of holiness, and thus sliding into lawlessness, or emphasizing holiness to the exclusion of "unique treasure," and thus sliding into legalism.

Semitists have connected Hebrew *sĕgullâ* with Akkadian *sakālu* (verb) and *sikiltum* (noun), "accumulate wealth" and "an accumulation of wealth," which seems to be the meaning of *sĕgullâ* in 1 Chron. 29:3 and Eccles. 2:8. In an Akkadian text from the mid-second millennium BC is a reference to Abban, king of Alalakh, in which he describes himself as "the servant of [the god] Adad, the beloved (*narum*) of Adad, the *sikiltum* of Adad." The coupling of *narum* ("beloved") with *sikiltum* suggests that the latter term describes the affection that the god has for his servant/devotee, and that *sikiltum* is not used by the king merely to describe the master/vassal hierarchy that exists between his god and himself.

We have a text from ancient Ugarit (much closer to the Hebrews than Mesopotamia, and dating to about 1200 BC) that also contains a possible Canaanite cognate to *sĕgullâ*. The Hittite king, who identifies himself as "the sun" (*shpsh*), wrote a letter to Hammurapi (*ʿmpri*), not the famous king (Hammurabi) connected with the law code, but the last king of Ugarit. He reminds Hammurapi, "You belong to the Sun, your master; you are his servant and his friend/personal property/treasure" (*ht* [ ] *l shpsh bʿlk ʿb*[*dh*] *sglth at*). "Servant" in this text does not suggest "lower rank, inferior," but is a term of endearment, as the word "servant" for Yahweh's Israel often is in the Bible. (I have been much enlightened about the meaning of *sĕgullâ* through the studies of Greenberg 1951; Held 1961; Loewenstamm 1992: 268–79; and the scattered comments of Dahood 1965: 313; 1966: 267; 1969: 341.)

One cannot avoid the fact that this phrase, and its positioning as the first in a list of three, highlights Israel's uniqueness and the special affection the Lord has for Israel (Kaminsky 2007: 85). Israel has a special relationship with the Lord that no other nation can claim or experience. Although Solomon does not use *sĕgullâ*, he expresses the same sentiment when he says, "For you singled them out from all the nations of the world to be your own inheritance" (1 Kings 8:53). I believe there is something of a parallel between *sĕgullâ mikkol haʿammîm* ("a unique treasure among all peoples") and what Gen. 3:1 says about the snake: *ʿārûm mikkol ḥayyat haśśādeh*. The Genesis verse does not say that all the animals of the field are crafty and the snake happens to be just a bit craftier than all the rest. Rather, *mikkol* suggests that the one character trait separating the snake from all other animals is its craftiness. Similarly, in Exod. 19:5 *mikkol* does not suggest that all the nations are Yahweh's *sĕgullâ* and that Israel is a little bit more his *sĕgullâ*. Rather, *mikkol* suggests that the one item setting Israel apart from other nations is that Israel alone is Yahweh's *sĕgullâ*. Not all commentators will appreciate this emphasis on exclusivity. Such an attitude, they suggest, breeds arrogance, bigotry, messianism, and eventually religious wars in the name of evangelism. So Lasine (2001: 210) says of Exod. 19:5, "This obsession with Israel being *special* is the most flagrant sign of Yahweh's parental narcissism."

As employed in v. 6, the second and third phrases to describe the Lord's covenant people are "a royalty/kingdom of priests" and "a holy nation." The first of these two, "a royalty/kingdom of priests," occurs only here in the OT. The NT's adaptation of these verses in Exod. 19 uses "royal priesthood" (1 Pet. 2:9; cf. also Rev. 1:6; 5:10; 20:6). But the idea is surely present in a verse like Isa. 61:6, "And you will be called priests of the Lord, you will be named ministers of our God," which anticipates the language of 1 Pet. 2:5. Perhaps we have an implementation of the phrase of Exod. 19:6 in 24:5. According to that verse, Moses sends "young Israelite men, and they offered burnt offerings and sacrificed young bulls as fellowship offerings to the Lord" (Rendtorff 1989: 389).

There are two possibilities for meaning here. First, priests enjoy a privileged relationship with God. They may enter his presence in a way that the laity cannot; they alone may go into the holy place, but the laity cannot. If that is the meaning, then "royalty/kingdom of priests" reinforces the significance of "unique treasure." Because they are the Lord's *sĕgullâ*, Israel is able to stand before God, to enter into his presence, in a way no other people can. See J. Davies 2004; synopsis in 2002.

The other possibility for interpretation of this phrase is that Israel is to play a mediatorial role between Yahweh and all the other nations. If we follow the Latin word for "priest" (*pontifex*, lit., "bridge-builder"), then the ministry of service is clear. Israel is the bridge between Yahweh and the nations. For sure, however, the Hebrew for priest, *kōhēn*, has no "bridge-builder" nuances inherent in the word.

What the phrase does accomplish is that it produces "a religion of supra-sacerdotalism, in which the traditional function of priesthood is collectivized and sublimated" (Terrien 1978: 125). Such a perspective is in line with classical Protestantism's emphasis on the priesthood of all believers. Not only does such a doctrine emphasize that every believer has direct access to God rather than being restricted to going through ordained priestly pipelines (Luther); the doctrine also affirms that God calls all his devotees to priestly, mediatorial ministry. This is one reason why the epistolary literature of the NT talks so much about the Spirit's gifting of Messiah's followers.

The third phrase is "a holy nation" (*gôy qādôš*). The equivalent phrase to this in Deuteronomy is "a holy people" (*ʿām qādôš*). See Deut. 7:6; 14:2, 21; 26:19; 28:9. Deuteronomy's phrase is the more expected because *ʿām* is generally used for Israel, while *gôy* is most often used for other nations. But not always (Cody 1964). God's first promise in Gen. 12:2 is to make Abram into "a great nation" (*gôy gādôl*), as also in 18:18. The Lord repeats the gist of that promise to Jacob in Gen. 35:11 and 46:3. God's passion is to make of the patriarch's descendants not only a *gôy gādôl*, but also a *gôy qādôš*. What is the value if there is only a growth in size and numbers, but not a corresponding growth in God-likeness? Size without sanctification produces only a big but empty balloon. Prick it, and it vanishes.

There is one difference between the emphasis on sanctification language in Exodus–Leviticus and that in Deuteronomy. In the former, Israel is challenged to be(come) holy (see Exod. 19:6; 22:31 [30]; Lev. 11:44–45; 19:2; 20:7, 26; 21:6). The text says either "you shall be holy" or "be holy." By contrast, most of the passages from Deuteronomy (7:6; 14:2, 21) say that Israel already *is* a holy people (e.g., 7:6, "For you *are* a people holy to the Lord your God"). Holiness language in Deut. 26:19 and 28:9 is perhaps closer to that in Exodus and Leviticus than to other similarly themed verses in Deuteronomy. So Exodus–Leviticus: "You shall be holy"; Deuteronomy: "You are holy." In one, holiness is a prospect; in the other, a possession. In one, holiness is a goal; in the other, a gain. That seems to square with NT teaching that already-holy believers are to pursue holiness, and the already-sanctified are to set their hearts on full sanctification.

I am not sure that the Israelites at the bottom of the mountain fully understand what they are saying when they respond in v. 8 to Moses with "Everything that the Lord has said we will do." Their enthusiasm is understandable, but their commitment to obedience is perhaps shallow and premature. Down the road a bit (Exod. 32), they jump at the first opportunity they see not to keep the covenant!

It will be a miracle that the people will be able to "hear" or "overhear" anybody **19:9**
speaking anything to anybody, and yet in v. 9 the Lord will speak to Moses and the people will be able to hear the conversation! How does one hear when there is a massive thunderstorm, flashes of lightning, and the ear-shattering blast of the ram's horn? They will surely be able to see, but what will they be able to hear that is comprehensible and not just noise? Later, when reflecting on this Sinai event, Moses says to his second-generation people, "You heard the sound of words but saw no form; there was only a voice" (Deut. 4:12).

It is important that the people be able to hear the Lord's talking with Moses, for such a hearing will credential Moses in the eyes of his congregants. It will establish him beyond dispute as the Lord's messenger. Israel is Yahweh's *sĕgullâ*, but Moses is his conduit for communicating with his *sĕgullâ*.

Recognition of Moses as one to whom the Lord uniquely speaks will then be an incentive for the people to "put their trust" in him for the long haul. The verb for "put one's trust in" is the Hiphil of *ʾāman*. It is the same verb (in the same stem) that Moses uses in 4:1 ("What if they do not *believe* me?"), and the one the Lord uses four times in responding to Moses's question about unbelief (4:1, 5, 8 [2x], 9). As I pointed out in my grammatical note on 4:1, the Hiphil of *ʾāman*, if it is referring to putting one's trust in the Lord, is usually followed by the preposition *bĕ*. If the verb refers to putting one's trust in a person, the following preposition is most often *lĕ* (as here in 19:9). But this is not a hard-and-fast rule. For example, Exod. 14:31, "The people . . . put their trust in the LORD and in Moses his servant," has (Hiphil of) *ʾāman bĕ . . . bĕ*. The Israelites have already put their trust in Moses (14:31). Now they need to do that again. They have put their trust in Moses when they see God act by the sea. Will they continue to put their trust in Moses when they hear God speak from a mountain through Moses?

Sailhamer (1995: 270n83) has observed that Exod. 19:9 is the last positive use of "believe/put one's trust in" in the Pentateuch. The remaining few are about somebody *not* believing (Num. 14:11; 20:12; Deut. 1:32; 9:23). This may be one reason, he argues, why Heb. 11, in its listing of First Testament models of faith and faithfulness, leaps from the sea crossing (Heb. 11:29) to the conquest of Jericho (Heb. 11:30).

I am not sure of the meaning of "And Moses announced the peoples' words to the LORD" at the end of v. 9. Verse 9b seems to repeat v. 8b. Plus, in v. 9 the people never speak, so how can Moses relay their speech?

19:10–15 This section is structured like vv. 3–8. There is a private communication to Moses (vv. 3b–6, 10–13). Moses descends the mountain and relays God's message (vv. 7, 14–15). What is missing here is any response from the people like that in v. 8.

One thing of interest here is the importance of preparing oneself for the coming of God's presence. Sometimes God shows up unannounced, and so preparation is impossible. But on preannounced or established occasions, prepare yourself for this sacred, transcendent moment. It was not uncommon all that long ago for Christian believers to bathe and prepare Sunday's dinner on Saturday so as to be ready with as few distractions as possible for the worshipful encounter on the Lord's Day. This is in line with Exod. 19.

The Lord's word to Moses to purify the people (Piel of *qādaš*) in v. 10 has a parallel in Job 1:5: "When a period of feasting had run its course, Job would send and have them [his children] purified" (again the Piel of *qādaš*). Joshua too is told to purify the people (Piel of *qādaš*) on another auspicious occasion (Josh. 7:13). Such verses cannot mean that Moses or Job or Joshua have the ability to make others holy. That is God's work. Perhaps these individuals consecrate their respective groups and ask God to cleanse them from any contamination. Or maybe Moses purifies his fellow Israelites simply by urging them to wash their clothes. (No water to drink was not a problem at Sinai as it was elsewhere, if there is not only enough for everybody to drink, but also enough for everybody to launder their clothes.)

Other Scripture passages mandate laundering and then bathing, in that order: Lev. 14:8, 9; 15:5, 6, 7, 8, 10, 11, 13, 21, 22, 27; 16:28; 17:15; and so on. Self-ablution is last for an obvious reason: the person laundering his clothes may have simply passed the impurities on the clothing onto his hands. For some reason Exod. 19 says nothing about bathing. To that degree, Exod. 19 is like Gen. 35:2, where Jacob, upon discovering idols with his family, says, "Get rid of the foreign gods, . . . and purify yourselves and change your clothes." It is possible, however, that the Hitpael of *qādaš* ("purify oneself"), used of the priests in Exod. 19:22, does refer to a ritual bath of purification. For example, David saw Bathsheba "bathing" (*rōḥeṣet*), and she "had purified herself [Hitpael of *qādaš*] from her uncleanness" (2 Sam. 11:2, 4).

Exodus 19 is one of four places where some form of the root *qdš* is used with "tomorrow/*māḥār*": (1) "Purify them [Piel perfect consecutive of *qādaš*] today and *tomorrow*"; (2) Num. 11:18, "Tell the people, 'Consecrate yourselves [Hitpael imperative of *qādaš*] in preparation for *tomorrow*, when you will eat meat'"; (3) Josh. 3:5, "Joshua told the people, 'Consecrate yourselves [Hitpael imperative of *qādaš*], for *tomorrow* the Lord will do amazing things among you'"; (4) Josh. 7:13,"Go, consecrate [Piel imperative of *qādaš*] the people. Tell them, 'Consecrate yourselves [Hitpael imperative of *qādaš*] in preparation for *tomorrow*.'" See Milgrom 1991: 965–66; De Vries 1975b.

In each of these four instances that speak of purifying/consecrating vis-à-vis "tomorrow," something of great importance is about to happen: (1) God is about to give the covenant and the law at Sinai; (2) God is about to give his hungry people food; (3) God is about to lead his people across the Jordan and into the promised land; (4) God is about to uproot the sin and the sinner (covetous Achan), which have caused so much setback in the larger community. Yes, Scripture tells us not to worry about tomorrow, but it also tells us to get ready for that special tomorrow when God is going to speak or act in some decisive way.

So filled with divine electricity is this mountain that Moses must establish boundaries around it (v. 12) lest the people touch it and perish. One would think that if the Israelites tremble in terror on this occasion because of what they see and hear, they would put as much distance between themselves and the mountain as possible. Not so. The Lord is not interested in doing something that will make his people hightail it out of there. As Gowan (1994: 27) has said, "It is important that they *can* take precautions, for this is not a danger to be escaped from, but to be approached as nearly as possible."

This account of Israel's meeting God at the mountain has some narrative analogies with Moses's meeting God at the bush (see Berman 2004 for the concept of "narrative analogy" in Scripture, and esp. p. 17 for the tie between Exod. 3 and 19). In both passages, revelation comes amid fire. In both there is an oscillation between attraction to and cowering from the source of revelation. In both there is a divine proscription against coming any closer. Finally and most telling, both accounts begin with a report of entering the desert and arriving at the mountain. Compare Exod. 3:1 with Exod. 19:1–2.

There is something about the electrifying presence of God that is both frightening and fascinating, both dangerous and delightful. To use the language of the early-twentieth-century German theologian Rudolf Otto (1923), in his famous book *The Idea of the Holy*, God is both *mysterium tremendum* and *mysterium fascinans*. Near his presence "we are lashed with terror," but "leashed with longing" (from "Orient Ode," by Francis Thompson [1859–1907]).

The same thing may be said, at a much, much lower level indeed, about people who enjoy activities that, if they go wrong, could swiftly cost them their lives: skydiving, swimming with sharks, rock climbing, bungee cord jumping. Yes, there is risk; yes, it is frightening—but the thrill of it makes it worthwhile. The experience takes your breath away, yet it is irresistible.

Keep in mind that Otto, whatever the shortcomings in his understanding of God's holiness, was aiming his gun at a European Christianity that had become sterile because, in its idolization of reason, it had lost or abandoned the concept of a God who defies our explanation and understanding, who transcends the categories in which we try to box him.

Today two groups exist. One I would call "Sinaiaholics"; the other I call "Sinaiphobics." The former wish to live on a diet of constant and steady Sinais. For them, nothing less than thunder and loud noise is really satisfying. God is not in the ordinary. God is in the spectacular. The latter group, by contrast, is very uncomfortable with the Sinai atmosphere. They prefer more normal, orderly worship, more meditation and less acoustics. Anything they cannot control makes them uneasy. Is there a happy meeting ground between the two? Yes, sometimes the voice of God is loud and overwhelming (Exod. 19), and yet sometimes the voice of God is not in the powerful wind, or the earthquake, or the fire, but is "a gentle whisper" (1 Kings 19:12). What God has joined together, let us not put asunder!

Touching things that ought not to be touched can be lethal (v. 12c). Eve thinks that even touching the forbidden fruit will bring the death penalty (Gen. 3:3), although that is not a part of the divine prohibition in 2:17. The Kohathite Levites would die if they "touch the holy things" (Num. 4:15). We recall Uzzah, who "took hold" (*'āḥaz*) of the ark when it looked as if it would fall off the cart (2 Sam. 6:6–7). Does that thinking explain why the woman who has just been healed of her bleeding and hears Jesus ask, "Who touched me?" comes to Jesus "trembling" (Luke 8:45, 47)?

Sometimes in Exodus it is appropriate to touch. Zipporah touches (*nāga' lĕ*) either Moses's feet or the feet of their firstborn, and so saves Moses's life (Exod. 4:25). At Passover the Israelites are to touch (*nāga' 'el*; NIV "put") the top and sides of the doorframe of their houses with blood (Exod. 12:22). The word for "plague" in Exod. 11:1 is *nega'*, the noun derived from the verb *nāga'*, and would literally mean "becoming touched." So a plague on Egypt is a touch by Yahweh. But in Exod. 19:12 there is to be no touching (*nāga' bĕ*) the mountain.

The tactile trespasser is to be stoned or arrowed to death (v. 13). By whom? Were guards posted at the base of Sinai to arrest violators? Elsewhere the Levites do guard duty around the sanctuary area, but not here. There is no trial, only instant death. Westbrook (1998b: 68) points to instances where a person can execute justice without going through normal procedures. For example, Exod. 22:2–3 [1–2] gives a homeowner the right to kill an intruder if the break-in comes at night. Zechariah 13:3 gives the parents of a false-prophet son the right to execute him. So who may kill the illicit toucher? Anybody nearby who can throw a stone or shoot an arrow.

There is another issue in v. 13 (and in 16 too) besides who is authorized to execute justice. Who blows the ram's horn? Is this just a metaphorical way of referring to an extraordinary howling of the wind (Goldingay 2003: 386n31)? Or is this blast "of celestial origin, probably blown by a member of God's angelic entourage to announce the awe-inspiring descent of the King of all the earth" (Alter 2004: 426)? Horns may introduce a theophany (Exod. 19:13, 16; 20:18), acclaim a king (2 Sam. 15:10; 20:1; 1 Kings 1:34, 39, 41), commence a cultic event like the Jubilee Year (Lev. 25:9), summon scattered people together (Isa. 27:13; Jer. 4:5). They are frequently used in battle scenes, to summon people to battle (Judg. 3:27; 6:34; 1 Sam. 13:3), to signal attack (Josh. 6:4, 5, 6, 8, 9, 13, 16, 20), to signal retreat or dismissal (2 Sam. 2:28; 18:16; 20:22). See D. Wright 2002: 210.

Verse 15 has Moses add an unusual word about the people preparing for/by the third day: "Do not go near a woman," which assumes, by the way, that Moses thought (incorrectly?) that only adult males were to go up to the mountain. The Lord had said nothing to Moses about sexual abstinence.

Leviticus 15:16–18 teaches that in marital intercourse both spouses become minimally impure. I say "minimally" because the impurity, brought on by genital discharges, lasts only until the following evening and is removed by bathing. Hence, should a couple wish to worship at the sanctuary, they must refrain from sexual intercourse on the evening before. In 1 Sam. 21:1–6, notice how David argues that he and his men have the right to eat holy bread because "indeed women have been kept from us." Paul encourages sexual abstinence, if it is brief and consensual, so that the married couple might devote themselves to prayer (1 Cor. 7:5). Somehow Moses already knows that the ejaculation of semen renders both partners ritually unclean, and that will keep them away from the mountain. So there are two restrictions: (1) do not go near the mountain; (2) do not go near a woman. One will get you killed. The other will render you unclean so you cannot come within an inch of dying.

19:16–25 Verses 10–15 have dealt with the necessary preparation of the people before the third day. These ten verses deal with what happens on the third day. Needless to say, "the third day" is a common phrase with as many as thirty occurrences in the historical writings of Scripture. When Paul says that Christ "was raised on the third day *according to the Scriptures*" (1 Cor. 15:4), there are numerous candidates, then, for which "third-day" Scripture Paul has in mind. There is no explicit OT passage that speaks of Messiah's resurrection on the third day. The most likely candidate is Gen. 22:4, "On the third day Abraham looked up and saw the place in the distance" (see Daly 1977: 71). To be sure, Isaac does not die, as Jesus does, but some Jewish traditions do have Isaac dying and being resurrected, possibly to provide a Jewish parallel to the Christian resurrection event.

It is crucial that Moses purifies the people and that they launder their clothes (v. 14) *before* he leads the people out of the camp to the base of the mountain (v. 17). As Ps. 24:3–4 asks, and then answers, "Who may ascend the hill of the LORD? Who may stand in his holy place? He who has clean hands and a pure heart." According to Jesus's teaching, it is the pure in heart who will see God (Matt. 5:8), a truth that reverberates in Heb. 12:14 ("Without holiness no one will see the Lord").

The pyrotechnic, acoustical manifestations of God's descent onto Sinai are matched in Scripture only by similar remarkable phenomena on the Day of Pentecost in Acts 2—the blowing of a violent wind, tongues of fire, and add to that scene the one in Acts 4, another coming of the Spirit: "After they prayed, the place where they were meeting was shaken" (4:31). As Wedderburn (1994: 29–30) and others have argued, Luke may be describing Pentecostal events with the help of features drawn from the giving of the covenant and law at Mount Sinai. That connection with Pentecost ("fifty") would be even clearer if we could prove that the Lord reveals his torah to Israel fifty days after the exodus.

At the base of the mountain are the laity and the priests (vv. 22, 24). Moses knows the people are not to have sexual congress with their spouses at such an auspicious moment long before any such law has come into existence. And here, we have priests long before the priestly office has been instituted. These cannot be Aaronic priests, but must be the young men who carry out cultic duties in 24:5, or maybe even some of the "elders" (19:7).

Verse 23 contains the only instance in the OT "in which an earlier command of God is cited as evidence that a later command of his is unnecessary" (Childs 1974: 362): "But Moses said to the Lord, 'The people are not able to come up to Mount Sinai, for you yourself warned us saying . . .'" Just as the people reminded Moses on a previous occasion of their earlier words to him (14:12), "Didn't we say to you in Egypt . . . ?" here Moses reminds the Lord of what the Lord has recently said about individuals ascending the mountain. Similarly, in 33:12 Moses calls God's attention to something God has previously said: "You have been telling me, 'Lead these people,' but you have not let me know whom you will send with me."

There is one graphic NT reference to these Sinai events, and that is Heb. 12:18–29. There are two discrete sections to it. In vv. 18–24 the writer draws a contrast between then and now, between old and new covenant. Then, it was a mountain burning with fire, storms, a trumpet's blaring, with death for contact. But now, we have Mount Zion, a heavenly Jerusalem, and Jesus; if we touch him, we need not fear dying.

In the second section (Heb. 12:25–28) the writer shifts from the contrast of vv. 18–24 to comparison, using his frequent "how much more/less" argument. The first covenant people do not escape the one who has warned them on earth. How much less will new covenant believers escape if they refuse the one who speaks from heaven? Then, to conclude in v. 29, the author of Hebrews says, "for our God is a consuming fire." God is a consuming fire at Sinai. God is a consuming fire at Calvary and at Pentecost. God will be a consuming fire at the parousia. Again to quote Childs (1974: 377), "The mode of his [God's] revelation has changed, but God has not. He remains a consuming fire." He "is the same yesterday and today and forever" (Heb. 13:8).

The Ten Commandments

(20:1–17)

Few passages of Scripture are as well known and identifiable to even the general populace as the portion now under consideration, Exod. 20:1–17. One may not be able to recite all of the commandments, or in proper sequence, but the expression itself is easily and widely recognizable. It is the singular passage of Scripture one may find, at least in America, on the front lawns of Christian believers who are convinced that observance of these Ten Words is the key to America's survival and that their abrogation is a sure harbinger of the country's demise. There is no other Scripture portion that has been so much debated vis-à-vis the constitutionality or nonconstitutionality of being displayed in public schools, courthouses, and city halls.

In the pages that follow, I plan first to make some preliminary observations about these commandments, and then proceed to translation/notes/commentary commandment by commandment.

1. When we use the expression "the Ten Commandments," we need to be aware of employing a term that the OT itself does not use for this collection of laws. The phrase it does use is "the Ten Words": (1) Exod. 34:28, "And he [Moses] wrote on the tablets the words of the covenant, *ʿăśeret haddĕbārîm*"; (2) Deut. 4:13, "He declared to you his covenant, *ʿăśeret haddĕbārîm*, which he commanded you to follow and then wrote them on two stone tablets"; (3) Deut. 10:4, "The Lord wrote on these tablets what he had written before, *ʿăśeret haddĕbārîm* he had proclaimed to you on the mountain." The Septuagint translates the Hebrew phrase in two of these three references literally, *deka logoi*, "ten words," the origin of the word "Decalogue," but for Deut. 4:13 it uses *deka rhēmata*.

To be sure, the NIV (and other modern translations) always render this thrice-used phrase "the Ten Commandments." But *dābār*/*dĕbārîm* is not the normal word for "commandment" and most commonly means "word/words." The word rendered "commandment" is *miṣwâ* (sg.), *miṣwôt* (pl.), two words now frequently written as *mitzvah* and *mitzvot*. Non-Hebrew readers will recognize the phrase *bar/bat mitzvah*, a term for the Jewish boy or girl who now officially passes into adulthood.

In fact, the words *miṣwâ/miṣwôt* occur only four times in Exodus, three of which are in the plural: 15:26, "If you indeed . . . give ear to his *commands*"; 16:28, "How long will you refuse to keep my *commands* and instructions?"; 20:6, "Those who love me and keep my *commandments*"; 24:12, "With the law and *commands* (sg.) I have written for their instruction." By contrast, the plural form of the word occurs twenty-one times in the lengthy Ps. 119 (vv. 6, 10, 19, 21, 32, 35, 47, 48, 60, 66, 73, 86, 98, 115, 127, 131, 143, 151, 166, 172, 176) and once in the singular (v. 96). Obviously, the writer of Ps. 119, when he speaks of the Lord's *miṣwôt*, is not thinking only of the ten laws of Exod. 20.

Perhaps we should not put too much weight on the fact that the "Ten Commandments" are really "Ten Words." Two items seem to suggest that. First, even if Exod. 20:1–17 is composed of ten "words," those utterances are still commands. They are not hints, or suggestions, or opinions, or ideas, but mandates. Second, to return to Ps. 119, in a chapter that meditates at length on God's decrees/laws/statutes/precepts, the expression "word/words" (either *dābār* or *ʾimrâ*) occurs more often than "commands," forty-two times (*dābār* 23x + *ʾimrâ* 19x) versus twenty-one times. In one verse (v. 172) they are used together: "May my tongue sing of your *word* [*ʾimrâ*], for all your *commands* are righteous." So, God's words are his commands, and his commands are his words.

2. If we stay with the traditional title, is it better to call them "the Ten Commandments" or "the Ten Commands"? Or is this much ado about nothing? The NIV, in the four Exodus passages cited above, uses "commands" for *miṣwâ/miṣwôt* in 15:26; 16:28; and 24:12 but translates it as "commandments" in 20:6. A command is more like an order, while a commandment is more like a rule. A command "is for a particular action by a specified addressee for one time only. . . . A commandment is . . . a rule of conduct that imposes an obligation on the addressee to the speaker" (Patrick 1999: 68). "You may not drive the car this weekend" is a parent's command, but "You are not to drive the car while text-messaging or talking on the cell phone" is a parent's commandment. Clearly the Ten Words of Exod. 20:1–17 fall into the category of commandments rather than commands.

3. The Decalogue of Exod. 20 is the one collection of laws that is repeated elsewhere in the same sequence. Compare Deut. 5:6–21. There are numerous examples of individual laws that resurface elsewhere, either in the same book or another book (e.g., the prohibition of boiling a kid in its mother's milk first appears in Exod. 23:19, then again in 34:26, and subsequently in Deut. 14:21). But the only legal corpus to have an encore is the Decalogue.

Yet, when the two recordings are placed side by side, differences become quite apparent, some significant, some insignificant:

Commandment	Verses	Description
1	Exod. 20:2–3; Deut. 5:6–7	No difference
2	Exod. 20:4–6; Deut. 5:8–10	(a) Exod. 20:4 prohibits the use of "any carved likeness and any image of what is in the heavens above" (*pesel wĕkol-tĕmûnâ*); Deut. 5:8 says "no carved likeness of an image" (*pesel kol-tĕmûnâ*, without *wāw* prefixed to *kol*).
		(b) "Third generation" (*ʿal šillēšîm*) in Exod. 20:5 lacks the "and" of Deut. 5:9 (*wĕʿal-šillēšîm*).
3	Exod. 20:7; Deut. 5:11	No difference
4	Exod. 20:8–11; Deut. 5:12–15	(a) "Remember" (*zākôr*) the Sabbath day in Exod. 20:8 versus "Keep" (*šāmôr*) the Sabbath day in Deut. 5:12.
		(b) "As the Lord your God has commanded you" in Deut. 5:12 is absent in Exod. 20:8.
		(c) "Your slave" appears in Exod. 20:10, but "*and* your slave" in Deut. 5:14.
		(d) "Nor your animals" (*ûbĕhemtekā*) stands in Exod 20:10 versus "nor your ox or donkey" (*wĕšôrĕkā waḥămōrĕkā*) in Deut. 5:14.
		(e) "So that your manservant and maidservant may rest as you do" in Deut. 5:14 is absent in Exod. 20:10.
		(f) The motive for Sabbath observance shifts from recalling what God did at creation (Exod. 20:11) to recalling what God did at the exodus (Deut. 5:15).
5	Exod. 20:12; Deut. 5:16	(a) "As the Lord your God has commanded you" in Deut. 5:16 is absent in Exod. 20:12.
		(b) "And that it may go well with you" in Deut. 5:16 is absent in Exod. 20:12.
6	Exod. 20:13; Deut. 5:17	No difference
7	Exod. 20:14; Deut. 5:18	Exod. 20:14 has "You shall not commit adultery" versus "*And* you shall not commit adultery" in Deut. 5:18.
8	Exod. 20:15; Deut. 5:19	"You shall not steal" appears in Exod. 20:15 versus "*And* you shall not steal" in Deut. 5:19.
9	Exod. 20:16; Deut. 5:20	(a) "You shall not bear" in Exod. 20:16 versus "*And* you shall not bear" in Deut. 5:20.
		(b) "False witness" (*ʿēd šāqer*) in Exod. 20:16 and "vain witness" (*ʿēd šāwĕʾ*) in Deut. 5:20, although NIV uses "false testimony" for both.
10	Exod. 20:17; Deut. 5:21	(a) "You shall not covet" in Exod. 20:17 versus "*And* you shall not covet" in Deut. 5:21.

Commandment	Verses	Description
		(b) Both verbs for "covet" in Exod. 20:17 are *ḥāmad*. In Deut. 5:21 the first verb for "covet" is *ḥāmad*, but the second verb for "set your desire on" is *ʾāwâ* ("covet, set one's desire on").
		(c) The order "your neighbor's house . . . wife" in Exod. 20:17 is "your neighbor's wife . . . house" in Deut. 5:21.
		(d) To Exod. 20:17's "you shall not set your desire on your neighbor's house," Deut. 5:21 adds "his field/land" (*śādēhû*).
		(e) "*And* his ox" in Exod. 20:17 is simply "his ox" in Deut. 5:21.

One observes that only three of the commandments (1, 3, and 6) are reproduced exactly the same. Others are reproduced almost exactly the same. The addition of "and/*waw*" at the beginning of commandments 7–10 in the Deuteronomy version does not appear all that significant.

The most significant differences are in commandments 4 (the Sabbath day) and 10 (coveting). Accordingly, I will speak to those when I come to the commentary section.

Just about everybody would agree on the centrality and importance of the Decalogue. Although the audience to whom the Decalogue is recited in Deut. 5 is different than that in Exod. 20 (second-generation Israelites versus first-generation Israelites), it is the same Decalogue with the same Author, still with ten and still the same sequence. For all the importance of the Decalogue, the Lord has not felt the need to produce a photocopy. When the Lord quotes an earlier word of his own, he does not always (for reasons that may escape us) quote himself verbatim.

4. In addition to its repetition elsewhere, there is another factor giving the Decalogue of Exod. 20 great importance. The introduction in v. 1, "And God spoke all these words, saying, . . ." seems to imply that God speaks these words directly to Israel. The emphasis in chap. 19 on God's speaking privately to Moses, who then in turn communicates that message to his people, may be absent in chap. 20.

The pattern of Moses's relaying divine revelation seems to be usual before and after chap. 20. Thus in the Passover chapter (12), the Lord speaks his will about these festivals privately to Moses (12:1–20), who in turn transmits those instructions to the Israelites (12:21–27). Even earlier, and on numerous occasions, the Lord speaks to Pharaoh only through Moses (and sometimes Aaron). In the provision-of-manna episode, the Lord speaks to Moses (16:4–5, 12), who in turn speaks to the Israelites (16:6–8, 15b–16). In chap. 20 itself, once we have gone beyond the Ten Commandments, the text moves from "And God spoke all these words, saying" (v. 1) to "And the Lord said to Moses, 'Thus you shall say to the Israelites'" (v. 22). Again, chap. 21 begins with, "And these are the laws you shall set before them" (21:1). The parade example of this pattern is the Lord's communicating to Moses at Sinai's summit, declaring his will for the building of the tabernacle and the institution of the priesthood (chaps. 25–30), and Moses's faithful transmission of those directives (35–40; 35:1, "And Moses assembled all the community of Israelites and said to them . . .").

Exodus 20:1–17 alone breaks that pattern, leading commentators to call this passage "The Decalogue as the Direct Address of God" (Nicholson 1977). The people's request in 20:19 that Moses, and not God, speak to them lest they die reinforces that fact, but not in an absolute way.

Deuteronomy's version suggests the same. In Deut. 5:4–5 Moses says, "The Lord spoke to you face to face . . . on the mountain. . . . And he said . . ." I take it that "face to face" means without mediation. However, we do have the problematic v. 5, which versions like NIV and NRSV put in parentheses and NJPS sets off by dashes. Such punctuation shows that "and he said" at the end of v. 5 is a continuation of v. 4, and everything else earlier in v. 5 is parenthetic: ("At that time I stood between the LORD and you to declare to you the word of the LORD"). So why mention in one verse the Lord's speaking face to face with Israel, and in the very next verse have Moses draw attention to his role as mediator? Perhaps this is splitting hairs, but Moses does not say, in v. 5, "At that time I stood between the Lord and you *and declared* to you the word of the LORD," but "*to declare* to you the word of the LORD." Possibly his intention never is implemented. Or maybe Moses is simply drawing attention to his normal role of mediator without specifically focusing on his mediation of the Ten Words.

The biggest argument in favor of God's speaking the Decalogue through Moses rather than directly is the last two words of the last verse of chap. 19, *wayyōʾmer ʾălēhem*, which I rendered, "and he [Moses] told them." However, the usual rendering of the Hebrew would be, "And he [Moses] said to them," with somebody's quoted words following. But no quoted words follow! Unless they are the words that God declares in vv. 2–17. See my grammatical note at 19:25 and the suggestion of Sailhamer. Interestingly, in her study of the eight patterns of commissioned communication in the Hebrew Bible, Vater (1980: 366) by my count cites thirty-seven illustrations from Exodus, but 20:1–17 is not one of them.

5. Yet a third evidence of the Decalogue's singular importance is its way of saying "You shall not." To begin with, one notes that eight of the Ten Commandments are prohibitive statements. This is not unexpected. Normally the purpose of law is to discourage (overtly) certain forms of behavior and by implication encourage others. A speed-limit sign by the road or highway says, in effect, "Do not drive faster then this, or risk the consequences." Where there is a chance to reverse one's direction of driving, but legally one should not do so, one will find a sign saying "No U turns permitted" but no sign that says

"Drive Straight Ahead Only." One will see "Wrong Way" but never "Right Way," and "Slower Drivers Keep Right" but never "Faster Drivers Keep Left."

Around a public swimming pool, one is likely to see a "swimming pool Decalogue": (1) no running; (2) no children unaccompanied by parent; (3) no swimming alone; (4) no diving in shallow end; (5) no glass allowed in the pool area; (6) no alcoholic beverages; (7) no immodest bathing attire; (8) no swimming unless lifeguard present; (9) no large floats or tubes may be used in the pool; (10) no food or drink may be consumed while one is in the water.

There are two ways in Hebrew to say "You shall not" or "Do not." One is *lōʾ* with the imperfect. The other is *ʾal* with the jussive. The LXX normally uses *ou* with the future indicative for *lōʾ* with the imperfect, and *mē* with the imperative for *ʾal* with the jussive.

There are two basic differences between these two ways of expressing a prohibition. First, while *lōʾ* with the imperfect is used almost exclusively for expressing commands, or commandments, only rarely does *ʾal* with the jussive have this function. Rather, it is used primarily to make a request, an exhortation, an entreaty, or a warning. When *ʾal* with the jussive does express a command, it is a command for the immediate situation but not for future occasions as well. The second difference flows from the first: *lōʾ* with the imperfect carries much stronger force than *ʾal* with the jussive. Bright (1973: 187) puts it succinctly: "Whereas the *ʾal* prohibitive expresses a specific command for a specific occasion, the *lōʾ* imperative expresses a categorical prohibition of binding validity both for the present and the future."

ʾAl with the jussive is common in Genesis–Exodus. Just a few examples will suffice: (1) Gen. 15:1, "Do not be afraid, Abram"; Gen. 22:12, "Do not lay a hand on the boy"; Gen. 50:19, "But Joseph said to them [his brothers], 'Don't be afraid'"; Exod. 3:5, "'Do not come any closer,' God said"; Exod. 12:9, "Do not eat the meat raw or cooked in water"; Exod. 19:15, "Do not go near a woman" (AT). One can easily observe that these references point to warnings, exhortations, statements of encouragement, or instruction rather than to commands. Where they have the force of a command, the command is limited to the addressee and to that specific occasion.

The Ten Commandments (Exod. 20 and Deut. 5) employ *lōʾ* with the imperfect to express a prohibition, suggesting that the Decalogue "expresses a categorical prohibition of binding validity both for the present and the future" (see Bright's quote above). Of course, *lōʾ* with the imperfect is not restricted to the Ten Commandments.

Bright (1973: 188) notes that in the legal sections of Exodus (20:1–17; 21:1–23:19; 34:17–26) there are 55 *lōʾ* prohibitives and only 2 with *ʾal*. In Leviticus there are 193 *lōʾ* prohibitives and only 11 with *ʾal*. In the legal corpus of Deuteronomy (12–26), the ratio of *lōʾ* versus *ʾal* is 125:0.

In the Wisdom literature of the OT, the situation reverses. There the *ʾal* prohibitive dominates: Proverbs has between 85 and 90 instances of *ʾal* with the jussive versus none (or at best, 2) with *lō'*; Job has about 23 with *'al*, none with *lō'*; Ecclesiastes has about 18 with *'al*, none with *lō'*.

Scholars call laws that begin with "you shall not" apodictic law. A dictionary will define the adjective "apodictic" as "absolutely certain or necessarily true." Such laws are to be distinguished from casuistic law, which usually is structured as an "if . . . then" law. Note, for example, how many of the laws in chaps. 21–23 begin with "If" rather than with "You shall not." I count about twenty-one verses or portions of a verse that begin with "if" just in chap. 21.

The basic difference between apodictic and casuistic laws is that the former are categorical imperatives of universal validity. Seldom if ever do they spell out punishment for their violation, unlike casuistic law. This difference is clear when one compares the apodictic law in Exod. 20:15 about stealing ("You shall not *steal*") with the casuistic law about stealing in Exod. 22:1 [21:37], "If a man *steals* an ox or a sheep and slaughters it or sells it, he must pay back five head of cattle for the ox and four sheep for the sheep." The absence of clearly stated sanctions from apodictic law suggests that the Decalogue was never intended to function as Israel's criminal code, although some have argued that it has functioned as such (e.g., Phillips 1970; 1983).

Almost all scholars of ancient law codes agree that while apodictic law appears here and there in ancient Near Eastern legal corpora, its presence there is not nearly as pervasive and prominent as it is in the Hebrew Bible. One who checks out other law codes (e.g., the Code of Hammurabi) discovers that they are for the most part composed entirely of casuistic/"if . . . then" laws.

The Ten Commandments do not exhaust apodictic law in Scripture. The last law in Exod. 21–23 (and several in chap. 22) is also an apodictic law: "Do not cook/You shall not cook [*lō'-tĕbaššēl*] a kid in its mother's milk" (23:19b). It is a second-person masculine singular imperfect with *lō'*, like the Ten Commandments, expressing an absolute truth, and it ignores any sanction (does not say what happens to you if you do boil a kid in its mother's milk). The first apodictic law in Scripture is the word of the Lord God to the primal man: "You must not eat [*lō' tō'kal*] from the tree of the knowledge of good and evil" (Gen. 2:17). The difference here is that Gen. 2:17 goes on to spell out a consequence for violation: "for when you eat of it you will surely die."

6. Who is the "you" that is addressed in eight of these Ten Commandments? In each of these eight is a masculine singular verb. The "you" is never plural or feminine. Similarly, the two imperatives, "remember" (v. 8) and "honor" (v. 12), are masculine singular in form. Hence, possibly the first conclusion to arrive at is that the Decalogue speaks to males. And since it is only Hebrew males who are present at Sinai (apart from the lingering "mixed multitude"), then a fuller answer would be that the Decalogue speaks to Israelite males.

In addition to the singular "you," the content of the commandments, especially those in the second half, suggests other answers. Clines (1995b: 102) opines that the narratee is "an individual, a male, an Israelite, employed, a house-owner, married, old enough to have children but young enough to have living parents, living in a 'city,' wealthy enough to possess an ox and an ass and slaves, important enough to be called to give evidence in a lawsuit." There are no commandments patently addressed to women, the poor, the slave, the homeless, and the unmarried.

Since chap. 19 indicates that the Lord speaks to the "people" and not to "males" (notwithstanding Moses's warning in 19:15 about not going near a woman), one still wonders whether groups like women or the unmarried feel left out. Were there women present who felt that it was all right for them to work on the Sabbath, but not their spouse, because the prohibition was directed to adult males and their children? That it was acceptable for them to covet their neighbor's husband because the commandment outlawed only coveting a neighbor's wife? Were there unmarried present who assumed fornicatory sex was okay because the prohibition addressed only adulterous sex? I think not.

To suggest that the grammatically masculine singular "you" includes only males is fallacious. To return to Exod. 23:19b cited above, it would be like using the masculine singular "you" in "You shall not cook a young goat in its mother's milk" to prove that in biblical Israel the husband (or adult male) did all the cooking. As we shall see in the next section, if God's moral law is written not only on two limestone tablets at Sinai, but also into the warp and woof of his creation, does this not suggest that the identity of the recipients of divine commands is an all-inclusive and all-embracing one?

7. This legal section in Exodus (both the Decalogue of 20:1–17 and the collection of laws in 20:22–23:19) is sandwiched between two chapters, both of which highlight covenant. In chap. 19 God offers the covenant to Israel, and in chap. 24 Israel accepts (done in a preliminary fashion in 19:8) and ratifies the covenant. Hence we have the sequence in this unit of covenant (Exod. 19) to law (most of 20–23) to covenant (24).

For that reason, at least in Exodus (and Deuteronomy), one cannot speak of covenant without law, nor can one speak of law without covenant. These are not two independent entities that just happen to stand side by side. Rather, each interacts with the other and gives the other its fullest, richest meaning.

It is intentional that chap. 19 (the offer of covenant) precedes chap. 20 (the offer of law). That order can never be reversed. And for this reason: the purpose of covenant is to institute or elevate a unique relationship between two parties. The purpose of law is to provide boundaries to that relationship that, if honored, will go a long way in perpetuating that relationship. What banks are to a river, law is to covenant. Take away the banks, and the river quickly becomes a swamp. Take away the regulations, and an athletic competition devolves into a melee. What vows and the faithful implementation of those vows are to marriage and the marriage ceremony, law is to covenant.

If a covenant is a means by which two parties create a new or deeper relationship with each other, those two parties may have one of two standings with each other. In one instance the parties may be equal in standing, and hence both parties submit to and abide by the regulations. The name for such a covenant is a parity covenant: each member of the covenant is on "par" with the other.

In another instance the parties may be nonequals, one stronger and more powerful, the other subordinate and less powerful. In this case, it is the stronger party who imposes the terms and obligations and regulations on the subordinate party. The name for such a covenant is a suzerainty covenant. A dictionary will define "suzerain" as "a sovereign or a state exercising political control over a dependent state, a feudal overlord." Yahweh is Israel's suzerain: Israel is Yahweh's vassal. Hence, it is the Lord alone who determines the boundaries in this covenant connection.

Still, one may ask whether there is a way to understand law theologically, without recourse to the category of covenant. Or must all law be subsumed under covenant, all law subsumed under gospel, all norms subsumed under narrative? To put it a bit differently, does not the OT root the good life, the ethical life, in the Lord's created order as well as in Sinaitic law?

The pharaoh of the Abraham story (Gen. 12:10–20) seems to be aware that one does not take the wife of another man and sleep with her, although he is not privy to Sinai's seventh commandment. The nations whom Amos upbraids in 1:3–2:3, before he turns his attention to Judah and Israel, are expected to know the difference between right and wrong modes of behavior, and yet they have never heard of the Decalogue. Isaiah offers the example of an ox and a donkey as models of how one is to relate to God (1:3). Jeremiah offers the stork, the dove, and the other migratory birds as models of how one is to know God (8:7). Proverbs encourages not more Bible reading or praying if one wants to be diligent and responsible, but rather observing the behavior of ants (6:6). As Provan (2001: 39) says, "There is an order in nature itself that is worthy of imitation by mankind" so that sin may be not only the transgression of a law but "the embrace of cosmic nonsense."

In Ps. 19, one of three torah psalms in the Psalter, the writer speaks about the sun in the first part (vv. 1–6) and the torah/law of the Lord in the second (vv. 7–13). In other words, David moves from creation to Sinai and draws a comparison between the two. The sun and the law are both sources of light and enlightenment. Nothing is "hidden" from the penetrating heat of the sun (v. 6 [7]), and the law can penetrate even down to exposing "hidden" faults (v. 12 [13]). It is as if David says, "What the regularities of the heavenly bodies are to what they govern, the commandments are to human communities." Thus the psalmist connects law with creation rather than with Sinai. In Jer. 33:20–22, 25–26 the Lord makes an analogy between the covenant he has made with Israel, David, and the Levites, on the one hand, and the covenant he has made with the day and with the night and the rest of his creation, on the other hand: "If you can break my covenant with the day and my covenant with the night . . . , then my covenant with David . . . can be broken." "If I have not established my covenant with the day and night and the fixed laws of heaven and earth . . . , then I will reject the descendants of Jacob." Covenant is inextricably connected with creation and Sinai. As Levenson (1980: 32) has said, "God's sovereignty is larger than his suzerainty."

8. Matthew 22:35–36 records one of Jesus's critics testing him with this question: "Teacher, what is the greatest commandment [or "the most important"] in the Law?" (Mark 12:28). The question is just a tad above another foolish question the disciples ask Jesus: "Who is the greatest in the kingdom of heaven?" (Matt. 18:1 = Mark 9:34; Luke 9:46). Why this penchant to know what is the greatest or who is the greatest?

Jesus answers his critic not by quoting any of the Ten Words, but rather first by quoting Deut. 6:5, "Love the Lord your God with all your heart and with all your soul and with all your mind" (Matt. 22:37). Then Jesus proceeds to overanswer the query by offering the answer to an unsolicited question: "And the second is like it: Love your neighbor as yourself" (Matt. 22:39; Lev. 19:18).

Jesus appears to be doing three things when he answers the question the way he does. First, he changes laws that are primarily prohibitive into ones that are performative, from "you shall not" to "you shall." Second, in the two parts of his answer, he is condensing the first four commandments (godward, vertical commandments) into one commandment, and contracting the remaining humanward, horizontal six commandments into one commandment. To love God that passionately rules out other gods and rules out the desecration of God's name and day. To love one's fellow neighbor unconditionally rules out disrespect, stealing, any violence against another, bearing false witness, or coveting. Third, Jesus is making the point that at the heart of obedience to God is love. One obeys not out of fear, but out of love. In so speaking, he anticipates Paul's "love is the fulfillment of the law" (Rom. 13:10).

Possibly the reason Jesus overanswers the question about which is the greatest commandment is because he is aware that to observe faithfully the first four, but ignore the last six, makes a mockery and charade of torah piety. How can anyone boast of loving God and then hating one's fellow human simultaneously, of loving God whom one cannot see, and withholding love from the brother or sister whom one can see (1 John 4:20–21)?

Anytime anybody in the NT quotes verbatim or paraphrases one of the commandments, it is one of the last six, not the first four. That is true of Jesus (Matt. 5:21–48; 15:4; 19:18, in his answer to the "rich young ruler's" question), of Paul (Rom. 7:7; 13:9; Eph. 6:2; Col. 3:5; 1 Tim. 1:9–10), of James (2:11). The brief reference in Heb. 4:4 to God's resting on the seventh day could as well refer back to Gen. 2:2–3 as to Exod. 20:11.

Translation

[1]And God spoke all these words, saying, [2]"I am the LORD your God, who brought you out from the land of Egypt, from the house of bondage. [3]You shall have no other gods in my presence.

[4]"You shall not make for yourself a sculptured image, nor any object like something in the heavens/sky above, or in the earth below, or in the subterranean waters. [5]You shall neither pay them homage nor serve them, because I, the LORD your God, am a jealous deity, reckoning the ancestors' iniquity to the sons, to the thirdlings and to the fourthlings of those who reject me, [6]but keeping faith even to the thousandth generation of those who are loyal to me and keep my commandments.

[7]"You shall not take the LORD your God's name frivolously/falsely, for the LORD will not leave unpunished the one who takes his name frivolously/falsely.

[8]"Remember the Sabbath day to hallow it. [9]Six days shall you labor and do all your work. [10]The seventh day, however, is a Sabbath to the LORD your God. You shall not do any work, you, and your son and your daughter, your male and female slave, and (any) draft animal, and the alien who is within your gates. [11]For in six days the LORD made the heavens/sky and the earth/land, the sea, and everything in them, then he rested on the seventh day. Therefore the LORD blessed the Sabbath day and hallowed it.

[12]"Show respect to your father and your mother so that your days may long endure upon the land that the LORD your God is giving to you.

[13]"You shall not murder/kill.

[14]"You shall not commit adultery.

[15]"You shall not steal.

[16]"You shall not testify against your neighbor as a false witness.

[17]"You shall not covet your neighbor's house(hold). You shall not covet your neighbor's wife, and his servant or maidservant, nor his ox and ass, indeed anything that belongs to your neighbor."

Grammatical and Lexical Notes

20:2. When "your" on "the LORD *your* God" is singular (*ʾĕlōhêkā*), the "I" on "*I* am the LORD" is *ʾānōkî* (Exod. 20:2, 5; Deut. 5:6, 9). When the "your" on "the LORD *your* God" is plural (*ʾĕlōhêkem*), the "I" on "*I* am the LORD" is *ʾănî* (Lev. 11:44; 18:2, 30; 19:2; 20:7, 24; 25:38, 55; 26:13; Num. 15:41). The reason for this use of *ʾănî* before "your God" (pl.) and *ʾānōkî* before "your God" (sg.) is not transparent.

20:3. Unlike the remaining negative commandments, this one does not start with a "You shall not." Rather, it opens with a third-person masculine singular verb: "There shall not be to you [*loʾ-yihyeh lĕkā*] other gods." The same construction (*hāyâ* + preposition *lĕ* + pronominal suffix) occurs in 19:5, "You shall be to me [*wihyîtem lî*] a unique treasure," and in 19:6, "You shall be to me [*wĕʾattem tihyû-lî*] a royalty of priests and a holy nation."

20:3. The expression "other gods" [*ʾĕlōhîm ʾăḥērîm*] occurs in Exodus only here and in 23:13. It occurs eighteen times in Deuteronomy, and eighteen times in Jeremiah (whose familiarity with Deuteronomy is well established). Exodus 34:14 does have "(no) other god" (*ʾēl ʾaḥēr*). See Hoffman 1994.

20:3. There is much discussion about the meaning of *ʿal-pānāy* ("in my presence"). Literally, the phrase says, "upon/on/over/against my face." The LXX reads the phrase in Exod. 20:3 as "except/but for me" (*plēn emou*), but the identical phrase in the Deuteronomic version of this commandment (Deut. 5:7) as "before my face" (*pro prosōpou mou*). If we translate the Hebrew as literally as possible, then we need to have an English counterpart composed of a preposition + pronominal adjective and noun, hence my "in my presence."

To demonstrate the possibility of numerous translations for *ʿal pĕnê*, with or without pronominal suffix, I shall cite several passages in which *ʿal pĕnê* occurs, and put in italics what language the NIV uses for the Hebrew phrase: (1) Gen. 16:12, "He [Esau] will *live in hostility toward* all his brothers"; (2) 25:18, "And they [Ishmael's descendants] *lived in hostility toward* all their brothers"; (3) 32:21 [22], "So Jacob's gifts went on *ahead of him*"; (4) Exod. 33:19, "I will cause all my goodness to pass *in front of you*"; (5) Lev. 10:3, "*In the sight of* all the people I will be honored"; (6) Deut. 21:16, "He must not give the rights of the firstborn to the son of the wife he loves *in preference to* his actual firstborn son"; (7) 1 Kings 6:3, "The portico *at the front of* the main hall"; (8) Job 1:11, "And he [Job] will curse you *to your face.*"

A few places where the *ʿal pānāy* of Exod. 20:3 occurs are (1) Isa. 65:3, "a people who continually provoke me to *my very face*"; (2) Jer. 6:7, "Her sickness and wounds are ever *before me*"; (3) those instances where somebody falls *face down/prostrate* [on my face] before the Lord in prayer and/or wonder (Ezek. 1:28; 3:23; 9:8; 11:13; Dan. 8:17).

20:4. The word for "sculptured image" is *pesel*. It is a carved image (cf. *pesel* translated in Lev. 26:1 LXX as *glypta*, "graven, carved"), and is usually representational. The word is one of several for "idols" in the vocabulary of the Hebrew Bible, but it appears only in the singular. One may "make" (*ʿāśâ*) a *pesel* (Exod. 20:4; Deut. 5:8; 27:15 [NIV, "carves"]; Judg. 17:3, 4); "fashion" (*yāṣar*) a *pesel* (Isa. 44:9 [NIV, "make"], 10 [NIV, "shapes"]); or "set up, erect" (*qûm*, Hiphil) a *pesel* (Judg. 18:30). The Akkadian equivalent of *ʿāśâ pesel* is *ṣalman epeshu*, "make an image."

20:5. "Serve them" is *tāʿobdēm* (as in Deut. 5:9). That is a Hophal of *ʿābad*, and the Hophal normally carries passive (or reflexive) meaning. If the verb were a Qal, the form would be *taʿabdēm*, as in Exod. 4:23, *wĕyaʿabdēnî* ("that he may serve me"). Weinfeld (1991: 277) suggests that the Hophal implies powerfully seductive, irresistible idolatry: "You shall not allow yourself to be brought to worship them."

20:5. The meaning of *qnʾ* (verb, "be jealous"; noun, "jealousy"; adjective, "jealous") is illuminated through a comparison with the Arabic and Syriac verb *qanaʾa*, which means "to become dark/ intensely red." The verb indicates the visible effects of anger on one's face.

20:5. The meaning of *pāqad ʿal* is open to debate: "reckoning to," "calling to account for," "punishing," or "visiting." The LXX uses three different verbs for *pāqad*: (1) and (2) when the verb means "punish, avenge, pay back," *ekdikeō* (27x), and *episkeptomai/episkopeō/episkepsis* (29x); (3) when the verb means "give, pay back," *apodidōmi* (4x, in Exod. 20:5; Lev. 18:25 [*antapodidōmi*]; Num. 14:18; Deut. 5:9). See Grossfeld 1984: 87, 95. *Pāqad ʿal* occurs (1) in participial form (*pōqēd*) in Exod. 20:5 = Deut. 5:9 ("punishing"); Exod. 34:7 (NIV, "he punishes"); Num. 14:18 (NIV, "he punishes"); (2) in imperfect verb form in Lev. 18:25 (*ʾeqōd*; NIV, "I punished it"); Num. 27:16 (*yipqōd*; NIV, "appoint"); (3) in infinitive construct form (*lipqōd*) in Isa. 26:21 (NIV, "to punish"); Amos 3:14 (NIV, "on the day I punish"). See André 1980: 261. Without any following preposition, *pāqad* may mean "visit" (NIV, "was gracious to"; Gen. 21:1); "was concerned about" (Exod. 4:31); "was gracious to" (1 Sam. 2:21).

The above raises an interesting question: how can a verb (without preposition) mean "be gracious to" or "be concerned about," but that same verb have the meaning "punish" when it is followed by a preposition (*ʿal* or *bĕ*)? B. Levine (1993: 367) suggests that the basic sense of the verb is "hand over, deliver, assign" and hence "turn one's thoughts/attention to somebody else." When God shows up for a "visit," you need to do one of two things: either welcome him, or run for cover.

20:5. "Thirdlings" and "fourthlings" are more commonly "third and fourth generation," but there is no word for "generation" here.

20:5. W. Roth (1962: 301) notes the phenomenon of "numerical sequence in Scripture," meaning a two-number sequence with the second being one unit higher than the first (X/X + 1). He finds thirty-two examples of this. For "three/third . . . four/fourth," see Exod. 20:5; 34:7; Num. 14:18; Deut. 5:9; Prov. 30:15b, 18, 21, 29; Jer. 36:23; Amos 1:3, 6, 9, 11, 13; 2:1, 4, 6. See also the study of Haran (1971), who describes this as "a contiguous pair of consecutive numbers in ascending order," and for whom "three/third . . . four/fourth" means not a specific number but an indefinite number, or approximately that number (1971: 238).

20:5. Does the punishment that is promised to last "to the third and fourth generations" start with the sinner or after the sinner? In other words, does the punishment extend four generations beyond the idolater (children>grandchildren>great-grandchildren>great-great-grandchildren) or three generations beyond the idolater (children>grandchildren>great-grandchildren)? The similar phrase in Exod. 34:7 seems to suggest four generations after the sinner (sons>sons of the sons>the third generation>the fourth generation), but 20:5 is a bit more ambiguous. Freedman and Overton (2002: 104–5) argue for the harmony of the two texts by suggesting haplography: in Exod. 20:5 the scribe's eye accidentally skipped from the first *bnym* to the second *bnym*, thus eliminating the intervening *bny-bnym* (as in 34:7).

20:5. "Those who reject me" may also be translated "Those who hate me." I take it that *šānēʾ* is used here as it is with the Lord in Mal. 1:2b–3a, "Jacob I have loved, but Esau I have *rejected/hated*."

There are a number of incidents in OT narrative where something happens three times, then a climactic fourth time: Noah sending out the raven, and three times a dove, who, on the last of these flights, does not return to the ark (Gen. 8:7, 8, 10, 12); Balaam's three misunderstandings of the donkey, followed by an understanding of the donkey (Num. 22:23, 25, 27, 28–30); Jotham's fable of the three trees that say no, followed by the fourth tree that says yes (Judg. 9:8–9, 10–11, 12–13, 14–15); Samson's sharing with Delilah three false secrets about his strength, followed by a fourth and true explanation of his strength (Judg. 16:7, 11, 13b, 17); the three times Samuel takes God's voice to be Eli's, followed by a fourth when he truly discerns the voice to be God's (1 Sam. 3:5, 6, 8, 10); Job's three tragedies, followed by a fourth that moves Job to affirm, even in suffering, God's control of the situation (Job. 1:15, 16, 17, 18–21).

We may also note Amos's repeated "For *three* sins of X, even for *four*" throughout chaps. 1 and 2 of his book. Paul (1991: 27–30) argues, cogently I believe, that such an expression emphasizes the length and finality of God's judgment against those who are guilty of overstepping moral boundaries against both humanity and God's revealed law.

20:6. For "keeping faith" (*ʿāśâ ḥesed*), see G. Clark 1993: 179, 249. The phrase can also be translated "showing kindness/love to" or something like "extending benevolence to."

20:6. If in v. 5 "hate" = "reject," then in this verse "love" = "be loyal to." See Moran (1963), who cites passages from both the Hebrew Bible and from other ancient Near Eastern texts in which "love" means "be loyal to," as subjects are loyal to their king. Moran draws attention to 1 Sam. 18:16; 2 Sam. 19:6–7; and 1 Kings 5:1 [15], and NIV's "on friendly terms with" seems a weak translation of *ʾōhēb*.

20:7. "Take" is the verb *nāśāʾ*, which most often means "carry, bear" or "lift." The verb appears again with "*spreading* false reports" (Exod. 23:1), "*uttering* an oracle" (Num. 23:7, 18; 24:3, 15, 20, 21, 23), "*swearing* an oath" (1 Kings 8:31), "*making* a prophecy" (2 Kings 9:25), "*beginning* music" (Ps. 81:2 [3]), "*lifting up* a prayer" (2 Kings 19:4 = Isa. 37:4), *taking up* a lament (Jer. 7:29). Given, then, the frequency of *nāśāʾ* with some kind of speech or sound, "to *nāśāʾ* the Lord's name," must be an elliptical way of saying, "take the Lord's name upon one's mouth/lips."

20:7. There remains a question about the meaning of *laššāwěʾ* ("frivolously, falsely"). I shall speak more about this in the commentary section. For now, note that the LXX uses *epi mataiō* both times in this verse and in Deut. 5:11. *Mataios* means "worthless, empty, vain." Compare James 1:26 for a NT use of *mataios*: "If anyone considers himself religious and yet does not keep a tight rein on his tongue, he deceives himself and his religion is *worthless*." See also 1 Cor. 3:20 ("the thoughts of the wise are *futile*") and Titus 3:9 ("*foolish* controversies and genealogies"). The Vulgate shows an interesting change of words. It translates the first *laššāwěʾ* of Exod. 20:7 with *in vanum*, but switches to *frustra* ("in deception") for the second one. In Deut. 5:11 the Vulgate uses *frustra* for the first *laššāwěʾ*, but *super re vana* ("over a vain matter") for the second.

20:7. The basic meaning of *nāqâ* ("leave unpunished") is "be clean, pure," but it comes also to mean "get off scot-free," or in legal contexts, "be acquitted." The verb *zaku* in Akkadian ("be clean") shares the same semantic range. See *CAD* Z:25–32. The verb appears in the Niphal stem in Exod. 21:19, "the one who struck the blow *will not be held responsible* [wĕniqqâ]," and in the Piel stem (as in 20:7) in 34:7 [2x], "maintaining love to thousands, . . . but by no means acquitting [*wĕnaqqēh lōʾ yĕnaqqeh*] the guilty" (NIV, "He does not *leave* the guilty *unpunished; he punishes* the children"). The verb is common in Proverbs, as in 6:29; 11:21; 16:5; 17:5; 19:5, 9; 28:20, all of which the NIV renders "(not) go unpunished." Exodus 20:7 and 34:7 both use the verb *nāśāʾ* and *nāqâ*. In both the verb *nāqâ* means the same, but *nāśāʾ* has the meaning "forgive/carry away" in 34:7 but "take up [on the lips]" in 20:7. See Fishbane 1980: 353.

20:8. Both the Exodus version of the Decalogue and the Deuteronomic one begin the fourth commandment by using the infinitive absolute for the imperative: *zākôr* (Exod. 20:8), *šāmôr* (Deut. 5:12). For a previous use of *zākôr* with imperative function, see Exod. 13:3 ("Remember [*zākôr*] this day on which you came out of the land of Egypt"). For later uses in the Torah, see Lev. 2:6 ("Crumble [*pātôt*] it and pour oil on it [the grain offering]"); Lev. 6:14 [7] ("Let Aaron's sons bring [*haqrēb*] it [the grain offering] before the LORD" [AT]); Num. 15:35 ("The man must die. Have the whole assembly pelt [*rāgôm*] him with stones" [AT]); Num. 25:17 ("Treat the Midianites as enemies [*ṣārôr*] and kill them"); Deut. 1:16 ("Hear [*šāmōaʿ*] the disputes and judge fairly"); Deut. 15:2 ("Let every creditor cancel [*šāmôṭ*] the loan he has made to his fellow Israelite" [AT]). Watts (1962) argues that the infinitive absolute never stands alone as a substitute for a finite verb form. Rather, the infinitive absolute is defined by a following verbal construction that carries an imperatival sense. He suggests that *zākôr* in Exod. 20:8 has gerundive force: "Remembering the Sabbath to hallow it, six days you shall labor."

20:8. The opening word in Exodus's version of this commandment is *zākôr* ("remember") and in Deuteronomy's version *šāmôr* ("keep, guard"). That these two verbs are not really all that different is seen in their use in parallelism elsewhere: Pss. 103:18, "with those who keep [*šāmar*] his covenant and remember [*zākar*] to obey his precepts"; 119:55, "In the night I remember [*zākar*] your name, O LORD, and I will keep [*šāmar*] your law." Additionally, *šāmar* . . . *ʿāšâ* ("keep . . . and do [all your work]") is a common pair of verbs, especially in Deuteronomy (e.g., 4:6; 5:1, 29; 7:12; 11:22, 32; 13:19; 15:5; 16:1). One also finds *zākar* . . . *ʿāšâ*: Num. 15:39, 40, "so you will remember [*zākar*] to obey [*ʿāšâ*]."

20:8. The most common rendering of *lĕqaddĕšô* is "to keep holy," but Childs (1974: 415) believes the Piel form of the infinitive is a "factitive" Piel, that is, not just "keep holy" but "make holy." He then adds, "The command to hallow is not identified simply with not working or resting, but over and above both of these is the positive action of making holy."

20:9. "Six days" is an accusative of time specifying the duration of an activity. See GKC §118i. It is similar to "Six years sow your fields" (Lev. 25:3).

20:10. For *bĕhēmâ* (normally, "cattle") Deut. 5:14 has *šôr* and *ḥămôr* ("ox" and "ass"). I have translated *bĕhēmâ* "(any) draft animal" rather than "cattle," for they are the animals rather than, say, sheep that "work" by pulling or carrying loads. For a similar meaning, see Isa. 46:1, "Bel bows down, Nebo stoops low; their idols are borne by beasts of burden [*laḥayyâ wĕlabbĕhēmâ*]."

20:12. There are two differences between the Exodus version of the fifth commandment and Deuteronomy's (Deut. 5:16). First, after "mother" Deut. 5:16 has "as the LORD your God has commanded you." Second, after "that your days may long endure" (Exod. 20:12), Deut. 5:16 adds "and that you may fare well" (AT; *ûlĕmaʿan yîṭab lāk*). The LXX includes the phrase *hina eu soi genētai* in both Exod. 20:12 and Deut. 5:16.

20:12. Biblical Hebrew can say only "father and mother" since it has no separate word for "parents," unlike Greek, which has the word *goneis* (Luke 2:27, 41, 43; 18:29; 21:16).

20:12. Weinfeld (1991: 282) points out that *ʾārak* in the Qal stem is a stative verb, "be long" (only three times: Gen. 26:8; Ezek. 12:22; 31:5). In the more common Hiphil stem, it has one of two meanings: a stative (as in the fifth commandment), equal to the Qal, or a causative ("make long, lengthen"). Only the Hiphil in the imperfect has stative force. GKC §53d calls such a Hiphil stative an "internal Hiphil."

20:13. There are two issues with this commandment and the three or two that follow it. In some editions of the Hebrew Bible, commandments 6 through 9 are recorded in one verse, v. 13. In such editions there will be only twenty-three verses in chap. 20 instead of twenty-six. Most editions of the Hebrew Bible assign one verse per commandment.

The second issue is the order of commandments 6 through 8: (a) murdering; (b) adultery; (c) stealing. In the LXX, however, the order is (a) adultery (*ou moicheuseis*); (b) stealing (*ou klepseis*); (c) killing (*ou phoneuseis*). Thus MT's *a-b-c* = LXX's *b-c-a*. Did the commandment about adultery originally follow the one about killing, or did it precede it? Jesus's words in Matt. 5:21 ("You have heard that it was said, . . . 'Do not murder'") and then in Matt. 5:27 ("You have heard that it was said, 'Do not commit adultery'") plus his words to the rich, young ruler ("Do not murder, do not commit adultery," Matt. 19:18 = Mark 10:19) follow the order of the MT. But Jesus's words to the young man in Luke's version ("Do not commit adultery, do not murder" [Luke 18:20]), plus Rom. 13:9 ("'Do not commit adultery,' 'Do not murder'") and James 2:11 ("For he who said, 'Do not commit adultery,' also said, 'Do not murder'") follow LXX's order. Apparently, there was some flexibility in the sequence of the commandments, especially murder and adultery. A copy of Deuteronomy from Qumran, for example, has the command against adultery precede the one against murder. We are not sure of the reason for switching the sequence, but one possibility is that the rearrangement allows for the two family-related commandments (honoring one's parents and being faithful to one's spouse) to appear consecutively (K. Thomas 1976: 208).

20:16. "Testify against" is *ʿānâ bĕ*. Without the preposition the verb means "to respond, answer." With the preposition it means "to respond as a witness," that is, "testify." Occasionally *ʿānâ bĕ* means "to testify on behalf of," as in Gen. 30:33, "And my honesty [Jacob's] *will testify for* me in the future." Much more often *ʿānâ bĕ* means "testify against." Compare Samuel's words to his people, "*Testify against* me in the presence of the LORD and his anointed" (1 Sam. 12:3); David's words to the Amalekite who claimed to have killed Saul, "Your own mouth *testified against* you when you said, 'I killed the LORD's anointed'" (2 Sam. 1:16); Eliphaz to Job, "Your own lips *testify against* you" (Job 15:6); "The look on their faces *testifies against* them" (Isa. 3:9); "And our sins *testify against* us" (Isa. 59:12); "Our sins *testify against* us" (Jer. 14:7); the end of Mic. 6:3 could be "Testify against me" (*ʿănēh bî*) instead of NIV's "Answer me."

20:16. For Exod. 20's *ʿēd šāqer* ("false witness"), Deut. 5:20 has *ʿēd šāwĕʾ*. The second word in each of these phrases appears in parallelism in Ps. 144:8 and 11 ("whose mouths are full of *lies* [*dibber-šāwĕʾ*], whose right hands are *deceitful* [*šāqer*]"). See also Zech. 10:2, "The idols speak deceit, diviners see visions that *lie* [*šeqer*], they tell dreams that are *false* [haššâwʾ]."

20:16. The Septuagint's *ou pseudomartyrēseis kata tou plēsion sou martyrian pseudē* ("You shall not false-witness a false witness against your neighbor") makes "false witness" sound like an activity of a perpetrator rather than the perpetrator himself. If that were the case in the Hebrew, it would read *ʿēdût šāqer* ("false testimony") rather than *ʿēd šāqer*. The Hebrew phrase is an accusative of manner, and so I translate it "*as* a false witness."

20:17. That Exod. 20 places "wife" after "house" suggests that "house" in v. 17 carries the meaning "household." The man's "household" includes his wife, servants, and animals. Deuteronomy 5:21 reverses the two nouns, leading instead with "wife," then following with "house." In this case "house" means "property" and does not include "wife" as "disposable property." Similarly, Block (2010: 462) suggests that the prohibition on coveting another's wife stands first and alone in Deuteronomy "to ensure the elevated status of the wife, and foreclose any temptation to use the Exodus version to justify men's treatment of their wives." If we stay with "house" in Exod. 20:17, what does this commandment mean for the Israelites at Sinai who have no houses? Phillips (1977: 3) has suggested that there is nothing in these short injunctions that is inapplicable to a desert setting. Accordingly, "house" includes "tents," to say nothing of the skill of using bricks in building that the Hebrews learned while in Egypt.

20:17. A second difference between Exod. 20:17 and Deut. 5:21 is that the former uses *ḥāmad* twice, while Deut. 5:21 employs *ḥāmad* in the first line, then the Hitpael of *ʾāwâ* in the second line. "You shall not *covet*. . . . You shall not *covet*" becomes "You shall not *covet*. . . . You shall not *crave*." The LXX translates all four with *epithymeō*. It also follows the sequence of "wife" and "house" of Deut. 5:21 in Exod. 20:17 (*ouk epithymēseis tēn gunaiki* . . . *tēn okian*) against MT's order. In Proverbs *ʾāwâ* (Hitpael) appears five times to describe an unhealthy craving (13:4; 21:26; 23:3, 6; 24:1) while *ḥāmad* appears three times (1:22; 6:25; 12:12; and in the Niphal in 21:20).

Commentary

If the understanding of the Decalogue as the direct speech of God can be **20:1**
sustained (see discussions above), then what gives the commandments their authority is not so much what is said as much as who says it, not so much the unique content as the unique speaker.

In calling this verse the "prologue" to what follows, I realize I am departing **20:2**
from those traditions, especially Judaism, that take v. 2 either as the first commandment or as part of the first commandment. What punctuation should one use to separate v. 2 from v. 3? The NIV uses a period, the NRSV a semicolon, but the NJPS a colon.

Throughout Scripture are frequent references to the Lord's delivering his people from Egypt. Two different verbs appear for the narration of this deliverance. Either it is *ʿālâ*, Hiphil ("bring up") or *yāṣāʾ*, Hiphil ("bring out"). See the study of these two verbs by Wijngaards (1965).

I note three basic differences between these two verbs for the exodus from Egypt. First, the verb *yāṣāʾ* (Hiphil) is used more often to describe the exodus from Egypt than is *ʿālâ* (Hiphil), about seventy-plus times (among them, Exod. 20:2) versus thirty-plus times for *ʿālâ*. Second, *ʿālâ* emphasizes the Lord's relocation geographically of his people from Egypt to elsewhere, while *yāṣāʾ* emphasizes that this is an act of liberation, a release from a hopeless situation of bondage, and not simply a relocation. Third, and springing from the second observation, is that the Lord is invariably the subject of *yāṣāʾ* (Hiphil) when the reference is to the exodus. The only exception I can find is Exod. 16:3, "You *have brought us out* into the desert to starve this entire assembly to death." (I do not count here those places where the Lord says to Moses something like, "I am sending you to Pharaoh to bring my people out of Egypt" in Exod. 3:10 and 6:26.)

By contrast, while the Lord is most always the subject of *ʿālâ* (Hiphil) too, the subject may be Moses (Exod. 17:3; 32:1, 7, 23; 33:1; Num. 16:13; 20:5; 21:5), or the golden calf (Exod. 32:4, 8; Neh. 9:18), or Jeroboam's two golden calves (1 Kings 12:28). Most frequently Moses is the subject of *ʿālâ* when his people are attacking him and bad-mouthing him about something. They do say, "Why did you bring us up from Egypt?" They do not say, "Why did you liberate us from Egypt's stranglehold on us?" And understandably so. As

Brichto (1992: 271) has said, "This sense of the liberating activity is reserved for the liberating Deity and denied to his agent, real or putative."

This prologue provides the reason why the Lord can now impose these ten laws. He is not only the one who has redeemed his people from slavery; now, having redeemed them, he also desires to begin to form his holy character in them. The one who has released Israel from Egyptian-imposed boundaries will now speak to Israel about Yahweh-imposed boundaries. There is a world of difference between boundaries that enslave and boundaries that energize, boundaries that destoy life and boundaries that direct life.

The only other place where such a prologue stands at the head of a legal pericope is Lev. 18:2, "Speak to the Israelites and say to them: 'I am the LORD your God.'" Even closer to Exod. 20:2 is Gen. 15:7, "I am the LORD, who brought you out of Ur of the Chaldeans to give you this land to take possession of it." Both are a self-introduction formula and use the Hiphil of *yāṣāʾ* in an *ʾăšer* clause. What the Lord has started with Abraham at the first exodus, he now is fulfilling with Abraham's descendants at the second exodus.

20:3 One thing that separates this commandment from the other nine is that it is the only one that "proscribes a relationship rather than an act" (Patrick 1999: 91).

One does not forbid something that people are unlikely to do anyway. What one does command (positively) is something that most, left to their own preferences, will not do. We do not need a command prohibiting the production of three-dollar bills or even two-dollar bills. Few parents ever have to say to their young children, "No vegetables unless you eat all your dessert." Is the reason Jesus gives his disciples "a new command"—a *mandatum novum* on Maundy Thursday of Passion Week, to "love one another" (John 13:34)—because he knows that, left to our own human nature, we will not love one another? We might ignore, use, manipulate, put down one another, but would we love one another? Probably not.

It is most likely that the prohibition of things like murder, adultery, and theft had been ethical norms for humanity long before God revealed them to Moses on Mount Sinai. At Sinai such already established norms are made part and parcel of revelation.

With respect to the first commandment, it appears that none of Israel's patriarchs or matriarchs have been enticed to worship other gods. Before they encounter Yahweh, yes (Josh. 24:14), but after Yahweh meets them, no. Adam through Noah through Joseph are all monotheists. Gods are a "dime a dozen" in Egypt, but the Israelites express absolutely no interest in them. Re or Amen/Amun or Thut never share the stage with Yahweh.

Hence, the first commandment cannot be designed to deter Israel from the polytheistic patterns of misbehavior practiced by its ancestors, prediluvian and postdiluvian. Every person from Adam to Joseph has kept the first commandment "since they were a lad."

Although Israel finds Egypt's gods irrelevant, they will find Canaan's gods irresistible. Hanging on by one's fingernails seldom makes polytheism attractive. But once the people are established, begin to put down roots, get a taste of the good life and the prosperity that goes with it, then maybe polytheism does begin to appear as an attractive addition or supplement to their core beliefs. The gods of the well-to-do usually outnumber the gods of the less fortunate (although they are not immune either).

Note that the command does not say, "You shall have no other gods, for no other gods exist." Other Scriptures do make that claim, especially in Isaiah: 45:14, "There is no other; there is no other god"; 45:18, "I am the LORD, and there is no other"; 45:21, "There is no God apart from me"; 45:22 and 46:9, "I am God, and there is no other." One does not need, however, to wait for references from later chapters in Isaiah for this truth about God to emerge. In the chapter in Deuteronomy just before the one containing the Decalogue, we read, ". . . so that you may know that the LORD is God; besides him there is no other" (4:35), and "The LORD is God in heaven above and on the earth below. There is no other" (4:39). Hence, without any sense of contradiction, Deuteronomy can say of the Lord, "There is no other," and seventeen verses later say, "You shall have no other gods." True, there are no other gods that have real existence, but in the world of human fantasy, there is no end to the number of gods the human mind can generate and to which humans may become devoted. What the Lord is calling for in this first commandment is an exclusive loyalty to him.

The second commandment prohibits the making of images (cf. 34:17). This **20:4–6**
is one difference between the first two commandments. The first speaks to possession ("you shall not have"), while the second speaks to manufacturing ("you shall not make"). That difference suggests that the first commandment in its proscription is broader than the second. Anybody and everybody can "have" an idol if they so choose, but not everybody can craft one. Surely not everybody has the prerequisite skills to melt down gold and silver and then cast the melted-down metals into a perfectly shaped small bovine.

There is another difference between vv. 3 and 4. Verse 3 prohibits other *ʾĕlōhîm*, while v. 4 prohibits making and using a *pesel*. That difference raises the question about what the *pesel* represents. Are the proscribed idols/images those connected with the other gods of the previous commandment? That is, "You shall have no other gods or even any images portraying those gods." Or are the proscribed idols images of Yahweh? This second possibility, if true, has given rise to the use of the word "aniconic" to describe Israelite religion. (The Greek influence on the English language is shown by the fact that a word in English converts into its opposite if an "a" is added to the beginning of the word. Think, for example, of "theist," somebody who believes in God, and its opposite, "atheist." If a word begins with a vowel, one adds "an" to a word instead of an "a," as here, "iconic," "images," and "aniconic," "no images.")

One might assume that v. 4 prohibits the representation of the Lord by images, for representation and worship of other deities have already been precluded in the first commandment. It is unlikely that the first commandment prohibits having other gods but forgets to say anything about also not having any physical representations of those deities. It is not the case that v. 3 is regrettably truncated.

However, it seems that it would be images of other gods rather than images of himself that would provoke the Lord's jealousy. Note that the antecedent of the plural "them" in v. 5 ("neither pay *them* homage nor serve *them*") is the singular "idol/*pesel*" of v. 4. I suggest one of two explanations for this. First, the word "idol," although grammatically singular, is expanded in v. 4 to include likeness to any celestial, terrestrial, or aquatic creature. This three-layered cosmological formula emphasizes that forbidden representations include "images of any being, wherever he might be found" (Vawter 1960: 73). The second possibility is that the "You shall neither pay them homage nor serve them" of v. 5 applies both to the "You shall have no other gods" of v. 3 and the "You shall not make a carved image" of v. 4. To that degree, commandments 1 and 2 have been fused. We have seen above that some religious traditions take vv. 3–6 as one commandment rather than as two distinct commandments, and there is some justification for that.

One can understand why the Israelites do not decorate their tabernacle, and later their temple, with statutes or busts of Yahweh, but what is so wrong about having a small figurine of him placed inconspicuously on the top of the dresser beside one's bed or on the kitchen table on festival days?

Surely it cannot be because the Bible wants to protect the understanding of God as nonbodied "spirit." If that is the case, why does the Bible so frequently picture God anthropomorphically? The Bible often speaks of his eyes, his arms, his feet, his nose, and his face. He is a God who talks, walks, rides, comes down, goes up, and so forth.

Actually the OT never provides an extensive explanation for this particular prohibition (or for most of its prohibitions). The closest it comes is in Deut. 4:11–20, part of Moses's homiletical address to the second-generation Israelites about what their parents experienced at Sinai. There Moses says twice that while the people heard the sound of words, they "saw no form" (Deut. 4:12, 15). The truth can be extrapolated from that: because God speaks from heaven without anything representing him being visible, there is no legitimacy for making any kind of an image of him. The coupling of these two truths is present in Exod. 20:22–23: (1) "You have seen for yourselves that I have spoken to you from heaven"; (2) "Do not make any gods to be alongside me." First, no visible form; then, no images to be made. The Sinai experience has become "a paradigm of Yahweh's self-disclosure to Israel" (E. Curtis 1985: 283–84).

Since at that holy mountain God does not manifest himself in an image, images are therefore excluded as a means by which God reveals himself. How God reveals himself on that august occasion has become the pattern by which he defines worship for his people in the ages to come.

One can imagine that other factors are at work here. The prohibition of idols/images will hopefully play a major role in resisting the influence of Canaanite religion, which was permissively iconic. Yet as we know, especially from the sermons of the prophets, the prohibition, if designed as a deterrent against imitation and borrowing the worship styles of others, was often not effective. For some a visible Baal was more appealing than an invisible Yahweh.

While outlawing idols/images, OT religion readily approves of the use of symbols. The inside of the tabernacle and the temple will never be confused with a four-bare-walls Quaker or Shaker meetinghouse. The ark of the covenant, for example, is a symbol of divine presence. So why prohibit idols but condone symbols?

Heschel (1954: 118) helpfully draws a distinction between "real" symbols and "conventional" symbols. For Heschel, a country's national flag serves as an illustration of a conventional symbol. The flag points to the honor and glory of a nation, not because it inherently possesses the qualities of that nation, but because of the association, or relationship, that particular flag has with the nation. A real symbol, by contrast, "is a visible object that represents something invisible, something present representing something absent. . . . He who has the image has the god." The last part of Heschel's statement ("He who has the image has the god") shows how easily symbols can become idols, how easily something that God has intended to be a conventional symbol can degenerate into a real symbol. The ark of the covenant, a conventional symbol of divine presence, becomes a real symbol when the Israelites think that the mere presence of the ark will turn the tide in the battle against the Philistines in 1 Sam. 4 (Where the ark is, God is). One thinks of Jeremiah's famous Temple Sermon (Jer. 7 and 26), where he preaches that it is not the simple presence of the temple in Jerusalem that will save the people from the Babylonians, but rather repentance and living with one another as God has planned. The temple is a symbol, not a talisman.

The second commandment is the first of three in the Decalogue (see also v. 7 [commandment 3] and vv. 8–11 [commandment 4]) that include a motive clause introduced by "for" (*kî*). A motive clause is a grammatically subordinate sentence that provides the motivation for the command. See the pioneering study of Gemser (1953) and the more extended study of Sonsino (1980). Gemser (1953: 50) identifies three motive clauses in the Exodus dialogue, while Sonsino (1980: 86) identifies four by including the "so that" of v. 12b in commandment 5.

The motive for avoiding idols, according to v. 5, is that Yahweh is a "jealous God/god/Deity" (*ʾēl qannāʾ*). To be sure, jealousy is not a characteristic we immediately associate with God. But it is a name or descriptor of God occurring elsewhere. See Exod. 34:14; Deut. 4:24; 5:9; 6:15; Josh. 24:19; Nah. 1:2 (the latter two written as *ʾēl qannôʾ* instead of *ʾēl qannāʾ*). For all of these the LXX uses *zēlōtēs* except for Josh. 24:19 (*zēlōsas*). The choice of the Greek word in the LXX raises the issue of whether to translate the noun as "jealousy" or "zeal," the adjective as "jealous" or "zealous," the verb as "be/make jealous," or "be/make zealous," or even "be/make envious."

A few times the Hebrew Bible uses *qnʾ* to denote jealousy in a pejorative sense, being jealous of another person who has something you do not have and to which you feel you are entitled. With such a meaning "You shall not be jealous" means "You shall not covet." Compare "When Rachel saw that she was not bearing Jacob any children, she *became jealous* [*wattĕqannēʾ*] of her sister" (Gen. 30:1), or "His brothers [Joseph's] *were jealous* [*wayĕqanʾû*] of him" (Gen. 37:11), or "*Do not envy* [*ʾal-tĕqannēʾ*] a violent man" (Prov. 3:31), a sentiment close to Ps. 37:1, "*Do not . . . be envious* of those who do wrong" (with the exact same verbal form). See also Prov. 24:1, 19.

A few individuals are marked out for their "zeal" for God because they eliminate those they believe to be lawbreakers and enemies of God: Phinehas (Num. 25:11), Elijah (1 Kings 19:10, 14), and Saul (2 Sam. 21:2). Undoubtedly it is this sense of holy rage inciting one to eradicate unbelief of which Paul speaks autobiographically in Gal. 1:13–14, "I persecuted the church . . . [and] was extremely *zealous* for the traditions of my fathers," and in Phil. 3:6, "as for *zeal*, persecuting the church." See Smiles 2002.

I am especially interested in the passages where *qnʾ* is connected with some aspect of marriage and/or love. Numbers 5:14 uses the root four times to express a spouse's indignation and passionate emotion over the companion's adulterous behavior, real or imagined. Proverbs 6:34 speaks of a "*jealousy* [that] arouses a husband's fury" when his wife has sex with another. Song 8:6 speaks of the love between two lovers as "strong as death, its *jealousy* unyielding as the grave."

These verses may supply the best clue in understanding what divine jealousy is all about. The Lord's relationship to Israel is a marital one. He has yoked himself to Israel in marriage, like a husband to a wife. Marriages succeed or falter at the point of faithfulness and exclusivity: "and forsaking all others shall be faithful to you alone." If there exists a juvenile, carnal jealousy, there also exists a holy jealousy. The opposite of this holy jealousy is indifference. To call God "jealous," or for God to refer to himself as "jealous," is simply to say that he does not ignore, or take lightly, or is not indifferent about his bride going after another. Idolatry becomes a form of adultery, violating that sacred nexus between lovers by substituting gods and images for God.

The manifestation of God's jealousy is cross-generational fallout on sons and daughters of three and four generations removed from the sins of their fathers and mothers (v. 5b), but endless and extensive benevolence on the offspring of commandment-keeping ancestors (v. 6). The Hebrew word for "iniquity" (NIV, "sin") is *ʿăôn*, and it mostly refers to deliberate, egregious sin. Among its more famous uses is its employment in connection with the Day of Atonement. On that day Aaron confesses all the "iniquities" (NIV, "wickedness") and rebellion of the people (Lev. 16:21), and then the live goat carries all their "iniquities" (NIV, "sins") on itself to a solitary place (Lev. 16:22). When the text says that God will "reckon the ancestors' iniquity" to their offspring, we need to understand that *ʿăôn* bears a consequential meaning: not primarily the iniquity itself, but the consequences of that iniquity, punishment. The best-known reference for this consequential use of *ʿăôn* is Cain's word to the Lord, "[The] punishment [for my iniquity—*ʿăônî*] is more than I can bear" (Gen. 4:13).

The expected question or mystery is why would God make children and grandchildren pay for the sins of fathers and grandfathers? Why not the culprit? Only Exod. 34:7b and Num. 14:18b state in an absolute, unqualified way that God punishes descendants for the sins of their forebears. Exodus 20:5 (= Deut. 5:9) tempers the phrase by adding "those who reject me" just as it adds "those who are loyal to me" in v. 6. That is to say, if the offspring walk in the way of their ancestors, for better or for worse, they will receive either God's blessing or judgment both because of their ancestors' behavior and their own behavior.

The idea of cross-generational, or vertical, retribution appears in some ancient Near Eastern texts. For instance, note this prayer of the Hittite king Mursilis: "My father sinned and transgressed against the word of the Hattian god, . . . but I have not sinned in any respect. It is only true, however, that the father's sin falls upon the son. So my father's sin has fallen upon me" (*ANET* 395). In contrast to this Hittite text, I am not aware of any text in the OT in which the recipient of the consequences of somebody else's misbehavior argues his own innocence and that he is, in fact, a scapegoat.

When we look at narratives in the Bible, we find numerous examples of somebody in a later generation paying the price for the foibles of somebody in an earlier generation. But we find not as many accounts of somebody later reaping the benefits of somebody's righteousness from an earlier era.

Some illustrations of the former include (1) Ham's "sin" (?) with his father Noah, and Noah's curse on Ham's son, Canaan (Gen. 9:20–27); (2) the children of first-generation Israelites "suffering for your [the first generation's] unfaithfulness" (Num. 14:33); (3) Moses and the Israelites: "Because of you the Lord became angry with me also" (Deut. 1:37); (4) Achan's children stoned for their father's sin (Josh. 7:25); (5) the child born of David's illicit union with Bathsheba died (2 Sam. 12:18); (6) the sons of Saul slain because of their father's sin against the Gibeonites (2 Sam. 21:8–9); (7) the sins of Jeroboam will be visited upon his son Abijah (1 Kings 14:10–18); (8) the sins of Baasha, king of Israel, will be visited upon his son Elah (1 Kings 16:1–12);

(9) the widow's words to Elijah: "What have you against me, man of God? Did you come to remind me of my sin and kill my son?" (1 Kings 17:18); (10) "They stood in their places and confessed their sins and the wickedness of their fathers" (Neh. 9:2). See also 1 Kings 21:29.

A few illustrations of transgenerational blessing would include the following: Noah's righteousness saves his entire family; Abraham's descendants receive Canaan because of Abraham's faithfulness to God; the Lord does not completely end Solomon's line because of David's following the Lord completely (1 Kings 11:6) and because of the Lord's promise to David (1 Kings 11:13).

It is commonly suggested that Jeremiah (Jer. 31:29–30) and Ezekiel (Ezek. 18) may be rejecting this idea of corporate/familial responsibility and be refuting the proverb "The fathers have eaten sour grapes, and the children's teeth are set on edge," and advancing in its place, "The soul who sins is the one who will die" (Ezek. 18:4). That this is hardly the case can be seen by observing that the Jeremiah who says "Everyone will die for his own sin" (31:30) also says (in the very next chapter!) "You show love to thousands but bring the punishment for the father's sins into the laps of the children after them" (32:18).

So which is it? Corporate responsibility or individualism? Or both? In my judgment, Kaminsky (1995) makes a compelling case for seeing the value of a more communitarian view in contrast to a strict, atomistic emphasis. How one behaves influences not only that person but also a much wider circle as well, possibly even the yet unborn. If God's covenant starts, but does not end, with Abraham (or David), why would it not be predictable that one's lifestyle, habits, and choices, and the fallout of all those, start with, but do not end with, the individual?

One final comment. In the Decalogue the statement about the extension of punishment for iniquity or the extension of benevolence is connected with the second commandment, or the first and second commandments, that is, idolatry. But few of the ten examples I put forward above have anything to do with idolatry (Jeroboam's calf would be one). Achan is guilty of theft, not idolatry. David is guilty of adultery (or worse), but not idolatry. Therefore, one is led to the conclusion that the motivation clause of vv. 5–6 could have been attached to just about any commandment: "You shall not steal, for I the LORD am . . . ," or, "You shall not commit adultery, for I the LORD am . . ." Its attachment to the first two demonstrates the crucial importance of proper worship. Mess up here, and you have the potential to mess up at many other places. A good case can be made for the fact that the key to faithful living, as far as the ten words are concerned, is the first two of them. As Kinlaw (2010: 136) has said, "The test of whether you are a believer is not in what you do with the third through the tenth commandments, but it is what you let the God of the first two commandments do with the good, the goods, in your life."

The meaning of the third commandment seems simple enough. Or is it? There 20:7
are greater differences among English versions in translating this commandment than for any of the other nine. Here is a sampling of the first half of the commandment: the familiar "Thou shalt not take the name of the LORD thy God in vain" (KJV; Alter 2004); "You shall not misuse the name of the LORD your God" (NIV); "You shall not utter the name of Yahweh your God to misuse it" (JB); "You shall not make wrong use of the name of the LORD your God" (NEB); "You shall not make wrongful use of the name of the LORD your God" (NRSV); "Do not use my name for evil purposes" (TEV); "You shall not abuse the name of the LORD your God" (Childs); "You shall not swear falsely by the name of the LORD your God" (NJPS); "You are not to take up the name of YHWH your God for emptiness" (E. Fox 1995: 371).

These different translations suggest that the third commandment prohibits either perjury (using God's name falsely when, for example, making a promise) or profanity. For this reason I have suggested both "falsely" and "frivolously" in my translation. That one and the same commandment might forbid two quite different illicit talks is not surprising. As Huffmon (1995: 364) has said, "An important feature of any fundamental or constitutional code is ambiguity. Explicitness is not a virtue; ambiguity that allows for clarification and adjustment to changing circumstances, while providing a basic direction of development, is a necessary quality of a fundamental code."

The main reason for understanding v. 7 as speaking of perjury (falsely swearing by God's name) is the verse's similarity to what Lev. 19:12 prohibits: "You [pl.] shall not swear falsely by my name and so profane the name of your God" (AT). The Hebrew verb for "swear" is *šāba'* (Niphal). It is used in parallelism with *nāśā' laššāwĕ'* in Ps. 24:4 in answer to questions about who may enter the Lord's presence: "he who has clean [the adjective *nĕqî*, related to the verb *nāqâ* in Exod. 20:7] hands and a pure heart, who does not lift up [*lō'-nāśā'*] his soul to an idol [*laššāwĕ'*] or swear [*wĕlō' nišba'*] by what is false." Thus Exod. 20:7 might be saying, "You shall not take/lift up the name of the LORD your God [upon your lips/mouth] falsely."

This interpretation, however, raises a problem with the interpretation of another passage. Exodus 20:7 says that the Lord will not acquit the one abusing his name. Then in Lev. 6:1–7 [5:20–26] we have a paragraph that deals with the forgiveness of one guilty of dishonesty, theft, or fraud who, exacerbating the crime, "swears falsely," *nišba' 'al-šāqqer* (Lev. 6:3, 5 [5:22, 24]), saying that he is not guilty of the charges. "To swear falsely" is to say, "As God is my witness, I swear that I never stole your wallet." So which is it? Can ritual expiation be offered (Lev. 6:1–7 [5:20–26]) for making an intentional false oath, or withheld (Exod. 20:7)? Perhaps forgiveness is granted if the individual on his own comes forward, confesses his sin, and makes restitution to the aggrieved party, a point Exod. 20:7 in its brevity does not make.

The Hebrew phrase *laššāwěʾ* ("in vain," KJV) carries several nuances in the Hebrew Bible. When it precedes the verb, it has adverbial force. There are five illustrations of this in Jeremiah: 2:30 ("*In vain* I punished your people"); 4:30 ("You adorn yourself *in vain*"); 6:29 ("But the refining goes on *in vain*"); 18:15 ("They burn incense to *worthless* idols"); 46:11 ("But you multiply remedies *in vain*").

When, however, *laššāwěʾ* follows the verb, as in Exod. 20:7/Deut. 5:11, the expression has nominal or adjectival force rather than adverbial force. Then *šāwěʾ* designates "emptiness, vanity," and for that reason sometimes takes on the meaning of "idol" (cf. NIV's "who does not lift up his soul *to an idol* [*laššāwěʾ*]" in Ps. 24:4). See also 26:4, "I do not sit with *deceitful men* [*mětê-šāwěʾ*]," or better, "with idol worshipers"; and 31:6 [7], "I hate those who cling to *worthless idols* [*hablê-šāwěʾ*]."

In sum, the third commandment cautions against using the Lord's name falsely to buttress a truth claim that is fabricated. By extension, it prohibits any use of the holy name that is without any real significance, any trivializing of the Tetragrammaton. I am not sure whether biblical Israel has any concept of "cussing" or using a collection of "four-letter words," but it is not a misunderstanding of this commandment to bring it to bear on the pervasive use today of "O my God" in every imaginable situation.

I am not totally convinced, however, that one must restrict this third word to actions involving verbal turpitude of some sort. I mentioned in the first grammatical and lexical note on 20:7 that the verb at the beginning, *nāśāʾ*, has the basic meaning "carry, bear." Hence, "you shall not carry/bear the name of the Lord your God *laššāwěʾ*." Two other passages in Exodus that speak of bearing, carrying a name are 28:12 ("Aaron is to bear the names [*wěnāśāʾ* . . . *ʾet-šěmôtām*] on his shoulders as a memorial before [*lifnê*] the Lord") and 28:29 ("he [Aaron] will bear the names [*wěnāśāʾ* . . . *ʾet-šěmôt*] of the sons of Israel over [*ʿal*] his heart"). Block (2011: 24) suggests that bearing or carrying somebody's name is rooted in the practice of marking or branding slaves as one would do to animals to indicate ownership. Thus, God has not only put his name on the place where he is to be worshiped (Deut. 12:5 and numerous other places in Deuteronomy), he has also put his name on Israel, his *sěgullâ* (possession, property). Recall the familiar 2 Chron. 7:14, "If my people, who are called by my name . . ." See also 1 Pet. 4:16, "If you suffer as a Christian, do not be ashamed, but praise God that *you bear* that name" (italics added). Accordingly, 20:7 may be saying, "Either honor my name, both by the way you live and by the way you talk, or else dissociate yourself from my name."

Unlike the second, or the first and second, commandment that speaks of the punishment of the sin of one generation on following generations, this one aims the punishment directly at the perpetrator.

The importance of the Sabbath in the OT is manifest in the following data. 20:8–11
First, it is mentioned more often in the Torah, from the time of Sinai and beyond, than any other commandment, eleven times in all (Exod. 20:8–11; 23:12; 31:13–17; 34:21; 35:2–3; Lev. 19:3, 30; 23:3; 26:2; Num. 28:9–10; Deut. 5:12–15), plus numerous other passing references to the Sabbath. Exodus and Leviticus account for nine of these. The Sabbath appears as a stated law only once in Numbers and only once in Deuteronomy, in the Decalogue chapter (5).

In conjunction with this, I note, second, that the Sabbath commandment is the only one of the ten that the Lord clearly sets forth even before the Israelites reach Sinai. As early as the manna episode in the wilderness, he is already teaching his people about the uniqueness of the seventh day, the Sabbath (Exod. 16:23, 27–30). Cooper and Goldstein (2003: 11) quote the Jewish exegete Bahya ben Asher (about AD 1300): "Know that the Sabbath commandment is the primary commandment given to Israel prior to the keeping of the Law, and that it is the first principle of faith."

Third, the Sabbath shares with the Day of Atonement and the Sabbatical Year two features that draw attention to its importance. First, these are the only three occasions that the Scripture styles as a *šabbat šabbātôn*, which the NIV always translates as a "S/sabbath of rest": the Sabbath (Exod. 31:15; 35:2; Lev. 23:3); the Sabbatical Year (Lev. 25:4); the Day of Atonement (Lev. 16:31; 23:32). The phrase might also be rendered "a most restful rest" to capture the back-to-back use of *šbt*. (The *-ôn* ending on *šabbātôn* changes the word from a noun ["rest"] to an adjective ["restful"], as in the noun *rōʾš* ["head"], which becomes the adjective "first" [*riʾšôn*] when *-ôn* is added to the end of the word. And "*most* restful" derives from the Hebrew way of expressing a superlative by using the same word twice in sequence, e.g., "holy of holies" = "most holy.")

Another feature the Sabbath shares with the Day of Atonement (but not with the Sabbatical Year) is that these are the only two days on which all and every kind of work is prohibited, whether more-demanding labor or even lighter/recreational work. Both are "most restful rest" days. This is the force of the forbidden *kol-mĕlāʾkâ* ("any [kind of] work") of Exod. 20:10 (= Deut. 5:14). Leviticus 23, a calendar of special days and festivals, highlights the difference between heavier ("job-related"?) and lighter work. Thus 23:3 and 31 prohibit any kind of work on the Sabbath and the Day of Atonement, using the exact same phrase as in the fourth commandment. For the other occasions the text forbids not *kol-mĕlāʾkâ*, but *kol-mĕlāʾkâ ʿăbōdâ*, which the NIV consistently renders "regular work": Lev. 23:7, 8 (Feast of Unleavened Bread); 23:21 (Feast of Weeks); 23:25 (Feast of Trumpets); 23:35, 36 (Feast of Tabernacles). Numbers 28–29, a parallel to the sacred calendar of Lev. 23, also prohibits "regular work" on festival days (Num. 28:18, 25 [Feast of Unleavened Bread]; 28:26 [Feast of Weeks]; 29:1 [Feast of Trumpets]; 29:12, 35 [Feast of Tabernacles]). Interestingly, Num. 29:7 also prohibits all and any kind of work on the Day of Atonement, using the *kol-mĕlāʾkâ* of Exod. 20/ Deut. 5/Lev. 23, but Num. 28:9–10, while speaking of the Sabbath, makes no mention of the work prohibition.

What Num. 28:9–10 does contribute to the conversation, something not seen in any other Sabbath text, is to spell out the Sabbath offerings: two yearling lambs and two-tenths of an ephah of fine flour. These unique offerings on the Sabbath are neither extravagant nor numerous. Other sacred days, yes, but not on the Sabbath.

Let me briefly mention three other items that underscore the importance of the Sabbath. First, the Sabbath and the Jubilee Year (Lev. 25:10) are the only two units of time that Israel is to "sanctify/hallow." Second, where the Sabbath appears in a sacred calendar, it always comes first (Exod. 23:12 and 14–19; Lev. 23:3 and 4–44; Num. 28:9–10 and Num. 28:11–29:40). Deuteronomy limits its Sabbath reference to the Decalogue, and hence the Sabbath day does not appear in the calendar of Deut. 16. Third, the first area in which one can demonstrate what it means "to be holy because I . . . am holy" (Lev. 19:2) is how one relates to parents and what one does with the Sabbath (Lev. 19:3).

Needless to say, there has been much debate over what "no kind of work" involves. Biblical examples of prohibited work include gathering food on the Sabbath (Exod. 16:29–30; Matt. 12:1–2; Mark 2:23–24), leaving one's home and community (Exod. 16:29b), plowing and harvesting (Exod. 34:21), building the tabernacle (Exod. 35:2ff.), lighting a fire (Exod. 35:3), gathering wood (Num. 15:32–36), marketing one's goods (Amos 8:5), carrying loads (Jer. 17:19–22; John 5:10), and healing (Luke 13:10–14).

Some activities are permissible on the seventh day. The priests need to replace the old loaves of bread with new ones in the sanctuary on the Sabbath (Lev. 24:8–9). A short trip to see Elisha in a time of dire need is acceptable (2 Kings 4:22–23). Palace and temple guards rotate on the Sabbath (2 Kings 11:4–8; 2 Chron. 23:4–7).

What about fighting in war on the Sabbath? There is no indication that the invading Israelites take the Sabbath off when they are in the process of conquering Canaan. Some Jews in the postbiblical period were bothered by their apparent inconsistency in fighting to defend their Mosaic torah against pagan Greek influences on one hand, and on the other hand fighting on the Sabbath against the pagans. See 1 Macc. 2:27–38. The book of *Jubilees* comes to a conclusion and climax (50.7–12) with a list of prohibited activities on the Sabbath, the last of which (50.12) is fighting on the Sabbath. *Jubilees* then ends (50.13) with the solemn warning, "Let any man who does any of these [works] on the day of the Sabbath die." Mattathias, the leader of the revolt against the pagans, argues that it is quite permissible to fight on the Sabbath to prevent being slaughtered, and his argument prevails (1 Macc. 2:40–41). Josephus (*Ant.* 14.4.2 §63) agrees with Mattathias: "The law permits [Jews on the Sabbath] to defend themselves against those who begin a battle and attack them, but it does not allow [Jews] to fight their military opponents if the latter are doing anything else."

The rationale for Sabbath observance is not primarily to give "a day off" to one's children, servants, work animals, and any stranger. To be sure, they are all beneficiaries of the Sabbath command. But if such a respite is the primary motive, then any day in the week would do just as well. Different days for different groups would serve the same purpose, maybe Mondays for offspring, Tuesdays for slaves, Wednesdays for the work animals, or mix them up or rotate them.

The primary purpose/motive for Sabbath observance is that in resting on this day, the Israelites take as their model the Lord, who rested on this day after his work of creation (Gen. 2:2–3). Thus the commandments are not only "Do as I say" but "Do as I did." The God who brooks no other god, the God who is provoked to jealousy by any human-made representation of him, the God who guards the sanctity of his name severely, here says, "Be like me." Nowhere in the Bible is the concept of *imitatio dei* as transparent as it is here. Leviticus 19:2b is another classic *imitatio dei* verse, "You shall be holy, for I the Lord your God am holy," but nowhere does Lev. 19 spell out anything God is or does that identifies him as holy and that we can do too.

God was not a workaholic. Don't you be one, says this fourth commandment. If the One who "will not grow tired or weary" (Isa. 40:28) rested on the seventh day, should not his followers follow in his footsteps? As Tsevat (1972: 455) has said, "Every seventh day the Israelite renounces his autonomy [over his time] and affirms God's dominion over him. Keeping the Sabbath is acceptance of the sovereignty of God." I also add that keeping the Sabbath is singing, "O, to Be Like Thee."

Perhaps the major difference between the Exod. 20 version of the Decalogue and that in Deut. 5 is that the latter roots the Sabbath observance in the exodus from Egypt: "Remember that you were slaves in Egypt and that the Lord your God brought you out of there with a mighty hand and an outstretched hand" (Deut. 5:15). I am not sure they are all that different. Both call the faithful to rest on the seventh day because of some beautiful work of God. That beautiful work of God is bringing something into existence that did not exist before, his cosmos and his covenant chosen. The addition of "as the Lord your God has commanded you" to "Observe the Sabbath day by keeping it holy" in Deut. 5:12 (but *not* in Exod. 20) demonstrates Deuteronomy's awareness of this command already pronounced in Exod. 20, and it is most unlikely that the writer of the code in Deut. 5 would have excised the original motivation clause and replaced it with a novel one. I argue that Deuteronomy does not replace the reason for Sabbath observance in Exod. 20, but rather accepts it and then extends it.

I agree with Greene-McCreight (1995) that for the Christian, Sunday is not a Christian Sabbath, but is the "Lord's Day." The Lord's Day is the first day of resurrection as well the day on which the Lord has created light. Hence, for the Christian who honors both Testaments, the first day speaks of light and resurrection, and all the darkness and chaos that was beaten back and overcome on those two "first" days. The Lord's Day, if it is the first day, is also the eighth day, that special day on which, through circumcision, a child becomes a member of the covenant community. Thus for both Jew and Christian, the eighth day speaks of a covenant/bonding that God establishes with his followers, thereby making them a new creation. Recall too the giving of the law at Sinai on the third day after the arrival at Sinai, and the resurrection of Christ on the third day (1 Cor. 15:4). With these connections in mind, Greene-McCreight (1995: 36) notes, "The Lord's Day is the first day, the eighth day, the third day, any and all of these, but it is not the Seventh Day."

Rest for the follower of Jesus is both a now reality and a not-yet reality, as are other realities such as "salvation." Those who have placed themselves under Christ's yoke have already experienced a most satisfying "rest" (Matt. 11:28). However, there is both possessively and prospectively a "Sabbath-rest for the people of God" (Heb. 4:9), which will become a full reality in the eschaton, when the faithful elect "will rest from their labor" (Rev. 14:13b).

20:12 There are three ways to introduce a positive command in Biblical Hebrew: a simple imperfect/*yiqṭōl* form, an infinitive absolute, and a second-person imperative. The fourth commandment illustrates the second of these (an infinitive absolute, *zākôr*). The fifth commandment illustrates the third of these (a second-person imperative, *kabbēd*). I am not aware of any explanation, apart from literary variety, to explain the switch from infinitive absolute to imperative in these two back-to-back positive commandments.

The command to "show respect to/honor" one's parents has its negative counterpart in Lev. 20:9, "If anyone curses [better, "dishonors"] his father or mother, he must be put to death." The verbs "honor/*kābēd*" and "curse, dishonor/*qālal*" are opposites. This can be observed by the fact that *kābēd* means "be heavy" and "honor," while *qālal* means "be light" and "dishonor." These two verbs occur in the same verse to describe the polar opposites of how one responds to the Lord: "Those who *honor* me I will *honor* [both times *kābēd*], but those who despise me will be *disdained/dishonored* [*qālal*]" (1 Sam. 2:30).

The Lev. 20:9 text indicates the importance of not dishonoring one's parents by following it in vv. 10–21 with a list of twelve illicit sexual unions: one wrong relationship that is nonsexual (20:9) followed by twelve that are sexual (20:10–21). Why put the parental one at the head of the list? Possibly Lev. 20 is suggesting that failure to honor appropriately one's progenitors opens the door to violating other relationships, using others rather than respecting and honoring others.

Another Levitical text that is even closer to Exod. 20:12 than Lev. 20:9 is Lev. 19:3: "Each of you must respect/revere [*yārē'*] his mother and father."

There are two differences between this text and the fifth commandment. Exodus's "show respect to/honor" (*kābēd*) is here "respect/revere" (*yārēʾ*). Also, Exodus's "father and mother" is here reversed to "mother and father." Normally "father" precedes "mother" in a patrilineal society, but the "mother" sometimes is the prior one, as here, and in Lev. 21:1–2, "A priest must not make himself ceremonially unclean for any of his people who die, except for a close relative, such as *his mother or father*." When Lev. 21:11 mentions the high priest's situation, it says, reverting to the more common order, "he must not make himself unclean even for *his father or mother*."

The most interesting thing about Lev. 19:3 is its coupling of commandments 5 and 4: "Each of you must respect his mother and father [v. 3a], and you must observe my Sabbaths [v. 3b]." All this after "Be holy [v. 2]." Holiness? Where does it shine forth? In how a person treats one's parents and how one treats the Sabbath. As Milgrom (2000b: 1608) says, "The fact that this one verse combines a quintessentially ethical commandment with a quintessentially cultic one is proof that . . . both ethics and ritual are of equal value."

It is well known that the Hebrew verb *kābēd* is also used in the Bible for honoring God. A good parallel to Exod. 20:12 (*kābēd* in the Piel imperative) is Prov. 3:9, "*Honor* the Lord with your wealth." See also the referencing above to 1 Sam. 2:30, "Those who *honor* me I will honor." Note the Lord's question to the people through Malachi: "A son honors [*yĕkabbēd*] his father, and a servant his master. If I am a father, where is the honor due me [*kĕbôdî*]. If I am a master, where is the respect due me [*môrāʾî*]?" (Mal. 1:6).

The Bible abounds with illustrations of those who do not honor the Lord; it also abounds with illustrations of those who do not honor their parents. One thinks of Jacob's tricking his father, Isaac, into believing he is Esau, or Jacob's sons' lying to their father about Joseph's death, or Samson's keeping his parents in the dark about the episode with the lion, or Michal's lying to her father, Saul, about David, or Absalom's orchestrating a coup against his father, David.

Mary and Joseph are not totally convinced that their twelve-year-old son is honoring them: "Son, why have you treated us like this? Your father and I have been anxiously searching for you" (Luke 2:48). And the Jesus who on one occasion can affirmatively quote the fifth commandment to his critics (Mark 7:9–13) also says on another occasion, "I have come to turn a man against his father" (Matt. 10:35), and "If anyone comes to me and does not hate his father and mother . . ." (Luke 14:26). It is possible, says Jesus, to honor and hate the same parental figure, as long as respect and reverence do not become worship. Parents are never meant to be *in loco dei* to their offspring. Parents make terrific teachers (Prov. 1:8, "Listen, my son, to your father's instruction") but terrible deities. The exception is for the very young, who are not able to imagine a God apart from their parents, as the story of young Samuel in the

Shiloh sanctuary illustrates: the voice of God and the voice of a parent (or parental figure) are indistinguishable.

The fifth commandment is addressed primarily to an adult son rather than to a school-age son. The son who is to honor his folks is also the person who is to give his slaves the seventh day off, not commit adultery, nor cast his eyes on his neighbor's wife. For that reason, it is possible that honoring one's parents includes not only while the parent is alive, but showing the necessary respect after the parent's death (Brichto 1973: 31).

The consequence of honoring one's parents is that the days (and years) of the commandment keeper will "long endure." The verb for "long endure" is *'ārak* (Hiphil). This is its only occurrence in Exodus, but in Deuteronomy it appears, apart from its use in the Decalogue (5:16), ten times. Eight times it is used positively to refer to the promise of long life for obedience (4:40; 5:33; 6:2; 11:9; 17:20; 22:7; 25:15; 32:47). Twice it is used negatively to refer to the loss of long life for disobedience (4:26; 30:18).

There is a very interesting use of this verb in one of the Servant Songs of Isaiah: "He will see his offspring and *prolong* [*'ārak*, Hiphil] his days" (Isa. 53:10). If this chapter ultimately speaks of Messiah Jesus, how can the verse refer to "his offspring," and how can one speak of an individual who lived only thirty-three years as "prolonging his days"? The answer must be that "offspring" means "disciples," and that "prolong his days" must mean that Messiah's followers will carry forth, implement, and finish Messiah's mission. In such a case, "long life," such as Deuteronomy holds out for the faithful, may not be restricted exclusively to the life of the individual, but may refer to realities continuing beyond the lifetime of the devotee.

Paul quotes the fifth commandment in Eph. 6:2 and then adds the interesting phrase "which is the first commandment with a promise." He then picks up the remainder of the commandment in v. 3 ("that it may go well with you and that you may enjoy long life on the earth"). As we saw in a grammatical note above, if Paul is quoting from his Hebrew Bible, he is citing Deut. 5:16, which alone has "that it may go well with you," but if he is quoting from his Greek Bible, then he could also be taking the words from Exod. 20:12.

Apparently Paul does not consider, and rightly so, the words about God's "showing kindness to . . ." in the previous commandment a promise. Or maybe he thinks of the fifth commandment as the first with a promise in the second half of the Decalogue, in those that cover relationships with other persons, from parents to neighbors.

What makes Paul's addition of "enjoying a long life" so interesting is that he himself did not seem to enjoy a long life, or maybe he did. He does say things like "I have fought the good fight" (2 Tim. 4:7). We do know that Paul speaks more about the rewards for faithfulness in the life to come, as does John in the Apocalypse (no more dying, no more tears, no more sickness; Rev. 21:4). And it would be interesting to reflect on Paul's referencing the promise of "long life" with his belief expressed elsewhere of Christ's imminent parousia (Rom. 13:12, "the day is almost here"; 1 Cor. 7:29, "the time is short"; Phil. 4:5, "The Lord is near"). See Lincoln 1982: 37–40. Yet the latter texts may simply demonstrate Paul's conviction that Jesus's death and resurrection have inaugurated "the last days."

And lest we think that Paul puts all blessing/reward "on hold" until entry into the new Jerusalem, let us recall his words to Timothy in 1 Tim. 4:8, "But godliness has value for all things, holding promise for both the present life and the life to come."

"You shall not *murder*" or "You shall not *kill*"? Which is the better translation? **20:13**
An examination of English versions shows that the decided preference is for "murder." Here is a sampling. The following translations opt for "murder": NIV; TNIV; NKJV; NLT; *Message*; NJPS; NEB; REB; NRSV; NASB; GNB; Weinfeld 1991: 275; E. Fox 1995: 372; Alter 2004: 431; Propp 2006: 103. These translations opt for "kill": KJV; JB; RSV; NAB; W. Bailey 2005. Several English Bibles that have replaced an older version with a new one have changed "kill" in the original translation to "murder" in the newer translation (KJV and NKJV; RSV and NRSV). I am not aware of any replacement translation that has made the change in the opposite direction, from "murder" to "kill."

The Hebrew verb in question is *rāṣaḥ*. It is one of four chief verbs that the Hebrew Bible employs to refer to ending somebody's life. The other three are *hārag*, *mût* (in the Hiphil, *hēmît*), and *qāṭal* (occurring only 4x: Job 13:15 ["slay"]; Job 24:14 ["kills"]; Ps. 139:19 ["slay"]; Obad. 9 ["in the slaughter"]). An illustration of *hārag* in Exodus is 2:14, the fellow Hebrew's question to Moses, "Are you thinking of *killing* me as you *killed* the Egyptian?" Among the verb's more illustrious uses is in Gen. 4:8, 14, 25, in conjunction with Cain's killing Abel. An illustration of *mût* (Hiphil) in Exodus is 1:16, "If it is a boy, *kill* him; but if it is a girl, let her live."

It is often argued that these three verbs mean "kill," while *rāṣaḥ* means "murder." I do not think it is that simple. To cite another example of *hārag* in Genesis, when Jacob's sons, Simeon and Levi, take revenge on the party who has violated their sister, do the brothers "kill" or "murder" the criminal party (Gen. 34:25, 26)? The difference between the two is obvious. The verb *hārag* denotes any act of "killing," whether laudable or culpable, while "murder" establishes culpability.

So what about *rāṣaḥ*? The sixth commandment provides the only appearance of the verb in Exodus. Far and away the verb occurs most often in those passages that deal with the cities of refuge for the "manslayer" (*hārôṣēaḥ*). There are four of these: (1) Num. 35, in which the verb appears twenty times, mostly in participial form; (2) Deut. 4:42; (3) Deut. 19:3, 4, 6; (4) Josh. 20:3, 5, 6; 21:13, 21, 27, 32, 38. These represent thirty-two of the forty-seven occurrences of *rāṣaḥ* in the Hebrew Bible.

Taking Num. 35 as our base for discussion, it is clear that *rāṣaḥ*, on the one hand, refers to deliberate murder (Num. 35:16–21), and the participle is correctly translated "murderer." But on the other hand, *rāṣaḥ* also refers to involuntary homicide (Num. 35:22–28), and the participle here is correctly translated "the one accused of murder" or "manslayer." Twice in Num. 35 (vv. 27, 30) the verb is used in perfect (v. 27) and imperfect (v. 30) form for the execution of a person, whether he has taken somebody's life deliberately or accidentally.

It is clear from these passages that *rāṣaḥ* refers to both intentional homicide ("murder") and accidental homicide ("kill"). As Tigay (1996: 357n106) says, "Since *rāṣaḥ* refers to intentional and accidental killing, and the latter, being unintentional, cannot be prohibited, the command must refer to the former, and 'you shall not murder' remains the best translation." The prefacing of *rāṣaḥ* with the negative particle *lōʾ*, I would add, makes "murder" more logical than "kill."

As with the Sabbath command, there are numerous other references in the Torah to taking the life of another. See Exod. 21:12, 14, 20–21; Lev. 24:17, 21; Num. 35:16–21, 30–34; Deut. 19:1–7; 11:13; 21:1–9; 27:24. Watts (1995: 545n13) has made the astute observation that whereas only one Sabbath text among a dozen or so mentions punishment for violation (Num. 15:32–36), all of the "murder" texts spell out quite strongly the punishment for violation (except in the Decalogue, and in Deut. 21:1–9 since it deals with the case of an unsolved murder).

The commandment against murder notwithstanding, there is hardly a historical book in the OT that does not narrate at least one instance of somebody murdering somebody. The books of 1 and 2 Samuel stand out as particularly violent and bloody. Judges is not far behind. As I wrote previously (Hamilton 2001: 169), "Every Israelite in Judges who dies violently at the hand of another dies at the hand of a fellow Israelite!"

Jesus extends the commandment about murder to include attitudinal and verbal homicide (Matt. 5:21–26). As with the other commandments of the Decalogue or elsewhere on which he expounds in the Sermon on the Mount, Jesus tends to expand them to include other areas (murder, adultery, the lex talionis, treating one's enemies and critics). The exception is divorce, which he restricts with his oft-debated "except for" clause. More than likely Jesus has the story of Cain's act of fratricide against Abel in mind when he speaks of "anyone who is angry with his brother" as a kind of killing, or something that, if not controlled, could lead to killing. The connection between Matt. 5:21–26 and Gen. 4 is made even more possible by the emphasis on a "gift" in both units. The Lord accepts the "gift" (Gen. 4:4 LXX, *dōron*) that Abel brings, but rejects the "sacrifice/offering" (*thysia*) that Cain presents. In this paragraph in which Jesus expands on the murder commandment, he three times uses the word "gift" (*dōron*, Matt. 5:23, 24 [2x]): "If you and your brother are at odds, leave your *dōron* at the altar, seek reconciliation, and only then present your *dōron*" (AT).

This seventh commandment prohibits adultery: a consensual sexual relationship between a man, either married or unmarried, and a married or engaged woman other than his spouse (if the man is himself married). It is not concerned with rape, homosexuality, sex with a prostitute, or sex between a married/unmarried man and an unmarried woman. **20:14**

The placement of this commandment after the one about murder may be intentional. Adultery can have the effect of murdering, and hence ending, the existence of the covenant relationships of two other people. It plunges a dagger deep into the sacred bonds of matrimony. Plus, Prov. 6:33–35 discourages adultery not primarily because the adulterer is sinful but because he is stupid. Should the husband ever get his hands on him, he will do everything physically violent to him short of killing him.

Also, this commandment looks forward to the eighth commandment, for adultery is a form of theft, and forward to part of the tenth commandment. Anyone who does "not covet his neighbor's wife" is unlikely to fall into an adulterous relationship. Adultery is more of an option for those who believe the grass is greener on the other side of the fence, that they are entitled to something/someone better, where desire trumps conscience rather than vice versa.

One would think that the more a society urges monogamy, the more one would expect to see violations of that standard via adultery. The more a society condones polygamy, the less one would expect to hear of adulterous liaisons. If Solomon has 700 wives, does he still need women, 300 concubines, for yet more trysts? Apparently the libido of even polygamists knows no limits. David's six wives (2 Sam. 3:2–5) do not deter him from hooking up with the married Bathsheba (2 Sam. 11).

The OT shares with other peoples of the ancient Near East a strong sentiment for the sanctity of the marriage relationship and a disgust at its dismantling through adultery. I know of no people, no code, that speaks of adultery as an excusable or virtuous act, and I put forward three facts to support this.

First, note the three scenes of potential adultery in Genesis, each of which involves a forefather of the Israelites and a non-Israelite. In two of these (20:9; 26:10) a non-Israelite king refers to adultery (which did not happen) as "sinning against" (NIV, "How have I wronged you?") the husband (20:9), and as "bringing [the consequences of] guilt" on the people of the perpetrator. In the third, 39:9, Joseph explains to Potiphar's wife that adultery would be a "sin against God," without having to explain to her why he considers adultery to be a sin. Also note that in two of these instances adultery is a sin against God rather than a sin against the husband: God's words to Abimelech, "And so I have kept you from *sinning against me*" (Gen. 20:6), and Joseph's, "How than could I do such a wicked thing and *sin against God*?" (Gen. 39:9).

Second, the phrase "great sin" (*ḥăṭāʾâ gĕdōlâ*) appears five times in the OT, once to refer to adultery (Gen. 20:9 [NIV, "great guilt"]), and four times to refer to idolatry (Exod. 32:21, 30, 31; 2 Kings 17:21), which is adultery at a religious level, leaving the God with whom you have yoked yourself to have an affair with another deity. Interestingly, the same expression, "great sin," has now appeared both in Egyptian marriage contracts (Rabinowitz 1959) and in a Canaanite text from Ugarit (Moran 1959) to refer to adultery. The idea of adultery as a sin against the god(s) and therefore carrying divinely sent consequences is rare, but not unheard of, in nonbiblical ancient Near Eastern literature. I shall refer to a legal text in the next paragraph. In what is known as the Shurpu text, we have a series of incantations addressed to the gods by sinners who are seeking relief from the suffering of divine punishment that has sickened them. Here are two of those sinners: the man "who entered the house of his companion, (sexually) approached the wife of his companion" (II 47–48), and the man whose peccadillo was "to go in secret to his friend's wife" (IV 6).

Third, as with the previous commandments, the topic resurfaces repeatedly in other legal collections (Lev. 18:20; 19:20–21; 20:10; Num. 5:11–31; Deut. 22:22). Almost every ancient Near Eastern law code likewise has an entry on adultery. Note how close the following three laws are (I draw my translations of texts in this section from Westbrook's [1990] interesting article on adultery in the ancient Near East):

1. Lev. 20:10, "If a man commits adultery with another man's wife—with the wife of his neighbor—both the adulterer and the adulteress must be put to death."
2. Deut. 22:22, "If a man is found sleeping with another man's wife, both the man who slept with her and the woman must die."

3a. Middle Assyrian Law A: 13 (about 1200 BC), "If the wife of a man goes out of her house and goes to a man where he is dwelling (and) he has intercourse with her, knowing that she is the wife of a man, the man and the woman shall be killed."

3b. Middle Assyrian Law A: 14, "If a man has intercourse with the wife of a man in a tavern or in the square, knowing that she is a man's wife, whatever the husband states is to be done to his wife shall be done to the paramour. If he has intercourse with her, not knowing that she is the man's wife, the paramour is free (of liability). The husband shall establish (the case against) his wife, and do to her as he wishes."

There is one significant difference between biblical and other Near Eastern law on adultery, but it is not an absolute difference. In the latter the husband of the adulteress may pardon, or seek revenge, or settle for damages (his "property" is now soiled). As more a civil crime than a religious crime, it is pardonable and commutable.

Like coveting, adultery is a private sin. Unlike theft or murder, adultery most often leaves no physical traces. With murder, you have a corpse or a missing person. With theft or robbery you have a missing wallet or purse, automobile, or somebody pointing a revolver at you. One would think that a couple wishing to engage in such a dalliance would want to do it as clandestinely as possible. Deuteronomy 22:22, however, suggests that the man and the woman could be apprehended *in coitu*. The law begins, "If a man is *found* [discovered, apprehended] sleeping with another man's wife." Similarly, the famous story of the adulterous woman, John 7:53–8:11, whatever its textual and canonical history, reveals the same. The Pharisees bring to Jesus "a woman caught in the act of adultery" (John 8:3–4). Numerous readers of this story have asked, "Why was the adulterer also not brought before Jesus?" Derrett (1963: 5–7) offers three suggestions, with the last the most likely: (1) the man has already been stoned to death; (2) the adulterer pays off the husband with hush money and vanishes into the night, or manages to escape capture; (3) the husband orchestrates the whole event even to the point of "planting" witnesses conveniently. Otherwise, how could the witnesses have observed the event? Thus it is his wife he wishes to trap, and not the wife's lover.

The opposite of adulterers caught in the act is the case in Num. 5:11–31. A husband is either unaware that his wife is in an adulterous relationship because it is "hidden" from him, there are "no witnesses," and she has not been "caught" (vv. 12–13), or else he suspects his wife is in such a relationship (v. 14). In the case of the nagging suspicion, he submits his wife to an ordeal that will establish either her guilt or innocence.

Two things are of interest about this legislation for our purposes. First, the woman is never said to be guilty of adultery, using the verb *nāʾap* of the seventh commandment. The wording that is used is that she has "gone astray" (*śāṭâ*) and has been "unfaithful" (*māʿălâ māʿal*). Milgrom (1990: 348–50; 2000a: 1748) explains the absence of explicit adultery vocabulary in Num. 5 as follows. The unapprehended criminal cannot be subject to the decisions of a human court, and so only God can mete out punishment. In not using *nāʾap*, the law wishes to dissociate this woman's fate from the death penalty imposed elsewhere for adultery.

This law does share one thing in common with some other "adultery" texts. The seriousness of the sin of adultery is brought out in Lev. 18 in that of all the illicit sexual relationships it mentions, the only ones that are said explicitly to bring "defilement" (*ṭāmēʾ*, a very common root in Leviticus) are adultery (v. 20) and bestiality (v. 23). The word *ṭāmēʾ* is used of the suspected woman in Num. 5:13, 14, 20, 27, 28, 29 and with other adulterers in Ezek. 18:6, 11, 15; 33:26. (Note from the summary paragraph in Lev. 18 [vv. 24–30] that all these illicit relationships defile [vv. 24 (2x), 25, 27, 28, 30].)

As with murder (Matt. 5:21–26), Jesus expands on the adultery commandment (5:27–30). A lustful leer at a woman produces heart adultery, and to that end he recommends ruthless damage control with oneself, including severance of an offending eye or a hand. In this hyperbolic counsel, Jesus is urging that those so tempted deal with the source of sin as immediately and drastically as possible. The problem, as Jesus phrases it, is "look[ing] at a woman *lustfully*." The Greek word behind "lustfully" is *epithymeō*, a strong, almost irresistible desire for weal or for woe. It is the word the LXX uses in the tenth commandment for not "coveting" one's neighbor's wife. Perhaps Paul comes close to what Jesus suggests in Matt. 5:27–30. In Col. 3:5 he urges, "*Put to death*, therefore, whatever belongs to your earthly nature." Among "what belongs to one's earthly nature," he includes immorality, impurity, lust/passion, and evil desires (*epithymian kakēn*), using the same word Jesus did in Matt. 5:28.

All this is not to say that Jesus frowns on a man or woman beholding physical beauty in another. Certainly Messiah never intends his followers to confuse a look with a leer.

20:15 What kind of stealing does the eighth commandment prohibit? Phillips (1970: 130–31), and others before him, have argued that the outlawed stealing is kidnapping. Indeed, the NIV translates the verb *gānab* correctly as "kidnap" in Exod. 21:16, "Anyone who *kidnaps* another and either sells him or still has him when he is caught must be put to death," and also Deut. 24:7 (2x). But these are the only three of sixty-eight uses of *gānab* in the Hebrew Bible that NIV translates "kidnap."

As both Weinfeld (1972: 536) and Jackson (1971: 203) have observed, there is no instance in the Hebrew Bible in which *gānab*, when standing alone, means "kidnap." The basic meaning of the verb is "to steal (property)." To mean anything else, it must be expressly qualified by an object or an obvious context.

The second issue here concerns two verbs that mean to take away from somebody something that does not belong to the perpetrator. One is the verb *gānab*, as in the eighth commandment and in the passages cited from Exod. 21 and Deut. 24. The other is the verb *gāzal*, which appears thirty times in the Bible (plus twelve more for the nouns related to *gāzal*), but the word never appears in Exodus.

The eighth commandment prohibits *gānab*, but not *gāzal*. What is the difference between the two? Milgrom (1976a: 89–93) reflects rabbinic teaching when he argues that *gāzal* refers to robbery (perpetrated by open force) and that *gānab* refers to theft (perpetrated by stealth). Breaking into a house, brandishing weapons, tying up and terrifying the occupants, and then looting that home would be *gāzal*, while breaking into a home while the occupants are away would be *gānab*. Robbing a bank would be *gāzal*, but embezzling funds would be *gānab*. This distinction is found in Akkadian, where *sharaqu* is the normal word for "theft," and *habātu* is used for "robbery."

Whether or not this distinction is correct, there must be some difference between the two because Lev. 19:11 ("Do not steal [*gānab*]") and 19:13 ("Do not defraud your neighbor or rob [*gāzal*] him") distinguish between them, so they cannot be completely synonymous.

There is an interesting use of *gānab* (7x) and *gāzal* (1x) in the story of Rachel stealing her father's gods (Gen. 31). The narrator tells us that Rachel "stole" Laban's gods while her father was away from home (v. 19). The narrator uses *gānab* again in v. 32b, "Now Jacob did not know that Rachel *had stolen* the gods." Laban accuses Jacob of "stealing" his gods (v. 30), and twice harangues Jacob for "stealing away" (vv. 26, 27, NIV "deceive me"), a point the narrator makes as well (v. 20). The one time Jacob uses *gānab* is in v. 39 ("And you [Laban] demanded payment from me for whatever *was stolen* by day or night").

The one place where *gāzal* occurs is in v. 31, "I [Jacob] was afraid, because I thought you [Laban] would *take* your daughters *away* from me *by force*." Thus *gānab* means "steal," while *gāzal*, at least in Gen. 31:31, means "take away by force." Jacob does not say, "I was afraid that you would take away *my wives*," but rather, "I was afraid that you would take away *your daughters*." Milgrom (1976a: 91) suggests that *gāzal* appears in v. 31 for Laban's actions "because as the *paterfamilias* he could move against Jacob forcibly." Westbrook (1988: 26) argues, more convincingly, that Jacob uses *gāzal* in v. 31 because he knows that Laban might abuse his authority and recognizes "that Laban might have a certain claim to take back Rachel and Leah in spite of their being married, perhaps if Jacob were guilty of some wrongdoing."

In sum, *gānab* (of the eighth commandment) does seem to point to theft (by stealth), while there are instances where *gāzal* means "rob, take by force." But there are places where *gāzal* cannot mean "rob," but rather something like "exploit (the poor and disadvantaged)." Abimelech's servants "seized" ("expropriated") Abraham's well, but they did not "rob" him (Gen. 21:25). See also Ps. 35:10, "You rescue the poor from these too strong for them, the poor and needy from those who *rob* [better, "exploit"] them." One does not normally "rob" the poor but the wealthy, unless even the poor has something the criminal would like to take away and have. Compare Prov. 22:22, "Do not exploit [*gāzal*] the poor."

For other references to *gānab* in Exodus apart from 20:15, see the following:

"Anyone who *kidnaps* another" (21:16)

"If a man *steals* an ox or a sheep . . ." (22:1 [21:37])

"If a *thief* is caught breaking in . . ." (22:2 [1])

"A *thief* must certainly make restitution" (22:3 [2])

"And they *are stolen* from the neighbor's house, the *thief*, if he is caught, must pay back double" (22:7 [6])

"But if the *thief* is not found . . ." (22:8 [7])
"But if the animal was *stolen* from the neighbor . . ." (22:12 [11])

There are obvious reasons why the Bible condemns unilateral stealing. It is hard to envision a scene where stealing would be a virtue, unless it is something like the very poor picking up coal that falls from trains speeding by and using it to warm their chilly and dilapidated houses (an example that Joseph Fletcher [1966] uses in his widely discussed book *Situation Ethics*). It is a behavioral pattern that needs to cease when one becomes a follower of Messiah, as Paul says in Eph. 4:28, "He who has been stealing must steal no longer."

C. Wright (1990: 137) puts this prohibition into a proper old-covenant perspective: "The thief robs his fellow Israelite, not merely of some of his economic prosperity, but [also] of part of what is his as a blessing and gift from God (as a person) and a part of his share in the inheritance of the people of Yahweh (as an Israelite). That is, stealing carries not only financial liabilities, but theological and spiritual liabilities as well."

20:16 The idea of a "false witness" must have been very pronounced in ancient Israel, for Biblical Hebrew has six different ways to say it: (1) *'ēd šāw'* (Deut. 5:20); (2) *'ēd šāqer* (Exod. 20:16; Deut. 19:18; Ps. 27:12; Prov. 6:19; 12:17; 14:5; 19:5, 9; 25:18); (3) *'ēd ḥāmās* (Exod. 23:1; Deut. 19:16; Ps. 35:11; NIV, the first two = "malicious witness," the third one = "ruthless witnesses"); (4) *'ēd ḥinnām* (Prov. 24:28, "Do not testify [*'al-tĕhî 'ēd-ḥinnām*] against your neighbor without cause"); (5) *'ēd bĕliyya'al* (Prov. 19:28, "A corrupt witness mocks at justice"); (6) *'ēd-kĕzābîm* (Prov. 21:28, "A false witness will perish"). Of these sixteen passages I have cited about "false witness," nine of them come from Proverbs.

More often than not the purpose of a witness is to affirm the truthfulness of something on which two other parties have already agreed. Thus the elders of Bethlehem are "witnesses" to the transactions between the relative of Ruth who backs off from his responsibilities to the widowed Ruth, and Boaz, who then accepts those responsibilities (Ruth 4:9–11). For another illustration of witnesses who are an affirming third party to an agreement between two other parties, see Jer. 32:10–15 and the witnesses who observe and hear the transference of property between Hanamel and Jeremiah.

Regrettably, witnesses may vouch for the "truthfulness" of false charges that have been brought by others against an innocent victim. To understand how destructive such a false witness can be, we need only ask Naboth (1 Kings 21:10, 13), David (Pss. 27:12; 35:11), Jesus (Matt. 26:60–61; Mark 14:55–61), or Stephen (Acts 6:13).

Only in the case of Naboth is a false witness made against one's "neighbor," for his property is adjacent to the king's. Those who concur with the charges against Jesus and Stephen are hardly "neighbors" of Jesus and Stephen. We need to recall that the ninth commandment is not only about lying, but also about lying to/about one's neighbor. What will such lying or gossip or rumor spreading do to one's neighbor? The concern is with the community fallout rather than with the individual consequence. The last two laws of the Decalogue especially highlight the neighbor and the healthy neighborhood. The late Mr. Rogers of afternoon children's television would sing, "It's a Beautiful Day in the Neighborhood." Yes, it will be and can be, says Exod. 20, when mature adults avoid behavior that is inimical to healthy, positive relationships with the neighbor.

The last commandment differs dramatically from the previous nine. The first **20:17**
nine prohibit certain activities or actions. The last prohibits an inner thought or desire. That desire can be for another's spouse or for another's property. The first line addresses sexual lust, while the second line addresses nonsexual lust. Vasholz (1987) would like to have the verb mean the same in both lines. Accordingly, for him the first line does not mean "You shall not covet your neighbor's wife's physical assets," but "You shall not covet your neighbor's wife's monetary assets [her dowry]." I think this is a bit of a stretch. In any case, adultery, or murder, or false witnessing are punishable, but how does one punish people for what they are thinking?

In an attempt to bring this last commandment more into line with the others, some commentators have suggested that *ḥāmad* refers not only to the thought, but also to the subsequent action that the thought precipitates. They observe that *ḥāmad* often is followed by a "doing" verb. Note these verses: Deut. 7:25, "Do not covet [*ḥāmad*] the silver and gold on them [the images of the gods], and do not take [*lāqaḥ*] it for yourselves"; Josh. 7:21, "When I [Achan] saw . . . I coveted [*ḥāmad*] them and took [*lāqaḥ*] them"; Mic. 2:2, "They covet [*ḥāmad*] fields and seize them [*gāzal*], and houses and take [*nāśā'*] them." When the woman in Paradise saw that the fruit of the tree was "pleasing [*neḥmād*] to the eye" (Gen. 2:9) and especially "pleasing [*ta'ăwâ*] to the eye[s] and desirable [*wĕneḥmād*] for gaining wisdom," she "took [*lāqaḥ*]" some (Gen. 3:6).

I suggest that the verbal sequence "coveted . . . took" is not parallelistic or synonymous, but sequential (coveting that leads to taking or seizing). I know of no instance where *ḥāmad* by itself means not only "covet" but also "take, misappropriate." The closest possibility for such an extended meaning is Exod. 34:24, a verse that speaks about worshipers leaving their homes vacant, and hence vulnerable to burglary, when they "go away to church": "I will drive out nations before you . . . and no one will *covet* [*ḥāmad*] your land when you go up three times each year to appear before the LORD your God." Even here God may be promising his people that in honoring him they will not even have to be concerned about anybody casting covetous eyes on their property or belongings. God will not only stymie brigandage, but also thoughts about brigandage. It is comforting to know that God can crawl inside the mind and emotions of those who pose a threat to one's possessions and can control the eruption of those thoughts. Baker (2005) correctly observes that although these two Hebrew verbs sometimes imply or explicitly refer to action, that does not mean that action is an integral part of the meaning of *ḥāmad* and *ʾāwâ*.

From the above, Jackson (1971: 207) draws two principles: "First, there is no evidence that liability for mere intention was ever applied in a human court. Second, . . . the idea did exist that merely to intend a wrong was itself wrong. It was a principle employed in God's justice, but not . . . in the jurisprudence of man." That is to say, the last commandment is more about a sin than about a crime.

Occasionally both the verb *ḥāmad* and *ʾāwâ*, and the nouns related to them, refer to a desire for something that is quite normal and healthy and appealing. One thinks of the phrase one often hears in church circles, "We covet an interest in your prayers." When God, according to Gen. 2:9, makes the fruit of the trees in the garden "pleasing to the eye" (*neḥmād lĕmarʾeh*), he is not producing an enticement to sin. If God can make things that are *ḥmd*, he can even *ḥāmad* himself: "Why gaze in envy, O rugged mountains, at the mountain where God *chooses/desires/covets* to reign?" (Ps. 68:16 [17]). The other verb, *ʾāwâ*, may be used of man's passionate feeling (in this case, the king) for his wife: "The king is *enthralled by* your beauty" (Ps. 45:11 [12]). See also Prov. 10:24, "What the righteous desire [*wĕtaʾʿăwat ṣaddîqîm*] will be granted." The reference to the "Suffering Servant" in Isa. 53:2b ("He had . . . nothing in his appearance that *we should desire* him") shows that *ḥāmad* might be used for the normal attraction to another individual's striking appearance. I suggest it is possible to have a "holy lust" for God, although that phrase might strike some as an unacceptable or confusing oxymoron.

Having said all that, it is correct to point out that the overwhelming number of uses of *ḥmd/ʾwh* refer to a wrongful desire. The same may be said of the verb *epithymeō* and the noun *epithymia* in the NT. Positive uses include: Luke 22:15 ("I have eagerly desired to eat this Passover with you"); Phil. 1:23 ("I desire to depart and be with Christ"); 1 Thess. 2:17 ("Out of our intense longing we made every effort to see you"). However, the negative sense is much more frequent: Mark 4:19; Rom. 6:12; 7:7–8; 13:14; Gal. 5:24; Col. 3:5; 1 Tim. 6:9; 2 Tim. 3:6; 4:3; Titus 3:3; James 1:14; 1 Pet. 1:14; 2 Pet. 2:10; 1 John 2:16–17; Jude 18.

It is not difficult to produce parallels from ancient Near Eastern literature to "You shall not murder" or "You shall not steal" and the like. It is impossible, I believe, to produce parallels from such literature to "You shall not covet." Gordon (1963; 1996: 59–61) has emphasized the tenth commandment's uniqueness among the laws of the ancient world by highlighting stories from Canaanite Ugarit in which gods and goddesses "covet" something to which they are not entitled (and the root is *ḥmd*). The narrators told such stories about their deities without a tinge of surprise or embarrassment. Jezebel, the

Tyrian wife of the Israelite king Ahab, says in effect to her husband about Naboth's vineyard: "You're the king. If you want it, take it" (1 Kings 21). As Gordon (1996: 60) says of this incident: "The tragedy was not that a good man (Ahab) was trapped in a marriage with a bad woman (Jezebel), but rather that a man and woman of opposing values were united in a hopelessly contradictory union."

Possibly the best way to avoid capitulating to a spirit of covetousness is to follow Paul's counsel in Phil. 4:11–12: "For I have learned to be content whatever the circumstances. I know what it is to be in need, and I know what it is to have plenty. I have learned the secret of being content in any and every situation." A contented spirit is the direct opposite of a covetous spirit.

Right Fear and Wrong Fear

(20:18–21)

Translation

[18]And all the people were beholding the thunderclaps and the lightning flashes, and the blast of the horn and the mountain smoking, and the people were fearful and drew back, and stood at a distance. [19]And they said to Moses, "Speak, you yourself, with us and we will listen, but let not God speak with us lest we die." [20]And Moses said to the people, "Do not be afraid for in order to test you God has come, and in order that fear of him may be on your faces to restrain you from sinning." [21]So the people stood at a distance while Moses approached the thick cloud where God was.

Grammatical and Lexical Notes

20:18. "All the people" (*kol-hāʿām*)—here and 19:16 (NIV, "everyone"); 24:3 (absent in NIV); 32:3; 33:8—does not carry the negative overtones of the same phrase when Moses uses it in Num. 11:11, "What have I done to displease you that you put the burden of *all these people* on me?"

20:18. The participle "were beholding" (*rōʾîm*) helps identify the first part of this verse as an introductory circumstantial clause, and it expresses action contemporaneous with what has transpired earlier in chap. 20 and in chap. 19. One can "see" lightning flashes, but one does not "see" thunderclaps. Biblical imagery in its sensory perceptions takes some liberties. Alter (2004: 432) refers to the description of the event in v. 18 as "one tremendous synesthetic experience."

20:18. Most ancient versions (LXX, Vulg., SP) render the Hebrew verb *wayyarʾ* ("were fearful") as a plural, *wayyirʾû*, to bring it into conformity with the very next word, which is a plural verb, *wayyānuʿû* ("and drew back").

20:18. The exact same form *wayyānuʿû* occurs as part of Isaiah's famous vision of the Lord in the temple, but there the NIV renders it "shook": "At the sound of their voices the doorposts and thresholds *shook*" (Isa. 6:4). The Qal participial form of *nûʿa* appears in Gen. 4:12 and 14 to describe Cain, "a restless *wanderer*" (*nāʿ wānād*), literally, "*a wanderer* and a fugitive." In Exod. 20:18 the people "drew back," or as easily "shook."

20:18. For other instances of *ʿāmad mērāḥōq* ("stood at a distance"), see v. 21; 1 Sam. 26:13, "Then David . . . stood on top of the hill some distance away"; 2 Kings 2:7, "Fifty men . . . went and stood at a distance"; Ps. 38:11b [12b], "My neighbors stay far away"; Isa. 59:14, "So justice is driven back and righteousness stands at a distance." The equivalent phrase (*ʿāmad bĕrāḥôq*) in Ps. 10:1 ("Why, O Lord, do you stand far off?"), with the preposition *bĕ* instead of *min*, demonstrates the interchangeability of these two prepositions (Sarna 1959: 312).

20:20. The negative particle *biltî* with prefixed preposition *lĕ* to introduce a clause expressing a negative purpose ("to restrain you from sinning") appears again only in 2 Sam. 14:14, the words of the wise woman of Tekoa to David, "But God does not take away life; instead, he devises ways *so that* [*lěbiltî*] a banished person may not remain estranged from him."

Commentary

20:18–21

Most commentators believe that these four verses belong more properly somewhere in chap. 19, most likely after v. 19, because of the heavy emphasis here on the powerful theophany of chap. 19 (lightning, thunder, a blaring horn, and the dread among the people that these generate). That may or may not be the case, but the bottom line is that this brief unit in the final form of the text follows the Decalogue and does not precede it. Whether the text is in its original position or transplanted, the interpreter must address why these few verses form a sequel to the revelation of the Decalogue in our canonical text.

If we connect these few verses solely with the theophany of chap. 19, then it severs the spoken word of God (the Decalogue) from the people's response in vv. 18–21. When God shows up electrifyingly, the people tremble (19:16b). When God speaks forth a powerful word (20:1–17), the people tremble (20:18–21). Savran (2005: 112) has tied the two together nicely when he speaks of "a growing sense of fear which begins with the disturbance of nature, increases as YHWH descends and 'speaks' with Moses in 19:19, and reaches its climax in their reaction to divine speech in 20:18. The people's anxiety in Exod. 20:19 is not a reaction which has been fixed at a single moment in time, but is the culmination of a series of responses which grow in intensity as the theophany proceeds." The visual and the verbal work in tandem to bring about the response that God desires: the people's healthy fear and reverence for God that will, hopefully, act as a deterrent against sinning.

But surely it is not God's will that his people "stand [perpetually] at a distance" from the divine presence. Worship is always about "drawing near" (*qrb*) to God, not distancing oneself (*rḥq*) from him. The root *rḥq* occurs 162 times in the Hebrew Bible, but as Lemke (1981: 547) has observed, *rḥq* never occurs in a cultic sense, and that is the blatant opposite of *qrb*. The closest it comes to such a meaning is in passages like Exod. 20:18, 21 and Josh. 3:4 ("But keep a distance of about a thousand yards between you and the ark"), but even here *rḥq* appears in its literal (and normal) sense: keep a safe distance between oneself and a holy object as a means of safeguarding against a lethal experience of the holy. The biblical dictum is "Come near to God and he will come near to you" (James 4:8).

There are two items in this unit that link Israel's encounter with God with Abraham's earlier encounter(s) with God. The first is some vocabulary similarity between Exod. 20 and Gen. 15 (the occasion on which the Lord enters into a covenant with the patriarch and his offspring). The reference in Exod. 20:18 to the "lightning flashes" (*hallappîdim*) recalls the role of the *lappîd ʾēš* ("a blazing torch") of Gen. 15:17. And the reference to the "mountain smoking" (*hāhār ʿāšēn*) in the same Exodus verse recalls the "smoking firepot" (*tannûr ʿāšān*) also of Gen. 15:17. Genesis 15 and Exod. 19–20 recount the Lord's graciously making a covenant with Abra(ha)m/Israel, and both in the context of a fiery, kratophanic (powerful theophanic) manifestation of God's presence.

The second connection with Abraham is that Gen. 22 and Exod. 20:20 provide the only two places where the verb *nāsâ* ("test") and the root *yrʾ* ("fear") occur together and in that sequence. The purpose of God's "testing" (*nāsâ*) Abraham in Gen. 22:1 is to provide irrefutable evidence that Abraham "fears" God (Gen. 22:12): "Now I know that you fear God [*kî-yĕrēʾ ʾĕlōhîm*]." In Exod. 20:20 the purpose of God's testing (*nassôt*) is that Israel's fear of him (*yirʾātô*) might be evident. Moberly (2000: 83, 84) nicely articulates the connection: "The story of Abraham has been deliberately told in the language of Israel's obedience to *torah* so that Abraham can be seen as a type or model for Israel. . . . Abraham now serves as the definitive example of the kind of obedient response that God seeks from Israel."

It is not a great test of whether Israel fears Yahweh when there is so much electricity in the air. Who would not tremble and feel overwhelmed? But what happens to that fear when the fireworks stop? The Lord is longing not only for that proper fear of him in Sinai's shadow, but for that fear that is faithful and consistent over the long haul. Goldingay (2009: 79) aptly remarks, "Will they let their fear in the realm of the emotions transmogrify into a revering in the realm of the will? . . . Yhwh wants to discover not only whether they will respond to the phenomena with the appropriate fear, but whether they will respond to the declaration of Yhwh's expectations with the appropriate revering."

In v. 20 Moses begins by telling the people not to be afraid (*ʾal-tîrāʾû*), a phrase he has used earlier, in 14:13, and which he will use again, in Num. 14:9 [2x]; Deut. 20:3; 31:6. In those passages the admonition is about the threat of adversaries. Here Moses is saying that Yahweh, regardless of how overwhelming his self-revelation may have been on this occasion, is not a God who desires that his devotees perpetually quail before him. He is not a God of whom one must be afraid. He is a God whose modus operandi is invitation rather than intimidation. Justified fear and reverence in his presence, yes; unjustified anxiety in his presence, no (and on the difference between the two, see Gruber 1990; Nissinen 2003: 122–26). There is, then, a fear that is unnecessary ("fear not") and a fear that is healthy ("that fear of him may be on your faces"). One is a phobic fear; the other is a passionate fear.

In an important study of "test" in Exod. 20:20, Greenberg (1960) has pointed out that many verbs appearing only in the Piel, but never in the Qal (as *nāsâ*/"test"), have a factitive/causative meaning (e.g., *māhar*, if in a Qal, would mean "go quickly," but in the Piel means "bring quickly"). Accordingly, he avoids "test" in Exod. 20:20 and translates, "God has come in order *to give you the experience* [of him] in order that the fear of him may be present with you to keep you from sinning." Greenberg resorts to some passages (e.g., 1 Sam. 17:39, David's words to Saul about Saul's armor, "He struggled in vain to go because he was *unused* [to them]. . . . I cannot go in these because I am *unused* to them") where he supplies readings that are questionable. Tellingly, he does not suggest this meaning for any other instances where *nāsâ* occurs in the Torah, except for Deut. 28:56. For other divine testings in the Pentateuch, see Gen. 22:1; Exod. 15:25; 16:4; Deut. 4:34; 8:2, 16; 13:3 [4]. And for Israel's "testing" Yahweh, see Exod. 17:7; Num. 14:22; Deut. 6:16; 33:8.

The fear of God, says Moses, is to help deter the people from sinning. Moses is not advocating some kind of sinless perfection. But neither is he excusing sin in believers nor suggesting that a little bit of sin is okay. One will look in vain here for any concept of *simul iustus et peccator* ("at the same time justified and a sinner"). Moses's words in Exod. 20:20 are very close to those of John in his First Epistle: "My dear children, I write this to you so that you will not sin" (1 John 2:1). Is a lapse possible? Surely, for John does go on to say, "but if anybody does sin. . . ." However, I think that both Moses and John would say that the possibility of a lapse must not become the norm, something with which we can be comfortable, and something we can tolerate and condone.

The Covenant Code

(20:22–23:33)

It is common to refer to this section of Scripture as the "Covenant Code" primarily because of the references in chap. 24 to Moses's telling the people "all the LORD's *words* [*dĕbārîm*] and *laws* [*mišpāṭîm*]" (24:3), and to Moses's reading to the people "the Book of the Covenant [*sēper habbĕrît*]" (24:7). Chapter 24 further highlights the Lord's "words" to Moses (v. 3a, "all the LORD's *words*"; v. 3b, "everything the LORD has said" is, literally, "all the *words* that the LORD has spoken we will do"). The same goes for v. 4a and v. 7b; also see v. 8. So chap. 24 contains five references to the Lord's *dĕbārîm* (3a, 3b, 4a, 7b, 8), but only one reference to the Lord's *mišpāṭîm* (v. 3).

Many scholars assert that the *mišpāṭîm* ("laws") of Exod. 24:3 refer to the prescriptions found in 21:2–22:17, most of which are framed as casuistic law ("If/Should . . . then . . ."). Then the *dĕbārîm* ("words") of Exod. 24:3 refer to the prescriptions of 20:22–26 and 22:18–23:19, most of which are framed as apodictic law ("Do not . . ."). However, neither section is consistent. Section 21:2–22:17 (the "If/Should . . ." laws) is punctuated with "Do not . . ." laws (21:12–17), and sections 20:22–26 and 22:18–23:19 (the "Do not . . ." laws) are punctuated with "If/Should . . ." laws (20:25; 22:25; 23:4).

I see no reason why "words" in 24:3 cannot refer back to the Ten Commandments, which after all begin with "And God spoke all these *words*" (20:1), in which case the "laws" of 24:3 refer to all of 20:22–23:33 rather than to just one portion of it. The fivefold use of "words" in chap. 24 versus the onetime use of "laws" would be that chapter's way of subordinating the Covenant Code to the Decalogue. The "laws" stand in the shadow of the "words." The "laws" are the sunrays, but the "words" are the sun. The "words" are the heart and the brain, while the "laws" are the other organs, which cannot function without the heart and the brain.

If that suggestion is anywhere on target, then one might expect the title "These are the laws you are to set before them" to come not at 21:1 but at the head of 20:22. By placing the title at the head of 21:1, the text for all practical purposes renders 20:22–26 as a transition from the Decalogue to the Covenant Code and a prologue introducing what follows. And if there is a prologue, then there should be a balancing epilogue at the end. That is exactly what we have:

Altar law as a prologue (20:22–26)
(Mostly) Case law (21:1–22:16)
(Mostly) Prohibitive law (22:17–23:19)
A divine sermonette as an epilogue (23:20–33)

Leaving aside the epilogue, one observes that the Covenant Code begins with apodictic law (20:22–26), shifts to casuistic law (21:1–22:16), and returns to apodictic law (22:17–23:19). This is an *a-b-a* structure. The structure is akin to that in the book of Job, which begins with (a) prose (chaps. 1–2), shifts to (b) poetry (3–41), and returns to (a) prose (42). The book of Daniel begins in (a) Hebrew (1:1–2:4a), shifts to (b) Aramaic (2:4b–7:28), and returns to using (a) Hebrew (Dan. 8–12). My observation is somewhat weakened by having to delete the epilogue (23:20–33) from this *a-b-a* grid. However, 20:22–26 (the prologue) is actually a law and so a part of 20:22–23:19, while the epilogue is not.

We are fortunate in having knowledge of several ancient Near Eastern law codes, most of which date from the first or second half of the second millennium BC (2000–1500 BC or 1500–1000 BC), or from the mid-first millennium BC. The most famous is Hammurabi's Code, but there are others: Eshnunna, Urnammu, Lipit-Ishtar, the Hittite Law Code, and the Middle Assyrian Law Code. At least so far, no Canaanite Code has been found.

When one compares some of the laws in these cuneiform codes with the laws in the Covenant Code, it would be hard, in some instances at least, to know whether one is reading from the Bible or from a Sumerian or Babylonian king's law code. The parallels range from identical, to close but not identical, to addressing the same issue but offering different legal treatment. Greengus (1976: 533–34) points to about fifty instances of parallels between Covenant Code law and other biblical law, on the one hand, and ancient Near Eastern law, on the other hand. See also the helpful chart in Childs (1974: 462–63), and the chart in Levinson (2008: 298), which focuses exclusively on parallels between the Covenant Code and the Laws of Hammurabi.

How does one explain such parallels, say, about female slaves or a goring ox? People in Scripture have connections with Mesopotamia at two different points: (1) the patriarchal period (Abraham hails from there, and Isaac and Jacob take wives from there), and (2) the exile in Babylon (late seventh century into the sixth century BC). If these points of contact explain the parallels, then one could argue for the antiquity of the Covenant Code laws, or for the relative lateness of the Covenant Code laws (with knowledge of the laws being brought back to Israel by the exiles returning from Babylon). More than likely, the parallels in content between biblical law and cuneiform law reflect a common Near Eastern legal tradition that was birthed in Mesopotamia and subsequently spread westward to Syria/Palestine and northward to Anatolia/Asia Minor.

If valid, this concept does not detract from Scripture's inspiration and authority. "Inspired" does not have to mean "unique, unheard of, unprecedented." One need only recall that in Exod. 18 it is Jethro, a Midianite priest, who instructs Moses on how best to handle the administration of justice. Yahweh does not suddenly inject himself into the conversation and say to Jethro: "Let me handle that." The old aphorism "All truth is God's truth" seems accurate here.

At times, probably at many times, some of the Covenant Code's laws seem morally and ethically more sensitive or compassionate than does nonbiblical law. But not always. One who investigates all these parallel laws carefully might find instances of nonbiblical law being more compassionate. So the contrast is not primarily between humane versus inhumane, ethically advanced versus primitive, charitable versus barbaric. On the one hand, even within the Covenant Code itself, certain laws almost make a modern believer say "Ouch!" such as the one that calls for the death penalty for the murder of a free citizen (21:12) versus the one that lets the slave owner off the hook if the slave survives a day or two before he expires after a savage beating by the slave's master (21:21). On the other hand, there are laws in the Covenant Code that could fit very nicely into the Sermon on the Mount, such as returning a lost animal of your enemy to your enemy (23:4) or leaving something growing in your field for the poor to eat (23:10–11; see Hanson 1977). If the laws of the Covenant Code often rise above those in Hammurabi's, then it is also true that the laws of this first "sermon on the mount" await a fuller word from the later Sermon on the Mount.

Two items set the Covenant Code apart from all other Near Eastern legal corpora. First, in none of these cuneiform law codes does any deity ever speak. To be sure, in Hammurabi's Code a bas-relief at the top of the stela on which the code is written shows the king's receiving the commission from Shamash, the sun god and the god of justice, to write the code. And both the code's prologue and epilogue appeal to the help and authority of Marduk and Shamash. But not once in any of the 282 laws does a deity speak. In contrast, the voice of Yahweh occurs at the beginning of the Covenant Code (20:22–26), at its conclusion (23:20–33), and throughout the Covenant Code (22:22–24, 27; 23:13, 15, 18). Unlike in Hammurabi's Code, God does not speak at the beginning, then disappear completely, only to appear briefly at the end. See Fensham 1976.

A second item sets the Covenant Code apart: unlike any of these cuneiform codes, the Covenant Code is set within a historical-narrative context, without which it would be shorn of much of its significance. That historical-narrative context is the Lord's mighty deliverance of his people from the paws of the most powerful "lion" in the world at that time, his gracious leading and provision for them as they charted an unknown future, and finally the compassionate offer of a covenant with Israel, the sealing and ratification of which chap. 24 will record.

In the comments that follow, I express my appreciation to the following scholars who are specialists in ancient Near Eastern law and biblical law, and even Greek and Roman law, and from whom I have learned much: Professors David Daube, F. C. Fensham, Bernard Jackson, Moshe Greenberg, Bernard Levinson, A. Phillips, Joe Sprinkle, and Raymond Westbrook, and for NT law, Professor J. D. M. Derrett.

The Altar Law

(20:22–26)

Translation

[22]The LORD said to Moses, "So shall you say to Israel's sons, 'You yourselves saw that from the heavens I spoke with (all of) you. [23]Do not fashion (anything to be) alongside me; neither gods of silver nor gods of gold shall you fashion for yourselves. [24]An altar of earth you shall fashion for me, and sacrifice upon it your whole burnt offerings and your fellowship offerings, your sheep and cattle. In any place where I allow my name to be invoked, I will come to you and grant you blessing. [25]And should you fashion for me a stone altar, do not construct them of hewn stone, for by wielding your sword upon such you have rendered it unfit. [26]Do not ascend by steps my altar in order that your nakedness not be exposed upon it.'"

Grammatical and Lexical Notes

20:23. The MT places an *ʾatnāḥ* under *ʾittî* ("alongside me"), hence ending the first half of the sentence here. Since by itself "Do not fashion/make alongside me" is without meaning, I have added parenthetically "(anything to be)" before *ʾittî*. The LXX ignores the Masoretic punctuation and reads the first half of the sentence, "Do not make alongside me gods of silver."

20:24. In v. 23 "fashion/make" (2x) is plural (*taʿăśûn, taʿăśû*), but in v. 24 "fashion/make" is singular (*taʿăśeh*). Possibly the reason for the shift from plural to singular (with the same verb) is that vv. 22–23 serve as a heading to all that follows and convey the words that the Lord has instructed Moses to speak to "Israel's sons" (pl.). Then, beginning with v. 24, we start with the laws that are addressed to each individual Israelite.

20:24. Verse 24 does not speak of four offerings but of two. The preposition *mēʾēt* should be understood in place of *et* ("your whole-burnt offerings and fellowship offerings *from* your sheep and cattle"). Note that SP reads not *ʾet-ṣōʾnkā wĕʾet-bĕqārekā* but *miṣṣōʾnkā ûmibbĕqārekā.*

20:24. This is the only place I am aware of where the verb *zābaḥ* ("sacrifice") is used with *ʿōlâ*, the whole-burnt offering. Normally *zābaḥ/zebaḥ* refers to "a slain offering whose meat is eaten by the worshiper" (Milgrom 1991: 218), and the *ʿōlâ* is burnt entirely (excepting the hide) on the altar. The parallel law in Deuteronomy (27:7) mentions only the "sacrifice" of the *šĕlāmîm*, which is eaten by the worshiper, while the *ʿōlâ* is "offered" (Deut. 27:6).

20:24. The expression *bĕkol-hammāqôm*, with the definite article *ha-* prefixed to *māqôm* ("In any place"), appears with a distributive sense in Gen. 20:13 ("This is how you can show your love to me: Everywhere [*ʾel kol-hammāqôm*] we go, say of me, 'He is my brother'"), and in Deut. 11:24 ("Every place [*kol-hammāqôm*] where you set your foot will be yours"). The SP simply deletes the word *kol* and reads *bmqm ʾšr* ("in the place where").

20:24. There are some differences in translations about how best to render *ʾazkîr*, the Hiphil of *zākar*: "I allow my name to be invoked"; "I reveal my name"; "I cause the remembrance of my name"; "I cause my name to be honored" (NIV); "I will pronounce my name"; and so forth. Uses of *zākar* in the Hiphil stem are much fewer than uses of the verb in the Qal stem. There are only three more in the Pentateuch: Gen. 40:14, "*Mention me* [*wĕhizkartanî*] to Pharaoh and get me out of this prison"; Gen. 41:9, "Today *I am reminded* [*ʾănî mazkîr*] of my shortcomings"; Exod. 23:13, "Do not *invoke* [*lōʾ tazkîrû*] the names of other gods; do not let them be heard on your lips." This last example is a close parallel to Exod. 20:24 since in both the object of *zākar* (Hiphil) is "name." For other instances of *ʾazkîr* in the Hebrew Bible, see Pss. 71:16 ("*I will proclaim* your righteousness, yours alone"); 77:11 [12], Ketib ("*I will remember* the deeds of the Lord"); 87:4 ("*I will record* Rahab and Babylon among those who acknowledge me"); Isa. 63:7 ("*I will tell* of the kindnesses of the Lord").

20:25. The Hebrew for "them" in "do not construct them" is *ʾethen* (fem.) and is a variant of *ʾōtān*.

20:25. *Gāzît* ("hewn stone") comes from the verb *gāzaz*. In the Torah *gāzaz* always refers to the "shearing" of sheep, cutting away their fleece (Gen. 31:19; 38:12, 13; Deut. 15:19). For other instances of *gāzît*, see 1 Kings 5:17 [31] ("dressed stone"); 6:36 ("dressed stone"); 7:9, 11 ("high-grade stone"); 7:12 ("dressed stone"); 1 Chron. 22:2 ("dressed stone"); Isa. 9:10 [9] ("dressed stone"); Lam. 3:9 ("blocks of stone"); Ezek. 40:42 ("dressed stone"); Amos 5:11 ("stone mansions").

20:25. I prefer to stay with "sword" for *ḥereb* for reasons I shall suggest in the commentary, although some translators opt for "chisel" or "tool." The LXX employs the rare word *encheiridion*, "hand-knife, dagger" (Caird 1968: 470).

20:25. The verb for "wielding" is *nûp*, Hiphil ("raise, lift"), and it is the verb behind the famous *tĕnûpâ*, the "wave" offering that an individual lifts up "before the Lord" (Exod. 29:24; Lev. 7:30; 8:27, 29; Num. 8:11, 21). The LXX translates *nûp* with the verb *epiballō* ("cast, throw"), suggesting using the *ḥereb* to hit or strike the stones.

20:25. The verb *ḥālal* III ("render unfit, desecrate, profane") occurs only one more time in Exodus (31:14: "Anyone who *desecrates* it [the Sabbath] must be put to death"). By contrast it occurs in Leviticus sixteen times, and in Ezekiel (which shares many affinities with Leviticus) thirty-two times.

20:26. While the word "altar" is a very common word in the Bible, "my altar" occurs only here and in 21:14; 1 Sam. 2:28, 33; Isa. 56:7; 60:7; Mal. 1:7, 10.

20:26. *ʾĂšer* is a conjunction of purpose in the phrase "in order that [*ʾăšer*] your nakedness not be exposed" (Gottstein 1949: 43). Holmstedt (2001: 8) argues for the retention of the relative use of *ʾăšer*: "You shall not go up by steps to my altar *which* your nakedness may not be exposed on it."

Commentary

This unit in Exodus introduces a series of laws that follow (see the discussion of the "Covenant Code" above), as does Lev. 17 and Deut. 12. All three commence with a law dealing with sacrifice/altars/worship (Exod. 20:22–26; Lev. 17:1–7; Deut. 12:1–3). All three collections end similarly, with a sacred calendar (Exod. 23:10–19; Lev. 25; Deut. 26:1–15). The latter, Deut. 26, may be more properly called liturgical, rather than calendrical, regulations, for it deals with the firstfruits ceremony (vv. 1–11) and the tithe (vv. 12–15). But note that the next-to-the-last law in the Covenant Code urges bringing the best of the firstfruits to the Lord's house (Exod. 23:19a), and the next-to-the-last law in the Deuteronomic Code addresses exactly the same topic (Deut. 26:1–11). 20:22–26

These five verses begin with apodictic law (v. 23, "Do not fashion . . ."), following the pattern of the Decalogue. Then the unit moves to casuistic law (v. 25, "Should you construct . . ."), anticipating the pattern that commences in chap. 21. It concludes by returning to apodictic law (v. 26, "Do not ascend . . ."). The *a-b-a* structure (apodictic>casuistic>apodictic) matches the *a-b-a* structure of the Decalogue (negative commands>positive commands>negative commands).

There is a deliberate connection between the veto on the people's making gods of silver and gold (v. 23) and the instruction about erecting soil or stone altars (vv. 24–26). What idols (v. 23) are to pagans, a symbol of a deity's presence, altars (v. 24) are to the Israelites (see Tigay [2004b] for this coherence between vv. 23 and 24). In highlighting the altar over the idol, this Exodus passage suggests that a few stones can become a shrine rather than needing to have a man-made humanlike or animal-like figure. While the Torah is filled with data about idols and idolatry (e.g., Exod. 20:4; Lev. 19:4; 26:1; Deut. 4:15–19, 23; 27:15), this is the only reference in that corpus to "gods of gold and silver," and more than likely an anticipation of the "golden" calf scenario in chap. 32. The prohibition on making gods out of such expensive metals is an appropriate prelude to a law that champions the building of a very simple altar. A wheelbarrow or two of soil and sod will do, as will a few undressed rocks piled on top of each other, much as the patriarchs in Genesis built. These altars can be of any size, any shape, and any place where God's name may be invoked (and where will that not be?), and these are altars that the laity as well as the clergy may approach. I suggest that because of the concern expressed in v. 26 that the nakedness of the one ascending the altar not be exposed. Exodus 28:42 and Lev. 6:10 [3] mandate that the priests wear linen breeches as a covering for the body whenever they approach the altar precisely to prevent such exposure. Outside of Gen. 2:25, nakedness is undesirable, for it almost always refers to the loss of dignity (see J. Bailey 1970: 45; and esp. Satlow 1997). Witness Noah's nakedness (Gen. 9:21), or David's when dancing (2 Sam. 6:20), the Ammonites humiliating David's ambassadors (2 Sam. 10:4), the adulterous wife (Hosea 2:3 [5]), or the treatment of prisoners of war (Isa. 20:3–4). Nakedness connotes nothingness and vulnerability (Job 1:21; 24:7; Eccles. 5:15 [14]). Only in 2 Sam. 11:2 does nakedness lead to sexual arousal.

There is not a lot of evidence in the Bible for altars having steps that one has to climb. I point to four other references: (1) 1 Sam. 9:25, Samuel and Saul "*came down* from the high place" after dining; (2) Lev. 9:22, "And having sacrificed the sin offering, . . . he [Aaron] *stepped down*"; (3) 2 Kings 16:12, "When the king [Ahaz] . . . saw the altar, he approached it and presented offerings on it" (better, "*went up* on it," *wayyaʿal ʿālāyw*); (4) Ezek. 43:17, "The *steps* of the altar face east."

The parallel law to vv. 24–26 in Deuteronomy is Deut. 27:5–8. There are some differences between the two (see Heger 1999: 58–76). Deuteronomy speaks only of an altar of stones, not an earthen altar. Exodus prohibits the use of a sword/chisel (*ḥereb*), while Deuteronomy prohibits any iron tool (*barzel*). Exodus prohibits the use of "hewn/dressed stone" (*gāzît*), while Deuteronomy allows the use only of "fieldstones" (NIV; *ʾăbānîm šĕlēmōt*), stones in their natural, uncut state. We could also render the phrase in Deut. 27:6 as "shalom stones." Building an altar in Exod. 20 is a possibility ("and should [*wĕʾim*] you construct . . ."), while in Deut. 27:5–6 it is a command ("Build there an altar to the Lord your God"). In Exod. 20:25 the phrase "for by wielding your sword upon such . . ." explains the preceding command ("Do not construct them of hewn stone"), while in Deut. 27:5 it is part of the command itself ("Do not use any iron tool upon them"). Last, the verb "render unfit/desecrate/profane" (*ḥālal* III) does not occur in Deuteronomy's altar law. It should be clear that the differences between the two accounts suggest a considerable difference in timing and place. The law in Exodus draws attention to any altar any Israelite could quickly put together in a few minutes even as he journeys through a barren, rocky wilderness. That in Deuteronomy anticipates settlement in the land and the erection, not of *an* altar, but of *the* altar at Mount Ebal.

Commentators are not sure why both accounts call for the use of undressed stone. Archaeologists have found Canaanite altars made of such stone, so that would rule out any anti-Canaanite polemic. Might we find a parallel between stones that have never been cut (by humans) and the bringing to God of a heifer on whom a man has never placed a yoke (Num. 19:2; Deut. 21:3; 1 Sam. 6:7)? That is, stones or animals are to be used for God only in their natural condition before they have been interfered with in any way by humans (Vaux 1961: 408). Might we draw a parallel between "uncut" stones and "unblemished" sacrificial animals? That is, bring to God and use for God that which is as "perfect" as possible (Olyan 1996). I think the most likely reason is that the emphasis is on the simplicity of worship. The Exodus law "repudiates . . . costly implements and icons" (Halpern 1983: 247). There is a place for adornment and opulence, as we see in Solomon's temple, or even in the hollow altar that one sees upon first entering the outer court area of the tabernacle (Exod. 27:1–8). No dirt or rocks are there, unless they are used for fill to give the altar stability. Rather, that altar is made of gold-embossed acacia wood. But there is also a place for the simple and the unadorned. Both a cathedral and a pile of dirt can become a holy place where we meet God. Regardless of which it is, the altar is the place where God shows up ("I will come to you") and the place where he blesses ("I will grant you blessing"). For that reason, the prayer of many who follow the Lord is, in the words of the hymn, "My heart an altar, and thy love the flame" (George Croly).

One obvious difference between the "simple" altar of Exod. 20 and the "ornate" altar of Exod. 27 is, as I indicated above, that the first is accessible by anybody, while the second one is accessible only by the clergy (on the possible implications of this, see Sailhamer 2009: 357–60). One is free and available to all; the other is off-limits to all but the ordained. One needs clean hands (hence the laver in the courtyard) and a pure heart (which no laver can provide) before approaching the second altar (Ps. 24:3–4). Clean hands are difficult to have when one is making an altar of earth or dirt or rough, uncut stone! But a pure heart is indispensable regardless of which altar one is approaching.

The Slave Law

(21:1–11)

Translation

[1]"And the following are the legal norms that you shall set before them. [2]Should you acquire/buy a Hebrew slave, six years he shall serve, but in the seventh year he shall go out free, owing nothing. [3]If by himself he comes in, by himself he shall go out. If a husband of a wife he is, his wife shall go out with him. [4]And should his master give him a woman, and she bears him sons or daughters, the woman and her children shall be her master's, and he shall go out by himself. [5]Should, however, the slave declare forthrightly, 'I love my master, my woman, and my sons; I will not go out free,' [6]his master shall have him approach God, and have him approach the door or the doorpost, and his master shall pierce his ear with an awl, and he shall serve him for life.

[7]"And should a man sell his daughter as a concubine-slave, she shall not go out as the male slaves go out. [8]If she is unacceptable in her master's eyes for whom she was intended, he shall let (anyone) redeem her. To a foreign people he has no authority to sell her, in so betraying her. [9]And if for his son he intended her, he shall do for her according to the norm for daughters. [10]If another woman he takes for himself, her food, her clothing—that is, her upkeep—he shall not withhold. [11]And if he does not do these three for her, she shall go out owing nothing, no payment."

Grammatical and Lexical Notes

21:1. I owe the translation "legal norms" for *hammišpāṭîm* to B. Levine 2000: 557.

21:2. *Qānâ* may mean "purchase, buy," but also "acquire." The verb's primary meaning is "create" and first appears in the Bible in Eve's declaration at Cain's birth, "With the help of the Lord *I have brought forth* a man" (Gen. 4:1). The only other occurrence of the verb in Exodus is in the Song at the Sea (15:16), ". . . until your people pass by, O Lord, until the people you *bought/created* pass by." Genesis 17:12, 13, 23, 27 uses the expression *miqnat-kesep* ("bought with money"), as does Exod. 12:44 ("Any slave you have bought"), so there is no doubt that *qānâ* means "buy" when used with *kesep*, "silver." Since "silver" is not used in Exod. 21:2, then possibly *qānâ* is a legal term referring to acquisition other than by purchase. See Falk 1967.

21:2. The law begins by using the second person ("Should *you* acquire a Hebrew slave"), then shifts to the third person ("should *his master* give him a woman" versus "should *you* give him a woman") in v. 4, and again in v. 6 ("*His master* shall have him approach God" [versus "*You* shall have him approach God"]). To make the grammar more "logical," some emend the MT to "if a Hebrew slave sells himself." Gevirtz (1961b: 157) has demonstrated, however, that such emendation is unnecessary. He quotes from several West Semitic curses to show that the shift from second to third person (in the protasis to apodosis) is quite common. Here is one example: "But if *you* do indeed open my [sarcophagus] lid, . . . may *he* get no seed."

21:2. There is no reason to believe that the Hebrew slave the master acquires is already a slave, as Van Seters (1996; 2003: 82–95) argues. The law is about freedom for the slave, not a change in his "ownership." Levinson (2006; 2008: 93–111) helpfully points out the difference between two types of objects that follow a transitive verb. An *affected* object exists before the action conveyed by the verb. An *effected* object is produced by the action contained in the verb. Before the individual is acquired as an *ʿebed*, he is a free man. Now, however, his status has changed.

21:2. The adjective *ḥopšî* ("free") occurs four times in this chapter, always in conjunction with slaves (vv. 2, 5, 26, 27); three times in the parallel slave law in Deuteronomy (15:12, 13, 18); and five times in Jeremiah in the prophet's discourse on the slave law of Exodus and Deuteronomy (34:9, 10, 11, 14, 16). See also 1 Sam. 17:25, the reward to any Hebrew fellow who dares take on Goliath: "The king will give great wealth. . . . He will also give him his daughter in marriage and *will exempt* his father's family *from taxes* [*ʿăśâ ḥopšî*]." This verse from 1 Sam. 17 suggests that *ḥopšî* means not freedom that is accorded to everybody (all must pay taxes), but a special and unique freedom (you have to pay no taxes at all). Such a use of *ḥopšî* should raise suspicions about the connection many orientalists make between this Hebrew word and the extrabiblical word *ḫupshi* from cuneiform documents, which refers to groups like peasants, serfs, and labor-gang workers (hardly free people). Given the difference between the two, Sternberg (1998: 447) can rightly say, "The *ḫupshi* in Mesopotamia and elsewhere had good reason to envy the *ḥopshi* in Israel."

21:2. "Owing nothing," here and in v. 11, is *ḥinnām*. Laban uses the word with Jacob: "Just because you are a relative of mine, should you work *for nothing*?" (Gen. 29:15). The origin of the word *ḥinnām* is *ḥēn* (from *ḥānan*), which is the Hebrew word for "grace." God's grace is free and does not come with a price tag to the recipient. That is what makes grace to be grace. One can see the same connection between the Latin words for "free" (*gratis*) and "favor, grace" (*gratia*).

21:3. "By himself/alone" (*bĕgappô*) occurs in the Hebrew Bible only in Exod. 21:3 [2x], 4. There is a word *gap* in Prov. 9:3 ("She [Wisdom] calls from the highest point [*gappê mĕrōmê*] of the city") with which the phrase in Exod. 21 may be connected. The "highest point" in the city stands "alone" and is thus apart from all other landmarks.

21:4. Although it is common to render *ʾiššâ* as "wife," I believe "woman" is better here, for the verse is about breeding, not about marriage.

21:4. Although the subject of "the woman and her children shall be her master's" is plural (or compound, feminine noun and masculine noun), the verb "shall be" is a third-person feminine-singular verb (*tihyeh*). See Ratner 1990: 242.

21:5. Throughout the Covenant Code, the absolute infinitive of nineteen different verbs appears twenty-seven times (references in Yaron 1995). For other instances of *ʾāmōr* before some finite form of *ʾāmar* ("declared forthrightly, said indeed"), see Judg. 15:2; 1 Sam. 2:30; 20:21; Jer. 23:17; Ezek. 28:9.

21:5. The Hebrew uses a perfect *ʾāhabtî* ("I loved") for a present-tense expression ("I love"). Hellers (1995: 764–65) suggests that the reason is because v. 5 is a legal transaction in which the servant is making a "performative utterance," here a declaration of loyalty rather than simply describing his emotional feelings for his master. Hellers points out an interesting use of the past tense with present meaning in the prayer that Jesus taught his followers. Luke 11:4 has Jesus use the (expected) present tense of the verb in "forgive [*aphiomen*] us our sins," but Matthew (Matt. 6:12) has Jesus use the (unexpected) past tense (*aphēkamen*) in "forgive us our debts."

21:6. The opening phrase of this verse, *wĕhiggîšô ʾădōnāyw ʾel-hā ʾĕlōhîm*, is far from clear. Here are the options: (1) "his master shall bring him to God" (Vannoy 1974); (2) "his master shall bring him to the gods" (Gordon 1935; Draffkorn 1957; even Luther's "vor die 'Götter'"); (3) "his master shall bring him to the judges" (KJV; NIV). Aquila (a translator of the Hebrew text into Greek in the second century AD) agrees with option 1 above with *pros tou theous*, as does the Vulgate (*diis*). The LXX combines options 1 and 3 with its *pros to kritērion tou theou* ("to God's judgment seat"). *Targum Onqelos* agrees with option 3 and employs *dyny*ʾ ("judges"). The phrase is conspicuously absent in the parallel slave law in Deut. 15:12–18. There are a few places in the Bible where X brings (Hiphil of *nāgaš*) Y to Z (in which Y and Z can be either a thing, a person, or a place): Lev. 2:8, the priest is to bring the grain offering to the altar; 2 Sam. 17:29, the people bring provisions to David; Amos 5:25 and Mal. 1:8; 3:3, the people bring sacrifices to the Lord; Mal. 2:12, they bring offerings to the Lord Almighty; 1 Kings 4:21 [5:1], nations bring tribute to Solomon. This is the one instance (Exod. 21:6) where one person brings another person to God/the gods. Both Fensham (1959) and Falk (1959) suggest that to bring someone to God means to bring that one to the sanctuary. Falk also observes that, according to some Babylonian texts, the release of slaves takes place before the god Shamash in the temple.

21:6. The verb *rāṣa*ʿ ("pierce") appears only here in the Hebrew Bible. The cognate noun *marṣēʿa* ("awl") appears twice, here and in Deut. 15:17. For "pierce," Deut. 15:17 uses *nātan bĕ* ("put/push through") for Exodus's *rāṣaʿ bĕ*.

21:7. Falk (1967: 242) argues for translating *mākar* as "transfer" when it is present in a legal context, rather than the usual "sell."

21:7. I translate *ʾāmâ* as "concubine-slave" rather than as something like "servant girl" or "female slave." This is the word's consistent use in Genesis (Gen. 20:17; 21:10, 12, 13; 30:3; 31:33).

21:8. "For whom" in "for whom she was intended" is *lô*, the Qereʾ (what is "read"), but the Ketib ("written") is the negative particle *lōʾ* ("who did *not* designate her"). For two other instances of Ketib and Qereʾ readings for *lōʾ* and *lô*, see Lev. 11:21 and 25:30.

21:8. On the verb *wāʿad*, versus the suggested *yāʿad* ("intend, designate, appoint"), see J. Thompson (1965), who observes that the Niphal, Hiphil, and Hophal uses of the verb demonstrate that the first radical is a *wāw* rather than a *yôd*.

21:8. Of the approximately fifty-five uses of *pādâ* ("redeem") in the Hebrew Bible, this is the only one in the Hiphil stem. The verb appears in the Qal in 13:13 [3x], 15 in reference to the "redemption" of the firstborn. As a translation of this causative from a transitive verb, Daube (1961: 262) offers either "and he let her redeem (herself)" or "and he let (anyone) redeem her," to illustrate direct or indirect causation. Daube (1947: 39) elsewhere observes the difference between the two Hebrew verbs for "redeem" (*gāʾal* and *pādâ*), which explains why the latter one is used in 21:8: "Whereas *gʾl* signifies the buying back of a man or thing that had once belonged to one's family but had got lost, *pdh* signifies the ransoming of a man or thing whose fate otherwise would be destruction, consecration or slavery. Thus *gʾl* primarily suggests the return of men or things into their old legitimate place, *pdh* the saving of men or things from their doom." For another use of *pādâ* for ransoming a "slave girl," see Lev. 19:20, "If a man sleeps with a woman who is a slave girl promised to another man but who has not been *ransomed* or given her freedom . . ."

21:8. Orlinsky (1947: 107–8) notes that the infinitive construct of verbs that have *ô* in the last syllable of the imperfect sometimes takes the form *qitl* before pronominal suffixes. So we have here *bĕbigdô-bāh* ("in his betraying her") rather than the expected *bĕbogdô-bāh*. For other examples, see 2 Sam. 1:10 ("because I knew that after he had fallen [*niplô* for the expected *noplô*]") and Amos 2:6 ("They sell [*mikrām* for the expected *mokrām*] the righteous for silver"). The infinitive construct may be spelled with the form *qotl* with pronominal suffixes, for in this same verse (Exod. 21:8) we have *lĕmokrāh* ("to sell her") rather than *lĕmikrāh*.

21:9. I render *kĕmišpaṭ* "according to the norm" to reflect the translation of the same noun in the plural in v. 1, *mišpāṭîm* ("legal norms"). Here *mišpaṭ* carries the idea of something that is normally and legally put into practice.

21:10. The Hebrew word *šĕʾēr* means both "food, meat" and "close relative" (e.g., Lev. 18:6). The same goes for a related word, *bāśār*, which also means both "meat, flesh, food," and a "blood relative" (e.g., in the phrase "[we are] your *flesh* and blood," in Judg. 9:2; Isa. 58:7).

21:10. There is much debate about the meaning of the word *ʿōnâ*, which occurs only here in the Hebrew Bible. One possibility is "marital rights" (NIV) as one of three things the master must not deny his concubine-slave after he has married another. To support this, one must posit the existence of a putative Hebrew verb *ʿānâ*, "to love," which is difficult to sustain. É. Levine (1999; 2000: 103–20) suggests the existence of a verb *ʿānâ* in Biblical Hebrew that in the Qal means "to open, plow the earth," and he points to the noun *maʿăniwtām* in Ps. 129:3 ("Plowmen have plowed my back and made *their furrows* long"). It is well known that the Piel of *ʿānâ* is used to refer to the "rape" of virgins (Gen. 34:2; 2 Sam. 13:14). Other Semitic languages may provide some support for "conjugal rights" in Exod. 21:10. In Arabic *ʿ(w)n* denotes "coitus." Margalit (1989: 372) points to a couple of lines in the Aqhat epic from Ugarit: *ʿn.larṣ.mṭr.bʿl/ wlshd.mṭr.ʿly/ nʿm.larṣ.mṭr.bʿl* ("The rain of Baal 'penetrates' [*ʿn*] the (female) earth / the rain of the mounter [penetrates] the field / Pleasure for the (female) earth is the rain of Baal"). For something of a possible parallel to Exod. 21:10, note that Exod. 23:24–26 promises, in return for Israel's devotion to God, Israel's sustenance and protection (v. 25) and fertility (v. 26, "none will miscarry or be barren in your land"). One wonders, however, why the covenant law says to the husband who has rejected this *ʾāmâ* as his bedmate, "Keep having sex with her."

A second possibility for understanding *ʿônâ* is advanced by Paul (1969). He takes as his clue the common threefold phrase in Akkadian *eprum*, *pishshatum*, *lubushtum*, "grain, oil/ointments, clothing." For Paul, Akkadian *eprum* = Heb. *šĕʾēr* ("food"), *lubushtum* = *kĕsût* ("clothing"), and therefore *pishshatum* ("oil/ointments") must = Heb. *ʿōnâ*. There are two problems with this. First, at best *ʿōnâ* = "oil/ointments" is only an inference. There is nothing in the Hebrew language itself to connect an *ʿnh* root with "oil." Second, if these are the three items that the man must "provide" or "give" the ex-bedmate, it seems strange that v. 11 would use the verb *ʿāśâ* ("make, do") for this benevolent act. Would not some verb like *nātan* ("give") be much more suited?

A third possibility for understanding *ʿōnâ*, and the one reflected in my translation, is that which Paradise (1997) has suggested. One may connect the hapax legomenon *ʿōnâ* with the Hebrew verb *ʿānâ*, which primarily means "to answer," but can also mean "provide, take care of, attend to the needs of" (Gen. 41:16; Eccles. 10:19; Hosea 2:21 [23]). Compare also the noun *ʿinyān* in Eccles. 2:26; 3:10; 4:8, which the NIV translates successively as "task," "burden," "(miserable) business," but which all could be rendered "care, concern." In Exod. 21:10 the word *ʿōnâ* would be a comprehensive term, and the *wāw* at the beginning of the word would be a *wāw explicativum*: "her food, her clothing—*that is, her upkeep.*" The reference to "these three" in v. 11 would refer not to "three" items of v. 10, but to the three possible scenarios this verse and the immediately preceding verses have spelled out, and by which the man must abide, a possible interpretation that Brin (1995: 351–52) also suggests in his discussion of the biblical phrase, "if he shall not (do)."

21:10. The verb *gāraʿ* ("withhold") has appeared back in 5:8, 11, 19 to refer to the nonpermitted "deduction" of bricks the Hebrew slaves were to make daily.

Commentary

21:1–11 The structure of this law is transparent. It covers two different, but related areas: (1) vv. 2–6, the male slave acquired for manual work and fathering a child, if given a woman for this purpose; (2) vv. 7–11, the female servant taken to be the concubine of her master. One servant provides labor and possibly a child; the other servant provides sexual and reproductive services. Verses 2–6 begin with a *kî* clause, which is followed by four clauses introduced with *ʾim* ("if"): vv. 3 [2x], 4, 5. Similarly, vv. 7–11 begin with a *kî* clause, which is followed by four clauses introduced with *ʾim* ("if"): vv. 8, 9, 10, 11.

The change in subject matter from the end of chap. 20 to the beginning of chap. 21 is abrupt and unexpected. We have just finished thinking about altars, worshiping the Lord with simple accoutrements, experiencing God's blessing, and now—slaves, either buying one or becoming one!

The Hebrew word *ʿebed* lends itself to two possible equivalents in English. Should we translate it "slave" or "servant"? When Paul describes himself as a *doulos* of Christ (Rom. 1:1; Phil. 1:1; Titus 1:1), is he referring to himself as Christ's "servant" or as Christ's "slave"? Other Hebrew words share the same ambiguity: *ʾādām*, "Adam" or "humankind"? *šāmayim*, "heaven" or "skies"? *ʾereṣ*, "earth" or "land"? One suspects that the ancient mind did not distinguish between servitude and servanthood.

Almost all commentators agree that the OT allows the practice of slavery. That is why Patrick (1973; 1985: 69–70) correctly points out the difference between casuistic laws that are remedial (e.g., stealing) and casuistic laws that govern rights and duties (e.g., slavery). The first describes illicit behavior, and the second describes licit behavior. There is no one verse in the Bible that says *lōʾ yihyeh-lĕkā ʿăbādîm* ("You shall not have slaves"); *lōʾ-yihyeh lĕkā ʾĕlōhîm ʾăḥērîm* ("You shall not have other gods"), yes, but not the other *lōʾ-yihyeh lĕkā*. At that point the reader will have one of two reactions (to verify this, just do an internet search on "Slavery in the Old Testament," and look at the numerous websites that appear on your screen). The cynical response will be to throw the OT and the God of the OT in with the despicable slave traders who brought African slaves to the West. They will suggest that abolitionists like Wilberforce of England turn their ammunition against the Bible as well for it was, they contend, the ultimate source for the justification of flesh peddling (and note the study of Giles [1994], who documents how many church fathers and even evangelical scholars up to the mid-twentieth century have justified slavery by appeal to Scripture). See also the thoughtful study of D. Thompson (1996: 340–48), who speaks of the direction in which the canonical debate regarding slavery was moving, although the canonical dialogue was never resolved.

The more "conservative" response will be to admit that while the Bible allows slavery, it has modified it and made it into a much more humane institution than that practiced by Israel's neighbors. To make this case, such readers will compare the slave laws of Scripture with those in other ancient Near Eastern law codes like the codes of Eshnunna (about 1770 BC) or Hammurabi (about 1750 BC), or the Hittite Laws (about 1600–1500 BC), or the Middle Assyrian Laws (about 1100 BC). The reader can find these codes translated into English in many different sources, but I recommend M. Roth 1997.

A comparison of these legal corpora, so it is maintained, shows that the Bible avoids the harshness and the cruelty these extrabiblical codes reserve for slaves. Sometimes this is true; I do not think anybody would deny that. But it is not always true. For example, the very last law in Hammurabi's Code allows the slave to go free after just "three" years of service to his master versus after "six" years of service in Exod. 21:2 and Deut. 15:12.

Many astute biblical scholars and orientalists have gone through these slave laws with a fine-tooth comb. I want to pay tribute to them and say how much I have learned from them. To name just a few, I am thinking of Mendelsohn (1935; 1949); Paul (1970); Lemche (1974; 1975; 1976); Phillips (1984); Turnbam (1987); Chirichigno (1993); Sprinkle (1994); Westbrook (1988; 1995; 1998a); Pressler (1998); Schenker (1998); Matthews (1994); Fleishman (2000).

Before turning to Exod. 21:1–11, let me state my own position. I reject the view that the Bible gives its imprimatur to slavery and looks the other way when ethical concerns raise their heads. Nor do I accept the view that the Bible endorses but tries to modify and ameliorate the practice of slavery. There are other things that the pagan nations did and the OT absolutely prohibits, like having idols, or cutting oneself, or eating pork, or working on Saturdays. The OT never tries to modify them. It exorcises them.

I believe the OT attempts, through its slave laws, to dissuade Israelites from the practice of slavery. I say this for two reasons. First, the most interesting slave law of all in the Bible is Deut. 23:15–16: "If a slave has taken refuge with you, do not hand him over to his master. Let him live among you wherever he likes and in whatever town he chooses" (and possibly the OT background to Paul's Letter to Philemon). That is to say, a slave can choose not to be a slave. To gain his freedom, he need not wait those six years. He can simply and legally run away, without consequence to either the fugitive or to the one who is harboring him. Here is one major difference between the codes. In the Laws of Eshnunna (laws 12–13) is a stiff fine for harboring a runaway slave, and Hammurabi's Code (numbers 15–16) makes it a capital offense. As Clines (1995a: 78, 81) has pointed out, "If a slave can choose not to be a slave, the concept of slavery does not exist as it once was thought to exist. . . . Slavery is in a sense abolished when it ceases to be a state that a person is forced into against their will."

Here is the second reason why I believe the OT tries to dissuade the practice of slavery (and I reference here to Sternberg [1998: 483–93] as the source of some of my thoughts). Exodus 21:2 begins with "When you buy [*qānâ*] a Hebrew slave [*ʿebed ʿibrî*]. . . ." These expressions appear in Genesis in conjunction with Joseph's slavery in Egypt. His brothers sell (*mākar*) him to some caravaners heading to Egypt (Gen. 37:28). Potiphar buys [*qānâ*] him from them (Gen. 39:1), and Potiphar's wife sneeringly refers to Joseph as "that Hebrew slave" (*hāʿebed hāʿibrî*) in Gen. 39:17. If Exod. 21:2 would say, "When you acquire/buy an *Israelite* slave," the parallel of the Exodus slave law with Joseph would be nonexistent. As it now stands, the slave law of Exod. 21 appears to hold out Potiphar and Mrs. Potiphar as the model of somebody who has "bought" a "Hebrew slave," resulting in all the tragic misfortunes that befall this Hebrew slave (years of imprisonment, character assassination, to name a few). As Sternberg (1998: 486) says, "The tacit Josephic precedent triggers its own, story-length prolepsis in the Mosaic audience's mind, with a view to deterring them from reenacting this follow-up in the world."

Another parallel with Genesis language is this. One may assume that a major reason why a person would voluntarily become a slave, or sell one's daughter into slavery, is because of staggering debt and poverty from which one cannot extricate oneself. The Egyptian people, because of their famine-ravaged land, say to Joseph, now their Egyptian prime minister, "Buy [*qānâ*] us." So Joseph "bought [*qānâ*] all the land of Egypt. . . . I have bought [*qanah*] you and your land" (Gen. 47:19, 20, 23), in return for which the people promised (Gen. 47:25) to be "slaves" (*ʿăbādîm*) to Pharaoh (NIV, "in bondage to Pharaoh"). Joseph, the one "bought," has become Joseph the "buyer." Joseph, once the *ʿebed*, "slave," has become the *ʾādôn*, "master." The enslaved has become the enslaver.

The Israelites now are only about three months out of Egypt. On three earlier occasions during those three months, slavery back in Egypt is their preferred option (Exod. 14:10–12; 16:2–3; 17:1–3), and here is the Lord speaking to his people about enslaving a Hebrew brother. In its own way Exod. 21:5's "I love my master" is a later form of an earlier "I love my Egypt (and all the security and comforts it provides)."

In a review of Sternberg's book, Cohn (2001: 740) catches the drift of the argument: "The texts aim to stigmatize an Israelite who would enslave another by coding him in the role of a Hamite [Egyptian] master, as well as tarring an Israelite who would choose servitude over liberty by coding him as a throwback to Egyptian slavery."

One might obtain slaves from several sources or circumstances: war captives, kidnapping, selling oneself voluntarily because of hunger or poverty, sold by one's parents, involuntarily through defaulting on a loan, and so forth. I believe it is on target to say that in Exod. 21 the concern is with a male debt-slave (vv. 2–6) and a female debt-slave (vv. 7–11). This is a law that would be more at home in the larger urban areas than in the more rural places. Knight (2000: 175) correctly points out that in most villages the average family would have neither the means nor the opportunity to purchase a slave. This particular law is aimed at the same kind of a person whom the fourth commandment addresses: somebody with the means to have male (*ʿebed*) and female (*ʾāmâ*) slaves, who are permitted to rest on the Sabbath.

Verses 2–6 address the rights of both the male slave buyer and the male slave. The buyer is entitled to six years of service. The slave is entitled to leave his master after these six years if he so chooses. If he chooses to leave, he takes his wife with him when he departs if he was married when he came in. That is to say, while the master has control over his male slave, he does not have absolute control. He cannot separate spouse from spouse as Saul does with Michal and David (1 Sam. 25:44).

The modern reader is rightly troubled by v. 4, which calls for the male servant to leave alone if the master has provided him with a woman and the couple has children. The woman the master supplies the male slave would be a female slave rather than one of his own daughters. As Westbrook (1998a: 224) says, "The master's property rights take precedence over the husband's marital rights," and for a parallel he quotes from the Laws of Eshnunna (law 4): "If a slave marries a slave-woman whom he loves and that slave is freed, she shall not go out from the house." Having said that, however, I believe very few Hebrew slaves would come into servitude single, unless very young. Bachelors are almost unheard of in the OT (Jeremiah excepted; see Jer. 16:2). Jackson (2007: 39) calls such a situation a "tripartite breeding relationship," which he describes as "an arrangement to use the reproductive capacities of two members of a household for the benefit of a third member."

To continue in servitude, the male servant merely says, "I love my master" and spouse and children (v. 5). If the slave's expression of "love" for his master, and his desire to stay with his master, is a genuine statement of the slave's affection, then we may parallel such sentiment with that expressed by Ruth to Naomi (A. Brenner 1999: 159). Like the male slave, Ruth choses to stay with her mother-in-law rather than return to her own home when she could have easily done so (Ruth 1:16–17). Perhaps "love" is not a genuine expression of affection for the master (J. Thompson 1977: 478; S. Ackerman 2002: 439). Maybe it is his love for his wife and children that is the real love, or his concern that, if on his own, he cannot provide for his family. As Phillips (1973: 357) points out, "There was, therefore, little point in exchanging security without freedom for freedom without security."

However, if the Israelites had followed that thinking, they would never have left Egypt. And that is why Egypt looks like a great and secure place to which to return. The freed are willing to surrender their freedom and return to bondage. How unexpected and tragic! This is precisely Paul's argument in Rom. 6:15–23: "Why would you want again to be slaves to sin when sin, as your master, brought only death?" (summary).

I am not clear about the significance of piercing the ear with an awl. If any part of the body is to be pierced, the earlobe provides the softest tissue possible, better, I think, than the nose, the lips, or some other anatomical part. For a parallel, another body mark that establishes and symbolizes a special and enduring relationship to which one has committed himself with another person is the mark of circumcision on male genitalia. Only male slaves have the ear pierced (in Exod. 21:6; yet females too in Deut. 15:17b: "Do the same for your maidservant"), and only males receive the mark of circumcision.

I have already noted one difference between the slave law in Exod. 21 and that in Deut. 15. In Exod. 21 the slave who desires to stay with his master is "brought to God," and "the door or doorpost" must be the door of a sanctuary near the master's home. As we have seen, "brought to God" is missing in Deut. 15, and so the "door" must be the door of the master's house rather than a sanctuary door.

Here is a second difference: On the one hand, Exod. 21 allows freedom after six years of service for only the male slave, not the female slave ("She shall not go out as the male slaves go out," v. 7b). On the other hand, Deut. 15:17b allows either to go free ("Do the same for your maidservant"). I am not convinced that the usual explanation of this difference is the correct one, counting Deuteronomy as an "ethical advance" over Exodus in that it treats women more fairly and equitably than does Exodus. Tigay (1996: 149) offers another explanation, which I think is preferable: "It is possible the two laws refer to different cases. Exodus refers to a minor sold conditionally by the father for the purpose of marriage [I would say, "for the purpose of concubinage"]; such a sale would naturally not be terminated after six years. . . . Deuteronomy, on the other hand, may refer only to an [older] girl or woman who became indentured because of insolvency or debt—her own or that of a husband or father—with no intention of marriage." That is to say, the female slave performs only domestic services and not sexual ones.

In the Exodus law, the one reason the slave woman may leave is if the master defaults in any way on his obligations to her (vv. 8–11).

It is clear that vv. 7–11 are about concubinage rather than marriage. Thus "another woman" in v. 10 would be "another concubine." Pressler (1998: 163) notes that (1) this slave girl is called an *ʾāmâ*, not an *ʾiššâ*; (2) she is "sold," not "given" (in marriage) to the man; and (3) the purchaser is her master (*ʾādôn*), not her husband (*baʿal*). A man could be the *ādôn* of a woman (or man), or the *baʿal* of a woman, but not *ʾādôn* and *baʿal* of the same woman simultaneously. Westbrook (1998a: 236–37) adds, "Rations are the stuff of servants and dependants, not wives. Were the slave-woman married to her master, she could have relied on the protection given by her status as a wife to ensure her sustenance, and would not have required special measures."

One hopes that this hypothetical slave woman is treated more sensitively, or if she leaves the master's home, with a bit more to hold her for the future than was another *ʾāmâ*, Hagar (Gen. 21). "Some food and a skin of water" (21:14) do not seem to be an overly generous parting gift for a single mother and her son as they head into a perilous wilderness, especially from a person as wealthy as Abraham.

Where can this released *ʾāmâ* go? I assume to her father's home, to the father who some time earlier has sold her to this man. What kind of meeting would that be? Instead of saying, "I am no longer worthy to be called your daughter," would she say, "You are no longer worthy to be called my father"? Or would she be like Hansel and Gretel, who—though left in the forest by their impoverished parents, hopefully to be found and raised by people with means or eaten by wild animals—rejoiced when reunited with their father?

Four Capital Offenses

(21:12–17)

Translation

[12]"A striker of a man who dies: he shall surely be put to death. [13]But he who did not lie in wait, but rather the Deity let him fall into his hand, I will establish a place to which he may flee. [14]Should, however, a man plot against his neighbor to kill him by craft, from my altar you shall take him to die.

[15]"A striker of his father or his mother: he shall surely be put to death.

[16]"A stealer of a man, whether he sells him or he is found in his hand: he shall surely be put to death.

[17]"And one who dishonors his father or his mother: he shall surely be put to death."

Grammatical and Lexical Notes

21:12. Verses 12, 15–17 all begin with a participle (*makkēh* [vv. 12, 15]; *gōnēb* [v. 16]; *mĕqallēl* [v. 17]). I have translated them all in a way to suggest that they introduce a *casus pendens*, and hence the reason for my punctuating these four verses with a colon. On the rarity of laws that begin with an indeterminate participle, see J. Williams 1964; 1965. On the use of the participle to express a future condition, see GKC §116b.

21:13. "Lie in wait" (*ṣādâ* I) occurs again in the Hebrew Bible only in 1 Sam. 24:11 [12], "I [David] have not wronged you [Saul], but you are *hunting me down* to take my life"; and maybe Lam. 4:18, "Men *stalked* us at every step."

21:13. The verb *ʾānâ* II (in the Piel) here means "let fall." It occurs three more times in the Hebrew Bible, twice in the Pual (Ps. 91:10, "Then no harm *will befall* you"; Prov. 12:21, "No harm *befalls* the righteous") and once in the Hitpael (2 Kings 5:7, "See how he is *trying to pick a quarrel* with me!").

21:14. The word for "craft" is *ʿormâ*. The noun *ʿormâ* ("craft, cunning") and the adjective *ʿārûm* ("crafty") are used for guile (the serpent in Gen. 3:1), and for scheming, plotting (Exod. 21:14; Josh. 9:4). Proverbs, however, uses these words to speak of cunning used legitimately (Prov. 1:4; 8:5, 12).

21:15. The *wāw* on *wĕʾimmô* in vv. 15 and 17 should be rendered "*or* his mother," not "*and* his mother." Thus here *wāw* = *ʾô*. Steiner (2000: 261–63) calls "or" a "pseudo-meaning" of *wāw*. The *wāw* should also be translated in v. 16 as "*or* he is found [*wĕnimṣāʾ*] in his hand." The LXX also uses "or" in vv. 15, 17 (*patera autou ē mētera autou*).

21:16. *Umĕkārô wĕnimṣāʾ bĕyādô* must be translated "*whether* he sells him *or* he is found in his hand." A translation like, "and sells him and he is found in his hand" makes no sense.

21:17. I shall comment below on whether one should stick with the usual rendering of *qālal* in the Piel as "curse," or employ a broader equivalent like "dishonor, abuse, neglect."

21:17. The LXX places v. 17 before v. 16 in order to have the two laws dealing with parents back to back.

Commentary

These three verses focus on two kinds of homicide, intentional (vv. 12, 14) 21:12–14
and unintentional (v. 13), and parallel the sixth commandment. "Man" as victim (*ʾîš*) refers not to all males but only to free citizens. This is clear by the fact that though anyone fatally striking a "man" is "to be put to death" (v. 12), someone who fatally beats his slave is "to be punished" (v. 20), but perhaps "be punished" is a synonym for "be put to death." The parallel verse in Leviticus (24:21) to Exod. 21:12 uses the more inclusive *ʾādām* rather than *ʾîš*: "But whoever kills a man [*ûmakkēh ʾādām*] must be put to death." *ʾĀdām* in Lev. 24:21 may be an *ʾîš* or an *ʿebed*, but in Exod. 21:12 *ʾîš* excludes the *ʿebed*.

The language of v. 13, the verse dealing with unintentional homicide, recalls the story of Saul's entering a cave to relieve himself, the very cave in which David is hiding from Saul (1 Sam. 24). As we saw in a grammatical note, Exod. 21:14 and 1 Sam. 24:11 [12] are the only two places in the Hebrew Bible (the text of Lam. 4:18 is debatable) that use the verb *ṣādâ* I for somebody "lying in wait for" or "hunting down" somebody with the intent of ending his life. Also, the phrase in Exod. 21:13 ("but the Deity [*hāʾĕlōhîm*] let him *fall into his hand*") is close to what David's men say to David about Saul ("This is the day the Lord spoke of when he said to you, 'I will *give* your enemy *into your hands* for you to deal with as you wish,'" 1 Sam. 24:4), and to what David himself says to Saul in 1 Sam. 24:10 ("This day you have seen with your own eyes how the Lord *delivered* you *into my hands* in the cave"). Like Exod. 21:13, David is not lying in wait for Saul, but he does not end Saul's life and, hence, does not need to flee.

For the intentional murderer, not even the altar provides a refuge (v. 14). I assume that this refers to any altar anywhere and not just to altars located in a "city of refuge." Note that Joab, in an (unsuccessful) attempt to save his life from Solomon's revenge, takes hold of the horns of the altar in Jerusalem, the city of David, which is neither a Levitical city nor an asylum city (1 Kings 2:28–34). Adonijah, Solomon's half brother and co-claimant to David's throne, does the same (1 Kings 1:50–53), but Solomon lets him go (for now), probably because Adonijah, unlike Joab, has no acts of homicide in his dossier.

To be sure, there are some basic differences between Exod. 21:12–14 and the altar asylum stories in 1 Kings 1–2. The most obvious difference is that Exod. 21:12–14 speaks to recent killings, not to ones that may have happened years and years ago as in the case of Joab. In discussing these two portions of Scripture, Burnside (2010: 420) raises the question of whether asylum may have been granted for criminal acts other than homicide (although Exod. 21:12–14 does restrict it to murder and killing) in later periods of Israelite history. For example, could the owner of a homicidal ox be granted asylum, or maybe a thief who believes his life is in danger for whatever reason, as Adonijah thought (1 Kings 1:51)?

All four laws end with "he shall surely be put to death" (v. 12, 15, 16, 17). When the Bible speaks of death for some infraction, it uses one of two forms. Either it is *môt yāmût* ("He shall surely die," infinitive absolute followed by the Qal of *mût*), or *môt yûmāt* ("He shall surely be put to death," infinitive absolute followed by the Hophal of *mût*). While the distinction between the two is not always maintained by the Hebrew Bible, as a general rule we can say that "He shall surely die" refers to death at God's hands, while "He shall surely be put to death" refers to death at human hands. By the way, the only other instance of *môt yûmāt* in the Covenant Code beside Exod. 21:12, 15, 16, 17 is 22:19 [18] ("Anyone who has sexual relations with an animal must be put to death").

There are two important issues here. First, should we translate *môt yûmāt* as "*must* be put to death" or "*may* be put to death"? Is the death penalty for these infractions a mandate or one possibility of several punishments? The Hebrew imperfect does not distinguish between "must" and "may," although the adding of the Qal infinitive absolute *môt* may tip the scales toward the former.

The second issue is this. The text is silent about *how* the guilty party is to be put to death, and silent about *who* is responsible for ending the life of the guilty party. One wonders if the "text's lack of interest in the details of how and by whom it is to be enforced suggest that the main intent [of these capital offenses] is less legal than moral" (Sprinkle 1994: 85). Noting the absence of any particulars of juridical procedure or any reference to the agents of the proposed measures, Gerstenberger (1995: 47, 49) observes that these "death sentences" are not "a legal sanction . . . but a signal of warning alerting people to the horrible consequences which are inherent in misconduct. . . . Death injunctions or death threats alert to the gravity of transgression; they are intended to preserve the basis of human life, but they must not be understood in legal terms."

21:15, 17 Just as vv. 12–14 reflect the sixth commandment, these two verses reflect the fifth one. The verses are close to Prov. 20:20, "If a man curses/dishonors [using the same participle, *mĕqallēl*, as Exod. 21:17] his father or mother, his lamp will be snuffed out in pitch darkness," and to Prov. 28:24, "He who robs [the participle *gôzēl*] his father and mother and says, 'It's not wrong'—he is a partner to him who destroys."

Verse 15 deals with a sin of commission against one's parent, physically and violently attacking them, while v. 17 deals more with a sin of omission against one's parents, failing to take care of them and provide for them, thus "dishonoring/neglecting" them. I prefer "dishonor" for the root *qālal* rather than "curse" (see Brichto 1963: 137–38, 165–66).

There are a wide variety of translations for this verb in the NIV. I cite three different stems: (1) Gen. 8:11, "Then Noah knew that the water *had receded* from the earth," and 1 Sam. 2:30, "Those who despise me *will be disdained*," both Qal; (2) Prov. 14:6, "Knowledge *comes easily* to the discerning," and 2 Sam. 6:22, "I will *become even more undignified* than this," both Niphals; (3) Exod. 18:22, "That will *make* your load *lighter*," and Isa. 23:9, "*to humble* all who are renowned on the earth," both Hiphils.

For the Piel stem of *qālal*, NIV most often has "curse," but that is debatable. Note this rendering in the NIV for Eli's sons: "His sons *made themselves contemptible*" (1 Sam. 3:13). The most concentrated use of *qālal* (Piel) is in 2 Sam. 6:5–14, Shimei's "cursing" David. The verb in Piel form occurs seven times (2 Sam. 16:5, 7, 9, 10 [2x], 11, 13), plus one time for the noun *qĕlālâ*, "cursing" (v. 12). The question for translation is this: does Shimei "curse" David, or does he "insult, dishonor" David?

I am not sure why these two laws are separated from each other by v. 16, which deals with kidnapping. Could it be that vv. 15–17 address the children (young or grown) of parents, while v. 16 addresses the kidnapping of children who are wrenched from their parents and on whom their parents depend? Or could it be another indication in chap. 21 of the move from topic A to topic B, then back to topic A. Note how the chapter alternates between laws about slaves and laws about free citizens: vv. 2–11 (slaves) >12–19 (free) >20–21 (slaves) >22–25 (free) >26–27 (slaves) >28–31 (free) >32 (slaves) >33–36 (free).

D. Wright (2009: 197–99) explains the order by appealing to a similar "disruption" of laws in the Code of Hammurabi. He notes that there is a series of laws (laws 192–93, 195) that deal with a child rebelling against parents. Intruding between them is a law (law 194) that deals with a completely different topic, the law of a wet-nurse who contracts for a second child. Eichler (2008: 22) argues for the logic of the sequence of all the capital cases in Exod. 21:12–17 by noting that the laws are arranged in descending order of the physical severity of the action committed, although I am not sure attacking one's parent (v. 15) is more severe than kidnapping (v. 16).

This law about the theft of persons has a parallel in Deut. 24:7, "If a man is **21:16**
caught/found kidnapping one of his brother Israelites and treats him as a slave or sells him, the kidnapper must die. You must purge the evil from among you." Both deal with stealing/kidnapping (*gānab*), and both use "found" and "sells." The one significant difference is that Deut. 24:7 restricts the law's application to one's "brother Israelite."

The language of both verses recalls similar language used in the Joseph story in Genesis. Joseph's brothers "sold" (*mākar*) him to Ishmaelites (Gen. 37:27–28), who in turn "sold" him to Potiphar (37:36). Thus Potiphar "bought" (*qānâ*) him (39:1). If Judah and his brothers were living after the revelation of the Covenant Code, they would be guilty of a capital offense. To make financial gain at the expense of one's brother, choosing fraternal enslavement over fratricide, brings death. Joseph's take on this is that he was "stolen" [*gānab*; NIV, "forcibly carried off"] from the land of the Hebrews" (40:15), using the same verb as in the kidnapping laws of Exod. 21:16 and Deut. 24:7.

A Fight Leading to a Nonpermanent Injury

(21:18–19)

Translation

18"When men quarrel (with one another), and one strikes the other with stone or with fist but he does not die, yet is bedridden, 19if he is gets up and walks outdoors on his cane, the striker shall be exonerated, except that he shall pay for the victim's loss of time and see to it that he completely recovers."

Grammatical and Lexical Notes

21:18. Limburg (1969: 295–96) notes that this is the only place where *rîb* has a reciprocal sense ("quarrel with one another"). Every other time the subject of *rîb* is only one of the parties to a dispute.

21:18. "Is bedridden" in the Hebrew is, literally, "he falls to bed" (*wĕnāpal lĕmiškāb*).

21:19. *Miš'enet* may designate a "cane, walking stick" (Exod. 21:19; Zech. 8:4), a shepherd's rod (Ps. 23:4), and a scepter or ceremonial staff (Num. 21:18; Judg. 6:21; 2 Kings 4:29, 31).

21:19. The verb *nāqâ* in the Niphal ("be exonerated") sometimes connotes vindication from guilt or erasure of obligation. Compare Gen. 24:8, "If the woman is unwilling to come back with you, then you will *be released from* this oath of mine." The same goes for the expression *nāqî min*: 24:41, "Then, when you go to my clan, you *will be released from* my oath"; 44:10, "Whoever is found to have it [Joseph's cup] will become my slave; the rest of you will be *free from blame*"; Num. 32:22, "Then when the land is subdued before the Lord, you may return and *be free from your obligation* to the Lord and to Israel"; Josh. 2:17, 19, 20, "This oath you made us swear will *not be binding*; . . . we *will not be responsible*; . . . we will be *released from* the oath you made us swear."

21:19. "Loss of time" is the Hebrew word *šebet*, which means "a sitting, resting." The progression in thought is from "sitting" to "staying at home" to "loss of time." For another possibility, see Fensham (1960), who renders *šebet* as "place, residence."

21:19. "Pay" is *nātan* ("give"), and v. 19 is one of several instances in this chapter where *nātan* = "pay" (vv. 22 [NIV, "allows"], 23 [NIV, "take"], 30 [lit., "pay/give for the redemption of"]). Together *sibto yittēn* means, literally, "He shall give him his sitting down."

21:19. "And see to it that he completely recovers" is, literally, "And he shall surely cure him" (*wĕrappō' yĕrappē'*).

Commentary

21:18–19 What starts out as a verbal altercation can develop, unfortunately, into a physical altercation. Words give way to blows, barbs give way to punches. The law presented here has a narrative parallel in Lev. 24:10, "Now the son of an Israelite mother and an Egyptian father went out among the Israelites, and a fight broke out in the camp between him and an Israelite." The verb for "a fight broke out" is *nāṣâ* II (Niphal), the same verb and stem Exod. 21:22 uses for "If men who are *fighting* hit a pregnant woman" and which Exod. 2:13 uses for Moses seeing two Hebrews *fighting*. In Lev. 24:10 at least, "quarreled" would be as good a translation as "fought." Surely words are exchanged before fists fly.

This law is not delivered to occupants of the local saloon, where fistfights are likely to break out among those who have had too much to drink. It is directed, rather, to the covenant people of God. Is this how the redeemed behave, quarreling and fighting, hitting one another with stones and bricks and anything else which an assailant can get hold of? Such actions must have been present in communities that claimed to be followers of Messiah Jesus, or else James would not have asked the question "What causes fights and quarrels among you?" (James 4:1). Instead of "fight[ing] the good fight of the faith" (1 Tim. 6:12), they are just fighting.

Those whom you wound, says v. 19, you must heal. Those whom you hurt, you must help. Costing somebody his living ("the victim's loss of time") will end up costing you. You may start out wishing the other guy were dead, but you will end up washing his feet.

But What if It's Your Slave You Beat?

(21:20–21)

Translation

[20]"Should a man strike his male slave or female slave with a rod and he dies on the spot, he must surely be avenged. [21]However, if a day or two he survives, he is not to be avenged for he (is/represents) his (master's) money-investment."

Grammatical and Lexical Notes

21:20. For other instances of *šēbeṭ* ("rod"), see Gen. 49:10 (NIV, "scepter"); 2 Sam. 18:14 (NIV, "javelin"); 23:21 (NIV, "club"); Prov. 13:24 and 23:13 (NIV, "rod"); Isa. 9:4 [3] (NIV, "rod"). Its most famous use is in Ps. 23:4b ("Your *rod* and staff, they comfort me"), one of three references that connect *šēbeṭ* with shepherding. In Lev. 27:32, the reference is most likely to a shepherd counting the sheep moving under his staff, designating every tenth one to be tithed. The third reference is Mic. 7:14: "Shepherd your people with your staff [*šēbeṭ*]."

21:20. "On the spot" or "Right there and then" is, literally, "under his hand" (*taḥat yādô*).

21:21. Yaron (1970: 553) notes that the phrase "X plus one" ("a day or two") may mean "some, several, a few," but in rules of law it has a stricter interpretation: "at least one day." Paul (1978) compares "a day or two" with a Mesopotamian medical text that reads, "If [the sick person] for a day or two (*ud.1.kam ud.2.kam*) recovers from his sickness and walks about . . ." (also see the language of Exod. 21:19 for "walks about/around").

21:21. The NIV softens the translation "If he *survives/lasts* a day or two" to "If the slave *gets up* after a day or two." The verb is *ya ʿămōd* ("he stands"). Both "survives" and "gets up" are unusual translations of *ʿāmad*.

21:21. "His money-investment" (*kaspô*) is, literally, "his money" or "his silver."

Commentary

If there is a law without which the OT would be none the less for wear, it could **21:20–21**
be this one, especially v. 21. The second verse teaches that if the battered slave survives at least twenty-four hours before he breathes his last, his master is off the hook for the massive beating he has given his slave. One would have to hit another quite hard and repeatedly to bring about the other's death. And is

the master's impunity because (1) his intentions were innocent or (2) because the slave is but his property and his master's money?

If the slave dies that day, he "must surely be avenged" (*nāqōm yinnāqēm*). If the slave lasts for twenty-four hours before he expires, he is "not to be avenged" (*lō' yuqqam*). What does *nāqōm yinnāqēm* mean, and is it the same as *môt yûmāt* ("he must surely be put to death") in the preceding laws? The SP simply reads *môt yûmāt*. The LXX renders it *dikē ekdikēthētō* ("Let him be justly punished") and *ouk ekdikēthēsetai* ("He shall not be punished"). But punished how? A number of suggestions for interpretation have been forthcoming: (1) "be punished" means the master must pay a fine (to somebody; see S. Driver 1911: 218; M. Klein 1979: 159); (2) "be punished" by Israelite justice since the (foreign) slave has no *gô'ēl haddām* (cf. Num. 35:19–27) to avenge his blood (see Greenberg 1962: 738)—even if the victim is an Israelite slave, the slave might not have a family near where his death has taken place, and often slaves live away from their native place (see Greenberg 1986: 13–14); (3) vicarious punishment, that is, an equivalent member of the master's household must be similarly punished (see Westbrook 1988: 89–100); (4) "be surely punished" is simply another way of saying "be surely put to death" as the SP has it (see Jackson 2006: 246–48).

The root *nqm* occurs seventy-nine times in the Hebrew Bible in fifty-nine texts. It never refers to private blood revenge but denotes a right execution of punishment forbidden to humans but exacted by God. He is the "God of vengeance" (*'ēl-nĕqāmôt* [Ps. 94:1]; *'ēl . . . nōqēm* [Nah. 1:2]). The true follower of the Lord leaves the taking of vengeance to God (1 Sam. 24:12; Jer. 11:20; 15:15; 20:12). Sometimes the Lord explicitly assigns the task of taking *nqm* to humans (Num. 31:2–3; Josh. 10:13). Where the framework of legitimacy is absent, *nqm* degenerates into something pejorative like "revenge" (Lev. 19:18; Pss. 8:2 [3]; 44:16 [17]; Jer. 20:10).

An Eye for an Eye

(21:22–25)

Translation

[22]"Should men fight and collide with a pregnant passerby and her fetus emerges, with no serious damage ensuing [to the mother? the fetus?], he [the culprit] shall surely be punished according to what the woman's husband imposes upon him, or he shall pay according to what the judges [establish]. [23]But if serious damage ensues [to the woman? the fetus?], you shall pay life as the penalty for life, [24]eye as the penalty for eye, tooth as the penalty for tooth, hand as the penalty for hand, foot as the penalty for foot, [25]burn as the penalty for burn, wound as the penalty for wound, bruise as the penalty for bruise."

Grammatical and Lexical Notes

21:22. The Hebrew does not designate how many men are brawling. It could be two or a melee. The LXX reads *duo andres* ("two men"), probably because the Hebrew word for "fight" (*nāṣâ*, Niphal) often refers to a fight involving two parties: two Hebrews (Exod. 2:13), a half-Egyptian and an Israelite (Lev. 24:10), two men (Deut. 25:11), two sons (2 Sam. 14:6), Dathan and Abiram (Num. 26:9, the Hiphil, for which NIV has "rebelled"). See N. Collins 1993: 299.

21:22. The verb for "collide with" is *nāgap*, which appears again in the law in 21:35 to refer to a bull/ox "injuring, kicking against" another bull/ox.

21:22. The literal Hebrew for "her fetus emerges" is "her children [pl.] come forth [*wĕyāṣĕʾû yĕlādêhā*]." Sprinkle (1994: 93) correctly calls it "the plural *yldyh* implying an abstract, 'child-product, fruit of the womb,' or the like, an apt term for a stillborn baby." The LXX has "and her little one comes forth not fully formed" (*kai exelthē to paidion autēs mē exeikonismenon*). GKC §124i and Gordis (1976b: 376) call it a "distributive plural." SP reads the phrase as a singular: "and her child comes out [*wĕyāṣāʾ wĕlādāh*]."

21:22. I leave commentary on *ʾāsôn* ("serious damage"), here and in v. 23, for below.

21:22. The verb for "punished" here is *ʿānaš* (with preceding infinitive absolute), as the verb for "avenged" in v. 20 was *nāqam* (with preceding absolute infinitive).

21:22. For the verb *šît*, meaning "to place," in a legal context referring to the imposition of a penalty, see Exod. 21:30 and Num. 12:11 (NIV, "hold against"). The LXX's translation of *šît* in Exod. 21:22 is *epiballō*, one that is used in classical Greek for imposing a fine or a penalty. See Rabinowitz 1961: 68n2.

21:22. As with *ʾāsōn* (see note above), there is much debate about the meaning of *biplilîm* ("as the judges [establish]"), on which I shall comment below.

21:23–24. Each of the "as the penalty for" in these verses is the preposition *taḥat* ("under"), as in *nepeš taḥat nepeš* ("life *as the penalty for* life"). The Leviticus version of the lex talionis also uses the preposition *taḥat* (Lev. 24:19–20), but the version in Deuteronomy (19:21) uses the preposition *bĕ*, the so-called *bêt pretii* (the *bêt* of price). I take it that *taḥat* and *bĕ* are synonymous in this instance. See also the use of *taḥat* with this sense in 21:26 (*taḥat ʿênô*); 21:27 (*taḥat šinnô*); 21:36 (*šôr taḥat haššôr*); and 22:1 [21:37] (*taḥat haššôr* and *taḥat haśśeh*).

Commentary

21:22–25 Once again we encounter in the Covenant Code the phenomenon of a seeming disruption in sequence of subject matter. Earlier, two laws appeared that focused on mistreating one's parents (Exod. 21:15, 17) with one about kidnapping coming in between (Exod. 21:16). Here, we have two laws that deal with abusing one's slave/servant (Exod. 21:20–21, 26–27). Sandwiched between them is this law on fighting men striking, inadvertently, a woman who is pregnant (Exod. 21:22–25).

More than likely most people of faith would never have heard, or thought much, about this particular old covenant law if Jesus had not quoted it and made commentary on it in Matt. 5:38–41, "You have heard that it was said, 'Eye for eye, and tooth for tooth.' But I tell you . . ." Scholars often refer to it as the lex talionis, "the law of the tooth" or "the law of the claw/talon." It does not appear that Jesus rejected out of hand either the basic legal principle of the penalty matching the offense or the legitimate desire for redress. His support of "an eye for an eye" appears to be reflected in his statement that those who do not forgive will not be forgiven (Matt. 6:15). Refuse to forgive? Then live with no forgiveness yourself. See Goldingay 2009: 446.

This law actually appears three times in the Pentateuch, but always in a different context. In Exodus it stands alone in the Covenant Code, between two laws dealing with injuries to slaves, one of which involves the slave's "eye" and "tooth" (21:26–27). In Leviticus it follows the law about the blasphemer (24:10–16, then 17–22). In Deuteronomy it appears in conjunction with a law about false testimony (19:15–21). This last formulation of the law intends to deter false testimony by saying the false witness will receive the same punishment that his testimony would have brought on the falsely accused.

Apart from the lex talionis, the only other law in Scripture that includes maiming as the punishment is the one dealing with the wife who grabs/damages the genitals of the man who is fighting with her husband (Deut. 25:11–12). The penalty: "you shall cut off her hand," and the Hebrew for the maimed part is *kap*, not *yād*. In Exod. 21 it is a woman who is hit, but in Deut. 25 it is a woman who does the hitting.

It is unlikely that the lex talionis was literally enforced, at least most parts of it. The exception is "a life for a life." There is only one clear or literal instance of its implementation in the Bible. In Judg. 1:6–7 the Judahites capture and pay back Adoni-Bezek, king of the Canaanites, who has cut off the thumbs and big toes of seventy kings, by slicing off his thumbs and big toes. Apart from homicide (for which there is no commutation of the death penalty), one would think that the law mandates financial compensation equivalent to the severity of the injury. Hartley (1992: lxii) puts it nicely: "This principle does not imply that punishment was carried out by inflicting bodily injury in kind, but that punishment for harm to a person is to be commensurate with the harm done, not greater as revenge dictates, nor less as indulgence desires." For the well-heeled and well-connected person, it cannot be "a tooth for a life." For the masses of the less-heeled and more vulnerable, it cannot be "a life for a tooth." It is, rather, the principle of equal justice for all, regardless of who they are and what their status is. Accordingly, the primary emphasis is not on the exacting of vengeance in kind, but on a limitation of such vengeance. It must not exceed the injury.

As we saw above, there are two Hebrew words in this law that are difficult to translate, on which skilled Hebraists have multiple opinions. The first is *ʾāsôn* in vv. 22–23, which I have rendered "serious damage." Even if that is the best English equivalent, do we understand the verses to refer to life-threatening or life-ending damage (1) to the fetus or (2) to the pregnant woman? If it is view 2, then v. 22 refers to some nonserious, nonfatal injury to the pregnant woman, while v. 23 refers to some serious, fatal blow to her that either severely harms her or ends her life. If it is view 1, then v. 22 refers to premature parturition, while v. 23 refers to miscarriage. Is the text deliberately vague so as to be multi-interpretational at this point? Can it be "both . . . and" rather than "either . . . or"? More-conservative interpreters lean toward view 1 (damage to the fetus), and such an interpretation lends much support to the value and the humanity of the fetus, strong ammunition in the abortion debate (see Kline 1977; House 1978). Some conservative interpreters, however, believe that *ʾāsôn* refers only to anything that happens to the woman (Sprinkle 1993; 1994: 89, 93). Even the ancient versions are uncertain. The Vulgate connects the word with the mother, while the LXX connects the word with the fetus.

Outside of these two verses in Exod. 21, the Hebrew word *ʾāsôn* occurs again only in Gen. 42:4, 38; 44:29, all of which express Jacob's concern that "harm" might come to Benjamin if he sends him off to Egypt. Here are three possibilities for *ʾāsôn* in Exod. 21 argued by informed scholarship: (1) *ʾāsôn* = "damage caused by an unknown perpetrator" (Westbrook 1986: 56–57); (2) *ʾāsôn* = the woman's death (Loewenstamm 1977: 358; D. Wright [2010: 548–49], whose study of this law and its relationship to corresponding laws in Hammurabi's Code is filled with much insight regarding similarities and differences); (3) *ʾāsôn* = the death of the fetus (Jackson 2006: 216–20).

One wonders, however, why this law uses the rare word *ʾāsôn* rather than the more common expression "and she dies," or "and he/it dies" as it did just before, in the law in vv. 18 and 20, and which is how *Targum Onqelos* has it. Here is where the three Genesis references cited above may help us. Jacob does not say, "What if Benjamin dies!" but "What if harm befalls him!" One can hear the angst, the emotion, and the breaking of his voice with the use of that vocabulary. Jacob uses emotionally charged phraseology rather than "objective language" ("he dies"). As Bartor (2007: 243–44) argues, the lawgiver has intentionally used an emotionally laden word to convey the deep pain and sorrow and shock the survivors of this family would surely experience, regardless of who dies. Bartor calls this "combined discourse": the narrator, through the use of such a noun, imbeds within his utterance the attitude and feelings of other characters.

The other word that is much debated in this law is the last one in v. 22, *biplilîm* "[or he shall pay] according to what the judges [establish]." The NIV has "and the court allows," and NRSV has "as the judges determine." The noun *pālîl* (plural in 21:22) occurs again only in Deut. 32:31b, for which NIV has "as even our enemies *concede*," and in Job 31:11 for which NIV has, "For that would have been shameful, a sin *to be judged*." But there are other possibilities for translating these two latter verses. For example, Speiser (1963b: 302–3) translates Deut. 32:31b as "even in our enemies' *estimation*," and so renders the end of Exod. 21:22 as "according to estimate," which is close to LXX's *meta axiōmatos* ("with judicial assessment"). Westbrook (1986: 58–61) has for the end of Exod. 21:22, "he shall pay *alone*," meaning that the term designates sole responsibility. Berlin (1989: 347) refines Westbrook's idea by suggesting that the basic meaning of *pll* is "be held accountable/responsible/liable," and so she has "he shall pay *as the culpable party*." Carmichael (1986: 35–36), followed by Jackson (2006: 226), renders the *wāw* on *wĕnātan* as "*or* he shall pay" rather than "*and* he shall pay," and comes up with the translation, "He [the one who struck her] shall be strictly fined according as the woman's husband shall lay upon him, *or he shall pay through judges*." That is the reading that makes most sense to me.

It is well known that *pālîl* and *pĕlilî* both derive from the verb *pālal*, which means "pray, intercede" in the Hitpallel stem, and which verb also produces the noun *tĕpillâ*, one of the Hebrew nouns for "prayer." The verb in this stem appears in the Pentateuch only in Gen. 20:7, 17; Num. 11:2; 21:7; Deut. 9:20, 26, with the meaning "pray for somebody," but is much more common in the books of Samuel and Kings. Both the Piel and Hitpallel stems of this verb appear in 1 Sam. 2:25, which in the NIV is, "If a man sins against another man, God *may mediate* [Piel] for him; but if a man sins against the Lord, who *will intercede* [Hitpallel] for him?"

So how does one get nouns meaning "judge, judgment" or an adjective like "punishable" from a verb meaning "pray, intercede"? Possibly the Hitpallel of this verb means "to open, submit oneself to God's judgment." One who prays is petitioning God, asking to be judged worthy, and accordingly, to have the prayer request answered.

Injuring One's Servant

(21:26–27)

Translation

[26]"Should a man strike the eye of his male slave or the eye of his female slave and destroy it, he must grant him his freedom in repayment for the eye. [27]And should he knock out the tooth of his male slave or female slave, he must grant him his freedom in repayment for the tooth."

Commentary

Conceivably this law might have been condensed into one sentence—"Should **21:26–27**
a man strike the eye or tooth of his . . ." But it contains two distinct sentences, one for the eye and one for the tooth. In both the beating is deliberate, but the injury is accidental, thus separating this law from the one in vv. 22–25, in which the hitting or colliding was accidental. All would agree that there is a significant difference between losing an eye and losing a tooth. If we need to choose between the two, the choice would not be difficult. But no such distinction is here. Either the infliction of a major injury or a minor injury wins freedom for the slave. Brichto (1998: 410) says this is so because the slave is not a slave. "He is not the property of his master. He belongs to himself. The only claim the master has upon him is not on his person but on his *time*. And the slightest impairment of his person, the slightest invasion—so to speak—of his capital, must eventuate in the end of his servitude."

The Injuring and Injured Ox

(21:28–36)

Translation

[28]"And should an ox gore a man or woman, and he dies, the ox shall surely be stoned. Its meat shall not be eaten, and the ox's owner is in the clear. [29]If the ox is a gorer from times past and was warned about to its owner, who nevertheless did not restrain it, and it killed a man or a woman, the ox shall be stoned, and also its owner put to death. [30]If expiation is established for him, he shall pay the redemption price of his life according to whatever is established for him. [31]Whether a son it gores or a daughter it gores, according to this principle it shall be done to him. [32]If a male slave the ox gores or a female slave, thirty shekels of silver he shall pay to its master, and the ox shall be stoned.

[33]"And should a man open a cistern or should a man excavate a well and does not put a cover on it and an ox or ass falls down it, [34]the cistern's owner shall make restitution with silver and so compensate its owner, but the dead animal remains his.

[35]"Should a man's ox collide with his neighbor's ox and it dies, they shall sell the live ox and divide equally its selling price, and the dead animal they shall also divide equally. [36]Or if it is known that the ox is a gorer from times past, but its owner did not restrain it, he must surely make restitution, ox in exchange for an ox, but the dead animal remains his."

Grammatical and Lexical Notes

21:28. Verses 28–32 and 35–36 account for six of thirteen uses of *nāgaḥ* ("gore") and *naggāḥ* ("gorer") in the Hebrew Bible (vv. 28, 29, 31 [2x], 32, 36).

21:28. "The ox shall surely be stoned, . . . *and* the ox's owner is in the clear" is an inclusive sentence rather than a contrastive one, and so I use "and" rather than "but." If it had been a contrastive sentence (*"but* the ox's owner is in the clear"), the Hebrew would have been *haššôr yissāqēl* . . . *ûbaʿal haššôr nāqî*. See Andersen 1974: 159–60.

21:29, 36. Both times the LXX reads "and did not destroy it" (*aphanisē auton*), rather than "and did not restrain it," taking the Hebrew verb as *šāmad* rather than as *šāmar*.

21:30. For other uses in the Pentateuch of *kōper* ("expiation, ransom, restitution") see Exod. 30:12; Num. 35:31, 32 (NIV has "ransom" for all three, but "payment" in Exod. 21:30).

21:30. For *šît ʿal* ("established for") at the start and end of the verse, see the same in v. 22 above ("impose upon").

21:30. *pidyōn* ("redemption price"), and again in Ps. 49:8 [9]. In Num. 3:49 the word is written *pidyōm* (with a final *m* instead of an *n*).

21:34. The sequence *yĕšallēm . . . yāšîb* ("He shall make restitution . . . compensate") appears in the goring-ox law in Hammurabi's Code (number 125): *u-sha-lam-ma . . . i-ri-a-ab*, "He shall make restitution . . . and restore (it)."

21:34, 36. Gordis (1976b: 347) points out that the accusative after *šālēm* generally represents the debt or obligation being discharged (Exod. 21:34, silver; Exod. 21:36, an ox; Exod. 22:6 [5], starting a spreading fire, *hammabʿir*; 2 Sam. 12:6, a lamb, *kibšâ*; 2 Kings 4:7, a debt, *nišyēk*; Prov. 19:17, a reward, *gĕmul*; Joel 2:25, years [the locust have eaten], *haššānîm*). Exodus 21:34 may be the one case where in a legal text the Piel of *šālēm* refers to restitution through a monetary equivalent rather than to a literal restoration either of the same object (ox for ox in v. 36) or in kind. See, however, Milgrom's (1976b) reservations.

21:34. This verse contains the first of fourteen uses of *šālēm* (Qal, "be whole"; Piel, "make whole, restore") in the following laws: 21:36; 22:1 [21:27], 3, 4, 5, 6, 7, 9, 11, 12, 13, 14, 15 [2, 3, 4, 5, 6, 8, 10, 11, 12, 13, 14]. In all instances the verb (in Piel) refers to an individual who must make good some loss for which he is responsible.

21:35. The word for "collide" (*nāgap*) is the same as that used back in v. 22 for fighting men who "collided" with a pregnant woman. In v. 28 the issue is the ox "goring [with its horn]" (*nāgaḥ*) a human. In v. 35 the issue is the ox "colliding" (*nāgap*) with another ox. The use of *nāgap*, rather than a repeat of *nāgaḥ*, would seem to allow for injuries other than those inflicted by goring.

21:35. The Hebrew verb for "divide equally" is *ḥāṣâ*; also see Num. 31:27 ("*Divide* the spoils between the soldiers who took part in the battle and the rest of the community"). From the verb comes the noun *ḥăṣî* ("half"). Naphtali's oldest son is Jahziel (*yaḥăṣîʾēl*, "God divides," 1 Chron. 7:13). See Falk 1969: 40–41.

21:35. Note the shift in the placement of the objects of the verbs: "they shall sell the live ox" (verb + object); "and divide equally its selling price" (verb + object); "and also the dead animal they shall divide equally" (object + verb), thus creating a chiasm.

21:36. This verse and v. 31 are two of the rare laws in the Code that contain a verse beginning with the word "or" (*ʾô*) rather than with *kî* or *ʾim*.

Commentary

Jackson (2006: 256) rightly says, "The goring ox must count as the most celebrated animal in legal history. . . . This beast has attracted an almost obsessive interest." To support that statement, I cite parallel laws from Hammurabi's Code and the Laws of Eshnunna (with translations from M. Roth 1997: 128 and 67 respectively): **21:28–36**

A. Hammurabi laws 250–52:

250. When an ox gores a man to death when it walks in the street, there is no reason for a process.
251. If a man's ox is known to gore, and his city has told him, and he does not cut its horns and control his ox, and this ox gores a man to death, he shall pay a half mina of silver.
252. If it is a man's slave, he shall pay a mina of silver.

B. Eshnunna Laws 53–55:

53. When an ox gores a(nother) ox to death, the owners of the oxen shall share the value of the living ox and the cadaver of the dead.
54. If an ox is (known as) a gorer, and the city has told its owner, but he has not looked after his ox, and it gores a man to death, he shall pay one-third of a mina of silver.
55. If it gores a slave to death, he shall pay fifteen shekels of silver.

There are obvious similarities about the Mesopotamian laws and Exod. 21: the goring ox that takes a human life, the carelessness of the owner in not protecting other citizens from an ox who has a history of injuring folk, and the set price if the ox kills a slave.

There are also some differences between the ox law of Exod. 21 and the other two. First, neither of these two say anything about the ox being stoned and its meat not eaten (Exod. 21:28). Only in the biblical law is there a significant economic loss for the owner of the ox. Second, only in biblical law is the negligent owner of the habitual gorer guilty of a capital crime, for which he must die or ransom himself (21:29–30). Third, the Exod. 21 law alone provides a subcase (21:31), one that deals with serious injury or death to a minor. And finally, the other two ancient Near Eastern laws say nothing about the ox's killing a woman or a daughter.

To provide a contemporary analogy, Brettler (2005: 69–71) compares the law in v. 28 to a person's driving a car with defective brakes, but of which he is totally unaware. If the driver of such an automobile hits and injures/kills a person, the driver's actions are unintentional, and he is not even negligent. In the law of v. 29, the driver has taken his car in for an inspection. The inspector has told him that the brakes are defective, and he should not drive until he has had them fixed. He drives his car anyway and is involved in a serious accident with a pedestrian because his brakes do not work adequately enough. Here there is negligence. One might also suggest that for mail deliverers, another analogy would be a dog who, otherwise so docile, one day nips at the leg of the mail carrier; because he is not on a leash or behind a fence, the mean-tempered, growling, teeth-baring dog is able to close his jaws on the mail carrier's leg.

There is an interesting structure to these nine verses: (1) a goring ox that causes serious injury or death to a human (vv. 28–32); (2) an ox falls into a hole somebody left uncovered and dies (vv. 33–34); (3) a goring ox that kills another ox (vv. 35–36). It seems that vv. 33–34 interrupt two laws about goring oxen (one ox that gores humans, and one ox that gores other oxen).

In two long essays on this law, Finkelstein (1973; 1981) explains the structure as follows. Verses 33–34 separate the law about an ox that kills a human from an ox that kills another ox (rather than running them together) to show that in the biblical way of thinking, the taking of human life is far more critical than the taking of any other form of life. Homicide is far more serious and carries greater consequences than bovicide, what Finkelstein calls a "Law of Persons" versus a "Law of Things."

That is certainly possible, but as Jackson (2006: 268) has observed, it may simply be a case of literary pattern: ox versus human (vv. 28–32); human versus ox (vv. 33–34); ox versus ox (vv. 35–36).

This may be the only time the Covenant Code mandates a specific form of lethal punishment. The goring ox is to be stoned (v. 29), the one time in Scripture where a killer is to be stoned. I assume that this means "stoned until it is dead," rather than simply "stoned" until it backs off the poor victim it is goring and runs away. Otherwise, why does the text add, "and its meat shall not be eaten"?

That raises a problem. How does one stone a half-ton, aggressive, homicidal ox whose testosterone flow is at flood level? He that is without fear, let him cast the first stone. An ox can weigh anywhere between five hundred and three thousand pounds, with an average weight somewhere between one thousand and two thousand pounds. Here we are not dealing with a voracious sheep that is nibbling its shepherd to death.

Perhaps it is the truth embedded in this law that is crucial rather than its actual implementation. It would be like the law in Deut. 22:8, which urges the building of a parapet around the roof of one's house to protect strollers on the roof from falling off. Take responsibility for what is yours. Keep Fido fenced in or on a leash, and put a fence around your swimming pool.

Thieves and Thievery

(22:1–4 [21:37–22:3])

Translation

[22:1 [21:37]] "Should a man steal an ox or kid and slaughter it or sell it, five cattle he shall repay in exchange for the ox, and four sheep in exchange for the kid. [22:2 [22:1]] If in the act of tunneling in, the thief is apprehended and struck dead, he [the homeowner?] has no bloodguilt. [3 [2]] If, however, the crime was perpetrated in broad daylight, he is liable. But [the thief] must make full restitution. If he is dirt poor, he shall be handed over to the person he was to pay for his thievery. [4 [3]] If what was stolen should indeed be discovered alive in his possession, any domesticated animal whether stock or draft, he shall pay double."

Grammatical and Lexical Notes

22:1 [21:37]. "Cattle" or "herd" (*bāqār*) is here a collective noun.

22:2 [1]. The noun *maḥteret* ("tunneling") appears again only in Jer. 2:34 ("though you did not catch them *breaking in*"). I will have more to say on this Jeremiah verse below. The verb *ḥātar* describes "digging, tunneling" activity in which Ezekiel engages (Ezek. 8:8; 12:5, 7, 12).

22:2 [1]. The antecedent of "he" in "he has no bloodguilt" could be either the thief or the homeowner, but v. 3 tilts it in favor of the latter.

22:3 [2]. Rather than translating *wĕnimkar bignēbātô* "he shall be sold for his theft," I render, "he shall be handed over for [*mākar bĕ*] his thievery," following Falk 1967: 243.

22:4 [3]. I take *miššôr ʿad-ḥămôr ʿad-śeh* as a merism ("any domesticated animal, whether stock or draft"). See Honeyman 1952: 13.

Commentary

22:1–4 [21:37–22:3] It is crystal clear that these four verses deal with thievery, either cattle rustling (22:1, 4 [21:37; 22:3]) or breaking and entering another domicile (22:2–3 [1–2]), and hence they expand on the eighth commandment. It is not as clear why the text starts with thievery of cattle, moves to thievery via housebreaking, then returns to thievery of cattle. Some modern translations try to make the text's movement more "logical." The RSV, for example, arranges the sequence of verses as 22:1, 4, 2, 3. The rearrangement in the NRSV is even more extensive:

22:1, 3b, 4, 2, 3a [21:37; 22:2b, 3, 1, 2a]. Sprinkle (1994: 130–34) nicely surveys the different suggestions scholars have offered and then presents a commonsense solution, noting that vv. 2–3a [1–2a] form a kind of parenthetical remark. Levinson (2008: 216) calls vv. 2–3a [1–2a] "an interpolation in which a redactor revises an original law to reflect upon the moral and ethical limits to self-help."

The text does not comment on the motive for stealing. The thief is described as possibly "dirt poor" (v. 3 [2]). There are very few thieves who are wealthy except those who engage in crimes like fraud and extortion. Normally they are paupers, either because they are lazy and irresponsible and so want the "easy buck" or because they are victims of circumstances over which they have no control, such as losing one's job or house and thus losing the ability to provide for one's family. Regardless, the text is clear that thievery is never justifiable. But not all acts of thievery are equally heinous. Here the assessed penalty for the apprehended thief is 300 or 400 percent (atop restitution) if he has irreparably damaged what he stole (22:1 [21:37]), and 200 percent if he has not damaged, either through slaughter or sale, what he stole (v. 4 [3]). In the case where the thief has stolen something and even lied about it under oath, but then returned the stolen material undamaged (Lev. 6:1–7 [5:20–26]), the penalty is 20 percent. The penalty slides downward for returning damaged versus undamaged goods and for apprehension versus voluntarily turning oneself in. Still, restitution is at the heart of every penalty for theft. Even forgiveness does not cancel the need for making amends.

There are two (or three) later portions of Scripture that reflect this particular law in the Covenant Code. One is Jer. 2:34 (alluded to above in the first grammatical note on 22:2 [1]). In this prophetic text God has caught Israel red-handed (*in flagrante delicto*) in the overt course of its covenant violation: "on your clothes men *find* the life*blood* of the innocent poor, though you did not catch them *breaking in*." I have put in italics three words Jer. 2:34 shares with Exod. 22:1–4: "find," *māṣāʾ*; "blood," *dām*; "breaking in, tunneling," *maḥteret*. The parallels suggest that what was, to begin with, a prophetic rebuke is now a legal indictment, in this case, the immoral abuse of the innocent (see Fishbane 1980: 351–52; 1985: 312–13).

The second reflection of this law is to be found in 2 Sam. 12:5–6, David's angry outburst to Nathan, "As surely as the LORD lives, the man who did this deserves to die. He must pay for that lamb *four times* over" (LXX has "seven" times over, and was possibly influenced by Prov. 6:30–31, "Yet if he [the thief] is caught, he must pay *sevenfold*," spoken in the larger context, ironically, of a section in Proverbs that deals with adultery à la David).

Close to David's words in 2 Sam. 12:6 [MT] are those of Zacchaeus in Luke 19:8, "And if I have cheated anybody out of anything, I will pay back *four times* the amount." Fitzmyer (1985: 1225) provides other illustrations of fourfold restitution from both Roman law and from Semitic texts near Qumran.

What makes Zacchaeus's words so refreshing is that he volunteers to do this. Jesus has not brought it up. That is surely one evidence of a moment of life change that comes from meeting Messiah. Thievery and following Jesus are mutually exclusive. To quote Paul (Eph. 4:28), "He who has been stealing must steal no longer."

Grazing Beasts and Spreading Fire

(22:5–6 [22:4–5])

Translation

5 [4] "Should a man trample down a field or vineyard [with cattle], having driven his cattle, and tramples in another's field, from the best of his field and from the best of his vineyard he shall make restitution.

6 [5] "When fire breaks out igniting thorn-bushes so that stacked or standing grain or the field is consumed, the one who lit the fire shall surely make restitution."

Grammatical and Lexical Notes

22:5 [4]. The two nouns "field [or] vineyard" (*śādeh ʾô-kerem*) are frequently paired in the Hebrew Bible (Num. 20:17; 21:22; 1 Sam. 8:14). They appear in parallel to each other in Job 24:6; Ps. 107:37; Prov. 24:30; Song 7:11a, 12a [12a, 13a]. These two words represent the two basic types of farming and productive land: sown fields of grain and areas for fruit-bearing vines and trees.

22:5 [4]. For the Piel of *šālaḥ* to refer to the "driving/dispatching" of animals or birds, see Gen. 8:7, 8, 10; Lev. 14:7, 53 (NIV, "sent/release" birds); Lev. 16:10 (NIV, "sending it [a live goat] into the wilderness"); Num. 21:6 (NIV, "sent . . . snakes").

22:5 [4]. It is possible to translate "having driven his cattle" as "when he lets his cattle graze." In such a case the *wāw* on *wĕšillaḥ* means "when," with the second verb (*šillaḥ*) preceding in time the first verb *yabʿer* ("trample down"). For another illustration of *wāw* = "when," compare elderly Jacob's words to Joseph in Gen. 47:30, "When I rest [*wĕšākabtî*] with my fathers, carry me out of Egypt."

Commentary

22:5–6 [4–5]

There are two reasons why these two laws are next to each other. One of these reasons is obvious to the person reading the text in English. Both laws deal with the same kind of issue: your animals or a fire you have started on your property ends up, through your negligence, damaging the property of a neighbor. Your cattle trample his field. What has started as controlled burning in your backyard becomes an out-of-control inferno, consuming everything in its path (Prov. 30:16, "And fire, which never says 'Enough!'").

There is another connection that is transparent only in the Hebrew. The Hebrew word for "trample [down]" (2x in v. 5 [4]) is *bāʿar*. It first is in the

Hiphil (*yabʿer*) and then in the Piel (*ûbiʿēr*). Also, the word for "his cattle" in v. 5 [4] is *bĕʿîrōh* (= *bĕʿîrô*), meaning beasts or animals capable of trampling good pastureland.

In the second law, v. 6 [5], the root *bʿr* occurs again, but this time with the meaning "light a fire" ("the one who lit the fire" [*hammabʿir ʾet-habbĕʿērâ*]). Thus in v. 5 [4] *bāʿar* = "trample," but in v. 6 [5] *bāʿar* = "light a fire." Both stamping hoofs and raging infernos have the capacity to destroy completely anything that is in their path. This idea of *bāʿar* to convey the idea of total destruction and riddance, by whatever means, may explain its metaphoric use in Deuteronomy for Moses's challenge to the people to "purge" all the evil inside and around them (Deut. 13:5 [6]; 17:7, 12; 19:13, 19; 21:21; 22:24; 24:7).

Depositors and Depositees

(22:7–13 [22:6–12])

Translation

[7 [6]]"Should a man give his neighbor money or goods to safekeep, and it is stolen from the man's house, if the thief is discovered, he shall make double restitution. [8 [7]]If the thief is not discovered, the house's owner shall be brought to the Deity [to prove] he has not laid his hand on his neighbor's property.

[9 [8]]"Concerning any kind of a trespass—an ox, a donkey, a kid, a cloak, or any missing thing—about which one may say, 'This is it,' the disputation of these two [a man and his neighbor] shall come to the Deity. The one whom God declares guilty shall make double restitution to his neighbor.

[10 [9]]"Should a man give his neighbor a donkey or an ox or a kid or any animal to safekeep, and it dies or is injured or carried off, but nobody was around to see anything, [11 [10]]there shall be an oath of the LORD between the two of them, [to prove] he has not laid his hand on his neighbor's property, and by which its owner must abide, and he [the neighbor] need not make any restitution. [12 [11]]If it was indeed stolen from him, he shall make restitution to its owner. [13 [12]]If it was mauled to pieces [by predators], he shall bring it as evidence. He need not make restitution with respect to what was mauled."

Grammatical and Lexical Notes

22:7 [6]. The verb "it is stolen" (*wĕgunnab*) is singular, but the subject of the verb is the plural, coordinated "money or goods." For other illustrations of this, see Lev. 25:49 (plural, coordinated subject "or his uncle or his cousin" + masculine, singular verb "may redeem him"); Deut. 13:2–3 (plural, coordinated subject "a miraculous sign or wonder" + masculine, singular verb "it takes place").

22:8 [7]. The verb *qārab* is used in two different stems in a juridical context: (1) Here, the Niphal (*niqrab*), "shall be brought before the Deity," appears, and also in Josh. 7:14, "in the morning *present yourselves* tribe by tribe." The Hiphil appears in Num. 27:5 for Moses's *bringing the case* of Zelophehad's daughters to the Lord.

22:8 [7]. *Ba῾al-habbayit* ("the house's owner") is the same as Akkadian *bêl biti(m)* and Ugaritic *b῾l bt*. Ugaritic also has the phrase *b῾it bhtm* ("Mistress of the House[s]") an epithet of a goddess and a title of honor for a free woman.

22:8 [7]. The more usual preposition after *qārab* for bringing somebody near somebody or something is *ʾel*. However, when one comes near God, the preposition tends to be *lipnê* ("near"), perhaps to soften the idea, conveyed by *qārab ʾel*, that one can go right up to deity (see Exod. 16:9; Lev. 3:1, 7; 6:14 [7]; 10:1; Num. 3:4; 6:16; 17:4). But *qārab ʾel* may be used too for coming near God (Exod. 22:8 [7]; 1 Sam. 14:36; Isa. 48:16; Ezek. 44:15).

22:8 [7]. The Hebrew word *mĕlāʾkâ* ("property"), here and in v. 11 [10], most often means "work, labor, service." In Gen. 33:14 the word refers to Jacob's "livestock [NIV, "droves"]." See also 1 Sam. 15:9, where *mĕlakah* refers to Agag's lesser-quality animals, which Saul does not spare. And 2 Chron. 17:13 uses the word to refer to the large "supplies" King Jehoshaphat has in the cities of Judah.

22:9 [8]. The words "an ox . . . or any missing thing" are in apposition to "concerning any kind of a trespass," and hence the reason why I set them off with hyphens. In such a list the preposition that governs the head noun (*ʿal-kol-dĕbar-pešaʿ*) is repeated before each item in the list (*ʿal-šôr*, *ʿal-ḥămôr*, etc.). See Lev. 1:2; Deut. 14:26; and 1 Kings 2:5 for other examples of this, and Joüon and Muraoka (1991: 131i).

22:9 [8]. "Declare guilty" is the Hiphil imperfect of *rāšaʿ*. The verb is a third-person plural (*yaršîʿun*, and appears without the final *-n* in Ps. 94:21, *yaršîʿû* [NIV, "condemn"]). For other instances where *ʾĕlōhîm* is used with plural verbs, see Gen. 20:13; 31:53; 35:7; 2 Sam. 7:23 (but the parallel verse in 1 Chron. 17:21 uses the singular, *hālak* versus *hālĕkû*). The noun *ʾĕlōhîm* appears with a plural participle in Ps. 58:11 [12] (*ʾĕlōhîm šôpĕṭîm*). Last, one finds the expression "living [pl.] God" (*ʾĕlōhîm ḥayyîm*) in Deut. 5:26 [23]; 1 Sam. 17:26, 36; Jer. 10:10.

22:10 [9]. Fishbane (1985: 170–71) suggests that "or any animal" is a secondary expansion since it shows a shift from naming specific stolen animals to a general statement ("or any animal"). But Avalos (1990) points out that one finds the same sequences in Akkadian laws with variants of the phrase *mimma shumshu* ("or anything else whatsoever"). He cites law 7 in Hammurabi's Code: "If a man silver or gold, or slave, or a girl, or an ox or a sheep, or an ass, or anything else whatsoever [*ù lu mi-im-ma shumshu*] from a man's son . . . buys or for safekeeping has received them . . ."

22:10 [9]. For other instances where the verb *šābar* is used to refer to animals that have suffered serious injury (here and in v. 14 [13], *nišbār* ["is injured"]), see Lev. 22:22; Ezek. 34:4; Zech. 11:16 (metaphorically understanding Israel as "injured sheep"). The cognate Akkadian verb *sheberu* also has the same semantic range: it may refer to seriously injured humans or animals. See *CAD* Sh/2:249–50.

22:10 [9]. The Niphal of *šābâ* ("carried off") is used earlier, in Gen. 14:14, "When Abram heard that his relative *had been taken captive*."

22:11 [10]. I take it that *šĕbuʿat YHWH* ("an oath of the Lord") means "an oath by the Lord," meaning one that employs his name. This is, admittedly, an odd way to say it. Normally oaths made to God or anyone else use *nišbaʿ lĕ* (e.g., Gen. 21:23; 25:33; 26:31; Josh. 2:12), while oaths made in God's name (whether by God or to God) use *nišbaʿ bĕ* (e.g., Gen. 22:16; Jer. 51:14; Amos 4:2; 6:8; 8:7).

22:11 [10]. I admit that "abide" in the phrase "and by which its owner must *abide*" is a rare English translation of *lāqaḥ* ("take").

22:13 [12]. The verb *ṭārap* means "to tear [by wild beasts]." Jacob uses this verb to describe the shredded animals he does not present to Laban (Gen. 31:39). It is the verb Jacob uses while believing that his beloved Joseph has been mauled to death (Gen. 37:33; 44:28). The noun *ṭĕrēpâ* ("what was mauled") appears in Exod. 22:31 [30] to refer to meat that the Israelites must not eat.

22:13 [12]. The LXX reads the Hebrew *yĕbiʾēhû ʿēd* ("you shall bring it [as] evidence") as "he shall take him to the prey" by reading the noun *ʿēd* ("evidence") as the preposition *ʿad* ("to"). Fensham (1962a) accepts this as the correct reading. Lending support to the LXX's reading is that the "it" in "he shall bring it" (*yĕbiʾēhû*) is a masculine suffix, but the antecedent of "it," *hû*, is the feminine word *haṭṭĕrēpâ* ("what was torn").

Commentary

This section continues the immediately preceding section's emphasis on thievery and thieves. The unique element here is the stress on how a situation is to be handled when one person (a depositor, a bailor) entrusts something of value to another (a depositee, a bailee), and something happens to the given thing while it is in possession of the latter. Did a thief abscond with it? Is the depositee the culprit? If not, how does he clear his name? What if there is no third-party witness and it comes down to the bailor's words versus the bailee's words? **22:7–13 [6–12]**

The lost items may be money or goods (v. 7 [6]), or some domestic animal (v. 10 [9]). In the case of the intervening law that deals with disputed ownership (v. 9 [8]), it includes both domestic animals and goods, in that order. Better to lose a shirt than an ox. Shirts are more easily replaced than oxen.

In all three subsections (vv. 7–8 [6–7]; v. 9 [8]; vv. 10–13 [9–12]), there is an emphasis on the role of God/the Deity (*hāʾĕlōhîm*) in arbitrating cases where there is disagreement or uncertainty about who is culpable or who is telling the truth. In the first subsection the bailee is "to be brought to God/the Deity." In the second subsection, the dispute over ownership is to come to God/the Deity, who will determine who is making a false claim of ownership. In the third subsection the depositor and depositee make an oath to the Lord to substantiate the latter's culpability or innocence.

There are two kinds of oaths in the Bible. The first kind of an oath is a promissory oath, in which the oath taker imposes some kind of an obligation on himself. See, for example, Lev. 5:4 ("Or if a person thoughtlessly takes an oath to do anything . . ."), or 1 Kings 1:13, 17, 30, where Bathsheba and Nathan successfully convince elderly David that he has earlier made an oath to the effect that Solomon is to succeed him. This oath is a self-imposed obligation, which explains why in Scripture the terms "oath" and "covenant" are interchangeable (see, e.g., the line "His oath, his covenant, his blood, support me in the whelming flood" from the hymn "The Solid Rock," by Edward Mote). In making a covenant with Israel, Yahweh places an obligation on himself to care for, provide, guide, and nurture his people. The covenant as oath emphasizes not only God's *control* of Israel, but also his *commitment* to Israel.

The second kind of oath we may call assertatory: an oath taken by an individual to exonerate oneself of a (false) charge brought against them and so clear their name. Clearly Exod. 22:8 [7] and 11 [10] fall into this category; see Num. 5:21 for another case. The depositee submits to an oath to prove that they did not steal or damage the item with which they were entrusted. The middle one in v. 9 [8] is a bit different. Both party A and party B claim to be the ox's owner. Who is a truth teller, and who is a fabricator? This particular law is like the situation on which Solomon has to make judgment: which woman is the mother of the baby (1 Kings 3:16–28)? How do you determine guilt/innocence without the benefits of modern technology like lie-detector polygraphs and DNA testing?

There is a passage in Leviticus (Lev. 6:1–7 [5:20–26]) that is close to this one. It too talks about somebody's deceiving his neighbor about "something entrusted to him or left in his care or stolen." The difference between the two is that Lev. 6:1–7 [5:20–26], unlike Exod. 22:7–13 [6–12], calls for the person suspected of and subsequently convicted of such illicit behavior first to make restitution plus 20 percent, and then offer up to the Lord a "guilt offering," a reparation offering (*ʾāšām*). The reason why a guilt offering is called for in Lev. 6 but not in Exod. 22 is that in the Lev. 6 the bailee "swore falsely" about his actions and needs forgiveness.

These laws in Exodus provide the legal background for passages like Ezek. 34, in which the Lord indicts Israel's shepherds (those responsible for providing stimulus and leadership) for not taking care of the flock with which he has entrusted them. The same truth spills over into the Second Testament. To quote but one example, note what elderly Paul says autobiographically in 2 Tim. 4:7: (1) life is a battle, and Paul has fought it ("I have fought the good fight"); (2) life is a race, and Paul has finished it ("I have finished the race"); (3) life is a trust, and Paul has kept and honored it ("I have kept the faith").

Injury to Borrowed Animals

(22:14–15 [22:13–14])

Translation

14 [13]"And should a man ask [for it]/borrow [it] from his neighbor, and it is injured or dies, its owner not being with it, he shall surely make restitution. 15 [14]If its owner is with it, he shall not make restitution. If it was hired, it came for its hire."

Grammatical and Lexical Notes

22:15 [14]. The last part of v. 15 [14] (*ʾim-śākîr hûʾ bāʾ biśkārô*) is very difficult to translate. I have settled on "If it was hired, it came for its hire." Part of the problem in translation is with the word *śākîr*, which normally means "hired man," a member of a certain profession, rather than an adjective referring to animals or some other kinds of property. Note the wide variety of options in the following translations: "If the animal was hired, the money paid for the hire covers the loss" (NIV); "If it was hired, only the hiring fee is due" (NRSV); "But if it was hired, he is entitled to the hire" (NJPS); close to NJPS is Paul (1970: 95), "But if it was hired [or "if he was a hirer"], he is entitled to the hiring fee (?)"; "If it was hired, its hiring-price is received" (E. Fox 1995: 381); "If he is hired, he gets his hire" (Alter 2004: 445); "If it was hired, it was reckoned in its hire" (Childs 1974: 444); "If he is a hired man [who caused the damage], it will come out of his wage," noted as a grammatically possible translation in Childs 1974: 449; "If it was hired, the risk [which eventuated] was already paid for in the value of the rent paid [by the borrower]" (Sprinkle 1994: 154); "If it was hired, it came for its hire" (Jackson 2006: 362). The ancient versions vary too: LXX, "But if he be one who hired it, it shall be his in lieu of his hire" (*ean de misthōtos ē, estai autō anti tou misthou autou*); Vulgate, ". . . especially if it were hired, and came for the hire of his work" (*maxime si conductum venerat pro mercede operis sui*).

Commentary

It is likely that few of us have ever borrowed an animal from a friend for **22:14–15 [13–14]**
some work in which we were engaged. Maybe it is some tool like a hammer or a drill, or maybe something like a lawnmower, and while we are using it, it breaks. Recall the lament of the individual who, while chopping down a tree, sees the axhead fly off and fall into the river. To Elisha he cries out, "Oh, my lord, . . . it was borrowed!" (2 Kings 6:5). What are the responsibilities of the borrower? Unlike a hirer, a borrower does not normally pay for the use of the thing borrowed. Jesus borrows the colt for Palm Sunday rather than hiring it

(see Derrett 1971: 250–53). But what if the colt steps in a hole, like the oxen pulling the cart with the ark on it (2 Sam. 6), and breaks its leg? Would Jesus, or the two disciples he sent to fetch it, be held responsible?

These three modern cases may be parallels: (1) If you borrow a neighbor's (uninsured) automobile and drive it solo and are involved in an accident, you are responsible for the damages (v. 14 [13]). (2) If you borrow a neighbor's automobile and he rides with you, if you are involved in an accident, he knows the accident was not your fault, regardless of who has to pay, because he has seen that you were driving carefully. You were not speeding or talking on your cell phone or text messaging (v. 15a [14a]). (3) If you rent the car from Avis or Enterprise and are involved in an accident, if you have paid for accident insurance or your own insurance policy covers you, you have to pay nothing. If you have not purchased accident insurance, and you have no policy, or the policy you have does not cover rentals, then the cost of the damages comes out of your own pocket (v. 15b [14b]).

Seduction of a Virgin Daughter

(22:16–17 [22:15–16])

Translation

16 [15]"Should a man seduce a virgin who has not been engaged and lie with her, he must surely pay the entire bride-price for a wife for himself. 17 [16]If her father absolutely refuses to give her to him, he shall pay money equivalent to the bride-price of virgins."

Grammatical and Lexical Notes

22:16 [15]. The verb *pātah* ("seduce") is used elsewhere with a sexual connotation, as in Judg. 14:15, "*Coax* your husband into explaining the riddle for us"; Judg. 16:5, "See if you can *lure* him into showing you the secret of his great strength"; Hosea 2:14 [16], "Therefore I am now going to *allure* her," and maybe in the oft-debated Jer. 20:7, the prophet's word of lament to Yahweh, "O Lord, you *deceived* me, and I *was deceived*." Compare also the line from a Ugaritic text *Il.attm.kypt*, "El cozens/deceives the two women [Asherah and Anat]" (Gibson 1978: 125n4). The exact verbal form as here—Piel, third-person masculine imperfect (*yěpatteh*)—occurs with the meaning "entice" in 1 Kings 22:20 (= 2 Chron. 18:19) and in Prov. 16:29, but in a context other than sexual.

22:16 [15]. The exact same phrase *bětûlâ ʾăšer lō-ʾōrāśâ* ("a virgin who has not been engaged") occurs in Deut. 22:28. Six of the eleven occurrences of the verb *ʾāraś* ("engage, betroth") are in Deuteronomy (20:7; 22:23, 25, 27, 28; 28:30).

22:16 [15]. The LXX translates the Hebrew "bride-price" (*mōhar*) with *phernē*, which often means "that which is brought by the wife," meaning a dowry. In LXX's *phernē pherniei autēn*, the pronoun *autēn* cannot be a direct object, but an adverbial accusative of respect, "for her." See Hiebert 1994: 206–10.

Commentary

I am not sure exactly why this law comes where it does, and how it follows along with the laws in the preceding verses of chap. 22. Is it that a virgin daughter is like an ox, a sheep, a donkey, silver or goods, as simply another item among the holdings or property of an adult male? Is the connection an equation between an injured ox and a deflowered daughter—both have lost their pristine form and so are less useful or marketable to their owner/father? Or does this particular law signal a shift in the Covenant Code laws, a shift away from property to an emphasis on people—a daughter, a sorceress, an **22:16–17 [15–16]** alien, a widow, an orphan, the poor? Note the blank line the NIV Study Bible leaves between vv. 15 and 16, and a heading in italics (*Social Responsibility*) for the laws commencing in v. 16.

One thing that sets this law apart from other laws is that it is one law where a third party's interference makes its fulfillment impossible. The father rejects out of hand giving his beloved daughter to this charming Casanova. Elsewhere, if an individual is unable to fulfill the law, it is because of one's own economic limitations. Compare Exod. 22:3 [2], "but if he has nothing . . ."; Lev. 5:7, "If he cannot afford a lamb . . ."; Lev. 5:11, "If he cannot afford two doves or two young pigeons . . ."; Lev. 27:8, "If anyone making the vow is too poor to pay the specified amount. . . ."

There are only two more references to a "bride-price" (*mōhar*) in the OT. Shechem asks Jacob and his sons to set the bride-price; he is willing to pay for Dinah at any level they wish (Gen. 34:12). Saul suggests to David that the bride-price for Michal is but a hundred Philistine foreskins (1 Sam. 18:25).

There is a law in Deuteronomy (22:28–29) that is close to this one. It too deals with a man having sex with an unengaged virgin, for which he must pay the girl's father "fifty shekels of silver." Maybe "fifty shekels of silver" is the bride-price, or more likely, some portion of the fifty shekels. This amount would be half of the "hundred shekels of silver" a husband has to pay as a fine for maliciously and falsely accusing his wife of nonvirginity at the time of their marriage (Deut. 22:19).

There are, however, major differences between the law in Exod. 22:16–17 [15–16] and the one in Deut. 22:28–29. In Exod. 22 the man "seduces" (*pātah*) and then "lies with" (*šākab ʿim*) the girl. In Deut. 22 the man "rapes" [NIV] (*tāpaś*) and "lies with" (*šākab ʿim*) the girl. Second, the law in Exod. 22 allows the father to withhold his daughter from the man who has slept with her, while the law in Deuteronomy does not. Furthermore, Deut. 22 alone adds that the man who has violated the girl cannot ever divorce her when he marries her. Nor does Deut. 22 use the word *mōhar*, "bride-price." Against most commentators, Pressler (1993: 35–41) opines, unconvincingly, I believe, that these are not two distinct laws, but are variants of the same law.

Is David's relationship with Bathsheba more like Exod. 22 or more like Deut. 22 (although Bathsheba is not a virgin, she is already married)? Does David "seduce" Bathsheba, or does he force himself on her? Is it consensual sex or coerced sex?

Regardless of how we come out in answering such questions, both the sexual laws of the Torah and the narrative of 2 Sam. 11 speak to the female and the male. To the female, they say, "Guard your virginity. It is priceless, and do not surrender it casually." To the male they say, "Put a lid on your libido, and act responsibly even when hormones rage."

The Sorceress

(22:18 [22:17])

Translation

[18] [17]"A sorceress you shall not let live."

Grammatical and Lexical Notes

22:18 [17]. The LXX renders this verse *pharmakous ou peripoiēsete* ("drug dispensers/potion enchanters you shall not protect/save [*peripateō*]"). The Vulgate makes its understanding of this verse transparent by rendering *maleficos non patieris vivere* ("Evildoers you shall not allow to live").

Commentary

The feminine word *měkaššēpâ* ("sorceress") is the feminine counterpart of masculine *měkaššēp* in Deut. 18:10 (NIV, "[one who] engages in witchcraft"). The difference between the two scriptural references, apart from gender, is that Deut. 18 only condemns the practice of sorcery, while Exod. 22 punishes its practice with death. **22:18 [17]**

One cannot be certain why the text singles out the "sorceress," and in lead position in the sentence at that, and not the "sorcerer"; see A. Brenner 1997: 84–86. Both females (Exod. 22:18 [17]; 1 Sam. 28; Isa. 47:9, 12; Ezek. 13:18; Nah. 3:4) and males (Exod. 7:11; Deut. 18:10; 2 Chron. 33:6; Jer. 27:9; Dan. 2:2) were practitioners of magic. It might be, to use a modern example, that one sees more "palm readers" who are women rather than men, more Berthas than Berts. The same situation existed in Mesopotamia. Sefati and Klein (2004: 180) note that in the *K* volume of *CAD* the entry for *kashshapu* ("sorcerer") fills up about two-thirds of a dictionary column, while the entry for *kashshaptu* ("sorceress") fills nearly two full columns. Like the OT, Mesopotamian texts frown on the practice of "black magic," such as sorcery, but unlike the OT, Mesopotamian texts are more accepting of the practice of "white magic," such as divination.

The two main forms that magic assumed in the biblical world were divination and sorcery. Milgrom (1990: 471) helpfully observes that the two differ in their objective. The purpose of divination, through whatever means the diviner uses, is to predict the future. The purpose of sorcery is to alter the future. Says Milgrom, "The magician who claims to curse or bless is a sorcerer, whereas the one who tells events but cannot affect them is a diviner." Such a distinction, if on target, puts the practice of sorcery in a more reprehensible position than the practice of divining. The divining person reaches conclusions passively. The practicing sorcerer reaches conclusions actively. One reports; the other programs. One prognosticates; the other manipulates.

The penalty phase of this law might have used stronger language, such as "She shall surely be put to death." Instead, it uses the softer "You shall not let [her] live." The Hebrew verb *tĕḥayyeh* can be parsed as a Piel second-person masculine singular imperfect ("You shall [not] let live") or as a Piel third-person feminine singular imperfect (see Eccles. 7:12 for the form); hence it can mean "A sorceress—she shall not cause [the dead] to live," shall not engage in magic like necromancy (Bretherton 2005). The verb is similar to that used by Jacob to Laban about the alleged theft of Laban's gods: "But if you find anyone who has your gods, *he shall not live*" (Gen. 31:32). The difference between the two verbs is that Jacob uses the Qal of "live" (*yiḥyeh*) while this law about the sorceress uses the Piel of "live" (*tĕḥayyeh*).

Bestiality

(22:19 [22:18])

Translation

[19 [18]]"Anybody lying with an animal shall surely be put to death."

Commentary

This law about bestiality reappears in Lev. 20:15, except instead of saying "lies with" (*šākab ʿim*), it says, literally, "places/gives his lying into" (*yittēn šĕkabtô bĕ*). Also, unlike Exod. 22:19 [18], the law in Lev. 20:15 mandates the death of the animal too, possibly because the animal is now considered irreversibly impure and contaminated. The ox that gores a human to death is to be put to death (21:28), but the animal with whom a human has sex is not (in Exod. 22). The reason is most likely because of the active versus the passive role of the animal. **22:19 [18]**

One would think that all law codes would outlaw the practice of bestiality. Almost all do. Thus Hittite law 187, "If a man does evil with a head of cattle, it is a capital crime and he shall be killed"; likewise law 188 begins, "If a man does evil with a sheep . . ."; and law 199, "If anyone does evil with a pig . . ." However, Hittite law 200(A) says, "If a man does evil with a horse or a mule, there shall be no punishment" (trans. A. Goetze, *ANET* 196–97). We do not know why the Hittite Law Code makes an exception with these two animals.

The Apostate

(22:20 [22:19])

Translation

[20 [19]]"One sacrificing to a deity shall be proscribed, except [it is] to the LORD alone."

Commentary

22:20 [19] The Hebrew verb for "proscribe" is *ḥāram* ("totally destroy, set apart for destruction, dedicate, devote"), which has generated much discussion. We are aware of its many appearances in the Hebrew Bible to describe what Israel is to do to the people of a foreign nation. In addition to uses in the book of Joshua (twenty-seven of eighty for verb and noun, and all but two of these in Josh. 6–11), see Num. 21:1–3; Deut. 7:2; 20:17–18; 1 Sam. 15 (8x).

What is not as well known is that *ḥerem* sometimes describes actions of an Israelite taken against a fellow Israelite: Exod. 22:20 [19]; Deut. 13:12–18 [13–19], esp. v. 15 [16]; Judg. 21:11. In the first two of these instances the reason for *ḥerem* is major religious compromise. In the last, Judg. 21:11, it is because of a petty grievance against the residents of Jabesh-Gilead who have failed to show up at the assembly at Mizpah to help out the women-deprived Benjamites. For not "*ḥerem*-ing" the images of gods, Israel runs the risk of being "*ḥerem*-ed" itself (Deut. 7:25–26).

Of these last three laws (sorcery/bestiality/apostasy), the last seems to be the most malefic. For violation of each, the language of penalty ranges from "not allowed to live" (sorcery) to "shall surely be put to death" (bestiality) to "shall be proscribed, totally destroyed" (apostasy).

The Alien, the Widow, the Orphan, the Poor

(22:21–27 [22:20–26])

Translation

21 [20]"A sojourner/alien you shall not mis-
treat or oppress, for you were sojourners/
aliens in the land of Egypt. 22 [21]No widow
nor orphan shall you mistreat. 23 [22]Should
you indeed mistreat him, when he cries
aloud to me, I shall indeed hear his cry,
24 [23]and my anger will flare, and I will kill
you with the sword, and your wives shall
become widows and your sons orphans.
25 [24]"If money you lend to my people, to
the indigent among you, you shall not be
to him like a creditor; you shall not impose
on him interest. 26 [25]If you indeed take as
security your neighbor's garment, before
the sun sets you should return it to him,
27 [26]because it is his only covering. It is his
garment for his skin. In what else can he
lie down? Should he cry out to me, I will
hear, for compassionate [am] I."

Grammatical and Lexical Notes

22:21 [20]. The Bible distinguishes between those non-Israelites who are in Israel permanently (*gēr*, "sojourner, alien,") and those who are there temporarily, say, on a trading mission (*nokrî*, "stranger"). With respect to the former, *gēr*, the Hebrew Bible uses the word for both non-Israelites and Israelites (or their ancestors). Here the LXX follows a consistent pattern. When *gēr* refers to a non-Israelite, LXX uses *prosēlytos* (72x). When *gēr* refers to an Israelite, or an Israelite ancestor (e.g., Gen. 15:13), LXX uses *paroikos* (11x). The Greek word *prosēlytos* is the origin of our English word "proselyte," but modern ideas of "convert" or "conversion" should not be read into the Greek word. To be sure, however, a *gēr* who settles in the land of Israel becomes in some ways a part of the life of the Israelite community. For further insight on the *gēr*/*gērîm* in Israel, see Houten 1991; Milgrom 2000a: 1493–1501.

22:21 [20]. Lev. 19:33 uses the same verb for "mistreating" the alien, *yānâ* (Hiphil), as does Exod. 22:21 [20].

22:21 [20]. The verb *lāḥaṣ* ("oppress") has appeared earlier, in 3:9, to refer to the abuse with which Pharaoh and the Egyptians oppress the Israelites.

22:22 [21]. "Widow" and "orphan" occur in parallelism in Ps. 68:5 [6], "A father to the *fatherless*, a defender of *widows*, is God in his holy dwelling." See the same pair ("orphan . . . widow") in Job 24:3; Isa. 1:17, 23; Jer. 49:11; Lam. 5:3. The reverse order "widow . . . orphan," as in Exod. 22:22 [21], is present in Job 22:9. Compare also the Ugaritic text (*CTA* [Aqhat 2] vv: 7–8) cited by Avishur (1975: 31–32): *ydn dn almnt yṯpṭ ṯpṭ ytm* ("He judges the cause of the widow, adjudicates the case of the fatherless"). For the threefold combination of "alien>orphan>widow," see Deut. 14:29; 16:11, 14; 24:17, 19–21; 27:19; Jer. 7:6; 22:3.

22:25 [24]. The verb *lāwâ* II (Hiphil = "lend"), with fourteen occurrences in the Hebrew Bible, appears again in the Torah only in Deuteronomy (28:12 [2x], 44 [2x]).

22:25 [24]. The noun "creditor" is the participle (*nōšeh*) of the verb *nāšâ* II, which occurs most famously in Jeremiah's claim, "I have neither *lent* nor borrowed" (Jer. 15:10).

22:25 [24]. The Hebrew word for "interest" is *nešek*, and derives from the verb *nāšak*, "bite," as in a snakebite (Num. 21:6, 8). Thus *nešek*, "interest," is a "bite" taken from another's wealth, a sum deducted before the loan is advanced. There is another Hebrew word for "interest/profit" (*tarbît*). *Nešek* may appear alone (Exod. 22:25 [24]; Deut. 23:19, 20 [20, 21]; Ps. 15:5). *Tarbît*, however, when it appears in conjunction with *nešek*, always comes after *nešek* (Lev. 25:36, 37; Prov. 28:8; Ezek. 18:8, 13, 17; 22:12). Loewenstamm (1969c) differentiates between the two by suggesting that *nešek* = interest on the loan of money, while *tarbît* = interest on the loan of food. I believe this distinction cannot be maintained, for Deut. 23:19 [20] says, "Do not charge your brother interest, whether on money [*nešek kesep*] or on food [*nešek ʾōkel*]"; also see Buch 2005.

22:26 [25]. For *ḥābal* I ("take as security"), see Deut. 24:6 ("Do not take a pair of millstones . . . as security for a debt"); 24:17 ("Do not . . . take the cloak of the widow as a pledge"); Amos 2:8 ("They lie down beside every altar on garments taken in pledge"); and others.

Commentary

22:21 [20] It is of no little interest that the Covenant Code can sandwich laws about the alien/widow/orphan/poor, the so-called *personae miserabilis*, between laws that focus on worshiping any God other than Yahweh (v. 20 [19]) and on blaspheming Yahweh (v. 28 [27]). There is no hint that the laws in vv. 21–27 [20–26] are subordinate to those in 20 [19] and 28 [27]. Idolatry or apostasy do not seem to be more detestable than riding roughshod over the most vulnerable people in a community. Maybe one way to blaspheme or vilify God (v. 28 [27]) is to abuse or ignore those less advantaged, but who nevertheless bear the divine image (vv. 21–27 [20–26]).

There must have been a large number of aliens residing in Israel at the time these Torah laws took shape. How else is one to explain the plethora of laws that deal with the *gēr*: Exod. 22:21 [20]; 23:9, 12; Lev. 19:33–34; 24:22; Num. 9:14; 15:14–16, 29–30; 35:15; Deut. 1:16; 10:19; 14:21, 29; 16:11, 14; 24:14, 17, 19, 21; 27:19 (about twenty by my count)? Some of these laws actually go beyond Exod. 22:21 [20], which simply says "not to mistreat or oppress him." But verses like Lev. 19:34 and Deut. 10:19 call on Israel to "love" the alien and to be charitable to the alien (Deut. 24:17–22). Those who have been redeemed by God's grace should be able to rise above the pitfall of xenophobia and be gracious and hospitable to all rather than just to "one's own."

22:22–24 [21–23] The concern for the widow and orphan is one that runs throughout ancient Near Eastern literature (see Fensham 1962b). It seems that in Israel there were two kinds of widows. Wherever the Hebrew word *ʾalmānâ* is juxtaposed with terms having to do with one's marital status, the best translation is "widow" (Lev. 21:14; 22:13; Num. 30:9 [10]). In the majority of instances, however, *'almānâ* has the nuance of "a once married woman who has no means of financial support, and who is thus in need of special legal protection" (Cohen 1973: 76–77). That is the case in Exod. 22:22 [21].

This distinction may explain why some women in Scripture who are widows are never called widows—Naomi, Orpah, Ruth, Abigail, Bathsheba. Even without their spouses, they have some means of support. However, Tamar (Gen. 38:11) is called a widow, and her only option is to return to live with her father, as her father-in-law Judah advises.

Modern readers of Scripture are, understandably, jolted when they hear the psalmist lash out at his malefactors with vitriolic language like "May his children be fatherless and his wife a widow" (Ps. 109:9). But what is one's response when essentially the same words come out of God's mouth, "Your wives shall become widows and your sons orphans" (Exod. 22:24b [23b])? Both the psalmist and especially God live by the lex talionis. The punishment matches the crime. Mistreat a spouseless woman or a parentless child, and watch what happens to your own spouse and child(ren).

22:25–27 [24–26] This law forbids (1) charging interest when lending money to the poor and (2) taking an article of clothing from the poor to whom you have made a loan as security or collateral for your loan, what Patrick (1973: 182) calls, "a means of enforcing repayment."

In contrast to biblical law, as G. Driver and Miles (1952: 174) note, "There is no trace of any attempt to prohibit the charging of interest in Akkadian law." This absence of proscribing lending on interest in the legal codes of the ancient Near Eastern world is helpfully traced in Maloney's article (1974). He reports that with some variation over time, the standard interest rates were 20 percent for loans of money and 33⅓ percent for those of grain.

The presence of such a restriction in biblical law and the absence of such a restriction in other ancient legal codes may be explained in two ways. First, using ancient Babylon as our example, we observe that such peoples had strong central governments and economies that included commerce, both internally and externally. In such a situation commercial loans are pervasive and fundamental, as in our own Western countries. In biblical Israel, by contrast, government and the economy were often locally/regionally administered, even when a king was on the throne, and hence the need for wide-sweeping commercial loans was either negligible or nonexistent (Neufeld 1955: 359). The other reason is theological rather than administrative. How could the people of God line their own pockets and feather their own nest at the expense of the poor? If Yahweh is "compassionate" (v. 27b [26b]) toward poor Israel, should not Yahweh's people be compassionate to the poor?

To be sure, this law does not encourage irresponsible borrowing by those unable to repay. The law does not condone unnecessary, extravagant indebtedness: "the creditor will eventually reduce or cancel my debt, so why worry?" If the Bible asks rhetorically, "Should we continue in sin so that grace may abound?" (Rom. 6:1 NRSV), it also asks rhetorically, "Should we continue to borrow so that indebtedness may abound?"

But that is not the thrust of this law. Its point is to urge generosity and fairness on the part of the lender vis-à-vis the borrower (who in most cases, if not all, would be poor). It does not ask whether the borrower is righteous or if he is responsible and trustworthy. Compassionate souls, such as the "compassionate" (*ḥannûn*) God, seldom ask such questions before opening up their pockets and their hearts. People of compassion are always philanthropic and risk takers (see Ap-Thomas 1957: 140–41).

Some form of this law appears in Exodus, Leviticus, and Deuteronomy in such a way as to suggest chronological sequence. Exodus 22:25–27 [24–26] forbids lending money at interest "to my people." Leviticus 25:35–38 forbids lending money at interest or food for profit to "one of your countrymen/brothers." Deuteronomy 23:19–20 [20–21] also prohibits charging interest on money or food to "your brother," but adds to money and food "anything else that may earn interest." Deuteronomy alone excludes the sojourner, *gēr*, from this proscription.

Archaeologists have uncovered an interesting Hebrew letter found at Masad Hashavyahu—on the southern coast of Palestine midway between Jaffa and Ashdod—and written sometime between 630 and 586 BC. It is a petition addressed by a reaper (*qṣr*) to a government official (*sr*). A foreman has confiscated the reaper's garment (see v. 26 [25] above), apparently for a supposed violation of reaping regulations or quotas, and has not returned it. I cite the original translation of Naveh (1960: 129–39):

1. Let my lord the governor hear
2. the word of his servant. Thy servant,
3. (behold) thy servant was reaping in Ha-
4. tsa-asam, and the servant reaped
5. and finished; I gathered in about a *ynm* before my
6. rest. When thy [se]rvant had fin[ished] his reaping, he gath-
7. ered in about a *ynm*, and there came Hashabiahu the son of Shoba-
8. i, and he took thy servant's garment. After I had finished
9. my reaping, that is a *ynm*, did he take thy servant's garment.
10. And all my brethren will witness on my behalf, they reap with me in the heat
11. [of the sun], my brethren will witness on my behalf "Verily," I am free of gu-
12. [ilt. Restore] my garment. And I will pay the governor in full to rest-

13. [ore my garment] _____(?)
14. ______ thy [se]rvant, and be not helpless to save.
15. _______

There is a NT text that is also close to this law. In Luke's version of the Sermon on the Mount/Plain, Jesus says, "If someone takes your cloak, do not stop him from taking your tunic. Give to everyone who asks you, and if anyone takes what belongs to you, do not demand it back" (Luke 6:29b–30). Luke's Jesus does not specify why the individual might take the cloak of another: (1) An act of a thief? (2) An act of a poor and needy person? (3) An act of seizure by a creditor? Matthew's Jesus, however, is quite specific about why the individual takes the cloak: "and if someone wants to sue you and take your tunic . . ." (Matt. 5:40), which seems close to reason 3 above. The word of Jesus is different from both that of Exod. 22 and the late Hebrew letter quoted above. Jesus focuses not on the person who takes the garment, but on the person from whom the garment is taken. "Don't take a cloak as surety," the law says. "Don't demand that the cloak be returned," Jesus says.

Proper Respect for God and Leaders

(22:28 [22:27])

Translation

[28 [27]] "God you shall not despise, nor a chieftain of your own kin shall you damn."

Grammatical and Lexical Notes

22:28 [27]. The LXX renders "you shall not despise/curse God" as "you shall not revile the gods" (*theous ou kakologēseis*). Daube (1990) has shown how both Philo and Josephus use the LXX's translation of this verse to show non-Jews of their day that Judaism is not inimical to other religions and the beliefs of those traditions, that Judaism is more tolerant than fundamentalistic.

22:28 [27]. Since the Hebrew Bible has no qualms about using the phrase "[not] curse/despise God" in its prohibitive laws, one wonders whether *bārak* ("bless") should be rendered "curse" in Job 1:5, 11; 2:5, 9, when God is the object of the verb (e.g., in Job 2:9, when Job's wife says to him, "*Bārak* God and die," does she counsel her husband to "*bless* God and die" or "*curse* God and die"?). See Linafelt (1996: 161–62), who registers reservations about such a euphemistic interpretation of *bārak*.

Commentary

22:28 [27] Unlike Exod. 21:17, which addresses "despising" one's parents (*ûmĕqallēl*; 22:28 [27], *lōʾ tĕqallēl*), this law does not spell out any penalty for its violation. Exodus 21:17 calls for the death penalty. But surely "cursing" God is as damnable as cursing one's parents, and so it too must have been a capital offense.

A passage in Leviticus close to this one is Lev. 24:10–16, the story of a man who "blasphemed the Name with a curse" (*wayyiqqōb . . . ʾet-haššēm wayĕqallēl*, Lev. 24:11). In Lev. 24:14 he is called the "blasphemer" (*hamĕqallēl*). Anybody who "curses" (*nōqēb*) the Lord's name or "blasphemes" it (*yĕqallēl*) is to be stoned (Lev. 24:15–16). The NIV tends to prefer "curse" for *nāqab* and "blaspheme" for *qālal*.

In some of these instances the LXX renders "blasphemed" by "named the name": Lev. 24:11, "he named the name and cursed" (*eponomasas . . . to onoma katērasato*); Lev. 24:16, "Anyone who names the name of the Lord . . ." (*onomazōn de to onoma kyriou . . .*).

Jesus, we know, is charged with the sin of blasphemy (Matt. 26:65–66; Mark 14:63–64; Luke 22:27; John 10:33, 36). How does Jesus, in the eyes of his critics, act blasphemously? It cannot simply be that Jesus "names the name." Rather, it must be in his claim that he is God's Son. What belongs to God by way of title and prerogative, he says belongs to him too. For members of the Sanhedrin and others, such claims are an insult and a brazen show of disrespect directed at their God. This is the thrust of Exod. 22:28 [27]: doing things or talking in such a way that derides or insults or shows disrespect for the Almighty. See the helpful comments on this topic in Brown 1994: 520–27.

Giving God the Firstborn

(22:29–30 [22:28–29])

Translation

[29][28]"Your first yield, as well as that from vats, you shall not put off. The firstborn of your sons you shall give to me. [30][29]Thus shall you do with your ox, with your sheep. Seven days they shall be with their mother; on the eighth day you shall give it to me."

Grammatical and Lexical Notes

22:29 [28]. The meaning of the word *mĕlēʾâ* ("first yield, first ripe fruits"?) is uncertain. A literal meaning would be "plenty, fullness." It occurs only three times (maybe four) in the Hebrew Bible, and each time NIV uses quite different words: Exod. 22:29 [28], "granaries"; Num. 18:27, "juice"; Deut. 22:9, "crops." The translation "juice" in Num. 18:27 is on target since the reference there is to liquid contents. Also, "crops" in Deut. 22:9 is correct.

22:29 [28]. Similarly, the word *demaʿ* ("vats"?) appears only here. The verb from which it is formed is present only in Jer. 13:17, "I will weep [*bākâ*] in secret because of your pride, my eyes will weep bitterly, overflowing with tears [*wĕdāmôʿa tidmaʿ wĕtērad ʿênî dimʿâ*]." How one moves from "tears" to "vats" is uncertain, although both suggest a liquid. Greenfield (1969: 101) suggests "the best, set apart portion," on the basis of the Samaritan Targum's translation of *ḥēleb* ("fat, best") in Gen. 45:18 and Deut. 32:9 as *dmʿ*. See also Barr 1961: 325n95.

22:29 [28]. The expression *lōʾ tĕʾaḥēr* ("you shall not put off") is like that in Eccles. 5:4 [3], "When you make a vow to God, *do not delay* [*ʾal-tĕʾaḥēr*] in fulfilling it." Note the choice of the *lōʾ* negative in the law, but the *ʾal* negative in Ecclesiastes.

Commentary

22:29–30 [28–29] The giving of the firstborn of animal and child to the Lord has already surfaced in Exodus (13:1–2, 11–13), and will appear later in 34:19–20. There is one major difference between the data in chap. 22 and that in chaps. 13 and 34. Both chaps. 13 and 34 urge the parent to "redeem" (with a sheep maybe?) every firstborn son (Exod. 13:13b; 34:20b). Exod. 22:29 [28] omits any reference to the "redemption" of the firstborn son. It simply says, "The firstborn of your sons you shall give to me." The language is very similar to that of the prophet Micah, "With what shall I come before the Lord. . . . Shall I offer/

give my firstborn for my transgression?" (Mic. 6:6–7). To be sure, there is no hint in the Exodus passage about giving one's firstborn son as a way of gaining access to God and winning his approval.

The absence of any reference to the redemption of the firstborn son in Exod. 22 has agitated some. Thus Levenson (1993: 3) says, "Of all the passages in the Bible that have been deemed offensive, none has been deemed so more often than this one, and none has generated greater resistance to a literal interpretation."

In response, I say that the primary emphasis in these two verses is on giving to the Lord the first and best of one's agricultural and animal products. The statement about the giving of the firstborn son is terse and almost parenthetical. Hence, the data is truncated and is to be "filled in" with the fuller data from chaps. 13 and 34.

Second, there are other passages in the Bible of individuals "given" to the Lord with no mention of their being "redeemed." For example, when Hannah prayerfully vows, "if you will . . . give [me] a son, then I will *give* him to the LORD all the days of his life" (1 Sam. 1:11), does she mean "sacrifice" the child, or dedicate/hand over the child? Similarly, Num. 8:16 refers to the Levites as those "who are to be given wholly to me" (*nĕtunîm nĕtunîm hēmâ lî*). "Wholly given" surely does not mean "sacrificed," but "dedicated."

What Not to Eat

(22:31 [22:30])

Translation

[31][30]"And men of holiness you shall be to me: meat in the field torn to pieces [by beasts] you shall not eat. To the dog throw it."

Commentary

22:31 [30] What is good for Spot to eat is not good for a human to eat. "Dogs" do not get good press in Scripture: 1 Kings 21:19; 2 Kings 9:36–37; Ps. 68:23 [24]; Prov. 26:11; Jer. 15:3; Matt. 7:6; Mark 7:27; Phil. 3:2; 2 Pet. 2:22; Rev. 22:15. Of course, these "dog" references are not to your friendly cocker spaniel, but to wild dogs who roam outside the city and eat carrion.

Like most laws in the Covenant Code, this one too reappears in other codes (see Lev. 17:15–16; Deut. 14:21). Exodus 22:31 [30] prohibits the consumption of animal meat "torn [by beasts] (*ṭĕrēpâ*)" in the open field. Deuteronomy 14:21 forbids the consumption of *nĕbēlâ* (NIV, "anything you find already dead"). Leviticus 17:15 forbids the eating of both *ṭĕrēpâ* and *nĕbēlâ*; also see Ezek. 4:14; 44:31. *Ṭĕrēpâ* refers to animals torn to pieces by powerful predators, say, as shepherds travel with their grazing flocks in open spaces. *Nĕbēlâ* reflects an agricultural/commercial society rather than a pastoral one, and the reference is to the death of animals who graze closer by the homestead.

Of interest here is the prefacing of this law about certain kinds of meat not to eat with "men of holiness" (or a "holy people") "you shall be to me." Almost every time the Torah introduces the subject of what foods one may or may not eat, it invariably connects it with holiness (Exod. 22:31 [30]; Lev. 11:44–45; 20:25–26; Deut. 14:21). As Milgrom (1991: 729) says, "Relatively few individual statutes of the Bible are coupled with the demand for holiness. And none of these present the demand with the same staccato emphasis and repetition as do the food prohibitions."

But who is to prevent a shepherd from barbecuing the remains of a dead lamb, or a farmer from cooking up the remains of a dead cow? There was no "food patrol" that policed or monitored their eating patterns. It is one thing to aspire to be holy when people are watching. It is another thing to aspire to be holy when nobody is watching, out in the field alone with one's flock, or around the dinner table with one's family. Such verses also teach that holiness includes letting the Lord be lord of all parts of one's life, and that includes the patterns of one's consumption.

This food prohibition is connected with the call to be holy (NIV, "You are to be my holy people"). By contrast, the food prohibition in Deut. 14:21 is tied in not with the call to be holy but with how the people are already holy (NIV, "But you are a people holy to the Lord your God"): Exodus, "You *shall be* holy"; Deuteronomy, "You *are* holy." In one, holiness is a goal; in the other, it is a present reality. Israel, who is holy, is always moving toward (more) holiness, or is challenged by God to move toward more holiness, as paradoxical as that may sound.

The pattern "You *shall be* holy" versus "You *are* holy" is consistent throughout Exodus, Leviticus, and Deuteronomy: "You shall be holy" (Exod. 19:6; 22:31 [30]; Lev. 11:44–45; 19:2; 20:7, 26; 21:8); "You are holy" (Deut. 7:6; 14:2, 21). Numbers uses both: Num. 15:40 ("And you *shall be* holy to your God" [NRSV]) and Num. 16:3 ("for all the congregation *are* holy" [NRSV], Korah's angry outburst at Moses and Aaron). In the two places where Deuteronomy breaks its own pattern of "You are holy" and instead has "You shall be holy" (Deut. 26:19; 28:9), the reference is back to the Sinai theophany recorded in Exodus.

Be Honest, and Be Helpful

(23:1–9)

Translation

1“You must not take up a false rumor. Do not be in league with a wicked one as a witness (bent on) violence. 2Do not go after the many for evil, nor distort the evidence in a dispute by tilting it in favor of the many. 3And a poor one you shall not show preference to in his dispute.

4“Should you encounter your enemy's ox or donkey wandering about, you shall surely return it to him.

5“Should you spot your enemy's donkey lying beneath his pack (unable to get back up), and desist from leaving (the scene), you shall surely help him (back on his feet).

6“You shall not pervert the justice due your indigent in his dispute. 7From a lying word distance yourself, and the guiltless and innocent you shall not kill, for I will not acquit the guilty. 8A bribe you shall not take, for the bribe blinds those able to see and perverts the words of the innocent.

9“A sojourner/alien you shall not oppress, for/and you yourselves know the sojourner's soul, for sojourners/aliens were you in Egypt land.”

Grammatical and Lexical Notes

23:1. The interchange of the imperative (via *lōʾ* with the imperfect; *lōʾ tiśśāʾ*, “You must not take up”) with the jussive (*ʾal-tašet*, “do not be in a league with”) is rare. Compare 1 Kings 20:8, “Don't listen [*ʾal-tišmaʿ*] or agree [*wělōʾ tōʾbeh*] to his demands”; Ezra 9:12, “Do not give [*ʾal-tittěnû*] your daughters in marriage to their sons, or take [*ʾal-tiśʾû*] their daughters for your sons. Do not seek [*wělōʾ-tidrěšû*] a treaty of friendship with them”; Amos 5:5, “Do not seek [*wěʾal-tidrěšû*] Bethel, do not go up [*lōʾ tābōʾû*] to Gilgal, do not journey [*lōʾ taʿăbōrû*] to Beersheba.”

23:1. The verb “take up” (*nāśāʾ*) by extension means “take up on your lips,” as in the third commandment, “You shall not *take up* [*lōʾ tiśśāʾ*] the name of the Lord your God” (20:7). See Pss. 16:4, “I will not . . . *take up* their names upon my lips”; and 50:16, “But to the wicked God says, ‘What right have you to . . . *take up* my covenant on your lips?’”

23:1. “Do not be in league with” is, literally, “Do not put your hand with” (*ʾal-tašet yāděkā ʿim*). The idiom is like a similar one, *śîm-yāděka ʿal-pîkā*, “put your hand on your mouth,” meaning “be quiet” (Judg. 18:19; Job 21:5b; Mic. 7:16).

23:1. For other instances of *ʿēd ḥāmās* (“a witness [bent on] violence”), see Deut. 19:16 (“a malicious witness”) and Ps. 35:11 (“Ruthless witnesses”). See also Ps. 27:12, “For false witnesses [*ʿēdê-šeqer*] rise up against me, breathing out violence [*ḥāmās*].”

23:2. *Rabbîm*, which I have translated as “the many,” both at the start and end of the verse, could also be rendered “the multitude,” “the great,” or “the majority.”

23:2. The phrase *lĕrāʿōt*, literally, "for evils," occurs only here. It may be compared with *bĕrāʿôt* in Ps. 88:3 [4], "For my soul is full *of troubles*."

23:2. The verb I have rendered "distort" is *ʿānâ* ("answer"). It is the exact verb and verb form used in the ninth commandment ("[not] bear false witness," Exod. 20:16; Deut. 5:20), except in the Decalogue it is *ʿānâ bĕ*, and here it is *ʿānâ ʿal*.

23:2. The use of the Qal infinitive construct of *nāṭâ* (*linṭōt*, "tilt"), followed later in the sentence by the use of the Hiphil infinitive construct of the same verb (*lĕhaṭṭōt*), is puzzling to me.

23:3. Leviticus 19:15 also uses the verb *hādar* ("[not] show preference to"), but there the object of the verb is the "great" (*pĕnê gādôl*) instead of "a poor one" (*dāl*).

23:4. For *pāgaʿ* to refer to chance encounters, see Gen. 28:11 ("when he [Jacob] *reached* a certain place"); 1 Sam. 10:5 ("As you approach the town, you will *meet* a procession of prophets" [AT]); Amos 5:19 ("It will be as though a man fled from a lion only to *meet* a bear" [AT]).

23:4. The word for "enemy" in this verse is *ʾōyēb*, but the word for "enemy" in v. 5 is *śōnēʾ* ("one who hates"); each is a participle with a pronominal suffix. Perhaps we can translate the first "your enemy" and the second "your adversary."

23:4. The verb for "wandering about" (*toʿeh*) is exactly the same as that used of Joseph: "A man found him [Joseph] *wandering around* in the fields and asked him, 'What are you looking for?'" (Gen. 37:15 AT). Hagar *wandered* in the desert near Beersheba (Gen. 21:14).

23:5. The word for "lying [beneath his pack]" is *rābaṣ*, the one most commonly used for animals in a slumbering or crouching position. It does not by itself mean "weighted down, crushed." Among its more famous uses, and in the same participial form, is God's word to Cain, "But if you do not do what is right, sin is *crouching* at your door" (Gen. 4:7 AT).

23:5. The Hebrew noun *maśśāʾ* ("pack") occurs sixty-five times in the Hebrew Bible (see Floyd 2002: 401–2). In thirty-three of these it refers to something that is literally carried or lifted, or to something that is weighty or burdensome. In about twenty-seven of these sixty-five places, *maśśāʾ* designates a speech or writing that most often pertains to prophets, and it is often rendered as "oracle." I am not sure how one Hebrew word equals both a "heavy burden" and an "oracle," but both are "weighty." The first is literally so; the second is metaphorically so because of its importance.

23:5. I render the first *ʿāzab* "leaving" (*mēʿăzōb*), and the second *ʿāzōb taʿăzōb* as "help." In the commentary section I shall present the arguments, pro and con, for an *ʿāzab* I ("leave, abandon") and an *ʿāzab* II ("lift up, help").

23:6. "Pervert/skew" (*taṭṭeh*, Hiphil) is the same verb (*nāṭâ*) used in the Qal and Hiphil infinitive constructs above in v. 2 ("distort, tilt").

23:7. The LXX uses the verb *dikaioō* to translate the Hiphil of *ṣādaq* (here, *ʾaṣdîk*, "I will [not] acquit") in this verse and in Deut. 25:1; Ps. 82:3 [81:3]; Isa. 5:23; 43:26. It is the verb for "justify" that Paul uses in some of his letters, especially in the opening chapters of Romans (2:13; 3:4, 20, 24, 26, 28, 30; 4:2, 5; 5:1, 9; 6:7; 8:30, 33).

23:8. *Sālap* (verb) and *selep* (noun) mean "pervert" and "perversion." The verb and noun together occur but nine times in the Hebrew Bible, six of which are in Proverbs (verb: 13:6 [NIV, "overthrows"]; 19:3 [NIV, "ruins"]; 21:12 [NIV, "*brings* to ruin"]; 22:12 [NIV, "frustrates"]; noun: 11:3 [NIV, "duplicity"]; 15:4 [NIV, "*deceitful* tongue"]).

23:8. In both sentences in this verse, the subject "bribe" (*šōḥad*) precedes the verb (usually it is the other way around): *wĕšōḥad lōʾ tiqqaḥ kî haššōḥad yĕʿawwēr*. Van der Merwe (1999: 177) cites this as an instance of "fronting" to connect the two parts of the sentence: what the constituent places before the verb in the second half of the sentence is identical to what the constituent places before the verb in the immediately preceding clause.

Commentary

23:1–3, 6–8 The laws in 23:1–9 begin (vv. 1–3) and end (vv. 6–9) with apodictic style laws: "you shall not/must not/do not." Sandwiched between them are laws that are casuistically framed (vv. 4–5): "Should (*kî*) you . . ." or "If you. . . ."

It is obvious that vv. 1–3 and 6–8 share a common theme, and that is a concern for truthfulness and justice. At least one scholar (McKay 1971) has suggested that these six verses have ten rules, and he dubs them "A Decalogue for the Administration of Justice in the City Gate," although McKay must make several textual changes to discover a Decalogue.

In any case, it may appear that the precepts of vv. 1–3 are for the benefit of witnesses, while those in vv. 6–8 are for the benefit of the judges. Unlike vv. 1–3, vv. 6–8 provide motive clauses for the encouraged behavior: "*for* I will not acquit the guilty"; "*for* the bribe binds those able to see." I am inclined to agree with Weisman (1995: 417–20), who fails to discern any clear-cut differentiation between witness and judge in these verses. He calls these apodictic instructions, "directives guiding anyone involved in the juridical process" (419). For example, a bribe (v. 8) could be a temptation either for a witness or for a judge. Either a witness or a judge could fail to be impartial (v. 3).

There are some interesting connections between these teachings and the story involving Abraham and Abimelech in Gen. 20 (see Hepner 2003: 144–45). In violation of Exod. 23:7, Abraham advances a "lying word" when he says to Abimelech about Sarah, "She is my sister" (Gen. 20:2). In reply to God, Abimelech says, "Lord, will you destroy [*hārag*, as in Exod. 23:7 ("kill")] an innocent [*ṣaddîq*, as in Exod. 23:7] nation?" (Gen. 20:4). He says to God that he has done all this with "clean [*niqyōn* like *nāqî*, "guiltless," in Exod. 23:7] hands" (Gen. 20:5). This Genesis narrative and Exod. 23:1–3, 6–8 say, "Fib on the truth, tell a lie, in or out of court, and nobody wins. It will end up hurting you and hurting everybody else." Dishonesty and untruthfulness end up destroying those who choose that path.

23:4–5 Both of these verses advocate kindness and sympathy on the part of the person who finds one of his enemy's animals straying (v. 4), or immobilized because of the weight it is carrying (v. 5).

There are no translation problems with v. 4. That is not the case, however, with v. 5, where we see at least two. The first is how best to render *ḥādal min* ("desist from"). Apart from Exod. 23:5, the only other place where *ḥādal min* followed by an infinitive occurs is 1 Kings 15:21 (= 2 Chron. 16:5), "When Baasha heard this, he stopped building [*wayyeḥdal mibbĕnôt*] Ramah." The phrase *ḥādal min* followed by a noun is more common, as in 1 Sam. 9:5, Saul's words to his servant, "Come, let's go back, or my father *will stop thinking about* the donkeys."

The second, and more complicated, translation problem is whether the two instances of *ʿāzab*—as *mēʿăzōb* on the one hand ("leaving"), and as *ʿāzōb taʿăzōb* on the other hand ("You shall surely help [him]")—are two uses of the same verb, or two homonymic verbs. The Septuagint apparently reads it as two different verbs: "You shall not pass it by/leave it [*ou parelousē*], but you shall raise it/lift it up [*synegereis*]." This rendering suggests the existence of an *ʿāzab* I ("leave, pass by, abandon") and an *ʿāzab* II ("help, raise up"). Williamson (1985: 82–85) argues for just one *ʿāzab* in Biblical Hebrew and so translates the passage, "and wouldest forbear *to release* it for him, thou shalt *surely release* it with him." Williamson has overlooked or has set aside the existence in Ugaritic of the verb *ʿdb* ("raise"), which seems to be the equivalent of Hebrew *ʿāzab* II. Scholars like Dahood (1959a), Margalit (1987: 396–97; 1989: 432), and Talmon and Fields (1989: 106n75) cite Canaanite texts like Aqhat 1.19, *ʿdb . . . mt.ydh*, "He [Dan'el] *picked up* his (walking-)stick as he set out on a journey," and a line from the Baal-Mot texts like 1.6.I.51, *lyʿdb.mrh.ʿm.bn.dgn*, "He cannot *raise* the staff like the son of Dagon." Cooper (1988: 16), like Williamson, rejects the existence of an *ʿāzab* II. He strikes off in a different direction with his rendering, "And would you refrain from *leaving* it [the load? the animal?], you *must leave alone* the animal." That is to say, one is to avoid any contact with the beast. You might do more harm than good. It would be like a passerby coming on an accident victim and administering anything more than basic first aid (covering the victim with a blanket, holding up the head of the victim so he can breathe, trying to stop the bleeding) without waiting for the paramedics to arrive. You can further injure the victim, and you can get sued.

In one sense, such laws as these in vv. 4–5 urge an individual not to extend his feelings of anger against an enemy to his enemy's animals. Your enemy's animals are not your enemy. So Carmichael (1974: 57) says, "It is doubtful if the lawgiver is at all concerned with lessening feelings of enmity between two human beings." But why, then, do other portions of Scripture, especially Wisdom literature, urge the putting of a lid on anger toward one's enemies and argue against gloating over an enemy's misfortune (Job 31:29; Prov. 20:22; 24:17; 25:21)? Dick (1983: 51) quotes several nearly identical aphoristic sayings from ancient Near Eastern literature. From a piece of Babylonian Wisdom literature ("Precepts and Admonitions") we have this counsel: "Do not return evil to the man who disputes with you; requite with kindness your evildoers, maintain justice to your enemy, smile on your adversary." And from an Egyptian Wisdom text (Papyrus Insinger 23.6) we have this: "It is better to bless than to curse someone who has injured you."

It is one thing to ask God to prepare a table for you in the presence of your enemies (Ps. 23:5). It is another thing to ask God to give you enough grace to prepare a table for your enemies. Surely it is of not little interest that the same Bible that contains both laws and precepts about being charitable to one's enemies also contains prayers in which the pray-er asks God to do horrible and unimaginable things to his enemies (e.g., Pss. 109; 137).

This verse essentially repeats 22:21 [20]. **24:9**

He Is the Lord of Your Property and Your Time

(23:10–19)

Translation

10"And six years you may sow your land and harvest its yield. 11But (in) the seventh year you shall let it lie fallow and abandon it, so that the indigent among your people may eat of it, and what is left over let the beasts of the field eat. You shall do likewise to your vineyard, to your olive grove.

12"Six days you may do your own work, but on the seventh day you must stop, so that your ox and your donkey may rest, and your bondman and the alien might catch a breather. 13Regarding everything I have said to you, take careful heed. The name of any other god you are not to utter; it shall not be heard in your mouth.

14"Three times in a year you shall observe a pilgrimage festival to me. 15The Pilgrimage Festival of Flatbread you shall observe seven days. You shall eat flatbread as I commanded you, at the fixed time of the month of Abib, for in it you left Egypt.

"None shall appear before my face empty-handed.

16"The Pilgrimage Festival of the Harvest, the firstfruits of your work that you sow in the field, and the Pilgrimage Festival of Ingathering at the going out of the year, when you harvest your work from the field, [you shall observe]. 17Three times in the year all your males shall appear before the face of the Master, the Lord.

18"You shall not sacrifice with anything leavened the blood of my sacrifice, nor shall the fat of my Pilgrimage Festival remain unto morning.

19"The best of the firstfruits of your ground you shall bring to the Lord your God's house.

"You shall not boil a kid in its mother's milk."

Grammatical and Lexical Notes

23:11. "Let it lie fallow" is the verb *šāmaṭ,* whose basic meaning is "release, let slip from one's hands." The related noun, *šĕmiṭṭâ,* is used in Deut. 15:1, 2 [2x], 9 not with land, as in Exod. 23, but with the releasing or remitting of debts at the end of seven years.

23:11. The Hebrew verb for "abandon" is *nāṭaš*. The verb means "drop, leave on the ground," here meaning that what grows on the ground naturally in the seventh year is "left on the ground." Numbers 11:31 says that "a wind . . . from the Lord . . . drove quail in from the sea. It *brought them down* [*nāṭaš*] all around on the camp," leaving them on the ground.

23:11. Fishbane (1980: 347–48) argues that "You shall do likewise to your vineyard, to your olive grove" is a later expansion of the verse. But the same formula (*kēn-tăʿăśeh*) is present in Exod. 22:30 [29]; 26:17; Deut. 20:15, and in all those instances it seems integral to the passage.

23:12. G. Robinson (1980: 37, 38, 39, 42) argues that in almost all instances *šābat* means "stop, desist" rather than "rest." And yet, stopping one's work inevitably leads to rest from one's work.

23:12. *Yinnāpēš* ("catch a breather") may also be rendered "be refreshed."

23:12. On "bondman" (*ben-ʾāmâ*), see Fensham 1969. It occurs six times in the Hebrew Bible (Gen. 21:10, 13; Exod. 23:12; Judg. 9:18; Pss. 86:16; 116:16). It is, at least in Exod. 23:12, a synonym for *ʿebed* ("servant").

23:13. "You are not to utter" is *lōʾ tazkîrû* (the Hiphil of *zākar*, "remember," in the Qal). The Hiphil of *zākar* takes *šēm*, "name," as the direct object six times: Exod. 20:24; 23:13; 2 Sam. 18:18 (NIV, "carry on the memory of"); Ps. 45:17 [18] (NIV, "perpetuate"); Isa. 26:13 (NIV, "honor"); Isa. 49:1 (NIV, "made mention of"). See Childs (1962: 11–15) for a study of the nuances of the Hiphil of *zākar*.

23:15. Both in this verse and in v. 17 "appear" is vocalized as a Niphal (v. 15, *yērāʾû*; v. 17, *yērāʾeh*), even though a proper translation calls for an active verb followed by a direct object ("appear before/see my face"; "all your males shall appear before/see my face"). See the same Niphal in Exod. 34:20b, which also speaks of a mortal's seeing God's face. Similarly, Exod. 34:23 and Deut. 16:16 also use the Niphal of *rāʾâ* in the same context, but they even include the accusative indicator *ʾet* after a passive verb and before the object "my face" (*ʾet-pĕnê hāʾādōn* and *ʾet-pĕnê YHWH*). Hebrew scholars suggest that the Qal of *rāʾâ* was the original vocalization, but the repointing of the verb to a Niphal toned down the idea of a mortal's beholding God's face. See C. McCarthy 1981: 337–38; Tov 2001: 274–75.

23:16. The LXX reads "The Pilgrimage Festival of Ingathering" (*hag hāʾāsip*) as "The Pilgrimage Festival of Finishing" (*heortēn synteleias*) by deriving *ʾāsip* not from the verb *ʾāsap* ("gather [in]"), as it does later in the verse when it translates *bĕʾospĕkā* ("when you harvest/gather in") by *en tē synagōgē*. Instead, it connects the first *ʾ-s-p* with the Hebrew verb *sûp* ("finish, complete"). See Tov 2008: 390.

23:16. Does *bĕṣēʾt haššānâ* ("at the going out of the year") refer to the *beginning* of the year or to the *end* of the year? Ginsberg (1982: 49) argues that it refers to the onset of the year and points to an analogy with the same verb *yāṣāʾ* used with the early morning "departure" of the sun from the east. However, when used with the "going forth" of the sun, the correlative of *yāṣāʾ* for the "setting/disappearance" of the sun is *bôʾ*. When used with the "going forth/the start" of the year, the correlative of *yāṣāʾ* is *šûb* ("return"). Hence, one finds the expression *tĕšûbat haššānâ* ("the return of the year") in 2 Sam. 11:1 and 1 Kings 20:22, 26, all of which refer to a king's undertaking a military campaign, and all of which NIV translates as "(next) spring." Another expression in the Hebrew Bible for the "start" of the year is *rēʾšît haššānâ* (Deut. 11:12). A parallel expression to *bĕṣēʾt haššānâ* in Exod. 23:16 is *tĕqûpat haššānâ* in 34:22.

It seems clear, then, that the phrase refers to the end of the year, the passing of the year. But the end of which year? Is there only one year? Today we speak of a calendar year, but also of an academic year or a fiscal year. Clines (1998: 373–78) has argued convincingly that the festivals are regulated not by a lunisolar calendar but by the agricultural seasons. So "at the end of the year" more likely means "at the end of the particular agricultural season" rather than "at the end of the calendar year."

23:17. For *hāʾādōn* ("Master, Sovereign"), see Exod. 34:23; Josh. 3:11, 13; Ps. 97:5; Isa. 1:24; 3:1; 10:16, 33; 19:4. Dahood (1965: 313–14), in reconsidering the baffling words of Ps. 68:17 [18], compares the Hebrew word *bām* with a Ugaritic root (*ybm*) and posits another use of *bām* by repointing and redividing from *ʾădōnāy bām* ("*The Lord* [*has come*?] from Sinai into his sanctuary") to *ʾādōn yābam* ("*The Lord created* Sinai as his sanctuary").

Commentary

23:10–13 There is a logical progression of thought in vv. 10–19. These first four focus on one's work, when to work and when not to work. Verses 14–17 focus on crucial times of worship throughout the year. Verse 11 highlights one special year, v. 12 one special day, vv. 14–17 three special occasions. Verses 18–19, in conclusion, offer a summary of how one worships God with sacrifice, outlined negatively in v. 18 and positively in v. 19a. The contrast between vv. 10–13 and 14–17 is brought out by the absence in vv. 10–13 and the presence in vv. 14–17 of not coming before God empty-handed.

Another possible way to divide these verses is to see the exhortation of v. 13 following the worship-related teachings of vv. 11–12 as parallel to the exhortation of vv. 18–19a following the worship-related teachings of vv. 14–17.

I think the connection between vv. 10–13 and vv. 14–17 is thematic. You don't control your work schedule (10–13). You don't control your worship schedule (14–17). Work does not displace worship, but neither does worship displace work. There is a time to harvest (*ʾāsap*, v. 10), with all the demanding labor that goes into that. There must also be a time to celebrate the Pilgrimage Festival of Ingathering (*ḥag hāʾāsip*, v. 16).

That this section begins with the seventh year (vv. 10–11) rather than with the seventh day, as one might expect (v. 12), places priority here on the year rather than on the day. To teach that in this year the farmer is to let his property "lie fallow and abandon it," means that once every heptad of years the farmer voluntarily releases and surrenders ownership of his land to the land's ultimate owner, Yahweh. Biblical Israelites, like moderns, are sensitive to the need to treat animals rightly ("and what is left over let the beasts of the field eat") and to treat the poor charitably ("so that the poor among your people may eat of it"). They could not have known, as moderns do, that continual cultivation of the soil may rob it of ingredients necessary for fertility. But maybe they knew something we moderns do not know: God is the real owner of the land. He is a Provider and a Farmer extraordinaire, and in that seventh year he will provide for the needs of the poor and the beasts of the land. Now take him as your model for the next six years.

23:14–17 Exod. 23:14–17 is one of five festival calendars in the Pentateuch. The other four are Exod. 34:18–26; Lev. 23; Num. 28–29; Deut. 16:1–17. One can readily admit that it is difficult, if not impossible, to make these five calendars consistent. Some are brief; others are longer. Some contain a festival and the details for its observance that another calendar in the Pentateuch totally ignores. A festival may be known by one Hebrew name in one of these calendars, yet by a completely different name in another of these calendars. And even when discussing the same festival, two of the calendars may go their own directions.

The calendar in Deut. 16:1–17 provides an interesting chiasm with Exod. 23:14–17, as Levinson (2000: 282–83; 2008: 27) has pointed out. Exodus 23 has "none shall appear before me/my face empty-handed" (23:15b) before "Three times a year all your males shall appear" (23:17). Deuteronomy 16 reverses the order of these two sentences: "Three times a year all your males shall appear" (Deut. 16:16a NRSV) and "No man should appear before the LORD empty-handed" (Deut. 16:16d).

The calendar closest to Exod. 23:14–17 is Exod. 34:18–26. It mentions the same three festivals, except that it calls the middle one the "Festival of Weeks" (*ḥag šābu'ōt*) rather than the "Festival of Harvest" (*ḥag haqqāṣîr*). Deuteronomy 16:10, 16 use the title of Exod. 34 rather than the phrase in Exod. 23. In addition to the mentioning of the three festivals, compare (1) the promise God makes in 23:20 with the one he makes in 34:10; (2) what he says he will do with the nations in 23:22–23 and in 34:11; (3) what he says about not making any covenant with the locals in 23:32–33 and in 34:12; (4) the emphasis in 23:15b and in 34:20b on not appearing before God empty-handed; (5) the importance of desisting from work on the seventh day, in 23:12 and 34:21; (6) the requirement that all males appear before the Lord thrice annually, in 23:17 and 34:23; (7) prohibition of the use of yeast in one's offerings, in 23:18a and 34:25a; (8) the command not to leave anything over until morning, in 23:18b and 34:25b; and (9) the warning not to boil a kid in its mother's milk, in 23:19b and 34:26b.

In light of these similarities, one might argue that Exod. 23 and 34 are variants of each other. But they differ in one respect. In chap. 23 the promise that God makes (see point 1 above) comes at the end of the cultic catalog (23:10–19 and 23:20–21). In chap. 34 the promise that God makes precedes and introduces the cultic catalog (34:10 and 34:18–26). Furthermore, one might argue that the divine promise of 23:20–21 is directed to the people of God ("I am sending an angel ahead of *you* to guard *you*, . . . to bring *you* to . . ."), while the divine promise of 34:10 is directed to Moses after Moses's prayer to God in 34:8–9 ("I am making a covenant with *you* before all *your* people"). On this point, see Brichto 1998: 402–3. Exodus 23, then, is a word for Israel, while Exod. 34 is a word for Moses.

Though it is impossible, as suggested above, to fix with certainty the months for these festivals, the following is a good approximation: (a) Festival of Flatbread/Unleavened Bread, April; (b) Festival of the Harvest, late May or early June; (c) Festival of Ingathering, late September or early October. The last two of these three (Harvest, Ingathering) might sound the same to the English reader. The first refers to the actual harvesting of the yield. The second refers to the processing and storage of the entire yield. One notes that there is a gap of a few months between the Festivals of Harvest and Ingathering. Surely it did not take, say, three months to store the harvest. One possibility is that the Festival of Harvest celebrates the harvesting of the grain crop. After that, and sometime later, would be the harvesting of other crops such as grapes or olives. The importance of this third festival is indicated by the fact that by the time it rolls around on the calendar, harvesting and storage of all crops have been completed. This may be one reason why everyone, including farmers, is able to congregate every seven years on this occasion for the public reading of the law (Deut. 31:10–13).

Two items are of special interest. First is the notice that on these special occasions no one is to enter God's presence empty-handed (23:15; 34:20b; Deut. 16:16b). The words of the old gospel song, "Nothing in my hands I bring," while apropos when reflecting on the salvation that Messiah offers ("simply to thy cross I cling" [Augustus M. Toplady, "Rock of Ages"]), do not fit OT patterns of worship. Here one does bring something in one's hands, a gift, and a way of thanking God for his benevolence. Expressing one's gratefulness to God is never confined to something verbal.

The second thing of interest is the command in 23:17 that on these occasions "all your *males/men* are to appear" in the sanctuary (again in 34:23; Deut. 16:16). First of all, does this include "all" males, infant to adult males, healthy and infirm? More important, why restrict this to males? Does this mean that women are excluded from participation in public worship? Pharaoh suggests to Moses earlier that women and children be left out of the pilgrimage on which Moses will take the Israelites (Exod. 10:8–11), either because he knows the men will return to Egypt to be with their wives and children, or because his Egyptian religion is a male-only religion.

I argue that this particular law does not prohibit the participation of women in community worship. Rather, it suggests that males are obligated to attend. Women are encouraged to attend but can be excused for any number of reasons: pregnancy, nursing, looking after elderly parents, and so forth. How can Scripture, on the one hand, exclude women from worship and, on the other hand, mandate the assembling of the people ("men, women, and children," Deut. 31:10–12) for the septennial reading of the Torah "before the LORD your God at the place he will choose"? Gruber (1992: 77) says succinctly, "Deuteronomy provides a ready answer for any insensitive male who may inquire 'why should she not leave her infant with a baby-sitter?' Deuteronomy's answer is that God Himself commands the baby herself to be present."

23:18–19a I am inclined to agree with Milgrom (2000b: 2070) that these verses refer not to the three festivals of the agricultural year, but are "general sacrificial requirements befitting the last line of a cultic catalog that lays emphasis on the offerer's responsibilities at the sanctuary."

The "fat" (or "suet") of the offering refers to the layers of fat beneath the skin of the animal and surrounding its organs. We are not sure why the "fat" of the animal is to be offered to God and is not for human consumption. A clue may be found in that the word "fat" (*ḥēleb*) can sometimes mean "the best," as in Gen. 45:18 ("I will give you the best [*ṭûb*] of the land of Egypt, and you can enjoy the fat [*ḥēleb*] of the land") and in Deut. 32:14 ("with the *finest* kernels of wheat [*'im-ḥēleb kilyôt ḥiṭṭâ*] . . ." [AT]). The best, the finest is what one offers to God.

"You shall not boil a kid in its mother's milk" is a verse, or a portion of a **23:19b**
verse, that reappears in Exod. 34:26b (also at the end of a cultic calendar), and in Deut. 14:21b (at the end of a list of edible and inedible food). It is a verse that has had tremendous influence in later Judaism in providing the biblical rationale for separating dairy products from meat products in a kosher food system. For example, *Targum Onqelos* simply renders the verse, "You shall not eat meat with/in milk."

It is also a verse that has attracted the attention of many biblical scholars who have tried to ascertain its meaning and significance. Among the more-recent studies from which I have gained much knowledge, I mention Carmichael 1976; Haran 1979; Ratner and Zuckerman 1986; Milgrom 1991: 737–42; Labuschagne 1992; J. Sasson 2002; 2003.

Before I get to three of the main interpretations of this law, let me briefly mention two recent and innovative suggestions. First, Labuschagne (1992) suggests that the reason for the prohibition is that when the new mother cow first gives her milk to her young, the milk has a yellowish or reddish tinge to it, making it look like blood. This is because of the cow's "beastings/beestings" or "colostrum," which my dictionary defines as "a yellow fluid rich in protein and immune factors, secreted by the mammary glands during the first few days of lactation." And we all know what the Bible says about not eating the blood (Gen. 9:4; Lev. 7:26–27; 17:10–12; Deut. 12:16, 23; 15:23; Acts 15:20). But it is not blood: the fluid only looks like blood.

A second innovative interpretation is offered by J. Sasson (2002; 2003). The Hebrew words for "fat" and "milk" have the same three consonants (*ḥ-l-b*), except that the vowels are different: *ḥēleb* ("fat") versus *ḥālāb* ("milk"). Sasson suggests that in Exod. 23:19b we read "fat" (*ḥēleb*) instead of "milk" (*ḥālāb*), and so the verse says, "You shall not boil a kid in its mother's *fat*." Would, then, boiling/cooking the kid in the father's fat be acceptable? And is not the fat of any animal, male or female, to be offered to the Lord (Lev. 7:23–24) and not for human consumption, unless it is wild game (17:13–14)?

Here are three other possibilities, more commonly suggested than the two above. First, maybe this verse is directed at a pagan, Canaanite cultic practice. Support for this view has come in a Ugaritic text from Ras Shamra (1400–1200 BC). It is a line in *CTA* 23.14, part of a larger text often identified as "The Gods Fair and Beautiful." The line is *ṭb*[*ḫ g*]*d bḥlb annḫ bḫmat*, "Coo[k a ki]d in milk, a lamb(?) in butter." As is seen with my square brackets, *ḫ* must be added to the first word and g to the second. Apart from the guess at filling in the missing letters is that (1) *ṭbḫ*, even if correct, means "slaughter" and not "cook," and (2) these Canaanite texts put a word divider between words that looks like a period, and such a word divider follows the *b* in *tb*, so the restoration cannot be *ṭbḥ*. Finally, if the proposed reading is correct, there is no mention about cooking the kid in its mother's milk, just cooking it in milk.

A second suggestion is humanitarian. It would be unnecessarily cruel to boil a kid in its mother's milk, as it would be to slaughter a mother and its young on the same day (Lev. 22:28), or to slaughter a newborn during the first week of its life (22:27), or take the mother bird together with her offspring (Deut. 22:6–7).

But if humanitarianism and kindness to animals is the motive, why is the prohibition not extended to all young animals? And true, one may not slaughter a mother and her young on the same day (Lev. 22:28), but one could slaughter them on successive days. True, one may not slaughter a newborn during the first week of its life (Lev. 22:27), but by the eighth day one may, even though the animal is still a suckling. So where is the kindness to young animals in these instances?

A third view, and the one I embrace, takes its start from a comment by Philo (*Virt.* 143): "[It is] grossly improper that the substance which fed the living animal should be used to season and flavor the same after its death. . . . Man [should not] misuse what has sustained its life." Do not use, says this law, something that brings life (milk for sustenance) to bring death (milk for cooking). Alter (2004: 452) calls "the mixture of the mother animal's nurturing milk with the slaughtered flesh of her offspring a promiscuous joining of life and death." What brought life now brings death, and that is not right. It is like religion, one of whose purposes is to bring life and tranquility and joy, but alas, it has often been used to bring death and chaos and sorrow.

You Obey Me; I Will Expel Them

(23:20–33)

Translation

[20]"Now I am about to send an angel/messenger before you, to guard you on the way, and to bring you to the region I have appointed. [21]Take care in his presence, listen to his voice. Do not play the rebel with him for he will not pardon your transgressions, for my name is within him.

[22]"If you will only listen to his voice and do everything I have said, I shall be an enemy to your enemies and a foe to your foes.

[23]"For my angel/messenger shall go before you and will bring you to the Amorites, the Hittites, the Perizzites, the Canaanites, the Hivites, and the Jebusites, and I shall wreak havoc among them. [24]You are not to bow down to their gods, or do them service, or follow their practices. You shall totally eradicate them and shatter to pieces their pillars. [25]You shall serve the LORD your God, and he will bless you (by providing) your bread and your water. And I will remove sickness from your midst. [26]None shall miscarry or be barren in your land. A full span of life I will give you. [27]My terror I shall send before you, and I shall throw into panic all the people against whom you will come. And I shall make all your enemies turn tail to you. [28]And I shall send the hornet before you, and it will drive out the Hivite, the Canaanite, and the Hittite from before you. [29]I will not drive them from before you in one year, lest the land become desolate and multiply against you the beasts of the field. [30]Little by little I shall drive them out from before you until you are fruitful and possess the land. [31]And I will fix your borders from the Red Sea to the Sea of the Philistines, and from the wilderness to the River, for I shall give into your hand the inhabitants of the land, and you will drive them out from before you. [32]You shall not make with them or with their gods a covenant. [33]They shall not dwell in your land lest they cause you to sin against me. Should you serve their gods, it will prove a snare for you."

Grammatical and Lexical Notes

23:20. It is not unexpected that, as here, the object of "guard" (*šāmar*) will be *derek* ("way, path, journey"), and again in Gen. 3:24; 18:19; Josh. 24:17; Job 23:11; Ps. 91:11; Prov. 2:8. Both an assigned mission and journeys are freighted with danger. Particularly close to Exod. 23:20 (*šāmar* + preposition *bĕ* prefixed to *derek*) is Jacob's vow in Gen. 28:20, "If God will be with me *and will watch over me on this journey . . .*"

23:21. The MT has pointed the verb *tamēr* as if it is from the verb *mārar* ("be bitter") rather than *temer* from the verb *mārâ* ("rebel"), which is LXX's reading (*apeithei*). A similar confusion between *mārar* and *mārâ*, but in the opposite direction, is present in 2 Kings 14:26, "The LORD has seen how 'bitterly' [*mōreh*, but read *hammar*] everyone in Israel . . . was suffering."

23:21. The "you" (3x) of v. 20 is a singular "you," and the imperatives of v. 21 are second-person singular. But the "your" on "your transgressions" is a plural "you."

23:22. A literal translation of "I shall be an enemy" is "I shall enemy your enemies and foe your foes." The Hebrew words *ʾoyeb* ("enemy") and *ṣar* ("foe") appear frequently in the Hebrew Bible. Gevirtz (1961a: 44) provides nine instances of *ʾoyeb* = *ṣar* in poetical passages, nine instances of the reverse sequence ("foe" = "enemy"), and four references where the two words are near each other but not in parallelism.

23:24. This verse contains the last of nineteen different verbs in the Covenant Code (twenty-five instances in all, counting the repeats) that use the infinitive absolute form of the verb along with the finite form of the same verb: *hārēs tĕhārĕsēm* ("you shall totally eradicate them") and *wĕšabbēr tĕšabbēr* ("and shatter to pieces"). Although the infinitive absolute is present in other Semitic languages, it never appears in any legal code.

23:25. In "He will bless you (by providing) your bread and your water," the words "by providing" are supplied for sense. See Mitchell (1987: 40).

23:26. For *mispar yāmêkā* ("a full span of life," or more literally, "the number of your days [I will make full]"), see Eccles. 2:3 ("during *the few days* of their lives"); 5:18 [17] ("during *the few days* of life God has given him"); 6:12 ("during *the few* and meaningless *days* he passes through like a shadow"). The phrase is semantically similar to Ps. 39:4 [5], "Show me, O Lord, my life's end and the number of my days [*ûmiddat yāmay*]."

23:27. The Hebrew word *ʿōrep* refers to the nape of the neck, the part of the body that the fleeing enemy shows to the one pursuing him.

23:28. There is still debate about the meaning of *ṣirʿâ* ("hornet, wasp"). It occurs again only in Deut. 7:20 and Josh. 24:12. All of the ancient versions are unanimous that the reference is to some kind of stinging insect. Sawyer (1976: 243–44) relates the word to *ṣāraʿat* ("leprosy" [?] or some kind of skin affliction), and argues that victims of such a disease look like they have been stung by a wasp or by a swarm of wasps. For a wasp/hornet presaging a panic among the people toward whom it flies, Sawyer notes the Greek *oistros* (Latin, *oestrus*), which means both "gadfly" and "panic, frenzy."

23:29. The ancient versions read *ʾăgārĕšennû* (and in v. 30 too) as *ʾăgārĕšēm* ("I will [not] drive them from before you"). R. Weiss (1963: 190) argues that such a reading is because the ligature *nûn* + *wāw* at the end of a word in square script has the appearance of a closed *mem*.

23:31. "The River" (*hannāhār*) is the Euphrates (Gen. 31:21; Num. 22:5; Josh. 24:2).

23:32. G. Driver (1966: 3) notes that three different prepositions may follow *kārat bĕrît* ("make/cut a covenant") when two human parties enter into such an agreement. One is *kārat bĕrît ʿim* when the subject of the verb is the suppliant (Gen. 26:28; 2 Chron. 23:3; Hosea 12:1 [2]). A second is *kārat bĕrît ʾet* when the covenant is between equals (2 Sam. 3:12, 13, 21; Jer. 34:8). The third, and the one used in Exod. 23:32, is *kārat bĕrît lĕ*. It is used when the agent who is the subject of the verb is the superior party, conferring a treaty as a favor or imposing some relationship (Josh. 9:6, 11, 15, 16; 24:25; 1 Sam. 11:1–2; 2 Sam. 5:3; 2 Kings 11:4). Hence, this latter form is used for Israel's not making a covenant with the nations (Exod. 23:32; 34:12; Deut. 7:2; Josh. 9:7; Judg. 2:2).

Commentary

22:20–33 It is common to refer to these fourteen verses as the epilogue to the Covenant Code/Collection, and rightly so. But it is striking that they do not call upon Israel to follow and adhere to the laws laid out in 20:22–23:19. From reading just 23:20–33 by itself, one would not know that preceding it were two and a half chapters of prescriptions. The equivalent chapters in Leviticus (chap. 26) and in Deuteronomy (chap. 28) do begin with such an emphasis: Lev. 26:3, "If you follow my decrees and are careful to obey my commands"; Deut. 28:1, "If you fully obey the LORD your God and carefully follow all his commands I give you today."

Rather, Exod. 23:20–33, or 23:20–26, strikes off in its own direction. Instead of urging obedience to a law, it urges obedience to a God-sent angel/messenger/agent: "Take care in *his* presence, listen to *his* voice. Do not play the rebel with *him*, . . . for my name is within *him*." In 20:22–23:19 Israel has access to the divine law. Now, and for times to come, they will have access to the divine presence, via the Lord's representative. Obey, says 20:22–23:33, both the written word and also the spoken word of the one who goes before you.

Who is this angel/messenger that the Lord promises to send at the vanguard of Israel's onward march to Canaan? And is this *mal'āk* the same as the "terror" (v. 27) and the "hornet" (v. 28) that God also promises to send ahead of his people?

There are a few modern commentators who believe this angel is none other than Moses himself (Brichto 1992: 110; Janzen 1997: 179–80). If that is so, one wonders if the people hearing this epilogue are discerning enough to say among themselves that *mōšeh* is really the *mal'āk*.

I am inclined to give *mal'āk* its normal meaning—a supernatural, nonhuman figure who is both distinguished from Yahweh and fused with Yahweh—and to connect this reference to a divine *mal'āk* with other references to him in Exodus (3:2; 14:19; 32:34; 33:2).

The promise of v. 20a anticipates the promise of Mal. 3:1, "See, I will send my angel/messenger, who will prepare the way before me." All three Synoptic Gospels pick up this word from Malachi and apply it to John the Baptist (Matt. 11:10; Mark 1:2–3; Luke 7:27). The Greek in the Synoptic passages is close to that of the LXX of Exod. 23:20: *idou egō apostellō ton angelon mou pro prosōpou sou*.

Perhaps there is a parallel not only between the angel who goes before and John the Baptist who goes before, but also between the angel and Jesus. According to John 14:2, Jesus goes ahead of his disciples to prepare a "place" for them. Similarly, the work of the angel is to go ahead and bring Israel to the "place/region" God has prepared (Exod. 23:20). The angel will guard Israel on "the way," and in the same Johannine context Jesus says, "I am the way" (John 14:6). The angel is to "guard/keep" Israel as it journeys. Jesus claims that he has "protected/guarded" (same Greek word as in LXX of Exod. 23:20) his own while he has been with them (John 17:12). Jesus's statement "I gave them the words you gave me" (John 17:8) seems close to "Listen to his voice" (Exod. 23:22), in that both refer to a message from God. Jesus speaks of "the name you gave me" (John 17:11), and of the angel the Lord says, "My name is within him" (Exod. 23:21b). As Bevan (2003: 581) has said, there is "a parallel between the angel's task in Exod. 23:20 of bringing Israel to Canaan and Jesus's task in John 14 of bringing the new Israel into the spiritual destination of which Canaan was a foreshadowing."

The promises that God makes in this portion of Exodus are much like those in Deuteronomy: "I will be your enemy's enemy" (v. 22) and "provide your bread and water" (v. 25); "I will remove sickness from your midst" (v. 25); "none shall miscarry or be barren; . . . a full span of life I will give you" (v. 26). All these are guarantees if only God's people "will listen to his voice and do everything I have said" (v. 22), and "not bow down to their gods" (v. 24) or "make with their gods a covenant" (v. 32). Accordingly, "Deuteronomic theology" (God honors obedience with blessing) is present in Exodus as well as in Deuteronomy.

In particular, as interpreters have pointed out (e.g., Van Seters 1972: 69; Weinfeld 1991: 380–84), Deut. 7 seems to have been formed out of Exod. 23:20–33. Here are the common emphases: (1) God will bring Israel into the land of six (Exod. 23:23) or seven (Deut. 7:1) Canaanite peoples; (2) God will destroy these peoples (Exod. 23:23), or Israel will destroy them with God's help (Deut. 7:2); (3) Israel is to be aware of the lure of apostasy and to that end destroy objects of foreign worship (Exod. 23:24; Deut. 7:3–5); (4) God will defeat the indigenous peoples by divine terror and wasps/hornets (Exod. 23:27–28; Deut. 7:20); (5) God will do this "little by little" (Exod. 23:30; Deut. 7:22); (6) Israel is not to enter into any kind of a pact with the Canaanites (Exod. 23:32; Deut. 7:2); (7) their gods have the potential to be a "snare" to Israel (Exod. 23:33; Deut. 7:16); (8) both speak of the danger "wild animals" would pose to Israel (Exod. 23:29; Deut. 7:22); finally, (9) both speak similarly of the divine promise that attends obedience. For example, compare the promise of no barrenness and freedom from disease in Exod. 23:25–26 and Deut. 7:14–15.

For all their similarities, there are also some differences between the two passages. First, there is no mention of an angel/messenger in Deut. 7. Though an angel shows up at key places in Exodus, angels are completely absent from Deuteronomy. Second, when Exod. 23 speaks of eliminating the Canaanite peoples, it uses the verb *gāraš* ("drive out") with the "hornet" as the subject of the verb in v. 28, God as the subject of the verb in vv. 29 and 30, Israel the subject of the verb in v. 31b. When Deut. 7 speaks of eliminating the Canaanite peoples, it uses the verb *ḥāram* ("totally destroy") in Deut. 7:2, or "destroy/devour" (*'ākal*) in 7:16, or "wipe out" (*'abad*, Hiphil) in 7:24. So in Exod. 23 God "drives out," while in Deut. 7 Israel "totally destroys" the locals, and I think we would agree there is a considerable difference between expulsion (Exod. 23) and extermination (Deut. 7). For the record, for better or for worse, the Canaanites were neither completely expelled nor exterminated, as passages like Judg. 1:21–33 and 1 Kings 9:20–21 attest.

Judges 2:2–3 seems to give a new spin on Exod. 23:29–30 (and Deut. 7:22) ("I will not drive them out from before you in one year. . . . Little by little I shall drive them out") by suggesting that God's refusal to drive out (*gāraš* again) the nations and allowing their gods to be a "snare" to Israel is a punishment inflicted on Israel due to its failure to fulfill the covenant. Israel has refused to keep the covenant, and so God has reneged on his promise. The fallout from either obedience or disobedience is enormous, and the latter is potentially catastrophic. What no Hivites or Hittites can do to God's plan, the Israelites do. For a completely different interpretation of Judg. 2:2–3, see Van der Kooij 1995: esp. 298–301.

A Ceremony of Covenant Ratification

(24:1–11)

Translation

[1]To Moses he had said, "Go up to the LORD, you and Aaron, Nadab and Abihu, and seventy of Israel's elders, and you shall bow down at a distance. [2]Moses alone shall come near the LORD, but they, they shall not come near, nor shall the people go up with him."

[3]Then Moses came and retold all of the LORD's words and all the legal norms; and all the people answered in unison and said, "Every last word the LORD has spoken we will do." [4]And Moses inscribed all of the LORD's words, and rising early in the morning he built an altar at the mountain's base with twelve pillars for the twelve tribes of Israel. [5]He sent acolytes of the Israelites, and they offered up burnt offerings and sacrificed well-being sacrifices to the LORD, bulls. [6]Moses took half of the blood and put it in basins and half of the blood he dashed against the altar. [7]He took the book of the covenant and read in the hearing of the people, and they said, "Everything about which the LORD has spoken we will do and obey." [8]Moses then took the blood and dashed (it) on the people and said, "Behold, the blood of the covenant that the LORD has made with you over all these words."

[9]And Moses went up, and Aaron, Nadab, and Abihu, and seventy of Israel's elders. [10]They saw the God of Israel, and beneath his feet something like a brick [made] of sapphire, and as pure as the heart of heaven. [11]Against/to Israel's spirited leaders he did not stretch forth his hand. They beheld the Divinity, and ate and drank.

Grammatical and Lexical Notes

24:1. If v. 1 began "To Moses God *said*," the form of the verb would be *wayyōʾmer*, as in v. 12. Instead, it is *ʾāmar*, and this suggests the pluperfect/the perfective, "*had* said." So maybe 24:1 really takes one back to chap. 19.

24:1. Although the imperative "go up" is directed to Moses and seventy-three others, it is a singular imperative (*ʿălēh*). The same goes for the verb in v. 9. Again the subject of "went up" is Moses and seventy-three others, but the verb is singular (*wayyaʿal*). In both cases, the use of a verb in the singular with multiple subjects, with Moses placed first, highlights the role of Moses. Moses stands in Yahweh's shadow; Aaron, his two sons, and the seventy elders stand in Moses's shadow.

24:2. The subject "they" (*hēm*) in *wĕhēm lōʾ yiggāšû* ("they did not approach") is grammatically not necessary since the subject is already in the verb form. Its use here is another way to set the seventy-three (*hēm*) apart from Moses (*hûʾ*, "*he*").

24:3. It is possible that *dibber* ("has spoken"), here and in v. 7, may carry a stronger meaning like "commanded" or "given instructions about" whenever the verb occurs in statements of compliance (as in Gen. 12:4, "as the Lord had *said to/commanded* him [Abraham]").

24:5. The word I have rendered as "acolytes" (*naʿărê*) could also be "young men, lads" or even "squires." In light of the function they perform, I chose a term with liturgical overtones.

24:5. The word "bulls" (*pārîm*) stands oddly at the end of the sentence. The Masoretes placed an *ʾatnāḥ* under *ʿōlōt* rather than some kind of disjunctive accent as their way of indicating that "bulls" referred only to the well-being sacrifices and not to the burnt offerings.

24:6. *ʾAggānōt* ("basins") is a synonym for *mizrākōt* ("basins, bowls, splashers") in Exod. 38:3. Exodus 24 uses the verb *zāraq* ("dash, splash") for Moses's handling of the blood in v. 6b and 8.

24:7. With regard to *sēper habbĕrît*, Haran (1985: 1n2) writes, "The substantive *sēper* denotes the scroll itself, upon which the work is written, without describing its contents. Otherwise, the character of the work is indicated by a construct case, the *nomen regens* of which describes the *sēper*." See *sēper tôlĕdōt ʾādām* ("the book of the generations of Adam/mankind," Gen. 5:1); *sēper kĕrîtut* ("the book of divorcement," Deut. 24:1, 3); *sēper hammiqnâ* ("the book of purchase," Jer. 32:11, 14).

24:10. The LXX softens the Hebrew "They saw the God of Israel" to "They saw the place where the God of Israel stood." The change is similar to that in v. 11 ("and they appeared in the place of God" [LXX]); and in 19:3, where "Moses went up to God" becomes "Moses went up the mountain of God" (LXX).

24:10. In "as pure as the heart of heaven" (*ûkĕʿeṣem haššāmayim lāṭōhar*), the word for "heart" (*ʿeṣem*) is, literally, "bone." The use of an anatomical term to denote "self/person/essence" is present in the frequent phrase *bĕʿeṣem hayyôm hazzeh*, "in/on this *very* day," (e.g., Gen. 7:13), which would translate literally as "in the bone of this day." Another anatomical term, *rōʾš*, "head," may appear with a similar nuance in a passage like 1 Sam. 25:39, "The Lord . . . has brought Nabal's wrongdoing down *on his own head/on himself*." Margalit (1989: 171, 450–51) points to the phrase in Ugaritic *ḥy.mḫ* and *ḥw.mḫ* ("[his] very life"), in which *mḫ* functions like Hebrew *ʿeṣem*. For some intriguing developments of this verse in postbiblical Judaism, see Fishbane (2003: 136–38). Such developments began with the observation of the similarity between the "brick" reference here and the recall of the "bricks" in the earlier chapters of Exodus, bricks the Egyptians forced the Hebrews to make.

24:11. The word for "spirited leaders" is *ʾăṣîlê*. The Hebrew word is drawn from the verb *ʾāṣal*, which is used in Num. 11:17, 25 for the withdrawal of some of the spirit from Moses and the conferring of that spirit on the elders. An *ʾāṣîl* is one who has received the spirit. As such, in Exod. 24 these charismatic leaders are not harmed in God's presence.

24:11. "He did not stretch forth his hand" is usually interpreted to mean, "He did not injure them," but G. Driver (1953: 38–39) takes the phrase to mean, "He did not beckon them to advance up to his throne." One might compare 2 Sam. 15:5, "Whenever anyone approached him [Absalom], . . . *he would reach out his hand*," but the phrase there lacks the preposition *ʾel*. The question is whether *šālaḥ ʾel* means "stretch against" or "stretch to(ward)."

24:11. The LXX has a different reading of this verse: "And not even one of the chosen of Israel perished [?]/went missing [?]. And they appeared in the place of God and were eating and drinking." The verb "perished" or "went missing" is *diaphōneō*. It is used to render the Niphal of *pāqad* in Num. 31:49 ("and not one *is missing*"), to render *nāpal* in Josh. 23:14 ("Not one of all the good promises the Lord your God gave you *has failed*. . . . Not one *has failed*"), and to render the Niphal of *ʿādar* in 1 Sam. 30:19 ("Nothing *was missing*").

24:11. Verse 10 uses *rāʾâ* for "seeing" God, while this verse uses *ḥāzâ* ("beheld") for "seeing" God. Avishur (1984: 75–76, 196, 241, 488, 650–51) provides instances of these two words together in the Hebrew Bible. They may occur in either order. Compare Isa. 30:10 ("They say to the seers [*rōʾîm*]. 'See [*rāʾâ*] no more visions!' and to the prophets [*ḥōzîm*], 'Give us no more visions [*ḥāzâ*] of what is right'") with Isa. 33:17 ("Your eyes will see [*ḥāzâ*] the king in his beauty and view [*rāʾâ*] a land that stretches afar"). Often *ḥāzâ* is used with somebody having a vision of God (Num. 24:4, 16) or seeing God (Pss. 11:7; 27:4; 63:2 [3]), or a prophet having a vision (Isa. 1:1; 2:1, although the prophet uses *rā'â* in 6:1 to describe his seeing God; Amos 1:1). And *ḥōzeh* is the word for "seer." Derrett (1998) has drawn attention to Jesus's use of two Greek words for "see" in John 16:16, and has suggested a parallel with the two Hebrew words for "see" in Exod. 24:10–11: "In a little while you will see [*theōreō* = *rā'â*] me no more, and then after a little while you will see me [*horaō* = *ḥāzâ*]." His paraphrase of the verse and its use of two verbs for "see" is "A little while and you *will observe* me no more, and again, after a little while *you shall inwardly apprehend me*" (italics mine).

Commentary

24:1–2 Many commentators have observed that the Lord's imperative to Moses to "go up" to his presence is not implemented until v. 9: "Go up to the LORD [v. 1]. . . . And Moses went up" [v. 9]. This has then led to the conclusion that vv. 3–8 are a later insert into vv. 1–2, 9–11. However, as I have argued in the first grammatical note, a better translation than "and he [God] said to Moses" would be,"and he [God] had said to Moses."

Nobody accompanied Moses when he "went up" the mountain in chap. 19 (vv. 3, 20), but here he is joined by his older brother, Aaron, two of Aaron's sons, and seventy of the elders. This, along with v. 9, is the final of several references in Exodus to Israel's elders (3:16; 4:29; 12:21; 17:6; 18:12), and 24:1, 9 are the only ones to designate seventy of them (as in Num. 11:24–25). They function as Israel's representatives. I take it that when Moses dashes the blood on the people (v. 8), he dashes it on these seventy. It would be challenging to dash blood on several million (or thousand) people!

Seventy-three of those who ascend the hill get a glimpse of the divine Shekinah, but only Moses observes the full glow. They receive a foretaste; Moses receives a taste. It is like the three disciples, Peter, James, and John, who are privileged to see Jesus in a way their nine colleagues do not (Matt. 17:1–2, another ascent up a sacred mountain; Matt. 26:37, a farther journey into a garden; Mark 5:37, a step inside a home to see Jesus manhandle death that has taken the life of a twelve-year-old). Apparently God has no favorites, but he does have intimates. The seventy-three left behind or the nine left out do not protest or complain that they are being cut out of the action.

24:3–8 Every covenant is solemnized by some kind of ceremony, be it elaborate or simple. Before Moses and his entourage leave the larger group, it is crucial that the masses hear from Moses what are the Lord's words and guidelines that will shape the way they are to live their lives. Additionally, it is important not only that they hear this word, but also that they respond to it by embracing it enthusiastically: "Everything the LORD has said we will do" (vv. 3b, 7b). That is exactly how they have responded even after they have heard precious little (19:8a). Their enthusiasm is commendable, the honesty and sincerity of their intention undeniable. Alas, it will not be too long (chap. 32) until we hear these same people saying, "All that the LORD has said not to do, we will do."

The scene is not unlike that in later biblical times when godly King Josiah reads the (newly rediscovered) "words of the Book of the Covenant" to his people (2 Kings 23:2b). The covenant is renewed, the hearers pledge a loyalty and faithfulness to this renewed covenant (23:3), and like Jesus, Josiah leads a temple cleansing, expunging anything improper from there (23:4–7). Alas, the moment of exile to Babylon is only a generation away. The covenant people of God, both of Moses's days and of the post-Josiah days, may have sung with Robert Robinson (in "Come, Thou Fount"), "Prone to wander, Lord, I feel it, prone to leave the God I love."

The dashing of the blood first on the altar (v. 6) and then on the people, or their representatives (v. 8a), is a symbolic act, binding both parties of this covenant to each other, Yahweh to Israel, and Israel to Yahweh. That in v. 5 the sacrifices offered on this occasion are the burnt offerings (*ʿōlōt*) and the well-being offerings (*zĕbāḥîm šĕlāmîm*) is significant. Nobody offers up a "sin" offering, a "guilt" offering, or any other kind of offering. Related sacrificial expressions occur in Exodus in 10:25, "sacrifices and burnt offerings" (*zĕbāḥîm wĕʿōlôt*); 18:12, "a burnt offering and sacrifices" (*ʿōlâ ûzĕbāḥîm*); 20:24, "your burnt offerings and fellowship offerings" (*ʿōlōttêkā . . . šĕlāmêkā*); 32:6, "burnt offerings . . . well-being offerings" (*ʿōlōt . . . šĕlāmîm*). Particularly apropos are Deut. 27:6–7 and Josh. 8:31, both of which involve covenant ratification, both of which take place on a mountain, and on both occasions the presider offers *ʿōlōt* and *šĕlāmîm*. According to Lev. 1 and 3, these are nonexpiatory sacrifices joyfully and spontaneously offered to God; they are either totally consumed in the altar's fire (the *ʿōlâ*), or partially consumed, with some of the meat, drained of its blood, going back to the donor (the *šĕlāmîm*).

This particular section of Exodus has contributed much to the soteriological language of the NT. For starters, Moses's phrase "This is the blood of the covenant" (v. 8) and Zech. 9:11 ("because of the blood of my covenant with you") provide the only two verses in the OT with the phrase "blood of the covenant" in them. Ezekiel 44:7 contains both nouns (but not in a construct relationship) but uses them negatively: "you desecrated my temple while you offered me . . . blood, and you broke my covenant" (AT). Jesus, taking the phrase from either Zech. 9:11, or more likely Exod. 24:8 (since it too deals with covenant), says over the cup, "This is my blood of the covenant" (Matt. 26:28; Mark 14:24). Luke has Jesus say, "This cup is the new covenant in my blood" (Luke 22:20). Matthew alone has Jesus add to the phrase "[which is poured out for many] *for the forgiveness of sin*."

The addition in Matthew of this note about sin's forgiveness as part of the cup-word leads us to a second NT passage heavily connected with Exod. 24, and that is Heb. 9:18–22, especially v. 20 ("He [Moses] said, 'This is the blood of the covenant, which God has commanded you to keep'"). Johnson (2006: 241) has noticed five differences between the LXX Greek of Exod. 24 and the Greek of Heb. 9:20. They are as follows: (1) Exod. 24:8, "*Behold* [*idou*], the blood of the covenant," versus Heb. 9:20, "*This* [*touto*] is the blood of the covenant"; (2) Exod. 24:8, "Behold the blood of the covenant, which the Lord has *made* [*dietheto*] with you," versus Heb. 9:20, "This is the blood of the covenant, which God *has commanded* (*eneteilato*) you to keep"; (3) Exod. 24:8, "which *the Lord* [*kyrios*] has made with you," versus Heb. 9:20, "which *God* [*ho theos*] has commanded you to keep"; (4) Heb. 9:20 reverses Exod. 24:8's *kyrios pros hymas* to *pros hymas ho theos*; (5) Heb. 9:20 omits the end of the verse in Exod. 24:8, "concerning all these words" (*peri panton tōn logōn toutōn*). Hebrews 9 also deletes any reference to Moses's building an altar, and the double response of the people's intention to hear and obey, and substitutes "calves" for "young bulls" (cf. Exod. 24). Hebrews 9 also adds items not mentioned in Exod. 24: water, scarlet wool, hyssop branches, and sprinkling the book itself.

Perhaps the most significant of these differences is the change from "*Behold* the blood of the covenant" to "*This* is the blood of the covenant," for it makes the words of Moses and the words of Jesus at the Last Supper over the cup almost identical (yet Moses cannot say "This is *my* blood of the covenant"). Also Heb. 9:22, like Matt. 26:28 but unlike Exod. 24, ascribes to the blood an expiatory function: "And without the shedding of blood there is no forgiveness."

24:9–11 Unlike v. 2, which sets Moses's privilege of access to the divine apart from his colleagues, the electrifying theophany recorded in these three verses is the privilege of all the seventy-five. No words are exchanged, either from God to mortals, or from mortals to God, or from mortals to mortals. When God shows up, sometimes it is that his voice may be heard. At other times when God shows up, it is simply that his glowing presence be enjoyed and experienced. Any conversation is out of place. God's verbal presence has come earlier. Now it is time to bask in his visual presence.

That this group is said to "see" (*rā'â*) God in v. 10 and "behold" (*ḥāzâ*) him in v. 11 is startling, especially when the same book of Exodus (33:20) has the Lord saying, "You cannot see my face, for no one may see me and live." No wonder the LXX tones the phrases down with "And they saw the place, there where the God of Israel stood" (*kai eidon ton topon ou eistēkei ekei ho theos tou Israēl*) in 24:10, and with "and they appeared in the place of God" (*kai ōphthēsan en tō topō tou theou*) in v. 11. Similarly Deut. 4:12 says, and this could refer to Exod. 19 rather than to Exod. 24, "You saw no form; there was only a voice."

But if this group actually sees God, nobody, then or later, describes what he sees, what God looks like. Immediately the camera of the text moves downward to capture what lies beneath the divine feet. And even here the narrator uses the language of analogy or approximation (as throughout Ezekiel's vision of God in Ezek. 1): "something like." The brick is described; God is not.

Who eats and drinks? Does God participate too? What do they eat and drink? Whose idea was it to bring food along, or is it God as host who provides the food and beverage? He does that earlier in Exodus for his people (chaps. 15–17). Is this a sacred covenant meal, or a happy, Sinaitic potluck? For Moses, at least, it will be forty days until he eats and drinks again (Exod. 34:28; Deut. 9:9, 18). Not so with the other participants.

Genesis 26:30 records the feast that Isaac makes with neighboring Philistines after a covenant is made, at which both parties "ate and drank." The same goes for the covenant that Jacob makes with Laban (31:44), which is followed by a meal (31:46; cf. v. 54). There are parallels too with Elijah in 1 Kings 18. As God tells Moses alone to come near (*nāgaš*) in v. 2, the prophet uses the same verb for his people (1 Kings 18:30). Moses builds an altar of twelve stone pillars (Exod. 24:4) and dashes blood on it, and Elijah repairs the broken altar using twelve stones, and swamps it with water (1 Kings 18:30–31). In Exod. 24:1 God says to Moses and the rest, "Go up," the same imperative Elijah uses with King Ahab in 1 Kings 18:41. Perhaps the best parallel is the one between the eating and the drinking in Exod. 24:11, and Elijah's telling Ahab to "go up, eat and drink. . . . So Ahab went up to eat and to drink" (1 Kings 18:41–42 NRSV). The supreme parallel to Exod. 24:11 is, of course, "the Last Supper." Maybe the wedding reception after the covenant of marriage is an extension of this. The holy hour and the happy hour flow together.

In addition to being a celebratory covenant meal, this partaking of food is "a sign that the weaker is taken into the family of the stronger, a reassuring gesture on the part of the superior toward the inferior, and not a pledge by the latter" (D. McCarthy 1981: 254). At Sinai, God has instituted a quasi-familial relationship with Israel, and healthy families eat together.

The Glory of the Lord Seen from Below

(24:12–18)

Translation

[12]And the LORD said to Moses, "Come up
to me to the mountain and be there. And
I will give you the tablets of stone, that
is, the teaching and commandment that
I have written to instruct them." [13]Moses
arose, and Joshua his attendant, and
Moses went up God's mountain. [14]To the
elders he had said, "Remain here for us
until we return to you. Aaron and Hur are
with you. Anybody with a grievance may
approach them."

[15]Moses went up the mountain, and the
cloud encased the mountain. [16]The LORD's
glory settled on Mount Sinai, and the cloud
encased it six days. He summoned Moses
on the seventh day from the cloud's midst.
[17]And the sight of the LORD's glory was like
consuming fire at the mountain's peak in
the sight of Israel's sons. [18]And Moses en-
tered into the midst of the cloud and went
up the mountain. Moses was on the moun-
tain forty days and forty nights.

Grammatical and Lexical Notes

24:12. The rendering "that is" before "teaching" is accomplished by reading the *wāw* on *wĕhattôrâ* as a *wāw explicativum,* rather than as a conjunctive *wāw* ("*and* the teaching"). "Teaching and commandment" is an anomalous, but not unexpected, term for the Ten Commandments.

24:13. For Joshua as Moses's "attendant," see Exod. 33:11; Num. 11:28; Josh. 1:1.

24:14. *Bāzeh* has the meaning "here" and is the equivalent of *pōh*. Compare Gen. 38:21, "There hasn't been any shrine prostitute *here* [*bāzeh*]."

24:14. *Mî-ba ʿal dĕbārîm* raise several translation issues. Literally, it says, "Who[ever] [is] possessor/master of words." To begin with, *mî* is the interrogative pronoun used as an indefinite ("whoever"), as in 32:26, "Whoever [*mî*] is for the LORD . . . ," and in 32:33, "Whoever [*mî*] has sinned against me . . ." See also Judg. 7:3; 2 Sam. 20:11; Eccles. 5:10 [9]; 9:4. Second, *dĕbārîm* does not have its normal meaning "words" but something like "accusation, charge, grievance." See BDB 182.1g. under *dābār* I. See, for example, Deut. 19:15, "A matter/accusation/grievance [*dābār*] must be established by the testimony of two or three witnesses," and Deut. 22:20, "If, however, the charge [*haddābār*] is true . . ." Rabinowitz (1954: 16) cites a similar use of *dābār* from Mishnah *Ketubbot* 10.6: *Dîn ûdĕbarîm ʾên lî ʿimmak*, "I have no lawsuit *or claim* against you."

24:17. *ʾĒš ʾōkelet*, "consuming fire," does not necessarily mean the fire was "eating up, destroying" everything in its path. When the verb *ʾākal* is used to describe the action of fire, the phrase can just as well mean "a blazing fire." For the Hebrew phrase, see Deut. 4:24; 9:3; Isa. 30:27. Avishur (1975: 15) finds a parallel in the Phoenician Kilamuwa inscription: "But I was in the hands of the kings like a fire that devours (*k mʾš ʾklt*) the beard, and like a fire that devours (*w[k m]ʾš ʾklt*) the hand."

Commentary

Verses 9–11 focused on what Moses and the seventy-three who ascend partway **24:12–18**
up Mount Sinai see. As Moses and Joshua ascend to the cloud perimeter, and then only Moses beyond that into the very cloud itself, the Israelites at the mountain's base behold the Lord's glory as a blazing fire (v. 17). The seventy-four see God. The masses see the glory of God. Earlier the seventy-four have seen God (vv. 10–11), but now not even the seventy-three nor Joshua can any longer see Moses. He has pulled a disappearing act.

Moses seems to have a sense that he will not reappear for a while. To that end, he has commissioned Aaron and Hur to handle any grievances or disputes that emerge while he is absent (v. 14). In such a holy place, at such a holy moment, with the Lord's magnificent glory within sight, and having gone on record as being obedient to the Lord, will the people still engage in disobedience, behavior that runs counter to everything they have just said and seen? Apparently yes.

The scene in 24:12–18 anticipates that at the very end of Exodus and into the first verse of Leviticus (Exod. 40:34–38; Lev. 1:1). Note these parallels: (1) "And the cloud encased the mountain" (24:15b) and "Then the cloud encased the tent of meeting" (40:34a); (2) "The LORD's glory settled on Mount Sinai" (24:16a) and "The LORD's glory filled the tabernacle" (40:34b); (3) "He summoned/called to Moses . . . from the cloud's midst" (24:16b) and "The LORD summoned/called to Moses . . . from the tent of meeting" (Lev. 1:1); (4) "like a consuming fire . . . in the sight of Israel's sons" (24:17b) and "fire was in the cloud by night, in the sight of all the house of Israel" (40:38b).

Yet, for all these similarities in concept and phraseology, there is one significant difference between the two passages. Exodus 24:18a says, "And Moses entered [*wayyābōʾ*] into the midst of the cloud." In contrast, Exod. 40:35a says, "Moses was not able to enter [*wĕlōʾ-yākōl mōšeh lābôʾ*] the tent of meeting." So we have Exod. 24, able to enter; yet Exod. 40, not able to enter. The cloud of Exod. 24, admission granted to Moses; the place of worship of Exod. 40, admission denied to Moses.

Maybe one reason for the denial in chap. 40 is that the glory that covers the tent of meeting is even greater than the glory that covers Sinai. To that end, one of the purposes of the tabernacle (as the dwelling place of God) is to intensify the Sinai experience: Israel will have more of God's glory right in the midst of its camp than Israel is able to observe at Sinai's top.

Milgrom (1991: 137) provides two other explanations. In the first place, the denial of permission for Moses to enter the tent in chap. 40 provides a parallel between Moses's first experience of God at Sinai (chap. 3), and his first experience of God at the tabernacle. In chap. 40 he is not allowed to enter, and in 3:5 at the burning bush God tells him, "Do not come any closer." A second explanation is that Moses's ability in chap. 24 to enter the cloud *this one time* underscores the uniqueness of the encounter with God at Sinai, just as the seventy-plus who "saw" and "beheld" God had a unique, onetime experience. They will never "see" God again, and Moses will never "enter" the cloud again. When he does enter the tent, it is to *hear* God, not to *see* God (Exod. 25:22). However, regardless of whether Moses has seen God or simply heard his voice, both situations produce a divine glow on his face when he rejoins his people (34:29–35). So "seeing" God's face is not more crucial than "hearing" his voice.

All three Synoptics record the cloud as covering the Mount of Transfiguration (Matt. 17:1–8; Mark 9:2–13; Luke 9:28–36). But only Luke (9:34b) has this part: "And they [Peter, James, and John] were afraid as they entered the cloud." What Moses has done, the three disciples do: they enter the cloud. Perhaps Moses's heartbeat also accelerates as he enters his own holy of holies.

PART 5

How to Build the Tabernacle

(25:1–31:18)

The previous part of Exodus (19:1–24:18) concludes with a ratification of the covenant between the Lord and Israel, with the latter pledging, not once but twice (24:3b, 7b), faithful obedience to this covenant as they had done in 19:8. Conceivably Exodus could conclude at this point. If the curtain falls here on the book, then the climactic message of Exodus would be that God has delivered Israel out of Egypt, entered into a covenant with the people at Sinai, and given the Israelites numerous stipulations, which they are to obey.

However, there are a couple of little paragraphs at the end of chap. 24 that shift the emphasis from what Israel "heard" at Sinai to what Israel "saw" at Sinai (see 24:9–11 and 12–18). Verses 9–10a inform us, amazingly, that Moses and seventy-four other leaders "saw the God of Israel," and v. 17 tells us that everybody saw the glory of God, which "looked like a consuming fire." To climb the mountain, to see God and eat there—all this suggests something about being in God's visible presence.

As such, the last portion of part 4 of Exodus forms a perfect bridge into part 5 (giving the tabernacle blueprint), for the tabernacle is surely about divine presence. It is a place where God "meets" with his people. It is now the closest one can get to "seeing" God. Because Exodus extends beyond chap. 24 into chaps. 25–31 (and the mostly parallel chaps. 35–40), the structure of the book of Exodus suggests that God desires not only his people's obedience but also their fellowship, not only their conformity but also their communion. God is not only holy (19–24); he is also host (25–31). Perhaps we should combine the two and call him Israel's "holy host." The first of these two words ("holy") prevents Israel from perceiving God as easily and always available and forever cozy and cuddly. The second of these two words ("host") prevents Israel from perceiving God as remote and disinterested.

One thing that stands out in part 5 (and 7) is the attention to every minor detail as God reveals to Moses how he wants Moses to build the tabernacle: the dimensions of each compartment and object, what different fabrics to use, what kind of wood, how many sockets and poles and hooks, gold and silver everywhere, an incense recipe, ephods, sashes, headbands, and so forth. It seems we have gone from the miraculous throughout chaps. 1–17, and from the mandates of chaps. 19–24, to the mundane and meticulous and minutiae of chaps. 25–31. To the low-church evangelical Protestant, it may all appear too Catholic, too structured, too liturgical, too sacramental, and not sufficiently ethical, too Johannine and not adequately enough Pauline.

Indeed, this place of worship is a beautiful place. Why should it not be aesthetically pleasing? It is a place of worship that appeals to the senses, and especially to visual sensibility. But what is it that gives this place its beauty? The high quality of craftsmanship under the supervision of Bezalel and Oholiab? The ornate holy furnishings, most of which are overlaid with pure gold? The curtains made from interweaving different kinds of beautiful fabrics? The odor of the incense?

No, all these beautiful items are but symbols, yet important symbols, to be sure. What makes this place of worship so compelling is the presence of God in its midst. No Israelite ever walks away from this tabernacle after a worship experience and says, "What a bronze altar!" or "What curtain flaps!" or "Best incense I've ever smelled!" or "Nice turban on the Reverend's head!" What they surely say after they exit the gate of the courtyard must be something like "What a God! And just think, he invited us into his residence to meet with him!"

The Tabernacle: An Overview

Exodus devotes approximately two chapters to narrating the exodus from Egypt, two-thirds of one chapter to the Decalogue, but thirteen to the tabernacle (sixteen if one includes the interlude in chaps. 32–34). That is about one-third of the entire book. That such a large portion should be assigned to one topic highlights the importance of worship in the life of the community, the importance of the presence of God among his people.

It is difficult, if not impossible, to think of Christianity without churches, Judaism without synagogues, Islam without mosques, Buddhism without temples. The same goes for ancient Near Eastern religion(s) as well. From Egypt to Mesopotamia, temples abounded. Fretheim (1991: 273) notes that sanctuaries and temples, but particularly the wilderness tabernacle, brought three dynamics to the worshiping community: (1) "a sanctuary brought *order* to the worship of God versus an anything-goes attitude"; (2) a sanctuary provided "a *tangible* sense of God's presence" (that is where you can find him); (3) a sanctuary provided "a point of *assurance* of God's presence and a point of *stability*" in the midst of an unstable and uncertain wilderness (italics original).

Hurowitz (1985) has drawn attention to three Near Eastern texts about temple building that have some affinity with the tabernacle. The first of these is a Sumerian text from near the end of the third millennium BC in which the god Ningirsu appears to Gudea, king of Lagash, and informs him of the plan of the temple he wishes Gudea to build, much as Yahweh does to Moses in chaps. 25–31. There is a double description of the temple's contents, one when Ningirsu first reveals it to Gudea, and a second one when the temple is actually being built, again like what we have in (a) chaps. 25–31 and (b) chaps. 35–40.

A second text with parallels, and perhaps the closest to Exodus, is the account in Akkadian by Samsuiluna, king of Babylon (1749–1712 BC), on building a temple. As in the Gudea cylinders and in Exodus, Samsuiluna builds the temple at the command of the god Enlil. The design and contents of the temple are described twice, first by Enlil, who mandates the project, and second by Samsuiluna, in his account of his fulfilling Enlil's order. When he finishes, Samsuiluna adds, "I did what was good to Samas, Adad, and

Aya. I fulfilled the command of Samas and Marduk." This sounds a lot like "and Moses did all that the Lord commanded him" scattered over the last two chapters of Exodus.

The third building project text is from Ugarit. Asherah represents Baal before El, the head of the Canaanite pantheon, asking El for permission for Baal to build a palace. When El gives the green light, Asherah sends Anat to Baal with the good news, and so Baal begins to build. For parallels between this Canaanite text and Exodus, see the chart in Hurowitz 1985: 29.

To a certain degree, then, some of Israel's fundamental institutions are not absolutely unique. As we saw earlier, it is Jethro, a "foreigner," a priest of Midian, who counsels Moses adroitly and marvelously about the nuts and bolts of the daily administration of justice (chap. 18). It is unlikely that only in Israel did one hear, "Honor your father and mother" or "You shall not kill" (chap. 20). Some of the laws from the Covenant Code, as we have seen, appear either almost verbatim or very similar in one or more of the law codes from the larger, biblical world (chaps. 21–23). Hence, the extension of some degree of parallelism into the last section of Exodus is not unexpected.

Most of the suggested parallels for the revelation of the tabernacle's design and construction come from the third and second millennia BC; yet many scholars tend to date the existence of the account of the Mosaic tabernacle (if the grand Exodus version ever existed) to the late exilic period. If the tabernacle is a Bronze Age artifact, it is a very modest and simple structure by contrast. Kitchen (1993: 123) compares the entire 75-foot by 150-foot area with the 1,200-foot by 600-foot temples of Rameses II and III at Medinet Habu near Thebes. To place the tabernacle beside one of those temples would be like placing a Quaker meetinghouse next to Notre Dame or Westminster Abbey.

What we have in Exodus—but in none of the three texts cited above, or in any other Near Eastern text—is that the tabernacle narrative is not an incident that exists by itself. It is part of a larger story, one that stretches from Gen. 1 to Exod. 40 (and beyond).

Note how it relates to what has immediately preceded: the theophany and the giving of the law and covenant at Sinai (19–24). I see several connections. First, the Sinai experience serves as a prototype of the tabernacle. Each is divided into three areas: (1) only Moses may ascend to the summit of Sinai, and only the high priest may enter the holy of holies; (2) only Aaron, his sons, and the seventy elders (and Joshua) may ascend Mount Sinai, and only the priests may enter the holy place; (3) the masses of laypeople gather at the base of the mountain, and the laity assemble in the outer courtyard, but go no farther.

Second, the tabernacle perpetuates the Mount Sinai experience. The glory of the Lord and the cloud that have settled on the mountain (24:16) now move to do the same with the tabernacle (40:34). Mountains do not move, but the glory of the Lord and his cloud can and do. There comes a time to leave mountains behind, however sacred (even if Peter wishes to remain on his), but that does not mean that one leaves God behind.

Third, the tabernacle intensifies the Mount Sinai experience. At the summit of Mount Sinai, Moses enters the cloud (24:18). But when the same glory covers the tabernacle, Moses is not able to enter it (40:35).

Fourth, the tabernacle relocates the Mount Sinai experience. The God whose presence has shrouded the top of Mount Sinai, far away from the Israelites at the base, will now dwell in the midst of his people, at the center of their encampment. The transcendent One becomes the incarnate One, with the result that every last Israelite will be able "to behold his glory" from a much closer vantage point. But the Holy One does not suddenly shift from being invisible to being visible to all. He remains, to use something of an oxymoron, an out-of-sight Immanuel. It is the truth that John articulates in his Gospel (John 1:14) about the eternal Word taking on flesh and "pitching his tent" (AT) among us that extends the degree of God's visibility. G. H. Davies (1962: 506) correctly ties together this latter section of Exodus and the teaching of the Second Testament when he says that the wilderness tabernacle is "the principal bridgehead in the OT to the doctrine of the Incarnation."

If there is a connection in chaps. 25–31, 35–40 with what immediately precedes it, then there is also a connection with what momentarily halts the building project and threatens to derail it: the golden-calf scenario and its aftermath in chaps. 32–34. The flow in these last chapters is from instruction (25–31) to interruption (32–34) to implementation (35–40). The contrast is between true worship (25–31, 35–40) and false worship (32–34). At the heart of either kind of worship is something that Israel builds, something God wants them to build (25–31) and something he does not want them to build (32). One thing that Israel builds brings his blessing. The calf that Israel builds brings his judgment.

There is also an emphasis on building at the beginning and end of Exodus. At the start of Exodus, the Israelites are building what Pharaoh and the Egyptians force them to build. This first building project was onerous and degrading. The second is joyous and uplifting.

Finally, one can observe some parallels between this building project at the end of Exodus and God's "building" project at the start of Genesis. For starters, Kearney (1977) has connected the Lord's seven speeches to Moses in Exod. 25–31 with the seven days of Gen. 1–2: (day 1) Exod. 25:1 and 25:2–30:10; (2) 30:11 and 30:12–16; (3) 30:17 and 30:18–21; (4) 30:22 and 30:23–33; (5) 30:34a and 30:34b–38; (6) 31:1 and 31:2–11; (7) 31:12 and 31:13–17. The most obvious parallel is between the Lord's seventh speech to Moses (31:12 and 31:13–17), which focuses on the Sabbath day as a day of cessation from labor and the emphasis on rest, and God's ceasing his labor and resting on the seventh day (Gen. 2:1–4a).

Other scholars (e.g., Blenkinsopp 1976: 280; 1977: 62) have noticed some similar phraseology in both sections of Scripture (his trans.):

"And God saw everything that he had made, and behold it was very good" (Gen. 1:31).	"And Moses saw all the work, and behold they had done it; as the LORD had commanded, so had they done it" (Exod. 39:43).
"Thus the heavens and the earth were finished" (Gen. 2:1).	"Thus all the work of the tabernacle . . . was finished" (Exod. 39:42).
"God finished the work which he had done" (Gen. 2:2).	"So Moses finished the work" (Exod. 40:33).
"So God blessed the seventh day" (Gen. 2:3).	"And Moses blessed them" (Exod. 39:43).

Possibly Exod. 32 functions in the book of Exodus much like Gen. 3 does in the opening chapters of Genesis. There is a monumental deviation in Gen. 3 and Exod. 32 from the divine norm, which only divine grace can resolve and heal.

In the commentary to follow, I shall focus primarily on chaps. 25–31 since much of 35–40 repeats its contents. I will note only those instances where there is something new in the latter portion. When we set the two sections side by side, some interesting items emerge (see the chart in Longacre 1995: 35, which I have modified somewhat):

A. Projected construction (25:1–30:38)	B. Narrated construction (36:8–39:31)
1. The ark (25:10–16)	5. The tent curtains (36:8–13)
2. The ark's cover (25:17–22)	6. The curtain over the tent (36:14–19)
3. The table (25:23–30)	7. The tent's framework (36:20–34)
4. The lampstand (25:31–40)	8. The veil (36:35–36)
5. The tent curtains (26:1–6)	9. The curtain before the holy place (36:37–38)
6. The curtain over the tent (26:7–14)	1. The ark (37:1–5)
7. The tent's framework (26:15–29)	2. The ark's cover (37:6–9)
8. The veil (26:31–33)	3. The table (37:10–16)
9. The curtain before the holy place (26:36–37)	4. The lampstand (37:17–24)
10. The outer altar (27:1–8)	18. The incense altar (37:25–28)
11. The courtyard (27:9–15)	20. Anointing oil (37:29)
12. The curtain before the courtyard (27:16–18)	10. The outer altar (38:1–7)
13. The ephod (28:6–14)	19. The laver (38:8)
14. The breastpiece (28:15–30)	11. The courtyard (38:9–17)

A. Projected construction (25:1–30:38)	**B. Narrated construction (36:8–39:31)**
15. The robe of the ephod (28:31–35)	12. The curtain before the courtyard (38:18–20)
16. The golden diadem (28:36–38)	13. The ephod (39:1–7)
17. Tunic, turban, sash (28:39–41)	14. The breastpiece (39:8–21)
x. (The undergarments) (28:42–43)	15. The robe of the ephod (39:22–26)
y. (Priests' ordination) (29:1–37)	17. Tunic, turban, sash (39:27–29)
z. (Daily offerings) (29:38–46)	16. The golden diadem (39:30–31)
18. The incense altar (30:1–10) (atonement money) (30:11–16)	
19. The laver (30:17–21)	
20. Anointing oil (30:22–33) (incense) (30:34–38)	

It is clear that the sequence does not match. For example, in part A the directions for how to build the inner altar of incense do not come until near the end of the unit (30:1–10), and they are separated from directions about other pieces of furniture. In part B, its actual construction comes on the heels of the construction of other pieces of furniture (37:25–28). A possible reason for this is offered by Milgrom (1991: 236–37). He observes that God's instructions to Moses fall into two sections: the tabernacle in blueprint (25:1–27:19) and the tabernacle in operation (27:20–30:38). Directions about the incense altar come in this second section because it is described functionally (see 30:7–8). The same explanation would apply to the delay of information about the laver (30:17–21).

Another difference in sequence is that part A begins with the items to be placed in the two inner, holy cubicles, excepting the incense altar (steps 1–4), then moves to a description of the facility in which they are to be housed (steps 5–9). Part B reverses that order and is the more logical one. Which does a first-time homebuyer do first: purchase or remodel a home and then get the furniture, or get the furniture and then purchase or remodel the home? By beginning with these "holy things," part A draws attention to the special significance of these sancta. If the entrance curtains and the framework curtains could speak, they would say of these sancta, "They must increase, but we must decrease" (cf. John 3:30).

Making a Sanctuary for God

(25:1–9; cf. 35:4–9)

Translation

[1]And the LORD spoke to Moses, saying: [2]"Speak to Israel's sons that they raise for me a contribution. From every man whose heart moves him you shall raise my contribution. [3]This is the contribution that you shall raise from them: gold and silver and bronze, [4]and blue, and purple, and crimson material, and linen and goat's hair, [5]and reddened ram's skins and dyed dolphin skins and acacia wood, [6]oil for the lamp, spices for the oil of unction, and for the perfumed incense, [7]onyx stones and stones for setting in the ephod and the breastpiece. [8]And they shall make me a sacred precinct, that I may dwell in their midst. [9]Exactly as I have shown you the replica of the dwelling place and the replica of all its furnishings, thus shall you make [it]."

Grammatical and Lexical Notes

25:2. The Hebrew word *tĕrûmâ* ("contribution, donation") is formed from the verb *rûm* ("lift, exalt") and literally means "what is lifted." Perhaps something in English like "levied contribution/donation" would fit. It is often associated with another similar-sounding word for "gift," *tĕnûpâ*. The two occur together in Exod. 29:27, "You shall consecrate the breast of the *tĕnûpâ* and the thigh of the *tĕrûmâ* that is waved (*hûnap*) and that is raised (*hûrām*)." The KJV renders *tĕnûpâ* as "wave offering" and *tĕrûmâ* as "heave offering." Whether these are the best translations is debatable. Thus, to call one offering "what is lifted" need not mean "lifted Godward," but "lifted," that is, "raised" from the donors. Churches still "raise" offerings. When coupled with YHWH as the object who receives the offering, one basic difference between the two offerings, as Milgrom (1991: 674) has pointed out, is that one makes a *tĕrûmâ "to* the LORD" (Exod. 25:2; 29:28; 30:13; 35:5; Lev. 7:14; Num. 15:19, 21), while one makes a *tĕnûpâ "before* the LORD" (Exod. 29:24; Lev. 7:30; 9:21; 10:15; 14:12; 23:11, 20; Num. 6:20; 8:11, 13, 15). This difference suggests that *tĕnûpâ* is associated with ritual and performed in the sanctuary, while *tĕrûmâ* can be offered anytime, anywhere. Normally, *tĕrûmâ* designates food gifts (Exod. 29:27–28; Lev. 7:12–14; Num. 15:19–21), but here the word refers to gifts of materials for building the tabernacle (Exod. 25:2–3; 35:21, 24; 36:3, 6).

25:2. The verb *nādab* ("moves") occurs again in the Qal only in 35:21, 29, both of which relate back to its initial use in 25:2. In later Biblical Hebrew (Ezra, Nehemiah, Chronicles) the verb reappears more than a dozen times in the Hitpael stem to refer to the peoples' readiness to donate freewill offerings (e.g., Ezra 1:6; 2:68). Compare also the lyrics of Deborah's song (Judg. 5:2, 9). See Hurvitz 1974: 29–32.

25:4. The word for "crimson" (*tôla ʿat*) occurs in the famous Isaiah passage, Isa. 1:18, "Though your sins are *like scarlet* [*kattôla ʿ*] . . ." The phrase *tôla ʿat šānî* ("crimson material") occurs in reverse order in Lev. 14:4: *šĕnî tôla ʿat*.

25:5. On *mĕʾādāmîm* ("reddened"), see A. Brenner's (1982: 110–12) study of this color term.

25:5. *Tĕḥāšîm* is still obscure (dolphin? porpoise? sea cow?), or is it a color term, "yellow-orange"? If it is the latter, then maybe Hebrew *taḥaš* is to be connected with Akkadian *tah-si-a*, which refers to leather dyed with some kind of pigment.

25:5. The LXX translates "acacia wood" (*ʿăṣê šiṭṭîm*) as "decay-resistant wood" (*xula asēpta*). Perhaps acacia wood is the equivalent of California redwood. In ancient Egypt it was considered a holy tree. A number of sites in the Bible have this tree as part of their name: Shittim (Num. 25:1; Josh. 2:1; 3:1); Abel Shittim (Num. 33:49); Beth Shittah (Judg. 7:22); Nahal Hashshittim (NIV, "the valley of acacias") in Joel 3:18 [4:18].

25:6. For *šemen hammišḥâ* ("the oil of unction"), see 29:7; Num. 4:16. Exodus 30:25, 31 call it "the sacred oil of unction," while Num. 35:25 calls it "the sacred oil."

25:8. The Hebrew word for "sacred precinct" is *miqdāš*. It refers not only to a sacred area but also to the sacred objects that are placed in that area, and hence v. 9 includes a reference to the "furnishings" as part of the *miqdāš*. The NIV translates the word as "sanctuary" every time it occurs in the Pentateuch, except for Num. 10:21 ("Then the Kohathites set out, carrying *the holy things* [*hammiqdāš*]"). The same double meaning goes for *qōdeš haqqŏdāšîm*: (a) "most holy place" or "holy of holies" and (b) "most holy things" as in Num. 4:4, "This is the work of the Kohathites: . . . the care of the *most holy things*." It is somewhat surprising that while derivatives of the root *qdš* ("holy") occur some eighty times in Exodus (mostly in 25–40), the word for this structure that contains this root, *miqdāš* (lit., "holy place" or "sanctuary") occurs only here in Exodus and back in 15:17. By contrast, in Exodus, *miškān* ("dwelling place") appears fifty-six times, and *ʾōhel môʿēd* ("tent of meeting") thirty-four times (statistics in Leder 1999: 29).

25:8. Once again the LXX tones down the Hebrew "that I may dwell in their midst" to "and I will appear among them" (*kai ophthēsomai en hymin*).

25:9. Should *tabnît* be translated as "design, model, pattern," or "replica"? Does God reveal a model, a blueprint, to Moses, or does he show him the heavenly sanctuary, and say, "Moses, make it exactly like that one"? Andersen and Freedman (1980: 631) comment on this word: "The thing made is the *tabnît* of what it is copied from. The original is not the pattern of the manufactured object. What Moses saw on the mount was not a plan of the tabernacle, but an *actual* tabernacle, the real or original one. What he made was the exact reproduction so that the glory of God could be housed in earth in a manner comparable to God's dwelling in heaven."

25:9. The first "you" in this verse, in "I have shown *you*," is a singular "you" (Moses). But the "you" in "thus *you* shall make [it]" at the end of the verse is a plural "you" (Israel). Both LXX and SP change MT's plural *taʿăśû* into singular *taʿăśeh*.

Commentary

The first verse of this unit introduces the longest divine speech in all of Exo- 25:1–9
dus, 25:2–30:10. Knierim (1995a: 115) nicely outlines it as follows (with my own slight modifications):

I. Narrative about Yahweh's speech to Moses (25:1–30:10)
  A. Formulaic narrative introduction (25:1)
  B. The speech—an instruction (25:2–30:10)
    1. The commission to Moses (25:2a)

2. The content of the speech (25:2b–30:10)
   a. The call for an offering . . . and its purpose (25:3–9)
   b. The instruction for manufacturing (25:10–30:10)

It is significant that God instructs Moses to relay these instructions to the Israelite people and not to the Israelite priests. The Torah clearly distinguishes between those occasions when Moses delivers a message to the laity (Exod. 25:2; 27:20; Lev. 1:2; 4:2; 7:23, 29; 12:2; Num. 5:2; 9:10; 15:2, 18; 28:2; 34:2; 35:2, 10), and when he delivers a message to the clergy (Lev. 6:9 [2], 25 [18]; 8:31; 9:2, 7; 10:3, 6, 8, 12; 16:2; 17:2; Num. 18:26). Priests serve in the sanctuary, but the laity construct it and will later worship in it. One wonders if Moses writes down any of these instructions for the people as he hears them from the Lord. After all, the details are extensive and quite minute. How much can we expect him to remember?

It is also significant that Moses first asks for donations to fund the project before he talks to the people about the tabernacle's design. One might expect that order to be reversed: first show them the plans, and then ask them to get behind it financially. Is that not how most religious communities wishing to construct a new building or expand and renovate an older building would go about it? Congregants tend to be more enthusiastic and generous when they can see, at least in blueprint, what their pledges and dollars are funding.

Moses's congregation is hardly skeptical. They do not adopt a cautious wait-and-see attitude. Exodus 36:6–7 describes a most unusual church problem! Moses has to issue an order instructing his people not to give any more, for more than enough is already on hand. I have often thought that 1 Cor. 15, Paul's breathtaking, marvelous chapter on Christ's resurrection and the believers' resurrection, would have been a great note on which to end this epistle. But there is a chap. 16, which begins, "Now about the collection . . ." Could anything be more anticlimactic, or is it a natural and necessary sequel to chap. 15?

Clearly the Israelites are carrying many valuables with them as they head to Canaan: not only precious metals like gold and silver, but also costly dyed materials. No wonder desert inhabitants like the Amalekites (17:8–16) lick their lips when they spot these mostly unarmed, vulnerable Israelites passing through their territory! Seizure of such goods will be like taking candy from a baby, so they think (wrongfully).

Verse 8 calls this place of worship a *miqdāš* ("sanctuary, sacred precinct"), while v. 9 calls it a *miškān* ("tabernacle, dwelling place"). Ezekiel 37:27–28 also uses these two words, but in reverse order, and with different following prepositions: "My dwelling place [*miškān*] will be *with/over* [*ʿal*] them. . . . Then the nations will know . . . when my sanctuary [*miqdāš*] is *among* [*bĕtôk*] them forever." Other passages, however, do use *bĕtôk* after *miškān*, as in Lev. 15:31 ("*my dwelling place*, which is *among* them") and Lev. 26:11 ("I will put *my dwelling place among* you"). Plus, the common phrase for God "to dwell among" his people is *šākan bĕtôk*: Exod. 25:8; 29:45–46; Num. 5:3; 35:34; 1 Kings 6:13; Ezek. 43:9; Zech. 2:10, 11 [14, 15].

It is this concept of "dwelling," as I said above, that makes the old covenant concept of the tabernacle an obvious connector with the new covenant's teaching about the incarnation. Says John 1:14, "The Word became flesh and made his dwelling among/tented among/tabernacled among us." In the old-covenant era, the Word never becomes flesh, but the Shekinah of Mount Sinai descends from Sinai's summit, enters into the encampment of the covenant people, and places itself at its very center as they make their journey to Canaan.

The Ark of the Covenant and Its Cover

(25:10–22; cf. 37:1–9)

Translation

10"And they shall make an ark of acacia wood, two and a half cubits its length, and a cubit and a half its width, and a cubit and a half its height. 11And you shall overlay it with pure gold, inside and outside you shall overlay it, and you shall make upon it a golden molding around it. 12And you shall cast for it four rings of gold, and place them on its four feet, two rings on its one side and two rings on its second side. 13And you shall make poles of acacia wood, and overlay them with gold, 14and you shall insert the poles into the rings through the ring on the sidewalls of the ark to carry the ark by them. 15In the rings of the ark the poles must be. They are not to be removed from it. 16And you shall place in the ark the testimony that I shall give you.

17"And you shall make a cover/propitiatory of pure gold, two and a half cubits its length, a cubit and a half its width 18And you shall make two cherubim of gold, from pounded work you shall make them at the two edges of the cover/propitiatory. 19And make one cherub at this one edge and one cherub at the other edge; from the cover/propitiatory you shall make the cherubim at both its edges. 20The cherubim shall have their wings spread out above, shielding with their wings the cover/propitiatory, and their faces pointing toward each other; in the direction of the cover/propitiatory shall the cherubim's faces be. 21And you shall place the cover/propitiatory over the ark from above, and in the ark you shall place the testimony that I shall give you. 22And I will meet with you there, and speak with you—from above the cover/propitiatory between the two cherubim that are on top of the ark of the testimony—all that I will command you concerning Israel's sons."

Grammatical and Lexical Notes

25:10. The "they shall make" of v. 10a and "From the cover *you shall make*" of v. 19b are the only plural "making" verbs in these thirteen verses. Every other "you" is a singular "you." The LXX and SP change "they shall make" of v. 10a into "you [sg.] shall make" (*wĕʿāśû* into *wĕʿāśîtā*), and the "you shall make" of v. 19b into a Niphal, "shall be made" (*taʿăśû* into *yēʿāśû*).

25:12. The Hebrew word for "side" (here and in v. 14, *ṣēlāʿ*) is the word famously translated as "rib" in Gen. 2:21.

25:15. Since the antecedent of "it" in "not removed from it" refers back to the word "ring" (sg., *ṭabbaʿat*; pl., *ṭabbāʿôt*), which is feminine, one would expect *mimmennâ* instead of *mimmennû* for "from it." The Masora gives five other instances where *mimmennû* is used where *mimmennâ* is expected (Lev. 6:15 [8]; 7:18; 27:9; Josh. 1:7; Judg. 11:34). Note especially Lev. 27:9, which uses first *mimmennâ*, then *mimmennû*, in reference to an animal/*bĕhēmâ* (feminine). Note also that Judg. 11:34 says of Jephthah's daughter: "Except for *her* [*mimmennû*!] he had neither son nor daughter."

25:16. *Hā ʿēdut* ("the testimony") is ellipsis for *luḥōt hā ʿēdut* ("the tablets of the testimony") in Exod. 31:18; 32:15; 34:29. Other expressions are (1) "The tablets of stone" (*luḥōt hā ʾeben*) in Exod. 24:12 and Deut. 9:9; (2) "The tablets of the stones" (*luḥōt hā ʾăbānîm*) in Deut. 4:13; 9:11; 1 Kings 8:9; and (3) "The tablets of the covenant" (*luḥōt habbĕrît*) in Deut. 9:9, 11.

25:17. I shall reserve comments on *kappōret* ("lid, cover, propitiatory") for below.

25:22. "The ark of the testimony" (*ʾărōn hā ʿēdut*) is one way of referring to this sacred chest (also Exod. 26:33–34; 30:6, 26; 39:35; 40:3, 5, 21; etc.). Others are (1) "the ark of God/the Lord" (Josh. 3:13; 4:5; 6:6, 7, 11, 13; 7:6; 1 Sam. 3:3; 4:6, 11, and throughout 2 Sam. 6); (2) "the ark of the covenant of the Lord" (Deut. 31:9, 25, 26; Josh. 3:3, 11, 17; 4:7, 18; 6:6, 8; 8:33; etc.); and (3) just "the ark of the covenant" (Josh. 3:6, 8, 14; 4:9).

Commentary

Leading off the description of this tent are directions on how to build the ark, **25:10–16** clearly the most sacred of all the pieces of furniture in the tabernacle. It is a simple box, open at the top, made of acacia wood, and overlaid with pure gold. To put cubits into approximate inches and feet equivalents, the ark is about 42–45 inches long (around 3½ feet) and about 27–30 inches wide and high (around 2½ feet). It has feet (v. 12) to keep its base from touching the floor, even of the most holy place. The note in v. 15 about never removing the poles from the rings also sets the ark apart. Numbers 4:5–6 calls for three coverings of the ark when it is time to dismantle the tent, break camp, and continue the journey: the veil, dolphin skins, and a blue cloth. The "table of the presence" also calls for three coverings (Num. 4:7–8), but the veil is reserved for the ark.

The implementation of 25:10–16 appears in 37:1–5. The two sections are very similar, but there are a few differences: (1) 37:1 informs the reader that it is Bezalel who builds the ark (cf. 31:2); (2) the command never to remove the poles is absent from chap. 37, as is (3) the command in chap. 25 to put the "testimony" in the ark, something that is done at the tabernacle's completion (40:20).

It is impossible to imagine OT religion without the ark. In some ways what the ark is to the old covenant, the cross is to the new covenant. Take out either, and you have removed the most sacred symbol of each. There are two great ark scenes later in Scripture that reinforce the ark's importance. One is in 1 Sam. 4–6, the occasion in which the Israelites believe that simply bringing the ark into the battlefield will reverse the course of the fight with the Philistines in their favor. After all, if they have the box, do they not have God's presence? Where the box goes, God goes, or does he? Can we turn what God intends to be a symbol into something magical?

The other scene is the one describing David's bringing the ark into Jerusalem, his new capital city (2 Sam. 6; 1 Chron. 13). For David, it is a festive occasion; for Uzzah, it is a fatal occasion. Uzzah dies, but David dances.

In light of passages like this that draw attention to the ark's significance and sanctity, one is hardly prepared for Jeremiah's pronouncement in Jer. 3:16, one of the most unique 3:16s in all the Bible, and one of several "The days are coming when it shall no longer be said . . ." scattered throughout Jeremiah: "In those days, when your numbers have greatly increased in the land," declares the LORD, "men will no longer say, 'The ark of the covenant of the LORD.' It will never enter their minds or be remembered; it will not be missed, nor will another one be made." The reason? Verse 17 says that Jerusalem will become "the Throne of the LORD." That's a big box! The divine glory and presence that once filled a receptacle will just as spectacularly and as powerfully fill his people, so that they will be a living, breathing ark.

25:17–22 Hebrew scholars are still undecided about how to translate *kappōret*: "lid, cover" (?) or something with more theological ingredients like "mercy seat" or "propitiatory" or "expiation lid/cover" or "atonement cover"? It is obviously formed from the verb *kāpar* (Piel, *kipper*), "make atonement." The LXX clearly favors these theological equivalents with its use of *hilastērion* (reproduced in the Vulgate as *propitiatorium*). The word occurs well over a dozen times in Exodus, about eight times in Leviticus, once in Numbers (7:89), and only one more time in the entire Hebrew Bible after that (1 Chron. 28:11). While there is broad consensus both in ancient and modern translations for understanding *kappōret* as having something to do with atonement, I see one problem here. To the best of my knowledge, there is no single text that assigns to the *kappōret* an explicit, expiatory function. On the Day of Atonement (Lev. 16), the high priest is to sprinkle blood on the *kappōret* (Lev. 16:15b), so perhaps this object came to be called *kappōret* because of what it received on *Yom Kippur*.

A suggestion has been made (Milgrom 1991: 1014) to connect Hebrew *kappōret* with Egyptian *kp(n)rdwy*, probably pronounced *kappuri(e)t*, "sole of the foot," and by extension "the place where the foot rests." The idea of "God's footstool" is known from 1 Chron. 28:2; Pss. 99:5; 132:7; and Isa. 60:13 has God saying, "I will glorify the place of my feet."

In any case, it is between the two cherubim that are on the sides of the *kappōret*, and on top of their outstretched wings, that God promises to "meet" with his people. Haran (1959) has argued that the outstretched wings of the cherubim are a throne for God. The Hebrew verb for "meet" is *yāʿad* (Niphal); also see 29:42; 30:6, 36 for the same verb in the same stem. The verb *yāʿad*, "to meet," provides another name for this tabernacle, *ʾōhel môʿēd*, "the tent of meeting" (as in 27:21). The tabernacle is a place where God both "dwells" (*šākan*) with his people and "meets" (*yāʿad*) with his people. Sommer (2001) calls this "conflicting constructions of divine presence," but I would call it "complementary constructions."

The "you" in "I will meet with *you* there" is a singular "you," and the pronoun must refer to Moses. The emphasis is not, as in chap. 24, on Moses (and others) seeing God, but on hearing God. What Moses will need from this point onward is what I shall call "the gift of ears."

The Table

(25:23–30; cf. 37:10–16)

Translation

23“And you shall make a table of acacia wood, two cubits its length and a cubit its width and a cubit and a half its height. 24And you shall overlay it with pure gold, and you shall make for it a golden molding all around. 25And you shall make for it a rim, a handbreadth all around, and you shall make a golden molding for its rim all around. 26And you shall make for it four gold rings, and place the rings at the four corners by its four feet. 27Close to the rim the rings shall be as housings for the poles to carry the table. 28And you shall make poles of acacia wood and overlay them with gold, and by them the table shall be carried. 29And you shall make its bowls, ladles, jars, and jugs by which to pour libations. Pure gold you shall make them. 30And you shall place on the table the bread of the Presence before me regularly.”

Grammatical and Lexical Notes

25:25. For *misgeret* (“rim, frame”) here and in v. 27, see 37:14. When used with Solomon’s temple, it is in the plural (1 Kings 7:28, 29 [NIV, “uprights”], 31, 32, 35, 36 [NIV “panels”]). The verb from which the noun is formed, *sāgar*, appears in Exod. 14:3 to refer to the wilderness that the Pharaoh thinks has “closed around”/“hemmed in” the fleeing Israelites.

25:25. *Ṭōpaḥ* (“a handbreadth”) occurs in the Pentateuch only twice, both in conjunction with the “rim/frame” of the table (25:25; 37:12). See also 1 Kings 7:26 (= 2 Chron. 4:5); Ezek. 40:5, 43; 43:13.

25:27. For *lĕʿummat* (“Close to”), see Exod. 28:27; 37:14; 39:20; Lev. 3:9; 1 Kings 7:20.

25:29. The word for “bowl(s),” *qĕʿārâ*, is formed from a Semitic verb, *qʿr* (“to be deep”), and suggests a vessel with a recession that is hollowed.

25:29. *Kappōt* are “ladles” fashioned in the form of one’s palm (*kap*).

25:29. *Qaśwâ* (“jar[s]”) appears again only in Exod. 37:16; Num. 4:7; and 1 Chron. 28:17. The LXX uses *spondeion*, a vessel used for the *spondē*, the libation.

25:29. The noun *mĕnaqqîyyōt* (“jugs”) is formed from the verb *nāqâ*, which carries the meaning “be clear” in 21:19 (Niphal) and “acquit” in 34:7 (Piel), and is related to the adjective *nāqî* (“clear” in 21:28; “guiltless” in 23:7). Or, it may be derived from an Akkadian verb *naqû*, “to offer a libation.”

25:29. It is likely that the preposition *b* on *bahēn* (“by which”) is the *bêt instrumenti*, although a translation “which shall be poured into them” (*ʾăšer yussak bahēn*) is also possible.

25:30. Sometimes the word *tāmîd* means “continually, nonstop,” as in Lev. 6:13 [6], “The fire must be kept burning on the altar continuously [*ʾēš tāmîd*]; it must not go out.” More often it means “regularly.”

Commentary

25:23–30 The table must be the second most important piece of furniture in the tabernacle, for it is always the first item mentioned after the ark (Exod. 25:10–22 and 25:23–30; 37:1–9 and 37:10–16; 40:3 and 40:4; Num. 4:4–6 and 4:7–8). Also, apart from the ark, it is the only furniture piece that has three coverings placed over it when the camp is on the move (Num. 4:7–8: a blue cloth, crimson cloth, and dolphin skins). All the remaining ones have only two covers (Num. 4:9–14).

Verse 30 has the full name for this item: *haššulḥān leḥem pānîm* ("the table for the bread of Presence" or "the table for the bread of display"). The shorter phrase in Num. 4:7, *šulḥan happānîm* ("the table of the [bread of] presence/display") is an ellipsis for the fuller phrase. Like the ark, it is made of acacia wood, which is plated with pure gold. It too has four gold rings near its feet through which poles are inserted for transport. It is a little shorter in length than the ark (2 cubits versus 2½ cubits, or 2½ feet versus 3 feet), a little shorter in width (1 cubit versus 1½ cubits, or 1½ feet versus 2 to 2½ feet), but equal in height (both 1½ cubits high, or 2-plus feet in height).

Primarily, this table, situated on the north side of the holy place, holds up the *leḥem pānîm* (traditionally called "the shewbread," but also "the bread of presence/display/face[s]"). I assume the bread is unleavened. It is not until Lev. 24:5–9 that the Lord gives Moses further data on the bread, which he is to transmit to his people. There one discovers that once a week twelve loaves (one for each tribe of Israel) are to be baked and placed in two rows of six on the table on the Sabbath. Presumably the priests eat the loaves that have been on the table for a week (Lev. 24:9).

Leviticus 24:8a calls this occasion with the bread "an everlasting/lasting covenant" (*bĕrît ʿôlām*). That is the phrase that God uses for his covenant with Noah (Gen. 9:16) and with Abraham (Gen. 17:7, 13, 19). See also Exod. 31:16; 2 Sam. 23:5; Isa. 24:5. Possibly one should draw a parallel between twelve loaves of bread placed in two rows of six with two other 2 × 6 = 12 scenes. Exodus 28:9–13 recounts the engraving of the names of the twelve sons of Jacob on two precious stones (six names to a stone) in the priest's shoulder pieces. Deuteronomy 27:12–13 says that six of the tribes shall stand on Mount Gerizim to bless the people, and six of the tribes shall stand on Mount Ebal to pronounce curses. The bread offering is the only offering in the Bible that is called *bĕrît ʿôlām*, and is the one ritual that is performed inside the tent weekly rather than daily. The Sabbath is a *bĕrît ʿôlām* (Exod. 31:16), and the bread offering is a *bĕrît ʿôlām*. The God who rests is also the God who nourishes. He hallows a day and he hallows bread.

Setting out edibles before one's deity for that deity to eat is a ubiquitous idea in the ancient Near East. Parallels from Egypt, Asia Minor, and Mesopotamia are readily available. Such a practice, however, was carried out on a daily basis, not a weekly basis, for such deities could not survive on one meal a week. In Israelite tradition, Yahweh "does not merely have a metabolism which functions at one-seventh the rate normal for deities: he does not consume the bread at all" (Gane 1992: 199). Thus in Ps. 50:12 Asaph has the Lord say, "If I were hungry I would not tell you, for the world is mine, and all that is in it."

The Lampstand

(25:31–40; cf. 37:17–24)

Translation

[31]"And you shall make a lampstand of pure gold; pounded work it shall be made. The lampstand, its base and stem, its cups, its calyxes, and its blossoms shall be of one piece with it; [32]six branches extending from its sides, three branches of the lampstand from one side, and three branches from its second side; [33]three cups shaped like almond blossoms on the one branch, calyx and blossom, and three cups shaped like almond blossoms on the one branch, calyx and blossom—and so for each of the six branches extending from the lampstand. [34]And on the lampstand four cups shaped like almond blossoms, their calyxes and their blossoms, [35]and a calyx of one piece with it under each pair of branches, a calyx of one piece of it under each pair of branches, for the six branches extending from the lampstand. [36]Their calyxes and their branches shall be of one piece with it, the whole of it one single pounded piece of pure gold. [37]And you shall make its seven lamps, and mount its lamps so that it gives forth light forwardly. [38]Its tongs and fire-pans [shall be] of pure gold. [39]With a talent of pure gold shall it be made together with all these furnishings. [40]And see, and make [it] by their replica that you viewed on the mountain."

Grammatical and Lexical Notes

25:31. The Hebrew word *mĕnōrâ* is formed from the noun *nēr*, "light," and the verb *nûr*, "to shine, blaze." Its form, with the prefixed *mem*, suggests the meaning "place of light," a lampstand.

25:31. The Hebrew uses an anatomical term for "base" (*yārēk*, lit., "thigh") and a botanical term for "stem" and "branches" (*qāneh*, "stem"). In the singular, *qāneh* refers to the central shaft of the lampstand that rests on the base, the *yārēk*. In the plural, *qāneh* refers to the six "branches" extending from the central stem or shaft.

25:31. *Gābîʿa*, "cup" or "bowl," is at the top of each of the branches.

25:31. All uses of *kaptōr* ("calyx[es]"), twelve of them, are in Exod. 25 and 37, except for Amos 9:1 ("the tops of the pillars") and Zeph. 2:14 ("will roost on her *columns*"). My dictionary defines "calyx" as "the outermost group of floral parts; the sepals collectively."

25:31. *Peraḥ* ("blossom[s]") is a floral component of the cup, the *gābîʿa*.

25:33. The plural, Pual participle *mĕšuqqādîm* ("shaped like almond blossoms") recalls Jeremiah's visions of the branch of an almond tree (*maqqēl šāqēd*) in Jer. 1:11.

25:37. The switch from the second-person "and *you* shall make" (*wĕʿāśîtā*) in the first half of the verse, to the third-person "and *he* shall mount" (*wĕheʿĕlâ*) in the second half of the verse—this switch is unexpected. The LXX and SP emend to *wĕhaʿălîtā* ("and you shall mount"). The reference is to placing the lamps (*nērōt*) atop the lampstand's six branches.

25:37. "So that it gives forth light forwardly" is *wĕhēʾîr ʿal-ʿēber pānêhā*. The equivalent phrase in Num. 8:2 is *ʾel-mul pĕnê hammĕnôrâ*, "[let the seven lamps cast light] toward the [area] *in front of* the lampstand" (AT). The meaning is that the menorah casts light northward, in the direction of the table and the incense altar.

25:38. The verse is a surprising nominal sentence, perhaps simply a continuation of something previous.

25:38. The word for "tongs" (*melqāḥayim*) is formed from the verb *lāqaḥ* ("take, carry off") and more than likely is used to hold the wicks as they are being inserted into the lamps.

25:38. The word for "firepans" (*maḥtōt*) could be a reference either to pans from which oil is poured into the lamps, or to pans used for removing the ashes from the lamps. In Lev. 10:1 they are containers for incense (NIV, "censers"), and in Num. 16:17–18 they are containers for incense and hot coals. The verb *ḥātâ* means to "snatch up" (NIV) in Ps. 52:5 [7] and "heap [burning coals]" (NIV) in Prov. 25:22.

25:39. For the use of "a talent of pure gold" (*kikkār zāhāb ṭāhôr*), compare 2 Sam. 12:30, "He [David] took the crown from the head of their king—its weight was a talent of gold (*kikkar zāhāb*)," approximately seventy-five pounds.

Commentary

We are fortunate in having an outstanding treatment of the tabernacle lamp- **25:31–40**
stand, which convincingly captures the essence of this item, how it looks and how the various parts are made. I highly recommend Meyers 1976.

Unlike the table, which is tended once weekly by the priests, the lampstand is tended to twice daily by the clergy (30:7–8). Aaron is to "tend" the lamps every morning (30:7), but "light" the lamps at twilight (30:8), suggesting that the lampstand is lit only during the darker hours of twilight, evening, and night (27:21b). Exodus 27:20–21 provides instructions for lighting the menorah. See also Exod. 25:6 and 35:8 ("oil for the lamp"); 40:4; Lev. 24:1–4; Num. 4:9–10; 8:1–4.

If the priests light and clean the lampstand in the tabernacle daily, then the priests of Solomon's temple must have been extra busy, for there were ten lampstands in that temple, two rows of five (1 Kings 7:49). The lampstand of the *miškān* is positioned on the south side of the holy place, opposite the table, with perhaps the incense altar nearly between them. There is no mention of any nocturnal light source for either the outer courtyard or the holy of holies. For the latter it is not needed because the high priest enters it only one day in the year.

Light is always something beneficent in Scripture, just as darkness is often something sinister. It is the first thing God creates (Gen. 1:4), and perhaps the only item he creates by fiat ("Let there be . . . And there was . . ."). Then on day 4 he creates, or allows to appear, a greater and lesser light (1:14–19), the sun and the moon, plus the stars. Is there any possible connection between the seven lamps/lights on the menorah and the seven celestial light sources visible to the eye: sun, moon, Mercury, Venus, Mars, Jupiter, Saturn (Trevaski 2009; referencing Poythress 1991: 18–19)?

Jesus is a Menorah, not just a menorah within a cubicle, but also the Menorah of the cosmos. Jesus calls himself the world's Menorah (John 8:12; 9:5; 12:46), and so does John the Baptizer (John 1:9). If Messiah is a Menorah, then Messiah's followers must also be a menorah (Matt. 5:14).

Yet without the olive oil as fuel, the lampstand remains only a beautiful but nonfunctioning apparatus. And without the oil of the Spirit, the follower of Messiah will never be a blazing menorah. Little did I know as a lad in Sunday school, singing the chorus, "Give me oil in my lamp, keep me burning, give me oil in my lamp, I pray" how biblical and vital those lyrics are.

The Curtains of the Tabernacle and the Curtains over the Tabernacle

(26:1–14; cf. 36:8–19)

Translation

1"The dwelling place you shall make of ten curtains of twisted linen, of blue and purple and scarlet, with cherubim; the work of a craftsman you shall make them. 2The length of each curtain is twenty-eight cubits, and a width of four cubits for each curtain, a single measure for all the curtains. 3Five of the curtains are to be joined to one another, and the other five curtains joined to one another. 4And you shall make blue loops on the edge of the outermost curtain in the first set, and do the same on the edge of the outermost curtain in the second set. 5Fifty loops you shall make on the one curtain, and fifty loops you shall make in the outermost curtain, which is in the second set, the loops opposite one another. 6And you shall make fifty gold clasps, and join the curtains to one another with the clasps, so that the dwelling place be one whole.

7"And you shall make curtains of goats' hair for a tent over the dwelling place; eleven curtains you shall make them. 8The length of one curtain, thirty cubits, and the width, four cubits for each curtain, a single measure for the eleven curtains. 9You shall join five of the curtains by themselves, and six of the curtains by themselves. And you shall double over the sixth curtain at the tent's front. 10And you shall make fifty loops on the edge of the outermost curtain of one set, and fifty loops on the edge of the curtain of the second set.

11"And you shall make fifty bronze clasps, and bring the clasps into the loops, and join the tent that it be one whole. 12And the overhang (that left over on the tent's curtains), the extra half-curtain you shall let overhang the rear of the dwelling place. 13And the cubit on one side and on the other in what is left over in the length of tent's curtains shall hang over the dwelling place's sides, this side and that side, to cover it. 14And you shall make a covering for the tent of reddened ram skins, and a covering of dolphin skins above that."

Grammatical and Lexical Notes

26:3. The phrase "to one another," twice in this verse and again in vv. 5, 6, 17, literally is "a woman to her sister" (*ʾiššâ ʾel-ʾăḥōtāh*). The idiom occurs again only in Ezek. 1:9, 23. Isaiah 34:15 uses *rĕʿûtâ* ("companion") in *ʾiššâ rĕʿûtāh* ("There also the falcons will gather, *each with its mate*"). The two nouns occur together with literal meaning in Lev. 18:18, "And a woman with her sister [*wĕʾiššâ ʾel-ʾăḥōtāh*] do not take as a rival wife" (AT).

26:9. For *kāpal* ("double"), see 28:16; 39:9. See also Isa. 40:2, "She has received from the LORD's hand *double* [*kiplayim*] for all her sins."

26:12. The Hebrew word for "overhang" is *sāraḥ* (verb, and v. 13), *seraḥ* (noun, occurring only in this verse), and is used for a *spreading* vine in Ezek. 17:6 and *flowing* turbans in Ezek. 23:15. Amos 6:4, 7 is the only time the root is used with humans, when the prophet speaks of Samaria's wealthy *lounging* on couches.

26:12. "That left over" is *hāʿōdēp*, the Qal participle of *ʿādap*. The same form has appeared in Exod. 16:23 to refer to the manna that was to be "left over" until the Sabbath. In 26:12 the root refers to size (what overreaches the edge), but in 16:23 it refers to quantity (how much remains after their eating the manna on the day before the Sabbath). Leviticus 25:27 uses the same to refer to the "balance" the man redeeming his own property is to pay to the man to whom he sold it.

Commentary

26:1–6 There is no doubt that these six verses and the following eight focus on the curtains for the walls of the inner two holy cubicles and over the top of the tabernacle. The Hebrew word for "curtain, panel" (*yĕrîʿâ*), in singular and plural, occurs twenty-four times in these fourteen verses.

Verses 1–2 inform the reader that the curtains around the tabernacle number ten in all (two rows of five), and each is 42 feet long by 6 feet wide. When the two rows are joined to each other, using the loops (*lulāʾâ*, *lulāʾôt*) and clasps (*qeres*, *qĕrāsîm*) of vv. 5–6, the two form a single fabric of 42 feet by 60 feet.

Verse 1 also tells us that these curtains are made of both (twisted) linen and colored wools (blue/purple/scarlet). Exodus 39:29 points out that the priests' sashes are made of the exact same combination of materials. The same goes for the priests' ephod (28:6). But other biblical laws forbid the laity to wear clothing that is a mixture of linen and wool: (1) Lev. 19:19, "Do not wear clothing woven of two kinds of material; (2) Deut. 22:11, "Do not wear clothes of wool and linen woven together." What is permissible in the tabernacle and for part of the priests' vestments is prohibited to the laity. It is like working on the Sabbath. The priest must work (e.g., changing the bread on the table and other activities), but the laity must not do any work of any kind.

Exodus 26:1 calls the construction of these curtains "the work of a craftsman" (*maʿăśēh ḥōšēb*). The latter word, *ḥōšēb*, "craftsman," appears again in v. 31; 28:6; 31:4 and 35:32 (NIV, "artistic designs"); 35:35; 36:8, 35; 38:23; 39:3, 8. More often than not, NIV uses "skilled craftsman" for this participial noun.

Of these, 35:35 is most interesting, for it lists three techniques of weaving in descending order: designing (*ḥōšēb*), embroidering (*rōqēm*), and weaving (*ʾōrēg*). The first two are mentioned when the material is made of three kinds of dyed wool and linen, as in 26:1. The third, weaving, is used only when the fabric is made of one kind of material, either linen or dyed wool (e.g., the robe of the ephod woven from blue wool only [28:31–32; 39:22]; or the priests' tunics, made of linen only [39:27]).

We are not entirely sure what the difference is between *ḥōšēb* and *rōqēm*, but the first, the one used in 26:1, appears when the text speaks of cherubim as part of the finished design of the material. Only the curtains surrounding the two holy places (26:1 and 36:8) and the veil in front of the holy of holies

(26:31 and 36:35) are called *kĕrubîm ma'ăśēh ḥōšēb* ("cherubim worked into them by a skilled craftsman"). See Haran (1965: 202–3) and Jensen (1992: 104–5), who calls *rōqēm* a "patterned weave" and *'ōrēg* a "simple weave."

For the curtain over the two holy places, the craftsmen use goats' hair, material **26:7–14**
that is less valuable than the dyed-wool/linen/cherubic curtains surrounding them (26:7 and 36:14). Also, while the clasps for the surrounding curtains are gold (26:6 and 36:13), the clasps for the upper covering are bronze (26:11 and 36:18). Finally, there is only one covering for the surrounding curtains, but three coverings for the upper curtains: goats' hair, rams' skins, and dolphin skins (26:14 and 36:19), possibly serving as tarpaulins to make the holy cubicles as waterproof as possible.

The Tabernacle Framework

(26:15–30; cf. 36:20–34)

Translation

[15]“And you shall make frames for the dwelling place of acacia wood, standing upright. [16]Ten cubits the length of the frame, and a cubit and a half of a cubit the width of each frame. [17]Two tenons in each frame joined together, each to the other; thus you shall do for every frame of the dwelling place. [18]And you shall make the frames for the dwelling place, twenty frames for the south side, [19]and forty silver sockets you shall make underneath the twenty frames, two sockets under each frame for its two tenons and two sockets underneath the other frame for its two tenons. [20]And for the second side of the dwelling place for the northern side, twenty frames, [21]with their forty silver sockets, two sockets under each frame and two sockets underneath the other frame. [22]For the hind part of the dwelling place, the west, you shall make six frames. [23]Two frames shall you make for the corners of the dwelling place at the hind part. [24]They shall be double at the bottom, but together they shall fit at the top into one ring: thus it shall be with both of them; they shall be for the two corners. [25]There shall be eight frames and sixteen silver sockets, two sockets under the first frame and two sockets under the other frame.

[26]“And you shall make crossbars of acacia wood, five for the frames of the one side of the dwelling place, [27]and five crossbars for the frames of the second side of the dwelling place, and five crossbars for the frames of the hind side of the dwelling place, the west. [28]And the central crossbar in the middle of the frames shall run from end to end. [29]And the frames you shall overlay with gold, and their rings you shall make of gold, housings for the crossbars, and you shall overlay the crossbars with gold. [30]And you shall erect the dwelling place according to the way that you were shown on the mountain.”

Commentary

26:15–30 Just as the word *yĕrîʿâ/yĕrîʿōt* (“curtain/s”) dominated vv. 1–4, the word *qeres/qĕrāsîm* (“frame/s”) dominates vv. 15–30. It occurs twenty-two times, at least once in every verse except for vv. 24 and 30.

These frames, or planks, are made of acacia wood (v. 15). Each is 15 feet high and a little over 2 feet wide, at least in their bottom half (v. 16). Rather than being solid planks of wood, it is likely that each frame is made of two sticks that are joined together by horizontal pieces of wood, giving each frame a ladder-like appearance. This is probably the reason for two sockets under each frame (vv. 19, 21). There are forty-eight frames in all, twenty each for the north and south sides, six for the west side, and two at the rear corners, most likely for added support (vv. 18, 20, 22, 23). Verse 24's information that at their top the two sides of each frame can fit into one ring suggests that each frame near its top narrows considerably from its base width of over 2 feet, maybe even down to a width in inches.

Providing support for all these frames are fifteen crossbars, five to a side (vv. 26–27), plus one central crossbar (v. 28). The crossbars, overlaid with gold, are held together by golden rings (v. 29).

Put all this material together, mostly heavy wooden beams, and it must add up to a considerable weight. It is the responsibility of the Merarite clan of Levites to transport this framework structure as Israel makes its way through the wilderness (Num. 3:36–37; 4:29–32). No wonder Moses gives four wagons and eight oxen to the Merarites for their transportation needs (7:8), while he gives only two wagons and four oxen to their sibling Gershonite clan (7:7) to assist them with the transportation of the various curtains and screens (3:25–26; 4:25–26). No Levites ever have to carry, thank God, several wooden beams on their shoulders.

The Veil and the Curtain before the Holy Place

(26:31–37; cf. 36:35–38)

Translation

[31]"And you shall make a veil of blue, purple, and crimson and twisted linen. [As] the work of a craftsman, he shall make it [with] cherubim. [32]And you shall set it on the four acacia posts overlaid [with] gold, their hooks gold, upon four silver bases. [33]And you shall set the veil under the clasps, and you shall bring there behind the veil the ark of the testimony, and the curtain shall divide for you the holy place from the most holy place. [34]And you shall set the cover/propitiatory over the ark of the testimony in the most holy place. [35]And you shall put the table outside the veil, and the lampstand facing the table on the south side of the dwelling place, and the table you shall set on the north side.

[36]"And you shall make a screen for the entrance of the tent, blue, purple, and crimson, and twisted linen, the work of an embroiderer. [37]And you shall make for the screen five acacia posts, and overlay them [with] gold, their hooks gold, and you shall cast for them five bronze bases."

Grammatical and Lexical Notes

26:31. The Hebrew word for "veil" is *pārōket* (LXX, *katapetasma*). It seems to be related to the Akkadian *parakku* ("shrine, a deity's residence"), and the related verb *parakku* ("go across, bar, block") is sometimes used with a curtain.

26:31. For the third-person verb "he shall make" after an initial "you shall make," the LXX predictably adjusts to a second-person verb.

26:33. The term *mibbêt* means "behind/inside," just as *miḥûṣ* in v. 35 means "outside." In Gen. 6:14, Noah is instructed to build an "ark" and "coat it with pitch *inside and out* [*mibbayit ûmiḥûṣ*]."

26:33. The verb *bādal* (Hiphil), when followed by *min*, means "set apart," e.g., "You are *to set* the Levites *apart from* the other Israelites" (Num. 8:14), or "The Lord will *single* him [the idolater] *out from* all the tribes of Israel for disaster" (Deut. 29:21 [20]). When *bādal* (Hiphil) is followed by *bên* . . . *bên* (as here in 26:33; also see Gen. 1:4, 7, 14, 18) or by *bên* . . . *lĕ* (Gen. 1:6) or by *bên* . . . *lĕbên* (Isa. 59:2), it has the meaning "divide" or "distinguish."

26:35. Verse 35 uses *nātan* ("set") in the second half of the verse (also 32, 33, 34), but v. 35a uses *śîm* ("put"). For *śîm*/*nātan*, see Avishur 1984: 640.

Commentary

The veil, which hangs by clasps on four acacia-wood pillars, separates the holy **26:31–35**
place from the most holy place. Behind it is the ark and the ark's cover. In front of it are the table on one side and the lampstand on the other. The altar of incense will end up there too, but it has not yet been mentioned (30:1–6).

Of the three entrance curtains (before the holy of holies, before the holy place, before the entrance into the outer courtyard), only the veil is called "holy" (Lev. 4:6, where *pārōket haqqōdeš* could be rendered "veil of holiness" [i.e., "the holy veil" or "veil of the holy place/sanctuary"]). Other terms for it besides just *pārōket* are (1) *pārōket hammāsāk*, "the screening curtain" (Exod. 35:12; 39:34; 40:21; Num. 4:5); (2) *hammāsāk*, "the screen" (Num. 3:31); (3) *pārōket hāʿēdut*, "the screen of the testimony" (Lev. 24:3).

Two items separate this middle entrance curtain from the veil. First, the veil **26:36–37**
is "the work of a craftsman" (*maʿăśēh ḥōšēb*, v. 31) while this curtain opening the way into the holy place is "the work of an embroiderer" (*maʿăśēh rōqēm*, v. 36). See my comments at the end of the commentary section of 26:1–6 for a possible distinction between *ḥōšēb* and *rōqēm*. Second, the "silver" bases for the pillars of the veil (v. 32) are here "bronze" (v. 37). One can imagine a sign hung on both these curtains: "authorized personnel only."

Solomon, by contrast, places "doors" in front of the entrance to the inner sanctuary of the temple (1 Kings 6:31). Curtains are easier to open than doors. One does not need a key; a simple brush of the hand will suffice. All the more reason, then, to pay attention to the "sign" on the curtains.

All three Synoptic Gospels mention the rending of the veil/curtain of the sanctuary in conjunction with Jesus's death (Matt. 27:51; Mark 15:38; Luke 23:45; John's Gospel does not record it). But there are some differences in the three verses. Perhaps the most striking one is that Matthew and Mark say this happens right after Jesus dies ("Jesus . . . gave up his spirit. At that moment the curtain of the temple was torn in two" [Matt. 27:50–51]), while Luke suggests it happens just before Jesus's death (23:45–46, "And the curtain . . . was torn in two. . . . When he said this, he breathed his last"). This location in Luke's account places the rending of the curtain between the deep darkness that engulfs the entire land, and Jesus's last recorded word from the cross to his Father (Luke 23:44–45a>45b>46). That placement means that the rending of the veil goes along with the thick darkness, and together both are a sign of the Father's displeasure at humanity's rejection of his Son. Or the rending of the veil is to be connected with what follows, Jesus's word committing himself to his Father, which, as we shall see, comes close to the emphasis on the veil in Hebrews. Jesus is soon to leave Golgotha's cruelties and enter the heavenly tent.

There are several items on which the Synoptics agree. First, they all use the word *naos* for the curtain of "the sanctuary" rather than *hieron*. The *naos* is the *miškān*, the dwelling place, the two inner holy places. Second, they all use the verb *schizō* for the "rending" of the curtain. That Greek term is the origin of our English word "schism" and "schismatic." They also use the passive of the verb ("was rent"), which must mean "was rent by God." It is the verb that Mark (but not Matthew or Luke, who use the less severe "were opened") employs for the "tearing open" of the heavens at Jesus's baptism (Mark 1:10). It is never a gentle, soft opening, but a violent, powerful, ripping apart of something.

The third thing they all agree on is that they do not specify which curtain is ripped into two. Is it the veil, the *pārōket* of Exod. 26:31–35? Or is it the curtain at the entrance to the holy place of Exod. 26:36–37? The Greek word that the Gospel writers use for this curtain is *katapetasma*, the same word that the LXX uses for both the veil (shielding the holy of holies; Exod. 26:31) and for the curtain at the entrance into the holy tent (26:37). The traditional answer is that the rent curtain is the veil, but there are some interpreters, ancient and modern, who argue for the second curtain. The reference in Heb. 6:19–20 to "the inner sanctuary behind the curtain" suggests the veil. If it is the inner curtain (and it is unlikely the question ever occurs to any of the Gospel writers), nobody would see it happening. You can see darkness and the sun's eclipse, and you can feel the earth tremble, but you cannot see the *pārōket* rent in twain unless you are a priest ministering in the holy place.

A final thing all Synoptic writers agree on is that they are content simply to record the incident. None comments on the significance of this. That is standard in Gospel narrative where the emphasis is on reporting and recording. For interpretation, we turn to the epistolary literature, specifically the Epistle to the Hebrews.

There are three references to the curtain/*katapetasma* in Hebrews. First, 6:19–20 speaks of Jesus, who enters the inner sanctuary behind the curtain on our behalf. Here the writer employs no less than three figures of speech: a nautical one ("hope as an anchor for the soul"); a cultic one (heaven is a sanctuary); an athletic one (Jesus has gone there as our "forerunner" [NIV, "who went before us"]).

The second is Heb. 9:3, which in its description of the wilderness tabernacle says, "Behind the second curtain was a room called the Most Holy Place." The third is 10:19–20. It speaks of the believers' confidence to enter through the curtain and into this most holy place because of Jesus and his blood, which has opened "a new and living way" and made it available for them. In such a case, the most holy place is not necessarily a reference to a heavenly sanctuary, as in 6:19–20, but is a phrase designating the immediate presence of God. So 10:22 begins by urging, "Let us draw near to God." Ephesians 2:13 reflects this truth: "But now in Christ Jesus you who were *once far away have been brought near* through the blood of Christ." Interestingly, Heb. 10:20 identifies the curtain as Jesus's body ("[a way he] opened for us through the curtain, that is, his body"). The sense may be that Jesus's body is something he has "to pass through" (i.e., his thirty-three years of human existence) in order to enter the heavenly tent.

So is the rending of the *pārōket*, as recorded in the Synoptic Gospels and the book of Hebrews, good news or bad news? It is both. On the one hand, the irreparable destruction of the *pārōket* portends a far greater destruction—not just of a piece of fabric but also of an entire edifice—for those who spurn Messiah. That is the thrust of the Gospel references. On the other hand, the ripping of the *pārōket* means that because of Jesus's death and resurrection, God's immediate presence is available to all who embrace Messiah, and one day they too will enter that heavenly tent, there to behold the Godhead in all of its revealed glory. That is the thrust of the emphases in Hebrews, and accordingly, none of its texts ever speak of the curtain's being rent or ripped apart as do all the Synoptics. (For further reflection on the NT's understanding of the parting of the tabernacle's curtain, one may consult commentaries on the Gospels and Hebrews. I found the analysis of Brown 1994: 1097–1118 very helpful.)

The Altar of Burnt Offering

(27:1–8; cf. 38:1–7)

Translation

1"And you shall make the altar of acacia wood, five cubits in length, and five cubits in width—the altar is a square—and three cubits its height. 2And you shall make its horns on its four corners, from the one piece its horns shall be, and you shall overlay it [with] bronze. 3And you shall make pots for its ash removal, and shovels and its basins and its forks and its firepans. All its utensils you shall make [of] bronze. 4And you shall make for it a meshed grating of bronze, and you shall make on the mesh four rings on its four corners. 5And you shall place it under the altar's ledge from below, and the mesh shall extend halfway up the altar. 6And you shall make poles for the altar, poles of acacia wood, and overlay them [with] bronze. 7And the poles shall be brought into the rings, and the poles shall be on the altar's two sides when it is carried. 8Hollow boarded you shall make it, just as he showed you on the mountain, thus they shall make [it]."

Grammatical and Lexical Notes

27:1. The altar of burnt offering is a "square" (*rābûaʿ*; also 38:1), as is the altar of incense (Exod. 30:2; 37:25) and the high priest's breastplate (Exod. 28:16; 39:9). Later biblical literature uses the related word *mĕrubbāʿ* for "square" (Ezek. 40:47; 45:2).

27:3. Apart from here and 38:3, *sîr* ("pot") appears in Exodus only in 16:3, which speaks of the Israelites recalling fondly how they sat by the "fleshpots" (*sîr habbāśār*) while still in Egypt. A "fleshpot" is a cauldron in which meat is cooked.

27:3. *Lĕdaššĕnô* ("for its ash removal") is the Piel infinitive construct of *dāšen* II with pronominal suffix. It is a denominative verb formed from the noun *dešen* ("ashes") and carries privative meaning: for the cleaning or removal of the suet ashes from the altar.

27:3. Again, as with other uncommon words in this verse, *yāʿ* ("shovel") appears in Exodus only in 27:3 and 38:3.

27:3. *Mizrāq* ("basin") is from the verb *zāraq* ("toss, throw") and so means a "tossing bowl." See Wiesenberg (1976: 156–58), who presents arguments in favor of understanding a *mizrāq* as a vessel *into* which contents (liquid, flour) flow or are poured, rather than a vessel *from* which contents flow or are poured.

27:3. *Mizlāgâ* ("fork") is present in Exodus here and in 38:3. See Num. 4:14 and 1 Sam. 2:13, 14. The word refers to an implement for removing cooked sections of the offerings from the altar. Kleven (1994: 197) notes *Targum Onqelos*'s translation of this word in Exod. 27:3; 38:3; and Num. 4:14 with *ṣinnôrta* ("flesh-hook") but downplays any connection with the *ṣinnôr* David uses to gain access to Jerusalem in 2 Sam. 5:8 (water shaft? some kind of hook used to scale the city walls?).

27:3. For *maḥtâ/maḥtōt* ("firepans"), see the comment at 25:38. All uses of *maḥtâ/mahtōt* are either with the lampstand (Exod. 25:38; 37:23; Num. 4:9) or with the sacrificial altar (Exod. 27:3; 38:3). The exception seems to be the "censers" in which Nadab and Abihu place fire and incense (Lev. 10:1), and also the censers of the Korah incident (Num. 16). They are most likely private or personal *maḥtōt* rather than the sanctuary *maḥtōt* of Exod. 25 and 38.

27:4. For *rešet* ("meshed," from the verb *yāraš*), see Pss. 57:6 [7], "They spread *a net* for my feet"; 140:5 [6], "They have spread out the cords of *their net*"; Prov. 1:17, "How useless to spread *a net* in full view of the birds!"

27:7. The LXX and SP change MT's third-person Hophal (*wĕhûbāʾ*) into a second-person Hiphil (*wĕhēbēʾtā*, "you shall bring").

27:8. For *nĕbûb*, here and in 38:7, "*hollow* [*of*] board," see Job 11:12 (NIV, "a *witless* man"), and Jer. 52:21, "Each of the pillars . . . was . . . *hollow*."

Commentary

The altar of burnt offering was 7½ feet square and 4½ feet high. It is also 27:1–8
called "the bronze altar" (Exod. 38:30; 2 Kings 16:14–15; Ezek. 9:2). It was hollow and therefore not heavy to carry. Since it lacked a roof, it would be filled with earth and rocks at each encampment.

Here we have the first mention of "horns" at the altar's four corners. They are not added to the altar, but are of one piece with it. Archaeologists have uncovered such four-horned altars throughout ancient Israel, especially at Beersheba and Arad (see Aharoni 1974; Rainey 1994; *ANEP* 192, #575).

Such horned altars were found throughout the ancient Near East, and there the horns served as emblems of the gods. In the Hebrew Bible a horn, a *qeren*, refers to the horns of a powerful animal, such as a ram or a bull, and so comes to be a symbol of strength and power (Deut. 33:17; 1 Sam. 2:1, 10; 2 Sam. 22:3; Pss. 75:4–5 [5–6]; 89:17 [18]; Jer. 48:25; Zech. 1:18–21). According to Amos 3:14, one manifestation of divine judgment is that God will cut off the horns of the altar, causing them to fall to the ground. That is to say, even the last refuge for a condemned individual (1 Kings 2:28–33) will be no more. Or maybe the hornless altar will be rendered useless because without horns it can no longer hold the sacrifice in place.

This bronze altar should be distinguished from the altar of incense. The first is bronze and is located in the courtyard. The second is gold and is located in the holy place in front of the veil. So we can call the first "the outer altar" and the second "the inner altar." The blood of whole-burnt and well-being offerings, both nonexpiatory, is splashed on the bronze altar (Lev. 1:5; 3:2). In the case of the sin offering of a priest or the community, the inner, incense altar receives the blood before the bronze altar does (Lev. 4:7, 18).

The Courtyard

(27:9–19; cf. 38:9–17)

Translation

[9]"And you shall make the dwelling place's court. On the south side hangings for the court of twisted linen, a hundred cubits in length for one side. [10]And its posts twenty, and their bases twenty, of bronze, the hooks of the posts and their bands silver. [11]And thus for the north side, in length hangings a hundred cubits, and its posts twenty and their bases twenty, of bronze, and the hooks of the posts and their bands silver. [12]And the width of the court on the west side, hangings [of] fifty cubits, their posts ten and their bases ten. [13]And the width of the court on the east side, fifty cubits. [14]And fifteen cubits of hangings on the one flank, their posts three and their bases three. [15]And for the second flank fifteen [cubits] of hangings, their posts three and their bases three. [16]And for the gate of the court a screen, twenty cubits, blue and purple and crimson and twisted linen, the work of an embroiderer, their posts four and their bases four. [17]All the posts surrounding the court shall be banded [with] silver, and their hooks silver and their bases silver. [18]The length of the court, a hundred cubits, and the width fifty cubits, and the height five cubits, twisted linen, and their bases bronze. [19]Thus for all the utensils of the dwelling place in all its ritual; and all its pegs and every peg of the court bronze."

Grammatical and Lexical Notes

27:10. The LXX reads "their posts" rather than "its posts."

27:11. The Masora provides a Qere᾿ reading for the Ketib's *wĕʿammudāw* with *wĕʿammudāyw* ("and its posts").

27:14. "Flank" (*kātēp*) elsewhere means "shoulder."

27:18. In "and the width fifty *cubits*," I follow the reading of the LXX (*eph' hekaton* = *bĕmēʾâ*) rather than MT's "fifty in fifty."

27:19. GKC §143e identifies the preposition *lĕ* on the first word *lĕkōl* as a *lāmedh* of inclusion: "*Thus* for all the utensils." GKC also cites *lĕkōl* in Gen. 9:10; 23:10; Exod. 27:3 (*lĕkol*) with the same meaning.

Commentary

27:9–19 These eleven verses describe the dimensions of and the materials surrounding the court(yard), Hebrew *ḥāṣēr* (LXX, *aulē*, "courtyard"; Vulg., *atrium*). Most uses of this word in the Hebrew Bible occur in Exod. 27:9–19 and 38:9–17 and in Ezekiel's vision of the temple he sees and describes, especially Ezek. 40:17–37.

When describing the curtains around the holy places, Exod. 26 uses *yĕrîʿōt* for the "curtains" and *qĕrāsîm* for the "frames." Exodus 27, when describing the materials around the court area, employs instead *qĕlāʿîm* ("hangings," 5x) and *ʿammudîm* ("post, pillars," 9x). Each "frame" is inserted into two bases/sockets (26:25), while each "post, pillar" is inserted into just one base/socket (27:11, 14), possibly indicating that the "frames" are heavier and larger than the "posts, pillars." Another difference between the two uprights is that the "frames" are overlaid with gold (26:29), while it appears that the "posts/pillars" are not. Presumably they are made of acacia wood, but that is not even stated as it is with the "frames" (26:15).

There are fifty-six of these *ʿammuddîm* ("posts"), twenty each on the north and south sides, ten on the west side, and two sets of three on the east side. The overall dimension of this court area is 150 feet long (vv. 9, 11) by 75 feet wide (vv. 12, 13), or 100 cubits by 50 cubits. At the entrance to the court is a screen 30 feet long, or 20 cubits, that is on four posts (v. 16). This particular curtain has tent pegs (*yātēd*, *yĕtēdōt*, v. 19), a feature not mentioned in connection with either the curtain at the entrance to the holy place or the curtain/veil at the entrance to the holy of holies, or with any of the curtains surrounding the two holy places. Maybe this indicates that the two latter curtains hang more loosely than this outer curtain, and are opened simply by lifting up the bottom of the curtain. It seems, however, that v. 19 places these tent pegs all around this outside perimeter hanging, and not just in conjunction with its entrance curtain.

The Oil for the Lamps

(27:20–21)

Translation

[20]"And you, you shall command Israel's sons to bring you pure oil of beaten olives for the light, to kindle a lamp regularly. [21]In the tent of meeting outside the veil which is before the testimony, Aaron, along with his sons, shall tend it from evening until morning before the LORD, an everlasting statute for their generations of Israel's sons."

Grammatical and Lexical Notes

27:20. The only previous references to *zayit* ("olive") in the Bible are Gen. 8:11, the "freshly plucked olive leaf" (*ʿălēh-zayit ṭārāp*) that the dove brings back to the ark, and Exod. 23:11, the command not to harvest one's olive grove (*lĕzêtekā*) in the seventh year so that the poor and wild animals may eat it.

27:20. The adjective *zāk* means "pure," and it occurs in a parallel passage, Lev. 24:2. It appears most often in wisdom literature (Job 8:6; 11:4; 16:17; 33:9; Prov. 16:2 [NIV, "innocent"]; 20:11; 21:8 [NIV, "innocent"]).

27:20. For other instances of *kātît* ("beaten, pounded") in reference to beaten/pressed olives, see Exod. 29:40; Lev. 24:2; Num. 28:5; 1 Kings 5:11 [25]. The verb *kātat* is the one Deut. 9:21 uses for Moses's "crushing" the idolatrous golden calf.

27:20. This is one certain instance where the Hiphil of *ʿālâ*, "go up" (*lĕhaʿălōt*), means "kindle," as it does in the parallel verse, Lev. 24:2. Other verses that also use the Hiphil of *ʿālâ* in conjunction with the lampstand may refer to the setting up of the lamps on the Menorah rather than lighting up the Menorah (Exod. 25:37; 40:25; Num. 8:2–3). Ezekiel 24:8 uses the phrase "to kindle/ignite [NIV, "stir up"] wrath" (*lĕhaʿălôt ḥēmâ*), again using the Hiphil infinitive construct of *ʿālâ* with the meaning "kindle," as in Exod. 27:20.

27:21. Does *ʿal-hāʿēdut* mean "*before* the testimony" or "*over* the testimony" or "*around* the testimony"?

27:21. The verb "attend" is singular (*yaʿărōk*) even though the subject is "Aaron and his sons." He is the liturgist; his sons are assistants. The parallel Lev. 24:3 does not even mention Aaron's sons (though Lev. 24:3 LXX does).

27:21. The verb *ʿārak* ("attend, arrange") appears in cultic texts with regard to arranging wood and sacrifice on the altar (Gen. 22:9; Lev. 1:7; 1 Kings 18:33), setting the bread on the table (Exod. 40:23; Lev. 24:8), and the lighting of the lamps on the lampstand (Exod. 27:21; Lev. 24:3–4).

27:21. The daily lighting of the lamps in the tabernacle is one of two items identified in Exodus as "an everlasting statute for their/your generations." The other is Exod. 12:17, the celebration of the Festival of Unleavened Bread. The phrase is much more common in Leviticus (3:17; 10:9; 16:31; 17:7; 23:14, 21, 31, 41; 24:3 [the parallel verse to Exod. 27:21]).

27:21. The LXX reads "for *your* generations" (*lĕdōrōtêkēm*) for MT's "for *their* generations" (*lĕdōrōtām*) in line with Lev. 24:3.

Commentary

Not only do the Israelite laity provide the gifts and materials necessary for **27:20–21**
the tabernacle's building; they also supply the olive oil necessary to keep the Menorah lamps burning through the night hours (v. 20a). Not just any kind of oil will do. It must be olive oil, which is a more valuable grade of oil than that derived from flax, sesame seed, or animal fats (which can be used for fuel). And it must be prepared in a certain way: pounded in a mortar and then passed through a strainer. It involves olives that are pure (*zāk*) and beaten/pressed (*kātît*). The latter word suggests being pounded with a pestle rather than crushed in a press, as if they are grapes.

The OT's teachings on keeping the lamps burning regularly may provide background for Jesus's admonition in Luke 12:35. There he says, "Be dressed ready for service and keep your lamps burning." For Jesus, keeping one's lamp burning continually is a symbol of watchfulness, being ready and waiting for the master's return.

One might expect this data on the anointing oil for the lamps on the lampstand to follow immediately after the Lord gives the data about the lampstand itself (25:31–40). Why delay it until the end of chap. 27? Possibly this arrangement reflects the fact that 25:1–27:19 focuses on the composition and dimensions of these sacred pieces of furniture, but beginning with 27:20–21 is a shift from the description of their appearance to a description of their function: Who provides the oil? What kind of oil is required? How does one prepare it? Who kindles the lamps, and when?

The Priestly Vestments

(28:1–5; cf. 39:1)

Translation

[1]"And you, present to me Aaron your brother and his sons with him from among Israel's sons to make him a priest for me—Aaron, Nadab, and Abihu, Eleazar and Ithamar, Aaron's sons, [2]And you shall make sacred vestments for Aaron, your brother, for honor and adornment. [3]And you, speak to every wise-hearted individual whom I have filled with a spirit of wisdom, that they make Aaron's vestments to consecrate him to serve me as priest. [4]These are the vestments that they are to make: a breastpiece, and ephod and robe, a plaited tunic, a turban and a sash. They shall make sacred vestments for Aaron, your brother, and for his sons to make him a priest for me. [5]And they, they shall take the gold, the blue and the purple and the crimson and the linen."

Grammatical and Lexical Notes

28:1. The expression *qārab* (Hiphil) *ʾel* ("present to") is used of bringing someone to God or someone coming near to God (Num. 16:5 [2x]); bringing something to the altar (Lev. 1:15; Num. 5:25); bringing something to a priest (Lev. 2:8; 9:9); bringing something or someone to the tent entrance (Exod. 29:4; 40:12). Close in meaning to Exod. 28:1, though using *qārab* (Hiphil) *lipnê* instead of *qārab ʾel*, is Num. 27:5, "So Moses *brought* their case [Zelophehad's daughters] *before* the LORD," presented their case before the Lord. Both Exod. 28:1 and Num. 27:5 involve a sense of presentation.

28:1. The infinitive construct with pronominal suffix (*lĕkahănô*, here and in v. 4) should be rendered "to make him a priest [for me]." Without the pronominal suffix it would be translated, "to serve as a priest [for me]."

28:2. The Hebrew word for "adornment, majesty, splendor" is *tipʾeret* (also see v. 40). The verb from which *tipʾāret* is formed, *pāʾar*, is used in the Piel stem for "adorning" the Lord's sanctuary (Isa. 60:13; Ezra 7:27 [NIV, "bring honor to"]). Three times we have the Hitpael of this verb followed by the preposition *ʿal*. Note NIV's different renderings for each passage: (1) Exod. 8:9 [5], "I *leave* to you *the honor*"; (2) Judg. 7:2, "in order that Israel may not *boast against* me"; (3) Isa. 10:15, "Does the ax *raise* itself *above* him who swings it?" The basic idea in these passages is "lord it over another," literally, "adorn oneself over another." Behind both the noun and the verb is the idea of "empowerment visually perceived as adornment" (Shedletsky and Levine 1999: 330–31).

28:3. For "wise-hearted" (*ḥakmê-lēb*), see 36:2, "And Moses called . . . every wise-hearted man in whose heart the LORD had given wisdom." Also, Exod. 35:25.

28:4. I shall comment on each of these sacred vestments throughout my discussion of 28:6–43. Note that the word "plaited" in "plaited tunic" is *tašbēṣ* (occurring only here), from the verb *šābaṣ*. It appears only twice in the Bible: Exod. 28:39, "And you shall *weave* the linen tunic"; and Exod. 28:20, *"framed* in gold in their settings." Later in the chapter (vv. 11, 13, 14, 25) we will find another word formed from *šābaṣ* and that is *mišbĕṣâ/mišbĕṣôt*, "frame(s)" or "plaited work" or "filigree," meaning a delicate ornamental work of fine silver, gold, or metal wires. So we have from the same verb a *tqtl* type of word (*tašbēṣ*), which is used with clothing, and a *mqtl* type of word (*mišbĕṣôt*), which is used with gold or other metals. Gevirtz (1982: 60–61) has collected an interesting number of *tqtl/mqtl* words that are formed from the same root, are similar in meaning, but are not equivalent. Two examples: (1) From the verb *šûb* ("[re]turn"), we have the nouns *tĕšûbâ* and *mĕšûbâ*. Both mean "turning," but the first means a circuit (1 Sam. 7:17), while the second means "a turning back, apostasy" (Jer. 3:6). (2) From the verb *ʾāwâ* ("desire"), we have the nouns *taʾăwâ* and *maʾăwâ*. Both mean "appetite," but the first refers to a physical appetite (Gen. 3:6), while the second refers to the appetite of the wicked (Ps. 140:8 [9]).

Commentary

It is fitting that just on the heels of the mention of Aaron's responsibility for **28:1–5**
keeping the lamps burning (27:20–21), the text should turn to how Aaron is to be clothed on such an occasion, or on all other occasions when he enters the dwelling place.

Those charged with the responsibility of making these sacred vestments are "wise-hearted" individuals whom God has filled with a "spirit of wisdom" (*rûaḥ ḥokmâ*). For other "wise" craftsmen/craftswomen, see Exod. 35:25 (women who are weavers); Jer. 10:9 (goldsmiths); Ezek. 27:8; Ps. 107:27 (sailors). Except for Ps. 107:27, NIV correctly renders "wise"/*ḥokmâ* in these passages as "skilled." The best example of this use of "wisdom"/*ḥokmâ* is what Exod. 35:30–31 says of Bezalel, foreman of the tabernacle's construction: "The Lord has chosen Bezalel . . . and has filled him with the Spirit of God, with *skill* [*ḥokmâ*, wisdom]." See also 36:1 ("every *skilled* person to whom the Lord has given *skill* and ability").

It is of some interest that the first "Spirit-filled" individual in the Bible is not Adam, Noah, or one of the patriarchs, or even Moses. It is a construction foreman, Bezalel. The Bible sanctifies the work and craftsmanship of the laborer as much as it does the work of patriarch, prophet, and priest. What one does with one's hands is as sacred as what one does with one's mind. Excellence in metalworking and fabric making, because of the Spirit, is no less vital than excellence in law-giving or preaching.

The Ephod

(28:6–14; cf. 39:1–7)

Translation

[6]"And they shall make the ephod gold, blue and purple, crimson and twisted linen, the work of a craftsman. [7]Two joining shoulder pieces it shall have at its two edges, joined. [8]And its fastening band that is on it shall be made the same—gold, blue and purple, crimson and twisted linen. [9]And you shall take two onyx stones and engrave on them the names of Israel's sons, [10]six of their names on the one stone and the names of the six remaining on the second stone in their birth order. [11]With carved stonework, the seal engravings you shall engrave on the two stones with the names of Israel's sons; encased in a plaited work of gold you shall make them. [12]And you shall set the two stones on the ephod's shoulder pieces, stones of remembrance for Israel's sons. And Aaron shall bear their names before the LORD upon his two shoulders for remembrance. [13]And you shall make plaited gold, [14]and two chains of pure gold, and by braiding you shall make them a cord. And you shall place the corded chains on the plaited work."

Grammatical and Lexical Notes

28:7. "Joining" is the Qal feminine-plural participle of *ḥābar* (*ḥōbĕrōt*; also see 26:3). "Joined" at the end of the sentence is the Pual perfect of *ḥābar* (*wĕhubbār*).

28:8. For *ḥēšeb* ("band") and *ʾăpuddâ* ("fastening/girding"), see 29:5, "And you shall gird [*ʾāpad*] him with the band [*bĕḥēšeb*] of the ephod." The words "fastening, gird" (noun and verb) and "ephod" share the same three radicals: *ʾ-p-d*. Mettinger (1971: 5) cites *pĕquddâ* in Num. 16:29, along with *ʾăpuddâ* in this verse, as rare instances of the nominal pattern *qĕtullah*, which are substantives with the function of an infinitive.

28:9. For *šōham* ("onyx"), see 25:7; 28:20. It was a material present even in Eden: Gen. 2:12, "And the gold of that land is good, bdellium is there, and a stone of onyx [*wĕʾeben haššōham*]" (AT). Its color was black.

28:9. The verb *pātaḥ* in the Qal means "open" as in Exod. 2:6, "and she [the princess] *opened* it [the ark/basket] and saw the child." In the Piel stem it takes the meaning "engrave, inscribe" (also 28:11, 36). This is not the only meaning for the Piel of *pātaḥ*. Thus Abraham's servant, upon reaching Rebekah's house, "unloaded" or "unharnessed" the camels (Gen. 24:32).

28:10. "In their birth order" (*kĕtôlĕdōtām*) is, literally, "according to their birthing."

28:11. For "seal engravings" (*pittûḥê ḥōtām*), see 28:21, 36; 39:6, 14, 30.

28:11. On "plaited work [of gold]" (*mišbĕṣôt*, and vv. 13, 14), see my comment above on *tašbēṣ* in v. 4. Both are formed from the verb *šābaṣ*.

28:14. For *šaršâ/šaršĕrōt* ("chain[s]"), see 39:15; 1 Kings 7:17; 2 Chron. 3:5, 16 [2x].

28:14. The Hebrew word *gablut* occurs only here, in v. 22, and in 39:15 ("braiding, intertwining").

28:14. The word for "cord" is *ʿăbōt*, which is in the feminine plural (*hāʿăbōtōt*) later in the sentence. It is the word for the "ropes" with which some seek to bind Samson, only there it is a masculine plural, *ʿăbōtîm* (Judg. 15:13; 16:11, 12).

Commentary

The ephod is the second most important item of clothing the high priest wears after the breastpiece. The reason for describing the ephod before the breastpiece may be because it provides the support for the breastpiece (Cassuto 1967: 373). We remain uncertain of the origin of the word *ʾēpōd*. Tvedtnes (1982) connects the Hebrew word with Egyptian *ifd/yfd* ("cloth"). Others suggest that the Hebrew word is cognate with Akkadian *epattu* ("a costly garment"). **28:6–14**

The ephod is shaped like an apron encircling the body and covers the loins (maybe from waist to thigh). It is kept in position on the body by means of two shoulder pieces (v. 7) and a fastening band (v. 8). Gold is its most dominant material and color. This is indicated by v. 6, which lists gold before it lists any fabrics.

Two onyx (or lapis lazuli) stones are each engraved with the names of six of Israel's twelve tribes (vv. 9–11), and attached to the two shoulder pieces (v. 12). The ephod is one of four garments that the high priest alone dons. The other three are the breastpiece, the ephod's robe, and the golden crown or diadem. The remaining four are donned by both high priest and ordinary priest (tunic, sash, some kind of a head covering, and linen breeches).

Verse 12 (and 39:7) calls these two stones "stones of remembrance" and goes on to say that when Aaron enters the holy place or the holiest place to minister, he is to bear these twelve names before the Lord "for remembrance" (*lĕzikkārōn*). Exodus 28:29 uses the same phraseology for the breastpiece, except that it adds a "continuing" remembrance/memorial before Yahweh. Exodus 30:16 and Num. 31:54 use *zikkārôn* for some gift of money or gold as a "remembrance, memorial" before the Lord. See also Num. 10:10 for this significance attached to the trumpet sounds at Israel's festivals.

In all these passages, what is brought or presented to the Lord apparently is for the benefit of the Lord's remembrance. These items or gifts or sounds serve as reminders to God, just as he said the rainbow after the flood would be a reminder to him (Gen. 9:14–15). In contrast, *zikkārôn* is to serve as a reminder to humans in a passage like Josh. 4:7, "These stones are to be a remembrance/memorial *to the people* of Israel forever" (AT). The use of the word in Num. 5:15 is not as clear: the husband who suspects his wife of adultery is to bring her to the priest and also an offering on her behalf. Such an offering is called "a grain offering of jealousy, a grain offering of remembrance [*minḥat zikkārôn*], a remembering of guilt [*mazkeret ʿāwōn*]" (AT). Here the NIV combines the two uses of *zākar* words with "a reminder offering to draw attention to guilt." I take it that the offering is a *zikkārôn* for the suspected adulteress. Again, the covering of the altar in Num. 16:40 [17:5] is a *zikkārôn* to the Israelites that nobody who is not a priest is to draw near to burn incense to the Lord.

But in the cases where the *zikkārôn* is for God's remembrance, as Childs (1962: 67) has said, these "cultic acts of Israel continually remind God of this eternal covenantal order. The cultic objects and rites act to guarantee that the covenant is not forgotten."

In particular, in wearing the ephod with its two stones, Aaron is "to bear/lift up the names" (*nāśāʾ ʾet-šĕmôtām*) of the twelve tribes before the Lord (v. 12b). The language is close to that of the third commandment, which forbids "lifting up the name" (*nāśāʾ ʾet-šēm*) of the Lord in vain (Exod. 20:7 = Deut. 5:11). In my discussion of the third commandment, I argued that "take up the name of the LORD" may be elliptical for "take up the name of the LORD on your lips," as in Ps. 16:4 ("or take up their names ["idolaters"] on my lips"). Is Aaron to bear and lift up on his lips the names of the twelve-tribed covenant people before Yahweh? If so, v. 12 is a classic illustration of priestly intercession ("Lord, remember Reuben, remember Levi, remember Judah, and so forth. They are your covenant people").

Subsequent references to this ephod may or may not be referring to the high priest's golden ephod (see P. Davies 1975: esp. 84–85). For example, the ephod Gideon "set up" (Judg. 8:27) seems to be a statue or an upright object rather than a garment (also see Judg. 18:18, "the statue/carved image of the ephod [*pesel hāʾēpôd*]"). And how do young Samuel (1 Sam. 2:18) and dancing David (2 Sam. 6:14) get away with wearing something that only the high priest is to wear? Maybe there is more than one kind of ephod. Or maybe all ephod references are to the same phenomenon, but a phenomenon that has different manifestations throughout Israel's history.

The Breastpiece

(28:15–30; cf. 39:8–21)

Translation

15“And you shall make a breastpiece of decision, the work of a craftsman; like the work of an ephod you shall make it—gold, blue and purple and crimson and twisted linen you shall make it. 16It shall be square, doubled, a handspan its length and a handspan its width. 17And you shall fill it with a filling of stone, four rows of stone: a row of ruby, topaz, and emerald the first row; 18the second row, turquoise, sapphire, and a crystal; 19and the third row, a jacinth, agate, and an amethyst; 20and the fourth row, beryl and an onyx and a jasper, gold-plaited in their fillings. 21The stones shall be according to the names of Israel's sons, twelve according to their names, seal engravings, each according to its name they shall be for the twelve tribes. 22And you shall make for the breastpiece woven chains, cord work, pure gold. 23And you shall make on the breastpiece two golden rings, and you shall place the two rings on the two edges of the breastpiece. 24And you shall place the two golden cords on the two rings at the edges of the breastpiece. 25And the two edges of the two cords you shall place in the two plaited frames, and place [them] on the ephod's shoulder pieces at the front. 26And you shall make two gold rings and set them on the two edges of the breastpiece, at its border that is beside the ephod on the inside. 27And you shall make two gold rings and place them on the ephod's two shoulder pieces below in the front, close to its joining point above the ephod's band. 28And they shall fasten the breastpiece from its rings to the ephod's rings by means of a blue cord to be on top of the ephod's band, that the breastpiece not come loose from the ephod. 29And Aaron will bear the names of Israel's sons in the breastpiece of decision over his heart/chest when he comes into the holy [place] for continual remembrance before the Lord. 30And you shall place in the breastpiece of decision the Urim and the T[h]ummim, that they be over Aaron's heart/chest when he comes before the Lord. Aaron shall bear Israel's judgment on his heart/chest before the Lord continually.”

Commentary

The importance of the breastpiece is obvious simply because of how much **28:15–30**
more space the text devotes to it (sixteen verses) than to any other priestly vestment. Meyers (2005: 242) notes that in the NRSV “196 words are devoted to the ephod and 400 to the breastpiece.” The ratio would be about the same in the NIV.

The Hebrew word for this article of clothing is *ḥōšen*. It never appears in the Hebrew Bible outside of Exod. 28:15–30 = 39:8–21 except for Lev. 8:8 (where the passage again lists the eight vestments that clothe the clergy).

The breastpiece, or the breastpiece of decision (*ḥōšen mišpāṭ*, Exod. 28:15, 29, 30), is made much like the ephod: gold, three mixed woolen fabrics, and linen (v. 15b). Along with the ephod (v. 6b), the breastpiece too is the work of a craftsman (*maʿăśēh ḥōšēb*, v. 15).

Haran (1965: 210) calls it "a cross between a square plate and a hollow pouch." It is worn over the area of the high priest's heart or chest (*lēb*); it is attached at its top to the ephod by means of gold cords/chains, which pass through and attach to gold rings (vv. 22–27); it is held at its bottom to the ephod by means of a blue cord that is drawn through two lower rings (v. 28).

In contrast to the two stones of the ephod on the shoulder pieces of the ephod, on each of which six tribal names are inscribed, here on the breastpiece are twelve stones. Each stone has one tribal name, and they must be much smaller stones than the two in the ephod. I am not sure I can vouch for the accuracy of the English equivalents I have used for these twelve stones in vv. 17–20. Alter (2004: 475) remarks, "For all the scholarly recourse to conjectured etymologies and comparative philology, it is virtually impossible to determine precisely what precious stones are referred to in this list of twelve terms. We can do little more than revel in the gorgeousness of the words, which is surely part of the intended response for the ancient audience."

Not only is the number of stones different for the ephod and breastpiece, but so is their placement. The ephod stones are on Aaron's shoulders, but the breastpiece stones are on Aaron's heart/chest area (vv. 29–30). The heart is the body's main organ, the seat of life. Placing the names of Israel's tribes "on/over the heart" (*ʿal lēb*) of Aaron may be compared with God's promise in the new covenant to write his words "on/over their heart" (*ʿal lēb*) in Jer. 31:33.

Verse 30 adds that the Urim and Thummim (or just "Tummim," without the *h*) are to be placed inside the breastpiece, and it does so without explaining what the Urim and Thummim are and what their function is. Moses does not say "the Ur . . . what?" And the parallel/fulfillment section (39:8–21) does not even mention them, but see Lev. 8:8. This is the first of only seven references in the Bible to their use. The remaining six are Lev. 8:8; Num. 27:21; Deut. 33:8; 1 Sam. 28:6; and Ezra 2:63 and the identical Neh. 7:65. Numbers 27:21 and 1 Sam. 28:6 use only "Urim," but the other five have "Urim and Thummim." Of these seven, the locus classicus for understanding their use is Num. 27:21, "He [Joshua] is to stand before Eleazar the priest, who will obtain decisions [*mišpāṭ*] for him by inquiring [*šāʾal*] of the Urim before the Lord." From this verse it is clear that use of these items, whatever they are, is a priestly function.

As one can imagine, there has been considerable debate about the meaning and function of the Urim and Thummim. I have profited greatly from the studies of Lindblom 1962; E. Robertson 1964; Lipinski 1970; Milgrom 1991:

507–11; W. Horowitz and V. Hurowitz 1992; de Tarragon 1995; Van Dam 1988; 1997; Kitz 1997.

There are several issues; for none of them is there a conclusive or consensual answer. First, what are they: flat stones? pebbles? sticks? arrows? dice? Second, what do the two words mean? The meaning of "Thummim" seems clear, deriving from a root meaning "be complete, innocent," as in Gen. 6:9, Noah is a "blameless" (*tāmîm*) man, or in Gen. 17:1, God's command to Abraham "to walk before me and be blameless [*tāmîm*]." The origin of Urim is debatable. It may come from the noun "light" (*ʾôr*) or from the verb *ʾārar* ("curse"). One would think that Urim should be the opposite of Thummim, thus tipping the scales in favor of a connection with *ʾārar*, "curse." Third, why are both words plural? Are there maybe two, or three, or four of each, or does the plural reflect the idea that the priest might cast these two or three times before a decision is forthcoming (Kitz 1997)? Fourth, can the Urim and Thummim give only a yes-or-no answer, or can they give a more detailed judgment? The answer to that question partially rests on what one does with many passages in Judges and the Samuels where somebody "inquired of the LORD" about something. See Judg. 1:1–2; 18:5; 20:18; 1 Sam. 10:22; 14:36; 22:10, 13, 15; 23:2, 4, 12; 28:6; 30:8; 2 Sam. 2:1; 5:19, 23; 16:23. How did these persons go about "inquiring of [*šāʾal bĕ*] the Lord"? None of these seventeen passages mentions the use of the priestly Urim and Thummim, but if that is understood, then the answer is that these items can provide much more than a simple yes-or-no response.

There was almost no end to the different devices people in the ancient Near Eastern world employed in order to divine the will of the gods. A few examples include necromancy (consulting the dead); lecanomancy (observing the water's reaction to dropped oil or stones); cleromancy (casting lots); extispicy (observing the entrails of sacrificed animals); hepatoscopy (examining the liver of sacrificed animals); psephomancy (drawing or throwing black stones and white stones from a bag). Divination literature is the most prevalent genre that Mesopotamia has produced. Most likely, Israel fell into the trap of using some of these same paganistic rituals. Are the Urim and Thummim an Israelite adoption, or adaptation, or innovation? Given the plethora of divinatory practices in the ancient Mediterranean world, "it is a significant indication of the spirit of Yahweh religion that it should never have absorbed into its system any but this, the simplest technical device for inquiring the will of God" (Eichrodt 1967: 114). Yet it is ironic that the only person in Exodus who ever engages in intercession for the people of God is not Aaron, when he has the chance to do so, but the "breastpiece-less" Moses (Exod. 32–33).

Other Vestments

(28:31–43; cf. 39:22–31)

Translation

[31]"And you shall make the ephod's robe entirely of blue. [32]And there shall be an opening for one's head in its middle; its neckline shall have an embroidered border around it, like the opening of a corselet [?] it shall be so that it not tear. [33]And you shall make on its hem pomegranates of blue and purple and crimson, on its hem all around, and gold bells among them all around. [34]A gold bell and pomegranate, a gold bell and pomegranate all around on the hem of the robe all around. [35]And Aaron shall have it on him to officiate so that its sound be heard when he enters the holy [place] before the LORD, and when he leaves, so that he will not die.

[36]"And you shall make a diadem of pure gold and engrave upon it seal engravings: 'Holy to the LORD.' [37]And you shall set it on a blue cord that it be on the turban, at the turban's front. [38]It shall be on Aaron's forehead, that Aaron may remove any iniquity arising from the holy things that Israel's sons consecrate with respect to any of their sacred donations, and it shall be on his forehead continually to win acceptance for them before the LORD.

[39]"And you shall weave the tunic with linen, and you shall make a linen turban, and a sash you shall make as the work of an embroiderer.

[40]"For Aaron's sons you shall make tunics, and you shall make for them sashes, and headgear you shall make them for glory and for adornment. [41]And you shall dress them, Aaron your brother and his sons, and you shall anoint them, and ordain them, and consecrate them that they may serve me as priests.

[42]"And make for them linen breeches to cover [their] nakedness; from the hips to the thighs they shall be. [43]And they shall be upon Aaron and upon his sons when they enter the tent of meeting or when they approach the altar to officiate in the holy [place], that they not bear guilt and not die—a perpetual statute for him and for his seed after him."

Grammatical and Lexical Notes

28:32. The meaning of *taḥrāʾ* remains a mystery: "collar" (NIV); "corselet" (Childs 1974); "coat of mail" (NJPS; Alter 2004). Lambdin (1953: 155) rejects an Egyptian origin for the Hebrew word and settles for the word's meaning some kind of unidentifiable garment that is slipped on over one's head like a poncho.

28:33. The word for "hem" (28:33, 34; 39:25, 26) is *šûl*. It is the same word in the famous Isaiah passage, 6:1, "And the *train* of his robe filled the temple." Eslinger (1995: esp. 170–72) offers a radically new translation of *šûl* in Isa. 6:1. The term refers, he says, not to the "hem" of Yahweh's garment but to his exposed nakedness, which Eslinger then ties in with Exod. 28:42, a reference to undergarments to cover the priest's nakedness.

28:33. The MT lacks any mention of "twisted linen" in conjunction with the ephod's robe, and 39:24 uses only the word *mošzār* ("twisted") rather than the fuller *šēš mošzār* ("twisted linen"). Both LXX and SP supply the missing words in 28:33 and 39:24.

28:34. Alter (2004: 476) notes, "The sheer splendor of the ornamentation is invoked in poetic incantation through the repetition of the phrase."

28:35. For *bôʾ* . . . *yāṣāʾ* ("enter" . . . "leave"), see Deut. 28:6, 19; 2 Kings 11:9; 2 Chron. 23:8; Jer. 37:4. For *yāṣāʾ* . . . *bôʾ* ("leave" . . . "enter"), see 2 Sam. 5:2 (= 1 Chron. 11:2). Krašovec (1983: 236) identifies each as a merism.

28:39. The word *kĕtōnet* ("tunic") may be spelled with one *t* in its center, as here, or with a doubled *t*. In Gen. 37:31, there are two references to Joseph's "robe." The first is spelled *kĕtōnet*, but the second *kuttōnet*. We have similar variation here: *kĕtōnet* (v. 39a), *kuttŏnōt* (v. 40a).

28:41. "And you shall ordain them" is, literally, "And you shall fill their hand" (*ûmillēʾtā ʾet-yādām*). More on this in the commentary section.

28:42. "To cover [their] nakedness" is, literally, "to cover the flesh of the nakedness" (*lĕkassôt bĕśar ʿerwâ*), in which *bĕśar* most likely refers to the genitalia.

28:43. The *wāw* on *wāmētû* ("and not die"), after the negative *wĕlōʾ-yiśʾû ʿāôn*, may be an instance where the *wāw* precedes a verb (or a noun) in place of the negative. See Tawil 1976: 411, 411nn51–52. It is more likely that *wĕlōʾ* negates both verbs, "not bear guilt and (not) die."

Commentary

The Robe of the Ephod (cf. 39:22–26)

This particular piece of clothing is called "the robe of the ephod" because **28:31–35**
the ephod is worn over it. It is made of blue wool, and perhaps twisted linen (see grammatical note on 28:33), and has an opening in the middle so it can be slipped over the high priest's head. Its ritual accessories include golden bells on its hem, alternating with ornaments in the shape of a pomegranate (see Houtman 1990).

Pomegranates are something one can see; bells are something one can see and hear. Pomegranates, along with grapes and figs, are the fruit that the scouts bring back from Canaan (Num. 13:23), which attest to the promised land's abundance and fertility. In Song 6:7 ("Your temples behind your veil are like the halves of a pomegranate") and 4:13 ("Your plants are an orchard of pomegranates"), the pomegranate is a symbol of the lady's beauty (beautifully shaped and colorful).

What about the bells? We do not know how many there are. We do know that somebody hears these bells when Aaron enters the shrine. Who hears them? The laity in the outer part of the forecourt? The priests and Levites waiting in the inner part of the forecourt? Aaron himself? God? This would be a very auspicious moment for any high priest as he leaves the area of less sanctity and enters the area of highest sanctity. Eslinger (1995: 171) finds a parallel in the hiker's use of a "bear bell" that he rings when he is in grizzly country lest he come upon and surprise one of those big bears, especially a mother with her cubs.

The Gold Diadem (cf. 39:30–31)

28:36–38 The Hebrew word for "diadem" is *ṣîṣ*. The word means "blossom, flower," suggesting some kind of floral decoration, and is cognate with Akkadian *ṣiṣṣatu* ("flower ornament"). The LXX renders the word "plate" (*petalon*) instead of "diadem." Like the stones of the ephod and the twelve stones of the breastpiece, it too has seal engravings, but whereas those sets of stones are engraved with the names of Israel's twelve tribes, the diadem bears the words "Holy to the LORD."

Exodus 29:6 calls this item a *nēzer haqqōdeš* ("a holy diadem"); 39:30, a *ṣîṣ nēzer-haqqōdeš zāhāb ṭāhôr* ("a diadem, a sacred crown of pure gold"); Lev. 8:9, a *ṣîṣ hazzāhāb nēzer haqqōdeš* ("the golden diadem, the holy crown"). From these passages it is clear that *ṣîṣ* and *nēzer* are synonyms. The latter word is related to the term *nāzîr*, Nazirite, "one who has been consecrated, set apart."

The purpose of the high priest's wearing the diadem is that Aaron "may remove the iniquity" (*nāśā' 'et-'ăôn*) connected with any offering an Israelite inadvertently brings as a gift to the Lord, such as a blemished animal (Exod. 28:38). The phrase *nāśā' 'ăôn/peša'/ḥaṭṭā't* has one of two meanings in Scripture. If the subject is a person, then the phrase normally, but not always, means "bear one's own punishment," as in Lev. 5:1, "If a person sins, . . . he will be held responsible," or "He must bear his punishment." In such a case, *'ăôn* refers not only to the sin but also to the wages of that sin, not only to the act but also to its consequence. See Lev. 5:17; 17:16; 22:9; Num. 18:1, 23 for the same meaning.

In other places the phrase means "forgive/remove one's iniquity/sin" rather than "be held responsible for the punishment of one's iniquity/sin" (as in Gen. 50:17 AT [with *peša'*, "transgression"]; Exod. 10:17 [*ḥaṭṭā't*, "sin"]; Exod. 34:7 ["wickedness"]; Lev. 10:17 ["guilt"]; Num. 14:18 ["sin and rebellion"]; 1 Sam. 15:25 ["sin"]; 25:28 ["offense"]; Isa. 33:24 ["sins"]; Hosea 14:2 [3] ["all our sins"]). In some instances the one doing the forgiving is God (Exod. 23:2; 34:7; Num. 14:18; Isa. 33:24; Hosea 14:2 [3]). In other instances the one doing the forgiving is a person (Joseph for his brothers, Gen. 50:17; Moses for Pharaoh, Exod. 10:17; the priests for the community, Lev. 10:17; Samuel for Saul, 1 Sam. 15:25; David for Nabal, 25:28).

I suggest that *nāśā' 'ăôn* in Exod. 28:38 has the second of these meanings, "remove iniquity," while the same phrase in v. 43 has the first of these meanings, "bear responsibility/guilt/punishment." In the case of v. 38, the diadem symbolically draws to itself any and all of the accidental impurities of any Israelite's offering to the Lord.

Tunic, Turban, Sash (cf. 39:27–29)

These three verses discuss the tunic (*kĕtōnet*), the turban (*miṣnepet*), and 28:39–41
the sash (*ʾaḇnēṭ*). The tunic, made wholly of linen, is the first garment to be donned after the linen breeches (*miknĕsê-bād*, v. 42; Lev. 6:10 [3]; 16:4). The high priest wears a "turban" (*miṣnepet*, Exod. 28:37), while an ordinary priest wears a "headgear" (*migbāʿôt*, v. 40). The first of these, *miṣnepet*, "turban," is formed from a root meaning "wind, bind," as in Akkadian *sanapu*/*sanabu*. In Isa. 62:3 and Ezek. 21:26 [31] it is parallel to "crown" (*ʿăṭeret*/*ʿăṭārâ*). Like the tunic, the sash is for all the priests. Like the tunic and the turban, its main constituent is linen. A later synonym for *ʾaḇnēṭ* is *ʾēzôr* (Job 12:18 [NIV, "loincloth"]; Jer. 13:2, 4, 6, 7, 11; Ezek. 23:15 [NIV, all "belt/s"]).

Once he has clothed the priests, Moses's responsibility is to anoint them (*māšaḥ*), ordain them (lit., "fill their hands") and consecrate them (*qādaš*, Hiphil). See v. 41b. Aaron is anointed (Lev. 8:12), as are ordinary priests (Exod. 28:41; 29:21; 30:30; 40:14–15; Lev. 7:35–36; 10:6–7; Num. 3:2–3). The anointing with oil can be either by *yāṣaq* (pouring, Lev. 8:12) or by *nāzâ* (sprinkling, Lev. 8:30).

The idiom for "ordain" is "fill the hands." It occurs in sections of the Bible dealing with the ordination of the clergy (Exod. 28:41; 29:9, 29, 35; 32:29 [NIV, "set apart"]; Lev. 8:33; 16:32; 21:10; Num. 3:3). See also Judg. 17:5, 12 (NIV, "installed"); 1 Kings 13:33 (NIV, "anyone who wanted to become a priest"); 1 Chron. 29:5 (NIV, "consecrate oneself"); 2 Chron. 13:9 (NIV, "consecrate oneself"); 29:31 (NIV, "dedicate oneself"). In all these instances the reference is to somebody's assuming a priestly function via consecration. "Ordination" itself may be expressed simply by the word *milluʾîm*, "filling(s)" (Lev. 8:22).

Many commentators have compared Hebrew *millēʾ yād* ("ordain," as in Exod. 28:41) with Akkadian *mullû ana*/*ina qatê* ("hand over, assign"), but as B. Levine (1989: 204n27) has observed, "To say in Akk. that someone 'filled' something *into* another's 'hand' is different from saying that someone was himself appointed to an office by having his hands filled." If some object was placed in the priest's hands, it remains a mystery what that object was. Note that in Exod. 29:24 and Lev. 8:27, Moses places the various ingredients of the ordination offering/sacrifice in the hands of Aaron and his sons. In any case, Aaron is fully clothed (except for his feet), and his hands are full.

Undergarments (No Parallel in Exod. 39)

The concern for modesty in the persons leading worship reflects the concern 28:42–43
first voiced in 20:26. I am not sure if the priests wear these undergarments always, or only when they are officiating. I am inclined to support the latter option. Leviticus 8:7–9, the fulfillment of Exod. 28, does not even mention the breeches (for surely each priest would put on his own underwear), but it does list all the other articles of clothing.

Yet failure to wear underpants is a serious enough sacrilege to bring about death (v. 43b). For other priestly violations that bring death, see Exod. 30:19–21, failure to wash hands before approaching the altar; Lev. 10:6, improper mourning; 10:9, drinking wine before going into the tent of meeting; 16:2, too frequent entry into the holy of holies; 16:13, failure to carry incense into the holy of holies; 22:8–9, failure to observe and enforce the laws of uncleanness; Num. 4:15, touching the holy things, or even looking at them (4:17–20); 18:3, allowing Levites to go where they are not supposed to.

All areas of the priest's body are covered, except for the feet. This suggests that the priests minister in the tabernacle barefoot. And it may explain why Moses (Exod. 3:5) and Joshua (Josh. 5:15) are told to remove their shoes in the presence of the Holy One.

This beautiful and elaborate clothing that the priests wear when officiating contrasts with the simple "cloak, mantle" (*'adderet*) that the prophet Elijah wears when he ministers (1 Kings 19:13, 19; 2 Kings 2:8, 13, 14), although such cloaks can also be very beautiful (it is what Achan covets and takes, Josh. 7:21, 24). One would not confuse the priest's clothing with what John the Baptizer wears (Matt. 3:4), although John too has a leather belt/sash around his waist.

Turning a Person into a Priest

(29:1–37)

Translation

[1]"And this is the thing that you shall do in order to consecrate them to be a priest to me: take one bull of the herd and two unblemished rams, [2]and flatbread and rounded loaves, flatbread mixed with oil and flat wafers daubed with oil; fine wheat flour you shall make them. [3]And you shall place them in one basket and bring them forward in the basket, along with the bull and the two rams. [4]Aaron and his sons you shall bring forward to the entrance of the tent of meeting, and wash them in water. [5]And you shall take the vestments and clothe Aaron with the tunic, and with the ephod's robe, and with the ephod, and with the breastpiece, and you shall gird him with the ephod's fastening band. [6]And you shall set the turban on his head, and place the holy diadem on the turban. [7]You shall take the oil of unction and pour it on his head, thereby anointing him. [8]And his sons you shall bring forward and clothe them with tunics. [9]And you shall belt them with a sash, Aaron and his sons, and fix headgear on them, and the priesthood shall be for them an everlasting statute, and you shall ordain Aaron and his sons.

[10]"And you shall bring forward the bull before the tent of meeting, and Aaron and his sons, too, shall lean their hands on the bull's head. [11]And you shall slaughter the bull before the LORD at the entrance to the tent of meeting. [12]And you shall take some of the bull's blood and place it on the altar's horns with your finger, and all [the rest of] the blood you shall pour out at the altar's base. [13]And you shall take all the suet that covers the entrails, and the lobe of the liver, and the two kidneys with the suet that is on them, and turn them into smoke on the altar. [14]But the bull's flesh and its hide and its dung you shall burn in the fire outside the camp. It is a sin/purification offering.

[15]"Then one of the rams you shall take, and Aaron and his sons shall lean their hands on the ram's head. [16]And you shall slaughter the ram, and take its blood, and dash [it] against the altar all around [17]And the ram you shall cut up into its quarters, and wash its entrails, and its shins, and place them on its quarters and on its head. [18]And you shall turn the entire ram into smoke on the altar; a burnt offering it is to the LORD, a pleasing fragrance, a food gift to the LORD.

[19]"And you shall take the second ram, and Aaron, and his sons too, shall lean their hands on the ram's head. [20]And you shall slaughter the ram and take some of its blood, and place it on Aaron's right earlobe and on his sons' right earlobe, and on the thumb of the right hand and on their big right toe, and you shall dash the [rest of] blood on the altar all around. [21]And you shall take some of the blood that is on the altar and some of the oil of unction, and sprinkle [it] on Aaron and on his vestments, and on his sons, and on his sons' vestments together with him. He and his vestments shall become holy, and his sons and his son's vestments together with him.

[22]"And you shall take from the ram the suet, and the broad tail and the fat that covers the entrails, and the lobe of the liver and the two kidneys and the fat that is on them, and the right thigh, for it is the ram of ordination, [23]and one flat loaf of bread and one rounded loaf made with oil, and one wafer from the basket of flatbread that is before the LORD. [24]And you shall set everything in Aaron's palms and in his sons' palms, and raise them as an elevation

offering to the LORD. [25]Then you shall take them from their hands and turn them to smoke on the altar, together with the burnt offering, as a pleasing fragrance before the LORD; it is a food gift to the LORD.

[26]"And you shall take the breast from the ram of ordination that is Aaron's, and raise it as an elevation offering to the LORD. It shall be your portion. [27]And you shall consecrate the breast of the elevation offering and the thigh of the contribution gift that is elevated and that is donated from the ram of ordination that is Aaron's and his sons'. [28]And it shall be for Aaron and his sons an everlasting statute from Israel's sons, for it is a donation, and a donation it shall be from Israel's sons, from their well-being offerings, their donation to the LORD.

[29]"And the sacred vestments that are Aaron's shall be for his sons after him for anointing in them and for ordaining in them. [30]Seven days the son who becomes priest instead of him shall wear them when he enters the tent of meeting to officiate in the holy [place].

[31]"The ram of ordination you shall take and cook its flesh in a holy place. [32]And Aaron, and his sons too, shall eat the ram's flesh and the bread that is in the basket at the entrance to the tent of meeting. [33]And those who were expiated by these things used to ordain them and to consecrate may eat them, but no stranger shall eat them, for they are holy. [34]And if any of the flesh of the ordination or any of the bread is left over until morning, you shall burn the remainder in the fire; it shall not be eaten, for it is holy.

[35]"And you shall do thus for Aaron and for his sons according to all I commanded you. Seven days you shall ordain them. [36]And the bull of the sin/purification offering you shall prepare for each day for atonement, and you shall decontaminate the altar by your performing purgation upon it, and you shall consecrate it by anointing it. [37]Seven days you are to make expiation upon the altar, and you shall consecrate it, and the altar shall be a holy of holies. Anyone/anything touching the altar must be holy/becomes holy."

Grammatical and Lexical Notes

29:1. The much more common imperative of *lāqaḥ* ("take") is *qaḥ/qāḥ* (without the first consonant). The longer form, *lĕqaḥ*, occurs only three times in the Hebrew Bible: here in Exod. 29:1 ("Take one bull"); in Prov. 20:16 ("Take the garment"); and again in Ezek. 37:16 ("Take a stick"). This last verse actually contains both forms of the imperative: "Take [*qaḥ*] a stick of wood. . . . Then take [*lĕqaḥ*] another stick of wood." As a parallel, Dahood (1965: 321) cites the imperative of *yāṣaq* ("pour"), which occurs as *ṣaq* (2 Kings 4:41) and *yĕṣōq* (Ezek. 24:3), which is parallel with the preceding imperative *šĕpōt* ("put"). Similarly, the usual imperative form of *yāšab* ("dwell, sit") is *šēb* (e.g., Gen. 20:15), but one finds the form *yōšĕbî* in Jer. 48:18 ("Come down from your glory and *sit* on the parched ground"), parallel with the preceding imperative *rĕdî* ("come down").

29:2. *Ḥallōt* refers to "rounded loaves," and they are the opposite of "flat wafers" later in the verse. The word appears only in cultic contexts (Lev. 2:4; Num. 15:20; 2 Sam. 6:19).

29:4. "The entrance to the tent of meeting" (also vv. 10–11) would be for the priestly ordinands the inner section of the courtyard, directly in front of the tent.

29:7. The recipe for the preparation of "the oil of unction" appears in 30:22–25.

29:7. The *wāw* on *ûmāšaḥtā* ("thereby anointing") is purposive and not the usual conjunctive "and." Otherwise the verse would speak of two anointings: pour and anoint.

29:10. It is usual to translate *sāmak yād*[*ayim*] *ʿal* as "lay hand[s] on," but I have used "lean hands on." The reason is because sometimes *sāmak ʿal* implies pressure, as in Judg. 16:29, "And [Samson] *leaned against* [NIV, "bracing himself against"] them [the two pillars]." See also 2 Kings 18:21 [= Isa. 36:6], "Egypt, that splintered reed of a staff, which pierces a man's hand and wounds him if *he leans on* it!"

29:11. *Šāḥaṭ* ("slaughter") in Exodus–Leviticus is a technical term for ritual slaughter that involves slitting the throat of the animal sacrifice. The verb appears seventy-nine times in the Hebrew Bible, the majority of which come in Exodus–Leviticus.

29:12. To the best of my knowledge, "at the base of the altar" (*ʾel-yĕsôd hammizbēaḥ*) occurs only in conjunction with the "sin/purification" offering (Exod. 29:12; Lev. 4:7, 18, 25, 30, 34; 5:9; 8:15; 9:9). The preferred verb with this expression is *šāpak* ("pour"), but Lev. 8:15 and 9:9 use *yāṣaq*.

29:13. *Ḥēleb* is "suet" or "fat." Milgrom (1991: 205) suggests that the term refers "to layers of fat beneath the surface of the animal's skin and around its organs, which can be peeled off, in contrast to the fat that is inextricably entwined in the musculature."

29:13. *Qereb* is "entrails" and is cognate with Akkadian *qerbu*. The word does not refer to all internal organs, but only to those having deposits of dung and thus being in need of washing (Lev. 1:9, 13).

29:13. *Yoteret* ("lobe [of the liver]") is formed from the noun *yeter*, "protuberance, excess." It is a fingerlike projection from the liver's lower end. In Latin this appendage is called the *lobus caudatus*.

29:13. The Hebrew word for "liver" (*kābēd*) is formed from the verb *kābad*, "be heavy." More than likely the ancients knew of the liver's large size, and according to Smith (1998: 433), the liver is an organ, "accounting for about 2 percent of body weight in human adults and about 5 percent in infants."

29:13. For *kĕlāyōt* ("kidneys"), compare Akkadian *kalītu* and Ugartic *klyt*. The word is often paired with "heart": Pss. 7:9 [10], "who searches *minds and hearts*"; 16:7, 9, "*my kidneys* [NIV, "heart"] instruct me. . . . Therefore my *heart* is glad"; Jer. 20:12, "you who . . . probe the *heart* and *mind*."

29:13. Hebrew *qāṭar* (Hiphil) is cognate with Akkadian *qutturu*. Both mean "turn into smoke." Its synonym, *śārap*, "burn" (see v. 14), is in these priestly sections of Scripture restricted to nonsacrificial burning. The verb is derived from the noun *qiṭēr/qîṭôr* ("smoke"). Also, the Hebrew word for "incense" (*qĕṭōret*) derives from the word "smoke," for it appears in the form of smoke.

29:14. There is no doubt that *ḥaṭṭāʾt* should be rendered "sin offering" throughout Lev. 4, but in some places it may be better translated "purification offering," especially in those instances where no (inadvertent) sin seems to be a part of the picture.

29:17. The verb *nātaḥ* ("cut up into quarters/sections") refers to the sectioning of living bodies, animal or even human (Lev. 1:6, 8, 12; 8:20; 9:13; 1 Sam. 11:7; 1 Kings 18:23, 33). For the verb's use for dismembering a human, see Judg. 19:29; 20:6.

29:17. *Kĕrāʿāyw* is better rendered "its shins" rather than "its legs," that is, the legs below the knees. This is the meaning of Akkadian *kuritu* ("between the knee and fetlock of the hind leg," according to *CAD* K:560). Among the cuneiform texts this entry in *CAD* cites is *shu muri . . . tashtebir ku-ri-is-śu*, "You broke *the shin* of the donkey." Amos 3:12 speaks of a shepherd having only "two leg bones" (*šĕtê kĕrāʿaim*) or a piece of an ear left over after one of his animals has been killed and eaten by a predator. The predator feasts on the upper meaty legs and leaves the shins behind.

29:18. Everywhere *rêaḥ nîḥôaḥ* occurs in Exodus (3x), Leviticus (16x), Numbers (13x), it means "a pleasing fragrance" to the Lord. In Ezekiel, however, the phrase is associated with pagan practices (6:13; 16:19; 20:28), but see 20:41.

29:18. Most versions of the Bible continue to translate *ʾiššeh* (and in v. 25) as "fire offering" by connecting it with Hebrew *ʾēš*, "fire." The term can be used (but is not necessarily used) with any offering as long as part of it is burned. Other scholars connect Hebrew *ʾiššeh* with a Ugaritic cognate, *iṯt* ("offering"). Interestingly, neither the LXX (*thysiasma*, "sacrifice") nor Vulgate use words that have anything to do with "fire" when they translate the word, and the Jewish Targums (*Neofiti, Onqelos, Pseudo-Jonathan*) always use *qrbn* ("gift") for *ʾiššeh*. For a defense of "fire offering," see B. Levine (1989: 7–8, 201n24). For a defense of "food gift," see Milgrom 1991: 161–62; Greenfield 1993: 33–34; Rendsburg 1998.

29:20. I have translated *tĕnûk* as "the lobe [of the ear]" (as in LXX, *lobon*), but *Targum Onqelos* has "the top [of the ear]."

29:20. In Hebrew the word *bōhen* is limited to "the thumb" and to "the big toe." The Akkadian *ubanu* may refer to any finger or to any toe.

29:21. The Qal perfect (with *wāw*) of *qādaš* (*wĕqādaš*) appears here, and the Qal imperfect of the same verb is present in v. 37 (*yiqdāš*). In the commentary section I shall discuss the arguments for translating the Qal of *qādaš* either as "shall become holy" or something like "must be in a holy state."

29:22. *ʾAlyâ* means "broad tail," which is generic only to the sheep family, here, the broad tail of a ram.

29:23. *Kikkar leḥem ʾaḥat* ("one flat loaf of bread"), like the following *ḥallat leḥem* ("one rounded loaf"), refers to a thick but flat and round loaf of bread.

29:23. *Rāqîq* ("wafer") is the opposite in shape of the two words discussed in the previous note: a thin, round cake as opposed to a thick, round cake.

29:26. *Mānâ* means "portion" or "prebend" (Lev. 7:33; 8:29; 1 Sam. 1:4; 9:23; 2 Chron. 31:19). It is a synonym for the word *ḥōq* ("due") and *mišḥâ* ("measure"). Note Lev. 7:33, 34, 35, which use the three words in succession for what is the priest's allotment (NIV, "share," v. 33; "regular share," v. 34; "portion," v. 35).

29:27. For "the breast of the elevation offering" (*ḥăzēh hattĕnûpâ*), see Lev. 7:34; 10:14, 15; Num. 6:20; 8:15. The expression "the thigh of the contribution gift" (*šôq hattĕrûmâ*) also appears in these same verses and always in the second position.

29:27. The Hophal forms of two different verbs are used for the action performed with the breast and the thigh. The breast of the elevation offering is "elevated" (the Hophal of *nûp*, and the only use of this verb in the Hophal in the Bible). The thigh of the contribution gift is "donated" (the Hophal of *rûm*). Milgrom (1991: 474–75) has argued persuasively that the causative stem of *rûm* in priestly texts should be rendered "donate[d], give[n] as a gift." The traditional translation of these two passive verb forms is "waved and raised."

29:28. I am not sure if there is a difference between *ḥoq-ʿôlām* ("an everlasting statute"), as here and elsewhere, and *ḥuqqat ʿôlām* (also "an everlasting statute"), as in Lev. 3:17 and many other times. The first (*ḥoq*) is the masculine form of the noun, and the second, *ḥuqqat*, is feminine in form. Milgrom (1991: 395, 618–19) argues that *ḥoq* in the priestly texts means "due, assigned portion," while *ḥuqqat* means "law, statute."

29:29. On the infinitive construct with an initial *o* vowel (*lĕmošḥâ*, "for anointing"), see Orlinsky 1947: 113–16.

29:29. Although the subject of "for ordaining them" is plural, Aaron's sons, the word "hand" in "fill their hand" is singular (*yādām*). See also vv. 33 and 35.

29:33. I shall have more to say in the commentary section on the root *kāpar*, here in the Pual, *kuppar*, followed by the preposition *bĕ* (*kuppar bāhem*), "[who were] expiated by them."

29:33. "Stranger" (*zār*) designates here somebody or anybody who is not of the seed of Aaron, that is, "layperson or Levite," as in Exod. 30:33; Lev. 22:10; and Num. 16:40 [17:5], where it refers to a nonpriest. The basic meaning of the word is "outsider, stranger."

29:34. For burning (on the following morning) what is left over, see Exod. 12:10; Lev. 7:15; 8:32 (the parallel verse to Exod. 29:34).

29:35. Note the form of the accusative with pronominal suffix *ʾōtākâ* ("I commanded *you*") versus more usual *ʾōtāk*. On uses of the plene (full) form of pronominal suffixes with the accusative indicator, see GKC §103b.

29:36. Although the word for "atonement" is plural (*hakkippurîm*), it is most likely an intensive plural (GKC §124e), meaning something like "full atonement." It is like the phrase *ḥaṭṭa't hakkippurîm* ("sin/purification offering of atonement") in 30:10.

29:36. The Piel of *ḥāṭā'* ("decontaminate") has the force of undoing or removing the effects of the action conveyed by the Qal stem. Hebrew grammarians call this the "privative" function of the Piel. Thus *ḥāṭā'* (Qal) means "sin, offend" whereas *ḥāṭā'* (Piel) means "remove the sin, the offense," meaning "purge, decontaminate." See Lev. 8:15 for the parallel verse.

29:37. I shall discuss below whether the last word in the verse, *yiqdāš*, means "shall become holy," "shall be holy," or "must be in a holy state."

Commentary

This long chapter on the procedure that Moses is to follow in ordaining Aaron **29:1–9**
to the high priesthood and his sons to the priesthood begins with a random inventory of the materials Moses will need—a young bull, two rams, and three types of flatbread made from choice wheat flour—without the Lord's yet saying anything about their purpose.

In requiring three kinds of flatbread or unleavened bread, v. 2 is like the requirement of the "peace" or "well-being" offering that also calls for three kinds of flatbread offered up to God as an act of thanksgiving (Lev. 7:12). Everything edible is to be eaten on the day it is offered (Lev. 7:15). With the ordination offering, anything edible left until the morning is to be incinerated (Exod. 29:34). Thus this ceremony of clergy ordination, however solemn it may be at times, begins by having a "thanksgiving-like" atmosphere.

Having presented the materials, Moses has three remaining responsibilities to commence the ordination ceremony. First, he "washes" Aaron and his sons (v. 4); second, he robes them (vv. 5–9). That the Hebrew of both Exod. 29:4 and Lev. 8:6 use "wash[ed] in" (*rāḥaṣ bě*) suggests that this is no mere light sprinkling of water, but more like what today we would call "total immersion." And probably this will be done somewhere in the outer courtyard, for the consecrands are still laity and nonordained. Third, Moses anoints Aaron (v. 7); on the practice in Syria-Palestine of anointing priests that can be documented from texts as early as the thirteenth or twelfth centuries BC, see Fleming (1998). So before the clergy enter into this sacred moment, they first need a washing; then second, a covering; and third, an anointing; Moses is the mediator of all three. One removes anything that should not be there. The second provides the clothing that the priests need to wear in order to expedite their priestly ministry. The third provides what is not there, a supernatural endowment, an anointing with oil. Note that 28:41 and 29:29 call all priests the *měšûḥîm*, "the anointed ones," whether they are sprinkled or immersed.

The first sacrifice to be presented is the sin/purification offering. Although **29:10–14**
listed fourth (of five) in the data about sacrifices in Lev. 1–5, here it comes

first. One will find the basic data on this sacrifice in Lev. 4. In line with Lev. 4:3, here Exod. 29:10 calls for the presentation of a bull for a priest's sin offering. Large cattle, like bulls, are used for purifying either a high priest or the entire community, whereas for other individuals smaller animals suffice: for a leader, a male goat (Lev. 4:23); for a lay member of the community, a female goat (Lev. 4:28).

There is one major difference between the high priest's sin/purification offering in Lev. 4:1–12 and here. In Lev. 4 one brings the bull's blood (some of it at least) into the holy place "before the LORD, in front of the curtain, . . . on the horns of the altar of fragrant incense" (Lev. 4:6–7). Here the bull's blood is splashed only on the horns of the outer altar, the brazen/bronze altar in the courtyard. The reason may be that on this occasion of holy ordination, any "sin" the priest may have committed inadvertently, and from which he needs purifying, would be a relatively insignificant offense.

Twice Aaron places both his hands on the head of the sacrifice. In Exod. 29:10a Aaron does it for himself, signifying that the bull is one that Aaron himself offers. In Lev. 16:21, on the Day of Atonement, Aaron lays both hands on the live goat's head and confesses over it the sin of his people. What later he will do for others (Lev. 16), he must first do for himself (Exod. 29). He who would become the human instrument of the people's purification must himself first be purified.

We remain uncertain as to why the text mandates the placing of the blood "on the altar's horns" rather than simply "on the altar." Possibly there is a parallel between placing the blood on part of the altar (v. 12), and placing the blood on parts of the priest's body: his (right) ear, thumb, and big toe (v. 20). What horns are to an altar, these body parts are to a person: their respective extremities. Perhaps the part represents the whole. Recall that on Passover the blood is placed on only part of the house (the top and sides of the door opening; Exod. 12:7, 22), again, another extremity, another point of entry.

I have consistently rendered *ḥaṭṭāʾt* as "sin/purification offering" (end of v. 14). The reason for rendering the Hebrew word as "sin" offering is obvious, for it comes from the verb *ḥāṭāʾ*, "sin, offend." It is the "missing-the-mark" sacrifice. Yet there are numerous instances in the Bible that call for somebody to present a *ḥaṭṭāʾt*, and yet the person has not committed any sin, such as the mother shortly after she has given birth to a child (Lev. 12:6), or the "short-term" Nazirite who is completing a term as a Nazirite (Num. 6:14, 16). Surely giving birth to a child is not a "sin." Is the new mother's immediate need forgiveness or purification (after her bleeding)?

Two phrases or words prominent in Lev. 4 and 5 are absent in Exod. 29:10–14, 35–37. First is "he/they shall be forgiven" (Lev. 4:20b, 26b, 31b). Second, 5:6 ("a penalty for the *sin* he has committed"); 5:7 ("as a penalty for his *sin*"); and 5:11 ("an offering for his *sin*") use language that does not appear in Exod.

29. Hence, I am inclined to go with "purification" offering rather than "sin" offering in this particular chapter.

29:15–18 The second sacrifice to be presented is the (whole) burnt offering, the *ʿōlâ* of Lev. 1, "the going-up" offering. The ram takes the place of the bull. There are two pieces of new data in Exod. 29:15–18 that are not present in vv. 10–14. One focuses on the animal. Verses 17–18a inform us that the animal is to be quartered, its entrails and skins washed, and then the whole ram is to be incinerated.

Second, v. 18b identifies this particular offering as "a pleasing fragrance" to the Lord. Regardless of whether one translates *ḥaṭṭāʾt* as "sin offering" or "purification offering," I can find only one place where it is called "a pleasing fragrance" (Lev. 4:31). By contrast, the *ʿōlâ* is frequently identified as such (Lev. 1:9, 13, 17; 8:21; Num. 15:10, 13, 14; 29:2, 6, 8, 13). The reason for this is that the *ʿōlâ*, unlike the *ḥaṭṭāʾt*, is a gift that is offered up to the Lord. And it is a gift that the Lord finds pleasant and enjoyable.

29:19–34 The third sacrifice to be presented is the ordination offering, and for this offering one is to use the second ram. It is different from all the other sacrifices/offerings in two respects. First, it is the only sacrifice that is exclusively for the benefit of the clergy. No Ephraimite or Naphtalite ever presents an ordination offering. Second, all other sacrifices are offered repeatedly: whenever one's heart moves a person in the case of the nonexpiatory ones, or whenever one needs forgiveness for something in the case of the expiatory ones. By contrast, the ordination offering is done only once, at the initial ordination of Aaron and his sons (described in Exod. 29, implemented in Lev. 8). As Exod. 29:29 indicates, the only other occasion when this particular offering will surface again is at the induction of one of Aaron's sons or distant offspring into the office of high priest.

The only other occasion on which blood is applied to part of one's right ear/thumb/big toe (v. 20) is for the individual healed and cleansed of some infectious skin disease (Lev. 14:14, 25). There it is the guilt offering (Lev. 14:14a, 25a) that supplies the blood. Here it is the ordination offering. These two occasions share two other things in common. First, in both, the individual is passing from one state to another, from unclean to clean, or from laity to clergy: from noncleric to being set apart.

Another common element in both is the use of the root *kāpar* (Piel), "expiate, purge, make atonement for," and both in situations where no palpable sin is identified. In Lev. 14 *kipper* (Piel) *ʿal* occurs four times (vv. 18, 19, 20, 29) to refer to the priest's "making expiation/atonement for" the one cleansed of his uncleanness. In Exod. 29 *kipper ʿal* occurs twice (v. 36, in infinitive construct form; v. 37, in imperfect form), and *kuppar bĕ* [Pual] occurs once (v. 33).

There is agreement among Hebrew scholars that the verb *kāpar* in the Piel means "rub, wipe." But does it mean "rub *on*/wipe *on*" or "rub *off*/wipe *off*," or both "smear, cover" or "remove"? One thing God can do with sin or iniquity is "cover it" (*kāsâ*; Neh. 4:5 [3:37]; Pss. 32:1; 85:2). Another thing God can do with sin or iniquity is "blot it out" (*māḥâ*; Neh. 4:5 [3:37]; Jer. 18:23) or "remove it" (*sûr* [Hiphil], Isa. 27:9; *rāḥaq* [Hiphil], Ps. 103:12). Supporting more this second possibility is that the Akkadian equivalent, *kuppuru*, the D stem or Doubled Stem (= Hebrew *kipper*, Piel) always means "wipe, rub off."

As one might expect, the object of *kipper* may be a person. When party A "makes atonement for" party B, the Hebrew expression is *kipper ʿal* ("make atonement on behalf of"). However, whenever party A "makes atonement on his own behalf," the Hebrew expression is *kipper bĕʿad* (Lev. 9:7; 16:6, 11, 24). Although it does not use *kipper*, Job 42:8 nicely brings out the difference between *ʿal* and *bĕʿad*: "Sacrifice a burnt offering *for yourselves* [*baʿadkem*]. My servant Job will pray *for you* [*ʿălêkem*]."

As one might not expect, the object of *kipper* may be an inanimate object. Thus, on the annual Day of Atonement, the high priest is "to make atonement for" the holy of holies (Lev. 16:16) and for the tent of meeting and for the altar of incense (16:20). In such cases the Hebrew can be *kipper ʿal/bĕ*, or have the direct object indicator *ʾet* before the direct object without any preposition after the verb. In some instances it may be debated whether *kipper ʿal* with an inanimate object means "make atonement *for* it" or "make atonement *upon* it" (Exod. 30:10; Lev. 8:15; 16:18). The NIV vacillates, rendering *kipper ʿal* in Exod. 30:10 "make atonement *on* its horns," but "make atonement *for* [the altar that is before the LORD]" in Lev. 16:18.

A verse that combines two kinds of impurity is Lev. 16:16, "In this way he will *make atonement for/purge* (*kipper ʿal*) the most holy place because of the uncleanness (*ṭumʾâ*) and rebellion (*pešaʿ*) of the Israelites, whatever their sins (*pešaʿ ḥaṭṭāʾat*) have been." Physical impurity (*ṭumʾâ*) is removed through purification (*ṭāhēr*). Moral impurity (*pešaʿ*, *ḥaṭṭāʾat*) is removed through forgiveness (*sālaḥ*, Niphal).

Whenever God is the subject of *kipper*, rather than a priest, the verb means "forgive" (Pss. 65:3 [4]; 78:38; 79:9; Isa. 6:7; Jer. 18:23; Ezek. 16:63).

To return to the four uses of *kipper* in Exod. 29, I am inclined to think we are dealing with the priest's physical impurity rather than any moral impurity. Thus v. 33 commands the ordinands to eat the offerings (the ordination offering and the breads), offerings by which they are expiated, meaning cleansed from any kind of impurity. In vv. 36–37 I lean toward reading the Hebrew something like "and you shall decontaminate [NIV, "purify"] the altar by performing purgation upon it [NIV, "by making atonement for it"], and anoint it to consecrate it."

With either persons or inanimate objects, the order is first to purify, and then to consecrate. Remove what should not be there, and then sanctify the person or object. The bottom line in all of this lengthy ordination ritual, much of which will seem strange to us, is this: before the priest can minister to the people, the Lord must first minister to the priest.

In grammatical notes to v. 21 and 37, I briefly noted the problem about how best to render the Qal of *qādaš* in those two verses and elsewhere: "shall become holy," or "shall be holy," or "must be in a holy state"? In particular, v. 37b says, "Anyone/anything touching the altar *yiqdāš*." The exact same phrase, with or without the word "altar," occurs three more times in the Bible: Exod. 30:29b; Lev. 6:18b [11b], 27a [20a].

This is the fourth "touching" scene in Exodus. Zipporah touches (*nāga' lĕ*) Moses or their son with the foreskin (Exod. 4:25). At Passover the Israelites touch the blood to (*nāga' 'el*) the doorposts of their houses (Exod. 12:22). At Sinai God frequently warns the people not to touch (*nāga' bĕ*) the mountain in Exod. 19:12. And here in 29:37 the text speaks of someone/something touching (*nāga' bĕ*) the altar. If one translates *yiqdāš* in v. 37 (with an understood human subject) as "becomes holy," then there is are considerably different results for touching the holy mountain and for touching the holy altar. Touch the mountain, and you are dead. Touch the altar, and you become holy!

Milgrom has led the way in arguing for "shall become holy" in all the four verses cited above (most noticeably in 1981: 278–99). In his favor are two facts. First, the opposite phrase of "whoever touches the altar *yiqdāš*" is "whoever touches [also *nāga' bĕ*] something unclean *yiṭmā'*." The latter phrase cannot mean "Whoever touches something unclean must be in a state of uncleanness." It can only mean "Whoever touches something unclean *is unclean/becomes unclean*" (Lev. 11:24, 26, 27, 31, 36, 39; 15:10, 11, 21, 23, 27). A second support in favor of this reading is to render *kol* in these four verses not as "anyone" but as "anything," or as "whatever" rather than "whoever." Thus holiness is contagious only for inanimate objects, but not for people. To maintain this point, Milgrom must translate *kol* as "whatever" when used with *yiqdāš*, but as "whoever" when used with *yiṭmā'*.

Grammatically, "shall become holy" is possible for *yiqdāš*. The main argument against this rendering is the idea that while the Bible suggests that impurity is highly communicable (simple physical contact can produce it), it does not seem to teach that holiness is also highly communicable (simply through physical contact). It is unlikely when God says, "Be holy, for I am holy" (cf. Lev. 19:2 NRSV, with the verb "be" plus the adjective "holy"), he means, "Go, touch an altar."

The Twice-Daily Offering

(29:38–46)

Translation

[38]"And this is what you shall sacrifice on the altar: two yearling lambs, each day, regularly. [39]The one lamb you shall sacrifice in the morning, and the second lamb you shall sacrifice at twilight. [40]And a tenth of a measure of fine flour mixed with a quarter-*hin* of pounded oil, and a quarter-*hin* libation of wine for the one lamb. [41]The second lamb you shall sacrifice at twilight, like the grain offering of the morning and its libation you shall sacrifice her as a pleasing fragrance, a food gift to the LORD, [42]a regular burnt offering for your generations [at] the entrance of the tent of meeting before the LORD, where I shall meet with you to speak to you there. [43]And I shall meet there with Israel's sons, and it shall be made holy by means of my glory. [44]And I shall make holy the tent of meeting and the altar, and Aaron and his sons I shall make holy to be priests to me. [45]And I shall dwell among Israel's sons and be to them as God. [46]And they shall know that I [am] the LORD their God, who brought them out of Egypt in order that my dwelling [might be] among them. I am the LORD their God."

Grammatical and Lexical Notes

29:38. The verb "sacrifice" in this verse (and in vv. 39 [2x], 41 [2x]) is *ʿāśâ*, normally meaning "do, make." In sacrificial texts *ʿāśâ* has the meaning "sacrifice" or "perform a sacrificial rite" (Lev. 4:20; 5:10; 14:19, 30; 15:15, 30; 16:24; 17:9; 22:23).

Commentary

29:38–46 The first thirty-seven verses of this chapter have focused on what the community does (Lev. 8:3) on very special days, particularly for the investiture of a high priest into that office. It is like a day on which the worldwide Roman Catholic community celebrates the selection and investiture of a new Holy Father. But what about days that are ordinary, days without fanfare, every day?

It is this issue that Exod. 29:38–46 (and Num. 28:3–4) addresses. There is to be a daily burnt offering consisting of two yearling lambs, one offered in the morning and the other in the evening. A grain offering and a libation accompany both the morning and evening offerings. The morning burnt offering is the first offering placed on the altar each day. The evening offering is left to burn on the altar during the night hours. First thing in the morning, a priest removes the ashes of the previous day's sacrifices and adds new firewood.

Leviticus 6:9 [2] calls this "the burnt offering [that] is to remain on the altar hearth throughout the night, till morning," and 9:17 calls it "the morning's burnt offering" (also see Num. 28:23; 2 Kings 16:15; Ezek. 46:15). This twice-daily offering parallels the twice-daily tending of the lampstand (Exod. 27:20–21), and the twice-daily burning of incense (30:7–8). Possibly all three priestly activities happen back-to-back—every morning and every evening: tend the lamps, offer the lamb, burn the incense. A priest may get so get caught up in his ministry on special and spectacular days that he loses his enthusiasm for the routines of daily ministry.

But it is in these ordinary, repetitious, perfunctory ministries that God promises to "meet" with his people (vv. 42b–43a). They are hallowed and hallowing moments (vv. 43b, 44). They provide the participants opportunity to reflect on whence they have come and on who is responsible for such a redemption (v. 46).

The Altar of Incense

(30:1–10; cf. 37:25–28)

Translation

[1]"And you shall make an altar for turning incense into smoke; of acacia wood make it. [2]A cubit its length and a cubit its width; a square it shall be, and two cubits in height; from the identical piece its horns. [3]And you shall overlay it with pure gold—its roof and its walls all around and its horns, and you shall make for it a gold molding all around. [4]And two gold rings you shall make for it beneath its molding on its two sides; you shall make (them) on the two opposite sides, and they shall be housings for the poles with which to carry it. [5]And you shall make the poles of acacia wood and overlay them (with) gold. [6]You shall place it before the veil that is by the ark of the testimony, before the propitiatory that is over the testimony, where I will meet with you. [7]And Aaron shall turn into smoke upon it perfumed incense; every morning, when he tends the lamps, he shall turn it into smoke. [8]And when Aaron lights the lamps at twilight, he shall turn it into smoke, a regular incense before the LORD for your generations. [9]You shall not offer up upon it any unauthorized incense, nor burnt offering, nor grain offering, nor shall you pour a libation on it. [10]And Aaron shall perform rites of expiation upon its horns one time a year; with (some) blood of the sin/purification offering of expiation, one time a year, he shall perform rites of expiation upon it for your generations. A holy of holies it (is) to the LORD."

Grammatical and Lexical Notes

30:4. "*They* shall be housings" is the reading of LXX and Vulgate, reading *wĕhāyû* rather that MT's singular *wĕhāyâ*.

30:9. The "*you*" in "*you* shall not offer . . . nor shall pour" is a plural "you," whereas the "you" verbs of vv. 5–6 are singular verbs. Both times the suffix on "for your generations" (vv. 8, 10) is plural (*-kem*).

Commentary

30:1–10 The dimensions of the incense altar, 1½ feet square and 3 feet high, indicate that this inner altar is smaller than the outer, bronze altar (7½ feet square and 4½ feet high; 27:1–8). That is so because the outer altar is the sacrificial altar and needs to be large enough to hold large animals. By contrast, this inner altar is the incense altar and therefore does not need to be as large. Unlike the hollow bronze altar, the incense altar has a roof (v. 3, *gaggô*). Whereas the outer altar's place is in the courtyard, the incense altar's place is directly in front of the veil, flanked by two other cultic objects: the table and the lampstand.

That, then, raises the question of why the description of this third piece of sacred furniture in the holy place is not presented and described back in chap. 25 (vv. 23–39) as are the other two objects in this holy cubicle. Chapter 37, by contrast, describes the construction of these three items together (table, vv. 10–16; lampstand, vv. 17–24; altar of incense, vv. 25–28). Why delay it until 30:1–10? One path to follow is Milgrom's suggestion (1991: 236–37), to which I drew attention earlier. He notes that "the description of the tabernacle is divided into two parts: Exod. 26:1–27:19, the tabernacle in blueprint, and Exod. 27:20–30:38, the tabernacle in operation. Because the incense altar is described functionally (Exod. 30:7–8), it therefore belongs in the latter section." Another possibility for the placement is Meyers's different take on it (1996; 2008: esp. 20–21). She notes that preceding the two chapters highlighting Aaron (his name appears thirteen times in chap. 28, sixteen times in chap. 29) is the notice about the oil for the lampstand (27:20–21). Immediately following these two chapters is the data about the altar of incense (30:1–10). The high priest is to carry out these two rituals twice every day, once in the morning and once in the evening. As Meyers states (2008: 21), "The mention of 'morning' before 'evening' in chap. 27 and vice versa in chap. 30 constitutes a chiasm that contributes to the ritual framing of Aaron as chief priest." Actually, the chiasm is the other way around: evening before morning in 27:21, and morning before evening in 30:7–8. One further fact of interest is that this chapter begins by presenting the data about the incense altar (vv. 1–10), but delays the data about the recipe for making the incense used on this altar until the end of the chapter (vv. 34–37), forming a nice inclusio.

It is easy to see why v. 9 bans the use of the burnt offering (i.e., meat), the grain offering (i.e., bread), and any libation (i.e., drink) on this inner altar, so close to the holy of holies and God's presence in that particular sanctum. Verse 9 is rejecting any idea, common among polytheistic religions, that one's duty is to place food and beverage in proximity to the deity for the divine consumption.

Verse 9 also prohibits the use of "unauthorized incense" (*qĕṭōret zārâ*). The Hebrew expression is like the *ʾēš zārâ*, "the unauthorized/strange" fire that Nadab and Abihu offer before the Lord (Lev. 10:1). Later, when discussing vv. 34–37, I shall have more to say on what "unauthorized incense" means. For now, let me suggest that the phrase simply designates incense that is unfit for the inner altar because of its composition, a kind of incense that is quite proper and legitimate on other occasions and places. The incense altar calls for *qĕṭōret sammîm* ("perfumed incense," Exod. 30:7). What verse 9 prohibits is the use of *qĕṭōret* instead of *qĕṭōret sammîm*.

The phrase "one time a year" (*ʾaḥat baššānâ*) occurs in v. 10 two times, and only one more time in the Hebrew Bible. That one time is Lev. 16:34,

"Atonement is to be made *once a year* for all the sins of the Israelites" (cf. Heb. 9:7). Only on this most sacred day of the year, the high priest alone performs some kind of expiation rite upon this inner altar (rather than "for" this inner altar). But twice every day the high priest burns the proper incense. Between this "once a year" and "twice every day," the altar of incense receives some of the sacrifice's blood when a sin offering is made for the high priest (Lev. 4:7) or for the entire community (4:18), as a witness to the seriousness of the offense.

This altar continues into NT times, for Luke 1:11 says that the angel of the Lord appeared to Zechariah, "standing at the right side of the altar of incense." That Luke mentions the "right" side of this altar, the favored side, may indicate that the angel's visit to the father-to-be of John the Baptizer is not an intimidating or threatening visit. Rather, it is a good-news visit. Hebrews 9:4 places this incense altar inside the holy of holies rather than in the holy place. An early manuscript of the NT from the fourth century AD, Codex Vaticanus, believes this to be a mistake, and in its translation places this altar back in the holy place! I can think of two reasons for the reading in Heb. 9:4. First, the Greek in the LXX of Exod. 30:6, which the writer of Hebrews probably uses, is sufficiently vague to allow either reading. Second, Aaron takes the incense from this altar on the Day of Atonement into the holy of holies, thus establishing a close relationship between this altar and the inner sanctum, a relationship allowed to no other piece of furniture outside of the holiest place.

Atonement Money

(30:11–16)

Translation

[11]And the LORD spoke to Moses, saying, [12]"When you carry out a head count of Israel's sons for their registration, each one shall give a ransom for his life to the LORD when he registers them, that there be no plague among them when he registers them. [13]This shall everyone give who passes through the registration: half shekel by the weight/shekel of the holy [place]—twenty *gerahs* to the shekel—a half shekel a donation to the LORD. [14]Everyone passing through the registration, from twenty years old and up, shall give the LORD's donation. [15]The rich man shall not pay more, and the poor man shall not give less than a half shekel, when giving the LORD's donation to atone for yourselves/to serve as ransom for your lives. [16]And you shall take the atonement money from Israel's sons, and assign it for the (construction) work on the tent of meeting, and it shall be for Israel's sons a remembrance before the LORD, to atone for yourselves/to serve as ransom for your lives."

Grammatical and Lexical Notes

30:12. "Carry out a head count" is sometimes translated "take a census of" (as in NRSV). The Hebrew says, literally, "when you lift up the head of" (*kî tiśśāʾ ʾet-rōʾš*). This Hebrew expression occurs nineteen times in the Bible. It appears seven times in Exodus and Numbers, each time meaning "take a head count/a census" (Exod. 30:12; Num. 1:2, 49; 4:2, 22; 26:2; 31:26). In none of the eleven passages outside of Exodus and Leviticus does the idiom have that meaning. For example, see the three uses of this phrase in Gen. 40: "Within three days Pharaoh will *lift up your head* [the chief cupbearer's]," v. 13; "Within three days Pharaoh *will lift off your head* [the chief baker's]," v. 19; "He [Pharaoh] *lifted up the heads* of the chief cupbearer and the chief baker," v. 20. Hence, in Gen. 40:13 the idiom means "grant a favor by sparing the life of a suppliant." In Gen. 40:19 the idiom means "withhold a favor and behead." In Gen. 40:20, where both courtiers are present, the idiom means "single out." This latter meaning is the one present in Exodus and Numbers: to single out somebody by registering that person in a census. The idiom may reflect the practice of the census taker's raising the bowed head as he counts someone. See Judg. 8:28; 2 Kings 25:27 (= Jer. 52:31); 1 Chron. 10:9; Job 10:15; Pss. 24:7, 9; 83:2 [3]; Zech. 1:21.

30:12. The root *pqd* in verbal form (*pāqad*, 2x) and nominal form (*happĕqudîm*, 3x) occurs five times in vv. 12–14 ("register" and "registration") in conjunction with this census. The root *pqd* also occurs with other census takings: numerous times in Num. 1–4; 26. The particular verb, *pāqad*, has many different meanings. It appears in Exod. 3:16 (NIV, "I have *watched over* you"); 4:31 (NIV, "the LORD *was concerned about* them"); 13:19 (NIV, "God will surely *come to your aid*"); 20:5 and 34:7 (NIV, "*punishing* the children for the sin of the fathers"); 32:34 (NIV, "when the time comes for me *to punish, I will punish* them for their sin"). So we have one verb in one book (Exodus) meaning "watch over," "be concerned about," "come to one's aid," "punish," and here in chap. 30 "enroll" or "register." The difference between *nāśā' rō'š* and *pāqad* may be that the first refers to the totals ("take the sum"), while *pāqad* refers to the individual count.

30:12. The meaning of *kōper* as "ransom" is established by its use with *pidyōn* ("redemption") in Exod. 21:30. The LXX's word for *kōper* is *lytron*, formed from the verb *lyō* ("release [from prison, from slavery, from a debt]"). *Lytron* is the word Mark 10:45 uses in "For even the Son of Man did not come to be served, but to serve, and to give his life as a *ransom* for many." The book of Exodus is already connecting ransom with atonement.

30:13–14. "Everyone passing through [the registration]" is *kol ha'ōbēr 'al[-happĕqudîm]*. In 2 Kings 12, in a passage with parallels to Exod. 30:11–16, we have the expression *kesep 'ōbēr* (2 Kings 12:4 [5]), which NIV renders "the money collected in the census," but another possibility could be "the silver of the census tax." In this rendering *kesep 'ōbēr* would be an ellipsis of the longer phrase *kesep ha'ōbēr 'al-happĕqudîm* (Fishbane 1995: 108).

30:13. The shekel is a weight unit rather than a coin. There are three different shekels: (1) the sanctuary weight (*šeqel haqqōdeš*), as here; (2) the royal weight (*šĕqālîm bĕ'eben hammelek*), 2 Sam. 14:26; and (3) the merchant's weight (*šeqel kesep 'ōbēr lassōḥēr*), Gen. 23:16.

30:13. For "gerah," see Lev. 27:25; Num. 3:47; 18:16; Ezek. 45:12. The sanctuary shekel contained twenty "grains" (*gerahs*) of silver.

30:15–16. I shall comment below on the phrase *lĕkappēr 'al-napšōtêkem*, which appears in both of these verses. In my translation I offer "to atone for yourselves" and "to serve as ransom for your lives."

Commentary

30:11–16 It is one thing to pay for the erection of a new building. It is another thing to have funds for its upkeep and maintenance over the long haul. In the case of the tabernacle, it is the people's voluntary offerings that pay for the construction of the tabernacle and its appurtenances (Exod. 25:1–7; 36:3–7). This temple tax of one-half shekel provides contingency funds for its upkeep. The offerings for construction are freewill. This temple tax is mandatory, but only for one time. It is difficult to know the value of "one-half shekel," but because v. 15 mandates the same tax for all, rich and poor, it must not be onerous for the poor or sacrificial for the wealthy. This absence of socioeconomic distinction stands in contrast to the sacrifices spelled out in Leviticus. For example, the offering of a (whole) burnt offering ranges from an animal from the herd (Lev. 1:3), to an animal from the flock (1:10), birds (1:14), or flour (Lev. 2). You have more, you offer more. If you have less, go to your pantry. The half-shekel offering was reduced in postexilic times. According to Neh. 10:32 [33], this tax amounts to "a third of a shekel." The reduction was probably due to the economic hardship experienced by the exiles as they returned to their homes from Babylon. (For further postbiblical references to the temple tax, see Liver 1963.)

These two kinds of offerings (freewill and mandatory) appear in the account of Joash (or Jehoash), king of Jerusalem, and his project to repair the temple (2 Kings 12). The king funds the project by appropriating several sources of revenue, three in fact. Two of those three are (1) "the money collected in the census" (as reflected in Exod. 30:11–16) and (2) "the money brought voluntarily to the temple" (2 Kings 12:4 [5]).

Perhaps unexpectedly to the modern reader, this temple tax is called a "ransom [*kōper*] for his life" (v. 12). Verse 16 speaks of "atonement money" (*kesep hakkippurîm*). And vv. 15 and 16 use the root *kpr* when they say that the giving of this half-shekel tax is *lĕkappēr ʿal-napšōtêkem*. As I indicated above, that Hebrew phrase may be translated, "to atone/make atonement for you/your lives," or "to serve as a ransom for you/your lives." Thus we have three uses of *kpr*: the singular noun *kōper* ("ransom"), the plural noun *kippurîm* ("atonement"), and the twice-used verb *kāpar ʿal* ("make atonement for/upon"). This fourfold use of the root *kpr* may be one reason 30:11–16 follows the data on the incense altar (30:1–10), which comes to a conclusion with a double use of the verb *kāpar ʿal* (v. 10).

The reason for using *kpr* with the temple tax may be because of the negative overtones often associated with census taking in Israel. Note the similarity between David's census taking in 2 Sam. 24 and Exod. 30:11–16. In response to David's act, God sends a plague (*deber*) among Israel (2 Sam. 24:15). According to Exod. 30:12, the purpose of the "ransom" is so that "there be no plague [*negep*] among them." There is, however, one major difference between the two, as Porter (1965: 374n1) has observed. In Exod. 30 the danger resides in each particular person who allows him- or herself to be counted, and there is no attribution of guilt to Moses the census taker, as there is to David the census taker.

Another parallel is in Num. 31, the account of Israel's war against Midian. Numbers 31:48–54, especially vv. 48–50, records that after the victory and after taking a census of their own troops (*nāśāʾ rōʾš*, Num. 31:49a, as in Exod. 30:12), they discover that not a single soldier is missing (*pāqad*, Num. 31:49b, as in Exod. 30:12). In response, the officers contribute to the sanctuary all the gold ornaments they have stripped off the slain Midianites, most likely to avoid any negative fallout for taking a count of their warriors. Their purpose for doing this, Num. 31:50 says, is *lĕkappēr ʿal-napšōtênū*, the exact same phrase as in Exod. 30:15–16, except for the change of the pronominal suffix, ransoming "our lives" versus "your lives." Finally, the gift of gold is a "reminder/remembrance" (*zikkārôn*) to the Lord as is the atonement money (Exod. 30:16 and Num. 31:54b).

There is no idea here of some OT form presaging medieval indulgences, of purchasing one's salvation. Forgiveness and atonement cannot be bought and paid for by the one in need of redemption. There is no "he who puts the most on the offering plate receives the greatest forgiveness." In both cases, Num. 31 and Exod. 30, the purpose is to prevent God's lethal punishment on Israel for taking a census. This would be a normal procedure when legitimately required, but one that could become an occasion for boasting in one's numbers rather than in one's Lord, an occasion for advancing military power as one's asset rather than divine power.

The temple tax is one that Jesus himself pays (Matt. 17:24–27) in order not to "offend" the Jewish authorities (see McEleney 1976). His onetime payment of this tax is unique to Jesus. Nobody else ever gets a half-shekel or four-drachma coin out of a fish's mouth. Also, any connection between this tax and atonement is absent from the verses in Matthew.

One might also see a connection between Exod. 30:11–16 and Cornelius in Acts 10. The giving of the half shekel for sanctuary maintenance is to be a "memorial" to the Lord (Exod. 30:16b). The angel says of Cornelius that his giving generously to those in need, to the poor, has come up as a "memorial offering" before God (Acts 10:4). A monetary gift has become a *mnēmosynon*, a memorial, a remembrance. When Jesus says, "Do this as a memorial [*anamnēsis*] for me" in Luke 22:19b (also see 1 Cor. 11:24–25), one wonders whether he is establishing a new ritual parallel to, and contrasting with, other cultic memorials (see Carpinelli 1999; Hamm 2003).

The Bronze Laver

(30:17–21; cf. 38:8; 40:7, 30)

Translation

[17]And the LORD spoke to Moses, saying, [18]"And you shall make a laver of bronze, and its base of bronze for washing, and place it between the tent of meeting and the altar, and place water there. [19]And Aaron and his sons shall wash from it their hands and their feet. [20]When they enter the tent of meeting, they shall wash [with] water that they not die, or when they approach the altar to officiate, to turn into smoke a food gift to the LORD. [21]And they shall wash their hands and their feet that they not die, and it shall be for them an everlasting statute, for him and for his seed, for their generations."

Grammatical and Lexical Notes

30:18. The Hebrew word for "laver" is *kiyyôr* (Lev. 8:11; 1 Kings 7:30; etc.).

30:19–20. The verb "shall wash" is the perfect form of the verb with initial *wāw* (*wĕrāḥăṣû*). The verb "shall wash" in v. 20 is the same verb, except there it is imperfect (*yirḥăṣû*). Haran (1989: 56–73) has observed this pattern of using the same verb, first in the perfect + *wāw* and then in the imperfect, throughout Exodus–Numbers. I cite a few of his examples: Exod. 12:14, "And you shall *celebrate* [*wĕḥaggōtem*]. . . . You shall *celebrate* it [*tĕḥagguhû*]"; Exod. 23:11, "Your people's poor may *eat* of it [*wĕʾākĕlû*]. . . . What is left the beast of the field will *eat* [*tōʾkal*]"; Num. 6:9, "He *shall shave* his head [*wĕgillaḥ*]. . . . on the seventh day he *shall shave* it [*yĕgallĕḥennû*]."

30:20. When "wash (with) water" occurs without a preposition on "water," as here (*yirḥăṣû-mayim*), then the phrase refers to washing only part of one's body. When the preposition *bĕ* occurs with "water" (*rāḥaṣ bammayim*), then the phrase refers to a washing of one's entire body, an immersion (e.g., Lev. 8:6; 14:9; 16:4, 24, 26, 28; 22:6; Num. 19:7, 8).

Commentary

The bronze laver is the sacrificial altar, and stands "between the tent of meeting **30:17–21**
and the altar" (v. 18), thus in the inner section of the tabernacle courtyard. The text provides no dimensions for this laver as it does for most other holy items.

Two things we do know are as follows. First, the laver exists for the benefit of the priest, to wash only his hands and feet before he enters the holy precincts for ministerial service. There is no reference to the priest having to wash his hands and feet after he conducts the ritual and leaves those holy precincts. The only occasion that calls for priestly washing after performing the ritual is on the Day of Atonement (Lev. 16:24). In rabbinic idiom (Mishnah *Yoma* 3.2), this limited washing is known as "the sanctification of hands and feet" (*kiddush yadayim be-raglayim*). Psalm 24:3–4a also reflects this idea: "Who may ascend the hill of the LORD? Who may stand in his holy place? He who has clean hands and a pure heart," one who is clean on the outside and clean on the inside.

The second thing we know about his laver is that if a priest fails to wash his hands and feet before entering the holy precincts, he will die (Exod. 30:20–21). The repetition of "that they not die" reinforces the importance of this ablution and raises it above a simply hygienic act.

This is one of eight instances of *mût* ("die") penalties that Exodus–Numbers lists for some kind of offense that relates to the sanctuary; see the chart in Milgrom (1991: 946). For the high priest, there is one *mût* violation, improper entry into the holy of holies (Lev. 16:2, 13). For the priests, there are three *mût* violations: (1) improper officiating, including failure to robe properly (Exod. 28:43), failure to wash hands and feet before entering the tent (Exod. 30:20–21), drinking wine or intoxicants before entering the tent (Lev. 10:9); (2) improper mourning (Lev. 10:6); (3) failure to keep faithfully God's requirements (Lev. 22:9). For the Levites, there are also three *mût* violations: (1) touching holy things they are not to touch (Num. 4:15); (2) viewing holy things that they are not to view (Num. 4:19–20); (3) going where only the priests are allowed to go in the tent (Num. 18:3). For the laity there is one *mût* violation, going where only the priests are allowed to enter inside the tent (Num. 17:13 [28]; 18:22).

Mark 7:1–13 records the incident of some Pharisees who are "gathered against Jesus" (not "gathered *around* Jesus," as in NIV). The Greek verb here is *synagō*, the very one that Ps. 2:2 LXX uses for kings and rulers "taking their stand against" the Lord and his Anointed One. The Pharisees want to know why Jesus's disciples do not wash their hands before they eat. There is no teaching anywhere in the First Testament about the necessity of laity's washing their hands before eating or before doing anything. Washing, as we have seen, is obligatory only for the priests, and that washing is only at times of priestly ministry. Apparently these Pharisees have extended the washing directives of the OT so that "every Jew should live like a priest, and every home become like the Temple" (Marcus 2000: 449).

The Anointing Oil

(30:22–33; cf. 37:29)

Translation

[22]And the LORD spoke to Moses, saying, [23]"And you, take for yourself fine spices: of free-flowing myrrh, five hundred (weight), of fragrant cinnamon, half as much, two hundred and fifty (weight), and of aromatic cane, two hundred and fifty (weight), [24]and cassia, five hundred (weight) by the sanctuary shekel, and olive oil, a *hin*. [25]And you shall make of it the sacred oil of unction; a perfumer's compound, the work of a perfumer; the sacred oil of unction it shall be. [26]And you shall anoint with it the tent of meeting, and the ark of the testimony, [27]and the table and all its furnishings, and the lampstand and its furnishings, and the altar of incense, [28]and the altar of burnt offering and all its furnishings, and the laver and its stand. [29]And you shall consecrate them, and they shall be holy of holies. Anybody/anything touching them becomes holy/must be holy. [30]Aaron and his sons you shall anoint, and you shall consecrate them to be priests to me. [31]And to Israel's sons you shall speak, saying, 'The sacred oil of unction this shall be to me for your generations. [32]On the flesh of a (lay)man it shall not be poured, and in its composition you shall not make anything like it. Holy it (is), holy it shall be to you. [33]The man who compounds its like and who places it on a stranger shall be cut off from his people.'"

Grammatical and Lexical Notes

30:23–24. It is difficult to identify with certainty all these different spices. The introductory phrase is "fine spices" (*bĕśāmîm rōʾš*). The form *beśem*, the singular of *bĕśāmîm*, occurs later in v. 23, the only time the singular form appears in the Bible ("and fragrant cinnamon," *wĕqinnĕmān-beśem*) apart from Song 5:1. A related word occurs even later in v. 23, *ûqĕnēh-bōśem* ("aromatic cane"). Like some other words for spices in these two verses, *bĕśāmîm* appears in the Song of Songs (4:10, 14, 16; 5:13; 6:2; 8:14).

"Free-flowing myrrh" is *mor-dĕrôr*. "Myrrh" (*mōr*) also occurs frequently in the Song of Solomon (1:13; 3:6; 4:6, 14; 5:5, 13). Pope (1977: 340) identifies *mōr* /myrrh as "an aromatic gum which exudes from cracks in the bark of the *Balsamodendron myrrha* which grows in Arabia, Abyssinia, and India." The only other use of *dĕrôr* in the Pentateuch is Lev. 25:10, the proclamation of "liberty, release" in the Jubilee Year for those bound by servitude. See the use of *dĕrôr* with this nuance in Isa. 61:1 ("The Spirit . . . has sent me to proclaim *freedom* for the captives"); in Jer. 34:8 ("to proclaim *freedom* for the slaves"); 34:15 ("Each of you proclaimed *freedom* to his countrymen"); 34:17 ("You have not proclaimed *freedom* to your fellow countrymen"). The Hebrew verb *dārar*, like Akkadian *darāru*, means "to move about freely," and hence my translation here, "free-flowing."

Qinnāmôn ("cinnamon") appears only three times in the Hebrew Bible: Exod. 30:23; Song 4:14; and Prov. 7:17. *Qāneh* ("cane") appears more often, but only once in the Song (4:14). The word occurs frequently in Exod. 25:31–39 and 37:17–24 to refer to the "shaft" or "branches" of the lampstand, if it is the same word. The noun *qiddâ* ("cassia") appears again only in Ezek. 27:19.

30:29. On *kol-hanōgēʿa bāhem yiqdāš*, see my earlier remarks on a similar phrase in 29:37.

30:32. "(Lay)man" in "on the flesh of a (lay)man" is *ʾādām* and may be rendered, "On the flesh of an ordinary/noncleric man." It is the equivalent of *zār* ("stranger") in v. 33.

30:32. *Yîsāk* ("it shall [not] be poured") provides the only use of the verb *yāsak* in the Hebrew Bible. The SP reads it *yûsak*, that is, the Hophal of *sûk* ("anoint").

Commentary

30:22–33 The Lord must like things in his dwelling that smell nice. Otherwise, why would he dictate the use of so many aromatic spices that together form the anointing oil to be used on the tent and its furnishings (vv. 26–29), and on Aaron and his sons (v. 30)?

The oil's composition is two parts liquid myrrh, one part each of cinnamon and cane, two parts cassia, with olive oil added (vv. 23–24). It is not just an aromatic anointing oil. Twice the text also calls it "the sacred oil of unction" (*šemen mišḥat-qōdeš*, vv. 25 [2x], 31), and v. 32b twice calls this oil "holy" (*qōdeš*). It is, therefore, different from "the log of oil" that is used on the individual with an infectious skin disease (Lev. 14:10b, 17–18).

According to v. 33, anybody who tries to duplicate this recipe or misuses it by pouring it on a layperson "shall be cut off from his people" (*wĕnikrat mēʿammāyw*). According to Milgrom (1991: 458), there are in Genesis–Numbers nineteen cases of violations for which the perpetrator is "cut off." The only one in Genesis is for neglecting circumcision (Gen. 17:14). The other three in Exodus are (1) for eating leavened bread during the Unleavened Bread Festival (12:15, 19); (2) duplicating and misusing sanctuary incense (30:38); (3) working on the Sabbath (31:14b). The remaining fourteen are in Leviticus and Numbers. This language does not occur outside of Genesis–Numbers.

"Cutting off" a person is a metaphor borrowed from the felling of trees, as in Jer. 11:19, what Jeremiah's enemies would like to do to him, "Let us destroy *the tree* and its fruit; let us *cut him off* from the land of the living, that his name be remembered no more." Since such sins (all the nineteen counted by Milgrom) are sins against God, it is God who cuts off. That can mean immediate death, premature death, the death of one's descendants, or even banishment and ostracism. See further B. Levine 1989: 241–42; Milgrom 1991: 457–60.

The Recipe for the Incense

(30:34–38; cf. 37:29b)

Translation

[34]And the LORD said to Moses, "Take for yourself the fragrant spices stacte, onycha, and galbanum, fragrant spices with pure frankincense in equal proportions, [35]and make of it incense, perfume, the work of a perfumer, salted, pure, holy. [36]And you shall pound some of it (into) finely ground powder, and place some of it before the testimony in the tent of meeting, where I shall meet with you. Most holy it shall be to you. [37]As for the incense that you will make, its same composition you shall not make for yourselves. Holy it shall be to you for the LORD. [38]A man who makes its like to smell it shall be cut off from his people."

Grammatical and Lexical Notes

30:34. The first spice or herb is *nāṭāp* ("stacte"). "Stacte" is a transliteration of the LXX's *staktē*. The word appears again only in Job 36:27 (NIV, "He draws up *the drops* of water"). Since the verb behind the noun *nāṭāp* is *nāṭap*, which means "drip," some have suggested that the noun might mean "resin, gum," any substance that drips from trees. The second spice or herb is *šĕḥēlet* ("onycha"), in LXX *onyx* and Vulgate *onycha*. It may come from the ocean, where it is a covering of a shellfish like the murex. The third spice or herb is *ḥelbĕnâ* ("galbanum"), in LXX *chalbanē*, in the Vulgate *galbanum*. My dictionary defines "galbanum" as "a gum resin with a pungent odor, obtained from certain Asian plants of the genus *Ferula*, or the parsley family: used in incense." The Hebrew word for "frankincense" is *lĕbōnâ*. The word literally means "white (stuff)," for frankincense looks whitish (*lābān*) when pounded into flakes or powder. It is a fragrant gum-resin from three species of the *Boswellia* tree found only in southern Arabia.

30:34. "In equal proportions" is *bad bĕbad*, an expression unique to this verse. *Lĕbad* occurs in Exod. 12:37 ("*besides* the children"), and in 26:9 ("join five of the panels *by themselves* and six of the panels *by themselves*" [AT]). See Rabin 1973: 57.

30:35. *Qĕṭōret* ("incense") literally means "that which goes up in smoke."

30:35. "Salted" is *mĕmullāḥ*, the Pual participle of *mālaḥ* II. The verb should be connected with the noun "salt" (*melaḥ*). See Lev. 2:13 for salt used with the cereal/grain. On "salted incense," see Hurowitz 1987.

30:36. *Šāḥaq* ("pound") appears again only in 2 Sam. 22:43 (= Ps. 18:42 [43]) ("beat") and in Job 14:19 ("wears away").

30:36. *Hādēq* ("finely ground powder") is the Hiphil infinitive absolute of *dāqaq*, with the infinitive used as an adverbial complement.

30:37. The first plural "you" in this paragraph is at the end of v. 36 ("Most holy it shall be to you [*lākem*]"). In v. 37 the first "you will make" is singular (*taʿăśeh*), while the second "you shall [not] make" is plural (*taʿăśû*), as is "for yourselves" (*lākem*) after it. Strangely, "Holy it shall be to you [*lĕkā*] for the LORD" at the end of v. 37 is a singular "you." Most ancient versions read *lākem* rather than MT's *lĕkā*.

Commentary

30:34–38 Chapter 30 begins by giving instructions for building the altar of incense (vv. 1–10). It concludes by outlining the recipe that one is to follow when preparing the incense used on or near this altar.

There are several parallels between the previous paragraph, which addresses the preparation of the anointing oil (v. 22–33), and this one, which addresses the preparation of incense. For the ingredients, each of these paragraphs uses a list of Hebrew words about whose English equivalents we are uncertain (vv. 23–24, 34). Both the oil and the incense are called "holy" (vv. 25, 31, 36, 37). Both use the expression "most holy" (*qōdeš qodāšîm*): v. 29 for the anointed furnishings in the place of worship; v. 36 for the incense itself. Both paragraphs end with a warning against misuse of either the anointing oil or incense, the penalty for which is being "cut off" (vv. 32–33, 37–38). Finally, just as there are two kinds of oil, the special anointing oil for the clergy and the oil placed on parts of the body of the person with some skin disease, there are two kinds of incense (Haran 1960b). Verses 34–38 describe the special kind of incense set apart for use in the tent. Verse 7 has spoken of *qĕṭōret sammîm*, whose preparation vv. 34–35 outline. Verse 9 has spoken of *qĕṭōret zārâ*, which does not designate "evil" or "idolatrous" incense. Rather, it simply designates ordinary incense whose composition is not identical with that of vv. 34–35 and thus is not restricted to be used by only the high priest and only in the holy place. For example, Lev. 2:2, 15–16 call for the use of this ordinary incense on the outer altar in conjunction with the cereal/grain offering.

Two occasions call for the use of this special incense. One is the daily incense offering by the high priest and only by the high priest, which Exod. 30:7–8 ordains. For a violation by a king's offering this incense rather than the high priest, see what King Uzziah attempts (2 Chron. 26:18). The other is on the Day of Atonement (Lev. 16:12–13). On this latter occasion the incense is not just ground "finely" (*hādēq*, Exod. 30:36), but ground "extra finely" (*qĕṭōret sammîm daqqâ*, Lev. 16:12). So Scripture speaks of three forms of incense: *qĕṭōret* for the outer altar; *qĕṭōret sammîm* for the inner altar with the daily incense offering; and *qĕṭōret sammîm daqqâ* on the Day of Atonement in the holy of holies.

At least four scriptural references connect incense with prayer: (1) Ps. 141:2 ("May my *prayer* be set before you like incense"); (2) Luke 1:10 ("And when the time for the burning of incense came, all the assembled worshipers *were praying* outside"); (3) Rev. 5:8 ("The four living creatures . . . were holding golden bowls full of incense, which are *the prayers* of the saints"); (4) Rev. 8:3–4 ("The smoke of the incense, together with *the prayers* of the saints, went up before God from the angel's hand"). Incense prayers are prayers that lift up an aromatic fragrance to God. They are not prayers of penitence or even intercession. They are prayers that flood heaven with all sorts of beautiful scents, prayers that activate one's olfactory sense.

Tabernacle Artisans

(31:1–11; cf. 35:30–36:7)

Translation

[1]And the LORD spoke to Moses, saying, [2]"See, I have called by name Bezalel, son of Uri, son of Hur, of the tribe of Judah. [3]And I have filled him with the Spirit of God, in wisdom, and in understanding, and in knowledge in every task, [4]in order to devise plans, to work in gold and in silver and in bronze, [5]and in cutting stone for settings, and in carving wood, in order to be able to do every task. [6]And I, behold, I have given him Oholiab son of Ahisamach, of the tribe of Dan; and into the heart of every wise-hearted one I have given wisdom, that they may make everything that I commanded you: [7]the tent of meeting, and the ark for the testimony, and the propitiatory, which is over it, and all the tent's furnishings, [8]and the table and its furnishings, and the pure lampstand and all its furnishings, and the altar of incense, [9]and the altar of burnt offering and all its furnishings, and the laver and its base, [10]and the vestments for service, that is, the sacred vestments for Aaron the priest and his sons' vestments to be a priest, [11]and the oil of unction, and the perfumed incense for the holy (place). As I have commanded you, they shall do."

Grammatical and Lexical Notes

31:2. *Rĕʾēh* ("see") often introduces declaration of gifts or, as here, appointments: Gen. 41:41 NRSV (Pharaoh to Joseph), "*See*, I have set you over all the land of Egypt"; Exod. 7:1 AT (God to Moses), "*See*, I have set you as a god to Pharaoh"; Deut. 1:8 AT (God to the Israelites), "*See*, I have given the land before you"; Deut. 1:21 AT (Moses to the Israelites), "*See*, the LORD your God has given the land before you"; Jer. 1:10 (God to Jeremiah), "*See*, today I appoint you over nations and kingdoms."

31:2. "Bezalel" (*bĕṣalʾēl*) means, "In the shadow of El" (*bĕ* + *ṣal* + *ʾēl*), a name he shares with a discredited Levite in the postexilic period (Ezra 10:30). For the idea of finding shelter in God's "shadow," see Pss. 91:1; 121:5 (NIV, "shade"). The use of "shadow" with theophoric names appears outside of Israel, as in the Akkadian transcription of the Philistine name "Tsilli-Bel," "My shade/shadow is Bel (Baal)." See further Huffmon 1965: 257.

31:6. "Oholiab" means "Father (is) my tent." For three other names in the Bible with "tent" as part of the name, see (1) Oholibama ("A high place [is] my tent"), one of Esau's Canaanite wives (Gen. 36:2, 14, 18); (2) Oholah ("Her tent," as though the final *he* were the feminine possessive suffix); and (3) Oholibah ("My tent [is] in her"). These last two forms are the metaphorical names Ezekiel uses for sinful Samaria and apostate Judah respectively (Ezek. 23:4, 5, 11).

31:6. "Ahisamach" means "My brother offers support," or "My brother has leaned [his hand for support]." The latter part of this name, the verb *sāmak*, appears in Exod. 29:10, 15, 19 for Aaron and his sons' laying or leaning their hands upon the various sacrifices at the time of their ordination.

31:10. There is uncertainty about the meaning of *bigdê haśśĕrād*, which I have rendered "vestments for service." Such a translation follows more the LXX and other ancient versions that read *haśśĕrād* as if it were *haššārēt*, from the verb *šārat* ("serve, officiate"). Margalith (1983) alone reads *haśśĕrād* as "fine linen," by citing a passage from the historian Herodotus (*Histories* 2.105), who speaks of a kind of fine linen from the far eastern part of the Middle East, a linen that the Greeks called *Sardōnikon* (the Sanskrit word for it is *çrath*, "fine linen") and is possibly the origin of the Hebrew *śĕrād* (in 31:10).

Commentary

Bezalel is one of the artisans who will oversee the construction of the tabernacle, all its furnishings, and the priestly vestments. He is from the tribe of Judah. We know Bezalel's father's name, Uri, and his grandfather's name, Hur, who may or may not be the same Hur of Exod. 17:10. **31:1–11**

Assisting Bezalel is Oholiab from the tribe of Dan (see further Bartusch 2003: 42–48). The tribe of Dan is the central tribe on the north side of the tent as Israel marches through the wilderness. This honor may be because Dan is the firstborn of all of Jacob's sons from his concubines (Gen. 30:4–6). Dan produces the most famous of all the judges, Samson. There is some kind of worship center there that is operated by a priestly line descended from Moses (Judg. 18:30). Finally, Dan provides two artisans who help respectively in the construction of the tabernacle (Oholiab) and in the construction of Solomon's temple (2 Chron. 2:13–14, "I [the king of Tyre] am sending you Hurami-Abi, a man of great skill, whose mother was from Dan"). Also, others besides these two have significant leadership roles, as v. 6b suggests.

This is the third time the phrase *rûaḥ ʾĕlōhîm* ("the Spirit of God") occurs in the Bible (v. 3a). The previous two are Gen. 1:2b, "And the *rûaḥ ʾĕlōhîm* was hovering over the waters," and Gen. 41:38, Pharaoh's words to his servants about Joseph, "Can we find anyone like this man, one in whom is the *rûaḥ ʾĕlōhîm*?" (Not wanting to make Pharaoh sound like a trinitarian monotheist, I believe we could render his words as "in whom is a divine spirit?")

What makes the use of this phrase stand out in v. 3 is that the Lord says he has "filled" (*waʾămallēʾ*) Bezalel with the Spirit of God. That means that the first "Spirit-filled" individual in the Bible is not some godly prediluvian or patriarch, or even the saintly Moses, but Bezalel, a layperson, a construction foreman. Such a calling is no less sacred and is no less in need of divine enablement than that of Moses the liberator and Aaron the supreme priest. His vestments may be overalls, a hard-hat, and steel-toe boots, but his vocation is from God, and his work is to honor God through the employment of his God-given skills.

I have translated *ḥokmâ* as "wisdom" in vv. 3 and 6 and as "wise-hearted" (*kol-ḥăkam-lēb*) in v. 6. Many modern translations correctly opt for "skill" as the English equivalent of *ḥokmâ* in vv. 3 and 6. Following M. Fox (2000: 32), I suggest the following nuances for *ḥokmâ* outside of Proverbs:

1. "Wisdom" = "expertise, craftsmanship, skill": Bezalel in Exod. 31:3; 35:31; Isa. 40:20, "a skilled craftsman" (*ḥārāš ḥākām*); Jer. 9:17 [16], "Call for the wailing women to come; send for the most skillful of them [*haḥăkāmôt*]"; Ezek. 28:5, "By your great skill [*bĕrōb ḥokmātĕkā*] in trading you have increased your wealth."
2. "Wisdom" = the learning and erudition gained from the study of books and lore: Eccles. 1:16, "Look, I have grown and increased in *wisdom* more than anyone"; Jer. 8:8, "How can you say, 'We are *wise*, for we have the law of the Lord'?"; Jer. 9:23 [22], "Let not the wise man boast in his *wisdom*"; Dan. 1:4, "Showing aptitude for every kind of learning [*bĕkol-ḥokmâ*]."
3. "Wisdom" = perceptiveness, astuteness, the ability to understand the implications of situations and interpret signs: 2 Sam. 14:20, "My lord [David] has *wisdom* like that of an angel of God—he knows everything that happens in the land"; Jer. 9:12 [11], "What man is *wise* enough to understand this?"; Ps. 107:43, "Whoever is *wise*, let him heed these things."
4. "Wisdom" = cleverness in devising plans and strategies: 2 Sam. 14:2, "Joab . . . had a *wise* woman brought from there"; 20:16, "A *wise* woman called from the city"; Job 5:13, "He catches the wise in their *craftiness*"; Eccles. 4:13, "Better a poor but *wise* youth than an old but foolish king."
5. "Wisdom" = prudence, good sense, exercising sound judgment in practical matters: 1 Kings 4:29 [5:9], "God gave Solomon *wisdom* and very great insight"; Eccles. 2:3, "My mind still guiding me with *wisdom*"; 7:10, "For it is not *wise* to ask such questions."

The Spirit of God that comes upon Bezalel and his colleagues enables them to work with metals, fabrics, wood, and stone. It is unlikely that Bezalel before this was clueless and all thumbs about how to make such items. Sometimes, to be sure, when the Spirit fills a human life, he gives new gifts and abilities not hitherto present. More often than not, I suspect, the Spirit takes gifts already present and refocuses and redirects them in ways of his choosing. For example, I think it is highly unlikely that when the Spirit comes mightily upon David (1 Sam. 16:13), the Spirit suddenly gives David the ability to play a lyre before Saul (16:18, 23). Rather, this is a gift, given by God and honed by practice, which the Lord is now able to use as David ministers encouragingly to a hurting Saul. The same goes for Bezalel. Those several areas of expertise that he has developed over years in Egypt—the Lord now is able to take and use that expertise to oversee the building of a holy dwelling place.

Guarding the Sabbath

(31:12–18; cf. 35:1–3)

Translation

[12]And the LORD said to Moses, saying, [13]"You, speak to Israel's sons, saying, 'For sure my Sabbaths you shall guard, for a sign it (is) between me and (all of) you for your generations to know that I (am) the LORD who sanctifies you. [14]And you shall guard the Sabbath, for holy (is) it to (all of) you. Whoever desecrates it shall certainly be put to death, for anybody who does any work on it, that person shall be cut off from the midst of his people. [15]Six days work may be done, but on the seventh day a most restful rest, holy to the LORD. Anybody who does any work on the seventh day shall certainly be put to death. [16]And Israel's sons shall guard the Sabbath in order to observe the Sabbath for their generations (as) an everlasting covenant. [17]Between me and Israel's sons a sign it (is) forever, for (in) six days the LORD made the heavens and the earth, but on the seventh day he was refreshed.'"

[18]And he gave Moses, when he had finished with him on Mount Sinai, the two tablets of the testimony, tablets of stone, written by God's finger.

Grammatical and Lexical Notes

31:13. *ʾAk* ("For sure"), while often meaning simply "yet," carries a sense of urgency when it introduces a law (Lev. 23:27, introducing legislation for the Day of Atonement; Lev. 23:39, introducing legislation for the Feast of Tabernacles; Num. 1:49, introducing God's directive to Moses not to include the Levites in the census).

31:13. Although many translations render *šāmar* as "keep" in vv. 13, 14, 16, I have chosen to go with "guard." The verb appears frequently with the Sabbath: Lev. 19:30; 26:2; Deut. 5:12; Isa. 56:2, 4, 6. Related to "keeping/guarding" the Sabbath is "keeping holy/sanctifying" (*qādaš*, Piel) the Sabbath (Exod. 20:8; Jer. 17:22; Ezek. 20:20; 44:24). Maybe *šāmar* appears in v. 13 lest *qādaš* appear twice in the verse ("You shall sanctify. . . . I am the LORD who sanctifies you").

31:14. *Môt yûmāt* [Hophal] ("shall certainly be put to death") refers to death carried out by other persons. By contrast, *môt yāmût* [Qal] ("shall certainly die," as in Gen. 2:17) means death at God's hands. The expression with the passive verb occurs in Exod. 19:12, and five times in the Covenant Code: Exod. 21:12 (homicide); 21:15 (attacking one's parents); 21:16 (kidnapping); 21:17 (dishonoring parents); 22:19 [18] (bestiality). The phrase is common in Leviticus–Numbers (esp. in Lev. 20), appearing in those two books eighteen times. Deuteronomy never uses *môt yûmāt*, even though there is no shortage of capital offenses listed in that book. *Yûmāt* ("shall be put to death") occurs without the preceding infinitive absolute in Deut. 13:5 [6]; 17:6.

31:14. Hebrew *ʿammêhā* ("his people") is unique to this verse, versus usual *ʿammāyw*.

31:15. Verses that prohibit "working" on the Sabbath may use the passive of the verb, *yēʿāseh* ("may [not] be done") as in Exod. 31:15; 35:2; Lev. 23:3. Or they may use the active form of the verb, *taʿăśeh* ("you shall [not] do") as in Exod. 20:10; 23:12; Deut. 5:14.

31:15. "A most restful rest" is *šabbat šabbātôn*. The expression is used with the Sabbath (Exod. 31:15; 35:2; Lev. 23:3), the Sabbatical Year (Lev. 25:4), the Day of Atonement (Lev. 16:31; 23:32). When used with the Sabbath, NIV has "a Sabbath of rest." When used with the Sabbatical Year or Day of Atonement, NIV has "a sabbath of rest." Hebrew expresses the superlative ("most restful") by repeating the word, usually in the plural: "vanity of vanities," "song of songs," "holy of holies."

31:16. "To observe the Sabbath" is, literally, "to do [*laʿăśôt*] the Sabbath."

31:17. For the Niphal of *nāpaš* (*wayyinnāpaš*), "he was refreshed," see Exod. 23:12 AT, "so that your ox . . . and the sojourner may be refreshed"; and 2 Sam. 16:14, "And there he [David] refreshed himself." Its use with God as subject is anthropomorphic, especially if one leans toward translating the verbal form "caught his breath" (Alter 2004: 492).

Commentary

31:12–17 This paragraph about the Sabbath follows immediately after the lengthy instructions about building the tabernacle and making the vestments for the clergy (25:1–31:11>31:12–17). There is a paragraph about the Sabbath that immediately precedes the actual building of the tabernacle (35:1–3>35:4–40:33). The placement of the notice about the Sabbath, first as a conclusion and then as an introduction, is a way of highlighting the Sabbath, signaling that work on the tabernacle must not trump it or ignore it. In two places where *šabbat* and *miqdāš* occur together (Lev. 19:30; 26:2), reverence for God's Sabbath(s) precedes reverence for God's sanctuary.

Exodus 31:12–17 is but one of several notices in the Pentateuch about the Sabbath. However, this is the only one (along with its parallel verse, 35:2) that spells out a penalty for Sabbath violation. In fact, it mandates two penalties. Verse 14 says that (1) the individual is to "be put to death" and (2) to "be cut off from the midst of his people." The only other violation that calls for this double consequence is giving one's children to Molech, a god of the Ammonites: "must be put to death. . . . I will cut him off from his people" (Lev. 20:2–3).

As we have seen earlier, "be put to death" means being put to death by other persons, but "being cut off" is something only God can do to a violator. That indicates that "be put to death" and "be cut off" are not two ways of expressing the same penalty. The first is obviously immediate death. The second could refer to banishment, premature death, the termination of one's line of descendants, no blissful afterlife, and so forth.

In light of the clear statement in Exod. 31:14 about the fate of the Sabbath breaker, it is puzzling why Moses and Aaron are uncertain about the destiny of the man who has broken the Sabbath by gathering wood on it (Num. 15:32–36, esp. v. 34: "and they kept him in custody, because it was not clear what should be done to him"). Are they uncertain about the method of execution? Or are they uncertain whether it would be God or themselves who would carry out the punishment?

Exodus 31:12–17 says nothing about worship on the Sabbath. The sole focus is on rest (v. 15), as God himself rested on the seventh day (v. 17). Neither does the fourth commandment ever mention worship on the seventh day (Exod. 20:8–11; Deut. 5:12–15); nor does Lev. 23:3 (although its use of the phrase "a holy convocation" would suggest some kind of community affair). This latter reference (Lev. 23) is most interesting. It lists seven special occasions on the calendar. On six of these seven, one is to give a food donation (traditionally "an offering made by fire") for the LORD: (1) Passover, Lev. 23:8; (2) Firstfruits, Lev. 23:13; (3) Weeks, Lev. 23:18; (4) Trumpets, Lev. 23:25; (5) Day of Atonement, Lev. 23:27; (6) Tabernacles, Lev. 23:36. The exception is the Sabbath. One does not present an *ʾiššeh* to the Lord on that day. Of all the Sabbath texts in the Pentateuch, the only one that calls for a sacrifice is Num. 28:9–10—two lambs, a grain offering, and a libation.

Surely the Sabbath must have called for some kind of celebration. When God enumerates the Sabbath as among Judah's "evil assemblies" (Isa. 1:13), he is not annoyed by the people's resting or slumbering on that day, but by their (hypocritical) celebrations on the Sabbath. In Hosea 2:11 [13] the Lord says of Ephraim, "I will stop all her celebrations, . . . her Sabbath days."

The reason for celebrating this day is that it is a once-weekly "sign" (vv. 13, 17) of the "everlasting covenant" (v. 16) that Yahweh has made with his people. "Everlasting/lasting covenant/sign" is a prominent phrase in the Bible (Gen. 9:16; 17:7, 13, 19; Exod. 31:16; Lev. 24:8; Num. 18:19; 25:13; 2 Sam. 23:5; Ps. 105:10; Isa. 55:3; 61:8; Jer. 32:40; Ezek. 16:60; 37:26). Tabernacles may come and go, but the Sabbath, a day of rest and celebration, abides forever.

In Exod. 24:4 Moses does the writing. Here it is God who does the writing, and **31:18**
with his finger at that (also see 32:16, "the writing was the writing of God"). The "finger" of God brought gnats upon Egypt (8:19 [15]). The "finger" of God conveys a powerful message to Israel from and about a holy God who has bound himself in responsible and eternal covenant to unworthy Israel. If God does the writing, then Moses's job is to hew the stone, to give the stone upon which God will write the shape it needs (Exod. 34:1, "Chisel out two stone tablets"). Moses does the carving; God does the incising.

PART 6

The Golden Calf and Covenant Renewal

(32:1–34:35)

Chapter 24 (the end of part 4) concludes by mentioning Moses's ascent and disappearance into the cloud-covered mountain, a disappearing act that lasts "forty days and forty nights." The directives the Lord gives to Moses for building the tabernacle (part 5, Exod. 25:1–31:18) occur during that forty-day period while Moses is in absentia.

It thus is understandable as the reader moves into part 6, and particularly into chap. 32, to note that the people are perplexed about Moses's lengthy absence. "Is he coming back at all?" they wonder. "Has he permanently abandoned us and left us to find our own way to God knows where?" they ask among themselves.

We notice the contrast (or comparison) in the peoples' response to Moses's absence at the beginning of part 6 with their response to Moses's presence at the end of part 6 (34:29–35). His absence leaves them with a lot of unanswered questions, and they eventually drift into idolatry. His presence (in 34:29–33) fills them with fear to be anywhere near him (34:30). Fearful without him, and fearful with him because they are fearful of him!

Two items join the beginning of part 6 with part 5, and the two are connected. First, the emphasis on true worship in chaps. 25–31 contrasts vividly with the emphasis on false, idolatrous worship in chap. 32. Second, both correct worship and false worship are funded by the gifts Israel brings to Moses (25:3–7) and to Aaron (32:2–3). The connections suggest that the golden calf is a kind of antiark or antitabernacle, or at least a surrogate for those structures.

The sin of Israel is egregious. It is one of only two occasions on which God is moved to wipe out that entire first generation of Hebrews as judgment for their sin. The other is the scout story of Num. 13–14. Compare Exod. 32:9–10 with Num. 14:22–23. In both scenes, Moses's intercessory prayer plays a major role in determining God's response to the idolaters in Exod. 32 and to the cynics in Num. 14. Compare Exod. 32:11–13 with Num. 14:13–19. Apparently few things get under God's skin as much as disloyalty and faithlessness.

The beginning of chap. 32 stresses absence versus presence (of Moses); this emphasis continues in chaps. 33–34, except that this time the issue is the absence/presence of the Lord: "I will not go with you" (33:3); "If I were to go with you even for a moment, I might destroy you" (33:5); "You have not let me know whom you will send with me" (33:12); "My Presence/Face will go with you" (33:14); "If your Presence/Face does not go with us, do not send us up from here" (33:15); "How will anyone know that you are pleased with me . . . unless you go with us?" (33:16); "O LORD, if I have found favor in your eyes, . . . then let the LORD go with us" (34:9). Here are two different evaluations on God's continuing presence with his people. From God's perspective, his presence represents a lethal threat to Israel (33:3, 5). From Moses's perspective, the Lord's presence is absolutely indispensable if Israel is to make it to Canaan (33:14).

Thus the tension between the Lord and Moses vis-à-vis Israel in chap. 32 ("I'm going to destroy them" versus "Don't destroy them") continues in chaps. 33–34 ("I'm not coming" versus "You must come").

Moses "wins" the standoff. God does not destroy Israel. And rather than send his angel/agent while he remains at Sinai, the Lord promises that his own "Presence/Face" will accompany them (and surely something of an anticipation of Moses's own "face" in 34:29–35).

Not only will the Lord continue with Israel, but he also will renew and reaffirm his covenant with Israel. This is the principal thrust of chap. 34. The reason God will do so is not because the people have repented of their sin. There is no evidence of any contrition on their part. They regret the Lord's threatened absence, but not their idolatry (33:4). Nor are Moses's prayers the determining issue, although they surely play a critical role in God's sorting out his options. The key factor is this: what kind of God is the Lord? While not oblivious to sin and its fallout (34:7b), he is "compassionate, gracious, slow to anger, abounding in love, faithful, . . . loving, . . . forgiving" (34:6–7a AT).

Making a Golden Calf

(32:1–6)

Translation

[1]When the people saw that Moses was lagging in coming down from the mountain, the people ganged up on Aaron and said to him, "Come, make for us a god who will go before us. For this Moses, the man who brought us up from the land of Egypt—we do not know what has happened to him." [2]And Aaron said to them, "Tear off the gold rings that are on the ears of your wives, your sons, and your daughters, and bring (them) to me." [3]So all the people tore off the gold rings that (were) in their ears, and brought (them) to Aaron. [4]He took (them/this) from their hand, and shaped it with the engraving tool, and made it (into) a molten calf. And they said, "This is your god, O Israel, who brought you up from the land of Egypt." [5]And Aaron saw, and built an altar before it. Aaron called out and said, "A festival to the LORD tomorrow." [6]They got up early the next day, and offered up burnt offerings, and presented well-being sacrifices. The people then sat down to eat and drink; then they arose to play.

Grammatical and Lexical Notes

32:1 *Bōšēš* ("was lagging") is a Polal third-person perfect of the verb *bôš*. Exodus 32:1 is the verb's only occurrence (in any stem) in the Pentateuch, except for Gen. 2:25 ("The man and his wife were both naked, and they were not ashamed [*yitbōšāšû*]"). The verb appears most often in the Qal stem, especially in the prophets, with a variety of meanings. Here is a sampling from Jeremiah with the NIV rendering: 2:36 [2x], "be disappointed by"; 6:15, "ashamed"; 8:12, "ashamed"; 9:19 [18], "our shame"; 10:14 (Hiphil), "is shamed"; 12:13, "bear the shame"; 14:3, 4, "dismayed"; 15:9, "disgraced"; 17:18, "be put to shame"; 20:11, "be disgraced." This verb's frequent coupling with "shame" allows the translation in 32:1, "Moses was *shamefully late*." The only other place where the Polal of *bōš* occurs is in Judg. 5:28, in a military context, and the exact same verbal form as in Exod. 32:1—"Why is his [Sisera's] chariot *so long* in coming? Why is the clatter of his chariots delayed?"

32:1. I have translated *qāhal* [Niphal] *ʿal* as "gang up on." The same phrase occurs in other wilderness rebellion stories such as Num. 16:3 AT ("rose up against"); Num. 16:19 (Hiphil; "gathered in opposition to"); Num. 16:42 [17:6] ("gathered in opposition to"); Num. 20:2 ("gathered in opposition to"). In these narratives *qāhal ʿal* is like *yāʿad* [Niphal] *ʿal*: Num. 14:35 ("banded together against me"); Num. 16:11 ("against the LORD you . . . have banded"); Num. 27:3 ("who banded against the LORD"). It looks odd that a verb that in two stems means "demonstrate against, beleaguer," when followed by the preposition *ʿal*, is cognate with the noun *qāhāl*, which is the Hebrew word for the duly constituted "community" of Israel. On a few occasions, however, *qāhāl* may refer to an unruly crowd or mob (Ezek. 16:40; 23:46; and probably Jer. 44:15, although NIV uses "assembly"). See also

Num. 22:4, in which the king of Moab refers to the approaching Israelites as "this *horde* [*qāhāl*] is going to lick up everything around us."

32:1. Although *ʾĕlōhîm* is a plural noun and *yēlĕkû* is a plural verb, I have chosen to translate both as singulars ("[Make for us] a god who will go before us"). I shall comment at length on this in the following section.

32:1. *Zeh mōšeh* ("this Moses") provides a rare instance of an adjectival demonstrative before a personal name. A parallel may be in Ezek. 5:5 if one reads, "This Jerusalem [*zōʾt yĕrûšālayim*] I have set in the center of the nations" rather than supply "is" and "which," as does NIV: "This is Jerusalem, which I have set in the center of the nations." In both Exod. 32:1 and Ezek. 5:5 the people/God are expressing disgust with and distancing themselves from Moses/Jerusalem, the sources of their disgust. For this negative, disparaging use of the demonstrative, see Joosten (1991).

32:1. Presumably the people could refer to Moses as "the *ʾādām*" who brought them out of Egypt. Referring to Moses as "the *ʾîš*" who brought them out of Egypt indicates either their subliminal respect for Moses or their sarcasm.

32:2. *Pāraq* ("tear off") is in the Qal in this verse, but in the Hitpael at the start of v. 3. We have the same Qal to Hitpael shift in Jon. 3:6, 8 ("And he [the king of Nineveh] covered himself [*wayĕkas*, Qal] with sackcloth. . . . Let man and beast be covered with [*wĕyitkassû*, Hitpael] sackcloth." In neither case is there any distinction of meaning, but simply what Ratner (1992: 145–46) calls "synonymous verbal pairs." *Pāraq* is an uncommon verb, one that first appears in Isaac's oracle to Esau about Jacob, "But when you grow restless, you will *throw off/break off* his yoke" (Gen. 27:40 AT). Dahood (1956: 367) has found a use of this verb in Ugaritic to refer to the removal of a piece of jewelry someone is wearing. He translates Aqhat A ii 10, *yprq lṣb wyṣḥq* as "He *takes off* his ring and laughs."

32:3. It is unlikely that "all the people," at least a million of them (women and children), give their earrings to Aaron! The same goes for *kol-hāʿām* in 19:16; 20:18; 24:3.

32:4. The Hebrew *wayyāṣar ʾōtô baḥereṭ* ("and shaped it with the engraving tool") has engendered much discussion and debate about its meaning, especially the last word *ḥereṭ* ("engraving tool"). The word appears in the singular again only in Isa. 8:1, "The Lord said to me, 'Take a large scroll and write on it with an ordinary *pen*.'" But how does one make a golden calf by using a pen or an engraving tool? The word appears in (unusual) plural form, *ḥăriṭîm* versus expected *ḥăraṭîm* in 2 Kings 5:23 ("He [Naaman] . . . then tied up the two talents of silver in two *bags*"), and *hāḥărîṭîm* in Isa. 3:22 ("the fine robes and the capes and cloaks, *the purses*"). So for *ḥereṭ*, we have (1) "engraving tool," (2) "pen," (3) "bags," (4) "purses." Are they all the same Hebrew word, or may we be dealing with homonyms?

Is there any possible connection between *ḥereṭ* in v. 4 and *ḥārût* (with a final *tāw* instead of a *têt*) in v. 16 ("The writing was the writing of God, *engraved* on the tablets")? Gevirtz (1967: 16n20) points to the interchange of emphatic and voiceless dentals in the verbs *ḥātap* with a *tāw* as the middle radical (Job 9:12; Prov. 23:28) and *ḥāṭap* with *ṭet* as the middle radical (Judg. 21:21; Ps. 10:9 [2x]), both of which mean "seize, snatch."

Another possibility is to render the Hebrew as "he fashioned it in *a mold*." This option is reached by appealing (1) to the Vulgate's *formavit opere fusorio* ("he fashioned [it] by a work of casting"); (2) the Syriac's Peshitta, which uses *ṭupsāʾ* ("form"); (3) *Targum Pseudo-Jonathan*, which as one of its translations for this phrase offers "and he threw it [the gold] into a mold"; and (4) an Arabic word for "mold" (*ḫirâṭah*). See G. Driver 1946: 208; Emerton 1997: 17–19.

A final possibility is to take *ḥereṭ* to mean some kind of apparel or garment. That is, Aaron places the collected gold into his cloak, then casts it into the fire, whereupon the calf emerges. See Loewenstamm 1967: 487–89; 1975: 337; Gevirtz 1984a (although Gevirtz [1967] previously opted for "[en]graving tool").

It is difficult to choose one option over the other, but I am inclined to go with "engraving tool" if only because of the use of the same word in Isa. 8:1.

32:4. The Hebrew word *ʿēgel* means "calf" or "young bull." The name of the king of Moab in Judg. 3:12, 14, 15, 17, Eglon, may be a mocking appellative, for his name means "calflike." Occasionally the calf is an acceptable sacrifice (Lev. 9:2–3, 8), but most often it is a common designation for an idol (Deut. 9:16, 21; 1 Kings 12:28, 32; 2 Kings 10:29; 17:16; 2 Chron. 11:15; 13:8; Neh. 9:18; Ps. 106:19; Hosea 8:5–6; 13:2).

32:6. The LXX reads "got up," "offered up," and "presented" as singular verbs, as something Aaron does rather than something the people do.

32:6. Although "burnt offering" (*ʿōlâ)* and "well-being offering" (*šĕlāmîm*) often appear together, sometimes different verbs are used with each, suggesting some kind of difference between the two. Thus here one "offers up" (*ʿālâ*, Hiphil) a burnt offering, but "presents" (*nāgaš*, Hiphil) a well-being offering. See also Deut. 27:6–7 and Josh. 8:31: one "offers up" the burnt offering, but "sacrifices" (*zābaḥ*) the well-being offering. In 1 Kings 3:15 Solomon "offered up" burnt offerings, but "made" (*ʿāśâ*) offerings of well-being.

32:6. Later I shall have more to say on the last word of the verse, *lĕṣaḥēq* ("to play"). The extremes are to understand it as referring to a sexual orgy or simply to playful celebration.

Commentary

The shift in atmosphere from Exod. 1–31 to Exod. 32 is jarring. The only **32:1–6**
notable "sin" any Israelite has committed while in Egypt or on the way to Canaan is by the group that defies God's directives about not gathering manna on the seventh day (chap. 16) or that grumbles about the lack of water (chaps. 15 and 17). But nobody suffers any consequences for these "sins" except for the Sabbath-manna searchers, who come up empty. The sinners who have paid a price for their sins in Exodus so far are non-Israelites: Egyptians and Amalekites.

That all changes in the postcovenant chap. 32. Fretheim (1991: 279) says of this incident, "It is Genesis 3 all over again." Similarly, Janzen (1997: 226) remarks, "It is Israel's version of the universal human turn in Genesis 2–3." Moberly (2008: 48) suggests that because Israel has just recently entered into a holy covenant with Yahweh at Sinai, where the people still remain, the sin of chap. 32 is "like committing adultery on one's wedding night."

Well, what exactly is Israel's sin? Polytheism or idolatry? Do they want to stop worshiping one God, called Yahweh, and instead begin to worship two or more unnamed Elohim? Or do they want Aaron to construct a visible form of Yahweh or of his long-gone servant Moses or of the invisible angel who is to go before them?

Now it is true that throughout chap. 32 the plural (in form) word *ʾĕlōhîm* is consistently used with a plural verb, suggesting the possible translation "gods who will go before you" or "gods who brought you up from Egypt." The people use a plural verb with *ʾĕlōhîm* (vv. 1, 4), as does the Lord in quoting the people (v. 8), and as does Aaron, who also quotes the people (v. 23).

Does all this suggest that the Israelites' sin is polytheism? Maybe so. For one thing, the OT sometimes uses *ʾĕlōhîm* with a plural verb when narrating a pagan understanding of deity. Thus, in speaking to the Philistine king Abimelech, Abraham says, "And when *God had made me wander* [*hitʿû*, plural verb] from my father's household . . ." (Gen. 20:13). When the Philistines hear the clamor associated with the arrival of the ark in the Israelite camp, they use with *ʾĕlōhîm* both a singular verb ("A god has come [*bāʾ*]") in 1 Sam. 4:7, and a plural participle ("they are the gods who struck [*hammakkîm*] the Egyptians") in 4:8.

Several factors, however, suggest that the sin is idolatry rather than polytheism (Sailhamer 1992: 311). First, the people's ultimatum that Aaron "make" them *ʾĕlōhîm* suggests an idol. In fact, the word "molten" in "molten calf" (*massēkâ*) in vv. 4 and 8 is a Hebrew word for "(cast) idol" (Exod. 34:17; Lev. 19:4; Deut. 9:12, 16; 27:15; Judg. 17:3, 4; 18:14; 2 Kings 17:16; Hosea 13:2; etc.). Second, it is unlikely that the *one* golden calf Aaron produces would be styled "gods." Hence, I conclude that the issue is not a false god(s), but a false perception of who the true one God is. Not only can you worship and obey him, but now you can also produce him! You can be responsible for his existence even if the product is intended only for surrogacy.

Three things stand out about Aaron's role in this scene. The first is the absence of any protest from him when the people make their request. No waving red flags, and no priestly fulminations against this way-out-of-line proposal. Second, if my translation of how Aaron makes the calf in v. 4 is on target, then it suggests that Aaron is some kind of a priestly Bezalel, gifted with the skill "to make artistic designs for work in gold, . . . and to engage in all kinds of craftsmanship" (31:4–5). Aaron can wear gold (28:6, 22, 34, 36) and work with gold. Third, his decision to proclaim "a festival to the Lord tomorrow" (v. 5b) is not an attempt to temper the Israelites' egregious sin as much as it is an act of baptizing blasphemy. Love may cover a multitude of sins (1 Pet. 4:8). Religious activity does not. This is the one time I am aware of in the Bible where somebody's building an altar gets him into a lot of hot water. A simple altar of dirt or undressed stones (Exod. 20:24–26), or a blood-spattered altar (24:6), yes. An altar on the heels of god-making, no. The contrast between Moses's building an altar (24:4) and Aaron's building an altar (32:5) is transparent. Understandably, Aaron does not use the altar that Moses has built for the ceremony of sealing the covenant.

It is clear how the NIV translators read the last word of v. 6, *lĕṣḥēq*, "to indulge in revelry." Childs (1974: 566) refers to "a religious orgy" that has begun, and Alter (2004: 495) speaks of "a bacchanalian celebration." Toorn (1989: 202) says that the verb is "an unmistakable euphemism for sexual activities, like Akkadian *ṣiāḫu*." For a quite different view of the Hebrew verb here, see the comment of J. Sasson (1973: 152): "Rather than wild abandoned acts, the scene that unfolds before the calf was probably an orderly ritual that followed practices well known to the ancient Near East, festivals that consisted of a (ritual) banquet followed by sports, miming, and antiphonal singing to honor the gods."

The verb *ṣāḥaq* is used in the Qal stem in connection with the birth of Isaac (Gen. 17:17; 18:12, 13, 15 [2x]; 21:6) and means "laugh, laughter." The name "Isaac" means "he laughs." The Piel stem, which we have in Exod. 32:6, has several meanings. In Gen. 19:14, Lot's sons-in-law think he is only "joking." In Gen. 21:9, Sarah observes Ishmael's "mocking" young Isaac, although there is much debate about the meaning of the verb in 21:9. In 26:8 the Philistine king sees Isaac "caressing" his wife. The last use of this verb in Piel stem in Genesis is 39:14 and 17, where Potiphar's wife claims that Joseph has tried "to make sport" of her. The last instance of the Piel of *ṣāḥaq* is Judg. 16:25, where the Philistines want the captured Samson to be brought out to entertain them (the related verb *śāḥaq*), and Samson "performed" for them.

The numbers for the verb are as follows: thirteen occurrences, six times in the Qal and seven times in the Piel. Divided by Scripture book, the number of occurrences are allocated as follows: eleven times in Genesis; once in Exodus; and once in Judges. Confining ourselves to the Piel uses, the NIV uses six different translations for the seven uses: (1) "joking" (Gen. 19:14); (2) "mocking" (Gen. 21:9); (3) "caressing" (Gen. 26:8); (4) "make sport of" (Gen. 39:14, 17): (5) "indulge in revelry" (Exod. 32:6); (6) "performed" (Judg. 16:25).

A sexual nuance for this verb is present in Gen. 26:8 and 39:14, 17, but not in the remaining three (Gen. 19:14; 21:9; Judg. 16:25). Is it present in Exod. 32:6 also? Stephen seems not to think so, for Luke quotes him in Acts 7:41b as saying, "they held a celebration in honor of what their hands had made." Paul is a bit more blunt. He quotes Exod. 32:6 in 1 Cor. 10:7, and then adds in v. 8, "we should not commit sexual immorality, as some of them did" (but that is a reference to Num. 25:1–9). The latter part of 1 Cor. 10:7 ("got up to indulge in pagan revelry") can just as accurately be translated as "rose up to play" (*paizein*). Where the Hebrew verb does have a sexual meaning, it means either normal sex or sexual play between spouses (Gen. 26:8) or sex that is illicit but not necessarily orgiastic (Gen. 39:14, 17).

Perhaps in quoting Exod. 32:6, Paul is more interested in the "sat down to eat and drink" part. Twice in Exodus the Israelites eat and drink. Once is in the context of a gracious divine provision for hungry and thirsty Israel (Exod. 15–17), and once is in the context of idolatry (Exod. 32:6). Since the larger context for 1 Cor. 10 is the issue of eating meat offered to idols (1 Cor. 8), a quotation from the First Testament about eating in the context of idolatry may contribute some light to that issue (see Hays 1989: 91–93).

Two later incidents in the Bible are closely connected with Exod. 32:1–6. The first is Judg. 8:24–26, the account of Gideon's ephod. In both, a cultic object (a calf, an ephod) is made from donated golden earrings. What Aaron does in Exod. 32, Gideon does in Judg. 8. If *ḥereṭ* is rendered "garment" in

Exod. 32 (see discussion above), it would provide another parallel, for Gideon has the people place their earrings in a garment, *śimlâ* (Judg. 8:25). In at least two ways Gideon's act is worse than Aaron's. First, unlike Aaron, he initiates the building project. Second, Israel's involvement with Gideon's ephod is greater than Israel's involvement with Aaron's calf. The only place where the Hebrew verb *zānâ* (KJV, "go a whoring after") occurs in Judges, apart from the introductory 2:17, is here in 8:27, "All Israel *prostituted themselves* by worshiping it [the ephod] there."

The second related incident is that recorded in 1 Kings 12:26–33, the account about how Jeroboam, northern Israel's first king, makes two golden calves, placing one at Bethel (the southernmost part of his domain) and one at Dan (the northernmost city). Even the language he uses is close to Exod. 32—"Here are your gods, O Israel, who brought you up out of Egypt" (1 Kings 12:28b). His motive is to provide two worship centers that might persuade his people to think that traveling south to the temple in Jerusalem is unnecessary. It is like congregants pulling out of First Baptist or First Presbyterian over some issue on which they disagree, then moving up the street and establishing Second Baptist or Second Presbyterian.

Jeroboam's design is not to set up one (visible) god at Bethel and another (visible) god at Dan. Rather, he sets up two identical idols at two different places for the worship of one God, Yahweh. Again, as in Exod. 32, the issue is not polytheism but idolatry.

Assuming that the narrative in Exod. 32 points to an event before 1 Kings 12 (and not all biblical scholars agree), it may look incredible to the reader that Jeroboam would choose Aaron's actions as his model to consolidate worship in his own backyard. He cannot build a second and third ark, so maybe the calf/bull is the most acceptable alternative, given that no animal more often represented gods in the ancient Near Eastern world than the bull, which was a symbol of both fertility and enormous power. (The name for something in the form of an animal is "theriomorphic"; cf. form of a human, "anthropomorphic"; of a woman, "gynomorphic"; of a man, "andromorphic.")

Jeroboam's actions serve as a reminder that when one chooses earlier models to follow and emulate, it is wise to choose models that are noble, inspiring, and holy rather than harmful, to choose God-honoring models rather than God-debasing ones.

Moses Prays, God Repents

(32:7–14)

Translation

[7]And the Lord spoke to Moses, "Leave! Go down! For your people whom you brought up from the land of Egypt have acted corruptibly. [8]They have quickly turned away from the path about which I commanded them. They have made for themselves a molten calf, have bowed down to it, have sacrificed to it, and have said, 'This is your god, O Israel, who brought you up from the land of Egypt.'" [9]And the Lord said to Moses, "I have seen this people, and indeed, it is a stiff-necked people. [10]So now, leave me be, so that my anger may blaze against them and annihilate them. But I will make of you a great nation."

[11]And Moses implored the face of the Lord his God, and said, "Why, O Lord, should your anger blaze against your people whom you brought out of the land of Egypt with great power and with a strong hand? [12]Why should the Egyptians say, 'For evil he brought them out, to kill them in the mountains, to annihilate them from off the face of the earth'? Turn away from your blazing anger and rescind the evil directed at your people. [13]Remember with respect to Abraham, to Isaac, and to Israel, your servants, to whom you swore by yourself, promising them, 'I will make your offspring as numerous as the stars of heaven, and all this land of which I said, I will give to your seed, and they shall possess it forever.'" [14]And the Lord rescinded the evil about which he had spoken to do to his people.

Grammatical and Lexical Notes

32:7. This is the second time at Sinai that the Lord has used the two imperatives *lek-rēd*, joined by a *maqqēp* ("Leave! Go down!") in addressing Moses (see 19:24). The LXX reads the two imperatives as *Badize to taxos enteuthen* ("Go down immediately"), probably in line with Deut. 9:12 AT, "Arise, go down quickly" (*qûm rēd mahēr*).

32:7. The verb for "has acted corruptibly" is *šāḥat* (Piel). It is the verb (and stem) for the Lord's "destroying" all life at the time of Noah (Gen. 6:17), or promising not to "destroy" all life by a flood again (9:11, 15). In the Niphal stem the verb describes the rampant "corruption" of humans in Noah's era (6:11, 12 [2x]).

32:8. "Turn away from" (*sûr min*) can be used of Israel's turning away from God, as here, or less often of God's turning away from somebody (Judg. 16:20, "He [Samson] did not know that the Lord *had left* him"; 1 Sam. 28:15, "The Philistines are fighting against me [Saul], and God *has turned away from* me").

32:9. "Stiff-necked" is *qěšēh-ʿōrep*. The expression occurs five more times in the Hebrew Bible, and all are in the Pentateuch (Exod. 33:3, 5; 34:9; Deut. 9:6, 13). See also Acts 7:51, where Stephen speaks of a "stiff-necked" people. Deut. 31:27 uses "your stiff neck." One also finds the expression "stiffen/harden the neck" (Deut. 10:16; 2 Kings 17:14; 2 Chron. 30:8; Neh. 9:16, 17; Prov. 29:1; Jer. 7:26; 17:23). In most of these references the text connects neck stiffening with Israel's "fathers," in the wilderness generation. Imagine one generation that has become the paradigm of obstinacy! To be stiff-necked is to be intractable, like a beast of burden in order to go its own way. Here is stiff-necked Israel wanting a calf to represent its God, and ironically the calf/the bull is the beast of burden, which is well known to stiffen its neck. On the phrase *qĕšēh-ʿōrep*, see R. Good 1983: 93–109, esp. 104–5.

32:10. The normal Hiphil imperative of *nûaḥ* ("leave [me] be") is *hannaḥ*, as in Exod. 16:33, "Take a jar [with manna] and place/set it before the LORD." Here we have the longer imperative form, *hannîḥâ*, a form that appears again only in Judg. 16:26 ("*Put* me [Samson] where I can feel the pillars"). The basic meaning of *nûaḥ* is "rest," as in Gen. 8:4, "The ark *came to rest* on the mountains of Ararat," or in Exod. 20:11, "But *he rested* on the seventh day."

A literal translation of *hannîḥâ lî* ("Leave me be") is "Let me rest." In his study of the lengthened imperative, Fassberg (1999) notes that it is often used when the imperative is directed at the speaker by means of a first-person pronominal suffix. With *hannîḥâ lî*, compare Gen. 21:23, "Swear to me" (*hiššābĕʿâ lî*); Gen. 27:3, "Hunt some wild game for me" (*ṣûdâ lî*); Gen. 27:7, "Bring me some game" (*hābîʾâ lî*); Gen. 29:15, "Tell me what your wages should be" (*haggîdâ lî*); Gen. 30:1 AT, "Give me children or I die" (*hābâ-lî*).

When Moses retells this episode in Deuteronomy, he recounts God's saying to him, "Let me alone" (9:14), *herep mimmennî* rather than *hannîḥâ lî*. The former expression translates literally as "Loosen [your grip] from me." It occurs in Judg. 11:37 AT, where Jephthah's daughter asks her father "to leave [her] alone" for two months of grieving; without *mimmennî* in 1 Sam. 11:3, where the residents of Jabesh Gilead ask the invading Amalekites "to leave [them] alone" for seven days to see if a deliverer will come for them; in 1 Sam. 15:16, where Samuel says to Saul, "*Stop*! Let me tell you"; and in Ps. 46:10 [11], "*Be still*, and know that I am God."

32:10. "But I will make of you a great nation" (*lĕgôy gādôl*) is the exact same wording the Lord uses with Abraham in Gen. 12:2. The promise that God makes to Moses in Num. 14:12 surpasses that here in Exod. 32:10. Numbers uses the comparative, not just *lĕgôy gādôl*, but *lĕgôy-gādôl wĕʿāṣûm mimmennû* ("a nation greater and stronger than they").

32:11. It is hard for me to believe that the verb *ḥālâ* ("implored") in the Qal is the same verb as *ḥālâ* in the Piel. *Ḥālâ* in the Qal most often means "be ill, diseased, weak" (e.g., Gen. 48:1; 1 Sam. 19:14; 1 Kings 14:1; 15:23; 17:17). *Ḥālâ* in the Piel most often means "implore, entreat" and frequently is followed by the word "face," as in Exod. 32:11 (also see 1 Sam. 13:12; 1 Kings 13:6 [2x]; 2 Kings 13:4; 2 Chron. 33:12; Job 11:19; Pss. 45:12 [13]; 119:58; Prov. 19:6; Jer. 26:19; Dan. 9:13; Zech. 7:2; 8:21, 22; Mal. 1:9). Might we have, then, *ḥālâ* I and *ḥālâ* II? *Ḥālâ* II would be cognate with Aramaic *hly*, "be sweet, pleasant." On the difficult *ʾăḥălê* in 2 Kings 5:3 ("Were I to *entreat for* my lord before the prophet of Samaria" [AT]), see Margalit 1989: 392–93.

32:11. On two why questions (*lāmâ*) back to back (vv. 11–12), see Gen. 4:6 (God to Cain); Gen. 12:18–19 (Pharaoh to Abraham); Gen. 47:15, 19 (the Egyptians to Joseph). Judges 5:28 has back-to-back why questions that use the other Hebrew word for "why?" (*maddûʿa*). See Barr 1985: 29. In Num. 11:11, Moses again asks the Lord two back-to-back why (*lāmâ*) questions, although NIV translates the second as "What?"

32:11. In v. 7, when God speaks of *Moses*'s bringing Israel from Egypt, he uses the Hiphil of *ʿālâ*. But in v. 11, when Moses speaks of *God*'s bringing Israel from Egypt, he uses the Hiphil of *yāṣāʾ*. Brichto (1992: 271n2) believes the reason for the change in verb is because the Hiphil of *ʿālâ* ("bring up") can be used for the exodus with any subject (God, Moses, the calf), while the Hiphil of *yāṣāʾ* ("bring out") can be used only with God. Brichto states, "The *yĕṣiʾa* from Egypt is thus not merely an ex-(h)odos but [also] a liberation from bondage. This sense, therefore, of the liberating activity is reserved for the liberating Deity and denied to his agent, real or putative." That may be a valid distinction in Exod. 32, but in Deut. 9:12, the parallel to Exod. 32:7, God uses the Hiphil of *yāṣāʾ* for *Moses's* "bringing out" the Israelites from Egypt.

32:12. I shall have much more to say below about *wĕhinnāḥēm* ("and *rescind* [the evil]") here and in v. 14. For now, note the following data. The verb *nāḥam*, when in the Niphal stem, occurs forty-eight times. In thirty-four of these, God is the subject of the verb, either implied or expressed: Gen. 6:6, 7; Exod. 32:12, 14; Judg. 2:18; 1 Sam. 15:11, 29 [2x], 35; 2 Sam. 24:16; 1 Chron. 21:15; Pss. 90:13; 106:45; 110:4; Isa. 1:24; 57:6; Jer. 4:28; 15:6; 18:8, 10; 20:16; 26:3, 13, 19; 42:10; Ezek. 24:14; Joel 2:13, 14; Amos 7:3, 6; Jon. 3:9, 10; 4:2; Zech. 8:14. The translator's challenge is to come to a conclusion how best to render *nāḥam* (Niphal) in these thirty-four instances: "repent" (KJV almost always); "relent" (NIV almost always); "change one's mind," and so forth. For Exod. 32:12, 14 I have gone with "rescind." In eighteen of these thirty-four the LXX uses one of the two verbs for "repent" in NT Greek (*metanoieō*, 13x; *metamelomai*, 5x). For *nāḥam* in Exod. 32:12, the LXX uses (the only time) *hileōs genou* ("become [from *ginomai*] merciful") and in 32:14 (the only time) *hilasthē* ("be merciful," imperative from *hilaskomai*).

32:12. In twelve of the above thirty-four uses, the Lord "repented" of "evil" (*hārāʿâ*): *nāḥam* (Niphal) *ʿal-hārāʿâ* (Exod. 32:12, 14; 1 Chron. 21:15; Jer. 18:8; Joel 2:13; Jon. 3:10; 4:2); *nāḥam* (Niphal) *ʾel-hārāʿâ* (2 Sam. 24:16; Jer. 26:3, 13, 19; 42:10). There seems to be no distinction in the choice of preposition, for 2 Sam. 24:16 uses *nāḥam ʾel*, and its parallel verse, 1 Chron. 21:15, uses *nāḥam ʿal*. Hebrew *rāʿâ* ("evil") is like Akkadian *lemnu* ("evil, morally bad") and *lemuttu* ("misfortune, calamity"). The same word carries an overtly ethical meaning ("evil") and the consequences for that malfeasance ("calamity, disaster, judgment"). See the examples cited in *CAD* L:128. Never in the Bible does God "repent" of sin, but he does "repent" of evil (that is, "evil" understood as judgment, calamity, or disaster).

32:13. For *zĕkōr lĕ* ("remember with respect to"), see Deut. 9:27; Neh. 5:19; 6:14; 13:14, 29; Ps. 137:7. Meek (1945: 13) calls the preposition after the imperative "the emphatic *lāmedh* of specification." Weinfeld (1991: 415) suggests that *zĕkōr lĕ* means, "to think in favor of someone," and cites 2 Chron. 6:42; Pss. 25:7; 132:1; 136:23; Jer. 2:2.

32:13. The LXX and SP, without warrant, change "to *Israel*" to "to *Jacob*," probably because "Abraham>Isaac>Jacob" is much more common than "Abraham>Isaac>Israel," which occurs only here, and because the parallel verse, Deut. 9:27, has, "Remember your servants, Abraham, Isaac and Jacob."

32:13. The only place in the Bible before this where "God swears by himself" is Gen. 22:16, *bî nišbaʿtî*; here it is *nišbaʿtā lāhem bāk* (Exod. 32:13). See also Isa. 45:23; Jer. 22:5; 49:13; 51:14; Amos 6:8; Heb. 6:13 ("Since there was no one greater to swear by, he swore by himself"). Mortals can say, "I promise . . . , so help me, God." Only the Lord God can say, "I promise, so help me, I." The Lord can also swear by his right hand and arm (Isa. 62:8), by his name (Jer. 44:26), by his holiness (Ps. 89:35 [36]; Amos 4:2), and by his faithfulness (Ps. 89:49 [50]).

Commentary

The Lord is able to see and hear what is transpiring at the bottom of the mountain, but Moses cannot. He orders Moses to descend, using a double imperative, to see for himself the apostate act below. Nowhere does the Lord bring up Aaron's role in this debacle. The entire focus of condemnation is on the Israelites, from whom the Lord wishes to dissociate himself, for he refers to them as "*your* people whom *you* brought up from . . . Egypt." 32:7–14

Both v. 7 and v. 9 begin with "And the LORD said/spoke to Moses," but Moses makes no response between these two divine speeches. Do we, then, have two addresses by God (vv. 7–8 and 9–10)? Or is it one address (vv. 7–10), making the second "And the Lord said to Moses" in v. 9 redundant? Perhaps the absence of any speech from Moses between vv. 7–8 and 9–10 is deliberate. Alter (2004: 495) suggests, "This repetition of the formula after the lack of an answer points to Moses's incapacity to respond, dumbfounded as he is by what God tells him."

God's third imperative to Moses is most interesting: "Leave me be" or "Let me alone" (v. 10). Cannot almighty God do what he wishes to do, whether Moses is at his side or not? Why would a God who has promised to never leave or forsake us now say, "Leave me alone"? God himself apparently believes that the presence of Moses at Sinai's summit might throw a roadblock into God's desired judgment on the idolaters. As Kinlaw (2010: 374) has put it, "He [God] is saying that all that needs to happen to prevent His just anger from having its appropriate effect on these covenant breakers is for Moses to step in and intercede for them"; to which Kinlaw adds, "Will we leave Yahweh alone?" Moses will pray, and God will then make some adjustment. Or maybe God is using reverse psychology. Balentine (1989: 606) calls the phrase "a form of invitation by prohibition." In his devotional book on prayer, Yancey (2006: 94) similarly says, "Moses hears that remark less as a command than as the sigh of a beleaguered parent who has reached the end of a tether yet somehow wants to be pulled back—in other words, an opening stance for negotiation."

Not only does Moses turn down the possibility of being Abraham number two ("I will make you into a great nation"; v. 10b), but he also intercedes fiercely and brazenly for idolatrous Israel. He chooses the role of intercessor over that of patriarch. There is nothing "Lucifer-like" in Moses that drives him to be something more or bigger than he is. If he choses to be the progenitor of a new nation, he will have only Abraham as a model. In choosing the role of intercessor, he connects with Abraham (Gen. 18:23–33; 20:7), Samuel (1 Sam. 7:5–9; 12:19; Jer. 15:1), Elijah (1 Kings 17:17–23; 18:24), Elisha (2 Kings 4:33; 5:11; 6:15–20), Job (Job 42:7–9). Moses again and again participates in a ministry of intercession (Exod. 32:31–34; 33:12–13, 15–16; 34:8–9; Num. 12:11–13; 14:13–19), yet he always places commitment to his people ahead of self-advancement and apparently never regrets that choice. He never says in hindsight, "Man, why did I turn down the chance to be number one?"

Moses offers three reasons why the Lord should temper his judgment: (1) Why save Israel, then destroy the people? (v. 11); (2) Why give the Egyptians an opportunity to gloat? (v. 12); (3) How can you ignore the promise of an eternal covenant that you made with our ancestors? (v. 13). In the retelling of this story in Deuteronomy, Moses repeats these three reasons but in a different order: 1-3-2 (Deut. 9:26–29). At no point does Moses excuse the people for their sin. He never suggests that God is overreacting with "much ado about nothing." His appeal is entirely directed to God, and to his character, his reputation, and his past actions. Moses prays the way he prays not because of what he knows about his people, but he prays the way he does because of what he knows about his God.

I am not aware of anybody in the First Testament, maybe the Second too, who speaks as bluntly to God as does Moses on this occasion. God has earlier spoken of Israel "turning away from" (*sûr min*) his commands (v. 8). Now Moses speaks of the Lord's need "to turn away from" (*šûb min*) his fierce anger (v. 12b). This latter expression, *šûb min*, is common, especially in prophetic literature when the prophet charges Israel with "turning away from" the way they are supposed to order their lives.

Furthermore, Moses asks God to repent/relent/change his mind (v. 12c). And God does as Moses asks (v. 14)! I believe this is the only instance in Scripture of a prophetic intercessor's asking God to *nāḥam*, only to read that God subsequently does *nāḥam*. The only other place where *šûb* (but not *šûb min* as in Exod. 32:12) and *nāḥam* (Niphal) occur together in the imperative is Ps. 90:13. NIV renders it, "Relent [*šûbâ*], O LORD! . . . Have compassion on [*wĕhinnāḥēm ʿal*] your servants." A more literal translation is "Return, O LORD, . . . and repent [?] concerning your servants." Interestingly, the superscription above that Ps. 90 is, "A Prayer of Moses, the man of God." I shall have more to say on this in the next paragraph. Hebrews 4:16 urges us "to come boldly unto the throne of grace" (KJV), but is Exod. 32:12b–c taking that truth a bit too far? I think not, if the pray-er is somebody like Moses. Only those who have stood for forty days and nights alone with a holy God, only those who are God's confidants, will pray at this depth and with this audacity. The rest, those closer to the margins of faith, will offer up more polite and orthodox prayers.

Presumably if Moses had left the Lord alone and not interceded for Israel, God would have carried through on what he tells Moses he intends to do (v. 10). This is the understanding of Ps. 106:23, "So he said he would destroy them—had not Moses, his chosen one, stood in the breach before him to keep his wrath from destroying them."

Whenever God repents/changes his mind about an intended, announced course of future action, it is because (1) some person or persons have changed their behavior, either from bad to good (Jer. 18:8) or from good to bad (18:10). In. Jer. 18:8 God moves from announced judgment to announced clemency. In Jer. 18:10 God moves from announced clemency to announced judgment. In at least two cases human repentance is expressed by a "turning from" (*šûb min*) evil, the same expression that Moses uses with God in Exod. 32:12. See Jer. 18:8; 26:3. (2) Or God may change his mind about something because party A has interceded before God for guilty party B (Exod. 32:12, 14; Amos 7:2–3, 5–6). I am aware of only one verse of the thirty-four listed earlier (see Grammatical and Lexical Notes) where God changes his mind without either human repentance or prophetic intercession, and that is 2 Sam. 24:16 (= 1 Chron. 21:15), for which NIV uses "was grieved."

I remain unconvinced that for those espousing "open theism" views (that God's foreknowledge is not absolute), passages like Exod. 32:12, 14 provide fuel for their argument. For example, see Sanders (1998: 53–75), who argues that if God's foreknowledge, or even omniscience, is absolute, how can he be said to change his mind about anything, or "be sorry" or "grieved" by something he has done or permitted?

As Master (2002) observes, Exod. 32 must be related to the rest of Exodus. For example, a God who is open to changing his mind and who is looking for a willing, enthusiastic, obedient candidate to lead his people would certainly change his mind about the Moses of Exod. 3–5, or the grumbling Israelites of Exod. 15–17. Hence, in Exod. 3–5 God does not do what Moses asks him to do ("Send somebody else"), but in Exod. 32 God does do what Moses asks him to do. Of his promised blessings or threatened punishment, God may *nāḥam* ("relent/rescind"), but of his decrees, he does not (see Ps. 110:4 KJV: the Lord "will not repent" that he has established a "house" for David [2 Sam. 7]). On the difference between divine decree and divine statement of intention, see Chisholm 1995.

Passages like Exod. 32:12, 14, however, remind the reader that God does not always operate unilaterally. He is a God who listens to our prayers, takes what we have to say seriously, and often adjusts his intentions. On such a case, it is appropriate to speak of "God's holy mutability" (Barth 1940: 496). The contemporary Jewish author Elie Wiesel (1978: 6) has written, "The Jew knows that he may oppose God as long as it is in defense of God's creation." A passage of Scripture like this one, or the one involving Sodom and Gomorrah (Gen. 18), demonstrates that within God's being there is tension between mercy and wrath. Accordingly, as C. Wright (1996: 140, quoted by Goldingay 2009: 269) has said, "Moses was not so much arguing *against* God . . . as participating in an argument *within* God."

I have benefited from many studies on "divine repentance," but two I single out for special appreciation because of their depth of insight are Fretheim (1988) and Freedman (1997).

From Intercession to Indignation

(32:15–20)

Translation

[15]And Moses turned and went down from the mountain, with the two tablets of the testimony in his hand, inscribed on both their sides, on one side and the other they were inscribed. [16]The tablets—God's work (were) they, and the writing—God's writing it (was), incised upon the tablets. [17]And Joshua heard the sound of the people in its shouting, and he said to Moses, "A sound of battle in the camp." [18]And he [Moses] said:

"It (is) not the tune of the song of
triumph,
Nor (is) it the tune of the song of
defeat.
It is the sound of debauchery I
hear."

[19]When he came close to the camp, and made out the calf and dancing, Moses's anger flared up. He flung from his hand the tablets, shattering them at the foot of the mountain. [20]He took the calf they had made, burned it in the fire, then ground it to powder, and scattered it over the water, which he forced the Israelites to drink.

Grammatical and Lexical Notes

32:15. The Hebrew *ʿebrêhem* ("their two sides") occurs only in this passage. Of all the references in the Bible to these two tablets of the testimony, this is the only one to comment on this particular feature about them. The technical term for an inscription with writing on both sides is an "opisthograph."

32:16. The first two-thirds of this verse begins with a subject as a *casus pendens*, and so my dashes: "The tablets—" and the "writing—." Then a nominal clause follows in which the predicate ("God's work"; "God's writing") precedes the resumptive personal pronoun ("[were] they," *hēmmâ*; "[was] it," *hûʾ*). Such a construction lends emphasis to the predicate. We have the same kind of nominal sentence in Exod. 3:5, "The place on which you are standing—holy ground (is) it [*hûʾ*]." See Zewi 1996: esp. 5–6; Geller 1991: esp. 25–26.

32:17. *Bĕrēʿōh* ("in its shouting") is formed from the verb *rûʿa*, "shout." In place of the Ketib's *bĕrēʿōh*, the Masora suggests the Qere's *bĕrēʿô*. As it is written, the word ends with the archaic spelling *-h* for the third-person masculine-singular pronominal suffix, and thus it provides an exact consonantal duplicate to "*For evil* he brought them out" in v. 12. Unvocalized, "for evil" and "in its shouting" are *brʿh*. See Rendsburg 2008: 96.

32:18. The speaker in v. 18 is Moses, not Joshua, and for clarification I have inserted "Moses" in square brackets.

32:18. The Hebrew Bible records the content of what Moses says to Joshua as a triadic line of poetry. The problem with translating it arises from the threefold use of the root *ʿ-n-h* in each line. In the first two lines, the word appears as a Qal infinitive construct, *ʿănôt* ("[the tune of the] song"), but in the third line the word appears as a Piel infinitive construct, *ʿannôt* ("[the sound of] music"). Further complicating the issue is that Biblical Hebrew has four verbs that share the radicals *ʿ-n-h*. There is *ʿānâ* I, which occurs mostly in the Qal, and most often means "answer, respond." However, a different root with the same letters (*ʿānâ* IV) connotes the utterance of sound, especially musical sound. In Ps. 147:7 it is parallel to *zāmar* (Piel): "*Sing* (*ʿānâ* IV, Qal) to the LORD with thanksgiving; *make music* (*zāmar*, Piel) to our God on the harp." Another verb with these letters (*ʿānâ* II) occurs mostly in the Piel and appears in Exod. 1:11, 12 for the Egyptians' "oppressing, abusing" the Israelites; in Exod. 10:3 for the Pharaoh's refusal "to humble" himself; and in Exod. 22:22 [21] with a warning not "to abuse" a widow or orphan. If lines 1 and 2 of Exod. 32:18 have the verb *ʿānâ* IV in the Qal ("sound of song"), could line 3 have the verb *ʿānâ* IV in the Piel ("sound of debauchery")?

There is a wide diversity of interpretations on this verse.

1. One may see forms of *ʿānâ* IV in all three lines and read, "It is not the sound of a *song* of triumph . . . nor the *song* of defeat, but the sound of an *orgy* I hear." This view is as old as the LXX, which renders the third line as "but the sound of those beginning with wine [*phōnēn exarchontōn oinou*]." See Deem 1978: 29; Rendsburg 2001: 192.
2. One may repoint the root in the third line from *ʿannôt* to *ʿănāt* and come up with the name of the Canaanite goddess of love and war, Anat: "It is the voice of Anat that I hear." See Edelman 1950; 1966; Whybray 1967.
3. Several have suggested that some word has dropped out, so that in line 3 we have "but it is the sound of *cultic singers* I hear" (Andersen 1966: 111).
4. R. Good (1987) appeals to Akkadian *enû* ("reverse") and Ugaritic *ʿny* to come up with "It's not the sound of a hero-song, nor the sound of a coward's taunt. I hear the sound of *reversal*" (a relationship with God that has broken down and apart).
5. Brichto (1992: 94, 271n7) suggests that paraphrase is unavoidable in all three lines. He draws this contrast between the last line and the first two: "It is not the sound of the victor's cry, nor the sound of the vanquished. The sound I hear I cannot make out."
6. B. Levine (2000: 96) suggests revocalizing the Piel infinitive construct in line 3 (*ʿannôt*) to the absolute form of the Qal-based noun *ʿānôt*, "music, song": "It is not the tune of the song of triumph, nor the tune of the song of defeat; it is the sound of *music* I hear."

In sum, it seems to me that option 2 is far-fetched. Option 3 is possible but unlikely and lacks any kind of supporting textual evidence. Choice 4 is inexplicable: what would the "sound of reversal" be? In option 5, Brichto is correct in noting the contrast, but I am not sure how he arrives at his translation, "The sound I hear I cannot make out." Hence, I believe the best options are 1 and 6, but I lean toward option 1 because it does not require emending the text as 6 does.

32:20. I shall comment on the verbs *šārap*, *ṭāḥan*, and *zārâ* below.

Commentary

32:15–20 I am not taken aback by Moses's sudden eruption of anger at seeing the calf and the celebration surrounding it, as are some commentators. Yes, God has already informed Moses of what the people are doing and saying at the foot of Sinai, but that does not make unexpected or unnecessary Moses's rage when he descends and actually sees what is going on. To hear about something is one thing; to see it is another. Job voices that truth when he says, "My ears had *heard* of you but now my eyes have *seen* you" (Job 42:5). Moses has heard; now he sees.

The first two verses describe the features of the two tablets more beautifully than any other passage. Not only are the two tablets inscribed on both sides, but v. 16 also says that God "made" these tablets, using the verb *ʿāśâ* for his making things, as does Gen. 1–2 (e.g., 1:7, 25, 26, 31; 2:4, 18; also 3:21). Then it adds that both tablets bear his handwriting. The emphasis on the divine origin of these tablets may be to draw a subtle contrast between something God makes—two tablets—and something the Israelites under Aaron's supervision make, one golden calf (Moberly 1983: 53). Both will be destroyed, the tablets through smashing, and the calf through burning and grinding.

That Joshua does not comprehend the nature of the sound he hears (v. 17) indicates that Moses has not passed on to Joshua what the Lord has told Moses. Joshua is closer to the action than is Moses, for he was camped at only the halfway point up to Sinai's summit. Moses has not heard anything since he was so far above the base. He would be coming down the mountain totally naive if God had not filled him in on the shenanigans below.

When Joshua misinterprets the noise, Moses immediately rules out either a victor's cry or a cry of the vanquished. How he identifies the noise depends on how one translates the last line of v. 18 (see the lengthy grammatical note above): "It is the sound of debauchery/an orgy I hear," or "it is the sound of music I hear," or "the sound I hear I cannot make out."

The scene is reminiscent of another one in Scripture: 1 Sam. 15 (see Grottanetti 1999: 59). In both Exod. 32 and 1 Sam. 15 a large group of people is about to engage in an erroneous and sinful (ritual) action, a sin of commission in Exod. 32, a sin of omission in 1 Sam. 15. Second, both happen under the supervision of a vicarious leader, Aaron and Saul, who previously have been anointed by the prophets Moses and Samuel respectively. Third, the prophet is absent both times when the sinful activities transpire, but finds out about it when God discloses it to him. Fourth, the prophet angrily confronts the leader of the crowd about his actions. Fifth, both times the prophet destroys quite violently the object of sinful behavior (the calf and Agag). Sixth, Aaron blames the people, and Saul blames the soldiers, while both proclaim their own innocence.

Moses earlier asks God about why he is so angry with his people (*lāmâ . . . yeḥĕreh ʾappĕkā*, v. 11), but then he himself becomes angry with them (*wayyiḥar-ʾap mōšeh*, v. 19). If such idolatry makes Moses's "nose turn red" (for this is what the Hebrew says), should it not also make the Lord's nose turn red?

Moses does three things with the calf (v. 20). First, he burns it (*śārap*). Second, he grinds it (*ṭāḥan*) until it is crushed fine (*ʿad ʾăšer-dāq*). Third, he scatters (*zārâ*) the dust left behind on the water and compels the people to drink it, without explaining why. That procedure raises at least three questions in the minds of readers: (1) How does one go about burning gold? (2) How does one go about grinding gold to powder? (3) How does one grind to powder what one has already burnt?

Almost all commentators are indebted to the connection the late Professor Loewenstamm has made between Exod. 32:20 and a Northwest Semitic text from Ugarit in his two articles (1967) and (1975). It is a text that describes the goddess Anat's vanquishing the god Mot. Seven lines are relevant:

> She seized divine Mot,
> With a sword she split him,
> With a sieve she winnowed him,
> With fire she *burnt* him,
> With millstones she *ground* him,
> In a field she *scattered* him,
> His flesh indeed the birds ate.

I have italicized the verbs in lines 4–6, for they are the same three in the same sequence as in Exod. 32:20: "burned . . . ground . . . scattered." The first two are the exact same words, *ś-r-p*, "burn"; and *ṭ-ḥ-n*, "ground." The Canaanite text uses *d-r-ʿ* for "scatter" while Exod. 32:20 uses *zārâ*. For Loewenstamm, both this Ugaritic text and Exod. 32:20 exhibit a picturesque, literary way of saying that someone totally destroys something or somebody else.

Frankel (1994) is one of the few to reject this explanation, and he offers an alternate explanation that he believes is more logical. He does so by significantly reordering the words in v. 20. He has v. 20 say, "And he ground them [the tablets] to powder and strewed it upon the water, and so made the Israelites drink it. He then took the calf they had made and burned it." So what the people were compelled to drink was water mixed with the ashes of the burnt tablets, not the dust left over from the burning of the calf mixed with water. That Frankel can offer this solution only by a radical reordering of the text is sufficient grounds for suspicion about its legitimacy.

The last part of v. 20 is very interesting, for it says that Moses forces everybody (a couple of million?) to drink the mixture. For what reason? The closest parallel we have is Num. 5:11–31, in which the wife whom her husband suspects of adultery has to drink "bitter water" that will prove, by what it does or does not do to her body, her guilt or innocence. In Exod. 32:20 it is Moses's way of determining who the ringleaders in this idolatrous act are. Otherwise, how else would the Levites, later in the chapter, be able to identify and punish the culpable parties? But we do not know what the symptoms of guilt are as is the case in the ordeal of Num. 5. Another reference to a similar water ordeal may be present in Jer. 8:14, "For the Lord our God has doomed us to perish and given us poisoned water to drink, because we have sinned against him." In any case, there is a powerful contrast between "the drinking scenes" in 15:22–25, 27; 17:1–6; and here in 32:20. Presumably, and maybe ironically too, the water into which Moses throws the dust of the calf must be the water that flows from the rock at Sinai/Horeb (17:6).

When Moses retells this event in Deuteronomy (9:1–10:11), he deletes this part about requiring the people to drink it (9:21). In Exod. 32:20 Moses scatters the ground calf on the water, while in Deut. 9:21 Moses throws (*šālak*) the calf's dust into a brook/stream (*hannaḥal*) flowing down the mountainside. That flowing stream will quickly carry away the dust, making it impossible for anybody to drink it. Does Moses have second thoughts about his earlier actions on the forced drinking? Moses deletes other items in the Deuteronomy account. For example, while he mentions his protracted intercession for fallen Israel (Deut. 9:25–29), he never repeats that he asked God "to change his mind" (*nāḥam*), or that in response God did change his mind.

And while Moses deletes items in the retelling, he also adds items. In Deut. 9:21 he calls the calf "that sinful thing," a word that appears later for Jeroboam's golden calves (1 Kings 12:30; 13:34; 14:16; 15:3, 26, 30, 34, although NIV renders the Hebrew word as "sin" or "sins" rather than "sinful thing" in these passages).

The emphasis in Deut. 9:21 on Moses's "throwing" the calf's dust into the stream, as opposed to "scattering" it on the water in Exod. 32:20, puts emphasis on a throwing scene that removes something, rather than on a drinking scene that proves something. It also anticipates subsequent throwing scenes where something illicit needs to be removed. See 2 Kings 23:6, 12 and what Josiah does. The passages are close to Exod. 32:20 and Deut. 9:21. In 2 Kings 23:6 Josiah brings out the pagan item to the brook Kidron, burns it (*śārap*), grinds it to ashes (*dāqaq lĕʿāpār*), and then throws (*šālak*) its ashes on the graves. In 2 Kings 23:12, Josiah destroys other idolatrous objects and throws their dust (*wĕhišlîk ʾet-ʿăpārām*) into the brook Kidron. Possibly Jesus's throwing items around and rearranging the furniture when he cleanses the temple is a reflection of this.

Moses Confronts Aaron

(32:21–24)

Translation

[21]And Moses said to Aaron, "What did these people do to you that you brought upon it such a great sin?" [22]And Aaron said, "Let not my lord's anger blaze. You yourself know the people, that in a bad way it (was). [23]They said to me, 'Make for us a god who will go before us; as for this Moses, the man who brought us up from the land of Egypt, we do not know what has become of him.' [24]And I said to them, 'Anyone having gold, take it off.' And they gave it to me. I threw it into the fire—and this calf came out."

Grammatical and Lexical Notes

32:21. Biblical Hebrew has two very similar words for "sin, offense." One, as here, is *ḥăṭāʾâ*. The other, as in 32:30, 32, 34; 34:7, is *ḥaṭṭāʾâ*, with the doubling of the middle consonant. I am not sure there is any important difference between them apart from the orthography, although the second one is much more common (296 times versus 8 times).

32:22. Aaron addresses Moses politely as "my lord" (*ʾădōnî*). Joshua speaks similarly to Moses (Num. 11:28), as do the chieftains of Gad and Reuben (Num. 32:25, 27) and of Gilead (Num. 36:2).

32:22. What is the best way to translate *bĕrāʿ*, the second last word in the verse? The versions are close: "prone to evil" (NIV); "bent on evil" (NRSV); "intent on evil" (Childs 1974); "determined on evil-doing" (Brichto 1992); "in an evil way" (Alter 2004). The exact same phrase, *bĕrāʿ*, occurs back in Exod. 5:19. Note the versions on this passage: "[The Israelite foremen] realized that they were *in trouble*" (NIV; NRSV; Childs 1974); "[And the Israelite foremen] saw themselves *coming to harm*" (Alter 2004). So why translate *bĕrāʿ* in chap. 32 as "intent on/prone to evil," but translate it as "in trouble" or "coming to harm" in chap. 5? To be consistent, should we not render *bĕrāʿ* in Exod. 32:22 something like "You know the people (were) in a bind, a fix"? See Janzen 1997: 238. Maybe *bĕrāʿ* is Biblical Hebrew's way of saying, "caught in a catch-22 situation," that is, in a no-win situation: damned if you do, and damned if you don't.

Commentary

32:21–24 Somehow in such a mass of people, Moses is able to locate Aaron and call him to accountability for his behavior. When he retells this event in Deuteronomy, Moses leaves out this altercation with Aaron, but he says something there that Exod. 32 does not record vis-à-vis Aaron: "And the LORD was angry enough with Aaron to destroy him, but at that time *I prayed for Aaron too*" (Deut. 9:20). The SP does add this at the end of Exod. 32:10, as does the Dead Sea Scroll text of Exod. 32:10–30 (4QpaleoEx^{m} = 4Q22) from Qumran (on which, see Skehan 1955).

Moses pulls no punches. He goes directly for Aaron's jugular: "You have brought [upon these people] such a great sin." The language is amazingly close to what Abimelech uses with Abraham in Gen. 20:9. Compare Abimelech's "What have you done [*meh-ʿāśîtā*] to us? How have I wronged you that you have brought [*kî-hēbēʾtā*] upon [*ʿal*] me and my kingdom such great guilt [*ḥăṭāʾâ gĕdōlâ*]?" with Moses's "What did these people do [*meh-ʿāśâ*] to you that you brought [*kî-hēbēʾtā*] upon [*ʿal*] it such a great sin [*ḥăṭāʾâ gĕdōlâ*]?" Three times in this chapter Moses labels what Israel has done as "a great sin" (vv. 21, 30, 31). In Gen. 20:9 the term refers to adultery. Here the term refers to idolatry, which is a form of adultery.

Moses's charge that Aaron is the one who has led the people into sin is the same as Abimelech's accusation that Abraham is the one who has almost led Abimelech into sin, if God had not intervened. Frequently the Bible speaks of the northern Israelite king, Jeroboam, "causing Israel to commit sin" (1 Kings 14:16; 15:30, 34; etc.), and of other kings, Israelite and Judean (like Manasseh, 2 Kings 21:16), who also cause Israel and Judah to commit sin. Verses like these teach the potential of individuals, especially of people of power and position, to exercise a negative influence on the behavior of others, be they charlatan, patriarch, priest, or king.

Aaron speaks to Moses the way Moses speaks to God. Moses says to God, "Why should your anger blaze [*yeḥĕreh ʾappĕkā*] against your people?" (v. 11), and Aaron says to Moses, "Let not my lord's anger blaze [*ʾal-yiḥar ʾap*]" (v. 22). Moses believes that God is overreacting; Aaron believes that Moses is overreacting. Aaron seems to suggest that Moses has forgotten that these very same people have already established a track record of grumbling, whining, and faultfinding. So why be shocked?

Aaron's explanation of how the calf has come into being (v. 24) challenges credulity: "I threw it into the fire—and this calf came out." Brichto (1992: 97) is the rare interpreter who believes that Aaron's words are accurate: "He flung an ingot into the fire; he waited confidently for its reduction to a liquid glob, ready to turn on the image-demanding instigators with this proof of their folly. Instead a miracle occurred. A miracle which could have been worked out only by the will of YHWH! . . . He [the Lord] suspended natural law, performed a miracle to demonstrate the dire consequences of faithlessness. . . ."

If that is the correct explanation, then Moses does not buy it and therefore gets it wrong. His wrath is not assuaged by now seeing that it is actually God who has made it. Nothing in the remainder of the chapter suggests a God-shaped calf. Accordingly, I stick with the traditional explanation Aaron offers:

"Blame it on the fire," to paraphrase a line from Phillips Brooks's famous sermon on this passage, "The Fire and the Calf" (Brooks 1989: 226).

I compare Moses's taking Aaron to task with Paul's taking Peter to task over his hypocrisy (Gal. 2:11–21). Aaron's behavior has led many to stumble, and Peter's behavior has led many to stumble (2:13). Paul "opposed him [Peter] to his face" as Moses does with Aaron. Unlike Aaron, Peter never has an opportunity to respond to Paul's accusation. But if he had responded, and if he had responded with an Aaron-like answer, it would have been something like this: "I don't know how my eating partners changed. I was eating with some gentiles, and suddenly I found myself, inexplicably, sharing a table with the circumcision crowd!"

Judgment on the Ringleaders

(32:25–29)

Translation

[25]And Moses saw the people that it (was) out of control because Aaron had let it get out of control to be helpless against any who would stand up (to) them. [26]And Moses stood in the gate of the camp, and said, "Whoever is for the LORD, (come) to me." All the sons of Levi gathered around him. [27]And he said to them, "Thus said the LORD God of Israel, 'Put each man his sword on his thigh, and cross the camp back and forth from gate to gate, and each man kill his brother, and each man his friend, and each man his kinsman.'" [28]The sons of Levi did according to Moses's word, and about three thousand of the people fell on that day. [29]And Moses said, "Dedicate your hands today to the LORD, for each man (is) against his son and against his brother, to give you today a blessing."

Grammatical and Lexical Notes

32:25. There is uncertainty about the meaning of the verb *pāraʿ*. It appears in this verse first as a Qal passive participle (*pāruʿa*), "out of control"; then as a Qal third-person perfect with pronominal suffix (*pĕrāʿōh*), "he had let it get out of control." In the Hiphil stem, *pāraʿ* appears in Exod. 5:4 (and only this one time in the Hebrew Bible): "Moses and Aaron, why are you *taking* the people *away* from their work?" (NIV), or "What do you mean by *distracting* the people from their work?" (Childs 1974), or "Why do you *disturb* the people from its tasks" (Alter 2004).

The basic meaning of the verb is "let go, let alone, disregard." Six of the sixteen occurrences of the verb are in Proverbs: (1) 1:25, "ignored advice"; (2) 4:15, "avoid" the way of the wicked; (3) 8:33, "ignore" instruction; (4) and (5) 13:18 and 15:32, "ignore" discipline; (6) 29:18 (Niphal), "cast off restraint." In all these instances the verb carries the idea of (not) neglecting or brushing aside something.

Sometimes the verb is used with one's hair, either letting it hang loosely or not trimming it: Lev. 10:6, "Do not let your hair/head *become unkempt* (in mourning)," or "Do not *bare* your head," or "Do not *dishevel* your hair"; Lev. 13:45, "Let his hair [the one with an infectious skin disease] *be unkempt*"; Lev. 21:10, "The high priest . . . must not let his hair become *unkempt*"; Num. 5:18, "He [the priest] shall *loosen* her hair [the wife suspected of adultery]"; and Num. 6:5, "He [the Nazirite] must let the hair of his head *grow long*." *Biprōʿa pĕrāʿôt* (verb + cognate noun in the plural) at the beginning of the Song of Deborah (Judg. 5:2) is almost impossible to translate, but one possibility is "when *locks go untrimmed* in Israel . . ." (NJPS). To be sure, this rendering of the start of Judg. 5:2 is considerably different from NIV's translation of the same portion of the verse, "When the princes in Israel take the lead. . . ."

If the basic meaning of the verb is "let go," then with hair the verb means to loosen the hair, letting it grow "wild." From that nuance we move to the verb as conveying the derivative idea of wild, disruptive, unruly behavior in Exod. 32. Brichto (1992: 98) has a graphic rendering of the passage: "Moses saw that the people *was deranged, deranged* by Aaron's act." Also, 2 Chron. 28:19 carries this nuance when it describes Ahaz as *promoting wickedness* (Hiphil) in Judah. The one time when the Lord is the subject of the verb is Ezek. 24:14, "The time has come for me to act. I will not *hold back*. I will not pity, nor will I relent [*nāḥam*, Niphal]." God's patience has reached the breaking point. Janzen (1989: 399–400) distances himself from the above interpretation of the verb in Exod. 32. He asserts that the verb means "set free" and argues that Aaron had "released" the Israelites from the prohibition against images of Yahweh in order to strike terror into their enemies, what Janzen (1989: 400) calls "a well-intentioned hermeneutical perversion of the covenant terms."

32:25. *Pĕrāʿōh* ("He had let it get out of control") contains the verb *pāraʿ* and the third-person masculine singular pronominal suffix *-ōh*. Though this suffix form appears with a noun thirty-seven times in the Hebrew Bible, there are only two other instances where it is the direct object of a verb: Num. 23:8, "How can I curse him [*qabbōh*] whom God has not cursed?" (AT); and 2 Kings 6:10, "Time and time again Elisha warned him [*wĕhizhîrōh*]" (AT). Statistics are in J. Curtis 1983: 557.

32:25. Another difficult word in this verse is *lĕšimṣâ*, which I have rendered "to be helpless." It occurs only here in the Hebrew Bible. There is a similar word in Job 4:12, *šemeṣ/šēmeṣ*, which NIV renders, "A word was secretly brought to me, my ears caught *a whisper* of it"; and in Job 26:14, "And these are but the outer fringe of his works; how faint *the whisper* we hear of him!" As we know, the Hebrew poetry of Job is complex. Clines (1989: 107, 111) renders *šemeṣ/šēmeṣ* in Job 4:12 as "My ears caught only *a fragment*"; Ginsberg (1969: 106n2)—by appealing to Arabic *šamaṣa* VII, "shudder with fear"—offers "*Terror* gripped me when I heard it."

32:26. The expression "in the gate of the camp" is odd. How does an open camp have a gate? The only parallel that comes to mind is 2 Chron. 31:2, "at the gates of the LORD's camp [AT; NIV, "dwelling"]."

32:26. *Mî* can mean "who" or the indefinite "whoever" (Judg. 7:3, "*Anyone* who trembles with fear"). The same goes for *mâ*, which means not only "what" but "whatever" (1 Sam. 20:4, "*Whatever* you want me to do, I'll do for you").

32:26. The Hebrew has Moses say, "Whoever (is) for the LORD, to me." The LXX has Moses ask, "Who is for the Lord?" and supplies the verb "come" before "to me" (*Tis pros kyrion? Itō pros mē*).

32:29. "Dedicate [fill] your hands" is the phrase used earlier for the "ordination" of the priests (28:41; 29:9, 29).

32:29. It is difficult to ascertain the function of the *wāw* on the infinitive *wĕlātēt* ("to give"). GKC §114p says the *wāw* is emphatic ("and that") and cites the first word of Lev. 10:10, also an infinitive with prefixed preposition *lĕ*, as a parallel (*ûlăhabdîl*).

Commentary

32:25–29 Earlier God has promised not to annihilate Israel in response to Moses's intercession, but that does not mean that all is forgotten and forgiven. In v. 27, Moses claims that the execution of the ringleaders is something God says to do, and hence he quotes the Lord in that verse. This is an instance of an unverifiable quotation, because Exod. 32 does not record the Lord's saying this to Moses. (For some other unverifiable quotations in the Bible, see Gen. 50:17, where Joseph's brothers quote words of their deceased father to Joseph, and 1 Kings 1:17, where Bathsheba quotes David about an earlier promise he made to Solomon establishing him as his successor.)

Now (some of) the Levites answer Moses's summons for the executioners to step forward. Moses himself is a Levite, as is Aaron (Exod. 2:1–10). At Moses's directive, they kill about three thousand of their kindred. Earlier the Israelites were spared the Lord's sword (5:3, "Or he may strike us with plagues or with the *sword*"); they were spared Pharaoh and his officials' sword (5:21, "You . . . have put a *sword* in their hand to kill us"); they were spared the Egyptians' sword (15:9, "The enemy boasted, . . . 'I will draw my *sword* and my hand will destroy them'"); they were spared Pharaoh's sword (18:4, "My fathers' God . . . saved me from the *sword* of Pharaoh"), but now they are not spared from the Levites' sword ("Put each man his *sword* on his thigh").

There are acts of fratricide in the Bible that are clearly wrong, such as Cain's killing Abel (Gen. 4) and Absalom's having his half brother Amnon killed (2 Sam. 13). The latter example may be understood as retributive justice, a "repayment" for what Amnon did to Tamar. Or it may also be self-motivated: with Amnon dead, Absalom is David's oldest living son, and hence the logical successor to his father's throne. Judah has the decency to ask his brothers about Joseph, "What will we gain if we kill our brother?" (Gen. 37:26).

Abimelech has no qualms about killing his seventy brothers (Judg. 9:5). And think of the other instances in Judges where one tribal brother violently turns on another tribal brother (Jephthah and 42,000 Ephraimites, Judg. 12:6; the Benjaminites and 40,030 Israelites, Judg. 20:21, 25, 31; the Israelites and 25,000 Benjaminites, Judg. 20:46). In Judges, every Israelite who dies violently at the hand of another dies at the hand of a fellow Israelite. No Israelite is said, explicitly, to die at the hand of any Midianite, Moabite, or Philistine.

Moses's words of blessing on the tribe of Levi in Deut. 33 seem to have Exod. 32:25–29 in mind when Moses remarks about Levi: "He said of his father and mother, 'I have no regard for them.' He did not recognize his brothers or acknowledge his own children, but he watched over your word and guarded your covenant." (By the way, one wonders how much Moses's words about Levi in Deut. 33:9 provide a backdrop for Jesus's words in Luke 14:26, "If anyone comes to me and does not hate his *father* and *mother*, his wife and *children*, his *brothers* and sisters . . ."; the shared words are in italics.) The problem with connecting Deut. 33:8–11 with Exod. 32:25–29 is that in Deut. 33 Moses says that this behavior of the Levites takes place at Massah and Meribah, not at Sinai. On the historical issues here, see Loewenstamm (1992: 55–65), an essay titled "The Investiture of Levi."

In return for their punishment of the idolaters, the Levites are instructed to "fill/consecrate their hands," to install themselves as priests. They are now to be the Lord's blessed ones. These crusading Levites anticipate Phinehas. For his zeal in suppressing apostasy and immorality (Num. 25:7–13), the Lord says of him, "He and his descendants will have a covenant of a lasting priesthood, because he was zealous for the honor of his God and made atonement for the Israelites" (25:13). Fight the good fight, and who knows what one will get. In retelling this in Deuteronomy, Moses leaves out all this messy stuff and simply states, "At that time the LORD set apart the tribe of Levi to carry the ark of the covenant of the LORD, to stand before the LORD to minister and to pronounce blessings in his name" (Deut. 10:8).

Some contemporary writers are offended by the contents of chap. 32, for it seems to validate massacre and other horrors, all done in the name of one's religion and all done with God's blessing. Hence, Whybray (1996: 112–19), in an essay provocatively titled, "The Immorality of God: Reflections on Some Passages in Genesis, Job, Exodus, and Numbers," homes in on Exod. 32. See also Lasine's essay (1994) that has a title beginning with "Levitic Violence, Fratricide . . ." Other writers see more positive lessons in this unit. For example, Fretheim (1991: 289) says, "Radical sin is believed to call for radical measures." While not in the least suggesting that Messiah's followers should similarly execute bloodbaths against apostates, Fretheim goes on to say, "The seriousness with which Israel takes the matter should occasion critical reflection by those of us who live in an age where virtually anything that goes by the name of religion is tolerated."

Moses's Further Intercession

(32:30–35)

Translation

[30]On the next day Moses said to the people,
"You have sinned a great sin, and now I
shall go up to the LORD. Perhaps I can make
atonement for your sin." [31]Moses returned
to the LORD and said, "I beg you! This
people has sinned a great sin, and have
made for themselves gods of gold. [32]And
now, if you will forgive their sin . . . , but if
not, wipe me out, please, from your book
that you have written." [33]And the LORD said
to Moses, "Whoever has sinned against me,
I shall wipe out from my book. [34]So now,
go! Lead the people to (the place) about
which I spoke to you. Indeed, my messen-
ger/angel shall go before you. And on the
day of my visiting, I shall visit punishment
upon them (for) their sins."

[35]And the LORD afflicted the people be-
cause they made the calf that Aaron made.

Grammatical and Lexical Notes

32:30. Moses's use of "perhaps" (*ʾûlay*) to introduce "I can make atonement for you" is telling. Moses's "perhaps" is closest to Amos's use of "perhaps" (Amos 5:15). Both introduce a note of uncertainty about how God will respond: "*Perhaps* the LORD God Almighty will have mercy on the remnant of Judah." See also Num. 23:3 ("*Perhaps* the LORD will come to meet with me"); 1 Sam. 14:6 ("*Perhaps* the LORD will act on our behalf"); 2 Sam. 16:12 ("*Perhaps* [NIV, "It may be that"] the LORD will see my distress"); Jer. 21:2 ("*Perhaps* the Lord will perform wonders for us"); Jon. 1:6 ("*Perhaps* [NIV, "maybe"] he will take notice of us, and we will not perish"); Zeph. 2:3 ("*Perhaps* you will be sheltered on the day of the LORD's anger"). In such passages "perhaps" is the same as "Who knows?" in other passages (2 Sam. 12:22; Joel 2:14; Jon. 3:9). Most interesting are the passages where the Lord himself or his spokesman uses "perhaps" (Isa. 47:12b; Jer. 26:2–3; 36:3, 7; 51:8; Ezek. 12:3). Note this punch line in the parable of the tenants that Jesus tells (Luke 20:9–19), "What shall I do? I will send my son, whom I love; *perhaps* they will respect him" (20:13). See further Fretheim 1984: 45–46.

32:30. The verb *kāpar* (mostly Piel) occurs often enough in the Hebrew Bible, but only three times in the first person. While "I can make atonement for" fits Exod. 32:30, that rendering does not fit the other two: (1) Gen. 32:20 [21], Jacob about Esau, "I will *pacify* him [NIV] with these gifts," or more literally, "I will cover [over] his face with these gifts"; (2) 2 Sam. 21:3, "How shall I *make amends* so that you will bless the LORD's inheritance?"

32:31. Earlier in the chapter, Moses uses *šûb min* (v. 12) for God's "turning from" his anger. Here he uses *šûb ʾel* for "returning" to God. Holladay (1958: 59–60) notes that there are 273 instances where *šûb* designates motion back to the point of departure. Somebody moves from point A to point B, and then back to point A again. In a number of these passages, *šûb ʾel* means "return to the LORD," "repent," especially in the prophetic literature. It is unlikely that there are many of these 273 uses of *šûb* that speak of somebody literally "returning" to the Lord (see 5:22). Note that Moses never prays for Pharaoh until he has "left" Pharaoh's presence to be alone (with God). See 8:8, 12 [4, 8]; 8:29, 30 [25, 26]; 10:17, 18. In 33:11 it is only after the Lord speaks to Moses face to face that Moses returns to his people.

32:31. I render *ʾānnāʾ* with "I beg you!" The NIV tends to render the word (also spelled *ʾānnâ*) as "O," especially in the phrase "O Lord!" (2 Kings 20:3 [= Isa. 38:3]; Neh. 1:5, 11; Pss. 116:4, 16; 118:25; Dan. 9:4; Jon. 1:14; 4:2), but uses "please" in Gen. 50:17 and "oh" in Exod. 32:31.

32:32. The three dots (. . .) after "And now, if you will forgive their sin . . ." represent Moses's unfinished sentence. The technical name for such a phenomenon is "aposiopesis," on which see Crown 1963.

32:32. The verb *māḥah* means to remove letters by washing. See the aquatic nuances of the verb in Isa. 44:22, "I have *swept away* your offenses like a cloud, your sins like the morning mist." It is the verb that Gen. 6:7; 7:4, 23 uses for the Lord's "wiping out" everything in the flood. The NIV properly translates the verb "wash" in Num. 5:23, "Write these curses on a scroll and then *wash* them off into the bitter water." See Haran 1982: 169, 169n19.

32:32. Moses's "but if not, wipe me out, please, from your book" uses language similar to Azitawaddu's Phoenician inscription, lines 12–14: "[12]And if a king among kings, or a prince among princes, if a man [13]who is a man of renown *shall wash out* the name of Azitawaddu [14]from this gate [*ʾš ymḥ šm ʾztwd bšʿr z*], and shall set [his own] name [in its place] . . ." Exodus 32:32 uses *mḥh min*, and the Phoenician text uses *mḥh b*.

32:34. I supply "place" in "to the [place] about which I spoke to you," following the LXX, which inserts the word. For Hebrew *ʾel-ʾăšer*, see Ruth 1:16, "Where [*ʾel ʾăšer*] you go I will go."

32:34. The basic meaning of *pāqad* is "visit, turn one's thoughts/attention" to somebody. See Gen. 21:1 KJV, "The Lord *visited* Sarah"; Exod. 4:31, the Lord *visited* (KJV; NIV, "was concerned about") his people in Egypt; 1 Sam. 2:21, the Lord *visited* (KJV; NIV, "was gracious to") Hannah. But when the preposition *ʿal* follows the verb, as here, it takes the meaning "punish, count against, hold accountable for." Hence, in the second commandment the Lord "punishes" (*pāqad ʿal*) the children for the sin of the fathers (Exod. 20:5; Deut. 5:9). See also the same language in Num. 14:18. A visit from God may be motivated either by his loving concern or by his jealous wrath. God may turn his attention to us when we most need him, or when he is the last individual we want around.

32:35. "Afflicted" (*nāgap*) is the verb Exod. 7:27 and 12:23, 27 use for the Lord's "afflicting/plaguing" Egypt. Does the verse refer to something that happens right there and then, or is it a prophetic word? Brichto (1992: 99) opts for the latter by prefacing v. 35 with "[A time did come when] . . ."

32:35. I see no need to adjust the literal reading of the last part of the verse: "because *they made* the calf that *Aaron made*." Both the people and Aaron play a role in the calf's manufacturing.

Commentary

32:30–35 Neither on this occasion nor on any other occasion when Moses intercedes for sinful Israel does he admonish them to repent of their sins. That will come later, in the Prophets. Moses in chap. 32 earlier has asked God to *šûb* and *nāḥam*, but he does not ask the people to *šûb* or *nāḥam*. He simply says, "Perhaps I can make atonement for your sin." That he begins with "Perhaps" indicates that Moses has no idea whether God is open to this. Earlier in the chapter he is bold with God to the point of being brazen. Here he hedges his approach with possibility-only language. To be sure, God is gracious and merciful, but his forgiveness cannot be presumed, as if God is duty bound to remove our sins anytime and anywhere we ask him. We cannot say, *Gott wird mir verzeihen, das ist sein Beruf* (attributed to the German writer Heinrich Heine [d. 1856] as he was on his deathbed, conversing with a priest), commonly translated into French as "*Dieu me pardonnera, c'est son métier*" ("God will forgive me; that's his job").

Yet Moses cannot make atonement for anybody. The priest, acting for God in God's name, can. Thus in Lev. 4 and 5, for example, the priest takes the blood of the sin and guilt offering and makes "atonement" for the offerer with the result that the offerer is "forgiven" (Lev. 4:20, 26, 31; 5:16, 18). There are so many similarities between Moses and Jesus, from birth to ministry, but at one crucial point the similarity breaks down. As Waltke (2007: 470) says, "But Moses unlike Christ cannot make atonement."

Moses petitions the Lord to forgive the people's sin (v. 32a). Hebrew has at least two ways to say "forgive" sin. The one used here is *nāśā' ḥāṭā'*, literally, "lift, carry, carry away sin." Normally the subject of the verb is God, but there are three instances where the text speaks of one person's forgiving another person and uses this phrase: Gen. 50:17 (Joseph and his brothers); Exod. 10:17 (Moses and Pharaoh); 1 Sam. 15:25 (Samuel and Saul). Another word for "forgive" is *sālaḥ*, which is used for forgiveness of sin in the verses from Lev. 4 and 5 cited in the previous paragraph. I do not believe there is much difference between them. Moses uses the two together in Num. 14:19, "In accordance with your great love, forgive (*sālaḥ*) the sin of these people just as you have pardoned (*nāśā'*) them from the time they left Egypt until now." If there is a difference, *nāśā'* [*ḥāṭā'*] suggests forgiveness through relieving or unburdening a person of their offense and consequent punishment. The forgiven person does not have to carry one's sin any more. God carries it (away). Since the cognate Akkadian word to Hebrew *sālaḥ* is *salahu*, which means "wash, sprinkle" (see *CAD* S:85–88), then this verb suggests forgiveness through removal by washing. Hence, God does two things with sin. Either he carries it away, or he washes it away. He removes our burden, and he cleans us up.

Moses then adds, "But if [you do] not [forgive], wash/wipe me out . . . from your book which you have written" (v. 32b). This is the first, but not the last, reference in Scripture to a celestial book, to one's name or deeds being recorded in heaven. See Pss. 40:7 [8]; 56:8 [9]; 69:28 [29]; 87:6; 139:16; Isa. 4:3; 34:16; 65:6; Jer. 22:30; Dan. 7:10; 10:21; 12:1; Mal. 3:16. Of these verses, the one closest to Exod. 32:32 is Ps. 69:28 [29], for it too uses the verb *māḥah* for the washing/blotting out of somebody's name—"May they *be blotted out* of the book of life and not be listed with the righteous." The opposite of having one's name written in the celestial book may be Jer. 17:13, which says, "Those who turn away from you *will be written in the dust*."

New Testament references to this heavenly book or register include Luke 10:20; Phil. 4:3; Heb. 12:23; Rev. 3:5; 13:8; 20:12, 15; 21:27. Ancient Sumerian and Assyrian records, as well as intertestamental literature (*Jubilees*, *1 Enoch*,

Qumran), also speak of this phenomenon. References may be found in Paul (1973).

Commentators often parallel this prayer of Moses with Paul's "I could wish that I myself were cursed and cut off from Christ for the sake of my brothers, those of my own race, the people of Israel" (Rom. 9:3–4). (Talk about being willing to go to hell, but for all the right reasons!) But the two are not similar. Paul is offering himself as a cursed, God-rejected substitute for the salvation of Israel. He would take perdition so Israel can have paradise. Moses, by contrast, says in effect, "If you don't let them play, take me off the team too."

The Lord could have responded in one of three ways: (1) "Yes, I will forgive them, but at the cost of blotting out your name from the book of life" (which would have been parallel to Rom. 9:3–4); (2) "Yes, I will forgive them, but there is no need to erase your name"; (3) "No, I will not forgive them, nor will I remove your name from my book." The Lord exercises the third option (vv. 33–35).

Thus it appears that while Moses is eminently successful with his intercession recorded in 32:11–13, he is not successful at all with his intercession recorded in vv. 31–32. To the first prayer, God says, "Yes!" To the second prayer, God says, "No!" He will *nāḥam* but not *nāśā'*. Israel will have continued existence, but not immediate expiation, at least not yet.

The language of vv. 34b–35 ("And on the day of my visiting . . .") is not easy to interpret, but its ominous tone is clear enough. Says Alter (2004: 500), "For this archetypal sin of the Golden Calf, a free-floating prospect of further retribution would seem to hover over the people like a dark shadow." We started this chapter by suggesting that Exod. 32 is the account of Israel's "original sin" and fall from grace. If, as Christian theology maintains, the effects or fallout from Adam's sin extend far beyond Adam, then the effects or fallouts from the sin of the calf makers extend far beyond the calf makers.

Israel to Move On, but without the Lord

(33:1–6)

Translation

[1]And the LORD said to Moses, "Go, go up from this (place), you and the people whom you brought up from the land of Egypt, to the land about which I swore to Abraham, to Isaac, and to Jacob, saying, 'To your seed I will give it,' [2]—And I shall send before you a messenger/angel, and I will drive out the Canaanite, the Amorite, and the Hittite and the Perizzite, the Hivite and the Jebusite—[3]to a land oozing with milk and sap, but I will not go up in your midst, for a stiff-necked people (are) you, lest I devour you on the way."

[4]When the people heard this ominous word, they mourned; not a person placed his jewelry on himself. [5](This came about in this way:) and the LORD said to Moses, "Say to Israel's sons, 'You (are) a stiff-necked people. Should I for one moment go up in your midst, I would annihilate you. And now, off with your jewelry until I decide what I shall do with you.'" [6]Israel's sons stripped themselves of their jewelry from (the time they were at) Mount Horeb (on).

Grammatical and Lexical Notes

33:3. For Canaan as a "land oozing with milk and sap," see Exod. 3:8, 17; 13:5; Num. 13:27; 14:8; 16:13–14; Deut. 6:3; 27:3.

33:3. The various Targums supply illustrations of "converse translation" in vv. 3 and 5. Thus, *Targum Onqelos* reads v. 3 of MT's "but I will not go up in your midst" as "for I shall not remove my presence from among you." Similarly, in v. 5 MT's "Should I for one moment go up in your midst" in *Targum Onqelos* becomes "For a single moment I shall remove my presence from among you." According to the various Targums, it is God's removal of his presence that is the punishment for Israel. See M. Klein (1976: 530–31).

33:4. For *šît* ("placed") referring to an article of clothing or adornment one might wear, see Prov. 7:10, "dressed like a prostitute [*šît zōnâ*]."

33:5. I have put "(This came about in this way:)" at the start of the sentence to show that vv. 5–6 are a "resumptive narrative technique." These last two verses explain how the reality of v. 4 happened, why the people removed their jewelry. Otherwise, v. 6 is a clumsy repetition: thus in v. 4 the people remove their jewelry on their own initiative, and then vv. 5–6 tell us that they have removed their jewelry because God told them to. See Brichto 1992: 102.

33:5. "For one moment" is *regaʿ ʾeḥād*. The Hebrew word *regaʿ* occurs elsewhere, in Num. 16:21 (*kĕrāgaʿ*, "[put an end to them] *at once/in an instant*"), and in Num. 16:45 [17:10] ("so I can put an end to them *at once/in an instant*"). See also Job 34:20, "They [the wicked] die *in an instant*"; and Ps. 73:19, "How *suddenly* are they [the wicked] destroyed."

33:5. The LXX translates the Hebrew word for "jewelry" in these verses with *kosmos*, for which the usual translation is "universe." The verb from which the noun *kosmos* derives, *kosmō*, means to "adorn," as in 1 Tim. 2:9, "I also want women to *dress* modestly"; and in Rev. 21:2, "I saw the Holy City, . . . prepared as a bride *beautifully dressed* for her husband."

33:6. "Stripped themselves" is the Hitpael of *nāṣal*. That verb appears in the Piel stem in 3:22 and 12:36 for Israel's "despoiling" the Egyptians, seizing their valuables.

33:6. The verse ends by saying "from Mount Horeb" (*mēhar ḥôrēb*). When temporal *m*(*n*) is prefixed to a place name, the place name represents the time spent at that place. Hence the addition of parentheses in my translation. Compare Ezek. 23:8, "She did not give up the prostitution *she began in Egypt* [*mimmiṣrayim*]"; and Hosea 13:4, "But I am the LORD your God from [the time you were in] Egypt [on] [*mē'ereṣ miṣrāyim*]." (Note how NIV supplements Hosea 13:4 with "who brought you" to give it sense.) See Greenberg 1997: 476.

Commentary

33:1–6 Israel is shortly to resume the journey to Canaan (v. 1), but with a messenger/angel going "before" the people (v. 2) as a surrogate for an absent, infuriated Yahweh who has dwelled "among" them (v. 3). There is a considerably different role for this messenger/angel in 33:3 than that mentioned in 23:20–23. In 23:20–23 the messenger/angel is a gracious provision of God for his people. In 33:3 the messenger/angel appears only because God has been deeply offended by his people's behavior. Such messengers/angels can represent either God's blessing (Exod. 23) or the withdrawal of God's presence (Exod. 33). Even in his wrath, however, the Lord is gracious. His presence with the Israelites means their possible annihilation. His absence from the people and limiting himself to a proxy means they have a future, another chance. If there is ever an occasion on which it is appropriate for the Lord to say that the gift of land has nothing to do with Israel's merits, but everything to do with his faithful promise to Israel's ancestors (v. 1a), this is it. Earlier it is Moses who raises with God the issue of God's earlier promise to the patriarchs (32:13). Here it is God who raises the issue with Moses of his earlier promise to the patriarchs.

Verse 4 (and 6) does not use the standard vocabulary of repentance: *šûb min* or *nāḥam* or *yādâ* (Hitpael), meaning to "turn from" sin or "repent of" sin or "confess" sin. But stripping oneself of jewelry or outer adornment may be a demonstrable way of renouncing one's sin. A parallel may be found in Gen. 35:4, where Jacob's household gets rid not only of all their foreign gods but also of "the rings in their ears," all of which Jacob subsequently buries. Hague (2001: 77) says, "In a setting of idol production, the nonuse of the ornaments alludes to a general background of purification and renunciation." See also Rodriguez (1997: 115, 118) in his essay on "Jewelry in the OT."

In some ways Exod. 33:1–6 is close to Num. 14. Both involve "sin scenes" with Moses pitted against sinful Israel, especially the ringleaders. The sin is idolatry in Exodus, rebellion in Numbers. In both cases, upon seeing what

Israel has done or what the Lord has done to the perpetrators, Israel "mourned" (Exod. 33:4 and Num. 14:39, both the Hitpael of *'ābal*). But there is one striking difference. In Exodus the mourning precedes God's decision to renew the covenant with Israel (chap. 34). In Num. 14 the mourning follows God's decision to wipe out the first adult generation, Caleb and Joshua excepted, and start over with a new generation.

This difference suggests two things. First, the mourning of Exod. 33 points to repentance, while the mourning of Num. 14 points to remorse. For his act of treachery, Judas Iscariot is remorseful (*metamelomai*, Matt. 27:3), but he never repents (*metanoeō*). Second, the likelihood that Israel goes beyond remorse to repentance in Exod. 33 seems to be reinforced by what they do with their jewelry or ornaments. No Israelite removes any article of clothing or body decoration in Num. 14. Tragically and regrettably, their confession of sin (Num. 14:40) comes too late, after the door of opportunity, so to speak, has been slammed shut by divine fiat.

Moses knows a thing or two about removing something from his body at "Mount Horeb" (3:1–6; 33:6b). While there and confronted by God, he removes his shoes (3:5). Here at Horeb his people remove their jewelry. Moses is moved to do what he does because of awe, while the Israelites are moved to do what they do because of guilt.

A Tent outside the Camp

(33:7–11)

Translation

[7]And Moses would take the tent and pitch it for himself outside the camp at a considerable distance from the camp, and he called it the tent of meeting. Anybody who was seeking the LORD would go out to the tent of meeting outside the camp. [8]Whenever Moses went out to the tent, all the people would get up and each man would station himself at his own tent opening, and they would watch Moses while he approached the tent. [9]Whenever Moses would approach the tent, the pillar of the cloud would descend and halt at the tent's entrance, and would speak with Moses. [10]All the people would see the pillar of the cloud halting at the tent's entrance. Thereupon all the people would rise and bow down, each man at his tent's entrance. [11]The LORD would speak to Moses face to face, the way a man speaks to his companion. Then he [Moses] would return to the camp, but his attendant, the lad Joshua son of Nun, would not budge from within the tent.

Grammatical and Lexical Notes

33:7. There are a lot of "woulds" in my translation, two in v. 7, three in v. 8, three in v. 9, two in v. 10, three in v. 11. This is my way of showing that most of the verbs in these five verses are what Hebrew grammarians call "frequentative" or "iterative" verbs: they refer to actions that someone repeatedly does (see, e.g., S. R. Driver 1998: 128, 147, 186; GKC §112e). I count twelve uses of the perfect with *wāw*- consecutive in these verses. If the unit is describing a onetime incident, the verb forms would be *wayyiqṭōl*.

33:7. The definite article in "the tent" (*hāʾōhel*) seems to point to some specific tent, maybe the one already mentioned in 18:7 ("And they [Moses and Jethro] went into the tent"). Or maybe the article is generic ("a tent").

33:7. The phrase "pitch one's tent" (*nāṭâ ʾōhel*) appears only here with Moses, and elsewhere in the Pentateuch with Abraham (Gen. 12:8), Isaac (Gen. 26:25), and Jacob (Gen. 33:19; 35:21). For other tent pitchers, see Judg. 4:11 (Heber the Kenite); 2 Sam. 6:17; 1 Chron. 15:1; 16:1; 2 Chron. 1:4 (David); 2 Sam. 16:22 (Absalom).

33:7. The pronominal suffix in *lô* after "he pitched" could be either direct object ("it"), or more likely a reflexive ("for himself").

33:7. Normally the expression "outside the camp" means "in the vicinity of the camp" (Lev. 4:12, 21; 9:11; 10:4–5; 13:46; 14:3, 7, 53; 16:10, 22, 27; 17:5; 24:14; Num. 5:2–4; 12:14–15). If a greater distance is intended, then an additional phrase is necessary, as here, "[outside the camp] at a considerable distance from the camp [*harḥēq min-hammaḥăneh*]."

33:7. For *kol-měbaqqēš YHWH* ("Anybody who was seeking the LORD"), see Deut. 4:29, "But if from there you *seek* the LORD your God . . ."; and Ps. 27:8, "My heart says of you, '*Seek* his face!' Your face, LORD, I will *seek*."

33:9. It is preferable to translate *ʿāmad*, here and in v. 10, as "halt" rather than "stand."

33:9. The grammatical subject of "and would speak" is "the pillar of the cloud." God is speaking from within the cloud, but from the people's position, they perceive it as the cloud speaking to Moses.

33:10. Here *kol-hāʿām* ("all the people") occurs with a singular verb (*wĕrāʾâ* and *wĕqām*). In v. 8 the same phrase is used with a plural verb (*yāqûmû*).

33:10. The verb *wĕhištaḥăwû* (MT *wĕhištaḥăûû*), "and bow down," is a *sht-* stem of *ḥāwâ*, rather than, as is commonly thought, a Hitpael stem of *šāḥah*. It may take a singular subject, as in Gen. 19:1, "And Lot . . . bowed [*wayyištaḥû*]"; 23:7, 12, "And Abraham bowed [*wayyištaḥû*]"; 24:26, "The servant of Abraham bowed [*wayyištaḥû*]." In such forms the *wāw* at the end is one of the radicals of the root.

33:11. Joshua is called Moses's "attendant" (*mĕšārēt*) in Exod. 24:13; Num. 11:28; Josh. 1:1. Elisha is a *mĕšārēt* to Elijah (1 Kings 19:21) and later has his own *mĕšārēt* (2 Kings 4:43; 6:15).

33:11. The verb for "[not] budge," *mûš* or *mîš*, has occurred in 13:22, "Neither the pillar of cloud by day nor the pillar of fire by night *left its place* [NIV]/*would budge* in front of the people." See also Num. 14:44, "The ark of the LORD's covenant did not *move/budge* from the camp."

Commentary

Apparently before there is a tent of meeting (described in chaps. 25–31, constructed in 35–40), there is a tent of meeting. Before God comes into the tent, he comes down to the/a tent. His presence may be outside the camp in a tent or in the midst of the camp in a tent. **33:7–11**

There are some obvious differences between the tent described here in vv. 7–11 and the sanctuary tent, or tabernacle, described in chaps. 25–31, 35–40. For one thing, this smaller "tent of meeting" is located far beyond the camp but not so far that the people cannot "see" Moses as he draws near the tent (v. 8) or "see" the descending cloud pillar (v. 10). By contrast, the sanctuary tent is located in the middle of the camp or inside the protective square formed by four groups of three tribes (Num. 2). Second, there is no explicit reference to the ark or to any other sacred object or to any sacrificial cult in the smaller tent of meeting, as there is in the sanctuary tent.

Third, what Aaron, or the Aaronide priests, do in the sanctuary tent, Moses does in this tent of meeting, and what the Levites do for the sanctuary tent, Joshua does for the tent of meeting (v. 11b). Anybody can approach the tent if they are on a God-seeking mission (v. 7b); at least they can go "out" to it, but not necessarily "into" it. Perhaps that is why Joshua seems to be a permanent resident in the tent: to prevent unauthorized entrance. Holy places and holy objects need to be guarded (cf. 1 Sam. 7:1, "And they consecrated Eleazar his son to *guard* the ark of the LORD").

A final difference is that this tent is a place for God's occasional appearance. He shows up when somebody seeks him and more spectacularly when Moses approaches the tent of meeting. The sanctuary tent, however, is God's permanent dwelling.

I am not so sure we should distinguish the tent of meeting from the sanctuary tent by suggesting that the function of the former is exclusively oracular (inquiring of God and hearing from God), while the function of the sanctuary tent is exclusively cultic (bringing offerings and sacrifices to God as an act of worship or for expiation). After all, even this tent at times is the place for a divine pronouncement (e.g., Exod. 25:22, "There above the cover between the two cherubim, . . . I will meet with you and *give you all my commands*"; Exod. 29:42, "There I will meet you *and speak to you*"; Num. 7:89, "When Moses entered the Tent of Meeting to speak with the LORD, he heard *the voice speaking to him*").

True, the Israelites have heard Moses just tell them that Yahweh will not accompany them on their journey (v. 3), that he will send a heavenly being to be his stand-in (v. 2). But God does not pull a disappearing act; rather, he relocates. Because of their sin with the calf, the Israelites now have God's partial presence rather than his full presence (vv. 1–6), his distant presence rather than his intimate presence (vv. 7–11).

But access to that presence they still have. At least the people can go out to the tent of meeting. They must not even touch the mountain, never mind climb it. Moses does not need to place a restraining fence or rope around the tent's perimeter. Yet that access is nothing like the access that Moses has. Nobody rises to their feet and stares when, say, an Ephraimite or Gadite goes out to this tent, but they all do when Moses goes out to it (v. 8). No pillar of cloud bursts forth from the heavens when, say, a Danite or Manassehite goes out to the tent, but the pillar does so when Moses approaches the tent (v. 9). And Moses is the only individual whose approach to this tent moves everybody else to genuflect (v. 10).

Finally, only with Moses does the Lord speak "face to face" (v. 11) at the entrance to this tent. The language is close to that of Deut. 34:10, "Since then, no prophet has risen in Israel, whom the LORD knew face to face"; and to Num. 12:8, "With him [Moses] I speak face to face." It is an experience that Moses shares with Jacob (Gen. 32:30 [31], "It is because I saw God face to face, and yet my life was spared"); with Gideon (Judg. 6:22, "I have seen the angel of the LORD face to face!"); and with Israel earlier (Deut. 5:4, "The LORD spoke to you face to face out of the fire on the mountain"). In the case of Deut. 5:4, "face to face" is *pānîm bĕpānîm* (literally, "face in face"), a tad different from the phrase used with Moses, *pānîm ʾel-pānîm*, and perhaps to distinguish God's speaking with Moses from God's speaking with Israel.

Later references to this outside-the-camp tent of meeting appear first in Num. 11, where Israel is complaining. In v. 24a Moses "went out [of the tent]" (*yāṣā'*) and "told the people what the LORD had said." The elders stand "around the tent," not in it (v. 24b). Two of the elders, Eldad and Medad, "remained in the camp" and did not "go out to the tent" (v. 26). Joshua is called a *naʿar* ("a lad") in Exod. 33:11, and here, "a young man" (*naʿar*) runs to Moses.

In Num. 12, Moses, Aaron, and Miriam "come out" to the tent (Num. 12:4). Then the Lord "descended in a pillar of cloud" (AT; as in Exod. 33:9) and stood at the entrance to the tent. Of Moses, God says, "With him I speak face to face" (Num. 12:8 = Exod. 33:11a).

Numbers 27:1–11 may also point to this tent. Zelophehad's daughters approach "the entrance to the Tent of Meeting" with a grievance (v. 2). They state their case before Moses (vv. 3–4). Moses brings their case before the Lord (v. 5). The Lord then gives an oracular response in favor of the daughters' concern (vv. 6–7).

In all of these "tent" stories, Moses functions as intercessor, whether it is for idolaters or complainers, or for those with a proper grievance. In 32:7–14 Moses intercedes most dramatically for idolatrous Israel. There is no mention of a specific intercession in 33:7–11, but one may see Moses's actions in these verses "as formalizing what he had done spontaneously in the preceding chapter" (Cooper and Goldstein 1997: 214). At the mountain, when Moses "goes up," God descends. At the tent, when Moses "goes out," God (in the pillar) comes down.

Moses Gets in God's Face about God's Face

(33:12–17)

Translation

[12]And Moses said to the LORD, "Look, you are the one saying to me, 'Bring up this people,' yet you, you have not let me know whom/what you will send with me. And you, you have said, 'I have known you by name, and also you have found favor in my eyes.' [13]So now, if, pray, I have found favor in your eyes, let me know, please, your way that I may know you so that I may find favor in your eyes. And see, for your people (is) this nation." [14]And he said, "My face will go with you, and I will give you rest." [15]And he said to him, "If your face is not going, do not take us up from this (place). [16]And how then will it ever be known that I have found favor in your eyes—I and your people—if not by your going with us, that I and your people be thus distinguished from every other people of the earth?" [17]And the LORD said to Moses, "Indeed, this matter about which you spoke I will do, for you have found favor in my eyes, and I have known you by name."

Grammatical and Lexical Notes

33:12. *ʾĒt ʾăšer-tišlaḥ ʿimmî* can just as well be translated "*what* you will send with me" as the more familiar "*whom* you will send with me."

33:12. The phrase "to find favor in the eyes of X" (*māṣāʾ ḥēn bĕʿênê*) occurs five times in this unit (vv. 12, 13 [2x], 16, 17). The expression occurs 43x in the Hebrew Bible, most often in Genesis (13x): 6:8; 18:3; 19:19; 30:27; 32:5 [6]; 33:8, 10, 15; 34:11; 39:4; 47:25, 29; 50:4. Apart from the five uses of the phrase in Exod. 33:12–17, it appears in Exodus again only in 34:9. A related phrase, *nātan ḥēn bĕʿênê*, "give grace in the eyes of," appears in Exod. 3:21; 11:3; 12:36 (NIV, "The LORD *made* the Egyptians *favorably disposed toward* his people"); also see Gen. 39:21; Ps. 84:11 [12]; Prov. 3:4; 13:15. Further references are listed in W. Clark 1971: 262, 262nn3–6; Ap-Thomas 1957: 132, 132n1. "To *find* favor/grace in the eyes of the LORD" does not mean "to *earn* favor/grace in the eyes of the LORD." Grace and divine favor can only be received, never achieved.

33:13. For "if, pray, I have found favor in your eyes" (*ʾim* or *ʾim-nāʾ* + perfect of *māṣāʾ*) in 33:13, see also Gen. 18:3; 30:27; 33:10; 47:29; 50:4; Exod. 34:9; Num. 11:15; 32:5; Judg. 6:17; 1 Sam. 20:29; 27:5; 2 Sam. 15:25; Esther 5:8; 7:3; 8:5.

33:13. If "find favor in the eyes of the LORD" appears 5x in this unit, the verb "know" appears 6x (vv. 12 [2x], 13 [2x], 16, 17). On the significance of six uses of "know" spread over six verses, see Muilenburg 1968: 176–81.

33:13. For the Hebrew "Let me know, please, your way," the Vulgate reads *Ostende mihi faciem tuam* ("Show me your face"), and LXX reads *Emphanison moi seauton* ("Show me yourself"). The Greek rendering is close to that of John 14:21, 22, "He who loves me . . . I too will love him and *show myself to him* [*emphanisō autō emauton*]. Then . . . Judas said . . . 'Why do you intend *to show yourself* [*emphanizein seauton*] to us and not to the world?'"

33:13. The last part of the verse, "for your people [is] this nation" (*kî ʿammĕkā haggôy hazzeh*) is one of the few places where the same verse refers to Israel as Yahweh's *ʿam* and *goy*. The expression "the people of the Lord" (*ʿam YHWH*) is common, but "the nation of the Lord" (*gôy YHWH*) never is used. And while there are hundreds of instances where "people," *ʿam*, has a pronominal suffix (as here, "*your* people"), there are only seven instances of "nation," *gôy*, with a pronominal suffix (Gen. 10:5, 20, 31, 32; Ezek. 36:13, 14, 15). See Speiser 1960.

33:14. "My face will go with you" is the way Biblical Hebrew says, "I will go with you in person." See Deut. 4:37, "He brought you out of Egypt by his face [i.e., in person] and his great strength" (AT); and Isa. 63:9, which LXX reads as "No messenger or angel but the Lord himself saved them" (and compare NIV's "and the angel of his presence [face] saved them," which follows the Hebrew text instead).

33:14. *Wahăniḥōtî* ("and I will give [you] rest") is a first-person Hiphil perfect of the verb *nûaḥ* (and compare the exact same verbal form in 2 Sam. 7:11; 1 Chron. 22:9; Ezek. 5:13 ["cease"]; 16:42 ["subside"]; 21:17 [22] ["subside"]), rather than a Hiphil form of *nāḥâ* ("lead, guide"). Both verbs occur in Exodus: *nûaḥ* in 10:14; 20:11; 23:12 (Qal); 17:11; 33:14 (Hiphil); *nāḥâ* in 13:17; 15:13; 32:34 (Qal). On the possible confusion of these two verbs in the Hebrew Bible, see Kselman 1981: esp. 540. God's promise to give rest recalls the famous words of Jesus, "Come to me, all you who are weary and burdened, and I will give you rest" (Matt. 11:28). God offers his people rest from weariness, on which topic see Brueggemann's (1972) fine essay, "Weariness, Exile and Chaos."

33:14. Brichto (1968: 46; 1992: 104), alone among modern commentators to the best of my knowledge, reads v. 14 as a question: "Suppose I go myself in the lead—will I satisfy you?" I do not believe such a reading is necessary to make sense of the verse.

33:15. The LXX reads the pronominal suffix on "take up" as a singular: "Do not take *me* up from this place" versus MT's "Do not take *us* up from this place."

33:16. Twice Moses uses the shorter form of the first-person independent pronoun, *ʾănî*, rather than the longer *ʾānōkî* ("*I* and your people . . . *I* and your people"). Revell (1995: 206–7) notes other instances of the use of *ʾănî* in a forceful and/or emotional presentation of a case: Gen. 31:44, 52 AT, Laban making a covenant with Jacob: "Come now, let's make a covenant, *I* [*ʾănî*] and you. . . . This heap is a witness . . . that I will not go past [*ʾănî lô*ʾ-ʾ*e*ʿ*ĕbôr*] this heap"; Num. 20:19 AT, Israel wanting passage through Moab: "We will go along the main road and should we drink your water, *I* and my livestock, we will pay for it"; Judg. 12:2, Jephthah justifying himself to the Ephraimites: "*I* and my people were engaged in a great struggle with the Ammonites." So with *ʾănî* we have "I and your people," "I and you," "I and my livestock," "I and my people."

33:16. *Pālâ* appears in the Niphal here and in Ps. 139:14 (NIV, "I am fearfully and *wonderfully made*") meaning "be separated, differentiated, distinguished," and in the Hiphil in Exod. 8:22 [18]; 9:4; 11:7 ("set apart, make a distinction"). *Pālâ* may be a phonetic variant of *pālāʾ* (e.g., Num. 6:2 AT, "If a man or woman *set apart* him/herself to make a special vow . . ."), although *pālāʾ* tends to focus on the wonderful, the extraordinary (as in Exod. 34:10, "I will do *wonders* [*niplāʾōt*]").

Commentary

This unit picks up immediately after the Lord's words to Moses in 33:1–3 **33:12–17**
about "going up," and after the "digression" of vv. 7–11. Brichto (1968: 45) calls the unit "the most astonishing (in sheer anthropomorphism) and the most opaque (in meaning) of biblical accounts of revelation." I suggest that vv. 12–17 are a fascinating illustration of the truth of v. 11a, "The Lord would speak to Moses face to face."

The structure of the passage is clear enough: (1) Moses airs his concerns to the Lord (vv. 12–13); (2) the Lord responds to those concerns (v. 14); (3) Moses airs a further concern (vv. 15–16); (4) the Lord addresses this concern (v. 17). So the movement is Moses>the Lord>Moses>the Lord, an *aba′b′* structure. It is clear that Moses does more talking and less listening, while the Lord does more listening and less talking.

Moses both underquotes and overquotes the Lord in v. 12. First, he quotes only a tiny portion of what the Lord has said in vv. 1–3, 5: "Bring up this people," but he omits any repeat of what the Lord has said about the angel, or his own absence, or the stubbornness of the people. Then he overquotes when he attributes to the Lord "I have known you by name." So Moses subtracts from God's words and adds to them. The Lord responds only to what Moses has said in v. 12a by saying, "My face will go with you" (v. 14), but ignores everything Moses has said in vv. 12b–13 (Irwin 1997: 630–31). In vv. 15–16 Moses ignores the Lord's ignoring his words in vv. 12b–13 and presses the Lord to include his people in the further journey. It is as if Moses says, "If it is just I you plan to go up with, forget it, but if your delivering grace includes your people, then count me in." As Childs (1974: 595) has said, "The effect [of Moses's words in v. 15] is to minimize the partial concession in order to press for the full request. . . . God's response [v. 14] had continued to attach to Moses himself. Moses shakes it off [vv. 15–16] and demands that the response include the people."

So understood, Moses comes off looking a whole lot better than the Lord! Israel owes as much a debt to Moses, and maybe more of a debt, as it does to Yahweh. Were it not for Moses, God would have wiped out Israel in chap. 32. Were it not for Moses, God would have been content with the deliverance of a solitary individual, Moses. Because of Moses's importunity, however, he will extend that grace to the multitudes, but not before Moses has convinced him of the same.

But surely Yahweh does not stand in the shadow of Moses. Surely the text is not designed to contrast Moses's passion with the Lord's parsimony, Moses's intercession with the Lord's indifference. One wonders if the text has the Lord answering the way he does in v. 14 as part of a deliberate divine strategy. It would be parallel to the Lord God's asking the in-hiding primal couple, "Where are you?" (Gen. 3:9), as if he is in the dark about their whereabouts. In the case of Gen. 3, the divine question provides Adam and Eve an opportunity freely to come forth on their own initiative, rather than wait to be flushed out from their hiding place. In the case of Exod. 33, the divine response provides Moses with the opportunity to bear Israel on his heart, to stand in the gap, to give Moses the opportunity to say to his Lord, "They need you much more than they need me," to say to Yahweh, "Israel (and I) need not only your 'present' presence, but also your 'active' presence." Individuals can be present, but do nothing or contribute nothing. Others can be present (God/Moses), and because they are, all the dynamics change for the better.

Wanting to See a Face, but Settling for a Back

(33:18–23)

Translation

[18]And he said, "Show me, please, your glory." [19]And he said, "I, I shall make all my benevolence pass over your face, and I shall proclaim the name LORD to your face. And I shall grant grace to whomever I grant grace, and have compassion on whomever I have compassion." [20]And he said, "You are not able to see my face, for an earthling cannot see me and survive." [21]And the LORD said, "Look, a place by me, and you position yourself on the crag. [22]And as my glory passes by, I shall place you in a fissure of the crag, and shield you with my palm until/at the time of my passing by. [23]Then I shall remove my palm so that you may see my back, but my face will not be seen."

Grammatical and Lexical Notes

33:18. The LXX's rendering of "show me your glory" (*deixon moi tēn seautou doxan*) recalls the Greek of John 14:8, "Show us the father" (*Deixon hēmin ton patera*). The Hiphil imperative of *rā ʾâ* occurs only four times in the Hebrew Bible, always with a pronominal suffix: here, "show me"; Judg. 1:24 ("show us"); Ps. 85:7 [8] ("show us"); Song 2:14 ("show me"). Twice earlier in this chapter (vv. 12, 13) Moses uses the Qal imperative of *rā ʾâ* (*rĕ ʾēh*, "Look") when speaking to God.

33:19. There are not many instances where the Hiphil of *ʿābar* is followed by the preposition *ʿal: ʾa ʿăbîr kol-ṭûbî ʿal-pānêkā* ("I shall make all my benevolence pass *over* your face"). One example is Gen. 8:1 AT, "And God caused a wind to pass over the earth" (*wayya ʿăbēr ʾĕlōhîm rûaḥ ʿal-hā ʾāreṣ*). See also Ezek. 5:1, "Take a sharp sword and use it as a barber's razor to shave your head" (lit., "and cause it to pass over your head [*wĕha ʿăbartā ʿal-rō ʾšĕkā*]"). Though the preposition does not follow the verb, the idea of God's "passing by" somebody is present with Elijah in 1 Kings 19:11, "Go out and stand on the mountain in the presence of the LORD, for the LORD is about to pass by [*wĕhinnēh YHWH ʿōbēr*]." During these experiences, Moses is in the cleft of a rock and Elijah is in a cave. See Cohn 1982: 342; B. Robinson 1991: 528.

33:19. For *qārā ʾ* (*bĕ*)*šēm* + object (here, "I shall invoke the name LORD"), see Gen. 4:26 AT, "And he called his name Enosh. . . . Men began to call on the name of the LORD." Smith (1993: 106) cites a number of passages with the phrase "call on my name, call on the name of the LORD," which he calls, "a cultic term for religious invocation and acknowledgment." See Gen. 4:26b; 2 Kings 5:11; Ps. 80:18 [19]; Isa. 65:1; Jer. 10:25; Joel 2:32 [3:5]; Zeph. 3:9; Zech. 13:9. What separates Exod. 33:19 from all these other references is that here the Lord does the invoking, and hence my translation in v. 19 as "proclaim."

33:21. "Position yourself on" is *nāṣab ʿal*, which refers either to standing "by" something/one or "on" something. So in Gen. 28:13 is the Lord "standing by" the ramp/ladder that Jacob sees in his dream, or "standing on" (top of) it? Or is he standing beside Jacob himself? The exact phrase is used in Gen. 18:2 ("Abraham looked up and saw three men *beside him* [NIV, "standing nearby"]") and with Joseph in Gen. 45:1: "Then Joseph could no longer control himself before all standing *beside him* [NIV, "all his attendants"]."

33:22. *Niqrâ* ("fissure, cleft, crevice") occurs only here and in Isa. 2:21, "They will flee to *caverns* in the rocks." The noun is formed from the uncommon verb *nāqar*, "gouge out" (Judg. 16:21; 1 Sam. 11:2).

33:22. *Kappî* is "my palm" rather than "my hand." The palm is the most tender part of the hand, an idea that is reflected in Isa. 49:16, "See, I have engraved you on the palms of my hands." Malul (1997: 356–60) has made a strong case for the reading "and shield you with my *wing/skirt* [*kānāp* instead of *kap*]." If we stay with traditional "palm," then this would be the only instance in the Bible where "hand" serves as a shield, a covering, a screen. The verb for "shield" (*śākak*, elsewhere *sākak*) is used with *kānāp* in Exod. 25:20 and 37:9 AT ("and the cherubim are to have their wings [*kānāp*] spread upward, shielding [*sōkĕkîm*] with their wings [*kānāp*] the propitiatory"). Also, the verb "*remove* my palm" in v. 23 (the Hiphil of *sûr*) frequently appears elsewhere for the removal of a garment (Exod. 34:34, a veil; Gen. 38:14, widow's clothes; Gen. 38:19, a veil; Esther 4:4, sackcloth; Deut. 21:13, clothes).

32:22. The last word of the verse, *ʿad-ʿobrî*, may be rendered "*until* my passing by" or "*at the time of* my passing by." For *ʿad* = "at the time of," see J. Thompson 1965: 223.

33:23. This is the only place in the Bible where God refers to his own back apart from Jer. 18:17, except that Exod. 33:23 uses *ʾăḥōrāy* while Jer. 18:17 uses *ʿōrep*, which is actually the back of the neck. Interesting is the scene Ezekiel sees (Ezek. 8:16) of twenty-five men with "their backs" toward the temple and their faces toward the east as they are bowing down to the sun. Note the translation NIV offers in a footnote to Gen. 16:13, the words of Hagar, "I have now seen the back of the One who sees me."

Commentary

33:18–23 One difference between vv. 18–23 and vv. 12–17 is that in vv. 12–17 Moses does more of the talking, and God does more of the listening. In vv. 18–23 that is reversed. God does more of the talking, and Moses does more of the listening. In these verses there is only one "he said" with Moses as the subject (v. 18), but three uninterrupted cases of "he said" with God as the subject (vv. 19, 20, 21). Using the NIV as our guide, note that vv. 12–17 record 118 words of Moses, but only 33 words of the Lord. By contrast, verses 18–23 record 116 words of the Lord, but only 5 words of Moses. (In the Hebrew, the total number of words is different, but the ratios are similar.)

All that Moses says in these six verses is "Show me, please, your glory" (v. 18). In v. 13 Moses asks to "know" God's way. Here he asks to "see" God's glory. The Scripture frequently mentions God's glory as something one can see: Exod. 16:7, "and in the morning you will *see* the glory of the Lord"; Isa. 35:2, "They will *see* the glory of the Lord, the splendor of our God"; Isa. 66:18, "And they will come and *see* my glory"; Ezek. 44:4, "I looked and *saw* the glory of the Lord filling the temple"; Matt. 24:30 (= Mark 13:26; Luke 21:27), "They will *see* the Son of Man coming on the clouds of the sky, with power and great glory"; Luke 9:32, "But when they [Peter, James, John] became fully awake, they *saw* his glory"; John 1:14, "We have *seen* his glory, the glory of the One and Only"; John 11:40, "Did I not tell you that if you believed, you would *see* the glory of God?"; John 12:41, "Isaiah said this because he *saw* Jesus' glory and spoke about him"; Acts 7:55, "But Stephen . . . looked up to heaven and *saw* the glory of God."

To return to Moses's request in v. 18, has he not already on several occasions observed God's glory? Note the references to the *kābôd*, glory, of God that Moses and all the Israelites could "see" (Exod. 16:7) when it "appeared" (16:10). Again, Moses and his people see the *kābôd* of God covering Mount Sinai (24:16–17), a "glory" that "looked like a consuming fire." In 40:34–35 Moses will get his fill of the Lord's *kābôd* when "it filled the tabernacle" with such intensity as to prohibit Moses's entrance.

In verse 18, however, when Moses requests to see God's glory, he may be asking for something other than another cloud or another thunderbolt or another flock of quail. In light of God's second word, v. 20, "You are not able to see my face," one suspects that Moses has asked to see God's face. It is not unreasonable for one with whom God speaks face to face to ask to see God's face. To be sure, there are places where "seeking God's face" is commendable: 1 Chron. 16:11, "Seek his face always"; 2 Chron. 7:14, "If my people, who are called by my name, . . . will seek my face . . ."; Pss. 27:8, "My heart says of you, 'Seek his face!' Your face, LORD, I will seek"; 105:4, "Look to the LORD and his strength; seek his face always." In these verses the language is highly figurative and speaks of the longing for intimacy with the Holy One. Do not just seek his hand, what he can give you; seek his face, himself.

Moses is after something more observable, the very divine visage. The problem with doing that does not lie with God (he does not say, "I am not able to do that"), but with the human mortal ("You are not able"). And here is the problem. As Barr (1960: 34) has said, "[The truth is] not so much that the deity is invisible, as that it is deadly for man to see him." Samson's father, Manoah, agrees with Yahweh: "We are doomed to die! We have seen God!" (Judg. 13:22). See also Deut. 4:33, "Has any other people heard the voice of God speaking out of fire, as you have, and lived/survived?"

What, then, of verses that speak of somebody's seeing God and living to tell about it? Examples include Jacob, who says, "I saw God face to face" (Gen. 32:30 [31]); or Moses, with whom God speaks or knows "face to face" (Exod. 33:11; Num. 12:8; Deut. 34:10). Hagar claims, "I have now seen the One who sees me" (Gen. 16:13; alternative reading in NIV note: "I have seen the back of the One who sees me," which is close to Exod. 33:23). In Isa. 6:1 the prophet says, "I saw the LORD seated on a throne." And finally, close to Exod. 33 is Exod. 24:10, which says that Moses, Aaron, two of his sons, and seventy elders "saw the God of Israel."

There are two ways to respond to this. One is to say that the verses cited in the above paragraph flatly contradict God's claim in Exod. 33:20. There must have been two mutually exclusive traditions in Israel that were never brought together: God cannot be seen. God can be seen. The other answer is to suggest that "saw" or "saw face to face," like "seek[ing] God's face," is the Bible's way of affirming the possibility and reality of an encounter or a relationship with God that is akin to a relationship between lovers. In such a case, the face of the Lord "must refer to his presence rather than his form" (Milgrom 1990: 368).

What Moses asks to see in v. 18 is God's glory. What he will get to see is God's goodness or benevolence, *kol-ṭûbî* (v. 19), and in 34:5–7 the Lord will expand further on what his goodness entails. In this instance, at least, God's glory is his goodness. It is not his power, his majesty, or his awesomeness that will pass by Moses, but his goodness. And Moses already has seen a lot of that. God has mercifully sustained his people in Egypt. That's his goodness. God has dramatically delivered his people from their captors. That's his goodness. God has graciously provided for his people in the wilderness and protected them. That's his goodness. God has lovingly entered into a covenant with his people at Sinai. That's his goodness. God has wisely given his people directives by which his people can best order their lives. That's his goodness. In 33:17, just before this unit, at Moses's urging God agrees to accompany Israel in its post-Sinai travels. That's his goodness. Commenting on the difference between seeing God's face and seeing God's goodness/benevolence, Kinlaw (2010: 175) says, "You can have a spiritual experience that is very exciting and yet is contentless. Or you can gain an insight into the character of the Eternal that will change you forever."

Twice in Exodus the Lord "passes" (*ʿābar*) by something. In conjunction with the Passover, he says in Exod. 12:12, "I will pass through Egypt" (*ʿābar bĕ*). Here, in 33:22, he will cause all his goodness to pass before Moses (*ʿābar ʿal*). The earlier "passing" was in judgment; the second passing is in benevolence. We have the same use of two different prepositions after *ʿābar* in Amos with opposite meanings. After describing a scene of judgment, the Lord says in Amos 5:17, "I will pass through [*ʿābar bĕ*] your midst." Then, after the vision of the plumb line and the basket of ripe fruit, the Lord says, "I will spare [*ʿābar lĕ*] them no longer" (Amos 7:8; 8:2).

The positive nuances conveyed by *ʿābar ʿal* or *ʿābar lĕ* and their translation in the LXX may illuminate a strange line in Mark 6. Jesus observes his disciples' difficulty in rowing against strong winds. Mark 6:48 records that Jesus, seeing their distress, "went out to them, walking on the lake." Then comes this phrase, "He was about to *pass by* them" (Mark 6:48c). Say what? Why walk on the water to help them, only to pass them by? (No wonder Matthew leaves this phrase out of his account [14:22–32]!) Is Jesus no different than the priest or Levite who "passes by" on the other side of the street rather than come to the aid of the battered crime victim (Luke 10:31–32)?

What we need to notice is that the verb for "pass by" in Mark 6:48c (*parerchomai*) is the one the LXX uses in Exod. 33:19, 22; 34:6 ("He passed in front of Moses"); and also for the Lord's word to Elijah in a passage that has parallels with Exod. 33:18–23, in 1 Kings 19:11, "Go out and stand on the mountain in the presence of the LORD, for the LORD is about to *pass by*." Far from meaning "ignore, be indifferent to," "pass by" in Mark 6:48 means "come to the aid of, graciously attend to the need of another." The disciples think Jesus is a ghost, but he is there when they need him. Moses may see only Yahweh's back, but Yahweh is there when Moses needs him. In both scenes the presence of a divine companion is real, yet elusive (Fleddermann 1983: esp. 391, 394).

There is a more obvious use of Exod. 33:18–23 in the NT than Mark 6, and that is Paul's quote of Exod. 33:19 in Rom. 9:15, "I will have mercy on whom I have mercy, and I will have compassion on whom I have compassion." While the apostle may be using this line from his Bible to lend further support to his argument in Rom. 9 supporting divine sovereignty in soteriology, it seems strange to suggest that this is its import in Exod. 33:19. I say "strange" because Exod. 33 (and 32), at best, soft-pedals the Holy One's acting unilaterally. On the contrary, there is much emphasis on the power of intercessory prayer and the Lord's saying to Moses words such as "Indeed, this matter about which you spoke I will do" (33:17).

Possibly the force of Paul's quote in Rom. 9 is not primarily to underscore divine sovereignty, as if God and God alone orchestrates who is in the kingdom and who misses it. It is God's willingness to forgive a sinful people and accompany them on their further trek that Exod. 32–34 highlights. We, if we were God, might not have been so gracious, but the Holy One will offer forgiving grace lavishly. As Birch (1991: 118) has said, "What is often mistaken in the church for a troublesome expression of divine arbitrariness is really an expression of divine freedom and a corrective to the tendency of religious institutions to define in their own terms who are deserving of God's mercy."

New Tablets, a Renewed Covenant, and New Wonders

(34:1–10)

Translation

[1]And the LORD said to Moses, "Carve for yourself two stone tablets similar to the original ones, and I shall inscribe on the tablets the words that were on the first tablets, which you shattered. [2]Be prepared by morning. You shall come up in the morning to Mount Sinai, and present yourself to me there on the mountain's peak. [3]Not a person shall come up with you; also not a person is to appear anywhere on the mountain, neither shall sheep nor cattle graze opposite that mountain." [4]And he carved two stone tablets similar to the original ones, and Moses rose early in the morning and went up to Mount Sinai just as the LORD had instructed him, and he took in his hand the two tablets of stone. [5]And the LORD came down in a cloud, [Moses] positioned himself with him there, and [the LORD] proclaimed the name LORD. [6]As the LORD passed before his face, he proclaimed, "The LORD, the LORD! A God compassionate and gracious, long-tempered, abounding in benevolence and trustworthiness, [7]who prolongs benevolence for millennia, who forgives iniquity and rebellion and sin, who, while surely not acquitting the guilty, assigns (the consequences of) the fathers' iniquity upon children and upon grandchildren, even upon descendants three and four generations removed." [8]Quickly Moses bowed groundward and prostrated himself. [9]He said, "If, pray, I have found favor in my Lord's eyes, may my Lord, please, go in our midst, however stiff-necked he is, and forgive our iniquities and our sin, and take us as yours."

[10]And he said, "For sure I am about to cut a covenant. Before all your people I shall work wonders that have not been created in all the earth and in all the nations. All the people in whose midst you (are) will witness the LORD's doings, how awesome it (is) what I am doing with you."

Grammatical and Lexical Notes

34:1. Hebrew grammarians often use the verb *šābar* to distinguish between the import of the Qal and Piel stems. In the Qal it means "to break," but in the Piel, as here, "smash, shatter." Thus the Piel intensifies the action conveyed by the Qal. For example, what can be broken simply by being snapped (such as a stick or rod, "The LORD has broken the rod/stick of the wicked" [Isa. 14:5], or a bone, "Do not break any of the bones" [Exod. 12:46]) needs only the Qal. But for something stronger, like stone tablets or bronze pillars (Jer. 52:17), the Hebrew uses the Piel. It is probably more complex than that. Possibly the choice between Qal and Piel of *šābar* depends on the range of effort: minimum>medium>more effort>maximum. The Piel of *šābar* is preferred where the object of the verb is plural and with larger objects. See Andersen and Freedman 1989: 250–52.

34:2. *Nākôn* ("be *prepared*"), the Niphal participle of *kûn* ("establish, prepare"), appears with the same stem and meaning but as a plural participle in Exod. 19:11, 15.

34:2. *Labbōqer* ("by morning") is different than *babbōqer* ("in the morning") two words later. The preposition *lĕ* prefixed to *labbōqer* is a temporal *lĕ* ("*by* morning"). See Meek 1948: 237; R. Williams 1976: §268; Waltke and O'Connor 1990: 206.

34:3. The verbs "appear" (*yērāʾ*) and "graze" (*yirʿû*) provide an instance of two words that are sound-alike (homophonic) pairs but are not root pairs. For examples of this elsewhere in the Hebrew Bible, see Berlin 2008: 109–10.

34:3. Throughout Exodus, the repeated references to Israel's sheep and cattle (Exod. 12:38; 17:3; 19:13; 34:3; also see Num. 14:33; 32:1) make their words in Num. 11:4 ("If only we had *meat* to eat") strange, hollow, and uncalled for.

34:5. It is debatable whether the subject of "positioned himself" (v. 5) and of "proclaimed" (vv. 5 and 6) is the Lord or Moses. Might Moses be the subject of one of the verbs ("positioned himself"), and Yahweh the subject of "proclaimed" in vv. 5 and 6? Or might Yahweh be the subject of "positioned himself" and Moses the subject of "proclaimed" in vv. 5 and 6? Exodus 33:21 and 34:2 use the Niphal of *nāṣab* for Moses's standing or positioning himself. Hence, it seems likely that "position himself" in Exod. 34:5 (Hitpael of *yāṣab*) would apply to Moses. Plus, every other time the latter form appears in Exodus, it has a human subject: 2:4 (Miriam); 8:20 [16]; 9:13 (Moses); 14:13; 19:17 (the Israelites). Finally, the use of *qārāʾ bĕšēm YHWH* in 33:19, in which the Lord is the speaker, certainly argues for the Lord's being the subject of the exact same phrase in Exod. 34:5. It is unlikely, therefore, that Yahweh would be the subject of *wayyiqrāʾ* ("proclaimed") in v. 5, but Moses the subject of *wayyiqrāʾ* in v. 6.

34:5. "To proclaim/invoke/call upon the name of the LORD" occurs about twenty-five times in the Bible. With only two prophets does the phrase appear: Elijah (1 Kings 18:24) and Elisha (2 Kings 5:11). So the phrase does not refer to an exclusively prophetic function, nor even to intercessory prayer. This is something humanity can do (Gen. 4:26), along with patriarchs (Abraham: Gen. 12:8; 13:4; 21:33; Isaac: Gen. 26:25), Israel (Isa. 12:4; 64:7 [6]; Joel 2:32 [3:5]; Zeph. 3:9; Zech. 13:9; etc.), and even "outsiders" (Isa. 41:25; and maybe Jer. 10:25). If my understanding of v. 5 is correct (see previous note), the Lord too employs the phrase (Exod. 33:19; 34:5). See Balentine 1984: 165–66.

34:6. In *wayyiqrāʾ YHWH YHWH*, it is possible to translate, "and the LORD proclaimed, 'The LORD!'" or "and he proclaimed, 'The LORD, the LORD!'" That is, the first *YHWH* may be either the subject of the verb or part of the proclamation. If it is the second, it parallels other repetitions of personal names: "Abraham! Abraham!" (Gen. 22:11); "Moses! Moses!" (Exod. 3:4); "Samuel! Samuel!" (1 Sam. 3:10); "My God, my God" (Matt. 27:46; Mark 15:34); "Martha, Martha" (Luke 10:41); "Simon, Simon" (Luke 22:31).

34:6. *Raḥûm wĕḥannûn* ("compassionate and gracious") is one of many instances in the Hebrew Bible of assonance as a means of expressing emphasis, according to Saydon (1955: esp. 296). For the same two adjectives in the same order, see Pss. 86:15; 103:8. For the opposite order, *ḥannûn wĕraḥûm*, see 2 Chron. 30:9; Neh. 9:17, 31; Pss. 111:4; 112:4; 145:8; Joel 2:13; Jon. 4:2.

34:6. Because of the etymological relationship between the adjective *raḥûm*, the verb *rāḥam*, and the noun *reḥem* ("womb"), many commentators believe that the *r-ḥ-m* root refers to motherly compassion (e.g., Trible 1978: 50, commenting on the root in Jer. 31:20). That may indeed be the case, but in all thirteen instances, *raḥûm* is a masculine adjective, and as Gruber (1983: 352n4) has reminded us, "Native speakers of a language tend to be far less conscious of the etymological history of words or the origin of idioms than are preachers, philologists, and students of Hebrew as a foreign language." So whether Moses or Jeremiah was aware that *r-ḥ-m* is a uterine metaphor referring to motherly love, womblike love, is open to question.

34:6. *ʾErek ʾappayim* ("long-tempered") is, literally, "long of nose/nostrils." Along with *rab-ḥesed weʾĕmet* ("abounding in benevolence and trustworthiness"), both expressions illustrate what grammarians call an epexegetical genitive: "long *with respect to* his nose" or "abounding *in respect to* benevolence." See Waltke and O'Connor 1990: 151; Arnold and Choi 2003: 10–11.

34:6. For *ʾerek . . . rab* ("long of . . . abounding in"), see Num. 14:18; Neh. 9:17; Pss. 86:15; 103:8; Prov. 14:29; Joel 2:13; Jon. 4:2. See also the Phoenician inscription of Azitawaddu from Karatepe in which he asks the gods that he be given "*length* of days [*ʾrk ymm*] *and a multitude* of years [*wrb šnt*]."

34:7. Outside of Exod. 34:7 and Ps. 31:23 [24], the singular participle *nōṣēr* ("who prolongs"), without any pronominal suffix, occurs only in Wisdom literature: Job 7:20 ("watcher"); 27:18 ("a watchman"); Prov. 13:3 ("guards"); 16:17 ("guards"); 24:12 ("guards"); 27:18 ("tends"); 28:7 ("keeps"). Dentan (1963) has traced many vocabulary links between Exod. 34:6–7 and the Wisdom literature of the Bible.

34:7. For *nāśāʾ ʿāôn* ("forgive iniquity"), see Num. 14:18; Pss. 32:5; 85:2 [3]; Isa. 33:24; Hosea 14:2 [3]; Mic. 7:18, all of which have the Lord as the subject of the verb. When a person is the subject of this expression, it means "bear responsibility for, be held responsible for" (Exod. 28:38, 43; Lev. 5:1, 17; 7:18; 17:16; 19:8; 20:17b, 19b, 20; Num. 18:1, 23).

34:7. When a negative particle is with a finite verb form and the infinitive absolute form of that verb, the negative particle comes after the infinitive absolute and before the finite verb (*wĕnaqqēh lôʾ yĕnaqqeh*), "while surely not acquitting the guilty." Compare Deut. 21:14, "You must not sell her [*ûmākōr lōʾ-timkĕrennâ*]."

34:7. The verb *nāqâ* ("acquit") carries the basic idea of clearing away guilt, or a debt, or some other kind of obligation. In the Piel, God is most often the subject of the verb (Exod. 20:7; 34:7; Num. 14:18; Deut. 5:11; Jer. 30:11; 46:28; Job 9:28; 10:14; Ps. 19:12 [13]). When a person is the subject (in the Niphal), the meaning is "(not) go unpunished," especially in Proverbs (Prov. 6:29; 11:21; 16:5; 17:5; 19:5, 9; 28:20).

34:7. *Pāqad ʿāôn* of X *ʿal* ("who assigns the iniquity of X upon . . .") is present in Exod. 20:5; Num. 14:18; Deut. 5:9. It is similar to *pāqad dām* of X *ʿal* in Hosea 1:4, "I will soon punish the house of Jehu for the massacre/blood of Jezreel."

34:8. For *wayyiqqōd*, "and he bowed" (from *qādad*), see Exod. 12:27b. What Moses does in v. 8 (both verbs), the Israelites do in 12:27b.

34:9. On whether *bĕʿênêkā ʾădōnāy* should be translated as "in your eyes, O Lord" (i.e., a vocative), or "in my Lord's eyes," see Andersen 1969, who opts for the latter.

34:9. "My Lord," instead of "the Lord," follows the LXX (*ho kyrios mou*).

34:9. I shall have more to say below on the conjunction *kî* in *kî ʿam-qĕšēh-ʿōrep*. How should it be translated? "*Because/for* it is a stiff-necked people" (i.e., a causative *kî*), or "*although* it is a stiff-necked people" (i.e., a concessive *kî*), or "*however much* it is a stiff-necked people" (i.e., an emphatic concessive *kî*)? I can find no reference to the use of *kî* in Exod. 34:9 in Muilenburg's (1961) detailed study of the linguistic and rhetorical uses of this particle. In his equally lengthy study of *kî*, Schoors (1981: esp. 272) cites *kî* in Exod. 34:9 as an emphatic concessive *kî* ("however much"). Yet he remarks that a concessive meaning of *kî* is defendable.

34:9. I have rendered *ûnĕḥaltānû* as "and take us as yours," a Qal, second-person perfect with pronominal suffix from the verb *nāḥal*. Deuteronomy uses *nāḥal* only in the Hiphil stem, the meaning of which is "*give/grant* an inheritance" (Deut. 1:38; 3:28; 12:10; 19:3; 21:16; 31:7; 32:8). The Qal of *nāḥal* means "*receive/take as* an inheritance."

34:10. To MT's "I am about to cut a covenant," the LXX adds, "I, the Lord, am about to cut/make a covenant with you [Moses]."

34:10. *Niplāʾōt* ("wonders") is a Niphal feminine-plural participle of *pālāʾ*. The word has occurred with pronominal suffix back in 3:20 ("And I will strike the Egyptians with all *my wonders* that I will perform among them").

Commentary

There are four clear subunits in these ten verses: (1) Moses prepares to go up the mountain to meet with the Lord (vv. 1–4); (2) the Lord appears and reveals to Moses privately what kind of a God he is (vv. 5–7); (3) Moses worships and once more makes intercession for his people (vv. 8–9); (4) the Lord promises to renew the covenant and to work wonders (v. 10).

It appears that the Lord has both carved and written on the first tablets (24:12 **34:1–4**
and esp. 32:16). Here he delegates the carving to Moses but reserves the inscribing for himself. That Moses is invited to participate in such a task is a testimony to his invaluable role and ministry in leading Israel through these uncertain times.

But why not go up immediately to meet with the Lord, once the carving work is completed? Why wait until morning of the next day (v. 2)? Emergencies, if they truly are that, cannot be postponed. One possibility is that the emphasis in chap. 34 on the morning of the next day (which is a day of renewal) balances the emphasis on "tomorrow" and "the next day" in 32:5–6 (which was a day of blasphemy). Again, one might suggest that the morning is a time of God's deliverance, when the forces of darkness are defeated (Gen. 19:27; Judg. 6:28; 1 Sam. 5:4; Isa. 37:36; Dan. 6:19). And where better are the forces of darkness defeated than at the empty tomb "early in the morning" (Luke 24:1)? The morning is also a great time to hear from God (Pss. 59:16; 90:14; 143:8).

More than likely, however, I believe that the Lord's instructions to Moses about ascending early on the morning of the next day have another explanation. In a number of passages, the Lord or his servant tells somebody "to consecrate/sanctify yourself, for tomorrow I/he will. . . ." See Exod. 19:10–15; Num. 11:18; Josh. 3:5; 7:13–14. The same idea may be present in Gen. 35:2–7, where Jacob has the people purify themselves and change their clothes after ridding themselves of foreign gods, before moving on to Bethel (presumably the next day) and erecting an altar. Note also that Job first has his sons purified, then early in the morning (of the next day) he offers appropriate sacrifices (Job 1:5). So in Exod. 34:2, 4, Moses must first purify himself (by means of washings or ablutions), then ascend the next day. In most of these passages (esp. from Exodus, Numbers, and Joshua), the Lord is planning to do something amazing the "next day." Here that something amazing is a renewal of the covenant.

I agree with interpreters who believe that the Lord is the speaker in vv. 6–7. **34:5–7**
Earlier, in chap. 32, Moses speaks to the Lord about the Lord. Here the Lord speaks to Moses about the Lord. Talking about oneself is a way of drawing attention to oneself. That exercise can be, to others, either helpful and illuminating, or obnoxious. Whether it is the first response or the second depends on *how* one talks about oneself. Does the individual describe himself in a way

that makes the listener feel inferior, or does the individual describe himself in a way that makes the listener grateful?

Nowhere in this litany does the Lord draw attention to his attributes of power, perfection, or holiness. Everything the Lord says autobiographically is something that God is or does for the benefit of others, especially his chosen people. For example, the first item listed is his "compassion, mercy." The LXX's word for this is *oiktirmōn*. In the "Sermon on the Mount," Matthew has Jesus say, "Be perfect, therefore, as your heavenly Father is perfect (*teleios*)" (5:48). The Lukan equivalent (6:36) has Jesus say, "Be merciful, just as your Father is merciful [*oiktirmōn*]." Although the NT describes God as "perfect, *teleios*," in the OT he is never called "perfect, *teleios*," or "blameless, *amōmos*." He is perfect. He is blameless, but that particular vocabulary does not appear there. *Teleios*, no! *Oiktirmōn*, yes!

The significance of vv. 6–7, the Lord's self-declaration, can be seen by observing how many other times the language of these two verses reappears in other passages. There are at least eight instances: Num. 14:18; Neh. 9:17b; Pss. 86:15; 103:8; 145:8; Joel 2:13; Jon. 4:2; Nah. 1:3. Six of these eight quote only the first part and do not quote the last part about God's not totally exonerating the people and making later generations bear some of the consequences of their ancestors' sins (the two exceptions are Num. 14:18 and Nah. 1:3). Slivers of Exod. 34:6–7 are also present in passages like Deut. 4:31; 2 Chron. 30:9; Neh. 9:31; Pss. 78:38; 86:5; 111:4; 112:4; 116:5.

While Exod. 20:5–6 does not use the language of God's attributes found in 34:6–7a, it does provide a striking parallel with 34:7b, for both speak of the fallout on later generations, either for weal or for woe. There are several contrasts between the two. First, 34:5–7, unlike 20:5–6, does *not* refer to God as a "jealous" God. Second, 20:5–6 begins by talking about punishment first (20:5b), then moves to talking about showing love (20:6). The later passage reverses that. It begins by talking about showing mercy (34:7a), then moves to talking about delayed punishment (34:7b). Third, Exod. 20:6a restricts God's show of mercy "to those who love me and keep my commandments." There is none of that language in 34:6–7. As Moberly (1983: 88) has put it so well, the absence in chap. 34 of any words like "to those who love me and keep my commandments" means "that Yahweh's mercy toward Israel is independent of their responding in the right way. Even when Israel is disobedient it is still the recipient of the divine goodness." Fourth, all the positive truths about God that 20:5–6 express are put within the larger context of a double prohibition (19:3, 4). There is not even a single prohibition in 34:5–7. Fifth, 34:7, when speaking of God's forgiveness, seems to search the Hebrew lexicon exhaustively to make sure to miss no "sin" family word—"who forgives *iniquities* and *rebellion* and *sin*." Janzen (2009: 36) has captured in powerful words the thrust of vv. 6–7, verses he refers to as "the settled character of God":

> It is easy to gain the impression that this proclamation [34:6–7] is integral to the Sinai covenant and its logic. If that is so, it is because the logic of the Sinai covenant, with its life-or-death sanctions, has become tempered by the compassionate ethos of the ancestral paradigm. And where the Sinai covenant, so to speak, "loses its temper" in the face of Israel's rebellions and idolatries, Israel's continuation before God turns on a reversion to the ethos of the ancestors.

It would be "nice" if this litany stopped after v. 7a. We have seen above that six of eight uses of Exod. 34:6–7 elsewhere do so stop! But although that would still be a glorious truth, it would only be part of the truth about the divine-human relationship. There is no such thing as iniquity without consequences, either for the perpetrator or for the perpetrator's kin. As Brueggemann (1997: 217–18) puts it, the truth of v. 7b, "indicates that Yahweh takes affront . . . very seriously, so seriously as to affect the relationship for as many as four generations. . . . It alerts Israel to the reality that Yahweh's full character is not subsumed under Yahweh's commitment to Israel in solidarity. There is something in Yahweh's sovereign rule . . . that is not compromised or conceded, even in the practice of solidarity."

Moses repeats two of the three "sin" words ("iniquity" and "sin") that the **34:8–9**
Lord in v. 7a has said he would forgive. Maybe he omits the third, "rebellion, transgression," because that is the strongest, most brazen word for "sin." As I indicated in a grammatical note above on 34:9, it is challenging to know how best to translate the *kî* in "*kî* stiff-necked he/it is." Most modern versions opt for the concessive *kî*: "*although/even though* it is a stiff-necked people" (NIV; NRSV; Childs 1974). A few opt for a causative *kî* (Alter 2004, "*for/because* it is a stiff-necked people"), or an emphatic concessive (Brichto 1992, "*however* stiff-necked a people it is"). The particle *kî* occurs about four thousand times in the Hebrew Bible with a very wide variety of nuances and uses, and so pinning down its meaning in v. 9 is difficult. Moberly (1983: 90) leans toward the emphatic concessive use and renders the phrase, "*Although* they are *indeed* a stiff-necked people, yet forgive our iniquities." So understood, Moberly says of this passage that it contains "a theology of the grace of God unsurpassed in the OT." See also NLT's "Yes, this is a stubborn and rebellious people, but please forgive our iniquity and our sins."

I believe the words "Before all *your* people" must refer to Moses. But in the **34:10**
second half of the verse, phrases like "in whose midst *you* are" and "I am doing with *you*" make more sense if we understand that in 10b "you" is the Israelites. Certainly throughout the following section, vv. 11–26, every "you" refers to Israelites.

The Lord's answer (in v. 10) to the prayer of Moses (in v. 9) is a promise to (re)make his covenant with Israel. To describe this, the Lord uses two similar, yet different, verbs. One is "*work* wonders" and "how awesome it is what I *am doing*," both of which are *ʿāśâ*. The second is "that have not *been created*," the Niphal of *bārāʾ*. The parade illustration of where the biblical text uses both *ʿāśâ* and *bārāʾ* for a divine work is the creation story in Gen. 1:1–2:4 (*ʿāśâ*: Gen. 1:7, 16, 25, 26, 31; 2:2, 4; *bārāʾ*: Gen. 1:1, 21, 27 [3x]; 2:4). One difference between these two verbs, and a difference that does not apply to their presence in Exod. 34:10, is that only the Lord is used as subject of *bārāʾ* in the Qal and Niphal stems, while both the Lord and a mortal may be the subject of *ʿāśâ*. What I am suggesting is that the use of these two verbs in Exod. 34:10, well known from the opening chapters of Genesis, may be the narrator's way of connecting creation with covenant renewal. Creation is a work of wonder. So is re-creation. Newness is a work of wonder. So is renewal.

The language of v. 10 (spoken by God) is close to that of Exod. 15:11c (sung to God). Compare 34:10, "work wonders" (*ʾeʿĕšeh niplāʾōt*) and "how awesome it is what I am doing with you" (*nôrāʾ hûʾ ʾăšer ʾănî ʿōśeh ʿimmāk*), with 15:11c, "Awesome in praise, worker of wonders" (*nôrāʾ tĕhillōt ʿōśēh peleʾ*). The passages share (1) *nôrāʾ*, the Niphal participle of *yārēʾ*; (2) the verb *ʿāśâ* in participial form; and (3) *niplāʾōt* and *peleʾ*, a Niphal participle used nominally and a noun respectively, both formed from the verb *palaʾ*. The Lord's capacity to do the wonderful, the amazing, the awesome does not terminate at the sea crossing. Rather, the wonders observed there are but a foretaste of the even more wonderful things to happen.

Commandments for Coping in Canaan

(34:11–26)

Translation

[11]"Take heed for yourself about that which I am instructing you today. Surely I am about to drive out from before you the Amorite and the Canaanite and the Hittite and the Perizzite and the Hivite and the Jebusite. [12]Be very careful lest you cut a covenant with the inhabitant of the land against whom you are coming lest he become a snare in your midst. [13]Instead, their altars you are to demolish and their pillars you are to shatter, and their sacred poles you are to cut down. [14]For you are not to prostrate to another god—for the LORD, Jealous One (is) his name, a jealous God (is) he—[15]lest, in your cutting a covenant with the inhabitant of the land, they lust after their gods and sacrifice to their gods, and invite you and you eat of his sacrifice, [16]and you take from among his daughters for your sons, and his daughters lust after their gods, and they cause your sons to lust after their gods.

[17]"Molten gods you shall not make for yourself.

[18]"The Pilgrimage Festival of Flatbread you shall observe. Seven days you shall eat flatbread, as I instructed you, at the set time of the month Abib, for in the month of Abib you came out of Egypt.

[19]"Every first issue of a womb is mine and all your livestock, the male first issue of ox and flock animal. [20]The first issue of a donkey you may redeem with a sheep, or if you do not redeem it, you shall break its neck. Every firstborn of your sons you must redeem, and they shall not see my face empty-handed.

[21]"Six days you may work, but on the seventh day you must desist; even at plowing time or harvesting time you must desist. [22]The Pilgrimage Festival of Weeks you shall keep for yourself, with the first yield of the wheat harvest; and the Pilgrimage Festival of Ingathering at the turn of the year. [23](These) three times a year, all your males shall see the face of the Master, the LORD, the God of Israel. [24]For I am about to dispossess nations from before you, and extend your border, and no person will covet your land when you go up to see the face of the LORD your God three times in the year.

[25]"You shall not slaughter together with any leavened bread the blood of my sacrifice, nor shall the sacrifice of the Pilgrimage Festival of Passover remain by morning.

[26]"The choice firstfruit of your soil you shall bring to the house of the LORD your God.

"You shall not boil a kid in its mother's milk."

Grammatical and Lexical Notes

34:11. The Qal imperative of *šāmar* begins this verse, *šĕmor-lĕkā* ("Take heed for yourself"), but the Niphal imperative of *šāmar* begins v. 12, *hiššāmer lĕkā*, "Be very careful," a form that has appeared in 10:28 and 23:21.

34:11. For earlier uses of *gāraš* ("drive out") in Exodus, see 2:17; 6:1; 10:11; 11:1 [2x]; 12:39; 23:28, 29, 30, 31; 33:2. Midianite shepherds are the subject of the verb in 2:17; Pharaoh in 6:1; 10:11; 11:1 [2x]; 12:39; the Lord in 23:28–30; 33:2. All are in the Qal stem except for 12:39 (Pual).

34:11. *Mippānêkā* ("from before you") most often has a geographical meaning, as here, but it may also carry a causative meaning, as in Josh. 2:10, "We have heard how the Lord dried up the water of the Red Sea *for you*" (i.e., "in your behalf, for your sake").

34:12. For *môqēš* ("snare"), see 23:33; Deut. 7:16; Judg. 2:3; 8:27; Ps. 106:36. Pharaoh's officials have accused Moses of being a "snare" to them (Exod. 10:7).

34:13. The verse is similar to Deut. 7:5. Both begin with adversative *kî* ("instead"). Both use *nātaṣ* for "demolishing" altars and *šābar* (Piel) for "shattering" pillars. Exodus 34:13 uses *kārat* for "cutting down" sacred poles while Deut. 7:5 uses *gāda*ʿ.

34:13. The LXX consistently translates *maṣṣēbâ* ("pillar," from the verb *nāṣab*) as *stēlē* ("stele"). This verse, Deut. 16:22; and Hosea 3:4; 10:1–2 suggest that the pillar was placed near an altar. The NIV tends to translate the Hebrew word as "sacred stone" rather than "pillar." Leviticus 26:1 and Deut. 16:22 label a "pillar" as idolatrous. But they are not always such. Exodus 24:4 has Moses setting up twelve stone pillars as a memorial of the covenant at Sinai (also see Josh. 4:20; 24:27). Jacob sets up a pillar three times, all with impunity (Gen. 28:18, 22; 31:45, 52; 35:20). The first memorializes his first encounter with God. The second is a boundary stone in his covenant with Laban. The third is a memorial for his deceased wife, Rachel.

34:13. The Hebrew word for "sacred pole" is *ʾăšērâ*. Hebrew "Asherah" is the equivalent of Ugaritic "Athirat," consort of the high god El. Sometimes she is called in those texts *ʾilt*, "goddess," or *qnyt ilm*, "the procreatress of the gods," or *ʾum ʾilm*, "mother of the gods," or *rbt ʾatrt ym*, either "Lady Athirat of the sea" or "the lady who traverses/treads on the sea." Most likely in a passage like Exod. 34:13, "Asherah" is a cult object, a wooden pole symbolizing the Canaanite goddess. See Day's fine study (1986).

34:14. "Another god" (*ʾēl ʾaḥēr*) occurs only here in the Hebrew Bible. The more usual expression is "other gods" (*ʾĕlōhîm ʾăḥērîm*), as in the first commandment (Exod. 20:3 and Deut. 5:7). The phrase *ʾēl ʾaḥēr* is similar to *ʾēl zār* ("foreign god") and *ʾēl nēkār* ("alien god") in Ps. 81:9 [10].

34:14. The opposite of *ʾēl ʾaḥēr* is Yahweh as *ʾēl qannāʾ*, "a jealous God." See also Exod. 20:5 (= Deut. 5:9); Deut. 4:24; 6:15; Josh. 24:19; Nah. 1:2. Exodus 34:14 is the one verse in which *qannāʾ* occurs twice ("Jealous One [is] his name, a jealous God [is] he").

34:15. *Kārat* ("cut") is used in this unit for the right kind of "cutting" (v. 13b), and the wrong kind of "cutting" (v. 15).

34:15. For *zānâ ʾaḥărê* ("lust after [false gods]"), here and in v. 16, see Lev. 17:7; 20:5, 6; Deut. 31:16; Judg. 2:17; Ezek. 6:9. Numbers 25:1 uses *zānâ ʾel* instead of *zānâ ʾaḥărê* (NIV, "indulge in sexual immorality with"). Ezekiel 16:26, 28 ("You engaged in prostitution with the Egyptians . . . with the Assyrians too") also uses *zānâ ʾel*, but in a figurative sense. Normally when *zānâ* refers to actual sexual activity, it takes a zero object (Gen. 38:24; Lev. 21:9; Hosea 2:5 [7]). The term need not be limited to prostitution, sex for hire, but may refer to any sex outside of a sanctioned relationship.

34:15. For "call/invite" (*qārāʾ*) to an immoral feast, see Num. 25:1–2, "Moabite women who *invited* them to the sacrifices to their gods."

34:15. Two wrong "eatings" (*ʾākal*)—32:6 in conjunction with the golden calf scenario, and 34:15 here in consort with the sacrifices of pagans—follow one good "eating" after the ratification of the covenant, in 24:11.

34:16. This verse, which prohibits marriage with non-Israelites, is much like Deut. 7:3, yet with one difference. Exodus 34:16 speaks only against Israelite men's marrying non-Israelite women, while

Deut. 7:3 includes this but adds to the prohibition Israelite women's marrying non-Israelite men (probably a less frequent occurrence).

34:17. *Massēkâ* ("molten [gods]") is the word Exod. 32:4 and 8 used for the golden calf. Thus *ʿēgel massēkâ* in chap. 32 parallels *ʾĕlōhê massēkâ* in 34:17. The exact same phrase (and prohibition) of 34:17 reappears in Lev. 19:4. The Hebrew word is frequently paired with *pesel* (e.g., Deut. 27:15, "Cursed is the man who carves an image/statue [*pesel*] or casts an idol/molten image [*massēkâ*])." The difference between the two is that *pesel* is a sculpted image (note the verb *pāsal*, "carve," in 34:1), while *massēkâ* is a molten image (from the verb *nāsak*, "forge, cast").

34:19. Obviously the phrase *peṭer reḥem* ("first issue of the womb") refers to the firstborn of the mother. The noun *peṭer* is formed from the verb *pāṭar*, which means, "loose, send forth, dismiss." For the phrase, see Exod. 13:2, 12, 13, 15. A much more common word for "firstborn" is *bĕkôr* (Exod. 6:14; 11:5; 12:12, 29; 13:2 [which uses both *bĕkôr* and *peṭer reḥem*]; 13:13 [with *peṭer* and *bĕkôr*]; 13:15 [using *bĕkôr* 3x and *peṭer reḥem*]).

34:19. *Tizzākār* may be an error for *hazzākār* ("male"). As it stands, *tizzākār* ("to be born a male") is a Niphal imperfect of the verb *zākar*, which appears only here and is not to be confused with the similarly written and common verb *zākar*, "remember."

34:20. The verb for "redeem" (3x) in this verse is *pādâ*. B. Levine (1989: 198) notes that throughout Lev. 27, a chapter wholly devoted to the topic of redemption, the verb for "redeem is *gāʾal* (10x—as Qal: Lev. 27:13 [2x], 15, 19 [2x], 20a, 31; as Niphal: Lev. 27:20b, 27b, 28, 33). By contrast, the other verb for "redeem," *pādâ* (and the one used 3x in Exod. 34:20), occurs only twice: Lev. 27:27a (Qal), 29 (Niphal). Levine believes that Lev. 27:27a chooses *pādâ* for the redemption of an unclean animal under the influence of Exod. 34:20a, which also uses *pādâ* for the same. Milgrom (2000b: 2390) offers another explanation. While granting that elsewhere in the Hebrew Bible *pādâ* and *gāʾal* are used in parallel, he suggests that in legal texts *pādâ* is the price set by the sanctuary for redemption, which others pay but not the owner. *Gāʾal*, however, is the price the owner himself pays to redeem something. I am not sure on what basis he is able to make such a distinction. Plus, Lev. 27:27 uses both verbs interchangeably. "If it is one of the unclean animals, he may redeem it [*pādâ*]. . . . If he does not redeem it [*gāʾal*], it is to be sold at its set value" (AT).

34:21. Dahood (1981: 414–15) discerns a poetic tricolon in this verse: "Six days shall you work / but on (*bĕ*) the seventh day shall you rest / from (*bĕ*) plowing and from (*bĕ*) harvesting you shall rest." Thus, for Dahood the preposition *bĕ* has two meanings in the same verse, "on" and "from." For *ḥārîš* ("plowing time") and *qāṣîr* ("harvesting time"), see Gen. 45:6 ("And for the next five years there will be no *plowing* and *reaping*"); 1 Sam. 8:12 ("Some [of your sons] he [the king] will assign . . . *to plow* his ground and *reap his harvest*").

34:22. *Ḥag šābuʿōt* ("Pilgrimage Festival of Weeks") is first identified by its Greek name "Pentecost" in two intertestamental books, Tob. 2:1 and 2 Macc. 12:31–32. Earlier Exod. 23:16 labeled this occasion "The Pilgrimage Festival of the Harvest [*ḥag haqqāṣîr*]." Numbers 28:26 calls it "The Day of Firstfruits [*yôm habbikkûrîm*]."

34:22. For *tĕqûpat haššānâ* ("the turn of the year"), Exod. 23:16 uses *ṣēʾt haššānâ* ("the going out of the year"); see my note at 23:16.

34:23. The verse is almost identical to 23:17 and Deut. 16:16a. Both Exod. 34:23 and Deut. 16:16a use *rāʾâ* (Niphal) *ʾet* for "show themselves to/see the face of/appear in the presence of," while Exod. 23:17 uses *rāʾâ* (Niphal) *ʾel* for the same. Gevirtz (1968: 275) points to Num. 6:25 ("The Lord make his face to shine upon you [*yāʾēr ʾel*]") and Ps. 67:1a [2a] ("May God . . . make his face shine upon us [*yāʾēr ʾet*]") as an instance of a particle (*ʾet*) functioning exactly as does a preposition (*ʾel*). Also, the word *hāʾādōn*, "the Master," is present in Exod. 23:17, but not in Deut. 16:16a.

34:24. The verb *yāraš* ("dispossess") occurs only here in Exodus apart from the last phrase in 15:9, where it refers to the destroying hand of Israel's enemy. By contrast, it appears numerous times in

Deuteronomy (seven times in the Qal; sixty-six times in the Hiphil). Both in the Qal and Hiphil stems the verb in Deuteronomy means "dispossess by extermination." A pointed illustration of that is Deut. 2:12, "Horites used to live in Seir, but the descendants of Esau *drove them out*. They destroyed [*šāmad*] the Horites."

34:24. The verb for "extend, widen" in "extend/widen your border" is *rāḥab* (Hiphil). Akkadian provides two verbs with a parallel meaning: (1) *ruppushu*: "I appointed governors over Egypt. I thus *enlarged* the territory of Assur, king of the gods" (*sha Ashshur shar ilani urappisha kishurrush*); (2) *shurbu*: "who *enlarges* the territory of Ashshur" (*musharbu miṣir mat Ashshur*). Texts are cited in Paul 1991: 69n244.

34:24. The verb for "covet" (*ḥāmad*) is the same as in the tenth commandment (Exod. 20:17 [2x]). Its use in 34:24 clearly shows that *ḥāmad*, at least sometimes, may convey more than simply desire or intention. The verse does not intend to say that nobody will find the land of the absent worshipers desirable. Rather, the Lord promises that no individuals will make plans to invade the property even though it is defenseless and attractive prey to others.

34:25. The opening verb in this verse is *lōʾ-tišḥat* ("you shall not *slaughter*"), while the opening verb in the parallel verse, 23:18, is *lōʾ-tizbaḥ* ("you shall not *sacrifice*"). Milgrom (2000b: 2070) suggests that the change is to show that only slaughter is permitted the laity, and that the actual offering of the sacrifice on the altar falls to the priests exclusively.

34:25. "The sacrifice of the Pilgrimage Festival of Passover" (*zebaḥ ḥag happāsaḥ*) is another way of saying, "The suet/fat of my festival offering" (*ḥēleb-ḥaggî*) in 23:18b.

34:25. For "not remain/be left over until/by morning," see its use with Passover (Exod. 12:10a; 23:18; 34:25; Num. 9:12; Deut. 16:4b); with the thanksgiving/fellowship offering (Lev. 7:15; 22:30); with the well-being/peace offering (Lev. 7:17; 19:6); with the ordination offering (Exod. 29:34; Lev. 8:32). All these injunctions are addressed to the laity, including the latter two, which involve laity in the process of ordination toward priesthood.

34:26. Milgrom (1991: 190) notes that *rēʾšît* refers to first-*processed* food while *bikkûrîm* refers to first-*ripe* food. Then again, *rēʾšît* in 34:26 (= 23:19) may simply mean "first" or "best, choice."

34:26. "The house of the Lord your God" need not necessarily refer to the central sanctuary (in Jerusalem). The reference may be simply to a regional sanctuary.

Commentary

34:11–26 The first thing one observes about 34:11–26 is that it is amazingly close to chap. 23. Here are the parallels:

Eliminating the nations (34:11 = 23:21)
Make no covenant with them (34:12 = 23:32)
They will lure you to serve their gods (34:13–16 = 23:33)
Pilgrimage Festival of Flatbread (34:18 = 23:15a)
Don't show up empty-handed (34:20b = 23:15b)
On the seventh day no work (34:21 = 23:12)
Pilgrimage Festival of Weeks/Harvest (34:22a = 23:16a)
Pilgrimage Festival of Ingathering (34:22b = 23:16b)
Males appear before God three times a year (34:23 = 23:17)

No blood with leaven, leave nothing over (34:25 = 23:18)
Bring the choice first yields to God's house (34:26 = 23:19)
A kid in its mother's milk (34:26b = 23:19b)

Two items are present in chap. 34, but absent in chap. 23. One is the data about the firstborn of animals clean and unclean, and of sons (34:19–20). The other is the prohibition about making molten gods (34:17). I cannot suggest a compelling reason for the omission of data about the firstborn in chap. 23 (or its insertion in chap. 34), but there is a good explanation for the omission in chap. 23 of the prohibition in 34:17. As we saw above in the grammatical note on v. 17, the Hebrew word for "molten (god)" was the one chap. 32 uses for the golden calf. A *massēkâ* has become an issue only after chap. 23, and hence its absence in chap. 23.

The data about the firstborn comes between laws dealing with worship (17>18>19–20 < 21–26). The flow of thought moves from special days (v. 18) to special animals and sons (vv. 19–20), and back to special days (vv. 21–26). Three times a year a male Israelite is to appear before the Lord. Every seventh day he is to cease from work. And one time in his lifetime an Israelite male is to redeem his wife's firstborn son. Thus Yahweh is Lord of one's calendar and Lord of one's children, Lord of festivals and Lord of families.

It is, nevertheless, quite a shift for modern (Christian) readers of Scripture to move from the "compassionate, gracious, long-tempered" Yahweh of v. 6 to the "jealous" Yahweh of v. 14. How does one move from an emphasis on a God who in v. 7 extends kindness transgenerationally almost interminably and forgives all kinds of sin to "be sure not to boil a kid in its mother's milk" of v. 26b?

G. Campbell Morgan, the famous London pulpiteer of yesteryear, expounded on Jesus's three temptations. Morgan notes that in the second temptation, as Matt. 4 records it, the devil says to Jesus, "It is written . . ." (Matt. 4:6). Jesus responds by saying, "It is written *again* . . ." (Matt. 4:7, KJV/NKJV). Seizing on the word "again," Morgan (1903: 181–82) points out that the truth never lies in simply "It is written" but also in "It is written" and "Again it is written." Thus one portion or verse of Scripture must be balanced with another portion or verse of Scripture to get at the whole truth.

Verses 6–7 focus on a God who exudes compassion, while vv. 11–26 focus on a God who issues commandments. Verse 10 focuses on a God who is about to "cut" a (renewed) covenant with Israel, while v. 13 challenges Israel to "cut" down the pagans' sacred poles. In v. 6 Israel's God is *ʾēl raḥûm wĕḥannûn* ("compassionate and gracious"), but in v. 14 Israel's God is *ʾēl qannāʾ* ("jealous"). The kindness that the Lord has extended and will extend to Israel (v. 7), Israel is not to extend to the peoples they encounter in Canaan (vv. 12–13). The firstborn son may bear some of the consequences of his father's sin (v. 7), but the father must redeem and dedicate him to the Lord anyway (v. 20), for the son is both his father's (v. 7) and the Lord's (v. 20).

In preparing to enter Canaan, Israel will need two things. For one, and this is by far the prior need, Israel will absolutely depend on the presence of a God, the likes of which vv. 6–10 declare. Israel is doomed to destruction and servility without that kind of a God.

But second, by God's help Israel needs to commit itself to living obedient, holy lives, lives that conform to divine regulations, which reveal God's likes and dislikes. That will not be easy or automatic. If Israel tragically fails when by itself in a wilderness, how will Israel fare when in the glare of "Canaanite lights"? It cannot be a case simply of "What happens in Canaan stays in Canaan." The function of vv. 11–26 is to provide divine guidelines for faithful living.

If one focuses only on vv. 1–10 to the exclusion of vv. 11–26, the result is antinomianism. If one focuses only on vv. 11–26 to the exclusion of vv. 1–10, the result is legalism. The Bible endorses neither unbridled freedom nor vacuous conformity. In the happy marriage of God's grace and believers' faithful living, there is the divine-human relationship the Lord intends. What God has brought together, let no one put asunder.

Moses the Writer and Yaḥweh the Writer

(34:27–28)

Translation

[27]And the Lord said to Moses, "Write down for yourself these words, for according to these words I have cut with you a covenant and with Israel." [28]And he was there with the Lord forty days and forty nights. Bread he did not eat and water he did not drink. And he [the Lord] wrote on the tablets the words of the covenant—the Ten Words.

Grammatical and Lexical Notes

34:28. One may "write" (*kātab*) on tablets (34:1b, 27, 28; Deut. 10:2, 4) or "inscribe" (*ḥārat*) on them (32:16) or "carve" (*pāsal*) them (34:1a) or "inscribe" (*ḥāraš*) on them (Jer. 17:1) or "make them plain" (*bāʾar*, Hab. 2:2).

34:28. It is clear that Moses is the subject of *kātab* in v. 27. I will discuss below why the Lord must be the understood subject of *kātab* in the next verse, v. 28. Hence I place [the Lord] in square brackets in my translation.

Commentary

For over a month Moses has been alone with the Lord, and during that period **34:27–28**
has neither eaten nor drunk anything. This is his second forty days and nights stay on the mountain for an audience with God (24:18). The first forty-day stay is not described as a time of fasting. The obvious parallel to Moses's forty-day fast is Jesus's forty-day fast (Matt. 4:2; Luke 4:2b). First Samuel 29:20 tells us that King Saul is wiped out after a one-day fast. How does Moses make it for forty, especially without water? The only explanation is the sustaining grace and power of God in the life of his servant who has seen bitter water turned sweet, and an almost interminable supply of water flowing out of the rock.

We are not told anything about any of Moses's activities during this forty-day period of solitary fasting. Brongers (1977), in his study of biblical references to fasting, suggests five different occasions for fasting and cites Exod. 34:28 (along with Judg. 20:26; 1 Sam. 28:20; 1 Kings 21:9; 2 Chron. 20:3; Esther 4:16) as illustrations of what he calls "preparatory/introductory fasting" (1977: 3, 8). Fasting is sometimes associated with praying (1 Sam. 7:5–6; 2 Sam. 12:16;

Neh. 1:4; also 2 Chron. 20:3; Joel 1:14; Acts 13:2) but not always. It could be that Moses spends much of these forty days writing down all the things the Lord tells him to write.

The words that the Lord instructs Moses to write down (v. 27) must be the words the Lord gives him in vv. 11–26. And it could include much more than that. After all, all the material in Leviticus and through Num. 10:10 that the Lord speaks to Moses he speaks while the Israelites are still encamped at Sinai. When does Moses put all those directives into writing? There is no account after Exod. 34 of Moses going up Sinai for another audience with God. To be sure, in Exod. 19 and 34 God speaks to Moses on the mountain top, but in Lev. 1:1 he speaks to Moses "from the tent of meeting."

If Moses is the writer referred to in v. 27, the Lord must be the subject referred to in v. 28b. There are several reasons for this (Moberly 1983: 103). First, in "*he* was there . . . *he* ate . . . *he* drank . . . *he* wrote," one might expect that because the first three subjects of the verb are Moses, then more than likely Moses is also the subject of the fourth "he." This is not necessarily so. Hebrew can shift the subject of third-person verb within the same sentence without clearly indicating so, such as we observed in 34:5 (see comments there). Second, making the Lord the subject of the verb in v. 28b makes the claim of that verse consistent with 34:1 (and with Deut. 10:4). Otherwise, there is a blatant inconsistency between the identity of the writer of the Decalogue in 34:1 and 34:28b. Third, in v. 27 the Lord tells Moses to write down "these words" (2x), while v. 28 uses other phraseology, "the words of the covenant—the Ten Words." If Moses is the writer in v. 28b, then one would expect the language to echo v. 27, that is, "And he [Moses] wrote *these words*." Fourth, the note in v. 28a (Moses's forty-day fast) would more than likely have followed v. 28b rather than preceded it, if Moses were the writer in v. 27 and 28b. Why break up two references to the same author's scribal activities through this parenthetical remark?

When Israel gets ready to leave Sinai, she will not depart with only word-of-mouth instructions. Rather, she will have the word of the Lord written down, written down by Moses, and written by the Lord himself. This does not imply that everybody is literate and so able to read these words, or even have access to them. Moses, Aaron, and selected others will be the readers and teachers.

The Veiled and Unveiled Moses

(34:29–35)

Translation

[29]And it happened when Moses came down from Mount Sinai—and two tablets of the testimony in Moses's hand when he came down from the mountain—that Moses was unaware that the skin of his face had become radiant when he spoke with him. [30]And Aaron saw, and all Israel's sons, Moses, and lo, the skin of his face was radiating light, and they were afraid to come near him. [31]But Moses called out to them, and Aaron and all the chieftains of the congregation came back to him and Moses spoke to them. [32]Afterward all Israel's sons came near, and he instructed them about what the LORD had spoken with him on Mount Sinai. [33]When Moses finished speaking with them, he placed over his face a veil. [34](And so it was that) whenever Moses came before the LORD to speak with him, he would remove the veil until he came out. He would then go out and speak to Israel about whatever he had been instructed. [35]Israel's sons would see Moses's face, that the skin of Moses's face radiated light. Only then would Moses place the veil back on his face until he came to speak with him.

Grammatical and Lexical Notes

34:29. Three times (vv. 29, 30, 35) this unit uses the verb *qāran* for Moses's face "radiating light" or "glowing." All three of these occurrences are in the Qal stem. The only other occurrence of this verb is once in the Hiphil, Ps. 69:31 [32]: NIV, "This will please the LORD more than an ox, more than a bull *with its horns* [*maqrin*, Hiphil participle, and so better "developing its horns"] and hoofs." The uncommon verb *qāran* provides the common related noun *qeren* which means "a horn." It occurs about a hundred times in the Bible, and refers to: (1) a projection on an altar, the altar's horns; (2) the horn of an animal; (3) as a metaphor for pride and vanity or for strength.

It is this cognate connection between the verb *qāran* and the noun *qeren* that has led to the idea that Moses's face developed horns, or hornlike phenomena that emanated from his face. Thus, among the ancient versions, LXX translates the verb nonliterally, Moses's face "shone" (*dedoxastai*), while Vulgate translates more literally, Moses's face "was horned," that is, v. 29, "he knew not that his face was horned [*ignorabat quad cornuta esset facies sua*]." I shall have more to say on this in the commentary section. See Kasher (1997), who documents instances in postbiblical literature of a "horned" Moses, and Propp (1987), who debates whether the biblical text suggests Moses's face was "transfigured" or "disfigured," and who opts for the latter.

34:29. Again there is a challenge to identify the subject and pronominal object at the end of the verse: "when he [the Lord?] spoke with him [Moses?]," or "when he [Moses?] spoke with him [the Lord?]." I lean toward the latter in light of the end of v. 35, which is more transparent.

34:33. The Hebrew word for "veil," here and in 34–35, is *masweh* and occurs only in these three verses. There are four other Hebrew words for "veil": (1) *ṣāʿîp*, worn by Rebekah (Gen. 24:65) and by Tamar (Gen. 38:14, 19); (2) *ṣammâ*, worn by the beloved woman in the Song (4:1, 3; 6:7) and by the "Daughter of Babylon" (Isa. 47:2); (3) *rādîd*, worn by the "women of Zion" (Isa. 3:23, NIV, "shawls") and by the beloved woman of Solomon's Song (5:7, NIV, "cloak"); (4) *rĕʿālâ*, worn by the "Daughters of Zion" (Isa. 3:19). Karl van der Toorn (1995) has helpfully discussed these five words for "veil" in his article in the Milgrom *Festschrift*. Exodus 34:33–35 appears to be the only time a man wore a veil.

We remain uncertain about the origin of Hebrew *masweh*. It appears to have some connection with the word *sût* in Gen. 49:11, a portion of Jacob's blessing on Judah: "He will wash his garments (*lĕbušô*) in wine, his *robes* (*sûtōh*) in the blood of grapes." Rendsburg (1999: 27) draws a parallel between *sût* (and by extension *masweh*) formed from the verb *swy*, and *rût* ("Ruth") formed from the verb *rwy*, "to refresh."

34:34. The verbs in vv. 34–35 have a frequentative sense. Hence, I insert at the start of v. 34, "(And so it was that"), thus making vv. 34–35 both parenthetical and proleptic.

34:34. *ʾEt ʾăšer* sometimes has an all-inclusive sense, "whatever" or "everything that": Ezek. 2:8, "But you, son of man listen to *what(ever)* I say to you . . . and eat *what(ever)* I give you"; Ezek. 3:1, "eat *what(ever)* is before you."

Commentary

34:29–35 The first few verses of this section (vv. 29–33) describe the uniqueness of Moses's final descent from Mount Sinai after an audience with the Lord. He has been up and down this mountain before, several times in fact, but never with such a divine facial glow to show for it like this time. Note, for example, his several ascents and descents mentioned throughout chap. 19, but in each his face, when he comes down, looks exactly like it did when he went up. Maybe there is some facial uniqueness when Moses descends from the mountain carrying the tablets after an earlier forty-day-and-night absence from the people (24:18b; 32:1, 19–20). On that occasion his face is red (with rage). Here his face is radiant (with divine glory). In 32:19 the emphasis is on what Moses sees after his descent ("When Moses . . . *saw* the calf and the dancing"). In 34:30 the emphasis is on what Aaron and his people see after Moses's descent ("When Aaron and the Israelites *saw* Moses . . ."). What Moses sees is blatant apostasy. What Aaron and Israel see is a beaming face. What Moses sees makes him throw a fit. What Aaron and his comrades see makes them fearful.

Verses 30a, 33, and by extension vv. 34–35, inform the reader that when Moses first descends the mountain his face is brilliantly radiant (but unveiled), and continues to be so as long as he is transmitting to them the laws the Lord has revealed to him. And later, whenever Moses enters the interior of the tent of meeting to meet with his God his face is again brilliantly radiant (but unveiled), and continues to be so as long as he imparts the message he has just received from God. At all other times (which probably would be most of the time), he places a veil over his face. The reason for donning the veil may be to conceal the facial brilliance at more "ordinary, common" times, but the text does not explicitly say that. Or maybe the veil covers the absence of that glow on Moses's visage, a glow that will not return until he reappears before the Lord to have the glory renewed and recharged. The text does not explicitly say that either. He needs no veil when he enters God's presence. He needs no veil when he speaks for God. But when he engages in banter and chitchat with neighbors, or shares dinner with Zipporah, or strolls through the camp with his grandchildren, out comes the veil.

One might think Moses's wearing a veil would be so curious as to be a conversation starter, especially among children: "Mommy, why is that man wearing a mask?" We are not even sure that the veil Moses wears is thick enough or large and dark enough to cover his face completely or just part of his face, akin to that worn by the Lone Ranger, or by Batman, or by a mime or jester or clown. They all wore/wear a mask when they are "at work." Moses puts on his veil when he is "off work." Possibly the veil is thin enough that if one looks closely at Moses he can make out the features of Moses's face behind the veil.

This veiling of Moses takes place while he and Israel are still at Sinai. Moses will be around for almost forty more years after they leave Sinai. How many times will Moses meet with God and subsequently mingle with his people during those several decades? And yet, there is not a single reference to his veil after Exod. 34 either by Moses himself, or by anybody contemporary with Moses, or by anybody else throughout OT history. The veil (*masweh*) that prevents anybody from gazing on Moses seems to be replaced by the veil (*pārōket*) that separates the holy place from the holiest place lest anyone gaze on the Holy One (see Dozeman 2000: 39–43). I do not know what would have happened to the person who tore off Moses's veil, but I do know what would have happened to the person who burst through the *pārōket*.

Another Hebrew verb that means "to shine, be bright" (Qal) or "make shine, make/give light" (Hiphil) is *ʾôr*. Had it been used here, it would have produced a good sound-alike effect with "the skin" of Moses's face (*ʾôr* and *ʿôr*). The verb *ʾôr* appears in Exod. 25:37 (Qal) to refer to the lamps of the lampstand "giving light," and 13:21 and 14:20 (both Hiphil) for a divine "lighting" of the night (see Gen. 1:15, 17). That *ʾôr* may describe the appearance of (part of) one's face is evidenced by 1 Sam. 14:27, 29, which uses *ʾôr* to refer to the "shining" or "brightening" of Jonathan's eyes. In a verse much like those in Exod. 34, the prophet says, "Arise, shine (*ʾôr*), for your light has come, and the glory of the Lord rises upon you" (Isa. 60:1).

So, why use the very rare verb *qāran* for "shine/was radiant" in Exod. 34 rather than the more common *ʾôr*? I am inclined to agree with those commentators who suggest the use of *qāran* (lit., "sprout/develop horns") is an echo of the molten calf story of chap. 32, and ties the two chapters together. Whom will God have to lead his people, the horned calf or bull of chap. 32, or the "horned" Moses of chap. 34? Will he go with the bovine of chap. 32 or with he-of-the-beaming-face of chap. 34? See Moberly 1983: 109; Sarna 1991: 221.

Not only does Exod. 34 provide the only reference to Moses's veil, but it also provides the only reference to his shining face. Two ideas come from his brilliant visage. First, the divine glow develops on Moses's face only after an extended stay in the presence of God, forty days and nights. Divine glory does not come upon those who treat time with God as a drive-through window. Second, when he descends the mountain he is completely in the dark about the light on his face. He does not descend pompously and say to his underlings, "What do you think of this?"

Several places in the NT connect with some of the data of Exod. 34:29–35. One is John 20:1–9, the story of Peter and the "other disciple" arriving at Jesus's tomb. When Peter enters the tomb, he too sees the linen strips just lying there, as does the disciple who remains outside, but he also sees "the burial cloth" (*soudarion*) neatly folded up by itself. This Greek word is used only four times in the NT, and translates as "a piece of cloth" or a "napkin" in Luke 19:20, and as "handkerchief" in Acts 19:12, but "face-veil" seems appropriate for its use with Jesus in John 20:7 and with Lazarus in John 11:44. Jesus, implies John, removes his face-veil, neatly wraps it and sets it by itself before he leaves the tomb to stay with his disciples before returning to his Father. Moses too removes his veil when he returns to the presence of God. Unlike Jesus, however, Moses has to put his veil back on repeatedly (see Schneiders 1983).

Another possible NT connection is the Mount of Transfiguration incident, especially the versions in Matthew and Luke. Mark notes only that Jesus's clothes become dazzling (Mark 9:3), but both Matthew (Matt. 17:2) and Luke (Luke 9:29) say his "face" shone too. In both cases Moses and Jesus are coming down a mountain. Compare the similarity of the LXX Greek of Exod. 34:29, *katabainontos de autou ek tou orous* ("when he came down from the mountain") with the Greek of Mark 9:9, *kai katabainonton autōn ek tou orous* ("as they were coming down the mountain"). We can also note the emphasis in 24:16 on the cloud covering the mountain "for six days" with Jesus's ascending the mountain "after six days" (Mark 9:2), or God's speaking from within a cloud (Exod. 24:16b; Mark 9:7). Marcus (2009: 1114) notes that when the people see Moses and his shining face at the foot of the mountain they are "afraid" (Exod. 34:30b LXX, *ephobēthēsan*), but when the people see Jesus and his shining face at the foot of the mountain, they are "overwhelmed" (NIV), better, "awestruck" (*ekthambeisthai*, Mark 9:15b). Marcus then adds, "Moses' radiance is terrifying. Jesus' is awe-inspiring and attractive."

The most obvious place where Exod. 35:29–35 surfaces in the NT is 2 Cor. 3:7–18. In the first section of this unit (vv. 7–11) Paul compares and contrasts the glory of the old covenant with the glory of the new covenant. The key word here is "glory" (*doxa*) and "be glorious" (*doxazein*). The noun appears 8x and the verb 2x (v. 10). Three times Paul's logical argument takes the form, "If A is true, how much more/less is B true" (for other instances of this form of rhetoric, see, e.g., Rom. 5:9; Heb. 9:14; 10:29; 12:25). Note the introductory "if" at or near the beginning of vv. 7, 9, 11. Yes, the ministry of the old covenant brought glory, but such glory pales in comparison to the glory the Spirit brings in the ministry of the new covenant.

Twice in 2 Cor. 3:7–11 (vv. 7b, 11a) and once in vv. 12–18 (v. 13b) Paul refers to the "fading" glory that was on Moses's face. "Fading" is the translation of the NIV, and of many other versions too. In my judgment that mistranslates the Greek verb *katargeō*, used in feminine, present passive participle form in v. 7 (*tēn katargoumenēn*), and used in neuter, present passive participle form in vv. 11 and 13 (*tou katargoumenon*).

The NIV does not use the word "fade" or "fading," or any other word like "fade," when it renders *katargeō* elsewhere. Here are some samples with the NIV translation: Rom. 3:3, 31 ("nullify"); Rom. 4:14 ("worthless"); Rom. 6:6 ("be done away with"); Rom. 7:2, 6 ("released from"); Eph. 2:15 ("abolishing"); 2 Thess. 2:8 ("destroy"). The verb means "to nullify, get rid of, terminate, render ineffective," and that nuance is much stronger than "fade" or "fading." Hence, the glory on Moses's face is "transient" or "transitory" glory, not because its glow gradually diminishes like a flashlight whose battery is running low, but because it has now forever been eclipsed and removed by the glory of the ministry of the new covenant.

In the second half of this section, 2 Cor. 3:12–18, Paul makes the point that he and any of Messiah's followers are both unlike Moses and like Moses. Paul and believers are unlike Moses in that they need no veil to conceal God's glory. Rather, they proclaim God's glory openly and boldly (vv. 12–13).

However, we are like Moses in the following way (thus making Moses not a type of Christ as he is elsewhere, but making him a type of the disciple of Christ). When he returns to the Lord's presence he removes his veil (Exod. 34:34). Paul broadens that idea in 2 Cor. 3:16 to say, "But whenever anyone [not just Moses!] turns to the Lord, the veil is taken away." Interestingly, the LXX of Exod. 34:34 uses *eisporeueto* (an imperfect indicative) for Moses's "returning to" the Lord, but Paul uses *epistrepsē* (an aorist subjunctive, i.e., not a narration of a past fact, but a statement of possibility) for anyone "turning to" the Lord. It is the same verb Paul uses to describe the conversion experience of the Thessalonians: "You *turned to* God from idols to serve the living and true God" (1 Thess. 1:9). With conversion comes the glory of God. And where is this glory better revealed than on the faces of those who have experienced and are experiencing such transformative grace (v. 18)? Followers of Jesus are both the light of the world and reflectors of the Light of the world. The better we do the second of these, the better we do the first. (For further analysis of this 2 Corinthians reference and its connections with Exod. 34, see the commentaries on this biblical book. I have learned much and have profited greatly from Hays's [1989: 131–53] insightful analysis of this Corinthian passage.)

PART 7

Tabernacle Built, God's Glory Fills

(35:1–40:38)

The Lord's revelation to Moses about how he wants Moses to erect the tabernacle (part 5, chaps. 25–31) almost never gets off the ground. That is because Israel's idolatrous sin (in the absence of Moses) nearly sabotages the plan before Moses can ever implement it. The Lord does not want a people who are engaging in unholy behavior building a holy place. Only the prayers of Moses, who stands in the gap (Ps. 106:23), and the Lord's compassion and graciousness to Israel prevent the tabernacle from being nothing more than a blueprint on paper, a plan and pattern but not a reality (part 6, chaps. 32–34). So fortunately, Exodus does not end with God or Moses disappointingly holding a rolled-up blueprint that is dead in the water.

The renewal of the Lord's covenant with his people now permits the instruction stage of the tabernacle (25–31) to move to the implementation stage of the tabernacle (35–40). There is an interesting parallel between the first verse of part 6 (32:1) and the first verse of part 7 (35:1). Both use the same Hebrew verb for "gather" (*qâal*), albeit in different stems. One would not observe this if reading the NIV, which renders the first *qāhal* in 32:1 as "they *gathered* around Aaron and said, 'Come, make us gods,'" and the second *qāhal* in 35:l as "Moses *assembled* the whole Israelite congregation." Both are quite acceptable translations of the Hebrew verb, but let us be a bit more literal: "they assembled against Aaron" (32:1) and "Moses *assembled* the whole Israelite congregation" (35:1). What a contrast between two kinds of assembling! The first, hostile and belligerent; the second, peaceful and instructive. The first, God-dishonoring; the second, God-honoring. The first, Israel talks; the second, Israel listens.

Interestingly, the *last* thing God speaks to Moses about in the instruction section is proper observance of the Sabbath with cessation from any and all kind of work (31:14–17). By contrast, the *first* thing Moses speaks to Israel about in the implementation section is proper observance of the Sabbath (35:2–3). The Sabbath emphasis has moved from the *omega* position to the *alpha* position.

Saving some topic for last can be a way of designating the last item a climactic one, or giving it the status of a tack-on. Perhaps Moses begins the way he does lest the people so focus on the magnitude of the directives he is about to give them that they miss the two-verse footnote on the Sabbath he adds at the end. Much better to get it wrong about the sea-cow hides than get it wrong about the Sabbath.

If in part 6 the Israelites do everything wrong, in part 7 they do everything right. How faithfully do they carry out the directives Moses gives them in 35:5–39:43? Chapter 39 tells us, not once but about ten times, that Israel does "just as the LORD had commanded Moses." So, the Moses who blasted wayward Israel in chap. 32 blesses faithful Israel in 39:43b. And no wonder! Compare what Moses "saw" in chap. 32 with what he "saw" in chap. 39.

And if chap. 39 highlights a faithful Israel, chap. 40 highlights a faithful Moses whose duty is to put all these materials together in their proper place. He too does, so the text tells us a half dozen times or so, just as the Lord instructs him.

Exodus 35:1–40:35 is all about the tabernacle. The last three verses of Exodus (40:36–38) begin and end by talking about "travels": "In all the *travels* of the Israelites . . . in the sight of all the house of Israel during all their *travels*." We move, then, from tabernacle to travels. As such, the ending in the book of Exodus does not lead so much into Lev. 1 as it does into Num. 10:11 and following when such "travels" resume.

The truth on which Exodus concludes is that wherever traveling Israel goes she will have a tabernacling God with her. The God of the mountain is now the God in the midst of the camp. Only time will tell whether Israel honors that divine immanence or acts contrariwise regardless.

A Holy Day and Holy Donations

(35:1–20)

Translation

[1]And Moses assembled the entire congregation of Israel's sons and said to them, "These are the words whose doing the LORD has commanded. [2]Six days work shall be done, but on the seventh day there shall be for you holiness, a most restful rest of the LORD. Anybody doing on it (any) work shall be put to death. [3]You shall not kindle a fire in any of your settlements on the day of the Sabbath."

[4]And Moses said to the entire congregation of Israel's sons, saying, "This (is) the word that the LORD commanded, saying, [5]'Take from what is with you a contribution to the LORD. Any whose heart moves him shall bring it (as) the LORD's contribution: gold and silver and bronze, [6]and blue and purple and crimson material, and linen and goat hair, [7]and reddened ram skins, dyed dolphin skins, and acacia wood, [8]and oil for the lamp, and spices for the oil of unction, and for the perfumed incense, [9]and onyx stones, and stones for being set in the ephod and in the breastpiece.

[10]"'And every wise-hearted one among you shall come and do everything that the LORD has commanded: [11]the dwelling place, its tent and its cover, its clasps and its boards, its bolts, its posts and its sockets; [12]the ark and its poles, the propitiatory and the propitiatory's cover, [13]the table and its poles, and all its furnishings, and the bread of the Presence; [14]and the lampstand for the light along with its furnishings, and its lamps and oil for the light, [15]and the altar of burnt offering and the bronze grating that goes with it, its poles and all its furnishings, the laver and its stand, [17]the hangings of the Court, the posts and sockets, and the screen for the Court's gate; [18]the pegs of the dwelling place, and the pegs of the Court and their cords; [19]the service-vestments to officiate in the holy place, the holy vestments for Aaron the priest, and his sons' vestments for priestly service.'"

[20]And the entire congregation of Israel's sons went out from before Moses.

Grammatical and Lexical Notes

35:1. "Assembled" is the Hebrew verb *qāhal* (Hiphil) followed by the accusative particle *ʾet*. It is the same verb Exod. 32:1 uses in the Niphal stem for Israel's "ganging up" on Aaron in light of Moses's protracted absence.

35:2. For other places that use the passive of *ʿāśâ* ("shall [not] be done") rather than the active in conjunction with prohibited Sabbath work, see Exod. 31:5; Lev. 23:3.

35:2. For *šabbat šabbātôn* ("a most restful rest") again with the Sabbath, see Exod. 31:15; Lev. 23:3; with the Day of Atonement (Lev. 16:31; 23:32); with the Sabbatical Year (Lev. 25:4). By contrast, the festivals are called simply *šabbātôn* (Lev. 23:24, trumpets; Lev. 23:39 [2x], tabernacles).

35:2. The preposition *lĕ* on the third word in *šabbat šabbātôn laYHWH* may be translated as "*to* the LORD," or as "*of* the LORD." See Milgrom 2000b: 1962, who argues strongly for the second option.

35:4. The occasions on which the Lord instructs Moses to assemble (v. 1) and speak to (v. 4) "the entire congregation of Israel" are few and far between, and hence are most likely times of very important revelations. See my comment on this phrase at 12:3.

35:5. For *tĕrûmâ* referring to the voluntary "contributions" given for the building of the tabernacle, see Exod. 25:2–3.

35:5. The Hebrew verb for the "moving" of one's heart is *nādab*. Some form of the root *n-d-b* occurs frequently with the giving of gifts for the sanctuary: the verb *nādab* (25:2; 35:21, 39); the adjective *nādîb* in construct form (35:5, 22); the noun *nĕdābâ* (35:29; 36:3). The meaning of the root can best be determined by noting the parallel words in Num. 21:17–18: "Spring up O well, Sing about it, about the well the princes (*śārîm*) dug, that the nobles of the people (*nĕdîbê hāʿām*) sank." In Judg. 5:2, 9 (the Song of Deborah) the Hitpael of *nādab* appears in participial form to refer to the individual of means who voluntarily answers the call to arms or who contributes his resources to the fighting enterprise. The bottom line is that a person who is described as *n-d-b* is magnanimous.

35:5. *Yĕbîʾehā ʾet tĕrûmat YHWH* ("he shall bring it [as] the Lord's contribution") demonstrates the use of a verbal pronominal suffix together with a nominal object in apposition. Compare for another example Lev. 13:57, *bāʾēš tiśrĕpennû ʾēt ʾăšer-bô hannāgaʿ*, "with fire you shall burn it, whatever has the mildew."

Commentary

35:1–20 This first unit in the "implementation" section about the tabernacle's construction has two parallels with earlier chapters in the "instruction" section. Verses 1–3 = 31:12–17 (keeping the Sabbath), and vv. 4–9 = 25:1–7 (the voluntary contribution of materials necessary for building the tabernacle). Verses 10–20 are similar to 31:6b–11, with both 31:6b and 35:10 speaking to the one "wise of heart" (*ḥăkam-lēb*). Most commentators take 35:1–19 as the unit, but I prefer 35:1–20. In v. 1 Moses assembles and addresses the people, and in v. 20, after hearing Moses's message, the people leave and return to their own tents to fetch the requested gifts. They say nothing. They simply retire to their own abode to donate willingly to the announced building program.

Note that while the Sabbath instruction concludes chaps. 25–31 (31:12–17), it introduces the data in chaps. 35–40 (35:1–3), albeit in briefer form (three verses versus six verses) and with one added instruction: "You shall not kindle a fire." Maybe the demands of building this edifice as quickly as possible will call for a seven-day workweek. May one put aside the prohibition about not working on the Sabbath Day when one is engaged in such a sacred enterprise? Apparently not. Under Pharaoh's supervision there was no respite from labor, no Sabbath. All that changes for the better when Pharaoh is out of the picture, and God speaks to his people about the need to halt all work once every seven days.

If 35:1–3 addresses Yahweh's lordship over one's time, 35:4–9 addresses his lordship over one's possessions. But there is a difference. Giving gifts for the sanctuary is voluntary. Observing properly the seventh day is anything but voluntary.

Like the Spirit's *charismata*, of which the NT speaks, not every family just happens to have in its tent a dyed dolphin skin, an ounce or two of gold, a couple of onyx stones, and so forth. Bring what *you* have, donate what *you* can donate. As Paul says, "Each man should give what he has decided in his heart to give, not reluctantly or under compulsion, for God loves a cheerful [lit., in the Greek, a "hilarious"] giver" (2 Cor. 9:7). Such a perspective changes a legal tithe or gift into a love tithe or gift.

Men and Women Give Generously

(35:21–29)

Translation

[21]And every man whose heart moved him, whose spirit urged him came—they brought the LORD's contribution for the work of the tent of meeting, and for all its ministries and for the sacred vestments. [22]And the men came, along with the women, all who were urgent of heart. They brought brooches, and earrings, and rings, gold ornaments of every kind, everyone dedicating an offering of gold to the LORD. [23]Every man who possessed blue, purple and crimson material and linen and goat hair and reddened ram skins and dyed dolphin skins they brought (it). [24]Everyone who donated a contribution of silver and bronze brought the LORD's contribution, and everyone who possessed acacia wood for all the work of the ministry brought (it). [25]All the wise-hearted women with her hands spun, and brought the spun stuff, the blue, and the purple, the crimson material, and the linen. [26]All the woman whose heart moved them with wisdom spun the goat hair. [27]The leaders brought onyx stone and stones to be set for the ephod and the breastpiece, [28]and spices, and oil for lighting, and for the oil of unction, and for the perfumed incense. [29]Every man and woman whose heart urged them to bring for all the work that the LORD had commanded to do by Moses's hand—Israel's sons brought a freewill gift to the LORD.

Grammatical and Lexical Notes

35:22. The preposition *ʿal* on *ʿal-hannāšîm* means "*along with, together with* the women."

35:22. The Hebrew word for "ornaments" (*kûmāz*) appears only here and in Num. 31:50. It may be cognate with the Arabic word *kumzat*, which means "bunch, heap" and so "a cluster of small ornaments."

35:22. The Hebrew word for "contribution" in vv. 21, 24 is *tĕrûmâ*. The word for "freewill gift" in v. 29 is *nĕdābâ*. The word for "offering" in v. 22 is *tĕnûpâ*. We observed earlier that one difference between a *tĕrûmâ* and *tĕnûpâ* is that the former is given/dedicated "to"/*lĕ* the Lord (e.g., 30:13; 35:5), while the latter is given/dedicated "in the presence of, before"/*lipnê* the Lord (e.g., Exod. 29:24–25; Lev. 7:30; 8:27, 29; 9:21; 10:15, all of which have some form of *nûp* [Hiphil] + *tĕnûpâ* + *lipnê* + *YHWH*). I can find only two instances that break this pattern: here in Exod. 35:22 (*hēnîp tĕnûpâ zāhāb laYHWH*), and in Num. 8:13, "Have the Levites stand in front of Aaron and his sons and then present them as a wave offering to the LORD [*wĕhēnaptā ʾōtām tĕnûpâ laYHWH*]" (NIV). Some ancient versions, alert to this distinction between the two similar nouns, changed *tĕnûpâ* in v. 22 to *tĕrûmâ* (see *Biblia Hebraica Stuttgartensia*, Exod. 35:22, note f).

Commentary

35:21–29 There is, of course, no parallel for these verses in chaps. 25–31 for they describe the gifts and offerings the people willingly bring for the tabernacle's construction in response to Moses's request (vv. 4–19). The novel element here is that both men and women respond to the plea with their gifts, resources, and talents (vv. 22, 25–26, 29).

We have not heard in Exodus from active women since Miriam's song in 15:21, and before that, since chaps. 2–4 (the two midwives, Moses's mother and sister, the Egyptian princess, Zipporah). Where women appear in the Sinai pericope, they are passive and merely spoken about (e.g., no sex with one's wife [19:15]; a father who sells his daughter as a slave [21:7–11]).

Verses 27–28 identify the "leaders" (*hanněśi'im*) as the ones who bring, among other items, the oil for lighting the menorah and the oil of unction for anointing. Lev. 24:2 assigns the responsibility for donating the oil to light the menorah's lamps to all "Israelites," not just to the chieftains or leaders of the Israelites. Possibly Exod. 35:27–28 refers to just the original supply of oil at Sinai, while Lev. 24:2 refers to what becomes standard procedure.

Bezalel and Aholiab

(35:30–36:1; cf. 31:1–6)

Translation

30And Moses said to Israel's sons, "See, the
LORD has called by name Bezalel son of Uri
son of Hur of the tribe of Judah. 31And he
has filled him with the Spirit of God, in wis-
dom in understanding, and in knowledge,
and in every work, 32and to devise plans, to
work in gold and in silver and in bronze,
33and in carving stones for settings, and
in carving wood, in order to be able to do
every task of devising. 34And to teach he
has placed in his heart—he and Aholiab
son of Ahisamach of the tribe of Dan. 35He
has filled them with heart-wisdom in order
to do every work done by a carver, and
designer and embroiderer in blue, and in
purple, in crimson material and in linen,
and by a weaver—those who are to do
every work and devisers of plans. 36:1And
Bezalel, along with Aholiab, and every
wise-hearted man to whom the LORD has
given wisdom and understanding in these
matters to know how to do every work
for the ministry of the holy place, shall do
everything that the LORD has commanded."

Commentary

35:30–36:1 This section is the fulfillment portion of the Lord's words to Moses in 31:1–6 about the divine appointment of Bezalel and Aholiab and others as the tabernacle artisans. Two items distinguish 35:30–36:1 from 31:1–11. First, 35:30–36:1 does not repeat all the individual items of 31:7–11 for whose making these two artisans are responsible. Moses has already mentioned them in 35:10–19. Second, the placement of the unit about the craftsmen is near the beginning of the fulfillment section rather than near the end as in the instruction section.

Three observations stand out about 35:30–36:1. First, the emphasis in 35:20–29 on the willingness of the donors (vv. 21, 22, 29) to bring their gifts voluntarily is replaced here with an emphasis on God's sovereign choice and gifting of those who will preside over the tabernacle's construction. God does not sovereignly pick the donors. There are no consequences for nonparticipation. If you wish not to part with your pendants or linens, then keep them. But Bezalel and Aholiab are God-appointed individuals who, unlike Moses, never say, "But who am I that I should go and build the ark," nor, "Send somebody else, for surely there are better craftsmen in the camp than we."

A second observation focuses on the emphasis on a God-given wisdom, whether in 25–31 or in 35–40, when the text mentions these artisans and their work with the gifts the people present. The Hebrew root *ḥ-k-m* occurs eighteen times in Exodus. Two of them appear earlier in Exodus. In 1:10 Pharaoh uses the verb "let us act wisely/prudently" to suggest to his people how best to deal with these Hebrews. And in 7:11 Pharaoh consults with his "wise men, sages." All the remaining sixteen occur with the God-given skill of Bezalel and Aholiab for doing the work on the tabernacle (28:3 [2x]; 31:3, 6 [2x]; 35:10, 25, 26, 31, 35; 36:1 [2x], 2 [2x], 4, 8). I am not so sure I can agree with Whybray (1974: 108–9) who sees no significance to the multiple uses of *ḥ-k-m* here, and chalks it up simply to the repetitive style of the author. Maybe, instead, there is a contrast between the employment of a wisdom that leads to the death and oppression of others, and a wisdom that leads one to use gratefully and artistically the skills God has given one for the sake of the larger community. The first is a wisdom from below; the second is a wisdom from above. Note that in Deut. 1:13, 15 Moses follows a similar procedure when he chooses "wise" leaders to assist him, and in Deut. 34:9 Joshua, the successor to Moses, is filled with a "spirit of *ḥokmâ*" after Moses lays hands on him.

Interestingly, nowhere does Exodus, or Leviticus through Deuteronomy, ever call or describe Moses as "wise." And that leads me to my third observation. If Moses is the individual we connect with tabernacle building, Solomon is the individual we connect with temple building. Moses makes or builds nothing. It is Bezalel and his crew who do that (36:8; 37:1, 10, etc.). He oversees, inspects, and sets up the tabernacle, yes, but he makes nothing. By contrast, throughout 1 Kings 6–7 we read repeatedly, "Solomon made/built." Furthermore, unlike Moses, the biblical text frequently describes Solomon as "wise" (1 Kings 3:12, 28; 4:29–31; 10:4; etc.). However, never once is Solomon's wisdom connected with temple building. The root *ḥ-k-m* occurs only once in the chapters describing the temple's construction (1 Kings 6–7), and there the reference is to the Phoenician craftsman from Tyre, Huram/Hiram whom Solomon has do much of the work on the temple: "King Solomon sent to Tyre and brought Huram. . . . He was highly skilled [*wayyimmālēʾ ʾet-haḥokmâ*]" (1 Kings 7:13–14). What the Israelites Bezalel and Aholiab are in Exodus, the non-Israelite Huram/Hiram is in 1 Kings. Of course, one does not find any reference to the Lord filling Hiram/Huram with his Spirit, as we have with Bezalel and Aholiab, but surely the Phoenician's craftsmanship is God-given too.

Generosity That Must Be Restrained!

(36:2–7)

Translation

[2]And Moses called to Bezalel and to Aholiab, and to every wise-hearted man to whom God had placed wisdom in his heart, every one whose heart moved him to approach the work to do it. [3]And they took from Moses every contribution that Israel's sons brought for the work of officiating at the holy place to do it, and they, they brought to him yet more freewill gifts morning after morning. [4]And all the wise ones who were doing all the work of the holy place came, each one from his work they were doing, [5]and they said to Moses, saying, "More than enough are the people bringing necessary for the construction of the work whose doing the LORD has commanded." [6]So Moses commanded the people, and they passed the word throughout the camp, saying, "Let no man or woman do any more work for the contribution of the holy place," with the result that the people were restrained from bringing. [7]The work was all that was needed for all the work to do it, and more.

Grammatical and Lexical Notes

36:2. "Everyone whose heart moved him" contains the phrase *nĕśāʾô libbô*, literally, "Everyone whose heart *lifted him up.*" The phrase first appears in 35:21, 26. See also 2 Kings 14:10 (= 2 Chron. 25:19), but with a different nuance for the idiom—"You [Amaziah, king of Judah] have indeed defeated Edom and now you *are arrogant* [*ûnĕśaʾăkā libbekā*]." "Lifting up one's heart" carries two diametrically different meanings as does "lifting up one's head."

36:2. Milgrom (1970: 77–80) wishes to translate *lĕqorbâ ʾel-hammĕlāʾkâ* not "to approach the work" but "to qualify for the project."

36:5. *Marbîm* ("more than enough") is the Hiphil masculine plural participle of *rābâ*. It appears in identical form in Neh. 6:17 to refer to the sending of many letters, in Eccles. 6:11 to refer to many words that increase vanity, and in 1 Chron. 8:40 to refer to producing many children. Hoftijzer (1970: 428–29n2) observes that *rābâ* (Hiphil) + prepostion *lĕ* + infinitive construct has three different nuances: (1) to underline the outcome of an action: Exod. 36:5, "More than enough are the people bringing [*marbîm hāʿām lĕhābîʾ*]"; 2 Sam. 18:8, "And the forest claimed more lives [*wayyyereb hayaʿar leʾĕkōl bāʿām*] that day than the sword"; (2) to refer to an action that is often done: 2 Kings 21:6, "He did much evil [*hirbâ laʿăśôt hāraʿ*] in the eyes of the LORD, provoking him to anger"; Amos 4:4, "Go to Bethel and sin; go to Gilgal and sin yet more [*harbû lipšōʿa*]"; (3) to emphasize the intensity of an action: Ezra 10:13, "Because we have sinned greatly [*kî-hirbînû lipšōʿa*] in this thing"; Isa. 55:7, "Let him return to the LORD . . . and to our God, for he will freely pardon [*kî-yarbeh lislôaḥ*]."

36:5. *Day* carries the meaning "sufficiency, enough, what is required." I have translated the word "more than is needed" here in vv. 5 and 7. Compare, for example, Lev. 25:26, "If, however a man has no one to redeem it for him but he himself prospers and acquires sufficient means [*ûmāṣāʾ kĕdê*] to redeem it"; and Prov. 25:16, "If you find honey, eat *just enough* [*dayyekā*]." See too Lev. 5:7 and 12:8, which speak of the poor who, when desiring to offer a sacrifice, cannot afford *the outlay* for a lamb.

36:6. For "they passed the word throughout the camp" (*wayyaʿăbîrû qôl bammahăneḥ*), see 2 Chron. 30:5, "They decided *to send a proclamation throughout* Israel"; 2 Chron. 36:22 (= Ezra 1:1), "The LORD moved the heart of Cyrus . . . *to make a proclamation throughout* his realm"; Ezra 10:7, "A *proclamation was then issued throughout* Judah"; Neh. 8:15, "and that they should *proclaim this word* and *spread it throughout* their towns." The phrase is similar to that in Lev. 25:9, "Then have the trumpet sounded [*wĕhaʿăbartā šôpar*] everywhere on the tenth day of the seventh month."

36:6. The verb *kālāʾ* in the Niphal stem + preposition *min* ["from"] ("were restrained from") also appears in Gen. 8:2, "And the rain had stopped falling from the sky [*wayyikkālēʾ haggešem min-haššāmāyim*]."

36:7. In vv. 6b and 7 "work" (*mĕlāʾkâ*) refers not to the actual construction of the tabernacle but to the gifts the people brought for its construction.

36:7. The Hebrew for "and more" at the end of the sentence is *wĕhôtēr*, the conjunction *wāw* + Hiphil infinitive absolute of *yātar*. As here, Hebrew may follow the perfect of one verb ("was"/*hāyĕtâ*) with *wāw* prefixed to an infinitive absolute of a second verb: Eccles. 8:9, "All this I saw [*rāʾîtî*] as I applied my mind [*wĕnātôn ʾet-libbî*] to everything under the sun"; Dan. 9:5, "We have sinned and done wrong. We have been wicked and have rebelled; we have turned away from [*ḥāṭāʾnû . . . wĕsôr min*] your commands and laws"; Zech. 7:5, "When you fasted and mourned [*ṣamtem wĕsāpôd*]." Blake (1946) has demonstrated that such uses of the infinitive absolute with *wāw* may follow other verb forms.

Commentary

It is not frequent that the leaders of congregations must order their congregants **36:2–7**
to cease giving for the treasury is overloaded and bursting. It is not a crisis most pastors, priests, or rabbis ever encounter and must resolve. But here it was a problem and an embarrassment stemming from too liberal amounts of donations. The very fact that Moses makes the offerings voluntary rather than compulsory more than likely contributes to the extravagant giving.

Of course, what the people are giving are fabric and metals the Egyptians earlier had given them. The Israelites do not have any problem with building a dwelling place for Yahweh that is made of precious jewelry, yarn, and linen that has "Egypt(ian)" written all over it. It is like the Salvation Army that believes there is no such thing, with very few exceptions, as tainted money that funds their ministries. Regardless of the source, if the monetary gifts help advance the cause of Christ and the further outreach of the Salvationists, then beat the drum and ask God's blessing on the gift.

The Tabernacle

(36:8–39:32)

Translation

Making the Curtains (36:8–19; cf. 26:1–14)

[8]And every one wise of heart among those doing the work made the dwelling place with ten curtains. Of twisted linen and blue and purple and crimson material, (with the design of) cherubim, the work of a craftsman. [9]The length of each curtain was twenty-eight cubits, and a width of four cubits for each curtain, a single measure for all the curtains.

[10]Five of the curtains he joined one to the other, and five (other) curtains he joined to one another. [11]And he made blue loops on the edge of the outermost curtain in the first set, and did the same on the edge of the outermost curtain in the second set. [12]Fifty loops he made on the one curtain and fifty loops he made in the outermost curtain which was in the second set, the loops opposite one another. [13]And he made fifty gold clasps, and joined the curtains to one another with the clasps, so that the dwelling place was one whole.

[14]And he made curtains of goat hair for a tent over the dwelling place; he made eleven curtains. [15]The length of one curtain was thirty cubits and the width was four cubits for each curtain, a single measure for the eleven curtains. [16]And he joined five of the curtains by themselves, and six of the curtains by themselves. [17]And he made fifty loops on the edge of the outermost curtain of one set, and fifty loops on the edge of the curtain of the second set. [18]And he made fifty bronze clasps to join the tent that it be one whole. [19]And he made a covering for the tent of reddened ram skins and a covering of dolphin skins above.

Making the Frames (36:20–34; cf. 26:15–30)

[20]And he made frames for the dwelling place of acacia wood, standing upright. [21]Ten cubits the length of the frame, and a cubit and a half the width of each frame. [22]Two tenons for each frame joined together, each to the other; thus he did for every frame of the dwelling place. [23]And he made the frames for the dwelling place, twenty frames for the south side, [24]and forty silver sockets he made for underneath the twenty frames, two sockets under each frame for its two tenons, and two sockets underneath the other frame for its two tenons. [25]And for the second side of the dwelling place, for the northern side, twenty frames, [26]with their forty silver sockets, two sockets under each frame, and two sockets underneath the other frame. [27]For the hind part of the dwelling place, the west, he made six frames. [28]Two frames he made for the corners of the dwelling place at the hind part. [29]They were double at the bottom, but together they fitted into one ring at its top. Thus it was for both of them at both corners. [30]And there were eight frames and sixteen silver sockets, two sockets under each frame.

[31]And he made crossbars of acacia wood, five for the frames of one side of the dwelling place, [32]and five crossbars for

the frames of the second side of the dwelling place, and five crossbars for the frames of the hind side of the dwelling place, the west. [33]And he made the central crossbar to run through the frames from end to end. [34]And the frames he overlaid with gold, and their rings he made of gold, housings for the crossbars. And he overlaid the crossbars with gold.

Making the Veil and Its Screen (36:35–38; cf. 26:31–37)

[35]And he made the veil of blue, purple and crimson material and twisted linen. (As) the work of a craftsman, he made it (in the design of) cherubim. [36]And he made for it four acacia posts and overlaid them with gold, and their hooks gold, and he cast for them four silver bases. [37]And he made a screen for the entrance of the tent, blue, purple and crimson material, and twisted linen, the work of an embroiderer, [38]and its five posts and their hooks. He overlaid their tops and their bands with gold, but their five bases were of bronze.

Making the Ark (37:1–5; cf. 25:10–16)

[37:1]And Bezalel made the ark of acacia wood, two and a half cubits its length, and a cubit and a half its width, and a cubit and half its height. [2]And he overlaid it with pure gold, inside and outside, and he made for it a gold molding around it. [3]And he cast for it four rings of gold on its four feet, and two rings on its one side and two rings on its second side. [4]And he made poles of acacia wood, and overlaid them with gold. [5]And he inserted the poles into the rings through the rings on the sidewalls of the ark to carry the ark.

Making the Ark's Cover (37:6–9; cf. 25:17–22)

[6]And he made a cover/propitiatory of pure gold, two and a half cubits its length, and a cubit and half its width. [7]And he made two cherubim of gold. From beaten work he made them at the two edges of the cover/propitiatory: [8]one cherub at this one edge and one cherub at the other edge. From the cover/propitiatory he made the cherubim at both its edges. [9]The cherubim had wings spread out above, shielding with their wings the cover/propitiatory, and their faces each toward the other. In the direction of the cover/propitiatory were the cherubim's faces.

Making the Table (37:10–16; cf. 25:23–30)

[10]And he made the table of acacia wood, two cubits its length and a cubit its width, and a cubit and a half its height. [11]And he overlaid it with pure gold, and made for it a gold molding all around. [12]And he made for it a rim, a hands breath all around, and he made a gold molding for its rim all around. [13]And he cast for it four gold rings, and placed the rings at the four corners by its four feet. [14]Close to the rim the rings were housings for the poles to carry the table. [15]And he made poles of acacia wood and overlaid them with gold to carry the table. [16]And he made the utensils that were on the table, its bowls, and its ladles and its jars and jugs by which to pour libations, of pure gold.

Making the Lampstand (37:17–24; cf. 25:31–40)

[17]And he made a lampstand of pure gold; of pounded work he made the lampstand, its base and stem, its cups, its calyxes and its blossoms were from one piece. [18]Six branches extending from its sides, three branches of the lampstand from one side, and three branches of the lampstand from its second side; [19]three cups shaped like

almond blossoms on the one branch, calyx and blossom, and three cups shaped like almond blossoms on the one branch, calyx and blossom—and so for each of the six branches extending from the lampstand. [20]And on the lampstand four cups shaped like almond blossoms, their calyxes and their blossoms, [21]and a calyx under the pair of branches of one piece of it, and a calyx under the pair of branches of one piece of it, for the six branches extending from the lampstand. [22]Their calyxes and branches were of one piece with it, the whole of it one single pounded piece of pure gold. [23]And he made its seven lamps, and its tongs and firepans of pure gold. [24]With a talent of pure gold he made it together with all its furnishings.

Making the Incense Altar (37:25–28; cf. 30:1–10)

[25]And he made an altar for turning incense into smoke of acacia wood, a cubit its length, and a cubit its width, a square, two cubits its height; from the identical piece were its horns. [26]And he overlaid it with pure gold—its roof and its walls all around, and its horns, and he made for it a gold molding all around. [27]And two gold rings he made for it beneath its molding on its two sides as housings for the poles with which to carry it. [28]And he made the poles of acacia wood and overlaid them with gold.

Making the Oil and Incense (37:29; cf. 30:22–38)

[29]And he made the oil of holy unction and the pure perfumed incense, the work of a perfumer.

Making the Bronze Altar (38:1–7; cf. 27:1–8)

[38:1]And he made the altar of burnt offering of acacia wood, five cubits its length and five cubits its width—a square—and three cubits its height. [2]And he made its horns on its four corners, from the one piece its horns shall be, and he overlaid it with bronze. [3]And he made all the utensils of the altar—the pots and the shovels and the basins, the forks and the firepans. All its utensils he made of bronze. [4]And he made for the altar a meshed grating of bronze under its ledge from below halfway up. [5]And he cast four rings on the four corners of the bronze mesh as housings for the poles. [6]And he made the poles of acacia wood and overlaid them with bronze. [7]And he inserted the poles into the rings on the sides of the altar to carry it by them. Hollow boarded he made it.

Making the Bronze Laver (38:8; cf. 30:17–21)

[8]And he made the laver of bronze and its base of bronze from the mirrors of the congregating women converging at the entrance to the tent of meeting.

Making the Court and Its Curtains (38:9–20; cf. 27:9–19)

[9]And he made the court, on the south side hangings for the court of twisted linen, a hundred cubits, [10]their posts twenty and their bases twenty, of bronze, and the hooks of the posts and their bands of silver. [11]And for the north side, a hundred cubits, their posts twenty and their bases twenty, of bronze, and the post's hooks and bands of silver. [12]On the west side hangings were a hundred cubits, their posts ten and their bases ten, and the posts' hooks and their bases of silver. [13]On the front side facing east fifty cubits, [14]hangings, fifteen cubits on [one] flank, their posts three and their bases three. [15]And for the second flank on each side of the court's gate were hangings

of fifteen cubits, their post three and their bases three. [16]All the court's hangings round about were of twisted linen. [17]And the posts' bases were of bronze, and the pillars' hooks and their bands of silver. The overlay of their heads was of silver, and they were banded with silver, all the court's posts. [18]The screen of the court's gate was the work of an embroiderer, blue and purple and crimson material and twisted linen, twenty cubits long and five cubits high in width exactly like the court's hangings. [19]And their posts were four and their bases four, of bronze, and their hooks of silver, and the overlay of their heads and of their bands of silver. [20]And all the pegs for the dwelling place and for the court all around were of bronze.

[21]These are the inventories of the dwelling place, the dwelling place of the testimony that were compiled by order of Moses, the ministry of the Levites under the supervision of Ithamar, the son of Aaron the priest. [22]And Bezalel, son of Uri, son of Hur, of the tribe of Judah, did everything that the LORD commanded Moses. [23]And with him was Aholiab, son of Ahisamach, of the tribe of Dan, a carver and designer and embroiderer in blue and purple and crimson material, and in linen.

[24]All the gold that was produced for the work in any kind of work of the holy place, the gold of the elevation offering, was twenty-nine talents or 730 shekels by the shekel of the holy place. [25]The silver of those registered in the congregation was a hundred talents or 1,775 shekels by the shekel of the holy place. [26]A *beka* to the head, half a shekel by the shekel of the holy place for anyone who passed through the registration, from twenty years old and above, for 603,550. [27]The hundred talents of silver were for casting the sockets of the holy place, and the veil's bases, a hundred bases for a hundred talents, a talent for a socket. [28]And the 1,775 shekels he made into hooks for the posts, and overlaid their heads and banded them. [29]And the bronze of the elevation offering was seventy talents, or 2,400 shekels. [30]And he made with it the sockets for the entrance to the tent of meeting, and the bronze altar and its bronze mesh, and all the altar's utensils, [31]and the court's sockets all around, and the sockets of the court's gate, and all the tabernacle's pegs, and all the pegs of the court all around.

Making the Priestly Vestments (39:1–32; cf. 28:1–43)

[39:1]And from the blue and purple and crimson material they made, they made service vestments for officiating in the holy place, and they made holy vestments for Aaron just as the LORD had commanded Moses.

Making the Ephod (39:2–7; cf. 28:6–14)

[2]And he made the ephod gold, blue and purple, crimson material and twisted linen. [3]And they hammered out the sheets of gold and he cut thin strips to work into the blue and into the purple and into the crimson material and into the linen, the work of a craftsman. [4]Shoulder-pieces they made for it, joined; at its two ends it was joined. [5]And its fastening band which is on it, and of one piece with it, was made like it—gold, blue, and purple and crimson material and twisted linen just as the LORD commanded Moses.

[6]And they made the onyx stones ringed with frames of gold, engraved with seal engravings of the names of Israel's sons. [7]And he set them on the ephod's shoulder-piece, stones of remembrance for Israel's sons, just as the LORD commanded Moses.

Making the Breastpiece (39:8–21; cf. 28:15–30)

[8]And he made the breastpiece, the work of a craftsman, like the work of the ephod—gold, blue, and purple, and crimson material, and twisted linen. [9]A square it was; doubled they made the breastpiece, a hand span its length and a hand span its width, doubled. [10]And they filled it with four rows of stones: a row of ruby, topaz

and emerald for the first row; [11]and the second row: turquoise, sapphire and crystal; [12]and the third row: a jacinth, agate and amethyst; [13]and the fourth row: beryl, onyx and jasper, ringed with gold frames in their fillings. [14]And the stones were according to the names of Israel's sons, twelve according to their names, seal engravings, each according to its name, for the twelve tribes. [15]And they made for the breastpiece woven chains like cords of pure gold. [16]And they made two gold frames and two gold rings, and placed the two rings on the breastpiece's two edges, [17]and they placed the two gold cords on the two rings on the breastpiece's edges. [18]And the two ends of the two cords they placed on the two frames, and placed them on the ephod's shoulder-pieces at its front. [19]And they made two gold rings and set them on the breastpiece's two edges, at its border which faced the ephod's inside. [20]And they made two gold rings and placed them on the ephod's two shoulder-pieces below in the front, close to its joining point above the ephod's band. [21]And they fastened the breastpiece from its rings to the ephod's rings by means of a blue cord to be on top of the ephod's band so that the breastpiece would not come loose from the ephod.

Making the Ephod's Robe (39:22–26; cf. 28:31–35)

[22]And he made the ephod's robe, the work of a weaver, entirely of blue. [23]And the robe's opening in its middle was like the opening of a corslet(?), a border for its opening all around so that it not tear. [24]And they made on the robe's hem the pomegranates of blue and purple and crimson material, twisted linen. [25]And they made bells of pure gold, and placed the bells in the middle of the pomegranates on the robe's hem, all around, in the middle of the pomegranates. [26](There was) a bell and a pomegranate, a bell and a pomegranate on the robe's hem all around for officiating, just as the LORD commanded Moses.

Making the Other Priestly Vestments (39:27–31; cf. 28:36–41)

[27]And they made tunics of linen, the work of an embroiderer, for Aaron and his sons, [28]and the turban of linen, and the decorated turbans of linen, and the linen breeches of fine twisted linen, [29]and the sash of twisted linen, blue and purple and crimson material, the work of an embroiderer, just as the LORD commanded Moses.

[30]And they made a diadem, a holy crown of pure gold, and wrote upon it an inscription of seal engravings: "Holy to the LORD." [31]And they placed on it a blue strip to attach on the turban above just as the LORD commanded Moses.

[32]All the labor on the tent of meeting's dwelling place was at an end. Israel's sons did according to all the Lord commanded Moses. Thus they did.

Grammatical and Lexical Notes

38:2. The LXX extends the end of the verse by adding, "and he overlaid it with bronze from the censers that belonged to the men who rebelled with the congregation of Korah" to harmonize the account in Exod. 38:1–2 with the account in Num. 16:38–39 [17:3–4] on how the outer altar comes to be overlaid with bronze.

38:8. There is an unexpected reference in 38:8b to the builders' making the bronze laver "from the mirrors of the congregating women converging [*bĕmarʾōt haṣṣōbĕʾōt ʾăšerṣābĕʾû*] at the entrance to the tent of Meeting." There is no reference to these women or to their (bronze) mirrors in the instruction section (30:17–21).

There are a number of issues here. First, Exod. 38:8 would be the only place where *marʾōt* means "mirrors." Everywhere else the plural noun occurs it means "visions" (Gen. 46:2; Ezek. 1:1; 8:3; 40:2; 43:3). Of course, a mirror is an object in which one observes a "vision" of oneself. And Akkadian supports the connection between the noun "mirror" formed from the verb "see" with *namaru* ("mirror") and *amaru* ("see"). If we go with "mirrors" then, I ask, what are these women doing with mirrors at the entrance to the tent, which, as of chap. 38, has not yet even been constructed? Furthermore, do these women freely donate these bronze mirrors as their gifts, or are they taken from them because of some kind of infraction?

The second issue is how best to render *haṣṣōbĕʾōt ʾăšer ṣābĕʾû*. My "the congregating women converging at . . ." is but one option. Alter (2004: 524) renders, "the women who flocked to . . ." A more common translation is something like, "the serving women who served at . . ." Such a translation, if correct, suggests that women played some legitimate cultic role in the tabernacle complex, a claim no other Scripture text supports, with one possible exception. The only other place the feminine, plural participle of *ṣābāʾ* (*ṣōbĕʾôt*) occurs is in 1 Sam. 2:22, "Now Eli . . . heard about everything his sons were doing . . . and how they slept with the women *who served* at the entrance to the tent of meeting." I shall return to this Samuel verse shortly.

The ancient versions were also uncertain about how to render the Hebrew in 38:8: "women fasting at . . ." (LXX); "women guarding the . . ." (Vulg.); "women praying at . . ." (*Targum Onqelos*). Kaplan (1967: 162) and Watson (1971: 46–47) believe they have solved the conundrum by reading *bĕmarʾōt* not as "from the mirrors" but as the preposition *bĕ* of intention affixed to the infinitive *marēʾ* ("feed, nourish") and by repointing *ṣōbĕʾôt* to *ṣĕbāʾôt*. Their reading is, "And he made the laver . . . to feed [with water] the ministers who served at the entrance to the tent of meeting." Such a reading removes women from the text altogether, but only at the high cost of disturbing the received text. Everhart (2004: 51), who wants to keep the women in the text, argues that while 38:8b may have more logically appeared somewhere in 35:22–29 (the list of gifts men and women brought), its presence in chap. 38 "is important enough that it warrants an interruption in the flow of the text."

Greenstein (2000: 171–73) has cogently observed that there is only one other instance in the Torah of an Israelite giving or surrendering, or having confiscated, a bronze utensil that is used on one of the pieces of holy furniture in the tabernacle. That is the account in Num. 16:37–39 [17:2–4] of Eleazar taking the censers of Korah and the other rebels, and then hammering them into sheets with which to overlay the outer altar (see my note on 38:2 above).

Given the close parallel between Exod. 38:8b and Num. 16:37–39 [17:2–4] on the one hand, and the parallel between Exod. 38:8b and 1 Sam. 2:22 on the other hand, one may surmise that these "serving women" are guilty of some cultic infraction, the nature of which the Torah has not spelled out.

38:21. Here is one brief notice that the Levites, under the supervision of Ithamar, play a role in the tabernacle's construction. See also Num. 4:29, 33, "This is the service of the Gershonite/Merarite clans as they work at the tent of meeting under the direction of Ithamar." However, it is his brother, Eleazar, who is the chief leader of the Kohathite clans, the Levitical branch that takes care of the tabernacle's "most holy things" (Num. 3:32; 4:16). After chaps. 3–4 Ithamar appears only in the second census (Num. 26:60). Eleazar, by contrast, appears frequently throughout Numbers (16:37–39 [17:2–4]; 26:1, 3; 27:2; 31:21, 26, 29, 31, 41, 51, 54), and it is his son, Phinehas, who is the high priest of the third-generation Israelites (Num. 25:10–13). Ithamar is to Eleazar as Jonathan is to David, or as Andrew is to Peter.

38:24–25, 29. It is difficult to convert into modern equivalents the amounts in weight of gold, silver, and bronze given for the sanctuary's construction. Part of the problem for calculation is whether to read in these three verses, "X number of talents of Y *and* X number of shekels," or "X number of talents of Y *or* X number of shekels." Childs (1974: 637), following the lead of others, settles on the following totals: gold, 1,900 pounds; silver, 6,437 pounds; bronze, 4,522 pounds. The NLT suggests higher equivalents: gold, 2,193 pounds; silver, 7,545 pounds; bronze, 5,310 pounds. Anyway you cut it, that's a lot of precious metals, especially considering today's market value for gold (over $1,000 per ounce)!

38:26. For "[a *beka*] to the head" (*laggulgōlet*), see Exod. 16:16, "an omer [of manna] to a head," and Num. 3:47, "you shall take five shekels for each head."

Commentary

36:8–39:32 Kudos to the readers of Scripture who patiently are able to plow their way through all the micrometric details vis-à-vis the tabernacle in chaps. 25–31, only to have to face an encore in chaps. 35–39. To be sure, chaps. 25–31 are about instructions and chaps. 35–39 are about the fulfillment of those instructions, or as Janzen (1997: 9) describes it, a move from "Planning a Place for Presence" to "Preparing a Place for Presence."

There are a number of places in Exodus where God delivers a message to Moses (for Israel or somebody else), which Moses in turn transmits to the Israelites or to Pharaoh. Such scenes may follow one of several patterns (see Vater 1980).

One pattern is: God delivers a message for Israel to Moses, and then there is a brief notice that Moses does so, without the text repeating the content of the message God gives him. An example of this is 19:3–7: 19:3–6, God's message to Moses for Israel, and v. 7, "So Moses . . . set before them all the words the Lord had commanded him to speak." See also 19:20–24 and v. 25 ("So Moses went down to the people and told them").

Another pattern is: God delivers a message for Israel to Moses, but there is no mention of Moses's delivering it. An example is 20:22–23:32, the so-called "Covenant Code," but no verse near its end like 19:7 or 25. See also 7:14–18 (the plague of blood); 8:1–4 [7:26–29] (the plague of frogs); 8:20–23 [16–19] (the plague of flies); 9:1–4 (the plague on livestock); 9:13–19 (the plague of hail), all of which are messages from God for Pharaoh to be delivered by Moses, but no verse or verses that describe their actual deliverance.

A third pattern is one in which both the message and the report of transmitting the message are similar, but there are some differences. The differences may be slight. Compare the Lord's message for Pharaoh in 3:18b with the notice of Moses's delivery of that message in 5:3 to which Moses adds, "or he may strike us with plagues or with the sword." Or the differences may be lengthier. Compare the Lord's message to Moses for Israel about the observance of Passover (12:1–11) with Moses's delivery of those directives to his people (12:21–27). Of the dozen or so items mentioned, about the only one reported in the actual delivery is what to do with the blood.

A fourth pattern is one that records only Moses's speaking for God to somebody without a previous reference that this is what God told him to say (see 10:3–6, the plague of locusts).

A final pattern, and the one we have in chaps. 25–31 and 35–39, is one in which the messages both in the commissioning and in the delivery of that commission are virtually identical. Nowhere does repetition operate on such a massive scale in Exodus as in these twelve chapters. And the repetition is almost verbatim, something that is rare in other repeated texts.

Presumably, near the end of Exod. 31 there could have been a brief notice, as in the first pattern above, to the effect that, "And Moses went to the people and told them what God told him." Or maybe at the beginning of chap. 35 there could have been a brief notice to the effect that, "And Moses told them what God had told him, they brought the necessary gifts, and built the tabernacle," then move to the summarizing section, 39:32–43, before ending with the magnificent chap. 40. In that way one deletes most of the repetitious, and some would say tedious, material in chaps. 35–39.

So what is accomplished by the repetition of all these minute details? For one thing, it draws attention to the faithfulness of Moses in transmitting accurately the message God gave him to deliver to his people. Moses the listener of chaps. 25–31 becomes Moses the mediator of chaps. 35–39. As Vater (1980: 373) has observed, when God gives a private message to Moses that Moses is to deliver to Israel or to Pharaoh, the overwhelming majority of such occasions (twenty-eight of thirty-eight) simply conclude with "And Moses told them/him" or with no reference at all to Moses passing on the message. In such instances the voice of the sender (God) is supreme, and the voice of the messenger (Moses) either miniscule or nonexistent. But in a situation like we have in chaps. 25–31 and 35–39 the voice of the messenger shares equal billing with the voice of the sender. Moses's much earlier concerns that none of his people might believe him (4:1), or that he is a bungling, tongue-tied speaker (4:10), have been put to rest, at least for a while.

Second, the repetition permits the contrast to emerge between what the people "made" in Exod. 32 under the supervision of Aaron with what the people "made" in Exod. 35–39 under the supervision of Bezalel, Aholiab, and other artisans. A key word in chaps. 25–40 is "make/made" (*ʿāśâ*). It occurs 323 times in Exodus, 236 of which are in chaps. 25–40 (Leder 2001: 260). There is also a contrast between what Israel builds at the beginning of Exodus and what Israel builds at the end of Exodus. While the English expressions "store cities" (1:11) and "dwelling place" (repeatedly in chaps. 25–31, 35–40) sound quite different, the Hebrew words for each are very similar, *miskĕnôt* and *miškān*. In chap. 1 Israel builds *miskĕnôt*; in chaps. 35–39 Israel builds a *miškān*.

Third, the repetition perpetuates the pattern in Exodus of things that happen or are narrated twice. God calls Moses twice to go to Egypt, first in 3:1–4:17 and then again in 6:2–8 after a miserable first audience with Pharaoh (5:1–23). Twice God gives his people the covenant and the tablets, first in chaps. 19–24, and a second time in chap. 34, punctuated again by the miserable scenario involving the calf in chap. 32. In particular, the repetition of the tabernacle data provides another striking illustration in Exodus of the move from promise/instruction to fulfillment. What God promises and predicts in

6:2–7 (the successful liberation of Israel from Egypt) comes to fulfillment in 12:31–14:31. The building of a shrine for whose erection God gives instructions in chaps. 25–31 comes to fulfillment in chaps. 35–39. What God says and predicts and outlines comes to pass in spite of an arrogant Pharaoh and calf-extolling Israelites.

Finally, the repetition of data in chaps. 35–39 moves the climactic message of Exodus beyond the concerns of chap. 34. Had Exodus concluded with chap. 34, then the book's final scene would have focused on forgiveness, restoration, and covenant renewal. Those emphases are vital, refreshing, and necessary to be sure. But Exodus concludes by inviting the reader to think about where God wants to take us after we have experienced forgiveness and reconciliation. Is forgiveness an end in itself or a means to an end? Exodus 35–40 suggests the latter. That end is the experience of God's gloriously taking up residence in the midst of his people (chap. 40) in the sanctuary his people have built for him (chaps. 35–39). While we give God our gifts and workmanship (chaps. 35–39), God gives us his presence (chap. 40).

Apart from the theological significance of the repetition of chaps. 25–31 in chaps. 35–39, one may observe also that the duplication of tabernacle data allows for the detection of a nice chiasm covering Exodus's last seventeen chapters (Milgrom 2000b: 1339):

A Theophany/Moses goes up the mountain (24:15–18)
  B Instructions for the tabernacle (25:1–31:11)
    C Sabbath (31:12–18)
      D Apostasy, forgiveness, covenant renewal (32–34)
    C′ Sabbath (35:1–3)
  B′ Implementation of the tabernacle instructions (35:4–40:33)
A′ Theophany/Moses cannot enter the tabernacle (40:34–38)

An Inventory of the Tabernacle's Furnishings

(39:33–43)

Translation

[33]And they brought the dwelling place to Moses, the tent and all its furnishings, its clasps, its frames, its crossbars, and its posts and bases, [34]and the covering of reddened ram skins, and the covering of dolphin skins, and the veil of the screen; [35]the ark of the testimony and its poles and the cover/propitiatory; [36]the table and all its furnishings, and the bread of the presence; [37]the pure lampstand, its lamps, lamps of array, and all its furnishings, and the oil for the light; [38]and the altar of gold and the oil of unction, and the perfumed incense, and the screen at the tent's entrance; [39]the bronze altar and the bronze meshing which goes with it, its poles and all its furnishings, the laver and its base; [40]the court's hangings and its posts and sockets, and the screen for the court's gate, its cords and pegs and all the furnishings for the dwelling place's construction, for the tent of meeting; [41]the vestments of officiation for officiating in the holy place, the holy vestments for Aaron, the priest, and his sons' vestments to be priests. [42]According to everything the LORD commanded Moses, thus Israel's sons accomplished the entire construction. [43]And Moses saw all the work, and behold, they had done it just as the LORD had commanded. Thus they had done it. And Moses blessed them.

Grammatical and Lexical Notes

39:43. While there are numerous instances of "X saw, and behold" (*wayyar᾽ wĕhinnēh*; e.g., Gen. 8:13; 18:2; 19:28; 24:63; 29:2; 33:1; Exod. 3:2; Josh. 5:13; Judg. 9:43; 2 Sam. 13:34), the pattern "X saw Y and behold, Z" is much less frequent. I can locate only three instances: (1) Gen. 1:31, "And God *saw* everything he had made, *and behold*, it was very good"; (2) Gen. 6:12, "And God *saw* the earth, *and behold*, it was corrupt"; (3) Exod. 39:43, "And Moses *saw* all the work, *and behold*, they had done it just as the LORD had commanded." Sometimes one sees things that are pleasant (instances 1 and 3). Sometimes one sees things that are revolting (instance 2). Moses's evaluation of the work on the tabernacle does not include the phrase, "it was good," as in Gen. 1:31, but if it was done just as the Lord had instructed, what else could it be but good?

Commentary

These verses constitute a summary of all the elements that went into the **39:33–43**
tabernacle's construction. The progression is from the holiest place (v. 35) to

the holy place (vv. 36–38), to the courtyard (v. 39), to the curtains (v. 40), to the priestly vestments (v. 41). Alter (2004: 530) says this summary "is rather like the recapitulation of themes at the end of the last movement of a classical symphony, pulling all the previously stated elements together as the piece moves toward satisfying closure."

A number of phrases in these last two chapters of Exodus recall similar phrases in the first two chapters of Genesis. Such parallels suggest some connection between God's building his world, and Moses and the Israelites' building the tabernacle. Here are four of those: (1) "And God saw everything he had made, and behold it was very good" (Gen. 1:31) with "And Moses saw all the work, and behold, they had done it; as the LORD commanded, so they had done it" (Exod. 39:43); (2) "Thus the heavens and the earth were finished" (Gen. 2:1) with "Thus all the work of the tabernacle of the tent of meeting was finished" (Exod. 39:32); (3) "God finished his work which he had done" (Gen. 2:2) with "So Moses finished the work" (Exod. 40:33); (4) "So God blessed the seventh day" (Gen. 2:3) with "And Moses blessed them" (Exod. 39:43). We might also include the extensive use of the Hebrew word for "skilled labor" (*mĕlākâ*) throughout chaps. 25–31 and 36–39 with the use of the same word in Gen. 2:2–3 to refer to the "work" from which God rests. Similarly, one may see a connection between the use of the verb "sanctify, consecrate" (*qādaš*, Piel) for what Moses is to do with the tabernacle's sancta and the priests (40:9–13), and the use of this verb, again in the Piel, for what God does with the seventh day at creation (Gen. 2:3). Many commentators have remarked on the Exod. 39–40 parallels with Gen. 1–2, taking their cue from the insightful study of Blenkinsopp (1976), but none have approached it more creatively than Josipovici (1988: 90–107, esp. 101–5).

Exodus 39:43 is the only occasion in Exodus in which Moses blesses anybody. It is doubtful if Moses honors Pharaoh's request to Moses to bless him (12:32). What a contrast between how Moses responds to Israel in chap. 32 and at the end of chap. 39! In chap. 32 he blasts them; here he blesses them. What he sees the people have done in chap. 32 incenses him; what he sees the people have done in chap. 39 inspires him.

God's Instructions to Moses about the Tabernacle and the Priests, and Moses's Fulfillment of the God-Given Instructions

(40:1–33)

Translation

1And the LORD spoke to Moses, saying, 2"On the day of the first month, on the first of the month, you shall erect the dwelling place (portion) of the tent of meeting. 3And you shall set there the ark of the testimony, and you shall screen the ark with the veil. 4And you shall bring in the table and lay out its arrangement, and you shall bring in the lampstand and kindle its lamps. 5And you shall place the gold altar for incense in front of the ark of the testimony, and set up the screen at the entrance to the dwelling place. 6And you shall place the gold altar for incense in front of the ark of the testimony, and set up the screen at the entrance to the dwelling place. 7And you shall place the laver between the tent of meeting and the altar, and pour water there. 8And you shall set up the courtyard all around, and place in position the screen of the courtyard's gate. 9And you shall take the oil of unction, and anoint the dwelling place and everything that goes with it, and you shall sanctify it and all its furnishings that it be holy. 10And you shall anoint the altar of burnt offering and all its furnishings, thus sanctifying the altar that it be a holy of holies. 11And you shall anoint the laver and its base, thus sanctifying it. 12And you shall bring near Aaron and his sons to the entrance of the tent of meeting, and wash them in water. 13And you shall clothe Aaron with holy vestments, and anoint him, thus sanctifying him, that he be a priest to me. 14And his sons you shall bring near and clothe them with tunics. 15And you shall anoint them just as you anointed their father, that they be priests to me, and their anointing shall become for them an everlasting priesthood for their generations." 16And Moses did according to everything the LORD commanded him; thus he did.

17In the first month in the second year, on the first of the month, the dwelling place was erected. 18And Moses erected the dwelling place and placed its sockets, and set up its frames, inserted its poles, and erected its posts. 19And he spread the tent over the dwelling place, and set up the covering of the tent over it from above, just as the LORD commanded Moses. 20And he took and placed the testimony in the ark, and set up the poles on the ark, and he placed the cover/propitiatory over the ark from above. 21And he brought the ark into the dwelling place, and set up the cover's/propitiatory's veil, and screened over the ark of the testimony just as the LORD commanded Moses. 22And he placed the table in the tent of meeting on the north side of the dwelling place outside the veil. 23And he laid out over it the arrangement of bread in front of the LORD, just as the LORD commanded Moses. 24And he set up the lampstand in the tent of meeting across from the table on the dwelling place's south side. 25He kindled the lamps in front of the LORD, just as the LORD commanded Moses. 26And he set up the gold altar in the tent of meeting in front of the veil. 27And he turned into smoke on it perfumed incense, just as the LORD commanded Moses. 28And he set up the screen at the entrance to the dwelling place. [29]The altar of burnt offering he set up at the entrance of the dwelling place (portion) of the tent of meeting, and offered up on it the burnt offering and the grain offering, just as the LORD commanded Moses. [30]And he set up the laver between the tent of meeting and the altar, and he poured water for washing. [31]From it Moses and Aaron and his sons washed their hands and their feet. [32]Whenever they went into the tent of meeting and approached the altar, they washed just as the LORD commanded Moses. [33]And he erected the courtyard all around the dwelling place and the altar, and placed in position the screen for the courtyard's gate. And Moses finished the work.

Grammatical and Lexical Notes

40:2. As in 39:32, *miškan ʾōhel môʿēd* needs to be rendered, "the dwelling place/tabernacle (portion) of the tent of meeting" (and in vv. 6, 29 too), to maintain the distinction between the inner shrine and the larger, surrounding tent.

40:4. The table must be the second most important sanctum in the tabernacle, for its mention always follows immediately after the mention of the ark: in the prescription section (35:10–22 and 35:23–30); in the construction section (37:1–9 and 37:10–16); in the directives to Moses for setting up the tabernacle (40:3 and 4); in the actual placement of the sancta in the tabernacle (40:21 and 22); and in the order of dismantlement when it is time to break camp and move on (Num. 4:5–6 and 7–8).

40:4. *ʿĀrak* is a common verb in Exodus–Leviticus to refer to the "laying out" or "setting up" of the tabernacle paraphernalia, or arranging the wood on the altar, or tending the lamps (Exod. 27:21; 40:4, 23; Lev. 1:7, 8, 12; 24:3; etc.). Its best known uses outside those related to the cult are (1) Abraham's "arranging" the wood atop the altar at Mount Moriah for Isaac (Gen. 22:9) and (2) David's famous word about God's "preparing" a table before him right before his enemies (Ps. 23:5).

40:7. For *nātan* meaning "pour," see also 30:18 (both have "water" as the object of the verb) and 1 Kings 8:36 (= 2 Chron. 6:27), which has "rain" as the object of the verb.

40:9. From v. 9 to v. 13 some form of the root *q-d-š* ("sanctify, consecrate, holy") occurs eight times (v. 9 [2x]; v. 10 [3x]; v. 11; v. 13 [2x]).

40:10. The reference to the outer altar as a "holy of holies," while all the other furnishings are but "holy" (v. 9), is surprising.

40:13. One major difference between the installation of priests and Levites into their respective offices is that the former are "sanctified, consecrated" (*qādaš*, Hiphil) according to v. 13, while the Levites are "given, dedicated" (*nātan*) according to Num. 8:16. Furthermore, there were no special sacred vestments for the Levites as there were for the priests.

40:15. *Kĕhunnâ* may refer, as an abstract noun, to "the priesthood" (e.g., Num. 25:13; Josh. 15:7) or to priestly groups (1 Sam. 2:36, "Appoint me to some *priestly group/office* so I can have food to eat").

40:17. In dating formulas the sequence month>year>day, as here, is rare. So is the sequence year>day>month (Zech. 9:1), month>day>year (2 Kings 25:8 [although NIV places day before month]; Jer. 52:13), and day>month>year (Num. 1:1; Ezra 6:15; Zech. 1:7). The most common sequence by far is year>month>day.

40:21. The ark is the first holy thing Moses places in the tabernacle. By contrast, it is the last holy thing Solomon places in the temple (1 Kings 8:3–5). In both instances, the appearance of the cloud follows the ark's placement, whether it is first or last (Exod. 40:34; 1 Kings 8:10–11).

40:25. Verses 25 and 29 both use the Hiphil imperfect of *ʿālâ* (*wayyaʿal*) for the "kindling" of the lamps on the lampstand (v. 25; also see v. 4), and for the "offering up" of the burnt offering (v. 29).

It is difficult to know with precision if the Hiphil of *ʿālâ*, when used with the lampstand, refers to "kindling" the lamps on it or to "placing atop" the lamps on its branches.

40:30–32. These three verses on "washing" before entering holy precincts recall the earlier warning in 30:20 that failure to wash one's hands in the laver would result in the death of the priestly official.

40:33. As I suggested above, there is a similarity between, "And Moses finished the work," and Gen. 2:2, "And God finished on the seventh day his work." But there is one difference in the Hebrew when one compares the two passages. The Genesis passage lacks the indicator of the direct object before the word "work," but Exod. 40:33b has it: *wayĕkal ʾĕlōhîm . . . mĕlaʾkĕtô* (Gen. 2:2); *wayĕkal mōšeh ʾet-hammĕlāʾkâ* (Exod. 40:33b). The absence of the definite article before "his work" in Gen. 2:2 is unexpected because I count about twenty-four instances in Gen. 1:1–2:4 where the indicator of the direct object (*ʾet*) is present after a transitive verb, either before the noun object or attached to a pronoun that is the object of the verb. Garr (2004a: 89) suggests that the presence of the object indicator in Exod. 40:33b indicates that Moses's work on the tabernacle is finished and concluded. Its absence from Gen. 2:2 indicates that while God's cessation from work is complete, the work itself is not necessarily complete.

Commentary

There is a parallel structure in chaps. 25–31 + 35–39 and 40:1–16 + 40:17–33. **40:1–33**
In the first part (25–31; 40:1–16), the Lord instructs Moses about what to pass on to his people about the tabernacle's construction (chaps. 25–31), and instructions for Moses himself on how to assemble the tabernacle's components (40:1–16). In the second part the text records Israel's (chaps. 35–39) and Moses's (40:17–33) faithful, obedient implementation of those divine directives.

The emphasis on the people and Moses faithfully following the will of God becomes even clearer when one observes the proliferation of the phrase "they/he did just as the Lord commanded Moses/him" in these last two chapters. It occurs seven times in conjunction with the making of the priestly garments (39:1, 5, 7, 21, 26, 29, 31), plus three more times in the summary section (39:32, 42, 43). It also occurs seven times in the account of Moses's assembling the tabernacle (40:19, 21, 23, 25, 27, 29, 32). For good measure we may note the occurrence of the phrase also seven times in Lev. 8, the account of the ordination of Aaron and his sons, and one that follows logically the end of Exodus (Lev. 8:4, 9, 13, 17, 21, 29, 36). One wonders if the "seven . . . seven . . . seven" pattern reflects a perfect conformity to the will of God. In any case, it is interesting to notice that while "Israel/Moses did just as the Lord commanded them/him" occurs seventeen times in the last two chapters (10 + 7), the phrase appears only twice in the first thirty-eight chapters of Exodus (7:10, 20). (Its presence in 36:1 is anticipatory rather than descriptive.) Whenever God's work is done in God's way for God's glory the brilliant presence of His Majesty is almost a given.

Verses 1 and 17 tell the reader that the tabernacle is set up "on the first day of the first month in the second year" (since leaving Egypt). The first month is also known as "Abib" or "Nisan," and points to a spring New Year's Day rather than to a fall New Year's Day now known as Rosh Hashanah. Israel has been camped at Sinai for about nine or ten months, for 19:1 tells us that Israel arrives at Sinai "in the third month" without specifying a day in that month. That means Israel's first Passover, celebrated while they were yet in Egypt, was about a year ago. Their next Passover is only several days away, observed as it is, along with the Festival of Unleavened Bread/Flatbread "in the month of Abib, for in that month you came out of Egypt" (Exod. 23:15; 34:18; Lev. 23:5–6; Num. 28:16–17; Deut. 16:1).

There is at least one other place in the Scripture where the "first day of the first month" is highlighted. That is Gen. 8:13, "By the first day of the first month of Noah's six hundred and first year, the water had dried up from the earth." Both Gen. 8:13 and Exod. 40:1, 17 point respectively to new beginnings for the postdiluvials who experience salvation from the deluge, and for the Israelites who experience salvation from the despot, Pharaoh. Noah's life moves from his salvation to something he builds (an altar) to worship God. Israel's life moves from her salvation to something she builds (a shrine) to worship God.

There is one other reference to this spring, first day of the year, and that is in a part of Esther not found in modern Protestant Bible versions since it is lacking in the Hebrew Bible, but present in some manuscripts of the LXX and Vulgate. There are six "additions" that expand the book of Esther from 163 verses to 271 verses. The first of these additions records Mordecai's dream (spread over seventeen verses). The dream begins this way, "In the second year of the reign of Artaxerxes, *on the first of Nisan*, Mordecai . . . had a dream." The addition then proceeds to describe Mordecai's revelatory dream of the rescue of the Jewish race from the lethal threat of extinction and the establishment of Mordecai in the king's court. So together we have: saved from a flood, saved from oppression and bondage, saved from genocide, and in one way or another all are connected with "the first day of the first month."

I have already drawn a parallel between "Moses finished the work" (40:33b) and "By the seventh day God had finished the work" (Gen. 2:2). There is, however, another great "finisher" in Scripture, maybe two. Near the end of his ministry Jesus is able to say, "I have finished the work you gave me to do" (John 17:4), or "Later, knowing that all was now finished . . . Jesus said, 'It is finished'" (John 19:28, 30). One may also add Paul's "I have fought the good fight, I have finished the race" (2 Tim. 4:7). Neither God nor Moses nor Jesus nor Paul is like the tower builder of whom Jesus speaks as a sorry example of one who "began to build but was not able to finish" (Luke 14:28–30).

Harry Emerson Fosdick, the irrepressible preacher of yeasteryear, preached and published a great sermon titled "The Importance of a Good Finish." That is true throughout Scripture, as we have seen, but it is also true in the holy, transformed life God desires to build and form in the believer's body, which is the Spirit's temple. To that end, we join with Charles Wesley in singing his robust hymn "Love Divine, All Loves Excelling": "Finish, then, thy new creation, pure and spotless, let us be."

God's Glory Fills the Tabernacle

(40:34–38)

Translation

[34]And the cloud covered the tent of meeting, and the LORD's glory filled the dwelling place. [35]And Moses was not able to enter into the tent of meeting because the cloud dwelt over it and the LORD's glory filled the dwelling place. [36]Whenever the cloud was lifted off from the dwelling place, Israel's sons would journey on in all their journeyings. [37]If the cloud was not lifted off, they would not journey on until the day of its being lifted. [38]For the LORD's cloud was over the dwelling place by day, and fire by night was in it, before the eyes of the entire house of Israel throughout all their journeyings.

Grammatical and Lexical Notes

40:34. Since I have from time to time connected phrases in chaps. 39–40 with similar phrases in Gen. 1–2, could we add to those examples the (uncommon) transitive use of *mālēʾ* ("filled") in vv. 34, 35 with the transitive use of *mālēʾ* in Gen. 1:22, 28 (and 9:1)?

40:35. The LXX translates the verb *šākan* ("the cloud *dwelt* over it") with *episkiazein*. That verb appears in at least two NT verses that may have some connection with this last unit in Exodus, apart from Acts 5:15 where the literal meaning "cast a shadow" occurs. The first of these is Luke 1:35, the angel's words to Mary: "The Holy Spirit will come upon you, and the power of the Most High will *overshadow* you." Surely this is a figurative way of speaking of God's reassuring, protecting presence with and over Mary. The other passage is in the Mount of Transfiguration scene in which we read that "a cloud came and *enveloped* them" (Matt. 17:5; Mark 9:7; Luke 9:34), with the "them" being Jesus, Moses, and Elijah, or the three disciples, Peter, James, and John, who witnessed the event. Both the closing scene in Exodus and the spectacle on the Mount of Transfiguration speak of a cloud that comes and covers.

40:36–37. The verb *ʿālâ* ("go, ascend, lift") appears often in the Qal and Hiphil stems, but only a few times in the Niphal stem. Three of those are here in vv. 36 and 37. The passive use of *ʿālâ* in chap. 40 anticipates its use again in Num. 9:17, "As the cloud was lifted off [*hēʿālōt*] from the tent, Israel's sons would journey on." The cloud has no ability to move on its own. It must be moved.

40:37–38. The verb *nāsaʿ* ("journey") and the plural noun *massāʿîm* ("journeyings") resurface in Exodus for the first time since Israel's earlier "journeyings" in Exodus (12:37; 13:20; 14:15; 16:1; 17:1 [verb and noun]; 19:2).

40:38. The expression "the LORD's cloud" (*ʿănan YHWH*) appears in the Bible only here and in Num. 10:34. In Num. 14:14 Moses speaks to the Lord about "your cloud" that hovers over the Israelites as they journey.

Commentary

40:34–38 The climax in the book of Exodus is the moving of the cloud that symbolizes divine presence from Mount Sinai's peak to over the tabernacle. Mountains cannot move and relocate. The divine *kābôd* ("glory") can. Just because the time must surely come for Israel to leave behind the holy Mount Sinai, that does not mean that Israel leaves behind the God of Sinai.

So intense is the divine effulgence that Moses is not able to enter the tent (v. 35). This is the second time in Exodus where God's hovering presence prevents somebody from entering something. The first is when Moses relays Passover guidelines to his people—"the LORD shall pass over the entrance (of your homes) and not allow the Destroyer to come into your houses" (12:23). Note the similarity in the Hebrew of "he will not allow . . . to come into" (*wĕlōʾ yittēn . . . lābōʾ ʾel*) of 12:23 with "And he was not able to enter" (*wĕlōʾ-yākōl . . . lābōʾ ʾel*) of 40:35. God's glory is thick enough and powerful enough to prevent any entry either by the "Destroyer" of chap. 12 or the Moses of chap. 40. Had the Destroyer penetrated the shield, the occupants of the home would have been doomed. Had Moses penetrated the shield, Moses would have been doomed. In chap. 12 salvation is for those on the inside looking out. In chap. 40 salvation is for one on the outside looking in.

Moses knows all about clouds and whether one may enter them or not. There is a striking contrast between the cloud on Mount Sinai and the cloud on the tabernacle. Exod. 24:16 speaks of both God's glory (*kābôd*) "dwelling" (*šākan*) on Mount Sinai and the cloud (*ʿānān*) "covering" (*kāšâ*) it for six days. These are the same nouns and verbs one finds in 40:34–38, except the emphasis has shifted from a mountain to a tabernacle.

But then there comes this stunning contrast: "And Moses entered into the cloud" (*wayyābōʾ mōšeh bĕtôk heʿānān*) in 24:18 with, "And Moses was unable to enter the tent of meeting" (*wĕlōʾ-yākōl mōšeh lābōʾ ʾel-ʾōhel môʿēd*) in 40:35. Permission granted in 24:18; permission denied in 40:35. I take it that when Leviticus begins by saying, "The LORD spoke to him [Moses] from the tent of meeting" (Lev. 1:1), Moses is standing somewhere in the tent's outer courtyard.

Milgrom (1991: 135–37) draws an intriguing parallel between Moses's first encounter with God at Sinai (Exod. 3) and his first encounter with God at the tabernacle (Exod. 40:34–35). The fire in the bush is like the cloud and glory over the shrine. And both phenomena make Moses want to move in more closely. But in neither case is he successful. Exodus 3:5, "Come no closer," matches Exod. 40:35a, "But Moses was not able to enter." Those two similar incidents imply that Moses's ability to enter the cloud in Exod. 24 is a rare exception, a onetime, unusual privilege.

There is a world of difference between Moses's not being able to enter the tent and his not being able to enter Canaan (again in *lōʾ bôʾ* [Hiphil] *ʾel*, Num.

20:12). In Num. 20 permission for entry is denied because of some sinful act on Moses's part. Not so in Exod. 40. There it is simply a case of knowing your limitations and respecting them. Honor the boundaries when the finite enters into the presence of the Infinite.

Exodus begins with a backward look, as it lists Jacob's sons who come to Egypt with their father, a replay of Gen. 46:8–27. It is appropriate, then, that Exodus concludes (40:36–38) with a forward look, anticipating those times in Numbers when the cloud will lift, signaling to the Israelites that it is time to close down the camp and continue the journey toward Canaan.

Works Cited

Ackerman, J. S. 1974. "The Literary Context of the Moses's Birth Story (Exodus 1–2)." In *Literary Interpretations of Biblical Narratives*, edited by K. R. R. Gros-Louis et al., 74–119. Nashville: Abingdon.

Ackerman, S. 1992. *Under Every Green Tree*. Atlanta: Scholars Press.

———. 2002. "The Personal Is Poetical: Covenantal and Affectionate Love (*ʾAhāb, ʾAhăbâ*)." *Vetus Testamentum* 52:437–58.

Ackroyd, P. R. 1951. "The Hebrew Root *Bʾsh*." *Journal of Theological Studies* 2:31–36.

Addinall, P. 1999. "Exodus III 19B and the Interpretation of Biblical Narrative." *Vetus Testamentum* 49:289–300.

Aejmelaeus, A. 1986. "Function and Interpretation of *Kî* in Biblical Hebrew." *Journal of Biblical Literature* 105:193–209.

Aharoni, Y. 1974. "The Horned Altar at Beersheba." *Biblical Archaeologist* 37:2–6.

Albright, W. F. 1957. *From the Stone Age to Christianity*. 2nd ed. Garden City, NY: Doubleday.

———. 1963. "Jethro, Hobab, and Reuel in Early Hebrew Tradition." *Catholic Biblical Quarterly* 25:1–11.

———. 1968. *Yahweh and the Gods of Canaan*. London: Athlone.

Albright, W. F., and T. Mann. 1971. *Matthew*. Anchor Bible. New York: Doubleday.

Alexander, T. D. 1999. "The Composition of the Sinai Narrative in Exodus xix 1–xxiv 11." *Vetus Testamentum* 49:2–20.

Allegro, J. N. 1955. "Uses of the Semitic Demonstrative *z* in Hebrew." *Vetus Testamentum* 5:309–12.

Allen, R. B. 1996. "The 'Bloody Bridegroom' in Exodus 4:24–26." *Bibliotheca sacra* 153:259–69.

Alter, R. 1981. *The Art of Biblical Narrative*. New York: Basic Books.

———. 1992. *The World of Biblical Literature*. San Francisco: Basic Books.

———. 2004. "Exodus." In *The Five Books of Moses. A Translation with Commentary*, 297–535. New York and London: Norton.

Althann, R. 1976. "A Note on Exodus 19,12aB–13." *Biblica* 57:242–46.

———. 1981. "*Mwl*, 'Circumcise' with the *Lamedh* of Agency." *Biblica* 62:239–40.

Andersen, F. I. 1966. "A Lexicographical Note on Exodus xxxii 18." *Vetus Testamentum* 16:108–11.

———. 1969. "A Short Note on Construct *K* in Hebrew." *Biblica* 50:68–69.

———. 1974. *The Sentence in Biblical Hebrew*. Janua linguarum, series practica 231. The Hague and Paris: Mouton.

Andersen, F. I., and D. N. Freedman. 1980. *Hosea*. Anchor Bible. Garden City, NY: Doubleday.

———. 1989. *Amos*. Anchor Bible. New York: Doubleday.

———. 2000. *Micah*. Anchor Bible. New York: Doubleday.

André, G. 1980. *Determining the Destiny PQD in the Old Testament*. Coniectanea biblica: Old Testament Series 16. Uppsala: Almquist & Wiksell.

Ap-Thomas, D. R. 1957. "Some Aspects of the Root *ḤNN* in the Old Testament." *Journal of Semitic Studies* 2:128–48.

Arichea, D. C., Jr. 1989. "The Ups and Downs of Moses: Locating Moses in Exodus 19–33." *The Bible Translator* 40:244–46.

Arnold, B. T., and J. H. Choi. 2003. *A Guide to Biblical Hebrew Syntax*. Cambridge: Cambridge University Press.

Avalos, H. 1990. "Exodus 22:9 and Akkadian Legal Formulae." *Journal of Biblical Literature* 109:116–17.

Avishur, Y. 1975. "Word Pairs Common to Phoenician and Biblical Hebrew." *Ugarit-Forschungen* 7:13–47.

———. 1980. "Expressions of the Type *BYN YDYM* in the Bible and Semitic Languages." *Ugarit-Forschungen* 12:125–33.

———. 1984. *Stylistic Studies of Word-Pairs in Biblical and Ancient Semitic Languages*. Alter Orient und Altes Testament 210. Neukirchen-Vluyn, Germany: Neukirchen Verlag.

Bailey, J. A. 1970. "Initiation and the Primal Woman in Gilgamesh and Genesis 2–3." *Journal of Biblical Literature* 89:137–50.

Bailey, W. A. 2005. *"You Shall Not Kill" or "You Shall Not Murder"? The Assault on a Biblical Text*. Collegeville, MN: Liturgical Press.

Baker, D. L. 2005. "Last but Not Least: The Tenth Commandment." *Hebrew Studies* 27:3–24.

Balentine, S. E. 1980. "A Description of the Semantic Field of Hebrew Words for 'Hide.'" *Vetus Testamentum* 30:137–53.

———. 1984. "The Prophet as Intercessor: A Reassessment." *Journal of Biblical Literature* 103:161–73.

———. 1985. "Prayer in the Wilderness Traditions: In Pursuit of Divine Justice." *Hebrew Annual Review* 9:53–74.

———. 1989. “Prayers for Justice in the Old Testament: Theodicy and Theology.” *Catholic Biblical Quarterly* 51:597–616.

Baloian, B. E. 1992. *Anger in the Old Testament*. American University Studies, Series VII, Theology and Religion 99. New York: Peter Lang.

Bar, S. 2008. “Who Were the Mixed Multitude?” *Hebrew Studies* 49:27–39.

Barclay, J. M. G. 1992. “Manipulating Moses: Exodus 2:10–15 in Egyptian Judaism and the New Testament.” In *Text as Pretext: Essays in Honour of Robert Davidson*, edited by R. P. Carroll, 28–46. Journal for the Study of the Old Testament: Supplement Series 138. Sheffield: Sheffield Academic Press.

Barr, J. 1960. “Theophany and Anthropomorphism in the Old Testament.” *Vetus Testamentum* 7:31–38.

———. 1961. *The Semantics of Biblical Language*. London: Oxford University Press.

———. 1968. *Comparative Philology and the Text of the Old Testament*. Oxford: Clarendon.

———. 1973. “An Aspect of Salvation in the Old Testament.” In *Man and His Salvation: Studies in Memory of S. G. F. Brandon*, edited by E. J. Sharpe and J. R. Hinnells, 39–52. Manchester, UK: Manchester University Press.

———. 1978. “Some Notes on *Ben* ‘between’ in Classical Hebrew.” *Journal of Semitic Studies* 23:1–22.

———. 1985. “‘Why?’ in Biblical Hebrew.” *Journal of Theological Studies* 36:1–33.

———. 1989. “Determination and the Definite Article in Biblical Hebrew.” *Journal of Semitic Studies* 34:307–35.

Barré, M. L. 1992. “My Strength, My Song in Exodus 15:2.” *Catholic Biblical Quarterly* 54:623–37.

———. 2000. “Textual and Rhetorical-Critical Observations on the Last Servant Song (Isaiah 52:13–53:12).” *Catholic Biblical Quarterly* 62:1–27.

Barth, K. 1940. *Church Dogmatics*. Vol. 2.1, *The Doctrine of God*. Edinburgh: T&T Clark.

Bartor, A. 2007. “The Representation of Speech in the Casuistic Laws of the Pentateuch: The Phenomenon of Combined Discourse.” *Journal of Biblical Literature* 126:231–49.

Bartusch, M. W. 2003. *Understanding Dan: An Exegetical Study of a Biblical City, Tribe and Ancestor*. Journal for the Study of the Old Testament: Supplement Series 379. Sheffield: Sheffield Academic Press.

Batto, B. F. 1983. “The Reed Sea: *Requiescat in Pace*.” *Journal of Biblical Literature* 102:27–35.

Bauckham, R. 2002. *Gospel Women: Studies of the Named Women in the Gospels*. Grand Rapids: Eerdmans.

Berlin, A. 1989. “On the Meaning of *Pll* in the Bible.” *Revue biblique* 96:345–51.

———. 2008. *The Dynamics of Biblical Parallelism*. Rev. and expanded ed. Grand Rapids: Eerdmans. Original ed., Bloomington: Indiana University Press, 1985.

Berman, J. A. 2004. *Narrative Analogy in the Hebrew Bible: Battle Stories and Their Equivalent Non-Battle Narratives*. Vetus Testamentum Supplements 103. Leiden: Brill.

Bevan, H. H. 2003. "Does 'Arise, Let Us Go Hence' (John 14:31D) Make Sense Where It Stands?" *Journal of Theological Studies* 54:576–84.

Beyerlin, W., ed. 1978. *Near Eastern Religious Texts Relating to the Old Testament*. Old Testament Library. Philadelphia: Westminster.

Biddle, M. E. 2002. "Ancestral Motifs in 1 Samuel 25: Intertextuality and Characterization." *Journal of Biblical Literature* 121:617–38.

Birch, B. C. 1991. *Let Justice Roll Down: The Old Testament, Ethics, and Christian Life*. Louisville: Westminster John Knox.

Birch, B. C., W. Brueggemann, T. E. Fretheim, and D. L. Peterson. 2005. *A Theological Introduction to the Old Testament*. 2nd ed. Nashville: Abingdon.

Bird, P. A. 1997. *Missing Persons and Mistaken Identities: Women and Gender in Ancient Israel*. Overtures to Biblical Theology. Minneapolis: Fortress.

Blake, F. R. 1946. "The Form of Verbs after *Wāw* in Hebrew." *Journal of Biblical Literature* 65:51–57.

Blenkinsopp, J. 1976. "The Structure of P." *Biblica* 38:275–92.

———. 1977. *Prophecy and Canon: A Contribution to the Study of Jewish Origins*. Studies of Judaism and Christianity in Antiquity 3. South Bend, IN: University of Notre Dame Press.

———. 2000. *Isaiah 40–55*. Anchor Bible. New York: Doubleday.

———. 2003. *Isaiah 56–66*. Anchor Bible. New York: Doubleday.

Block, D. I. 2010. "'You Shall Not Covet Your Neighbor's Wife': A Study in Deuteronomic Domestic Ideology." *Journal of the Evangelical Theological Society* 53:449–74.

———. 2011. "Bearing the Name of the Lord with Honor." *Bibliotheca sacra* 168:20–31.

Breasted, J. H. 1967. *A History of Egypt*. New York: Bantam.

Brenner, A. 1982. *Colour Terms in the Old Testament*. Journal for the Study of the Old Testament: Supplement Series 21. Sheffield: Almond.

———. 1985. *The Israelite Women: Social Role and Literary Type in Biblical Narrative*. Sheffield: JSOT Press.

———, ed. 1993. *A Feminist Companion to Exodus to Deuteronomy*. Feminist Companion to the Bible 6. Sheffield: Sheffield Academic Press.

———. 1997. *The Intercourse of Knowledge: On Gendering Desire and "Sexuality" in the Hebrew Bible*. Biblical Interpretation Series 26. Leiden: Brill.

———. 1999. *Ruth and Esther: A Feminist Companion to the Bible*. 2nd ed. Sheffield: Sheffield Academic Press.

Brenner, A., and F. van Dijk-Hemmes. 1993. *On Gendering Texts: Female and Male Voices in the Hebrew Bible*. Leiden: Brill.

Brenner, M. L. 1991. *The Song of the Sea: Ex. 15:1–21*. Beihefte zur Zeitschrift für die alttestamentliche Wissenschaft 198. New York: de Gruyter.

Bretherton, D. J. 2005. "An Invitation to Murder? A Re-interpretation of Exodus 22:18." *Expository Times* 116:145–52.

Brettler, M. Z. 2005. *How to Read the Bible*. Philadelphia: Jewish Publication Society.

Brichto, H. C. 1963. *The Problem of "Curse" in the Hebrew Bible*. Philadelphia: Society of Biblical Literature.

———. 1968. "On Faith and Revelation in the Hebrew Bible." *Hebrew Union College Annual* 39:35–53.

———. 1973. "Kin, Cult, Land and Afterlife—a Biblical Complex." *Hebrew Union College Annual* 44:1–54.

———. 1992. *Toward a Grammar of Biblical Poetics: Tales of the Prophets*. New York and Oxford: Oxford University Press.

———. 1998. *The Names of God: Poetic Readings in Biblical Beginnings*. New York: Oxford University Press.

Bright, J. 1973. "The Apodictic Prohibition: Some Observations." *Journal of Biblical Literature* 92:185–204.

Brin, G. 1994. *Studies in Biblical Law: From the Hebrew Bible to the Dead Sea Scrolls*. Translated by J. Chipman. Journal for the Study of the Old Testament: Supplement Series 176. Sheffield: Sheffield Academic Press.

———. 1995. "The Formula 'If He Shall Not (Do)' and the Problem of Sanctions in Biblical Law." In *Pomegranates and Golden Bells: Studies in Biblical, Jewish, and Near Eastern Ritual, Law, and Literature in Honor of Jacob Milgrom*, edited by D. P. Wright et al., 341–62. Winona Lake, IN: Eisenbrauns.

———. 2001. *The Concept of Time in the Bible and the Dead Sea Scrolls*. Leiden: Brill.

Brongers, H. A. 1977. "Fasting in Israel in Biblical and Post-biblical Times." *Oudtestamentische Studiën* 20:1–21.

Brooks, Phillips. 1989. *The Joy of Preaching*. Reprinted, Grand Rapids: Kregel.

Brown, R. E. 1966–70. *The Gospel according to John: Introduction, Translation, and Notes*. 2 vols. Anchor Bible. Garden City, NY: Doubleday.

———. 1994. *The Death of the Messiah: From Gethsemane to the Grave; A Commentary on the Passion Narrative in the Four Gospels*. 2 vols. New York: Doubleday.

Brueggemann, W. 1972. "Weariness, Exile and Chaos." *Catholic Biblical Quarterly* 34:19–38.

———. 1994. "Exodus." In *The New Interpreter's Bible*, edited by L. E. Keck et al., 1:675–981. Nashville: Abingdon.

———. 1997. *Theology of the Old Testament: Testimony, Dispute, Advocacy*. Minneapolis: Augsburg.

Buch, J. 2005. "*Neshekh* and *Tarbit*: Usury from Bible to Modern Finance." *Jewish Biblical Quarterly* 33:13–22.

Burnside, J. 2010. "Flight of the Fugitives: Rethinking the Relationship between Biblical Law (Exodus 21:12–14) and the Davidic Succession Narrative (1 Kings 1–2)." *Journal of Biblical Literature* 129:418–31.

Burrows, E. 1936. "The Number Seventy in Semitic." *Orientalia* 5:389–92.

Butts, A. M. 2010. "A Note on *Nĕʾdārî* in Ex. 15:6." *Vetus Testamentum* 60:167–71.

Caird, G. B. 1968. "Toward a Lexicon of the Septuagint I." *Journal of Theological Studies* 19:453–75.

———. 1980. *The Language and Imagery of the Bible*. Philadelphia: Westminster.

Carmichael, C. M. 1967. "Laws, Wisdom, and Historical Traditions." *Journal of Semitic Studies* 12:198–206.

———. 1974. "A Time for War and a Time for Peace: The Influence of the Distinction upon Some Legal and Literary Material." *Journal of Jewish Studies* 25:50–63.

———. 1976. "On Separating Life and Death: An Explanation of Some Biblical Laws." *Harvard Theological Review* 69:1–7.

———. 1986. *Biblical Laws of Talion*, 21–39. Oxford: Oxford Centre for Post-graduate Studies. Originally in *Hebrew Annual Review* 9 (1985): 107–26.

———. 1996. "Joseph, Moses, and the Institution of the Israelite Judicature." In *"Go to the Land I Will Show You": Studies in Honor of Dwight W. Young*, edited by J. E. Coleson and V. H. Matthews, 15–25. Winona Lake, IN: Eisenbrauns.

Carpinelli, F. G. 1999. "'Do This as *My* Memorial' (Luke 22:19): Lucan Soteriology of Atonement." *Catholic Biblical Quarterly* 61:74–91.

Carroll, R. P. 1994. "Strange Fire: Abstract of Presence Absent in the Text; Meditations on Exodus 3." *Journal for the Study of the Old Testament* 61:39–58.

Cassuto, U. 1967. *A Commentary on the Book of Exodus*. Jerusalem: Magnes.

Cave, C. H. 1964. "The Obedience of Unclean Spirits." *New Testament Studies* 11:93–97.

Ceresko, A. R. 1975. "The A:B::B:A Word Pattern in Hebrew and Northwest Semitic with Special Reference to the Book of Job." *Ugarit-Forschungen* 7:73–88.

Chavel, S. 2003. "Compositry and Creativity in 2 Samuel 21:1–14." *Journal of Biblical Literature* 122:23–52.

Childs, B. S. 1962. *Memory and Tradition in Israel*. Studies in Biblical Theology 37. Naperville, IL: Allenson.

———. 1963. "A Study of the Formula, 'Until This Day.'" *Journal of Biblical Literature* 82:279–92.

———. 1974. *The Book of Exodus: A Critical, Theological Commentary*. Old Testament Library. Philadelphia: Westminster.

Chirichigno, G. C. 1993. *Debt-Slavery in Israel and in the Ancient Near East*. Sheffield: JSOT Press.

Chisholm, R. 1995. "Does God 'Change His Mind'?" *Bibliotheca sacra* 152:387–99.

Christiansen, B. 2009. "A Linguistic Analysis of the Biblical Hebrew Particle *nāʾ*: A Test Case." *Vetus Testamentum* 59:379–93.

Clark, G. 1993. *The Word Ḥesed in the Hebrew Bible*. Journal for the Study of the Old Testament: Supplement Series 157. Sheffield: Sheffield Academic Press.

Clark, W. M. 1971. "The Righteousness of Noah." *Vetus Testamentum* 21:261–80.

Clines, D. J. A. 1989. *Job*. Vol. 1. Word Biblical Commentary. Dallas: Word.

———. 1995a. "Ethics as Deconstruction, and, the Ethics of Deconstruction." In *The Bible in Ethics: The Second Sheffield Colloquium*, edited by J. W. Rogerson et al., 77–106. Journal for the Study of the Old Testament: Supplement Series 207. Sheffield: Sheffield Academic Press.

———. 1995b. "The Ten Commandments, Reading from Left to Right." In *Words Remembered, Texts Renewed: Essays in Honour of John F. A. Sawyer*, edited by

J. Davies et al., 97–112. Journal for the Study of the Old Testament: Supplement Series 195. Sheffield: Sheffield Academic Press.

———. 1998. "The Evidence for an Autumnal New Year in Pre-exilic Israel Reconsidered." In *On The Way to the Postmodern: Old Testament Essays, 1967–1998*, 1:371–94. Journal for the Study of the Old Testament: Supplement Series 292. Sheffield: Sheffield Academic Press.

———. 2006. *Job*. Vol. 2. Word Biblical Commentary. Dallas: Word.

Coats, G. W. 1968. "Despoiling the Egyptians." *Vetus Testamentum* 18:450–57.

———. 1970. "Self-Abasement and Insult Formulas." *Journal of Biblical Literature* 89:14–26.

———. 1975. "Moses versus Amalek: Aetiology and Legend in Exod. 17:8–16." In *Congress Volume Edinburgh 1974*, edited by G. W. Anderson et al., 29–41. Vetus Testamentum Supplements 28. Leiden: Brill.

———. 1998. *Exodus 1–18*. Forms of the Old Testament Literature 2A. Grand Rapids: Eerdmans.

Cody, W. 1964. "When Is the Chosen People Called a *Goy*?" *Vetus Testamentum* 14:1–6.

Cogan, M. 1968. "A Technical Term for Exposure." *Journal of Near Eastern Studies* 27:133–35.

Cohen, C. 1972. "Hebrew *tbh*: Proposed Etymologies." *Journal of the Ancient Near Eastern Society* 4:36–45.

———. 1973. "The 'Widowed' City." *Journal of the Ancient Near Eastern Society* 5:75–81.

———. 1975. "Studies in Early Israelite Poetry I: An Unrecognized Case of Three-Line Staircase Parallelism in the Song of the Sea." *Journal of the Ancient Near Eastern Society* 7:13–17.

Cohn, R. L. 1982. "The Literary Logic of 1 Kings 17–19." *Journal of Biblical Literature* 101:333–50.

———. 2001. Review of *Hebrews between Cultures: Group Portraits and National Literature*, by M. Sternberg. *Journal of Biblical Literature* 120:739–41.

Collins, A. 2008. "The Biblical Pithom and Tell el-Maskhuta: A Critique of Some Recent Theories on Exodus 1,11." *Scandinavian Journal of the Old Testament* 22:576–83.

Collins, N. L. 1993. "Notes on the Text of Exodus xxi 22." *Vetus Testamentum* 43:289–301.

———. 1994. "Evidence in the Septuagint of a Tradition in Which the Israelites Left Egypt without Pharaoh's Consent." *Catholic Biblical Quarterly* 56:442–48.

Cooper, A. 1988. "The Plain Sense of Exodus 23:5." *Hebrew Union College Annual* 59:1–22.

Cooper, A., and B. R. Goldstein. 1992. "Exodus and *Maṣṣot* in History and Tradition." *Maarav* 8:15–38.

———. 1997. "At the Entrance to the Tent: More Cultic Resonances in Biblical Narrative." *Journal of Biblical Literature* 116:201–15.

———. 2003. "The Development of the Priestly Calendars (I): The Daily Sacrifice and the Sabbath." *Hebrew Union College Annual* 74:1–20.

Cowley, A. E. 1923. *Aramaic Papyri of the Fifth Century BC*. Oxford: Oxford University Press.

Cranfield, C. E. B. 1975. *A Critical and Exegetical Commentary on the Epistle to the Romans*. Vol. 1. International Critical Commentary. Edinburgh: T&T Clark.

———. 1979. *A Critical and Exegetical Commentary on the Epistle to the Romans*. Vol. 2. International Critical Commentary. Edinburgh: T&T Clark.

Cross, F. M., Jr., and D. N. Freedman. 1955. "The Song of Miriam." *Journal of Near Eastern Studies* 14:237–50.

Crown, A. D. 1963. "Aposiopesis in the Old Testament and the Hebrew Conditional Oath." *Abr-Nahrain* 4:96–111.

———. 1974. "An Alternative Meaning of *ʾIš* in the Old Testament." *Vetus Testamentum* 24:110–12.

Culley, R. C. 1976. *Studies in the Structure of Hebrew Narrative*. Philadelphia: Fortress.

Curtis, E. M. 1985. "The Theological Basis for the Prohibition of Images in the Old Testament." *Journal of the Evangelical Theological Society* 28:277–87.

Curtis, J. B. 1983. "On Job's Witness in Heaven." *Journal of Biblical Literature* 102:549–62.

Dahood, M. J. 1956. Review of *Ancient Near Eastern Texts Relating to the Old Testament*, by J. B. Pritchard. *Biblica* 37:365–67.

———. 1958. "Qoheleth and Recent Discoveries." *Biblica* 39:302–18.

———. 1959a. "The Root *ʿZb* in Job." *Journal of Biblical Literature* 78:303–9.

———. 1959b. "The Value of Ugaritic for Textual Criticism." *Biblica* 40:160–70.

———. 1962. "*Nādâ* 'to Hurl' in Ex 15,16." *Biblica* 43:248–49.

———. 1963. "Zacharia 9,1 *ʿÊn ʾĀdām*." *Catholic Biblical Quarterly* 25:123–24.

———. 1965. "Hebrew-Ugaritic Lexicography III." *Biblica* 46:311–32.

———. 1966. "The Phoenician Background of Qoheleth." *Biblica* 47:264–82.

———. 1967. "Hebrew-Ugaritic Lexicography V." *Biblica* 48:421–38.

———. 1969. "Hebrew-Ugaritic Lexicography VII." *Biblica* 50:337–56.

———. 1971. "Hebrew-Ugaritic Lexicography IX." *Biblica* 52:337–56.

———. 1972. "Hebrew-Ugaritic Lexicography X." *Biblica* 53:386–403.

———. 1974a. "Hebrew-Ugaritic Lexicography XII." *Biblica* 55:381–93.

———. 1974b. "Northwest Semitic Notes on Genesis." *Biblica* 55:76–82.

———. 1975. "Isaiah 51,19 and Sefire III 22." *Biblica* 56:94–95.

———. 1977. "Ebla, Ugarit and the Old Testament." *Vetus Testamentum* 29:81–112.

———. 1978. "Exodus 15,2 *ʾAnwēhû* and Ugaritic *Shnwt*." *Biblica* 59:260–61.

———. 1979. "Scripto Defectiva in Judges 1,19." *Biblica* 60:570.

———. 1981. "Vocative *Lamedh* in Exodus 2,14 and Merismus in 34,21." *Biblica* 62:413–15.

———. 1982. "Eblaite and Biblical Hebrew." *Catholic Biblical Quarterly* 44:1–24.

———. 1987. "Love and Death at Ebla and Their Biblical Reflections." In *Love and Death in the Ancient Near East: Essays in Honor of Marvin H. Pope*, edited by J. H. Marks and R. M. Good, 93–99. Guilford, CT: Four Quarters.

Daly, R. J. 1977. "The Soteriological Significance of the Sacrifice of Isaac." *Catholic Biblical Quarterly* 39:45–75.

Damrosch, D. 1987. *The Narrative Content: Transformation of Genre in the Growth of Biblical Literature*. San Francisco: Harper & Row.

Daube, D. 1947. *Studies in Biblical Law*. Cambridge: Cambridge University Press.

———. 1961. "Direct and Indirect Causation in Biblical Law." *Vetus Testamentum* 11:246–69.

———. 1963. *The Exodus Pattern in the Bible*. London: Faber & Faber.

———. 1990. "Heine's Belsatzar." *Journal of Jewish Studies* 41:254–58.

Davies, G. H. 1962. "Tabernacle." In *Interpreter's Dictionary of the Bible*, edited by G. A. Buttrick, 4:498–506. Nashville: Abingdon.

Davies, G. I. 1974. "The Hebrew Text of Exodus viii 19." *Vetus Testamentum* 24:489–92.

———. 1999. "The Theology of Exodus." In *In Search of True Wisdom: Essays in Honour of Ronald E. Clements*, edited by E. Ball, 137–52. Journal for the Study of the Old Testament: Supplement Series 300. Sheffield: Sheffield Academic Press.

Davies, J. A. 2004. *A Royal Priesthood: Literary and Intertextual Perspectives on an Image of Israel in Exodus 19:6*. Journal for the Study of the Old Testament: Supplement Series 395. London: T&T Clark. A synopsis of the dissertation is in *Tyndale Bulletin* 53 (2002): 157–59.

Davies, N. de G. 1943. *The Tomb of Rekh-mi-Rē at Thebes*. New York: Plantin.

Davies, P. R. 1975. "Ark or Ephod in 1 Sam xiv 18?" *Journal of Theological Studies* 26:82–87.

Day, J. 1986. "Asherah in the Hebrew Bible and Northwest Semitic Literature." *Journal of Biblical Literature* 105:385–408.

Deem, A. 1978. "The Goddess Anath and Some Biblical Hebrew Cruces." *Journal of Semitic Studies* 23:25–30.

De Moor, J. C. 1993. "The Twelve Tribes in the Song of Deborah." *Vetus Testamentum* 43:483–93.

DeNeff, S. 2002. *More Than Forgiveness: A Contemporary Call to Holiness Based on the Life of Jesus Christ*. Indianapolis: Wesleyan Publishing House.

Dentan, R. C. 1963. "The Literary Affinities of Exodus xxxiv 6f." *Vetus Testamentum* 13:34–51.

Derrett, J. D. M. 1963. "Law in the New Testament: The Story of the Woman Taken in Adultery." *New Testament Studies* 10:1–26.

———. 1971. "Law in the New Testament: The Palm Sunday Colt." *Novum Testamentum* 13:241–58.

———. 1979. "Contributions to the Study of the Gerasene Demoniac." *Journal for the Study of the New Testament* 3:2–17.

———. 1996. "'On That Night': Luke 17:34." *Evangelical Quarterly* 68:35–46.

———. 1998. "Not Seeing and Later Seeing (John 16:16)." *Expository Times* 109:208–9.

De Vries, S. J. 1975a. "Temporal Terms as Structural Elements in Holy-Word Tradition." *Vetus Testamentum* 25:80–115.

———. 1975b. "The Time Word *Mahar* as a Key to Tradition Development." *Zeitschrift für die alttestamentliche Wissenschaft* 87:73–77.

———. 1975c. *Yesterday, Today, and Tomorrow: Time and History in the Old Testament*. Grand Rapids: Eerdmans.

Dick, M. B. 1983. "Job 31, the Oath of Innocence, and the Sage." *Zeitschrift für die alttestamentliche Wissenschaft* 95:31–53.

Dickson, J. R., and B. S. Rosner. 2004. "Humility as a Social Virtue in the Hebrew Bible." *Vetus Testamentum* 54:459–79.

Donaldson T. L. 1981. "Moses Typology and the Sectarian Nature of Early Christian Anti-Judaism: A Study in Acts 7." *Journal for the Study of the New Testament* 12:27–52.

Dozeman, T. B. 1996. *God at War: Power in the Exodus Tradition*. Oxford: Oxford University Press.

———. 2000. "Masking Moses and Mosaic Authority in Torah." *Journal of Biblical Literature* 119:21–45.

———. 2006. "The Commission of Moses and the Book of Genesis." In *A Farewell to the Yahwist? The Composition of the Pentateuch in Recent European Interpretation*, 107–29. Society of Biblical Literature Symposium Series 34. Atlanta: Society of Biblical Literature.

———. 2009. *Exodus*. Eerdmans Critical Commentary. Grand Rapids: Eerdmans.

Draffkorn, A. E. 1957. "*ILĀNI/ELOHIM*." *Journal of Biblical Literature* 76:216–24.

Driver, G. R. 1946. Review of *The Hebrew-Arabic Dictionary of the Bible, Known as Kitāb-Jāmiʿ al-Alfāẓ of David ben Abraham al-Fāsī the Karaite*, edited by S. L. Skoss. *Journal of Theological Studies* 47:208–11.

———. 1953. "Hebrew Poetic Diction." *Vetus Testamentum* 1:26–39.

———. 1954a. "Ezekiel: Linguistic and Textual Problems." *Biblica* 35:145–59, 299–312.

———. 1954b. "Reflections on Recent Articles." *Journal of Biblical Literature* 73:125–36.

———. 1966. "Forgotten Hebrew Idioms." *Zeitschrift für die alttestamentliche Wissenschaft* 78:1–7.

———. 1968. "Old Problems Re-examined." *Zeitschrift für die alttestamentliche Wissenschaft* 80:174–83.

———. 1973. "Affirmation by Exclamatory Negation." *Journal of the Ancient Near Eastern Society* 5:107–22.

Driver, G. R., and J. C. Miles. 1952. *The Babylonians*. Vol. 1. Oxford: Clarendon.

Driver, S. R. 1889. "Notes on Three Passages in St. Paul's Epistles." *The Expositor*, 3rd series, 9:15–23.

———. 1911. *The Book of Exodus*. Cambridge Bible for Schools and Colleges. Cambridge: Cambridge University Press.

———. 1998 [1874]. *A Treatise on the Use of Tenses in Hebrew and Some Other Syntactical Questions*. London: Oxford University Press. 3rd ed., 1892. Reprinted, Grand Rapids: Eerdmans.

Dumbrell, W. J. 1975. "Midian—a Land or a League?" *Vetus Testamentum* 25:323–27.

Edelman, R. 1950. "Exodus 32:18." *Journal of Theological Studies* 1:56.

———. 1966. "To *ʿAnnôt* Exodus xxxii 18." *Vetus Testamentum* 16:355.

Ehrensvärd, M. 2000. "Determination of the Noun in Biblical Hebrew." *Scandinavian Journal of the Old Testament* 15:301–14.

Ehrlich, C. S. 1985. "The Text of Hosea 1:9." *Journal of Biblical Literature* 104:13–19.

Eichler, B. L. 2008. "Exodus 21:22–25 Revisited: Methodological Considerations." In *Birkat Shalom: Studies in the Bible, Ancient Near Eastern Literature, and Post-biblical Judaism Presented to Shalom M. Paul on the Occasion of His Seventieth Birthday*, edited by C. Cohen et al., 1:11–29. Winona Lake, IN: Eisenbrauns.

Eichrodt, W. 1961. *Theology of the Old Testament*. Vol. 1. Translated by J. A. Baker. Philadelphia: Westminster.

———. 1967. *Theology of the Old Testament*. Vol. 2. Translated by J. A. Baker. Philadelphia: Westminster.

Elman, Y. 1976. "The Akkadian Cognate of Hebrew *Shĕḥîn*." *Journal of the Ancient Near Eastern Society* 8:33–36.

Elwode, J. 1990. "Non-biblical Supplements to Classical Hebrew *ʾim*." *Vetus Testamentum* 40:221–23.

———. 1994. "The Use of *ʾEt* in Non-Biblical Hebrew Texts." *Vetus Testamentum* 44:170–82.

Embry, B. 2010. "The Endangerment of Moses: Towards a New Reading of Exodus 4:24–26." *Vetus Testamentum* 60:177–96.

Emerton, J. A. 1996. "Are There Examples of Enclitic *Mem* in the Hebrew Bible?" In *Texts, Temples, and Tradition: A Tribute to Menachem Haran*, edited by M. V. Fox et al., 321–38. Winona Lake, IN: Eisenbrauns.

———. 1997. "Comparative Semitic Philology and Hebrew Lexicography." In *Congress Volume: Cambridge 1995*, edited by J. A Emerton, 1–24. Vetus Testamentum Supplements 66. Leiden: Brill.

Enns, P. 1996. "The 'Moveable Well' in 1 Corinthians 10:4: An Extra-biblical Tradition in an Apostolic Text." *Bulletin for Biblical Research* 6:23–38.

———. 2000. *Exodus*. NIV Application Commentary. Grand Rapids: Zondervan.

———. 2005. *Inspiration and Incarnation: Evangelicals and the Problem of the Old Testament*. Grand Rapids: Baker Academic.

Eslinger, L. 1995. "The Infinite in a Finite Organical Perception (Isaiah vi 5)." *Vetus Testamentum* 45:145–72.

———. 1996. "Knowing Yahweh: Exodus 6:3 in the Context of Genesis 1–Exodus 15." In *Literary Structure and Rhetorical Strategies in the Hebrew Bible*, edited by L. J. de Regt et al., 188–98. Assen, Netherlands: Van Gorcum.

Everhart, J. S. 2004. "Serving Women and Their Mirrors: A Feminist Reading of Exodus 38:8b." *Catholic Biblical Quarterly* 66:44–54.

Exum, J. C. 1994. "'You Shall Let Every Daughter Live': A Study of Exodus 1:8–2:10." In *The Feminist Companion to the Bible*, vol. 6, *Exodus to Deuteronomy*, edited by A. Brenner, 37–61. Sheffield: Sheffield Academic Press.

Falk, Z. W. 1959. "Exodus xii 6." *Vetus Testamentum* 9:86–88.

———. 1960. "Hebrew Legal Terms." *Journal of Semitic Studies* 5:340–54.

———. 1967. "Hebrew Legal Terms: II." *Journal of Semitic Studies* 12:241–44.

———. 1969. "Hebrew Legal Terms: III." *Journal of Semitic Studies* 14:39–44.

Fassberg, S. E. 1999. "The Lengthened Imperative *Qaṭĕlah* in Biblical Hebrew." *Hebrew Studies* 40:7–13.

Fee, G. D. 1987. *The First Epistle to the Corinthians*. New International Commentary on the New Testament. Grand Rapids: Eerdmans.

Feldman, L. H. 1997. "Josephus' Portrait of Jethro." In *The Quest for Context and Meaning: Studies in Biblical Intertextuality in Honor of James A. Sanders*, edited by C. A. Evans and S. Talmon, 573–94. Leiden: Brill.

Fensham, F. C. 1959. "New Light on Exodus 21:6 and 22:7 from the Laws of Eshnunna." *Journal of Biblical Literature* 78:160–61.

———. 1960. "Exodus xxi 18–19 in the Light of Hittite Law #10." *Vetus Testamentum* 10:333–35.

———. 1962a. "*ʿD* in Exodus xxii 12." *Vetus Testamentum* 12:337–39.

———. 1962b. "Widow, Orphan, and the Poor in Ancient Near Eastern Legal and Wisdom Literature." *Journal of Near Eastern Studies* 21:129–39.

———. 1969. "The Son of a Handmaid in Northwest Semitic." *Vetus Testamentum* 19:312–21.

———. 1976. "The Role of the Lord in the Legal Sections of the Covenant Code." *Vetus Testamentum* 26:262–74.

Fewell, D. N., and D. M. Gunn. 1993. *Gender Power and Promise: The Subject of the Bible's First Story*. Nashville: Abingdon.

Finkelstein, J. J. 1973. "The Goring Ox: Some Historical Perspectives on Deodands, Forfeitures, Wrongful Death and the Western Notion of Sovereignty." *Temple Law Quarterly* 46:169–290.

———. 1981. *The Ox That Gored*. Transactions of the American Philosophical Society 71, part 2. Philadelphia: American Philosophical Society.

Fishbane, M. 1980. "Revelation and Tradition: Aspects of Inner-Biblical Exegesis." *Journal of Biblical Literature* 99:343–61.

———. 1985. *Biblical Interpretation in Ancient Israel*. Oxford: Clarendon.

———. 1995. "Census and Intercession in a Priestly Text (Exodus 30:11–16) and Its Midrashic Transformation." In *Pomegranates and Golden Bells: Studies in Biblical, Jewish, and Near Eastern Ritual, Law, and Literature in Honor of Jacob Milgrom*, edited by D. P. Wright et al., 103–11. Winona Lake, IN: Eisenbrauns.

———. 2003. *Biblical Myth and Rabbinic Mythmaking*. Oxford: Oxford University Press.

Fitzmyer, J. A. 1981. *The Gospel according to Luke*. Vol. 1. Anchor Bible. Garden City, NY: Doubleday.

———. 1985. *The Gospel according to Luke*. Vol. 2. Anchor Bible. Garden City, NY: Doubleday.

Fleddermann, H. 1983. "'And He Wanted to Pass by Them' (Mark 6:48c)." *Catholic Biblical Quarterly* 45:389–95.

Fleishman, J. 1992. "The Age of Legal Maturity in Biblical Law." *Journal of the Ancient Near Eastern Society* 21:35–48.

———. 2000. "Does the Law of Exodus 21:7–11 Permit a Father to Sell His Daughter as a Slave?" *Jewish Law Annual* 13:47–64.

Fleming, D. E. 1993. "The Etymological Origins of the Hebrew *Nabiʾ*: The One Who Invokes God." *Catholic Biblical Quarterly* 55:217–24.

———. 1998. "The Biblical Tradition of Anointing Priests." *Journal of Biblical Literature* 117:401–14.

Fletcher, J. F. 1966. *Situation Ethics: The New Morality*. Philadelphia: Westminster.

Floyd, M. H. 2002. "The מַשָּׂא [*Maśśāʾ*] as a Type of Prophetic Book." *Journal of Biblical Literature* 121:401–22.

Fokkelman, J. P. 1987. "Exodus." In *The Literary Guide to the Bible*, edited by R. Alter and F. Kermode, 56–65. Cambridge, MA: Belknap.

———. 1998. *Major Poems of the Hebrew Bible: At the Interface of Hermeneutics and Structural Analysis*. Vol. 1, *Ex 15, Deut. 32, and Job 3*. Studia semitica neerlandica 37. Assen, Netherlands: Van Gorcum.

Fontaine, C. E. 1982. *Traditional Sayings in the Old Testament*. Bible and Literature Series 5. Sheffield: Almond.

Forti, T. 2006. "Bee's Honey—From Realia to Metaphor in Biblical Wisdom Literature." *Vetus Testamentum* 56:327–41.

Foster, R. 1992. *Prayer: Finding the Heart's True Home*. San Francisco: HarperSanFrancisco.

Fowler, M. D. 1987. "The Meaning of *Lipnê YHWH* in the Old Testament." *Zeitschrift für die alttestamentliche Wissenschaft* 99:384–90.

Fox, E. 1995. *The Five Books of Moses: Genesis, Exodus, Leviticus, Numbers, Deuteronomy; A New Translation with Introductions, Commentary, and Notes*. New York: Schocken Books.

Fox, M. V. 1980. "The Identification of Quotations in Biblical Literature." *Zeitschrift für die alttestamentliche Wissenschaft* 92:416–31.

———. 2000. *Proverbs*. Vol. 1. Anchor Bible. New York: Doubleday.

———. 2009. *Proverbs*. Vol. 2. Anchor Bible. New York: Doubleday.

Frankel, D. 1994. "The Destruction of the Golden Calf: A New Solution." *Vetus Testamentum* 44:330–39.

Freedman, D. N. 1960. "Archaic Forms in Early Hebrew Poetry." *Zeitschrift für die alttestamentliche Wissenschaft* 72:101–7.

———. 1969. "The Burning Bush." *Biblica* 50:245–46.

———. 1997. "When God Repents." In *Divine Commitment and Human Obligation: Selected Writings of David Noel Freedman*, edited by J. R. Huddleston, 1:409–46. Grand Rapids: Eerdmans.

Freedman, D. N., and S. D. Overton. 2002. "Omitting the Omissions: The Case for Haplography in the Transmission of Biblical Texts." In *"Imagining" Biblical Worlds: Studies in Spatial, Social and Historical Constructs in Honor of James W. Flanagan*, edited by D. M. Gunn and P. M. McNutt, 99–116. Journal for the Study of the Old Testament: Supplement Series 359. Sheffield: Sheffield Academic Press.

Fretheim, T. E. 1984. *The Suffering of God: An Old Testament Perspective*. Philadelphia: Fortress.

———. 1988. "The Repentance of God: A Key to Evaluating Old Testament God-Talk." *Horizons in Biblical Theology* 10:47–70.

———. 1991. *Exodus*. Interpretation: A Bible Commentary for Preaching and Teaching. Louisville: John Knox.

Frick, F. S. 1977. *The City in Ancient Israel*. Society of Biblical Literature Dissertation Series 36. Missoula, MT: Scholars Press.

Frisch, A. 1996. "'For I Feared the People and I Yielded to Them' (1 Sam. 15,24)—Is Saul's Guilt Attenuated or Intensified?" *Zeitschrift für die alttestamentliche Wissenschaft* 108:98–104.

Frolov, S. 1996. "The Hero as Bloody Bridegroom." *Biblica* 76:520–23.

Frymer-Kensky, T. 2002. *Reading the Women of the Bible: A New Interpretation of Their Stories*. New York: Schocken Books.

Fuchs, E. 2000. *Sexual Politics in the Biblical Narrative: Reading the Hebrew Bible as a Woman*. Journal for the Study of the Old Testament: Supplement Series 310. Sheffield: Sheffield Academic Press.

Gane, R. 1992. "'Bread of the Presence' and Creator-in-Residence." *Vetus Testamentum* 42:179–203.

Gardiner, A. H. 1920. "The Ancient Military Route between Egypt and Palestine." *Journal of Egyptian Archaeology* 6:99–116 plus plates.

———. 1952. *Egyptian Grammar*. 2nd ed. Oxford: Published on behalf of the Griffith Institute, Ashmolean Museum, by Oxford University Press.

———. 1957. *Egyptian Grammar*. 3rd ed. Oxford: Published on behalf of the Griffith Institute, Ashmolean Museum, by Oxford University Press.

———. 1961. *Egypt of the Pharaohs*. Oxford: Clarendon.

Garr, W. R. 1992. "The Grammar and Interpretation of Exodus 6:3." *Journal of Biblical Literature* 111:385–408.

———. 2004a. "God's Creation: *Br'* in the Priestly Source." *Harvard Theological Review* 97:83–90.

———. 2004b. "*Hen*." *Revue biblique* 111:321–44.

Garsiel, M. 1991. *Biblical Names: A Literary Study of Midrashic Derivations and Puns*. Translated by P. Hackett. Rumat Gan: Bar-Ilan University Press.

———. 2002. "Revealing and Concealing as a Narrative Strategy in Solomon's Judgment (1 Kings 3:16–25)." *Catholic Biblical Quarterly* 64:229–47.

Gaster, T. H. 1936–37. "Notes on 'The Song of the Sea' (Exodus xv)." *Expository Times* 48:45.

Geller, S. 1991. "Cleft Sentences with Pleonastic Pronoun: A Syntactic Construction of Biblical Hebrew and Some of Its Literary Uses." *Journal of the Ancient Near Eastern Society* 20:15–33.

Gemser, B. 1953. "The Importance of the Motive Clause in Old Testament Law." *Vetus Testamentum* 1:50–66.

Geoghegan, J. C. 2004. "The Abrahamic Passover." In *Le-David Maskil: A Birthday Tribute for David Noel Freedman*, edited by R. E. Friedman and W. H. C. Propp, 47–62. Biblical and Judaic Studies 9. Winona Lake, IN: Eisenbrauns.

Gerstenberger, E. 1995. "'. . . He/They Shall Be Put to Death': Life-Preserving Divine Threats in the Old Testament." *Ex auditu* 11:43–61.

Gevirtz, S. 1961a. "The Ugaritic Parallel to Jeremiah 8:23." *Journal of Near Eastern Studies* 20:41–46.

———. 1961b. "West-Semitic Curses and the Problem of the Origin of Hebrew Law." *Vetus Testamentum* 11:137–58.

———. 1963. *Patterns in the Early Poetry of Israel*. Studies in Ancient Oriental Civilization 32. Chicago: University of Chicago Press.

———. 1967. "A Spindle Whorl with Phoenician Inscription." *Journal of Near Eastern Studies* 26:13–16.

———. 1968. "A New Look at an Old Crux: Amos 5:26." *Journal of Biblical Literature* 87:267–76.

———. 1982. "Formative *ʿAyin* in Biblical Hebrew." *Eretz-Israel* 16:57–66.

———. 1984a. "*Ḥereṭ* in the Manufacture of the Golden Calf." *Biblica* 65:377–81.

———. 1984b. "'Naphtali' in the Blessing of Jacob." *Journal of Biblical Literature* 103:513–21.

———. 1986. "Of Syntax and Style in 'Late Biblical Hebrew'—'Old Canaanite' Connection." *Journal of the Ancient Near Eastern Society* 18:25–29.

Gibson J. C. L. 1978. *Canaanite Myths and Legends*. Edinburgh: T&T Clark.

Giles, K. 1994. "The Biblical Argument for Slavery: Can the Bible Mislead? A Case Study in Hermeneutics." *Evangelical Quarterly* 66:3–17.

Ginsberg, H. L. 1969. "Job the Patient and Job the Impatient." *Vetus Testamentum* 17:88–111.

———. 1973. "Ugaritico-Phoenicia." *Journal of the Ancient Near Eastern Society* 4:131–47.

———. 1982. *The Israelian Heritage of Judaism*. New York: Jewish Theological Seminary.

Globe, A. 1974. "The Literary Structure and Unity of the Song of Deborah." *Journal of Biblical Literature* 93:493–512.

Gnuse, R. K. 2000. "Redefining the Elohist?" *Journal of Biblical Literature* 119:201–20.

Goldbaum, F. 1964. "Two Hebrew Quasi-Adverbs: *Lkn* and *ʾKn*." *Journal of Near Eastern Studies* 23:132–35.

Goldingay, J. 1993. "*Kayyôm Hazzeh* 'On This Very Day'; *Kayyôm* 'On the Very Day'; *Kāʿēt* 'At the Very Time.'" *Vetus Testamentum* 43:112–15.

———. 2003. *Israel's Gospel*. Vol. 1 of *Old Testament Theology*. Downers Grove, IL: InterVarsity.

———. 2006. *Israel's Faith*. Vol. 2 of *Old Testament Theology*. Downers Grove, IL: InterVarsity.

———. 2009. *Israel's Life*. Vol. 3 of *Old Testament Theology*. Downers Grove, IL: InterVarsity.

Goldstein, B. R., and A. Cooper. 1990. "The Festivals of Israel and Judah and the Literary History of the Pentateuch." *Journal of the American Oriental Society* 110:19–31.

Good, E. M. 1970. "Exodus xv 2." *Vetus Testamentum* 20:358–59.

Good, R. M. 1983. *The Sheep of His Pasture: A Study of the Hebrew Noun ʿAm(m) and Its Semitic Cognates*. Harvard Semitic Monographs 29. Chico, CA: Scholars Press.

———. 1987. "Exodus 32:18." In *Love and Death in the Ancient Near East: Essays in Honor of Marvin H. Pope*, edited by J. H. Marks and R. M. Good, 137–42. Guilford, CT: Four Quarters.

Gordis, R. 1949. "Quotations as a Literary Usage in Biblical, Oriental and Rabbinic Literature." *Hebrew Union College Annual* 22:157–219.

———. 1955. "Was Qoheleth a Phoenician?" *Journal of Biblical Literature* 74:103–14.

———. 1971. *Poets, Prophets, and Sages: Essays in Biblical Interpretation*. Bloomington: Indiana University Press.

———. 1976a. "Studies in the Esther Narrative." *Journal of Biblical Literature* 95:43–58.

———. 1976b. *The Word and the Book: Studies in Biblical Language and Literature*. New York: Ktav.

———. 1981. "Virtual Quotations in Job, Sumer and Qumran." *Vetus Testamentum* 31:410–27.

Gordon, C. H. 1935. "*ʾĔlōhîm* in Its Reputed Meaning of *Rulers, Judges*." *Journal of Biblical Literature* 54:139–44.

———. 1963. "A Note on the Tenth Commandment." *Journal of Bible and Religion* 31:208–9.

———. 1965. *Ugaritic Textbook*. Analecta orientalia 38. Rome: Pontifical Biblical Institute.

———. 1996. "The Background of Some Distinctive Values in the Hebrew Bible." In "*Go to the Land I Will Show You": Studies in Honor of Dwight W. Young*, edited by J. E. Coleson and V. H. Matthews, 57–68. Winona Lake, IN: Eisenbrauns.

Gottstein, M. H. 1949. "Afterthought and the Syntax of Relative Clauses in Biblical Hebrew." *Journal of Biblical Literature* 68:35–47.

Gottwald, N. 1979. *The Tribes of Yahweh: A Sociology of the Religion of Liberated Israel 1250–1050 BCE*. Maryknoll, NY: Orbis Books.

Gowan, D. E. 1994. *Theology in Exodus: Biblical Theology in the Form of a Commentary*. Louisville: Westminster John Knox.

Grabbe, L. L. 1993. "Comparative Philology and Exodus 15,8: Did the Egyptians Die in a Storm?" *Scandinavian Journal of the Old Testament* 7 (2): 263–69.

Greenberg, M. 1951. "Hebrew *Sĕgullah*: Akkadian *Sikiltu*." *Journal of the American Oriental Society* 71:172–74.

———. 1960. "*Nsh* in Exodus 20,20 and the Purpose of the Sinaitic Theophanies." *Journal of Biblical Literature* 79:273–76.

———. 1962. "Crimes and Punishments." In *The Interpreter's Dictionary of the Bible*, edited by G. A. Buttrick et al., 1:733–44. Nashville: Abingdon.

———. 1969. *Understanding Exodus*. New York: Behrman.

———. 1983. *Ezekiel 1–20: A New Translation with Introduction and Commentary.* Anchor Bible. Garden City, NY: Doubleday.

———. 1986. "More Reflections on Biblical Criminal Law." *Scripta hierosolymitana* 31:1–17.

———. 1997. *Ezekiel 21–37: A New Translation with Introduction and Commentary.* Anchor Bible. Garden City, NY: Doubleday.

Greene-McCreight, K. 1995. "Restless Until We Rest in God: The Fourth Commandment as Test Case in Christian-Biblical Interpretation." *Ex auditu* 11:29–41.

Greenfield, J. C. 1969. Review of *The Literary and Oral Tradition of Hebrew and Aramaic amongst the Samaritans*, vol. 3, part 2, by Z. Ben-Hayyim. *Biblica* 50:98–102.

———. 1993. "Etymological Semantics." *Zeitschrift für Althebräistik* 6:26–37.

Greengus, S. 1976. "Law in the OT." In *The Interpreter's Dictionary of the Bible: Supplementary Volume*, edited by K. Crim et al., 532–37. Nashville: Abingdon.

Greenstein, E. L. 1988. "On the Prefixed Preterite in Biblical Hebrew." *Hebrew Studies* 29:7–17.

———. 1989. "The Syntax of Saying 'Yes' in Biblical Hebrew." *Journal of the Ancient Near Eastern Society* 19:51–59.

———. 1995. "The Firstborn Plague and the Reading Process." In *Pomegranates and Golden Bells: Studies in Biblical, Jewish, and Near Eastern Ritual, Law, and Literature in Honor of Jacob Milgrom*, edited by D. P. Wright et al., 555–68. Winona Lake, IN: Eisenbrauns.

———. 2000. "Recovering 'The Women Who Served at the Entrance.'" In *Studies in Historical Geography and Biblical Historiography Presented to Zecharia Kallai*, edited by G. Galil and M. Weinfeld, 165–73. Vetus Testamentum Supplements 81. Leiden: Brill.

Griffiths, J. G. 1953. "The Egyptian Derivation of the Name Moses." *Journal of Near Eastern Studies* 12:225–31.

Grossfeld, B. 1984. "The Translation of Biblical Hebrew *pqd* in the Targum, Peshitta, Vulgate and Septuagint." *Zeitschrift für die alttestamentliche Wissenschaft* 96:83–101.

Grottanetti, C. 1999. *Kings and Prophets: Monarchic Power, Inspired Leadership and Sacred Text in Biblical Literature.* New York and Oxford: Oxford University Press.

Gruber, M. I. 1983. "The Motherhood of God in Second Isaiah." *Revue biblique* 90:351–59.

———. 1990. "Fear, Anxiety and Reverence in Akkadian, Biblical Hebrew and Other North-West Semitic Languages." *Vetus Testamentum* 40:411–22.

———. 1992. *The Motherhood of God and Other Studies.* South Florida Studies in the History of Judaism 57. Atlanta: Scholars Press.

Guillaume, A. 1963. "The Use of *Ḥlš* in Exod. XVII,13, Isa. XIV,12, and Job XIV,10." *Journal of Theological Studies* 14:91–92.

Guillaume, P. 2004. "Metamorphosis of a Ferocious Pharaoh." *Biblica* 85:232–36.

Haak, P. D. 1982. "A Study and New Interpretation of *qṣr npš*." *Journal of Biblical Literature* 101:161–67.

Habel, N. C. 1965. "The Form and Significance of the Call Narratives." *Zeitschrift für die alttestamentliche Wissenschaft* 77:297–323.

———. 1976. "Appeal to Tradition as a Literary Form." *Zeitschrift für die alttestamentliche Wissenschaft* 85:253–72.

Hague, M. R. 2001. *The Descent from the Mountain: Narrative Patterns in Exodus 19–40*. Journal for the Study of the Old Testament: Supplement Series 323. Sheffield: Sheffield Academic Press.

Halpern, B. 1983. *The Emergence of Israel in Canaan*. Society of Biblical Literature Monograph Series 29. Chico, CA: Scholars Press.

Halpern, B., and R. E. Friedman. 1980. "Composition and Paronomasia in the Book of Jonah." *Hebrew Annual Review* 4:79–92.

Hamilton, V. P. 1990. *The Book of Genesis: Chapters 1–17*. New International Commentary on the Old Testament. Grand Rapids: Eerdmans.

———. 1995. *The Book of Genesis: Chapters 18–50*. New International Commentary on the Old Testament. Grand Rapids: Eerdmans.

———. 2001. *Handbook on the Historical Books*. Grand Rapids: Baker Academic.

Hamm, D. 2003. "The Tamid Service in Luke-Acts: The Cultic Background behind Luke's Theology of Worship (Luke 1:5–25; 18:9–14; 24:50–53; Acts 3:1; 10:3, 30)." *Catholic Biblical Quarterly* 65:215–31.

Hanson, P. D. 1977. "The Theological Significance of Contradiction within the Book of the Covenant." In *Canon and Authority*, edited by G. W. Coats and B. O. Long, 110–31. Philadelphia: Fortress.

Haran, M. 1959. "The Ark and the Cherubim: Their Symbolic Significance in Biblical Ritual." *Israel Exploration Journal* 9:30–38.

———. 1960a. "The Nature of the '*'Ohel Mo'edh*' in Pentateuchal Sources." *Journal of Semitic Studies* 5:50–65.

———. 1960b. "The Uses of Incense in the Ancient Israelite Ritual." *Vetus Testamentum* 10:113–29.

———. 1965. "The Priestly Image of the Tabernacle." *Hebrew Union College Annual* 36:191–226.

———. 1971. "The Graded Numerical Sequence and the Phenomenon of 'Automatism' in Biblical Poetry." *Vetus Testamentum* 22:238–67.

———. 1978. *Temples and Temple-Service in Ancient Israel: An Inquiry into the Character of Cult Phenomena and the Historical Setting of the Priestly School*. Oxford: Clarendon.

———. 1979. "Seething a Kid in Its Mother's Milk." *Journal of Jewish Studies* 30:23–35.

———. 1982. "Book-Scrolls in Israel in Pre-exilic Times." *Journal of Semitic Studies* 33:161–73.

———. 1984. "The Shining of Moses's Face." In *In the Shelter of El Elyon: Essays on Ancient Palestinian Life and Literature in Honor of G. W. Ahlstrom*, edited by W. B. Barrick and J. R. Spencer, 159–73. Journal for the Study of the Old Testament: Supplement Series 31. Sheffield: JSOT Press.

———. 1985. "Book-Size and the Device of Catch Lines in the Biblical Canon." *Journal of Jewish Studies* 36:1–11.

———. 1989. *Forms of the Priestly Style in the Pentateuch*. Jerusalem: Magnes.

Harland, P. J. 1996. "Robber or Violent Man? A Note on the Word *Pārîṣ*." *Vetus Testamentum* 46:530–34.

———. 2000. "*Bṣ*ʿ: Bribe, Extortion or Profit?" *Vetus Testamentum* 50:310–21.

Hartley, J. E. 1992. *Leviticus*. Word Biblical Commentary. Waco: Word Books.

Hays, R. B. 1989. *Echoes of Scripture in the Letters of Paul*. New Haven: Yale University Press.

Heger, P. 1999. *The Three Biblical Altar Laws*. Beihefte zur Zeitschrift für die alttestamentliche Wissenschaft 279. Berlin: De Gruyter.

Held, M. 1961. "A Faithful Lover in an Old Babylonian Dialogue." *Journal of Cuneiform Studies* 15:1–26.

———. 1965. "The Action-Result (Factitive-Passive) Sequence of Identical Verbs in Biblical Hebrew and Ugaritic." *Journal of Biblical Literature* 84:272–82.

———. 1968. "The Root *ZBL/SBL* in Akkadian, Ugaritic and Biblical Hebrew." *Journal of the American Oriental Society* 88:90–96.

Hellers, D. 1995. "Some Performative Utterances in the Bible." In *Pomegranates and Golden Bells: Studies in Biblical, Jewish, and Near Eastern Ritual, Law, and Literature in Honor of Jacob Milgrom*, edited by D. P. Wright et al., 757–66. Winona Lake, IN: Eisenbrauns.

Hendel, R. S. 2000. "'Begetting' and 'Being Born' in the Pentateuch: Notes on Historical Linguistics and Source Criticism." *Vetus Testamentum* 50:38–46.

Hepner, G. 2003. "Abraham's Incestuous Marriage with Sarah: A Violation of the Holiness Code." *Vetus Testamentum* 53:143–55.

Heschel, A. J. 1954. *Man's Quest for God: Studies in Prayer and Symbolism*. New York: Scribner.

Hess, R. S. 1990. "Splitting the Adam: The Usage of *ʾAdam* in Genesis i–iv." *Vetus Testamentum* 41:1–15.

Hiebert, R. J. V. 1994. "Deuteronomy 22:28–29 and Its Premishnaic Interpretations." *Catholic Biblical Quarterly* 56:203–20.

Hoffman, Y. 1994. "The Conception of 'Other Gods' in Deuteronomic Literature." In *Israel Oriental Studies xiv*, edited by Ilai Alon et al., 103–18. Leiden: Brill.

Hoffmeier, J. K. F. 1986. "The Arm of God versus the Arm of Pharaoh in the Exodus Narratives." *Biblica* 67:378–87.

———. 1997. *Israel in Egypt: The Evidence for the Authenticity of the Exodus Tradition*. New York: Oxford University Press.

———. 2007. "What Is the Biblical Date for the Exodus? A Response to Bryant Wood." *Journal of the Evangelical Theological Society* 50:225–47.

Hoftijzer, J. 1965. "The Particle *ʾt* in Classical Hebrew." *Oudtestamentische Studiën* 14:1–99.

———. 1970. "David and the Tekoite Woman." *Vetus Testamentum* 20:419–44.

———. 1973. "The Nominal Clause Reconsidered." *Vetus Testamentum* 23:446–510.

Holladay, W. L. 1958. *The Root "Shubh" in the Old Testament*. Leiden: Brill.

———. 1964. "The Background of Jeremiah's Self-Understanding: Moses, Samuel, and Psalm 22." *Journal of Biblical Literature* 83:153–64.

Holmstedt, R. 2001. "Headlessness and Extraposition: Another Look at the Syntax of Relative Clauses in Biblical Hebrew." *Journal of Northwest Semitic Languages* 27 (1): 1–16.

Honeyman, A. M. 1952. "*Merismus* in Biblical Hebrew." *Journal of Biblical Literature* 71:11–18.

Horowitz, W., and V. Horowitz. 1992. "Urim and Thummim in Light of a Psephomancy Ritual from Assur (LKA 137)." *Journal of the Ancient Near Eastern Society* 21:95–115.

Hort, G. 1957. "The Plagues of Egypt I." *Zeitschrift für die alttestamentliche Wissenschaft* 69:84–103.

———. 1958. "The Plagues of Egypt II." *Zeitschrift für die alttestamentliche Wissenschaft* 70:48–59.

House, H. W. 1978. "Miscarriage or Premature Birth: Additional Thoughts on Exodus 21:22–25." *Westminster Theological Journal* 41:108–23.

Houten, C. van. 1991. *The Alien in Israelite Law*. Journal for the Study of the Old Testament: Supplement Series 107. Sheffield: JSOT Press.

Houtman, C. 1985. "A Note on the LXX Version of Exodus 4,6." *Zeitschrift für die alttestamentliche Wissenschaft* 97:253–54.

———. 1986. "On the Meaning *Ûbāʿēṣîm Ûbāʾăbānîm* in Exodus VII 19." *Vetus Testamentum* 36:347–51.

———. 1989. "'YHWH Is My Banner'—a 'Hand' on the 'Throne' of YH: Exodus xvii 15b, 16a and Their Interpretation." *Oudtestamentische Studiën* 25:110–21.

———. 1990. "On the Pomegranate and Golden Bells of the High Priest's Mantle." *Vetus Testamentum* 40:223–29.

———. 1993–2000. *Exodus*. 4 vols. Historical Commentary on the Old Testament. Kampen: Kok; Leuven: Peeters.

Howell, A. J. 2010. "The Firstborn Son of Moses as the 'Relative of Blood' in Exodus." *Journal for the Study of the Old Testament* 35:63–76.

Huffmon, H. B. 1965. *Amorite Personal Names in the Mari Texts: A Structural and Lexical Study*. Baltimore: Johns Hopkins University Press.

———. 1974. "Exodus 23:4–5: A Comparative Study." In *A Light unto My Path: Old Testament Studies in Honor of Jacob M. Myers*, edited by H. N. Bream et al., 271–78. Philadelphia: Temple University Press.

———. 1995. "The Fundamental Code Illustrated: The Third Commandment." In *Pomegranates and Golden Bells: Studies in Biblical, Jewish, and Near Eastern Ritual, Law, and Literature in Honor of Jacob Milgrom*, edited by D. P. Wright et al., 363–71. Winona Lake, IN: Eisenbrauns.

Hughes, J. A. 1970. "Another Look at the Hebrew Tenses." *Journal of Near Eastern Studies* 29:12–24.

Hummel, H. H. 1957. "Enclitic *Mem* in Early Northwest Semitic, Especially Hebrew." *Journal of Biblical Literature* 75:85–107.

Humphreys, W. L. 2001. *The Character of God in the Book of Genesis*. Louisville: Westminster John Knox.

Hurowitz, V. A. 1985. "The Priestly Account of the Building of the Tabernacle." *Journal of the American Oriental Society* 105:21–30.

———. 1987. "Salted Incense—Exodus 30,35; Maqlu vi 111–113; ix 118–120." *Biblica* 68:178–94.

———. 1992. "'His Master Shall Pierce His Ear with an Awl' (Exodus 21:6): Marking Slaves in the Bible in the Light of Akkadian Sources." *Proceedings of the American Academy of Jewish Research* 58:47–77.

———. 1998. "Spanning the Generations: Aspects of Oral and Written Transmission in the Bible and Ancient Mesopotamia." In *Freedom and Responsibility*, edited by R. M. Griffen and M. B. Edelman, 11–30. New York: Ktav.

Hurvitz, A. 1974. "The Evidence of Language in Dating the Priestly Code: A Linguistic Study in Technical Idioms and Terminology." *Revue biblique* 81:24–56.

———. 1985. "Originals and Imitations in Biblical Poetry: A Comparative Examination of 1 Sam 2:1–10 and Ps 113:5–9." In *Biblical and Related Studies Presented to Samuel Iwry*, edited by A. Kort and S. Morschauser, 115–21. Winona Lake, IN: Eisenbrauns.

Irwin, W. A. 1961. "Where Shall Wisdom Be Found?" *Journal of Biblical Literature* 80:133–42.

———. 1997. "The Course of the Dialogue between Moses and Yhwh in Exodus 33:12–17." *Catholic Biblical Quarterly* 59:629–36.

Isbell, C. 1978. "The Divine Name *'Ehyeh* as a Symbol of Presence in Israelite Tradition." *Hebrew Annual Review* 2:101–18.

———. 1982. "Exodus 1–2 in the Context of Exodus 1–14: Story Lines and Key Words." In *Art and Meaning: Rhetoric in Biblical Narrative*, edited by D. J. A. Clines et al., 37–61. Journal for the Study of the Old Testament: Supplement Series 19. Sheffield: JSOT Press.

Ishida, T. 1979. "The Structure and Historical Implications of All the Lists of Pre-Israelite Nations." *Biblica* 60:461–90.

Jackson, B. S. 1971. "Liability for Mere Intention in Early Jewish Law." *Hebrew Union College Annual* 42:197–225.

———. 2006. *Wisdom-Laws. A Study of the "Mishpaṭim" of Exodus 21:1–22:16*. Oxford: Oxford University Press.

———. 2007. "Gender Critical Observations on Tripartite Breeding Relationships in the Hebrew Bible." In *A Question of Sex? Gender and Difference in the Hebrew Bible and Beyond*, edited by D. W. Rooke, 39–52. Hebrew Bible Monographs 14. Sheffield: Sheffield Phoenix.

Jacobs, L. 1972. "The *Qal Va-Ḥomer* Argument in the Old Testament." *Bulletin of the School of Oriental and African Studies* 35:221–26.

Janzen, J. G. 1985. "Resurrection and Hermeneutics: On Exodus 3:6 and Mark 12:26." *Journal for the Study of the New Testament* 23:43–58.

———. 1989. "The Root *pr*ʿ in Judges v,2 and Deuteronomy xxxii,42." *Vetus Testamentum* 39:393–406.

———. 1990. "The Character of the Calf and Its Cult." *Catholic Biblical Quarterly* 52:597–607.

———. 1992. "Song of Moses, Song of Miriam: Who Is Seconding Whom?" *Catholic Biblical Quarterly* 54:211–20.

———. 1994. "The 'Wandering Aramean' Reconsidered." *Vetus Testamentum* 44:359–75.

———. 1997. *Exodus*. Westminster Bible Companion. Louisville: Westminster John Knox.

———. 2009. *At the Scent of Water: The Ground of Hope in the Book of Job*. Grand Rapids: Eerdmans.

Japhet, S. 2003. "Insights from Job 3, from a Medieval Commentary: Rabbi Samuel Ben Meir (Rashbam) on the Book of Job." In *Reading from Right to Left: Essays on the Hebrew Bible in Honour of David J. A. Clines*, edited by J. C. Exum and H. G. M. Williamson, 241–53. Journal for the Study of the Old Testament: Supplement Series 373. Sheffield: Sheffield Academic Press.

———. 2006. "Periodization between History and Ideology II: Chronology and Ideology in Ezra–Nehemiah." In *Judah and the Judeans in the Persian Period*, edited by O. Lipschits and M. Oeming, 491–508. Winona Lake, IN: Eisenbrauns.

Jenson, P. P. 1992. *Graded Holiness: A Key to the Priestly Conception of the World*. Sheffield: JSOT Press.

Johnson, L. T. 2006. *Hebrews: A Commentary*. New Testament Library. Louisville: Westminster John Knox.

Joosten, J. 1991. "The Syntax of *Zeh Mosheh* (Ex 32.1, 23)." *Zeitschrift für die alttestamentliche Wissenschaft* 103:412–15.

Josipovici, G. 1988. *The Book of God*. New Haven: Yale University Press.

Joüon, P., and T. Muraoka. 1991. *A Grammar of the Hebrew Bible*. Rome: Pontifical Biblical Institute.

Kaiser, W. C., Jr. 1990. "Exodus." In *The Expositor's Bible Commentary*, edited by F. E. Gaebelein, 2:287–437. Grand Rapids: Zondervan.

Kaminsky, J. S. 1995. *Corporate Responsibility in the Hebrew Bible*. Journal for the Study of the Old Testament: Supplement Series 196. Sheffield: Sheffield Academic Press.

———. 2007. *Yet I Loved Jacob: Reclaiming the Biblical Concept of Election*. Nashville: Abingdon.

Kaplan, J. 1967. "Two Samaritan Amulets." *Israel Exploration Journal* 17:158–62.

Kasher, R. 1997. "The Mythological Figure of Moses in Light of Some Unpublished Midrashic Fragments." *Jewish Quarterly Review* 88:19–42.

Kaufmann, Y. 1972. *The Religion of Israel*. Edited and translated by M. Greenberg. New York: Schocken.

Kearney, P. J. 1977. "Creation and Liturgy: The P Redaction of Exodus 25–40." *Zeitschrift für die alttestamentliche Wissenschaft* 89:375–87.

Keil, C. F., and F. Delitzsch. 1865. *Biblical Commentary on the Old Testament*, vol. 1, *The Pentateuch*. Translated by J. Martin. Edinburgh: T&T Clark. Reprinted, Grand Rapids: Eerdmans, 1971.

Kidd, J., and E. Ramirez. 1999. *Alterity and Identity in Israel*. Beihefte zur Zeitschrift für die alttestamentliche Wissenschaft 283. Berlin: De Gruyter.

Kiessling, N. K. 1970. "Antecedents of the Medieval Dragon in Sacred History." *Journal of Biblical Literature* 89:167–75.

Kim, H. C. P. 2000. "Gender Complementarity in the Hebrew Bible." In *Reading the Hebrew Bible for a New Millennium: Form, Concept, and Theological Perspective*, edited by W. Kim et al., 1:263–91. Harrisburg, PA: Trinity.

Kinlaw, D. F. 2010. *Lectures in Old Testament Theology: Yahweh Is God Alone*. Wilmore, KY: Francis Asbury Society.

Kirsch, J. 1997. *The Harlot by the Side of the Road: Forbidden Tales of the Bible*, 145–79. New York: Ballantine Books.

Kitchen, K. A. 1993. "The Tabernacle—a Bronze Age Artifact." *Eretz-Israel* 24:119–29.

———. 2003. *On the Reliability of the Old Testament*. Grand Rapids: Eerdmans.

Kitz, A. M. 1997. "The Plural Forms of *ʾUrim* and *Tummim*." *Journal of Biblical Literature* 116:401–10.

Klein, M. L. 1976. "Converse Translation: A Targumic Technique." *Biblica* 57:515–37.

———. 1979. "Nine Fragments of Palestinian Targum to the Pentateuch from the Cairo Genizah (Additions to MS A)." *Hebrew Union College Annual* 50:149–64.

Klein, R. 1974. *Textual Criticism of the Old Testament: From the Septuagint to Qumran*. Philadelphia: Fortress.

Kleven, T. 1994. "The Use of *Ṣnr* in Ugaritic and 2 Samuel 5:8." *Vetus Testamentum* 44:195–204.

Kline, M. G. 1977. "*Lex Talionis* and the Human Fetus." *Journal of the Evangelical Theological Society* 20:193–201.

Klingbeil, G. A. 1997. "Ritual Time in Leviticus 8 with Special Reference to the Seven-Day Period in the Old Testament." *Zeitschrift für die alttestamentliche Wissenschaft* 109:501–13.

———. 2000. "The Finger of God in the Old Testament." *Zeitschrift für die alttestamentliche Wissenschaft* 112:409–15.

Knierim, R. P. 1995a. "Conceptual Aspects in Exodus 25:1–9." In *Pomegranates and Golden Bells: Studies in Biblical, Jewish, and Near Eastern Ritual, Law, and Literature in Honor of Jacob Milgrom*, edited by D. P. Wright et al., 113–23. Winona Lake, IN: Eisenbrauns.

———. 1995b. *The Task of Old Testament Theology: Method and Cases*. Grand Rapids: Eerdmans.

Knight, D. A. 2000. "Village Law and the Book of the Covenant." In *"A Wise and Discerning Mind": Essays in Honor of Burke O. Long*, edited by S. Olyan and R. C. Culley, 163–79. Brown Judaic Studies 325. Providence: Brown University Press.

Knoppers, G. N. 1994. "Jehoshaphat's Judiciary and 'The Scroll of YHWH's Torah.'" *Journal of Biblical Literature* 113:59–80.

Knowles, M. D. 2004. "Pilgrimage Imagery in the Return of Ezra." *Journal of Biblical Literature* 123:57–74.

Krašovec, J. 1983. "Merism-Polar Expressions in Biblical Hebrew." *Biblica* 64:231–39.

Kroeze, J. H. 2001. "Alternatives for the Nominative in Biblical Hebrew." *Journal of Semitic Studies* 46:33–50.

Kselman, J. S. 1978. "The Recovery of Poetic Fragments from the Pentateuchal Priestly Source." *Journal of Biblical Literature* 97:161–73.

———. 1981. "A Note on *W'nḥhw* in Isa. 57:18." *Catholic Biblical Quarterly* 43:539–41.

Kutler, L. 1984. "A 'Strong' Case for Hebrew *Mar*." *Ugarit-Forschungen* 16:111–18.

Labuschagne, C. J. 1966. "The Emphasizing Particle *Gam* and Its Connotations." In *Studia Biblica et Semitica: Theodoro Christiano Vriezen*, edited by W. C. van Unnik and A. S. van der Woude, 193–203. Wageningen, Netherlands: Veenman.

———. 1973. "The Particles *Hen* and *Hinneh*." *Oudtestamentische Studiën* 18:1–14.

———. 1982a. "The Meaning of *Bĕyād Rāmā* in the Old Testament." In *Von Kanaan bis Kerala: Festschrift für Prof. Mag. Dr. Dr. J. P. M. van der Ploeg O.P.*, edited by W. C. Delsman et al., 143–48. Alter Orient und Altes Testament 211. Neukirchen-Vluyn, Germany: Neukirchener Verlag.

———. 1982b. "The Pattern of Divine Speech Formulas in the Pentateuch: The Key to Literary Structure." *Vetus Testamentum* 32:268–81.

———. 1992. "'You Shall Not Boil a Kid in Its Mother's Milk': A New Proposal for the Origin of the Prohibition." *Vetus Testamentum* 49:6–17.

Lambdin, T. O. 1953. "Egyptian Loan Words in the Old Testament." *Journal of the American Oriental Society* 73:145–55.

Larsson, G. 1983. "The Chronology of the Pentateuch: A Comparison of the MT and LXX." *Journal of Biblical Literature* 102:401–9.

Lasine, S. 1994. "Levitic Violence, Fratricide, and Sacrifice in the Bible and Later Revolutionary Rhetoric." In *Curing Violence*, edited by M. I. Wallace and T. H. Smith, 204–29. Sonoma, CA: Polebridge.

———. 2001. *Knowing Kings: Knowledge, Power, and Narcissism in the Hebrew Bible*. Semeia Studies 40. Atlanta: Society of Biblical Literature Press.

Layton, S. C. 1990. *Archaic Features of Canaanite Personal Names in the Hebrew Bible*. Harvard Semitic Monographs 47. Atlanta: Scholars Press.

Leder, A. C. 1999. "Reading Exodus to Learn and Learning to Read Exodus." *Calvin Theological Journal* 34:11–35.

———. 2001. "The Coherence of Exodus: Narrative Unity and Meaning." *Calvin Theological Journal* 36:251–69.

Lee, J. A. L. 1972. "*Aposkeuē* in the Septuagint." *Journal of Theological Studies* 23:430–37.

Lemche, N. P. 1974. "*Ḥpšy* in 1 Sam. xvii. 25." *Vetus Testamentum* 24:373–74.

———. 1975. "The 'Hebrew Slave': Comments on the Slave Law—Ex xxi 2–11." *Vetus Testamentum* 25:129–44.

———. 1976. "The Manumission of Slaves—the Fallow Year—the Sabbatical Year—the Jobel Year." *Vetus Testamentum* 26:38–59.

———. 1991. *The Canaanites and Their Land*. Journal for the Study of the Old Testament: Supplement Series 110. Sheffield: JSOT Press.

Lemke, W. E. 1981. "The Near and Distant God: A Study of Jer. 23:23–24 in Its Biblical, Theological Context." *Journal of Biblical Literature* 100:541–55.

Lemmelijn, B. 1999. "The Phrase *Ub'ṣym Ub'bnym* in Exod. 7,19." *Biblica* 80:264–68.

Leonard, J. M. 2008. "Identifying Inner-Biblical Allusions: Psalm 78 as a Test Case." *Journal of Biblical Literature* 127:241–65.

Levenson, J. D. 1980. "The Theologies of Commandment in Biblical Times." *Harvard Theological Review* 73:17–33.

———. 1993. *The Death and Resurrection of the Beloved Son: The Transformation of Child Sacrifice in Judaism and Christianity*. New Haven: Yale University Press.

Levine, B. A. 1974. *In the Presence of the Lord: A Study of Cult and Some Cultic Terms in Ancient Israel*. Leiden: Brill.

———. 1981. "The Deir ʿAlla Plaster Inscriptions." *Journal of the American Oriental Society* 101:195–205.

———. 1989. *Leviticus: The Traditional Hebrew Text with the New JPS Translation*. JPS Torah Commentary. Philadelphia: Jewish Publication Society.

———. 1993. *Numbers*. Vol. 1. Anchor Bible. New York: Doubleday.

———. 2000. *Numbers*. Vol. 2. Anchor Bible. New York: Doubleday.

Levine, É. 1999. "On Exodus 21,10 *ʿOnah* and Biblical Marriage." *Zeitschrift für altorientalische und biblische Rechtgeschichte* 51:133–64.

———. 2000. *Heaven and Earth, Law and Love: Studies in Biblical Thought*. Beihefte zur Zeitschrift für die alttestamentliche Wissenschaft 303. Berlin: De Gruyter.

Levinson, B. M. 2000. "The Hermeneutics of Tradition in Deuteronomy: A Reply to J. G. McConville." *Journal of Biblical Literature* 119:269–86.

———. 2005. "The Birth of the Lemma: The Restrictive Reinterpretation of the Covenant Code's Manumission Law by the Holiness Code (Leviticus 25:44–46)." *Journal of Biblical Literature* 124:617–39.

———. 2006. "The 'Effected Object' in Contractual Legal Language: The Semantics of 'If You Purchase a Hebrew Slave' (Exod. xxi 2)." *Vetus Testamentum* 56:485–504.

———. 2008. *"The Right Chorale": Studies in Biblical Law and Interpretation*. Forschungen zum Alten Testament 54. Tübingen: Mohr Siebeck.

Limburg, J. 1969. "The Root *Riv* and the Prophetic Lawsuit Speeches." *Journal of Biblical Literature* 88:291–304.

Linafelt, T. 1996. "The Undecidability of *brk* in the Prologue of Job and Beyond." *Biblical Interpretation* 4:154–72.

Lincoln, A. T. 1982. "The Use of the Old Testament in Ephesians." *Journal for the Study of the New Testament* 14:16–57.

Lindblom, J. 1962. "Lot-casting in the Old Testament." *Vetus Testamentum* 12:164–78.

Lindstrom, F. 1983. *God and the Origin of Evil: A Contextual Analysis of Alleged Monistic Evidence in the Old Testament*. Translated by F. H. Cryer. Coniectanea biblica: Old Testament Series 21. Lund, Sweden: CWK Gleerup.

Lipinski, E. 1970. "*ʾÛrîm* and *Tummîm*." *Vetus Testamentum* 20:495–96.

Liver, J. 1963. "The Half-Shekel Offering in Biblical and Post-biblical Literature." *Harvard Theological Review* 56:173–98.

Loewenstamm, S. E. 1967. "The Making and Destruction of the Golden Calf." *Biblica* 48:481–90.

———. 1969a. "The Expanded Colon in Ugaritic and in Biblical Verse." *Journal of Semitic Studies* 14:176–96.

———. 1969b. "The Lord Is My Strength and My Glory." *Vetus Testamentum* 19:464–70.

———. 1969c. "*Nshk* and *M/trbyt*." *Journal of Biblical Literature* 88:78–80.

———. 1975. "The Making and Destruction of the Golden Calf—a Rejoinder." *Biblica* 56:330–43.

———. 1977. "Exodus 21:22–25." *Vetus Testamentum* 27:352–60. Reprinted in *Comparative Studies in Biblical and Ancient Oriental Literatures*, 517–25. Neukirchen-Vluyn, Germany: Neukirchener-Verlag, 1980.

———. 1992. *From Babylon to Canaan: Studies in the Bible and Its Oriental Background*. Jerusalem: Magnes.

Lohfink, N. 1994. "'I Am Yahweh, Your Physician' (Exodus 15:26)." In *Theology of the Pentateuch: Themes of the Priestly Narrative and Deuteronomy*, translated by L. M. Maloney, 35–94. Minneapolis: Fortress.

Long, B. O. 1968. *The Problem of Etiological Narrative in the Old Testament*. Beihefte zur Zeitschrift für die alttestamentliche Wissenschaft 108. Berlin: Topelmann.

———. 1973. "The Effect of Divination upon Israelite Literature." *Journal of Biblical Literature* 92:489–97.

———. 1976. "The Stylistic Components of Jeremiah 3:1–5." *Zeitschrift für die alttestamentliche Wissenschaft* 88:386–90.

———. 1997. *Planting and Reaping Albright: Politics, Ideology, and Interpreting the Bible*. University Park: Pennsylvania State University Press.

Longacre, R. E. 1995. "Building for the Worship of God: Exodus 25:1–30:10." In *Discourse Analysis of Biblical Literature: What It Is and What It Offers*, edited by W. R. Bodine, 21–49. Semeia Studies. Atlanta: Scholars Press.

Longman, T., III. 2009. *How to Read Exodus*. Downers Grove, IL: InterVarsity.

Lundbom, J. R. 1999. *Jeremiah*. Vol. 1. Anchor Bible. New York: Doubleday.

———. 2004a. *Jeremiah*. Vol. 2. Anchor Bible. New York: Doubleday.

———. 2004b. *Jeremiah*. Vol. 3. Anchor Bible. New York: Doubleday.

Macdonald, J. 1976. "The Status and Role of the *Naʿar* in Israelite Society." *Journal of Near Eastern Studies* 33:147–70.

Magonet, J. 1975. "The Bush That Never Burnt (Narrative Technique in Exodus 3 and 6)." *Heythrop Journal* 16:304–11.

———. 1997. *The Subversive Bible*. London: SCM Press.

Malamat, A. 1962. "Mari and the Bible: Some Patterns of Tribal Organization and Institutions." *Journal of the American Oriental Society* 82:143–50.

Maloney, R. 1974. "Usury and Restriction on Interest Taking in the Ancient Near East." *Catholic Biblical Quarterly* 36:1–20.

Malul, M. 1997. "*Kappî* (Ex 33,22) and *Bĕḥāpnāyw* (Prov. 30,4): Hand or Skirt?" *Zeitschrift für die alttestamentliche Wissenschaft* 109:356–68.

Mankowski, P. V. 2000. *Akkadian Loanwords in Biblical Hebrew*. Harvard Semitic Studies 47. Winona Lake, IN: Eisenbrauns.

Marcus, J. 2000. *Mark*. Vol. 1. Anchor Bible. New York: Doubleday.

———. 2009. *Mark*. Vol. 2. Anchor Bible. New York: Doubleday.

Margalit, B. 1987. "Ugaritic Contributions to Hebrew Lexicography." *Zeitschrift für die alttestamentliche Wissenschaft* 99:391–404.

———. 1989. *The Ugaritic Poem of Aqht*. Beihefte zur Zeitschrift für die alttestamentliche Wissenschaft 182. Berlin: De Gruyter.

———. 1992. "The Day the Sun Did Not Stand Still: A New Look at Joshua x 8–19." *Vetus Testamentum* 42:466–91.

Margalith, O. 1983. "*Śĕrād Bigdê* = Fine Linen from Colchis? [Exod. 31:10]." *Zeitschrift für die alttestamentliche Wissenschaft* 95:430–31.

Marks, H. 1995. "Biblical Naming and Poetic Etymology." *Journal of Biblical Literature* 114:21–42.

Master, J. 2002. "Exodus 32 as an Argument for Traditional Theism." *Journal of the Evangelical Theological Society* 45:585–98.

Mastin, B. A. 1979. "Was the *Shalish* the Third Man in the Chariot?" *Vetus Testamentum* 30:125–54.

Matthews, V. H. 1994. "The Anthropology of Slavery in the Covenant Code." In *Theory and Method in Biblical and Cuneiform Law*, edited by B. M. Levinson et al., 119–35. Sheffield: Sheffield Academic Press.

Mazar, B. 1965. "The Sanctuary of Arad and the Family of Hobab the Kenite." *Journal of Near Eastern Studies* 24:297–303.

McAffee, M. 2010. "The Heart of Pharaoh in Exodus 4–15." *Bulletin of Biblical Research* 20:331–53.

McCarthy, C. M. 1981. *The "Tiqqune Sopherim" and Other Theological Corrections in the Masoretic Text of the Old Testament*. Orbis biblicus et orientalis 36. Freiburg: Göttingen.

McCarthy, D. J. 1967. "'Creation' Motifs in Ancient Hebrew Poetry." *Catholic Biblical Quarterly* 29:87–100, 393–406.

———. 1981. *Treaty and Covenant: A Study in Form in the Ancient Oriental Documents and in the Old Testament*. New ed. Analecta biblica 21a. Rome: Pontifical Biblical Institute.

McEleney, N. J. 1976. "Matthew 17:24–27: Who Paid the Temple Tax? A Lesson in Avoidance of a Scandal." *Catholic Biblical Quarterly* 38:178–92.

McKay, J. W. 1970. "Helel and the Dawn-Goddess." *Vetus Testamentum* 20:451–64.

———. 1971. "Exodus xxiii 1–3, 6–8: A Decalogue for the Administration of Justice in the City Gate." *Vetus Testamentum* 21:311–25.

Meek, T. J. 1930. "The Translation of *GER* in the Hexateuch and Its Bearing on the Documentary Hypothesis." *Journal of Biblical Literature* 49:172–80.

———. 1945. "The Syntax of the Sentence in Hebrew." *Journal of Biblical Literature* 64:1–13.

———. 1948. "Old Testament Roots." *Journal of Biblical Literature* 67:233–39.

———. 1963. "A New Bible Translation." *Journal of Biblical Literature* 82:265–71.

Meier, J. P. 2000. "The Debate on the Resurrection of the Dead: An Incident from the Ministry of the Historical Jesus." *Journal for the Study of the New Testament* 77:3–24.

Melamed, E. Z. 1961. "Break-Up of Stereotype Phrases as an Artistic Device in Biblical Poetry." *Scripta hierosolymitana* 8:115–53.

Mendelsohn, I. 1935. "The Conditional Sale into Slavery of Free-Born Daughters in Nuzi and the Law of Ex. 21:7–11." *Journal of the American Oriental Society* 55:190–95.

———. 1949. *Slavery in the Ancient Near East: A Comparative Study of Slavery in Babylonia, Assyria, Syria and Palestine from the Middle of the Third Millennium to the End of the First Millennium.* New York: Oxford University Press.

———. 1962. "Slavery in the Old Testament." In *The Interpreter's Dictionary of the Bible*, edited by G. A. Buttrick et al., 4:383–91. Nashville: Abingdon.

Mendenhall, G. E. 1958. "The Census Lists of Numbers 1 and 26." *Journal of Biblical Literature* 77:52–66.

Mettinger, T. N. D. 1971. "The Nominal Pattern 'Qetullah' in Biblical Hebrew." *Journal of Semitic Studies* 16:2–14.

Meyers, C. L. 1976. *The Tabernacle Menorah: A Synthetic Study of a Symbol from the Biblical Cult.* Dissertation Series, American Schools of Oriental Research 2. Missoula, MT: Scholars Press.

———. 1996. "Realms of Sanctity: The Case of the 'Misplaced' Incense Altar in the Tabernacle Texts of Exodus." In *Texts, Temples, and Traditions: A Tribute to Menachem Haran*, edited by M. Fox et al., 33–46. Winona Lake, IN: Eisenbrauns.

———. 2005. *Exodus.* New Cambridge Bible Commentary. Cambridge: Cambridge University Press.

———. 2008. "Framing Aaron: Incense Altar and Lamp Oil in the Tabernacle Texts." In *Sacred History, Sacred Literature: Essays on Ancient Israel, the Bible, and Religion in Honor of R. E. Friedman on His Sixtieth Birthday*, edited by S. Dolansky, 13–21. Winona Lake, IN: Eisenbrauns.

Milgrom, J. 1970. *Studies in Levitical Terminology: The Encroacher and the Levite; The Term ʿAboda.* Berkeley: University of California Press.

———. 1976a. *Cult and Conscience: The "Asham" and the Priestly Doctrine of Repentance.* Studies in Judaism in Late Antiquity 18. Leiden: Brill.

———. 1976b. "The Legal Terms *Shlm* and *Brʾshw* in the Bible." *Journal of Near Eastern Studies* 35:271–73.

———. 1976c. "Profane Slaughter and a Formulaic Key to the Composition of Deuteronomy." *Hebrew Union College Annual* 47:1–17.

———. 1981. "Sancta Contagion and Altar/City Asylum." *Vetus Testamentum* 32:278–310.

———. 1982. "Religious Conversion and the Revolt Model for the Transformation of Israel." *Journal of Biblical Literature* 101:169–76.

———. 1990. *Numbers.* JPS Torah Commentary. Philadelphia: Jewish Publication Society.

———. 1991. *Leviticus*. Vol. 1. Anchor Bible. New York: Doubleday.

———. 2000a. *Leviticus*. Vol. 2. Anchor Bible. New York: Doubleday.

———. 2000b. *Leviticus*. Vol. 3. Anchor Bible. New York: Doubleday.

Miller, P. D. 1970. "Animal Names as Designations in Ugarit and Hebrew." *Ugarit-Forschungen* 2:181–82.

Mitchell, C. W. 1987. *The Meaning of* BRK *"To Bless" in the Old Testament*. Society of Biblical Literature Dissertation Series 95. Atlanta: Scholars Press.

Moberly, R. W. L. 1983. *At the Mountain of God: Story and Theology in Exodus 32–34*. Journal for the Study of the Old Testament: Supplement Series 22. Sheffield: Sheffield Academic Press.

———. 1992. *The Old Testament of the Old Testament: Patriarchal Narratives and Mosaic Yahwism*. Overtures to Biblical Theology. Minneapolis: Fortress.

———. 2000. *The Bible, Theology, and Faith: A Study of Abraham and Jesus*. Cambridge: Cambridge University Press.

———. 2008. "Exodus." In *Theological Interpretation of the Old Testament: A Book-by-Book Survey*, edited by K. J. Vanhoozer et al., 42–51. Grand Rapids: Baker Academic.

Moo, D. J. 1983. *The Old Testament in the Gospel Passion Narratives*. Sheffield: Almond.

Moore, M. S. 1998. "Ruth the Moabite and the Blessing of Foreigners." *Catholic Biblical Quarterly* 60:203–17.

Moran, W. L. 1959. "The Scandal of the 'Great Sin' at Ugarit." *Journal of Near Eastern Studies* 18:280–81.

———. 1963. "The Ancient Near Eastern Background of the Love of God in Deuteronomy." *Catholic Biblical Quarterly* 25:77–87.

———. 1967. "The Conclusion to the Decalogue (Ex 20,17 = Dt 5,21)." *Catholic Biblical Quarterly* 29:543–54.

Morgan, G. C. 1903. *The Crises of the Christ*. New York: Revell.

Morgenstern, J. 1949. "The Despoiling of the Egyptians." *Journal of Biblical Literature* 68:1–28.

Morrow, W. 1986. "Consolation, Rejection, and Repentance in Job 42:6." *Journal of Biblical Literature* 105:211–25.

Mowinckel, S. 1962. "Drive and/or Ride in the Old Testament." *Vetus Testamentum* 12:278–99.

Muilenburg, J. 1953. "A Study in Hebrew Rhetoric: Repetition and Style." *Vetus Testamentum* 1:97–111.

———. 1961. "The Linguistic and Rhetorical Usages of the Particle *Kî* in the Old Testament." *Hebrew Union College Annual* 32:135–60.

———. 1966. "A Liturgy on the Triumphs of Yahweh." In *Studia Biblica et Semitica: Theodora Christiano Vriezen*, 233–51. Wageningen: Veenman. Reprinted in *Hearing and Speaking the Word: Selections from the Works of James Muilenburg*, 151–69. Chico, CA: Scholars Press, 1984.

———. 1968. "The Intercession of the Covenant Mediator (Exodus 33:1a, 12–17)." In *Words and Meanings: Essays Presented to David Winton Thomas*, edited by P. R. Ackroyd and B. Lindars, 159–81. Cambridge: Cambridge University Press.

Muraoka, T. 1978. "On the So-Called *Dativus Ethicus* in Hebrew." *Journal of Theological Studies* 29:495–98.

Muraoka, T., and M. Ragland. 1998. "The *Wāw* Consecutive in Old Aramaic? A Rejoinder to Victor Sasson." *Vetus Testamentum* 48:99–104.

Na'aman, N. 1988. "The List of David's Officers (*Šalîšîm*)." *Vetus Testamentum* 38:72–79.

Naude, J. A. 1977. "Syntactic Aspects of Co-ordinate Subjects with Independent Personal Pronouns." *Journal of Northwest Semitic Languages* 25 (2): 75–99.

Naveh, J. 1960. "A Hebrew Letter from the Seventh Century BC." *Israel Exploration Journal* 10:129–39.

Neufeld, E. 1955. "The Prohibitions against Loans at Interest in Ancient Hebrew Law." *Hebrew Union College Annual* 26:355–412.

Neusner, J. 1977–86. *The Tosefta*. 6 vols. New York: Ktav.

Niccacci, A. 1996. "Finite Verb in the Second Position of the Sentence Coherence of the Hebrew Verbal System." *Zeitschrift für die alttestamentliche Wissenschaft* 108:434–40.

Nicholson, E. 1965. "The Meaning of the Expression *ʿAm Haʾareṣ* in the Old Testament." *Journal of Semitic Studies* 10:59–66.

———. 1977. "The Decalogue as the Direct Address of God." *Vetus Testamentum* 27:422–33.

Nigosian, S. A. 1993. "Moses as They Saw Him." *Vetus Testamentum* 43:339–50.

Nissinen, M. 2003. "Fear Not: A Study of an Ancient Near Eastern Phrase." In *The Changing Face of Form Criticism for the Twenty-First Century*, edited by M. A. Sweeney and E. Ben Zvi, 122–61. Grand Rapids: Eerdmans.

Noble, P. R. 1997. "Amos' Absolute 'No.'" *Vetus Testamentum* 47:329–40.

Noth, M. 1962. *Exodus: A Commentary*. Old Testament Library. Philadelphia: Westminster.

Novak, D. 1998. *Natural Law in Judaism*. Cambridge: Cambridge University Press.

Novick, T. 2009. "*Hʾmyn* in Jud 11,20 and the Semantics of Assent." *Zeitschrift für die alttestamentliche Wissenschaft* 121:577–83.

Ogden, G. S. 1967. "Notes on the Use of *Hwyh* in Exodus ix 3." *Vetus Testamentum* 17:483–84.

———. 1971. "Time, and the Verb *Hyh* in Old Testament Prose." *Vetus Testamentum* 21:451–69.

Olyan, S. M. 1996. "Why an Altar of Unfinished Stones? Some Thoughts on Ex 20,25 and Dtn 27,5–6." *Zeitschrift für die alttestamentliche Wissenschaft* 108:161–71.

Orlinsky, H. M. 1947. "The Infinitive Construct and the Verbal Noun in Biblical Hebrew." *Journal of the American Oriental Society* 67:107–26.

Oswalt, J. N. 1977. "The Myth of the Dragon and Old Testament Faith." *Evangelical Quarterly* 49:163–72.

———. 2008a. "Exodus." In *Cornerstone Biblical Commentary*, edited by P. W. Comfort, 1:259–560. Carol Stream, IL: Tyndale House.

———. 2008b. "Exodus." In *NLT Study Bible*, 122–91. Carol Stream, IL: Tyndale House.

Otto, R. 1923. *The Idea of the Holy: An Inquiry into the Non-rational Factor in the Idea of the Divine and Its Relation to the Rational*. Translated by J. W. Harvey. Reprinted, London: Oxford University Press, 1980.

Paradise, J. 1997. "What Did Laban Demand of Jacob? A New Rereading of Genesis 31:50 and Exodus 21:10." In *Tĕhillah lĕ-Moshe: Biblical and Judaic Studies in Honor of Moshe Greenberg*, edited by M. Cogan et al., 91–98. Winona Lake, IN: Eisenbrauns.

Pardee, D. 1978. "The Semitic Root *MRR* and Etymology of Ugaritic *Mr(r)//Brk*." *Ugarit-Forschungen* 10:249–88.

Pardes, I. 2000. *The Biography of Ancient Israel: National Narratives in the Bible*. Berkeley: University of California Press.

Parker, S. B. 1971. "Exodus xv 2 Again." *Vetus Testamentum* 21:373–79.

———. 1997. *Stories in Scripture and Inscriptions: Comparative Studies on Narratives in Northwest Semitic Inscriptions and the Hebrew Bible*. New York and Oxford: Oxford University Press.

Parunak, H. Van Dyke. 1975. "A Semantic Survey of *NḤM*." *Biblica* 56:512–32.

Patrick, D. 1973. "Casuistic Law Governing Primary Rights and Duties." *Journal of Biblical Literature* 92:180–84.

———. 1985. *Old Testament Law*. Atlanta: John Knox.

———. 1999. *The Rhetoric of Revelation in the Hebrew Bible*. Minneapolis: Fortress.

Paul, S. 1969. "Exod. 21:10: A Threefold Maintenance Clause." *Journal of Near Eastern Studies* 28:48–53.

———. 1970. *Studies in the Book of the Covenant in the Light of Cuneiform and Biblical Law*. Vetus Testamentum Supplements 18. Leiden: Brill.

———. 1973. "Heavenly Tablets and the Book of Life." *Journal of the Ancient Near Eastern Society* 5:345–54. Reprinted in *Divrei Shalom: Collected Studies of Shalom M. Paul on the Bible and the Ancient Near East, 1967–2005*, 59–70. Leiden: Brill, 2005.

———. 1978. "An Unrecognized Medical Idiom in Canticles 6,12 and Job 9,21." *Biblica* 59:545–47.

———. 1980. "Adoption Formulae: A Study of Cuneiform and Legal Clauses." *Maarav* 2:173–85.

———. 1991. *Amos: A Critical and Historical Commentary on the Bible*. Hermeneia. Minneapolis: Fortress.

———. 1992. "Exodus 1:21: 'To Found a Family'; A Biblical and Akkadian Idiom." *Maarav* 8:139–42.

Peels, H. G. L. 1994. "On the Wings of the Eagle (Dtn 32,11): An Old Misunderstanding." *Zeitschrift für die alttestamentliche Wissenschaft* 106:300–303.

Penchansky, D. 1999. *What Rough Beast? Images of God in the Hebrew Bible*. Louisville: Westminster John Knox.

Perles, F. 1926–27. "On the Strophic Form of Exodus 15." *Jewish Quarterly Review* 17:403–4.

Phillips, A. 1970. *Ancient Israel's Criminal Law: A New Approach to the Decalogue*. Oxford: Blackwell.

———. 1973. "Family Law in Pre-exilic Israel." *Vetus Testamentum* 23:349–61.

———. 1977. *God B.C.* Oxford: Oxford University Press.

———. 1981. "Another Look at Adultery." *Journal for the Study of the Old Testament* 20:3–25.

———. 1983. "The Decalogue—Ancient Israel's Criminal Law." *Journal of Jewish Studies* 34:1–20. Reprinted in *Essays on Biblical Law*, 2–24. Journal for the Study of the Old Testament: Supplement Series 344. Sheffield: Sheffield Academic Press, 2002.

———. 1984. "The Law of Slavery: Exodus 21:2–11." *Journal for the Study of the Old Testament* 30:51–66.

Pope, M. H. 1977. *Song of Songs: A New Translation with Introduction and Commentary*. Anchor Bible. New York: Doubleday.

———. 1992. "Euphemism and Dysphemism in the Bible." In *The Anchor Bible Dictionary*, edited by D. N. Freedman, 1:720–25. New York: Doubleday.

———. 1994a. "Euphemism and Dysphemism in the Bible." In *Probative Pontificating in Ugaritic and Biblical Literature: Collected Essays*, edited by M. S. Smith, 279–91. Ugaritisch-biblische Literatur 10. Münster, Germany: Ugarit-Verlag.

———. 1994b. "Mid Rock and Scrub: A Ugaritic Parallel to Exodus 7:19." In *Probative Pontificating in Ugaritic and Biblical Literature: Collected Essays*, edited by M. S. Smith, 41–46. Ugaritisch-biblische Literatur 10. Münster: Ugarit-Verlag. Reprinted from *Biblical and Near Eastern Studies: Essays in Honor of William Sanford LaSor*, edited by G. A. Tuttle, 146–50. Grand Rapids: Eerdmans, 1978.

Porten, B., and J. C. Greenfield. 1968. "The Aramaic Papyri from Hermopolis." *Zeitschrift für die alttestamentliche Wissenschaft* 80:216–31.

Porten, B., and U. Ruppaport. 1971. "Poetic Structure in Genesis ix." *Vetus Testamentum* 21:363–69.

Porter, J. R. 1965. "The Legal Aspects of the Concept of 'Corporate Personality' in the Old Testament." *Vetus Testamentum* 15:361–80.

Poythress, V. S. 1991. *The Shadow of Christ in the Law of Moses*. Phillipsburg, NJ: Presbyterian & Reformed.

Pressler, C. 1993. *The View of Women Found in Deuteronomic Family Laws*. Beihefte zur Zeitschrift für die alttestamentliche Wissenschaft 216. Berlin and New York: De Gruyter.

———. 1998. "Wives and Daughters, Bond and Free: Views of Women in the Slave Laws of Exodus 21:2–11." In *Gender and Law in the Hebrew Bible and the Ancient Near East*, edited by V. H. Matthews et al., 147–72. Journal for the Study of the Old Testament: Supplement Series 262. Sheffield: Sheffield Academic Press.

Propp, W. H. C. 1987. "The Skin of Moses's Face—Transfigured or Disfigured?" *Catholic Biblical Quarterly* 49:375–86.

———. 1996. "The Priestly Source Recovered Intact?" *Vetus Testamentum* 46:458–78.

———. 1999. *Exodus 1–18: A New Translation with Introduction and Commentary*. Anchor Bible. New York: Doubleday.

———. 2006. *Exodus 19–40: A New Translation with Introduction and Commentary*. Anchor Bible. New York: Doubleday.

Provan, I. 2001. "'All These I Have Kept Since I Was a Boy' (Luke 18:21): Creation, Covenant, and the Commandments of God." *Ex auditu* 17:31–46.

Rabin, C. 1961. "Etymological Miscellanea." *Scripta hierosolymitana* 8:384–400.

———. 1973. "Hebrew *Baddīm* 'Power.'" *Journal of Semitic Studies* 18:52–58.

Rabinowitz, J. J. 1954. "Some Notes on an Aramaic Contract from the Dead Sea Region." *Bulletin of the American Schools of Oriental Research* 136:15–16.

———. 1959. "The 'Great Sin' in Ancient Egyptian Contracts." *Journal of Near Eastern Studies* 18:73.

———. 1961. "The Susa Tablets, the Bible and the Aramaic Papyri." *Vetus Testamentum* 11:55–76.

Rainey, A. 1988. "Further Remarks on the Hebrew Verbal System." *Hebrew Studies* 29:35–42.

———. 1994. "Hezekiah's Reform and the Altars of Beersheba and Arad." In *Scripture and Other Artifacts: Essays in Honor of Phillip J. King*, edited by M. D. Coogan et al., 333–54. Louisville: Westminster John Knox.

———. 1996. *Canaanite in the Amarna Tablets: A Linguistic Analysis of the Mixed Dialect Used by the Scribes from Canaan*. 3 vols. Leiden: Brill.

———. 2003. "The Suffix Conjugation Pattern in Ancient Hebrew Tense and Modal Functions." *Ancient Near Eastern Studies* 40:3–42.

Ratner, R. 1990. "The 'Feminine Takes Precedence' Syntagm and Job 19,15." *Zeitschrift für die alttestamentliche Wissenschaft* 102:238–51.

———. 1992. "Morphological Variation in Biblical Hebrew Rhetoric." *Maarav* 8:143–59.

Ratner, R., and B. Zuckerman. 1986. "A Kid in Milk?" *Hebrew Union College Annual* 57:15–60.

Redford, D. B. 1963. "Exodus I 11." *Vetus Testamentum* 13:401–18.

———. 1970. *A Study of the Biblical Story of Joseph (Genesis 37–50)*. Vetus Testamentum Supplements 20. Leiden: Brill.

———. 1987. "An Egyptological Perspective on the Exodus Narrative." In *Egypt, Israel and Sinai: Archaeological and Historical Relationships in the Biblical Period*, edited by A. Rainey, 137–61. Tel Aviv: Tel Aviv University.

Reider, J. 1952. "Miscellanea Hebraica." *Journal of Jewish Studies* 3:78–86.

Reif, S. 1983. "A Root to Look Up? A Study of the Hebrew *Nś' 'Yn*." *Vetus Testamentum* 36:230–44.

Reinhartz, A. 1998. *"Why Ask My Name?" Anonymity and Identity in Biblical Narrative*. New York: Oxford University Press.

Rendsburg, G. A. 1988. "Bilingual Wordplay in the Bible." *Vetus Testamentum* 38:354–57.

———. 1989. Review of *Die Inkongruenz im biblischen Hebraisch*, by J. Levi. *Journal of Biblical Literature* 108:500.

———. 1992. "Israelian Hebrew Features in Genesis 49." *Maarav* 8:161–70.

———. 1998. Review of *Targum Neofiti I: Numbers; Targum Pseudo-Jonathan: Numbers*, translated by M. McNamara and E. G. Clarke. *Journal of Biblical Literature* 117:547.

———. 1999. "Hebrew Philological Notes (I)." *Hebrew Studies* 40:27–32.

———. 2001. "Hebrew Philological Notes (II)." *Hebrew Studies* 42:187–95.

———. 2008. "Alliteration in the Exodus Narrative." In *Birkat Shalom: Studies in the Bible, Ancient Near Eastern Literature, and Postbiblical Judaism Presented to Shalom M. Paul on the Occasion of His Seventieth Birthday*, edited by C. Cohen et al., 83–100. Winona Lake, IN: Eisenbrauns.

Rendtorff, R. 1989. "'Covenant' as a Structuring Concept in Genesis and Exodus." *Journal of Biblical Literature* 108:385–93.

Revell, E. J. 1995. "The Two Forms of First Person Singular Pronoun in Biblical Hebrew: Redundancy or Expressive Contrast." *Journal of Semitic Studies* 40:199–217.

Reviv, H. 1989. *The Elders in Ancient Israel: A Study of a Biblical Institution*. Jerusalem: Magnes.

Richardson, H. N. 1971. "The Last Words of David: Some Notes on II Samuel 23:1–7." *Journal of Biblical Literature* 90:257–66.

Robertson, D. A. 1969. "The Morphemes *-y* (-ī) and *-w* (-ō) in Biblical Hebrew." *Vetus Testamentum* 19:211–23.

———. 1972. *Linguistic Evidence in Dating Early Hebrew Poetry*. Society of Biblical Literature Dissertation Series 33. Missoula, MT: Scholars Press.

Robertson, E. 1964. "The Urim and Tummim: What Are They?" *Vetus Testamentum* 14:67–74.

Robinson, B. P. 1986. "Zipporah to the Rescue: A Contextual Study of Exodus iv 24–26." *Vetus Testamentum* 36:447–61.

———. 1987. "Symbolism in Exod. 15:22–27." *Revue biblique* 94:376–88.

———. 1991. "Elijah at Horeb, 1 Kings 19:1–18: A Coherent Narrative." *Revue biblique* 98:513–36.

———. 1997. "Burning Bush." *Journal for the Study of the Old Testament* 75:107–22.

Robinson, G. 1980. "The Idea of Rest in the Old Testament." *Zeitschrift für die alttestamentliche Wissenschaft* 92:32–42.

Rodriguez, A. M. 1997. "Jewelry in the Old Testament: A Description of Its Functions." In *To Understand the Scripture: Essays in Honor of William H. Shea*, edited by D. Meerling, 103–25. Berrien Springs, MI: Institute of Archaeology, Siegfried H. Horn Archaeological Museum.

Rofé, A. 1997a. "From Tradition to Criticism: Jewish Sources as an Aid to the Critical Study of the Bible." *Vetus Testamentum* 66:235–47.

———. 1997b. "The Methods of Late Biblical Scribes as Evidenced by the Septuagint Compared with the Other Textual Witnesses." In *Tĕhillah lĕ-Moshe: Biblical and Judaic Studies in Honor of Moshe Greenberg*, edited by M. Cogan et al., 259–70. Winona Lake, IN: Eisenbrauns.

Ron, Z. 2010. "'What Is It?' Interpreting Exodus 16:15." *Jewish Biblical Quarterly* 38:230–34.

Roth, M. T. 1997. *Law Collections from Mesopotamia and Asia Minor*. With H. A. Hoffner Jr. Edited by P. Michalowski. 2nd ed. Writings from the Ancient World 6. Atlanta: Scholars Press.

Roth, W. M. W. 1962. "The Numerical Sequence X/X + 1 in the Old Testament." *Vetus Testamentum* 12:300–311.

Rubinstein, A. 1952. "A Finite Verb Continued by an Infinitive Absolute in Biblical Hebrew." *Vetus Testamentum* 2:362–67.

Russell, B. D. 2007. *The Song of the Sea: The Date of Composition and Influence of Exodus 15:1–21*. Studies in Biblical Literature 101. New York: Peter Lang.

Russell, S. C. 2009. *Images of Egypt in Early Biblical Literature: Cisjordan-Israelite, Transjordan-Israelite, and Judahite Portrayals*. Beihefte zur Zeitschrift für die alttestamentliche Wissenschaft 403. Berlin and New York: de Gruyter.

Sadka, Y. 2001. "*Hinneh* in Biblical Hebrew." *Ugarit-Forschungen* 33:479–93.

Sæbø, M. 1981. "Offenbarung oder Verhüllung? Bemerkungen zum Charakter des Gottesnamens in Ex 3,13–15." In *Die Botschaft und die Boten: Festschrift für Hans Walter Wolff zum 70. Geburtstag*, edited by J. Jeremias and L. Perlitt, 43–55. Neukirchen-Vluyn, Germany: Neukirchener Verlag.

———. 1998. "God's Name in Exodus 3:13–15: An Expression of Revelation or of Veiling?" In *On the Way to Canon: Creative History in the Old Testament*, 78–92. Journal for the Study of the Old Testament: Supplement Series 191. Sheffield: Sheffield Academic Press.

Sailhamer, J. H. 1992. *The Pentateuch as Narrative: A Biblical-Theological Commentary*. Grand Rapids: Zondervan.

———. 1995. *Introduction to Old Testament Theology: A Canonical Approach*. Grand Rapids: Zondervan.

———. 2009. *The Meaning of the Pentateuch: Revelation, Composition and Interpretation*. Downers Grove, IL: InterVarsity.

Sakenfeld, K. D. 1978. *The Meaning of* Hesed *in the Hebrew Bible: A New Inquiry*. Harvard Semitic Monographs 17. Missoula, MT: Scholars Press.

Sanders, J. 1998. *The God Who Risks: A Theology of Providence*. Downers Grove, IL: InterVarsity.

Sandmel, S. 1961. "The Haggada within Scripture." *Journal of Biblical Literature* 80:105–22.

Särkiö, P. 1993. "The 'Third Man'—David's Heroes in 2 Sam. 23,8–29." *Scandinavian Journal of the Old Testament* 7:108–24.

Sarna, N. 1959. "The Interchange of the Prepositions *Beth* and *Min* in Biblical Hebrew." *Journal of Biblical Literature* 78:310–16.

———. 1986. *Exploring Exodus: The Heritage of Biblical Israel*. New York: Schocken.

———. 1991. *Exodus*. JPS Torah Commentary. Philadelphia: Jewish Publication Society.

Sasson, J. M. 1973. "The Worship of the Golden Calf." In *Orient and Occident: Essays Presented to Cyrus H. Gordon on the Occasion of His Sixty-Fifth Birthday*, edited by H. A. Hoffner, 151–59. Alter Orient und Altes Testament 22. Kevelaer, Germany: Verlag Butzon & Bercker; Neukirchen-Vluyn, Germany: Neukirchener Verlag.

———. 1990. *Jonah*. Anchor Bible. New York: Doubleday.

———. 2002. "Ritual Wisdom? On 'Seething a Kid in Its Mother's Milk.'" In *Kein Land für sich allein: Studien zum Kulturkontakt in Kanaan, Israel/Palästina und Ebirnari für Manfred Weippert zum 65. Geburtstag*, edited by U. Hübner and E. A. Knauf, 294–308. Orbis biblicus et orientalis 186. Freiburg, Germany: Universitätsverlag; Göttingen, Germany: Vandenhoeck & Ruprecht.

———. 2003. "Should Cheeseburgers Be Kosher?" *Biblical Archaeology Review* 19 (6): 40–43, 50–51.

Sasson, V. 1986. "The Book of Oracular Visions of Balaam from Deir ʿAlla." *Ugarit-Forschungen* 17:283–306.

———. 1997. "Some Observations on the Use and Original Purpose of the *Wāw* Consecutive in Old Aramaic and in Biblical Hebrew." *Vetus Testamentum* 47:111–27.

———. 2001. "The *Wāw* Consecutive/*Wāw* Contrastive and the Perfect Verb Tense, Context, and Texture in Old Aramaic and Biblical Hebrew with Comments on the Deir ʿAlla Dialect and Post-Biblical Hebrew." *Zeitschrift für die alttestamentliche Wissenschaft* 113:602–17.

Satlow, M. L. 1997. "Jewish Constructions of Nakedness in Late Antiquity." *Journal of Biblical Literature* 116:429–54.

Savran, G. W. 2005. *Encountering the Divine: Theophany in Biblical Narrative*. London: T&T Clark.

Sawyer, J. F. A. 1976. "A Note on the Etymology of *Ṣāraʿat*." *Vetus Testamentum* 26:241–45.

Saydon, P. P. 1955. "Assonance in Hebrew as a Means of Expressing Emphasis." *Biblica* 36:36–50, 287–304.

Schenker, A. 1998. "The Biblical Legislation on the Release of Slaves: The Road from Exodus to Leviticus." *Journal for the Study of the Old Testament* 78:23–41.

Schley, D. G. 1990. "The *Shalishim*: Officers or Special Three-Man Squads?" *Vetus Testamentum* 40:321–26.

Schneiders, S. M. 1983. "The Face Veil: A Johannine Sign (John 20:1–10)." *Biblical Theology Bulletin* 13 (3): 94–97.

Schoors, A. 1981. "The Particle *Kî*." *Oudtestamentische Studiën* 21:240–76.

Scott, R. B. Y. 1949. "Secondary Meanings of *ʾĀḥar*, After, Behind." *Journal of Theological Studies* 50:178–79.

Seely, D. R. 2004. "The Image of the Hand of God in the Book of Exodus." In *God's Word for Our World: Biblical Studies in Honor of Simon John De Vries*, edited by J. H. Ellens et al., 38–54. Journal for the Study of the Old Testament: Supplement Series 388. London: T&T Clark.

Sefati, Y., and J. Klein. 2004. "The Law of the Sorceress (Exodus 22:17 [18]) in the Light of Biblical and Mesopotamian Parallels." In *Sefer Moshe: The Moshe Weinfeld Jubilee Volume; Studies in the Bible and the Ancient Near East, Qumran, and Post-biblical Judaism*, edited by C. Chaim et al., 171–90. Winona Lake, IN: Eisenbrauns.

Segal, M. 2008. "*Wyʾr ʾt hlylh* (Exodus 14,20): New Light on an Old Problem." *Zeitschrift für die alttestamentliche Wissenschaft* 120:254–61.

Segal, P. 1989. "The Divine Verdict of Leviticus x 3." *Vetus Testamentum* 39:91–95.

Seitz, C. 1999. "The Call of Moses and the 'Revelation' of the Divine Name: Source-Critical Logic and Its Legacy [Exodus 3,1–4, 17; 6,2–9]." In *Theological Exegesis: Essays in Honor of Brevard S. Childs*, edited by C. Seitz et al., 145–61. Grand Rapids: Eerdmans.

Shafer, B. E. 1977. "The Root *bḥr* and Pre-exilic Concepts of Chosenness in the Hebrew Bible." *Zeitschrift für die alttestamentliche Wissenschaft* 89:20–42.

Shedletsky, L., and B. Levine. 1999. "The *Mšr* of the Sons and Daughters of Ugarit." *Revue biblique* 106:321–44.

Shemesh, Y. 2005. "Punishment of the Offending Organ in Biblical Literature." *Vetus Testamentum* 55:343–65.

Sheppard, G. T. 1985. "The Anti-Assyrian Redaction and the Canonical Context of Isaiah 1–39." *Journal of Biblical Literature* 104:193–216.

Sivan, D., and W. M. Schniedewind. 1993. "Letting Your 'Yes' Be 'No' in Ancient Israel: A Study of the Asseverative *Loʾ* and *Hălo ʾ*." *Journal of Semitic Studies* 38 (2): 209–26.

Skehan, P. W. 1955. "Exodus in the Samaritan Rescension from Qumran." *Journal of Biblical Literature* 74:182–87.

———. 1963. "The Hand of Judith." *Catholic Biblical Quarterly* 25:94–110.

Sklba, R. J. 1972. "The Redeemer of Israel." *Catholic Biblical Quarterly* 34:1–18.

Smiles, V. M. 2002. "The Concept of 'Zeal' in Second-Temple Judaism and Paul's Critique of It in Romans 10:2." *Catholic Biblical Quarterly* 64:282–99.

Smith, M. S. 1993. "The Invocation of Deceased Ancestors." *Journal of Biblical Literature* 112:105–7.

———. 1997. *The Pilgrimage Pattern in Exodus*. Journal for the Study of the Old Testament: Supplement Series 239. Sheffield: Sheffield Academic Press.

———. 1998. "The Heart and Innards in Israelite Emotional Expressions: Notes from Anthropology and Psychobiology." *Journal of Biblical Literature* 117:427–36.

———. 1999. "Matters of Space and Time in Exodus and Numbers." In *Theological Exegesis: Essays in Honor of Brevard S. Childs*, edited by C. Seitz et al., 182–207. Grand Rapids: Eerdmans.

———. 2001. "The Poetics of Exodus 15 and Its Position in the Book of Exodus." In *Imagery and Imagination in Biblical Literature: Essays in Honor of Aloysius Fitzgerald, F.S.C.*, edited by L. Boadt and M. S. Smith, 23–34. Catholic Biblical Quarterly Monograph Series 32. Washington, DC: Catholic Biblical Association of America.

———. 2010. *Exodus*. New Collegeville Bible Commentary: Old Testament 3. Collegeville, MN: Liturgical Press.

Sohn, S.-T. 1999. "'I Will Be Your God and You Will Be My People': The Origin and Background of the Covenant Formula." In *Ki Baruch Hu: Ancient Near Eastern, Biblical and Judaic Studies in Honor of Baruch A. Levine*, edited by R. Chazan et al., 355–72. Winona Lake, IN: Eisenbrauns.

Sommer, B. D. 2001. "Conflicting Constructions of Divine Presence in the Priestly Tabernacle." *Biblical Interpretation* 9:41–63.

Sonsino, R. 1980. *Motive Clauses in Hebrew Law Biblical Forms and Near Eastern Parallels*. Society of Biblical Literature Dissertation Series 45. Chico, CA: Scholars Press.

Speiser, E. A. 1960. "An Angelic 'Curse': Exodus 14:20." *Journal of the American Oriental Society* 80:198–200.

———. 1963a. "Background and Function of the Biblical *Nāśi'*." *Catholic Biblical Quarterly* 25:111–17.

———. 1963b. "The Stem *PLL* in Hebrew." *Journal of Biblical Literature* 82:301–6.

Sprinkle, J. M. 1993. "The Interpretation of Exodus 21:22–25 (Lex Talionis) and Abortion." *Westminster Theological Journal* 55:233–53.

———. 1994. *The Book of the Covenant: A Literary Approach*. Sheffield: JSOT Press.

———. 2004. "Law and Narrative in Exodus 19–24." *Journal of the Evangelical Theological Society* 47:235–52.

———. 2006. *Biblical Law and Its Relevance: A Christian Understanding and Ethical Application for Today of the Mosaic Regulations*. Lanham, MD: University Press of America.

Stec, D. M. 1987. "The Use of *Hen* in Conditional Clauses." *Vetus Testamentum* 37:478–86.

Steiner, R. C. 2000. "Does the Biblical Hebrew Conjunction *Wāw* Have Many Meanings, One Meaning, or No Meaning at All?" *Journal of Biblical Literature* 119:249–67.

Stern, P. D. 1992. "The Origin and Significance of 'The Land Flowing with Milk and Honey.'" *Vetus Testamentum* 42:554–57.

Sternberg, M. 1987. *The Poetics of Biblical Narrative: Ideological Literature and the Drama of Reading*. Bloomington: Indiana University Press.

———. 1998. *Hebrews between Cultures: Group Portraits and National Literature*. Indiana Studies in Biblical Literature. Bloomington: Indiana University Press.

Strawn, B. 2002. "*Wĕnil'a(h)*, 'O Victorious One' in Ps 68,10." *Ugarit-Forschungen* 34:785–98.

Talmon, S. 1954. "*Ḥatan Damim*." *Eretz-Yisrael* 3:93–95.

———. 1961. "Synonymous Readings in the Textual Traditions of the Old Testament." *Scripta hierosolymitana* 8:335–83.

———. 1963. "The Gezer Calendar and the Seasonal Cycles of Ancient Canaan." *Journal of the American Oriental Society* 83:177–87.

———. 1978. "The Presentation of Synchroneity and Simultaneity in Biblical Narrative." *Scripta hierosolymitana* 27:9–26.

———. 1985. "The Ancient Hebrew Alphabet and Biblical Text Criticism." In *Mélanges bibliques et orientaux en l'honneur de M. Mathias Delcor*, edited by A. Caquot et al., 387–402. Kevelaer, Germany: Butzon & Bercker; Neukirchen-Vluyn, Germany: Neukirchener Verlag.

———. 1992. "The 'Topped Triad': A Biblical Literary Convention and the 'Ascending Numerical Pattern,'" *Maarav* 9:181–98.

———. 1997. "The Significance of *Shalom* and Its Semantic Field." In *The Quest for Context and Meaning: Studies in Biblical Intertextuality in Honor of James A. Sanders*, edited by C. A. Evans and S. Talmon, 75–115. Leiden: Brill.

Talmon, S., and W. W. Fields. 1989. "The Collocation *Mshtyn Bqyr W'ṣwr W'zwb*." *Zeitschrift für die alttestamentliche Wissenschaft* 101:85–114.

Tarragon, J.-M. de. 1995. "Witchcraft, Magic and Divination in Canaan and Ancient Israel." In *Civilizations of the Ancient Near East*, edited by J. Sasson, 3:2071–81. 4 vols. New York: Scribner.

Tawil, H. 1976. "Hebrew *Ḥṣlḥ/Ṣlḥ*, Akkadian *Esheru/Shushuru*: A Lexicographical Note." *Journal of Biblical Literature* 95:405–13.

Terrien, S. 1978. *The Elusive Presence: Toward a New Biblical Theology*. San Francisco: Harper & Row.

Thomas, D. W. 1934. "The Root *Yd'* in Hebrew." *Journal of Theological Studies* 35:298–301.

———. 1948. "A Note on *Wayyeda' 'Elohim* in Exod. II, 5." *Journal of Theological Studies* 49:143–44.

———. 1956. "Some Observations on the Hebrew Root *Ḥdl*." *Vetus Testamentum* 4:8–16.

Thomas, K. J. 1976. "Liturgical Citations in the Synoptics." *New Testament Studies* 22:205–14.

Thompson, D. L. 1996. "Women, Men, Slaves and the Bible: Hermeneutical Inquiries." *Christian Scholar's Review* 25 (3): 326–49.

Thompson, J. A. 1965. "Expansions of the *'D* Root." *Journal of Semitic Studies* 10:222–40.

———. 1977. "Israel's Lovers." *Vetus Testamentum* 27:475–81.

Thompson, P. E. 1971. "The Yahwist Creation Story." *Vetus Testamentum* 21:197–208.

Tigay, J. H. 1975. "An Empirical Basis for the Documentary Hypothesis." *Journal of Biblical Literature* 94:329–42.

———. 1978. "'Heavy of Mouth' and 'Heavy of Tongue': On Moses's Speech Difficulty." *Bulletin of the American Schools of Oriental Research* 231:557–67.

———. 1982. "On the Meaning of *Ṭ(W)ṬPT*." *Journal of Biblical Literature* 101:321–31.

———. 1996. *Deuteronomy*. JPS Torah Commentary. Philadelphia: Jewish Publication Society.

———. 2004a. "Exodus." In *The Jewish Study Bible*, edited by A. Berlin and M. Z. Brettler, 102–202. Oxford: Oxford University Press.

———. 2004b. "The Presence of God and the Coherence of Exodus 20:22–26." In *Sefer Moshe: The Moshe Weinfeld Jubilee Volume; Studies in the Bible and the Ancient Near East, Qumran, and Post-biblical Judaism*, edited by C. Chaim et al., 195–211. Winona Lake, IN: Eisenbrauns.

Toorn, K. van der. 1989. "Female Prostitution in Payment of Vows in Ancient Israel." *Journal of Biblical Literature* 108:193–205.

———. 1995. "The Significance of the Veil in the Ancient Near East." In *Pomegranates and Golden Bells: Studies in Biblical, Jewish, and Near Eastern Ritual, Law, and Literature in Honor of Jacob Milgrom*, edited by D. P. Wright et al., 327–39. Winona Lake, IN: Eisenbrauns.

Tov, E. 2001. *Textual Criticism of the Hebrew Bible*. 2nd ed. Minneapolis: Fortress.

———. 2008. "Biliteral Exegesis of Hebrew Roots in the Septuagint?" In *Hebrew Bible, Greek Bible, and Qumran: Collected Essays*, 378–97. Texts and Studies in Ancient Judaism 121. Tübingen: Mohr Siebeck.

Towner, W. S. 1968. "'Blessed be YHWH' and 'Blessed Art Thou, YHWH': The Modulation of a Biblical Formula." *Catholic Biblical Quarterly* 30:386–99.

Trevaskis, L. M. 2009. "The Purpose of Leviticus 24 within Its Literary Context." *Vetus Testamentum* 59:295–312.

Trible, P. 1978. *God and the Rhetoric of Sexuality*. Philadelphia: Fortress.

———. 1984. *Texts of Terror: Literary-Feminist Readings of Biblical Narrative*. Overtures to Biblical Theology. Philadelphia: Fortress.

———. 1989. "Bringing Miriam out of the Shadows." *Bible Review* 5 (1): 14–25, 34.

Tsevat, M. 1972. "The Basic Meaning of the Biblical Sabbath." *Zeitschrift für die alttestamentliche Wissenschaft* 84:447–59.

———. 1994. "The Hebrew Slave according to Deuteronomy 15:12–18: His Lot and the Value of His Work, with Special Attention to the Meaning of *Mishneh*." *Journal of Biblical Literature* 113:587–95.

Turnbam, T. J. 1987. "Male and Female Slaves in the Sabbath Year Laws of Exodus 21:1–11." In *SBL Seminar Papers 1987*, edited by K. H. Richards, 545–49. Atlanta: Scholars Press.

Tvedtnes, J. A. 1982. "Egyptian Etymology for Biblical Cultic Paraphernalia." *Scripta hierosolymitana* 28:215–21.

Unterman, J. 1995. "The Social-Legal Origin for the Image of God as Redeemer *Gōʾel* of Israel." In *Pomegranates and Golden Bells: Studies in Biblical, Jewish, and Near Eastern Ritual, Law, and Literature in Honor of Jacob Milgrom*, edited by D. P. Wright et al., 399–405. Winona Lake, IN: Eisenbrauns.

Uphill, E. P. 1968. "Pithom and Raamses: Their Location and Significance, Part 1." *Journal of Near Eastern Studies* 27:291–316.

———. 1969. "Pithom and Raamses: Their Location and Significance, Part 2." *Journal of Near Eastern Studies* 28:15–39.

Van Dam, C. 1988. "Urim and Thummim." In *The International Standard Bible Encyclopedia*, edited by G. W. Bromiley et al., 4:957–59. Grand Rapids: Eerdmans.

———. 1997. *The Urim and Thummim: A Means of Revelation in Ancient Israel*. Winona Lake, IN: Eisenbrauns.

Van der Kooij, A. 1995. "'And I Also Said': A New Interpretation of Judges ii 3." *Vetus Testamentum* 45:294–306.

Van der Merwe, C. H. J. 1999. "Explaining Fronting in Biblical Hebrew." *Journal of Northwest Semitic Languages* 25 (2): 173–86.

———. 2009. "Another Look at the Biblical Hebrew Focus Particle *Gam*." *Journal of Semitic Studies* 54:313–32.

Van Leeuwen, R. C. 1980. "Isaiah 14:12, *Hôlesh ʿAl Gwym* and Gilgamesh xi,6." *Journal of Biblical Literature* 99:173–84.

Vannoy, J. R. 1974. "The Use of the Word *Hāʾĕlōhîm* in Exodus 21:6 and 22:7, 8." In *The Law and the Prophets: Old Testament Studies Prepared in Honor of Oswald*

Thompson Allis, edited by J. H. Skilton, 225–41. Philadelphia: Presbyterian & Reformed.

Van Seters, J. 1972. "The Terms 'Amorite' and 'Hittite.'" *Vetus Testamentum* 22:64–81.

———. 1986. "The Plagues of Egypt: Ancient Tradition or Literary Invention?" *Zeitschrift für die alttestamentliche Wissenschaft* 98:31–39.

———. 1994. *The Life of Moses: The Yahwist as Historian in Exodus–Numbers*. Louisville: Westminster John Knox.

———. 1996. "The Law of the Hebrew Slave." *Zeitschrift für die alttestamentliche Wissenschaft* 108:534–46.

———. 2003. *A Law Book for the Diaspora: Revision in the Study of the Covenant Code*. Oxford and New York: Oxford University Press.

Vasholz, R. I. 1987. "You Shall Not Covet Your Neighbor's Wife." *Westminster Theological Journal* 49:397–403.

Vater, A. M. 1980. "Narrative Patterns for the Story of Commissioned Communication in the Old Testament." *Journal of Biblical Literature* 99:365–82.

Vaux, R. de. 1961. *Ancient Israel*. Translated by J. McHugh. 2 vols. New York: McGraw Hill.

Vawter, B. 1960. "A Note on 'The Waters beneath the Earth.'" *Catholic Biblical Quarterly* 22:71–73.

———. 1986. "Prov 8:22: Wisdom and Creation." *Journal of Biblical Literature* 48:461–67.

Vermès, G. 1963. "Haggadah in the Onkelos Targum." *Journal of Semitic Studies* 8:159–69.

———. 1975. *Post-biblical Jewish Studies*. Leiden: Brill.

Vervenne, M. 1987. "Hebrew *Shalish*—Ugaritic *ṮLṮ*." *Ugarit-Forschungen* 19:355–73.

Wakeman, M. K. 1969. "The Biblical Earth Monster in the Cosmogonic Combat Myth." *Journal of Biblical Literature* 88:313–20.

———. 1973. *God's Battle with the Monster*. Leiden: Brill.

Walsh, J. T. 2001. *Style and Structure in Biblical Hebrew Narrative*. Collegeville, MN: Liturgical Press.

Walters, J. A. 2002. "Moses at the Lodging Place: The Devil Is in the Ambiguities." *Encounter* 63:407–25.

Waltke, B. K. 2007. *An Old Testament Theology: An Exegetical, Canonical, and Thematic Approach*, 346–478. Grand Rapids: Zondervan.

Waltke, B. K., and M. O'Connor. 1990. *An Introduction to Biblical Hebrew Syntax*. Winona Lake, IN: Eisenbrauns.

Ward, W. A. 1974. "The Semitic Biconsonantal Root *SP* and the Common Origin of Egyptian *CWF* and Hebrew *SP*: 'Marsh(-plant).'" *Vetus Testamentum* 24:339–49.

Watson, W. G. E. 1971. "More on Shared Consonants." *Biblica* 52:44–50.

———. 1989. "Internal or Half-Line Parallelism in Classical Hebrew Again." *Vetus Testamentum* 39:44–66.

Watts, J. D. W. 1962. "Infinite Absolute as Imperative and the Interpretation of Exodus 20,8." *Zeitschrift für die alttestamentliche Wissenschaft* 74:141–45.

———. 1964. *A Survey of Syntax in the Old Testament*. Grand Rapids: Eerdmans.

———. 1995. "Public Readings and Pentateuchal Law." *Vetus Testamentum* 45:540–57.

Wedderburn, A. J. M. 1994. "Traditions and Redaction in Acts 2:1–13." *Journal for the Study of the New Testament* 55:27–54.

Weinberg, W. 1980. "Language Consciousness in the Old Testament." *Zeitschrift für die alttestamentliche Wissenschaft* 92:185–204.

Weinfeld, M. 1972. Review of *Ancient Israel's Criminal Law: A New Approach to the Decalogue*, by A. Phillips. *Journal of Biblical Literature* 91:535–38.

———. 1977. "Ancient Near Eastern Patterns in Prophetic Literature." *Vetus Testamentum* 27:178–95.

———. 1980. "Old Testament—the Discipline and Its Goals." *Vetus Testamentum* 32:423–34.

———. 1991. *Deuteronomy 1–11*. Anchor Bible. New York: Doubleday.

Weisman, Z. 1995. "The Place of the People in the Making of Law and Judgment." In *Pomegranates and Golden Bells: Studies in Biblical, Jewish, and Near Eastern Ritual, Law, and Literature in Honor of Jacob Milgrom*, edited by D. P. Wright et al., 407–20. Winona Lake, IN: Eisenbrauns.

Weiss, A. L. 2006. *Figurative Language in Biblical Prose Narrative: Metaphor in the Book of Samuel*. Vetus Testamentum Supplements 107. Leiden: Brill.

Weiss, R. 1963. "On Ligatures in the Hebrew Bible (*nu* = *m*)." *Journal of Biblical Literature* 82:188–94.

———. 1964. "A Note on *ʾŌtâ* in Ex 10,11." *Zeitschrift für die alttestamentliche Wissenschaft* 76:188.

Weitzman, S. 1997. *Song and Story in Biblical Narrative: The History of a Literary Convention in Ancient Israel*. Bloomington: Indiana University Press.

Westbrook, R. W. 1986. "Lex Talionis and Exodus 21,22–25." *Revue biblique* 93:52–69.

———. 1988. *Studies in Biblical and Cuneiform Law*. Cahiers de la Revue biblique 26. Paris: Gabalda.

———. 1990. "Adultery in Ancient Near Eastern Law." *Revue biblique* 97:542–80.

———. 1995. "Slave and Master in Ancient Near Eastern Law." *Chicago-Kent Law Review* 70:1631–76.

———. 1998a. "The Female Slave." In *Gender and Law in the Hebrew Bible and the Ancient Near East*, edited by V. H. Matthews et al., 214–38. Journal for the Study of the Old Testament: Supplement Series 262. Sheffield: Sheffield Academic Press.

———. 1998b. "A Matter of Life and Death." *Journal of the Ancient Near Eastern Society* 25:61–70.

Westermann, C. 1967. *Handbook to the Old Testament*. Translated by R. H. Boyd. Minneapolis: Augsburg.

Wevers, J. W. 2004. "Two Reflections on the Greek Exodus." In *God's Word for Our World: Biblical Studies in Honor of Simon John De Vries*, edited by J. H. Ellens et al., 1:21–37. London: T&T Clark.

Whedbee, J. W. 1998. *The Bible and the Comic Vision*. Cambridge: Cambridge University Press.

White, H. C. 1975. "The Initiation Legend of Ishmael." *Zeitschrift für die alttestamentliche Wissenschaft* 87:267–305.

Whybray, R. N. 1967. "*'Annôt* in Exodus xxxii 18." *Vetus Testamentum* 17:122.

———. 1974. *The Intellectual Tradition of the Old Testament*. Beihefte zur Zeitschrift für die alttestamentliche Wissenschaft 135. Berlin: De Gruyter.

———. 1996. "The Immorality of God: Reflections on Some Passages in Genesis, Job, Exodus, and Numbers." *Journal for the Study of the Old Testament* 21:89–120.

Wiesel, E. 1978. *A Jew Today*. New York: Vintage.

Wiesenberg, E. J. 1976. "Exposition of the Rare Words *Rḥt* and *Mzrh*." *Hebrew Union College Annual* 47:143–80.

Wijngaards, J. 1965. "*Hôṣî'* and *He'elâ*: A Twofold Approach to the Exodus." *Vetus Testamentum* 15:91–102.

Williams, J. G. 1964. "Concerning One of the Apodictic Formulas." *Vetus Testamentum* 14:484–89.

———. 1965. "Addenda to 'Concerning One of the Apodictic Formulas.'" *Vetus Testamentum* 15:113–15.

Williams, R. J. 1976. *Hebrew Syntax: An Outline*. 2nd ed. Toronto: University of Toronto Press.

Williamson, H. G. M. 1985. "A Reconsideration of *'Zb* in Biblical Hebrew." *Zeitschrift für die alttestamentliche Wissenschaft* 97:74–85.

Wiseman, D. J. 1982. "'Is It Peace?'—Covenant and Diplomacy." *Vetus Testamentum* 32:311–26.

Wolters, A. 1990. "Not Rescue but Destruction: Rereading Exodus 15:8." *Catholic Biblical Quarterly* 52:223–40.

Wood, B. 2005. "The Rise and Fall of the Thirteenth-Century Exodus—Conquest Theory." *Journal of the Evangelical Theological Society* 48:475–89.

———. 2007. "The Biblical Date for the Exodus Is 1446 BC: A Response to James Hoffmeier." *Journal of the Evangelical Theological Society* 50:249–58.

Wright, C. J. H. 1990. *God's People in God's Land: Family, Land, and Property in the Old Testament*. Grand Rapids: Eerdmans.

———. 1996. *Deuteronomy*. New International Biblical Commentary. Peabody, MA: Hendrickson.

Wright, D. P. 1987. "Deuteronomy 21:1–9 as a Rite of Elimination." *Catholic Biblical Quarterly* 49:387–403.

———. 2002. "Music and Dance in 2 Samuel 6." *Journal of Biblical Literature* 121:201–25.

———. 2009. *Inventing God's Law: How the Covenant Code of the Bible Used and Revised the Laws of Hammurabi*. New York: Oxford University Press.

———. 2010. "Miscarriage, Talion, and Slave Injury in the Covenant Code and Hammurabi's Laws." In *Gazing on the Deep: Ancient Near Eastern and Other Studies in Honor of Tzvi Abusch*, edited by J. Stackert et al., 539–64. Bethesda, MD: CDL Press.

Wright, N. T. 2003. *The Resurrection of the Son of God*. Vol. 3 of *Christian Origins and the Question of God*. Minneapolis: Fortress.

———. 2004. *Paul for Everyone: 1 Corinthians*. London: SPCK; Louisville: Westminster John Knox.

Würthwein, E. 1979. *The Text of the Old Testament*. Translated by E. F. Rhodes. Grand Rapids: Eerdmans.

Wyatt, N. 1979. "The Development of the Tradition in Exodus 3." *Zeitschrift für die alttestamentliche Wissenschaft* 91:437–42.

———. 1986. "The Significance of the Burning Bush." *Vetus Testamentum* 36:361–65.

———. 2009. "Circumcision and Circumstance: Male Genital Mutilation in Ancient Israel and Ugarit." *Journal for the Study of the Old Testament* 33:405–31.

Yadin, A. 2003. "*Qol* as Hypostasis in the Hebrew Bible." *Journal of Biblical Literature* 122:601–26.

Yancey, P. 2006. *Prayer: Does It Make Any Difference?* Grand Rapids: Zondervan.

Yaron, R. 1970. "The Middle Assyrian Laws and the Bible." *Catholic Biblical Quarterly* 51:549–57.

———. 1993. "Stylistic Conceits: The Negated Antonym." *Journal of the Ancient Near Eastern Society* 22:141–48.

———. 1995. "The Absolute Infinitive in Biblical Law." In *Pomegranates and Golden Bells: Studies in Biblical, Jewish, and Near Eastern Ritual, Law, and Literature in Honor of Jacob Milgrom*, edited by D. P. Wright et al., 449–60. Winona Lake: IN: Eisenbrauns.

Yee, G. A. 2009. "'Take This Child and Suckle It for Me': Wet Nurses and Resistance in Ancient Israel." *Biblical Theology Bulletin* 39:180–89.

Young, I. M. 1998. "Israelite Literacy: Interpreting the Evidence." *Vetus Testamentum* 48:238–53.

Zevit, Z. 1998. *The Anterior Construction in Classical Hebrew*. Society of Biblical Literature Monograph Series 50. Atlanta: Scholars Press.

———. 2007. "The First Halleluyah." In *Milk and Honey: Essays on Ancient Israel and the Bible in Appreciation of the Judaic Studies Program at the University of California, San Diego*, edited by S. Malena and D. Miano, 157–64. Winona Lake, IN: Eisenbrauns.

Zewi, T. 1996. "Subordinate Nominal Sentences Involving Prolepsis in Biblical Hebrew." *Journal of Semitic Studies* 41:1–20.

———. 1998. "On Similar Syntactical Roles of *Inuma* in El Amarna, and *Hnh*, *Whnh* and *Hn* in Biblical Hebrew." *Journal of the Ancient Near Eastern Society* 25:71–86.

———. 2000. "Tripartite Nominal Sentences in Biblical Hebrew." *Journal of Northwest Semitic Languages* 26 (2): 51–63.

Author Index

Scripture and Ancient Sources Index

Old Testament

Genesis

Leviticus

Deuteronomy

Joshua

Judges

Ruth

1 Samuel

2 Samuel

1 Kings

2 Kings

1 Chronicles

2 Chronicles

Ezra

Proverbs

Ecclesiastes

Song of Songs

Isaiah

Jeremiah

Lamentations

Ezekiel

Daniel

Hosea

John

Acts

Romans

Subject Index